Contemporary Authors®

ISSN 0010-7468

Contemporary Authors®

A Bio-Bibliographical Guide to
Current Writers in Fiction, General Nonfiction,
Poetry, Journalism, Drama, Motion Pictures,
Television, and Other Fields

volume 206

GALE®

THOMSON
—★—™
GALE

Detroit • New York • San Diego • San Francisco • Cleveland • New Haven, Conn. • Waterville, Maine • London • Munich

Contemporary Authors, Vol. 206

Project Editor
Scot Peacock

Editorial
Katy Balcer, Sara Constantakis, Anna Marie Dahn, Alana Joli Foster, Natalie Fulkerson, Arlene M. Johnson, Michelle Kazensky, Julie Keppen, Jennifer Kilian, Joshua Kondek, Lisa Kumar, Thomas McMahon, Jenai A. Mynatt, Judith L. Pyko, Mary Ruby, Lemma Shomali, Susan Strickland, Anita Sundaresan, Maikue Vang, Tracey Watson, Denay L. Wilding, Thomas Wiloch, Emiene Shija Wright

Research
Tamara C. Nott, Sarah Genik, Nicodemus Ford, Michelle Campbell

Permissions
Lori Hines

Imaging and Multimedia
Dean Dauphinais, Robert Duncan, Leitha Etheridge-Sims, Mary K. Grimes, Lezlie Light, Dan Newell, David G. Oblender, Christine O'Bryan, Kelly A. Quin, Luke Rademacher

Composition and Electronic Capture
Carolyn A. Roney

Manufacturing
Stacy L. Melson

LIBRARY OF CONGRESS CATALOG CARD NUMBER 62-52046

ISBN 0-7876-5199-0
ISSN 0010-7468

Printed in the United States of America
10 9 8 7 6 5 4 3 2 1

Contents

Indexing note: All *Contemporary Authors* entries are indexed in the *Contemporary Authors* cumulative index, which is published separately and distributed twice a year.

As always, the most recent Contemporary Authors cumulative index continues to be the user's guide to the location of an individual author's listing.

Preface

Contemporary Authors (CA) provides information on approximately 100,000 writers in a wide range of media, including:

- Current writers of fiction, nonfiction, poetry, and drama whose works have been issued by commercial publishers, risk publishers, or university presses (authors whose books have been published only by known vanity or author-subsidized firms are ordinarily not included)

- Prominent print and broadcast journalists, editors, photojournalists, syndicated cartoonists, graphic novelists, screenwriters, television scriptwriters, and other media people

- Notable international authors

- Literary greats of the early twentieth century whose works are popular in today's high school and college curriculums and continue to elicit critical attention

A *CA* listing entails no charge or obligation. Authors are included on the basis of the above criteria and their interest to *CA* users. Sources of potential listees include trade periodicals, publishers' catalogs, librarians, and other users of the series.

How to Get the Most out of *CA*: Use the Index

The key to locating an author's most recent entry is the *CA* cumulative index, which is published separately and distributed twice a year. It provides access to *all* entries in *CA* and *Contemporary Authors New Revision Series (CANR)*. Always consult the latest index to find an author's most recent entry.

For the convenience of users, the *CA* cumulative index also includes references to all entries in these Gale literary series: *Authors and Artists for Young Adults, Authors in the News, Bestsellers, Black Literature Criticism, Black Literature Criticism Supplement, Black Writers, Children's Literature Review, Concise Dictionary of American Literary Biography, Concise Dictionary of British Literary Biography, Contemporary Authors Autobiography Series, Contemporary Authors Bibliographical Series, Contemporary Dramatists, Contemporary Literary Criticism, Contemporary Novelists, Contemporary Poets, Contemporary Popular Writers, Contemporary Southern Writers, Contemporary Women Poets, Dictionary of Literary Biography, Dictionary of Literary Biography Documentary Series, Dictionary of Literary Biography Yearbook, DISCovering Authors, DISCovering Authors: British, DISCovering Authors: Canadian, DISCovering Authors: Modules* (including modules for Dramatists, Most-Studied Authors, Multicultural Authors, Novelists, Poets, and Popular/ Genre Authors), *DISCovering Authors 3.0, Drama Criticism, Drama for Students, Feminist Writers, Hispanic Literature Criticism, Hispanic Writers, Junior DISCovering Authors, Major Authors and Illustrators for Children and Young Adults, Major 20th-Century Writers, Native North American Literature, Novels for Students, Poetry Criticism, Poetry for Students, Short Stories for Students, Short Story Criticism, Something about the Author, Something about the Author Autobiography Series, St. James Guide to Children's Writers, St. James Guide to Crime & Mystery Writers, St. James Guide to Fantasy Writers, St. James Guide to Horror, Ghost & Gothic Writers, St. James Guide to Science Fiction Writers, St. James Guide to Young Adult Writers, Twentieth-Century Literary Criticism, 20th Century Romance and Historical Writers, World Literature Criticism,* and *Yesterday's Authors of Books for Children.*

A Sample Index Entry:

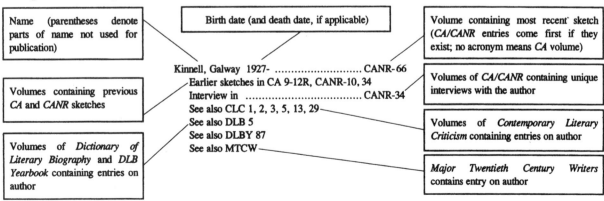

How Are Entries Compiled?

The editors make every effort to secure new information directly from the authors; listees' responses to our questionnaires and query letters provide most of the information featured in *CA*. For deceased writers, or those who fail to reply to requests for data, we consult other reliable biographical sources, such as those indexed in Gale's *Biography and Genealogy Master Index,* and bibliographical sources, including *National Union Catalog, LC MARC,* and *British National Bibliography.* Further details come from published interviews, feature stories, and book reviews, as well as information supplied by the authors' publishers and agents.

An asterisk (*) at the end of a sketch indicates that the listing has been compiled from secondary sources believed to be reliable but has not been personally verified for this edition by the author sketched.

What Kinds of Information Does An Entry Provide?

Sketches in *CA* contain the following biographical and bibliographical information:

- **Entry heading:** the most complete form of author's name, plus any pseudonyms or name variations used for writing

- **Personal information:** author's date and place of birth, family data, ethnicity, educational background, political and religious affiliations, and hobbies and leisure interests

- **Addresses:** author's home, office, or agent's addresses, plus e-mail and fax numbers, as available

- **Career summary:** name of employer, position, and dates held for each career post; resume of other vocational achievements; military service

- **Membership information:** professional, civic, and other association memberships and any official posts held

- **Awards and honors:** military and civic citations, major prizes and nominations, fellowships, grants, and honorary degrees

- **Writings:** a comprehensive, chronological list of titles, publishers, dates of original publication and revised editions, and production information for plays, television scripts, and screenplays

- **Adaptations:** a list of films, plays, and other media which have been adapted from the author's work

- **Work in progress:** current or planned projects, with dates of completion and/or publication, and expected publisher, when known

- **Sidelights:** a biographical portrait of the author's development; information about the critical reception of the author's works; revealing comments, often by the author, on personal interests, aspirations, motivations, and thoughts on writing

- **Interview:** a one-on-one discussion with authors conducted especially for *CA*, offering insight into authors' thoughts about their craft

- **Autobiographical essay:** an original essay written by noted authors for *CA*, a forum in which writers may present themselves, on their own terms, to their audience

- **Photographs:** portraits and personal photographs of notable authors

- **Biographical and critical sources:** a list of books and periodicals in which additional information on an author's life and/or writings appears

- **Obituary Notices** in *CA* provide date and place of birth as well as death information about authors whose full-length sketches appeared in the series before their deaths. The entries also summarize the authors' careers and writings and list other sources of biographical and death information.

Related Titles in the *CA* Series

Contemporary Authors Autobiography Series complements *CA* original and revised volumes with specially commissioned autobiographical essays by important current authors, illustrated with personal photographs they provide. Common topics include their motivations for writing, the people and experiences that shaped their careers, the rewards they derive from their work, and their impressions of the current literary scene.

Contemporary Authors Bibliographical Series surveys writings by and about important American authors since World War II. Each volume concentrates on a specific genre and features approximately ten writers; entries list works written by and about the author and contain a bibliographical essay discussing the merits and deficiencies of major critical and scholarly studies in detail.

Available in Electronic Formats

GaleNet. *CA* is available on a subscription basis through GaleNet, an online information resource that features an easy-to-use end-user interface, powerful search capabilities, and ease of access through the World-Wide Web. For more information, call 1-800-877-GALE.

Licensing. *CA* is available for licensing. The complete database is provided in a fielded format and is deliverable on such media as disk, CD-ROM, or tape. For more information, contact Gale's Business Development Group at 1-800-877-GALE, or visit us on our website at www.galegroup.com/bizdev.

Suggestions Are Welcome

The editors welcome comments and suggestions from users on any aspect of the *CA* series. If readers would like to recommend authors for inclusion in future volumes of the series, they are cordially invited to write the Editors at *Contemporary Authors*, Gale Group, 27500 Drake Rd., Farmington Hills, MI 48331-3535; or call at 1-248-699-4253; or fax at 1-248-699-8054.

Contemporary Authors Product Advisory Board

The editors of *Contemporary Authors* are dedicated to maintaining a high standard of excellence by publishing comprehensive, accurate, and highly readable entries on a wide array of writers. In addition to the quality of the content, the editors take pride in the graphic design of the series, which is intended to be orderly yet inviting, allowing readers to utilize the pages of *CA* easily and with efficiency. Despite the longevity of the *CA* print series, and the success of its format, we are mindful that the vitality of a literary reference product is dependent on its ability to serve its users over time. As literature, and attitudes about literature, constantly evolve, so do the reference needs of students, teachers, scholars, journalists, researchers, and book club members. To be certain that we continue to keep pace with the expectations of our customers, the editors of *CA* listen carefully to their comments regarding the value, utility, and quality of the series. Librarians, who have firsthand knowledge of the needs of library users, are a valuable resource for us. The *Contemporary Authors* Product Advisory Board, made up of school, public, and academic librarians, is a forum to promote focused feedback about *CA* on a regular basis. The seven-member advisory board includes the following individuals, whom the editors wish to thank for sharing their expertise:

- **Anne M. Christensen,** Librarian II, Phoenix Public Library, Phoenix, Arizona.

- **Barbara C. Chumard,** Reference/Adult Services Librarian, Middletown Thrall Library, Middletown, New York.

- **Eva M. Davis,** Teen Services Librarian, Plymouth District Library, Plymouth, Michigan.

- **Adam Janowski, Jr.,** Library Media Specialist, Naples High School Library Media Center, Naples, Florida.

- **Robert Reginald,** Head of Technical Services and Collection Development, California State University, San Bernadino, California.

- **Katharine E. Rubin,** Head of Information and Reference Division, New Orleans Public Library, New Orleans, Louisiana.

- **Barbara A. Wencl,** Media Specialist, Como Park High School, St. Paul, Minnesota.

International Advisory Board

Well-represented among the 100,000 author entries published in *Contemporary Authors* are sketches on notable writers from many non-English-speaking countries. The primary criteria for inclusion of such authors has traditionally been the publication of at least one title in English, either as an original work or as a translation. However, the editors of *Contemporary Authors* came to observe that many important international writers were being overlooked due to a strict adherence to our inclusion criteria. In addition, writers who were publishing in languages other than English were not being covered in the traditional sources we used for identifying new listees. Intent on increasing our coverage of international authors, including those who write only in their native language and have not been translated into English, the editors enlisted the aid of a board of advisors, each of whom is an expert on the literature of a particular country or region. Among the countries we focused attention on are Mexico, Puerto Rico, Germany, Luxembourg, Belgium, the Netherlands, Norway, Sweden, Denmark, Finland, Taiwan, Singapore, Spain, Italy, South Africa, Israel, and Japan, as well as England, Scotland, Wales, Ireland, Australia, and New Zealand. The sixteen-member advisory board includes the following individuals, whom the editors wish to thank for sharing their expertise:

- **Lowell A. Bangerter,** Professor of German, University of Wyoming, Laramie, Wyoming.

- **Nancy E. Berg,** Associate Professor of Hebrew and Comparative Literature, Washington University, St. Louis, Missouri.

- **David William Foster,** Regent's Professor of Spanish, Interdisciplinary Humanities, and Women's Studies, Arizona State University, Tempe, Arizona.

- **Frances Devlin-Glass,** Associate Professor, School of Literary and Communication Studies, Deakin University, Burwood, Victoria, Australia.

- **Hosea Hirata,** Director of the Japanese Program, Associate Professor of Japanese, Tufts University, Medford, Massachusetts.

- **Jack Kolbert,** Professor Emeritus of French Literature, Susquehanna University, Selinsgrove, Pennsylvania.

- **Mark Libin,** Professor, University of Manitoba, Winnipeg, Manitoba, Canada.

- **C. S. Lim,** Professor, University of Malaya, Kuala Lumpur, Malaysia.

- **Eloy E. Merino,** Assistant Professor of Spanish, Northern Illinois University, DeKalb, Illinois.

- **Linda M. Rodríguez Guglielmoni,** Associate Professor, University of Puerto Rico—Mayagüez, Puerto Rico.

- **Sven Hakon Rossel,** Professor and Chair of Scandinavian Studies, University of Vienna, Vienna, Austria.

- **Steven R. Serafin,** Director, Writing Center, Hunter College of the City University of New York, New York City.

- **David Smyth,** Lecturer in Thai, School of Oriental and African Studies, University of London, England.

- **Ismail S. Talib,** Senior Lecturer, Department of English Language and Literature, National University of Singapore, Singapore.

- **Dionisio Viscarri,** Assistant Professor, Ohio State University, Columbus, Ohio.

- **Mark Williams,** Associate Professor, English Department, University of Canterbury, Christchurch, New Zealand.

CA Numbering System and Volume Update Chart

Occasionally questions arise about the *CA* numbering system and which volumes, if any, can be discarded. Despite numbers like " 29-32R," " 97-100" and "205," the entire *CA* print series consists of only 248 physical volumes with the publication of *CA* Volume 206. The following charts note changes in the numbering system and cover design, and indicate which volumes are essential for the most complete, up-to-date coverage.

***CA* First Revision**	• 1-4R through 41-44R (11 books) *Cover:* Brown with black and gold trim. There will be no further First Revision volumes because revised entries are now being handled exclusively through the more efficient *New Revision Series* mentioned below.
***CA* Original Volumes**	• 45-48 through 97-100 (14 books) *Cover:* Brown with black and gold trim. 101 through 206 (106 books) *Cover:* Blue and black with orange bands. The same as previous *CA* original volumes but with a new, simplified numbering system and new cover design.
***CA* Permanent Series**	• *CAP*-1 and *CAP*-2 (2 books) *Cover:* Brown with red and gold trim. There will be no further Permanent Series volumes because revised entries are now being handled exclusively through the more efficient *New Revision Series* mentioned below.
***CA* New Revision Series**	• CANR-1 through CANR-115 (115 books) *Cover:* Blue and black with green bands. Includes only sketches requiring significant changes; **sketches are taken from any previously published CA, CAP, or CANR volume.**

If You Have:	You May Discard:
CA First Revision Volumes 1-4R through 41-44R and *CA Permanent Series* Volumes 1 and 2	*CA* Original Volumes 1, 2, 3, 4 Volumes 5-6 through 41-44
CA Original Volumes 45-48 through 97-100 and 101 through 206	**NONE:** These volumes will not be superseded by corresponding revised volumes. Individual entries from these and all other volumes appearing in the left column of this chart may be revised and included in the various volumes of the *New Revision Series*.
CA New Revision Series Volumes *CANR*-1 through *CANR*-115	**NONE:** The *New Revision Series* does not replace any single volume of *CA*. Instead, volumes of *CANR* include entries from many previous *CA* series volumes. All *New Revision Series* volumes must be retained for full coverage.

A Sampling of Authors and Media People Featured in This Volume

Charlie Kaufman

California-based Kaufman received much recognition for the inventive original screenplays *Being John Malkovich* and *Adaptation*. Released in 1999, *Being John Malkovich* is a bizarre saga about a shy puppeteer who stumbles upon a trap door that lets him spend fifteen minutes at a time inside the mind of actor John Malkovich. *Adaptation*, released in 2002, is a highly metatextual movie loosely based on Kaufman's own life, specifically his attempts to adapt Susan Orlean's nonfiction book *The Orchid Thief* to film.

Anita Nair

Nair, an Indian novelist and author of short stories, worked for twelve years writing advertising copy before she was able to devote herself to the self-described addiction of writing. Her works include *Satyr of the Subway: And Eleven Other Stories, The Better Man,* and *Ladies Coupé: A Novel in Parts.* Nair's debut novel, *The Better Man,* centers on the bachelor Mukundan Nair, who retires to his birthplace in a remote village in Kerala. A popular and critical hit in India, *The Better Man* earned mostly positive critical response in the United States.

Geoff Nicholson

British novelist Nicholson, who was a finalist for the prestigious Whitbread Prize, aims to be "a serious comic writer." His protagonists, such as the characters in *Hunters and Gatherers* who are consumed by collecting, frequently take their interests to the point of obsession. In the novel *Everything and More,* Nicholson turns a jaundiced eye on materialism with a tale centering on a fictional London department store. An autobiographical essay by Nicholson is included in this volume of *CA.*

Dan Pagis

An immigrant to Israel, a poet, and a scholar of medieval Hebrew poetry, Pagis is recognized for providing fresh insights into the study of ancient Hebrew poetic texts. He has been described as a poet of displacement and survival, having been born in the politically destabilized province of Bukovina, Romania, and later imprisoned in a Nazi concentration camp. Pagis was a leading modernist, and his works are often characterized by their intellectual and ironic detachment. In addition to the five books of poetry published during his lifetime, Pagis also issued numerous scholarly texts, and one children's book, *Ha'beitzh She'hithapsa.*

Marcel Reich-Ranicki

Also known as "der Literaturpapst," or the pope of literature, Reich-Ranicki is a literary critic whose highbrow intellect, irreverent manner, and unforgiving reviews have made him a household name in Germany. He is also the author of numerous volumes of criticism about German and Polish literature as well as the memoir *The Author of Himself.* Well known for disparaging books written by Günter Grass, Heinrich Böll, and other literary giants, Reich-Ranicki is considered by many to be Germany's preeminent literary critic. In 2002 he was honored with the prestigious Goethe Prize in recognition of his life's work.

Emilie Schindler

During World War II, Schindler helped her industrialist husband Oskar save over 1,200 Jewish people from being killed in Nazi death camps. Their work was commemorated in the Thomas Keneally book *Schindler's List,* later adapted to film by Steven Spielberg. In 1996 Schindler wrote *Memorias,* which was translated from the original Spanish into English as *Where Light and Shadow Meet.* In this memoir she describes Oskar as a self-serving womanizer, and presents her own recollections of scavenging food and medicine for the Jewish people whom she and her husband helped.

Eric-Emmanuel Schmitt

Schmitt is one of France's most prolific and acclaimed playwrights. His dramas, including *Enigma Variations,* perhaps his best-known stage play, have been performed in countries all over the world, including the United States. Schmitt has garnered many premier national writing honors, including Moliére Awards for individual plays and the Prix de l'Académie Française for the whole of his theatrical work. Schmitt is also a novelist, and his titles in this genre include *L'Evangile selon Pilate* and *La Part de l'autre.*

Tavis Smiley

A television and radio personality as well as an author, Smiley is known for his commentary on social and political issues, particularly those affecting African Americans. His first job in talk radio, a sixty-second syndicated program called *The Smiley Report,* resulted in the 1993 book *Just a Thought: The Smiley Report.* He went on to host a television show on Black Entertainment Television and see the launch of his own radio show on National Public Radio. Smiley is also the author of *Keeping the Faith: Stories of Love, Courage, Healing, and Hope from Black America.*

Acknowledgments

Grateful acknowledgment is made to those publishers, photographers, and artists whose work appear with these authors' essays. Following is a list of the copyright holders who have granted us permission to reproduce material in this volume of *CA*. Every effort has been made to trace copyright, but if omissions have been made, please let us know.

Text

Robert Sward: Poem "On My Way to the Korean War," first appeared in *Ambit 106*. Poems "Scarf Gobble Wallow Inventory," "Mr. Amnesia," "Honey Bear," "The Three Roberts," and "For Gloria on Her 60th Birthday" from *Four Incarnations: New and Selected Poems, 1957-1991*. Poem "Ten Years under the Eucalyptus Tree—The Tree that Destroyed California," unpublished. All reprinted by permission of Robert Sward. / Poem "Rosicrucian in the Basement" from *Rosicrucian in the Basement,* by Robert Sward. Black Moss Press, 2001. Copyright © 2001 by Black Moss Press. Poems "The Rosicrucian One Dollar Bill" and "After the Bypass" from *Heavenly Sex,* by Robert Sward. Black Moss Press, 2002. Copyright © 2002 by Black Moss Press. All reprinted by permission of Black Moss Press.

Photographs/Art

Geoff Nicholson: All photos reproduced by permission of the author, except as noted: portrait of Nicholson (dark shirt and jacket), © Jerry Bauer. Reproduced by permission.

Robert Sward: All photos reproduced by permission of the author, except as noted: portrait of Sward (wearing hat), by Paul Schraub. Reproduced by permission.

A

* Indicates that a listing has been compiled from secondary sources believed to be reliable, but has not been personally verified for this edition by the author sketched.

ABELLÁN, José Luis 1933-

PERSONAL: Born May 19, 1933, in Madrid, Spain; son of José M. Abellán and Angela M. Gonzalez. *Education:* University Complutense de Madrid, M.U., 1960, Ph.D., 1961. *Hobbies and other interests:* Walking, photography.

ADDRESSES: Home—Gravina 7, 28004 Madrid, Spain. *Office*—Facultad de Filosofía, Universidad Complutense de Madrid, 28040 Madrid, Spain. *E-mail*—jabellan@filos.ucm.es.

CAREER: Philosopher, author, and journalist. University of Puerto Rico, professor, 1961-63; University of Belfast, Belfast, Ireland, professor, 1963-65; University of Madrid, Madrid, Spain, professor, 1966—. Representative of Spain to executive board of United Nations Educational, Scientific, and Cultural Organization (UNESCO), 1983-85; member of editorial committee, Espasa-Calpe Publishers.

MEMBER: North American Academy of the Spanish Language, PEN (Spain), Asociacion Internacional de Hispanistas, Ateneo de Madrid, Sociedad Española de Filosofía.

AWARDS, HONORS: Fellow, Spanish and Spanish-American Studies, University of Nebraska; grantee, Juan March Fund, 1976; National Essay prize, 1976, for *El erasmismo española;* Medalla Alfonso X el sabio.

WRITINGS:

Miguel de Unamuno a la luz de la psicología, Tecnos (Madrid, Spain), 1964.

Ortega y Gasset en la filosofía española, Tecnos (Madrid, Spain), 1966.

Filosofía española en América, 1936-1966, Seminario y Ediciones (Madrid, Spain), 1967.

La cultura en España (ensayos para un diagnóstico), Edicusa (Madrid, Spain), 1971.

La idea de América. Origen y evolución, Istmo (Madrid, Spain) 1972.

Sociología del 98, Península (Barcelona, Spain), 1974.

La industria cultural in España, Edicusa (Madrid, Spain), 1975.

El erasmismo española, Gafica el Espejo (Madrid, Spain), 1976.

El pensamiento española: de Seneca a Zubiri, UNED (Madrid, Spain), 1977.

El exilio español de 1939, 6 volumes, Taurus (Madrid, Spain), 1976-78.

Panorama de la filosofía española actual: una situacion escandalosa, Espasa-Calpe (Madrid, Spain), 1979.

Historia de posguerra (narraciones), Ambit Literario (Barcelona, Spain), 1979.

Historia crítica del pensamiento español, seven volumes, Espasa-Calpe (Madrid, Spain), 1979-1991.

De la guerra civil al exilio republicana, Mezquita (Madrid, Spain), 1982.

París o el mundo es un palacio, Anthropos (Barcelona, Spain), 1987.

(With Antonio Monclús) *El pensamiento español contemporáneo y la idea de América,* two volumes, Anthropos (Barcelona, Spain), 1989.

(With Tomas Mallo) *La escuela de Madrid, un ensayo de filosofía,* Asamblea de Madrid (Madrid, Spain), 1991.

Ideas para el siglo XXI, Libertarias/Prodhufi (Madrid, Spain), 1994.

Historia del pensamiento español, Espasa-Calpe (Madrid, Spain), 1996.

George Santayana (1863-1952), Ediciones del Orto (Madrid, Spain), 1996.

El exilio filosófico en América: Los transterrados del 39, F.C.E. (México City, México), 1998.

El 98: cien años después, Aldebarán (Madrid, Spain), 2000.

Ortega y Gasset y los orígenes de la transición democrática, Espasa-Calpe (Madrid, Spain), 2000.

El exilio como constante y como alegoría, Biblioteca Nueva (Madrid, Spain), 2001.

José Gaos, introducción y antología, Ediciones Cultura Hispánica (Madrid, Spain), 2001.

Editor of several textbooks and collections, including *Biblioteca de pensamiento;* author of numerous articles in national and foreign journals.

SIDELIGHTS: José Luis Abellán is a tenured professor of philosophy at the University Complutense in Madrid, Spain. Abellán specializes in the history of ideas in Spain and Latin America and lectures extensively worldwide.*

*   *   *

ABRAHAMSEN, David 1903-2002

OBITUARY NOTICE—See index for *CA* sketch: Born June 23, 1903, in Trondheim, Norway; died May 24, 2002, in Hamden, CT. Psychiatrist and author. Highly respected in his field of psychiatry and as a psychoanalyst, Abrahamsen was more popularly known as the author of biographies about David Berkowitz, the "Son of Sam" killer, and U.S. President Richard Nixon. Born to a Jewish family in Norway, Abrahamsen later wrote about his experiences of being a minority in that country in his *Jeg er jode* ("I Am a Jew"). He earned his medical degree at Royal Frederick University in 1929, followed by additional study at the London School of Economics and Political Science and the State University of New York, where he earned another M.D. in 1943. While still in Norway in the 1930s, he practiced psychiatry and worked at a clinic. His first experience in criminal psychiatry came in the late 1930s with his work at the Department of Justice in Oslo. After moving to the United States, Abrahamsen continued his interest in criminal psychology when he worked at St. Elizabeth's Hospital in Washington, D.C., from 1940 to 1941 and for the Illinois State Penitentiary from 1941 to 1942. During the 1940s and 1950s, he was affiliated with a number of hospitals and clinics—including the Menninger Clinic—and taught at universities such as Columbia, where he worked at the New York State Psychiatric Institute, and the New School for Social Research. He also gained additional experience in criminal psychopathology at the Sing Sing Correctional Facility in Ossining, New York. Abrahamsen's experience with the criminal mind led him to be retained by the district attorney's office in Brooklyn to analyze Berkowitiz, who was accused of shooting six young women. Abrahamsen determined that Berkowitz was fit to stand trial, even though he was mentally disturbed. Berkowitz pleaded guilty to the charges and was imprisoned without a trial, but the relationship between him and Abrahamsen did not end there. The two continued to correspond, resulting in Abrahamsen's biography *Confessions of Son of Sam* (1985), in which he writes about Berkowitz's delusions. Abrahamsen is also well known for his somewhat controversial biography *Nixon versus Nixon* (1977), in which he describes the former president as "screwed up." Although criticized for analyzing Nixon without ever interviewing him, Abrahamsen argued that he had sufficient evidence from secondary sources to reach his conclusions. In addition to these works, Abrahamsen was also the author of numerous books on psychology, including *The Road to Emotional Maturity* (1958), *Our Violent Society* (1970), and *Murder & Madness: The Secret Life of Jack the Ripper* (1992).

OBITUARIES AND OTHER SOURCES:

BOOKS

Who's Who in America, 50th edition, Marquis, 1995.

PERIODICALS

Los Angeles Times, May 24, 2002, p. B17.
New York Times, May 22, 2002, p. A23.
Washington Post, May 25, 2002, p. B6.

ADAMS, Clinton 1918-2002

OBITUARY NOTICE—See index for *CA* sketch: Born December 11, 1918, in Glendale, CA; died of cancer May 13, 2002, in Albuquerque, NM. Artist, educator, and author. Adams was a highly influential lithographer credited by many for revitalizing the art of printmaking in the United States. He studied art at the University of California, Los Angeles, where he earned a master's degree in 1942 before serving as a warrant officer in the U.S. Air Force during World War II. Returning to Los Angeles in 1946, he taught art at his alma mater until 1954, when he moved on to the University of Kentucky and the University of Florida at Gainesville. Adams returned to Los Angeles in 1960 to become associate director of the Tamarind Lithography Workshop. Although he joined the faculty of the University of New Mexico, Albuquerque, in 1961, he remained a program consultant for the workshop. In his work for Tamarind, Adams helped teach artists how to create lithographic pieces. In 1970 the workshop ran out of funds, and Adams helped move it to the University of New Mexico, where it became the Tamarind Institute. Adams remained associated with Tamarind until his retirement in 1985. In addition to creating many of his own works of art, which were displayed in over sixty shows, Adams published several art books, including *The Tamarind Book of Lithography: Art and Techniques,* written with Garo Z. Antreasian in 1971, *American Lithographers, 1900-1960* (1983), *Printmaking in New Mexico, 1880-1990* (1991), and *Nineteenth-Century Lithography in Europe* (1998). He also edited *Second Impressions: Modern Prints and Printmakers Reconsidered* (1996).

OBITUARIES AND OTHER SOURCES:

BOOKS

Who's Who in America, 54th edition, Marquis, 2000.

PERIODICALS

Los Angeles Times, May 30, 2002, p. B13.
New York Times, June 2, 2002, p. A31.

*   *   *

ADAMS, Rachel (Elizabeth) 1968-

PERSONAL: Born November 9, 1968. *Education:* University of California-Berkeley, B.A., 1990; University of Michigan, M.A., 1992; University of California-Santa Barbara, Ph.D., 1997.

ADDRESSES: Office—Department of English and Comparative Literature, Columbia University, 602 Philosophy Hall, Mail Code 4927, New York, NY 10027. *E-mail*—real5@columbia.edu.

CAREER: Camera Obscura, Santa Barbara, CA, managing editor for three years; Columbia University, New York, NY, assistant professor of English and comparative literature, 1997—.

WRITINGS:

Sideshow U.S.A.: Freaks and the American Cultural Imagination, University of Chicago Press (Chicago, IL), 2001.
(Editor, with David Savran) *The Masculinity Studies Reader,* Blackwell Press (London, England), 2001.
(Editor) Kate Chopin, *The Awakening,* Fine Publications, 2002.

Contributor to periodicals, including *American Literature, Camera Obscura, American Quarterly, Minnesota Review, GLQ,* and *Signs.* Contributor to books, including *Freakery: Cultural Spectacles of the Extraordinary Body.*

SIDELIGHTS: Rachel Adams is an assistant professor of English at Columbia University in New York City. In *Sideshow U.S.A.: Freaks and the American Cultural Imagination,* she explores the cultural perception of people regarded as "freaks," including carnival performers, people with disabilities, people who cross gender boundaries, those from various subcultures, and those from unfamiliar cultures. Adams examines the use of freaks in literature, such as in Carson McCullers's *The Member of the Wedding* and Toni Morrison's *Beloved;* in photography, including Diane Arbus's photographs; and in American culture at large. She also offers studies of other books and films on freaks, including Katherine Dunn's novel *Geek Love,* Tod Browning's 1932 film *Freaks,* and Leslie Fiedler's study of Browning's film. Adams includes commentary from freaks themselves, who discuss their role in American culture and their work to "reclaim" their image.

Adams did extensive research for the book, and presents sometimes shocking facts about events in the history of freaks—for example, in 1906 a man from

Central Africa was placed in the same cage as an orangutan at the Bronx Zoo. In *Publishers Weekly,* a reviewer called the book "wide-ranging, wonderfully imaginative and often startlingly provocative."

BIOGRAPHICAL AND CRITICAL SOURCES:

PERIODICALS

Publishers Weekly, November 12, 2001, review of *Sideshow U.S.A.: Freaks and the American Cultural Imagination,* p. 49.*

*   *   *

ADICKES, Roland 1930-

PERSONAL: Surname is pronounced *A-diks*; born March 12, 1930, in Tübingen, Germany; naturalized U.S. citizen; son of Franz (a pharmaceutical researcher) and Gertrud (de Reuter) Adickes; children: Erich. *Education:* University of Chicago, M.A., 1958, J.D., 1961. *Politics:*" I have voted Republican ever since the Democrats botched Vietnam." *Religion:*" Inactive Lutheran." *Hobbies and other interests:* Gardening, photography.

ADDRESSES: Home—8267 Maxwell Lane, Dixon, CA 95620-9662.

CAREER: Worked as lawyer for state government agencies in California. Admitted to the California State Bar.

WRITINGS:

The United States Constitution and Citizens' Rights: The Interpretation and MIS-Interpretation of the American Contract for Governance, McFarland & Co. (Jefferson, NC), 2002.

Contributor to law journals, including *California Law Review* and *Southern California Law Review.*

SIDELIGHTS: Roland Adickes told *CA:* "My primary motivation for writing is that I feel I have something worthwhile to say about the law and the United States Constitution. I am trying to avoid legalese and to write in plain English, in order to reach fellow citizens who are not trained in the law. I am appealing to their common sense. My experience in government service and my readings in American history have shown me how often the law, beginning with rules that make sense, diverges over time from common sense and the plain English meaning of words. Legal fictions tend to be substituted for what used to be plain English which every citizen could understand.

"In my writing process I draw on thoughts that I have held in my mind, often for decades, sometimes written down, sometimes just mulled over the years. As these begin to accumulate and crystalize into current expression, I find they lead me sometimes in new directions, which then requires new research and a process of reconciliation with my previous lines of thought. After the passage of much time, things fall into place.

"As to my book, *The United States Constitution and Citizens' Rights,* my readings in constitutional law over the years, including in particular *The Founders' Constitution,* a compilation edited by the late Philip Kurland, my constitutional law teacher at the University of Chicago, made me realize that we are at a watershed; we are close to abandoning the federal government of enumerated powers that the founders gave us and which was still preserved in the constitutional amendments after the U.S. Civil War. The process of abandoning the founders' concept began in the 1930s, during the second administration of President Franklin D. Roosevelt, by substituting legal fictions for the plain English of the Constitution. By now we have progressed far toward a central government with unlimited powers of legislation that is close to turning the states into mere administrative agencies of the federal government. At the time of this writing, the U.S. Supreme Court is holding out for our traditional Constitution by the vote of one justice.

"The aim of my book is to give my fellow citizens a procedure by which the trend toward a centralized, all-powerful government could be halted and partially reversed, if the citizens want to stay with the founders' concept. The proposed 'Declaration of True Meaning' procedure would make it possible for citizens to focus on one 'special interest' at a time and vote it up or down. This cannot be done by electing congressional representatives, because such elections cannot be limited to a single issue."

*   *   *

AGUINIS, Marcos 1935-

PERSONAL: Born January 13, 1935, in Cordoba, Argentina; married Ana María (Marita) Meirovich (deceased); children: Hernán, Gerardo David, Ileana Ethel, Luciana Beatriz. *Religion:* Jewish.

ADDRESSES: Agent—Editorial Planeta, S.A., C/ Corsega, 273-279, Departamento Literario, 08008 Barcelona, Spain.

CAREER: Doctor, author, and lecturer. International Psychoanalytic Association, London, England, teacher; Government of Argentina, Buenos Aires, Argentina, vice-secretary then secretary of Culture. Lecturer at seminars for educational, artistic, scientific and political institutions in Germany, Spain, the United States, Israel, Russia, Italy, and in Latin America; creator of national program for democratization of culture (PRONDEC), for UNESCO and the United Nations.

AWARDS, HONORS: Planeta award (Spain); honorable commendation, Sociedad Argentina de Escritores; Reforma Universitaria award, La Plata University; Fernando Jeno award, Mexico; National Sociology award; Lobo de Mar award; Swami Pranavananda award; annual Silver Plaque, EFE Agency, for contributions to the strengthening of the Iberoamerican language and culture; named knight of letters and arts (France), award from Sociedad Argentina de Escritores, 1995, for life's work.

WRITINGS:

Maimónides, un sabio de avanzada, IWO-Instituto científico judío (Buenos Aires, Argentina), 1963.
La cruz invertida, Losada S.A. (Buenos Aires, Argentina), 1969.
Refugiados, Losada S.A. (Buenos Aires, Argentina), 1969.

Cantata de los diablos, Planeta (Barcelona, Spain), 1972.
Brown, Ediciones Daia (Buenos Aires, Argentina), 1977.
Operativo siesta, Biblioteca Universal Planeta (Buenos Aires, Argentina), 1977.
El combate perpetuo, Sudamericana-Planeta (Buenos Aires, Argentina), 1981.
Carta esperanzada a un general: puente sobre el abismo, Sudamericana-Planeta (Buenos Aires, Argentina), 1981.
Profanación del amor, Planeta (Barcelona, Spain), 1982.
La conspiración de los idiotas, 3rd edition, Emecé (Buenos Aires, Argentina), 1982.
El valor de escribir, Sudamericana-Planeta (Buenos Aires, Argentina), 1985.
Y la rama llena de frutos: todos los cuentos, Sudamericana-Planeta (Buenos Aires, Argentina), 1986.
Un país de novela, viaje hacia la mentalidad de los argentinos, Planeta (Buenos Aires, Argentina), 1988.
Memorias de una siembra: utopía y práctica del PRONDEC (Programa Nacional de Democratización de la Cultura), Planeta (Buenos Aires, Argentina), 1990.
La gesta del marrano, Planeta (Buenos Aires, Argentina), 1991.
Importancia por contacto, 2nd edition, Biblioteca Universal Planeta (Buenos Aires, Argentina), 1993.
Elogio de la culpa, Planeta (Buenos Aires, Argentina), 1993.
Todos los cuentos, Sudamericana (Buenos Aires, Argentina), 1995.
(With Monseñor Justo Laguna) *Diálogos sobre la Argentina y el fin del milenio,* Sudamericana (Buenos Aires, Argentina), 1996.
Nueva carta esperanzada a un general, Sudamericana (Buenos Aires, Argentina), 1996.
La matriz del infierno, Sudamericana (Buenos Aires, Argentina), 1997.
(With Monseñor Justo Laguna) *Nuevos diálogos,* Sudamericana (Buenos Aires, Argentina), 1998.
El atroz encanto de ser argentinos, Planeta (Buenos Aires, Argentina), 2001.

SIDELIGHTS: Marcos Aguinis is both Jewish and Argentine. As an author and cultural intellectual he has always publicly recognized and reconciled both identities. Although his work encompasses many other subjects, his lifelong themes are oppression, identity, and the cultural frontiers of the Jewish community. These themes are found in the sprouting of a Judeo-Argentine literature that, as Naomi Lindstrom wrote in *Jewish Issues in Argentine Literature: From Gerchunoff to Szichman,* "arises as a result of the efforts of the Delegation of Argentine Israelite Associations: With the emergence in the 1930s of fascism and renewed anti-Semitism, the number of Jewish leaders and intellectuals began to show to greater readiness to admit publicly that the Argentine special Jewish community needed care and advocacy beyond the general protection offered by the pluralism of the national melting pot."

Although Aguinis's first careers were in neurosurgery and psychoanalysis, his first love was literature. When asked about the beginnings of his writing, the author explained that he began at twelve with an unpublished novel and several short stories. At age thirteen he wrote a long article about peace, influenced by the books of Stefan Zweig. Attending the university in Cordoba, Aguinis chose to study medicine over literature; as he wrote in an autobiographical essay in Stephen Sadow's *King David's Harp: Autobiographical Essays by Jewish Latin American Writers,* "I didn't enroll in Literature or Philosophy or History because those schools—in my native Cordoba—were controlled by backwards figures, steeped with a Catholicism closer to the Inquisition than the Gospels. I decided on medicine because nothing would bring me closer to man."

"I must confess," Aguinis concluded in his essay, "that I never was comfortable with the choice. It had positive aspects, among them the ability to get closer to the pain, anguish, desperation, and also the gratitude of human beings." Missing the world of literature, Aguinis was encouraged to learn that many of his favorite authors throughout history, such as Rabelais, Chekov, Pio Baroja, Somerset Maugham, Axel Munthe, and Arthur Conan Doyle, were also physicians. Soon afterwards he published his first novel, a biography of the Jewish physician and humanist Maimonides. The study's title, *Maimonides: A Priest for the Oppressed,* conveys Aguinis's view that Jews have developed a special sensibility to the exploitation of others.

Like Alberto Gerchunoff before him, Aguinis was convinced that a Jew can also be a patriotic Argentine. In this spirit he wrote *Carta esperanzada a un general,* a critique of the oppressive role played by the military in Argentina. The book left open the possibility of dialogue and reconciliation between the civilian population and the military in the aftermath of a dictatorship; this was one of Aguinis's objectives when he held a government position in the Alfonsín administration. Aguinis's concerns with human rights, his strong patriotism, and his sensitivity derived from his Jewish heritage led him toward the composition of works like *La cruz invertida,* which in turn gave Aguinis a reputation as an international voice for human rights. Inspired by German priests who prepared revolutionary documents for the Second Vatican Council, *La cruz invertida* was praised for its denunciation of human rights abuses and its forecasting the repressive dictatorships in Chile and Argentina in the 1970s.

La cruz invertida faced a unique situation upon publication. At the time, both the author's own country and the country in which the work was published were dictatorships with histories of suppressing publications which advocated the themes expressed in Aguinis's book. *La cruz invertida* also created a problem for both the Spanish and Argentine governments when it received the Planeta prize in Spain, at that time the most important literary award in the Spanish language. The government of Francisco Franco intended to ban the volume, but since its author was Argentine, the book was allowed to be published. The Argentine military government also intended to ban the book, but after it was given a prize in Spain they abstained from censoring it. As Aguinis wrote in *King David's Harp,* "Isn't it humorous that the two tyrannies had worked together to guarantee the liberty of expression?"

BIOGRAPHICAL AND CRITICAL SOURCES:

BOOKS

King David's Harp: Autobiographical Essays by Jewish Latin American Writers, edited by Stephen Sadow, University of New Mexico Press (Albuquerque, NM), 2000.

PERIODICALS

Alba de America, July, 1998, "El profetismo en la Matriz," pp. 107-114; March, 1999, interview with Marcos Aguinis, pp. 395-404.

Folio, Volume 17, 1987, "Controversial Argentine Jewish Writer," pp. 25-63.

Reflejos, December, 1996, "De Maimónides a Marranos," p. 25.

Revista Signos, November, 1992, Augusto Cesar Sarrocchi Carreno, "'Camisa limpia' y 'La gesta del marrano,' dos voces para una misma problematica," pp. 155-165.

Salina, November, 1998, review of *La cruz invertida,* p. 185.*

*   *   *

AICHELE, George, Jr. 1944-

PERSONAL: Born June 12, 1944, in Washington, DC; son of George (a patent lawyer) and Helen (a homemaker; maiden name, Pauschert) Aichele; married, June 1, 1968; wife's name, Connie (a teacher); children: Sara Aichele Castle, Daniel. *Ethnicity:*" Euro-American." *Education:* University of Illinois, B.A. (with honors), 1965; Garrett Theological Seminary, B.D. (highest honors and distinction), 1969; Northwestern University, Ph.D., 1974. *Politics:* Left-Socialist. *Religion:* "Post-Christian." *Hobbies and other interests:* Bicycling.

ADDRESSES: Home—2248 Shannon Dr., Adrian, MI 49221. *Office*—Adrian College, Adrian, MI 49221; fax: 517-264-3827. *E-mail*—gaichele@adrian.edu or gcaichele@attbi.com.

CAREER: Theologian and educator. Northwestern University, Evanston, IL, interim chaplain and teacher, 1974-75; North Iowa Area Community College, Mason City, instructor in philosophy and social sciences, 1976-77; Upper Iowa University, Mason City, instructor in philosophy and literature, 1977-78; Adrian College, Adrian, MI, 1978—, chair of department of philosophy and religion, 1980-85, 1993-98, became professor, 1990. The Bible and Culture Collective, founding member.

MEMBER: Society of Biblical Literature, International Association for Fantasy in Art and Literature.

AWARDS, HONORS: Teacher/scholar grant, Adrian College, 1989, for research on translation and narrative; AAR grants, 1990, 1991, for *The Postmodern Bible.*

WRITINGS:

Theology as Comedy: Critical and Theoretical Implications, University Press of America (Lanham, MD), 1980.

The Limits of Story ("Semeia Studies" series), Scholars Press (Chico, CA), 1985.

(With others from the Bible and Culture Collective) *The Postmodern Bible,* Yale University Press (New Haven, CT), 1995.

Jesus Framed ("Biblical Limits" series), Routledge (New York, NY), 1996.

The Control of Biblical Meaning: Canon as Semiotic Mechanism, Trinity Press International (Harrisburg, PA), 2001.

EDITOR

(With Tina Pippin) *Semeia 60: Fantasy and the Bible,* Scholars Press (Chico, CA), 1992.

(With Gary Phillips) *Semeia 69/70: Intertextuality and the Bible,* Scholars Press (Chico, CA), 1995.

(With Tina Pippin) *The Monstrous and the Unspeakable: The Bible as Fantastic Literature,* Sheffield Academic Press (Sheffield, England), 1997.

(With Tina Pippin; and contributor) *Violence, Utopia, and the Kingdom of God: Fantasy and Ideology in the Bible,* Routledge (New York, NY), 1998.

Culture, Entertainment, and the Bible, Sheffield Academic Press (Sheffield, England), 2000.

(With Richard Walsh) *Screening Scripture: Intertextual Connections between Scripture and Film,* Trinity Press International (Harrisburg, PA), 2002.

Contributor to periodicals, including *Journal of the American Academy of Religion, Christian Century, Journal for the Fantastic in the Arts, Forum, Anglican Theological Review, Journal for the Study of the New Testament,* and *Neotestamentica* and to books, including *Handbook of Postmodern Biblical Interpretation,* edited by A. K. M. Adam, Chalice Publishing, 2000, and *The Postmodern Bible Reader,* edited by David Jobling, Tina Pippin, and Ronald Schleifer, Basil Blackwell, 2001. Series editor of "Playing the Text," Sheffield Academic Press.

SIDELIGHTS: George Aichele, Jr. is a theologian and educator who has moved away from Christianity, but who is drawn to biblical texts as literature and as a student of their non-biblical interpretations. His *Jesus Framed* is the first volume in Routledge's "Biblical Limits" series, described by *National Catholic Reporter*'s William C. Graham as having the intention of combining "the traditional field of biblical studies with literary criticism, anthropology, and gender-based approaches in search of a new way to understand biblical texts." Stephen D. Moore wrote in the *Journal of Theological Studies* that "this is an auspicious first volume in a significant series." Moore said the book "is less an evolving series of tightly linked chapters than a congeries of loosely connected essays. Trenchant theoretical reflections on the act of reading alternate with readings of selected Markan texts—the parables discourse, the trial narrative, the ending(s)—or textual fragments." Moore wrote that Aichele "undoubtedly possesses one of the most sophisticated minds in contemporary New Testament studies.... There is scarcely a page of this book that fails to stimulate or provoke."

Aichele is editor, with Tina Peppin, of *Violence, Utopia, and the Kingdom of God: Fantasy and Ideology in the Bible*. Each coeditor contributed one of the eight essays, which link the Bible and contemporary culture, but also apply contemporary viewpoints to biblical events. Pippin's contribution, "They might be giants: Genesis 6:1-4 and women's encounter with the supernatural," is an attempt to understand the divine from a feminist perspective.

The theme of *Violence, Utopia, and the Kingdom of God* is the "dialogue between fantasy theorists and biblical scholars and theologians," wrote Derk Visser in *Utopian Studies,* and the work focuses on contemporary culture rather than biblical tradition. Visser commented that "this volume deserves our study; the more so as several authors provide useful models for introducing topics that may grab the attention of our students." Visser cited as an example Michel Desjardins's "Retrofitting Gnosticism: Philip K. Dick and Christian Origins." Visser said that "the tone of the volume is set in the preface by Jack Zipes who sees a parallel in the 'faith and hope' of serious fantasy literature and the writers of the Bible that coped imaginatively with 'suffering and violence to project the possibilities for a more compassionate and humane world.'" Gene Doty's "Blasphemy and the Recovery of the Sacred" is a discussion of both God and a triumphant Satan in the novels of James Blish and of the works of C. S. Lewis and Frank Peretti. Other

contributions include Jorunn Jacobsen Buckley's "Presenting the Poison in the Gospel of John" and W. Doty's "Imagining the Future—Possible." Visser noted that in Aichele's contribution, "he quotes Matthew 11:12-14 that the violent have seized the Kingdom of Heaven ... and he scrutinizes the gospel of Mark for evidence of Christ's violent words and actions. But Aichele insists on seeing Mark's Jesus as a person of uncertain identity and raises the question whether Jesus may not be himself the aggressor against the Kingdom." Visser called *Violence, Utopia, and the Kingdom of God* "an interesting collection."

Aichele told *CA:* "Neutral, objective biblical interpretation—the tradition ideal of exegesis—simply does not exist, and never has. All exegesis is also eisegesis—the interpreter is always personally involved in the act of interpretation—and the ethics of interpretation mandate that the interpreter own up to that involvement. My readings of texts always come from the specific realties of my situation and experience. Nevertheless, I begin with some words from Roland Barthes, from the autobiographical pages that begin his book, *Roland Barthes:* 'Once I produce, once I write, it is the Text itself which (fortunately) dispossesses me of my narrative continuity. The Text can recount nothing.'. I write this in the fear but also the hope that this text will replace me or stand in my place, speak for me but also speak instead of me, interrupt my story, separate me from that story.

"I grew up when rock 'n' roll was young, and I graduated into the hippie counterculture. My father was a Chicago patent lawyer, and my mother was a lawyer's wife, both of them Eisenhower Republicans. We lived in a lily-white, affluent suburb, but I also went to a large public high school with a diverse student body, and I was very much aware of the sprawling West Side ghettos just a few miles to the east. My family was active in a Methodist church where, probably because many of its members were well-educated professionals, and also because there is no significant theological tradition in American Methodism, we young folks were allowed to talk and think as we pleased. We questioned God, and the meaning of life, and even our suburban privilege.

"This was during the post-*Sputnik* period, at the height of the cold war. I did honors study in math and science, and got so far ahead in course work that it only took me three years to finish college. But by the time I graduated from high school I was burned out on math and science. In college I majored in philosophy, with minors in sociology and psychology, and had a growing interest in literature of all sorts. I read Marx, Sartre, Nietzsche, Freud, and Durkheim. I went on peace marches and civil rights marches. I rebelled against my bourgeois roots.

"I went to seminary with thoughts of an academic career or maybe institutional chaplaincy. But I was becoming alienated from the church, which I saw aligned with the privilege of the white upper middle class. I looked, with Dietrich Bonhoeffer and Albert Camus and the 'death of God' thinkers among others for a post-Christian church for the 'secular city,' or even a revolutionary religion. I got married, lived in a couple of different communes, got involved in street ministry in the inner city, and eventually helped shut down the Northwestern University campus during the great student strike of 1970. I entered a Ph.D. program with a major in theology and minors in New Testament and literary theory—the sort of thing that was then called 'theology and literature.' Since Northwestern did not have a program of this sort in place, I pretty much designed my own curriculum, with the help of a supportive committee, and I did a dissertation exploring comedic aspects of contemporary theology. I was already thinking of theological discourse as narrative, and as fiction.

"It wasn't until I was nearly done with my dissertation that I encountered semiotic theory and poststructuralism—both of them at the same time, so that it took me a while to sort out some of the relationships. I started reading Michel Foucault and Barthes, and then Jacques Derrida, Julia Kristeva, Umberto Eco, and others. It was then that I also discovered some interesting things happening in biblical studies. I received my Ph.D. in 1974, the same year that the journal *Semeia* was first published. I had studied at Garrett Seminary with William Doty, who was involved in the early *Semeias* and was himself one of Robert Funk's students. But my seminary and graduate coursework in the Bible concerned older forms of historical criticism, with form criticism and the new hermeneutic presented as the latest thing. When I came across the early writings of scholars such as John Dominic Crossan and Dan Via, their views resonated strongly with my own interests—particularly Via's book, *Kerygma and Comedy in the New Testament.* This eventually led me to revise my dissertation and publish it under the title *Theology as Comedy.*

"As a student, I had been disappointed by the highly speculative historical studies that passed as biblical scholarship, making assumptions and then drawing conclusions that coincided, it seemed, with the view of liberal Protestantism. Likewise, the New Criticism that was still fashionable in secular literary circles seemed hermeneutically deficient to me. I could not understand how meaning could be somehow contained 'in' the text. It appeared that what both biblical historians and New Critics saw in the text was mostly themselves. The early structuralists also wanted to find meaning 'in' the text, but as that method evolved and indeed mutated, the answers became more and more sensitive to the problematic of meaning. Barthes's essay on Genesis 32 showed me that meaning was something that the reader, in the present moment, negotiates with the text, not something hidden in the text at its point of origin.

"Meanwhile, after several years of academic un(der)employment, I was offered a job at Adrian College. During this period, I had worked at various different jobs, including campus minister, bus driver, psychiatric orderly, part-time college teacher (of everything but biblical studies!), and finally, home care giver to my own small children. It was also during this period that I began writing for publication. The job at Adrian arose by chance, and I thought it might not last very long, but I have been there now since 1978. It is a small department, three full-time people, and a double department at that, both philosophy and religion.

"My second book, *The Limits of Story,* was provoked by a National Endowment for the Humanities (NEH) summer seminar during which I studied intensively with the poststructuralist critic Paul de Man. This remarkable experience encouraged me to explore the metaphysical and linguistic underpinnings of narrative, especially in relation to biblical genres such as myth and parable. In *The Limits of Story,* I examined the relation between literary genre and linguistic reference, and this then continued into a study of literary fantasy, a genre which has fascinated me ever since I was a child. I understand fantasy, following Tzvetan Todorov, Rosemary Jackson, and Jack Zipes, as a literature that unsettles the reader's assumptions and beliefs and thus opens the possibility of new perceptions, new thoughts, and new values. Fantasy is basically a revolutionary literature. In the fantastic narrative, the text's reference to reality somehow becomes uncertain, and the fictionality of the text is thereby made explicit.

"In essays focusing primarily on the gospel of Mark (that most uncertain of gospels), I have explored ways in which the fantastic operates within biblical narratives. I have also written about the fantastic in nonbiblical literature, television shows, and films. One goal of my editing and writing partnership with Tina Pippin has been to open up a wider dialog between biblical scholars and serious students of fantastic narratives, and this has resulted in four collections of essays involving dozens of contributors, *Semeia 60,* an issue of the *Journal for the Fantastic in the Arts,* and two books, *The Monstrous and the Unspeakable* and *Violence, Utopia, and the Kingdom of God.*

"I understand the fantastic as a point at which ancient and contemporary texts resonate with one another. They 'translate' one another, in the sense that Walter Benjamin speaks of the tangential point at which the original text and its translation touch one another. It is not a transfer of meaning but rather a point at which what Benjamin called 'pure language' becomes apparent. Indeed, translation theory has been another major interest of mine. Following Benjamin, de Man, and Derrida, but also logicians such as John Stuart Mill, Gottlob Frege, and Willard van Orman Quine, I reject the notion of 'dynamic equivalence' that is widely accepted in Bible translation societies and other Christian circles and only recently challenged in some Society of Biblical Literature sessions. The task of translation serves as a topic (much like fantastic) through which the text's resistance to meaning becomes apparent. Through my studies in literary fantasy and in translation theory I have become more and more aware of the text as a physical object, an other that is not an 'Other' in any theological sense (á la Paul Ricoeur or Emmanuel Levinas) but simply an inert physical thing that says nothing.

"In recent writings, such as *Jesus Framed* and *Sign, Text, Scripture,* I have attempted to make the physicality of the text an important aspect of my readings of biblical and nonbiblical narratives and my understanding of semiotic theory. My goal has been to bring to light the silent, inert materiality of the text, and to become aware of how that materiality lets the text speak, and how it also keeps the text from speaking. Since I can only do this through yet another text, the task inevitably defeats itself—as Barthes says, 'the

Text can recount nothing'—but this failure continues to instruct me.

"A second NEH seminar, this one with the postmodernism expert Ihab Hassan, further refined my interests along these lines, for postmodernism is very much concerned with the problem of meaning. Shortly thereafter I was invited to become part of the 'Literary Facets' unit of the Westar Institute, a group of people that rather quickly metamorphosed itself into the Bible and Culture Collective (BCC). Ten people of different genders, ages, religious orientations, and academic affiliations spent several years working closely together in order to write a book, *The Postmodern Bible,* and to explore in brave new ways the brave new world of postmodern biblical scholarship. I am proud to have been part of that experiment, and I don't think the full consequence of what we achieved has yet been realized. I cannot begin to estimate the value, for my own thinking and scholarship, of being so closely involved with these nine brilliant people, focusing on the same task over a considerable period of time.

"Another theme that has emerged in my research and writings, and that was very much stimulated by my involvement with the BCC, is the question of ideology. In relation to texts, ideology takes the form of intertextuality. Intertextuality is the meaning that arises when two or more texts are brought together—again, the task of translation. This returns me to the question of the physicality of the text, and of how texts come to be regarded as meaningful. How can texts acquire the meanings that seem obvious and natural and unquestionable to some people, even though these meanings are not at all obvious to others? I have played with a 'reading from the outside' inspired in part by Isaiah 6:9-10 and Mark 4:11-12: 'for those outside everything is in parables; so that they may indeed see but not perceive, and may indeed hear but not understand.' Reading from the outside counters a widespread belief that only those within the faith community can properly understand the scriptures. Reading from the outside is the 'stupid' reading of those who are not privy to the institutionalized understanding passed down through catechisms and creeds, i.e., though ideology. As one who is himself estranged from the believing community, but still fascinated by the biblical texts, reading from the outside is both my only option as a biblical critic, and an intellectually provocative exercise.

"Although my formal ties to Christianity have largely withered away, I am still drawn to biblical texts and the semiotic and ideological questions that they stimulate in me. I still regard myself as a theologian, albeit a post-ecclesiastical theologian. I study biblical texts because I still want to read them and to understand them. For me these texts serve as an irritant, a provocation, and a cause for wonder; I find them both beautiful and horrible. As I have drifted away from Christianity, I have become more and more aware of the church's claim to ownership of these texts, and have wanted to dispute that claim, to steal the texts and allow them to sink or float on their own in the cultural currents of our times, just like any other text. One result of this has been my book, *The Control of Biblical Meaning.* Since that book was published, I have been engaged in a series of articles, published in various sources, in which I pursue the problem of how various biblical texts might be read in post-canonical contexts.

"In the Christian Bible, the New Testament appropriates the Jewish scriptures and turns them into something else, namely, the Christian Old Testament. This happens at different levels of the biblical texts, from the macro level of a single codex binding together two Testaments into one unified object, to the micro level of numerous references to 'the scriptures,' 'the law and the prophets,' 'what Moses says,' as well as unmarked citations and allusions. It also happens within each of the biblical canons, in what Michael Fishbane calls inner-biblical exegesis. However, when the canon loses its authority, a much wider variety of intertextual contexts becomes possible.

"The canon of scripture appears because a religious community desires an intertextual web through which the scriptures completely explain each other. The entire collection of writings restricts the reading of any one of the texts. The canon results from the ideological desire to secure the text against the threat of loss, to possess the text and to confine its meaning. In my writings, I have attempted to 'liberate' the canonical texts from this hermeneutical control of the Bible through a critique of the semiotic mechanism of canon. I do not think that my desire to break the canon is any less ideological, or theological, than the desire of believers to defend the canon. It merely seeks a quite different result."

BIOGRAPHICAL AND CRITICAL SOURCES:

PERIODICALS

Catholic Biblical Quarterly, January, 1998, Fernando F. Segovia, review of *The Postmodern Bible: The*

Bible and Culture Collective, p. 137; January, 1999, Walter A. Vogels, review of *Sign, Text, Scripture: Semiotics of the Bible,* p. 145.

Choice, September, 2001, P. S. Spalding, review of *The Control of Biblical Meaning: Canon as Semiotic Mechanism,* p. 134.

National Catholic Reporter, May 9, 1997, William C. Graham, review of *Jesus Framed,* p. 14.

Journal of Biblical Literature, winter, 2000, Stephen Moore, review of *Sign, Text, Scripture,* p. 747.

Journal of Religion, January, 1987, Rowland A. Sherrill, review of *The Limits of Story,* p. 148.

Journal of Religious History, October, 1988, Katrina M. Poetker, review of *Jesus Framed,* p. 337.

Journal of Theological Studies, October, 1997, Stephen D. Moore, review of *Jesus Framed,* p. 582.

Theology, March, 1997, Bridget Upton, review of *Jesus Framed,* p. 138; January, 2002, David Jasper, review of *Culture, Entertainment, and the Bible,* p. 53.

Utopian Studies, spring, 1999, Derk Visser, review of *Violence, Utopia, and the Kingdom of God: Fantasy and Ideology in the Bible,* p. 209.

OTHER

George Aichele Home Page, http://home.attbi.com/~gcaichele (August 24, 2002).

*   *   *

ALBERS, Patricia 1949-

PERSONAL: Born October 4, 1949, in Ames, IA; daughter of Henry H. (a professor) and Marjorie (an interior designer; maiden name, Klein) Albers; married Joel Spiewak, 1973 (divorced, 1981); married Benjamin W. McKendall, Jr. (a dean), October 8, 1988; children: (first marriage) Sam. *Education:* University of Iowa, B.A. (magna cum laude), 1971; Middlebury College, M.A., 1972. *Hobbies and other interests:* Traveling, rowing.

ADDRESSES: Home—280 North Orchard Ave., Mountain View, CA 94043. *Agent*—Laurie Fox, Linda Chester and Associates, 1678 Shattuck Ave., Ste. 331, Berkeley, CA 94709. *E-mail*—palbers2@earthlink.net.

CAREER: Art critic, curator, and writer. *Le Nouveau Photo-Cinema,* Paris, France, columnist, 1978-82; Euphrat Museum of Art, Cupertino, CA, director of special programs, 1989-94; independent curator in the San Francisco Bay Area, San Francisco, CA, 1994—; School of Art and Design, San Jose University, San Jose, CA, lecturer, 2000—.

MEMBER: ArtTable (member of executive committee, northern California), International Association of Art Critics.

AWARDS, HONORS: Shadows, Fire, Snow: The Life of Tina Modotti was named a Best Book of 1999 by Library Journal.

WRITINGS:

Shadows, Fire, Snow: The Life of Tina Modotti, Clarkson Potter (New York, NY), 1999.
Tina Modotti and the Mexican Renaissance, Editions Jean-Michel Place (Paris, France), 2000.

Contributor to periodicals, including *San Jose Mercury News* and *San Francisco Focus.*

WORK IN PROGRESS: Sauvage: The Life of Joan Mitchell.

SIDELIGHTS: Patricia Albers writes of art and artists. Her *Shadows, Fire, Snow: The Life of Tina Modotti* was called the "first truly satisfying biography" of Modotti by a *Publishers Weekly* contributor. In a *Library Journal* review, Rebecca Miller commented that Albers "portrays a complex woman who made extraordinary life choices in an attempt to unite personal desires with the social realities of her time." Ted Loos noted in the *New York Times Book Review* that Modotti "threw herself into causes of all sorts, from love affairs to revolutions, with a scorched-earth intensity."

Modotti (1896-1942) was the friend of the most creative people of her time, as well as the lover of some of the era's most extraordinary men. She was born to a large, poor family in Udine, Italy, and her father was a factory worker and labor organizer. As a young girl, Modotti worked in sweatshops, which gave her insight into the plight of workers and which would later color her politics. She came to California when her father moved to San Francisco hoping to find a better job and she began acting in Italian theater, writing poetry, and creating her own clothes.

Modotti moved to Los Angeles with artist Roubaix de l'Abrie (Robo) Richey and was a successful stage and silent film actress when she met Edward Weston, whose portraits of her made her famous and who introduced her to photography. Albers discovered the papers of Richey, and she uses these to flesh out the years he and Modotti were together.

New Criterion writer Stephen Schwartz wrote that "Richey died of smallpox in Mexico City, leaving Modotti to commandeer Weston's salon, already dominated by Communist intellectuals, and which thanks to her soon included the American Comintern agents Bertram and Ella Wolfe. This circle included the prominent artists and activists Diego Rivera and David Siqueiros. Modotti attached herself to Rivera as well as Frida Kahlo. Modotti also joined a Mexican neofuturist avant-garde group, Los Estridentistas and, influenced as much by their interest in technological images as by the revolutionary chatter swirling around her, Modotti began producing 'modernist' photographs of an openly propagandist character."

Loos wrote that "in analyzing Modotti's work, Albers puts her professional eye to good use. She pinpoints what is worthy about Modotti's photographs, particularly how they capture 'the sensual materiality of life, its textures and tones,' while putting into perspective a fitful career that lasted less than a decade." Loos continued, "At her best Modotti had a knack for turning the ordinary into the iconic, and she developed her own style quite quickly. Her intensely creative period of the mid 1920s saw a thematic evolution—pictures of telephone wires and spare architectural spaces gave way to workers' parades as Modotti tried to combine formalism with anti-Fascism."

Modotti was drawn to the Communist Party where she met her soulmate, Julio Antonio Mella, a handsome Cuban revolutionary and exile. When Mella was assassinated while the two were walking together, Modotti was blamed by the press for Mella's death, an accusation that haunted her. After she was deported in 1930, Modotti traveled back and forth in Europe, spending time in Berlin, Paris, and Moscow, while she worked as a spy, writer, and office worker for the party. She wrote propaganda during the Spanish Civil War and was a hospital administrator. She eventually returned to Mexico City, where she died at age forty-six from heart disease, alone in a taxi cab. However, some contend that she was killed by Stalinists. *Booklist*'s Donna Seaman wrote that "Albers's fascinating portrait elevates Modotti to her rightful place beside Frida Kahlo and Georgia O'Keeffe."

BIOGRAPHICAL AND CRITICAL SOURCES:

PERIODICALS

Booklist, April 1, 1999, Donna Seaman, review of *Shadows, Fire, Snow: The Life of Tina Modotti,* p. 1375.
Choice, January, 2000, J. A. Day, review of *Shadows, Fire, Snow,* p. 921.
Library Journal, April 15, 1999, Rebecca Miller, review of *Shadows, Fire, Snow,* p. 82.
New Criterion, October, 1999, Stephen Schwartz, review of *Shadows, Fire, Snow,* p. 70.
New York Times Book Review, May 2, 1999, Ted Loos, review of *Shadows, Fire, Snow,* p. 24.
Publishers Weekly, March 1, 1999, review of *Shadows, Fire, Snow,* p. 50.
Women's Review of Books, December, 1999, Helen Yglesias, review of *Shadows, Fire, Snow,* p. 19.

*   *   *

ALDECOA, Ignacio 1925-1969

PERSONAL: Born 1925, in Victoria, Álava, Spain; died 1969; married Josefina Rodriguez. *Education:* Studied philosophy and letters at universities of Madrid and Salamanca, Spain.

CAREER: Novelist and short-story writer.

WRITINGS:

El fulgor y la sangre (novel; title means "The Lightning and the Blood"), Planeta (Barcelona, Spain), 1954, reprinted, Espasa-Calpe (Madrid, Spain), 1996.

El mercado, Cid (Madrid, Spain), 1954.
Vísperas del silencio (short stories; title means "On the Verge of Silence"), Taurus (Madrid, Spain), 1955.
Espera de tercera clase (short stories; title means "Third-Class Waiting Room"), Puerta del Sol (Madrid, Spain), 1955.
Con el viento solano (novel; title means "With the Easterly Wind"), Planeta (Barcelona, Spain), 1956, reprinted, 1994.
Gran sol (novel; title means "Great Sun"), Noguer (Barcelona, Spain), 1957, reprinted, Alfaguara (Madrid, Spain), 2001.
El corazón y otros frutos amargos (short stories; title means "The Heart and Other Bitter Fruits"), Arién (Madrid, Spain), 1959, reprinted, Alianza (Madrid, Spain), 1995.
Caballo de pica (short stories; title means "Picador's Horse"), Taurus (Madrid, Spain), 1961.
Arqueología, relatos, Rocas (Barcelona, Spain), 1961.
Cuaderno de godo (travel essays; title means "Gothic Notebook"), Arién (Madrid, Spain), 1961.
Neutral Corner (short story), illustrated by Ramón Masats, Lumen (Barcelona, Spain), 1962, reprinted, Alfaguara (Madrid, Spain), 1996.
El país vasco (travel), Noguer (Barcelona, Spain), 1962, translation by Doireann MacDermott published as *The Basque Country,* 1963.
Pájaros y espantapájaros (short stories), Bullón (Madrid, Spain), 1963.
Los pájaros de Baden-Baden (short stories), Cid (Madrid, Spain), 1965, reprinted, Iberia (Madrid, Spain), 1989, translation by Susana Heringman published as *The Birds of Baden-Baden,* Iberia (Madrid, Spain), 1986.
Parte de una historia (collection), Noguer (Barcelona, Spain), 1967, reprinted, Alianza (Madrid, Spain), 1995.
Santa Olaja de acero y otras historias (short stories), Alianza (Madrid, Spain), 1968.
La tierra de nadie y otros relatos (short stories), Salvat (Barcelona, Spain), 1970.
Cuentos completos, two volumes, Alianza (Madrid, Spain), 1973, published as *Cuentos completos: 1949-1969,* edited by Josefina Rodriguez de Aldecoa, Cátedra (Madrid, Spain), 1977, reprinted, Santillano (Madrid, Spain), 1996.
Cuentos escogidos, edited by Gloria Ray Faraldos, Alhambra (Madrid, Spain), 1988.
Seguir de pobres, edited by Maliano Peraile, Diptongo (Madrid, Spain), 1993.

Tres cuentos inéditos, prologue by Josefina Rodriguez de Aldecoa, Alfaguara (Buenos Aires, Argentina), 1995.

Also wrote *En el kilo 400,* 1959. Work included in anthologies, including *Historias de la gente,* Editorial Popular (Madrid, Spain), 1989; and *Tres de cuadrilla,* Espasa-Calpe (Madrid, Spain), 1990.

Aldecoa's writings have been translated into several languages, including French, English, German, Romanian, and Czech.

SIDELIGHTS: Ignacio Aldecoa's first stories appeared in several Spanish literary journals. Known for recounting the lives of ordinary people such as fishermen, gypsies, and civil guards in his many short stories, Aldecoa also penned the novels *El fulgor y la sangre, Con el viento,* and *Gran sol.* Published in 1954, *El fulgor y la sangre* is set in a ruined castle which overlooks an unnamed town in Castile. According to Gustavo Pérez Firmat, writing in *Hispanic Review,* the novel's "action transpires in one afternoon segmented into seven temporal units, each corresponding to a chapter." Firmat noted that although the duration of the action takes place in a single afternoon, "Aldecoa manages to build up considerable suspense." Firmat added, "suspense is also sustained by the way in which the uncertainty of the leader is channeled into the expectation of alternative endings."

Firmat concluded of the author's work, "Aldecoa's art . . . cannot be represented by the mirror which copies life, but by the 'lupa' [or magnifying glass] which recovers its apparently negligible aspects." Janet Winecoff Díaz, a contributor to *Modern Spanish and Portuguese Literatures,* noted that "the helplessness of those who can only wait—one of Aldecoa's most insistent themes—is masterfully presented, with the suspense maintained until the final moment" in *El fulgor y la sangre.*

Santa Olaja de acero y otras historias is an anthology of previously published short fiction, and draws from Aldecoa's collections *Vísperas de silencio, Espera de tercera clase, En el kilo 400,* and *Caballo de pica.* C. W. Butler, reviewing the work in *Hispania,* stated that most of the characters in *Santa Olaja* are "part of an endless parade of humanity enduring drudgery and hopelessness from birth to death." Butler added that "nature plays a very important role . . . and is [so] skillfully woven into the impressionistic tapestries of plot, situation, and character that it becomes incidental music." David Ross Gerling commented in *World Literature Today:* "*Santa Olaja de acero* should be in every Spanish short-story anthology because of the flash point produced by its carefully coordinated blending of plot and crescendo." Gerling concluded, "Aldecoa's stories of humble people enlighten, entertain, even enrage, but they never degenerate into sentimentality."

BIOGRAPHICAL AND CRITICAL SOURCES:

BOOKS

Garcia Vino, Manuel, *Ignacio Aldecoa,* EPESA (Madrid, Spain), 1972.

Landeira, Ricardo, and Carlos Melllizo, editors, *Ignacio Aldecoa: A Collection of Critical Essays,* University of Wyoming Department of Modern and Classical Languages, 1999.

Lytra, Drosoula, *Soledad y conviviencia en las novelas de Ignacio Aldecoa,* Fundacion Universidaria Española (Madrid, Spain), 1978.

Marrero Henriquez, José Manuel, *Documentacion y lirismo en la narrativa de Ignacio Aldecoa,* Universidad de Las Palmas de Gran Canaria (Las Palmas de Gran Canaria, Spain), 1997.

Martin Gaite, Carmen, *Esperando el porvenir: homenaje a Ignacio Aldecoa,* Ediciones Siruela (Madrid, Spain), 1994.

Schneider, Marshall J., and Irwin Stern, editors, *Modern Spanish and Portuguese Literatures,* Continuum (New York, NY), 1988.

PERIODICALS

Cincinatti Romance Review, Volume 7, 1988, pp. 85-96.

Cuadernos Hispanoamericanos, Volume 241, 1970, pp. 188-196; Volume 363, 1980, pp. 589-595; January-February, 1981, pp. 287-299.

Hispania, December, 1969, C. W. Butler, review of *Santa Alaja de acero y otras historias,* pp. 967-968; March, 1987, Clark W. Zlotchew, "Toward a Glossary for Ingacio Aldecoa's *Gran sol,*" pp. 155-159.

Hispanic Journal, fall, 1980, Janet Diaz, "Recursos artisticos nada objetivos de un escritor objetivista: Ignacio Aldecoa," pp. 17-25.

Hispanic Review, winter, 1977, Gustavo Perez Firmat, "The Structure of *El fulgor y la sangre,*" pp. 1-12.

Insula, Volumes 396-397, 1979, p. 14; April, 1995, pp. 13-15.

Letras peninsulares, fall-winter, 1999-2000, Jennifer Lowe, "Partial Accounts: Invention and Narration in Two Novels by Unamuno and Aldecoa," pp. 361-372.

Revista Hispanica Moderna, December, 1994, pp. 459-475.

Rocky Mountain Review of Language and Literature, Volume 26, 1972, pp. 83-88.

Romance Notes, spring, 1970, Janet Winecoff Diaz, "The Novels of Ignacio Aldecoa," pp. 475-481.

World Literature Today, spring, 1996, David Ross Gerling, review of *Cuentos completos: 1949-1969,* p. 366.*

* * *

ALEXANDER, L(ouis) G(eorge) 1932-2002

OBITUARY NOTICE—See index for *CA* sketch: Born January 15, 1932, in London, England; died June 17, 2002, in Chambery, France. Educator, curriculum designer, and author. Alexander is said to have achieved greater celebrity around the world than he did in his native England, for his specialty was teaching English as a foreign language. He was venerated from China to Egypt as he traveled the world to present his very popular lectures, primarily to teachers. In the 1960s Alexander was praised for breaking new ground in the field of teaching English as a foreign language, notably with the adult course *New Concept English* and the children's series *Look Listen Learn.* As his field of specialization grew in popularity and importance in an increasingly global world, Alexander eagerly adapted emerging technologies into his teaching approach. In the 1970s he collaborated on the design of television and video courses. In the 1980s, the early days of the personal computer revolution, he created computer-based courses in Spanish and French for the Atari computer system; they were among the first of their kind. In the 1990's Alexander went even further with *Direct English,* which integrated concepts of CD-ROM, video, and various Internet tools into the process of foreign-language learning. Best known for his long affiliation with the publisher now known as the Longman Group, Alexander had also taught English at a school in Greece for several years prior to 1965. He later served as a member of the Council of Europe threshold level committee on modern-language teaching and chaired the educational writers group of the Society of Authors. In addition, Alexander wrote grammar books for the native speaker of English, works that were praised as both meticulous and comprehensive. These include *The Essential English Grammar* and *Right Word Wrong Word: Words and Structures Confused and Misused by Learners of English.*

OBITUARIES AND OTHER SOURCES:

PERIODICALS

Guardian (London, England), July 9, 2002, obituary by David Mortimer, p. 18.

Independent (London, England), July 11, 2002, obituary by Tim Rix, p. 18.

Times (London, England), June 27, 2002, p. 36.

* * *

ALLEN, Jo Harvey 1943-

PERSONAL: Born 1943; daughter of a carpenter and a dress shop manager; married Terry Allen (an artist, musician, writer, and director), 1961; children: Bukka, Bale (sons). *Education:* Attended high school in Lubbock, TX.

ADDRESSES: Agent—Pakula/King and Associates, 9229 West Sunset Blvd., Suite 315, West Hollywood, CA 90069.

CAREER: Performance artist, actress, writer, and songwriter. Anderson Ranch, guest artist.

Film appearances include *True Stories,* Warner Studios, 1986; *Tapeheads,* Pacific Arts, 1988; *Checking Out,* Warner Bros., 1989; *Fried Green Tomatoes,* Universal, 1991; *Floundering,* A-pix Entertainment, 1994; *The Client,* Warner Bros., 1994; *Chicken Run* (animated), DreamWorks Distribution, 2000; and *All the Pretty Horses,* Columbia/Tristar, 2000.

Television movie appearances include *Cold Sassy Tree,* TNT, 1989; *Floating Away,* Showtime, 1998; *Scattering Dad,* CBS, 1998; and *The Outfitters,* Sundance Channel, 1999. Appearances in television specials include *Elysian Fields,* CBS, 1989. Appearances on episodic television include *The Road,* TNN, 1994.

Stage appearances include *Do You Know Where Your Children Are Tonight?,* 1985; *Pioneer* (opera), Theatre Artaud, San Francisco, CA, 1991; *Chippy: Diaries of a West Texas Hooker,* American Music Theatre Festival, Philadelphia, PA, 1994; and *Homerun* (solo show), DiverseWorks Art Space, Houston, TX, 1998. Appearances on major tours include *Pioneer* (opera), U.S. cities, 1992; *Homerun* (solo show), U.S. cities, 1998. Also performed in *As It Is in Texas* and *Counter Angel* (solo shows) and in *Hally Lou.* Radio appearances include *Every Three Minutes,* New American Radio, 1989; *Bleeder,* New American Radio, 1990; *Reunion* 1992; and *Dug-Out,* New American Radio, 1993.

WRITINGS:

Cheek to Cheek: Poems and Excerpts from Interviews, Duck Down (Fallon, NV), 1983.
(With Terry Allen) *Pioneer* (opera), produced at Theatre Artaud, 1991.
(With Terry Allen and others) *Chippy: Diaries of a West Texas Hooker* (play), produced at American Music Theatre Festival, 1994.
The Beautiful Waitress, Bemis Center for Contemporary Arts (Omaha, NE), 2000.

Also author (with Terry Allen, Bukka Allen, and Bale Allen) of *Do You Know Where Your Children Are Tonight?,* 1985. Author of *As It Is in Texas, Homerun,* and *Counter Angel* (solo shows) and *Hally Lou.*

Contributor to magazines.

SIDELIGHTS: Known to film buffs for roles such as that of "the lying woman" in *True Stories* (1986) and the women's awareness teacher in *Fried Green Tomatoes* (1991), Jo Harvey Allen is also a presence on the stage both in her native Lubbock, Texas and points beyond. She has cowritten a number of works with husband Terry Allen, most notable among these being

Chippy: Diaries of a West Texas Hooker, a musical play the couple conceived and wrote with other players in the original 1994 production. Based on the journals of an actual west Texas prostitute from the early twentieth century, "The musical's themes of resilience and compassion through hard times might be universal," Joe Nick Patoski wrote in *Texas Monthly,* "but its High Plains Panhandle imagery is so vivid you can almost hear the squeak of the oil pumps and smell the dirt after a rain." Discussing the title character, whom she portrayed, Allen said, "Chippy had a hard life, but she really had fun. She had over six thousand men . . . and she really enjoyed sex."

Allen has also written and appeared in a number of one-woman shows, among them *Homerun.* Discussing her performance at the DiverseWorks Art Space in Houston in November 1998, Patoski described both the writer and her character as "the brash, bighearted, hilarious embodiment of a West Texas goddess." Her home region plays a major role in virtually all of Allen's work, as she explained in an online interview with Chris Oglesby for *Virtualubbock.com.* Growing up in Lubbock, Allen said, her life was filled with paradoxes. For instance, "there were three books on the bookshelf in our house: There was *Emily Post Etiquette,* and *The Bible,* and *The Girl Scout Handbook.* Those three books were on the bookshelf. . . . And *Lady Chatterly's Lover* was in the cedar chest. And it was the most read. [Laughs] It was the most worn."

BIOGRAPHICAL AND CRITICAL SOURCES:

BOOKS

Contemporary Theatre, Film, and Television, Gale (Detroit, MI), volume 32, 2000.

PERIODICALS

Texas Monthly, July, 1994, Joe Nick Patoski, review of *Chippy,* pp. 60-61; November, 1998, Joe Nick Patoski, review of *Homerun,* p. 50.
Village Voice, August 9, 1994, review of *Chippy,* p. 86.

OTHER

Virtualubbock.com, http://www.virtualubbock.com/ (June 17, 1998), Chris Oglesby, interview with Jo Harvey Allen.*

ALTOBELLO, Brian J. 1948-

PERSONAL: Born February 20, 1948, in New Orleans, LA. *Education:* Louisiana State University, B.S., 1970, M.A., 1975.

ADDRESSES: Home—628 Chambertin Dr., Kenner, LA 70065. *E-mail*—baltobel@yahoo.com.

CAREER: Louisiana State Department of Education, Baton Rouge, consultant. *Military service:* Served in U.S. Army.

MEMBER: Organization of American Historians.

AWARDS, HONORS: Finalist for Distinguished Book Award, Military Historical Foundation.

WRITINGS:

Into the Shadows Furious: The Brutal Battle for New Georgia, Presidio Press (Novato, CA), 2000.

*   *   *

AMOROSO LIMA, Alceu 1893-1983
(Tristão de Athayde)

PERSONAL: Born December 11, 1893, in Laranjeiras, Brazil; died of a heart attack, August 15, 1983, in Rio de Janeiro, Brazil; son of Manuel José Amoroso Lima (a businessman); married Maria Teresa Faria, c. 1919. *Education:* Studied Brazilian literature with Coelho Neto; Faculdade de Direito e Ciencias Juridicas e Sociais in Rio de Janeiro, law degree, c. 1913; studied at the Collège de France, c. 1914. *Religion:* Catholic.

CAREER: Administrator in his father's business, beginning c. 1919; professor at several universities in Rio de Janeiro, Brazil; writer and literary and social critic, c. 1919-83; literary critic for *O Jornal* under pseudonym Tristão de Athayde, 1919-45; editor of *A Ordem,* 1928-68; president of Centro Dom Vital, Rio de Janeiro, Brazil.

MEMBER: Christian Democratic Movement of Latin America (cofounder, 1947), Brazilian Academy of Philosophy, Brazilian Catholic Action (president of national committee, 1934), Brazilian Catholic Coalition (founder, 1932), Grupo Goethe (founder, c. 1919), Appointed to Pope Paul VI's pontifical commission on justice and peace, 1967.

AWARDS, HONORS: Elected to Brazilian Academy of Letters, 1935; Mary Moors Cabot prize for contribution to continental understanding in international journalism, 1969; honorary doctoral degrees, Catholic University in Washington, DC, and New York University.

WRITINGS:

NONFICTION

Affonso Arinos, Annuario do Brasil (Rio de Janeiro, Brazil), 1922.
Estudos (title means "Studies"), five volumes, Terra de Sol (Rio de Janeiro, Brazil), 1927-1933.
Tentativa de Itinerario, [Rio de Janeiro, Brazil], 1928.
De Pio VI a Pio XI, [Rio de Janeiro, Brazil], 1929.
Freud, [Rio de Janeiro, Brazil], 1929.
Esboco de Uma Introdução a Economia Moderna, [Rio de Janeiro, Brazil], 1930, 2nd edition published as *Introdução à Economia Moderna,* Civilização Brasileira (Rio de Janeiro, Brazil), 1933.
Debates Pedagogicos, Schmidt (Rio de Janeiro, Brazil), 1931.
Preparação à Sociologia, [Rio de Janeiro, Brazil], 1931.
Problema da Burguezia (title means "A Problem of the Bourgeoisie"), Schmidt (Rio de Janeiro, Brazil), 1932.
Economia Pre-politica, Livraria Catholica (Rio de Janeiro, Brazil), 1932.
Politica, Livraria Catholica (Rio de Janeiro, Brazil), 1932.
Introdução ao Direito Moderno, Edição de Centro D. Vital (Rio de Janeiro, Brazil), 1933.
A Materialismo Juridico e Suas Fontes, [Rio de Janeiro, Brazil], 1933.
Contra-revolução Espiritual, Spinola & Fusco (Cataguases, Brazil), 1933.
Pela Reforma Social, Spinola & Fusco (Cataguases, Brazil), 1933.

Da Tribuna e da Imprensa, [Rio de Janeiro, Brazil], 1935.

No Limiar da Idade Nova (title means "At the Threshold of the New Age"), J. Olympio (Rio de Janeiro, Brazil), 1935.

Pela Ação Católica, Biblioteca Anchieta (Rio de Janeiro, Brazil), 1935.

O Espírito e o Mundo, J. Olympio (Rio de Janeiro, Brazil), 1936.

Indicações Politicas, Civilisacão Brasileira (Rio de Janeiro, Brazil), 1936.

Elementos da Ação Catolica, [Rio de Janeiro, Brazil], 1938.

Idade, Sexo e Tempo: Três Aspectos da Psicologia Humana (title means "Age, Sex, and Time"), J. Olympio (Rio de Janeiro, Brazil), 1938.

Contribuição à História do Modernismo 1: O Premodernismo, J. Olympio (Rio de Janeiro, Brazil), 1939.

Poesia Brasileira Contemporânea (title means "Contemporary Brazilian Poetry"), P. Bluhm (Belo Horizonte, Brazil), 1941.

Trés Ensaios sôbre Machado de Assis, P. Bluhm (Belo Horizonte, Brazil), 1941.

Pela União Nacional, J. Olympio (Rio de Janeiro, Brazil), 1942.

Meditação sobre o Mundo Moderno, J. Olympio (Rio de Janeiro, Brazil), 1942.

Mitos do Nosso Tempo, [Rio de Janeiro, Brazil], 1943.

O Cardeal Leme, J. Olympio (Rio de Janeiro, Brazil), 1943.

A Igreja e o Novo Mundo (title means "The Church and the New World"), Z. Valverde (Rio de Janeiro, Brazil), 1943.

Humanismo Pedagógico: Estudos de Filosofía da Educação, Stella Editora (Rio de Janeiro, Brazil), 1944.

O Crítico Literário (title means "The Literary Critic"), AGIR (Rio de Janeiro, Brazil), 1945.

Voz de Minas, AGIR (Rio de Janeiro, Brazil), 1945.

A Estética Literária y o Critico (title means "Literary and Critical Aesthetics"), Americ.-Edit. (Rio de Janeiro, Brazil), 1945.

Pela Cristianização da Idade Nova, two volumes, Livraria Agir (Rio de Janeiro, Brazil), 1946.

O Problema do Trabalho, AGIR (Rio de Janeiro, Brazil), 1947.

Primeiros Estudos: Contribuição a Historia do Modernismo Literario, AGIR (Rio de Janeiro, Brazil), 1948.

Obras Completas de Alceu Amoroso Lima, thirty-five volumes, [Rio de Janeiro, Brazil], 1948-1955.

Manhãs de S. Lourenço, AGIR (Rio de Janeiro, Brazil), 1950.

Mensagem de Roma, AGIR (Rio de Janeiro, Brazil), 1950.

O Existencialismo, AGIR (Rio de Janeiro, Brazil), 1951.

Europa de Hoje, AGIR (Rio de Janeiro, Brazil), 1951.

O Sentido da Uniao Pan Americana, [Rio de Janeiro, Brazil], 1953.

Meditação sobre o Mundo Interior, J. Olympio (Rio de Janeiro, Brazil), 1954.

A Realidade Americana: Ensaio de Interpretação dos Estados Unidos (title means "The American Reality"), AGIR (Rio de Janeiro, Brazil), 1954.

Pela América do Norte (title means "Passing through North America"), two volumes, Ministério da Educação e Cultura, Serviço de Documentação (Rio de Janeiro, Brazil), 1955-1956.

O Existencialismo e Outros Mitos do Nosso Tempo, AGIR (Rio de Janeiro, Brazil), 1956.

A Vida Sobrenatural e o Mundo Moderno, AGIR (Rio de Janeiro, Brazil), 1956.

Introdução à Literatura Brasileira (title means "Introduction to Brazilian Literature"), AGIR (Rio de Janeiro, Brazil), 1956.

Quadro Sintético da Literatura Brasileira (title means "A Schematic View of Brazilian Literature"), AGIR (Rio de Janeiro, Brazil), 1956.

A Segunda Revolução Industrial, AGIR (Rio de Janeiro, Brazil), 1958.

O Espirto Universitario, [Rio de Janeiro, Brazil], 1959.

A Crítica Literária no Brasil, [Rio de Janeiro, Brazil], 1959.

O Trabalho no Mundo Moderno, AGIR (Rio de Janeiro, Brazil), 1959.

O Teatro Claudeliano, AGIR (Rio de Janeiro, Brazil), 1959.

O Jornalismo como Gênero Literário, AGIR (Rio de Janeiro, Brazil), 1960.

Problemas de estética, [Rio de Janeiro, Brazil], 1960.

A Familia no Mundo Moderno, AGIR (Rio de Janeiro, Brazil), 1960.

Visão do Nordeste, AGIR (Rio de Janeiro, Brazil), 1960.

Europa e America: Duas Culturas (title means "Europe and America: Two Cultures"), AGIR (Rio de Janeiro, Brazil), 1962.

Cultura Interamericana, AGIR (Rio de Janeiro, Brazil), 1962.

O Gigantismo Econômico, AGIR (Rio de Janeiro, Brazil), 1962.

Da Inteligência à Palavra, AGIR (Rio de Janeiro, Brazil), 1962.

A Missão de São Paulo, AGIR (Rio de Janeiro, Brazil), 1962.

Revolução, Reação ou Reforma? (title means "Revolution, Reaction or Reform?"), Tempo Brasileiro (Rio de Janeiro, Brazil), 1964.

Pelo Humanismo Ameaçado (title means "In Defense of Threatened Humanism"), Tempo Brasileiro (Rio de Janeiro, Brazil), 1965.

João XXIII, J. Olympio (Rio de Janeiro, Brazil), 1966.

A Experiência Reacionária (title means "The Reactionary Experience"), Tempo Brasileiro (Rio de Janeiro, Brazil), 1968.

Adeus à Disponibilidade e Outros Adeuses (title means "A Farewell to Availability and Other Farewells"), AGIR (Rio de Janeiro, Brazil), 1969.

Meio Século de Presença Literária (title means "Half a Century of Literary Presence"), J. Olympio (Rio de Janeiro, Brazil), 1969.

Comentários à Populorum Progressio, Editôra Vozes (Petrópolis, Brazil), 1969.

Violência ou Não?, Editôra Vozes (Petrópolis, Brazil), 1969.

Companheiros de Viagem, J. Olympio (Rio de Janeiro, Brazil), 1971.

Em Busca da Liberdad (title means "In Search of Freedom"), Paz e Terra (Rio de Janeiro, Brazil), 1975.

Tristão de Athayde: Teoria, crítica e história literária, edited with an introduction by Gilberto Mendonca Teles, [Rio de Janeiro, Brazil], 1980.

Tudo é Mistério 1: Pecado. 2: Dons do Espírito Santo. 3: Virtudes, Editôra Vozes (Petrópolis, Brazil), 1983.

Also author of *Os Direitos do Homem e o Homen sem Direitos* (title means "The Rights of Man and the Man without Rights"), 1974.

Contributor to Brazilian periodicals, frequently under the pseudonym Tristão de Athayde, including *O Journal, Diario de Noticias, Jornal do Brasil, Jornal do Comercio, Revista do Brasil, O Estado de Minas,* and *La Prensa.*

SIDELIGHTS: Alceu Amoroso Lima was one of Brazil's most important literary and social critics. Vera Regina Teixetra in *Latin American Writers* praised Amoroso Lima as "a champion of social justice and an unrelenting fighter for political and intellectual freedom."

Amoroso Lima began his writing career under the pseudonym Tristão de Athayde, but used it less frequently after converting to Catholicism in 1928. His Catholicism influenced most of his writings thereafter. Among his titles are *Affonso Arinos, Problema da Burguesia, No Limiar da Idade Nova, A Igreja e o Novo Mundo, Pela América do Norte, Quadro Sintético da Literatura Brasileira, Pelo Humanismo Ameaçado,* and *Meio Século de Presença Literária.*

Amoroso Lima was born to affluent parents. His father had his own business, and was active in his country's political and cultural life. According to Teixetra, Amoroso Lima's family knew such prominent writers as Joaquim Maria Machado de Assis and Affonso Arinos, as well as minister of finance Ruy Barbosa, an orator who drafted the 1890 Brazilian constitution. Amoroso Lima's first published book dealt with Arinos and his works. Before he began his writing career, he graduated from law school at the Faculdade de Direito e Ciencias Juridicas e Sociais in Rio de Janeiro. There he met many of his strongest intellectual influences, including Silvio Romero. After graduation, he traveled in Europe, primarily in Italy and France. In France he studied philosophy with Henri Bergson at the Collège de France. Teixetra wrote, "Bergson's lessons, during those formative years, left an indelible mark on Amoroso Lima's philosophical posture."

Amoroso Lima returned to Rio de Janeiro by 1919, married Maria Teresa Faria, and began working at his father's business. When offered to become the literary critic for *O Jornal,* he decided to use the pseudonym Tristão de Athayde because, as Teixetra put it, he was "afraid that such a task might not be compatible with his image of entrepreneur." He used this identity for most of his periodical contributions, and even after he began concentrating on works of philosophy and criticism while teaching at various Rio de Janeiro universities, his books often appeared under both names.

According to Teixetra, the drowning of Christian leader Jackson de Figueiredo figured as heavily into Amoroso Lima's writing as his religious conversion. "That untimely death and Amoroso Lima's sense of loyalty, led him to chart for himself a new course in life in order to carry on Jackson's interrupted mission," Teixetra said.

Teixetra described *A Igreja e o Novo Mundo* as "a philosophical analysis of man and religion since the discovery of America," and *Idade, Sexo e Tempo: Tres*

Aspectos da Psicologia Humana as, "in the writer's own estimation" "his most important book." Addressing the backlash against sexual taboos in *Idade, Sexo,* Amoroso Lima condoned sexuality as a basic instinct, but railed against its excesses, according to Teixetra.

The writer's Catholicism also inspired his interest in and commitment to human rights. Such works as *Revolução, Reação ou Reforma?, Pelo Humanismo Ameaçado,* and *A Experiência Reacionária,* Teixetra said, "confirmed Amoroso Lima's self-imposed mission to denounce the military regime." *Os Direitos do Homem e o Homen sem Direitos* and *Em Busca da Liberdade* also reflect his disdain for tyranny. Amoroso Lima received the Mary Moors Cabot prize in 1969 for his contribution to continental understanding in international journalism. Two years earlier, he had been appointed by Pope Paul VI's commission on justice and peace.

BIOGRAPHICAL AND CRITICAL SOURCES:

BOOKS

Latin American Lives, Macmillan (New York, NY), 1996-1998.
Sole, Carlos A., editor, *Latin American Writers,* Scribner's (New York, NY), 1989.

PERIODICALS

Books Abroad, Volume 21, number 4, Samuel Putnam, "Alceu Amoroso Lima."*

*   *   *

ANDĚL, Jiří 1939-

PERSONAL: Born March 7, 1939, in Jenišovice, Czechoslovakia (now Czech Republic); son of Josef (a farmer) and Marta (a farmer) Anděl; married June 6, 1962; wife's name Vlasta; children: Petr, Martin. *Ethnicity:* "Czech." *Education:* Charles University, M.Sc., 1961. *Religion:* Roman Catholic. *Hobbies and other interests:* Playing the organ.

ADDRESSES: Office—Faculty of Mathematics and Physics, Charles University, Sokolovská 83, 18600 Prague, Czech Republic. *E-mail*—andel@karlin.mff.cuni.cz.

CAREER: Educator. Charles University, Prague, Czech Republic, assistant professor, 1961-77, associate professor, 1977-85, professor of mathematics, 1986—, vice dean of faculty of mathematics and physics, 1993—.

MEMBER: Biometric Society, Bernoulli Society, Czech Statistical Society.

AWARDS, HONORS: Czech National Prize, 1990.

WRITINGS:

Statistical Analysis of Time Series (in Czech), SNTL (Prague, Czechoslovakia), 1976.
Mathematical Statistics (in Czech), SNTL (Prague, Czechoslovakia), 1978, revised, 1985.
Statistical Methods (in Czech), Matfyspress (Prague, Czech Republic), 1993, 1998.
Mathematics of Chance, Wiley Publishing Group (New York, NY), 2001.

Contributor of more than 150 articles to academic journals.

Author's work has been translated into German.

WORK IN PROGRESS: Research on "statistical models of non-linear time" series.

SIDELIGHTS: Jiří Anděl told *CA:* "I have been a teacher at Charles University in Prague since 1961. My specialization is mathematical statistics. During my professional career I have published some 157 scientific papers and four books. The books were originally published in the Czech language; later one of them was translated into German, and the last one, *Mathematics of Chance,* was translated into English and published by Wiley. The main motivation for writing is to present new scientific results and to prepare textbooks for students.

"My work was particularly influenced by Professor Jaroslav Hásek (1926-1974), a famous scientist. Although he died young some thirty years ago, his papers and books are still very frequently cited. He was my supervisor during my postgraduate study.

"My writing process has changed dramatically since I began to use the computer. For example, before preparing the final version of *Mathematics of Chance,* I wrote eight complete earlier versions of the text. I prepared preprints in the form of books and sent them to my professional colleagues. Their critical remarks and proposals helped to improve both the content and presentation of the material.

"I have collected interesting examples from probability theory and mathematical statistics for many years. Some of them have unexpected and surprising solutions, and some are solved using interesting mathematical methods. Typically, they are connected with everyday situations where people must make decisions under uncertainty. Such examples, when presented in lectures, concentrate the interest of the students and lead them to a deeper study of probability theory and mathematical statistics.

*   *   *

ANGLEY, Ernest (W.) 1921-

PERSONAL: Born 1921, in Gastonia, NC; father, a textile worker; married Esther Lee Sykes (an evangelist preacher; died 1970). *Education:* Attended Church of God Bible Training School (now Lee College), 1941.

ADDRESSES: Agent—c/o Author Mail, Winston Press, P.O. Box 2091, Akron, OH 44309.

CAREER: Church of God, evangelist preacher in the southern United States, prior to 1952; Healing Stripes Evangelistic Association, cofounder, 1952; preacher in Akron, OH, 1952-57; Grace Cathedral, Akron, OH, founder and preacher, 1957-70; touring preacher at revival meetings, beginning 1970. Ernest Angley Ministries, founder and presenter of weekly television series. Also worked in rubber industry.

WRITINGS:

Raptured, Carolina Press (Wilmington, NC), 1950.
Miracles Are Real—I Got One!, Manna Christian Outreach (Greensburg, PA), 1975.

Faith in God Can Heal the Sick, Winston Press (Akron, OH), 1983.
Cell 15, Winston Press (Akron, OH), 1984.
The Deceit of Lucifer, Winston Press (Akron, OH), 1989.
Weeds in Eden, Winston Press (Akron, OH), 1998.
The Unforgivable Sin, Winston Press (Akron, OH), 1999.

Founder, *Power of the Holy Ghost* (magazine).*

*   *   *

APATOW, Judd 1968-

PERSONAL: Born 1968, in Queens, NY.

ADDRESSES: Agent—United Talent Agency, 9560 Wilshire Blvd., #500, Beverly Hills, CA 90212-2427.

CAREER: Producer, television series creator, writer, director, and actor.

Film work includes (associate producer) *Crossing the Bridge,* Buena Vista, 1992; (executive producer) *Heavyweights,* Buena Vista, 1995; (executive producer) *Celtic Pride,* Buena Vista, 1996; (producer) *The Cable Guy,* Columbia TriStar, 1996; and (producer) *The Whistleblower,* 1999. Film appearances include *Heavyweights,* Buena Vista, 1995.

Television series work includes (creator and executive producer) *The Ben Stiller Show,* MTV, 1992, 1995; (consulting producer) *The Larry Sanders Show,* HBO, 1992-95; (consulting producer) *The Critic* (animated), Fox, 1994; (co-executive producer) *The Larry Sanders Show,* HBO, 1997-98; (executive producer) *Freaks and Geeks,* NBC, 1999-2000; and (executive producer), *Life on Parole,* 2002. Episodic television work as director includes *The Larry Sanders Show,* HBO, 1992; and "I'm with the Band," "Carded and Discarded," "Dead Dogs and Gym Teachers," *Freaks and Geeks,* NBC, 1999.

Work on television specials includes (co-producer) *The Road Warriors,* HBO, 1992; (segment producer) *"Ben Stiller," Rock the Vote,* MTV, 1992; (co-producer) *Roseanne Arnold*, ABC, 1992; (co-producer) *Tom Arnold: The Naked Truth 2*, HBO, 1992; and (co-producer) *Tom Arnold: The Naked Truth 3*, HBO, 1993. Appearances on television specials includes *The 15th Annual Young Comedians Show—Hosted by Dana Carvey*, 1992; (host) *Canned Ham: The Cable Guy*, Comedy Central, 1996; and *Jim Carrey: The Joker's Wild*, Romance Classics, 1996.

Episodic television appearances include "Episode with Bobcat Goldthwait," and as Foxy the Fox, *The Ben Stiller Show*, MTV, 1992; "A Few Good Scouts," *The Ben Stiller Show*, MTV, 1993; "Goofy Ball," *Newsradio*, NBC, 1995; and as himself, *The Ben Stiller Show*, MTV, 1995.

Appearances on recordings include *Adam Sandler's What the Hell Happened to Me?*, 1996.

AWARDS, HONORS: Shared several Cable ACE awards for *The Larry Sanders Show*.

WRITINGS:

(With Harriet Grey and Lou Holtz) *The Cable Guy* (novel; see also below), St. Martin's Press (New York, NY), 1996.

SCREENPLAYS

(With Roger Birnbaum) *Heavyweights*, Buena Vista, 1995.
(Uncredited) *Happy Gilmore*, Universal, 1996.
(With Colin Quinn) *Celtic Pride*, Buena Vista, 1996.
(Uncredited) *The Cable Guy*, Columbia TriStar, 1996.
(With Tim Herlihy and Carrie Fisher) *The Wedding Singer*, New Line Cinema, 1998.

TELEVISION EPISODES

(And co-creator, executive producer, and actor) *The Ben Stiller Show*, MTV, 1992, 1995.
The Larry Sanders Show, HBO, 1992, 1997.
(And consulting producer) *The Critic*, Fox, 1994.
(And creator, executive producer, and director) *Freaks and Geeks*, NBC, 1999.

(And executive producer) *Undeclared*, NBC, 2001-2002.
Life on Parole, 2002.

TELEVISION SPECIALS

Tom Arnold: The Naked Truth, HBO, 1991.
(Segment writer), *Class Clowns*, ABC, 1992.
The Road Warriors, HBO, 1992.
Tom Arnold: The Naked Truth 2, HBO, 1992.
(With Dana Carvey and others) *The 15th Annual Young Comedians Show*, United American Video (Charlotte, NC), 1992.
Baseball Relief: An All-Star Comedy Salute, Fox, 1993.
Tom Arnold: The Naked Truth 3, HBO, 1993.
The 36th Annual Grammy Awards, 1994.
(Author of special material for Jim Carrey), *American Film Institute Salute to Clint Eastwood*, 1996.

Also writer for *The TV Wheel*, 1995.

SIDELIGHTS: Judd Apatow has worked in numerous capacities in the entertainment industry, from conception to the screen, bringing films and television series to life. Not only did he create the highly acclaimed series *Freaks and Geeks* and work on the follow-up, *Undeclared*, he has written or cowritten a number of screenplays, including the Adam Sandler vehicles *Happy Gilmore* and *The Wedding Singer*. During the early 1990s, Apatow paid his dues as a writer on various TV specials, as well as on series that included *The Ben Stiller Show* and *The Larry Sanders Show*.

Apatow's career is a tribute to persistence: not only have many of his efforts earned critical acclaim only to suffer commercially, but not all of his work has won high marks from critics. Such was the case with *Celtic Pride*, a film Jack Mathews described in the *Los Angeles Times* as "a comedy about the [Boston] Celtics that's even worse than the team. And not half as funny." Yet Apatow has enjoyed numerous triumphs, beginning with his award-winning work on the *Larry Sanders Show* and continuing with two highly acclaimed comedy series in the late 1990s and early 2000s.

Like *Star Trek* in its initial run, *Freaks and Geeks* was cancelled due to poor ratings only to become a cult favorite in reruns. Discussing the genesis of the show in an interview with Daniel Radosh for *Modern Humorist,* Apatow said, "The teen show craze was at its peak, and people were beginning to get irritated with it, so the time was right for a show that went the other way." Rather than playing down the unglamorous characteristics of teenagers, *Freaks and Geeks*—as its title suggests—emphasizes those aspects.

With *Undeclared* two years later, Apatow had another critical success that was cancelled during its first, abbreviated season. After praising its predecessor, Ken Tucker in *Entertainment Weekly* noted approvingly that actor Seth Rogen from *Freaks and Geeks* was back on *Undeclared,* a fact that in Tucker's opinion suggested "that Apatow felt he was on the right track and want[ed] to find the proper format to continue exploring his belief that young people are as complicated as they are confused and silly." Set at the fictional University of North Eastern California, *Undeclared* also starred musician Loudon Wainwright III, a personal favorite of Apatow's from his younger days. After the show's cancellation, Apatow addressed fans on his Web site, commenting, "I am proud of what everyone at 'Undeclared' accomplished. I hope you enjoyed it. We certainly put our hearts into every moment. I appreciate your support and look forward to making something else in the future that, hopefully, you will like as well."

BIOGRAPHICAL AND CRITICAL SOURCES:

BOOKS

Contemporary Theatre, Film, and Television, volume 32, Gale (Detroit, MI), 2000.

PERIODICALS

Entertainment Weekly, September 21, 2001, Dan Snierson, review of *Undeclared,* p. 48, Ken Tucker, "Honor Roles? Ken Tucker Thinks the Aging *That '70s Show* Could Learn a Few Lessons from the Well-rounded New College Sitcom *Undeclared,*" p. 67.
Los Angeles Times, April 19, 1996, Jack Mathews, review of *Celtic Pride,* p. 6; September 25, 2001, Howard Rosenberg, review of *Undeclared,* p. F2.

People Weekly, May 6, 1996, Ralph Novak, review of *Celtic Pride,* p. 20.
Variety, September 20, 1999, review of *Freaks and Geeks.*
Washington Post, September 25, 2001, Tom Shales, review of *Undeclared,* p. C1.

OTHER

Modern Humorist, http://www.modernhumorist.com/ (August 13, 2001), Daniel Radosh, "The Freakiest Geek: An Interview with Judd Apatow, Producer of *Undeclared* and *Freaks and Geeks.*"
Onion A.V. Club, http://www.theonionavclub.com/ (October 3, 2001), Keith Phipps, interview with Judd Apatow.
Undeclared Online, http://www.undeclaredonline.com/ (December 28, 2002), Judd Apatow, "Judd Speaks."*

*   *   *

ARMAS MARCELO, J(uan) J(esú) 1946-

PERSONAL: Born 1946, in Las Palmas de Gran Cararia, Spain. *Education:* Graduated from University Complutense, Madrid, Spain.

ADDRESSES: Agent—c/o Ediciones Alfaguara, 60 Torrelaguna, 28043 Madrid, Spain.

CAREER: Novelist, teacher, and editor. Lectured at Instituto de Agüimes, funda Inventarios Provisionales Editores, Canary Islands; edited Spanish and Latin-American poetry. Editora Regional Canaria, director, 1975-79; Cabildo Insular de Gran Canaria, director.

AWARDS, HONORS: Premio Galdós, 1975, for *El camaleâon sobre la alfombra;* Premio International de Novela, Plaza & Janés, 1996, for *Los dioses de sí mismos.*

WRITINGS:

Scherzos pour Nathalie, Inventarios Provisionales (Las Palmas, Gran Canaria, Spain), 1972.
El camaleâon sobre la alfombra, Plaza & Janés (Barcelona, Spain), 1974.

Estado de coma, Plaza & Janés (Barcelona, Spain), 1976.

Calima, Sedmay Edicions (Barcelona, Spain), 1978.

Guía secreta de Canarias, Sedmay Edicions (Barcelona, Spain), 1979.

Las naves quemadas, Editorial Ergos Vergara (Barcelona, Spain), 1982, translation by Sarah Arvio published as *Ships Afire,* Avon Books (New York, NY), 1988.

El árbol del bien y del mal, Plaza & Janés (Barcelona, Spain), 1985.

Tirios, troyanos y contemporáneos, Editorial Playor (Madrid, Spain), 1987.

Los dioses de sí mismos, Plaza & Janés (Barcelona, Spain), 1989.

Vargas Llosa: el vicio de escribir, Temas de Hoy (Madrid, Spain), 1991.

Exposición Eduardo Urculo: el viajero, la ciudad y el equipaje: pintura, escultura, dibujo, Ayuntamiento de Oviedo (Oviedo, Spain), 1994.

Madrid, Distrito Federal, Seix Barral (Barcelona, Spain), 1994.

García Alvarez: José Antonio García Alvarez, Vice-consejería de Cultura y Deporte de Las Palmas (Las Palmas, Gran Canaria, Spain), 1995.

Los años que fuimos Marilyn, Espasa Calpe (Madrid, Spain), 1995.

Tal como somos, Espasa Calpe (Madrid, Spain), 1996.

Cuando éramos los mejores, Temas de Hoy (Madrid, Spain), 1997.

Así en La Habana como en el cielo, Alfaguara (Madrid, Spain), 1998.

Cuba en el corazón, photographs by Pedro F. Palazuelos, Creática (Santander, Cantabria, Spain), 1998.

Los mares de Iberia, Pabellón de España (Lisbon, Portugal), 1998.

El niño de luto y el cocinero del Papa, Alfaguara (Madrid, Spain), 2001.

SIDELIGHTS: J. J. Armas Marcelo was born in Las Palmas de Gran Canarias, Spain. After earning a degree in Spanish literature at the University Complutense of Madrid, Armas Marcelo returned to the Canaries and began lecturing at the Instituto de Agüimes, where he also edited Spanish and Latin American poetry and worked with groups to promote cultural life throughout the Canaries.

In 1972, toward the end of the dictatorship of Spanish ruler Ferdinand Franco and its censorship campaigns, Armas Marcelo was reprimanded by the central government in Madrid for having published the collection of poetry *Número trece* by José Ángel Valente because it was deemed injurious to the character of a general of the Spanish army. He continued his work, however, as the first director of Editora Regional Canaria and from 1975 to 1979 was director of the group Cabildo Insular de Gran Canaria.

In 1979 Armas Marcelo organized the first Spanish-language congress, bringing together more than two hundred writers and journalists from throughout the Spanish-speaking world. During this period he put special emphasis on developing relations between the Canaries and the countries of Latin America, especially Venezuela and Cuba, which had strong historical, literary, and anthropological ties.

In 1978 Armas Marcelo moved to Madrid, but he remained connected with the Canaries by writing a weekly column, "Madrid, Distrito Federal," in the Las Palmas newspaper *La Provincia* and in *Canarias 7* a column called "Tal como somos." Each of these columns was later collected and published in book form.

The first novels of Armas Marcelo describe the insular world of the Canaries and the internal social and political conflicts. The third of these, *Calima,* however, was the most influential in forming the author's evolving style since it is based on an historical incident: the kidnapping the tobacco grower Eufemiano Fuentes. A lone, hooded gunman took Fuentes from his bed at 4:30 in the morning, and his wife found a ransom note demanding $900,000, but Fuentes was never seen again. To complicate the investigation was the implication that Antonio Cubillo, the leader of the Canary Island separatist movement (MPAIAC), was responsible, a charge he never confirmed or denied. This was 1976, the year Franco died and a confusing period in which Spain's transitional democracy was taking power. Five members of Cubillo's family were also detained and one of them, Angel Cabrera, alias El Rubio, was accused of the crime, but the body of Fuentes was never found. El Rubio went underground. In 1980 the case was still being investigated, and Cabrera was on the point of being captured. During the attempt to arrest him one police officer and a student bystander were killed.

Armas Marcelo's novels *El árbol del bien y del mal* and *Las naves quemadas* follow his continuing interest in Latin America expressed here in the imaginary country of Salbago. *Las naves quemadas,* published in English as *Ships Afire,* examines, in a style redolent of the Latin American magic realism, the period of Spanish conquest in the New World. The protagonist, Juan Réjon, and his buccaneer crew settle on Sabalgo, a fictitious Caribbean island, and nearly wipe out the indigenous population. Over the next generation the anything-goes city of Royal is built, and Juan's son Alvaro heads off to Santo Domingo and becomes rich as a slaver. Eventually he returns to Sabalgo, half crazed from years of searching for El Dorado and well addicted to coca. A reviewer for *Publishers Weekly* wrote, "First published in Spain, Armas Marcelo's wild epic explores the fine line between reality and fantasy, the point at which obsessive greed and lust twist into madness. This exaggerated adventure tale also embodies a biting criticism of conquest, epitomized by the 16th century Spanish Empire and its destructive craze for power." The conquistadors, both father and son, end their days as lunatics as the Dutch raid and pillage Sabalgo. The *Publishers Weekly* writer concluded, "The author's luscious style matches the exotic content: every page erupts with rococo exotic language, with lengthy, convoluted, enticing constructions, all admirably translated by Arvio."

In 1991 Armas Marcelo wrote a literary biography of his close friend Peruvian novelist Mario Vargas Llosa, *El vicio de escribir.* The Spanish Web site *Cultura* wrote, "*El vicio de escribir* is one of the most in-depth political and literary biographies on this important Hispano-Peruvian novelist published to date."

Así en la Habana como en el cielo is a close look at Cuba from the standpoint of a Spaniard (and in some ways even more as Canarian) with deep ethnic ties to the Cuban people. A. Jesús Garcia Calero noted in his introduction to an interview with Armas Marcelo published on the *Pearson College* Web site, "J. J. Armas Marcelo has managed to write a very astute novel that clearly shows the in certitudes and the hopes of the fin-de-regime Castro Cuba. In his scrupulously described 'ruined sanctuary' that is Havana, the author has drawn a community that feels itself isolated, tired of Fidel and the embargo, with half its heart in exile and the other contemplating a future as complicated as its present, defending itself with sarcasm, resistance, illusions, and santería."

Despite declarations to the contrary, Armas Marcelo returned to Cuba and published *El Niño de Luto y el cocinero del Papa,* a novel based on the historic visit of Pope John Paul II to Cuba. In this novel told in the form of a far-reaching thriller, the reader discovers the secrets of Diosmediante Malaspina, a lawyer, deeply religious Catholic, and active homosexual better known in Havana as Niño de Luto, whose religious faith leads him to believe that John Paul II is divinely sent to end the communist dictatorship in Cuba.

The second equally eccentric character is Angelo Ferri, the pope's personal chef, who decides to stay behind and live in Havana with Mauro Manfreddi, a well-known ex-member of the Red Brigades, and open La Creazione, an Italian restaurant in Havana's Paseo del Prado. Armas Marcelo continues the narration in a Balzacian fashion, introducing many peripheral characters to create a rich portrait of Havana. A contributor to *Exodusltd.com,* wrote that *El Niño de Luto y el cocinero del Papa* "confirms that Armas Marcelo is the most Latin American of the Spanish novelists and the most Spanish of the Latin Americans."

In addition to his writing and journalism, Armas Marcelo is the director of the literary television program *Los Libros* broadcast on TVE (Television España).

BIOGRAPHICAL AND CRITICAL SOURCES:

PERIODICALS

Booklist, May 1, 1999, Elinor Ibanez Takenaga, review of *Así en la Habana como en el cielo,* p. 1583.

Village Voice Literary Supplement, October 1988, review of *Ships Afire,* p. 7.

Publishers Weekly, May 13, 1988, review of *Ships Afire,* p. 269.

Washington Post Book World, October 13, 1991, Gustavo Perez Firmat, review of *Ships Afire,* p. 14.

OTHER

Exodusltd., http://www.exodusltd.com/ (February 28, 2002), review of *El Niño de Luto y el cocinero del Papa.*

Pearson College Spanish Department Web site, http://www.pearson-college.uwc.ca/ (May 9, 2002), interview with J. J. Armas Marcelo.

Portalatino, http://www.portalatino.com/ (February 28, 2002).

Terra, http://www.terra.es/cultura/ (February 19, 2001); (May 9, 2002) Lola Canales, review of *El niño de luto y el cocinero del Papa;* (May 9, 2002) interview with J. J. Armas Marcelo.*

*   *   *

ATKINS, Ace

PERSONAL: Born in Alabama. *Education:* Received degree from Auburn University.

ADDRESSES: Home—Mississippi. *Agent*—c/o Author Mail, St. Martin's Press, 175 Fifth Ave., New York, NY 10010. *E-mail*—atkinsace@aol.com.

CAREER: Author. *St. Petersburg Times,* St. Petersburg, FL, former correspondent; *Tampa Tribune,* Tampa, FL, former crime reporter.

AWARDS, HONORS: Livingston Award for outstanding journalism, 1999, 2000; Pulitzer Prize nomination for journalism, 2000.

WRITINGS:

"NICK TRAVERS" SERIES; MYSTERY NOVELS

Crossroad Blues, St. Martin's (New York, NY), 1998.
Leavin' Trunk Blues, Thomas Dunne Books (New York, NY), 2000.
Dark End of the Street, HarperCollins (New York, NY), 2002.

SIDELIGHTS: Former crime reporter Ace Atkins's first novel is *Crossroad Blues.* The story follows Nick—an ex-New Orleans Saints football player, blues historian, part-time Tulane University instructor, Guitar Slim biographer, and regular harmonica player at JoJo's Blues Bar—as he wades through a sea of psychopaths while investigating the disappearance of Michael Baker, another music history professor at Tulane. Baker was hunting down unknown recordings of Robert Johnson, a legendary jazz musician who disappeared in the 1930s. "Despite the weight of two overused [mystery] genre staples (The New Orleans setting and an ex-sports star as hero)," said a *Publishers Weekly* critic, *Crossroad Blues* is "lively" and "a pleasure" to read. The critic hoped Nick Travers would reappear in future mysteries. Likewise, *Booklist* reviewer Bill Ott proclaimed that "Atkins has combined several recurring [genre] themes . . . but he's stirred them in his own special way, producing one of the year's most promising new series." *Crossroad Blues'* "plotting is endlessly confusing, and the narration heavily laden with raw language and raw sex," according to a contributor to *Kirkus Reviews,* who nevertheless added that "the author's energy, talent, and deep love of music" compensate for any shortcomings. And Marilyn Stasio implied in her *New York Times Book Review* that, stylistically, Atkins would benefit from being less "fancy and more emotionally attuned," but she complimented this "frisky debut mystery." Stasio concluded that "when his old guys open up you can really hear the music everybody talks about so reverently."

Nick Travers returns in *Leavin' Trunk Blues,* a novel one *Publishers Weekly* critic called "even darker, sadder and much colder" than the first book. This time Travers goes to Chicago to help former blues singer Ruby Walker. Ruby has been imprisoned for forty years for the murder of her husband, Billy Lyons, but she still claims she is innocent. When Travers agrees to help her he finds himself pursued by a ruthless killer named Stagger Lee. "Nick suffers almost more pain than the book's short length can bear," said the *Publishers Weekly* reviewer, but the story is made enjoyable nevertheless by Atkins's strong characterizations and "contagious love for the blues."

In 2001 Atkins signed a six-figure deal to write two more "Nick Travers" novels, one of which, *Dark End of the Street,* was published in 2002.

BIOGRAPHICAL AND CRITICAL SOURCES:

PERIODICALS

Booklist, August, 1998, Bill Ott, review of *Crossroad Blues,* p. 1972.
Entertainment Weekly, December 11, 1998.

Kirkus Reviews, September 15, 1998, review of *Crossroad Blues,* p. 1332.

Library Journal, October 1, 1998, review of *Crossroad Blues,* p. 139.

New York Times Book Review, November 8, 1998, Marilyn Stasio, review of *Crossroad Blues,* p. 32.

Publishers Weekly, August 31, 1998, review of *Crossroad Blues,* p. 51; May 29, 2000, review of *Leavin' Trunk Blues,* p. 54.

OTHER

Ace Atkins Web site, http://www.aceatkins.com/ (August 25, 2002).*

* * *

ATKINS, Eileen 1934-

PERSONAL: Born June 16, 1934, in London, England; daughter of Arthur Thomas (a utility meter reader) and Annie Ellen (a seamstress; maiden name, Elkins) Atkins; married Julian Glover (an actor; divorced); married Bill Shepherd (a television producer), 1977. *Education:* Attended Guildhall School of Music and Drama.

ADDRESSES: Agent—Jonathan Altaras Associates, 2 Goodwin's Ct., London WC2N 4LL, England.

CAREER: Actress and writer.

Film appearances include *Inadmissible Evidence,* Paramount, 1968; *The Devil within Her* (also known as *The Baby, I Don't Want to Be Born, It's Growing inside Her, The Monster,* and *Sharon's Baby*), American International Pictures, 1975; *Equus,* United Artists, 1977; *Raku Fire,* 1977; *The Dresser,* Columbia, 1983; *Nelly's Version,* Channel 4 Films, 1983; *The Vision,* 1987; *Let Him Have It,* Fine Line Features, 1991; *Wolf,* Columbia, 1994; *Jack and Sarah,* Gramercy Pictures, 1995; *The Avengers,* Warner Bros., 1998; *Women Talking Dirty,* 1999; *Gosford Park,* 2001; *The Hours,* 2002; *American Girl,* 2003; and *Cold Mountain,* 2003.

Television movie appearances include *The Big Man Coughed and . . .* (also known as *The Wednesday Play: The Big Man Coughed and . . .*), BBC, 1966; *Oliver Twist,* CBS, 1982; *Roman Holiday,* NBC, 1987; *A Hazard of Hearts,* CBS, 1987; *Cold Comfort Farm,* BBC, 1995; *The Sleeper,* 2000; *Wit,* HBO, 2001; and *Bertie and Elizabeth,* 2002.

Television series appearances include *In My Defence,* 1990. Television miniseries appearances include *Smiley's People,* syndicated, 1982; *The Modern World: Ten Great Writers,* 1988; *China Rising: The Epic History of Twentieth-Century China,* 1992; *A Dance to the Music of Time,* 1997; and "The Hand of God," *Talking Heads 2,* BBC, 1998. Appearances on episodic television include *Tales* (also known as *Patricia Highsmith's Tales* and *Cadavres exquis*), Antenne 6. Other television appearances include *The Burston Rebellion,* BBC, 1985; *The Stuff of Madness,* Harlech Television, 1990; *The Maitlands,* 1993; and *David Copperfield,* 2000. Also appeared in *Breaking Up* and *Shades of Darkness.*

Appearances on television specials include *Hilda Lessways,* BBC, 1959; *An Age of Kings,* BBC, 1960; *The Three Sisters,* BBC, 1969; *A Midsummer Night's Dream* BBC, 1971; *The Lady's Not for Burning,* PBS, 1974; *The Lady from the Sea,* 1974; *Electra,* 1974; "She Fell among Thieves," *Play of the Week,* BBC-2, 1978; *Titus Andronicus* BBC-2, 1985; *The Madonna of Medjugorje,* PBS, 1988; *A Room of One's Own,* 1990; "The Lost Language of Cranes," *Great Performances,* PBS, 1992; and *Madame Bovary,* PBS, 2000.

Television series work includes (creator, with Jean Marsh) *Upstairs, Downstairs,* London Weekend Television, 1971-75, broadcast on *Masterpiece Theatre,* PBS, 1974-77; and (creator, with Marsh), *The House of Elliott,* BBC, 1991-94.

Stage appearances include *Harvey,* Repertory Theatre, Bangor, Ireland, 1952; *Love's Labour's Lost,* Open Air Theatre, London, England, 1953; *Roots,* Old Vic Theatre, London, 1960; *The Square,* Bromley Theatre, London, 1961; *Twelfth Night,* Old Vic Company, 1962; *Richard III,* Old Vic Company, 1962; *The Tempest,* Old Vic Company, 1962; *Semi-Detached,* Saville Theatre, London, 1962; *The Provok'd Wife,* Vaudeville Theatre, London, 1963; *Exit the King,* Edinburgh Festival, Edinburgh, Scotland, then Royal Court Theatre, London, 1963; *Twelfth Night,* Ravinia Festival, 1964; *Hamlet,* Ravinia Festival, 1964; *The Killing of Sister George,* Old Vic Theatre, then Duke of York's Theatre, London, 1965 later Belasco Theatre, New York City, 1966; *The Restoration of Arnold Middleton,* Royal Court Theatre, 1966; *The Promise,* Henry Miller's Theatre, New York City, 1967; *The Cocktail Party,* Chichester Festival, Chichester, England, then Wyndham's Theatre, London, 1968; *The Sleeper's Den,* Royal Court Theatre, 1969; *Vivat! Vivat Regina!,* Chichester Festival, then Picadilly Theatre, London, 1970, later Broadhurst Theatre, New York City, 1972; *Suzanna Andler,* Aldwych Theatre, London, 1973; *As You Like It,* Royal Shakespeare Company, Stratford-upon-Avon, England, 1973; *Heartbreak House,* National Theatre Company, Old Vic Theatre, 1975; *Saint Joan,* Old Vic Theatre, 1977; *The Night of the Tribades,* Helen Hayes Theatre, New York City, 1977; *Twelfth Night,* Old Vic Theatre, 1978; *The Lady's Not for Burning,* Old Vic Theatre, 1978; *Mary Barnes,* Long Wharf Theatre, New Haven, CT, 1980; *Passion Play,* Royal Shakespeare Company, Aldwych Theatre, 1981; *Sergeant Musgrave's Dance,* Old Vic Theatre, 1984; *Medea,* Young Vic Theatre, London, 1986; *Let Us Go Then, You and I: The Life and Poetry of T. S. Eliot,* Lyric Theatre, London, 1986; *Tuesday's Child,* Stratford East Theatre, London, 1986; *Thursday's Ladies,* Apollo Theatre, London, 1987; *The Winter's Tale,* National Theatre Company, Cottesloe Theatre, 1988; *Cymbeline,* National Theatre Company, 1988; *Mountain Language,* Lyttelton Theatre, London, 1988; *Exclusive,* Strand Theatre, London, 1989; *A Room of One's Own,* Hampstead Theatre, London, 1989, then Arena Stage, Washington, D.C., 1993-94; *Prin,* Manhattan Theatre Club, New York City, 1990; *The Night of the Iguana,* National Theatre Company, 1992; *Vita and Virginia,* Ambassadors' Theatre, London, 1993; *Gypsy of the Year,* St. James Theatre, New York City, 1994; *Indiscretions* Ethel Barrymore Theatre, New York City, 1995; *John Gabriel Borkman,* National Theatre Company, 1996; and *A Delicate Balance,* Theatre Royale, London, 1997. Also appeared in productions with Memorial Theatre Company, Stratford-upon-Avon, 1957-59.

Taped readings include *King John,* Arkangel, 1998; and *Romeo and Juliet,* 1998. Videotaped performances include *Virginia Woolf: A Room of One's Own* (solo reading), Films for the Humanities and Sciences, 1997.

AWARDS, HONORS: Evening Standard Award, best actress, 1965, 1967 for *The Killing of Sister George;* Drama Desk Award, outstanding performance, and *Variety* Award, 1972, both for *Vivat! Vivat Regina!;* Drama Desk Award, best featured actress in a play, 1978, for *The Night of the Tribades;* British Academy Award, 1985; Olivier Award, Society of West End Theatre, 1988, for *Cymbeline;* named Commander, Order of the British Empire, 1990; Drama Desk Award, best solo performance, 1991, for *A Room of One's Own; Evening Standard* British Film Award, best screenplay, 1997, for *Mrs. Dalloway.*

WRITINGS:

Vita and Virginia (play, based on correspondence between Vita Sackville-West and Virginia Woolf, produced at Ambassadors' Theatre, 1993), Samuel French (London, England), 1995.
Mrs. Dalloway (also known as *Virginia Woolf's Mrs. Dalloway;* based on the novel by Virginia Woolf), First Look Pictures, 1997.

Co-creator, with Jean Marsh, of *Upstairs, Downstairs,* London Weekend Television, 1971-75, and *The House of Elliott,* BBC, 1991-94.

SIDELIGHTS: Eileen Atkins is considered one of the most prominent women in contemporary British theatre. Well known for her portrayal of writer Virginia Woolf in such productions as *Vita and Virginia* and *A Room of One's Own,* Atkins grew up in an atmosphere much different from that of Woolf. Atkins was raised in a housing project in London, but on the basis of her talent she earned a scholarship to study drama, after which she embarked on a successful career with the Royal Shakespeare Company and Britain's National Theatre. Along with her many performances in films, television, and on stage, she is also known as the co-creator (with Jean Marsh) of the highly successful television series *Upstairs, Downstairs.*

In addition to portraying Woolf in the one-woman show *A Room of One's Own,* Atkins wrote *Vita and Virginia,* which is drawn from Woolf's correspondence with her lesbian lover, the novelist Vita Sackville-West. Reviewing the New York production, with Atkins as Woolf and Vanessa Redgrave as Sackville-West, Lloyd Rose of the *Washington Post* questioned the need for such distinguished actresses in what he called "a slight vehicle." The problem, he wrote, was that "while Woolf is fascinating, Sackville-West, though full of joie de vivre, is not very interesting. Emotionally, she's high-strung and gushy, and as a novelist she produces things with titles such as 'Seducers in Ecuador.'" Likewise a reviewer in *Time* faulted the raw material from which the story was extracted: "The words are beautiful, but the subject matter—auto trips, Virginia's health, contemporaries unknown to us—becomes tedious." On the other hand, David Patrick Stearns in *USA Today* maintained that the production "shows that two radiant actresses and minimal scenery can be quite enough." The writing itself he called "a discreetly intimate pairing of minds."

With *Mrs. Dalloway,* Atkins set herself to an even greater task. This time around, she sought to write a screenplay for a work that many critics have compared to James Joyce's *Ulysses* with regard to the difficulties involved in translating it to the screen. Woolf's novel is a chronicle of a single day (in this case, June 13, 1923), in which the protagonist undertakes a series of seemingly unremarkable activities around London. Mrs. Dalloway, portrayed by Vanessa Redgrave in the film, spends the day preparing for a party she is to host that evening, but as with Joyce's Leopold Bloom, the Jewish advertising salesman making his rounds in Dublin, the story takes place primarily in the protagonist's head, in thoughts portrayed on the page by the use of stream-of-consciousness techniques.

Countenancing the challenge to which Atkins had set herself, some critics were more than a little skeptical as to the results—though again, they faulted the material more than the writer herself—while others expressed admiration for the sheer ambition of the undertaking. "In a movie universe clanking with special effects," wrote Jack Kroll in *Newsweek*, "*Mrs. Dalloway* dares to luxuriate in art's greatest special effect: language." Lisa Schwarzbaum of *Entertainment Weekly,* after confessing that she had thought the book "unfilmable," credited Atkins and director Marleen Gorris for "a remarkable job of suggesting the inner mental jumble Woolf strove to convey."

BIOGRAPHICAL AND CRITICAL SOURCES:

BOOKS

Contemporary Theatre, Film, and Television, volume 32, Gale (Detroit, MI), 2000.

Zucker, Carole. *In the Company of Actors: Reflections on the Craft of Acting.* Theatre Arts Book/ Routledge (New York, NY), 1999.

PERIODICALS

Advocate, March 3, 1998, Jan Stuart, review of *Mrs. Dalloway,* pp. 55-56.
Entertainment Weekly, March 6, 1998, Lisa Schwarzbaum, review of *Mrs. Dalloway,* p. 55.
Los Angeles Times, February 15, 1998, Susan Salter Reynolds, "A Woolf at Her Door: Actress-Screenwriter Eileen Atkins, Bowing to Her Muse, Takes *Mrs. Dalloway* to the Movies" (profile), p. 4.
National Review, March 23, 1998, John Simon, review of *Mrs. Dalloway,* pp. 57-58.
New Republic, March 9, 1998, Stanley Kauffmann, review of *Mrs. Dalloway,* pp. 28-29.
Newsweek, March 2, 1998, Jack Kroll, review of *Mrs. Dalloway,* p. 80.
Time, December 5, 1994, review of *Vita and Virginia,* p. 94.
USA Today, November 25, 1994, David Patrick Stearns, review of *Vita and Virginia,* p. D4.
Washington Post, May 15, 1994, Elizabeth Kastor, "Eileen Atkins, Reveling in the Habit of Freedom" (profile), p. G4; November 22, 1994, Lloyd Rose, review of *Vita and Virginia,* p. D2.*

*   *   *

AVALOS, Luis 1946-

PERSONAL: Surname is pronounced with accent on the first "A"; born September 2, 1946, in Havana, Cuba; immigrated with his family to the United States, 1946; son of Jose Antonio (a sugar refiner) and Estrella (a dressmaker; maiden name, De Leon) Avalos. *Hobbies and other interests:* Swimming, tennis.

ADDRESSES: Agent—SDB Partners, Inc., 1801 Avenue of the Stars #902, Los Angeles, CA 90067-5981.

CAREER: Actor and writer. Resident actor at Lincoln Center Repertory Company, New York, NY, 1969-73. Film appearances include *Badge 373,* Paramount,

1973; *Hot Stuff,* Columbia, 1979; *Sunday Lovers* United Artists, 1980; *The Hunter,* 1980; *Stir Crazy,* Columbia, 1980; *Love Child,* 1982; *Ghost Fever,* 1987; *Criminal Act* 1989; *Fires Within,* 1991; *The Butcher's Wife,* 1991; *Lone Justice 2,* 1995; *Jungle2Jungle,* Buena Vista, 1997; *and Love Stinks,* Independent Artists, 1999.

Appearances in television series include *The Electric Company,* 1973-78; *Highcliffe Manor,* NBC, 1979; *E/R,* CBS, 1984; *I Had Three Wives,* CBS, 1985; *You Again?,* 1986; *Hangin' with Mr. Cooper,* ABC, 1992; and *Ned Blessing: The Story of My Life and Times,* CBS, 1993.

TV movie appearances include *The Ghost of Flight 401,* 1978; *Long Journey Back,* 1978; *Not Just Another Affair,* 1982; *The Fantastic World of D. C. Collins,* NBC, 1984; *Perry Mason: The Case of the Musical Murder,* NBC, 1989; *The Story Lady,* NBC, 1991; *Ned Blessing: The True Story of My Life* (also known as *Lone Justice* and *Ned Blessing*), CBS, 1992; *Gambler V: Playing for Keeps,* 1994; *The Rockford Files: If It Bleeds . . . It Leads,* CBS, 1999; *Noriega: God's Favorite,* Showtime, 2000; and *Columbo: Murder with Too Many Notes,* 2000.

Appearances in television miniseries include *Fresno,* CBS, 1986; *Changes* NBC, 1991; and *OP Center* (also known as *Tom Clancy's "OP Center"*), ABC, 1995. Appearances on television specials include *Side by Side,* 1976; *Pals,* 1981; *The Boys in Blue,* CBS, 1984; *George Burns Comedy Hour,* CBS, 1985; *Slickers,* NBC, 1987; *Camp California,* ABC, 1989; and *Belles of Bleecker Street,* ABC, 1991. Appearances in TV pilots *Condo,* 1983; *Hacienda Heights,* NBC, 1996; and *Comfort, Texas,* ABC, 1997.

Appearances on episodic television include "The Condemned," *Kojak,* 1977; *Barney Miller,* ABC, 1978; *The Jeffersons,* CBS, 1979; "The Lottery," *The Incredible Hulk,* CBS, 1980; *Soap,* 1981; *Fame,* NBC, 1981; "Up in Arms," *Hill Street Blues,* ABC, 1981; "Your Kind, My Kind, Humankind," *Hill Street Blues,* ABC, 1981; *Making a Living,* ABC, 1981; *Archie Bunker's Place,* CBS, 1982; *Mama's Family,* CBS, 1982; *Second Family Tree,* CBS, 1982; *Jennifer Slept Here,* NBC, 1983; "Grand Illusion," *Simon & Simon,* CBS, 1983; *Benson,* ABC, 1984; *You Again?,* NBC, 1986; "Button

Your Beau," *Marblehead Manor,* 1988; *Empty Nest,* NBC, 1988; *Full House,* ABC, 1988; *Trial and Error,* CBS, 1988; "Hell and High Water," *ER,* NBC, 1995; "War Cries," *JAG,* CBS, 1995; "Red Cadillac," *Land's End,* 1996; "Pieces of 8 Is Enough," *Land's End,* 1996; "Where's 'Swaldo," *NYPD Blue,* ABC, 1996; *Good News,* UPN, 1997; *Head over Heels,* UPN, 1997; *Texas Ranger,* CBS, 1999; and *Resurrection Blvd.,* Showtime, 2000.

Stage appearances include *Never Jam Today,* City Center Theatre, New York City, 1968; *Camino Real,* Lincoln Center Repertory Company, New York City, 1969; *El Grande de Coca-Cola,* Plaza Nine Theatre, New York City, 1975; and *As You Like It,* New York Shakespeare Festival, New York City, 1976. Also appeared in *The Good Woman of Setzuan, Kool Aid, Armedians, Payment as Pledged, Save Grand Central, Marco Polo, Beggar on Horseback, Antigone, A Streetcar Named Desire, Don Juan in Hell,* and *Twelve Angry Men,* all Lincoln Center Repertory Company.

AWARDS, HONORS: Named Best Actor in Theatre, Association of Hispanic Critics, 1974; Hispanic of the Year, *Caminos* magazine, 1984; La Palma Espinada, Cuban American Cultural Institute, 1999; NOSOTROS Golden Eagle for Outstanding Achievement in Film and Television, for *Condo.* Recipient of numerous other awards from community organizations; commended by the California state senate, the Consulate general of Mexico, and the mayor, county, and city council of Los Angeles.

WRITINGS:

(With others) *Ghost Fever* (screenplay), 1986.
(With Julio Vera) *Diplomatic Ties,* Procter & Gamble, 1987.

Wrote *El Regalo de Paquito* and translated it into English as *Paquito's Christmas* (musical); wrote *Ay Caramba.*

SIDELIGHTS: Recognized for his work in the community—not only the Cuban-American and Hispanic-American communities, but his adopted hometown, Los Angeles—Luis Avalos has appeared in numerous television programs. In addition to some 600 segments of Public Television's *The Electric Company,* he has performed in shows ranging from *Rockford Files* to *Soap* to *NYPD Blue.*

Avalos has written for film as well as for the stage. His play *El Regalo de Paquito,* presented in English as *Paquito's Christmas,* has become a holiday tradition at the Los Angeles Theatre Center. Avalos's screenwriting credits include his work as cowriter of the script for *Ghost Fever,* a 1987 comedy in which he also starred opposite Sherman Helmsley. Set in Georgia, the movie tells the story of police officers who are sent to serve an eviction notice on two elderly sisters living in an old mansion. Instead, the patrolmen find two gorgeous young women, but that is only the beginning of the mysteries they uncover in what turns out to be a haunted house.

BIOGRAPHICAL AND CRITICAL SOURCES:

BOOKS

Contemporary Theatre, Film, and Television, volume 35, Gale (Detroit, MI), 2001.

PERIODICALS

Los Angeles Times, September 16, 1987, Leonard Klady, review of *Ghost Fever,* p. 7; December 16, 1994, F. Kathleen Foley, review of *Paquito's Christmas,* p. F28.*

B

BADOVINAC, Zdenka 1958-

PERSONAL: Born May 20, 1958, in Novo Mesto, Slovenia; parents' names, Niko and Mira. *Ethnicity:* "Slovenian."

ADDRESSES: Home—Gregorčičeva 19, Ljubljana, Slovenia. *Office*—Moderna Galerija Ljubljana, Tomšičeva 14, 1000 Ljubljana, Slovenia; fax: +386-1-2514120. *E-mail*—zdenka.badovinac@mg-lj.si.

CAREER: Moderna Galerija Ljubljana, Ljubljana, Slovenia, exhibitions curator, 1987-92, director, 1992—.

WRITINGS:

(Editor, with Mika Briski and Iara Boubnova, and contributor) *Body and the East: From the 1960s to the Present* (bilingual in English and Slovenian), MIT Press (Cambridge, MA), 1999.

*   *   *

BAKER, G. P.
   See BAKER, Gordon (Park)

*   *   *

BAKER, Gordon (Park) 1938-2002
   (G. P. Baker)

OBITUARY NOTICE—See index for *CA* sketch: Born April 20, 1938, in Englewood, NJ; died of melanoma, June 25, 2002, in Woodstock, Oxfordshire, England.

Philosopher, educator, and author. Baker went to England as a Marshall Scholar in 1960 and settled in that country for the rest of his career. Except for a brief time at the University of Kent at Canterbury, his base of operations was Oxford University, where he served as a fellow and tutor in philosophy and an enthusiastic and popular lecturer at St. John's College. It was there that Baker met Peter M. S. Hacker, and the two began a collaboration which resulted in the books for which Baker may be best remembered. Baker's original focus was on the philosophy of Ludwig Wittgenstein, whose writings are difficult to interpret and easy to misunderstand. Baker and Hacker's weighty two-volume interpretation, *Wittgenstein: Understanding and Meaning* and *Wittgenstein: Rules, Grammar, and Necessity,* was highly commended for the rigor of the authors' research as well as the clarity of the published work. Baker's other collaborations with Hacker include an interpretation of the philosophy of Wittgenstein's predecessor Gottlob Frege and a critical volume titled *Language, Sense, and Nonsense: A Critical Investigation into Modern Theories of Language.* In later years Baker turned his attention to the French mathematician and philosopher René Descartes. With his companion at the time, Kathleen Morris, he wrote *Descartes' Dualism,* published in 1996, as well as a second work on Descartes and his own *Meditations,* which remained unpublished at the time of Baker's death. Some of Baker's writings appeared under the name G. P. Baker.

OBITUARIES AND OTHER SOURCES:

PERIODICALS

Independent (London, England), July 3, 2002, obituary by Peter Hacker, p. 18.
Times (London, England), July 18, 2002.

BALABAN, Bob
　See BALABAN, Robert Elmer

＊　　＊　　＊

BALABAN, Robert Elmer 1945-
　(Bob Balaban)

PERSONAL: Born August 16, 1945, in Chicago, IL; son of Elmer (a movie theater chain co-owner) and Eleanor (maiden name, Pottasch) Balaban; married Lynn Grossman (a writer), April 1, 1977; children: Mariah, Hazel.

ADDRESSES: Agent—Susan Smith & Associates, 121 North San Vicente Blvd., Beverly Hills, CA 90211.

CAREER: Writer, director, and actor. Stage appearances include *You're a Good Man, Charlie Brown,* Theatre 80 St. Mark's, New York City, 1967; "Visit from Mamaroneck," and Borden Eisler, "Visitor from Forest Hills," *Plaza Suite,* Plymouth Theatre, 1968; *Up Eden,* Jan Hus Playhouse, New York City, 1968; *The White House Murder Case,* Circle in the Square, New York City, 1970; *The Basic Training of Pavlo Hummel,* New York Shakespeare Festival, Public Theatre, New York City, 1971; *Who Wants to Be the Lone Ranger?,* Center Theatre Group, New Theatre for Now, Los Angeles, 1971; *The Children,* New York Shakespeare Festival, Public Theatre, 1972; *Some of My Best Friends,* Longacre Theatre, New York City, 1977; *The Inspector General,* Circle in the Square, 1978; *Marie and Bruce,* New York Shakespeare Festival, Public Theatre, 1980; *The Three Sisters,* Manhattan Theatre; Club, New York City, 1982; *The Boys Next Door,* McCarter Theatre, Princeton, NJ, 1986; *Speed the Plow,* Broadway production, 1991; *Some Americans Abroad,* off-Broadway production, 1991; and *The Water Engine & Mr. Happiness,* Atlantic Theater Company, New York City, 1999. Work as stage director includes *Girls, Girls, Girls,* New York Shakespeare Festival, Public Theatre, 1980; *Vick's Boy,* Theater Off Park, New York City, 1999; and *Y2K,* Humana Theatre Festiville, 1999, then Lucille Lortel Theatre, New York City, 1999-2000. Also directed *Tennessee and Me,* Ensemble Studio Theatre, New York City.

Film appearances include *Midnight Cowboy,* United Artists, 1969; *Me Natalie,* National General, 1969; *The Strawberry Statement,* Metro-Goldwyn-Mayer, 1970; *Catch 22,* Paramount, 1970; *Making It,* Twentieth Century-Fox, 1971; *Day for Night,* Columbia, 1973; *Bank Shot,* United Artists, 1974; *Report to the Commissioner,* United Artists, 1975; *Close Encounters of the Third Kind,* Columbia, 1977; *Girlfriends,* Warner Bros., 1978; *First Love,* 1979; *Altered States,* Warner Bros., 1980; *Absence of Malice,* Columbia, 1981; *Prince of the City,* Warner Bros., 1981; *Whose Life Is It, Anyway?,* Metro-Goldwyn-Mayer/United Artists, 1981; *In Our Hands,* Almi Classics, 1984; *2010,* Metro-Goldwyn-Mayer/United Artists, 1984; *End of the Line,* Orion Classics, 1987; "Buy Your Slippers" and "The Whale Sandwich," *Funny,* 1988; *Dead Bang,* 1989; *Alice,* 1990; *Little Man Tate,* 1991; *Bob Roberts,* 1992; *For Love or Money,* 1993; *Amos & Andrew,* 1993; *Greedy,* 1994; *City Slickers II: The Legend of Curly's Gold,* 1994; *Pie in the Sky,* Fine Line, 1996; *Waiting for Guffman,* Sony Pictures Classics, 1996; *Conversation with the Beast,* 1996; *Clockwatchers,* Artistic License, 1997; *Deconstructing Harry,* Fine Line, 1997; *The Definite Maybe,* 1997; *The Making of "Close Encounters of the Third Kind,"* 1998; *Cradle Will Rock,* 1999; *Jakob the Liar,* Buena Vista, 1999; *Three to Tango,* Warner Bros., 1999; *Natural Selection,* 1999; *Best in Show,* Warner Bros., 2000; *Tex, the Passive-Aggressive Gunslinger,* 2000; *The Mexican,* 2001; *Plan B,* 2001; *Gosford Park,* 2001; *Ghost World,* 2001; *The Majestic,* 2001; *5-25-77,* 2003.

Television movie appearances include *Marriage: Year One,* NBC, 1971; *The Face of Fear,* CBS, 1990; *Unnatural Pursuits,* Arts and Entertainment, 1994; *The Late Shift,* HBO, 1996; *Giving up the Ghost,* Lifetime, 1998; and *Swing Vote,* ABC, 1999. Television movie work as director includes *The Brass Ring,* 1983; and "The 5:24," *Subway Stories: Tales from the Underground,* HBO, 1997. Episodic television work as director includes "Trick or Treat," *Tales from the Darkside,* syndicated, 1983; "Fine Tuning," *Amazing Stories,* NBC, 1985; *Eerie, Indiana,* 1991; *Legend,* UPN, 1995; "Great Men," *Oz,* HBO, 1997; *Lateline,* ABC, 1999; *Now and Again,* ABC, 1999; *Strangers with Candy,* Comedy Central, 1999; and *Deadline,* 2000. Work as a director on television specials includes *Penn and Teller's Invisible Thread,* PBS, 1987.

Episodic television appearances include "Back in the World," *Miami Vice,* 1985; "Stone's War," *Miami Vice,* 1986; "Gershwin's Trunk," *Amazing Stories,* 1987;

"The Pitch," "The Ticket," "The Watch: Part 2," "The Shoes," "The Pilot," *Seinfeld,* NBC, 1992-93; *Legend,* UPN, 1995; "The One with Joey's Bag," *Friends,* NBC, 1999; "20 Hours in L.A.," *West Wing,* NBC, 2000; and Frederick Lizzard, "Lizzard's Tale," *Now and Again,* 2000. Made television debut in *The Mod Squad,* ABC; also appeared as Ambrose Riley, "Maude's Ex-Convict," *Maude.* Appearances in television specials include *Invisible Thread,* PBS, 1987.

Appearances on recordings includes original-cast album for *You're a Good Man, Charlie Brown.*

WRITINGS:

The Last Good Time (screenplay), Samuel Goldwyn Company/Apogee Films, 1994.
Close Encounters of the Third Kind Diary, Fromm International (New York, NY), 1997.
(Contributor of story idea) *Gosford Park,* Capitol Films, 2001.
Beware of Dog (juvenile), Scholastic (New York, NY), 2002.

SIDELIGHTS: Writer, actor, and director Bob Balaban has a long history with the movies—one that goes back, quite literally, to before his birth. His father, Elmer, was the last of the seven Balaban brothers who, from a center of power in Chicago, controlled the theatre business throughout much of the Midwest during the first half of the twentieth century. Elmer Balaban is said to have developed an early version of pay television with his idea of using a set-top box into which viewers would insert quarters to receive first-run movies broadcast into the home.

Son Bob got his start with Chicago's Second City troupe and made his off-Broadway debut as Linus in *You're a Good Man, Charlie Brown.* He made an impression on filmgoers in *Midnight Cowboy* (1969) as a nervous youth who purchases Jon Voigt's sexual favors in a public bathroom, and again as an excitable cartographer and translator in *Close Encounters of the Third Kind* (1978). Nearly two decades later, Balaban wrote a memoir of his work on the picture.

In the intervening years and since, Balaban "has been in more movies than Leo the Lion," the trademark of Metro Goldwyn Mayer, according to Luaine Lee in the *Pittsburgh Post-Gazette,* almost always playing "the nerdy egghead or the hyper businessman programming somebody's downfall." In *Gosford Park* (2001), the story of which he helped create, he portrays a 1930s Hollywood producer visiting an English country home at the time of a murder.

Balaban wrote and directed *The Last Good Time* (1995), in which an aging widower (Armin Mueller-Stahl) befriends, and ultimately embarks on a May-December romance with, a beautiful young woman played by Olivia D'Abo. Balaban also wrote *Beware of Dog,* a novel for readers age eight to eleven. In the story, friends Thomas and Violet take Thomas's dog McGrowl for a walk; McGrowl saves their lives but is hit by a truck in the process. The children take the dog to a man they believe is a veterinarian, but who is in fact a villain who turns McGrowl into a robot he intends to use for his own evil purposes. *Beware of Dog* is the first in a series of "McGrowl" books.

BIOGRAPHICAL AND CRITICAL SOURCES:

BOOKS

Contemporary Theatre, Film, and Television, Volume 33, Gale (Detroit, MI), 2001.

PERIODICALS

Atlanta Constitution, April 28, 1995, Eleanor Ringel, review of *The Last Good Time,* p. P4.
Chicago Tribune, May 5, 1995, John Petrakis, review of *The Last Good Time,* p. F7.
Los Angeles Times, April 14, 1995, Peter Rainer, review of *The Last Good Time,* p. 6; December 30, 2001, Kenneth Turan, review of *Gosford Park,* p. F1.
People Weekly, May 22, 1995, Tom Gliatto, review of *The Last Good Time,* p. 18.
Pittsburgh Post-Gazette, December 26, 2001, Luaine Lee, "That's That Guy! Actor Makes Name for Himself as 'The Smart, Efficient Person,'" p. C2.
Publishers Weekly, August 5, 2002, Diane Roback, review of *Beware of Dog,* p. 73.
San Francisco Chronicle, April 28, 1995, Mick LaSalle, review of *The Last Good Time,* p. C3; December 30, 2001, Edward Guthmann, "Bob Balaban Gives the Scoop on 'Gosford Park,'" p. 29.
Video Magazine, January, 1996, Sol Louis, review of *The Last Good Time,* p. 101.*

BARAN, Susan

PERSONAL: Born in New York, NY.

ADDRESSES: Home—New York, NY, and Sag Harbor, NY. *Agent*—c/o Painted Leaf Press, P.O. Box 2480, New York, NY 10109-2480.

CAREER: Dickinson School, founder and director.

WRITINGS:

Harmonious Whole (poetry), Groundwater Press (New York, NY), 1989.
The Necessary Boat (poetry), Painted Leaf Press (New York, NY), 2000.*

*   *   *

BARNETT, Le Roy G. 1941-

PERSONAL: Born February 19, 1941, in St. Louis, MO; son of Lee and Kathleen (Rasmussen) Barnett; married Dorothy Potter (a teacher), June 10, 1972. *Education:* Michigan State University, B.A. (geography), 1972; Western Michigan University, M.L.S. (information science), 1983, Ph.D. (geography), 1979.

ADDRESSES: Home—9713 Looking Glass Brook Rd., Grand Ledge, MI 48837-9270. *E-mail*—dbarnett@arq. net.

CAREER: Motor Wheel Corp., Lansing, MI, inspector, 1973-74; State of Michigan, Lansing, archivist, 1974-97. *Military service:* U.S. Army, 1959-63; became E-5.

WRITINGS:

Checklist of Printed Maps of the Middle West-Michigan, G. K. Hall, 1981.
Mining in Michigan, Northern Michigan University Press, 1983.
Railroads in Michigan, Northern Michigan University Press, 1986.

Shipping Literature of the Great Lakes, Michigan State University Press (Lansing, MI), 1992.
Michigan's Early Military Forces, Wayne State University Press (Detroit, MI), 2002.

Contributor of articles to periodicals. Contributing editor, *Michigan History Magazine,* 1991—.

WORK IN PROGRESS: Roads of Remembrance: The State and Federal Memorial Highways of Michigan; continuing research on Michigan history.

SIDELIGHTS: Lee Roy G. Barnett told *CA:* "As a former reference archivist/librarian, I enjoy preparing union lists and similar access tools that help information providers quickly find facts of interest to their clients. I am also stimulated to write articles about aspects of Michigan's past that are not commonly known by the citizens of this state."

*   *   *

BARRETT, Harrison D(elivan) 1863-1911

PERSONAL: Born April 25, 1863, in Canaan, ME; died January 12, 1911, in Canaan, ME. *Education:* Unitarian Theological Seminary, Meadville, PA, graduated, 1889.

CAREER: Worked as a schoolteacher in Minnesota and Wyoming; became spiritualist lecturer and medium; National Spiritualist Association (now National Spiritualist Association of Churches), founding president, 1893-1911.

WRITINGS:

(Compiler, with A. W. McCoy) *Cassadaga: Its History and Its Teachings,* Gazette Printing (Meadville, PA), 1891.
(Compiler) *Life Work of Mrs. Cora L. V. Richmond,* Hack & Anderson (Chicago, IL), 1895.
Pantheistic Idealism, Glass & Prudhomme (Portland, OR), 1910.

Editor, *Banner of Light,* 1897-1904.*

BAU, Joseph 1920-2002

OBITUARY NOTICE—See index for *CA* sketch: Born June 18, 1920, in Krakow, Poland; died of pneumonia May 24, 2002, in Tel Aviv, Israel. Animator and author. Sometimes called the "Israeli Walt Disney" for his animation work, Bau was immortalized in the movie *Schindler's List,* which documented his secret wedding in a German concentration camp. Bau displayed an early talent for art and attended the University of Plastic Arts in Krakow before the German invasion. Along with his family, he was moved to a Jewish ghetto and then to a concentration camp. Fortunately for him, his artistic skills saved his life when the Germans decided to use him to make maps and signs. What the Nazis did not know, however, was that Bau also employed his skills to forge hundreds of documents which saved many Jewish lives. While in the camp, Bau met his future wife, Rebecca, and the two were secretly married at great risk to their lives. Their fortunes turned when Rebecca managed to have both their names put on the list of Oscar Schindler, who, through bribes and manipulation, managed to save many Jews by having them transferred to be workers in his factory in Czechoslovakia. After the war, Bau reunited with his wife and returned to the university to complete his studies. He then moved to Israel with his family and worked at the Brandwein Institute in Haifa as a graphic artist. Opening his own studio in 1956, Bau began to work on animated films and is credited by many for bringing that art form to Israel. He also produced public service announcements and did the credits for the majority of Israeli films produced during the 1950s, 1960s, and 1970s. In addition, Bau was a highly acclaimed painter and author of the memoir *Dear God, Have You Ever Gone Hungry?* (1982), which was translated into English in 1998. For his work, Bau received a nomination for the 1998 Israel Prize.

OBITUARIES AND OTHER SOURCES:

PERIODICALS

Chicago Tribune, June 14, 2002, section 2, p. 11.
Daily Telegraph (London, England), June 7, 2002, p. 2.
Los Angeles Times, June 13, 2002, p. B12.
Washington Post, June 15, 2002, p. B7.

BAUER, Peter (Thomas) 1915-2002

OBITUARY NOTICE—See index for *CA* sketch: Born November 6, 1915, in Budapest, Hungary; died May 3, 2002, in London, England. Economist, educator, and author. Bauer was a conservative economist who taught at the London School of Economics and was an advisor to former British Prime Minister Margaret Thatcher. The son of a bookmaker, Bauer attended the Scholae Piae in Budapest; when a friend of the family offered to finance his education, he traveled to England, where he managed to matriculate at Gonville and Caius College, Cambridge, despite his limited English. During breaks at Cambridge, Bauer returned to Hungary where he studied law. He completed his economics degree in 1937, returning to Budapest to complete his law degree and serve with the Imperial Hussars. Returning to England, he completed doctoral studies in economics and began teaching at the University of London. This was followed by work as a Cambridge University lecturer in economics from 1948 to 1956 and as the Smuts Reader in Commonwealth Studies from 1956 to 1960. He joined the London School of Economics in 1960, retiring as professor emeritus in 1983. Bauer's interest in Third-World economies had started years earlier when he joined the trading firm Guthrie & Company in the 1940s. The company was involved in the rubber industry in Malaysia, and Bauer was fascinated by the success of small proprietors there. He also studied trade in West Africa through research funded by the Colonial Office. This research led Bauer to conclude, contrary to the popular Keynesian school, that government involvement in business—and especially large infusions of money from foreign nations into Third-World economies—actually helped prolong poverty. Instead, Bauer recommended that poverty could be eased by encouraging governments to grant more freedoms to businesses and individuals so that they could more easily pursue their own initiatives. After being elevated to the House of Lords by Thatcher in 1982, Bauer gained wider attention for his views and became more politically influential as a voice against foreign aid for economic development. He also wrote about his theories in such books as *Economic Analysis and Policy in Underdeveloped Countries* (1958) and *Equality, the Third World, and Economic Delusion* (1981). Though unpopular at first, some of Bauer's ideas gained authority as they were adopted by the Thatcher and Reagan administrations. Bauer was recognized for his achievements in economics with the Milton Friedman Prize for Advancing Liberty. Unfortunately, the award came after his death, and the $500,000 award was given to his estate.

OBITUARIES AND OTHER SOURCES:

PERIODICALS

Guardian (London, England), May 6, 2002.
Los Angeles Times, May 19, 2002, p. B18.
New York Times, May 14, 2002, p. C19.
Times (London, England), May 6, 2002.

*   *   *

BEASLEY, David 1931-

PERSONAL: Born May 4, 1931, in Hamilton, Ontario, Canada; son of James Davis and Marjorie Marcella (Zealand) Beasley; married Violet Esther Nicholas, October 25, 1958 (died November 10, 1999); companion of Michelle Rustan. *Education:* McMaster University, B.A., 1953; Pratt Institute, M.L.S., 1965; New School for Social Research (now New School University), Ph.D., 1982. *Politics:* "Social Democrat."

ADDRESSES: Home and office—150 Norfolk St. S., Simcoe, Ontario, Canada N3Y 2W2; fax: 519-426-0105. *E-mail*—davus@kwic.com.

CAREER: New York Public Research Library, New York, NY, reference librarian, 1965-92; writer, 1992—.

MEMBER: Writers Union of Canada, United Empire Loyalists Association, New York Library Guild (president of local chapter), Phi Beta Mu.

WRITINGS:

The Canadian Don Quixote: The Life and Works of Major John Richardson, Canada's First Novelist, Porcupine's Quill (Erin, Ontario, Canada), 1977.
Through Paphlagonia with a Donkey: A Journey through the Turkish Isfendyars (travel journal), Davus (New York, NY), 1983.
(Editor and author of introduction) *Major Richardson's Short Stories,* Theytus (Penticton, British Columbia, Canada), 1986.
The Suppression of the Automobile, Greenwood Press (Westport, CT), 1988, revised edition published as *Who Really Invented the Automobile?,* Davus (Simcoe, Ontario, Canada), 1997.
How to Use a Research Library, Oxford University Press (New York, NY), 1988, revised edition published as *Beasley's Guide to Library Research,* University of Toronto Press (Toronto, Ontario, Canada), 2000.
That Other God (novel), Davus (Simcoe, Ontario, Canada), 1993.
The Jenny: A New York Library Detective Novel, Davus (Simcoe, Ontario, Canada), 1994.
Hamilton Romance: A Hamilton-Toronto Nexus (fiction), Davus (Simcoe, Ontario, Canada), 1996.
Chocolate for the Poor: A Story of Rape in 1805 (fiction), Davus (Simcoe, Ontario, Canada), 1996.
The Grand Conspiracy: A New York Library Mystery (fiction), Davus (Simcoe, Ontario, Canada), 1997.
Douglas MacAgy and the Foundations of Modern Art Curatorship, Davus (Simcoe, Ontario, Canada), 1998.
Pagan Summer (fiction), Davus (Simcoe, Ontario, Canada), 1998.
Understanding Modern Art: The Boundless Spirit of Clay Edgar Spohn, Davus (Simcoe, Ontario, Canada), 1999.
Aspects of Love: Helen, Caravetti, Adam (fiction), Davus (Simcoe, Ontario, Canada), 2000.
McKee Rankin and the Heyday of the American Theatre, Wilfrid Laurier University Press (Waterloo, Ontario, Canada), 2002.

Consulting editor, *Index to Current Urban Documents,* 1971—.

WORK IN PROGRESS: A historical novel about an escaped slave in Canada; research on American-Canadian history, 1720-1900.

SIDELIGHTS: David Beasley told *CA:* "I am motivated to write by getting as close to the truth of an experience or a subject as possible through the act of writing. In the early days I was interested in the ideas of Gustave Flaubert, the atmospherics of Jean Giano, and other French writers. Lately I have found my ideas about art in accord with my late close friend, the artist Clay Spohn, whose biography I wrote."

"My writing process varies according to the subject. I have written a novel all day every day for six weeks, and written a novel for half-an-hour every morning before going to a job for months. Presently, when writing historical fiction I write in the morning and research in the afternoon.

"I wrote *The Canadian Don Quixote: The Life and Works of Major John Richardson, Canada's First Novelist* because I wanted to show that there was a tradition in Canadian writing and there was a progenitor. Also, I hoped that, by doing this, my Canadian novels and the works of other Canadians would be published. My inspiration in general comes from curiosity about a place, a time, and a subject.

*   *   *

BEEMAN, Randal S(cott) 1963-

PERSONAL: Born July 20, 1963, in Frankfort, KS; son of Keith (a professor of veterinary medicine) and Janet (a homemaker; maiden name, Bonar) Beeman; married Monica Quirarte; children: Augustine, Everett, Winston. *Education:* Kansas State University, B.S., 1987; M.A., 1989; Iowa State University, Ph.D., 1995. *Politics:* "Democrat." *Religion:* Roman Catholic. *Hobbies and other interests:* Poetry.

ADDRESSES: Home—1405 Radcliffe Ave., Bakersfield, CA 93305. *Office*—Department of History, Bakersfield College, 1801 Panorama Dr., Bakersfield, CA 93305. *E-mail*—rbeeman@bc.cc.ca.us.

CAREER: Educator. National Agricultural Center and Hall of Fame, Bonner Springs, KS, curator and assistant director, 1990; Kansas State University, Manhattan, instructor in history, 1990; Metropolitan Community Colleges, Kansas City, MO, adjunct instructor in history, 1990-91; Iowa State University, Ames, instructor in history, 1994; University of Nevada—Las Vegas, visiting assistant professor of history, 1995-96; Bakersfield College, Bakersfield, CA, professor of history, 1996—. Community College of Southern Nevada, adjunct instructor, 1996. Keep Bakersfield Beautiful Foundation, past member of board of directors. Coach of youth baseball and soccer teams.

MEMBER: Organization of American Historians, American Historical Association, California Council for the Promotion of History, Kern County Historical Society (member of board of directors).

WRITINGS:

(With James A. Pritchard) *A Green and Permanent Land: Ecology and Agriculture in the Twentieth Century,* University Press of Kansas (Lawrence, KS), 2001.

Contributor of articles and reviews to periodicals, including *Environmental History, Journal of Sustainable Agriculture, Agricultural History, Journal of Agricultural and Environmental Ethics,* and *Californian.*

WORK IN PROGRESS: Cesar Chavez: Reassessing the Legacy.

BIOGRAPHICAL AND CRITICAL SOURCES:

PERIODICALS

Agricultural History, fall, 2001, James E. Hansen II, review of *A Green and Permanent Land: Ecology and Agriculture in the Twentieth Century,* p. 498.
Choice, September, 2001, M. Taylor, review of *A Green and Permanent Land,* p. 145.

*   *   *

BEHDAD, Ali 1961-

PERSONAL: Born May 22, 1961, in Sabzevar, Iran; naturalized U.S. citizen; son of Hassan (a banker) and Fatemeh (a homemaker; maiden name, Oskovi) Behdad. *Ethnicity:* "Persian." *Education:* University of California, Berkeley, B.A., 1983; University of Michigan, Ann Arbor, M.A., 1986, Ph.D. (comparative literature), 1990, Middlebury College, M.A. (French), 1988. *Politics:* Democrat. *Religion:* Muslim. *Hobbies and other interests:* Swimming, interior design.

ADDRESSES: Home—3425 Inglewood Blvd., Los Angeles, CA 90066. *Office*—Department of English, Rolfe Hall, Rm 3321, University of California, Los Angeles, Los Angeles, CA 90066; fax: 310-206-5093. *E-mail*—behdad@humnet.ucla.edu.

CAREER: University of California, Los Angeles, associate professor, then professor of English, beginning c. 1993.

MEMBER: Modern Language Association, MESA.

AWARDS, HONORS: University of California, Los Angeles President's fellowship; HIR fellowship, UCI.

WRITINGS:

Belated Travelers: Orientalism in the Age of Colonial Dissolution, Duke University Press (Durham, NC), 1994.

Contributor of articles to periodicals, including *L'Esprit Createur, Diaspora,* and *Aztlan.* Contributor to anthologies, including *Centuries' Ends, Narrative Means,* edited by Robert Newman, Stanford University Press, 1996; *Identity, Violence, and Self-Determination,* edited by Samuel Weber and Peter van der Veer, Stanford University Press, 1997; and *New Directions in the Postcolonial Theory,* edited by Fawzia Afzal-Khan, Duke University Press, 1998.*

*   *   *

BELZER, Richard 1944-

PERSONAL: Born August 4, 1944, in Bridgeport, CT; son of Charles (a candy and tobacco retailer) and Francis Belzer; married Gail Susan Ross (divorced); married Dalia Danoch (divorced); married Harlee McBride (an actress), 1983; children: (third marriage) two. *Education:* Attended Dean Junior College, Franklin, MA, for one year. *Hobbies and other interests:* Reading newspapers.

ADDRESSES: Agent—Panacea Entertainment, 2705 Glendower Ave., Los Angeles, CA 90027.

CAREER: Actor, stand-up comedian, producer, and writer. Previously worked as a newspaper writer, jewelry salesperson, dock worker, census taker, disk jockey, and teacher. *Military service:* Served briefly in the U.S. Army during the early 1960s; discharged on July 22, 1964.

Film appearances include *The Groove Tube,* Levitt-Pickman, 1974; *Fame,* Metro-Goldwyn-Mayer/United Artists, 1980; *Author! Author!,* Twentieth Century-Fox, 1982; *Night Shift,* Warner Bros., 1982; *Café Flesh,* 1982; *Scarface,* Universal, 1983; *Horror House on Highway 5,* 1985; *Gypsy Beam, America,* ASA, 1986; *The Tommy Chong Roast,* 1986; *Flicks,* United Artists, 1987; *The Wrong Guys,* New World, 1988; *Freeway,* New World, 1988; *The Big Picture,* Columbia, 1989; *Fletch Lives,* Universal, 1989; *Bonfire of the Vanities,* Warner Bros., 1990; *Off and Running* HBO Video, 1991; *Missing Pieces,* Orion, 1992; *Mad Dog and Glory,* Universal, 1993; *Dangerous Game,* Metro-Goldwyn-Mayer, 1993; *The Puppet Masters,* Buena Vista, 1994; *North,* Columbia, 1994; *Get on the Bus,* Columbia, 1996; *A Very Brady Sequel,* Paramount, 1996; *Girl 6,* Twentieth Century-Fox, 1996; *The Bar Channel,* 1998; *Species II,* Metro-Goldwyn-Mayer/United Artists, 1998; *Man on the Moon,* Universal, 1999; and *Arrow,* 1999.

Television series appearances include *Thicke of the Night,* syndicated, 1983; *The Late Show,* Fox, 1986; *The Beach Boys: Endless Summer,* syndicated, 1989; *Caroline's Comedy Hour,* Arts and Entertainment, 1990; *London Underground,* Comedy Central, 1991; *Comics Only,* Comedy Central, 1991; *The A-List,* Comedy Central, 1992; *Lois and Clark: The New Adventures of Superman,* ABC, 1993-94; *Homicide: Life on the Street,* NBC, 1993-99; *Crime Stories,* Court TV, 1999; and *Law & Order: Special Victims Unit,* NBC, 1999—. Also appeared as host, *Hot Properties,* Lifetime; and on *The Richard Belzer Show,* Cinemax.

Appearances on television specials include *The Young Comedians All-Star Reunion,* HBO, 1986; *Just for Laughs II,* Showtime, 1987; *Funny, You Don't Look 200,* ABC, 1987; *American Video Awards,* syndicated, 1987; *The Comedy Club Special,* syndicated, 1988; *Belzer on Broadway,* Showtime, 1992; *The Please Watch the Jon Lovitz Special,* Showtime, 1992; *Free to Laugh: A Comedy and Music Special for Amnesty International,* Lifetime, 1992; *A Tribute to Sam Kinison,* Fox, 1993; *Harley-Davidson's 90th Birthday*

Blast, 1993; *It's Just a Ride,* Comedy Central, 1994; *Comic Relief VI,* HBO, 1994; *But . . . Seriously,* Showtime, 1994; *Lifetime Applauds: The Fight against Breast Cancer,* Lifetime, 1995; *A Comedy Salute to Andy Kaufman,* NBC, 1995; *But Seriously '94,* Showtime, 1995; *The 9th Annual American Comedy Awards,* 1995; *Comic Relief American Comedy Festival,* ABC, 1996; *Comedy Club Superstars,* ABC, 1996; *Catch a Rising Star 50th Anniversary—Give or Take 26 Years,* CBS, 1996; *Cutting Edge: The Future of Crime Fighting,* NBC, 1996; "Richard Belzer: Another Lone Nut," *HBO Comedy Hour,* HBO, 1997; *Town Hall,* Comedy Central, 1997; *Nissan Presents: The 2nd Annual Celebration of America's Music,* ABC, 1998; *The 25th International Emmy Awards,* 1998; *The 12th Annual American Comedy Awards,* 1998; *The American Comedy Awards Viewer's Choice,* 1998; *Andy Kaufman: The E! True Hollywood Story,* E! Entertainment Television, 1998; *Elmopalooza,* ABC, 1998; *John Belushi: The E! True Hollywood Story,* E! Entertainment Television, 1998; *When Cars Attack,* ABC, 1998; *Barry Levinson on the Future in the 20th Century: Yesterday's Tomorrows,* 1999; *The Capture and Trial of Adolf Eichmann,* 1999; *Comedy Central Presents Behind-the-Scenes at the American Comedy Awards,* 1999; *Fatal Passion,* Court TV, 1999; *Inside the Criminal Mind,* Court TV, 1999; *The Kennedy Center Mark Twain Prize Celebrating the Humor of Richard Pryor,* 1999; *People v. Simpson: Unfinished Business,* Court TV, 1999; *The 14th Annual American Comedy Awards,* 2000; and *Comedy Central Presents the Second Annual Kennedy Center Mark Twain Prize,* Comedy Central, 2000. TV appearances in pilots include *The Facts,* CBS, 1982. Appearances in television miniseries include *The Invaders,* Fox, 1995.

Episodic television appearances include "'Twas the Episode before Christmas," *Moonlighting,* ABC, 1985; "Richard Belzer in Concert," *On Location,* HBO, 1986; "Trust Fund Pirates," *Miami Vice,* 1986; *Hot Properties,* 1986; *The Flash,* CBS, 1990; "Into the Night," *Studio 59,* ABC, 1991; "Doubt of the Benefit," *The Larry Sanders Show,* HBO, 1994; *Nurses,* NBC, 1994; *Lois & Clark: The New Adventures of Superman,* ABC, 1994; "Charm City: Part 1," *Law & Order,* NBC, 1996, "Baby, It's You: Part 1," 1997; "Unusual Suspects," *The X-Files,* Fox, 1997; "Stealing Burt's Car," *Mad about You,* NBC, 1998; "Sideshow," *Law & Order,* NBC, 1999, "Entitled," 2000; "They Say It's Your Birthday," *The Beat,* UPN, 2000; and *South Park,* Comedy Central, 2000. Also appeared on *The Late Show with David Letterman,* CBS; *The Tonight Show Starring Johnny Carson,* NBC; and *Good Sports,* CBS.

Television movie appearances include *Hart to Hart: Crimes of the Heart,* NBC, 1994; *Bandit: Bandit, Bandit,* syndicated, 1994; "Not of This Earth," *Roger Corman Presents,* Showtime, 1995; *Prince for a Day,* NBC, 1995; *Deadly Pursuits,* NBC, 1996; and *Homicide: The Movie,* NBC, 2000.

Stage appearances include *The Comedy Crusade against Diabetes,* Joyce Theatre, New York City, 1988. Appeared off-Broadway in *The National Lampoon Show.* Has been a frequent guest on Howard Stern's radio program. Recordings include *Another Lone Nut,* University of Puerto Rico Press, 1998, and audio version of *UFOs, JFK, and Elvis* (see below), New Star/Dove, 1999.

WRITINGS:

"Richard Belzer in Concert" (television episode), *On Location,* HBO, 1986.

(With Larry Charles and Rick Newman) *How to Be a Standup Comic,* Villard Books (New York, NY), 1988.

Belzer on Broadway (television special), Showtime, 1992.

UFOs, JFK, and Elvis: Conspiracies You Don't Have to Be Crazy to Believe, Ballantine Books (New York, NY), 1999.

SIDELIGHTS: Emerging from a bitter, painful childhood and an early adulthood marked by tragedy and numerous false starts, Richard Belzer in his fifth decade finally achieved the career success that had long eluded him. The son of an abusive mother, Belzer was beaten often as a child, but found that he could sometimes escape the abuse by making his mother laugh. This was his first venture into the world of comedy, and subsequent events—his mother's death from cancer in 1963, his father's suicide four years later, and a number of dead-end jobs—served to inform what became a trademark mordant style, characterized by put-downs and black humor.

During the 1970s, Belzer watched a number of his friends emerge onto the national stage while he remained relatively obscure, but when his good friend Freddie Prinze committed suicide at the age of twenty-two, this only served to call into question the value of that fame. During the early 1980s, by which time

Belzer had been married and divorced twice, he weathered a bout with cancer and emerged a kinder, gentler comedian and human being. Instead of drinking to relax, he meditated, and instead of using his stand-up routine to poke bitter fun at audience members, he began making himself the focal point of the jokes.

Belzer's career turned around in the 1990s with his memorable stint as Detective John Munch on television's long-running and celebrated series *Homicide.* Like Belzer, Munch had several failed marriages and had lost friends to suicide and other tragedies. At the end of the decade, readers discovered another similarity between Belzer and Munch: a fascination with conspiracies, which the comedian discusses in his book *UFOs, JFK, and Elvis: Conspiracies You Don't Have to Be Crazy to Believe.*

"Just for the record," wrote Irene Lacher in the *Los Angeles Times,* "you do have to be crazy to believe Elvis is alive." In fact, the reference to Elvis Presley in the title — and the implied reference to the fringe belief that the great performer is still alive — probably is there more to attract attention than for any other reason. The book is actually concerned with the other two phenomena referred to in the title: the idea that President John F. Kennedy's assassination was an act of conspiracy whose particulars have been obscured in an even more sinister cover-up; and that aliens have visited Earth and continue to do so. Reviewing the book, several critics noted that most of the "information" Belzer brings into his work is either of questionable value —much of it, particularly on the UFOs, being from sources that command little respect in the scientific or journalistic communities—, or simply not very original. On the other hand, several writers found the book entertaining. A commentator in *Publishers Weekly,* discussing the audio version read by the author, observed that, Belzer "comes across as a friendly guy with a healthy anti-authority streak." Brian Bethune in *Maclean's* found the book "savagely hilarious," and in *USA Today* Richard Willing called it "a platform for the scouring pad that is Belzer's sense of humor."

BIOGRAPHICAL AND CRITICAL SOURCES:

BOOKS

Contemporary Newsmakers 1985, Gale (Detroit, MI), 1986.
Contemporary Theatre, Film, and Television, volume 32, Gale (Detroit, MI), 2000.

PERIODICALS

Booklist, May 15, 1999, Ilene Cooper, review of *UFOs, JFK, and Elvis: Conspiracies You Don't Have to Be Crazy to Believe,* p. 1644.
Boston Globe, June 11, 1999, Michael Blowen, review of *UFOs, JFK, and Elvis,* p. D9.
Library Journal, May 1, 1999, Joe J. Accardi, review of *UFOs, JFK, and Elvis,* p. 74.
Los Angeles Times, June 28, 1999, Irene Lacher, "Conspiring with Comedian Richard Belzer," p. 2.
Maclean's, August 2, 1999, Brian Bethune, "Look Who's Paranoid Now: Nonfiction Titles Bring Conspiracy Theories in from the Cold," p. 41.
People Weekly, June 14, 1999, Mike Lipton, review of *UFOs, JFK, and Elvis,* p. 54.
Publishers Weekly, March 22, 1999, review of *UFOs, JFK, and Elvis,* p. 76; July 5, 1999, review of *UFOs, JFK and Elvis* (audio version), p. 35.
USA Today, June 15, 1999, Richard Willing, review of *UFOs, JFK, and Elvis,* p. D8.*

*　　*　　*

BENTIVOGLIO, Fabrizio 1957-

PERSONAL: Born January 4, 1957, in Milan, Italy. *Education:* Attended school of the Piccolo Teatro, Milan.

ADDRESSES: Office—Tipota Movie Company, Lungotevere Flaminio 66, 00196 Rome RM, Italy. *Agent*—Gianni Antonangeli, Studio Antonangeli srl, Via Lutezia 5, 00198 Rome RM, Italy.

CAREER: Actor, director, and writer.

Film appearances include *Masoch,* 1980; *La dame aux Camelias,* 1981; *La festa perduta,* 1981; *Morte in Vaticano,* 1982; *Il bandito dagli occhi azzurri,* 1982; *La donna delle meraviglie,* 1985; *Salome,* 1986; *Monte Napoleone,* 1986; *Regina,* 1986; *Apartment Zero,* Skouras Pictures, 1988; *Rebus,* 1989; *Marrakech Express,* 1989; *Turnè,* 1990; *Italia Germania 4 a 3,* B.I.M., 1990; *L'aria serena dell'ovest,* 1990; *Un americano rosso,* 1991; *Un'anima divisa in due,* 1993; *La fine e nota,* 1993; *Come due coccodrilli,* 1994; *La scuola* 1995; *Un eroe borghese,* 1995; *I sfagi tou kokora,*

1996; *Pianese Nunzio, 14 anni a maggio,* Medusa Distribuzione, 1996; *Le affinita elettive,* AMA Films, 1996; *Testimone a rischio,* 1996; *L'avventura di un uomo tranquillo,* 1996; *Marianna Ucria,* 1996; Trimark Pictures, 1997; *Le acrobate,* Mikado, 1997; *Mia eoniotita ke mia mera,* Artistic License, 1998; *La parola amore esiste,* Mikado, 1998; *Del perduto amore,* CDI; Buena Vista International, 1998; *La balia,* Instituto Luce, 1999; *The Missing,* Roadshow, 1999; *Denti,* Cecchi Gori Distribuzione, 2000; *La lingua del santo,* Medusa Distribuzione, 2000; *Magicians,* 2000; *Hotel,* 2001; *A cavallo della tigre,* 2001; and *Ricordati di me,* 2003.

Other film work includes (casting director) *Turnè,* 1990; (director) *Tipota,* International Movie Company, 1999. Stage appearances include *Timone d'Atene* and *La tempesta,* both 1978; *I parenti terribili,* 1979; *Prima del silenzio,* 1980; *L'avaro,* 1981; *La vera storia* and *Gli amanti dei miei amanti sono miei amaniti,* both 1982; *Metti una sera a cena,* 1983; *D'amore si muore,* 1985; *Italia Germania 4 a 3,* 1987; and *La guerra vista dalla luna* and *La tempesta,* both 2000.

AWARDS, HONORS: Coppa Volpi, 1993, and Ciak d'oro, 1994, both for best actor, for *A Soul Split in Two*; Grolla d'oro, 1993, both for best actor, for *The End Is Known*; Montreal World Film Festival awards, 1995, for best actor, for *Ordinary Hero*; Premio Pasinetti, 1996, for *Pianese Nunzio, Fourteen in May*; David di Donatello, 1996-97, Sacher d'oro, and Ciak d'oro, both 1997, both for best actor, both for *An Eyewitness Account*; Sao Paulo International Film Festival audience award, 1999, for best short, for *Tipota*; David di Donatello, 1998-99, for best supporting actor, for *Del perduto amore.*

WRITINGS:

Turnè (screenplay; also known as *Strada Blues*), 1990.
Tipota (screenplay), International Movie Company, 1999.

SIDELIGHTS: The name of Italian actor Fabrizio Bentivoglio, according to girlfriend Valeria Golino in *USA Today,* "means 'I care for you.'" The beautiful Golino—"all curly hair and curvy mouth," as a *USA Today* writer described her—is well known to American viewers from her work in films such as *Rain Man*;

Bentivoglio, on the other hand, is much better known on the other side of the Atlantic. Most of his films have appeared in Italian only, though the acclaimed *Apartment Zero* (1988) is an exception.

Bentivoglio has also written screenplays, among them *Turnè* (1990). *Turnè* is the story of two actors who belong to a touring theatre company staging a Chekhov play in towns throughout Italy. One of the two players pines for the lover he has left behind, only to learn that his friend is having an affair with her. What ensues is a confrontation of egos punctuated by moments of great humor and emotion.

BIOGRAPHICAL AND CRITICAL SOURCES:

BOOKS

Contemporary Theatre, Film, and Television, volume 34, Gale (Detroit, MI), 2001.

PERIODICALS

American Spectator, July, 1990, Bruce Bawer, review of *Turnè,* p. 34.
USA Today, May 5, 1994, "Golino Gets a Hot Shot at Comedy," p. D2.

OTHER

Pietrobo, http://www.pietrobo.com/ (December 29, 2002), "Life and Works of Fabrizio Bentivoglio."*

*   *   *

BEN-YITZHAK, Avraham 1883-1950

PERSONAL: Born September 13, 1883, in Przemysl, Austria-Hungary; died of tuberculosis, May 29, 1950, in Ramatayim, Israel. *Education:* University of Berlin, University of Vienna. *Politics:* Zionist. *Religion:* Jewish.

CAREER: Writer and teacher.

WRITINGS:

(With Dov. Dahary and I. M. Lask) *Yeladim bi-temunot,* Yonah (Tel Aviv, Israel), 1963.

Shirim (poetry), Sifre Tarshish (Jerusalem, Israel), 1952.

Kol ha-shirim (title means "Complete Poetry"), edited by Hanan Haver, ha-Kibuts ha-me'uhad (Tel Aviv, Israel), 1992.

'Al Avraham Ben-Yitzhak bi-melot shanah le-moto (sound recording of radio program broadcast in 1975), Kol Yisra'el (Jerusalem, Israel), 1993.

Es entfernten sich die Dinge. Gedichte und Fragmente. Gedichte in Deutch und Hebraisch (title means "Poems and Fragments in German and Hebrew"), edited by Efrat Gel-Ed and Christoph Meckel, 1994.

ADAPTATIONS: Ben-Yitzhak's poetry was set to music by Noa Blass, and published as *Yetsirot le-kol ule-fesanter,* c. 1983; lyrics by Ben-Yitzhak are included in *Ich kannte meine Seele nicht: 2 sopranos, contralto, tenor, baryton, basse,* [Ottignies, Belgium], 1990.

SIDELIGHTS: The first modernist poet to write in Hebrew, Avraham Ben-Yitzhak also wrote literary criticism. During his lifetime he published only twelve poems. One poem he later repudiated, citing a disagreement with editorial changes made to it by his editor. Although considered by many Hebrew poetry scholars to be a gifted writer, Ben-Yitzhak appears to have spent more time in cafés theorizing about literature than producing it. Despite the encouragement of many writers and editors, he likely suffered from a depression that interfered with his ability to write. He frequently failed to deliver commissioned essays. He chose to live a hermit-like existence, and although well known among Hebrew intelligentsia, in his later years he seldom spoke. Despite his unconventional approach to both life and his own writing career, Ben-Yitzhak attracted a loyal following whose belief in his writing was unshakable. He was also known as a devoted Zionist.

Born in the small village of Przemysl in the Galicia region of what was at the time Austria-Hungary, Ben-Yitzhak was raised by his maternal grandparents. His father died when he was very young. Educated in the tradition of Orthodox Judaism, he also received private instruction from secular tutors. Among them was Eleizer Lipshitz, a scholar from Lvov who urged him to work harder and achieve more. Post cards from Lipshitz urged the young Ben-Yitzhak to take his exams more seriously, to go to the cultural center of Berlin, to write more poetry, and to publish. Ben-Yitzhak published little, and usually preferred to publish anonymously. It took the well-known German theologian and philosopher Martin Buber to persuade Ben-Yitzhak to include his name on an essay.

Ben-Yitzhak traveled a good deal and lived in several European cities, including London and Copenhagen, before settling in Israel. He studied at universities in Berlin and Vienna, as well as Lvov, although he never completed a degree. Nonetheless, he was invited to teach Hebrew literature and psychology at the Hevrat Ezra Teachers College in Jerusalem in 1913. The venture was doomed to failure from the start, however. The very day Ben-Yitzhak arrived in Jerusalem, he was injured in a road accident and spent three months in hospital. He returned to Vienna to recuperate.

Ben-Yitzhak was in Vienna when World War I began. He became involved briefly in Zionist politics before taking a teaching position at the Hebrew Pedagogical Institute in Vienna, which sapped all his energy and provided only a modest income. He fell ill with tuberculosis and stopped writing. When his native town of Przemysl fell to the Russians in 1915, Ben-Yitzhak lost all the writings he had left in his mother's house. He fell into a depression from which he never fully recovered. He also refused to publish any more poetry. Eventually he continued to write, albeit at a very slow rate.

Ben-Yitzhak never achieved the promise as a writer that many saw in him. Instead, he frequented literary cafés, discussing ideas with such major modernist literary figures as James Joyce, Arnold Schoenberg, and Elias Canetti. Wealthy friends became his patrons, and Ben-Yitzhak depended upon them for his livelihood even after he escaped the Nazi occupation of Vienna in 1938 and fled to Jerusalem. His tuberculosis worsened and he died in Jerusalem soon after the State of Israel was founded in 1948.

Ben-Yitzhak's writing career lasted only from the early 1900s until World War I, and he published his final poem around 1930. "Happy are they that sow and will not reap/They shall wander afar," he wrote in lines of varying length. In this work reminiscent of Old Testament poetry, he employs repetition throughout. Inverting traditional expectations of happiness, the poem has a distinctly modern flavor that disrupts cultural norms and praises silence over speech. The poem appears to borrow from Psalms 126, but it reverses the biblical text.

One of his earliest poems, "Bright Winter," written in February and March, 1903, describes a northern landscape of ice, snow, and fog. "The world is pure and hard and white," he wrote. The river, however, moves deep beneath the frozen landscape. Seen in psychological terms, the contrasting imagery of icy stillness and brisk movement of hidden waters illustrates conflicting impulses toward inaction and action. The poet sees his heart as "a diamond" that "would flow with the currents/Running beneath the icy skin." Ultimately, the poem extols the virtues of purity, which is aligned with the icy stillness of the landscape. The only evidence of movement lies hidden in submerged waters, creating a tension between life as movement and life as a frozen landscape.

Other poems by Ben-Yitzhak speak of the secrets of nature, of harvests that are mighty, and of winds that produce voice. The poems focus on the changing seasons and images from the natural world, including sunsets and storms, the seas, and the stars. Very much in the tradition of French symbolists and the *imagistes* of the early twentieth century, the poems represent early stages of modernism. According to a contributor to *Cassell's Encyclopedia of World Literature*, Ben-Yitzhak introduced such Symbolist techniques as color symbolism into Hebrew poetry, moving it "away from rational to lyrical, symbolical themes." Although published individually, Ben-Yitzhak's poems were not published as a collection until 1957. His entire *oeuvre* consists of eleven poems and fifteen fragments of poems and essays. They were published in a dual German-Hebrew language edition that includes supplemental essays by poets Leah Goldberg, Tuvia Rubner, and Robert Weltsch. Karsten Sand Iversen wrote, "This small volume provides the kernel of an entire folk legend."

BIOGRAPHICAL AND CRITICAL SOURCES:

BOOKS

Cassell's Encyclopedia of World Literature, William Morrow & Company (New York, NY), 1973, p. 144.

OTHER

Litteraturmagasinet Standart, http://www.sb.aau.dk/ (September 13, 2002), Karsten Sand Iversen, "Avraham Ben-Yitzhak."*

*   *   *

BERRY, Sheila Martin 1947-

PERSONAL: Born 1947; married Doug Berry (an author); children.

ADDRESSES: Home—9808 Alfaree Rd., Richmond, VA 23237. *E-mail*—dberry@i2020.net.

CAREER: Novelist and numerologer. Worked as a crime victim advocate.

WRITINGS:

My Name Is Legion (novel), Archer Books (Santa Maria, CA), 1999.
(Coauthor, with Lynn M. Copen and Linda M. Pucci), *Getting Ready for Court: Civil Court Edition* (juvenile nonfiction), Sage Publications, 2000.
(With husband, Doug Berry) *Circumstantial Evidence: Anatomy of a Midwestern Murder,* Public Eye Publications, 2002.

Author of novel *The Spy Who Never Was.*

ADAPTATIONS: The Spy Who Never Was was adapted as a TNT cable television film, 1999.

BIOGRAPHICAL AND CRITICAL SOURCES:

PERIODICALS

Publishers Weekly, August 16, 1999, review of *My Name Is Legion,* p. 63.

OTHER

Harriet Klausner's Review Archive, http://harriet klausner.wwwi.com/ (January 14, 2003), review of *My Name Is Legion.*

BIANCIARDI, Luciano 1922-1971

PERSONAL: Born 1922, in Grosseto, Italy; died November 14, 1971, of complications from alcoholism. *Education:* Attended Scuola Normale di Pisa.

CAREER: Novelist, translator, journalist, sportswriter, and social critic. Taught high school for three years in Grosseto, Italy; Feltrinelli (publishing house), Milan, Italy, member of editorial staff; *Il Contemporaneo,* founder; translator and columnist, 1957-71.

WRITINGS:

(With Carlo Cassola) *I minatori della Maremma* (title means "Maremma's Miners"), Laterza (Bari, Italy), 1956, reprinted, Hestia (Cernusco, Italy), 1995.

Il lavoro culturale (title means "Cultural Work"), Feltrinelli (Milan, Italy), 1957.

L'ospite americana, Feltrinelli (Milan, Italy), 1958.

L'integrazione (title means "Integration"), Bompiani (Milan, Italy), 1960.

Da quarto a Torino: breve storia della spedizione dei Mille (title means "From Quarto to Turin"), Feltrinelli (Milan, Italy), 1960.

La vita agra, Rizzoli (Milan, Italy), 1962, reprinted, Bompiani (Milan, Italy), 1998, translation by Eric Mosbacher published as *It's a Hard Life,* Viking (New York, NY), 1965.

La battaglia soda (title means "Real Battle"), Rizzoli (Milan, Italy), 1964, reprinted, Bompiani (Milan, Italy), 1997.

(With Pepi Merisio) *Floriano Bodini,* Li Castello (Milan, Italy), 1964.

Aprire il fuoco (title means "Open Fire"), Rizzoli (Milan, Italy), 1969, reprinted, ExCogita (Milan, Italy), 2001.

Daghela avanti un passo! (title means "Step Lively"), Bietti (Milan, Italy), 1969, reprinted, Longanesi (Milan, Italy), 1992.

Viaggio in Barberia (title means "Travels in Barberia"), L'Editrice dell'Automobile (Rome, Italy), 1969, reprinted, EDT (Turin, Italy), 1997.

(With Mario Terrosi) *Bianciardi com'era (Lettere di Luciano Bianciardi ad un amico grossetano),* Il Paese Reale (Grosseto, Italy), 1974.

Il peripatetico e altre storie, Rizzoli (Milan, Italy), 1976.

Garibaldi, Mondadori (Milan, Italy), 1982.

(With Mario Terrosi and Alberto Gessani) *L'intellettuale disintegrato,* Ianua (Rome, Italy), 1985.

La solita zuppa e altre storie, Bompiani (Milan, Italy), 1994.

(Editor) *Chiese escatollo e nessuno raddoppiò: diario in pubblico 1952-1971,* Baldini & Castoldi (Milan, Italy), 1995.

La nascita dei Minatori della Maremma: il carteggio Bianciardi, Cassola, Laterza e altri scritti, edited by Velio Abati, Giunti (Florence, Italy), 1998.

L'alibi del progresso: scritti giornalistici ed elzeviri, preface by Dario Fo, ExCogita (Milan, Italy), 2000.

TRANSLATOR

Aldous Huxley, *Ritorno al mondo nuovo,* Mondadori (Milan, Italy), 1961.

Saul Bellow, *Il re della pioggia,* Garzanti (Milan, Italy), 1966.

(With Marcella Monsanti) Osamu Dazai, *Il soleil si spegne,* Feltrinelli (Milan, Italy), 1966.

William Faulkner, *Una favola,* Mondadori (Milan, Italy), 1971.

Also translator of *Narratori della generazione alienata,* 1961; *Tropic of Cancer* by Henry Miller, 1962; *Tropic of Capricorn* by Henry Miller, 1962; and *A Confederate General from Big Sur* by Richard Brautigan.

ADAPTATIONS: La vita agra was adapted for film.

SIDELIGHTS: Luciano Bianciardi was part of the generation of left-wing intellectuals who worked in Italian publishing in the 1950s and 1960s. He wrote and translated novels expressing his anger and frustration with modern industrialized life, protesting society's lack of purpose and values. A number of his translations were of the works of "beat" writers such as Henry Miller and Richard Brautigan, and their work tremendously influenced his own. In the end, he lost his own sense of purpose and died of alcoholism.

Bianciardi was born and grew up in Grosseto, Italy. He attended the Scuola Normale in Pisa, where he earned a degree in philosophy with a thesis on John

Dewey. After finishing his education, he taught in Grosseto for three years; during this time, he also reorganized the city library's material on the Risorgimento. In the 1950s, he contributed articles to many progressive periodicals. He was one of the original editorial staff of the publishing house Feltrinelli, and he worked with the periodical *Il Contemporaneo* from its beginning.

Beginning in 1957, Bianciardi earned all his living from working as a translator and columnist. He was known for his incisive criticism and analysis of contemporary culture. Much of his work is autobiographical and satirical. His work is eclectic, ranging from social inquiry to history to travel writing, such as the travelogue *Viaggio in Barberia.*

Bianciardi wrote a number of works on industrial culture. In *I minatori della Maremma* he examines the Tuscan mining industry over the nineteenth and twetieth centuries. He focuses in particular on the Ribolla lignite mine near his hometown of Grosseto, where an explosion in 1954 killed forty-three miners. The satirical *Il lavoro culturale,* published in 1957, is a story about two intellectual brothers who attempt to promote culture in the provinces. *L'integrazione* is a sequel to *Il lavoro culturale* in which the two brothers travel to the city and work in publishing during the industry's boom in the 1950s. They become alienated to one another and go their separate ways; the narrator decides to integrate himself with society while his brother chooses to drop out. Bianciardi tells his story derisively, with a humor that approaches the grotesque.

La vita agra is considered Bianciardi's most successful novel; it was translated into several languages and made into a film. The main character, an idealistic intellectual, travels to the city planning to blow up the high-rise office buildings of an industrial conglomerate. He hopes to prevent the industrialization which has overtaken Milan from possessing the rest of the country. He is constantly frustrated by industrialized modern life and becomes increasingly alienated from society, full of anger and feelings of isolation in his world of existential angst.

Bianciardi wrote a number of historical works, several of them focusing on Garibaldi and the Risorgimento. *Da quarto a Torino* tells the story of the Mille expedition. *La battaglia soda* begins with the capture of Capua in November 1860 and progresses to the second battle of Custoza in June 1866. In *Daghela,* Bianciardi examines the most important figures and events in Italian unification. He combines historical and industrial themes in *Aprire il fuoco,* a novel in which he mixes up Risogimento events with later ones; the main character is a paranoid political exile who works as a translator, and the novel is told through his fantasies, reminiscences, and daily routine.

Bianciardi also translated a number of English works into Italian. His particular specialty was works by beat writers and "angry" novelists; he favored the writings of Henry Miller and Jack Keruoac, as well as William Faulkner. He was very attracted to works that question and rebel against the status quo and majority values. His translations of Henry Miller's *Tropic of Cancer* and *Tropic of Capricorn* earned him legal battles and scandals over content and language. The year before he published *La vita agra,* he translated the anthology *The Beat Generation and the Angry Young Men* as *Narratori della generazione alienata.* After writing *La vita agra,* he translated Richard Brautigan's *A Confederate General from Big Sur.* His novel *Aprire il fuoco,* written after this translation, features characters who, like Brautigan's, seek to escape from the city and find refuge near the sea; also like Brautigan, one of the main characters feels that there are no values left in which he can believe.

The influence of beat writing is present throughout *La vita agra.* Like beat heroes, Bianciardi's protagonists all seem to live in the present. Ironically, after writing *La vita agra,* his big protest novel, Bianciardi lost his sense of purpose and he went into a self-imposed exile at Rapallo. Critics have suggested that his subsequent books about the Risorgimento were Bianciardi's attempt to cope with the industrialized present and vent his anger. He still felt the need to oppose organized authority. In some ways, his work on the Risorgimento was an attempt to raise Italy's conflict to the level of something like the U.S. Civil War. He felt that the values present in the Risorgimento had been lost and distorted in the present.

In addition to writing, Bianciardi was very interested in the cinema. From 1950 until his death he organized cinema clubs, wrote film criticism, and collaborated on a number of film projects. Bianciardi was increasingly isolated at the end of his life and took to drinking heavily. He died alone on November 14, 1971.

After his death, a foundation was created in his name to examine contemporary culture.

BIOGRAPHICAL AND CRITICAL SOURCES:

BOOKS

Bede, Jean-Albert, and William B. Edgerton, *Columbia Dictionary of Modern European Literature,* 2nd edition, Columbia University Press (New York, NY), 1980.
Falaschi, Francesco, editor, *Scrittori e Cinema tragli anni '50 e '60,* Giunti Gruppo Editoriale (Florence, Italy), 1997.
Perosa, Sergio, editor, *Le traduzioni italiani de William Faulkner,* Istituto Veneto di scienze, lettere ed arti (Venice, Italy), 1998.
Rinaldi, Rinaldo, *Il Romanzo come deformazione,* Mursia (Milan, Italy), 1985.

PERIODICALS

Cristallo, December, 1987, "Il risorgimento di Luciano Bianciardi," pp. 61-68.
Cuadernos Hispanoamericanos, February, 1972, "Bianciardi: La revoluzione como fabula," pp. 388-391.
Romance Languages Annual, 1998, Mark Pietralunga, "Luciano Bianciardi Translates Richard Brautigan: *Rebellion at Big Sur,*" pp. 345-349.

OTHER

Brera, http://www.brera.net/ (March 21, 2002), Alessandro Mazzola, "Luciano Bianciardi, un suicidio a Brera."
Dadascanner, http://www.dadascanner.com/ (March 21, 2002), "Monni torna su Bianciardi."*

*   *   *

BIRO, Brian D. 1954-

PERSONAL: Born October 5, 1954, in Santa Monica, CA; son of Louis P. (a police officer) and Miriam (a museum curator) Biro; married, September 21, 1985; wife's name, Carole (a health practitioner); children: Kelsey, Jenna. *Education:* Stanford University, B.A., 1976; University of California, Los Angeles, M.B.A., 1985. *Religion:* Christian. *Hobbies and other interests:* Sports, family activities, reading, exercise, the outdoors.

ADDRESSES: Home and office—204 Weston Way, Asheville, NC 28803; fax: 828-654-8853. *Agent*—Deidre Knight, Knight Agency, P.O. Box 550648, Atlanta, GA 30355. *E-mail*—bbiro@att.net.

CAREER: U.S. Swim Coach, Woodland Hills, CA, owner and head coach, 1976-83; Lynden Air Freight, Seattle, WA, vice president, 1986-91; Robbins Research, San Diego, CA, vice president, 1991-93; professional speaker and writer in Asheville, NC, and Hamilton, MT, 1993—.

WRITINGS:

Beyond Success: The Fifteen Secrets of a Winning Life!, Pygmalion Press (Hamilton, MT), 1995, 3rd edition published as *Beyond Success: The Fifteen Secrets to Effective Leadership and Life Based on Legendary Coach John Wooden's Pyramid of Success,* Berkley (New York, NY), 2001.
The Joyful Spirit: How to Become the Happiest Person You Know!, Pygmalion Press (San Diego, CA), 1998.

WORK IN PROGRESS: A companion book to *Beyond Success.*

SIDELIGHTS: Brian D. Biro told *CA:* "I absolutely love what I do! My work as a speaker and author focuses on personal leadership, breaking through fears and doubts, possibility thinking, and team building. I relish the opportunity through my writing to help readers improve the quality of their personal, family, and professional lives. I am a principle-based author and teacher, so the ideas I share reach into the core of each human being. I also love storytelling.

"One of my primary mentors has been the great coach, John Wooden. I am also deeply influenced by Gandhi, Mother Teresa, Jesus, and my family. Often my greatest teachers are my children!

"The first step for me in writing a book is a clear outline leading to my ultimate theme. I write a chapter at a time and never try to force a section. Sometimes that means I 'percolate' for several days until the writing flows.

"Throughout my life I have been fascinated by people—first as a coach, then as a business executive, and finally as a writer and speaker. I have focused always on seeking to bring out the best in others—to help them build joyful, productive, and fulfilling lives."

*   *   *

BISCHOF, Guenter
   See BISCHOF, Günter

*   *   *

BISCHOF, Günter 1953-

PERSONAL: Born October 6, 1953, in Mellau, Austria; son of Josef (a store manager) and Leopoldine (a homemaker; maiden name, Feurstein) Bischof; married Melanie Boulet (a grant writer and consultant), May, 1991; children: Andrea Julia, Marcus Christopher, Alexander Carroll. *Education:* University of New Orleans, M.A., 1980; University of Innsbruck, M.Phil., 1982; Harvard University, M.A., 1983, Ph.D., 1989. *Religion:* Roman Catholic. *Hobbies and other interests:* Gardening, fishing, hiking, reading, classical music.

ADDRESSES: Office—Department of History, University of New Orleans, New Orleans, LA 70148; fax: 985-280-6882. *E-mail*—gjbhi@mobiletel.com.

CAREER: Educator. University of New Orleans, New Orleans, LA, began as assistant professor, became professor of history, 1989—, associate director, then executive director of Center for Austrian Culture and Commerce, 1997—, associate director of Eisenhower Center for Leadership Studies, 1989-97. Guest professor at University of Munich, 1992-94, University of Innsbruck, 1993-94, University of Salzburg, 1998, and University of Vienna, 1998; Institute of Human Sciences, Vienna, Austria, guest scholar, 1998. H-German, member of board of directors, 1995—; Austrian Commission on the Future of Austria, member, 1998; Austrian Marshall Plan Foundation, founding chair, 2000—. City of New Orleans, member of board of directors, Council for International Visitors, 1990-92. American Field Service—Austria, member. *Military service:* Austrian Army, 1973-74.

MEMBER: American Historical Association, German Studies Association, Society of American Historians of Foreign Relations, Austrian Association for American Studies, German Association for World War II Studies, Harvard Club of Louisiana.

AWARDS, HONORS: Early Career Achievement Award, University of New Orleans Alumni Association, 1990.

WRITINGS:

(Editor, with Josef Leidenfrost) *Die bevormundete Nation: Österreich und die Alliierten, 1945-1949,* Haymon (Innsbruck, Austria), 1988.

(Editor, with Charles S. Maier) *The Marshall Plan and Germany: West German Development within the Framework of the European Recovery Program,* Berg Publishers (New York, NY), 1991.

(Editor, with Stephen E. Ambrose) *Facts against Falsehood: Eisenhower and the German P.O.W.'s,* Louisiana State University Press (Baton Rouge, LA), 1992.

(Editor, with Rolf Steininger and others) *Die Doppelte Eindämmung: Europäische Sicherheit und deutsche Frage in den Fünfzigern,* Hase & Koehler (Munich, Germany), 1993.

(Editor, with Stephen E. Ambrose) *Eisenhower: A Centenary Assessment,* Louisiana State University Press (Baton Rouge, LA), 1995.

(Editor, with Robert Dupont) *The Pacific War Revisited,* Louisiana State University Press (Baton Rouge, LA), 1997.

(Editor, with Dieter Stiefel) *80 Dollar: 50 Jahre ERP-Fonds und Marshall-Plan in Österreich,* Überreuther (Vienna, Austria), 1999.

Austria in the First Cold War, 1945-1955: The Leverage of the Weak, St. Martin's Press (New York, NY), 1999.

(Editor, with Rüdiger Overmans) *Kriegsgefangenschaft im Zweiten Weltkrieg: eine Vergleichende Perspektive,* Gerhard Höller (Ternitz, Austria), 1999.

(Editor, with Saki Dockrill) *Cold War Respite: The Geneva Summit of 1955,* Louisiana State University Press (Baton Rouge, LA), 2000.

(Editor, with Wolfgang Krieger) *Normandieinvasion 6. Juni 1944: Internationale Perspektiven,* Studien (Innsbruck, Austria), 2001.

Founding coeditor of "Contemporary Austrian Studies" series, Transaction Books, 1993—. Contributor to books, including *The German Economy, 1945-1947:*

Charles P. Kindleberger's Letters from the Field, Meckler Corp. (Westport, CT), 1989. Contributor of articles and reviews to periodicals, including *Die Furche.* Founding coeditor, *Eisenhower Center Studies of War and Peace.*

WORK IN PROGRESS: A textbook on Austrian history; research on U.S.-Austrian relations in the twentieth century and on the militarization of American society in the cold war.

SIDELIGHTS: Günter Bischof told *CA:* "In every writer's career there comes a point of transition from *reading* the classics to picking up the pen and giving it a shot yourself. As a youngster I was an avid reader of American cartoons (in German!) and stories of Catholic missionaries all over the world. In high school I read the great German and Austrian classics like Goethe, Schiller, and Grillparzer, as well as Shakespeare and Hemingway. In college I studied American literature and European history and devoured Hawthorne, Melville, Faulkner, and the nonfiction 'new journalists' Tom Wolfe and Gay Talese. When specializing in American history, the great historical narratives of Lord Bullock, Bernard Bailyn, David Herbert Donald, David Kennedy, and Stephen Ambrose, but also Barbara Tuchman and memoirs such as George Kennan's became my daily fare. From these historians I drew inspiration for my own writing, which has concentrated exclusively in historical analysis.

"After dabbling with some smaller historical portraits and reviews in the Austrian intellectual weekly *Die Furche* in the early 1980s, my writing career began with publishing my own research in scholarly articles in the mid-1980s in both German and English. I have continued to do so ever since. While I still write in both languages, I have come to prefer to write in English. German academic language is ponderous, pretentious, and gets the reader lost in subordinate clauses; it seldom aspires to the grand historical narrative. The grand tradition of the sweeping historical narrative is alive and well in the Anglo-American tradition. English is expressive and pithy and highly adaptable to changes in larger society. It's the language I prefer for writing.

"I have cofounded one book series and one journal to cultivate and shepherd along a younger generation of historians in my research fields of cold war studies and contemporary Austrian studies.

"I like to pen newspaper commentaries on critical contemporary issues. Sometimes I act as conscience for truthful Austrian and American historical memories of World War II. Historians have to remind national communities that the good and the bad of difficult historical pasts need to be faced squarely and not willfully forgotten or transferred into streamlined, pious, patriotic history. Some pasts may be unmasterable, but they need to be confronted. Historians of contemporary history cannot only hide in archives; they have a public duty for providing historical contexts to political debates that move a nation."

*   *   *

BLACK, J. L. 1937-

PERSONAL: Born January 16, 1937, in Sackville, New Brunswick, Canada; son of Laurie (a merchant and soldier) and Gwendolyn (a musician) Black; married 1961; wife's name Janice. *Ethnicity:* "Scot." *Education:* Mount Allison University, B.A., 1958; Boston University, M.A., 1961; McGill University, Ph.D., 1967.

ADDRESSES: Home—Ottawa, Ontario, Canada. *Office*—Centre for Research on Canadian-Russian Relations, Carleton University, Ottawa, Ontario, Canada; fax 613-520-4439. *E-mail*—lblack@carleton.ca.

CAREER: Laurentian University, Sudbury, Ontario, Canada, professor, 1967-76; Carleton University, Ottawa, Ontario, professor, 1976—, director of Centre for Research on Canadian-Russian Relations, 1990—.

WRITINGS:

Nicholas Karamzin and Nineteenth-Century Russian Society: A Study in Russian Political and Historical Thought, University of Toronto Press (Toronto, Ontario, Canada), 1975.
(Editor) *Essays on Karamzin: Russian Man-of-Letters, Political Thinker, Historian, 1766-1826,* Mouton (The Hague, Netherlands), 1975.
Citizens for the Fatherland: Education, Educators, and Pedagogical Ideals in Eighteenth-Century Russia, East European Quarterly Press (Boulder, CO), 1979.

G.-F. Müller and the Imperial Russian Academy, 1725-1783, McGill-Queen?s University Press (Kingston, Ontario, Canada), 1986.

(Editor with J. W. Strong) *Sisyphus and Poland: Observations on Martial Law,* Ronald B. Frye Publishers (Winnipeg, Manitoba, Canada), 1986.

(Editor) *The Origins, Evolution, and Nature of the Cold War: An Annotated Bibliographic Guide,* American Bibliographical Center-Clio Press (Santa Barbara, CA), 1986.

(Editor with N. Hillmer) *Nearly Neighbours: Canada and the Soviet Union from Cold War to Détente and Beyond,* Frye Publishers (Kingston, Ontario, Canada), 1989.

(Editor and translator, with D. K. Buse and V. J. Moessner, and coauthor of introduction) *G.-F. Müller and Siberia,* Limestone Press (Fairbanks, AK), 1989.

Into the Dustbin of History: The USSR from August Coup to Commonwealth, 1991, Academic International Press (Gulf Breeze, FL), 1993.

(Editor with P. Stavrakis and J. DeBardeleben) *Beyond the Monolith: The Emergence of Regionalism in Post-Soviet Russia,* Johns Hopkins University Press (Baltimore, MD), 1997.

Canada in the Soviet Mirror: Ideology and Perception in Soviet Foreign Affairs, 1917-1991, Carleton University Press (Ottawa, Ontario, Canada), 1998.

Russia Faces NATO Expansion: Bearing Gifts or Bearing Arms?, Rowman & Littlefield (Lanham, MD), 1999.

Editor of *Russia and Eurasia Documents Annual* (formerly *USSR Documents Annual*), Academic International Press, 1988-2000.

WORK IN PROGRESS: Research on Russia and "the new world order."*

*　　*　　*

BLACKER, Terence

PERSONAL: Male. *Education:* Attended Cambridge.

ADDRESSES: Home—Suffolk, England. *Office*—c/o Author Mail, St. Martin's Press, 175 Fifth Ave., New York, NY 10010.

CAREER: Writer.

AWARDS, HONORS: Award for Teenage Book of the Year for *Homebird;* writing fellowship, University of East Anglia, 1994.

WRITINGS:

Fixx (novel), Bloomsbury (London, England), 1989.

The Fame Hotel (novel), Bloomsbury (London, England), 1992.

Revenance (novel), Bloomsbury (London, England), 1996.

(Editor with William Donaldson) *The Meaning of Cantona,* Mainstream (Edinburgh, Scotland), 1997.

Kill Your Darlings (novel), Weidenfeld & Nicolson (London, England), 2000, St. Martin's (New York, NY), 2001.

Columnist, *Independent.* Contributor to periodicals, including London *Times.*

"HOTSHOTS" SERIES; CHILDREN'S BOOKS

Pride and Penalties, Pan Macmillan (London, England), 1997.

Shooting Star, Pan Macmillan (London, England), 1997.

On the Wing, Pan Macmillan (London, England), 1997.

"MS. WIZ" SERIES; CHILDREN'S BOOKS

Ms. Wiz Spells Trouble, illustrations by Toni Goffe, Piccadilly (London, England), 1988.

In Stitches with Ms. Wiz, Piccadilly (London, England), 1990.

In Control, Ms. Wiz?, illustrations by Kate Simpson, Piccadilly (London, England), 1990.

You're Nicked Ms. Wiz, illustrations by Toni Goffe, Piccadilly (London, England), 1991.

Ms. Wiz Loves Dracula, illustrations by Kate Simpson, Piccadilly (London, England), 1993.

Time Flies for Ms. Wiz, illustrations by Kate Simpson, 1993.

You're Kidding, Ms. Wiz, illustrations by Tony Ross, Macmillan (London, England), 1996.

Ms. Wiz Supermodel, Macmillan (London, England), 1997.

OTHER CHILDREN'S BOOKS

If I Could Work, illustrations by Chris Winn, Lippincott (Philadelphia, PA), 1988.

Henry and the Frights, illustrations by Adriano Gon, Piccadilly (London, England), 1989.

Herbie Hamster, Where Are You?, illustrations by Pippa Uwin, Random (New York, NY), 1990, published as *Houdini, the Disappearing Hamster,* Andersen (London, England), 1990.

The Surprising Adventures of Baron Munchausen, illustrations by William Rushton, Knight, 1991.

The Great Denture Adventure, illustrations by John Eastwood, Pan (London, England), 1992.

Homebird (novel), Bradbury, 1993.

The Transfer (novel), Macmillan (London, England), 1998.

SIDELIGHTS: Terence Blacker is an acclaimed English writer whose publications include both mainstream novels and various children's books. Blacker's first novel, *Fixx,* concerns a deceitful opportunist who becomes an arms dealer at the behest of the administration of Prime Minister Margaret Thatcher. The hero, Jonathan Fixx, had engaged in criminal activities in the 1950s and worked in the music business in the 1960s. In the ensuing decade, after entering high society via a marriage made through coercion and blackmail, Fixx becomes an arms dealer, and he eventually engages in espionage on behalf of both the British and Soviet governments. Sean French, writing in *New Statesman & Society,* described *Fixx* as "undoubtedly something of a tour de force, consisting of 250 pages of deliberately repellent, clichéd prose." Another reviewer, John Spurling, acknowledged *Fixx,* in a London *Observer* assessment, as "an amusing, if never quite a hilarious book," and Jane Dorrel, in a *Books* analysis, hailed the novel as a "chilling and witty account." John Melmoth, meanwhile, wrote in the *Times Literary Supplement* that *Fixx* is "flawless and funny."

In his next novel, *The Fame Hotel,* Blacker relates the police investigation that ensues following the fetishistic murder of a ghost writer whose journal provides unappealing insights into the lives of various public figures. A *Books* reviewer called *The Fame Hotel* a "beautifully written book" and added that it constitutes a "sheer delight from start to finish." Less impressed, Mark Sanderson declared in the *Times Literary Supple-*

ment that Blacker's book "seems distinctly secondhand." Ruth Pavey, however, wrote in the London *Observer* that *The Fame Hotel* offers its readers "plenty of opportunities for laughing."

Blacker's third novel, *Revenance,* relates events in a small village plagued by the ghost of a woman who suffered rejection from her lover, poet John Skelton, who died in 1529. The ghost troubles various citizens, including a child molester and promiscuous teens. Patrick Skene Catling, writing in *Spectator,* proclaimed *Revenance* "very funny." He added, "In the matter of all the best fantasists, Blacker writes realistically, establishing believable ordinariness to maximise the impact of an outbreak of the extraordinary." *New Statesman & Society* critic Laurie Taylor, meanwhile, called *Revenance* a "hectically enjoyable fantasy," and *Times Literary Supplement* reviewer Roz Kaveney deemed Blacker's book "an intelligent novel."

Kill Your Darlings, Blacker's next novel, tells of an unproductive writing teacher who drives a promising student to suicide, then appropriates his manuscript with intentions of assuming authorship. *Booklist* reviewer Emily Melton summarized Blacker's novel as "literate, clever, and entertaining," and she noted its "witty digs at the world of the literary glitterati." Another reviewer, writing in the London *Times,* noted "the scythe [Blacker] wittily takes to the fads of the book world." Hugo Barnacle concluded in *New Statesman* that Blacker's "perverse humour exerts a horrible fascination," and Sam Gilpin observed in the *Times Literary Supplement* that *Kill Your Darlings* is "skilfully managed." He described the novel as a "dark study of writerly self-delusion." Sheila Riley, meanwhile, observed in *Library Journal* that Blacker "delves . . . deeply and convincingly into the pit of narcissism, mayhem, and soul-destroying Faustian bargains," and a *Kirkus Reviews* critic stated that "Blacker . . . reveals far more than anyone should know about a writer's inner and outer lives." Still another critic, writing in *Publishers Weekly,* concluded that "Blacker should take a bow."

Blacker has also written novels for younger readers. In 1993 he published *Homebird,* the story of a teenager who flees from boarding school after meeting with violence from a vicious bully. As a runaway, the hero encounters a host of memorable individuals, including a thief, a drug dealer, and a prostitute, and he finds himself framed for robbery. The novel ends with the youth returned home, though he still suffers from nightmares involving the cruel classmate. A *Voice of Youth* reviewer deemed *Homebird* "short but potent," and Jacqueline Rose praised it in *School Library Journal* as "riveting" and added that it generates "plenty of action and suspense." Similarly, Ellen Fader wrote in *Horn Book* of the novel's "can't-put-it-down quality" and "fast-paced action," and a *Publishers Weekly* critic concluded that the "wisecracking . . . narrative" helps render *Homebird* "an ideal book for reluctant readers."

The Transfer, another of Blacker's novels for teenage readers, tells of a fanatical soccer fan who magically transforms himself into a computer-generated player capable of saving a professional team from relegation to a lower division. The boy's plans go horribly awry, however, after he loses the magical device necessary for his extraordinary play. Further exacerbating matters, the hero discovers that his own teacher has become infatuated with his alter-ego. *Books for Keeps* reviewer Andrew Kidd stated that "this comic fantasy really hits the target," and he called special attention to Blacker's "high quality writing." Another critic, Linda Saunders, wrote in *School Librarian* that *The Transfer* "offers action, humour and a few lessons about life," and Geoff Fox declared in the *Times Literary Supplement* that "Blacker plays wittily with ideas and language."

Blacker also writes of soccer in the "Hotshots" series of novels recounting the trials and tribulations endured by members of a girls' team. A *Times Educational Reviewer* proclaimed the series "tosh" but nonetheless "fine."

Among Blacker's writings for schoolchildren is a series of tales featuring Ms. Wiz, a plucky witch who works as a teacher. Pamela Cleaver, writing in *Books,* called Ms. Wiz "cool and clever," and Chris Stephenson, in a *School Librarian* assessment, found the heroine "dashing." In addition to the "Ms. Wiz" stories, Blacker has written such children's books as *If I Could Work,* wherein a boy imagines himself in jobs ranging from firefighter to film actor. Nancy A. Gifford, writing in *School Library Journal,* contended that the book "just doesn't work," but a *Booklist* critic deemed it "a good choice for preschool story hours." Another tale, *Henry and the Frights,* concerns a boy who overcomes his nighttime fears through the aid of kindly nocturnal creatures. Jill Bennett, in her *Times Educational Supplement* analysis, found *Henry and the Frights* "appealing and accessible."

A more demanding book, *Herbie Hamster, Where Are You?* — published in England as *Houdini, the Disappearing Hamster* —, features illustrations where the main character is hidden; readers are instructed to find the hamster in various settings. *Booklist* reviewer Denise Wilms proclaimed the volume "a fun exercise." Cliff Moon noted in *School Librarian* that the book calls for "rapt attention," and Pearl Herscovitch reported in *School Library Journal* that "children are challenged."

Blacker's writings for younger children also include *The Surprising Adventures of Baron Münchausen,* a recounting of the German folk hero's preposterous exploits. A *Books for Keeps* reviewer recommended the book as "irrepressible fun." Similarly, *The Great Denture Adventure,* wherein a grandmother accidentally expels her false teeth, thus sending them on a series of unlikely but amusing travels—impressed a *School Librarian* critic as "entertaining and enjoyable."

Other publications by Blacker include *The Meaning of Cantona,* a collection of reflections on French soccer player Eric Cantona, who led Manchester United to several Premier League championships and English Cup victories in the 1990s. A *Books* reviewer recommended *The Meaning of Cantona* as a "hilarious compilation."

BIOGRAPHICAL AND CRITICAL SOURCES:

PERIODICALS

Booklist, June 1, 1988, review of *If I Could Work,* p. 1672; August, 1990, Denise Wilms, review of *Herbie Hamster, Where Are You?,* p. 2169; November 1, 2001, Emily Melton, review of *Kill Your Darlings,* p. 461; December 1, 2001, Anna Rich, review of *Ms. Wiz Supermodel,* p. 64.

Books, March, 1989, Jane Dorrell, review of *Fixx,* p. 22; October, 1989, Pamela Cleaver, reviews of *Ms. Wiz Spells Trouble, In Stitches with Ms. Wiz,* and *You're Nicked Ms. Wiz,* p. 22; September, 1992, review of *The Fame Hotel,* p. 27; October, 1997, review of *The Meaning of Cantona,* p. 17.

Books for Keeps, July, 1990, review of *In Stitches with Ms. Wiz,* p. 10; March, 1992, review of *The Surprising Adventures of Baron Munchausen,* p. 10; July, 1993, review of *Time Flies for Ms.*

Wiz, p. 13; May, 1994, review of *Ms. Wiz Loves Dracula,* p. 12; November, 1996, review of *You're Kidding, Ms. Wiz,* p. 9; May, 1998, Andrew Kidd, review of *The Transfer,* p. 27.

Books for Your Children, spring, 1991, C. Haydn Jones, review of *You're Nicked Ms. Wiz,* p. 21.

Children's Book Service Review, October, 1990, review of *Herbie Hamster, Where Are You?,* p. 13.

Horn Book, July-August, 1993, Ellen Fader, review of *Homebird,* p. 464.

Junior Bookshelf, October, 1989, review of *Henry and the Frights,* p. 210.

Kirkus Reviews, October 1, 2001, review of *Kill Your Darlings,* p. 1378.

New Statesman, July 10, 2000, Hugo Barnacle, review of *Kill Your Darlings,* p. 57.

New Statesman & Society, February 17, 1989, Sean French, "First-Person Thatcherism," p. 39; January 19, 1996, Laurie Taylor, review of *Revenance,* p. 40.

Observer (London, England), February 12, 1989, John Spurling, review of *Fixx,* p. 50; August 30, 1992, Ruth Pavey, review of *The Fame Hotel,* p. 50.

Publishers Weekly, April 5, 1993, review of *Homebird,* p. 79; October 15, 2001, review of *Kill Your Darlings,* p. 44.

School Librarian, February, 1989, Chris Stephenson, review of *Ms. Wiz Spells Trouble,* pp. 19-20; August, 1990, Shona Walton, review of *In Control, Ms. Wiz?,* p. 106; November, 1990, Cliff Moon, review of *Houdini, the Disappearing Hamster,* p. 141; May, 1993, Katherine Moule, review of *The Great Denture Adventure,* p. 53; August, 1993, Chris Stephenson, review of *Ms. Wiz Loves Dracula,* p. 105; summer, 1998, Linda Saunders, review of *The Transfer,* p. 76.

School Library Journal, August, 1988, Nancy A. Gifford, review of *If I Could Work,* p. 78; November, 1990, Peal Herscovitch, review of *Herbie Hamster, Where Are You?,* p. 85; April, 1993, Jacqueline Rose, review of *Homebird,* p. 140.

Spectator, February 17, 1996, Patrick Skene Catling, "Let Me Go, Lover," p. 32.

Times (London, England), October 28, 2001, Trevor Lewis, review of *Kill Your Darlings,* p. 46.

Times Educational Supplement, June 2, 1989, Jill Bennett, "Means of Escape," p. B8; April 18, 1997, reviews of *Pride and Penalties, On the Wing,* and *Shooting Star,* p. 12; October 31, 1997, Geraldine Brennan, "Wild and Wonderous Witchery," p. 8; February 27, 1998, Geoff Fox, "Call of the Wild," p. 10.

Times Literary Supplement, May 5, 1990, John Melmoth, "Up and on the Make," p. 483; October 2, 1992, Mark Sanderson, "Trash by the Tranche," p. 21; February 2, 1996, Roz Kaveney, "Little Local Difficulties," p. 23; July 21, 2000, Sam Gilpin, "Creative Writing," p. 22.

Voice of Youth Advocate, August, 1993, Eleanor Klopp, review of *Homebird,* p. 148.*

*　　*　　*

BLISCHKE, Wallace R. 1934-

PERSONAL: Born April 20, 1934, in Oak Park, IL; son of Walter H. (a tool maker) and Mabel E. (a homemaker) Blischke; married Rosemary Case (divorced, 1973); married Beverly Williams (died March 10, 1987); married Carol Mowell, August 5, 1995; children: Elizabeth Case, Scott, Michael; stepchildren: Douglas Satterblom, Carol Satterblom, Julia M. Hata, Kathryn Kinslow. *Education:* Elmhurst College, B.S., 1956; Cornell University, M.S., 1958, Ph.D., 1961. *Religion:* Lutheran.

ADDRESSES: Home—5401 Katherine Ave., Sherman Oaks, CA 91401-4922. *Office*—Marshall School of Business, University of Southern California, Los Angeles, CA 90089-1421. *E-mail*—blischke@marshall.usc.edu.

CAREER: North Carolina College of Agriculture and Engineering (now North Carolina State University), Raleigh, faculty member, 1961-62; worked for Space Technology Laboratories of TRW Systems, 1962-64; Control Data Corp., Beverly Hills, CA, principal scientist for C-E-I-R Professional Services, 1964-70; private consultant in statistical analysis, 1970-72; University of Southern California, Los Angeles, associate professor of statistics, 1972-98, associate professor emeritus and consultant, 1998—. Presenter of seminars and classes at universities, corporations, and other institutions in the United States and abroad; consultant to government agencies, business, and industry, including Blue Chip Stamps, Ford Motor Company, Shell Oil, and National Aeronautics and Space Administration.

MEMBER: American Statistical Association (fellow), Institute of Mathematical Statistics, Biometric Society, INFORMS, Sigma Xi, Phi Kappa Phi.

WRITINGS:

(With D. N. P. Murthy) *Warranty Cost Analysis,* Marcel Dekker (New York, NY), 1994.

(With D. N. P. Murthy) *Product Warranty Handbook,* Marcel Dekker (New York, NY), 1996.

(With D. N. P. Murthy) *Reliability: Modeling, Prediction, and Optimization,* Wiley Publishing Group (New York, NY), 2000.

Case Studies in Reliability and Maintenance, Wiley Publishing Group (New York, NY), 2002.

Contributor to books, including *Linear Models,* edited by S. R. Searle, Wiley Publishing Group (New York, NY), 1972; *The Theory and Applications of Reliability, with Emphasis on Bayesian and Nonparametric Methods,* Volume 2, edited by Chris Tsokos and I. N. Shimi, Academic Press (New York, NY), 1977; and *Statistics of Quality,* edited by S. Ghosh, W. R. Schucany, and W. B. Smith, Marcel Dekker (New York, NY), 1996. Contributor to periodicals, including *Journal of Spacecraft and Rockets, European Journal of Operational Research, International Journal of Production Economics, Mathematical and Computer Modeling, Journal of Information and Optimization Sciences, Technometrics, Health Services Research, Biometrics, Annals of Mathematical Statistics,* and *Naval Research Logistics Quarterly.* Associate editor, *American Journal of Mathematical and Management Sciences* and *Communications in Statistics.*

WORK IN PROGRESS: Warranty Management; research on warranty analysis and reliability.

*   *   *

BOBORYKIN, Petr Dmitrievich 1836-1921

PERSONAL: Born August 15, 1836, in Nizhnii Novgorod, Russia; died following a stroke, August 12, 1921, in Lugano, Switzerland; married Sofiia Aleksandrovna (Kalmykova) Zborzhevskaia (an actress), November, 1872. *Education:* Attended University of Kazan, 1853-55; attended University of Derpt in Tartu, Estonia, 1855-60; University of St. Petersburg, degree, 1861.

CAREER: Writer, c. 1861-1921; land owner, c. 1861-c. 1917; *Biblioteka dlia chteniia* (library), owner and editor, 1863-65.

MEMBER: St. Petersburg Actors Club.

AWARDS, HONORS: Imperial Academy of Sciences, honorary membership, 1902.

WRITINGS:

(Translator) Johann-Gottlieb Lehmann, *Khimiia: Polnoe karmannoe rukovodstvo k teoreticheskoi i prakticheskoi khimii,* three volumes, M. O. Vol'f (St. Petersburg, Russia), 1860-1867.

Odnodvorets (play; title means "The Smallholder"), first published in *Biblioteka dlia chteniia,* [Russia], 1860, produced at the Malyi Theatre, Moscow, Russia, 1861.

Rebenok (play; title means "The Infant"), first published in *Biblioteka dlia chteniia,* [Russia], 1861, produced at the Malyi Theatre, Moscow, Russia, 1862.

V put'-dorogu! (novel; title means "On the Road!"), first published in *Biblioteka dlia chteniia,* numbers 1-5, 9, 12, 1862, numbers 5-8, 12, 1863, numbers 9-12, 1864, reprinted, Vnutrenniaia strazha i E. Arnol'd (St. Petersburg, Russia), 1864.

Zemskie sily (novel; title means "The Powers of the Land"), first published in *Biblioteka dlia chteniia,* numbers 1-8, 1865, reprinted, Akademiia nauk (St. Petersburg, Russia), 1865.

V chuzhom pole, first published in *Russkii vestnik,* numbers 10, 12, 1866, reprinted, A. M. Kotomin (St. Petersburg, Russia), 1872.

Zhertva vecherniaia (novel; title means "Victim of the Night"), first published in *Vsemirnyi trud,* numbers 1-2, 4-5, 7, 1868, reprinted, M. Khan (St. Petersburg, Russia), 1868, revised and enlarged edition, N. A. Shigin (St. Petersburg, Russia), 1872.

Na sud, first published in *Vsemirnyi trud,* numbers 1-5, 1869, reprinted, [St. Petersburg, Russia], 1869.

Solidnye dobrodeteli (novel; title means "Solid Virtues"), first published in *Otechestvennye zapiski,* numbers 9-12, 1870, reprinted, E. P. Pechatkin (St. Petersburg, Russia), 1871.

Povesti, M. O. Vol'f (St. Petersburg, Russia), c. 1871.

Povesti i rasskazy, Moriegerovsky (St. Petersburg, Russia), 1872, compiled, edited, and annotated by Sergei I. Chuprinin, Sovetskaia Rossia (Moscow, USSR), 1984.

Teatral'noe iskusstvo (lectures), N. Nekliudov (St. Petersburg, Russia), 1872.

Del'tsy (novel; title means "The Operators"), first published in *Otechestvennye zapiski,* numbers 4-12, 1872, numbers 1-5, 1873, reprinted, V. Tushkov (St. Petersburg, Russia), 1874.

Polzhizni (novel; title means "Half a Life"), first published in *Vestnik Evropy,* numbers 11-12, 1873, reprinted, Kekhribardzhi (St. Petersburg, Russia), 1874.

Doktor Tsybul'ka (novel), first published in *Otechestvennye zapiski,* numbers 3-6, 1874, reprinted, Salaev (Moscow, Russia), 1875.

V usad'be i na poriadke, Dolgo-li? Povesti (novellas), Kekhribardzhi (St. Petersburg, Russia), 1876.

Likhie bolesti (novel; title means "Grave Disorders"), first published in *Otechestvennye zapiski,* numbers 10-11, 1876, reprinted, [St. Petersburg, Russia], 1877.

Ne u del (play; title means "Out of Office"), published in *Slovo,* number 1, 1878.

Sami po sebe (novel; title means "All by Themselves"), published in *Slovo,* numbers 9-12, 1878.

Sytye: P'esa v 5-i aktakh (play; title means "Fat Cats"), first published in *Slovo,* number 11, 1879, reprinted, V. Demakov (St. Petersburg, Russia), 1879.

Iskusstvo chteniia, V. Demakov (St. Petersburg, Russia), 1882.

Kitai-gorod (novel), first published in *Vestnik Evropy,* numbers 1-5, 1882, reprinted, Goslitizdat (Moscow, USSR), 1957.

Teoriia teatral'nogo iskusstva (nonfiction), V. S. Kurochkin (St. Petersburg, Russia), 1882.

Doktor Moshkov: P'esa v 4-kh aktakh (play), first published in *Izvestiia Literatury,* number 2, 1884, reprinted, A. E. Landau (St. Petersburg, Russia), 1885.

Sochineniia, twelve volumes, M. O. Vol'f (St. Petersburg, Russia), 1884-1886.

Za rabotu (novel; title means "To Work!"), published in *Nov',* numbers 13-18, 1885.

Kleimo: Drama v 4-kh aktakh (play), E. N. Rassokhina (Moscow, Russia), 1886.

Narodnyi teatr, Novostoi (Moscow, Russia), 1886.

Iz novykh (novel; title means "The New Men"), published in *Vestnik Evropy,* numbers 1-6, 1887.

Na ushcherbe (novel; title means "On the Wane"), published in *Vestnik Evropy,* numbers 1-6, 1890.

Poumnel (novella; title means "Older and Wiser"), published in *Russkaia mysl',* numbers 10-12, 1890.

Povesti dlia vzroslykh, V. I. Az (Moscow, Russia), 1891.

S boiu (play; title means "Pitched Battle"), published in *Artist,* number 13, 1891.

Vasilii Terkin, published in *Vestnik Evropy,* numbers 1-6, 1892, I. D. Sytin (Moscow, Russia), 1895.

Trup: Povest', published in *Severnyi vestnik,* number 4, 1892, Posrednik (Moscow, Russia), 1893.

Pered chem-to, published in *Severnyi vestnik,* numbers 10-11, 1892, Karl Malkomes (Stuttgart, Germany), 1893.

Pereval (novel; title means "The Pass"), published in *Vestnik Evropy,* numbers 1-6, 1894.

Khodok (novel; title means "The Go-between"), published in *Vestnik Evropy,* numbers 1-6, 1895.

Kniaginia (novel; title means "The Princess"), published in *Vestnik Evropy,* numbers 1-6, 1896.

Po-drugomu (novel; title means "Another Way"), published in *Vestnik Evropy,* numbers 1-4, 1897.

Sobranie romanov, povestei i rasskazov, twelve volumes, A. F. Marks (St. Petersburg, Russia), 1897.

Tiaga (novel; title means "Drawing Force"), published in *Vestnik Evropy,* numbers 1-5, 1898.

Kuda idti? (novel; title means "Whither Now?"), published in *Vestnik Evropy,* numbers 1-4, 1899.

Nakip': Komediia v 4-kh aktakh (play; title means "Froth on the Surface"; produced at the Aleksandrinskii Theatre, St. Petersburg, Russia, 1899), [St. Petersburg, Russia], 1899, published as *Povetrie,* in *Theatr i iskusstvo,* number 1, 1900.

Evropeiskii roman v XIX stoletti: Roman na zapade za dve treti veka (nonfiction; title means "The European Novel of the Nineteenth Century: The Novel in the West over Two-thirds of a Century"), M. Stasiulevich (St. Petersburg, Russia), 1900.

Zhestokie (novel; title means "The Cruel Ones"), published in *Russkaia mysl',* numbers 1-6, 1901.

Istinno-nauchnoe znanie: Otvet moim kritikam, I. N. Kushnerev (Moscow, Russia), 1901.

Vechnyi gorod (itogi perezhitogo), I. N. Kushnerev (Moscow, Russia), 1903.

Uprazdniteli, published in *Russkaia mysl',* number 11, 1904.

Za polveka: Moie vospominaniia (memoirs; title means "Half a Century"), first published in installments in *Russkaia mysl', Golos minuvshego, Minuvshie gody,* and *Russkaia starina,* 1906-1913, edited with introduction and notes by B. P. Koz'min, Zemlia i fabrika (Moscow, USSR), 1929.

Velikaia razrukha (novel; title means "Rack and Ruin"), V. I. Sablin (Moscow, Russia), 1908.

Ne pervye, ne poslednie: Rasskazy dlia detei srednego vozrasta, M. O. Vol'f (St. Petersburg, Russia), 1908.

Stolitsy mira: Tridsat' let vospominanii (nonfiction; title means "Capitals of the World"), Sfinks (Moscow, Russia), 1911.

Obmirshchenie (novel; title means "Profanation"), Sfinks (Moscow, Russia), 1912.

Odna dusha: Rasskaz, Universal'naia biblioteka (Moscow, Russia), 1918.

Vospominaniia, two volumes, edited and annotated by E. Vilenskaia and L. Roitberg, Khudozhestvennaia literatura (Moscow, USSR), 1965.

Sochineniia, three volumes, edited and annotated by Sergei I. Chuprinin, Khudozhestvennaia literatura (Moscow, Russia), 1993.

Contributor of essays and fiction to periodicals, including *Vsemirnyi trud, Philosophie positive, Fortnightly Review, Rivista europea, Otechestvennye zapiski, Slovo, Voprosy filosofii i psikhologii, Severnyi vestnik, Contemporary Review, L'Humanite nouvelle,* and *Russkaia mysl'.*

SIDELIGHTS: Russian novelist, dramatist, and critic Petr Dmitrievich Boborykin wrote so prolifically during the late nineteenth and early twentieth centuries that rivals and detractors derived two Russian verbs from his last name. According to John McNair in *Dictionary of Literary Biography, boborykat* means "to write immoderately and tediously," and *oboborykinit'sia* means "to become dazed from a surfeit of Boborykin." Though many contemporary Russian literature readers have overlooked him, Mc-Nair said "some of his novels, stories, and plays had in their day considerable impact on the reading (and theatergoing) public."

While no single work stands out, Boborykin's volume and variety are impressive. He wrote twenty-six novels, including *Polzhizni* and *Kitai-gorod;* about thirty plays, including *Odnodvorets* and *Nakip';* and volumes of criticism such as *Teatral'noe iskusstvo* and *Evropeiskii roman v XIX stoletti: Roman na zapade za dve treti veka.* After decades of neglect, the Russian publisher Khudozhestvennaia literatura issued *Sochineniia,* a three-volume collection of some of Boborykin's writings, in 1993.

Boborykin's parents had already separated before his birth, and he lived most of his childhood and adolescence with his grandparents. His grandfather was a retired general and owned estates. While attending the local secondary school, he took interest in Russian and European literature. After enrolling at the university in Kazan, intending to pursue administrative studies,

Boborykin soon transferred to the University of Derpt in Estonia, where he emphasized chemistry, physiology, and medicine. There, he began work on his first published book, a translation into Russian of a chemistry textbook by German geologist Johann Gottlob Lehmann.

After several years at Derpt, he transferred to the university in St. Petersburg, where he completed his administrative studies work in 1861. By then Boborykin had decided to become a professional writer; inheriting his grandfather's estates soon afterward gave him even more economic freedom to work toward this goal.

Boborykin first published his work in serial form, as did most of his Russian contemporaries. His first original piece was the play *Odnodvorets,* which appeared in print in *Biblioteka dlia chteniia* in 1860 and which was produced in Moscow a year later. Boborykin's first novel, *V put'-dorogu!,* also became available to readers in *Biblioteka dlia chteniia,* and the owner of that publication eventually convinced Boborykin to purchase the journal. The young writer did not realize the extent of the journal's financial problems, but he kept *Biblioteka dlia chteniia* afloat until, as McNair reported, disaster struck.

Boborykin allowed the publication of *Nekuda* by Nikolai Semenovich Leskov in an 1864 issue of *Biblioteka dlia chteniia,* and, in McNair's words, this novel was so "widely regarded as an attack on Russian radicalism" that it "provoked outrage, much of it directed at *Biblioteka dlia chteniia* and its unfortunate editor. Contributions were withdrawn and subscriptions canceled." Boborykin had to stop publishing *Biblioteka dlia chteniia* in 1865, and he wrote prolifically for more than twenty years just to pay off related debts. McNair wrote, "the opprobrium attaching to him from the *Nekuda* episode was never wholly forgotten and was certainly a factor in his failure to win the critical recognition he believed to be his due."

According to McNair, some of Boborykin's plays, especially *Nakip',* were successful in their time. Boborykin took a great interest in theatrical matters and dramatic techniques. He married an actress, lectured on dramatic performance, and wrote articles and books on the subject. He also called for better training for Russian actors.

After Boborykin penned *Velikaia razruka,* he concentrated on shorter works of fiction and memoirs. Boborykin, who frequently traveled throughout Europe, was vacationing in Italy in 1914 when a doctor advised him not to return to Russia for health reasons. He eventually settled in Switzerland, where he watched from afar as his native Russia struggled through war and revolution.

He continued to write for the periodicals of other nations, however, until he had a stroke in June, 1921. Boborykin died a few months later.

BIOGRAPHICAL AND CRITICAL SOURCES:

BOOKS

Dictionary of Literary Biography, Volume 238: *Russian Novelists in the Age of Tolstoy and Dostoevsky,* Gale (Detroit, MI), 2001.
Offord, Derek, editor, *The Golden Age of Russian Literature and Thought,* St. Martin's Press (Detroit, MI), 1992.

PERIODICALS

Slavonic and East European Review, Volume 63, number 4, 1985, John McNair, "A Russian European: Boborykin in England," pp. 540-559; Volume 70, number 2, 1992, John McNair, "*The Reading Library* and the Reading Public: The Decline and Fall of *Biblioteka dlia chteniia,*" pp. 213-227.*

*   *   *

BORGESE, Giuseppe Antonio 1882-1952

PERSONAL: Born November 12, 1882, in Polizzi Generosa, Palermo province, Italy; immigrated to the United States, 1931, naturalized citizen 1938; died, of cerebral thrombosis in Fiesole, Italy, December 2, 1952; son of a lawyer; married Maria Freschi (divorced); married Elisabeth Mann, 1939; children: (first marriage) Leonardo, Giovanni. *Education:* University of Florence, Ph.D. 1903.

CAREER: Novelist and literary critic; professor of literature. La Stampa, Turin, Italy, literary editor; University of Rome, professor of German literature, 1910-17; Press and Propaganda Bureau, head; Roman Congress, organizer, 1919; Interallied Conference, London, England, delegate, August 1918; *Corriere della Sera,* Milan, Italy, foreign editor; University of Milan, professor of German literature and aesthetics, 1919-31, 1948-52; University of California, visiting professor, 1931; University of Chicago, professor of Italian literature, 1936-48; University of Chicago, Committee to Frame a World Constitution, founder, 1946. *Military service:* Officer in Italian army, diplomat in France and Switzerland during World War I.

WRITINGS:

Storia della critica romantica in Italia (title means "History of Romantic Criticism in Italy"), 1905, Mondadori (Milan, Italy), 1949.
La nuova Germania, Fratelli Treves (Milan, Italy), 1917.
La vita e il libro (title means "Life and Books"), 1913.
Rubè, 1921, translated by I. Goldberg, 1923.
A Poetics of Unity, 1934.
Atlante americano, Guanda Editore (Modena, Italy), 1936.
Benedetto Croce, Edizoni Controcorrento (Boston, MA), 1945.
Golia: Marcia del fascismo (title means "Goliath: The March of Fascism"), Mondadori (Milan, Italy), 1949.
(With H. Agar) *The City of Man: A Declaration of World Democracy,* 1940.
(With Harold Deutsch and Louis Gottschalk) *Italy: A Radio Discussion,* University of Chicago Press (Chicago, IL), 1943.
(Editor) *Italian Short Stories of Today,* 1946.
(Librettist) *Montezuma: Opera in Three Acts,* music by R. Sessions, 1964.
Schoonheden, Goossens (Tricht), 1988.
Beautiful Women, translated by John Shepley, Northwestern University Press (Evanston, IL), 2001.

Wrote a number of critical articles for journals and the literary pages of newspapers; wrote novels and several plays in the 1920s; wrote feature articles for *Corriere della sera.*

SIDELIGHTS: Giuseppe Antonio Borgese was one of the most important figures in Italian literature in the first half of the twentieth century. Linguist, novelist, journalist, and academic, he participated fully in Italian literary and political life, serving as a professor and a diplomat. Driven away from Italy by the rise of fascism, he fled to the United States where he continued to fight against the movement that had overtaken his homeland. Borgese was ultimately a romantic; though he admired classical thought, in his work and ideology, he tended to come down on the side of idealism and aesthetic transcendence. All his activities, whether scholarly, creative, or political, were informed by his concept of spiritual unity, which he called "syntax."

Borgese was born in a small town in the mountains near Palermo, Sicily, the third child of a lawyer and his wife. He went to Palermo in 1888, where he lived with uncles and aunts while attending school. His favorite authors at the time were Tolstoy and De Sanctis. In 1900 he went to Florence, where he completed his studies, earning a Ph.D. in 1903. During this time, he became very interested in the work of poet Gabriele D'Annunzio and Benedetto Croce. Borgese was fascinated by criticism and aesthetics. His first book, *Storia della critica romantica in Italia,* was an adaptation of his doctoral thesis and was published in 1905. It was widely praised, but, like many of his essays, showed the influence of Croce and therefore earned him some notoriety in literary circles.

Borgese spent the next several years in Naples, the Lombard Lakes, Berlin (where he lived from 1907 to 1909), and Turin. He took an interest in Johann Wolfgang von Goethe, who was to remain one of his favorite writers. In Turin, Borgese was appointed literary editor of the daily *La Scala.* He met Maria Freschi, a poet from Florence; they married and had two sons.

In 1909, after he returned from Germany, the University of Rome offered Borgese the chair of German literature. He taught German literature at the University of Rome from 1910 until 1917. He delivered lectures and essays on Goethe that revealed his love of creative criticism, and almost seemed to say that critics needed to compete with authors in creativity. After World War I, however, he tired of that competition and began to write creatively himself.

Politically, Borgese was generally liberal and progressive, though he did have a brief period (1904-1908) of reactive nationalism. Though he was raised in the Catholic faith and his sentiments lay there, his main desire was for a rational and universal religion. During his younger years, he corresponded with other young men about the best way to reestablish religion's former cultural primacy and modernize its intellectual life, an ambitious and occasionally contradictory task. Though he started out as something of a rebel, he gradually resumed more traditional ground and found it a good place from which to fight for his goals.

In the years before World War I, Borgese wrote hundreds of essays and articles on Italian and European literatures for *Corriere della Sera* and other periodicals. Some of these early essays were published in the 1913 collection *La vita e il libro.* Borgese wrote on D'Annunzio and wrote an essay on Goethe's *Faust* that illustrated the intellectual and structural unity of Goethe's work; his work on Goethe also illuminated his own innate preference for romanticism. He was an advocate for such writers as Federigo Tozzi and Alberto Moravia.

Though he had initially admired D'Annunzio's work, in 1909 Borgese changed his mind and repudiated both the poet and the literary trend of "dannunzianesimo." He also changed his opinion about Croce's aesthetics and critical methods. He wrote essays that opposed Croce's philosophy's fragmentism; these essays and others on aesthetics and the history of criticism were later collected in the 1934 anthology *A Poetics of Unity.*

During World War I, Borgese served as an officer on the front and as a diplomat in France and Switzerland. He wrote that this experience unleashed his imagination and his urge toward poetry; he wrote a number of plays, short stories, novels, and poems in the next decade, while continuing to write on aesthetics, politics, history, and translating the work of Goethe and Chamisso. He also became directly involved in politics at this time. He headed the bureau of Press and Propaganda under Orlando and participated in the Roman Congress and the Interallied Conference in 1918. In those positions and in his role as foreign editor of *Corriere della Sera* he did what he could to encourage the formation of a unified and democratic Europe, in line with U.S. President Woodrow Wilson's intention. This political position did not endear him to the subsequent fascist regime led by Benito Mussolini.

Rubè, Borgese's most famous novel, was published in 1921. This is the tale of a young, amoral Sicilian lawyer, a European "hollow man" who lives a meaningless life and dies a meaningless death. Borgese's primary concerns in writing the novel were philosophical rather than aesthetic. The protagonist's angst anticipates the anguished fictional characters who pervaded European literature in subsequent years. *Rubè* captured the attention of the Italian literary world of its time and did much to bring Italian fiction out of its contemporary provincialism; critics had more or less relegated the novel as a form to the literary trash heap, but Borgese's book injected some vigor back into the genre.

Sergio Pacifici in *The Modern Italian Novel: From Capuana to Tozzi* described *Rubè* as "less a well-made novel, or a well-written narrative, than a work that anticipates certain vital trends in literature and politics alike that were to blossom in the years following its publication, while simultaneously offering an accurate reflection of the mood of despair pervading the first decades of our century." Two years later, Borgese published *I vivi e i morti,* a continuation of the themes introduced in *Rubè* but less despairing. This book was also successful, though less so than its predecessor.

Borgese wrote a number of other works of fiction, poetry, drama, and criticism in the 1920s, but none of them has been widely read outside Italy. His best work at the time was his shorter pieces, especially his feature articles for *Corriere della Sera* and some short stories. A collection of translations of his stories titled *Beautiful Women* was published in 2001. All of these stories describe women, wives, mothers, lovers, with "melancholy fervor." In the first of the eighteen stories, a woman catches her husband with her maid and jumps off a balcony. In others, a beautiful girl drowns in a river, and a man fights over a woman with his best friend.

Borgese lived in Milan from 1919 to 1931, teaching German literature and aesthetics at the University of Milan. The growth of fascism made his life increasingly difficult, and he chose to move to the United States in 1931, where he took a position as a visiting professor at the University of California. He meant this move to be temporary, but soon after he left, all Italian professors were required to take the fascist oath; Borgese refused and stayed on in the United States.

In the following years, Borgese taught modern literature at several U.S. institutions, including Dr. Johnson's New School in New York and Smith College in Northampton, Massachusetts. His students were somewhat afraid of him due to his exotic demeanor and passionate convictions, but many of them learned to love and respect him. In 1936 he took a position at the University of Chicago, teaching Italian literature and political science. He began writing in English instead of Italian and continued to produce numerous essays and articles.

Borgese remained active among European exiles. His book *Goliath: The March of Fascism* was published in 1937; it was immediately translated into several languages, though it did not appear in Italian until 1946. Perhaps Borgeese's most important work in English, it is an impassioned attack on Mussolini's tyranny, to which Borgese contrasts what he considers Italy's "true face."

Borgese became a U.S. citizen in 1938. While in the United States he met German novelist Thomas Mann and fell in love with Mann's daughter Elizabeth. He divorced his first wife and married Elizabeth Mann in 1939.

In 1942 Borgese wrote, "Unity, across all separations, has been the leading inspiration of my life and work. . . . To this inspiration I hope to devote whatever is left of time and vigor to me." He spent his later years working to replace all kinds of tyranny with democracy. In 1946 he and Mortimer Adler worked at the University of Chicago to found the Committee to Frame a World Constitution. Borgese served as secretary general of the committee and contributed to a "Preliminary Draft of a World Constitution." He also edited the committee's monthly publication, *Common Cause.*

Borgese returned to Italy in 1948. He went back to the University of Milan where he resumed his post teaching aesthetics. He continued criticizing Croce's approach to literary history and worked to restore Francesco De Sanctis' poetry to a proper reading in light of culture and history, particularly De Sanctis' concept of the descent from the ideal into the real. At the same time, he had difficulty refuting Croce's theories convincingly; in the end, his own theories of poetry were quite similar to Croce's aesthetic theory of transcendence; though he tried to side with the classicists, Borgese was at heart a romantic. He died in Fiesole in 1952 of cerebral thrombosis.

BIOGRAPHICAL AND CRITICAL SOURCES:

BOOKS

Bede, Jean-Albert, and William B. Edgerton, *Columbia Dictionary of Modern European Literature,* 2nd edition, Columbia University Press (New York, NY), 1980.

Pacifici, Sergio, *The Modern Italian Novel: From Capuana to Tozzi,* Southern Illinois University Press (Carbondale, IL), 1973.

PERIODICALS

Annali della Facolta di Magistero dell'Universita di Bari, 1972-73, "Evoluzione ideologica . . . ," pp. 273-322.

Belfagor, January 31, 1997, "Giuseppe Antonio Borgese Politico," pp. 43-69.

Esperienze Letterarie, October, 1999, "Gli scritti politici di Giuseppe Antonio Borgese," pp. 53-69.

Italian Studies, 1999, Luciano Parisi, "La critica militante di Giuseppe Antonio Borgese," pp. 102-117.

Italianist, 1997, "I vivi e i morti," pp. 60-73.

Italica, summer, 1979, Gian-Paolo Biasin, "Il rosso o il nero: testo e ideologia in *Rubè,*" pp. 172-197.

Modern Language Notes, January, 1997, Luciano Parisi, "Borgese e Manzoni," pp. 38-56.

Publishers Weekly, May 28, 2001, p. 50.

OTHER

Bartleby, http://www.bartleby.com/ (March 21, 2002), "Borgese, Giuseppe Antonio."

Italialibri, http://www.italialibri.net/ (March 21, 2002), "Giuseppe Antonio Borgese (1882-1952)."

Letteratura Italiana, http://www.digilander.iol.it/ (March 21, 2002), "Giuseppe Antonio Borgese."*

*   *   *

BRANHAM, William M(arrion) 1909-1965

PERSONAL: Born April 6, 1909, in Burkesville, KY; died in a car crash, December 24, 1965, in Amarillo, TX; father, a logger; married Hope Brumbech, 1934 (died, 1937); children: one (died, 1937).

CAREER: Independent healing evangelist, beginning 1933. Branham Tabernacle (also known as Branham Tabernacle and Related Assemblies), founder; affiliated with Spoken Word Publications and Voice of God Recordings. Toured Africa and Europe in healing revivals, c. 1950s.

WRITINGS:

The Revelation of the Seven Seals, Spoken Word Publications (Tucson, AZ), 1967.

Conduct, Order, Doctrine of the Church, two volumes, Spoken Word Publications (Jeffersonville, IN), 1974.

Subject Encyclopedia of Sermons by Rev. William M. Branham, compiled by David Mamalis, William Branham Library (Mesa, AZ), 1978.

Biographie de William Branham, edited by André Morin, Editions Sermons William Branham (Warden, Québec, Canada), 1983.

Author of "An Exposition of the Seven Church Ages," Branham Campaigns (Jeffersonville, IN) and "Footprints on the Sands of Time," Spoken Word Publications (Jeffersonville, IN). Founder, *Voice of Healing,* 1948.

BIOGRAPHICAL AND CRITICAL SOURCES:

BOOKS

Lindsey, Gordon, *William Branham: A Man Sent from God,* William M. Branham (Jeffersonville, IN), 1950.

Pement, Eric, *An Annotated Bibliography of Material by and about William Marrion Branham,* Cornerstone Magazine (Chicago, IL), 1986.

Weaver, C. Douglas, *The Healer-Prophet, William Marrion Branham,* Mercer University Press (Macon, GA), 1987.*

*   *   *

BRATTON, Daniel L(ance) 1950-

PERSONAL: Born July 8, 1950, in Cleveland, OH; son of David and Shirley (a journalist; maiden name, Gremb) Bratton; married Genevieve Thomas, May, 1973 (marriage ended, c. 1983); married Carol Williams, February, 2001. *Education:* University of Lethbridge, B.A. (with distinction), 1972; University of Toronto, M.A., 1975, Ph.D., 1983; also attended Bluffton College, Harvard University, and University of Saskatchewan. *Politics:* "Jeffersonian Democrat." *Religion:* "Pantheist." *Hobbies and other interests:* Gardening, equestrian pursuits, collecting Far Eastern antiquities and arts-and-crafts furniture, architectural history.

ADDRESSES: Home—P.O. Box 548, Elora, Ontario, Canada N0B 1S0. *Office*—Faculty of Comparative Literature, Miyozaki International College, 1405 Kano Kiyotake-cho, Miyazaki-gun, Japan 889-1605; fax: (Canada) 519-846-9845 and (Japan) 011-82-985-84-3396. *E-mail*—dbratton@miyazaki-mic.ac.jp.

CAREER: Educator. Ryerson Polytechnic University, Toronto, Ontario, Canada, instructor in English, 1977-89, coordinator of evening studies, 1988-89; University of Toronto, Toronto, instructor in English, 1990-93; Youngdong University, Youngdong, South Korea, assistant professor, 1995-98, associate professor of English, 1998; Miyazaki International College, Miyazaki, Japan, professor of literature, 1999—. Guest lecturer at other institutions, including University of Salford, Manchester Metropolitan University, and Salve Regina University.

MEMBER: Edith Wharton Society, Writers Union of Canada.

AWARDS, HONORS: Canada Council grant.

WRITINGS:

Thirty-two Short Views of Mazo de la Roche: A Biographical Essay, ECW Press (Canada), 1996.
(Editor and author of introduction) *Yrs. Ever Affly: The Correspondence of Edith Wharton and Louis Bromfield,* Michigan State University Press (East Lansing, MI), 2000.

Contributor of articles and reviews to periodicals, including *Comparative Culture* and *Edith Wharton Review.*

WORK IN PROGRESS: A biography of actress Dora Sayers.

SIDELIGHTS: Daniel L. Bratton told *CA:* "My primary motivation for writing at this time is to explore the theoretical possibilities inherent to the practice of life writing. For example, in composing a biography of the Canadian writer Mazo de la Roche, I interspersed my account of the chapters in my subject?s life with critical discussion of her works; photographs (both old and contemporary); passages from—and actual reproduction of—old letters; conversations with the last living contacts with de la Roche and her cousin, Caroline Clement; and an interview with Timothy Findley, who had been a scriptwriter for the Canadian Broadcasting Company program *Whiteoaks of Jalna.* I plan to follow a similar approach in presenting the life story of Dora Sayers, a Broadway actress of the 1930s-1940s who belonged to a distinguished Canadian family and lived, in her formative years, in close proximity to de la Roche and the poet Dorothy Livesay."

BIOGRAPHICAL AND CRITICAL SOURCES:

PERIODICALS

Booklist, December 15, 2000, Mary Carroll, review of *Yrs. Ever Affly: The Correspondence of Edith Wharton and Louis Bromfield,* p. 781.
Canadian Literature, summer-autumn, 1999, Joy Henley, review of *Thirty-two Short Views of Mazo de la Roche: A Biographical Essay,* p. 222.
University of Toronto Quarterly, winter, 1997, John Orange, review of *Thirty-two Short Views of Mazo de la Roche,* p. 296.

*   *   *

BUCKLEY, James Monroe 1836-1920

PERSONAL: Born December 16, 1836, in Rahway, NJ; died February 8, 1920, in Morristown, NJ; son of John and Abbie Lonsdale (Monroe) Buckley; married Eliza A. Burns, August 2, 1864 (marriage ended); married Sarah Isabella French Staples, April 22, 1874 (marriage ended); married Adelaide Shackford Hill, August 23, 1886. *Education:* Attended Wesleyan University, Middletown, CT, c. 1856-57; attended medical school, 1866-69.

CAREER: Pastor of Methodist Episcopal churches in Exeter, NH, Dover, NH, and Manchester, NH, between 1859 and 1866; Methodist minister in Detroit, MI,

1870s; pastor of Methodist churches in Brooklyn, NY, and Stamford, CT, late 1870s; *New York Christian Advocate* (also known as *Christian Advocate*), editor, 1880-1912. Also worked as a schoolteacher. Delegate to general conferences of the Methodist Episcopal church, beginning 1872; International Ecumenical Methodist Conference, delegate, 1881, 1891, 1901.

WRITINGS:

Christians and the Theater, 1875.
Oats or Wild Oats?, 1885.
The Midnight Sun, the Tsar, and the Nihilist, 1886.
Faith Healing, Century Co. (New York, NY), 1892, published as *Faith Healing, Christian Science, and Kindred Phenomena,* 1906.
A Hereditary Consumptive's Successful Battle for Life, Hunt & Eaton (New York, NY), 1892.
Travels in Three Continents: Europe, Africa, Asia, Hunt & Eaton (New York, NY), 1895.
A History of Methodists in the United States, Christian Literature Co. (New York, NY), 1896.
A History of Methodism in the United States, two volumes, Harper (New York, NY), 1898.
Christian Science and Other Superstitions, Century Co. (New York, NY), 1899.
The Fundamentals and Their Contrasts, Publishing House of the Methodist Episcopal Church (Nashville, TN), 1906.
(Editor, with Daniel Ayres Goodsell and Joseph Beaumont Hingeley) *The Doctrines and Discipline of the Methodist Episcopal Church,* Jennings & Graham (Cincinnati, OH), 1908.
The Wrong and Peril of Woman's Suffrage, 1909.
Theory and Practice of Foreign Missions, 1911.
Constitutional and Parliamentary History of the Methodist Episcopal Church, Jennings & Graham (New York, NY), 1912.

Author of booklets, including "Two Weeks in the Yosemite and Vicinity," Nelson & Phillips (New York, NY), 1873. Also author of hymns. Contributor to Methodist periodicals.

BIOGRAPHICAL AND CRITICAL SOURCES:

BOOKS

Mains, George Preston, *James Monroe Buckley,* Methodist Book Concern (New York, NY), 1917.

OBITUARIES:

PERIODICALS

Christian Advocate, February 19, 1920.
New York Times, February 9, 1920.
Outlook, February 18, 1920.*

*   *   *

BURDEN, Michael 1960-

PERSONAL: Born 1960.

ADDRESSES: Office—New Chamber Opera, 4 Mansfield Rd., Oxford OX1 3TA, England.

CAREER: New College, Oxford University, Oxford, England, lecturer in music, 1989—; Oxford University, fellow in music and lecturer in opera studies, 1995—. Founder, with Gary Cooper, New Chamber Opera, 1990.

WRITINGS:

Lost Adelaide: A Photographic Record, Oxford University Press (New York, NY), 1983.
Garrick, Arne, and the Masque of Alfred: A Case Study in National, Theatrical, and Musical Politic, Edwin Mellen Press (Lewiston, NY), 1994.
The Purcell Companion, Amadeus Press (Portland, OR), 1995.
Purcell Remembered, Amadeus Press (Portland, OR), 1995.

EDITOR

Performing the Music of Henry Purcell, Oxford University Press (New York, NY), 1996.
A Woman Scorn'd: Responses to the Dido Myth, Faber (New York, NY), 1998.
Henry Purcell's Operas: The Complete Texts, Oxford University Press (New York, NY), 1999.

SIDELIGHTS: Michael Burden is best known for his studies of seventeenth-century music composer Henry Purcell, including *The Purcell Companion, Purcell Remembered, Performing the Music of Henry Purcell, A Woman Scorn'd: Responses to the Dido Myth,* and *Henry Purcell's Operas: The Complete Texts.* Though Purcell is often treated as a solitary figure in music history, Burden has worked both as an editor and as a scholar to find Purcell's connections to other composers.

In *The Purcell Companion,* for example, Burden combines the work of ten disparate Purcell experts, including Andrew Pinnock, Eric van Tassel, Peter Holman, and Bruce Wood. In Burden's own essay, "Purcell's Contemporaries," he focuses on the much-overlooked question of Purcell's relationship to other artists of the period. As William Gatens explained in *American Record Guide:* "One of the most serious issues [facing Purcell scholarship] has been a tendency to study Purcell in isolation, largely neglecting his contemporaries and immediate predecessors. Michael Burden addresses this issue directly." Gatens concluded, "It is a fine collection that will be of immense value to the serious student, though the more casual reader may find it rough going in places." Paul Griffiths, writing for the *Times Literary Supplement,* similarly concluded that "*The Purcell Companion . . .* is also thoroughly worthwhile."

In another Purcell study by Burden, *Purcell Remembered,* Burden collects disparate documents related to the composer's life. Mark A. Radice, writing in *Notes,* called the book "extraordinarily engaging both for the scholar and the amateur," and added that "Michael Burden's editorial remarks are helpful, interesting, and carefully researched." Gatens, however, said, "While a good deal of scholarship went into the preparation of this book, it does not seem to be addressed primarily to other scholars, though many of them will want to have it handy." He added, "This is not a book to displace the still-standard Purcell biography of Franklin B. Zimmerman, but rather a volume to delight the general reader and point the serious student toward a wealth of fascinating sources."

Burden's more recent Purcell studies, *Performing the Music of Henry Purcell* and *A Woman Scorn'd,* each place Purcell in an interdisciplinary context. In the former volume, Burden brings together the work of both performers and scholars to discuss the traditions of performing Purcell; in the latter volume, Burden places Purcell's Dido opera in the context of other interpretations of the Dido myth. *Notes* contributor Judith Milhous commented on *Performing the Music of Henry Purcell:* "Coordination is not a characteristic of this volume. . . . Many of the essays represent sound scholarship, but they do not really form a coherent book, and the quality ranges from admirable to extremely disappointing." In *A Woman Scorn'd,* however, the interdisciplinary approach pleased several critics somewhat better. Peter Porter, writing in the *Times Literary Supplement,* welcomed the book: "This erudite but wayward assembly of commentary on *Dido and Aeneas* does modern readers one good service—it reminds them that the classics have not come down to us in some impeccably hermetic package."

Often, scholars have treated Purcell as a sort of "hermetic package" himself. But through his editorial duties and scholarship, Burden has managed to find the cultural connections to Henry Purcell, firmly placing the composer in his proper place in cultural history.

BIOGRAPHICAL AND CRITICAL SOURCES:

PERIODICALS

American Record Guide, November-December, 1995, William Gatens, review of *The Purcell Companion,* p. 312; September-October, 1996, William J. Gatens, review of *Purcell Remembered,* p. 283.
Music & Letters, August, 1996, Rebecca Herissone, review of *Purcell Remembered,* p. 460; May, 1997, Ian Spink, review of *Performing the Music of Henry Purcell,* p. 262.
Notes, March, 1997, Mark A. Radice, review of *Purcell Remembered,* pp. 791-795; March, 1998, Judith Milhouse, review of *Performing the Music of Henry Purcell,* pp. 688-691.
Observer Review, April 30, 1995, Jeremy Noble, "The Supple, Youthful, Perennial Purcell," p. 20.
Times Literary Supplement, September 15, 1995, Paul Griffiths, "How the Linnet Sings," pp. 3-4; December 25, 1998, Peter Porter, "Bad Conscience about Carthage," p. 18.*

*   *   *

BUSI, Aldo 1948-

PERSONAL: Born February 25, 1948, in Montichiari, Italy. *Education:* University of Verona, graduated 1981.

ADDRESSES: Agent—c/o Antiche Olura, 8, 25018 Montichiari Brescia, Milan, Italy.

CAREER: Novelist. Has worked in Milan, elsewhere in Europe, and in the United States as a sanitation worker, a real estate agent, and a waiter.

WRITINGS:

Seminario sulla gioventù, Adelphi, Mondadori (Milan, Italy), 1984, translation by Stuart Hood published as *Seminar on Youth,* Carcanet (Manchester, England), 1988.

Vita standard di un ventidore provvisorio di collant, Mondadori (Milan, Italy), 1985, translation by Raymond Rosenthal published as *The Standard Life of a Temporary Pantyhose Salesman,* Farrar, Straus, Giroux (New York, NY), 1988.

La delphina bizantina, Mondadori (Milan, Italy), 1986.

Una pioggia Angelica, Mondadori (Milan, Italy), 1987.

Sodomie in corpo 11: non viaggio, non sesso e scrittura, Mondadori (Milan, Italy), 1988, translation by Stuart Hood published as *Sodomies in Elevenpoint,* Faber (London, England), 1992.

(With Dario Cioli) *Pâté d'homme: tragoedia Peninsulare in tre atti uno strappo, due estrazioni e taglio finale,* Mondadori (Milan, Italy), 1989.

Altri abusi: viaggi, sonnambulismi e giri dell'oca, Mondadori (Milan, Italy), 1989, translation by Stuart Hood published as *Uses and Abuses: Journeys, Sleepwalking, and Fool's Errands,* Faber & Faber (London, England), 1995.

Pazza, Bompiani (Milan, Italy), 1990.

L'amore è una budella gentile: flirt con Liala, Leonardo (Milan, Italy), 1990.

Sentire le donne, Mondadori (Milan, Italy), 1991.

Le persone normali, Mondadori (Milan, Italy), 1992.

Manuale del perfetto gentilomo, Sperling & Kupfer (Milan, Italy), 1992.

La delfina bizantina, Mondadori (Milan, Italy), 1992.

Vendita galline Km 2, Mondadori (Milan, Italy), 1993.

Manuale della perfetta gentildonna, Sperling & Kupfer (Milan, Italy), 1994.

Cazzi e canguri, Frassinelli (Milan, Italy), 1994.

Madre Asdrubala: all'asilo si stà bene e s'imparan tante cose!, Mondadori (Milan, Italy), 1995.

Grazie del pensiero, Mondadori (Milan, Italy), 1995.

La vergine Alatiel: che con otto uomini forse diecimila volte giaciuta era, Mondadori (Milan, Italy), 1996.

Suicidi dovuti, Frassinelli (Milan, Italy), 1996.

Nudo di madre: manuale del perfetto scrittore, Bompiani (Milan, Italy), 1997.

L'amore trasparente: canzoniere, Mondadori (Milan, Italy), 1997.

Frangi: 1996-1997, Galleria Poggiali & Forconi (Florence, Italy), 1997.

(With Marco Lodola and Laura Cherubini) *Marco Lodola: frames,* Electra (Milan, Italy), 1997.

Aloha!!!!!: gli uomini, le donne e le Hawaii, Bompiani (Milan, Italy), 1998.

Disidentico: maschile, femminile e oltre, Panepinto Arte (Rome, Italy), 1998.

Per un'Apocalisse più svelta, Bompiani (Milan, Italy), 1999.

Casanova di se stessi, Mondadori (Milan, Italy), 2000.

Manuale della perfetta manna: con qualche contrazione anche per il papà, Mondadori (Milan, Italy), 2000.

Cucchi: chi cucca chi, Cucchi?, Galleria Poggiali & Forconi (Florence, Italy), 2000.

Possenti: Arthur Rimbaud occasioni e suggestioni, Bandecchi & Vivaldi (Pontedera, Italy), 2000.

Manuale del perfetto papà: beati gli orfani!, Mondadori (Milan, Italy), 2001.

Un cuore di troppo, Bompiani (Milan, Italy), 2001.

TRANSLATOR

Lewis Carrol, *Alice nel Paese delle Meraviglie,* Mondadori (Milan, Italy), 1989.

Giovanni Boccacio, *Decamerone da un italiano all'altro: cinquanta novelle,* Rizzoli (Milan, Italy), 1990.

(With Carmen Covito), Baldassare Castiglione, *Carmen Covito e Aldo Busi traducono il cortigiano di Baldassar Castiglione,* Rizzoli (Milan, Italy), 1993.

Also translated Goethe's *I dolori del giovane Werther,* 1983; (with Carmen Covito) *Il Novellino,* 1992; Friederich Schiller's *Intrigo e amore,* 1994; and the Brothers Grimm's *La vecchia nel bosco,* 1996; translator of additional works by John Ashbery, Heimitovon Doderer, Meg Wolitzer, Chistina Stead, and Paul Bailey.

Contributor to the magazine *Epoca.*

SIDELIGHTS: Aldo Busi has been called "the most inventive linguistic conjurer in the new Italian novel." His novels display an unabashed view of his homosexuality, and his persona is widely described as "outrageous." He constantly challenges the reader to decide what is "normal" and what is not and asks why anyone would want to be normal anyway.

Busi grew up in a provincial Italian town in the 1950s. He decided he was a homosexual in his youth and went to each of his neighbors in turn to announce this fact. They chased him out of town; Busi left home at the age of fourteen and studied languages while working in hotels and restaurants, notably the Pinguino Bar in Milan. After graduating from high school in Florence, he enrolled at the University of Verona, from which he graduated in 1981 with a thesis on the American poet John Ashbery. During his youth, he learned three languages and lived in London, Paris, and Berlin. He received most of his education at private schools paid for by a wealthy and beautiful German woman who later became the inspiration for the character Arlette in *Vita standard di un venditore provvisorio di collant.*

Busi's first two novels are full of autobiographical elements, though the protagonists are fictional. *Seminario sulla gioventù* tells of the adventures of Barbino, a young man from rural northern Italy who hates his mother and whose father is gone. He moves to Milan, where he supports himself as a homosexual prostitute and a menial worker. He soon takes off for Paris, where he studies French at the Alliance Française and falls in with three French women; one of them in particular, Arlette, becomes his protector. His relationship with Arlette is stressful, and the two of them torture one another: she wants to domesticate him and he desperately resists. To Barbino, women mean dependence; he worries that a sexual relationship with a woman can make him "too human." Finally the tension becomes too much, and Barbino escapes to England, where he studies English and continues to live in poverty. Boyd Tonkin, reviewing the novel for *New Statesman,* wrote, "A lush stylist, full of flourish and nuance, Busi digressively explores his own version of philosophy in the boudoir. Though absent in the lives and on the lips of his characters, the anarchic rage that dropped from sight after 1968 nonetheless drives Barbino's mission to puncture the watertight selfhood of his tricks."

Busi's next novel, *Vita standard di un ventitore provvisorio di collant,* is a kind of continuation of *Seminario sulla gioventù.* This novel features a slightly older protagonist, Angelo Bazarovi, who is living with his mother, working on his graduate thesis and spending time on the homosexual beaches of Lake Garda. He takes a job as a translator for Cesare Lometto, the head of a pantyhose company, an impossible tyrant who represents the capitalist as evil. Angelo accompanies his boss on forays through the Common Market countries and then travels to America with Lometto's wife; she is about to give birth to her fourth child, and Lometto wants the baby to be an American citizen who could become president. She unfortunately gives birth to a daughter with Down's syndrome, whom Lometto orders destroyed. Angelo cannot allow this to happen and saves the child whose misfortune it is to be different. This book was very well received by critics. Luca Fontana, reviewing it for *New Statesman,* wrote that Busi's second book "established him as the most inventive linguistic conjurer in the new Italian novel. . . . His is a rich, narcissistic, complacent prose, but extremely vivid and, as often with our best writers, very hard to translate."

In more recent novels, including *Sodomie in corpo 11* and *Altri abusi,* Busi abandons his fictional protagonists and instead introduces a first-person narrator, "Io" ("I"). This new character is a traveling writer with no home, no family, and no lover who is totally dedicated to the act of writing. He travels all over the world, visiting Finland, Iceland, Tunisia, Korea, Colombia, and points in between. Rather than recording his observations as a journalist, he writes and comments on everything he sees, filling his prose with stream-of-consciousness literary criticism and social commentary. Homosexuality is constantly present, with vivid descriptions of sexual encounters. But Busi does not write as an activist; homosexuality is simply a fact of life for him.

Altri abusi is a collection of memoirs and travel writings and a search for fellow outsiders. Busi muses on the difficulties of helping street children in Bogotà, swaps fashion tips with the president of Iceland, and gets arrested in England. The reviewer for the London *Observer* wrote, "along the way, Busi displays an impressive erudition which he occasionally dismantles to reveal the loneliness he finds mirrored in the world's dispossessed."

In *Sodomie in corpo 11,* Busi's narrator travels about allowing his homosexuality free rein. He confronts the reader with meticulous and expansive descriptions of his physical encounters, but the sum of the story seems to be that life is sad. Franco Ricci, reviewing the novel for *World Literature Today,* wrote that "as the reader follows the author's philosophical, literary, and psychological peregrinations, he realizes that the external world offers little solace and that the human heart may only ponder with temerity the ravages of one's own sexual proclivities."

La delfina bizantina is set in Ravenna in an unspecified future, and describes the activities of an organization called the Sindaco, which works for the Mafia by promoting its big-business concerns from the United States and the Vatican's male-dominated power politics. A horde of feminists is about to set fire to the Ravenna Palace of Justice. In the midst of this, three witch-like women found a new feminist group as an alternative to the world of masculine capitalism; they make their headquarters at the Byzantine Dolphin, a luxurious local campsite. One of the three, Signorina Scontrino, totally dominates the other two. This female collective quickly turns into an equivalent of Dallas, a city that represents everything Busi hates about the United States, and the three founding women turn on one another. *La delfina bizantina* is full of Busi's trademark linguistic virtuosity; Ian Thomson, reviewing it for *Times Literary Supplement,* wrote, "as a compendium of literary forms and styles (gothic, baroque, satire, elegy, mock-philosophical) *La delfina bizantina* is at times genuinely exhilarating, and one has to admire Busi's virtuosity with the Italian language—turning it inside out, twisting, deforming, and generally bashing it over the head."

The protagonist of *Vendita galline km 2* is also named Delfina. She is the ghost of a lesbian who narrated the events of the people in her family. She sees herself as an outcast because she was named after dolphins, victims of Western capitalism. In the end, she convinces her former lover Caterina to write a novel titled *Vendita galline km 2.*

Suicidi dovuti was supposed to be Busi's final novel; the writer told interviewers for years that he would write five novels, and this was the fifth. Though that ultimately proved not to be true, the novel does contain a sense of closure. It is set in a town that represents Busi's hometown of Montichiari, which his earlier protagonist Barbino left to explore the world. The novel is a monologue criticizing provincial Italian capitalism, told in the words of a poor bell-ringer.

Le persone normali is both a thriller and a meditation on the nature of "normal" people. Busi sets his story at a weight-control clinic and spa in Liguria where someone is stealing the jewelry of the corpulent clientele. The women are tended by several strange men, including a dwarf in riding breeches, a middle-aged man called the "Latin Love" and a pair of gangster types. The author asks exactly what is normal and why anyone should aspire to the condition and argues that in fact so-called normal people are slaves to sexual repression. The dialogue is outrageous and the language inventive, and in the end all mysteries are solved.

The narrator of *Casanova di se stessi* is Aldo Subi, a famous Italian author and television personality. The story opens with the deaths of two men, Eros and Amato, who are found naked in bed after drinking hemlock in a double suicide; between them is a book of the *Memoirs of Giacomo Casanova*. Busi then goes back to their childhoods to begin the narrative of their lives. Eros was a wealthy judge and Amato a poor teacher. They have competed with one another their whole lives, with Eros usually holding the upper hand. Amato marries a woman named Carita, who also becomes Eros's mistress; Eros marries Amato's sister. The two men appear to be friendly to one another, but in fact their relationship is full of anger, jealousy, and revenge; nevertheless, they also have a clandestine sexual relationship.

Busi has also put his talents to work as a translator. His translations include Lewis Carroll's *Alice in Wonderland* and Boccacio's *Decameron*. Busi's *Decameron* omits the narrative framework and moralizing discussions of the original but follows the rest of the work more or less line by line, enlivening the language with modernisms and anachronisms of his own. David Robey, a reviewer for the *Times Literary Supplement,* found Busi's translation quite readable and amusing, if a bit silly. He noted that Busi uses language to highlight the clash of cultures and values in Boccacio's text; Boccacio had veiled his radically discordant story with a veneer of classical polish, but Busi has swept away the polish and dramatized the discord beneath it.

In addition to novels and translations, Busi has also published several "manuals," collections of articles written for newspapers and magazines, and a play that has never been performed because it is too obscene. *Pazza* is a multimedia production; its cover features

Busi wearing a red dress. *Grazie del pensiero* is a collection of letters and answers from his column in the gay magazine *Hot Line*. *L'amore e una budella gentile (flirt con Liala)* is an interview between Busi and Liala, the famous Italian writer Amaliana Cambiasi Negretti. He has also directed the translation of a series of classic texts for the publisher Frassinelli.

Many observers have described Busi as "outrageous." He tries to shock the public, appearing in drag and describing himself as "gorgeous." He also claims that he produces nothing but masterpieces. Whether that is true or not, his works have been through many printings and have been translated into several languages. He has appeared on many Italian talk shows and is famous in his native land for his positions on controversial topics.

Busi once commented, "I am not a gay writer because if I had been straight I wouldn't have been a heterosexual writer: I would have been exactly the writer I am now, let's say, a writer. I don't see any specific link between one's own sexuality and the laws of true, not targeted literature."

BIOGRAPHICAL AND CRITICAL SOURCES:

BOOKS

Gay & Lesbian Literature, St. James Press (Detroit, MI), 1994.

PERIODICALS

Choice, January, 1989, review of *The Standard Life of a Temporary Pantyhose Salesman,* p. 810.

Kirkus Reviews, April 15, 1989, review of *Seminar on Youth,* p. 566.

London Review of Books, February 16, 1989, Michael Wood, review of *The Standard Life of a Temporary Pantyhose Salesman,* pp. 22-23.

Nation, December 26, 1988, James Marcus, review of *The Standard Life of a Temporary Pantyhose Salesman,* pp. 728-729.

New Statesman, March 27, 1987, Luca Fontana, "Italy: The Names and the Prose," pp. 29-30; April 27, 1988, Boyd Tonkin, "No Pity He's a Whore," pp. 26-27.

Observer, February 16, 1997, Jay Rayner, review of *Uses and Abuses: Journeys, Sleepwalking, and Fool's Errands,* p. 18.

Review of Contemporary Fiction, fall, 1992, "Aldo Busi," pp. 57-69.

Times Literary Supplement, May 9, 1986, Peter Hainsworth, review of *Seminario sulla gioventù,* p. 497; October 9, 1987, Ian Thomson, "Ravenna Rococo," p. 1115; August 11, 1989, Paul Bailey, "The Assuefaction Principle," p. 878; October 4, 1991, David Robey, "Candid Decamerone," p. 30; June 19, 1992, Julian Duplain, "Setting off for the Unexpected," p. 20.

World Literature Today, winter 1988, Luigi Monga, review of *La delfina bizantina,* p. 110; spring, 1989, Franco Ricci, review of *Sodomie in corpo 11,* p. 290; spring, 1993, Charles Klopp, review of *Le persone normali,* p. 350; spring, 1997, Eugenio Giusti, "Aldo Busi: Writer, Translator, Celebrity," pp. 325-331; summer, 2000, Rufus S. Crane, review of *Casanova di se stessi,* p. 657.

OTHER

Carmen Covito, http://www.carmencovito.com/ (March 21, 2002), "La riposta di Aldo Busi."

Italica, http://www.italica.rai.it/ (March 21, 2002), "Bibliografia di Aldo Busi."

Libreria di Dora, http://www.italialibri.net/ (March 21, 2002), "Aldo Busi," "Almeno essere stati italiani per qualcosa! Intervista con Aldo Busi."*

C

CABOT, Laurie 1933-

PERSONAL: Born March 3, 1933, in Wewoka, OK. *Education:* Attended Fullerton Junior College, Massachusetts College of Art, and Rhode Island School of Design.

ADDRESSES: Agent—c/o Author Mail, Delta, Bantam Dell Publishing Group, Random House, 1540 Broadway, New York, NY 10036.

CAREER: Founder of Temple of Isis, Salem, MA, grove of the Council of Isis Community, and Witches' League for Public Awareness. Teacher of witchcraft as a science, beginning c. 1960s, including classes at Salem State College.

AWARDS, HONORS: Paul Revere Patriots Award, governor of Massachusetts, 1977.

WRITINGS:

(With Tom Cowan) *Power of the Witch: The Earth, the Moon, and the Magical Path to Enlightenment,* Delacorte Press (New York, NY), 1989.
(With Tom Cowan) *Love Magic: The Way to Love through Rituals, Spells, and the Magical Life,* Delta (New York, NY), 1992.
(With Jean Mills) *Celebrate the Earth: A Year of Holidays in the Pagan Tradition,* Delta (New York, NY), 1994.

(With Jean Mills) *The Witch in Every Woman: Reawakening the Magical Nature of the Feminine to Heal, Protect, Create, and Empower,* Delta (New York, NY), 1997.

BIOGRAPHICAL AND CRITICAL SOURCES:

PERIODICALS

Booklist, October 15, 1997, Patricia Monaghan, review of *The Witch in Every Woman: Reawakening the Magical Nature of the Feminine to Heal, Protect, Create, and Empower,* p. 364.*

* * *

CALDERS, Pere 1912-1994

PERSONAL: Born 1912, in Barcelona, Spain; died July 21, 1994, in Barcelona, Spain; son of Vicencs Calders i Arús (a dramatist); married second wife, Rosa Artís; children: three sons. *Education:* Barcelona School of Fine Arts, 1927-29. *Politics:* Republican.

CAREER: Novelist, journalist, short story writer, and essayist. *Military service:* Spanish Republican Army, 1936-39, served as a cartographer.

MEMBER: Association of Catalan Language Writers.

AWARDS, HONORS: Victor Català Prize, 1954, for *Cròniques de la veritat oculta;* Sant Jordi Prize, 1964, for *L'ombra de l'atzavara;* Premi de la Crítica Serra d'Or, 1969, for *Tots els contes;* Premi de la Crítica Serra d'Or and Premi Lletra d'Or, both 1979, both for *Invasió subtil;* Premi a la Creació de la Generalitat, 1984, for *Tot s'aprofita;* Award of Honor in Catalan Letters, 1986; Spanish prize for journalism, 1993.

WRITINGS:

Unitats de Xoc (title means "Shock Troops"), Edició Patrocinada per la Institució de les lletres catalanes (Barcelona, Spain), 1938, reprinted, Observador (Barcelona, Spain), 1991.

Cròniques de la veritat oculta (title means "Chronicles of Hidden Truth"), Editorial Selecta (Barcelona, Spain), 1955, reprinted, Edicions 62 (Barcelona, Spain), 1998.

Gent de l'alta Vall, seguit de Tres reportatges especials, Albertí (Barcelona, Spain), 1957.

Demà, a les tres de la matinada (title means "Tomorrow at Three in the Morning"), Albertí (Barcelona, Spain), 1959, reprinted, Observador (Barcelona, Spain), 1991.

L'ombra de l'atzavara, Editorial Selecta (Barcelona, Spain), 1964, reprinted, Observador (Barcelona, Spain), 1991.

Josep Carner, Editorial Alcides (Barcelona, Spain), 1964, reprinted, L'Aixernador (Argentona, Spain), 1991.

Ronda naval sota la boira, Editorial Selecta (Barcelona, Spain), 1966, reprinted, Edicions 62 (Barcelona, Spain), 1982.

Aquí descansa Nevares, Alfaguara (Orense, Spain), 1967, reprinted, Edicions 62 (Barcelona, Spain), 1997.

Tots els contes, 1936-1967, Llibres de Sinera (Barcelona, Spain), 1968.

Antología de los cuentos de Pere Calders, Polígrafa (Barcelona, Spain), 1969.

Invasió subtil i altres contes, Edicions 62 (Barcelona, Spain), 1978, reprinted, 1996.

Antaviana, Edicions 62 (Barcelona, Spain), 1979, reprinted, 2000.

Una curiositat Americana i altres contes, Sontex (Barcelona, Spain), 1980.

Aquí descansa Nevares i altres narracions mexicanes, Edicions 62 (Barcelona, Spain), 1980.

Obres completes, Edicions 62 (Barcelona, Spain), 1980.

Cepillo, Ediciones Hymsa (Barcelona, Spain), 1981, translation by Marguerite Feitlowitz published as *Brush,* Kane/Miller, 1986.

Tot s'aprofita, Editorial Prometeo (Valencia, Spain), 1981.

El primer arlequí, Edicions de la Magrana (Barcelona, Spain), 1983.

De teves a meves, Editorial Laia (Barcelona, Spain), 1984.

Tria personal, Edicions 62 (Barcelona, Spain), 1984.

Los niños voladores, Argos Vergara (Barcelona, Spain), 1984.

Ver Barcelona, Ediciones Destino (Barcelona, Spain), 1984.

La revolta del terrat i altres contes, Editorial Laia (Barcelona, Spain), 1984.

Ruleta rusa: y otros cuentos, Editorial Anagrama (Barcelona, Spain), 1984.

Aquí descansa Nevares y otros relatos mexicanos, Grijalbo (Barcelona, Spain), 1985.

El desordre public, Empúries (Barcelona, Spain), 1985.

Un estrany al jardí, Edicions de la Magrana (Barcelona, Spain), 1985.

Ronda naval bajo la niebla, Editorial Anagrama (Barcelona, Spain), 1985.

Contes, Dalmau (Barcelona, Spain), 1985.

Gaeli i l'home déu, Edicions 62 (Barcelona, Spain), 1986.

De lo tuyo a lo mío, Editorial Laia (Barcelona, Spain), 1986.

El principio de la sabiduría, Edicions del Mall (Barcelona, Spain), 1986.

Raspall, Edicions Hymsa (Barcelona, Spain), 1987.

El sabeu, aquell?, Casals (Barcelona, Spain), 1987.

El primer Arlequín, Crónicas de la verdad oculta, Gente del alto valle, Alianza Editorial (Madrid, Spain), 1988.

Fumar o no fumar: vet aquí la qüestió, Ediciones Destino (Barcelona, Spain), 1988.

Todo se aprovecha, Ediciones B (Barcelona, Spain), 1988.

Fumar o no fumar: ésa es la cuestión, Ediciones Destino (Barcelona, Spain), 1988.

Porta d'agua, Lunwerg Editores (Barcelona, Spain), 1989.

Contes diversos, Observador (Barcelona, Spain), 1991.

Gent de l'alta vall; Aquí descansa Nevares, Observador (Barcelona, Spain), 1991.

Dibuixos de guerra a l'esquella de la Torratxa, Edicions La Campana (Barcelona, Spain), 1991.

L'honor a la deriva, Edicions 62 (Barcelona, Spain), 1992.

Histories de la mà esquerra, Edicions de la Magrana (Barcelona, Spain), 1993.

Els millors contes de Pere Calders, Avui (Barcelona, Spain), 1994.

La glòria del doctor Larén, Edicions 62 (Barcelona, Spain), 1994.

Mesures, alarmes i prodigis, Edicions 62 (Barcelona, Spain), 1994.

La lluna a casa i altres contes, Abadia de Montserrat (Barcelona, Spain), 1995.

Un crim, Edicions 62 (Barcelona, Spain), 1995.

Cartes d'amor, Edicions 62 (Barcelona, Spain), 1996.

Demà, a les tres de la matinada; seguit de Tres reportatges especials, Ediciones 62 (Barcelona, Spain), 1997.

Cuentos increíbles, Editorial Popular (Madrid, Spain), 1998.

La meva àvia, la planta, Pagès Editors (Lleida, Spain), 2000.

Calders: els miralls de la ficció, Centre de Cultura Contemporània de Barcelona (Barcelona, Spain), 2000.

Contributor to numerous publications, including *Esquella de la Torratxa, Avui, Diario Mercantil, La Rambla, Treball, Nostra Revista, Pont Blau, Revista de Catalunya, Serra d'Or,* and *Tele-estel.*

Calders' works have been translated into German, English, Bulgarian, Spanish, Italian, and Japanese.

ADAPTATIONS: Some of Calders' stories were adapted for the stage presentation *Antaviana* and performed by the Dagoll Dagom theater company.

SIDELIGHTS: Pere Calders is considered by many critics to be one of the finest prose writers to emerge from the province of Catalonia. "Calders is . . . Catalonia's foremost short-fiction writer," wrote Jaume Martí-Olivella in *World Literature Today.* His work is a forerunner of the those pieces that would, in more recent years, have been categorized as "magical realism." In her book, *Pere Calders: ideari i ficció,* Amanda Bath wrote that Calders considers the human condition to be the only topic worthy of consideration in literature. She also noted that Calders' juxtaposition of fantasy as a diametrically opposed concept to bureaucratic oppression, materialism, and superficial perspective is a constant source of humor and relief. "Pere Calders has earned a well-deserved renown as master of the strange and the fantastic," said Peter Cocozzella in *World Literature Today.* "The appearance of the unusual, the magical, or the fantastic as something totally natural in the midst of everyday life," is characteristic of the author's stories, wrote Joan J. Gilabert in the *Encyclopedia of World Literature in the Twentieth Century.*

Calders was born in 1912 in Barcelona, Spain. After his elementary school years, he attended the city's school of fine arts. His first jobs consisted of working as an artist for an advertising firm and writing for such publications as *El Diario Mercantil* and *Avui.* In those early years, Calders considered drawing and illustration to be his primary occupation, for he recognized the difficulty of earning a living as a professional writer, especially one who wrote in the Catalan dialect. Yet, despite his initial hesitation, Calders published his first two books in 1936: *El primer arlequí,* a short story collection, and *La glòria del doctor Larén,* a novel.

During the following year, Calders enlisted as a volunteer in the Republican Army, serving as a cartographer. In addition to his military work, he recorded his personal impressions of the Spanish Civil War and transformed them into the novel *Unitats de Xoc,* which was published in 1938. This book, written in the form of a war journal, recounts the adventures of a group of Catalan volunteers in the Spanish Civil War. The men begin their military duty as cartographers for the Republican Army, but are gradually swept toward the front lines of battle. "*Unitats de Xoc* offers a direct testimony of what it meant to be a Catalan soldier on the front line," wrote Martí-Olivella in *World Literature Today.* The critic mentioned that Calders uses a sincere and "morally uplifting tone" in a work that discusses the threat posed by the government of Francisco Franco toward the author's native province, Catalonia. Martí-Olivella also noted that the book is "written with the tenderness and ironic counterpoint" that are characteristic of Calders' work. "His artistry reaches unforgettable heights in painterly description . . . of the loneliness, mystery, absurdity [and] cruelty" of a war that pits brother against brother, said Cocozzella in *World Literature Today.* In his prologue to the first edition of *Unitats de Xoc,* Carles Riba observed that Calders' work constitutes one of the most significant literary documents of the Spanish Civil War.

At the end of the Spanish Civil War Calders fled from Catalonia, but was captured and sent to a concentration camp at the base of the Pyrenees Mountains. He soon left the camp and traveled to Mexico, where he lived in exile for the next twenty-three years. During his exile, Calders worked for a Mexican publishing firm and, whenever possible, wrote articles for Catalan magazines published in that country. He also wrote several short story collections: *Memòries especials, Cròniques de la veritat oculta, Gent de l'alta vall,* and *Demà a les tres de la matinada.* The stories in the last two collections exhibit Calders' typical "combination of humor with fantasy or absurdity," wrote Janet W. Díaz in an article in *World Literature Today.*

The Mexican publishers that employed Calders made it possible for him to return to Spain in 1962, when they purchased the Barcelona firm of Montaner i Simon. He worked for that company until he retired in the 1970s, and continued to write, a task that would occupy him throughout the rest of his life.

L'ombra de l'atzavara appeared soon after Calders' return to Spain, and was awarded the Sant Jordi Prize. It was so commercially successful that it was reprinted twice during that year. The novel provides a look at the exiled Catalans who sought political asylum in Mexico and discusses the problems encountered by a group of refugees that tries to maintain its cultural heritage in a land that "demanded complete fidelity" in exchange for the right to live there. Joan Daltell, the chief protagonist, yearns to return to his native Catalonia. He marries a Mexican woman and has a son, but neither of them understands his longing, nor is interested in Daltell's homeland. One day, it seems that Daltell will suddenly receive the money to return to Spain, when he is asked to run a small publishing company. His attempts to build a successful business are foiled, however, by a corrupt government bureaucracy. By the end of the novel, Daltell returns to his former job and hopes for another lucky chance in the future. Albert M. Forcadas, writing in *World Literature Today,* remarked that *L'ombra de l'atzavara* "follows a linear plot line and a traditional mode of narration." He commented that the novel's continued success "proves that a good story . . . still holds the greatest appeal."

Ronda naval sota la boira was published in 1966. "A clever hybrid of short-story and soap-opera narratives enhanced by an ironic tone, [it] is the author's best work," said Forcadas in *World Literature Today.* The novel appears in the form of a diary, written by Oleguer Sureda, who is taking a cruise on the ocean liner,

Panoràmic, when it springs a serious leak during a voyage in the middle of the Atlantic Ocean. When the captain, Maurici, tries to signal for help, he discovers that the radio is broken. Calders describes some of the eccentric personalities who are aboard the ship in scenes that could easily have occurred in either "the Theater of the Absurd . . . . [or] The Twilight Zone," Forcadas remarked. He continued by saying: "Calders attains an original and profound literary product" in this book. "In *Ronda,* the author tackles metafiction in dead earnest with consummate artistry," stated Cocozzella.

Calders' next work, *Aquí descansa Nevares i altres narracions mexicanes,* contains six short stories. The title piece—which describes two members of the Nevares family who live in one of the mausoleums in Mexico City because their house was destroyed in a torrential rain—is based upon an actual situation. Forcadas considered the collection to be filled with "fine psychological studies." The critic also praised the introduction, written by Joan Melción, as a valuable contribution toward understanding Calders and his works.

Invasió subtil i altres contes, another short story collection, was published in 1978. The stories comprise "a masterful display of ingenuity," Forcadas remarked in *World Literature Today,* and range in subject from a Catalan-speaking extraterrestrial who meets a human being in a forest to a tale of an elderly man who desires to buried in the style of an Egyptian pharaoh after his death. "Calders achiev[es] a perfect balance between humor and fantasy" in these stories, noted Forcadas.

In 1981 Calders made a brief foray into the field of children's literature. *Brush* is the tale of a little boy who owns a mischievous dog. When his parents insist that the puppy leave their household, the lad tries to find another companion. He discovers an unusual substitute in a brush that lives in the broom closet. The boy's new "pet" soon proves his worth by making himself invaluable to the family. A critic from *Horn Book* wrote that the plot is filled with "absurd fantasy at its best." Patricia Dooley, on the other hand, felt that the book was disappointing because a brush could never take the place of a lively animal. In *Publishers Weekly,* the writer noted that Calders' work "builds effortlessly" and is imbued with "child-like directness and feeling."

With *Tot s'aprofita,* a volume of thirty-six stories of varying length, Calders returns to his "unusual approaches" to adult literature and life. The story which lends its name to the collection describes a woman who murders her tyrannical spouse. After her arrest, the medical establishment convinces the police to release her because she actually committed a good deed in the sense that her husband's vital organs became available to needy transplant recipients. Forcadas felt that this collection, which combines "skeptical tenderness and cruel irony, is a real treat for the readers."

At the age of seventy-two, Calders selected his personal favorites from among all his writings and published these pieces in *Tria personal.* The author chose only one story written before the Spanish Civil War, "L'imprevist a la casa nùmero 10," a tale that previously appeared in *El primer arlequí.* His work from *Cròniques de la veritat oculta* is amply represented by eleven short stories which exhibit Calders' lifelong preoccupation with everyday lives infused with fantastic, inexplicable, and occult happenings. Tales are also included from *Demà a les tres de la matinada, Contes diversos, Invasió subtil i altres contes,* and *Aquí descansa Nevares i altres narracions mexicanes.* "*Tria personal* emphasizes that vein of Calders . . . [which is similar to] the early Asimov, a science fiction which reminds man of his limitations in the vast universe," wrote Janet Pérez in *World Literature Today.*

L'honor a la deriva, published in 1992, contains twenty-five stories, some of which are exceedingly short; Martí-Olivella called it a "small but important" work. Some of the stories are based upon a literal misunderstanding or distortion of a particular idiomatic phrase that causes immense chaos and confusion in the lives of human beings. "Calders's witty use of idiolectal humor" is an outstanding feature of this work, according to Martí-Olivella. Cocozzella noted that the plot of the title story "unravels with clockwork precision."

A final work, *Mesures, alarmes i prodigis,* appeared after Calders' death in 1994. It is a collection of various articles Calders wrote for the daily Catalan newspaper *Avui. Mesures, alarmes i prodigis* is notable for its broad range of topics, and the editor, professor Xavier Luna, has chosen several articles that emphasize Calders' particular concern about "the dangers confronting the Catalan language." In his appraisal of the collection, Martí-Olivella wrote, "As usual, Calders manages to establish his point by means of a remarkable sense of humor and a subtle capacity to displace rather trivial facts into significant events."

BIOGRAPHICAL AND CRITICAL SOURCES:

BOOKS

Encyclopedia of World Literature in the Twentieth Century, St. James Press (Detroit, MI), 1999.

PERIODICALS

Children's Book Review Service, July, 1986, review of *Brush,* p. 138.
Horn Book, July-August, 1986, Anita Silvey, review of *Brush,* pp. 439-440.
Publishers Weekly, June 27, 1986, review of *Brush,* p. 87-88.
School Library Journal, November, 1986, Patricia Dooley, review of *Brush,* p. 73.
World Literature Today, autumn, 1979, Albert M. Forcadas, review of *Invasió subtil i altres contes,* p. 664; summer, 1981, Albert M. Forcadas, review of *L'ombra de l'atzavara,* pp. 455-456; autumn, 1981, Albert M. Forcadas, review of *Aquí descansa Nevares i altres narracions mexicanes,* pp. 657-658; winter, 1981, Janet W. Díaz, review of *Demà a les tres de la matinada,* p. 85-86; spring, 1984, Albert M. Forcadas, review of *Tot s'aprofita,* pp. 255-256; summer, 1984, Peter Cocozzella, review of *Unitats de Xoc,* p. 402; winter, 1985, Janet Pérez, review of *Tria personal,* p. 77; autumn, 1991, Jaume Martí-Olivella, review of *Unitats de Xoc,* p. 65; autumn, 1993, Peter Cocozzella, review of *Obres completes, Volume 5,* pp. 803-804; autumn, 1993, Jaume Martí-Olivella, review of *L'honor a la deriva,* p. 803; autumn, 1995, Albert M. Forcadas, review of *Ronda naval sota la boira,* pp. 774-775, review of *Mesures, alarmes i prodigis,* pp. 775-776.

OTHER

Associació d'Escriptors Catalanas Web site, http://www.escriptors.com/autors/ (March 21, 2002).

OBITUARIES:

Independent, July 27, 1994, p. 12.*

*   *   *

CAPPAS, Alberto O.

PERSONAL: Male. *Education:* State University of New York—Buffalo, graduated.

ADDRESSES: Home—85 Fourth Ave., No. 3JJ, New York, NY 10003.

CAREER: New York State Division for Youth, deputy commissioner of communications and special projects, 1982-87; City of New York, New York, NY, director of community affairs and assistant deputy administrator for Human Resources Administration. *Latino Village Press,* publisher and editor (with others); *Place for Poets,* founder; *Latinos in Government,* founder and general manager; gives readings from his works and other cultural presentations, including appearances at Pratt Institute, Schenectady Community College, New York University, Ithaca College, Nuyorican's Poets' Cafe, and Harlem Hospital Center. A & L Speakers and Consultants Bureau, founder and president; Don Pedro Enterprises, founder and president.

AWARDS, HONORS: Keepers of Our Culture Award for literature, New York State Hispanic Heritage Month Committee, 1994; Charles Evans Hughes Award for Creative Writing, New York Urban League.

WRITINGS:

Echos (poetry chapbook), Place for Poets (New York, NY), 1987.
Echolalia: Verse and Vibrations (poetry), Calton Press (New York, NY), 1989.
The Disintegration of the Puerto Ricans (poetry), Don Pedro Enterprises (New York, NY), 1997.
The Pledge: A Guide for Our Children and Youth (juvenile), privately printed, 2001.

Work represented in anthologies.

CARAM, Eve (La Salle) 1934-

PERSONAL: Born May 11, 1934, in Hot Springs, AR; daughter of Raymond Briggs (a La Salle Extension University of Arkansas state manager) and Lois Elizabeth (a professional organist and pianist; maiden name, Merritt) La Salle; married Richard George Caram, April 19, 1965 (divorced April 19, 1978); children: Bethel Eve. *Education:* Attended University of Texas, 1952; Bard College, B.A. (world literature), 1956; University of Missouri, M.A. (English and writing), 1977. *Politics:* Democrat. *Religion:* "Liberal wing of Episcopal Church. Though I am *NOT* a regular attendee, spirituality is, however, an *important* force in my life." *Hobbies and other interests:* Outdoors (beach, swimming), music, classic films from Golden Era.

ADDRESSES: Home—3400 Ben Lomond Place 121, Los Angeles, CA 90027. *Office*—The Writers' Program, UCLA Extension, 1099 LeConte, Los Angeles, CA 90024; and Department of English, California State University at Northridge, 1811 Nordhoff, Northridge, CA 91330.

CAREER: Author and educator. Stephens College, Columbia, MO, English instructor, 1974 and 1979-82; University of Southern California, Los Angeles, instructor in fiction writing, 1982-87; Writers' Program, University of California-Los Angeles Extension, senior instructor in fiction writing, 1983—; California State University, Northridge, professor of English and writing, 1983—. Yacklo, Saratoga Springs, NY, writer-in-residence, 1976, 1982, and 1992-93; Los Angeles City College, instructor; judge in fiction contests; speaker at conferences.

MEMBER: Association of American University Professors, PEN Center USA West, National Association of Teachers of English, Association of California State Professors, Poets and Writers, Austin Writers' League.

WRITINGS:

Dear Corpus Christi (novel), Plain View Press (Austin, TX), 1991.
Wintershine (short novel), Plain View Press (Austin, TX), 1994.

(Editor) *Palm Readings: Stories from Southern California,* Plain View Press (Austin, TX), 1998.

Rena a Late Journey (novel), Plain View Press (Austin, TX), 1999.

Fiction editor, *West/Word,* 1991.

WORK IN PROGRESS: The Blue Geography, a novel; *Places of Leaves,* "a reading memoir"; articles for anthologies.

SIDELIGHTS: Eve Caram told *CA:* "Writing has always been a compulsion, and a way for me. In writing I clear a way for myself to proceed on the journey of living, (and I write constantly of journeys of one sort or another). I am interested in the past as it intersects with and illuminates the present, the way it affects actions and thought, relationships, growth. I don't think we leave the past behind us, or that it is behind us; we take it with us as we live. For many of my characters time isn't linear at all, each moment is an eternal one. (I have no philosophy about this, only a feeling, but like most fiction writers I am interested in the uses of time and believe that the way a writer uses time is a crucial element in his or her art.) We write out of memory—we recollect to grasp what is happening to us now, and to make bearable what we may feel may be passing away. Jayne Anne Phillips has said that fiction often begins in memory and ends in dreams. Certainly this had been true of the fiction I write.

"I write from memory and from imagination. I almost always start with a landscape and the people that come out of it. (My first published novel, *Dear Corpus Christi,* began with a letter my central character was writing back to the place where she was young.) The story comes out of both the place and the people who have been shaped by it, their aspirations, the choices they must make to attain what they want or what they feel they must accomplish. The landscape itself is often an influence. When I'm stuck I just go back to it (sometimes even to weather), as if it can tell my characters what direction to take. (And often it does!)

"People I have known and loved have inspired my writing, as have many other writers (Willa Cather, Katherine Anne Porter, and William Goyen just to name a few). Many of my characters have sprung out of people in my mother's family, most of whom have now departed. My characters, however, almost always turn out to be astonishingly different from the people they were modeled after. This pleases me because I have never set out to write or wanted to write a mere reminiscence. I have always written with the hope of transcending the personal and to join my own experience and that of those I have known to something greater, something that connects to the experience of many."

*   *   *

CARDELLA, Lara 1969-

PERSONAL: Born 1969, in Licata, Sicily, Italy.

ADDRESSES: Agent—c/o Author Mail, Penguin Books Ltd., Hamish Hamilton, 80 Strand, London WC2R 0RL, England.

CAREER: Novelist.

AWARDS, HONORS: Literary prize, 1989, for *Volevo i pantaloni.*

WRITINGS:

Volevo i pantaloni, Mondadori (Milan, Italy), 1989, translation by Diana di Caraci published as *Good Girls Don't Wear Trousers,* Hamish Hamilton (London, England), 1993, Arcade (New York, NY), 1994.

Intorno a Laura, Mondadori (Milan, Italy), 1991.

Una ragazza normale, Mondadori (Milan, Italy), 1994.

Volevo i pantaloni 2, with Ferruccio Parazzoli, Mondadori (Milan, Italy), 1995.

Detesto il soft, Rizzoli (Milan, Italy), 1997.

Finestre accese, Biblioteca Universale Rizzoli (Milan, Italy), 2000.

Contributor to *Jo's Girls: Tomboy Tales of High Adventure, True Grit, and Real Life,* Beacon, 1997.

ADAPTATIONS: Volevo i pantaloni was adapted for film and released by Penta Video, 1990.

SIDELIGHTS: Lara Cardella hit the top of the literary charts at the age of nineteen with her first novel, *Volevo i pantaloni,* about a girl in traditional Sicily who shocks her family by wanting to wear pants. The book scandalized Cardella's Sicilian hometown but became a bestseller on the European continent.

In *Volevo i pantaloni* Cardella depicts her hometown of Licata, Sicily, as a destitute village full of gossipy inhabitants and hypocritical adults, a present-day Italian town still stuck in a medieval mindset. Her teenage protagonist, Anna, wishes that she could wear pants instead of the skirts which all women in her town are obliged to wear. She is not allowed to wear pants because her traditional parents believe that only men and whores wear trousers. To Anna, pants symbolize the independence enjoyed by men in a society that still discriminates against females; her efforts to wear pants constitute the beginning of her efforts to define her own individuality.

Anna pursues her dream through several phases of experimentation. She first decides to be a nun and enters a convent, mistakenly believing that nuns wear trousers beneath their habits. Next she tries to be a man, imitating a male cousin to learn how males behave; she practices spitting, scratching, and strutting but then discovers in a sordid episode that males are physically different from females, which ends that avenue of experimentation.

Because being a man is not possible, Anna decides that she will have to be a whore if she wants her pants. She apprentices herself to a school friend who instructs her in the arts of flirtation and seduction, and Anna succeeds so well that the morning after her first party, her uncle finds her on a park bench in the embrace of a young man. He drags her home, where her family beats her unconscious and confines her to her room, keeping her out of school and other public places while they decide how to handle the dishonor she has brought on them. The family ultimately send Anna to live with another aunt and uncle, even though that uncle is an alcoholic who has already sexually abused the girl. Anna finds herself living in a domestic hell where violence is tolerated as long as it remains within the family. Her only comfort is her aunt, who shares her diary with the girl and opens up a world of romantic secrets to her.

Though the inhabitants of Cardella's hometown were offended by the book, which they thought was an inaccurate depiction of them, the novel's widespread success paved the way for Cardella's subsequent literary career. *Volevo i pantaloni,* was translated into a number of languages, including French, German, Spanish, Portuguese, Greek, and Japanese. Cardella won a prize for her novel, as well as critical acclaim.

Ann Caesar, reviewing the English translation for the *Times Literary Supplement,* wrote, "The virtues of Cardella's style lie in its lightness of touch and in her ready, slapdash humor. She has written a youthful and fundamentally optimistic book that quickly veers away from the disturbing underside of the society she describes." A reviewer for *Kirkus Reviews* called *Volevo i pantaloni* "a remarkably open, if occasionally amateurish, representation of a place where 'women can be wives and mothers but they can never be people.'" A reviewer for *Babelguides* noted that the book became a cause celebre in Europe because "it reveals that the Southern tradition of bringing up girls in an atmosphere of coercion and self-negation is continuing."

Some reviewers found the novel somewhat overblown and clumsy but suggested that the blame could be placed on the translation; the English title, *Good Girls Don't Wear Trousers,* is not quite the same as the Italian one, which simply means "I wanted trousers." The novel was made into a film in 1990. An excerpt from the book was also included in a 1997 collection of short stories about tomboys, *Jo's Girls: Tomboy Tales of High Adventure, True Grit, and Real Life,* which put Cardella in the company of such authors as Willa Cather, Toni Morrison, and Virginia Woolf.

Cardella has followed her promising debut with several other novels. *Una ragazza normale* is about a young woman's fears of not being normal, and the compromises she makes to ensure that she will be accepted and loved. *Detesto il soft* describes a young woman's problems with the opposite sex. Cardella's more recent novels have not generated the notoriety of her first one, but they have continued the author's exploration of the themes of normality and the difficulty of living as an independent individual.

BIOGRAPHICAL AND CRITICAL SOURCES:

PERIODICALS

Booklist, September 1, 1994, Gilbert Taylor, review of *Good Girls Don't Wear Trousers,* p. 22; December

1, 1994, Sylvia S. Goldberg, review of *Una ragazza normale,* p. 658; October 15, 1998, Sylvia S. Goldberg, review of *Detesto il soft,* p. 408.

Kirkus Reviews, July 1, 1994, review of *Good Girls Don't Wear Trousers,* p. 682.

Publishers Weekly, August 1, 1994, review of *Good Girls Don't Wear Trousers,* p. 72; April 28, 1997, review of *Jo's Girls: Tomboy Tales of High Adventure, True Grit, and Real Life,* p. 58.

Times Literary Supplement, October 6, 1989, review of *Volevo i pantaloni,* p. 19; May 28, 1993, Ann Caesar, review of *Good Girls Don't Wear Trousers,* p. 23.

OTHER

Babelguides, http://www.babelguides.com/ (March 21, 2002), review of *Good Girls Don't Wear Trousers.**

*   *   *

CARRADINE, David 1936-
(John Arthur Carradine)

PERSONAL: Born December 8, 1936, in Hollywood, CA; son of John Richmond Reed (an actor) and Ardanelle Abigail (McCool) Carradine; half-brother of Keith Carradine and Robert Carradine (both actors); uncle of Martha Plimpton and Ever Carradine (both actresses); married Donna Lee Becht (an actress; divorced); companion of Barbara Hershey (an actress; also known as Barbara Seagull), 1972-75; married Linda Gilbert, 1977 (divorced, 1983); married Gail Jensen (a manager, producer, and songwriter), 1986 (divorced, 1997); married Marina Benjamin (an actress and producer), February, 1997; children: (first marriage) Calista; (with Barbara Hershey) Tom; (second marriage) Kansas. *Education:* Attended Oakland Junior College, San Francisco State College (now San Francisco State University), and University of California, Berkeley; studied acting, dialects, voice, piano, tap, ballet, martial arts, fencing, aerobatic flying, horsemanship, and fast draws. *Politics:* "Jeffersonian Democrat." *Religion:* Christian Scientist. *Hobbies and other interests:* Music, songwriting, filmmaking, sculpting, painting, creating computer art, philosophy, art, science, horses, children, French, the American Revolution, tai chi, baseball, coaching athletes of the Special Olympics.

ADDRESSES: Agent—Gilla Roos West, 9744 Wilshire Blvd., Beverly Hills, CA 90212.

CAREER: Actor, director, producer, and writer. Composer of more than seventy songs for the publishing company of Catahoula and Carlin. Affiliated with Art House. Also worked as a commercial illustrator and at the Lucky Lager Brewery. *Military service:* U.S. Army, 1960-62.

Film appearances include *Taggart,* Universal, 1964; *Bus Riley's Back in Town,* Universal, 1965; *The Violent Ones,* Feature Film, 1967; *Too Many Thieves,* Metro-Goldwyn-Mayer, 1968; *Heaven with a Gun,* Metro-Goldwyn-Mayer, 1969; *Young Billy Young,* United Artists, 1969; *The Good Guys and the Bad Guys,* Warner Bros., 1969; *Macho Callahan,* Avco-Embassy, 1970; *The McMasters,* Chevron, 1970; *Boxcar Bertha,* American International Pictures, 1972; *House of Dracula's Daughter,* 1973; *Mean Streets,* Warner Bros., 1973; *The Long Goodbye,* United Artists, 1973; *You and Me,* 1975; *Death Race 2000,* New World Pictures, 1975; *Cannonball,* New World Pictures, 1976; *Bound for Glory,* United Artists, 1976; *The Serpent's Egg,* Paramount, 1977; *Thunder and Lightning,* Twentieth Century-Fox, 1977; *A Look at Liv,* Win Kao Productions, 1977; *Roger Corman: Hollywood's Wild Angel,* Blackwood Films, 1978; *Gray Lady Down,* Universal, 1978; *Deathsport,* New World Pictures, 1978; *Cloud Dancer,* Blossom Pictures, 1979; *Circle of Iron,* Avco-Embassy, 1979; *Fast Charlie, the Moonbeam Rider,* Universal, 1979; *The Long Riders,* United Artists, 1980; *Americana,* Crown International, 1981; *The Best of Sex and Violence,* Wizard Video, 1981; *Q,* United Film Distributors, 1982; *Safari 3000,* Metro-Goldwyn-Mayer/United Artists, 1982; *Trick or Treats,* Lone Star International Pictures, 1982; *Lone Wolf McQuade,* Orion, 1983; *On the Line,* El Iman/Amber, 1984; *Kain of the Dark Planet,* 1984; *The Warrior and the Sorceress,* New World Pictures, 1984; *Labyrinth,* TriStar, 1986; *P.O.W.: The Escape,* Cannon, 1986; *Armed Response,* CineTel, 1986; *Wheels of Terror,* Manley, 1986 (released as *The Misfit Brigade,* Trans World, 1988); *Marathon,* 1987; *Run for Your Life,* Multivideo, 1987; *Animal Protector,* Producers Corporation, 1988; *Wizards of the Lost Kingdom II,* Concorde-New Horizons, 1988; *Warlords,* American International Pictures, 1988; *Open Fire,* 1988; *Fatal Secret,* Swedish Action Film Force, 1988; *Maniac Cop,* Shapiro-Glickenhaus, 1988; *Crime of Crimes,* Trident Releasing, 1989; *Las huellas del lince,* A. G. Films/Casablanca Films/Tripode Films,

1989; *Ministry of Vengeance,* Concorde Pictures, 1989; *Sauf votre respect,* Candice Productions, 1989; *Nowhere to Run,* Concorde Pictures, 1989; *Crime Zone,* Concorde Pictures, 1989; *Sundown: The Vampire in Retreat,* Vestron Video, 1989; *Tropical Snow,* 1989; *The Mad Bunch,* Swedish Action Film Force, 1989; *Martial Law,* Media Home Entertainment, 1990; *Bird on a Wire,* Universal, 1990; *Think Big,* Concorde Pictures, 1990; *Sonny Boy,* Triumph Releasing, 1990; *Omega Cop II: The Challenge,* Romarc, 1991; *Dune Warriors,* Concorde Pictures, 1991; *Project Eliminator,* Victory Pictures, 1991; *Night Children,* Columbia/TriStar Home Video, 1992; *Waxwork II: Lost in Time,* LIVE Home Video, 1992; *Field of Fire,* Concorde Pictures, 1992; *Evil Toons,* American Independent Pictures, 1992; *Midnight Fear,* Rhino Home Video, 1992; *Distant Justice,* Columbia/TriStar Home Video, 1992; *Animal Instincts,* Academy, 1992; *Double Trouble,* Motion Picture Corporation of America, 1992; *Roadside Prophets,* New Line Cinema, 1992; *Night Rhythms,* Imperial Entertainment, 1992; *Frontera Sur,* 1993; *Kill Zone,* New Horizons Home Video, 1993; *Dead Center,* 21st Century Film Corporation, 1994; *Capital Punishment,* Screen Pix Home Video, 1996; *Full Blast,* Showcase Entertainment, 1997; *Knocking on Death's Door,* Concorde Pictures, 1997; *The Defectors,* 1998; *Light Speed,* Santelmo Entertainment, 1998; *Nosferatu: The First Vampire,* 1998; *Natural Selection,* Rio Bravo Entertainment, 1998; *Stray Bullet II,* New Horizons Home Video, 1998; *The Rage,* Miramax, 1998; *Children of the Corn V: Field of Terror,* Dimension Films, 1998; *Sublet,* Krasko Productions, 1998; *Lovers and Liars,* 1998; *Drop-Dead,* Libra Pictures/Regent Entertainment, 1998; *Crossroads of Destiny,* Concorde Pictures, 1999; *Zoo,* Pilgrims 5, 1999; *American Reel,* KiMina Entertainment/North by Northwest Entertainment, 1999; *Kiss of a Stranger,* Libra Pictures/Regent Entertainment, 1999; *Shepherd,* 1999; *The Donor,* RGH/Lions Share Pictures, 2000; *Down and Dirty,* Golden Lion Productions, 2000; *Nightfall,* Concorde-New Horizons, 2000; *G.O.D.,* Amsell Entertainment, 2000; and *An American Tail: The Treasure of Manhattan Island,* Universal Pictures Home Video, 2000. Appeared in the documentary *Shows of Strength: David Carradine's Martial Arts Adventure.* Also appeared in *Action Force Team* and *Caddo Lake.*

Film work includes (director) *You and Me,* 1975; (director, producer, and editor) *Americana,* Crown International, 1981; and (associate producer) *Project Eliminator,* Victory Pictures, 1991.

Television appearances include (series) *Shane,* ABC, 1966; *Kung Fu,* ABC, 1972-75; *Kung Fu: The Legend Continues,* syndicated, 1993-97; and *Walking after Midnight,* 1999. Television appearances include (miniseries) *Mr. Horn,* CBS, 1979; *North and South,* ABC, 1985; *North and South, Book II,* ABC, 1986. Also appeared in *Confessional.* Television movies include *Maybe I'll Come Home in the Spring,* ABC, 1970; *High Noon, Part II: The Return of Will Kane,* CBS, 1980; *Gauguin the Savage,* CBS, 1980; *Jealousy,* ABC, 1984; *The Bad Seed,* ABC, 1985; *Oceans of Fire,* CBS, 1986; *Kung Fu: The Movie,* CBS, 1986; *Six against the Rock,* NBC, 1987; *The Cup,* 1988; *I Saw What You Did,* CBS, 1988; *The Cover Girl and the Cop,* NBC, 1989; *Future Force,* syndicated, 1990; *Brotherhood of the Gun,* CBS, 1991; *Future Zone,* syndicated, 1991; *Luck of the Draw: The Gambler Returns,* NBC, 1991; *Deadly Surveillance,* Showtime, 1991; *Last Stand at Saber River,* TNT, 1997; *Lost Treasure of Dos Santos,* The Family Channel, 1997; *Martian Law,* 1998; *Out of the Wilderness,* 1998; *The New Swiss Family Robinson,* ABC, 1998; *The Warden,* syndicated, 2000; *By Dawn's Early Light,* Showtime, 2000. Appearances on television specials include *Johnny Belinda,* ABC, 1967; *Don Johnson's Music Video Feature and Heartbeat,* HBO, 1987; and *Too Hot to Skate,* CBS, 1997.

Appearances on episodic television include "The Eli Bancroft Story," *Wagon Train,* ABC, 1963; "Go Fight City Hall," *East Side, West Side,* CBS, 1963; "The Intruders," *The Virginian,* NBC, 1964; "Thou Still Unravished Bride," *The Alfred Hitchcock Hour,* NBC, 1965; "The War and Eric Kurtz," *Bob Hope Presents the Chrysler Theater,* NBC, 1965; "The Greatest Game," *Trials of O'Brien,* CBS, 1966; "Cortez and the Legend," *Saga of Western Man,* NBC, 1967; "The Hunted," *Cimarron Strip,* CBS, 1967; "The Rebels," *Coronet Blue,* CBS, 1967; "Due Process of Law," *Ironside,* NBC, 1968; "Tarot," *The Name of the Game,* NBC, 1970; "License to Kill," *Ironside,* NBC, 1971; "The Quincunx," *Ironside,* NBC, 1971; "Lavery," *Gunsmoke,* CBS, 1971; "The Phantom Farmhouse," *Night Gallery,* NBC, 1971; "The Long Way Home," *The Family Holvak,* CBS, 1975; *Saturday Night Live,* NBC, 1980; "Hostage," *Today's F.B.I.,* ABC, 1981; "Partnership," *Darkroom,* ABC, 1981; "To the Finish," *The Fall Guy,* ABC, 1983; "Mind of the Machine," *Airwolf,* CBS, 1984; "Paddles Up," *Partners in Crime,* NBC, 1984; "October the 31st," *The Fall Guy,* ABC, 1984; "A Distant Scream," *Hammer House of Mystery and Suspense,* Associated Television and Hammer Film

Productions, 1984; "Dead Ringer," *The Fall Guy,* ABC, 1985; "Thanksgiving," *Amazing Stories,* NBC, 1986; "And the Moon Be Still as Bright," *The Ray Bradbury Theater,* USA Network, 1987; "Tell Me a Story," *Night Heat,* CBS, 1987; "The Country Boy," *Matlock,* NBC, 1987; "The Prisoner," *Matlock,* NBC, 1989; "Ghosts," *The Young Riders,* ABC, 1990; "Hostage," *Dr. Quinn, Medicine Woman,* CBS, 1996; "Ape-pocalypse. . . A Little Later!," *Captain Simian and the Space Monkeys,* syndicated, 1997; "The Mandrill Who Knew Too Much," *Captain Simian and the Space Monkeys,* syndicated, 1997; *Profiler,* NBC, 1999; and "Deja Vu All over Again," *Charmed,* The WB, 1999. Also appeared in an episode of *Armstrong Circle Theater,* NBC and CBS. Appearances on television pilots include *Kung Fu,* ABC, 1972; and *Kung Fu: The Legend Continues,* syndicated, 1993. Appearances on music videos include "Heartbeat" by Don Johnson, 1987.

Television work includes (series; director) *Kung Fu,* ABC, 1972-75; (producer) *Kung Fu: The Legend Continues,* syndicated, 1993-97; (producer) *Kung Fu: The Movie,* CBS, 1986; and (associate producer) *Future Force,* syndicated, 1990.

Stage appearances include *Othello,* San Francisco State College, San Francisco, CA, 1958; *The Royal Hunt of the Sun,* American National Theatre and Academy, New York City, 1965; *The Transgressor Rides Again,* 1969; and *The Ballad of Johnny Pot,* 1970. Appeared in *Romeo and Juliet,* Playbox Theatre, Berkeley, CA; *Black Elk Speaks,* American Indian Theatre, Tulsa, OK; and in productions of other Shakespearian plays, including *Hamlet.* Stage work includes (producer) *Othello,* San Francisco State College, 1958.

Recordings include (videos) *David Carradine's Tai Chi Workout,* Boxtree, 1994, produced as *David Carradine's Tai Chi Workout: The Beginner's Program for a Healthier Mind and Body,* Henry Holt, 1995; and (with David Nakahara) *David Carradine's Introduction to Chi Kung: The Beginner's Program for Physical, Emotional, and Spiritual Well-Being,* Henry Holt, 1997.

MEMBER: Screen Actors Guild, American Federation of Television and Radio Artists, Actors' Equity Association, Directors Guild of America, Writers Guild of America, Muscular Dystrophy Association, National Rifle Association, Fraternal Order of Police (honorary member), 1199 Club.

AWARDS, HONORS: Theatre World Award, most promising personality, 1965, for *The Royal Hunt of the Sun;* Emmy Award nomination, outstanding continued performance by an actor in a leading role in a drama series, 1972, and Golden Globe Award nomination, best television actor—drama, 1974, both for *Kung Fu;* National Board of Review Award, best actor, and Golden Globe Award nomination, best motion picture actor—drama, both 1976, both for *Bound for Glory;* Man of the Year Award, Fraternal Order of Police, 1985; Golden Globe Award nomination, best performance by an actor in a supporting role in a series, miniseries, or motion picture made for television, 1986, for *North and South;* received a star on the Hollywood Walk of Fame, 1997; Directors Fortnight Award, Cannes International Film Festival, for the score of *Mata Hari.*

WRITINGS:

Americana (screenplay), Crown International, 1981.
The Spirit of Shaolin, Charles E. Tuttle (Boston, MA), 1991.
Endless Highway (autobiography), Journey Editions (Boston, MA), 1995.

Also wrote (with Christopher Sergel) the book *Troublemaker.* Wrote episodes for the TV series *Kung Fu: The Legend Continues* (1993-97). Composer of songs and music for dramatic productions, including the films *Americana,* Crown International, 1981; and *American Reel,* KiMina Entertainment/North by Northwest Entertainment, 1999. Composed the score of *Mata Hari.* Composed music for the annual revues of the Drama Department, San Francisco State College (now San Francisco State University).

SIDELIGHTS: In what must surely have come as a shock to millions of fans from the 1970s, David Carradine admitted in *Spirit of Shaolin,* "I was a fake. When I left the [television] series [*Kung Fu*] after four years I knew nothing about kung fu. At the time I did not understand it at all, and I was faking it all the time even though I knew the moves. I am an actor. We just thought we had a good story." Carradine had clearly fooled an entire nation: in the enormously popular television series, which ran from 1972 to 1975, he played Kwai Chang Caine, a nineteenth-century Chinese immigrant to America who—despite his meek demeanor and unassuming appearance—is a master of the martial arts. Moreover, as Ty Burr noted in *Entertainment Weekly*, Caine embodied an "ass-kicking hippie Zen" ethic that was perfectly suited to the moment. The series, along with the films of Bruce Lee, helped popularize kung fu and other martial arts in the West, but Carradine himself, as he revealed in *Spirit of Shaolin*, only studied the skills and philosophy of Eastern self-defense much later. However, by the time he returned to the small screen in a reprise of his most popular role, playing Caine's grandson in *Kung Fu: The Legend Continues*, he had not only learned aspects of the discipline, but had made several instructional videotapes on the subject.

With the autobiography *Endless Highway*, Carradine delineates what a reviewer in *Publishers Weekly* called a "dreary catalogue of human disaster"—that is, his own life story. Though he enjoyed a seemingly charmed youth as son of veteran character actor John Carradine, he reveals that he tried to kill himself as early as the age of five. Things became much worse after his parents divorced: once his mother, her mind addled by alcohol, mistook him for his father and tried to seduce him. Burr of *Entertainment Weekly* noted that it is "hard to muster sympathy" over some of Carradine's romantic problems, such as choosing between two beautiful actresses—Barbara Hershey, mother of a son by Carradine, and Season Hubley—and several reviewers faulted Carradine for placing the blame for all his problems on others. Yet even these critics extolled the writing and Carradine's storytelling ability: *Publishers Weekly* called *Endless Highway* "breezy and anecdotal and . . . good-natured," while Burr pronounced it "a pithy, occasionally stirring read." Mike Tribby in *Booklist* was unqualified in his praise for what he called an "exhaustive and intensely personal" book containing "600-plus pages of good reading."

BIOGRAPHICAL AND CRITICAL SOURCES:

BOOKS

Contemporary Theatre, Film, and Television, volume 32, Gale (Detroit, MI), 2000.

PERIODICALS

Booklist, December 1, 1995, Mike Tribby, review of *Endless Highway*, p. 603.

Entertainment Weekly, December 8, 1995, Ty Burr, review of *Endless Highway*, p. 59.
Library Journal, December, 1991, Jennifer Langlois, review of *Spirit of Shaolin*, p. 156; November 15, 1995, Richard W. Grefath, review of *Endless Highway*, p. 75.
New York Times Book Review, February 11, 1996, Kathryn Shattuck, review of *Endless Highway*, pp. 723-724.
Publishers Weekly, October 16, 1995, review of *Endless Highway*, p. 49.
Seattle Post-Intelligencer, November 14, 1991, "David Carradine Was a Kung-Fu Faker," p. A3.
St. Louis Post-Dispatch, December 3, 1995, review of *Endless Highway*, p. 2A.
USA Today, January 27, 1993, Brian Donlon, "Caine's New Kicks: 'Kung Fu' Carradine's Reincarnation," p. D3.

*   *   *

CARRADINE, John Arthur
See CARRADINE, David

*   *   *

CASSAVETES, Nick 1959-

PERSONAL: Born May 21, 1959, New York, NY; son of John Cassavetes (an actor and director) and Gena Rowlands (an actress); children: Sasha, Virginia. *Education:* Attended Syracuse University, 1976.

ADDRESSES: Agent—United Talent Agency, 9560 Wilshire Blvd., Suite 500, Beverly Hills, CA 90212.

CAREER: Actor, director, and writer. Also worked on television commercials and worked as a janitor.

Film appearances include *Husbands*, Columbia, 1970; *A Woman under the Influence*, Castle Hill, 1974; *Mask*, Universal, 1985; *Black Moon Rising*, New World Pictures, 1986; *The Wraith*, New Century, 1986; *Quiet Cool*, New Line Cinema, 1986; *Assault of the Killer Bimbos*, Empire, 1988; *Desperation Rising*, 1989; *Blind Fury*, TriStar, 1989; *Under the Gun*, Marquis, 1989; *Backstreet Dreams*, Vidmark Entertainment,

1990; *Young Commandos,* Cannon, 1991; *Twogether,* Columbia/TriStar Home Video, 1992; *Broken Trust,* Monarch Home Video, 1993; *Gypsy Eyes,* 1993; *Sins of Desire,* Columbia/TriStar Home Video, 1993; *Body of Influence,* Academy Entertainment, 1993; *Sins of the Night,* Academy Entertainment, 1993; *Class of 1999 II: The Substitute,* Vidmark Entertainment, 1994; *Mrs. Parker and the Vicious Circle,* Fine Line Features, 1994; *Black Rose of Harlem,* New Horizons, 1996; *Me and the Gods,* Cinequanon Pictures International, 1997; *Face/Off,* Paramount, 1997; *Limbo Productions,* 1998; *The Astronaut's Wife,* New Line Cinema, 1999; *Life,* Universal, 1999; *Panic,* Artisan Entertainment, 2000; and *The Independent,* United Lotus Group, 2000. Film work as director includes *Unhook the Stars,* Miramax, 1996; *She's So Lovely,* Miramax, 1997; *Going after Cacciato,* Evolution Entertainment, 2001; *John Q,* New Line Cinema, 2001; and *The Killing of a Chinese Bookie,* New Line Cinema, 2002.

Television movie appearances include *Reunion,* CBS, 1980; *Shooter,* NBC, 1988; and *Just like Dad,* The Disney Channel, 1996. Appearances on episodic television include *L.A. Law,* NBC, 1986; "The Convict," *Matlock,* NBC, 1987; "Double Identity—November 9, 1965," *Quantum Leap,* NBC, 1989; and *Crime and Punishment,* NBC, 1993. Appearances on TV pilots include *The Marshall Chronicles,* ABC, 1990.

AWARDS, HONORS: Directors' Week Award for best film, Fantasporto, 1997, for *Unhook the Stars;* Golden Palm nomination, Cannes International Film Festival, 1997, for *She's So Lovely.*

WRITINGS:

SCREENPLAYS

(With Helen Caldwell) *Unhook the Stars,* Miramax, 1996.
(With David McKenna) *Blow* (based on the book by George Jung, as told to Bruce Porter), New Line Cinema, 2000.

Also author of the screenplays for *Going after Cacciato* (based on the novel by Tim O'Brien), 2001; and *The Notebook* and *Godforsaken,* both 2003.

SIDELIGHTS: Interviewed by Kristine McKenna of the *New York Times,* Nick Cassavetes began by saying, "Are we gonna talk about my parents?" His concern to separate his identity from those of his mother and father is understandable. Though his work was scorned during his lifetime, in the years since his death in 1989, Nick's father, John Cassavetes, has become revered as one of the seminal figures in American independent film. Eight of his films starred his wife and Nick's mother, the actress Gena Rowlands.

Despite his desire to separate his identity from that of his parents, Cassavetes chose his mother for the leading role in his directorial debut, *Unhook the Stars.* No less a critic than Roger Ebert praised the script, which Cassavetes wrote with Helen Caldwell, for its evenness and lack of over-the-top emotional or dramatic pyrotechnics—precisely those qualities for which the elder Cassavetes was known. *Unhook the Stars,* Ebert wrote, "doesn't create a lot of contrived plot problems and then resolve them with dramatic developments. Each element of the screenplay . . . is taken only as far as it will willingly go. . . . The outcome is nicely open-ended, instead of insisting that Mildred [Rowlands's character] do something concrete to provide a happy ending." Ebert concluded that "Like his father, Nick Cassavetes has made a movie about a slice of life." But in contrast to the films of John Cassavetes, whose characters drank and smoked too much and approached their many problems with an insistence that passed over the borderline into mania, *Unhook the Stars* "is about manageable, not unmanageable, life. It has an underlying contentment."

Cassavetes also wrote the script for *Blow,* the 2001 film directed by Ted Demme, who died of a heart attack later that year. The film stars Johnny Depp as George Jung, a middleman in the drug trade who helped introduce cocaine to the United States. The tale, wrote Malcolm Johnson in the *Hartford Courant,* "reworks the American rise-and-fall story in a strange way" by "cross-pollinat[ing] a period rock saga like 'The Doors' with a modern gangster story like 'Scarface.' What begins as a larkish comedy ends as a wispy tragedy."

BIOGRAPHICAL AND CRITICAL SOURCES:

BOOKS

Contemporary Theatre, Film, and Television, volume 32, Gale (Detroit, MI), 2000.

PERIODICALS

Atlanta Journal, February 14, 1997, Eleanor Ringel, review of *Unhook the Stars,* p. 11.

Chicago Sun-Times, February 14, 1997, Roger Ebert, review of *Unhook the Stars,* p. 38; April 6, 2001, review of *Blow,* p. 31.

Hartford Courant, April 6, 2001, Malcolm Johnson, review of *Blow,* p. D4.

Los Angeles Times, October 27, 1996, Kristine McKenna, review of *Unhook the Stars,* p. 33.

New York Times, April 6, 2001, A. O. Scott, review of *Blow,* p. E1.

Wall Street Journal, April 6, 2001, Joe Morgenstern, review of *Blow,* p. W1.

Washington Post, April 6, 2001, review of *Blow,* p. T41.*

*   *   *

CELA, José Camilo 1916-2002

OBITUARY NOTICE—See index for *CA* sketch: Born May 11, 1916, in Iria de Flavia, Spain; died of a heart ailment January 17, 2002, in Madrid, Spain. Author. Cela was one of Spain's most notable novelists and the recipient of the 1989 Nobel Prize in Literature. He attended the University of Madrid in the 1930s, but his studies were interrupted by the Spanish Civil War. Although he fought on the side of future dictator Francisco Franco from 1936 until 1939, Cela would later denounce fascism in his writings. Wounded, he returned to university study until 1943. While still in school, he began writing novels, the first to be published being *La familia de Pascual Duarte* (1942). Though criticized for its violent content and banned by the Franco government, the book, translated in 1964 as *The Family of Pascual Duarte,* became widely read in Spain and Latin America and has been called the most translated Spanish novel since Miguel Cervantes' *Don Quixote.* Cela met with similar censorship with novels such as *The Hive* (*Caminos inciertos: la colmena;* 1951), which many subsequent critics have judged to be his greatest work. Cela's straightforward and blunt writing style helped bring about a rebirth in Spanish fiction writing, and he is also credited with creating a new cinematic technique in his books. Other novels in his extensive oeuvre include *Rest Home* (1943), *Mrs. Caldwell Speaks to Her Son* (1953), *Tobogan de hambrientos* (1962), and *Cristo versus Arizona* (1988). The author also published numerous short story collections, essays, and travel books. His many awards, in addition to the Nobel Prize, include the 1984 Spanish National Prize for Literature and the 1994 Cervantes Prize.

OBITUARIES AND OTHER SOURCES:

BOOKS

Contemporary Literary Criticism, Gale (Detroit, MI), Volume 4, 1975, Volume 13, 1980, Volume 59, 1990, Volume 122, 2000.

Dictionary of Hispanic Biography, Gale (Detroit, MI), 1996.

Dictionary of Literary Biography: 1989 Yearbook, Gale (Detroit, MI), 1990.

Reference Guide to Short Fiction, 2nd edition, Gale (Detroit, MI), 1999.

PERIODICALS

Chicago Tribune, January 19, 2002, sec. 1, p. 25.

Los Angeles Times, January 18, 2002, p. B15.

New York Times, January 18, 2002, p. A23.

Times (London, England), January 18, 2002, p. 23.

Washington Post, January 19, 2002, p. B7.

*   *   *

CHAMBERLAIN, Safford 1926-

PERSONAL: Born October 7, 1926, in Oklahoma City, OK; son of Ernest R. (in public relations) and Ethel (a homemaker; maiden name, Everingham) Chamberlain; married LaVonne Krefting, 1967 (died 1983); married Sharyn Crane (an archaeologist), 1997; children: (first marriage) Thornton Louis, Desiree C. Chamberlain Palmer. *Education:* Attended Pasadena Junior College, 1944, 1947, Pomona College, 1947-50, and Cornell University, 1950-51. *Politics:* "Democratic Socialist." *Religion:* Unitarian-Universalist. *Hobbies and other interests:* Jazz saxophone.

ADDRESSES: Home—1118 Fremont Ave., South Pasadena, CA 91030. *E-mail*—saffordC@aol.com.

CAREER: East Los Angeles College, Monterey Park, CA, associate professor, 1947-50, associate professor, 1963-89; ; KPFK-FM Radio, Los Angeles, CA, literature and drama director, 1960-63; writer. *Military service:* U.S. Army, 1944-46.

AWARDS, HONORS: John Dye Award for Creative Writing, Pomona College, 1950; Certificate of Merit in Historical Recorded Sound Research, Association for Recorded Sound Collections, 2001.

WRITINGS:

An Unsung Cat: The Life and Music of Warne Marsh, Scarecrow Press (Lanham, MD), 2000.

Contributor of short stories to periodicals, including *Miscellaneous Man.*

WORK IN PROGRESS: Short stories.

SIDELIGHTS: Safford Chamberlain told *CA:* "My primary motivation for writing, especially for writing fiction, is to make sense of my life. Influences on my writing include Hemingway, for his mastery of understatement, Faulkner, who did what I wish I could do in entering the minds of all his characters, and Robert Stone, for everything.

"My writing process for nonfiction is gathering and organizing facts, outlining, writing, and rewriting. For the biography *An Unsung Cat: The Life and Music of Warne Marsh,* the hard part was interviewing, the easy part was writing. For fiction, the process is similar. I try to marshal my ideas, including facts I have put down from life in journals. Then I find a point of view, or voice, and structure the facts as fiction. Usually the greatest fiction is that the story is fiction. The computerized word-processor is a godsend for me, enabling me to rewrite every time I sit down at the keyboard. I can't stop myself from rewriting.

"My inspiration is to make sense of my life, specifically aspects or events of my life that have been a part of my emotional and moral becoming. Writing is my prayer for forgiveness."

CHERNICK, Michael R(oss) 1947-

PERSONAL: Born March 11, 1947, in Havre de Grace, MD; son of Jack (a nuclear engineer) and Norma (a nurse; maiden name, Wiener) Chernick; married Deborah Ann Lewandowski, February 29, 1988; children: Nicholas Alexander, Daniel Stephen. *Education:* State University of New York at Stony Brook, B.S., 1969; University of Maryland, M.A., 1973; Stanford University, M.S., 1976, Ph.D., 1978. *Politics:* Democrat. *Religion:* Jewish. *Hobbies and other interests:* Chess, bowling, coin collecting, managing Little League.

ADDRESSES: Home—15 Quail Dr., Holland, PA 18966-1645. *Office*—Novo Nordisk Pharmaceuticals, Inc., 100 College Rd. W., Princeton, NJ 08540. *E-mail*—mchernic@yahoo.com.

CAREER: Statistician and educator. Risk Data Corp., Irvine, CA, chief of statistical research for workers' compensation insurance, 1992-95; St. Jude Medical, Inc., Sylmar, CA, senior biostatistician for medical devices, 1995-98; Biosense Webster, Diamond Bar, CA, senior biostatistician for medical devices, 1998-2001; Novo Nordisk Pharmaceuticals, Inc., Princeton, NJ, assistant director of biostatistics for drug development, 2001—. Institute for Professional Education, instructor in mathematics and statistics; instructor at other institutions, including California State University, Long Beach; independent statistical consultant.

MEMBER: International Biometrics Society, American Statistical Association (fellow; past president of Southern California chapter; representative to council of chapters, 2000-01; program chair for sports statistics section, 2002), Institute of Mathematical Statistics, Society for Clinical Trials, Society for Industrial and Applied Mathematics.

AWARDS, HONORS: Jacob Wolfowitz Prize, *American Journal of Mathematical and Management Sciences,* 1983.

WRITINGS:

Bootstrap Methods: A Practitioner's Guide (statistics book), Wiley Publishing Group (New York, NY), 1999.
Introductory Biostatistics for the Health Sciences: Modern Applications including Bootstrap, John Wiley (Hoboken, NJ), 2003.

Contributor to professional journals, including *American Journal of Mathematical and Management Sciences.*

WORK IN PROGRESS: Research on extreme value theory, biostatistics, outlier methods, bootstrap, and time series.

SIDELIGHTS: Michael R. Chernick told *CA:* "I have been an industrial statistician for the last twenty-three years. In the course of my career I have worked on problems in diverse areas, including pattern recognition and classification, image processing, target tracking algorithm, insurance claim cost predictions, time series modeling and forecasting, survival analysis, statistical design, expert system development, and clinical trial design and analysis. In the course of this work I have also published numerous papers in the leading journals of probability and statistics. I have a strong interest in statistical methodology. A small collection of powerful techniques are remarkably useful in a wide variety of applications.

"My motivation for the book I published on bootstrap methods was to provide statisticians and applied researchers with an understanding of the general applicability of bootstrap methods and to provide reference to the large volume of papers on the theory and application of the bootstrap. I also wanted to alert people about situations where the method fails and modifications that work in special cases.

"The introductory book on biostatistics provides an improved text for the introductory course Bob Friis and I have taught to health science majors at California State University at Long Beach."

*   *   *

CHRISTENBURY, Leila 1950-

PERSONAL: Born March 6, 1950, in Washington, DC; daughter of Paul Scarborough (a stockbroker) and Leila Boyd (Simpson) Davis (in personnel). *Education:* Hollins College, B.A., 1972; University of Virginia, M.A., 1973; Virginia Polytechnic Institute and State University, Ed.D., 1980. *Politics:* Democrat. *Religion:* Roman Catholic.

ADDRESSES: Home—214 Old Orchard Lane, Richmond, VA 23226. *Office*—School of Education, Virginia Commonwealth University, P.O. Box 842020, Richmond, VA 23284; fax: 804-828-1326. *E-mail*—lchrist@saturn.vcu.edu.

CAREER: University of Northern Iowa, Cedar Falls, assistant professor of English, 1979-80; James Madison University, Harrisonburg, VA, assistant professor of English, 1980-82; Hollins College, Roanoke, VA, director of publications, 1982-86; Virginia Commonwealth University, Richmond, professor of English education, 1986—, director of Capital Writing Project, 1988-94. Virginia Polytechnic Institute and State University, associate director of Southwest Virginia Writing Project, 1981; Youngstown State University, visiting lecturer, 1994.

MEMBER: National Council of Teachers of English (member of board of directors, 1993—; chair for Literacy Award, 1999-2000; member of executive committee, 1999—; vice president, 1999-2000; president, 2001-02), Conference on English Education (member of executive committee, 1990-94; chair of Richard A. Meade Award committee, 1994), National Conference on Research in Language and Literacy, Assembly on Literature for Adolescents (director, 1982-86; chair of intellectual freedom committee, 1988-89), Assembly on Appalachian Literature, Assembly on Women in Life and Literature, Gay/Straight Educators Assembly, Virginia Association of Teachers of English (district president, 1977-78; member of state executive board, 1977-93 and 1998—), Virginia Conference of English Educators (chair, 1986-88), Virginia Writers Club, Phi Beta Kappa (president of Roanoke Valley chapter, 1983), Phi Delta Kappa, Phi Kappa Phi, Delta Kappa Gamma, Omicron Delta Kappa.

AWARDS, HONORS: Extraordinary Sacrifice and Service Award, Virginia Association of Teachers of English, 1984; Council for the Advancement and Support of Education, gold medal, 1984, and bronze medal, 1985, and gold medal, 1986, both for *Hollins;* Rewey Belle Inglis Award for outstanding woman in English education, National Council of Teachers of English, 1997; University Award of Excellence, Virginia Commonwealth University, 2001.

WRITINGS:

(With Patricia P. Kelly) *Questioning: A Path to Critical Thinking,* National Council of Teachers of English (Urbana, IL), 1983.

Books for You, National Council of Teachers of English (Urbana, IL), 1995.

Making the Journey: Being and Becoming a Teacher of English Language Arts, Heinemann (Portsmouth, NH), 1994, 2nd edition, 2000.

(With Diana Mitchell) *Both Art and Craft: Teaching Ideas That Spark Learning,* National Council of Teachers of English (Urbana, IL), 2000.

Contributor to books, including *Teaching Shakespeare into the Twenty-first Century,* edited by Ronald E. Salomone and James E. Davis, Ohio University Press (Athens, OH), 1997; *Reader Response in Secondary and College Classrooms,* edited by Nicholas J. Karolides, Lawrence Erlbaum (Mahwah, NJ), 2000; and *Reading Their World: The Young-Adult Novel in the Classroom,* 2nd edition, edited by Virginia Monseau and Gary Salvner, Boynton/Cook (Portsmouth, NH), 2000.

*   *   *

CLARK, Katharine
   See FLORA, Kate Clark

*   *   *

CLARKE, Gerald

PERSONAL: Born in CA. *Education:* Yale University, B.A.; postgraduate study at Heidelberg University, Oxford University, and Harvard University.

ADDRESSES: Home—Long Island, NY. *Agent*—c/o Author Mail, Random House, 201 East 50th St., New York, NY 10022. *E-mail*—geraldclarke@geraldclarke. com.

CAREER: Journalist. *New Haven Journal-Courier,* New Haven, CT, former writer; *Baltimore Sun,* Baltimore, MD, former writer; *Time,* New York, NY, former political writer, former entertainment reporter.

WRITINGS:

Capote (biography), Simon & Schuster (New York, NY), 1988.

Get Happy: The Life of Judy Garland (biography), Random House (New York, NY), 2000.

Contributor to periodicals, including *Architectural Digest, Esquire,* and *Time.*

SIDELIGHTS: Gerald Clarke is a journalist whose publications include biographies of fellow writer Truman Capote and entertainer Judy Garland. *Capote,* Clarke's first book, concerns the literary figure who realized significant success with works such as *Other Voices, Other Rooms* and *In Cold Blood,* then succumbed to substance abuse and exploited his own celebrity before dying in middle age. As Michael Wood affirmed in the *Times Literary Supplement:* "Truman Capote became so famous for being famous . . . that it was possible to forget he was a writer. People remembered the glittering parties and the ritzy friendships, but not the books." Wood added: "Gerald Clarke worked on his book for more than nine years. . . . He spent much time with Capote, and seems to have spoken to everyone who knew him, which was everyone. But Clarke is neither charmed nor spooked." Wood proclaimed *Capote* a "very good biography."

Many reviewers seconded Wood's appraisal of *Capote.* Mary Vespa wrote in *People* that *Capote* serves as a "gracefully written, well-researched biography," and Molly Haskell stated in the *New York Times Book Review* that the biography proves "rich in intelligence and compassion." Further praise came from *Wall Street Journal* reviewer Bruce Bawer, who hailed *Capote* as "a masterpiece," and *Washington Post Book World* critic John Lahr, who acknowledged it as "exceptionally satisfying." With similar enthusiasm, Larry Lee wrote in the *San Francisco Chronicle* that "*Capote* is engrossing, vivid, beautifully written," and a *Publishers Weekly* critic remarked that "*Capote* is a superb portrait." An *Economist* reviewer, meanwhile, called Clarke an "indefatigable biographer," and John Skow declared in *Time* that Clarke "sorts out the nonsense, the brilliance and the bitchiness of Capote's life in what is the liveliest and rowdiest literary biography in recent memory."

Clarke followed *Capote* with *Get Happy: The Life of Judy Garland,* a biography of the forlorn singer and actress, who enjoyed fame and success from childhood—perhaps most memorably in *The Wizard of Oz*—but ultimately fell victim to drug addiction. He told a *Beatrice* interviewer: "After I finished *Capote,* I searched for a subject of equal interest—which, to my mind, meant a life of achievement on one hand and drama on the other. Someone had suggested Judy Garland to me, and it clicked. . . . So, I sat down, and I read the biographies that had already been written and came up with no real impression of Judy. I had a lot of facts, but I didn't . . . get a clear picture of who she was." At his online home page, Clarke also disclosed, "In *Get Happy*, I try to tell the real story of Judy Garland." "I think—I hope—I've succeeded." *Time* reviewer Terry Teachout is among those readers who believe Clarke succeeded in his endeavor. Teachout noted Garland's "sad life and squalid death," and insisted that *Get Happy* "is the Garland 'biography' to read if you're reading only one."

Upon publication in 2000, *Get Happy* won widespread acclaim as an impressive, if disturbing, biography. William J. Mann wrote in *Advocate:* "Understanding the magical connection Judy had with her audiences is a prize that's eluded chroniclers up to now. . . . To this end, Clarke . . . succeeds admirably, possibly even brilliantly." George Hodgman, meanwhile, deemed *Get Happy*, in an *Entertainment Weekly* appraisal, a "compelling read," and Rosellen Brewer, in a *Library Journal* analysis, contended that the biography "could possibly stand as the definitive work on the troubled actress/singer." Less impressed, *Newsweek* reviewer David Gates described *Get Happy* as "a weird mix of deep dish and high-toned prose," and *Booklist* critic Ray Olson noted the book's "boilerplate phrasing calculated to press sentimental buttons." However, a *Publishers Weekly* critic found *Get Happy* to be "a detailed, respectful and haunting portrait," and even Olson conceded in *Booklist* that the biography is "impressively thorough." Favorable reactions also came from the *Hollywood Reporter,* where Ellen Jaffe-Gill called *Get Happy* "a compelling, tragic book," and *Entertainment Weekly,* where George Hodgman lauded the book as a "big, gutsy biography." *January* reviewer Monica Stark expressed still further praise, recommending *Get Happy* as "an absorbing, if depressing, journey."

BIOGRAPHICAL AND CRITICAL SOURCES:

PERIODICALS

Advocate, April 11, 2000, William J. Mann, review of *Get Happy: The Life of Judy Garland,* p. 64.
Booklist, February 1, 2000, Ray Olson, review of *Get Happy,* p. 995.

Economist, August 27, 1988, review of *Capote.*
Entertainment Weekly, April 7, 2000, George Hodgman, "Judy, Judy, Judy."
Hollywood Reporter, April 17, 2000, Ellen Jaffe-Gill, review of *Get Happy.*
Library Journal, April 1, 2000, Rosellen Brewer, review of *Get Happy,* p. 104.
Newsweek, March 27, 2000, David Gates, "Wrong End of the Rainbow," p. 72.
New York Times Book Review, June 12, 1988, Molly Haskell, review of *Capote.*
People, June 20, 1988, Mary Vespa, review of *Capote.*
Publishers Weekly, May 13, 1988, review of *Capote;* February 14, 2000, review of *Get Happy,* p. 180.
San Francisco Chronicle, May 22, 1988, Larry Lee, review of *Capote.*
Time, May 30, 1988, John Skow, review of *Capote;* April 10, 2000, Terry Teachout, "The Hole in Judy's Heart," p. 132.
Times Literary Supplement, May 2, 1988, Michael Wood, "Immortality at a Price," p. 950.
Wall Street Journal, June 2, 1988, Bruce Bawer, review of *Capote.*
Washington Post Book World, May 29, 1988, John Lahr, review of *Capote.*

OTHER

Beatrice, http://www.beatrice.com/ (December 2, 2001), Ron Hogan, interview with Gerald Clarke.
Gerald Clarke Home Page, http://www.geraldclarke.com/ (December 2, 2001).
January, http://www.januarymagazine.com/ (December 2, 2001), Monica Stark, "Not So Happy."*

*   *   *

COATES, Lawrence 1956-

PERSONAL: Born September 7, 1956, in Berkeley, CA; son of Howard (an accountant) and Betty (a drafter; maiden name, Bertelsen) Coates; married Kimberly Engdahl, August 9, 1997. *Education:* University of California—Santa Cruz, B.A., 1990; University of California—Berkeley, M.A., 1992; University of Utah, Ph.D., 1997.

ADDRESSES: Home—514 North Prospect St., Bowling Green, OH 43402. *Agent*—Alison Bond Ltd., 155 West 72nd St., New York, NY 10023. *E-mail*—coatesl@bgnet.bgsu.edu.

CAREER: U.S. Merchant Marine, sailor, 1979-82; Southern Utah University, Cedar City, professor, 1997-2001; Bowling Green State University, Bowling Green, OH, professor, 2001-02. *Military service:* U.S. Coast Guard, quartermaster, 1974-78.

AWARDS, HONORS: Western States Book Award in fiction, and Utah Book Award, both 1999, both for *The Blossom Festival;* fellow, National Endowment for the Arts, 2000-01.

WRITINGS:

The Blossom Festival (novel), University of Nevada Press (Reno, NV), 1999.

* * *

COCA, Jordi 1947-

PERSONAL: Born October 20, 1947, in Barcelona, Spain.

ADDRESSES: Agent—c/o Author Mail, Edicions Proa, Diputació 250, 08007 Barcelona, Spain.

CAREER: Writer of novels, poetry, essays, and children's literature; University of California at Berkeley, visiting professor, 1992. Also worked variously in the theater.

AWARDS, HONORS: Documenta prize, 1988, for *Mal de lluna;* Josep Pla prize, 1992, for *La japonesa;* critic prize, 1993, for *Louise (un conte sobre la felicitat);* Ciutat de Palma prize, 1996, for *Dies meravellosos;* children's literature prize, 1997, for *La faula dels ocells grecs;* Sant Jordi novel prize, 2000, for *Sota la pols.*

WRITINGS:

PROSE

Un d'aquells estius (Els Lluïsos) (title means "One of Those Summers"), Edicions 62 (Barcelona, Spain), 1971.
Alta comèdia (title means "High Comedy"), Pòrtic (Barcelona, Spain), 1973.

Exòtiques (title means "Exotics"), Pòrtic (Barcelona, Spain), 1975.
Selva i Salonet (title means "Selva and Salonet"), Robrenyo (Mataró, Spain), 1978.
El detectiu, el soldat i la negra (title means "The Detective, the Soldier, and the Black Woman"), Laia (Barcelona, Spain), 1980.
Les coses febles (title means "Weak Things"), Edicions del Mall (Barcelona, Spain), 1983.
Ni àngels ni dimonis (title means "Neither Angels nor Demons"), Publicacions de l'Abadia de Montserrat (Barcelona, Spain), 1983.
Sopàrem a Royal (title means "We Will Dine at the Royal"), Èczema (Sabadell, Spain), 1983.
Incidents a l'horitzó (title means "Incidents on the Horizon"), Edicions dels Dies (Sabadell, Spain), 1983.
Mal de lluna (title means "Moon Sick"), Edicions 62 (Barcelona, Spain), 1988.
La japonesa (title means "The Japanese Woman"), Destino (Barcelona, Spain), 1992.
Louise (un conte sobre la felicitat) [title means "Louise (A Story about Happiness")], Destino (Barcelona, Spain), 1993.
Paisatges de Hopper (title means "Hopper's Landscapes"), Edicions 62 (Barcelona, Spain), 1995.
El cor de les coses (title means "The Heart of Things"), Empúries (Barcelona, Spain), 1995.
Dies meravellosos (title means "Wonderful Days"), third edition, Edicions 62 (Barcelona, Spain) 1996.
L'Emperador (title means "The Emperor"), Destino (Barcelona, Spain), 1997.
La faula dels ocells grecs (title means "The Fable of the Greek Birds"), Empúries (Barcelona, Spain), 1997.
De nit, sota les estrelles (title means "At Night, under the Stars"), Proa (Barcelona, Spain), 1999.
Biblioteca Jordi Coca (title means "Jordi Coca's Library"), Proa (Barcelona, Spain), 2000.
Sota la pols (title means "Under the Sand"), Proa (Barcelona, Spain), 2001.

POETRY

Cel de nuit / Cel de nit (title means "Nuit Sky/Night Sky"), Editorial NahuJa Livres (Ceret, Spain), 1997.
Terres grogues (title means "Yellow Lands"), Proa (Barcelona, Spain), 1998.

ESSAYS

Pedrolo perillós? (title means "Dangerous Pedrolo?"), Dopesa (Barcelona, Spain), 1973.

Joan Brossa: oblidar i caminar (title means "Joan Brossa: To Forget and to Walk"), Pòrtic (Barcelona, Spain), 1973, published as *Joan Brossa o el pedestal són les sabates* (title means "Joan Brossa; or, The Pedestal Are the Shoes"), La Magrana (Barcelona, Spain) 1992.

L'Agrupació Dramàtica de Barcelona. intent de Teatre Nacional Català 1955-1963 (title means "Barcelona Drama Group. Project of Catalan National Theatre 1955-1963"), Edicions 62/Institut del Teatre (Barcelona, Spain), 1982.

(Coauthor with E. Gallén and A. Vázquez) *La Generalitat republicana i el teatre (1931-1939): legislació* [title means "The Republican Catalan Government and Theatre (1931-1939)"], Edicions 62/Institut del Teatre (Barcelona, Spain), 1982.

Qüestions de Teatre (title means "Theater Matters"), Edicions 62/Institut del Teatre (Barcelona, Spain), 1985.

(Coauthor) C. Batlle and I. Bravo, *Adrià Gual. Mitja vida de Modernisme,* (title means "Adrià Gual. Half a Life of Modernism"), Diputació de Barcelona (Barcelona, Spain), 1992.

SIDELIGHTS: Spanish poet and novelist Jordi Coca started writing around the age of fourteen while he studied dramatic arts. He did not finish the two university degrees he started, one in literature the other in business, because his love for theater soon called him, and he started working in various ways at the Institut del Teatre where he spent much of his professional time until 1992.

An avid traveler, he discovered the East block countries at the end of the 1960s and was invited to Baghdad as an observer during the Iran-Iraq war. As a direct consequence of his travels, he was led into politics where he ran for the Iniciativa per Catalunya party, a leftist political group.

As a writer, Coca is acknowledged to have revitalized the world of Catalan literature in the early seventies. As a young man, he studied and wrote about two of his most direct influences: Joan Brossa and Manuel Pedrolo. His first novel, *Un d'aquells estius (Els Lluïsos),* is a coming-of-age story that takes place after the Spanish Civil War. As Guillem-Jordi Graells noted in *Escriptors,* in all of Coca's novels there is a need to discover and unravel both the individual and the collective origins. In Coca's narrations, there is always a yearning to resolve different literary tendencies. He addresses the most important authors of the twentieth century—Marcel Proust, Cesare Pavese, Juan Rulfo, and Franz Kafka among others—and mixes them with the pivotal writers of the nineteenth century, the classics, and/or Chinese poetry. One novel, however, influenced him deeply: Peter Handke's *Die Angst des Tormanns beim Elfmeter* which was published in 1970. Thanks to this German novel, and the works of Alain Robbe-Grillet, Coca was able to conceptualize what he wanted to achieve in his prose. The best example of the style that developed is *El detectiu, el soldat i la negra.* After this novel, Coca explored different options, resulting in a series of radical works which are difficult to classify.

Coca stopped publishing fiction until 1986. *Mal de lluna,* a short novel, opened a new period in Coca's work. His style was now clean and brief, while the story is deceptively simple: a young girl goes to visit her father, with whom she has only an epistolary relationship. After 1986, he worked relentlessly on expanding short story ideas into full-fledged novels such as *La japonesa* and *Louise (un conte sobre la felicitat).* The year 1996 marked yet another shift in Coca's narrative style. *Dies Meravellosos* is a realistic social novel that depicts the years of political transition between Carrero Blanco's assassination and the failed coup-d'état in 1981.

BIOGRAPHICAL AND CRITICAL SOURCES:

BOOKS

Broch, Alex, *Jordi Coca,* Institució de les Lletres Catalanes (Barcelona, Spain), 1994.

PERIODICALS

World Literature Today, Volume 53, 1979, George E. Wellwarth, review of *L'Agrupació Dramàtica de Barcelona. intent de Teatre Nacional Català 1955-1963,* p. 494.

OTHER

Escriptors, http://www.escriptors.com/autors/ (March 21, 2002), "Jordi Coca—Catalan Writer."*

*   *   *

COLBERT, Edwin Harris 1905-2001

OBITUARY NOTICE—See index for *CA* sketch: Born September 28, 1905, in Clarinda, IA; died November 16, 2001, in Flagstaff, AZ. Paleontologist and author. Colbert, an esteemed paleontologist who discovered a fossil that helped advance the theory that the continents were once an entire mass of land, also was a scientist able to make the general public appreciate the importance of dinosaurs. Colbert received a bachelor's degree in 1928 from the University of Nebraska and followed with a master's and doctorate from Columbia University in 1930 and 1935, respectively. He worked in a variety of curator positions at the American Museum of Natural History in New York City from 1930 until his retirement in 1970 and lectured at schools around the country, including the University of Pennsylvania, Bryn Mawr, and Columbia. Colbert was also a researcher who traveled around the globe. During a 1969 expedition to Antarctica he was part of a team which found a fossil of a Lystrosaurus, a non-swimming mammal. Similar fossils had been located in South Africa, so this discovery led credence to the theory that the continents were previously one mass of land. Throughout his long career Colbert wrote than twenty books. His most popular, *The Dinosaur Book: The Ruling Reptiles and Their Relatives,* was published in 1945 and remained in print for more than twenty years. He also wrote the classic paleontology and evolutionary biology text *Colbert's Evolution of the Vertebrates: A History of the Backboned Animals through Time,* first published in 1955 and reprinted five times. Other titles include *The World of Dinosaurs, The Age of Reptiles,* and *Continental Drift and the Distribution of Fossil Reptiles.* After he retired from the natural history museum he moved west and was the curator of vertebrate paleontology at the Museum of Northern Arizona. His last book, *The Little Dinosaurs of Ghost Ranch,* was published in 1995.

OBITUARIES AND OTHER SOURCES:

PERIODICALS

Chicago Tribune, November 26, 2001, sec. 2, p. 6.
New York Times, November 25, 2001, p. A30.
Washington Post, November 23, 2001, p. B6.

COOK, Olive 1912-2002

OBITUARY NOTICE—See index for *CA* sketch: Born February 20, 1912, in Cambridge, England; died May 2, 2002, in Saffron Walden, Essex, England. Artist and author. Although a talented artist in her own right, Cook was most well known for her many books on English architecture. She was a graduate of Newnham College, Cambridge, where she earned a master's degree in 1937. During World War II she was a supervisor of publications for the National Gallery in London, as well as an air raid warden. Fascinated by the beauty of English architecture, she set out with her husband, photographer Edwin Smith, to produce several books on the subject, including *English Cottages and Farmhouses* (1954), *English Abbeys and Priories* (1961), *The English House through Seven Centuries* (1968), and *England* (1971), although she also produced similar books about Ireland and Italy. After her husband's death in 1971, Cook maintained his photography collection, which she edited into the book *Edwin Smith, Photographer, 1935-1971* (1984). She also remained active in the art world, working at festivals and helping to establish the Fry Art Gallery.

OBITUARIES AND OTHER SOURCES:

PERIODICALS

Independent (London, England), May 8, 2002, p. 18.
Times (London, England), June 14, 2002.

*   *   *

CORDELIER, John
    See UNDERHILL, Evelyn

*   *   *

COWPER, Richard
    See MIDDLETON-MURRY, John (Jr.)

*   *   *

CRAIN, Caleb

PERSONAL: Education: Harvard University, A.B., 1989; Columbia University, Ph.D., 1999.

ADDRESSES: Home—Brooklyn, NY. *Agent*—c/o Publicity Department, Yale University Press, P.O. Box 209040, New Haven, CT 06520-9040.

CAREER: Freelance writer and translator. *Lingua Franca,* senior editor, 1999-2000, reporter, 1997-2001; Columbia University, New York, NY, adjunct assistant professor of English. New York Public Library Center for Scholars and Writers, fellow, 2002-03.

WRITINGS:

(Translator) Eda Kriseova, *Vaclav Havel: The Authorized Biography,* St. Martin's Press (New York, NY), 1993.

(Translator, with Káca Poláckova-Henley and Peter Kussi) Josef Skvoreck, *The Tenor Saxophonist's Story,* Ecco Press (Hopewell, NJ), 1997.

American Sympathy: Men, Friendship and Literature in the New Nation, Yale University Press (New Haven, CT), 2001.

Also contributor to periodicals, including *Lingua Franca, Nation, New York Times Book Review, Newsday,* and *New Republic.* Wrote introductions for two Modern Library editions, *Wieland and Other Stories* by Charles Brockden Brown and *The Algerine Captive* by Royall Tyler.

SIDELIGHTS: Caleb Crain is a writer and translator. In *American Sympathy: Men, Friendship, and Literature in the New Nation,* Crain examines the views of male friendship and closeness in early U.S. literature and society. Considering novels by Charles Brockden Brown, Ralph Waldo Emerson, and Herman Melville, Crain discusses how male closeness was fostered in friendship, art, and personal life. He also surveys letters and diaries of the period, presenting a history of men's friendships and the changes they underwent. In the *New York Times Book Review,* Graham Robb called the book a "rambling but evocative study," and noted that Crain shows that "expressions of love do change from one generation to the next." A *Virginia Quarterly Review* critic wrote that the book displays a "wit and pleasing style that can be rare these days in literary criticism," and a *Choice* reviewer called it "a fascinating, if quirky, depiction" of male bonds in early America.

BIOGRAPHICAL AND CRITICAL SOURCES:

PERIODICALS

Choice, December, 2001, review of *American Sympathy: Men, Friendship, and Literature in the New Nation,* p. 682.

Library Journal, June 1, 2001, Gene Shaw review of *American Sympathy,* p. 156.

New York Times Book Review, June 3, 2001, Graham Robb, "Bosom Buddies," p. 18.

Publishers Weekly, July 12, 1993, review of *Vaclav Havel: The Authorized Biography,* p. 61.

Review of Contemporary Fiction, summer, 1997, Steve Horowitz, review of *The Tenor Saxophonist's Story,* p. 281.

Virginia Quarterly Review, winter, 2002, review of *American Sympathy,* pp. 12-13.*

*　　　*　　　*

CUNNINGHAM, Agnes 1909-
(Sis Cunningham)

PERSONAL: Born 1909, in Oklahoma; married Gordon Friesen (a performer and publisher), 1941 (died 1996). *Education:* Attended Commonwealth College, Mena, AR.

ADDRESSES: Agent—c/o University of Massachusetts Press, P. O. Box 429, Amherst, MA 01004.

CAREER: Red Dust Players, performer and union organizer, under name Sis Cunningham, beginning in Oklahoma, 1939; *Broadside,* New York, NY, founder (with Gordon Friesen) and publisher. Also worked for Southern Tenant Farmers Union and Veterans of Industry of America; Southern Summer School for Women Workers, Asheville, NC, teacher. Performer on recordings, including (with Bob Norman) *Brownwater and Blood,* Folkways, 1979.

WRITINGS:

(Editor) *Songs of Our Times, from the Pages of "Broadside" Magazine,* three volumes, Oak Publications (New York, NY), 1964-70.

(With husband Gordon Friesen) *Red Dust and Broadsides: A Joint Autobiography,* edited by Ronald D. Cohen, foreword by Pete Seeger, University of Massachusetts Press (Amherst, MA), 1999.

BIOGRAPHICAL AND CRITICAL SOURCES:

PERIODICALS

Choice, January, 2000, W. K. McNeil, review of *Red Dust and Broadsides,* pp. 945-946.

OTHER

Culturefront Online, http://www.culturefront.org/ (February 24, 2000), summer, 1999.*

*   *   *

CUNNINGHAM, Sis
    See CUNNINGHAM, Agnes

*   *   *

CUSSONS, Sheila 1922-

PERSONAL: Born August 9, 1922, in Piketburg, Cape Province, South Africa. *Education:* University of Natal (Natal, South Africa), B.A.; attended Camberwell Polytechnic (now Camberwell College of Art, London, England). *Religion:* Roman Catholic.

ADDRESSES: Home—Cape Town, South Africa. *Agent*—c/o Tafelberg Publishers, Box 879, Cape Town, South Africa.

CAREER: Poet and painter.

AWARDS, HONORS: Eugene Marais Debut Prize, 1971; Ingrid Jonker Prize, 1971; Hofmeyer Prize, 1972; South African Central New Agency prize, for *Die woedende brood.*

WRITINGS:

Plektrum (title means "Plectrum"), 1970.
Die swart kombuis (title means "The Black Kitchen"), Tafelberg (Cape Town, South Africa), 1978.

Verf en vlam (title means "Paint and Flame"), Tafelberg (Cape Town, South Africa), 1978.
Die Skitterende wond (title means "The Brilliant Wound"), Tafelberg (Cape Town, South Africa), 1979.
Die Sagte sprong (title means "The Gentle Leap"), Tafelberg (Cape Town, South Africa), 1979.
Die Somerjood (title means "The Summer Jew"), 1980.
Omtoorvuur (title means "Transfiguring Fire"), Tafelberg (Cape Town, South Africa), 1982.
(Translator) Jorge Luis Borges, *Die Vorm van die Swaard en Ander Verhale* (title means "The Shape of the Sword and Other Stories"), 1981.
Die woedende brood (title means "The Angry Bread"), Tafelberg (Cape Town, South Africa), 1981.
Gestaltes 1947 (title means "Configurations"), Tafelberg (Cape Town, South Africa), 1982.
Verwikkelde lyn, Tafelberg (Cape Town, South Africa), 1983.
Membraan, Tafelberg (Cape Town, South Africa), 1984.
Poems: A Selection (in English and Afrikaans), Tafelberg (Cape Town, South Africa), 1985.
Die heilige modder (title means "The Holy Mud"), Tafelberg (Cape Town, South Africa), 1988.
Die knetterende woord (title means "The Crackling Word"; includes some poems in English), Tafelberg (Cape Town, South Africa), 1990.
'n Engel deur my kop, Tafelberg (Cape Town, South Africa), 1997.
Die asem wat ekstase is, Tafelberg (Cape Town, South Africa), 2000.

Some of Cussons's poems appear in English translation in *The Penguin Book of South African Verse,* Penguin Books (New York, NY), 1968; her poems are also published in *Standpunte* and *Tydskrif vir Letterkunde.*

SIDELIGHTS: A South African who writes almost exclusively in Afrikaans, Sheila Cussons is among the most prominent poets from her homeland. Unpublished until her late forties, Cussons received critical acclaim when she used her poetry to respond to the life-changing experience of being seriously burned by an exploding gas stove. Following this accident, she became a prolific writer and produced numerous volumes of predominantly mystical, religious poetry. Other elements important in her work are the frequent use of humor and a painterly attention to visual detail. Cussons is also an artist and has contributed illustrations to some of her publications. Barend J. Toerien noted in a review of *Die heilige modder* in *World Literature Today* that Cussons falls outside of the largely Protestant South African tradition, given the influence of her conversion to Roman Catholicism and the many years she lived in Barcelona, Spain. Other works by Cussons include the poetry collections *Di swart kombuis* and *Verwikkelde lyn,* both of which, in Toerien's opinion, contain some of her finest writing. Other works include Afrikaans translations of stories by Jorge Luis Borges, and the autobiographical account *Gestaltes 1946.*

After studying art in Pietermaritzburg, South Africa, as well as in London and Amsterdam, Cussons settled in Spain for more than thirty years. Her first collection of poetry, *Plektrum,* offers work done during a quarter of a century and includes many poems responding to Afrikaans poet N. P. van Wyk Louw. This volume predates Cussons's disfiguring burns and arduous recovery which included two years of hospitalization. She subsequently developed a mystical style and frequently wrote about religious experiences in everyday life.

The poet's altered style of writing and increased volume attracted the attention of critics including Toerien, who reviewed a number of Cussons's collections for *World Literature Today.* An early review considers *Di swart kombuis,* which Cussons published in her mid-fifties. The title refers to the mythical "black kitchen" of Hera, which Cussons depicts as a place where religious and marital struggles are played out. Toerien called the volume "rich and copious," and considered it evidence that its author was "a major poet." The critic described how Cussons connects her own suffering with that of Christ, portraying life as "a scorching, cleansing crucible." He commended the structure of the poems and pointed to Cussons's voice as a key attraction, with its "absolutely impersonal quality without a grain of self-pity."

Di swart kombuis was promptly followed by *Verf en vlam,* a volume Toerien valued as "very good" if not quite as excellent as its predecessor. The critic sensed an "intensity" attributable to the thirty years Cussons lived in Barcelona. The critic found that in this collection the poet "expresses mostly ecstatic religious experiences or celebrates the natural beauty of the world with a painter's eye." A celebration of the world in its most minute details, the poems led Toerien to conclude that Cussons not only possesses great range and a courageous approach to writing, but that she is "one of the three major living poets in Afrikaans."

Toerien found resemblances to the works of William Blake and George Herbert in *Die woedende brood,* a collection titled after a poem that describes eating bread as a religious act. He found a "childlike wonder" akin to Blake's work and a penchant for the metaphysical resembling that of Herbert. "Mostly meditative, her poetry has a rare intensity and reflects the immediacy of religious experience in everyday things," he explained. The critic also noted that Cussons did not write directly about her accident, but that she did frequently write about fire. He admired the poetic portraits of the poet's friends and mother that he characterized as "drenched in Spain" and showing little South African influence.

Cussons continued her fire theme in the content and title of *Omtoorvuur,* a selection of poems published to coincide with her sixtieth birthday. The collection, which also includes ten previously unpublished poems, was valued by Toerien as "a very beautiful volume . . . in every way." His comment encompasses the writer's own etchings and line drawings, which reflect a continuum in the poems. The early illustrations show a conflict with an angel, while more recent images are more peaceful. In his review of the collection, Toerien regretted that the portrait poems are not included as well as other favorites, but was happy to see that Cussons's "fine sense of humor" is well represented.

The collection *Membraan* marked Cussons's return to South Africa. She continues to write about religious themes, but, according to Toerien, does so here in a more "serene" manner. The sonnets in the volume stimulated his greatest enthusiasm and he judged that there are "many excellent poems," albeit with the qualification that "some are conspicuously slight."

Further evidence of Cussons's relocation is found in *Die heilige modder,* a small collection of poems that refers to Cape Town's landmarks and its flora and fauna. Toerien sensed "a feeling of restricted space, a shrinking world" that he credited to the poet's age and characteristic mysticism. He most admired her descriptions of the city and concluded that the book portrays "a small spectrum of life in a technically good and satisfying manner."

When Toerien reviewed *'n Engel deur my kop,* a selection of religious poems published to mark the poet's seventy-fifth birthday, Cussons had published no new work since 1990. This collection included poems from all of her existing volumes. The occasion gave Toerien opportunity to reflect on the span of Cussons's career. He described her early works as showing "intense agony, physical yet sublimated into the spiritual in clear and sharp diction." Poems written after her return to South Africa are said to be "quieter, less intense." Finally, he wrote that Cussons has created a body of work "remarkable for its straightforward, immediate diction, for its ability to make the abstract tangible, for its spare but apt use of metaphors."

BIOGRAPHICAL AND CRITICAL SOURCES:

PERIODICALS

World Literature Today, spring, 1979, Barend J. Toerien, review of *Die swart kombuis,* pp. 337-338; autumn, 1979, Barend J. Toerien, review of *Verf en vlam,* p. 734; autumn, 1982, Barend J. Toerien, review of *Die woedende brood,* p. 740; summer, 1983, Barend J. Toerien, review of *Omtoorvuur,* p. 504; spring, 1985, Barend J. Toerien, review of *Membraan,* p. 312; spring, 1989, Barend J. Toerien, review of *Die heilige modder,* p. 354; autumn, 1998, Barend J. Toerien, review of *'n Engel deur my kop,* p. 886.*

CUTLER, William W. III 1941-

PERSONAL: Born May 28, 1941 in Boston, MA; married Penelope Cope Cutler. *Ethnicity:* "Caucasian/ Anglo Irish." *Education:* Harvard University, B.A., 1963; Cornell University, Ph.D., 1968.

ADDRESSES: Office—Department of History, Temple University, 1115 West Berks St., Rm. 913, Philadelphia, PA 19122.

CAREER: Temple University, Philadelphia, PA, professor, 1968—. Member and vice president, board of school directors, Jenkintown, PA, school district.

WRITINGS:

(Co-editor with Howard Gillette, Jr.) *The Divided Metropolis,* Greenwood Press (Westport, CT), 1980.
Parents and Schools, University of Chicago Press (Chicago, IL), 2000.

WORK IN PROGRESS: A book on student culture and school life, forthcoming 2006.

D

DANESHVAR, Simin 1921-

PERSONAL: Born April 23, 1921, in Shiraz, Iran; daughter of a physician; married Jalal Al-e Ahmad (a writer and social critic), 1950 (died, 1969). *Education:* University of Tehran, Ph.D., 1949; attended Stanford University as a Fulbright fellow, 1952.

ADDRESSES: Agent—c/o Author Mail, Mage Publishers, 1032 29th St. NW, Washington, DC 20007.

CAREER: Writer and educator. Radio Tehran, Tehran, Iran, writer, became director of foreign news, 1940s; *Iran* (newspaper), journalist, 1941-45; Tehran Conservatory, Tehran, instructor; University of Tehran, Tehran, associate professor of art history until the late 1970s, became chairman of the Department of Art History and Archaeology; Writers' Association of Tehran, co-founder.

WRITINGS:

Atash-e khamoush (stories; title means *The Quenched Fire*), 1948.
Shahri chon behesht (stories; title means *A City as Paradise*), 1961.
Savushun (novel), Kharazmi (Tehran, Iran), 1969, translation by M. R. Ghanoonparvar with an introduction by Brian Spooner, Mage Publishers (Washington, DC), 1990, translation by Roxane Zand published as *A Persian Requiem,* Braziller (New York, NY), 1992.

Be ki salam konam? (title means "To Whom Can I Say Hello?"), Kharazmi (Tehran, Iran), 1980.
Ghorub-e-Jalal (title means "Jalal's Sunset"), 1981.
Dih kay salam kunam?, Tehran, 1981.
Daneshvar's Playhouse (stories), translation by Maryam Mafi, Mage Publishers (Washington, DC), 1989.
Sutra and Other Stories, translation by Hasan Javadi and Amin Neshati, Mage Publishers (Washington, DC), 1994.
Az parandah'ha-yi muh ajir-i bipurs, (Tehran, Iran), c. 1997.

Translator of works by George Bernard Shaw, Anton Chekhov, Nathaniel Hawthorne, William Saroyan, Alan Paton, and Arthur Schnitzler; contributor to periodicals, including *Pacific Spectator.*

SIDELIGHTS: Simin Daneshvar was the first woman to have a collection of short stories published in Iran. Daneshvar, who was married to established novelist Jalal Al-e Ahmad, surpassed her husband in literary importance with the publication of her novel *Savushun,* which was first translated under its original title, then again as *A Persian Requiem.* Her husband died shortly after the original was published, and Daneshvar continued to write and to promote the work of young writers, assisting them both academically and financially, an effort she and her husband had begun through the Writers' Association of Tehran.

Daneshvar was born into a middle-class family and educated in a missionary school where she became fluent in English, a skill that opened doors for her as she pursued a career as a radio and print journalist and which afforded her the opportunity to study at Stanford University. When she returned to Iran, Daneshvar became an associate professor at the University of Tehran, but she was never offered a full professorship, she later learned because of the intervention of SAVAK, the secret police, who opposed the appointment of such an outspoken woman.

The stories of *Atash-e khamoush* deal with the issues of life, death, love, and sacrifice and resemble the stories of U.S. author O. Henry, whose work Daneshvar had read and admired. Her second collection, *Shahri chon behesht,* reflects a more mature style and focuses on the lives of Persian women.

Savushun was first published in 1969 but not translated or reviewed in English until twenty years later. *Choice* reviewer M. C. Hillman observed that because Daneshvar's groundbreaking novel is written from a feminine perspective, it "can serve as an important window into a room in Iranian culture not often visited or accurately described." The title is taken from the term that describes the mourning of Iran's pre-Islamic hero Siyavush, who went through an ordeal by fire and was killed by foreigners.

Daneshvar's husband was best known for his polemic essay "Gharbzadagi," an angry criticism of Western influence and ideas. "Al-i Ahmad died (or was he murdered by Savak?) in the year of *Savushun*'s publication, and the novel gives fictional form to some of the concerns of 'Gharbzadagi,'" wrote Robert Irwin in the *Times Literary Supplement.* "Al-i Ahmad had urged his fellow-intellectuals to turn away from Europe and find in Iran's own culture sources of self-respect. He was inclined, though only half-inclined, to look for future salvation in the religious establishment and traditional Iranian Shi'ism. Daneshvar too seems to be advocating a return to traditional roots, though not to a rigorous religious fundamentalism."

The story, based on historical fact, is set in Shiraz during the World War II Allied occupation of Iran and is narrated by Zari, whose concerns are to care for her husband, Yusof, their children, and her garden. Her country is occupied in the north by Russia and by Britain in the south, with the occupying countries concerned over Reza Shah's suspected Nazi sympathies. Hoarding and rising prices of food are brought on by the demands of the troops, and disease, particularly typhus, is blamed on the British. The people of Shiraz, like Zari and her husband, listen to Berlin radio and wonder if perhaps Hitler may be "the Imam of the Age." Yusof, a landowner, refuses to gives his crops to the armies, since this would mean the starvation of the peasants. His older brother Khan, is politically ambitious and cooperates with the requests for food. Yusof is killed, and the book ends with a funeral procession that threatens to become a mass demonstration until the police step in and disperse the crowds.

Persis M. Karim wrote in *San Francisco Review of Books* that although the story "concerns the war and the influence of capitalist and communist ideologies in an Islamic country, the main field of action is Zari's development as she encounters the injustices of her society and dares to question them. Initially aroused by her rebellious but essentially decent husband, who challenges the government and is martyred for his efforts, Zari comes into her own as a woman of conscience despite her traditional prescribed roles of wife, mother, and provider of charity."

"Unfolding within this large tapestry are a variety of other fascinating stories," noted Victoria Amador in *Belles Lettres,* "the coming to manhood of Zari's son; her interactions with a Machiavellian old crone intent on revenge for Zari's rejection of her son's advances; Zari's regular visits to prisoners and insane asylum residents . . . and Zari's tender relationship with her husband."

Both Karim and Nasrin Rahimieh of *World Literature Today* noted that the first English translation preserves not only the original title, but also a more accurate rendition of the original, a glossary, and an introduction by Brian Spooner. Rahimieh said that the second translation, titled *A Persian Requiem,* "attempts to bridge linguistic and cultural gaps between the novel and its English-language readers." *Choice* reviewer M. Cook said *A Persian Requiem* "weaves an absorbing tale sensitively and elegantly translated by Roxane Zand." "This very human novel avoids ideological cant while revealing complex political insights, particularly in light of the 1979 Iranian revolution," wrote a *Publishers Weekly* reviewer.

Daneshvar's Playhouse is a collection of six stories written over the years and which are representative of the author's writings of life in Iran. Rahimieh felt that

Maryam Mafi's translations "make the stories accessible even to readers unfamiliar with the social and cultural setting of Daneshvar's texts. Without losing too much of the flavor of the original, Mafi has, when possible, found idiomatic equivalents for Persian terms and customs."

"The formal detachment of Daneshvar's prose reinforces her subtle revelation of repressive features in Iranian society," wrote Sybil Steinberg in *Publishers Weekly.* Each of the characters in these stories is trapped in his or her own metaphorical playhouse and has little control over their own lives. The characters include a nanny in "Vakil Bazaar," the housewife of "The Accident," a lonely wife in "To Whom Can I Say Hello?," and a retired colonel in "Traitor's Intrigue."

"The portrayal of the deprived classes of society through black characters is an important feature of Daneshvar's fiction," noted Parvin Loloi in *Contemporary World Writers.* "'The Playhouse' particularly displays her typical wit and perception, presenting the life of a lower class actor, whose job is to blacken his face every night and play the role of either a servant or a guard, but whose true sensibility is demonstrated in his improvised jokes, which are somewhat reminiscent of the wisdom of Shakespeare's fools." The final essay, "The Loss of Jalal," is Daneshvar's account of the death of her husband and is followed by a letter to her readers in which Daneshvar talks about the difficulties she has had to face as a woman writer and professor in a patriarchal system, as well as a criticism of Western society.

Mafi writes in the afterword to *Daneshvar's Playhouse* that Daneshvar's stories "reflect reality rather than fantasy. They contain themes such as child theft, adultery, marriage, childbirth, sickness, death, treason, profiteering, illiteracy, ignorance, poverty, and loneliness. . . . Daneshvar depicts the lifestyles of the lower classes, the traditional middle class, and the bourgeoisie with equal clarity." Mafi continued, saying that Daneshvar "is particularly concerned with elderly single women who have worked their entire lives to earn a living, but find themselves poor and brokenhearted in their final years. . . . Daneshvar, who has adopted the plight of the lower classes, especially that of poor women, considers their economic dependence on men as the source of all their misfortune." "Although Daneshvar underscores the social factors

contributing to the unfortunate situation of women," added Mafi, "she nevertheless maintains her objectivity, at times turning her critical eye upon the individual."

The six tales in *Sutra and Other Stories* were called "vibrant" by a *Publishers Weekly* contributor, who said they "chronicle the vicissitudes of life—its horror, unfairness, humor, and fleeting beauty." The title story is about a former sea captain and smuggler who recalls his life and the wife and daughter he forced into prostitution, then abandoned. Rahimieh noted that these translations are not preceded by an introduction, nor are they accompanied by a glossary. Rahimieh felt that Daneshvar's writings in English have become familiar enough that these are no longer necessary. "The stories themselves take us into the innermost thoughts of characters often tragically caught between harsh realities with which they must contend and pleasant dreams they have little hope of seeing realized. Now and then we glimpse traces of Daneshvar's persistent social critique and personal hopes for the future."

BIOGRAPHICAL AND CRITICAL SOURCES:

BOOKS

Contemporary World Writers, St. James Press (Detroit, MI), 1993.
Daneshvar, Simin, *Daneshvar's Playhouse,* translated and with an afterword by Maryam Mafi, Mage Publishers (Washington, D.C.), 1989.

PERIODICALS

Belles Lettres, summer, 1992, Victoria Amador, review of *A Persian Requiem,* p. 59.
Booklist, February 15, 1992, Ivy Burrowes, review of *A Persian Requiem,* p. 1087.
Choice, June, 1991, M. C. Hillman, review of *Savushun,* p. 1646; September, 1992, M. Cooke, review of *A Persian Requiem,* p. 124.
International Journal of Middle East Studies, May, 1993, Paul Sprachman, review of *A Persian Requiem,* p. 347; November, 1995, G. Michael Wickens, review of *Sutra and Other Stories,* p. 527.

Library Journal, December, 1990, Paula I. Nielson, review of *Savushun,* p. 160.

Middle East Journal, autumn, 1991, Ahmad Karimi-Hakkak, review of *Savushun,* p. 699; winter, 1991, William L. Hanaway, review of *Daneshvar's Playhouse,* p. 148.

Middle East Policy, April, 1995, Robert Brenton Betts, review of *A Persian Requiem,* p. 146.

Publishers Weekly, September 1, 1989, Sybil Steinberg, review of *Daneshvar's Playhouse,* p. 74; January 20, 1992, review of *A Persian Requiem,* p. 57; September 19, 1994, review of *Sutra and Other Stories,* p. 52.

San Francisco Review of Books, January, 1992, Persis M. Karim, review of *Savushun,* p. 57.

Times Literary Supplement, March 1, 1991, Robert Irwin, review of *Savushun,* p. 20.

World Literature Today, autumn, 1990, Nasrin Rahimieh, review of *Daneshvar's Playhouse,* pp. 690-691; summer, 1992, Nasrin Rahimieh, review of *A Persian Requiem,* p. 574; winter, 1995, Nasrin Rahimieh, review of *Sutra and Other Stories,* pp. 214-215.

OTHER

Mage Publishers Web Site, http://www.mage.com/ (June 28, 2002). *

*   *   *

DANTE, Joe 1946-

PERSONAL: Born November 28, 1946, in Morristown, NJ.

ADDRESSES: Agent—David Gersh, The Gersh Agency, 232 North Canon Dr., Beverly Hills, CA 90210-5302.

CAREER: Director, editor, producer, screenwriter, and actor.

Film appearances include *Cannonball,* New World, 1976; *Roger Corman: Hollywood's Wild Angel,* Cinegate, 1978; *Piranha,* New World, 1978; *The Slumber Party Massacre,* 1981; *The Fantasy Film Worlds of George Pal,* 1985; *Gremlins 2: The New Batch,* 1990; *Oscar,* 1991; *Sleepwalkers,* 1992; *The Magic World of Chuck Jones,* 1992; *Flying Saucers over Hollywood: The Plan 9 Companion,* 1992: *Il silenzio dei proscutti,* 1994; and *Beverly Hills Cop III,* 1994.

Film work includes (dialogue director) *Fly Me,* 1982; (editor) *The Arena,* 1983; (director and editor) *Hollywood Boulevard,* New World, 1976; (editor) *Grand Theft Auto,* New World, 1977; (director and editor) *Piranha,* New World, 1978; (director) *Rock n' Roll High School,* 1979; (director and editor) *The Howling,* AVCO-Embassy, 1981; (director) "It's a Good Life," *Twilight Zone—The Movie,* Warner Bros., 1983; (director) *Gremlins,* Warner Bros., 1984; (director) *Explorers,* Paramount, 1985; (director) "Hairlooming," "Bullshit or Not," "Critics Corner," "Roast Your Loved One," and "Reckless Youth," *Amazon Women on the Moon,* Universal, 1987; (director) *Innerspace,* Warner Bros., 1987; (director) *The 'Burbs,* Universal, 1989; (executive producer) *The Phantom,* Paramount, 1996; (director) *Gremlins 2: The New Batch,* 1990; (director) *Matinee,* 1993; (director) *Small Soldiers,* DreamWorks Distribution L.L.C., 1998; and (producer) *Malevolence,* 1999.

Appearances on television specials include *The Horror Hall of Fame,* syndicated, 1990; *Flesh and Blood: The Hammer Heritage of Horror,* 1994; *Hollywood Stars: A Century of Cinema,* Disney Channel, 1995; *The Roger Corman Special,* Showtime, 1995; and *Masters of Fantasy: Industrial Light & Magic,* Sci-Fi Channel, 1998. Appearances on episodic television include *Naked Hollywood,* Arts and Entertainment, 1991. Television series work as director includes *Eerie, Indiana,* NBC, 1991 (also creative consultant). Television movie work includes *Runaway Daughters,* Showtime, 1994; *The Second Civil War,* HBO, 1997; and *The Warlord: Battle for the Galaxy,* UPN, 1998. Work on television pilots includes *Eerie, Indiana,* NBC, 1991; and *The Warlord: Battle for the Galaxy,* CBS, 1995 (and executive producer). Work on episodic television includes *Police Squad!,* ABC, 1982; "The Shadow Man," *The Twilight Zone,* CBS, 1985; "Boo!" *Amazing Stories,* NBC, 1986; "The Greibble," *Amazing Stories,* NBC, 1986; "Lightning," *Pictures Windows,* Showtime, 1995; "The Occupant," *Night Visions,* 2000; and "Quiet Please," *Night Visions,* 2000.

WRITINGS:

(With others) *Rock n' Roll High School,* New World Pictures, 1979.

SIDELIGHTS: Protégé of legendary B-movie film-maker Roger Corman, Joe Dante came up through the ranks, developing a catalogue that included some memorable movies of his own. First among these was *Hollywood Boulevard* (1976), which he made with fellow Corman student Allan Arkush. Eventually he attracted the attention of Steven Spielberg, who put him to work on a segment of *Twilight Zone—The Movie* (1983). This led to more impressive engagements, beginning with *Gremlins* (1984), and continuing through the animated *Small Soldiers* (1998) and beyond.

Long before he won acceptance from mainstream Hollywood, however, Dante cowrote and co-directed what was destined to become a cult classic among film and music fans alike: *Rock n' Roll High School* (1979). Jointly directed by Dante, Arkush, and Jerry Zucker, with a screenplay by Dante, Arkush, Richard Whitley, Russ Dvonch, and Joseph McBride, the film was an inadvertent vehicle for one of the great unsung acts of rock history, the Ramones. Often regarded as the fathers of American punk, the Ramones never attracted the following of their more noisy British counterparts, the Sex Pistols. In *Rock n' Roll High School,* however, they were the stars of the show.

In many ways, *Rock n' Roll High School* is the prototype for the joyful and sometimes raunchy films of the 1980s that celebrate teenage abandon. The tale itself is built on a fittingly slender thread involving an attempt by mean-spirited adults to put an end to rock n' roll at Vince Lombardi High School by burning a pile of records. Music fan and student Riff Randell (P. J. Soles) organizes the student resistance, and in this she is supported by the Ramones themselves. The kids take over the school, the Ramones become honorary students, and the film ends with a bang.

BIOGRAPHICAL AND CRITICAL SOURCES:

BOOKS

Contemporary Theatre, Film, and Television, volume 33, Gale (Detroit, MI), 2001.
Roberts, Jerry, and Steven Gaydos, *Movie Talk from the Front Lines: Filmmakers Discuss Their Works with the Los Angeles Film Critics Association,* McFarland & Co. (Jefferson, NC), 1999.

Singer, Michael. *A Cut Above: Fifty Film Directors Talk about Their Craft,* Lone Eagle (Los Angeles, CA), 1998.*

*　　*　　*

DAVIES, A(rthur) Powell 1902-1957

PERSONAL: Born June 5, 1902, in Birkenhead, England; immigrated to United States, 1928; died September 26, 1957, in Washington, DC. *Education:* Richmond College, London, B.D., 1925.

CAREER: Methodist lay minister prior to World War I; pastor of Methodist church in Oxford, England, c. 1925-28; pastor of Methodist Episcopal churches in Goodwin Mills and Clarks Mills, ME, 1928-29, and Portland ME, 1929-32; pastor of Unitarian church in Summit, NJ, 1933-44; All Souls Church, Washington, DC, pastor, 1944-57. Unitarian Advance, member; Americans for Democratic Action, founding member.

WRITINGS:

American Destiny, Beacon Press (Boston, MA), 1942.
Man's Vast Future: A Definition of Democracy, Farrar, Straus & Young (New York, NY), 1951.
The Urge to Persecute, Beacon Press (Boston, MA), 1953.
The Meaning of the Dead Sea Scrolls, New American Library (New York, NY), 1956.
The First Christian: A Study of St. Paul and Christian Origins, Farrar, Straus & Cudahy (New York, NY), 1957.

Author of pamphlets, including "The Man from Nazareth," Community Church (Summit, NJ), 1937. Sermons recorded on album *The Voice of A. Powell Davies,* three volumes, Publications Committee, All Souls Church (Washington, DC), 1957-59.

BIOGRAPHICAL AND CRITICAL SOURCES:

BOOKS

Religious Leaders of America, 2nd edition, Gale (Detroit, MI), 1999.*

DAY, Barry (Leonard) 1934-

PERSONAL: Born April 27, 1934, in Lincoln, England; immigrated to the United States, 1979; son of Samuel and Marguerite (Bell) Day. *Education:* Balliol College, Oxford, B.A., 1956, M.A., 1957.

ADDRESSES: Home—New York, NY. *Office*—Lintas Worldwide, 1 Dag Hammarskjold Plaza, New York, NY 10017-2201.

CAREER: Lintas, Ltd., London, England, creative director, 1956-59; worked for McCann-Erikson and its affiliates, beginning 1970; McCann-Erikson International, New York, NY, vice chairman, 1979-81; McCann-Erikson Worldwide, New York, NY, vice chairman, 1981-88; Interpublic Group of Cos., New York, NY, director, 1988-89; Lintas Worldwide, New York, NY, vice chairman and director of international development, 1989—. Member of Institute of Practitioners in Advertising; director of International Shakespeare's Globe Theatre board. Former political media advisor to British Prime Minister Margaret Thatcher.

MEMBER: Royal Society of Arts (fellow).

WRITINGS:

The Message of Marshall McLuhan, Lintas (London, England), 1967.
What We Have Here Is a Failure to Communicate, McCann-Erikson Advertising (London, England), 1975.
It Depends on How You Look at It, McCann-Erikson Advertising (London, England), 1978.
(Editor) *One hundred Great Advertisements,* 1978.
Political Communications, 1982.
And You Call That Creative?, 1983.
You Have Thirty Seconds Starting . . . Now, 1987.
Perspectives: Europe, 1992.
(With Graham Payn) *My Life with Noël Coward,* Applause (New York, NY), 1994.
This Wooden "O": Shakespeare's Globe Reborn: Achieving an American's Dream, foreword by John Gielgud, Oberon Books (London, England), 1996, Limelight Editions (New York, NY), 1998.

(Editor and annotator) Noël Coward, *Noël Coward: The Complete Lyrics,* Overlook Press (Woodstock, NY), 1998.
(Editor, with Tony Ring) P. G. Wodehouse, *P. G. Wodehouse, in His Own Words,* Hutchinson (London, England), 2001.

Also consulting editor to *A Complete Guide to Advertising,* 1985.

SIDELIGHTS: Advertising executive Barry Day has written about both advertising and the theater. In America the Englishman is best known for his work as an editor and co-author of two books on Noël Coward: *My Life with Noël Coward* and *Noël Coward: The Complete Lyrics.* Both have been praised by critics for their readability and their catchy subject matter.

During his long and successful career as an advertising executive, Day served as the vice chairman of the firm of McCann-Erikson, where he handled the company's creative, research, media, and strategic planning departments. Anthony Vagnoni commented on Day's impressive position at McCann-Erikson in *Back Stage:* "His title is vice-chairman, world-wide director of professional services, but his function seems to be that of a combination mentor, counselor, prophet, and statesman. He's McCann's minister without portfolio, a worldly and wizened advisor to kings and presidents whose task it is to guide his charges through the pitfalls of the present, warn them of the dangers of the future and remind them of the lessons of the past."

Through his work in the advertising field, Day developed a reputation for creating ad campaigns which established long-lived brand identities. He explained in *Back Stage,* "Advertisers by and large don't seem to understand that when you're creating a real brand campaign, like the Esso tiger or the Martini world or the Coke feeling, that you're creating something for the long haul." He added, "There's a difference between an advertisement and advertising—one is one of something, the other is a process . . . and the process is by far the hard part. It means creating a long-term relationship, so that everything else you do and everything you've done is a cumulative investment with a cumulative payoff."

Day has written and edited a number of books about advertising, including *What We Have Here Is a Failure to Communicate,* but he also enjoys writing about the theater. His first book on the subject is *My Life with Noël Coward,* which was written with Graham Payn, a longtime companion to Coward who also was an actor in many of Coward's plays. Although Jack Helbig noted in *Booklist* that readers of *My Life with Noël Coward* will gain no new revelations on the playwright, the critic did feel it was imminently "readable" and provides an "interesting, often tartly witty portrait of Coward." In addition to Payn's reminiscences, the book includes bonuses such as "a transcript of a 1961 conversation between Coward and Judy Garland, as well as previously unpublished essays by Coward on the theater," according to a *Publishers Weekly* reviewer.

Day has also been praised for his book about the reconstruction of the Globe Theater, *This Wooden "O": Shakespeare's Globe Reborn.* Stephen Patterson, writing in *Back Stage,* recommended it as an "enjoyable read about a pushy American who helped save a priceless piece of British history, and more importantly, world theater history. This story of Sam Wanamaker's obsession with the rebuilding of William Shakespeare's Globe Theater is a big Broadway musical waiting to happen. It is a uniquely American tale of an outsider coming in and telling everyone else, 'I'm gonna see to it that my dream of what is best for you is the dream that you will eventually envision and embrace for yourself.'"

BIOGRAPHICAL AND CRITICAL SOURCES:

PERIODICALS

Back Stage, July 29, 1988, Anthony Vagnoni, "Barry Day's Expansive View," p. 10B; August 14, 1998, Stephen Patterson, "Off the Bookshelf," p. 41.

Booklist, November 15, 1994, Jack Helbig, review of *My Life with Noël Coward,* p, 573; April 15, 1999, Ray Olson, review of *The Complete Lyrics,* p. 1498.

Publishers Weekly, October 17, 1994, review of *My Life with Noël Coward,* p. 74.*

*　　　*　　　*

de ATHAYDE, Tristão
See AMOROSO LIMA, Alceu

De-la-NOY (WALKER), Michael 1934-2002

OBITUARY NOTICE—Born April 3, 1934, in Hessle, Yorkshire, England; died of cancer, August 12, 2002, in Kettering, Northamptonshire, England. Journalist and author. De-la-Noy's celebrity rests on his biographies and historical works. Described by some as an outspoken, colorful, and sometimes nettlesome personality, he was at the same time praised for the journalistic clarity of his writings and for his sympathetic biographies of people whose lives often lay outside the conventions of their times. De-la-Noy spent the first part of his career as a journalist and occasional magazine editor. He also spent some years representing the laity of his diocese at what later became the General Synod of the Anglican Church, and he served briefly in the 1960s as press secretary to then-Archbishop of Canterbury Michael Ramsey. De-la-Noy was nearly fifty years old when his attention turned to nonfiction writing and the most prolific phase of his career began. He originally focused on the work of writer Denton Welsh, editing the author's journals for unexpurgated publication and producing the biography *Denton Welch: The Making of a Writer.* His other biographies include *Merwyn Stockwood: A Lonely Life,* a sympathetic portrayal of a celibate homosexual Anglican bishop. De-la-Noy, whose early religious faith had reportedly faded as he aged, penned *The Church of England: A Portrait* in the 1990s; in it, he recalled the values of the church of his youth and voiced his concern for the future of Anglican Christianity. His books on the royal family include *The Honours System, The Queen behind the Throne,* a biography of the late Queen Mother Elizabeth that became a bestseller when it was published in 1994, and *The King Who Never Was: The Story of Frederick, Prince of Wales.*

OBITUARIES AND OTHER SOURCES:

PERIODICALS

Independent (London, England), August 13, 2002, p. 14.
Times (London, England), August 13, 2002, p. 28.

*　　　*　　　*

DEVI, Indra 1899-2002
(Eugenie Vasilievna Peterson)

OBITUARY NOTICE—See index for *CA* sketch: Born May 12, 1899, in Riga, Latvia; died April 25, 2002, in Buenos Aires, Argentina. Yoga instructor and author.

Devi, believed to be the first Westerner to teach yoga in India, was a teacher to Hollywood stars and encouraged Russian leaders to legalize the practice in their country. Her influence stretched from Europe to South America. She grew up in Moscow and left with her mother for Berlin when the communists took over the country. She began acting and dancing, and developed an interest in India when she read a book by an Indian poet. Peterson left for India in 1927 and took the stage name Indra Devi. While there she met and married her first husband, Jan Strakaty, commercial attaché to the Czechoslovak Consulate in Bombay. He introduced her to the maharaja and his wife, who then introduced her to Sri Krishnamacharya, a yoga guru who taught in the royal palace. Devi studied with Krishnamacharya and trained to be a teacher. When she and her husband were transferred to China she taught yoga classes in the home of Madame Chiang Kaishek. Around that time she wrote her first of twelve books, titled *Yoga—The Technique of Health and Happiness.* Other titles include *Forever Young, Forever Healthy, Yoga for Americans,* and *Renew Your Life through Yoga: The Indra Devi Method for Relaxation through Rhythmic Breathing.* After her husband's death in 1946 Devi moved to the United States and headed for Hollywood, where she became yoga instructor and helped teach breath control to such stars as Gloria Swanson, Greta Garbo, and Jennifer Jones. She also taught at Elizabeth Arden spas. She eventually moved to Tecate, Mexico with her second husband, and held training classes for yoga teachers in her home. Devi is credited with creating a new form of yoga called Sai yoga, named for the guru Satya Sai Baba. After the death of her second husband, Devi moved to Argentina and continued offering yoga classes, maintaining her ability to teach well into her nineties at the Fundacion Indra Devi.

OBITUARIES AND OTHER SOURCES:

PERIODICALS

Los Angeles Times, May 5, 2002, p. B19.
New York Times, April 30, 2002, p. C18.
Times (London, England), May 13, 2002.
Washington Post, May 7, 2002, p. B6.

*   *   *

de VRIES, Abraham H. 1937-
(Thuys van der Vyfer, a pseudonym)

PERSONAL: Born February 9, 1937, in Ladismith, Cape Town, South Africa. *Education:* Attended University of Stellenbosch, South Africa; Gemeen-

telijke Universiteit van Amsterdam, D.Lit (Afrikaans language and literature); University of Stellenbosch, D.Lit, 1986.

ADDRESSES: Home—South Africa. *Office*—c/o Human & Rousseau Publishers, Waalburg Building 1st Floor, 28 Wale Street, P.O. Box 5050, Cape Town, South Africa 8000.

CAREER: Writer, poet, and lecturer. *Die Vaderland,* Johannesburg, South Africa, arts editor, 1963-65; Peninsula Technikon, Cape Town, South Africa, head of Department of Languages and Communication, retired 1997; University of Port Elizabeth, University of Rhodes, University of Natal, visiting lecturer.

AWARDS, HONORS: Reina Prinsen Geerligs prize, 1962, for *Hoog teen die Heunningkrans, Verlore Erwe,* and *Proegoed;* Eugene Marais prize, 1967, for *Vliegoog;* Perskor prize, 1974, for *Briekwa;* De Kat/ Potpourri prize, 1989, for the short story *Die Bruid.*

WRITINGS:

Hoog teen die Heunningkrans, Culemborg (Kaapstad, South Africa), 1956.
Verlore Erwe, Culemborg (Kaapstad, South Africa), 1957.
Proegoed (poems), H.A.U.M. (Kaapstad, South Africa), 1959.
Vetkers en Neonlig, H.A.U.M. (Kaapstad, South Africa), 1961.
Dubblleldoor, Tafelberg-uitgewers (Kaapstad, South Africa), 1964.
Vliegoog, Tafelberg-uitgewers (Kaapstad, South Africa), 1965.
Die Rustelose Sjalom (travel), Human & Rousseau (Kaapstad, South Africa), 1965.
Afspraak met Eergister, Tafelberg-uitgewers (Kaapstad, South Africa), 1966.
Dor in die Klein Karoo, Afrikaanse Pers-Boekhandel (Johannesburg, South Africa), 1966.
Kruispadu (novel), Tafelberg-uitgewers (Kaapstad, South Africa), 1966.
Joernaal uit 'n Gragtehuis (journal), Tafelberg-uitgewers (Kaapstad, South Africa), 1968.
Twee Maal om di Son, Tafelberg-uitgewers (Kaapstad, South Africa), 1969.
Volmoed se Gasie, Human & Rousseau (Kaapstad, South Africa), 1972.

Briekwa, Perskor (Johannesburg, South Africa), 1973.

Bliksoldate Bloie Nie, Human & Rousseau (Kaapstad, South Africa), 1975.

Die Klein Karoo, Tafelberg-uitgewers (Kaapstad, South Africa), 1977.

Uur van die Idiote, Human & Rousseau (Kaapstad, South Africa), 1980.

Soms op 'n reis (title means "At Times When Traveling"), edited by André Brink, Human & Rousseau (Kaapstad, South Africa), 1987.

Nag van die Clown (title means "Night of the Clown"), Human & Rousseau (Kaapstad, South Africa), 1989.

'n Plaaswinkel naby Oral, Human & Rousseau (Kaapstad, South Africa), 1994.

Skaduwees tussen Skaduweesu (title means "Shadows among Shadows"), Human & Rousseau (Kaapstad, South Africa), 1997.

(Editor) *Uit die Kontreie Vandaan,* Human & Rousseau (Kaapstad, South Africa), 2000.

Op die wye oop Karoo, Human & Rousseau (Kaapstad, South Africa), 2002.

ANTHOLOGIES

(Compiler) *Kort Keur* (short stories), Human & Rousseau (Kaapstad, South Africa), 1977.

(Compiler) *Die Afrikaanse Kortverhaalboek* (short stories), Human & Rousseau (Kaapstad, South Africa), 1978.

Steekbaars, Klipbok-uitgewers (Kaapstad, South Africa), 1989.

Op die wyse van die taal, Vlaeberg (Kaapstad, South Africa), 1989.

Ons kom van ver af, Prog Uitgewers, 1995.

(Compiler) *Eue,* Human & Rousseau/Tafelberg-uitgewers (Kaapstad, South Africa), 1996.

Kort Vertel: Aspekte van die Afrikaanse Kortverhaal, Suid-Afrikaanse Instituut (Amsterdam, Netherlands), 1998.

(Editor) *Uit die Kontreie Vandaan,* Human & Rousseau (Kaapstad, South Africa), 2000.

Also author of three thrillers under pseudonym Thuys van der Vyfer: *Die swart sikkel,* 1961; *Mesne agter glas,* 1965; and *Alibi van 'n verdagte,* 1972. Translator of numerous books into Afrikaans, including *Zorba die Griek* by Nikos Kazantzakis, *Jojakim van Babilon* by Marnix Gijsen, *Die Vonnis* by Somerset Maugham, *Die Blinde uil* by Sadegh Hedayat, and *Palmwyn* by Adriaan van Dis.

SIDELIGHTS: Considered one of the most important writers of modern South Africa, Abraham H. de Vries writes in Afrikaans, one of the eleven official languages of South Africa. His books include literary criticisms, short stories, poems, and a novel. He has also written travel books about Holland, Greece, and Israel and three thrillers under the pseudonym Thuys van der Vyfer. In addition to his writing, de Vries, who has a special expertise in Afrikaans short-story writing, lectures on Afrikaans literature at various universities throughout the world.

As with most South African writers, de Vries often comments on the racist policy of apartheid through his stories and writings, focusing primarily on the Little Karoo and Western Cape of South Africa. For example, in the short story "Tin Soldiers Don't Bleed," which was written before the end of South African apartheid, de Vries writes an indictment of the South African government's fostering of racial separatism in its school system.

In a review of the 1987 collection of ten de Vries short stories titled *Soms op 'n reis,* Barend J. Toerien, writing in *World Literature Today,* called de Vries a "clever" but "unassuming and deceptively simple writer." In this collection of short stories, de Vries focuses on how the powerful perpetrate injustices on ordinary people, including stories about the German occupation of the Netherlands during World War II and South African apartheid. "He underplays the stresses his characters undergo," wrote Toerien. "These are largely simple people whose loneliness, even in the midst of company is no more than suggested."

In his 1998 collection of short stories, *Skaduwees tussen Skaduwees,* de Vries once again writes about oppression, apartheid in South Africa, and the aftermath of apartheid. "In contrast to many of his South African contemporaries," wrote Martinus A. Bakker in a review in *World Literature Today,* "de Vries does not shun the description, in graphic detail, of the not-always-so-glorious consequences of the political revolution of 1994, which terminated the apartheid era." Pointing out that "irony and double entendre" are "two major components of de Vries's style," Bakker noted that de Vries accomplishes these stylistic aspects by incorporating characters, like clowns and magicians, "whose activities, whose comings and goings, are as mysterious, obscure, and susceptible to different interpretations as their actions."

Throughout his writings, de Vries acts as both a writer and a critic, making his stories, according to Bakker, "both literary works and essays." Many critics place de Vries's short stories in the realm of postmodernism, a complicated and controversial academic term, that, in its simplest interpretation, refers to works that reject rigid genre distinctions and emphasize parody, irony, and even playfulness. For example, in one of the stories in *Skaduwees tussen Skaduwees,* de Vries as narrator-author writes a postscript to his ending, saying that "nothing happened like it does in a story" and then goes on to provide another ending. As Bakker pointed out, this device "intentionally leaves the reader wondering what 'really happened'" while creating a competing "new or additional story." Perhaps de Vries's view of the short story is best summed up by the narrator-writer in one of the stories in *Skaduwees tussen Skaduwees,* who stated, "Make facts into a story and then people suddenly believe."

BIOGRAPHICAL AND CRITICAL SOURCES:

PERIODICALS

Literator, April, 1993, Martie Muller, "Die Rol van Bioptemie in die Postmodernistiese Teks," pp. 77-87.
World Literature Today, summer, 1988, Barend J. Toerien, review of *Soms op 'n reis,* p. 502; spring, 1998, Martinus A. Bakker, review of *Skaduwees tussen Skaduwees,* p. 447.*

*　　*　　*

DEWAR, Elaine Ruth 1948-

PERSONAL: Born June 18, 1948, in Saskatoon, Saskatchewan, Canada; daughter of Sam (a physician) and Petty Sarah (Davidner) Landa; married Stephen Dewar, June 1, 1969; children: Anna Esther, Danielle Sarah Nicole. *Education:* Nutana C.I., 1966; York University; University of Toronto, B.A., 1970. *Religion:* Jewish. *Hobbies and other interests:* Swimming, tennis, drawing, reading.

ADDRESSES: Agent—c/o Random House of Canada Limited, Publicity Dept., 1 Toronto St., Unit 300, Toronto, Ontario M5C 2V6, Canada.

CAREER: Journalist and author. Me and My Friends Gallery, founder, 1970-72; *Maclean's,* researcher, assistant editor, and associate editor, 1973-77; freelance journalist, editor, and story editor, 1977—; *City Woman* (magazine), contributing editor, 1978-82; *Toronto Life* (magazine), contributing editor, 1984-94; *Lorne Green's New Wilderness,* writer and story editor, 1982-85; Ryerson Polytechnical Institute, instructor in magazine journalism, 1985-86; Writers to Reform Libel Law, cofounder, 1990—; Dewar Productions, Inc., director and vicepresident, 1988—.

AWARDS, HONORS: A. C. Forrest Memorial Award; Mutual Life of Canada Award for business writing; Jackman Foundation Award for investigative journalism; University of Western Ontario President's Medal; Outdoor Writer's Association of America Two-Star Award; Foundation for the Advancement of Canadian Letters Author's Award; University of Kansas School of Journalism White Award for investigative journalism.

WRITINGS:

Cloak of Green, J. Lorimer (Toronto, Ontario, Canada), 1995.
Bones: Discovering the First Americans, Random House Canada (Toronto, Ontario, Canada), 2001.

SIDELIGHTS: Elaine Ruth Dewar is a Canadian investigative journalist. In *Cloak of Green,* she presents a study of the environmental movement in various places around the world and shows that, like many other organizations, the environmental movement is connected to government agencies and to businesses and works to promote and protect its own interests. Dewar also theorizes that environmental groups are linked in a conspiratorial effort to destroy nationalism and create a new world order, which Dewar calls the "Global Governance Agenda."

In *Books in Canada,* Jeb Blount praised Dewar's description of the Green movement's tactics, goals, and claims, as well as her commentary on the links between government and environmental groups. However, he disagreed with her analysis that the actions and words of environmentalists provide evidence, in Blount's words, of a "huge and sinister conspiracy" in which environmentalist and business interests are allied to transfer power to supranational organizations. Mark Nichols wrote in *Maclean's* that Dewar's "arguments and conclusions are often contradictory and hard to follow" and noted that she "fails to prove" the existence of this massive plot.

Bones: Discovering the First Americans provides profiles of several scientists who disagree with the prevailing theory that the ancestors of the Native Americans came to North America on foot over the Bering Strait during the last Ice Age. Dewar also presents controversial evidence from archeology, folklore, and genetics that some scientists say suggests that humans settled in South America as many as fifty thousand years ago. She examines such issues as the Kennewick Man, a skeleton found in a Washington State riverbed, that has been described as Paleo-Indian, Caucasoid, or Ainu-Polynesian; some have suggested that these remains indicate that Europeans, Polynesians, or other groups beat the Native Americans to North America. Dewar describes this controversy, as well as the ensuing battle between native groups, scientists, and the U.S. Army Corp of Engineers over whether these remains should be studied or reburied.

Other indications of an early link to Europe include textiles found in Spirit Cave in Nevada, that are similar to those found at central European archeological sites. On the other hand, a 13,500-year-old skull named "Luzia," found in southern Brazil, has been described as having "African" or "Aboriginal" features.

A *Publishers Weekly* reviewer wrote of *Bones*, "Dewar is a keen observer of place and personality," and commented that "the scientists she interviews are the real heart of the story she wishes to tell." In *Canadian Geographic,* Heather Pringle stated, "A gifted science writer, Dewar weaves a mesmerizing tale from all this intrigue," but noted that Dewar's central argument, that the New World's first inhabitants might have been African or Asian seafarers, is unconvincing. *Report Newsmagazine* reviewer Martin Loney commented that "Dewar is at her best in taking the reader with her across the Americas to remote sites and museums, and to the offices and laboratories of the principal protagonists." He noted that he found her thesis unconvincing, perhaps because the scientists involved could not agree on the issue. Loney also commented, "[Dewar's] book is clearly attracting interest outside academic and political circles."

BIOGRAPHICAL AND CRITICAL SOURCES:

PERIODICALS

Booklist, January 1, 2002, Philip Herbst, review of *Bones: Discovering the First Americans,* p. 785.

Books in Canada, March, 1996, Jeb Blount, "Cheating on Mother Nature," p. 27.

Canadian Book Review Annual, 1995, Simon Dalby, review of *Cloak of Green,* p. 432.

Canadian Geographic, March, 2001, Heather Pringle, "Bones of Contention," p. 83.

Maclean's, July 24, 1995, Mark Nichols, review of *Cloak of Green,* p. 51; March 19, 2001, Brian Bethune, "Mystery of the First North Americans," p. 24.

Publishers Weekly, January 28, 2002, review of *Bones,* p. 280.

Quill and Quire, September, 1995, Stephanie Thorson, review of *Cloak of Green,* p. 63.

Report Newsmagazine, July 30, 2001, Martin Loney, "Aboriginal Origins: New Finds Cast Doubt on the Long-dominant Theory of Settlement in the Americas," p. NA.*

*   *   *

DIOMEDE, John K.
   See EFFINGER, George Alec

*   *   *

DOENIM, Susan
   See EFFINGER, George Alec

*   *   *

DÖNHOFF, Marion (Hedda Ilse Countess) 1909-2002

OBITUARY NOTICE—See index for CA sketch: Born December 2, 1909, at Castle Friedrichstein near Löwenhagen, East Prussia (now Poland); died March 11, 2002, in Germany. Newspaper editor, publisher, and author. Dönhoff was an influential political commentator who ran the weekly German newspaper *Die Zeit.*

The daughter of Prussian aristocrats, the countess— or *gräfin* as she was known in her native tongue—was educated at the University of Frankfurt and Basle University, where she earned a Ph.D. in political science. She lost her inheritance during World War II when German Chancellor Adolf Hitler took over her father's land, and fled to Switzerland, where she secretly joined the anti-Nazi movement. After the war she became a writer for *Die Zeit* and rose to political editor in 1955, editor-in-chief in 1968, and publisher in 1973. As the editor and head of the newspaper, she became a highly influential figure, swaying the opinions of half a million German readers and becoming the voice of the liberal intelligentsia. Her many books also voice her strong viewpoints, including tolerance for the communist East and a mistrust for what she called the American arms race. Among her more than thirty books are *Die Bundesrepublik in der Ara Adenauer, Von Gestern nach Übermorgen, Gestalten unserer Zeit: Politische Portraits, Der Effendi wunscht zu beten,* and *Macht und Moral.* Dönhoff was also the recipient of numerous awards, including the Theodor Heuss Prize, the Peace Price of the German Book Trade, the Heinrich Heine Prize, and the Roosevelt Freedom Prize.

OBITUARIES AND OTHER SOURCES:

PERIODICALS

New York Times, March 12, 2002, p. A27.
Times (London, England), March 12, 2002.

*   *   *

DOR, Moshe 1932-

PERSONAL: Born December 9, 1932, in Tel Aviv, Israel; married Ziona Dor, March 29, 1955; children: two sons. *Education:* Attended Hebrew University of Jerusalem, 1949-52; University of Tel Aviv, B.A., 1956.

ADDRESSES: Home—11 Brodetsky Street, Tel Aviv, Israel, 69051. *Agent*—c/o Lynne Rienner Publishers, 1800 30th Street, Suite 314, Boulder, CO 80301.

CAREER: Poet and journalist. *Maariv,* Israel, editorial staff. *Likrat,* founder and editor. Embassy of Israel, London, England, counselor for cultural affairs, 1975-77; American University, Washington, DC, writer-in-residence, 1987.

MEMBER: Association of Hebrew Writers, National Federation of Israeli Journalists, Israel PEN (president, 1988-90).

AWARDS, HONORS: Honorable mention, International Hans Christian Andersen Prize, 1975; Holon prize for literature, 1981; Israeli prime minister's award for creative writing, 1986; Bialik prize for literature, 1987.

WRITINGS:

Beroshim Levanim, Li-kerat (Israel), 1954.
Tsav 'ikul: Shirim (title means "Order of Attachment: Poems"), Hadar (Tel Aviv, Israel), 1960.
Ma'avar hatsiyah: Shirim (title means "Cross the Street: Poems"), Hadar (Tel Aviv, Israel), 1962.
Sirpad u-matekhet: Shirim, Agudat ha-sofrim be-Yi'sra'el le-yad Masadah (Tel Aviv, Israel), 1965.
Ikarus ha-'olam (title means "Icarus the World"), Hadar (Tel Aviv, Israel), 1966.
Baron Porst'eli bi-Yerushalayim: Shirim, Tarbut ve-hinukh (Tel Aviv, Israel), 1968.
Sefinah mi-tavlot shokolad, Masadah (Ramat Gan, Israel), 1968.
Ha-Armon shel Amir, Sifriyat po 'alim (Merhavya, Israel), 1970.
Keri'ah rishonah, keri'ah sheniyah (essays; title means "Reading and Rereading"), Tarbut ve-hinukh (Tel Aviv, Israel), 1970.
Torat Erets-Yisra'el be-Bavel, Devir (Tel Aviv, Israel), 1971.
Mapot ha-zeman: Shirim (title means "Maps of Time: Poems"), ha-Kibuts ha-me'uhad (Tel Aviv, Israel), 1975, translation by John Bakti and Dor published as *Maps of Time,* introduction by Alan Sillitoe, Menard Press (London, England), 1978.
(Editor, with Natan Zach) *The Burning Bush: Poems from Modern Israel,* introduction by Alan Sillitoe, Allen (London, England), 1977.
'Afifonim be-Hemsted Hit: Shirim (title means "Kites in Hampstead Heath: Poems"), Sifriyat po 'alim (Tel Aviv, Israel), 1980.
Be-rosh ha-shunit: mivhar shirim, 1954-1986, (title means "On top of the Cliff"), Sifriyat Ma 'ariv (Tel Aviv, Israel), 1986.
Crossing the River: Selected Poems, edited by Seymour Mayne, Mosaic Press (Lanham MD), 1989.
(Editor, with Barbara Goldberg and Giora Leshem) *The Stones Remember: Native Israeli Poety,* Word Works (Washington, DC), 1991.

Ahava u-she'ar pur'anuyot: Shirim (title means "Love and Other Calamities: Poems"), ha-Kibuts ha-me'uhad (Tel Aviv, Israel), 1993.

Khamsin: Memoirs and Poetry by a Native Israeli, Lynne Rienner Publishers (Boulder, CO), 1994.

Gehalim ba-peh: pirke otobiyografyah (title means "Coals in the Mouth"), Tag (Israel), 1995.

Ekh 'ishnah ha-livyetanit mikteret: sipure-'am (title means "Why the Whale Smoked a Pipe), Yedi 'ot ahronot: Sifre hemed (Tel Aviv, Israel), 1996.

Shetikat ha-banai (title means "Silence of the Builder"), Zemorah-Bitan (Tel Aviv, Israel), 1996.

(Editor, with Barbara Goldberg) *After the First Rain: Israeli Poems on War,* forward by Shimon Peres, Syracuse University Press in association with Dryad Press (Syracuse, NY), 1998.

SIDELIGHTS: The author of numerous books of poetry, children's verse, literary essays, and literary interviews, Moshe Dor is also well known throughout Israel for his appearances on television and radio as a commentator on literature and other topics. Dor's father migrated to Israel from Russia, and Dor grew up in Tel Aviv's Workers' Quarters. A stutterer, Dor immersed himself in reading at a young age and was interested not only in literature but in history and political science. In the early 1950s, Dor helped establish *Likrat,* which served as a forum the young vanguard of Israeli writers and commentators who were vocal in their views against the Soviet Union and their anti-bureaucratic beliefs. As one of the editors of *Likrat,* Dor helped to promote a new generation of Israeli authors and poets who went against the status quo and readily embraced Western literature.

Winner of Israel's prestigious Bialik prize, Dor has written numerous poems that are well known in Israel. In addition to his own writing, Dor has served as editor of several volumes of Israeli poetry that have been translated into English, including *The Stones Remember,* a volume of contemporary Hebrew poetry published in 1992.

Dor's first book of poems to be translated into English was *Maps of Time,* published in England in 1978. More than a decade later, *Crossing the River* was translated to English. The volume covers several decades of Dor's poetry. Another compilation of Dor's poetry, *Khamsin: Memoirs and Poetry by a Native Israeli,* is available in English and also includes several autobiographical essays. Together, the poems and essays reveal Dor's development as an artist and as an individual. Divided into two sections, the book begins with the autobiographical prose section called "This Parched Land." Writing in *Publishers Weekly,* a reviewer said that Dor "describes with lyrical precision" his "struggle to become an artist during Israel's fight for independence, recapturing his childhood in 'little whit town' of Tel Aviv in the 1930s, his sexual maturation, his youthful activities in the Hagana [a Jewish self-defense organization] in the 1940s, the publication of his first poems and his evolution into a student-intellectual and modernist Israeli writer." As noted by Jean Berrett in *Iowa Review,* Dor writes of Israel, the "motherland, in longing and nostalgia, in praise and disappointment."

The second part of *Khamsin,* called "More Distant than Lunacy, than Love?," comes from a poem Dor wrote to his father recounting his father's immigration to Israel. The poem goes on to compare Dor's own life to his father's. Berrett described the poem as "the poet's attempt to understand the strange separation between father and son." The poems throughout this section continue with many of themes presented in the initial autobiographical prose section. "In fact," wrote Berrett, "the sensuous present counterpoises throughout the poems in *Khamsin*—against politics and business, against memory and changes in time, against death." Berrett also noted that throughout the poems Dor continues to ask "*unanswerable* questions," such as "How shall I ever find peace . . . ?" and "What more is left?" Berrett went on to say: "The questions are crying out from the human condition, a protest and invocation, voiced plainly and incorrigibly, as if to God above."

BIOGRAPHICAL AND CRITICAL SOURCES:

PERIODICALS

Choice, November, 1990, review of *Crossing the River,* p. 494; July-August, 1992, review of *The Stones Remember: Native Israeli Poetry,* p. 1687.

Iowa Review, fall, 1996, Jean Berrett, review of *Khamsin: Memoirs and Poetry by a Native Israeli,* pp. 194-200.

Publishers Weekly, August 9, 1991, review of *The Stones Remember,* p. 53; November 21, 1994, review of *Khamsin,* p. 74.

Translation Review Supplement, December, 1999, review of *After the First Rain,* p. 5.

OTHER

Moshe Dor (audio recording), New Letters on Air (Kansas City, MO), 1990.

Israeli Poet Moshe Dor Reading from His Works in the Recording Laboratory (audio recording), Library of Congress Archive of Recorded Poetry and Literature, 1995.*

* * *

DORFMAN, Robert 1916-2002

OBITUARY NOTICE—See index for *CA* sketch: Born October 27, 1916, in New York, NY; died June 24, 2002, in Belmont, MA. Statistician, political economist, educator, and author. Dorfman began his career as a statistician, but during a ten-year affiliation with various agencies of the federal government he changed his focus to economics. In that field he established a respected career through his research on linear programming (a statistical tool for modeling quantitative decision-making) and his work in the field of environmental economics. Dorfman was a professor of economics at Harvard University from 1955 until his retirement in 1987. He also served on environmental boards of the Environmental Protection Agency and the National Research Council, as well as U.S. presidential commissions on natural resources and employment statistics. Dorfman was a consultant to the RAND Corporation, the Brookings Institution, and the International Bank for Reconstruction and Development. His books on linear programming include *Linear Programming and the Theory of the Firm* and *On Quadratic Programming.* Environmental writings include *Models for Managing Regional Water Quality* and *Economics of the Environment: Selected Readings.* In his later years Dorfman developed an interest in economic history. In 1997 he published *Economic Theory and Public Decisions: Selected Essays of Robert Dorfman.*

OBITUARIES AND OTHER SOURCES:

PERIODICALS

Chicago Tribune, June 27, 2002, pp. 2-8.
Los Angeles Times, June 28, 2002, p. B12.
New York Times, June 24, 2002, p. A14.
Washington Post, June 29, 2002, p. B6.

DOUVAN, Elizabeth (Ann Malcolm) 1926-2002

OBITUARY NOTICE—See index for *CA* sketch: Born November 23, 1926, in South Bend, IN; died of congestive heart failure, June 15, 2002, in Ann Arbor, MI. Social psychologist, educator, administrator, and author. Douvan is remembered as a pioneer in the field of women's studies. Affiliated with the University of Michigan from 1950 to 1996, she was named the Kellogg Professor of Psychology in 1965 and appointed program director at the Institute for Social Research in 1974. Within her Family and Sex Role Program, Douvan was able to study the ways in which women's roles developed and changed over the years. Her writings include *The Adolescent Experience, Feminist Personality and Conflict, The Inner American,* and in 1997, *A New Outline of Social Psychology.* Douvan served as the founding president of the American Psychological Association division on the psychology of women. A strong proponent of the importance of a stable marriage, but also a staunch defender of women's rights, Douvan published *Marital Instability: A Social and Behavioral Study of the Early Years.*

OBITUARIES AND OTHER SOURCES:

PERIODICALS

Los Angeles Times, June 26, 2002, p. B11.
Washington Post, June 29, 2002, p. B6.

* * *

du BOUCHET, André 1924-

PERSONAL: Born 1924, in Paris, France. *Education:* Earned degrees from Amherst College and Harvard University.

ADDRESSES: Agent—c/o Fata Morgana, Freecyb, 28 rue Hermel, 75018 Paris, France.

CAREER: Poet, critic, and journalist. Harvard University, Cambridge, MA, former instructor; *L'Ephémère* (journal), Paris, France, editor, 1966-72.

AWARDS, HONORS: Prix des Critiques, 1962; Prix Nationale de la Poésie, 1986.

WRITINGS:

Air (poetry), J. Aubier (Paris, France), 1946, revised edition published as *Air: 1950-1953,* Clivages (Paris, France), 1977, English translation by the author published as *Air,* 1951.

Sans couvercle (poetry), GLM (Paris, France), 1953.

(Author of text with Henri Maldiney) *Tal Coat,* Maeght (Paris, France), 1954.

Le moteur blanc (poetry and prose; title means "White Motor"), GLM (Paris, France), 1956.

Au deuxième étage (poetry; title means "On the Second Floor"), Dragon (Paris, France), 1956.

Sol de la montagne (poetry; title means "Mountain Soil"), J. Hugues (Paris, France), 1956.

Cette surface, illustrated by Pierre Tal-Coat, PAB (Alés, France), 1956.

(Editor) Victor Hugo, *L'oeil égaré dans les plis de l'obéissance au vent,* GLM (Paris, France), 1956, bound with *L'infini et l'inachevé,* Seghers (Paris, France), 2001.

Sur le pas, illustrated by Pierre Tal-Coat, Maeght (Paris, France), 1959.

Ajournement, illustrated by Jacques Villon, Iliazd (Paris, France), 1960.

Dans la chaleur vacante, Mercure de France (Paris, France), 1961, reprinted, 1978, translation by David Mus published as *Where Heat Looms,* Sun & Moon Press (Los Angeles, CA), 1996.

(Translator) Paul Celan, *Poémes,* Jean Hugues (Paris, France), 1961, reprinted, Clivages (Paris, France), 1978.

(Translator) James Joyce, *Finnegans Wake,* Gallimard (Paris, France), 1962.

La lumière de la lame, etchings by Joan Miró, Maeght (Paris, France), 1962.

(Author of text) Gaston-Louis Roux) *L'avril* (etchings), Janine Hao (Paris, France), 1963.

(Translator) Friedrich Hölderlin, *Poèmes,* illustrations by Max Ernst, Mercure de France (Paris, France), 1963, reprinted, 1986.

(Translator) William Shakespeare, *La tempête* (translation of *The Tempest*), Réalisé pour le compt d'un (Paris, France), 1965.

L'inhabité, Jean Hugues (Paris, France), 1967.

Où le soleil (poetry; title means "Where Is the Sun?"), Mercure de France (Paris, France), 1967.

(Author of text) Alberto Giacometti, *Dessins, 1914-1965,* Galerie Claude Bernard (Paris, France), 1968.

Qui n'est pas tourné vers nous?, Mercure de France (Paris, France), 1972.

(Translator) Richard Ellmann, *Giacomo Joyce* (translation of *James Joyce*), Gallimard (Paris, France), 1973.

(Translator) William Faulkner, *Le gambit du cavalier* (translation of *Knight's Gambit*), Rombaldi (Paris, France), 1973, reprinted, Gallimard (Paris, France), 1995.

(Translator, with others) Friedrich Hölderlin, *L'unique* (translation of *Der Einzige*), Maeght (Paris, France), 1973.

La Coleur, Le Collet de buffle (Paris, France), 1975.

Laisses, illustrated by Pierre Tal-Coat, Françoise Simecek (Lausanne, France), 1975.

Hölderlin aujourd'hui (criticism), Le Collet de buffle (Paris, France), 1976.

The Uninhabited: Selected Poems of André du Bouchet, translation by Paul Auster, Living Hand (New York, NY), 1976.

Un jour de plus augmenté d'un jour, Le Collet de buffle (Paris, France), 1977.

Sous le linteau en forme de joug, Clivages (Paris, France), 1978.

L'incoherencé (poetry), Hachette (Paris, France), 1979.

Rapides (poetry; title means "Rapids"), Hachette (Paris, France), 1980.

Défets, Clivages (Paris, France), 1981.

(With Gilles du Bouchet) *Fraichir,* Clivages (Paris, France), 1981.

Ice en deux (also see below), illustrated by Geneviève Asse, Quentin (Geneva, Switzerland), 1982.

Peinture, Fata Morgana (St. Clement La Riviere, France), 1983.

L'avril précédé de fraîchir, Thierry Bouchard (Paris, France), 1983.

Aujourd'hui c'est, Fata Morgana (St. Clement La Riviere, France), 1983, translation by Cid Corman published as *Today It's,* Origin Press (St. Paul, MN), 1985.

Ici en deux (collected verse), Mercure de France (Paris, France), 1986.

Cendre tirant sur le bleu, Clivages (Paris, France), 1986.

Une tache, Fata Morgana (St. Clement L Riviere, France), 1988.

Désaccordée comme par de la neige: et Tübingen, le 22 mai 1986 (lecture), Mercure de France (Paris, France), 1989.

Des "Hauts-de-Buhl," Fourbis (Paris, France), 1989.

(Translator) Ossip Emilievitch Mandelchtam, *Psysiologie de la lecture,* Fourbis (Paris, France), 1989.

Le surcroît (poetry; title means "The Increase"), Fourbis (Paris, France), 1990.

De plusieurs déchirements dans les parages de la piénture, Unes (Le Muy, France), 1990.

Verses, Unes (Le Muy, France), 1990.

Carnets, 1952-1956, Plon (Paris, France), 1990.

Axiales, Mercure de France (Paris, France), 1992.

Matière de l'interlocuteur, Fata Morgana (St. Clement La Riviere, France), 1992.

Baudelaire irrémédiable (criticism), Deyrolle (Paris, France), 1993.

Retours dur le vent, Fourbis (Paris, France), 1994.

Poèmes et proses, Mercure de France (Paris, France), 1995.

Pourquoi si calmes, Fata Morgana (St. Clement La Riviere, France), 1996.

Andains, photographs by Francis Helgorsky, Editions a Die (Die, France), 1996.

D'un trait qui figure et défigure, Fata Morgana (St. Clement La Riviere, France), 1997.

L'ajour (poetry), Gallimard (Paris, France), 1998.

Carnet 2, Fata Morgana (St. Clement La Riviere, France), 1998.

Carnet 3: Annotations sur l'espace, Fata Morgana (St. Clement La Riviere, France), 2000.

L'emportement du muet (poems and essays), Mercure de France (Paris, France), 2000.

Annotations sur l'espace: non datés, Fata Morgana (St. Clement La Riviere, France), 2000.

Tumulte, Fata Morgana (St. Clement La Riviere, France), 2001.

Contributor to periodicals, including *Prevue, Courier du centre internationale d'études, Le Temps moderns,* and *Botteghe Oscure.* Work included in anthologies, including *Prácticas poéticas contemporáneas, Italia y Francia: Giuseppi Ungaretti y André du Bouchet,* Centro de Estudios Literarios (Guadalajara, Mexico), 1988; and *Translations,* Marsilio Publishers (New York, NY), 1997. Du Bouchet's work has been translated into German, English, Italian, and Spanish.

SIDELIGHTS: "Of the three or four French poets who first came to prominence in the early 1950s," wrote Mark Hutchinson in a *Times Literary Supplement* article, "André du Bouchet is probably the least familiar to English readers." Unlike his peers Yves Bonnefoy and Jacques Dupin, du Bouchet largely remained untranslated through the last decades of the twentieth century. The poet, influenced by the works of Friedrich Hölderlin and Pierre Reverdy, belonged to the avant-garde school "l'ephémère", which was born out of the cultural climate that followed World War II. Taking its cue from poet Jacques Dupin's characterization of postwar France as "a desert," the l'ephémère poets reflected that view in their sometimes surrealistic imagery. In his *Postwar Figures of L'Ephémère: Yves Bonnefoy, Louis-René des Forêts, Jacques Dupin, André du Bouchet,* James Petterson noted that the l'ephémère poets "represent a literary movement through their own refusal to be restricted to any one definition of their writings. They speak of and perhaps with the voice of the ephemeral, a voice . . . that, for André du Bouchet, utters 'words of rupture.'"

Born in Paris between the two world wars, du Bouchet followed his family in their flight from France when German occupation threatened. He lived in the United States for several years and was educated there, returning to France in 1948. Eight years later du Bouchet translated a poem by eighteenth-century German writer Hölderlin; the writer's own poetry would soon follow. In *French Studies,* critic John Stout noted that while du Bouchet's early work clearly reveals the influence of Reverdy, "the younger man . . . also diverged from his predecessor's example." Stout quoted critic Robert W. Greene, who commented: "Du Bouchet's poems have a perceptively harder, less nuanced and more peremptory quality about them than Reverdy's and possess a stark, elemental lyricism that seems peculiar to Du Bouchet alone."

Another distinguishing feature about du Bouchet is the poet's "rejection," as Stout put it, of closure. "A Reverdy poems rarely lasts longer than one page," Stout elaborated, going on to note that du Bouchet "emphasizes openness and ceaseless motion. His words constantly push forward from one page to the next, refusing the limits imposed by each page. Their dynamic language expresses his desire to sustain motion, forcing the reader's eye forward before the words can solidify into a fixed meaning."

While limited translation of du Bouchet's work reached English readers during the late twentieth century, most of the poet's works can be read only in their original French, among them the poetry collections *L'ajour* and *Axiales,* and du Bouchet's "Carnet" series. In *L'ajour*, according to Judy Cochran of *World Literature Today*, the poet "continues to explore the relationship between man and the elements begun in earlier works." The title refers to a lacemaking technique used to make decorative table linens; the intricate weaving of threads and open spaces is reflected in the format of du Bouchet's poems in which words "are unraveled line by line to be rewoven at another time," according to Cochran. *World Literature Today* contributor Michael Bishop assessed *Axiales* as "a book of pluralities, of infinite direction, of ideality and shifting, 'orbital' alignment." Bishop pronounced du Bouchet "one of the great poets of our time, and *Axiales* . . . a book of simple, though complicated, profundity." Du Bouchet's notebooks were published in three volumes over several decades as the "Carnet" series. Bishop found that in *Carnet 2* the author "steps boldly outside the conventional diaristic limits," adding in *World Literature Today* that "this is perhaps really not surprising in a poet who has deemed his entire written enterprise to be but one vast unfinishable sentence."

"Like other poets of his generation," noted Glenn Fetzer in *Nottingham French Studies*, du Bouchet "engages in an ongoing attempt to accede to some reality which is external to oneself, which is unknown, and which remains nameless." Fetzer also acknowledged du Bouchet as a poet of "endless discontinuity and decelerated expression, of shapeless and colourless expanse," and his "attention to sight and to seeing self permits an often-overlooked perspective on his poetics."

BIOGRAPHICAL AND CRITICAL SOURCES:

BOOKS

Chappuis, Pierre, *André du Bouchet*, Seghers (Paris, France), 1979.

Gavronsky, Serge, *Poems and Texts*, October House (New York, NY), 1969.

Hommage an André du Bouchet (in German), Schirn Kunsthalle (Frankfurt, Germany), 1989.

Petterson, James, *Postwar Figures of L'Ephémère: Yves Bonnefoy, Louis-René des Forêts, Jacques Dupin, André du Bouchet*, Associated University Press (Cranbury, NJ), 2000, pp. 151-195.

PERIODICALS

French Studies, October, 1992, John Stout, "'Ici Reverdit La Pierre': Pierre Reverdy and Contemporary French Poetics," pp. 424-433.

Language Quarterly, winter-spring, 1991, Glenn Fetzer, "Jacques Dupin, André du Bouchet, and the Space of Poetry," pp. 115-128.

Monde des Livres, June 10, 1983, Monique Petillon, interview with du Bouchet, p. 10.

Nottingham French Studies, autumn, 1996, Glenn Fetzer, "André du Bouchet: Imaging the Real, Seeing the Unseeable," pp. 76-83.

Pacific Coast Philology, Volume 32, number 1, 1997, Eric D. Friedman, "André du Bouchet and the Infinite Book of Painting," pp. 66-75.

Times Literary Supplement, February 14, 1992, Mark Hutchinson, "The Restless 'Je,'" p. 13.

World Literature Today, summer, 1993, Michael Bishop, review of *Axiales*, p. 587; winter, 2000, Judy Cochran, review of *L'ajour*, p. 108; summer, 2000, M. Bishop, review of *Carnet 2*, p. 629; summer-autumn, 2001, M. Bishop, review of *L'emportement du muet*, p. 174.*

*   *   *

DUDLEY, Guilford, Jr. 1907-2002

OBITUARY NOTICE—See index for *CA* sketch: Born June 23, 1907, in Nashville, TN; died June 13, 2002, in Nashville, TN. Diplomat, administrator, insurance executive, horse breeder, and author. Dudley was most widely recognized as the chair of the Campaign Liquidation Trust established after the resignation of U.S. President Richard M. Nixon in 1974. It was Dudley's responsibility to monitor the disbursement of several million dollars remaining in Nixon's re-election campaign fund, an obligation that would last for more than ten years. He had previously served as Nixon's ambassador to Denmark. Dudley came to the Nixon administration from the insurance industry, where he had served as the president of the Life and Casualty Insurance Company of Tennessee throughout the 1950s and 1960s. He had been active in Republican politics in Tennessee for several years, including a stint as chair of the state Republican finance committee. After accomplishing the objectives of the Campaign Liquidation Trust in 1985, Dudley returned to the insurance business, but he remained active in Republican social circles in the nation's capital and in his native Tennessee, where he was also involved with various philanthropic organizations. He also bred race horses that competed throughout the United States and Europe. Dudley was the author of *The Skyline Is a Promise: A Chief Executive's Blueprint for Personal Success.*

OBITUARIES AND OTHER SOURCES:

PERIODICALS

Los Angeles Times, June 22, 2002, p. B19.
New York Times, June 20, 2002, p. C14.
Washington Post, June 21, 2002, p. B7.

E-F

EARLY, H(enry) C(lay) 1855-1941

PERSONAL: Born May 11, 1855, in Augusta County, VA; died September 1, 1941, in Harrisonburg, VA; son of Noah and Sarah (Kidd) Early; married Mary Ann Showalter, 1876. *Education:* Attended Shenandoah Valley Normal School (now Bridgewater College).

CAREER: Worked as public schoolteacher; elected minister, Church of the Brethren, 1880; Brethren Congregation of Mill Creek, evangelistic preacher, 1884-98, pastor, beginning 1898. Church of the Brethren, member of general mission board, 1901-10, chair, 1910-24, member of annual conference standing committee and moderator of annual conference, 1899-1925. Also worked as developer of neglected farm property.

WRITINGS:

Contributor to books, including *Bridgewater Brethren,* edited by R. E. Sappington, 1978. Contributor to periodicals, including *Gospel Messenger.*

BIOGRAPHICAL AND CRITICAL SOURCES:

BOOKS

Flory, J. S., *H. C. Early: Christian Statesman,* Brethren Press (Elgin, IL), 1943.
Religious Leaders of America, 2nd edition, Gale (Detroit, MI), 1999.*

EFFINGER, George Alec 1947-2002
John K. Diomede, Susan Doenim

OBITUARY NOTICE—See index for *CA* sketch: Born January 10, 1947, in Cleveland, OH; died April 26, 2002, in New Orleans, LA. Science-fiction author. Effinger earned a scholarship to Yale University but dropped out of the Ivy League institution and found fame at age twenty-five with his first novel, *What Entropy Means to Me.* The book is not easily categorized. It combines aspects of science fiction, episodic novels, and morality tales into a story about the eldest son of the ruling family of a planet named Home. The son searches for his lost father but disappears and his younger brother must piece together what happened to the older sibling. The book, published in 1972, was followed by several other science-fiction works, including *Those Gentle Voices: A Promethean Romance of the Spaceways, The Nick of Time,* and *When Gravity Fails.* Effinger also wrote a four-volume "Planet of the Apes" series, the nonfiction piece *Blood Pinball,* and several novels. Considered by critics to be both witty and ironic in his work, Effinger penned a series of stories about a teenager obsessed with shopping who finds herself in situations which mock science fiction. The stories were published in one volume in 1993 as *Maureen Birnbaum, Barbarian Swordsperson.*

OBITUARIES AND OTHER SOURCES:

PERIODICALS

New York Times, May 2, 2002, p. A25.
Washington Post, May 1, 2002, p. B5.

ENFIELD, Harry 1961-

PERSONAL: Born May 30, 1961, in Sussex, England; son of Edward Enfield and Deirdre Enfield; married Lucy Caroline Lyster, February 22, 1997; children: one daughter, one son. *Education:* Worth Abbey, University of York.

ADDRESSES: Agent—c/o PBJ Management Ltd, 7 Soho St., London W1D 3DQ, England.

CAREER: Writer, actor, and comedian. Film appearances include *Barney's Christmas Surprise,* 1988; *Bob's Birthday,* 1993; *What Rats Won't Do,* PolyGram Filmed Entertainment, 1998; *Comic Relief: Doctor Who and the Curse of the Fatal Death,* 1999; and *Kevin & Perry Go Large,* Icon Film Distribution, 2000. Film work includes (producer and song performer) *Kevin & Perry Go Large,* Icon Film Distribution, 2000. Recordings include an appearance in the video of Elvis Costello's "This Town."

Television series appearances include *Spitting Image,* 1984; *Saturday Live,* 1986; *Friday Night Live,* 1988; *Harry Enfield's Television Programme,* 1990; *Men Behaving Badly,* 1992; *Harry Enfield and Chums,* 1994; *Sermon from St. Albion's,* 1998; and *Brand Spanking New Show,* 2000. Appearances in TV movies include *Smashey and Nicey, the End of an Era,* 1994; *Norman Ormal: A Very Political Turtle,* 1998; *Live from the Lighthouse,* 1998; *Hooves of Fire,* 1999; *The Nearly Complete and Utter History of Everything,* 1999; and *Top Ten Comedy Records,* 2000. Appearances on TV specials include *Just for Laughs II,* Showtime, 1987; and *Norbert Smith, a Life,* PBS, 1989. Appearances on episodic television include "Mr. Fluffy Knows Too Much," *Girls on Top,* 1986; "Neighbourhood Watch," *Lenny Harry Tonite,* 1986; *Filthy, Rich, and Catflap,* 1987; *French and Saunders,* 1987; *Have I Got News for You,* 1991; "Barcelona, May 1917," *The Young Indiana Jones Chronicles,* 1992; *Sunday Night Clive,* 1994; *Clive James,* PBS, 1994; *Clive Anderson All Talk,* 1997, 1998; *Parkinson,* 1999, 2000; and *Rove Live,* 2000.

AWARDS, HONORS: Gold Rockie Banff Award, 1989; Silver Rose of Montreux, 1990, 1995, and 1998; International Emmy for Popular Arts Programs, 1991; Writers Guild Award for Best Entertainment Series, 1995; RTS Award for Best Entertainment Program, 1997; Silver Rose of Montreux 1998; Television and Radio Industry Award for Satellite and Digital TV Programme of the Year, 2001; Quality Street Award for Best Comedy Film, 2001.

WRITINGS:

Norbert Smith, a Life, (also known as *Sir Norbert Smith: A Life,* PBS, 1989.
Harry Enfield and His Humorous Chums, Penguin (London, England), 1997.
Kevin & Perry Go Large (screenplay), Icon Film Distribution, 2000.

Wrote screenplay for *Smashey and Nicey, the End of an Era,* 1994. Wrote episodes of *Saturday Live, Friday Night Live, Harry Enfield's Television Programme,* and *Harry Enfield and Chums.*

SIDELIGHTS: British comedian, actor, and writer Harry Enfield operates across an entire spectrum of comedy, from spoofs of distinguished actors to the kind of gross-out humor familiar to fans of *Dumb and Dumber.* His television show *Harry Enfield and Chums,* according to Simon Hoggart in the *Spectator,* is "quite without political correctness." With characters such as a homophobic father who celebrates the fact that his son's "'special friend' died in a car crash rather than of AIDS," Hoggart wrote, the show "could never, ever appear on American television."

By contrast, *Sir Norbert Smith: A Life* appeared on PBS in 1990. A takeoff on that network's own *Masterpiece Theatre, Sir Norbert* is a mock biography of an allegedly distinguished, aged, and now senile British thespian. Sir Norbert, played by Enfield himself, has portrayed characters from Mozart to Nelson Mandela, playing everything from Shakespeare to Westerns with the same lack of talent.

At the opposite end of the humor spectrum is *Kevin & Perry Go Large,* which likewise stars Enfield as one half of the eponymous pair. Kevin & Perry, the latter played by actress Kathy Burke, are two teenage boys with a dilemma familiar to viewers of such movies, as well as TV shows such as *Beavis and Butthead.* Each boy's principal ambition in life is to lose his virginity, and in this quest, there are plenty of opportunities for jokes about acne, body hair, intestinal gas, and erections. Kevin's failure to control an erection, in fact, is a major driving force in the plot: an involuntary bodily reaction sets off an alarm, inadvertently foiling a robbery, and winning the boys reward money that facilitates a trip to a sexy Spanish beach. Mayna Bergmann of *Video Business* called *Kevin & Perry Go Large* "Silly, gross, and amusing."

BIOGRAPHICAL AND CRITICAL SOURCES:

BOOKS

Contemporary Theatre, Film, and Television, volume 34, Gale (Detroit, MI), 2001.

PERIODICALS

New Statesman, April 10, 1987, Hugo Williams, review of *Saturday Live,* p. 24.
New York Times, November 16, 1990, John J. O'Connor, review of *Sir Norbert Smith: A Life,* p. B5.
People Weekly, November 19, 1990, David Hiltbrand, review of *Sir Norbert Smith: A Life,* pp. 13-14.
Spectator, January 18, 1997, Simon Hoggart, review of *Harry Enfield and Chums,* p. 44.
Variety, May 1, 2000, Derek Elley, review of *Kevin & Perry Go Large,* p. 32.
Video Business, April 1, 2002, Derek Elley and Mayna Bergmann, review of *Kevin & Perry Go Large,* p. 20.

OTHER

Harry Enfield, http://www.geocities.com/harryenf/harry.htm (October 23, 2002).
Harry Enfield and Chums, http://www.powerage.demon.co.uk/enfield/home.htm (October 23, 2002).*

*   *   *

FABBRI, Diego 1911-1980

PERSONAL: Born July 2, 1911, in Forli, Italy; died August 14, 1980, in Riccione, Italy; son of Augusto Fabbri (a factory worker) and Itala Camporesi (a seamstress); married 1937. *Education:* University of Bologna, D. Jur., 1936.

CAREER: Playwright and screenwriter. Worked for Catholic publications, 1936-40; Centro Cattolico Cinimatografico, secretary-general, 1940-50; *La Fiera Litteria,* editor and contributor, 1945-68; Sindicato Nazionale degli Autori Drammatici, cofounder, 1945; Rome, Teatro la Cometa, director, 1960-62; Confédération Internationale des Sociétés des Auteurs et des Compositeurs, chairman, 1973-75; *Il Dramma,* editor, 1977.

MEMBER: Christian Democrats.

AWARDS, HONORS: National theater prize, for *Inquisizione,* 1950; Marzotto International Prize, for *Portrait of a Young Man;* Théâtre des Nations prize, 1959, for *Figli d'arte;* Feltrinelli prize for theater, 1977.

WRITINGS:

COLLECTIONS

Teatro, three volumes, Vallecchi (Florence, Italy), 1959-1964.
Tre commedie d'amore, U. Mursia (Milan, Italy), 1972.
Tutto il teatro, two volumes, Rusconi (Milan, Italy), 1984.
Mastro Don Gesualdo/I vicere, Ente dello Spettacolo (Rome, Italy), 1988.
Diego Fabbri tra seduzione e rivelazione: antologia teatrale, San Paolo (Turin, Italy), 1996.

STAGE WORKS

I fiori del dolore (title means "The Flowers of Grief"), published in *Controcorrente,* 1931, revised edition, 1933.
Ritorno, 1933.
I loro peccati, 1935.
Il fanciullo sconosciuto, 1935.
Il nodo (title means "The Knot"), published in *Controcorrente,* 1936, revised as *Paludi* (title means "Marshes"), in *Spettacolo,* 1942.
Ricordo, 1937.
Rifiorirà la terra, 1937.
Miraggi, 1937.
Orbite (title means "Orbits"), 1941, published in *Paloscenico,* 1950.

Il prato, 1943, published in *Teatro 1,* Vallecchi (Florence, Italy), 1959.

La libreria del sole, 1943.

Rancore, 1950, published in *Sipario,* 1950.

Inquisizione, 1950, Garzanti (Milan, Italy), 1952.

Il seduttore, published in *Scena,* 1951.

Processo di famiglia (title means "Family Trial"), 1953, published in *Il dramma,* 1954, reprinted in *Tutti il teatro,* Rusconi (Milan, Italy), 1984.

Processo a Gesù (title means "Trial of Jesus"), published in *Il dramma,* 1955, translation by Adele Fiske published as *Retrial of Christ,* [Purchase, NY], 1959, new translation published as *Between Two Thieves,* 1967, M. Boni (Bologna, Italy), 1978.

La bugiarda (title means "The Liar"), published in *Il dramma,* 1956, reprinted in *Tutti il teatro,* Rusconi (Milan, Italy), 1984.

Veglia d'armi (title means "Vigil of Arms"), Vallecchi (Florence, Italy), 1957.

Delirio, 1958.

I demoni, Vallecchi (Florence, Italy),1960.

Processo Karamazov: La leggenda del Grande Inquisitore, 1960, revised as opera libretto *Leggenda del ritorno,* music by Renzo Rossellini, G. Ricordi (Milan, Italy), 1966.

Figli d'arte (title means "Sons of Art"), Vallecchi (Florence, Italy), 1960.

Divertimento, published in *Teatro 2,* Vallecchi (Florence, Italy), 1960.

Contemplazione, published in *Teatro 2,* Vallecchi (Florence, Italy), 1960.

I testimoni, published in *Teatro 2,* Vallecchi (Florence, Italy), 1960.

Teresa Desqueyroux, published in *Il dramma,* 1961.

Ritratto d'ignoto, Vallecchi (Florence, Italy), 1962.

Lo scoiattolo, published in *Teatro 3,* Vallecchi (Florence, Italy), 1964.

A tavola non si parla d'amore, 1963, published in *Teatro 3,* Vallecchi (Florence, Italy), 1964.

Il confidente, Vallecchi (Florence, Italy), 1964.

L'avvenimento, Vallecchi (Florence, Italy), 1968.

Lascio all mie donne, 1969, published in *Il dramma,* 1971.

Non è per scherzo dhe ti ho amato, published in *Tre commedie d'amore,* 1972.

Area fabbricabile, published in *Tre commedie d'amore,* 1972, revised edition published as *Il cedro del libano* in *Tutti il teatro,* Rusconi (Milan, Italy), 1984.

Il vizio assurdo, Rizzoli (Milan, Italy), 1974.

Il commedione di Giuseppe Gioacchino belli poeta e impiegato pontificio, 1978.

L'hai mai vista in scena . . . ?, 1979.

Al Dio ignoto, 1980, published in *Tutto il teatro,* Rusconi (Milan, Italy), 1984.

Gli assenti, published in *Tutto il teatro,* Rusconi (Milan, Italy), 1984.

L'avventuriero, published in *Tutto il teatro,* Rusconi (Milan, Italy), 1984.

Incontro al parco delle terme, Edizioni Logos (Rome, Italy), 1982.

Mastro Don Gesualdo, Ente dello Spettacolo (Rome, Italy), 1988.

I vicere, 1988.

Works have been translated into French and Spanish.

SCREENPLAYS

(With others) *La porta del cielo,* 1945.

(With others) *Un giorno nella vita,* 1946.

(With others) *Il testimone,* 1946.

(With others) *Daniele Cortis,* 1947.

Guerra alla guerra, 1948.

Fabiola, 1950.

La belleza del diavolo, 1950.

Verginita, 1952.

Processa alla città, 1952.

(With others) *Europa '51,* 1952.

Il mondo le Condanna, 1953.

La passeggiata, 1953.

I vinti, 1953.

Il seduttore (based on his novel), 1954.

(With others) *Generale della Rovere,* 1960.

OTHER

Il prato (radio play), 1941.

Trio (radio play), 1949, published in *Tutti il teatro,* Rusconi (Milan, Italy), 1984.

Christo tradito, Macchia (Rome, Italy), 1949.

Pane vivo (television script), 1952.

Ambiguità Christiana, F. Cappelli (Rocca San Casciano, Italy), 1954, reprinted, Edizioni Studium (Rome, Italy), 1994.

Qualcuno fra voi (television script), Vallecchi (Florence, Italy), 1963.

Paolo VI: testimoianze e interpretazioni, M. Boni (Bologna, Italy), 1978.

Il commedione di Giuseppe Gioachino Belli, poeta e impiegato ponticio, Emila Romagna Teatro (Rome, Italy) 1979.

SIDELIGHTS: Diego Fabbri was one of the best-known playwrights in Italy in the twentieth century, especially in the postwar era. A Christian moralist, in his plays he juxtaposed the perfect divine against the imperfect mortal and explored humanity's moral dilemmas and search for grace. These themes won his plays a wide following among Catholics in Italy and the rest of the world.

Fabbri was born in 1911 in the town of Forli, in the Emilia-Romagna region of Italy. His parents were devoutly Catholic and raised him in their religious tradition. His father was a factory worker and a republican who taught his son to love freedom and to hate fascism. His mother loved the theater, and Fabbri inherited this love from her. He began performing in local plays at the age of eight, joining the amateur company "Ricreativo di S. Liugi." He wrote several plays for the parish troupe while he was in his teens; the earliest of these, *I fiori del dolore,* was written when he was seventeen. This play, like most of his earliest work, is quite serious and pessimistic. Fabbri went to the University of Bologna to study law and business and continued to indulge his passion for drama, writing a number of plays for an all-male acting group.

Fabbri graduated from the university in 1936 and immediately attempted to produce his play *Il nodo,* but the fascist government banned it for its "extreme pessimism." He opened his own private school and ran it for several years, reluctant to pursue any sort of public career under Italian dictator Benito Mussolini. He wrote for several Catholic newspapers and periodical from 1936 until 1940. He moved to Rome in 1939, telling everyone that he meant to work in a Catholic publishing house; what he really wanted to do was to succeed as a playwright, and he brought along three scripts he had already written to get himself started. His early plays were notable not only for their pessimism but also their anti-fascist views and their emphasis on social reform and intellectual and spiritual involvement with Catholicism. His views were certainly in conflict with orthodox doctrine, and conservative Catholics found him irreverent.

In 1940 he became secretary-general of the Catholic Film Center, a position he held until 1950. He worked on liberalizing the Church's attitude toward film and cinema, particularly on limiting its efforts to censor dramatic works.

In 1941 Fabbri's play *Orbite* was produced in Rome. *Orbite* explores the themes of human isolation and suggests that people can escape from their solitary orbits by poetry, music, and sacrifice. Later that year, Fabbri produced a revised edition of *Il nodo* called *Paludi.* The public was not wild about the pessimistic play, but it did add to Fabbri's growing reputation as a playwright. *Paludi* is clearly an anti-fascist criticism of dictatorship. The hero, Carlo, tries to rebel against the corrupt system and is murdered by his fellow workers, who cannot understand Carlo's quest for freedom and instead interpret his rebellion as greed. The anguish expressed in this play is similar to that in the works of Ugo Betti, one of the key influences on Fabbri's work.

La libreria del sole, produced in Rome in 1943, examined the relationship between priests and their parishioners. Anselmo, a priest in the midst of a spiritual crisis, goes to visit his family; this makes him realize that to be a good priest, he must enter the world of real people and accept them instead of merely devoting himself to priestly religious devotion.

During the war, Fabbri became active with the Christian Democrats. He delivered a number of speeches for them, shocking his listeners with his sympathy toward Marxism and his questioning of the Church's official positions. His most famous speech, "Christo Tradito," recommended that Marxism and Christianity reconcile with one another. Some of his comments about the Church anticipated controversies which materialized later and resulted in the reforms Pope John XXIII made at Vatican Council II. For example, Fabbri suggested that the Church stop blaming Jews for the death of Jesus, that it should get more in touch with the lives of common parishioners, and that it should make peace with the Orthodox East. He explored these themes in some of his later plays.

When the war ended, he wrote a number of screenplays and produced religious films. He also worked with the magazines *La fiera litteraria* and *Il dramma,* writing a number of critical essays on the dramatists Cesare Ludovici, Rossi di San Secondo, and Ugo Betti that were widely praised.

In the late 1940s Fabbri returned to writing plays and reaffirmed the reputation he had begun to make several years earlier. His works of this period are still very pessimistic. Interestingly, several of his plays from this period take the form of legal trials; these include *Inquisizione, Processo di famiglia,* and *Processo di Gesù.* During this period, Fabbri began to enjoy international attention, especially in France, where he spent part of every year.

His 1950 play *Inquisizione,* his first real success, won a national prize for its portrayal of a young priest's crisis of faith. In this play, the young priest is counseling a couple who are having marital difficulties, and an older priest helps him to see that his efforts are in fact full of hypocrisy and selfishness. Gradually he helps the younger man understand compassion and humility, and the couple ends up reconciled; the older priest has always wanted to see a miracle, and he believes that this is one. The actual Church did not appreciate this portrayal of their institution.

Fabbri explores the disjuncture between Christianity and communism in Italy in *Processo di famiglia.* In this play, a mother, father, foster parents, and a priest all fight for the custody of a young boy. The boy kills himself rather than face these irreconcilable forces.

The Church also failed to approve of Fabbri's play *Il seduttore* because his protagonist commits suicide rather than choose between his three lovers, and suicide is considered a heretical act. In this play, which was directed by Luchino Visconti, the hero Eugenio has affairs with three women at the same time; he is not a Don Juan character, but instead simply lets the women seduce him; he takes lovers because he sees it all as a sort of game, a game he wants to win. In the 1951 version, the protagonist ends the play by ending his own life. Fabbri re-wrote the ending to satisfy the Vatican, and in the 1956 version, he only simulates suicide.

With 1956's *Processo a Gesù,* his most famous play, Fabbri began to abandon his pessimistic attitude and instead fill his works with irony, wry humor, and irreverence. He was inspired to write the play by the news that some English-speaking jurists in Jerusalem had enacted a trial of Jesus. In this play, a family of German-Jewish actors enact a drama in which they try Jesus; they want to determine his guilt or innocence

and then to determine who was responsible for his death. They draw lots to assign parts, which include Mary and Joseph, Mary Magalene, Judas Iscariot, Pontius Pilate, and Caiaphas. The character Elias, whose son has been killed by anti-Semites, takes on the role of judge; after examining the facts, he finds Pilate guilty of murder. Other members of the acting troupe seated in the audience stand up and tell the house what they think of Jesus, either expressing their need for him or denouncing them; they include a prostitute, an intellectual, a blind man, and a priest, and they represent modern people and all of their varied opinions. Giancarlo Vigorelli pointed out that the character of Mary Magdalene is the key to this play, emphasizing that Christ returns only to people who come together in his name and that Christianity celebrates community, not individuality.

In an introductory note to *I demoni,* Fabbri said that the key to his work lies in his characters; he suggested that all of his plays were "trials," in which his characters must prove their guilt or innocence, save themselves or not.

In *Vegli d'armi,* a group of Jesuits discusses Christianity while their founder St. Ignatius, disguised as a butler, serves them. In *La bugiarda,* a woman lies to both her husband and her lover. Isabella, a courtesan, strings along two men in this aggressive light comedy. Though this play was at first censored, it was a great success in London. Conservatives criticized it for its irreverence, but Fabbri responded that it was a work of pure invention. The performance of 1959's *Figli d'art,* directed by Luchino Visconti, won a prize in Paris at the Theatre of the Nations Festival.

Fabbri's plays were influenced by the work of Pirandello, Ugo Betti, Ibsen, and Chekov. He used his dramas to investigate the place of religion in modern life, and he did not suggest easy answers to his own questions. He held the view that human existence is lonely and painful, alleviated only by spiritual means such as faith in God, loving others, and art.

Fabbri was keenly interested in bringing theater to the people and worked in theatrical institutions in addition to writing his own plays. He and Vito Pandolfi signed a "Manifesto per un teatro del popolo" in 1943, calling for a national and popular theater. In 1945, he and Ugo Betti and other dramatists founded the Sindacato

Nazionale degli Autori Drammatici. He directed the Teatro la Cometa in Rome from 1960 to 1962. He was particularly involved with *La fiera litteraria,* which he managed from 1959 to 1968. His works have been performed in a number of other countries, especially France and Spain, but also in Switzerland, Argentina, Brazil, England, Ireland, and Belgium.

Fabbri adapted a number of works by French authors and by Dostoevsky for the Italian stage. These include *I demoni* and *Processo Karamazov,* both by Dostoevsky, and *Teresa Desqueyroux,* from a work by Mauriac. Late in his career, Fabbri wrote mostly for television. He died in Riccione in 1980. He left his manuscripts and books to the town of Forli, where he had grown up, and in return the town created a study center in his honor.

BIOGRAPHICAL AND CRITICAL SOURCES:

BOOKS

International Dictionary of Theatre, Volume 2: *Playwrights,* St. James Press (Detroit, MI), 1994.

PERIODICALS

Il Baretti, 1966, "Il teatro di diego fabbri, pp. 7-66.
Cultura e Scuola, July-September, 1988, "Figure femminili nel teatro," pp. 198-204.
Filosofia Psicologia Humanides, 1963, "Umanita di Diego Fabbri," pp. 448-469.
Nuova Antologia, 1969, "Il teatro di Diego Fabbri," pp. 228-251.
Revista de Letras da Faculdade de Filosofia Ciencias e Letras de Assis, 1973, "L'avvenimento de Diego Fabbri," pp. 81-112.
Revista Italiana di Drammaturgia, September, 1980, "Diego Fabbri," pp. 101-117.
Sipario, October, 1990, "Uomo di cultura . . . ," pp. 11-15, "Motivi processuali," pp. 16-19.
Studi Novecenteschi, June, 1995, Paolo di Sacco, "Diego Fabbri (1911-1980), pp. 7-43.
Vita e Pensiero, March, 1995, Paolo di Sacco, "Processo a Gesù e il metateatro processuale e cristologico di Diego Fabbri," pp. 183-196.

OTHER

In ricordo di Diego Fabbri, http://www.grtv.it/ (April 22, 2002), "Gli eredi donano alla città natale tutti gli scritti in ricordo di Diego Fabbri."*

FIENNES, William 1971-

PERSONAL: Born 1971 in Oxford, England; son of Saye and Sele Fiennes. *Education:* Attended Oxford University.

ADDRESSES: Agent—c/o Author Mail, Random House, 1540 Broadway, New York, NY 10036.

CAREER: Writer.

WRITINGS:

The Snow Geese: A Story of Home, Random House (New York, NY), 2002.

Contributor to periodicals, including *Granta, Times Literary Supplement, Daily Telegraph, London Review of Books,* and *Observer.*

SIDELIGHTS: The name William Fiennes may sound familiar—he is the distant cousin of the actors Ralph and Joseph Fiennes—because he made a name for himself with his first book, *The Snow Geese: A Story of Home.* According to Mark Cocker of the *Guardian,* "*The Snow Geese* is the debut of a striking talent." The book chronicles Fiennes's journey across America and into Canada as he follows the path of snow geese on their 3,000-mile spring migration from their winter home in southern Texas to their breeding grounds in the Canadian Arctic.

Fiennes's graduate studies at Oxford were disrupted when a long-term illness caused him to undergo several operations. While on convalescence at his family's estate in Oxford, Fiennes re-read a favorite childhood book, *The Snow Goose* which prompted his desire to track the geese. "The pang of nostalgia, the intense longing to go home that I had experienced in the hospital, had now been supplanted by an equally intense longing for adventure, for strange horizons," he told Stephen J. Lyons of *BookPage.*

Fiennes tracks the geese by car, Greyhound bus, small plane, and train. He describes everything in meticulous detail along his trip, including a host of quirky characters he meets along the way: Jean, the ex-nun who plays tennis and loves doing other people's laundry, Ruth the quilter, Ken, the Texan rice farmer who leads him to his first flock of geese, and non-English speaking Intuits who take him to the wilderness to hunt for the geese.

Some critics felt that occasionally Fiennes was a bit excessive with his generous use of adjectives. A writer from *Kirkus Reviews* wrote, "The author has a tendency to over portray his human traveling companions . . . but he can turn a lovely phrase: 'the books on either side of it leaned together like hands in prayer.'" Tom Fort from the *Financial Times* commented, "Occasionally he strives overmuch—lady golfers with calves like 'fresh tench', a hunting print showing 'the lope and fealty of labradors'." Other reviewers believed that Fiennes's descriptive prose is not only justifiable but essential to bringing his characters to life. Mark Cocker of the *Guardian* was particularly impressed by Fiennes's "ability to capture with such seeming ease the inaccessible yet highly expressive sounds created by birds moving in large flocks." Sharyn Wizda Vane from the *Austin American-Statesman* noted, "Fiennes . . . has a poet's eye for detail that elevates his recollections far above mere travelogue."

Fiennes explores several underlying themes in recounting his three-month voyage. He discovers how snow geese being driven to travel north in spring and south in winter symbolize the importance of home and the need for it. Fiennes "writes powerfully of the sense of belonging that his family home in the English countryside gives him, of the illness which seems to have precipitated his decision to follow the geese, of his longing to return," Fort commented.

The Snow Geese has been classified as a travel memoir, a natural history book on birds, an autobiography, and a meditation on home and nostalgia. Fiennes has his own take on the book. "All of these stories are about the human condition, the longing to find home," he told Quentin Mills-Fenn during an interview for *Style Manitoba*. "The whole book, the journey, is about a series of almost homes, providing some of the features of home."

BIOGRAPHICAL AND CRITICAL SOURCES:

PERIODICALS

Austin American-Statesman, March 14, 2002, Sharyn Wizda Vane, "North toward Home: Author Wil-

liam Fiennes Followed Snow Geese from Texas to Canada—and Discovered What It Means to Belong," p. E1.

Booklist, February 1, 2002, Gilbert Taylor, review of *The Snow Geese: A Story of Home,* p. 912.

Canadian Geographic, March, 2002, Jeanie McFarlane, "A Fanciful Flight to Recovery," p. 97.

Daily Telegraph, June 7, 2002, Nigel Reynolds, "Jenkins in Book Prize Battle with Newcomer," p. NA; August 23, 2002, Charlie Methven, "Bird-brained."

Financial Times, March 16, 2002, Tom Fort, review of *The Snow Geese: A Story of Home,* p. 5.

Guardian, August 29, 2002, Mark Cocker, "Stairway to Heaven."

Independent, March 23, 2002, Salley Vickers, "The Odyssey with Ornithology," p. 12.

Kirkus Reviews, December 15, 2001, review of *The Snow Geese: A Story of Home,* p. 1734.

Library Journal, February 1, 2002, Maureen J. Delaney-Lehman, review of *The Snow Geese: A Story of Home,* p. 126.

National Geographic Adventurer, March, 2002, Anthony Brandt, review of *The Snow Geese: A Story of Home,* p. 45.

New Statesman, March 4, 2002, Robert McFarlane, "Wings of Desire," p. 53.

New York Times, February 20, 2002, Richard Eder, "A Recovering Soul Takes Wing as It Migrates on Nature's Draft," p. B8.

New York Times Book Review, June 23, 2002, Drake Bennet, review of *The Snow Geese: A Story of Home,* p. 21.

Observer, March 17, 2002, Hermione Lee, "Solace for the Goose," p. 250.

Publishers Weekly, February 4, 2002, review of *The Snow Geese: A Story of Home,* p. 71.

Scotsman, July 13, 2002, "A Mild Goose Chaser," p. 10.

Spectator, March 16, 2002, Steve King, review of *The Snow Geese: A Story of Home,* p. 53.

Star Tribune, August 29, 2002, Pamela Miller, review of *The Snow Geese: A Story of Home.*

Tampa Tribune, June 9, 2002, Amy Smith Linton, "Curiosity Follows Flock Home," p. 4.

Times Literary Supplement, March 22, 2002, William Ashworth, "Flight Paths and Homing Instincts," p. 12.

OTHER

BookPage, http://www.bookpage.com/ (August 29, 2002), Stephen J. Lyons, "A Road Trip of Discovery."

Sally Vickers, http://www.salleyvickers.com/ (August 29, 2002), review of *The Snow Geese: A Story of Home.*

Style Manitoba, http://www.stylemanitoba.com/ (November 11, 2002), Quentin Mills-Fenn, "The Long Way Home: An Interview with William Fiennes.*"

*   *   *

FINDLEY, Timothy (Irving Frederick) 1930-2002

OBITUARY NOTICE—See index for *CA* sketch: Born October 30, 1930, in Toronto, Ontario, Canada; died of complications from a pelvic fracture June 20, 2002, in France. Actor, novelist, playwright, and author. As a novelist and playwright, Findley was widely admired throughout his native Canada. His audience was diverse, perhaps because his fiction mingled elements of mystery, horror, science fiction, suspense, and other genres without falling permanently into any single genre or literary style. Critics have noted the dramatic flair that enlivens much of his writing. Findley began his career as a professional actor; he was an original member of the Stratford Festival in Ontario, Canada, in 1953. His first bestseller was the novel *The Wars,* about the emotional disintegration of a young soldier during World War I, which earned the author his first Governor General's Award, among several other honors. Many of Findley's writings, as he himself once suggested, are about ordinary people thrust into extraordinary circumstances, and critics noted his frequent focus on the most basic of human fears. Others suggested that Findley's writing, whether novel, short story, stage play, memoir, or television script, reflects a layer of social criticism. The novel *Not Wanted on the Voyage* was described by some as an interpretation of the biblical story of Noah and the flood that casts Noah as an evil man with ulterior motives and the flood itself as a horrific act of holy vengeance. Findley's other novels include *The Telling of Lies: A Mystery,* which was honored in the United States by the Edgar Allan Poe Award of the Mystery Writers of America, and the 2001 novel *Spadework,* set in the town of Stratford, Ontario, where Findley's career began a half-century earlier. His plays include *Elizabeth Rex,* featuring as characters William Shakespeare and Queen Elizabeth I, which play earned Findley his second Governor General's Award in 2000; and the award-winning *The Stillborn Lover.* Findley was decorated an officer of the Order of Canada and made a knight of the French Order of Arts and Letters.

OBITUARIES AND OTHER SOURCES:

BOOKS

Contemporary Literary Criticism, Volume 102, Gale (Detroit, MI), 1998.
Contemporary Novelists, 7th edition, St. James Press (Detroit, MI), 2001.
Findley, Timothy, *Inside Memory: Pages from a Writer's Workbook,* HarperCollins (New York, NY), 1990.
Findley, Timothy, *From Stone Orchard: A Collection of Memories,* HarperCollins (New York, NY), 1998.

PERIODICALS

Chicago Tribune, June 22, 2002, pp. 1-19.
Los Angeles Times, June 23, 2002, obituary by Jon Thurber, p. B16.
New York Times, June 22, 2002, obituary by Anthony DePalma, p. B21.
Times (London, England), July 31, 2002.
Washington Post, June 23, 2002, p. C8.

*   *   *

FISHER, Antwone Quenton 1959-

PERSONAL: Born 1959, in Ohio; son of Eddie Elkins and Eva Mae Fisher; married; children: one daughter.

ADDRESSES: Home—Los Angeles, CA. *Agent*—c/o Author Mail, William Morrow, 10 East 53rd St., 7th Floor, New York, NY 10022.

CAREER: Served in the U.S. Navy for eleven years; Sony Pictures Entertainment, security guard.

WRITINGS:

(With Mim Eichler Rivas) *Finding Fish* (memoir), Morrow (New York, NY), 2001.
The Antwone Fisher Story (screenplay), Twentieth Century-Fox Film Corporation, 2002.
Who Will Cry for the Little Boy?: Poems, Morrow (New York, NY), 2003.

ADAPTATIONS: Finding Fish was adapted as an audiobook, narrated by Alton Fitzgerald White, Harper Audio, 2001.

SIDELIGHTS: Antwone Quenton Fisher is the author of both a book and a screenplay based on his life. *Finding Fish,* the book, and *The Antwone Fisher Story,* the movie, both cover his childhood, which he largely spent in an abusive foster home. Fisher was born to a seventeen-year-old prison inmate named Eva Mae Fisher in 1959, and since his father was dead Fisher was put into foster care. His first foster home was loving, but when he was two he was transferred to the home of Reverend and Mrs. Pickett (called the Tates in the film version). It was in this home that he became subject to abuse so horrendous that it would scarcely be believable if Fisher did not include in his book excerpts from actual case files that confirm his tales. Fisher left the Picketts' home at age sixteen and spent a year at a reform school before becoming homeless. Finally, at age nineteen he joined the U.S. Navy, where he spent eleven years, found trust, camaraderie, and self-respect, and became a decorated sailor. He reunited with his birth family at the age of thirty-three, and has found success as a husband, a father, and a full-time screenwriter. "If a major feature of survival memoirs is their ability to impress readers with the subject's long, steady climb to redemption and excellence, then this engrossing book is a classic," concluded a *Publishers Weekly* contributor.

The film version of *Finding Fish* frames the story of Fisher's childhood with that of his early adulthood in the U.S. Navy. In the film, Fisher (played by Derek Luke) is sent to a Navy psychologist named Jerome Davenport, played by Denzel Washington, to learn how to deal with the uncontrollable anger, stemming from his previous abuse, that threatens to sink his military career. The film threatens to be typical inspirational fare, where Fisher confronts his past and settles into a healthy new life with the Davenports as surrogate parents and with his love interest, fellow sailor Cheryl (played by Joy Bryant), "but the movie's smarter than that," Eleanor Ringel Gillespie wrote in the *Atlanta Journal-Constitution.* As Karen Durbin noted in her film review for the *New York Times,* "Maybe one reason audiences applaud this movie is for raising their spirits without insulting their intelligence."

Reversing the usual process, Fisher penned his screenplay first, writing it while holding down a day

job as a security guard at Sony Pictures and only later adapting it into book form. "It was cathartic to write the movie," he explained to *Black Issues Book Review* interviewer Lisa Kennedy. "But when you write movies you can't have all the characters you want, and you have to write 120 pages. So I decided I'd write the book and then I'd be able to say everything I wanted to say."

BIOGRAPHICAL AND CRITICAL SOURCES:

PERIODICALS

Atlanta Journal-Constitution, December 20, 2002, Eleanor Ringel Gillespie, review of *The Antwone Fisher Story.*

Black Issues Book Review, May-June, 2002, Cynthia Roby, review of *Finding Fish* (audio book), p. 26; July-August, 2002, Lisa Kennedy, "Role Reversal: Hollywood Writers Take Their Act from Print to Screen and Vice Versa," pp. 24-27.

Book, March, 2001, "Denzel Washington Goes Fishing in Directorial Debut," p. 14.

Ebony, April, 2001, review of *Finding Fish,* p. 16.

Library Journal, January 1, 2001, Antoinette Brinkman, review of *Finding Fish,* p. 136; August, 2001, Danna Bell-Russel, review of *Finding Fish,* p. 188.

New York Times, December 19, 2002, Stephen Holden, "A Director and His Hero Find Answers in the Details"; December 22, 2002, Karen Durbin, "With a Brain as Well as a Heart."

Publishers Weekly, November 27, 2000, review of *Finding Fish,* p. 61.

Time, February 26, 2001, Lise Funderberg, review of *Finding Fish,* p. 72.

OTHER

Onion A.V. Club, http://www.theonionavclub.com/ (December 19, 2002), Tasha Robinson, review of *Finding Fish.**

*   *   *

FITZPATRICK, Tom 1927-2002

OBITUARY NOTICE—See index for *CA* sketch: Born February 2, 1927, in New York, NY; died of lung cancer June 25, 2002, in Phoenix, AZ. Journalist. Fitzpatrick won the Pulitzer Prize for spot news coverage in 1970 for his eyewitness account of a radical

Students for a Democratic Society (SDS) rampage through urban Chicago a year earlier. As a reporter for the *Chicago Sun-Times,* he followed the protestors on foot through Lincoln Park and witnessed their violent behavior and clashes with police at close range. A few years prior to that, Fitzpatrick had received the Edward Scott Beck Award of the *Chicago Tribune* for his series on a rescue effort to reach coal miners trapped in a cave. Fitzpatrick was a lifelong journalist, admired for his versatile demeanor that enabled him to pursue a story in whatever manner would accomplish his goal, and for his evocative columns, which could move his readers to laughter, anger, or tears. Fitzpatrick began his career with newspapers in Ohio, including the *Cleveland Plain Dealer.* In the 1960s he worked for several Chicago-area newspapers, originally as a sports writer, then as a news reporter. In 1979 he became a columnist with the *Arizona Republic,* and over the next fifteen years he rotated between jobs in Phoenix and Chicago. Fitzpatrick's career was not without controversy. The same tenacity and assertiveness that won him the stories he covered sometimes led to colorful confrontations with his editors and colleagues. His final assignment was said to be with an alternative newspaper in Phoenix called the *New Times.* Fitzpatrick's collected columns from the *Chicago Sun-Times* were published as *Fitz: All Together Now.*

OBITUARIES AND OTHER SOURCES:

PERIODICALS

Chicago Tribune, June 26, 2002, obituary by Matthew Walberg, pp. 2-9; July 10, 2002, pp. 2-7.
Cleveland Plain Dealer, June 27, 2002, obituary by Angela D. Chatman, p. B7.
Washington Post, June 29, 2002, p. B6.

* * *

FitzSIMONS, Peter

PERSONAL: Born in Peats Ridge, Australia; married, 1992; wife's name Lisa; children: two sons. *Education:* Sydney University, Sydney, Australia, B.A.

ADDRESSES: Agent—c/o HarperCollins, 10 East 53rd Street, 7th Floor, New York, NY 10022.

CAREER: Journalist and writer. *Sydney Morning Herald,* Sydney, Australia, journalist, 1989—. Television commentator for Australian *Today Show* and *Wide World of Sports.*

WRITINGS:

Little Theories of Life, cartoons by Brian Kogler, Allen & Unwin (North Sydney, New South Wales, Australia), 1991.
Basking in Beirut and Other Adventures with Peter FitzSimons, Allen & Unwin (North Sydney, New South Wales, Australia), 1991.
Nick Farr-Jones: The Authorised Biography, Random House Australia (Milsons Point, New South Wales, Australia), 1993.
Rugby Stories: Some Rucking Good Yarns, Allen & Unwin (St. Leonards, New South Wales, Australia), 1993.
Hitchhiking for Ugly People: And Other Life Experiences, Random House (Milsons Point, New South Wales, Australia), 1994.
The Sporting Greats, Random House Australia (Milsons Point, New South Wales, Australia), 1995.
The Rugby War, HarperSports (Sydney, New South Wales, Australia), 1996.
Beazley: A Biography, HarperCollins (Pymble, New South Wales, Australia), 1998.
Everyone but Phar Lap: Face to Face with the Best of Australian Sport, HarperSports (Pymble, New South Wales, Australia), 1997.
FitzSimons on Rugby: Loose in the Tight Five, Allen & Unwin (St. Leonards, New South Wales, Australia), 1999.
Nancy Wake: A Biography of Our Greatest War Heroine, HarperCollins (New York, NY), 2001.
John Eales: The Biography, Queen Anne (Harpenden, Australia), 2001.

Also columnist for London *Daily Telegraph* and contributor to *Ruby Heaven.*

SIDELIGHTS: Peter FitzSimons grew up on a farm north of Sydney, Australia, and was a noted tough Australian rugby player who also played professionally for Italy and France before turning to writing. A long-time journalist with the *Sydney Morning Herald,* FitzSimons is noted in journalism for his humor and sports writing but has also interviewed numerous dignitaries, including former U.S. president George Bush and Mother Theresa. FitzSimons has also hosted his own Australian television show and is a professional speaker specializing in humor and motivation.

FitzSimons' first two books, *Little Theories of Life* and *Basking in Beirut and Other Adventures with Peter FitzSimons,* are humor books based on his personal experiences and outlook on life. He has also written several books focusing on the sport of rugby, including biographies of Australian rugby stars Nick Farr-Jones and John Eales. *Nick Farr-Jones: The Authorised Biography,* which was FitzSimons' first full biography, tells the life story of the legendary Australian rugby player who captained the 1991 World Cup champion Australian team. Writing in *Australian Book Review,* Rafe Champion noted that FitzSimons, who was once a teammate of Farr-Jones, "has managed to avoid hagiography" and "has made an effective transition to the more demanding form of the biography."

FitzSimons' next biography focuses on Kim Beazley, a leading member of Australia's Labor Party (ALP) who was elected opposition leader in 1996. "The book is more than a simple telling of Beazley's rise to power or a background study of his character," wrote Trevor Warren in the *Journal of Australian Studies.* "FitzSimons provides us with a useful look into politics and policy processes of the Hawke and Keating governments; it is also in part a social history, both of Australia and the ALP." Writing in the *Australian Book Review,* Joe Rich called the book a "strongly etched, well-rounded portrait." Rich also noted: "The account benefits from FitzSimons' flair for evoking ambiance by picking out the ordinary, commonplace details comprising the background of the action—the physical surroundings, the posturing as tensions mounted in various power struggles, the body language of participants (such as Beazley slumping back on learning of the start of the Gulf War) and their idiosyncrasies."

In *Nancy Wake: A Biography of Australia's Greatest War Heroine,* FitzSimons tells the story of Wake, a member of the French Resistance during World War II. Wake had gone to France to work as a journalist and eventually married a rich Frenchman. Appalled by German treatment of the Jews, she quickly joined the French Resistance when Germany occupied France.

Her heroic deeds became legendary. Known as the "White Mouse" by the Germans, Wake once bicycled for seventy-two hours through numerous German checkpoints to make her delivery. She also was adept at combat, once killing a German soldier with a karate chop and lobbing grenades in a Gestapo headquarters. Although Wake survived the war, her husband was executed by the Gestapo. Nearing the age of ninety and living in Port Macquarie in Australia at the time of the book's publication, Wake was remembered by the members of the Resistance for her beauty, high spirits, and rebellious nature. Writing in the *Age,* Brenda Niall noted that in FitzSimons' biography "Wake herself speaks to us, forthright, and matter-of-fact." Although Niall found FitzSimons style "irritatingly bouncy" and "over-emphatic," she noted that the book emphasizes Wake's "larrikin humor, her zest for danger, and her casual impudence in the face of authority."

BIOGRAPHICAL AND CRITICAL SOURCES:

PERIODICALS

Age (Melbourne, Australia), June 4, 2001, Brenda Niall, "Better Ways to Take Our Nancy."

Australian Book Review, February, 1994, Rafe Champion, "The Politics of Sport," p. 49; November, 1998, Joe Rich, "The Man Who Would Have Been," pp. 7-8.

Journal of Australian Studies, March, 1999, Trevor Warren, review of *Beazley,* p. 185.*

*   *   *

FLANAGAN, Thomas (James Bonner) 1923-2002

OBITUARY NOTICE—See index for *CA* sketch: Born November 5, 1923, in Greenwich, CT; died of a heart attack March 21, 2002, in Berkeley, CA. Educator and author. Flanagan received recognition for his historical novels set in Ireland. He was a graduate of Amherst College, where he earned a B.A. in 1945 after serving in the U.S. Naval Reserve from 1942 to 1944, and Columbia University, where he received his Ph.D. in 1958. Flanagan was a teacher at Columbia during the 1950s before moving on to the University of California—Berkeley, where he was an English professor from 1960 until 1992, retiring as a distinguished professor. After publishing a nonfiction work, *The Irish Novelists, 1800-1850,* in 1959, Flanagan moved on to fiction and was highly praised for his historical novel of the 1798 Irish rebellion, *The Year of the French,* which won the National Book Critics Circle award. His subsequent novels *The Tenants of Time* and *The End of the Hunt* similarly describe Irish struggles against the English. The recipient of the American Irish Historical Society's gold medal in 1982, Flanagan was also the author of the books *Louis David' Riel: Prophet of the New World* and *Dangerous Edge of the Thing,* as well as a number of mystery stories published in such magazines as *Ellery Queen's Mystery Magazine,* which gave him the best story of the year award in 1957.

OBITUARIES AND OTHER SOURCES:

BOOKS

Writers Directory, 16th edition, St. James Press (Detroit, MI), 2001.

PERIODICALS

Los Angeles Times, March 29, 2002, p. B12.
New York Times, March 29, 2002, p. A22.
Washington Post, March 30, 2002, p. B6.

*   *   *

FLORA, Kate Clark
(Katharine Clark)

PERSONAL: Born in Maine; daughter of a farmer and a writer; married an attorney and law professor; children: Jake, Max. *Education:* Northeastern University, LL.D.

ADDRESSES: Home—Concord, MA. *Agent*—c/o Author Mail, St. Martin's Press, 175 Fifth Ave., New York, NY 10010. *E-mail*—kozak@tiac.net.

CAREER: Author and attorney. Represented the Department of Human Services for the office of Maine's attorney general; maintained a private practice. Cambridge Center for Adult Education, Cambridge, MA, writing teacher; radio personality.

MEMBER: Sisters in Crime (New England chapter president).

WRITINGS:

"THEA KOZAK" SERIES

Chosen for Death, Forge (New York, NY), 1994.
Death in a Funhouse Mirror, Forge (New York, NY), 1995.
Death at the Wheel, Forge (New York, NY), 1996.
An Educated Death, Forge (New York, NY), 1997.
Death in Paradise, Forge (New York, NY), 1998.

OTHER

(As Katharine Clark) *Steal Away,* Fawcett Books (New York, NY), 1998.

SIDELIGHTS: Kate Clark Flora was born in Maine where she later worked for the attorney general's office, before leaving to become a full-time writer. She has written a number of mysteries featuring Thea Kozak, a Massachusetts educational consultant and amateur private investigator who, in *Chosen for Death,* loses her husband in a car crash and her sister to murder. In the second book of the series, *Death in a Funhouse Mirror,* Thea is in a relationship with detective Andre Lemieux and looking into the death of Helene Streeter, the mother of a good friend. Eve Paris thinks her father Clifford killed Helene so that he could be with his gay lover, but there is no evidence to prove it. *Booklist*'s Emily Melton felt the ending is obvious but called the story "terrific," based on its "deft characterizations, the wonderfully original humor" and Thea's "in-your-face charm and chutzpah." A *Publishers Weekly* contributor noted that Flora "wraps things up satisfactorily in a story that is successfully carried forward by the strength of its characters."

In *Death at the Wheel,* Thea's mother introduces her to Julie Bass, whose cheating husband has died in a racing accident. When the police suspect that someone tampered with Calvin's car, they arrest Julie on suspicion. Thea agrees to help her but soon discovers that the widow has been having an affair with a local doctor and that there are a number of people who disliked Calvin. "Despite Flora's tight pacing, the finale is disappointingly convenient," said a *Publishers Weekly* reviewer. Melton called the story "funny, suspenseful, playful, and moving" and described Thea as "honest and genuine."

In reviewing *An Educated Death,* a *Publishers Weekly* writer commented that Flora "rings some new changes on the academic mystery with her contemporary private school settings." *Library Journal*'s Rex E. Klett called this the "fourth in a fine series." Thea is asked to help by a friend who is the headmistress of the private school where a female student has drowned. Thea discovers that Laney Taggert was pregnant, possibly by a member of the faculty, and that an employee has a suspicious background. When she interferes with the police investigation, Thea nearly becomes a victim herself. Melton called this "another notable entry in an entertaining series."

Death in Paradise is set in Hawaii, where Thea is assisted in solving a crime by eleven-year-old Laura Mitchell, called a "bright spot" by a *Publishers Weekly* contributor. Thea is handling a conference for an association of girls' schools and being frustrated by her incompetent coworkers and the executive director, Martina Pullman, who has many enemies, including the first wife of her husband. When Martina is murdered, strangled with her own stocking, Thea tries to find the killer before he or she strikes again and in the process is nearly drowned while scuba diving. Klett described the book as "an exciting series addition." *Booklist*'s John Rowen called it "a trifle long but smoothly written, solidly plotted, and populated with strong characters."

Flora wrote her next book, *Steal Away,* as Katharine Clark. When asked about her use of a pseudonym by Jon Jordan for *Mystery One* online, she said, "When Ballantine bought *Steal Away,* which is a suspense novel rather than a mystery, they were trying to create an opportunity for it to be a 'break out' book. . . . The usual marketing solution is to create a 'brand new author' to promote to bookstores, and that author gets a new name. That being said, I rather like the idea of being Katharine Clark."

A *Publishers Weekly* contributor called *Steal Away* a "mannered novel of suspense." Nine-year-old David Stark disappears on his way home from school, and his estranged parents, Rachel and Stephen, must work together to try to find him. The couple lost their first son to a genetic disease carried by Stephen, after which he underwent a vasectomy. David was, in fact, conceived through a sperm donation from a doctor who has contracted AIDS, thus posing the question of whether Rachel was infected. Stephen, who has been

having an affair with Rachel's sister, turns to a child rescue group for help, while Rachel relies on a seemingly psychic connection with David to discover his whereabouts. A *Kirkus Reviews* contributor wrote that "though many twists, turns, and nailbiting moments remain as David's danger increases, Rachel's intuition will finally come to the rescue. A fine addition to the genre, and a promising debut." In a *Booklist* review, David Pitt noted that "fans of family-crisis novels featuring realistic characters in tough situations . . . should be well pleased." *Library Journal*'s Alice DiNizo called *Steal Away* a "first-rate thriller. Readers will look forward to more from first novelist Clark."

BIOGRAPHICAL AND CRITICAL SOURCES:

PERIODICALS

Booklist, October 15, 1995, Emily Melton, review of *Death in a Funhouse Mirror,* p. 387; October 15, 1996, Emily Melton, review of *Death at the Wheel,* p. 406; October 1, 1997, Emily Melton, review of *An Educated Death,* p. 310; September 15, 1998, John Rowen, review of *Death in Paradise,* p. 202; October 15, 1998, David Pitt, review of *Steal Away,* pp. 405-406.

Kirkus Reviews, September 15, 1998, review of *Steal Away,* p. 1304.

Library Journal, October 1, 1994, Rex E. Klett, review of *Chosen for Death,* p. 118; October 1, 1996, Rex E. Klett, review of *Death at the Wheel,* p. 131; October 1, 1997, Rex E. Klett, review of *An Educated Death,* p. 130; September 1, 1998, Rex E. Klett, review of *Death in Paradise,* p. 220; October 15, 1998, Alice DiNizo, review of *Steal Away,* p. 95.

Publishers Weekly, November 14, 1994, review of *Chosen for Death,* p. 56; September 18, 1995, review of *Death in a Funhouse Mirror,* p. 117; September 23, 1996, review of *Death at the Wheel,* p. 59; July 21, 1997, review of *An Educated Death,* p. 187; July 20, 1998, review of *Death in Paradise,* p. 211; September 28, 1998, review of *Steal Away,* p. 71.

OTHER

Kate Clark Flora Home Page, http://www.kate flora.com (June 25, 2002).

Katharine Clark Home Page, http://www.katharine clark.com (June 25, 2002).

Mystery One, http://www.mysteryone.com/ (October 17, 2001), Jon Jordan, interview.*

FRASER, Dawn 1937-

PERSONAL: Born September 4, 1937, in Balmain, Sydney, New South Wales, Australia; daughter of Kenneth George and Rose Christina (Miranda) Fraser; married Gary Ware, 1965 (divorced); children: Dawn-Lorraine. *Hobbies and other interests:* Sports.

ADDRESSES: Home—403 Darling St., Balmain, Sydney, New South Wales 2041, Australia. *Agent*—c/o Hodder Headline Australia, Level 22, 201 Kent St., Sydney, New South Wales 2000, Australia.

CAREER: Olympic swimmer, politician, and author. House of Representatives, New South Wales, member of Parliament representing Balmain, Australia, 1988-91. Worked as a swim coach and ran a cheese shop and a pub in Balmain. Beachwatch, chair; Australia Day Council, vice president; World Masters Swimming, patron; member of Leichardt Committee of Red Cross, New South Wales division, Lyndon Community. Member, International Sporting Events advisory committee, and Sydney 2000 Olympic bid committee. Sponsor, National Community Awareness Campaign on Aid and Development.

MEMBER: Australians Abroad Council, Advertising Standards Council.

AWARDS, HONORS: Olympic gold medalist, 100-meter freestyle, 1956, 1960, 1964; Olympic gold medalist, 4 x 100-meter freestyle relay, 1956; Helms Award, 1961; named Australian ABC Sportsman of the Year, Australian Broadcasting Corporation, 1962; Australian of the Year, 1964; named to International Swimming Hall of Fame, Fort Lauderdale, FL, 1965; Australia's Best Sportsperson for the last twenty-five years, Australian Broadcasting Corporation, 1975; named to Hall of Fame, American Women's Sports Foundation, 1985; named to Australia's Sports Hall of Fame, 1985.

WRITINGS:

(Coauthor, with Harry Gordon) *Below the Surface: The Confessions of an Olympic Champion,* Morrow (New York, NY), 1965.
(Coauthor, with Harry Gordon) *Dawn Fraser,* Circus Books (Melbourne, Victoria, Australia), 1979.

Our Dawn: A Pictorial Biography, Sally Miner Publisher (Birchgrove, New South Wales, Australia), 1991.
Dawn: One Hell of a Life, Hodder Headline Australia (Sydney, New South Wales, Australia), 2001.

SIDELIGHTS: An Olympic swimming legend considered by many to be Australia's greatest female athlete, Dawn Fraser was the youngest of eight children and grew up in a working-class family. Suffering from asthma, she took up swimming at a young age to help counteract the disease's effects and the rest, as they say, is history. Although Fraser has authored or co-authored several books about her swimming career and life, she wrote her 2001 book, *Dawn Fraser: One Hell of a Life,* to set the record straight. "I've tried to show people that Dawn Fraser is a human being like the other great icons of this country of ours," Fraser said in a *Time International* article.

Fraser's book recounts many of her well-known exploits as a swimmer as well as her infamous clashes with authority. Fraser quit school at the age of thirteen and began working in a dress factory. The following year, she was spotted by a leading Australian swimming coach, Harry Gallagher, as she swam in a local pool. Gallagher was so impressed by Fraser's talent that he waived his coaching fees. Fraser later moved from her hometown of Balmain near Sydney to Adelaide so she could train intensively under Gallagher's tutelage. Another important booster in her swimming career was her brother Don, who encouraged her to swim. Don became ill and was sent to the hospital, where he died at the age of thirteen. However, before he died he told Fraser that she had a "gift" and that she should "keep training for [him]."

During her training with Gallagher, Fraser trained primarily with male swimmers, which she believes helped her competitively. She quickly progressed and qualified for the 1956 Olympic games held in Melbourne, Australia, where she went on to win a gold medal in the 100-meter freestyle and as a member of the 4 x 100-meter freestyle relay team. She went on to take the gold medal for the 100-meter freestyle in the 1960 Olympic Games in Rome and the 1964 Olympics in Tokyo. During her career, Fraser won eight Olympic medals—four gold and four silver—and set at least twenty-seven world records. Fraser was the first woman to break the one-minute barrier for the 100 meters, and the first woman swimmer to win gold medals in three consecutive Olympic Games.

Fraser was a strong-willed, independent person who often found herself in trouble with the authorities. At the age of twelve she was banned from competition for twelve months by the Australian Swimming Union, which deemed her a "professional" for taking a token amount of money for a race during a football club picnic. In the 1960 Rome games, she refused to swim the butterfly leg of the 4 x 100-meters medley during a qualifying heat because she had not been told earlier that she would have to swim. She also rebelled by wearing unofficial tracksuits and swimsuits during official events and was banned for two years from international events because of charges of drunkenness and other offenses.

Fraser's trouble with authority culminated during the 1964 Tokyo Olympic games. Although she was in a car wreck that had killed her mother and severely injured Fraser's spine and neck, she still won the gold medal in the 100-meter freestyle event. But trouble followed Fraser as she insisted on marching in the Olympic opening ceremonies despite an edict by a coach that banned anyone who had to compete within forty-eight hours of the opening ceremony. "Now I had worked very, very hard after the car accident in which my mother was killed, to get to that Olympic Games, there was nothing, nothing that was going to stand in my way of winning a Gold Medal," Fraser said in an interview for the Australian Radio National's program the *Sports Factor*. Fraser ended up marching, much to the chagrin of many Australian Olympic officials. Fraser further upset officials when she wore her own swimming suit. Fraser had made her own suit because she found the official suit uncomfortable.

In her book, Fraser also writes about her final confrontation with swimming officials. After a night of celebration, she and some friends took an Olympic flag from the Japanese Imperial Palace. Although she was caught by the Japanese police, they didn't press charges and actually gave her the flag in return for her autograph. Fraser, who had injured her ankle while trying to evade capture, carried the national flag for the Australian team during the closing ceremonies, walking the entire way in an ankle cast. Nevertheless, the Australian Swimming Union banned her for ten years from any competition following the Olympics, effectively ending her career as a competitive swimmer.

During the interview on *Sports Factor*, Fraser commented that she tried to find out why the Australian Swimming Union seemed so intent on ending her career. But she never came up with an answer. "I could have been at fault by standing up for my rights," she said in the interview.

Fraser's autobiography also contains little-known facts about her life, including one extremely disturbing incident that occurred outside the sports arena when she was raped at knife point by a Polish sailor on a ship in Sydney harbor. Although the judge suppressed any news leaks about Fraser's rape, he also dismissed the charges against the sailor for lack of evidence. "In those days women were not sort of really recognized and it was such an embarrassing situation to go through," she said during a television interview on Australia's *Lateline*.

After ending her swimming career, Fraser earned a living by working in a number of areas, from coaching and running her own businesses to serving as an independent member of Australia's New South Wales Legislative Assembly. Throughout, she continued to speak her mind, both in politics and on issues concerning the Olympics. For example, she has questioned the integrity of the Olympic Committee and athletes who take performance-enhancing drugs.

Fraser has remained a swimming legend and Australian icon. As for her own days as a swimmer, Fraser recalled her feelings for the sport during the *Sports Factor* interview. "Mine was a complete love affair," she said, remembering that the initial training periods involved "a lot of pain and cold water." She added, "But all of a sudden when you start getting fit, it's a beautiful thing, diving into the cool crisp water and then just sort of being able to pull your body through the water and the water opening up for you. And to have that feel and touch on your fingertips and your body, it's just beautiful."

BIOGRAPHICAL AND CRITICAL SOURCES:

PERIODICALS

New York Times, July 23, 1996, "Fraser Is Hospitalized," p. B15.
Rodale's Fitness Swimmer, July, 2000, "Dawn of a New Era," p. 17.
Time International, June 25, 2001, Daniel Williams, "Beyond Stardom: Two Lives Brought to Book Highlight the Gulf between Celebrity and Heroism."

OTHER

Australian Broadcasting Corporation Web site, http:// www.abc.net.au/ (September 12, 2002), transcript from *Lateline,* "Dawn's Hell of a Life."
The Australians (video tribute to Australian sportspersons), Paramount Pictures (Hollywood, CA), 1988.
Radio National's The Sports Factor Web site, http:// www.abc.net.au/ (Sept. 12, 2002), Amanda Smith, interview with Dawn Fraser.*

*   *   *

FRAZIER, Allie M. 1932-2002

OBITUARY NOTICE—See index for *CA* sketch: Born March 20, 1932, in Shaw, MS; died June 4, 2002, in Roanoke, VA. Philosopher, theologian, educator, administrator, and editor. Frazier taught philosophy and religion at Hollins College from 1964 until his retirement in 1997. He also established a master's degree program in liberal studies and directed the program for several years. Frazier was appointed to the Camp-Youts Chair of Ethics in 1993, the same year he was named professor of the year by the Association of Graduate Liberal Studies Programs. Frazier pursued a broad range of scholarly interests, from the history of philosophy to Asian religions to Holocaust studies. He edited the anthologies *Readings in Eastern Religious Thought* and *Issues in Religion: A Book of Readings.* Frazier, who had earned a bachelor's degree in sacred theology at Boston University, was also an occasional pastor at a Unitarian-Universalist church in Roanoke, Virginia.

OBITUARIES AND OTHER SOURCES:

PERIODICALS

Roanoke Times, June 6, 2002, obituary by Cody Lowe, p. B3.
Washington Post, June 8, 2002, p. B7.

*   *   *

FREEMAN, Thomas 1919-2002

OBITUARY NOTICE—See index for *CA* sketch: Born November 16, 1919, in Glasgow, Scotland; died May 12, 2002, in Ireland. Psychiatrist and author. Freeman's work as a psychoanalyst helped the medical profession to better understand the causes and potential cures of such illnesses as schizophrenia and manic depression. Receiving his medical degree from Queen's University of Belfast in 1942, Freeman was in the Royal Medical Corps during the war, training as a parachutist and attaining the rank of major by the time he left the army in 1947. After working as a senior registrar for a hospital and a clinic in England, Freeman became a consultant in psychiatry at the Glasgow Royal Mental Hospital from 1952 to 1954, impressing the staff with his ability to diagnose difficult cases. He was next assigned as a consultant at the Hampstead Child Therapy Clinic (which was later renamed the Anna Freud Centre), where he collaborated with Anna Freud, the granddaughter of Sigmund Freud. Together they worked on diagnosing disturbed children and formulating a ways to create accurate psychological profiles that were later also used on adult patients. After leaving the clinic, Freeman went into private practice while also continuing to serve as a consultant to hospitals. Some of his important publications include *A Psychoanalytic Study of the Psychoses* (1973), *Childhood Psychopathology and Adult Psychoses* (1976), *The Psychoanalyst in Psychiatry* (1988), *Development and Psychopathology,* written with Stanley Wiseberg and Clifford Yorke (1988), and *But Facts Exist* (1998).

OBITUARIES AND OTHER SOURCES:

BOOKS

Who's Who, 152nd edition, St. Martin's Press (New York, NY), 2000.

PERIODICALS

Scotsman (Edinburgh, Scotland), June 10, 2002, p. 14.
Times (London, England), May 31, 2002, p. 39.

*   *   *

FRIEDRICHS, David O. 1944-

PERSONAL: Born October 31, 1944, in White Plains, NY; son of K. O. (a professor of mathematics) and Nellie (a homemaker and teacher; maiden name, Bruell) Friedrichs; married Jean L. Richards, August 7, 1971 (divorced, October, 1994); married Jeanne

Windle; children: (second marriage) Jessica, Bryan. *Education:* New York University, A.B., 1966, M.A., 1970. *Politics:* "Progressive." *Hobbies and other interests:* International travel, collecting photographic documentary books, family history.

ADDRESSES: Home—510 Clark St., Clarks Green, PA 18411. *Office*—Department of Sociology, University of Scranton, Scranton, PA 18510-4605; fax: 570-941-6485. *E-mail*—friedrichsd1@uofs.edu.

CAREER: Educator. College of Staten Island of the City University of New York, began as instructor, became assistant professor of sociology, 1969-77; University of Scranton, Scranton, PA, began as assistant professor, became professor of sociology and criminal justice, 1977—. Ohio University, Rufus Putnam Lecturer, 1991. Consultant to National Science Foundation and National Institute of Justice.

MEMBER: White Collar Crime Research Consortium (president, 2002-04), American Society of Criminology (vice chair of division on critical criminology, 1995-96; member of executive board, 2001-03), Association for Humanist Sociology (vice president, 1986), Academy of Criminal Justice Sciences, Society for the Study of Social Problems, Law and Society Association, American Sociological Association.

AWARDS, HONORS: Frank Brown Scholarship Medal, 1984.

WRITINGS:

Trusted Criminals: White Collar Crime in Contemporary Society, Wadsworth Publishing (Belmont, CA), 1996, 2nd edition, 2002.

(Editor) *State Crime,* Volumes 1: *Defining, Delineating, and Explaining State Crime,* Volume 2: *Exposing, Sanctioning, and Preventing State Crime,* Ashgate (Brookfield, VT), 1998.

Law in Our Lives: An Introduction, Roxbury Publishing (Los Angeles, CA), 2001.

Contributor of numerous articles and reviews to periodicals. Editor, *Legal Studies Forum,* 1985-89; associate editor or member of editorial board of professional journals.

WORK IN PROGRESS: Research on crimes of the state and on transitional justice.

SIDELIGHTS: David O. Friedrichs told *CA:* "It gives me considerable satisfaction to work through, organize, and make sense of a body of literature on some significant and relatively neglected scholarly terrain—for example, white-collar crime, state crime, socio-legal scholarship—and to address issues of conceptual clarification. I like to think that my writing contributes to generating wider awareness of some enduring sources of injustice.

"I do not regard myself as a disciple of any great thinker or school of thought, and I have been influenced by a rather eclectic mix of intellectual movements and writers. At different times existentialism, neo-Marxist conflict theory, radical and critical criminology, and interactionism have been important to me. German sociologist Max Weber and American sociologist C. Wright Mills have in quite different ways been sources of inspiration. In terms of substantive interests, E. H. Sutherland's pioneering work on white-collar crime has been important. My former professor, Richard Quinney, has produced work that has provoked and moved me over a period of decades. My interest in law and society scholarship, and my approach to addressing scholarly fields, owes something to the work of sociologist Edwin Schur.

"My writing process? For many years I could only compose original drafts in handwriting on yellow legal pads; in recent years I can only do so on a word processor. Perhaps atypically for academics, I do almost all of my writing in my university office, not at home. I build up large files and notes on topics of interest, and then work my way through them quite systematically. I prefer to work hard on a first draft, as I prefer to avoid endless rewriting. But I also take the approach of throwing in almost everything I imagine I can use, and then cutting out sections as needed further down the line.

"I came of age during the 1960s—the civil rights and anti-Vietnam War era—and accordingly developed an enduring interest in the use and misuse of power, and law. I am about as far removed as one can be from a narrow specialist. Indeed, I am almost fatally attracted to ambitious topics of broad scope (such as state crime)."

BIOGRAPHICAL AND CRITICAL SOURCES:

PERIODICALS

Caribbean Journal of Criminology and Social Psychology, January, 1996, Jagan Lingamneni, review of *Trusted Criminals: White Collar Crime in Contemporary Society.*

Choice, September, 1996, R. T. Sigler, review of *Trusted Criminals.*

Criminal Justice Review, spring, 1996, Michael Lynch, review of *Trusted Criminals.*

Social Pathology, fall, 1996, Ronald Burns, review of *Trusted Criminals.*

*   *   *

FULDA, Joseph S. 1958-

PERSONAL: Born February 13, 1958, in New York, NY; son of Manfred (a professor) and Naomi (a teacher) Fulda. *Education:* Attended Yeshiva R.S.R. Hirsch, 1975-77; City College of the City University of New York, B.S. (summa cum laude), 1979; New York University, M.S., 1981; Columbia University, C.S.E., 1986; Graduate School of the City University of New York, M.Phil. and Ph.D., both 1990.

ADDRESSES: Home—701 West 177th St., No. 21, New York, NY 10033. *E-mail*—fulda@acm.org.

CAREER: New York University, New York, NY, research assistant at Courant Institute of Mathematical Sciences, 1979-80; Polytechnic Institute of New York, Brooklyn, instructor in computer science, 1982-83; Hofstra University, Hempstead, NY, assistant professor of computer science, 1984-88; Mount Sinai School of Medicine of the City University of New York, research assistant professor of biomathematical sciences, 1988-90; Columbia University, New York, NY, instructor in computer technology and applications, 1992; Fairleigh Dickinson University, Rutherford, NJ, adjunct professor of computer science, 1994; American College Testing, examiner for Law School Admission Test, 1995—. Guest on radio and television programs; public speaker.

MEMBER: Sigma Xi, City College of New York Alumni Association (member of board of directors, 1981-82).

AWARDS, HONORS: Editor's Choice Award, National Library of Poetry, 1994.

WRITINGS:

Are There Too Many Lawyers? and Other Vexatious Questions, Foundation for Economic Education, 1993.

Eight Steps toward Libertarianism, Free Enterprise Press (Bellevue, WA), 1997.

Contributor to books, including *Reflections of Light,* National Library of Poetry, 1995. Contributor of articles, reviews, and poetry to journals, including *Journal of Value Inquiry, Journal of Law and Information Science, Lincoln Review, Jewish Monthly, Computer and Society, Thought, International Journal of Intelligent Systems, Journal of Theoretical Biology,* and *Journal of the International Society for Ecological Modeling.* Contributing editor, *Freeman: Monthly Journal of Ideas on Liberty,* 1994—; associate editor, *Sexuality and Culture: An Interdisciplinary Journal,* 1997—.

G

GADAMER, Hans-Georg 1900-2002

OBITUARY NOTICE—See index for *CA* sketch: Born February 11, 1900, in Marburg an der Lahn, Germany; died March 13, 2002, in Heidelberg, Germany. Philosopher, educator, and author. Gadamer made his name in philosophical hermeneutics, the study of human understanding and meaning. He was educated at the University of Marburg, where he earned a Ph.D. in 1922, and also studied under Martin Heidegger at Heidelberg University. During the 1930s he taught philosophy at his alma mater and then moved on to the University of Leipzig in 1939, where he later served as dean of the philosophy faculty and chancellor after World War II. Because he declared himself apolitical, his teaching career was largely uninterrupted by the Nazi and communist governments and when he was offered a position at the University of Frankfurt, he was allowed to leave East Germany. Gadamer spent the 1950s and 1960s at the University of Heidelberg, where he was the chair of the philosophy department, retiring as a professor emeritus in 1968. Although retired, he continued to write philosophy books for the rest of the twentieth century. As a philosopher, he objected to the notion that truth can be discovered through pure science, and in his work on the interpretation of written texts he asserted that meanings are not fixed but rather subject to the understanding of the reader. He was also an opponent of globalization, which he felt denies the existence of very real social and economic borders, and of the spread of information technology, which he felt puts people under the dangerous delusion that since they are informed they do not need to understand. Among Gadamer's more than seventy books are *Philosophische Systematik, Idee und Zahl, Truth and Historicity, Rhetorik und Hermeneutik, Was ist Literatur?, Literature and Philosophy in Dialogue: Essays in German Literary Theory, Language and Linguisticality in Gadamer's Hermeneutics,* and the autobiography *Philosophical Apprenticeship.* Among his awards are the 1971 German Order of Merit and the Hegel Prize from the City of Stuttgart, the latter which he received in 1979.

OBITUARIES AND OTHER SOURCES:

BOOKS

Encyclopedia of World Biography, second edition, Gale (Detroit, MI), 1998.
International Who's Who, 63rd edition, Europa Publications (London, England), 2000.

PERIODICALS

Guardian (London, England), March 18, 2002, p. 20.
Independent (London, England), March 26, 2002, p. 6.
Los Angeles Times, March 26, 2002, p. B10.
New York Times, March 25, 2002, p. A23.
Times (London, England), March 16, 2002, p. 40.
Washington Post, March 16, 2002, p. B5.

*   *   *

GAO, (Sonya) Xiongya 1955-

PERSONAL: Born December 19, 1955, in China; naturalized U.S. citizen; daughter of Yi and Jianhong (Wang) Gao; children: Sharon Xiaging Chen. *Ethnicity:* "Chinese." *Education:* Xi'an Foreign Languages University, B.A., 1979, M.A. (translation), 1986; Ball State University, M.A. (English), 1987, Ph.D., 1993.

ADDRESSES: Home—3908 Courtland Dr., Metairie, LA 70002. *Office*—Department of English, Southern University—New Orleans, 6400 Press Dr., New Orleans, LA 70126. *E-mail*—xiongya@hotmail.com.

CAREER: Xi'an Foreign Languages University, Xi'an, China, lecturer in English, 1979-83; San Bernardino Valley College, San Bernardino, CA, instructor in English, 1993-96; Southern University—New Orleans, New Orleans, LA, assistant professor of English, 1996—. Lecturer at University of Redlands, California State University—San Bernardino, and University of California—Riverside, all 1993-96.

AWARDS, HONORS: Carol Ann Kendrick Memorial Research Scholar, Ball State University, 1990; Twenty-first Century Award for Achievement, 2000.

WRITINGS:

Pearl S. Buck's Chinese Women Characters, Susquehanna University Press (Cranbury, NJ), 2000.

*   *   *

GARDNER, John W(illiam) 1912-2002

OBITUARY NOTICE—See index for *CA* sketch: Born October 8, 1912, in Los Angeles, CA; died of complications from prostate cancer February 16, 2002, in Stanford, CA. Lobbyist, cabinet official, foundation executive, educator, and author. Gardner pursued many careers in his lifetime, but he is probably best known as the founder and chair of Common Cause, the citizens' lobby dedicated to protect the integrity of the process and practices of government. In that role, he addressed issues of campaign finance reform, ethics and conflict of interest, civil rights, and voter participation, among others. Gardner was also the secretary of the U.S. Department of Health, Education, and Welfare under President Lyndon Johnson, with responsibilities that included launching the new Medicare program and the 1964 Civil Rights Act and creating the Corporation for Public Broadcasting. For twenty years prior to that, Gardner had been affiliated with the Carnegie Corporation of New York, where he worked to improve the quality and effectiveness of American public education; he also served as president of the

Carnegie Foundation for the Advancement of Teaching. After retirement from Common Cause, he cofounded and chaired the Independent Sector, an organization to support volunteerism, followed by a stint as chair of the National Civic League. Gardner was also a professor of psychology, and from 1989 to 1996 he served as Haas Centennial Professor of Public Service at Stanford University. Among other honors he was awarded the Presidential Medal of Freedom and the Public Welfare Medal of the National Academy of Sciences. Gardner authored more than a half-dozen books, including *Excellence: Can We Be Equal and Excellent Too?* and *Self-Renewal: The Individual and the Innovative Society.* He was the editor of *To Turn the Tide,* a collection of speeches by former President John F. Kennedy.

OBITUARIES AND OTHER SOURCES:

PERIODICALS

Los Angeles Times, February 18, 2002, obituary by Myrna Oliver, p. B11.
New York Times, February 18, 2002, obituary by Robert D. McFadden, p. A16.
Washington Post, February 18, 2002, obituary by Richard Pearson, p. B6.

*   *   *

GATEWARD, Frances 1963-

PERSONAL: Born February 11, 1963, in Columbia, SC; daughter of Franklin L. and Won Yon (Kim) Gateward. *Ethnicity:* "African American/Asian." *Education:* Temple University, B.A., 1986; University of Maryland—College Park, M.A., 1989, Ph.D., 2000.

ADDRESSES: Office—Program in Film and Video Studies, University of Michigan, Ann Arbor, MI 48109.

CAREER: University of Michigan, Ann Arbor, assistant professor of film and video studies, 2001—.

WRITINGS:

(Editor) *Zhang Yimou: Interviews,* University Press of Mississippi (Jackson, MS), 2001.
(Editor with Murray Pomerance) *Sugar, Spice, and Everything Nice: Cinemas of Girlhood,* Wayne State University Press (Detroit, MI), 2002.

GENAUER, Emily 1911(?)-2002

OBITUARY NOTICE—Born July 19, 1911 (some sources cite 1910), in New York, NY; died August 23, 2002, in NY. Art critic, journalist, columnist, and author. Genauer is remembered for award-winning art criticism, particularly through her weekly column for the Newsday Syndicate for which she earned a Pulitzer Prize in 1974. Her career had begun nearly fifty years earlier, however, when she became a reporter and art critic for the *New York World.* Genauer was a vocal admirer of modern art and a supporter of newly emerging and little-known artists. Her respect for the work of then-controversial artists like Pablo Picasso and Diego Rivera was unequivocal; it was also sometimes unsettling to her employers, especially during the conservative, anti-communist years following World War II. Genauer worked successively for the *New York World-Telegram* and the *New York Herald Tribune,* finally joining the Newsday Syndicate in 1967. She also appeared as an art commentator on various television programs, including some thirteen years with the public television series *City Edition.* Her writings include biographies of artists Marc Chagall and Rufino Tamayo and critical works such as *Chagall at the Met.* Genauer's appreciation for the arts also extended to the world of modern dance; she was a board member of the Martha Graham School of Contemporary Dance and the School of Dance at Connecticut College.

OBITUARIES AND OTHER SOURCES:

PERIODICALS

Los Angeles Times, August 27, 2002, p. B11.
New York Times, August 26, 2002, obituary by Robert F. Worth, p. A17.
Washington Post, August 26, 2002, p. B4.

*   *   *

GENOVESE, Vincent J. 1945-

PERSONAL: Born September 10, 1945, in Minersville, PA; son of James (a coal miner) and Sophy (Duash) Genovese; married Geraldine Artz, February 1, 1969; children: Jennifer, Jason, Jody Genovese Kensey. *Ethnicity:* "Italian/American." *Education:* West Chester University, B.S., 1967; Kutztown University, M.S., 1968; also attended Lehigh University and Texas Tech University. *Politics:* "Registered Democrat (consider myself independent)." *Religion:* Roman Catholic. *Hobbies and other interests:* Fly-fishing, reading, travel.

ADDRESSES: Home and office—252 South Fourth St., Minersville, PA 17954. *E-mail*—vicandgeri@webtv. net.

CAREER: Worked as high school guidance counselor, 1968-99; retired. Also worked as personnel consultant and marriage counselor. Past member of board of directors for civic organizations.

WRITINGS:

The Angel of Ashland (biography), Prometheus Books (Amherst, NY), 2000.

WORK IN PROGRESS: Billy Heath: The Lazarus of Little Big Horn, "the stunning discovery of a man who survived Custer's last stand"; research on the life of Henry Pleasant, "the architect of the Civil War battle of Petersburg."

SIDELIGHTS: Vincent J. Genovese told *CA:* "My love for reading (all genres) probably gave me the motivation to start writing. I wrote *The Angel of Ashland* thirty-one years ago and left it to gather dust, feeling it was too controversial to print. By today's standards that sounds ludicrous. I have two novels completed that I will seek to publish in the near future. At the present all my energy is directed to getting my newest work on the shelves. *Billy Heath: The Lazarus of Little Big Horn* is an unbelievable (but true) story of one man, perhaps the only man, who survived the Battle of Little Big Horn. Though it is destined to be extremely controversial, I am determined (despite the opposition of the Custer scholars) to see it come to print."

*   *   *

GERMINO, Dante (Lee) 1931-2002

OBITUARY NOTICE—See index for *CA* sketch: Born June 9, 1931, in Durham, NC; died after being hit by a train May 25, 2002, in Amsterdam, Netherlands. Educator and author. Germino was a well-regarded professor of government. He graduated from Duke

University in 1952 with an A.B., and went on to Harvard University, where he received his Ph.D. in 1956. His first academic post was as an instructor at Wellesley College, where he eventually became an associate professor of political science from 1964 to 1966. After traveling to the University of Philippines as a Rockefeller Foundation visiting professor of government and foreign affairs, he joined the University of Virginia in 1968 and was a professor there at the time of his death. Germino was particularly well versed in Italian politics, writing about the subject in such books as *The Italian Fascist Party in Power* (1959) and *The Government of Italy,* written with Stefano Passigli (1968). During the 1960s Germino was an active political protester against Vietnam, and later also argued against the university's practice of having investments in South Africa, where apartheid was practiced. Some of his other publications include *Political Philosophy and the Open Society* (1982) and *Antonio Gramsci: Architect of a New Politics* (1990).

OBITUARIES AND OTHER SOURCES:

PERIODICALS

Washington Post, May 31, 2002, p. B6.

*   *   *

GIARD, Robert 1939-2002

OBITUARY NOTICE—Born July 22, 1939, in Hartford, CT; died July 16, 2002. Photographer. Giard became a professional photographer in 1971; his typical subjects were landscape and nude photography. After attending a play about the AIDS crisis in 1985, he dedicated his life to becoming what he once described to *CA* as "an archivist, a preservationist" of gay and lesbian life. For more than fifteen years, until the moment of his death on a bus trip to Chicago, Giard pursued his mission throughout the United States, collecting hundreds of photographs of gay and lesbian writers. His black-and-white portraits depict literary figures of the stature of Allen Ginsberg and Andrea Dworkin, and his subjects quite often posed informally among their most treasured possessions. Nearly two hundred of Giard's photographs were displayed in an exhibition at the New York Public Library and collected in the book *Particular Voices: Portraits of Gay and Lesbian Writers,* for which he received a Lambda Literary Award in 1997.

OBITUARIES AND OTHER SOURCES:

PERIODICALS

Los Angeles Times, July 29, 2002, p. B8.
New York Times, July 26, 2002, p. C15.

*   *   *

GRIFFITHS, Andy 1961-

PERSONAL: Born September 3, 1961, in Melbourne, Victoria, Australia; partner of Jill Groves (an editor); children: Jasmine, Sarah.

ADDRESSES: Agent—Fiona Inglis, Curtis Brown (Australia), P.O. Box 19, Paddington, New South Wales 2021, Australia; fax: (02) 9360 3935.

CAREER: Writer. Has worked as a musician, English teacher, and book editor and publisher.

AWARDS, HONORS: Victorian YABBA and New South Wales KOALA children's choice awards, both 1999, both for *Just Annoying!*

WRITINGS:

Progressive Rock Drumming: For Beginner to Advanced Student, Koala Publications (Costa Mesa, CA), 1990.
Swinging on the Clothesline, Longman (Melbourne, Victoria, Australia), 1993.
Rubbish Bins in Space, Longman (Melbourne, Victoria, Australia), 1995.
Just Annoying!, illustrated by Terry Denton, Pan Macmillan (Sydney, New South Wales, Australia), 1998.
Just Tricking!, illustrated by Terry Denton, Pan Macmillan (Sydney, New South Wales, Australia), 1998, published as *Just Kidding!,* Macmillan Children's Books (London, England), 2001.
Just Crazy!, illustrated by Terry Denton, Macmillan Children's Books (London, England), 2001.
Just Stupid!, illustrated by Terry Denton, Macmillan Children's Books (London, England), 2001.

The Day My Bum Went Psycho, Macmillan Children's Books (London, England), 2002.
Just Disgusting!, Pan Macmillan (Sydney, New South Wales, Australia), 2002.

Also author of "Stinky Stories" series illustrated by Jeff Raglus: *Banana Boy, Hamburger Man, Jelly Bean Girl,* and *Rose Petal Fairy;* editor of "Blasters" series of short-story anthologies, including *Fears and Fantasies, Animal Tails,* and *Risks and Challenges,* all 1997.

ADAPTATIONS: Just Tricking!, Just Stupid!, and *Just Annoying* were adapted for audio cassette, Bolinda Audio (Newport Beach, CA). The "Just" series of books was adapted for twenty-six segments of a half-hour animated television series called *What's with Andy?* by Cinegroupe for the TELETOON network in Canada.

WORK IN PROGRESS: Zombie Bums from Uranus, sequel to *The Day My Bum Went Psycho,* and *The One That Goes Kerching,* an adult novel about a father and his adventures as he tries to find an old toy cash register for his daughter.

SIDELIGHTS: With a 1920s Underwood typewriter he bought at a school "fête," Australian children's writer Andy Griffiths wrote his first published story when he was in year eight at school. Called "Lost in Time," it appeared in *Pursuit* magazine. Despite this early success, Griffiths was more interested in rock music and spent most of his creative talents in school writing rock songs. After high school when several of the punk rock bands he had formed disbanded, he decided to return to school and earned a degree in education. He then became an English high school teacher and editor and publisher of educational books focusing on English and writing.

The urge to write stories never left Griffiths however, and he returned to writing short stories when he became a stay-at-home dad in the early 1990s. When he tried to get a book of short stories published, eight publishers rejected it until one finally suggested turning it into a textbook with writing exercises. The result was *Swinging on the Clothesline,* which Griffiths followed with *Rubbish Bins in Space.* Both collections feature stories and writing exercises focusing on different genres, styles, and subject matter, all designed to inspire and stimulate students to write.

The books, which became widely used in schools throughout Australia, also incorporate large doses of humor, fun, and play, such as suggestions for annoying parents, instructions on riding spiders without getting bitten, and the real story behind the demise of dinosaurs. In these books, Griffiths focuses on eliminating routine, which he sees as the "greatest enemy" in the classroom. He writes in the introduction to *Rubbish Bins in Space:* "The teacher must be very vigilant for ways to shock that routine, to rediscover the freshness of the moment, to uncover the raw wonder lurking underneath the surface of the 'ordinary,' and to unleash the potential energy in the most predictable of response."

Griffiths is also the author of the "Just!" series of books, all illustrated by Terry Denton. The books are a series of short stories about the young Andy, billed as the world's greatest, craziest, most annoying, and most stupid practical joker. In *Just Tricking!,* the first in the series, Andy's adventures—which usually involve his best friend Danny—include playing dead so he can get out of school, convincing a friend that he's invisible, and getting stuck in a gorilla suit and nearly winding up in a zoo. In *Just Annoying!* Andy continues to annoy friends and family to the point that his parents dump him from their car and drive away. Writing in *Magpie,* Margaret Phillips noted: "I suspect Terry Denton and Andy Griffiths had a great time dreaming them [the stories] up and I suspect numerous readers are going to have a great time poring over them." In *Just Stupid!* Andy does . . . well . . . just stupid things, like cramming twenty marshmallows into his mouth. Commenting on Griffiths' "effective" use of the first person, present tense to tell the stories, Russ Merrin, writing in *Magpies,* noted that the style "lends immediacy to the author's conversational anecdotes. As the reader, you rather get the feeling that Andy's prank has only just happened a few minutes ago, and you have just stumbled into its aftermath." In a *Magpies* review of *Just Crazy!,* Neville Barnard commented on the basis of the success of the *Just!* Series of books: "As in most of the *Just . . .* series, the content of the stories is only a minor detail. It is the extravagant humour and imagery that Griffiths creates that ensnares the reader."

Griffiths created a new character for his juvenile novel *The Day My Bum Went Psycho,* the story of Zack Freeman and his crazy "runaway bum" that tries to unite all bums to conquer the world. Writing in the *Age,*

Michelle Griffin described the book as a "carefully plotted comedy thriller, one part Lara Croft adventure and two parts Monty Python daftness." The book also includes a glossary of "bum" terms, including "bum-plug," which is "used to cork bums for the purpose of harnessing their gas power," and "runaway bum," which is "a bum that has sprouted arms and legs, detached itself from its owner's body and run away." And, in case his readers are worried about the intentions of their own bums, Griffiths includes a test to determine whether their bums are "psycho," with questions like "Has your bum ever embarrassed you in public?"

Although *The Day My Bum Went Psycho* delighted young readers, it also gained attention from a more adult contingent and, as a result, made headline news throughout Australia and the British Broadcasting Corporation's (BBC) World Service. The book's cover photo featuring buttocks was used on a poster promoting Australia's National Literacy Week. Thinking it might be offensive to some people, the Department of Education, Training, and Youth Affairs decided to remove the poster from the campaign. As a result, Griffiths and his publisher decided to withdraw the book entirely from the campaign. The education minister eventually denied authorizing the ban and had the poster reinstated. "I always dreamed of being banned," Griffiths told Griffin. "I just didn't think it would be this easy." Griffiths went on to say: "It always annoyed me that children's literature has been so polite. The world of literature should be really wild and free like rock 'n' roll. That's where I take a lot of my inspiration. That's where I came from."

Although he enjoys writing for children, Griffiths is also planning on writing for adults. "I have to cut so much when I'm writing for kids to make it acceptable," Griffiths said in the *Age.* "I can think up really great plots, but they're too risky or grim. It's a fine line writing for kids."

In addition to his writing, Griffiths spends about six months a year fulfilling speaking engagements at schools throughout Australia. To make his presentation more interesting, he attended a stand-up comedy school. "I am driven," Griffiths said in the *Age* article. "I can never quite relax."

On his personal Web page, Griffiths ruminated about writing: "Why did I write then? Because it came easily, I guess, because it was a way of expressing myself, to entertain my friends, to shock, because it was a way of having fun." He goes on to say that he continues to write for the same reasons plus a few more such as "it's a way of making a living out of something I would do even if nobody was paying me and because I've discovered it's a way of staying awake—of keeping a small part of my mind detached and observing experience—it's a way of finding value in the most mundane and boring places and experiences—a way to recapture that childlike sense of wonder that can so easily get sidelined in the day-to-day grind of being a practical goal-oriented grownup."

As for his subject matter, Griffiths added: "I sometimes wonder if that's the writer's job—to have the courage to come out and say the things that other people only think."

BIOGRAPHICAL AND CRITICAL SOURCES:

PERIODICALS

Age (Melbourne, Victoria, Australia), September 8, 2001, Michelle Griffin, "The Bottom of the Matter."

Australian Book Review, November, 1998, Ruth Starke, "Infectious Laughter," p. 44.

Magpies, September, 1997, review of *Just Tricking!,* p. 33; September, 1998, Margaret Phillips, review of *Just Annoying!,* pp. 34-35; July, 1999, Russ Merrin, review of *Just Stupid!,* p. 24; November, 2000, Neville Barnard, review of *Just Crazy!,* pp. 33-34.

OTHER

Andy Griffiths Home Page, http://www.andygriffiths. com.au (September 12, 2002).*

　　　　　*　　*　　*

GUATTARI, Félix 1930-1992

PERSONAL: Born 1930; died 1992. *Education:* University study of pharmacology and philosophy; studied psychoanalysis with Jacques Lacan.

CAREER: Psychoanalyst. Associated with Clinique de la Borde, Courcheverney, France, beginning 1953; *Le voie communist,* editor, beginning 1958; *Recherches* (journal), founder. Member, Centre d'Initiative pour de Nouveaux Espaces de Liberté.

WRITINGS:

(With Mikel Dufresne and Marthe Robert) *Anthropologie,* Groupes d'études de philosophe de l'Université de Paris (Paris, France), 1966.

Psychoanalyse et transversalité: essais d'analyse instituitonnelle, Maspero (Paris, France), 1972.

(With Gilles Deleuze) *L'anti-oedipe: capitalisme et schizophrénie,* Minuit (Paris, France), 1972, translation by Robert Hurley, Mark Seem, and Helen R. Lane published as *Anti-Oedipus: Capitalism and Schizophrenia,* Viking (New York, NY), 1977.

(With Gilles Deleuze) *Kafka: pour un litterature mineure,* Minuit (Paris, France), 1975, translation by Marie Maclean published as *Kafka: Toward a Minor Literature,* Johns Hopkins University Press (Baltimore, MD), 1985.

(With Gilles Deleuze) *Rhizome: introduction,* Minuit (Paris, France), 1976, translation by John Johnston published as *On the Line,* Semiotext(e) (New York, NY), 1983.

La révolution moléculaire, Recherches (Fontenay-sous-Bois, France), 1977, translation by Rosemary Sheed published as *Molecular Revolution: Psychiatry and Politics,* Penguin (New York, NY), 1984.

(With Gilles Deleuze) *Politique et Psychoanalyse,* Des Mots Persus (France), 1977.

L'inconsicient machinique: essais de schizo-analyse, Recherches (Fontenay-sous-Bois, France), 1979.

(With Gilles Deleuze) *Mille plateaux: capitalisme et schizophrénie,* [France], 1980, translation by Brian Massumi published as *A Thousand Plateaus: Capitalism and Schizophrenia,* University of Minnesota Press (Minneapolis, MN), 1987.

(With others) *Les nouveaux espaces de liberté,* D. Bedou (Gourdon, France), 1985, translation by Michael Ryan published as *Communists like Us: New Spaces of Liberty, New Lines of Alliance,* Semiotext(e) (New York, NY), 1990.

(With Jean Oury and François Tosquelles) *Pratique de l'institutionnel et politque,* Matrice (Vigneux, France), 1985.

Les années d'hiver, 1980-1985, Barrault (Paris, France), 1986.

Traité de namadologie, [France], translation by Brian Massumi published as *Nomadology: The War Machine,* Semiotext(e) (New York, NY), 1986.

(With Suely Rolnik) *Micropolítca: cartografias do desejo* (in Portuguese), Vozes (Petrópolis, Portugal), 1986.

(With others) *Sarenco: la triptyque du cinéma mobile, 1983-1987,* H. Veyrier (Paris, France), 1988.

Cartographies schizoanalytiques, Galilée (Paris, France), 1989.

Les trois écologies, Galilée (Paris, France), 1989, translation by Ian Pindar and Paul Sutton published as *Three Ecologies,* Athlone Press (New Brunswick, NJ), 2000.

(With Gilles Deleuze) *Qu'est-ce que la philosophie?,* Minuit (Paris, France), 1991, translation by Hugh Tomlinson and Graham Burchell published as *What Is Philosophy?,* Columbia University Press (New York, NY), 1994.

Chaosmose, Galilée (Paris, France), 1992, translation by Paul Bains and Julian Pefanis published as *Chaosmosis: An Ethico-Aesthetic Paradigm,* Indiana University Press (Bloomington, IN), 1995, selections translated by Sylvère Lotringer as *Chaosophy,* Semiotext(e) (New York, NY), 1995.

The Guattari Reader, edited by Gary Genosko, Blackwell (Cambridge, MA), 1996.

Architettura della sparizione, architettura totale: spaesamenti metropolitani (in Italian), Mimesis (Milan, Italy), 1996.

Piano sul pianeta: captitale mondiale integrato e globalizzazione (in Italian), Ombre Corte (Verona, Italy), 1997.

Author's works have been translated into other languages, including Japanese, English, German, Spanish, Italian, and Portuguese.

SIDELIGHTS: Psychoanalyst and philosopher-turned-activist Félix Guattari began his political life as a member of a French Trotskyist splinter group. He worked for a time with the French Communist Party before breaking these political ties to edit the dissident newspaper *La voie communiste* in 1958. Ian Pindar, writing in the *Times Literary Supplement,* noted that by 1968 Guattari "was an active supporter of the student-worker alliance" and was "described as embodying the spirit of the 1960s." During the 1960s

Guattari joined forces with his longtime collaborator, Gilles Deleuze; the two of them would produce several influential works.

Indeed, Guattari and Deleuze became something of a philosophical package-deal. They were, in Pindar's words, "the Odd Couple of twentieth-century thought: [Deleuze] a reclusive professor of philosophy, married with two children, and [Guattari] a militant, homosexual activist-intellectual who insisted on making a noise." For the two, collaboration provided a "kind of collective memory," as Pindar quoted them as once remarking. They even saw themselves as two sides of the same figure, once noting that the only reason they kept their real names was "habit, purely out of habit." While Deleuze cast the longer shadow of the pair, toward the end of Guattari's life he was sometimes referred to as an "accompanist rather than . . . accomplice," according to Pindar.

Guattari and Deleuze are credited with four influential philosophical works. The first, *L'anti-oedipe: capitalisme et schizophrénie,* was released in 1972 to acclaim and controversy. *L'anti-oedipe* takes up the cause of French postmodern psychoanalyst Jacques Lacan, who was famous for his staunch criticism of American psychological methods and with whom Guattari had studied. The root of the work is the Oedipus complex, a psychological condition characterized by the impulse of a small boy to kill his father and sexually possess his mother. "The theory of anti-Oedipus rests on the concept of a machinic universe and the recognition of a machinic self," explained *Seton Hall Law Review* writer Steven Carras. "It is a machine whose function is not to function, and whose longevity is determined not by the flawless movement of its durable parts, but rather by the constant disruption of the operation."

L'anti-oedipe has been viewed as a critique of modern social and institutional structures. In the authors' view, twentieth-century men and women were allowed to take a new direction, eschewing traditional roles and becoming "nomads" constantly in a state of transformation. A *Times Literary Supplement* writer described *L'anti-oedipe* as an "attack on the 'familialisme' of psychoanalysis, which obsessively reduces the whole of psychic life to a 'dirty secret,' involved with our immediate family and its smallest cell," that being the mother, father, and child. "But a secret is constituted not by its subject-matter, but by the fact that it is not told; since this is an important

theme in the book, one must not give the impression that psychology can be simply disposed of by sweeping it under the carpet."

Guattari and Deleuze's *Mille plateaux: capitalisme et schizophrénie* bears the same subtitle as *Anti-oedipe.* In *Mille plateaux,* translated as *A Thousand Plateaus: Capitalism and Schizophrenia,* the authors argue that capitalism is a form of mental illness because within it a person's worth is gauged by their profitability as opposed to criteria based upon their participation in church, family, or community. To Sander Gilman, writing in *Journal of Interdisciplinary History, Mille plateaux* "simply replaces one dogma (Marxism) with another, even more confining one (psychoanalysis)." Despite his criticism of the authors' viewpoint, Gilman concluded that *A Thousand Plateaus* "provides much material for thought. . . . It is full of insights which anger, such as [the authors'] discussion of the delusional structure of psychosis without any empathy for the psychic pain which these delusions represent But it is also full of brilliant insights, such as their rereading of Levi-Straus' image of the tool in psychological terms."

Guattari produced other notable books, including *Les trois écologies* and *Qu'st-ce que la philosophie?,* before his death in 1992. Longtime collaborator Deleuze committed suicide three years later. According to Pindar, the two men were "more talked about than read, more misrepresented than understood, which they would probaby regard as no bad thing. They never tired of inisting that their work doesn't mean anything."

BIOGRAPHICAL AND CRITICAL SOURCES:

PERIODICALS

Artforum International, summer, 1994, John Rajchman, review of *What Is Philosophy?,* p. S22.

Choice, December, 1994, review of *What Is Philosophy?,* p. 614; September, 2001, M. Uebel, review of *The Three Ecologies,* p. 132.

College Literature, winter, 1994, Stanley Corngold, "Kafka and the Dialect of Minor Literature," pp. 89-101.

Cultural Studies, April, 2000, J. Macgregor Wise, "Home: Territory and Identity," p. 295.

Hypatia, spring, 1999, Pelagia Goulimari, "A Minoritarian Feminism? Things to Do with Deleuze and Guattari," p. 97.

Journal of Interdisciplinary History, spring, 1989, Sander Gilman, review of *A Thousand Plateaus: Capitalism and Schizophrenia,* p. 657.

Modern Fiction Studies, summer, 1987, Clayton Koelb, review of *Kafka: Toward a Minor Literature,* pp. 376-378.

New Statesman, September 2, 1994, Roger Caldwell, review of *What Is Philosophy?,* p. 37.

Partisan Review, fall, 1988, William Phillips, "Kafka and His Text," p. 675.

Philosophy Today, winter, 2001, Bruce Janz, "The Territory Is Not the Map," p. 392.

Seton Hall Law Review, spring, 1984, Steven Carras, review of *Anti-Oedipus: Capitalism and Schizophrenia,* p. 477.

Times Literary Supplement, March 16, 1973, "In the Factory of the Unconscious," p. 295; June 23, 1995, Paul Patton, review of *What Is Philosophy?,* pp. 10-12; January 2, 1998, Ian Pindar, review of *The Guattari Reader,* p. 7; April 27, 2001, Robin Buss, review of *The Three Ecologies,* p. 33.

OTHER

Deleuze & Guattari on the Web, http://www.uta.edu/ english/ (May 8, 2002), Charles Stivale, "Pragmatic/Machinic" (interview).

Sociology Online, http://www.sociologyonline.co.uk/ (July 16, 2002).*

*   *   *

GUTERL, Matthew Pratt 1970-

PERSONAL: Born June 15, 1970, in Somerville, NJ; son of Robert Edward (a judge) and Sheryl Pratt (a teacher and guidance counselor) Guterl; married Sandra Latcha (a dental hygienist), September 16, 1995. *Education:* Richard Stockton College of New Jersey, B.A., 1993; Rutgers University, Ph.D., in U.S. history, 1999. *Politics:* "Radical Contrarian." *Religion:* Catholic.

ADDRESSES: Home—21 Grant Ave., Somerville, NJ 08876. *Office*—Center for the Study of Race and Ethnicity in America, Brown University, Dyer House, 150 Power St., Providence, RI 02912-1886. *E-mail*—matthewguterl@cs.com.

CAREER: St. John's University, adjunct assistant professor, department of history, 1999-2000; Brown University, teaching and research fellow, 2001—; Washington State University, assistant professor, department of comparative American cultures, 2000—.

MEMBER: Washington State University scholarship committee, College of Liberal Arts, and curriculum and publicity committees, Department of Comparative American Cultures.

AWARDS, HONORS: Black Atlantic Project fellowship, Rutgers Center for Historical Analysis, 1997-98; dissertation fellowship, Rutgers University, 1997-98; predoctoral fellowship, National Museum of American History, Smithsonian Institution, 1998; excellence fellowship, Rutgers University, 1998, associate postdoctoral fellowship in the Slavery Abolition, and Resistance Program, Yale University, 2001; Andrew W. Mellon Foundation fellowship, 2001; postdoctoral fellowship, Center for the Study of Race and Ethnicity in America, Brown University, 2001-03; grants from American Historical Association, 2000, John Hope Franklin Research Center for African and African-American Documentation, Duke University, 2001, and Washington State University, 2001.

WRITINGS:

The Color of Race in America 1900-1940, Harvard University Press (Cambridge, MA), 2001.

Also contributed article "The New Race-Consciousness: Race, Nation, and Empire in American Culture," to *Journal of World History,* September, 1999; contributed chapter to *Fear Itself: Enemies Real and Imagined in American Culture,* edited by Nancy L. Schultz, Purdue University Press, 1998.

WORK IN PROGRESS: A World without Slaves: Race and Work in the Age of Emancipation, for Harvard University Press (Cambridge, MA), 2006.

SIDELIGHTS: Matthew Pratt Guterl has spent most of his academic career examining the complex issues surrounding racial identity in the United States. His doctoral dissertation at Rutgers University was titled *Investing in Color: A Cultural History of Race in*

Modern America, 1910-1940, and he has presented papers at conferences on topics concerning Asian, Irish, and African laborers in America and their relationships with various aspects of U.S. culture.

Guterl has also published articles examining the subject, including "After Slavery: Asian Labor, Immigration, and Emancipation in the United States and Cuba, 1940-1880" and "The New Race-Consciousness: Race, Nation, and Empire in American Culture, 1910-1930," both in the *Journal of World History.*

His book, *The Color of Race in America, 1900-1940,* explores how concepts of race developed in the early twentieth century. Thomas J. Davis wrote in *Library Journal,* "In four notably nuanced essays, Guterl suggests a parallel between U.S. problems of racial classification at the turn of the 20th and 21st centuries." Vernon Ford commented in *Booklist,* "Guterl . . . highlights the lives and work of a number of personalities during the early part of the twentieth century who reflect the transformation of racial identity in the U.S."

The essays in *The Color of Race in America, 1900-1940* concentrate primarily on four New Yorkers: Daniel Cohalan, an Irish-American nationalist prominent in New York politics; Madison Grant, an eugenicist and white supremacist principally opposed to southern and eastern European immigrants; W. E. B. Du Bois, the famous African-American intellectual-turned-Marxist; and mixed-race novelist Jean Toomer, who struggled against the label affixed to him as a black man. A reviewer for the *Economist* said, "Race here is a much broader idea than the simple two-term notion derived from considering just black-white relations."

BIOGRAPHICAL AND CRITICAL SOURCES:

PERIODICALS

Booklist, September 1, 2001, Vernon Ford, review of *The Color of Race in America, 1900-1940,* p. 256.
Economist, April 6, 2002, review of *The Color of Race in America, 1900-1940.*
Library Journal, October 15, 2001, Thomas J. Davis, review of *The Color of Race in America, 1900-1940,* pp. 91-92.*

GUTMANN, Stephanie

PERSONAL: Born in Chicago, IL. *Education:* Roosevelt University, B.A.; Columbia University, M.A. (journalism).

ADDRESSES: Agent—c/o Author Mail, Simon & Schuster, 1230 Avenue of the Americas, New York, NY 10020.

CAREER: New York Post, New York, NY, former reporter; also former staff member for the *Wilkes-Barre, Times Leader,* and *Los Angeles Times.*

WRITINGS:

The Kinder, Gentler Military: Can America's Gender-Neutral Fighting Force Still Win Wars?, Scribner (New York, NY), 2000.

Contributor to periodicals, including *Cosmopolitan, New Republic, Newsday, Penthouse, Playboy, New York Times,* and *Washington Post.*

SIDELIGHTS: Journalist Stephanie Gutmann is the author of *The Kinder, Gentler Military: Can America's Gender-Neutral Fighting Force Still Win Wars?,* in which she argues, as a *Publishers Weekly* reviewer noted, that "the U.S. military has been seriously handicapped by attempts to integrate women into the fighting force." Gutmann, however, summarized the book, in a *Book Notes* interview, as "mostly a look at what the . . . often called new military looks like." She added, "I really wanted people to see."

In *The Kinder, Gentler Military,* Gutmann writes that training-camp standards have been modified to allow for the allegedly inferior strength and stamina of female trainees. She also reports on the military's own discovery that hospitalization rates increased tenfold with female recruits. Gutmann's aim, however, is not to advocate a ban on female soldiers. "She does not oppose the presence of women in the military, she says," observed a *Chicago Tribune* writer. "She only quarrels with the turbo-charged zeal with which the services . . . have pursued gender neutrality and President Clinton's desire for a force that looks like America." In the book, Gutmann calls for sexual segregation in training, and she recommends the dropping of recruitment quotas based on sexes. The *Publishers Weekly* critic described the proposals as "common-sense solutions" but conceded that Gutmann "is not subtle in making her argument."

Upon its publication in 2000, *The Kinder, Gentler Military* received recognition as a compelling analysis of the American military with regard to female soldiers. *Commentary* reviewer Francis Fukuyama hailed the book as "first-rate reporting on the reality of the contemporary military," and Cathy Young wrote in *National Review* that Gutmann's work constitutes a "passionate polemic, based on research and observation." But not all reviewers were entirely impressed. *Nation* reviewer Michael Kimmel, for example, called *The Kinder, Gentler Military* a "shrill and strident antifeminist polemic." Some critics noted the book's potential to spark debate. Cathy Young, for example, concluded her *National Review* appraisal by stating that "it is to be hoped that [*The Kinder, Gentler Military*] . . . will reinject some tough questions into the often sugercoated discussion of women in the military, even if the answers may be different from the ones proposed here." Don Feder, in a *Town Hall* online piece, was more vigorous in his support of Gutmann's analysis: "Now, the warrior culture is dying," he declared. "Feminists, sensitivity trainers . . . are tugging on the life supports." He ended his article by stating: "National security will be the ultimate casualty. Try fighting the next war with troops who are used to calling a time-out when they're stressed."

Gutmann, meanwhile, observed, in a *National Review* interview that change is already occurring within the military. "I think we have already started cycling back to a more traditional military in one sense: A lot of women tried the military in the early '90s when there was such a huge push," she contended. "A lot of women tried it and weren't so crazy about it. They are also not jumping into the sort of vaunted jobs that supposedly they were pining for—the jobs that are closer to combat."

BIOGRAPHICAL AND CRITICAL SOURCES:

PERIODICALS

Commentary, February 2000, Francis Fukuyama, "G. I. Jane."
Nation, June 19, 2000, Michael Kimmel, "Janey Got Her Gun."
National Review, April 17, 2000, Cathy Young, "Killing Me Softly."
Publishers Weekly, February 7, 2000, review of *The Kinder, Gentler Military: Can America's Gender-Neutral Fighting Force Still Win Wars?*, p. 76.
Wilson Quarterly, summer, 2000, Andrew J. Bacevich, review of *The Kinder, Gentler Military*, p. 135.

OTHER

Book Notes, http://ww.booknotes.org/ (June 15, 2001), Brian Lamb, interview with Stephanie Gutmann.
Chicago Tribune, http://chicagotribune.com/ (April 5, 2000), "Don't Blame Women for the Ills of the Military."
Home, http://home.satx.rr.com (June 15, 2001), review of *The Kinder, Gentler Military*.
Town Hall, http://www.townhall.com/ (June 14, 2000), Don Feder, "Death of Warrior Culture Dooms Military."
National Review, http://www.nationalreview.com/ (April 7, 2000), Kate Dwyer, "Stephanie Gutmann Says."*

H

HAAG, Herbert 1915-2001

PERSONAL: Born 1915 in Singen, Germany; died August 23, 2001, in Lucerne, Switzerland; buried in Lucerne, Switzerland. *Education:* University of Fribourg, Switzerland, doctorate. *Religion:* Roman Catholic.

CAREER: Priest, theologian, educator, and author. Ordained Catholic priest, 1940; University of Lucerne, Lucerne, Switzerland, professor of theology, 1948-60; University of Tübingen, Tübingen, Germany, professor of Old Testament, 1960-80.

AWARDS, HONORS: Prix Courage, 2000.

WRITINGS:

Was lehrt die literarische Untersuchung des Ezechiel-Textes? Eine philologisch-theologische Studie, Paulusdruckerei (Freiburg, Switzerland), 1943.

Biblische Schöpfungslehre und kirchliche Erbsündenlehre, Verlag Katholisches Bibelwerk (Stuttgart, Germany), 1966, translations by Dorothy Thompson published as *Is Original Sin in Scripture?,* Sheed and Ward (New York, NY), 1969.

Bibel-Lexikon, Benziger (Zürich, Switzerland), 1968.

(Editor, with Franz Peter Möhres) *Ursprung und Wesen des Menschen,* Mohr (Tübingen, Germany), 1968.

Abschied vom Teufel, Benziger (Zürich, Switzerland), 1969.

Der Tag ist Nahe: Adventsgedanken, Rex-Verlag (Lucerne, Switzerland), 1969.

Er tut kund sein Wort, Rex-Verlag (Lucerne, Switzerland), 1970.

Gelten die Zehn Gebote noch?, Rex-Verlag (Lucerne, Switzerland), 1970.

Biblisches Wörterbuch, Herderbücherei (Freiburg, Germany), 1971.

Menschen im Alten Testament, Verlag Katholisches Bibelwerk (Stuttgart, Germany), 1971.

Vom alten zum neuen Pascha: Geschichte und Theologie des Osterfestes, KBW Verlag (Stuttgart, Germany), 1971.

Gott und Mensch in den Psalmen, Benziger (Zürich, Switzerland), 1972.

Teufelsglaube, with articles by Katharina Elliger, Bernhard Lang, and Meinrad Limbeck, Katzmann (Tübingen, Germany), 1974.

Das Land der Bibel: Gestalt, Geschichte, Erforschung, Pattloch (Aschaffenburg, Germany), 1976.

(With Katharina Elliger and Winfried Elliger) *Vor dem Bösen ratlos?,* R. Piper (Munich, Germany), 1978.

Des Buch des Bundes: Aufsätze zur Bibel und zu ihrer Welt (article collection), edited by Bernhard Lang, Patmos Verlag (Düsseldorf, Germany), 1980.

(With Hans Küng and Norbert Greinacher) *Der Fall Küng: ein Dokumentation,* Piper (Zürich, Switzerland), 1980.

Du hast mich verzaubert: Liebe unde Sexualität in der Bibel, Benziger (Zürich, Switzerland), 1980.

Der Gottesknecht bei Deuterojasaja, Wissenschaftliche Buchgesellschaft (Darmstadt, Germany), 1985.

Stört nicht die Liebe: die Diskriminierung der Sexualität: ein Verrat an der Bibel, Walter-Verlag (Olten, Germany), 1986.

Mein Weg mit der Kirche, with an afterword by Rudolf Zihlmann, Benziger (Zürich, Switzerland), 1991.

Den Christen die Freiheit: Erfahrungen und widerspenstige Hoffnungen, Herder (Freiburg, Germany), 1995.

Am Morgen der Zeit: das Hohelied der Schöpfung, with photographs by Werner Richner, second edition, Verlag Benziger (Düsseldorf, Germany), 1995, translation by Hans Küng of original edition published as *The God of the Beginnings and of Today,* in *The Unknown God?,* Sheed and Ward (New York, NY), 1967.

Worauf es ankommt: wollte Jesus eine Zwei-Stande-Kirche?, Herder (Freiburg, Germany), 1997, translation by Robert Nowell published as *Upstairs, Downstairs: Did Jesus Want a Two-Class Church?,* Crossroad Publications (New York, NY), 1997.

Nur wer sich ändert, bleibt sich true; für eine Verfassung der katholischen Kirche, Herder (Freiburg, Germany), 2000.

SIDELIGHTS: Herbert Haag was a Swiss theologian and Old Testament scholar who argued that one need not be ordained as a priest to celebrate the Catholic Mass. He also campaigned for the ordination of women and for the right of priests to marry. His views made him a controversial figure in the Catholic Church.

Haag studied philosophy, languages, and Asian culture before earning a doctoral degree in theology at the University of Fribourg, Switzerland. He was ordained as a priest in the diocese of Basel, Switzerland in 1940, and taught theology in Lucerne, Switzerland from 1948 to 1960, and in Tübingen, Germany from 1960 to 1980.

In 1966 Haag published *Biblische Schöpfungslehre und kirchliche Erbsündenlehre,* which was translated in 1969 into English as *Is Original Sin in Scripture?* The book examines the Catholic doctrine of original sin, and concludes that there is no scriptural basis for this teaching. The belief, according to Haas, is based on early interpretations of scripture, not what the scriptures actually say. In *Choice,* a reviewer noted that the implications of this finding are "enormous" and that the book should be read by "all students of scripture." In *America,* Dennis Hamm wrote, "although

Haag's treatment of the question is extremely brief, his ample notes lead the reader to the pertinent literature available in German, French and English."

Haag wrote an open letter to Swiss newspapers in 1981 that defended Hans Küng, a controversial Catholic theologian who had challenged church doctrine. Because of his controversial views, Küng had been deprived by Pope John Paul II of his right to teach as a Catholic theologian.

In 1985 Haag created the Herbert Haag Foundation with the goal of fostering openness in the church. The foundation supported organizations that opposed priestly celibacy, as well as those opposing church rules that did not allow women to be priests.

In 1997 Haag published *Worauf es ankommt: wollte Jesus eine Zwei-Stande-Kirche?,* which was translated the same year into English as *Upstairs, Downstairs: Did Jesus Want a Two-Class Church?* The book examines the historical origins of the separation between clergy and lay people in the Catholic Church. Haag contended that this separation is at the root of many problems in the church, and that this rigid separation should be abolished. Haag's conclusions are based on his examination of scripture, which show that the notion of an ordained ministry is a historical development that is not based in biblical authority; it is also contradicted by the actions of Jesus, who did not differentiate between his disciples and other people. Haag also examines the role of ordinary people in the church, noting that the church reforms instigated by Vatican II did not really address this issue. In *Catholic Library World,* Lucien Richard wrote that the book is "challenging" and that although it is obviously "one-sided," it provides "important insights on an important debate in the Church."

In reaction to Haag's contention that ordained priests are not necessary to celebrate Mass, the Swiss Bishops Conference issued a declaration stating that the conference officially withdrew its confidence in Haag. Kurt Koch, bishop of Basel, Switzerland, said that Haag's opinions were "self-centered and destructive," according to Eric Pace in an obituary for Haag in the *New York Times.*

In contrast, Haag received the Swiss Prix Courage in 2000 in recognition of his controversial views. The prize is awarded annually to a person who shows heroism or courage in everyday life. Haag died in 2001 after a short illness. He was buried in Lucerne, Switzerland.

BIOGRAPHICAL AND CRITICAL SOURCES:

PERIODICALS

America, April 12, 1969, Dennis Hamm, review of *Is Original Sin in Scripture?,* p. 454.
Catholic Library World, September, 1999, Lucien Richard, review of *Upstairs, Downstairs: Did Jesus Want a Two-Class Church?,* p. 38.
Choice, January, 1970, review of *Is Original Sin in Scripture?,* p. 1590.
Religious Studies Review, July, 1981, David Jobling, review of *Das Buch des Bundes: Aufsätze zur Bibel und zu ihrer Welt,* p. 253; January, 1997, Marvin A. Sweeney, review of *Des Gottesknecht bei Deuterojasaja,* p. 59.
Swiss News, November, 2000, Michael Maupin, "Prix Courage," p. 5.

OBITUARIES:

PERIODICALS

National Catholic Reporter, September 7, 2001, p. 10.
New York Times, August 30, 2001, Eric Pace, "Herbert Haag, 86, Priest Who Challenged Vatican," p. A17.*

*   *   *

HAMEIRI, Avigdor 1890(?)-1970

PERSONAL: Born c. 1890, in Hungary; died 1970.

CAREER: Writer, poet, translator, and journalist. *Military service:* Austro-Hungarian Army, World War I.

WRITINGS:

Mi-shire Avigdor Foyershtayn: kovets rishon, J. Schlesinger (Budapest, Hungary), 1911.
(Coauthor, with Josef Milet) *Kibuts galuyot apotiyozah,* defus ha-Po'el ha-Tsayir (Tel Aviv, Israel), 1920, published as *Kibuts galuyot apotiyozah le-*

Yom ha-zikaron ha-'esrim le-nishmat Dr. Hertsl, Hotsa'at Kupat ha-sefer veha-Keren ha-kayemet le-Yisra'el (Tel Aviv, Israel), 1980.
Lev hadash, [Tel Aviv, Israel], 1921.
Hazon ha-adam, A. Y. Stibl, 1924.
Halev em: 663-669, Haktav (Jerusalem, Israel), 1925.
Tahat shamayim adumim. Sipure Milhamah 1, Hotsa'at "ha-Ketav" (Jersualem, Israel), 1925.
Shire Avigdor Hame'iri, Hotsa'at "ha-Ketav" (Jersualem, Israel), 1925.
Keshet Ya'akov, sipure milhamah 2, Hotsa'at "ha-Ketav" (Jersualem, Israel), 1925.
'Ets ha-sadeh: sipur, P. Ginzberg (Tel Aviv, Israel), 1926.
Be-shem Rabi Yeshu mi-Aatseret: sipure milhamah III, Hotsa'at "le-ma'an ha-sefer" mi-ta'am Va'ad "ha-ketav" (Jerusalem, Israel), 1928.
Ha-Shiga'on ha-gadol: reshimot katsin 'Ivr ba-milhamah ha-gedolah, "Mitspeh" (Tel Aviv, Israel), 1928, reprinted, Devir (Tel Aviv, Israel), 1989.
Ben shine ha-adam: re'ini'-Odesah 679-680, Hotsa'at "Hashahar" (Tel Aviv, Israel), 1929.
Sefer ha-shirim, 'Am-ha-sefer (Tel Aviv, Israel), 1931-32.
Be-gehinom shel matah: reshimot ketsin 'Ivri bi-shevi Rusyah, Mistpeh (Tel Aviv, Israel), 1932, reprinted, Devir (Tel Aviv, Israel), 1989.
Tenuvah, roman, Hotsa'at "Mitspeh" (Tel Aviv, Israel), 1933.
Hokhmat ha-behemot (children's stories), illustrated by Aryeh Navon, Hotsa'at "erets" (Tel Aviv, Israel), 1933, reprinted, 1982.
Shirat ha-damim: kovets shirim . . . 'al me'ora'ot 696, Hots'at Sifrut la-'am (Tel Aviv, Israel), 1936.
'Al ha-dam, Lev hadash (Tel Aviv, Israel), 1936.
Ha-Mukhsharim anu le-malkhut?, [Tel Aviv, Israel], 1937.
Li-kerat medinah ivrit o galut Yehuday?, Hotsa'at "ha-Mahar mi-ta'am ha-Sifriyah da'at (Tel Aviv, Israel), 1937.
Masa' be-Eropha ha-pera'it: (rishmi-egev anakroniyim), Va'ad ha-Yovel (Tel Aviv, Israel), 1938.
Pinokyo be-erets Yisra'el, Mitspah (Tel Aviv, Israel), 1940.
Ha-'Ivri ha-kadmon, "Yavneh" (Tel Aviv, Israel), 1942.
Ben lailah le-lailah, novelot (short stories), Yavneh (Tel Aviv, Israel), 1944.
Ha-Moked ha-ran: shirim (poetry), Mosad Byalik 'al-yede Devir (Tel Aviv, Israel), 1944.

Halomot shel bet raban: mahazor shirim, Sifriyat po'alim (Merhavyah, Israel), 1945.

Sheker: Sipur, Yedi'ot aharonot (Hefah, Israel), 1946.

Ha-Mashiah ha-lavan: roman, Y. Sreberk (Tel Aviv, Israel), 1947.

Frantsisko Goya; 32 temunot be-tseruf mavo u-ve'urim, Sinai (Tel Aviv, Israel), 1949.

Ha-Yekum: Astronomiyah la-no'ar vela-kol: 'im temunot ve-tsiurim (astronomy), Hotsa'at Sinay (Tel Aviv, Israel), 1950.

Yeladim ve-hagim be Yisra'el, illustrated by Miryam Bartov, Sinai (Tel Aviv, Israel), 1950.

Ha-Guf ha-ge'oni: sipurim, 'Ayin (Tel Aviv, Israel), 1951.

Ha-Mahapekhah be-ya'ar-'ad: 'eser ma'aiyot u-ma'asiyah . . . (juvenile; title means "The Jungle Revolt"), illustrated by Shemuel Katz, N. Tverski (Tel Aviv, Israel), 1951, reprinted, Misrad ha-bitahon (Tel Aviv, Israel), 1980.

Ha-Impresyonim: 32 temunot 'im mavo u-ve'urim, Sinai (Tel Aviv, Israel), 1951.

Omanut Sin-Yapan 32 temunot be-tseruf mavo u-ve'urim, Sinai (Tel Aviv, Israel), 1951.

The Great Madness, translated by Jacob Freedman, Vantage Press (New York, NY), 1952, new edition translated by Yael Lotan, Or-Ron (Haifa, Israel), 1984.

Maks Liberman: 32 temunot be-tseruf mavo u-ve'urim, Sinai (Tel Aviv, Israel), 1952.

(Coauthor, with Margot Klausner) *Mekorot ha-dramah,* Masadah (Tel Aviv, Israel), 1953.

Mivhar sipure Avigdor Hame'iri, 'Idit (Tel Aviv, Israel), 1954.

Sodo shel Sokrates: roman me-tekufat Yavan ha'atikah, 'Idit (Tel Aviv, Israel), 1955.

Ashre ha-gafrur: hazon ha-gevurah veha-tehilah shel Hanah Senesh: Mahazeh be-sheva' hitgaluyot (play), Hotsa'at "Niv" (Tel Aviv, Israel), 1958.

Be-livnat ha-sapir: shirim (vocalized poetry), Bialik Institute (Jerusalem, Israel), 1962.

Yosili Teglashi: shir-gevurah (poems), Masadah (Ramat Gan, Israel), 1967.

Sipurai ha-milhamah, 'Am 'oved (Tel Aviv, Israel), 1970.

Ha-Guf ha-ge'oni: (16 sipurim) (short stories), Ketsin hinukh rasshi, 'Anaf hasbarah, Misra ha-bitahon (Tel Aviv, Israel), 1951.

TRANSLATOR

Rudolf Erich Raspe, *Mase ha-Baron ish Minkhhozen ve-mots'otav* (title means "The Adventures of Baron Munchausen"), Hotsa'at Omanut (Frankfurt an Main, Germany), 1900.

Imre Madách, *Hazon ha-adam,* A. Y. Stibl, 1924.

Max Brod, *Harpatkah be-Yhapan: roman,* Masadah be-siyu'a Mosad Byalik (Tel Aviv, Israel), 1943.

(With Rapheal Patai) Jószsef Patai, *Hotsa'at ha-yovel shel mivhar kitve Yosef Patai,* Yavneh (Tel Aviv, Israel), 1943.

Malka Locker, *ha'Olam le-lo shomer,* [Tel Aviv, Israel], 1945.

Raphael Mahler, *Toldo ha-Yehudim be-Polin: 'ad ha-me'ah ha-19 . . . ,* Sifiyat po'alim (Merhavyah, Israel), 1946.

Vladimir Talaktionovich Korolenko, *Yalde ha-martef,* Yizre'el (Tel Aviv, Israel), 1948.

Heinrich Heine, *Ne'imot 'Ivriyot,* Sinai (Tel Aviv, Israel), 1949.

Stefan Zweig, *Yirmeyahu: piyut deramati be-tesha'temunot,* ha-Mahiakah le-'inyene ha-no'ar veha-haluts shel ha-Histradrut ha-tsiyonit (Jerusalem, Israel), 1949.

Sándor Petofi, *Mi-shire Sandor Petefi,* Hotsa'at Sinai, 1952.

George Barath, *ha-Historyah mitpalelet,* Defus "Nesher" (Jerusalem, Israel), 1954.

Albert Katz, *Ba'ale terisin me-haye ha-kedushah veha-hulin shel gedole 'amenu bi-tekufat ha-Talmud,* P. Feldhaym (New York, NY), 1956.

Bo'u le-ekhol: sipur katan le-yalde ha-gan (juvenile), illustrated by Miryam Bartov, Sinai (Tel Aviv, Israel), 1957.

Mór Jókai, *I ha-osher: korot helek tevel ha-shishi she-yarad tehomah,* Yosef Sreberk (Tel Aviv, Israel), 1960.

Bela Szenes, *Ts'ibi,* ha-Kibuts ha-me'uhad (Tel Aviv, Israel), 1976.

(With Hannah Senesh and Itamar Ya'oz-Kest), *Le-lo safah: shirim* (vocalized poems), ha-Kibuts ha-me'uhad (Tel Aviv, Israel), 1978.

Author and translator of lyrics for musical scores. Stories and poetry have appeared in anthologies, including *Hatne Peras Yisra'el: mivhar sipurim* (stories), Misrad ha-hinukh veha-tarbut, be-shitfu Yahdav (Jerusalem, Israel), 1970, and *Fogóddz a semmibe: lágerversek* (poetry), Eked (Tel Aviv, Israel), 1989.

Contributor to Hebrew periodicals.

ADAPTATIONS: Many of Hameiri's poems have been set to music.

SIDELIGHTS: Hebrew poet, writer, and translator Avigdor Hameiri was born in Hungary and moved to Palestine in 1921. A leading intellectual in the Yashuv (the early Jewish settlement in Palestine) and a staunch anti-communist, he wrote several novels. He was one of the first Hebrew poets considered to be an "Expressionist," and his poems often depict the trials and suffering of the Jewish people. Many of his poems have been set to music.

Hameiri served in the Austro-Hungarian Army during World War I, was captured by the Russians, and became a prisoner of war. *The Great Madness,* Hameiri's autobiographical war novel, takes place in Austrian Galicia (Poland). Hameiri often wrote about Jews who had to fight other peoples' war and how they often were the scapegoat. His novel *Be-gehinom shel matah* is about a Jewish officer in World War II in the Soviet Union. In addition to poetry and novels, Hameiri wrote many short stories and books for children. Writing in *Booklist,* Sylvia S. Goldberg said that in Hameiri's collection *Sipurai ha-milhamah,* the short stories "present a frightening image" of the war. Goldberg also noted that Hameiri's stories "admirably capture the tragedy experienced by Jewish soldiers who fought in World War I."

BIOGRAPHICAL AND CRITICAL SOURCES:

PERIODICALS

Booklist, July 15, 1972, Sylvia S. Goldberg, review of *Sipurai ha-milhamah,* p. 981.

OTHER

Avigdor Hameiri Reading His Poems and a Short Story in Hebrew in the Recording Laboratory, July 18, 1952, Archive of Recorded Poetry and Literature, Library of Congress (Washington, DC), 1952.*

*　　　*　　　*

HAMILTON, Virginia (Esther) 1936-2002

OBITUARY NOTICE—See index for *CA* sketch: Born March 12, 1936, in Yellow Springs, OH; died of breast cancer February 19, 2002, in Dayton, OH. Author. Hamilton wrote more than thirty children's books that covered many genres, from mysteries, science fiction, and mainstream fiction to biographies and collections of folk tales. What critics and readers alike appreciated in her fiction was that her characters were African-American children living in a mainstream world. Her focus was less on African-American issues and more on the universal issues that affect all young people, whatever race they happen to be. She gave African-American children a multitude of characters through which they could see themselves and their lives. Hamilton was the first African-American author to receive the prestigious Newbery Award for her novel *M. C. Higgins, the Great,* which also received a National Book Award in 1975. She won an Edgar Allan Poe Award from the Mystery Writers of America for *The House of Dies Drear.* The American Library Association honored Hamilton with many awards, including several Coretta Scott King awards and the Laura Ingalls Wilder Medal for lifetime achievement in 1995. In the same year she became the first children's author to receive the coveted "genius grant" of the John D. and Catherine T. MacArthur Foundation. Hamilton combined her successful career as a novelist with her interest in black oral tradition, folk tales, and history in several nonfiction works. Her *Many Thousands Gone: African Americans from Slavery to Freedom* celebrates the lives of the famous and the unknown with equal respect, while her folktale collections include *The People Could Fly: American Black Folktales* and *Her Stories: African American Folktales, Fairy Tales, and True Tales.* In the year of her death Hamilton published *Time Pieces,* a work that has been described as a semi-autobiographical novel.

OBITUARIES AND OTHER SOURCES:

BOOKS

Mikkelsen, Nina, *Virginia Hamilton,* Twayne (New York, NY), 1994.
Wheeler, Jill C., *Virginia Hamilton,* Abdo & Daughters (Minneapolis, MN), 1997.

PERIODICALS

Chicago Tribune, February 21, 2002, pp. 2-8.
Los Angeles Times, February 23, 2002, obituary by Maria Elena Fernandez, p. B16.
New York Times, February 20, 2002, obituary by Margalit Fox, p. A21.
Washington Post, February 22, 2002, p. B8.

HAN Shaogong, 1953-

PERSONAL: Born January 1, 1953, in Chang Sha, Hunan Province, China; son of Han Ke Xian and Zhang Jing Xin; married Liang Yu Li, 1980; children: one daughter. *Education:* Diploma in Chinese studies, 1982. *Hobbies and other interests:* Chinese calligraphy.

ADDRESSES: Home—First Building, Hainan Plaza, 69 Guoxing Rd., Haikou, People's Republic of China. *Office*—Room 2-602, Hainan Teachers' University, Haikou 571100, Hainan, People's Republic of China. *E-mail*—hanshaog@public.hk.hi.cn.

CAREER: Associated with Hainan Teachers' University; writer.

MEMBER: Chinese Writer's Association (member of council), Hunan Youth Union (vice chair), Hunan Literature Correspondence Collective (president), Hainan Writers Association (chair), Hunan Province branch, Federation of Literature and Art Circles (member of council).

AWARDS, HONORS: Awards for best Chinese story, 1980, 1981.

WRITINGS:

Shi niu yang, Ren ming (Shanghai, China), 1973.

(With Zhengwen Gan) *Ren Bishi* (biography), Hunan ran min chu ban she (Changsha, China), 1979.

Yuelan: zhong duan bian xiao shuo ji, Guangdong ren min chu ban she (Canton, China), 1981.

Fei guo lan tian (short stories), Hunan ran min chu ban she (Changsha, China), 1983.

You huo (short stories; title means "Lure"), Hunan ran min chu ban she (Changsha, China), 1985.

Kong cheng (short stories), Linbai chu ban she (Taipei, China), 1988.

Mou sha, Tuan jing chu ban shi ye gong si (Taipei, China), 1989.

(Translator with Gang Han) Milan Kundera, *Sheng ming zhong bu neng cheng shoul zhi qing* (translation of *The Unbearable Lightness of Being*), Shi bao wen hua chu ban qi ye you xian gong si (Taipei, China), 1990.

Homecoming?, and Other Stories, translated by Martha Cheung, Renditions (Hong Kong, China), 1992.

Pa pa pa, Zuo jia chu ban she (Beijing, China), 1993.

Ye xing zhe men yu, Zhi shi chu ban she (Shanghai, China), 1994.

Sheng zhan yu you xi, Nuijin da xue chu ban she (Xianggang, China), 1994.

Hai nian (essays), Hainan chu ban she (Haikou, China), 1994.

Han Shaogong (short stories), Ren min wen xue chu ban she (Beijing, China), 1994.

Xie pi (short stories), Changjiang wen yi chu ban she (Wuhan, China), 1994.

Nan ren di yi ban shi nü ren, Shi dai wen yi chu ban she (Changchung, China), 1994.

Han Shaogong sang wen: hai nian (essays), Hainan chu ban she (Haikou, China), 1995.

Zhen yao chu shi, Zhong gong zhong yang dang xiao chu ban she (Beijing, China), 1995.

Deng lan se chen ru hei an, Zhongguo she hui ke xue chu ban she (Beijing, China), 1995.

Bei men kou yu yan, Nan hai chu ban gong si (Haikou, China), 1995.

Han Shaogong xiao shuo jing xuan (short stories), Tai bai wen yi chu ban she (Xi'an, China), 1996.

Ling hun di sheng yin, Jilin ren min chu ban she (Changchun, China), 1996.

Xin xiang, Tianjin ren min chu ban she (Tianjin, China), 1996.

Xue se=xu se, Dunhuang wen yi chu ban she (Lanzhou, China), 1996.

Wan mei di jia ding (essays), Zuo jia chu ban she (Beijing, China), 1996.

Shi jie, Hunan wen yi chu ban she (Changsha, China), 1996.

Maqiao ci dian: Han Shaogong zi xuan ji, Zuo jia chu ban she (Beijing, China), 1996.

Gui chu lai: duan pian ji (fiction), Zuo jia chu ban she (Beijing, China), 1996.

Fo you yi nian jian, Bei yue wen yi chu ban she (Taiwan, China), 1996.

(With Ma Lihua and Shi Tiesheng) *Wu jia zhi ren: Ma Lihua, Shi Tiesheng, Han Shaogong jia zuo ji hui,* Hai tian chu ban she (Shenzhen, China), 1996.

Han Shaogong zuo pin zi xuan ji, Li jiang chu ban she (Guangxi Guililn, China), 1997.

(With Guoping Zhou and Jinjing Zhong) *Han Shaogong san wen* (essays), Zhongguo guang bo dian shi chu ban she (Beijing, China), 1998.

Zhu quing sha bai, Zhongguo dui wa fan yi chu ban gong si (Beijing, China), 1998.

Gu ren (short stories), Hunan shi fan da xue chu ban she (Changsha, China), 1998.

Wo men yi qi zou gou: bai ming zhi ing xie zhi qing, Hunan wen yi chu ban she (Changsha, China), 1998.

(With Yanhou) *Han Shaogong,* Ming bao yue kan (Xianggang, China), 1999.

Fernando Pessoa, *Huang ran lu* (translation of *The Book of Disquiet*), Shanghai wen yi chu ban she (Shanghai, China), 1999.

Xin xiang, Xi yuan chu ban she (Beijing, China), 2000.

Meng an, Shandong wen yi chu ban she (Jinan, China), 2001.

Xi wang mao cao di, Shandong wen yi chu ban she (Jinan, China), 2001.

Xing er shang de mi shi, Shandong wen yi chu ban she (Jinan, China), 2001.

Ran hou, Shandong wen yi chu ban she (Jinan, China), 2001.

Wen xue de gen, Shandong wen yi chu ban she (Jinan, China), 2001.

Ba ba ba, Shandong wen yi chu ban she (Jinan, China), 2001.

Zai xiao shou de hou tai, Shandong wen yi chu ban she (Jinan, China), 2001.

Ling xiu zhi si, Bei yue wen yi chu ban she (Taiwan, China), 2001.

Also author of *Nu nu nu* (title means "Wife, Wife, Wife"), 1986. Chief editor, *Hainan Review,* beginning 1988.

Author's works have been translated into several languages, including Czech, English, and French.

SIDELIGHTS: Han Shaogong came of age during a turbulent time in modern Chinese history, an era that saw government crackdowns on urban populations that demanded greater democracy and freedom of expression. During the so-called "Cultural Revolution" the young Han was sent to the rural Hunan Province, where he was forced to live and work for six years. With the decline of the Mao regime, Han began to write; his forté became the short story and the novella. In his first years of publishing, Han characteristically waxed polemic against his country's political orthodoxy, but by the mid-1980s another side of his character was revealed. Han founded the "In Search of Roots" movement and dedicated himself to rediscovering and celebrating his homeland's ancient cultural values.

In the *New York Times Book Review,* contributors Judith Shapiro and Liang Heng placed Han alongside peers Gao Xiaosheng and Gu Cheng as exemplars of a "new" Chinese literature. According to the critics, China's post-Mao generation of writers "are in a unique position, having lived, during what should have been their school years, in a cultural desert. Their break with ancient traditions has made them both relatively free and greatly deprived. Some of them fiercely reject a heritage they do not really understand. Others are trying to redefine and rediscover what they have lost, tapping China's folk roots to develop a distinct but nonpolitical literature." The essayists placed Han in the second category, noting that the author had "visited local ethnic minorities in the hill areas, where he wrote down legends and superstitions."

An admirer of Milos Kundera and Franz Kafka, Han invests some of his fiction with a variety of Germanesque expressionism characterized by "the sordid ugliness of human nature, conveyed incisively in a visceral and deeply moving language," according to Bettina Knapp in *World Literature Today.* Writing about the novella *Pa pa pa,* Knapp noted that the title character is one of society's castoffs, a mentally disabled manchild of no determinate age who can pronounce only the three syllables "pa pa pa." Abandoned by his father at birth, the man is still cared for by his mother with "a love that is massed with sorrow," as Knapp wrote. Some of the townspeople take advantage of the character's slow mind; others revere him as an oracle endowed with supernatural powers. This conflicted character, in Knapp's view, is Han's "constant reminder of a backward, mutilated, and emotionally deprived land."

Reviewing the English translation of Han's stories published as *Homecoming?* for *Far Eastern Economic Review,* David Clive Price dubbed the title story weak, with "vaguely Kafkaesque prose [bearing] the weight of an awsome historical responsibility." While Price concluded that Han has "an enigmatic side to [his] writing that needs space and time to develop," the stories struck *World Literature Today* contributor Shang-Tai Chang as "a welcome addition to English resources in contemporary Chinese fiction." *Homecoming?,* added Sheng-Tai, "is about the discovery of a repressed inner self through an apparent case of mistaken identity." In one story, "The Blue Bottle-Cap," a labor camp worker named Chen goes mad; his only connection to sanity is a missing bottlecap for which he searches ceaselessly. "Only the narrator has a secret sympathy for Chen, whose madness is an indictment not merely of evil but of the prevalent moral apathy which passes for sanity and normalcy in Chinese society," Shang-Tai maintained. The critic also praised Han's use of language, which, even in translation, "sometimes rises to an epic grandeur, with a breathless rhythm suggesting an anxious soul in quest of meaning."

BIOGRAPHICAL AND CRITICAL SOURCES:

PERIODICALS

Choice, April, 1994, Jeffrey Kinkley, "The New Chinese Literature: The Mainland and Beyond," pp. 1249-1263.
Far Eastern Economic Review, October 29, 1992, David Clive Price, "Old Characters, New Voices," p. 60.
New York Times Book Review, January 11, 1987, Judith Shapiro and Liang Heng, "Letter from China—Young Writers Test the Limits," p. 3.
World Literature Today, summer, 1991, Bettina Knapp, review of *Pa pa pa,* p. 546; winter, 1994, Sheng-Tai Chang, review of *Homecoming?, and Other Stories,* pp. 211-212; autumn, 2000, p. 802.* HAN

*   *   *

HARRELL, Thomas Willard 1911-2002

OBITUARY NOTICE—See index for *CA* sketch: Born in 1911, in Troup County, GA; died of colon cancer April 17, 2002, in Portola Valley (some sources say Palo Alto), CA. Psychologist, professor, and author. Harrell is best known for several studies he conducted with Stanford University graduates who received M.B.A. degrees, noting friendly people tended to earn more; women earned less; and marriage was a good thing for men's careers but not for women's. Harrell received his bachelor's degree in 1932 and his master's degree in 1933 from the University of Georgia and followed with a doctorate from Johns Hopkins University in 1936. He joined the staff at the University of Illinois at Urbana until World War II interrupted his academic career. Serving in the U.S. Army for four years, he was promoted to lieutenant colonel. When he

returned from the army Harrell rejoined the staff at Urbana, where he stayed until 1952 when he moved to Stanford University. During his long tenure at Stanford he wrote *Industrial Psychology* and *Manager's Performance and Personality,* and coauthored *A Casebook in Industrial and Personal Psychology.*

OBITUARIES AND OTHER SOURCES:

PERIODICALS

Los Angeles Times, May 10, 2002, p. B13.
Washington Post, May 12, 2002, p. C9.

*   *   *

HARRISON, Molly (Hodgett) 1909-2002

OBITUARY NOTICE—Born September 23, 1909, in Stevenage (some sources cite Great Wymondley), Hertfordshire, England; died August 7, 2002, in Whitchurch-on-Thames, Oxfordshire, England. Museum curator, educator, historian, and author. Harrison spent nearly her entire career at the Geffrye Museum in London, arriving there as a teacher or assistant in 1939 and serving as curator from 1941 to 1969. Trained as a teacher and mandated to focus on the museum as a teaching aid, she is credited as a pioneer in her field. Harrison assumed her position during World War II, when the city of London was abandoned by most of the families who could afford to leave. The Geffrye Museum, located in one of the poorest parts of the city, played host to large numbers of impoverished neighborhood children. With this audience, as she described in the book *Museum Adventures: The Story of the Geffrye Museum,* Harrison implemented a philosophy wherein museums exist as much for learning as for preserving antiquities; no one is excluded from attendance, not the poor or culturally deprived, and especially not the children; and true learning emerges more successfully from active involvement than passive observation. To that end, she instituted activity sessions, craft workshops, free films and concerts, and myriad eye-catching displays. She also wrote several adult and children's books. One of the highlights of the Geffrye Museum is a collection devoted to home interiors, and as a writer Harrison demonstrated an interest in the history of everyday life. Her books include such titles as *The Kitchen in History, Growing up in Victorian Days,* and *People and Furniture: A Social Background to the English Home.* Harrison was a fellow of the Museums Association and the Royal Society of Arts; in 1967, she was decorated a member of the Order of the British Empire.

OBITUARIES AND OTHER SOURCES:

PERIODICALS

Guardian (London, England), August 23, 2002, obituary by Gene Adams, p. 20.
Independent (London, England), August 28, 2002, obituary by David Dewing, p. 14.
Times (London, England), August 14, 2002, p. 27.

*   *   *

HARRISON, Royden John 1927-2002

OBITUARY NOTICE—See index for *CA* sketch: Born March 3, 1927, in London, England; died June 29 (some sources cite June 30), 2002, in Sheffield, England. Historian, political scientist, educator, and author. Harrison was a staunch supporter of the British Labour party, an esteemed Labour historian, and a prolific writer on socialist ideology. As a socialist, Harrison was convinced that education was necessary for all people, and he directed substantial effort toward the education of trade union members and advocacy on the behalf of public service workers. During his fifteen-year affiliation with the University of Sheffield, Harrison created extramural day-release classes for minors and other working-class people that broke new ground in the field of formal training for union members. He also served as their delegate to the Sheffield Trades and Labour Council. He was a founding member of the Society for the Study of Labour History in 1960 and a longtime editor of the *Labour History Journal.* Harrison began his writing career with histories that have been hailed as masterpieces of Labour scholarship and intellectual integrity. These include *Before the Socialists: Studies in Labour and Politics, 1861-1881* and *The Life and Times of Sidney and Beatrice Webb: 1858-1905, the Formative Years,* the companion volume to which was still in progress

at the time of his death. In 1970 Harrison accepted a professorship and chair of social history at the University of Warwick. There he collaborated on creating the massive collection of the Modern Records Centre and *The Warwick Guide to British Labour Periodicals, 1790-1970: A Checklist.* He trained graduate students and lectured abroad, including appearances in Japan. The fruit of his teamwork approach to graduate training includes the volumes *Independent Collier: The Coal Miner as Archetypal Proletarian Reconsidered* and *Divisions of Labour: Skilled Workers and Technological Change in Nineteenth-Century England,* both of which Harrison edited. Harrison retired in 1982 to devote the rest of his life to the Webb biography.

OBITUARIES AND OTHER SOURCES:

PERIODICALS

Guardian (London, England), July 3, 2002, obituary by Michael Barratt Brown and John Halstead, p. 18.
Independent (London, England), July 20, 2002, obituary by John Halstead, p. 14.
Times (London, England), July 22, 2002, p. 29.

*   *   *

HASKINS, Caryl P(arker) 1908-2001

PERSONAL: Born August 12, 1908, in Schenectady, NY; died of cardiac arrest, October 8, 2001, in Westport, CT; son of Caryl Davis (an engineer) and Frances Julia Parker; married Edna Ferrell (a scientist), July 12, 1940. *Education:* Yale University, Ph.D., 1930; Harvard University, Ph.D. (physiology), 1935.

CAREER: Biophysicist and author. General Electric, 1931-53; Massachusetts Insitute of Tecnology, Cambridge, MA, research associate, 1935-44; Union College, Schenectady, NY, research professor in biophysics, 1937-55, liaison officer, 1940-43, executive assistant to the chair, 1943-44, deputy executive officer, 1944-45; National Defense Research Committee, scientific advisor to the Policy Council, 1947; Research and Development Board of the National Military Establishment, scientific advisor, 1948-51; Advisory

Committee, Secretary of Defense on Special Weapons, chair, 1948-49; Secretary of Defense, consultant, 1948-60; Secretary of State, consultant, 1950-60; President's Science advisory committee, 1955-58, consultant, 1959-70; Center for Advanced Study in Behavioral Sciences, director, 1960-75; El. du Pont de Nemours & CO., director, 1971-81; Haskins Laboratories Inc., New Haven, CT (originally based in New York, NY), president and research director, 1935-55, director, 1935-2001, chair, 1969-2001; Carnegie Institute, Washington, DC, president, 1956-71, trustee, 1949-2001.

Naval Advisory Committee on Naval History, member, 1971-84, vice chair, 1975-84; Thomas Jefferson Memorial Foundation, director, 1972-79; Wildlife Preservation Trust International, director, 1976-2001; Carnegie Corporation of New York, trustee, 1955-80, honorary trustee, 1980-2001; Smithsonian Institution, regent, 1956-80, regent emeritus, 1980-2001; RAND Corporation, trustee, 1955-75, advisory trustee, 1988-2001. Served on numerous political and scientific councils and boards.

AWARDS, HONORS: Presidential Certificate of Merit; King's Medal for Service in the Cause of Freedom; Joseph Henry Medal; Smithsonian Institution Centenary Medal, Harvard University, 1992; honorary degrees from many colleges and universities.

WRITINGS:

Of Ants and Men, Prentice-Hall (New York, NY), 1939.
The Amazon: The Life History of a Mighty River, Doubleday, Doran (Garden City, NY), 1943.
Of Societies and Men, Norton (New York, NY), 1951.
The Scientific Revolution and World Politics, Greenwood Press (Westport, CT), 1964.
(Editor) *The Search for Understanding: Selected Writings of Scientists of the Carnegie Institution,* M.I.T. Press (Cambridge, MA), 1967.
The Testament of the Years Between, Edinburgh University Press (Edinburgh, Scotland), 1969.

Also authored hundreds of scientific articles.

SIDELIGHTS: Caryl P. Haskins was a biophysicist with a strong interest in entomology, in particular the study of ants. He served as scientific advisor to many government organizations and boards.

Haskins's father, Caryl Davis Haskins, was an engineer for General Electric Company and helped to create the self-guiding torpedo. He died when Haskins was three years old, and Haskins was raised by his mother, who was very protective of him. When he enrolled at Yale University in New Haven, Connecticut, she rented an apartment in New Haven to remain close to him.

Haskins published his first scientific paper when he was eighteen years old. Like his father, he first worked for General Electric. Within a few years he began research on the effects of radiation on living tissue. He initially conducted his research in a garage, but eventually found space at the Massachusetts Institute of Technology and at Union College in Schenectady, New York; he taught at both schools.

As a biophysicist, Haskins applied his knowledge of physics to the study of biological processes and structures. However, he ranged far from this relatively narrow field, studying many areas of science, most notably entomology and genetics. He was the author of several books and hundreds of scientific articles. His wife coauthored several scientific papers with him.

In 1935 Haskins co-founded Haskins Laboratories, a private organization that studied the biological foundations of speech, hearing, and language. The lab later created a "reading machine," or photoelectric scanning device, as well as a supersonic guidance device. In the 1940s Haskins worked in wartime defense, researching radar and proximity fuses for the Office of Scientific Research and Development. After World War II, he continued to act as advisor to government and military groups, including the President's Science advisory committee. In 1956 Haskins became president of the Carnegie Institution, a non-profit, private scientific research group.

Haskins' books—particularly *Of Ants and Men,* which compares ant societies to human ones, and *The Amazon: The Life History of a Mighty River,* which describes the river and its ecology—won him a wide audience outside his scientific field. *Of Ants and Men* was also widely translated.

According to Carla Baranauckas in a *New York Times* obituary, Haskins once wrote of ants, "They are fascinating creatures. When they go to war they stab each other, spray poison and cut off each other's heads. They subjugate weak races and keep slaves. But they can be kind, too. Nothing they like to have around more than a pet beetle." His interest in ants led him to make about fifty trips to Australia to study them; these expeditions were financed by money he inherited from a wealthy aunt.

According to an obituary in the *Washington Post,* Haskins "was known for an eloquent and sometimes elegiac turn of phrase, even when arguing for basic funding or the societal value of scientists." When he was not working, Haskins studied genetics in a greenhouse on his Westport, Connecticut property. He also bred exotic fish and kept a colony of poisonous ants.

BIOGRAPHICAL AND CRITICAL SOURCES:

PERIODICALS

Choice, January, 1969, review of *The Search for Understanding: Selected Writings of Scientists of the Carnegie Institution,* p. 1459; January, 1973, V. V. Raman, review of *The Scientific Revolution and World Politics,* p. 1404.

OBITUARIES:

PERIODICALS

Los Angeles Times, October 13, 2001, p. B17.
New York Times, October 13, 2001 obituary by Carla Baranauckas, p. A9.
Washington Post, October 10, 2001, p. B6.*

*   *   *

HAYFORD, Jack W. 1934-

PERSONAL: Born 1934; married Anna Marie Smith, 1954; children: Rebecca Hayford Bauer, Jack, Mark, Christa Hayford Andersen. *Education:* LIFE Bible College, (with honors), 1956; Attended Azusa Pacific University, 1970. *Religion:* Pentacostalist.

ADDRESSES: Office—The Church on the Way, 14300 Sherman Way, Van Nuys, CA 91405-2403.

CAREER: Foursquare Church, Fort Wayne, IN, minister, 1956-60; International Church of the Foursquare Gospel, Los Angeles, CA, national youth director, 1960-65; LIFE Bible College, Los Angeles, CA, faculty member, 1965-73, dean of students, 1965-70, president, 1977-82; The Church on the Way, Van Nuys, CA, founding pastor, 1969—; The King's College and Seminary, Van Nuys, CA, founder and chancellor, 1999—.

MEMBER: Lausanne Committee for World Evangelization.

AWARDS, HONORS: D.D. from LIFE Bible College, 1977; D.D. from Oral Roberts University, 1984; Litt.D. from California Graduate School of Theology, 1985; Clergyman of the Year, Religion in Media, 1985; California Community Award, Religious Heritage of America, 1988; Sally Award, Salvation Army Southern California, 2001.

WRITINGS:

The Church on the Way, Chosen Books, 1983.
Early Flight: Healing Hope for Parents of the Miscarried or Aborted, Living Ways Ministries (Van Nuys, CA), 1986.
I'll Hold You in Heaven: Healings and Hope for the Parent of a Miscarried, Aborted, or Stillborn Child, Regal Books (Ventura, CA), 1990.
The Key to Everything, Word Publishing, 1994.
My Life Story, Creation House (Orlando, FL), 1994.
Worship His Majesty: How Praising the King of Kings Will Change Your Life, 2000.
The Leading Edge, Charisma House (Lake Mary, FL), 2001.
Grounds for Living: Sound Teaching for Sure Footing in Growth and Grace, Regal Books (Ventura, CA), 2001.
How to Live through a Bad Day: Seven Powerful Insights from Christ's Words on the Cross, Thomas Nelson (Nashville, TN), 2001.

Author of numerous other books on Christian devotion, including *Taking Hold of Tomorrow, Rebuilding the Real You,* and *A Passion for Fullness.* General editor of *Spirit Filled Life Bible.* Also composer of more than five hundred hymns, songs, and choruses.

SIDELIGHTS: When Jack W. Hayford founded The Church on the Way in 1969 in Van Nuys, California, his congregation consisted of eighteen Pentecostalist members of the Foursquare denomination founded by Aimee Semple McPherson. Today, that congregation has grown into a 10,000-member "mega-church," and "Hayford's flawless personal reputation and a self-effacing, conversational manner of preaching also has revitalized the Foursquare denomination," according to a *Los Angeles Times* reporter. "Pastor Jack" has emerged as a major figure within Pentecostalism and a bridge-builder to more traditionalist evangelical and fundamentalist churches. He hosts the interdenominational Pastors Seminar every year, co-hosts Love L.A. with the Rev. Lloyd Ogilvie of the Hollywood Presbyterian Church, and in 1989 addressed the World Conference on Evangelism on behalf of Pentecostalism, a "watershed event . . . introducing the Pentecostalist experience to mainstream evangelicals," according to Vinson Synan, a prominent historian of the movement.

Hayford's nearly three dozen books focus on his ministry and the life lessons he's drawn from it. In 1983, he published *The Church on the Way,* more as "a case study in principles of New Testament spirituality" than a simple success story, according to a *Library Journal* reviewer. Other titles address the grief of parents after miscarriage or abortion, how to see worship as a gift rather than a demand, and other spiritual questions. Just a week before the tragedy of September 11, 2001, Hayford's publishers released *How to Live through a Bad Day: Seven Powerful Insights from Christ's Words on the Cross.* Since then, according to a *Publishers Weekly* report, the publisher, Thomas Nelson, has given away caseloads of the book.

BIOGRAPHICAL AND CRITICAL SOURCES:

PERIODICALS

Library Journal, January 15, 1983, review of *The Church on the Way,* p. 138.
Los Angeles Times, December 15, 1991, John Dart, "His Way: Pastor Sparks Rebirth of Pentecostal Church," pp. B1, B6.
Publishers Weekly, September 24, 2001, Lynn Garrett, "Religion Publishers Respond to the Tragedy," p. 19.*

H'DOUBLER, Margaret (Newell) 1889-1982

PERSONAL: Original name Margaret Newell Hougen Doubler; pronounced "doe-blur"; born 1889, in Beloit, KS; died March 26, 1982, in Springfield, MO; daughter of Charles Hougen-Doubler (a photographer and inventor) and Sarah Todd; married Wayne L. Claxon (a college art teacher), 1934. *Education:* University of Wisconsin (Madison, WI), graduated with a biology major and philosophy minor, 1906-10; attended Teachers College of Columbia University (New York, NY), 1916-17.

CAREER: Educator and writer. University of Wisconsin at Madison, physical education teacher, 1910-16, dance teacher, 1917-54, professor emeritus, beginning in 1954. Founded extracurricular dance group Orchesis.

AWARDS, HONORS: Outstanding Woman of the Community Award, University League of Wisconsin, 1945; honorary award, 1953, and Luther Halsey Gulick Award, 1971, both from the American Association of Health, Physical Education, and Recreation; Wisconsin Governor's Council Award for Distinguished Achievement in the Performing Arts, 1964; *Dance Magazine* award, 1965.

WRITINGS:

A Manual for Dancing, [Madison, WI], 1921.
The Dance and Its Place in Education, Harcourt, Brace and Company (New York, NY), 1925.
Rhythmic Form and Analysis, J. M. Rider (Madison, WI), 1932.
Dance: A Creative Art Experience, F. S. Crofts and Company (New York, NY), 1940, third edition, University of Wisconsin Press (Madison, WI), c. 1998.
Movement and Its Rhythmic Structure, [Madison, Wisconsin], 1946.
A Guide for the Analysis of Movement, [Madison, Wisconsin], 1950.

SIDELIGHTS: The existence of degree programs in dance at U.S. colleges and universities is directly linked to the work of educator Margaret H'Doubler. Working at the University of Wisconsin at Madison, she embraced modern dance as a beneficial activity for all students, although at first she had to teach men in secret. She created a method of teaching dance that focuses on understanding physiology and allowing self-discovery rather than following the movements of an instructor. During her forty-four years of teaching, she developed new theories about dance, which she detailed in several publications. Her textbook *Dance: A Creative Art Experience* was once the most widely used work of its kind and was still being reprinted almost sixty years after its initial publication. And although she was not interested in preparing students for careers as dancers, she precipitated the profession's continued focus on self-expression.

H'Doubler's own education included very little dance training. After earning a degree in biology and philosophy, she began teaching physical education courses at the University of Wisconsin. In 1916-1917 she did graduate work at Columbia University, where she studied with philosopher John Dewey. His influence convinced her that creative arts experiences were important to all citizens in a democracy. She did not, however, admire traditional dance schools; the work that most interested her was being done by Alys Bentley, who taught music and dance to children. H'Doubler returned to Wisconsin to create classes combining the study of music visualization, creative expression, and anatomical function. Her students did perform on an annual basis, which led her to create the extracurricular group Orchesis to organize these events. This organization has been emulated in universities in the United States, Canada, and Europe.

In addition to teaching, H'Doubler regularly wrote about the theories she was developing. Her books reflect her ideological evolution, which began with an emphasis on music visualization and defined dance as an activity. *A Manual for Dancing* and *Dance and Its Place in Education* were written during this period. By 1940 she assigned greater importance to how the body functions and elevated dance to an entity, ideas that are reflected in *Dance: A Creative Art Experience.* Throughout, H'Doubler separated the practices of educational and professional dancing. She believed that studying dance has intellectual, emotional, and physical benefits, and thus is an end in itself. She did, however, encourage her students to consider becoming dance teachers.

At the end of the twentieth century, dance critic and scholar Janice Ross wrote extensively about H'Doubler's achievements in the book *Moving Les-*

sons: Margaret H'Doubler and the Beginning of Dance in American Education and in *DanceTeacher* magazine. Ross reminded readers of the radical nature of H'Doubler's approach to dance, which challenged artistic and social traditions. Writing in *DanceTeacher,* Ross explained, "Precisely because H'Doubler was not a dancer, she was able to radically re-imagine dance . . . [it] became a novel way for the woman college student to find her expressive side and to explore the physical self that was denied the majority of women in early twentieth-century America." According to Ross, H'Doubler freed dance students from "negative associations of dance as sinful, sexually promiscuous social practice, designed to display women's bodies."

BIOGRAPHICAL AND CRITICAL SOURCES:

BOOKS

International Dictionary of Modern Dance, St. James Press (Detroit, MI), 1998.

PERIODICALS

DanceTeacher, October, 2000, Janice Ross, "The Non-Dancing Mother of Dance Education."*

*   *   *

HENDERSON, David 1927-

PERSONAL: Male. Born 1927.

ADDRESSES: Agent—c/o Author Mail, The Brookings Institution, 1775 Massachusetts Ave., NW, Washington, DC 20036.

CAREER: Economist and educator. Government of Great Britain, Office of Aviation, chief economist, economic advisor to Office of the Treasury; special adviser to the Secretary of State for Wales; Royal Institute of International Affairs, visiting fellow.

WRITINGS:

Innocence and Design: The Influence of Economic Ideas on Policy, Basil Blackwell (Oxford, England), 1986.

The Changing Fortunes of Economic Liberalism: Yesterday, Today and Tomorrow, New Zealand Business Roundtable (Wellington, New Zealand), 1999.

The MAI Affair: A Story and Its Lessons, The Brookings Institution (Washington, DC), 2000.

Misguided Virtue: False Notions of Corporate Social Responsibility, New Zealand Business Roundtable (Wellington, New Zealand), 2001.

SIDELIGHTS: David Henderson's *Innocence and Design: The Influence of Economic Ideas on Policy* is a compilation of the Reith lectures he presented in his native England in 1985. In general, the lectures addressed what Henderson calls "do-it-yourself economics," or "DIYE": the province of special interest groups such as trade unionists, politicians, and business people who want governments to make economic decisions which benefit their particular sector.

Henderson contrasts orthodox supply-and-demand economics—free trade ideas—with later theories of government regulation of the economy as exemplified by John Maynard Keynes' "General Theory of Employment, Interest, and Money." Keynesian ideas have influenced many democratic governments, including those of Great Britain and the United States, to arrange governmental interference in the economy in order to better regulate employment, supply, and demand. Ernest Gellner, in a *Times Literary Supplement* review, explained that "Keynesianism meant a switch of focus in economics, away from the problem of how wealth is distributed among various factors in the economy, to the question of how the total output is determined."

Gellner called Henderson a kind of modified Keynesian who, after working in a number of political posts, now understands more fully the "world in which competing interests fight for a share of the cake." Unlike Keynes, who saw economic mistakes being made because of certain unconscious, dated ideas about how economies worked, Henderson sees the DIYE-ers as the new, misguided shakers and movers for government economic tinkering. He cites, for example, many workers' fears about free trade and their insistence on government protection from foreign competition. "Or, again," as a reviewer in the *Economist* wrote, "should not a government help its exporters with subsidised credit or tax breaks, especially if every other country

is doing so?" Henderson writes, "DIYE . . . is apt to see the world in terms of sharp contrasts, switches and discontinuities." Still, Henderson understands fully that the complex economy in today's Western democracies can never be free from government involvement. According to Gellner, "The infrastructure cannot but be centrally maintained and supervised. . . . [Non-economic factors lead] to an inescapable involvement of the polity in the economy." Henderson himself asserts that trade policies "form the central core of resource-allocation questions."

Gellner called *Innocence and Design* "elegant, serious and symptomatic . . . a kind of intellectual autobiography." He described Henderson as "an urbane and civilized writer who does not raise his voice" while at the same time offering trenchant criticism of the DIYE-ers. Yet Gellner felt that Henderson is somewhat inconsistent in wishing to apply "sound economic theory" to independent sectors of a free economy: "You cannot advise those who are in the market," the critic noted. Gellner also said that Henderson gives too little attention to the so-called "sociological tradition which explores the social roots and limits of market behaviour. . . . This book is meant to make us heed economics more, but its failure to show any understanding of the ideas it is opposing may lead us to trust economics less." The *Economist* reviewer, on the other hand, concluded by saying that "every professional economist who [reads this book] . . . will come away more convinced than ever than his work is worth doing."

BIOGRAPHICAL AND CRITICAL SOURCES:

PERIODICALS

Economist, March 22, 1986, pp. 92-93.
Times Literary Supplement, July 4, 1986, Ernest Gellner, review of *Innocence and Design: The Influence of Economic Ideas on Policy,* pp. 743-744.*

* * *

HENDERSON, Hamish 1919-2002

OBITUARY NOTICE—See index for *CA* sketch: Born November 11, 1919, in Blairgowrie, Perthshire, Scotland; died March 8, 2002, in Edinburgh, Scotland. Song writer, poet, and author. Henderson was renowned as an award-winning poet, folklorist, and translator who helped preserve Scottish oral and musical traditions. Henderson gained an appreciation for languages and music from his mother, who taught him French and Gaelic. He studied modern languages at Downing College, Cambridge, where he earned his master's degree and developed a love of Italian. After university, in 1939 he went to Germany, where he worked with a Quaker group to help Jews escape from the Nazis. When World War II started, he joined the Highland Division, where he reached the rank of captain while serving in Egypt, Tunisia, Libya, and Italy. It was of his experiences fighting in the North African desserts, specifically at the Battle of El Alamein, that inspired his Someset Maugham Award-winning 1948 poetry collection *Elegies for the Dead in Cyrenaica*. Around the same time he also edited *Ballads of World War II, Collected by Seamus Mor Maceanruig*. The money Henderson won for the Maugham award was used to conduct research in Italy, where he translated Antonio Gramsci's *Prison Letters,* though this work was not published until 1996. When he returned to Scotland, Henderson began a long association with the University of Edinburgh, where he was a senior lecturer and research fellow from 1951 to 1987, and an honorary fellow thereafter. Henderson was inspired by U.S. musicologist Alan Lomax to help with a collection of international folk songs; he loved collecting the stories and music of the local people, and wrote a number of songs himself, including "Freedom Call-All-Ye," which has been adopted by many as the unofficial national anthem of Scotland. In addition to his songs, the poet also organized the People's Festival Ceilidhs from 1951 to 1954. The purpose of the festival was to organize local musicians to perform native music during the Edinburgh Festival. Henderson's festival later became known as the Edinburgh Fringe Festival. Many of Henderson's poems, songs, and essays are collected in his 1990 book *Alias MacAlias: Writings on Songs, Folk, and Literature.*

OBITUARIES AND OTHER SOURCES:

BOOKS

Writers Directory, 16th edition, St. James Press (Detroit, MI), 2001.

PERIODICALS

Independent (London, England), March 12, 2002, p. 6.
Los Angeles Times, March 12, 2002, p. B11.
Times (London, England), March 11, 2002.

HENZE, Paul B(ernard) 1924-

PERSONAL: Born August 29, 1924, in Redwood Falls, MN; son of Paul Henry and Elizabeth Ann (Rush) Henze; married Martha Elaine Heck, September 15, 1951; children: John, Elizabeth, Martin, Mary, Alexander, Samuel. *Education:* St. Olaf College, A.B., 1947; Harvard University, A.M., 1948; University of Nebraska, postgraduate work, 1943-44; University of Maine, postgraduate work, 1947; University of Minnesota, postgraduate work, 1948.

ADDRESSES: Home—6014 Namakagan Rd., Bethesda, MD 20816-3118.

CAREER: Author, and government official. Department of Defense, Washington, DC, foreign affairs officer, 1950-51; Radio Free Europe, Munich, Germany, policy advisor, 1952-58; Turkey, communications advisor, 1958-59; Operations Research Office, Johns Hopkins University, Baltimore, MD, research staff, 1960-61; Department of Defense, Washington, DC, executive, 1961-68; American embassy, Addis Ababa, Ethiopia, first secretary, 1969-72; Department of State, 1973; American embassy, Ankara, Turkey, first secretary, 1974-77; National Security Council, head of Nationality Working Group, 1977-80; Smithsonian Institution, Wilson fellow, 1981-82; RAND Corporation, resident consultant, 1982—. Foreign Area Research, Inc., vice-president; Central Asian Foundation, vice president; American Turkish Foundation, trustee. Military service: Served in U.S. Army during World War II.

MEMBER: American Association for the Advancement of Science, British Institute for Archaeology at Ankara, Archeological Institute of America, French Society for Ethiopian Studies, American Association for the Advancement of Slavic Studies, National Parks Association, Royal Society for Asian Affairs, American-Turkish Society, East African Wildlife Society, Society for Central Asian Studies, British Institute in East Africa, Hakluyt Society, Mongolia Society, Society for Study of Caucasia, Georgian Association,U.S.-Uzbekistan Council.

WRITINGS:

Ethiopian Journeys: Travels in Ethiopia, 1969-72, E. Benn (London, England), 1977.
The Plot to Kill the Pope, Scribner (New York, NY), 1983.

Rebels and Separatists in Ethiopia: Regional Resistance to a Marxist Regime, RAND (Santa Monica, CA), 1986.

Is There Hope for the Horn of Africa? Reflections on the Political and Economic Impasses, RAND (Santa Monica, CA), 1988.

Contrasts in African Development: The Economies of Kenya and Ethiopia, 1975-1984, RAND Corporation (Santa Monica, CA), 1989.

(Editor, with others) *Soviet Strategy and Islam,* Palgrave MacMillan (New York, NY), 1989.

Eritrean Options and Ethiopia's Future, RAND (Santa Monica, CA), 1989.

Ethiopia, Crisis of a Marxist Economy: Analysis and Text of a Soviet Report, RAND (Santa Monica, CA), 1989.

Ethiopia in Early 1989: Deepening Crisis, RAND (Santa Monica, CA), 1989.

Ethiopia's Economic Prospects for the 1990s, RAND (Santa Monica, CA), 1989.

Mengistu's Ethiopian Marxist State in Terminal Crisis: How Long Can It Survive? What Will Be Its Legacy?, RAND (Santa Monica, CA), 1989.

Glasnost about Building Socialism in Ethiopia: Analysis of a Critical Soviet Article, RAND (Santa Monica, CA), 1990.

Impressions and Conversations in Uzbekistan and Kazakhstan, September 1988, RAND (Santa Monica, CA), 1990.

The United States and the Horn of Africa: History and Current Challenge, RAND (Santa Monica, CA), 1990.

Ethnic Dynamics and Dilemmas of the Russian Republic, RAND (Santa Monica, CA), 1991.

Ethiopia in 1990: The Revolution Unraveling, RAND (Santa Monica, CA), 1991.

The Horn of Africa: From War to Peace, St. Martin's Press (New York, NY), 1991.

Ethiopia in 1991: Peace through Struggle, RAND (Santa Monica, CA), 1991.

The Transcaucasus in Transition, RAND (Santa Monica, CA), 1991.

Turkey: Toward the Twenty-first Century, RAND (Santa Monica, CA), 1992.

Whither Turkestan?, RAND (Santa Monica, CA), 1992.

(With Graham E. Fuller, Ian O. Lesser, and J. F. Brown) *Turkey's New Geopolitics: From the Balkans to China,* Westview Press (Boulder, CO), 1993.

Turkish Democracy and the American Alliance, RAND (Santa Monica, CA), 1993.

Ethiopia: The Collapse of Communism and the Transition to Democracy: Adjustment to Eritrean Independence, RAND (Santa Monica, CA), 1995.

Ethiopia: The Fall of the Derg and the Beginning of Recovery under the EPRDF (March 1990-March 1992), RAND (Santa Monica, CA), 1995.

Ethiopia and Eritrea in Transition: The Impact of Ethnicity on Politics and Development, RAND (Santa Monica, CA), 1995.

Russia and the Caucasus, RAND (Santa Monica, CA), 1996.

The Russian Duma Elections of December 1995, RAND (Santa Monica, CA), 1996.

Turkey and Attaturk's Legacy, with a foreword by Zbigniew Brzezinski, SOTA (Haarlem, Netherlands), 1998.

Layers of Time: A History of Ethiopia, St. Martin's Press (New York, NY), 2000.

SIDELIGHTS: A former government official, Paul B. Henze has been a consultant with the RAND Corporation since 1982. He served with the U.S. Department of State in Ethiopia and Turkey, and was a member of the National Security Council staff during the administration of President Jimmy Carter. He has written numerous books on Ethiopia, Russia, Turkey, and other nations.

In *The Plot to Kill the Pope,* Henze discusses the attempted assassination of Pope John Paul II in May 1981. The would-be assassin, a young Turkish man named Mehmet Ali Agca, was directed by the Bulgarian secret service, then under the control of the Soviet Union's secret service and at the direction of Soviet leader Yuri Andropov. Henze describes terrorism in Turkey at the time of the assassination attempt, and tells how terrorist groups there were aided by the Soviet Union, which funneled arms through Bulgaria and Syria. He also discusses the fact that Agca was a member of a terrorist organization known as the "Grey Wolves," and had connections to a Turkish crime organization. Henze proposes that the Soviets wished to kill the pope because the pope, as a Polish citizen, was a source of inspiration for members of the Polish Catholic Church, historically the major center of spiritual, intellectual, and political resistance to Soviet communism. The church in Poland was allied with Solidarity, a Polish labor union that placed itself squarely against Communist rule, and the first free trade union that forced a communist regime to recognize it; thus, the Soviets were eager to neutralize its power.

Henze, who speaks fluent Turkish, conducted research in Turkey for this book, and used Turkish, Italian, and Bulgarian sources to reconstruct Agca's background; travels through Iran, Bulgaria, and Germany; activities in those countries; and connections with terrorist and criminal elements there. In the *New York Times Book Review,* Carol Gilligan wrote that Henze "provides a brilliant and completely original analysis of sponsored terrorism in Turkey."

In *Layers of Time: A History of Ethiopia,* Henze presents a history of the African nation, from its origins two thousand years ago to the present day. He emphasizes the Ethiopian tradition of strong leaders, independence, and self-government, as well as the nation's pride in its culture and people. In *Choice,* B. Harris, Jr. described the book as "impressive, comprehensive, and documented." A *Kirkus Reviews* writer called it "a timely study of a country still much in the news." In the *Times Literary Supplement,* Christopher Clapham wrote, "Henze's familiarity with the country is encyclopedic, and over the years he must have traveled more widely in Ethiopia than any other foreigner." Clapham also commented that the book is "thoroughly accessible" and that "the author's personal accounts of his explorations are . . . interwoven with the events that he describes."

The Horn of Africa: From War to Peace describes why this region has become so politically and economically troubled, and gives recommendations to help resolve some of the area's problems. The first part of the book provides a history of the region, focusing on Ethiopia, Sudan, and Somalia, including a discussion of American and Soviet involvement in these countries. In the second section, Henze traces the effects of arms imports, largely from the Soviet Union, on these countries since World War II, as well as the legacy of conflicts waged with these weapons. The third part of the book lists Henze's recommendations for achieving peace and progress, including political pluralism, extensive local government, and a federation of the nations in the Horn of Africa, as well as aid from other nations. In the *Times Literary Supplement,* Richard Pankhurst called this "a scholarly and well-documented work." In the *International Journal of African Historical Studies,* Zbigniew Konczacki wrote, "His observations and suggestions are usually apt and constructive."

BIOGRAPHICAL AND CRITICAL SOURCES:

PERIODICALS

America, February 25, 1984, Thurston Davis, review of *The Plot to Kill the Pope,* p. 138.

American Spectator, June, 1984, Paul Seabury, review of *The Plot to Kill the Pope,* p. 36.

Annals of the American Academy of Political and Social Science, May, 1995, Frederick W. Frey, review of *Turkey's New Geopolitics: From the Balkans to China,* p. 188.

Asian Affairs, October, 1990, R. A. Longmire, review of *Soviet Strategy and Islam,* p. 381.

Booklist, May 15, 2000, Jay Freeman, review of *Layers of Time: A History of Ethiopia,* p. 1724.

Choice, April, 2001, B. Harris, Jr., review of *Layers of Time,* p. 1513.

Commentary, April, 1984, Roger Kaplan, review of *The Plot to Kill the Pope,* p. 79.

International Affairs, July, 1992, David Pool, review of *The Horn of Africa: From War to Peace,* p. 561.

International Journal of African Historical Studies, winter, 1992, Zbigniew Konczacki, review of *The Horn of Africa,* p. 198.

Journal of International Affairs, summer, 1995, Michael A. Reynolds, review of *Turkey's New Geopolitics,* p. 266.

Kirkus Reviews, May, 2000, review of *Layers of Time,* p. 691.

New York Times Book Review, January 15, 1984, Edward Jay Epstein, review of *The Plot to Kill the Pope,* p. 6.

Times Higher Education Supplement, January, 1992, Richard Pankhurst, review of *The Horn of Africa,* p. 19.

Times Literary Supplement, November 23, 2001, Christopher Clapham, review of *Layers of Time,* p. 20.*

*   *   *

HERBERT, W. N. 1961-

PERSONAL: Born 1961, in Dundee, Scotland.

ADDRESSES: Agent—c/o Author Mail, Bloodaxe Books Ltd., Highgreen, Tarset, Northumberland NE48 1RP, England.

CAREER: Poet and author.

WRITINGS:

POETRY

Dundee Doldrums, Galliard (Edinburgh, Scotland), 1992.

(Editor and contributor) *Contraflow on the Super Highway,* Southfields Press and Gairfish (London, England), 1994.

Forked Tongue, Bloodaxe (Newcastle upon Tyne, England), 1994.

The Testament of the Reverend Thomas Dick, Arc (Todmorden, Lancaster, England), 1994.

Cabaret McGonagall, Bloodaxe (Newcastle Upon Tyne, England), 1996.

The Laurelude, Bloodaxe (Newcastle upon Tyne, England), 1998.

(Editor, with Matthew Hollis) *Strong Words: Modern Poets on Modern Poetry,* Bloodaxe (Northumberland, England), 2000.

OTHER

To Circumjack MacDiarmid: The Poetry and Prose of Hugh MacDiarmid, Oxford University Press (New York, NY), 1992.

SIDELIGHTS: Scottish poet W. N. Herbert has produced many collections of poetry, much of it written in literary Scots. In reviewing his *Dundee Doldrums, Times Literary Supplement* reviewer Eva Salzman wrote that "the dialect often possesses an irony and a distinctive music that would be simply absent in English gloss."

To Circumjack MacDiarmid: The Poetry and Prose of Hugh MacDiarmid, is Herbert's study of Scottish poet Christopher Murray Grieve, who wrote under the name Hugh MacDiarmid. Herbert analyses his poems and criticism. *Choice* reviewer M. Tucker wrote that "Herbert's singleness of view reduces the poet's majestic work to a psychological struggle against emotional insecurity and fear of public failure." Herbert goes into detail about MacDiarmid's controversial career, including his tendency to use other writers' ideas. He concludes by suggesting that because of the love of Valda Grieve, MacDiarmid reached a point of "holy poverty," a state of existence which enabled him to escape his self-loathing.

Herbert's *Forked Tongue* is a collection of his poems. They range from recollections of his past to comment on language and make references to Dante, El Greco, Fra Angelico, Andrew Cruickshank, Fanny Wright, Epicurus, and others. Herbert's homeland is central to poems such as "Dingle Dell" and "Scotland the Twit." He focuses on his own past in "The Cortina of the Isles" and "The Beano Elegies." His references to language can be found in "Other Tongues," "Keaton's Blues," and "Parolla di Cavallo." "The Cortina Sonata" is the section that contains his English poems, and poems in Scots are contained in the section titled "The Landfish: and Other Poems." His "Three Sonnets by Raphael" is written in modern Scots. "Omnegaddrums" contains his previously published Scots poems, and poems about the closing of the Timex factory in his native Dundee are found in "Ticka Ticka."

Times Literary Supplement reviewer Bernard O'Donoghue wrote that "in many ways this is the book's most impressive achievement. It can sound rather pious. . . . But this shaded gravity comes as something of a relief after the dazzle of the earlier pyrotechnics, as indeed does its political engagement in the context of much contemporary poetry." O'Donoghue noted that the 1985 *Concise Scots Dictionary* can be used to decipher Herbert's Scots. O'Donoghue noted that the "New Generation Poets" of Britain are dominated by the Irish and that the title of this collection is reminiscent of John Montague's "Grafted Tongue" and Thomas Kinsella's "gapped tradition in Irish-English." *World Literature Today* reviewer Robert L. Kindrick wrote that "even the poems without linguistic hurdles require thought and reflection, not only on the verse at hand but on other poems in the collection and on the words to which the poet alludes. The poetry and the experience Herbert offers are well worth the effort." Adam Thorpe wrote in the *Observer* that the "Cortina Sonata" "falls howling" between the English and the Scots, and that in the Scots, he discovered "a great McGonagall-haunted poem . . . amongst many other delights."

In reviewing Herbert's *The Testament of the Reverend Thomas Dick, Quadrant* reviewer David Kennedy noted the recent emphasis on and popularity of the New Generation Poets and the claim that rock music is critical to its members, including Herbert. Kennedy admitted that Herbert is an Iggy Pop fan, that he relied on a Doors song as a model for some of the poems in *Forked Tongue,* and that he makes references to Jimi

Hendrix's *Voodoo Chili.* "However," said Kennedy, "taken as part of a published oeuvre in English and Scots that also engages with Allen Ginsberg, Italian culture, classical mythology, ethnographic artifacts, and nineteenth-century Scottish science, the presence of rock music seems merely typical of a highly original and restless intelligence that writes poetry about whatever it chooses. . . . However, this should not be taken as a suggestion that Herbert is an out-and-out postmodernist: rather, as *The Testament of the Reverend Thomas Dick* makes abundantly clear, his best work is analogous to musical form, particularly the sonata with its development of two distinct themes."

G. Ross Roy wrote in *World Literature Today* that "it takes a brave man to use the name McGonagall in the title of a poem, and a book, considering that *Punch* called William McGonagall (c. 1825-1902) `the greatest Bad Verse writer of his age.'" Roy said that the difference between the verse of Herbert and that of McGonagall is that McGonagall "took his absurdities absolutely seriously, whereas Herbert knows better." Roy called Herbert's *Cabaret McGonagall* "the meeting place for all the misfits of Scotland." Roy said that Herbert "maintains" his "high standards." The poems are both comic and serious, in both English and Scots. The book is divided into four sections that represent the points of the compass, with subtitles such as "East of Auden" and "Gone West." The poems include "The Ballad of Scrapie Powrie," about a man who scrapes out the skulls of his victims along with his accomplice, Monstrous Meg. In "Postcards of Scotland," Herbert holds up the false images of Scotland offered to tourists. "The Ballad of Technofear" projects into cyberspace, and Herbert writes of love in "The Ballad of Success." In "Ballad of the King's New Dialect," Herbert addresses the decline of Scots when James VI of Scotland became James I of England. Robert Burns is mentioned in "Lammer Wine," which is also written in the Standard Habbie stanza attributable to Burns.

Times Literary Supplement reviewer Patrick Crotty said the collection "comes at the reader from all angles, strutting and wheedling and with its fists flying. . . . Herbert's cultural cornucopia of deep-fried Mars bars, cowboy movies, literary tourist attractions, chips, microchips, and answerphones elicits in response a baffling variety of styles, as the fetishism of commodities hits the means of poetic production." Crotty said that like the "more considered pieces," including "Roadkill," "Corbandie," "August in the La-

ich," "Looking up from Aeroplanes," the "Featherhood" sequence "conducts its business quietly, indeed almost shyly. . . . The ratio of reflective to uproarious poems . . . however, suggests that Herbertsville is going to be a noisy neighbourhood for some time to come."

In reviewing Herbert's *The Laurelude, Times Literary Supplement* reviewer Stephen Knight wrote that Herbert "is simply more comfortable with the texture of Scots, at ease with its greater freedom." The title poem spans thirty-eight pages and includes over one thousand lines. Knight noted that Herbert's tribute, "In Memoriam Bill Burroughs" is his "chief attempt in *The Laurelude* to render English more pliable." Knight said "To a Mousse" and "Letterbomb," both contained in *The Laurelude,* are "welcome additions to the canon." Knight wrote "that the quality of the versification can so vary within a single poem is an example of Herbert's attachment to chaos. . . . *The Laurelede* is an exasperating book, solipsistic and hectoring, recondite and direct, cadenced to perfection and cloth-eared, formally accomplished and slapdash. This is, no doubt, precisely how its author intended it to be."

BIOGRAPHICAL AND CRITICAL SOURCES:

PERIODICALS

Choice, October, 1993, M. Tucker, review of *To Circumjack MacDiarmid,* p. 289.

Observer, May 8, 1994, Adam Thorpe, "Mirror-land, Soul-shingle," p. 21.

Quadrant, September, 1994, David Kennedy, "Quaternities," pp. 77-79.

Times Literary Supplement, July 3, 1992, Eva Salzman, "The Formal and the Fast-Food," p. 28; August 5, 1994, Bernard O'Donoghue, "Whae Dae Ye Think Ye Ur?," p. 19; December 27, 1996, Patrick Crotty, "More Deeds of Scrapie," p. 25.

World Literature Today, spring, 1995, Robert L. Kindrick, review of *Forked Tongue,* pp. 411-412; spring, 1997, G. Ross Roy, review of *Cabaret McGonagall,* p. 432.*

*   *   *

HERZOG, Whitey 1931-

PERSONAL: Born November 9, 1931, in New Athens, IL; married; wife's name, Mary Lou.

ADDRESSES: Home—MO. *Agent*—c/o Author Mail, Simon & Schuster, 1230 Avenue of the Americas, New York, NY 10020.

CAREER: Washington Senators, infielder, outfielder, 1956-58; played for Kansas City Athletics, 1958-60, Baltimore Orioles, 1961-62, Detroit Tigers, 1963; Kansas City Athletics, scout, 1964, coach, 1965; New York Mets, coach, 1966, director of player development, 1967-72; Texas Rangers, manager, 1973; California Angels, coach, 1974-75, senior vice president, director of players, 1991-94; Kansas City Royals, manager, 1975-79; St. Louis Cardinals, manager, 1980-90, vice president, 1990; retired, 1994; writer, 1987—.

AWARDS, HONORS: American League Manager of the Year, 1976; UPI Executive of the Year, 1981, 1982; *Sporting News* Man of the Year, 1982; National League Manager of the Year, 1982, 1985, 1987; Baseball Writers' Association of America, Manager of the Year, 1985.

WRITINGS:

(With Kevin Horrigan) *White Rat: A Life in Baseball,* Harper & Row (New York, NY), 1987.
(With Mike Shropshire) *Seasons in Hell: With Billy Martin, Whitey Herzog, and "the Worst Baseball Teams in History," the 1973-1975 Texas Rangers,* D. I. Fine (New York, NY), 1996.
(With Jonathan Pitts) *You're Missin' a Great Game: From Casey to Ozzie, the Magic of Baseball and How to Get It Back,* Simon & Schuster (New York, NY), 1999.

SIDELIGHTS: Whitey Herzog, also known as the "White Rat," has been the manager of five different baseball teams, including nine full seasons as manager and general manager for the St. Louis Cardinals, and four seasons with the Kansas City Royals. Herzog was born Dorrel Norman Elvert Herzog on November 9, 1931, in New Athens, Illinois. He began as a minor-league player with a lackluster record, but when he turned to managing in the big leagues his career soared. In his career as a manager he had 1281 victories. *Sports Illustrated* declared Herzog manager of the decade for the 1980s, and he has been inducted into the Baseball Hall of Fame.

Herzog began his baseball career playing as an infielder and an outfielder for the Washington Senators from 1956 to 1958. For the next five years he bounced around among a number of teams, returning in 1964 to the Kansas City Athletics, this time as a scout, and the next year as a coach.

Herzog met with his first major success as the manager for the Kansas City Royals. The team won three straight division titles and one second-place finish in only four years. Herzog was named Manager of the Year in 1976 by UPI and the Baseball Bulletin. But 1982 would prove an even more exciting year; The St. Louis Cardinals won the league championship and the World Series. UPI named Herzog Manager of the Year again and Executive of the Year. The *Sporting News* also named Herzog Manager of the Year, as well as Man of the Year. In 1985, when the St. Louis Cardinals were predicted to finish last, they played to the seventh game of the World Series and won the National League title. That year the Baseball Writers' Association of America named Herzog Manager of the Year. The Cardinals won the title again in 1987.

Herzog has written three books about his experiences in baseball. His first, written with Kevin Horrigan, was *White Rat: A Life in Baseball,* an autobiography. Herzog tells his story, explaining some of the mysteries of his career, such as why he traded Keith Hernandez for Ozzie Smith. He also addresses some of the banes of baseball, such as drugs and expansion, and suggests solutions. Wes Lukowsky noted in his review for *Booklist* that Herzog provides a special perspective into the world of baseball because of the range of his involvement in major-league baseball. "His broad viewpoint provides a rare three-dimensional glimpse into the workings of a team," remarked Lukowsky. The first 200 pages of *You're Missin' a Great Game: From Casey to Ozzie, the Magic of Baseball and How to Get It Back,* give affectionate one-paragraph to two-page character sketches of Herzog's baseball colleagues. Then he launches into a discourse of what is wrong with modern baseball, from its economic structure to some of the rules, and again offers suggestions. Some of his solutions are more realistic than others, but the issues he raises are noteworthy. Bill James wrote in the *New York Times Book Review,* "And yet, even when he reaches, I have tremendous respect for what Herzog is trying to accomplish. He is trying to have a serious discussion about what is wrong with modern baseball and what can be done about it. . . . What makes the book work is that Herzog wants to talk about the things that people don't like to talk about."

Herzog got his nickname "White Rat" from former Boston Red Sox player Johnny Pesky, who named him so because of his white-blond hair. In an interview for the *New York Times,* Whitey was asked if he minded the nickname. "No . . . I don't mind the nickname. I even have a white rat on my front lawn at home." He is referring to a rat made of wood. "'With that rat, everyone knows who lives there.'"

BIOGRAPHICAL AND CRITICAL SOURCES:

PERIODICALS

Booklist, April 1, 1987, p. 1169; March 15, 1999, Wes Lukowsky, review of *You're Missin' a Great Game: From Casey to Ozzie, the Magic of Baseball and How to Get It Back,* p. 1283.
Library Journal, February 1, 1999, Paul Kaplan, Morey Berger, review of *You're Missin' a Great Game,* p. 95.
New York Times, September 3, 1985.
New York Times Book Review, May 30, 1999, p. 8.
Playboy, August, 1990, Thomas Boswell, "The Autocrat of Astroturf," p. 115.*

*   *   *

HILLENBRAND, Laura 1967-

PERSONAL: Born 1967, in Fairfax, VA. *Education:* Kenyon College, Gambier, OH.

ADDRESSES: Agent—Tina Bennett, Janklow/Nesbit Associates, 445 Park Ave., New York, NY 10022.

CAREER: Contributing editor/writer, *Equus Magazine,* 1989—. Consultant for PBS documentary on Seabiscuit, 2002

AWARDS, HONORS: Eclipse Awards for magazine writing, 1998, 2001; Booksense Nonfiction Book of the Year, 2001, William Hill Sports Book of the Year, 2001, and National Book Critics Circle Award finalist,

2001, all for *Seabiscuit: An American Legend*; Los Angeles Book Prize finalist; second prize, Barnes & Noble Discover Award; finalist, Borders Original Voices Award.

WRITINGS:

Seabiscuit: An American Legend, Random House (New York, NY), 2001.

ADAPTATIONS: Laura Hillenbrand is currently serving as consultant on a Universal Studios movie based on the book *Seabiscuit: An American Legend.* An audiobook version of *Seabiscuit,* was released by Random AudioBooks, 2001.

SIDELIGHTS: In her debut book, *Seabiscuit: An American Legend,* Laura Hillenbrand has written an exciting book that has already won the Triple Crown of publishing: runaway sales of a nonfiction sports book, nomination for the National Book Award Critics Circle Award, and a movie in production by Universal Studios.

The first paragraph of the preface sets the tone of the book. "In 1938, near the end of the decade of monumental turmoil, the year's number-one newsmaker was not Franklin Delano Roosevelt, Hitler, or Mussolini. It wasn't Pope Pius XI, nor was it Lou Gehrig, Howard Hughes, or Clark Gable. The subject of the most newspaper column inches in 1938 wasn't even a person. It was an undersized, crooked-legged racehorse named Seabiscuit. In the latter half of the Depression, Seabiscuit was nothing short of a cultural icon in America, enjoying adulation so intense and broad-based that it transcended sport.

The heroes in Seabiscuit's story include the burned-out, knobby-kneed racehorse; his jockeys, Red Pollard, down and out and half blind, and George Woolf, cool and cocky but doomed; the aging western trainer Tom Smith, and horseman Charles S. Howard, a Buick dealer and self-made man. Their story played out against the backdrop of the Great Depression. One in four breadwinners were unemployed, foreclosure was common, thousands were hungry. Spectator sports, radio programming, and movie theaters offered an escape and created instant celebrity, even for horses.

Enamored of the rags-to-riches myth, Americans were quick to idolize those who exemplified it. Driven by hunger, hope, and heart, Seabiscuit and his crew lived the rags-to-riches dream.

Between 1935 and 1940, Seabiscuit traveled over 50,000 miles by train and was mobbed at every whistle stop. Jim Squires, reviewing the book for the *New York Times,* says that "as the most popular and most watched personality in the world, he was the 30's era equivalent of Elvis or the Beatles, and, as a sports attraction, could draw bigger crowds than Tiger Woods."

Charles Howard embodied the entrepreneurial spirit of the age. A one-time bicycle repairman, he became a millionaire selling "horseless carriages" to the western United States. He fell in love with racehorses and hired Tom Smith, a closed-mouthed old mustang breaker from the High Plains, as his trainer. It was Smith who saw something in this horse that had run seventeen races before he won. Small, mud-colored and knock-kneed, Charles Howard bought him at auction in 1936 for $8,000 and hired Red Pollard, a one eyed, over-the-hill boxer, Red Pollard, as his jockey.

"Silent" Tom Smith set about transforming an animal everyone else called lazy, awkward, and hostile into a great racehorse. Even if no one from the Eastern establishment world of thoroughbreds had ever seen his frontier style of training, everyone agreed that the "Lone Plainsman," as Smith was called, could "talk horse." A newspaper reporter once quipped that "Tom Smith says almost nothing, constantly." Hillenbrand describes Smith, who'd trained rodeo horses and learned his craft from Plains Indians, "[as having] the ethereal quality of hoof prints in windblown snow."

Hillenbrand interviewed aging jockeys and horsemen to give the book plenty of local color. Racing scenes in California in the '30s and her characterization of Pollard and George Woolf were especially praised by the critics.

Pollard is remembered as the poet laureate of jockeys, known for his seemingly telepathic understanding of difficult horses and his love for Emerson's poetry. Hillenbrand description of Pollard's tumble, which kept him out of a great match race, is especially good: "Jockeys say there is a small, bright sound when

hooves clip against each other, a cheery portent of the wreck that is likely to follow . . . Pollard must have heard it. Fair Knightess' forelegs were kicked out from under her. Unable to catch herself, she pitched into a somersault at 40 miles per hour . . . Pollard went down with her, his helpless form following the line of her fall, over her back and neck and vanishing under her crashing body. She came down onto him with terrific force and skidded to a stop."

George Woolf was no less competitive as a jockey: In one race, recounts Hillenbrand, "The wire was looming overhead, and Ligaroti was lunging for the lead. Woolf could not move Seabiscuit up. With just a few yards to go, Woolf was frantic . . . . He had to move Ligaroti back. With twenty yards to go, Woolf tore his hand free, threw out his right arm and grabbed Ligaroti's bridle, just above the bit. Just as the wire passed overhead, he pulled back, lifting the horse's head up and to the left as Seabiscuit's head bobbed forward. Seabiscuit flew under the wire." As Jane Smiley wrote in the *Washington Post,* Hillenbrand's "effort shows in the details and the energy of her story; her historical figures, horses and people, live and breathe in a lively, lovely way."

All of America was listening to the long-awaited race between Seabiscuit and his arch rival, War Admiral. It was a classic match-up. Seabiscuit was the new West, War Admiral represented the Eastern establishment. The country had waited for more than a year to see them race. In the climax of the book, Hillenbrand recounts "the greatest race in history," run at Pimlico Race Track in Maryland on November 1, 1938, with all the excitement of first class sports reporting.

That *Seabiscuit: An American Legend* was written at all is a story of courage all its own. In 1987, a virulent case of food poisoning left Hillenbrand bedridden for ten months, fighting fevers, chills, and profound exhaustion. Doctors could not make a definitive diagnosis: some thought she had contracted AIDS, others suspected multiple sclerosis. Since there was no clear diagnosis, some doctors, as well as some friends, thought it was merely psychosomatic. "I had difficulties with just about everyone taking it seriously at first," she said. Finally she was diagnosed with Chronic Fatigue Syndrome (CFS). Hillenbrand felt then—and still does now—that it is a ridiculous name for such a debilitating disease.

CFS is a disease that leaves many of its victims completely disabled and unable to take care of themselves. "This illness is to fatigue what a nuclear bomb is to a match," she says. "It's an absurd mischaracterization." In a *Washington Post* interview, Jennifer Frey wrote that "she is thirty-three years old and can't walk a block without becoming incredibly tired. Her morning shower exhausts her. Vertigo causes the words on the computer screen to dip and weave as she types."

"Random House editor Jon Karp once said that *Seabiscuit* is a metaphor for my life, and he's right," Hillenbrand commented. "The subjects that I've written about—the men and the horse—were radically different individuals, but the one thread that pulls through all of their lives and through the events that they live through together is the struggle between overwhelming hardship and the will to overcome it."

BIOGRAPHICAL AND CRITICAL SOURCES:

BOOKS

Hillenbrand, Laura, *Seabiscuit: An American Legend,* Random House, 2001.

PERIODICALS

Atlanta Journal-Constitution, May 3, 2001, Eleanor Ringel Gillespie, review of *Seabiscuit: An American Legend,* p. D4.
Booklist, September, 1, 2001, Bill Ott, review of *Seabiscuit,* p. 35; January 1, 2001, Dennis Dodge, review of *Seabiscuit,* p. 900.
Boston Herald, August 10, 2001, review of *Seabiscuit,* p. 42.
Business Week, March 26, 2001, review of *Seabiscuit,* p. 27.
Entertainment Weekly, March 26, 2001, review of *Seabiscuit,* p. 62.
Forbes, March 5, 2001, Mark Rotella, review of *Seabiscuit,* p. 116.
Guardian (London), August 4, 2001, Stephen Moss, review of *Seabiscuit,* p. 9.
Library Journal, April 1, 2001, Patsy E. Gray, review of *Seabiscuit,* p. 106.
London Review of Books, October 4, 2001, Marjorie Garber, review of *Seabiscuit,* p. 35.

Los Angeles Times, March 18, 2001, Susan Salter, review of *Seabiscuit,* p. 11; July 1, 2001, review of audio version of *Seabiscuit.*
New York Review of Books, July 19, 2001, Elizabeth Hardwick, review of *Seabiscuit,* p. 4.
New York Times, March 6, 2001, Michiko Katutani, "No Beauty, but They Had the Right Horse There," p. B7.
New York Times Book Review, March 11, 2001, Jim Squires, "Can Do! Once upon a Time There Was a Knock-kneed, Mud-colored Runt of a Horse. His Name Was Seabiscuit . . . ," p. 12.
Publishers Weekly, March 26, 2001, Daisy Maryles, review of *Seabiscuit,* p. 24; January 1, 2001, review of *Seabiscuit,* p. 75.
Sunday Telegraph (London, England), Max Davidson, review of *Seabiscuit.*
Time, April 2, 2001, Jesse Birnbaum, review of *Seabiscuit,* p. 72.
Times (London, England), Allan Mallinson, review of *Seabiscuit,* p. 15.
Times Literary Supplement, July 20, 2001, Alan Lee, review of *Seabiscuit,* p. 10.
US Weekly, May 7, 2001, Phoebe Hoban, review of *Seabiscuit,* p. 48; April 2, 2001, Sarah Goodyear, review of *Seabiscuit,* p. 74.
Wall Street Journal, March 9, 2001, Frederick C. Klein, review of *Seabiscuit,* p. W9.
Washington Post, March 9, 2001, Jennifer Frey, "Against the Odds: Laura Hillenbrand Surmounts Illness to Cross the Finish Line with 'Seabiscuit'," p. C01.
Washington Post Book World, March 18, 2001, Jane Smiley, "Track Star," p. T05.

OTHER

Romance Reader, http://theromancereader.com/ (December 2, 2001), Cathy Sova, review of *Seabiscuit.*

*   *   *

HOLMES, Marjorie (Rose) 1910-2002

OBITUARY NOTICE—See index for *CA* sketch: Born September 22, 1910, in Storm Lake, IA; died March 13, 2002, in Manassas, VA. Columnist and author. Holmes became famous as the author of numerous columns and books that make Christian themes more accessible to the average reader. After earning a bachelor's degree from Cornell College, Holmes first earned a living as a Texas farmer. She next tried radio, working on fashion and children's programs at stations in Illinois and Ohio. By the early 1940s she had turned to writing, publishing her first novel, *World by the Tail,* in 1943. In 1959 she began writing a domestic-themed column, "Love and Laughter," for the Washington, D.C. *Star,* which she continued to author until 1973; her articles, which were collected in *Love and Laughter,* were especially popular with women homemakers and earned the author the unofficial title of "patron saint of housewives." Holmes also wrote the monthly column "A Woman's Conversation with God" from 1971 to 1977. Her books were immensely popular, especially her fictionalized account of Mary, Joseph, and Jesus in the trilogy that includes *Two from Galilee, Three from Galilee: The Young Man from Nazareth,* and *The Messiah.* With the death of her first husband, Holmes began writing books about grief and healing, including *God and Vitamins: How Exercise, Diet, and Faith Can Change Your Life, To Help You through the Hurting,* and *Still by Your Side: How I Know a Great Love Never Dies.* Holmes also taught writing at a number of workshops and conferences and published a book on the subject, *Writing Articles from the Heart: How to Write and Sell Your Life Experiences.* In addition, she is the author of six young adult books, contributed to magazines such as *McCall's* and *Reader's Digest,* and completed an ouvre of over thirty books that have sold millions of copies.

OBITUARIES AND OTHER SOURCES:

BOOKS

Writers Directory, 16th edition, St. James Press (Detroit, MI), 2001.

PERIODICALS

Los Angeles Times, April 2, 2002, p. B11.
Washington Post, April 1, 2002, p. B5.

J

JAMISON, Judith 1943(?)-

PERSONAL: Born May 10, 1943 (some sources say 1944), in Philadelphia, PA; daughter of John (a sheet metal worker) and Tessie (a teacher, maiden name Bell) Jamison; married and divorced Miguel Godreau (a dancer), 1972. *Education:* Attended Fisk University (Nashville, TN); studied dance at the Philadelphia Dance Academy (now University of the Arts).

ADDRESSES: Home and office—Alvin Ailey American Dance Theatre, 211 West 61st St., Third Floor, New York, NY 10023-7832.

CAREER: Alvin Ailey American Dance Theatre, New York, NY, principal dancer, 1965-80; Jamison Project, founder and artistic director, 1988-91; Alvin Ailey American Dance Theatre, artistic director, 1989—. Danced with the Harkness Ballet, 1966-67, and appeared as guest artist with Swedish Royal Ballet, 1972, American Ballet Theatre, 1976, Vienna State Opera, 1977, and Béjart's Ballet of the Twentieth Century, 1979. Also appeared on television, including *Dance in America* (PBS); as dancer for television film *Memories and Visions,* 1973; *Ailey Celebrates Ellington* (CBS), 1974; *The Cosby Show* (NBC), 1986; *Alvin Ailey Television Special* (NBC), 1988; and *The Dancemaker: Judith Jamison* (PBS), 1988. Starred in Broadway show *Sophisticated Ladies,* 1980. Choreographed works, including *Divining* and *Just Call Me Dance,* 1984; *Time Out* and *Time In,* 1986; *Into the Life,* 1987; *Tease,* 1988; *Forgotten Time* and *Read Matthew 11:28,* 1989; *Rift,* 1991; and *Hymn,* 1993.

National Endowment for the Arts, board member, 1972-76; Jacob's Pillow, board member; Harkness Center for Dance Injuries, advisory board member.

AWARDS, HONORS: Dance Magazine Award, 1972; Distinguished Service Award, Harvard University, 1982; Distinguished Service Award, mayor of New York, 1982; Candace Award, 1990; Frontrunner Award, 1992; Women of the Arts Award, 1992; Dance USA Award, 1998; Kennedy Center Honors, President Bill Clinton, 1999; Prime Time Emmy Award, 2001, for outstanding choreography in PBS *Dance in America* documentary "A Hymn for Alvin Ailey"; National Medal of Arts, 2001; Philadelphia Arts Alliance Award; Franklin Mint Award; Ebony Black Achievement Award; Outstanding Achievement in the Arts Award, Big Brothers/Big Sisters of New York City; Spirit of Achievement Award, National Women's Division of Yeshiva University's Albert Einstein College of Medicine; Golden Plate Award, American Academy of Achievement; Distinguished Artists Multicultural Award, Club 100 of the Los Angeles Music Center; Isabella Graham Award, Graham-Windham Services to Families and Children; Dean's fellow, Columbia College; honorary doctorate degrees from numerous universities.

WRITINGS:

(With Howard Kaplan) *Dancing Spirit: An Autobiography,* Doubleday (New York, NY), 1993.

SIDELIGHTS: Judith Jamison has made important contributions to American modern dance as dancer, choreographer, and artistic director. She began studying dance at a time when there were few black role models for her to follow and was made famous in the 1970s in conjunction with the rise of the Alvin Ailey

American Dance Theatre (AAADT). A tall, strong, graceful, and emotive dancer, she starred in productions including the solo *Cry, Pas de Duke* with Mikhail Baryshnikov, and the Broadway show *Sophisticated Ladies* with Gregory Hines. She was hand picked by Ailey to succeed him as artistic director of AAADT, at a time when it was critically acclaimed but crippled by debts. She has since put her own mark on the company by improving its finances, embracing new choreographic styles, and otherwise adding her own personal vision to the guiding principles of her mentor. A few years after taking the helm at AAADT, Jamison wrote the memoir *Dancing Spirit: An Autobiography,* which reviews and comments on these experiences. The book was welcomed for its insight into Ailey's dynamic character and Jamison's own growth as a multi-talented figure in the world of dance.

Born and raised in Philadelphia, Jamison began studying dance at age six, when her parents enrolled her in dance class with the hope of making their unusually tall child more graceful. She made her formal debut in 1959, dancing in *Giselle.* After high school, Jamison began studying psychology at Fisk University, but after her freshman year left to attend dance school. In her autobiography, Jamison remembers not fitting in at Fisk, where classmates were perplexed by her dancing on pointe during halftime at basketball games. At the Philadelphia Dance Academy, Jamison exhibited exceptional talents. While attending a master class, she came under the eye of Agnes de Mille, who asked her to perform with the American Ballet Theatre in the *Four Marys.*

Once in New York City, Jamison decided to look for work as a professional dancer. She operated rides at the World's Fair before being spotted by Ailey at an audition for a Harry Belafonte television special. She failed to properly execute the jazz steps being taught at the tryout but nevertheless impressed Ailey, who asked her to join his modern dance company. With the AAADT she embarked on a rigorous touring schedule and traveled as far as western Europe and Senegal. Jamison became a principal dancer in the 1970s. Among her most notable dances is the solo *Cry,* which Ailey choreographed for Jamison. The piece is a tribute to black mothers which dramatizes their fortitude throughout generations of hardship. Another important role was in Ailey's *Pas de Duke,* part of a tribute to Duke Ellington that partnered Jamison with Mikhail Baryshnikov, the premiere male ballet dancer of the era.

During the fifteen years that she danced with AAADT, Jamison and Ailey became good friends. She left the company in 1980 to star in the Broadway show *Sophisticated Ladies,* but their ties remained strong. A few years later, Jamison's first work as a choreographer, *Divining,* was premiered by the Ailey company. In 1988 Jamison created her own dance company, the Jamison Project, which was based in Detroit and Philadelphia. Ailey was fatally ill when, in 1989, he asked Jamison to become his successor as artistic director of AAADT. She accepted and eventually merged her own company with his. Her new assignment included the challenge of saving AAADT from enormous debts. With a new board of directors, Jamison has solidified the company's financial footing and expanded its operations. Her innovations include a national dance program for underprivileged children, the Women's Choreography Initiative, performances at the Olympic Arts Festival in 1996, appearances in American Express commercials, and collaborating with Fordham University on a B.F.A program.

Writing her autobiography gave Jamison the opportunity to reflect on the challenges and rewards of her long involvement with dance. With its focus on professional rather than personal issues, *Dancing Spirit* reveals her to be a private person who is immersed in her work. One exception is the loving portrait Jamison draws of her parents, who instilled a love of the arts in their daughter. More frequently, Jamison concentrates on the life of a professional dancer, including the grind of touring, the physical demands of performing, and the heartbreak of injuries. She also writes about her relationships with other important dance figures, most importantly Ailey.

Critics enjoyed Jamison's first-hand knowledge of the dance world but often found the autobiography fails to illuminate the author's inner workings. *Dance Magazine* writer Doris Hering commented that the book is marred by a lack of editorial oversight, which resulted in factual and grammatical errors. She commended the book's photographs but felt that the disorganized material falls far short of a definitive biography.

Stronger reviews included comments from a *Publishers Weekly* writer, who described the memoir as an "engaging" account with a wider scope than Jamison's own experiences. "Above all, her portrait of the complicated Ailey himself is of interest," the critic said; "Welcoming, intelligent and chatty—sometimes, too chatty—she also brings down to earth the experience of performing." According to a *Kirkus Reviews* writer, *Dancing Spirit* provides a "good understanding . . . of her development and sense of purpose" and shows her to be woman with a strong religious faith. The critic judged that "Her narrative is sometimes sketchy and bewildering as she skips around the years" and that in the end Jamison "remains an enigma." Introducing an excerpt from the book, an *American Visions* writer noted that the book privileges professional experiences over personal ones, and thereby "melds the two images into one." Regarding the book's tone, the commentator said, "[Jamison] writes with a certain innocence, in a simple, direct style."

BIOGRAPHICAL AND CRITICAL SOURCES:

BOOKS

Contemporary Black Biography, Volume 7, Gale (Detroit, MI), 1994.
International Dictionary of Modern Dance, St. James Press (Detroit, MI), 1998.
Newsmakers 1990, Issue 3, Gale (Detroit, MI), 1990.
Notable Black American Women, Gale (Detroit, MI), 1992.

PERIODICALS

American Visions, October-November, 1993, "Judith Jamison Dances Her Way Through Life," p. 14.
Dance Magazine, July, 1994, Doris Hering, review of Dancing Spirit, p. 78.
Kirkus Reviews, October 1, 1993, review of *Dancing Spirit.*
Publishers Weekly, October 18, 1993, review of *Dancing Spirit,* p. 59.*

* * *

JENKINS, Daniel T(homas) 1914-2002

OBITUARY NOTICE—See index for *CA* sketch: Born June 9, 1914, in Merthyr Tydfil, Wales; died June 22, 2002, in London, England. Theologian, minister, edu-

cator, and author. Jenkins maintained two vocations on two continents, often simultaneously, for most of his working life. As an ordained Congregational minister, he preached at churches throughout England and Wales and in the United States. As a theologian, he taught for more than ten years at the University of Chicago, then at the newly created University of Sussex in England in the 1960s, ending his academic career as Weyerhaeuser Professor of Systematic Theology at Princeton Theological Seminary in New Jersey in the 1980s. Jenkins was powerfully drawn to the invigorating spirit of ecumenism in America, it was reported, as a contrast to the narrower and sometimes political divisiveness of Protestant denominations in England. His preaching, teaching, and writing all reflected his views on the importance of bringing people together rather than dividing them, which he explored in the book *Europe and America: Their Contributions to the World Church;* the relationship of Protestant theology to daily ministry, which he addressed in many books, including *The Gift of Ministry* and *The Nature of Catholicity;* and the relationship between Christian faith and public life. He worked with the Christian Frontier Council in London, an organization dedicated to that end, and authored books like *Equality and Excellence: A Christian Comment on Britain's Life* and *The Educated Society.* Another of Jenkins's concerns, particularly during the 1960s, was the increasingly secular society around him, especially at the university and within the Christian community. His concern prompted the book *Beyond Religion: The Truth and Error in "Religionless Christianity."*

OBITUARIES AND OTHER SOURCES:

PERIODICALS

Herald (Glasgow, Scotland), July 6, 2002, obituary by W. Gerald Jones, p. 18.
Independent (London, England), July 2, 2002, obituary by Elaine Kaye, p. 16.
Times (London, England), June 24, 2002, p. 35.

* * *

JONES, Bill T.
See JONES, William T.

JONES, William T. 1952-
(Bill T. Jones)

PERSONAL: Born February 15, 1952, in Bunnell, FL; son of Augustus (a migrant farm worker) and Estella (a migrant farm worker) Jones; partner of Arnie Zane (died 1988). *Education:* Attended the State University of New York (SUNY) at Binghamton, 1970. *Hobbies and other interests:* Gardening.

ADDRESSES: Home—Rockland County, NY. *Office*—Bill T. Jones/Arnie Zane Dance Company, 853 Broadway, Suite 1706, New York, NY 10003-4703.

CAREER: Dancer, choreographer, and company artistic director. American Dance Asylum, co-founder, 1973; Bill T. Jones/Arnie Zane & Company (later Bill T. Jones/Arnie Zane Dance Co.), co-founder and artistic director, 1982—; Lyon Opera Ballet, resident choreographer, 1994—. Has done commissioned works for modern dance, ballet, and opera companies, including the Alvin Ailey American Dance Company, Berkshire Ballet, Berlin Opera Ballet, Brooklyn Academy of Music's Next Wave Festival, Boston Ballet, Boston Lyric Opera, Diversions Dance Company, Glyndebourne Festival Opera, Houston Grand Opera, Lyon Opera Ballet, New York City Opera, and St. Luke's Chamber Orchestra.

AWARDS, HONORS: Fellowship for choreography, Artists Public Service, 1979; choreographic fellowships, National Endowment for the Arts, 1980, 1981, and 1982; New York Dance and Performance Award, 1989; Izzy award, 1990, for *Perfect Courage;* Dorothy B. Chandler Performing Arts Award, 1991; *Dance Magazine* award, 1993; MacArthur Foundation fellowship, 1994; *Boston Globe-Horn Book* picture book honor award, 1999, for *Dance.* With Arnie Zane, German Critics Award, 1980, for *Blauvelt Mountain;* New York Dance and Performance Award (Bessie) for choreographers/creators, 1986.

WRITINGS:

(With Arnie Zane) *Body Against Body: The Dance and Other Collaborations of Bill T. Jones and Arnie Zane,* edited by Elizabeth Zimmer and Susan Quasha, Station Hill Press (Barrytown, NY), 1989.

(With Peggy Gillespie) *Last Night on Earth,* Pantheon Books (New York, NY), 1995.

(With Susan Kuklin) *Dance,* photographed by Susan Kuklin, Hyperion Books for Children (New York, NY), 1998.

Wrote introduction to *Continuous Replay: The Photographs of Arnie Zane,* 1999.

SIDELIGHTS: The bold, innovative work of dancer and choreographer Bill T. Jones has made him a popular if sometimes controversial figure in American dance. As a gay, African-American artist, he has often treated themes of personal importance, including sexuality, racism, and terminal illness. He is creative director of the Bill T. Jones/Arnie Zane Dance Company, which he co-founded with his lover Arnie Zane. Since Zane's death of AIDS-related illness in 1988, it has grown to be an internationally acclaimed company. It is known for staging large-scale, postmodern productions that utilize vocalization, mime, and spontaneous movement as well as dance. With his tall, strong, graceful form, Jones has continued to perform into his fifties. He too is HIV-positive, but is asymptomatic. His other work includes serving as resident choreographer of the Lyons Opera Ballet and directing opera and theater. Jones has published *Body Against Body: The Dance and Other Collaborations of Bill T. Jones and Arnie Zane,* the autobiography *Last Night on Earth,* and the children's book *Dance,* which features photographs of Jones.

Jones enrolled at the State University of New York (SUNY) at Binghamton to run track and study theater, but he soon found a new passion after seeing a Martha Graham Company dance performance. Jones and Zane met at SUNY and soon became lovers and dance partners. Together, they discovered the contact improvisation classes that would form a basis for their later professional work. After a period that included living in Amsterdam and doing things other than dance, the pair formed Bill T. Jones/Arnie Zane & Company in 1982. Like their own early duet work, which highlighted their contrasting personalities and physical types—(with Jones being tall and black, and Zane shorter and white)—their company became known as a collection of dancers of all sizes, shapes, and races.

Among the most famous of Jones's works is the evening-length piece *Last Supper at Uncles Tom's Cabin/The Promised Land* (1990). It includes a narrative that retells Harriet Beecher Stowe's slave story *Uncle Tom's Cabin,* injects contemporary questions about faith and Christianity, and depicts humanity as a unified, vulnerable entity by placing some fifty naked non-dancers on stage, holding hands. The dance was denounced by the Vatican and earned some other negative responses, but was very successful. Another work that made headlines for Jones was *Still/Here* (1994), which used video from workshops that he held for terminally ill patients. Considerable debate was prompted when New York Times dance critic Arlene Croce denounced the piece as "victim art." She refused to review the work, saying that such material was undiscussible.

The dramatic turns of Jones's personal and professional life provided ample material for his autobiography, *Last Night on Earth.* Given Jones's notoriety, reviewers welcomed hearing his own reflections on his life and art. This includes commentary on his childhood, his early search for sexual and artistic identity, his volatile relationship with Zane, and the "survival workshops" he conducted after Zane's death. Writing for *Booklist,* Donna Seaman said the book is written with expected "eloquence" and "candor," and that the "cathartic narrative" reveals much about the author's purpose as an artist, "thus deepening our appreciation for his challenging creations." Another reviewer commented in *Publishers Weekly* that Jones "writes affectingly" of the various phases of his life and concluded that this was "an eloquent and moving autobiography."

In the children's book *Dance,* Jones teamed with co-author and photographer Susan Kuklin to create a work about why dancers dance. In an article for the *Horn Book Magazine* Kuklin revealed that Jones had wondered if he would appeal to children, and that she knew his boundless creativity was a perfect fit. "I didn't worry one bit, because children respond to honesty, and Bill is an honest artist. Creating this book was never short of wonderful," she said. The resulting book features simple but evocative text by the co-authors and photos by Kuklin that show Jones dancing across white pages. Also in the *Horn Book Magazine,* a reviewer described how "The spare and poetic text . . . moves in balanced harmony with the figure or figures on each page." The writer judged that more than other works showing young male dance students, Jones proved that everyone can share the joy of dance. *Booklist* writer Carolyn Phelan admired this "unusual" offering and considered it a good gift for dancers as

well as a welcome way to "broaden children's horizons" about dancing. A *Publishers Weekly* critic was especially pleased by the book's visual appeal, noting that "striking as the text is, the visuals win the highest accolades" in a book that was "marvelously designed."

Yet another reviewer addressed the question of what a controversial figure like Jones is doing in a children's book. In an article for *American Visions,* Kevin Brown advised that *Dance* is not only "a prudently wholesome affair," but that it is "a book that anyone can dream to . . . you close it having collaborated in a kind of imaginative duet." Brown also noted that it is just one of the diverse pursuits of an artist who will not be a dancer forever.

BIOGRAPHICAL AND CRITICAL SOURCES:

BOOKS

International Dictionary of Modern Dance, St. James Press (Detroit, MI), 1998.
Lesbian & Gay Biography, St. James Press (Detroit, MI), 1997.

PERIODICALS

American Visions, December, 1998, Kevin Brown, "Bill T. Jones Makes Curves," p. 34.
Booklist, September 1, 1995, Donna Seaman, review of *Last Night on Earth,* p. 26; November 15, 1998, Carolyn Phelan, review of *Dance,* p. 593.
Horn Book Magazine, January, 1999, review of *Dance,* p. 79; January, 2000, Susan Kuklin, "Creating Dance," p. 7.
Publishers Weekly, June 26, 1995, review of *Last Night on Earth,* p. 97; October 5, 1998, review of *Dance,* p. 91.*

*   *   *

JORDAN, June (Meyer) 1936-2002
June Meyer

OBITUARY NOTICE—See index for *CA* sketch: Born July 9, 1936, in New York, NY; died of breast cancer, June 14, 2002, in Berkeley, CA. Educator, poet, playwright, librettist, and author. Jordan has been described as a writer for every person who ever felt like an outsider. The prolific, award-winning author wrote from a perspective distinctly African-American, in a voice resoundingly female, but her themes and her message of hope were directed at everyone willing to listen and learn. Jordan was born in Harlem and grew up in Brooklyn. She began her teaching career in the 1960s. At the State University of New York at Stony Brook in the 1980s, she directed the Poetry Center. At the University of California at Berkeley in the 1990s, Jordan taught African-American studies and women's studies. She also founded the Poetry for the People program, where undergraduate students learned how to teach poetry and reach out to the community, at schools or prisons, among the poor and homeless, wherever they found people in need of a voice. Jordan championed the cause of women, children, and the African-American community above all. She often employed the dialect of "Black English," and her poetry in particular has been described as alternately blunt and exquisitely tender. Jordan was nominated for the National Book Award in 1971 for the children's book *His Own Where—,* and she won the Herald Angel Award from the Edinburgh Arts Festival in 1995 for the opera libretto *I Was Looking at the Ceiling and Then I Saw the Sky.* She was also a playwright. Critics have been especially drawn to Jordan's essay collections, in which she discussed her views on many subjects, often controversial and always rooted in her experience as an African-American woman. These collections include *Technical Difficulties: African-American Notes on the State of the Union* and *Affirmative Acts: New Political Essays.* In all, Jordan penned nearly thirty books, including *The Haruko: Love Poetry of June Jordan* and *Kissing God Goodbye: New Poems.* Prior to 1969 she wrote under the name June Meyer.

OBITUARIES AND OTHER SOURCES:

BOOKS

Contemporary Poets, 7th edition, St. James Press (Detroit, MI), 2001.
Jordan, June, *Civil Wars: Selected Essays, 1963-1980,* Beacon Press, 1981, revised edition, Scribner (New York, NY), 1996.
Jordan, June, *Soldier: A Poet's Childhood,* Basic Civitas Books, 1999.

PERIODICALS

Los Angeles Times, June 15, 2002, obituary by Jon Thurber, p. B19.

New York Times, June 18, 2002, obituary by Dinitia Smith, p. A23.
Washington Post, June 16, 2002, obituary by Jon Thurber, p. C8.

*   *   *

JURAFSKY, Daniel 1962-

PERSONAL: Born 1962 in Yonkers, NY. *Education:* University of California, Berkeley, B.A. (with honors), 1983, Ph.D., 1992. *Hobbies and other interests:* Playing jazz (drums), performing in plays and musicals.

ADDRESSES: Home—734 Maxwell Ave., Boulder, CO 80304. *Office*—Department of Linguistics, 290 Hellems, University of Colorado, Boulder, CO 80309; fax: 303-492-4416. *E-mail*—jurafsky@colorado.edu.

CAREER: Freelance engineer and consultant, 1983-92; International Computer Science Institute, post-doctoral researcher, 1992-95; University of California, Berkeley, adjunct assistant professor of linguistics, 1993-94; University of Colorado, Boulder, assistant professor, 1996-2001, associate professor of linguistics and computer science, 2001—.

MEMBER: Association for Computational Linguistics (executive committee member), Linguistic Society of America (chair of computing, 2000), Computer Speech and Language (editorial board member.)

AWARDS, HONORS: National Science Foundation Career Award, 1997; MacArthur fellow, John D. and Catherine T. MacArthur Foundation, 2002.

WRITINGS:

(Editor, with Barbara A. Fox and Laura A. Michaelis) *Cognition and Function in Language,* Center for the Study of Language and Information Publications (Stanford, CA), 1999.
(With James H. Martin) *Speech and Language Processing: An Introduction to Natural Language Processing, Speech Recognition, and Computational Linguistics,* Prentice Hall (Upper Saddle, NJ), 2002.

Contributor to journals including *Cognitive Science, Language and Speech, Studies in the Linguistic Sciences, Probabilistic Linguistics, Computational Linguistics,* and *Computer Speech and Language* (editorial board member.)

Contributor to books including *Frequency and the Emergence of Linguistic Structure,* John Benjamins, 2001; *Handbook of Pragmatics,* Blackwell, 2002; *Probability Theory in Linguistics,* MIT Press, 2002; *The Lexical Basis of Sentence Processing: Formal, Computational, and Experimental Issues,* John Benjamins, 2002; *Papers in Laboratory Phonology VII,* Mouton de Gruyter, 2002; and *Exploring AI in the New Millenium,* Morgan Kaufmann, 2002.

SIDELIGHTS: Daniel Jurafsky was shocked when he heard the news that he was one of twenty-four Americans to receive the prestigious MacArthur Fellowship—the honor comes with a $500,000 grant. Jurafsky is the sixth University of Colorado professor to be chosen as a MacArthur fellow since the John D. and Catherine T. MacArthur Foundation introduced the awards in 1981. The grant is awarded to writers, scientists, artists and, humanists who have excelled in their respective fields with exceptional originality, creativity, and dedication to future advances.

Jurafsky, a computational linguist, won for his research on "improving the capacity for computers to process natural language by analyzing the syntax and usage of ordinary sentences," he told the *Denver Post.*

Jurafsky has been teaching at the University of Colorado since 1996 in the Department of Linguistics, the Department of Computer Science, and the Institute of Cognitive Science. He is coauthor of the book *Speech and Language Processing: An Introduction to Natural Language Processing,* a comprehensive reference book that covers how algorithms from different domains—computer science and linguistics—can be tied together. He is also coeditor of *Cognition and Function in Language.**

BIOGRAPHICAL AND CRITICAL SOURCES:

PERIODICALS

Denver Post, September 25, 2002, "CU Professor Is Awarded 'Genius Grant' of $500,000," p. P-01.
Rocky Mountain News, September 25, 2002, Barry Gutierrez, "CU Professor Chosen for 'Genius Award' MacArthur Fellow to Receive $500,000 to Spend as He Likes," p. 4A.

OTHER

Daniel Jurafsky Home Page, http://www.colorado.edu/ (September 30, 2002).
MacArthur Fellows Web Site, http://www.macfound. org/ (September 30, 2002).

K

KAMEN, Martin D(avid) 1913-2002

OBITUARY NOTICE—Born August 17, 1913, in Toronto, Ontario, Canada; died of pneumonia, August 31, 2002, in Santa Barbara, CA. Biochemist, educator, and author. In 1940 Kamen and a colleague at the University of California in Berkeley discovered the radioactive isotope Carbon-14, a key that opened the door to the emerging field of biochemistry. It is also the discovery that most people associate with the later development of the carbon-dating technique that revolutionized modern archaeology. It would be many years, however, before he began to accumulate the accolades due an achievement of such magnitude. During World War II Kamen worked on the Manhattan Project in Oak Ridge, Tennessee, where he accidentally stumbled upon and reported evidence of a secret nuclear reactor at the site. Later, in an unrelated incident, he was observed dining with representatives of the Soviet Union, and the ensuing scandal nearly ruined his career. Kamen was fired from his job in Berkeley, hauled before the House Un-American Activities Committee, denied a United States passport, and vilified in the press as a spy. Eventually Kamen was exonerated and resumed his scientific career, but as he described in his book, *Radiant Science, Dark Politics: A Memoir of the Nuclear Age,* the experience nearly drove him to suicide. Kamen later taught at various universities, retiring from both the University of California at San Diego and the University of Southern California in the 1970s. An accomplished chamber musician, he continued to play the viola in retirement. Kamen's many, if belated, honors include the Enrico Fermi Award of the United States Department of Energy, the C. F. Kettering Award of the American Society of Plant Physiologists, and the Merck Award of the American Society of Biological Chemists.

OBITUARIES AND OTHER SOURCES:

BOOKS

Kamen, Martin D., *Radiant Science, Dark Politics: A Memoir of the Nuclear Age,* University of California Press (Berkeley, CA), 1985.

PERIODICALS

Chicago Tribune, September 7, 2002, pp. 1-23.
Los Angeles Times, September 6, 2002, obituary by Thomas H. Maugh II, p. B12.
New York Times, September 5, 2002, obituary by Kenneth Chang, p. A21.
Washington Post, September 8, 2002, p. C7.

*　　*　　*

KAMIN, Blair 1957-

PERSONAL: Born August 6, 1957, in Red Bank, NJ; son of Arthur Z. and Virginia P. Kamin; married Barbara Mahany (a reporter); children: Willie. *Education:* Amherst College, B.A., 1979; Yale University, M.A. (environmental design,) 1984.

ADDRESSES: Office—Chicago Tribune, 435 North Michigan Ave., Chicago, IL 60611.

CAREER: Des Moines Register, Des Moines, IA, reporter, 1984-87; *Chicago Tribune,* Chicago, IL, reporter, 1987-88, suburban affairs writer, 1988-92, culture news reporter, 1992, architecture critic, 1992—. Franke Institute for the Humanities, University of Chicago, visiting fellow, 1999.

AWARDS, HONORS: National Education Reporting Award, Education Writers Association, 1985; Edward Scott Beck Award, *Chicago Tribune,* 1990; Pulitzer Prize for Criticism, 1999, for writings about redevelopment efforts on the Chicago waterfront; Polk Award for criticism; American Institute of Architects' Institute Honor for Collaborative Achievement; eight-time recipient of the Peter Lisagor Award for Exemplary Journalism.

WRITINGS:

Tribune Tower: American Landmark: History, Architecture, and Design, photography by Bob Fila, Tribune Company (Chicago, IL), 2000.
Why Architecture Matters: Lessons from Chicago, University of Chicago Press (Chicago, IL), 2001.

SIDELIGHTS: Architecture critic Blair Kamin has been a *Chicago Tribune* fixture for more than a decade, publishing nearly 1,000 bylined articles. In 2001, Kamin collected sixty-one of his "piercing, often witty columns," to quote *Austin American-Statesman*'s Jeanne Claire Van Ryzin, in *Why Architecture Matters: Lessons from Chicago.* These articles include his Pulitzer Prize-winning columns.

Withold Rybczynski, in the *Times Literary Supplement,* noted the impact of *New York Times* architecture critic Paul Goldberger on Kamin, who attended a seminar at Yale University that featured Goldberger. "Goldberger's influence is clearly visible in Kamin's writing, which steers clear of obscure jargon and aims to situate architecture in a broader cultural setting." Rybczynski cited Kamin's "affection for his city [which] colours every page of *Why Architecture Matters.*"

John King wrote in the *San Francisco Chronicle,* "This is no abstract dissertation on Ionic columns; rather, it tackles how architecture shapes the way we live."

Choice reviewer R.W. Liscombe called Kamin's article on the Sears Tower "masterly," and said *Why Architecture Matters* would appeal to specialists and general readers alike.

Kamin, in his *Chicago Tribune* column, weighs in on everything from rebuilding plans for the devastated World Trade Center site in New York to a stadium proposal for Chicago's professional football team, the Bears.

As an example of Kamin's influence, *Sports Illustrated's* Lester Munson, citing opposition to an "extravagant lakefront colossus" proposed for the Bears, said Kamin called it a "monstrosity" and an "eyesore."

BIOGRAPHICAL AND CRITICAL SOURCES:

PERIODICALS

American Statesman (Austin, TX), November 18, 2001, Jeanne Claire Van Ryzin, "Critic Looks beyond the Bricks and Beams," p. L7.
Choice, March, 2002, R.W. Liscombe, review of *Why Architecture Matters: Lessons from Chicago,* p. 1229.
San Francisco Chronicle, October 14, 2001, John King, "Architecture—The Art We Live With," p. R3.
Times Literary Supplement, November 2, 2001, pp. 13-15.

OTHER

CNN-Sports Illustrated Web site, http://sports illustrated.cnn.com/ (September 27, 2001), Lester Munson, "Bears May Lose Stadium Deal."
Metropolis Magazine, http://www.metropolismag.com/ (April 10, 2002), Julie Lasky, "The Great American Exaggeration."
New York Observer Web site, http://www.observer. com/ (August 8, 2002), Tom McGeveran, "At Tower Site Vast Top Seen as Memorial."*

*   *   *

KATZEN, Halbert

PERSONAL: Male. *Education:* Brandeis University, B.A.; University of Colorado, M.B.A. and J.D.

ADDRESSES: Agent—c/o Insights Out Publishing, P.O. Box 11286, Boulder, CO 80301. *E-mail*—halbert7@aol.com.

CAREER: Lawyer, spiritual educator, writer, and public speaker.

WRITINGS:

The Logic of Love: Finding Faith through the Heart-Mind Connection, Insights Out Publishing (Boulder, CO), 2000.

Contributor of articles to journals.

BIOGRAPHICAL AND CRITICAL SOURCES:

PERIODICALS

Publishers Weekly, November 29, 1999, review of *The Logic of Love,* p. 68.*

* * *

KAUFMAN, Charlie 1958-

PERSONAL: Full name, Charles Stewart Kaufman; born November, 1958, in NY; son of Myron (an engineer) and Helen (a homemaker) Kaufman; married, wife's name Denise. *Education:* Attended Boston University and New York University.

ADDRESSES: Home—Pasadena, CA. *Agent*—c/o Marty Bowen, United Talent Agency, 9560 Wilshire Blvd., 5th Floor, Beverly Hills, CA 90212.

CAREER: Producer and author of screenplays for film and television. Staff writer for television shows, including *Get a Life!,* 1990-92, *The Edge,* 1992-93, *The Dana Carvey Show,* 1996, and *Ned and Stacey,* 1996-97; producer of television shows, including *Ned and Stacey* and *Misery Loves Company.*

AWARDS, HONORS: Academy Award nomination for Best Screenplay Written Directly for the Screen, Academy of Motion Picture Arts and Sciences, Golden Globe nominations for best motion picture, musical or comedy, and best screenplay, Hollywood Foreign Press Association, Golden Satellite awards for best picture, comedy, best picture (tie), and best screenplay, National Society of Film Critics, and best original screenplay designations from Online Film Critics Society and Los Angeles Film Critics Association, all 1999, all for *Being John Malkovich;* best screenwriter citations, National Board of Review, Boston Film Critics Association, New York Film Critics Circle, and Toronto Film Critics Association, all 2002, all for *Adaptation.*

WRITINGS:

SCREENPLAYS

(And executive producer) *Being John Malkovich* (USA Films, 1999), Faber & Faber (New York, NY), 2000.
(And producer) *Human Nature,* New Line Cinema, 2001.
Confessions of a Dangerous Mind, Miramax, 2002.
(And executive producer) *Adaptation* (Columbia Pictures Industries, Inc., 2002), Newmarket Press (New York, NY), 2002.
Eternal Sunshine of the Spotless Mind, USA Films, 2003.

SIDELIGHTS: California-based writer Charlie Kaufman has gained a high profile in the film world for his work on such quirky, mind-bending screenplays as *Being John Malkovich* and *Adaptation.* These films in particular, which offer viewers a "funhouse ride through Kaufman's cerebral cortex" in the words of film reviewer Brian D. Johnson in *Maclean's,* have proved popular with critics and audiences alike.

"I don't know how a movie this original got made today, but thank God for wonderful aberrations," David Ansen commented in *Newsweek* after seeing Kaufman's first film. Released in 1999, *Being John Malkovich* is a bizarre saga about a shy, depressed puppeteer named Craig—played by John Cusack—who stumbles upon a trap door that lets him spend fifteen minutes at a time inside the mind of middle-aged actor—and film costar—John Malkovich. Craig and his coworker, Maxine start charging people 200 dollars each for the fifteen-minute Malkovich ride. *Be-*

ing John Malkovich "toys with the mutual yearning that binds actor and audience," Jan Stuart noted in his review for the *Advocate.* "The actor thrives by inhabiting all manner of people, while the little people they emulate burn to know, if not be, them." However, this is not the only message of the film: the puppeteer also finds that a real human being is the ultimate puppet as he, his frumpy, repressed wife—played by Cameron Diaz—and Maxine play out their fantasies—including sexual ones—through the body of the actor Malkovich.

The more recent film *Adaptation* is a highly metatextual film loosely based on Kaufman's own life. In 1998, after completing *Being John Malkovich,* Kaufman was asked to write a screenplay based on journalist Susan Orlean's book *The Orchid Thief: A True Story of Beauty and Obsession.* This book, inspired by an actual theft of rare orchids in Florida but largely consisting of meditations on the nature of obsession, offered little for Kaufman to work with. To make matters worse, Kaufman had sold the idea for a separate project, *Eternal Sunshine of the Spotless Mind,* to another production company, so he was facing two script deadlines. Frustrated by his inability to adapt *The Orchid Thief* and unable to quit the project since he had already been paid, Kaufman began to write himself into the story.

Adaptation begins with Charlie Kaufman, played by actor Nicholas Cage, on the set of *Being John Malkovich.* Just like the real Kaufman, Cage is attempting to write a script based on *The Orchid Thief* and is frustrated and in danger of being mentally and emotionally consumed by his task. He is also obsessed with the beautiful Susan Orlean, played by Meryl Streep. Unlike the real Kaufman, the film version of the screenwriter has a twin brother named Donald Kaufman—also played by Cage—who writes a formulaic Hollywood blockbuster full of sex, drugs, and violence wherein the protagonists learn neatly packaged life lessons and live happily ever after. In collaboration with Donald, Charlie begins to include crowd-pleasing features into his own script, which is the screenplay for the movie that the viewer is now watching. The end result, David Ansen explained in *Newsweek,* is "an inspired flight of fancy, an oddly poignant examination of the creative process, a rumination on adaptation (orchids to their environment, books to the screen and misfits like Charlie to life) and, in its ultimate irony, a story in which our hero learns a life-altering lesson." Viewers of *Adapta-*

tion may be forgiven for not realizing that there is no Donald Kaufman in real life; in the film's credits the fictional twin is named as a coauthor of the film.

"I intentionally don't do anything or write anything or think anything that I don't feel is risky," Kaufman said in an interview with Anthony Kaufman for indieWIRE online. "Not even if I've taken a job, if I can't see what the risk is or danger is or how it could fail miserably, then I can't do it. Because I feel like that's cheating and it's not worth anything. You're not giving anybody anything. You're not doing anything. And I want to do something," Kaufman added. "I want to put something interesting, as interesting as I can be, into the world."

BIOGRAPHICAL AND CRITICAL SOURCES:

PERIODICALS

Advocate, Jan Stuart, review of *Being John Malkovich,* p. 67.

Daily Variety, November 15, 2002, Michael Fleming, "The Truth about Charlie," p. 2.

Entertainment Weekly, April 19, 2002, Owen Gleiberman, review of *Human Nature,* p. 47; November 15, 2002, Dan Snierson, review of *Adaptation,* p. 53; December 6, 2002, Lisa Schwarzbaum, review of *Adaptation.*

Esquire, April, 2002, interview with Kaufman, p. 30; December, 2002, Mike Sager, interview with Kaufman, pp. 139-140; January, 2003, Tom Carson, review of *Adaptation,* pp. 36-37.

Film Comment, September, 1999, Chris Chang, review of *Being John Malkovich,* p. 6; March-April, 2002, Alice Lovejoy, review of *Human Nature,* pp. 73-74.

Hollywood Reporter, November 11, 2002, Kirk Honeycutt, review of *Adaptation,* pp. 7-8.

Interview, April, 2002, Scott Lyle Cohen, review of *Human Nature,* p. 74.

Maclean's, November 15, 1999, Brian D. Johnson, review of *Being John Malkovich,* p. 152; December 9, 2002, Brian D. Johnson, review of *Adaptation,* p. 78.

Nation, December 23, 2002, Stuart Klawans, review of *Adaptation,* p. 42.

Newsweek, November 1, 1999, David Ansen, review of *Being John Malkovich,* p. 85; April 15, 2002, Devin Gordon, review of *Human Nature,* p. 56; December 9, 2002, Devin Gordon, interview with Kaufman, p. 82, David Ansen, review of *Adaptation,* p. 83.

New York, November 8, 1999, Peter Rainer, review of *Being John Malkovich,* pp. 63-64.

New York Times, December 6, 2002, A. O. Scott, review of *Adaptation;* December 9, 2002, Sarah Boxer, review of *Adaptation.*

People, April 22, 2002, Leah Rozen, review of *Human Nature,* p. 35; December 16, 2002, Leah Rozen, review of *Adaptation,* p. 45.

Time, April 29, 2002, Belinda Luscombe, profile of Kaufman, p. 16.

Variety, September 6, 1999, David Rooney, review of *Being John Malkovich,* p. 61; May 28, 2001, Todd McCarthy, review of *Human Nature,* p. 19.

OTHER

Audience, http://www.audiencemag.com/ (December 19, 2002), J. Rentilly, interview with Kaufman.

Being Charlie Kaufman, http://www.beingcharlie kaufman.tripod.com (December 19, 2002).

Chicago Sun-Times, http://www.suntimes.com/ (December 19, 2002), Roger Ebert, review of *Being John Malkovich.*

Hollywood.com, http://www.hollywood.com/ (December 19, 2002), biography of Kaufman.

indieWIRE, http://www.indiewire.com/ (December 19, 2002), Anthony Kaufman, interview with Kaufman.

NuReel.com, http://www.nureel.com/ (March 26, 2002), interview with Kaufman.*

*   *   *

KEACH, James 1948-

PERSONAL: Born December 7, 1948, in Flushing, NY; son of Walter Stacy Keach, Sr. (a producer, actor, writer, and drama coach); married Holly Collins (divorced); married Mimi Maynard (divorced, 1993); married Jane Seymour (an actress and producer), May 15, 1993; children: (first marriage) Kalen; (third marriage) twin sons, John Stacy and Kristopher Steven.

ADDRESSES: Agent—Metropolitan Talent Agency, 4526 Wilshire Blvd., Los Angeles, CA 90010.

CAREER: Actor, producer, director, writer. Film appearances include *Sunburst,* CFA, 1975; *New World,* 1976; *Death Play,* New Line Cinema, 1976; *FM,*

Universal, 1977; *God Bless Dr. Shagetz,* 1977; *Comes a Horseman,* United Artists, 1978; *Hurricane,* Paramount, 1979; *The Long Riders,* United Artists, 1980; *Smokey and the Hotwire Gang,* 1980; *The Legend of the Lone Ranger,* 1981; *Love Letters,* New World, 1983; *National Lampoon's Summer Vacation,* Warner Bros., 1983; *Moving Violations,* Twentieth Century-Fox, 1984; *Stand Alone,* New World, 1984; *The Razor's Edge,* Columbia, 1984; *Wildcats,* Columbia, 1985; *Evil Town,* Trans World Entertainment, 1987; *The Experts,* 1989; *Options,* 1989; *The Dance Goes On,* 1992; *The New Swiss Family Robinson,* 1998. Film work includes (executive producer) *The Long Riders,* United Artists, 1980; (producer) *Armed and Dangerous,* Columbia, 1986; (producer) *The Experts,* 1989; (associate producer and director) *False Identity,* 1990; (director) *The Stars Fell on Henrietta,* 1995; (director) *Camouflage,* Sunland Studios, 1999.

Television movie appearances include *Orville and Wilbur,* PBS, 1972; *The Hatfields and the McCoys,* ABC, 1975; *Miles to Go before I Sleep,* CBS, 1975; *Kill Me If You Can,* NBC, 1977; *The Blue Hotel,* PBS, 1977; *Nowhere to Run,* NBC, 1978; *Like Normal People,* ABC, 1979; *The Great Cash Giveaway Getaway,* NBC, 1980; *Thou Shall Not Kill,* NBC, 1982; *The Man Who Broke 1,000 Chains,* HBO, 1987; *Good Cops, Bad Cops,* NBC, 1990; *Murder in High Places,* NBC, 1991; *The New Swiss Family Robinson,* ABC, 1998; *Enslavement: The True Story of Fanny Kemble,* Showtime, 2000. Appearances on episodic television include "The Assassin," *Kung Fu,* 1973; "The Man Who Couldn't Forget," *Cannon,* 1974; "A Coven of Killers," *S.W.A.T.,* 1975; "Lady Blue," *Starsky and Hutch,* 1975; "Trouble at Fort Apache," *Baa Baa Black Sheep,* 1976; "Cry Wolf," *Cannon,* 1976; "Day of Outrage," *The Quest,* 1976; "I Love You, Rosey Malone," *Starsky and Hutch,* 1977; "Hostage," *Dr. Quinn, Medicine Woman,* CBS, 1997. Appearances on TV specials include *Spotlight with Phyllis George,* The Nashville Network, 1996; *Marry Me!,* The Family Channel, 1997; *Intimate Portrait: Jane Seymour,* Lifetime, 1998; *Disney's Animal Kingdom: The First Adventure,* ABC, 1998; Appeared in *Six Characters in Search of an Author.* Appearances in TV pilots include *Lacy and the Mississippi Queen,* NBC, 1978; *Big Bend Country,* CBS, 1981; *Wishman,* ABC, 1983. Other television appearances include *Till Death Do Us Part,* 1982. Television movie work as director (unless otherwise noted) includes *Sunstroke,* USA Network, 1992; *Praying Mantis,* USA Network, 1993; *A Passion for Justice: The Hazel Brannon Smith Story,* ABC, 1994; *The Absolute Truth,* CBS, 1997; *A Marriage of Convenience,* Lifetime, 1998; *Dr. Quinn, Medicine Woman: The Movie,* CBS, 1999; (executive producer) *A Memory in My Heart,* CBS, 1999; *Enslavement: The True Story of Fanny Kemble,* Showtime, 2000; *Murder in the Mirror,* CBS, 2000; *Blackout,* 2001; *Submerged,* 2001; *Moms on Strike,* 2002. Work on episodic television as director includes *The Young Riders,* ABC, 1989; *Covington Cross,* ABC, 1992; *Jack's Place,* ABC, 1993; *Dr. Quinn, Medicine Woman,* CBS, 1993-1998. Other television work includes (producer) *A Winner Never Quits,* ABC, 1986; (producer) *The Young Riders,* ABC, 1991-92; (director) *Blackout,* 2001.

Stage appearances include *Henry IV, Part I,* in *The Wars of the Roses,* New York Shakespeare Festival, Delacorte Theatre, New York City, 1970; *Henry IV, Part II,* in *The Wars of the Roses,* New York Shakespeare Festival, Delacorte Theatre, 1970; *Richard III,* in *The Wars of the Roses,* New York Shakespeare Festival, Delacorte Theatre, 1970; *The Outcry,* Lyceum Theatre, New York City, 1973; *The Tooth of Crime,* Center Theatre Group, New Theatre for Now, Mark Taper Forum, Los Angeles, 1973; *What Have You Done for Me Lately?,* Callboard Theatre, Hollywood, CA, 1984. Appeared in *Hamlet, Romeo and Juliet, The Tempest,* and *Troilus and Cressida,* all New York Shakespeare Festival; also appeared in *Metamorphosis* and *Grimm's Fairytales,* both in Paul Sills' Story Theatre.

WRITINGS:

(With William Bryden, Steven Phillip Smith, and Stacy Keach) *The Long Riders* (screenplay), United Artists, 1980.
The Forgotten (television movie script), USA Network, 1989.

CHILDREN'S BOOKS

(With wife, Jane Seymour) *Splat! The Tale of a Colorful Cat,* illustrated by Geoffrey Planer, G. P. Putnam's Sons (New York, NY), 1998.
(With Jane Seymour) *Yum! A Tale of Two Cookies,* illustrated by Planer, G. P. Putnam's Sons (New York, NY), 1998.

(With Jane Seymour) *Boing! No Bouncing on the Bed,* illustrated by Planer, G. P. Putnam's Sons (New York, NY), 1998.

ADAPTATIONS: The film *Armed and Dangerous,* released by Columbia in 1986, is based on a story by Keach.

SIDELIGHTS: With his brother, Stacy Keach, and two others, James Keach wrote the screenplay of *The Long Riders,* an acclaimed 1980 film in which three sets of actor brothers—the Keaches, the Carradines, and the Quaids—play the notorious James, Younger, and Miller brothers of the Old West. More recently, Keach and wife Jane Seymour have written a series of children's books inspired by their twin sons John Stacy and Kristopher Steven. G. P. Putnam's Sons printed some 90,000 copies of the first two, *Splat! The Tale of a Colorful Cat* and *Yum! A Tale of Two Cookies,* released simultaneously in 1998, and by November of that year, the two books had gone into a second printing.

These tales center on the twin kittens This One and That One, offspring of Big Jim and Lady Jane, who live in Malibu, California. In *Splat!,* the mother goes shopping and leaves the father in charge of the kittens. Big Jim lets them use their mother's paintbrushes, and when they ask him what they should paint, he says, "Don't be furbrained—use your imagination. Pablo Picatso and Henri Catisse didn't ask their dad for ideas." Just before he dozes off in his armchair, Big Jim suggests that they paint him—a suggestion that, as misinterpreted by the twins, results in much mischief, mayhem, and mess.

Yum! begins as Lady Jane is baking cookies. After putting the twins to bed, she takes a basket of cookies to Big Jim, who is fishing under the moonlight, but unbeknownst to her, This One and That One have stowed away in her basket and eaten the cookies. The book ends with the entire family dancing "on the sand. By the sea. By the light of the moon." *Boing! No Bouncing on the Bed* is a "no-jumping-on-the-bed" tale in the tradition of the classic rhyme about "ten little monkeys jumping on the bed." This time, however, after repeated attempts to stop the twins from jumping on the bed, Lady Jane finally joins them, and when Big Jim discovers them at play, he joins in too. "Though hardly essential purr-chases," wrote a reviewer in *Publishers Weekly,* discussing the first two books, "these are cheerful little capers."

BIOGRAPHICAL AND CRITICAL SOURCES:

BOOKS

Contemporary Theatre, Film, and Television, volume 34, Gale (Detroit, MI), 2001.

PERIODICALS

Christian Century, July 16, 1980, James M. Wall, review of *The Long Riders,* p. 739.

Dallas Morning News, November 2, 1998, Nancy Churnin, "Real-Life Twins Inspired Books by Seymour, Keach," p. C3.

Horizon, July, 1980, Timothy Lovejoy, review of *The Long Riders,* p. 71.

Ladies Home Journal, August, 1980, Gene Shalit, review of *The Long Riders,* p. 24.

New Republic, May 31, 1980, Stanley Kauffmann, review of *The Long Riders,* pp. 24-25.

New Statesman, September 5, 1980, Sean Hignett, review of *The Long Riders,* pp. 26-27.

New York, May 26, 1980, David Denby, review of *The Long Riders,* pp. 68-69.

New Yorker, May 19, 1980, Roger Angell, review of *The Long Riders,* pp. 143-145.

People Weekly, June 16, 1980, review of *The Long Riders,* p. 28.

Publishers Weekly, September 28, 1998, review of *Splat! The Tale of a Colorful Cat* and *Yum! A Tale of Two Cookies,* p. 100.

School Library Journal, February, 1999, Blair Christolon, review of *Splat! The Tale of a Colorful Cat* and *Yum! A Tale of Two Cookies,* pp. 88-89; November, 1999, Roxanne Burg, review of *Boing! No Bouncing on the Bed,* p. 130.

Time, June 16, 1980, Richard Schickel, review of *The Long Riders,* p. 51.

Washingtonian, July, 1980, Dan Rottenberg, review of *The Long Riders,* p. 49.*

KUKRIT PRAMOJ, M. R.
See PRAMOJ, M(on) R(ajawong) Kukrit

*   *   *

KUSCH, Robert 1934-

PERSONAL: Born 1934. *Education:* Valparaiso University, B.A.; Northwestern University, M.A. and Ph.D.

ADDRESSES: Office—Department of English, 51 Murray Hall, Rutgers University, 510 George St., New Brunswick, NJ 08901-1167.

CAREER: Rutgers University, New Brunswick, NJ, associate professor of English.

WRITINGS:

My Toughest Mentor: Theodore Roethke and William Carlos Williams (1940-1948), Bucknell University Press (Lewisburg, PA), 1999.

Contributor of articles and poetry to periodicals, including *Contemporary Poetry, Journal of Modern Literature, Chicago Review, California Quarterly, Critical Quarterly, Pembroke, Sewanee Review,* and *Yale Review.*

BIOGRAPHICAL AND CRITICAL SOURCES:

PERIODICALS

Choice, January, 2000, G. Grieve-Carlson, review of *My Toughest Mentor: Theodore Roethke and William Carlos Williams (1940-1948),* p. 933.*

L

La DUE, William J. 1928-

PERSONAL: Born March 15, 1928, in Milwaukee, WI; son of Charles S. (an engraver) and Agnes May (O'Rourke) La Due; married Margaret L. Halbur (a teacher of humanities), July 1, 1977. *Education:* St. Francis Seminary, Milwaukee, WI, B.A., 1951; Gregorian University, Rome, Italy, L.Th., 1955; Lateran University, Rome, Italy, D.C.L., 1960. *Religion:* Roman Catholic.

ADDRESSES: Home and office—7536 East Camino de Querabi, Tucson, AZ 85715-4264.

CAREER: Ordained Roman Catholic priest, 1954, laicized, 1976; St. Francis Seminary, Milwaukee, WI, professor of canon law, 1963-76, dean of studies, 1965-70; First Wisconsin Bank (now U.S. Bancorp), Milwaukee, vice president and district manager, beginning 1976; First Interstate Bank (now Wells Fargo Bank), Tucson, AZ, vice president and district manager, until 1993; freelance writer, 1993—. Alverno College, member of board of trustees, 1968-70; Catholic University of America, visiting assistant professor, 1972-74, acting department chair, 1973-74.

MEMBER: American Academy of Religion, Canon Law Society of America.

WRITINGS:

The Chair of Saint Peter: A Short History of the Papacy, Orbis Books (Maryknoll, NY), 1999.
Jesus among the Theologians: Contemporary Interpretations of Christ, Trinity Press International (Harrisburg, PA), 2001.
The Journey to the Trinity: An Introduction to Trinitarian Belief, Trinity Press International (Harrisburg, PA), 2003.

Contributor to periodicals, including *Jurist, Pastoral Life, American Ecclesiastical Review, Studia Canonica,* and *Living Light.*

WORK IN PROGRESS: A manuscript on Christian eschatology, "concentrating on the data contained in the Old and New Testaments, the patristic and medieval contributions, and summaries of recent scholars on the subject."

SIDELIGHTS: William J. La Due told *CA:* "On the basis of my religious and secular professional backgrounds, my aim is to communicate in popular and readable terms the basic tenets of the Christian tradition, so that men and women in secular as well as religious life may be able to explore recent developments in these critical religious areas. My emphasis is on contemporary contributions in Christian theology from Protestant, Catholic, and Orthodox points of view."

*   *   *

LAKE, Don(ald) 1953-

PERSONAL: Born July 19, 1953, in Toronto, Canada.

ADDRESSES: Agent—Abrams Artists Agency, 9200 West Sunset Blvd., #1125, West Hollywood, CA 90069-3606.

CAREER: Actor, screenwriter, film editor, and producer. Worked on *Second City TV,* Chicago. Film appearances include *Don't Answer the Phone!,* Crown International Pictures, 1980; *Lookin' to Get Out,* Paramount, 1982; *Police Academy,* Warner Bros., 1984; *The Pink Chiquitas,* 1986; *Blue Monkey,* International Spectrafilm, 1987; *The Big Town,* Columbia Pictures, 1987; *Short Circuit 2,* RCA Home Video, 1988; *Something about Love,* 1988; *Speed Zone!,* Media Home Entertainment, 1989; *Terminator 2: Judgment Day,* TriStar Pictures, 1991; *Hot Shots!,* Twentieth Century-Fox, 1991; *Super Mario Bros.,* Warner Espanola, S.A., 1993; *Beethoven's 2nd,* United International Pictures, 1993; *Wagons East,* TriStar, 1994; *Waiting for Guffman,* Sony Pictures Classics, 1996; *Rocket Man,* Buena Vista, 1997; *Almost Heroes,* Warner Bros., 1998; *The Extreme Adventures of Super Dave,* Metro-Goldwyn-Mayer, 2000; *Return to Me,* Metro-Goldwyn-Mayer, 2000; and *Best in Show,* Warner Bros., 2000.

Television series appearances include *Bizarre,* 1980; *Bill & Ted's Excellent Adventures,* Fox, 1992; *The Building,* CBS, 1993; *The Bonnie Hunt Show,* CBS, 1995; and *Pepper Ann,* ABC, 1997. Appearances on TV movies include *Really Weird Tales,* 1987; *Hostage for a Day,* Fox, 1994; and *Sodbusters,* Showtime, 1994. Appearances in TV miniseries include *Hands of a Stranger,* NBC, 1987. Appearances on TV specials include *Out of Our Minds,* syndicated, 1984; *The Dave Thomas Comedy Show,* CBS, 1990; *Lola,* ABC, 1990; and *Larry David: Curb Your Enthusiasm,* 1999.

Appearances on episodic television include "The Five Labours of Hercules: Parts 1 & 2," *The Littlest Hobo,* 1983; *Hot Shots,* CBS, 1986; "Diamonds Aren't Forever," *Alfred Hitchcock Presents,* 1989; "The Morning Show," *Murphy Brown,* CBS, 1989; "Good Doc, Bad Doc: Part 1" and "Malpractice Makes Imperfect: Part 2," *Doctor Doctor,* 1990; "Teens from a Mall," *Parker Lewis Can't Lose,* Fox, 1990; "Older and Wiser," *The Golden Girls,* CBS, 1991; "Three o'Clock and All Is Hell," *Blossom,* NBC, 1991; "Food for Thought" *Empty Nest,* NBC, 1991; "Double-breasted Suit," *L. A. Law,* NBC, 1991; *Camp Wilder,* ABC, 1992; *Likely Suspects,* Fox, 1992; *Super Dave,* Showtime, 1992; *Love & War,* CBS, 1993; *The Boys Are Back,* CBS, 1994; "Will Is from Mars . . . ," *The Fresh Prince of Bel-Air,* NBC, 1994; *The Martin Short Show,* NBC, 1994; "The Class Reunion," *Ellen,* ABC, 1994; *Super Dave's Vegas Spectacular,* Showtime, 1995; *Goode Behavior,* UPN, 1996; "Johnny and the Pacemakers," *Double Rush,* 1995; *Sparks,* UPN, 1996; *Murder One,* ABC, 1997; "Playing Doctor," *Men Behaving Badly,* 1997; "Chimp off the Old Block," *The Wild Thornberrys,* Nickelodeon, 1999; *The List,* VH1, 1999; and *Watching Ellie,* 2002.

Television work includes (remote editor) *The Bonnie Hunt Show,* CBS, 1995; (associate producer) *Superfest: A Celebration of Ability,* PBS, 1988; and (producer) *Life with Bonnie,* ABC, 2002.

WRITINGS:

Maniac Mansion (television episode), The Family Channel, 1990.
(Story only) *The Extreme Adventures of Super Dave* (screenplay), Metro-Goldwyn-Mayer, 2000.
(With Bonnie Hunt; and story) *Return to Me,* Metro-Goldwyn-Mayer, 2000.
Life with Bonnie (TV series), ABC, 2002.

SIDELIGHTS: Much of Don Lake's career has been tied to that of actress and comedienne Bonnie Hunt, who is perhaps best known for her role as Laurel in *Jerry Maguire.* Nearly two years earlier, however, in 1995, Hunt was facing the cancellation of yet another miniseries—her fourth. *The Bonnie Hunt Show* also featured Lake and Holly Wortell, the three having known each other since their days of working with the *Second City TV* comedy troupe Chicago. Hunt, who Robert Bianco called "the best celebrity talk-show guest in America," is almost universally beloved of critics, who bemoaned the demise of *The Bonnie Hunt Show,* and enthusiastically greeted Hunt's 2002 return at the helm of *Life with Bonnie.* According to Michael Speier of *Daily Variety,* the show, on which Lake worked as a writer, "may very well signal the beginning of the end of ABC's doldrums."

Lake and Hunt also worked on the screenplay of *Return to Me,* which Hunt directed. The 2000 film marks, as many reviewers noted, a return to the style of Hollywood romances from the 1930s and 1940s. Keith Simanton in *Seattle Times* wrote that Hunt—and, by extension, her cowriter Lake—attempt "to perform a heart transplant, on the ailing, arrhythmic [genre of] romantic comedy" by infusing it with the heart of "what would have historically been called 'a woman's weepie'—great, pillowed, swooning heaps of melodrama like *Dark Victory* or *An Affair to Remember.* The operation is, in most respects, a success." Simanton's extended metaphor is apt, as a look at the script reveals. *Return to Me* is the story of a widower, architect Bob Rueland (David Duchovny), who meets a waitress, Grace Briggs (Minnie Driver). From the beginning, Bob finds himself strangely drawn to Grace, who is recovering from heart-transplant surgery. Eventually the two come to the realization that Grace quite literally has his dead wife's heart.

Such a plot twist, naturally, runs the risk of becoming a bit maudlin or at least too precious, and Kevin Thomas in the *Los Angeles Times* noted that "the gimmick is out-and-out shameless, but Hunt follows the Hitchcock dictum of letting the audience know what it is upfront, letting suspense build as to how her key people will . . . [deal] with it." In any case, "What makes it all a little spooky," maintained Jay Carr of the *Boston Globe,* "is first seeing [Bob and] his zoologist wife, living hectically and happily before her abrupt demise." Wrote Thomas, "*Return to Me* is the kind of big romantic movie Hollywood used to make with such seeming ease. This means you actually can care about the lovers, there's a fine sense of balance between humor and pathos in their story, and far from existing in a vacuum, they are surrounded by a substantial number of endearing types who recall the beloved character actors of the studio era."

BIOGRAPHICAL AND CRITICAL SOURCES:

BOOKS

Contemporary Theatre, Film, and Television, volume 33, Gale (Detroit, MI), 2001.

PERIODICALS

Boston Globe, April 7, 2000, Jay Carr, review of *Return to Me,* p. D6.
Daily Variety, September 13, 2002, Michael Speier, review of *Life with Bonnie,* p. 5.
Hartford Courant, September 22, 1995, James Endrst, "'Bonnie Hunt' May Need Its Angels to Survive," p. E1; April 7, 2000, Malcolm Johnson, review of *Return to Me,* p. D4.

Los Angeles Times, April 7, 2000, Kevin Thomas, review of *Return to Me,* p. F6.
Seattle Times, April 7, 2000, Keith Simanton, review of *Return to Me,* p. J5.
USA Today, September 17, 2002, Robert Bianco, review of *Life with Bonnie,* p. D6.
Variety, March 27, 2000, Emanuel Levy, review of *Return to Me,* p. 19.*

*　　　*　　　*

LANDAU, Tina

PERSONAL: Born in New York, NY. *Education:* Attended Yale University and Harvard University.

ADDRESSES: Agent—Helen Merrill, Helen Merrill Ltd., 295 Lafayette St., Suite 915, New York, NY 10012-2700.

CAREER: Writer and director. Steppenwolf Theatre Company, Chicago, IL, ensemble member, 1998—.

Stage work as director includes *Floyd Collins,* American Music Theater Festival, Philadelphia, PA, 1993 then Playwrights Horizons, New York City, 1996; *Ain: The Outcast,* Majestic Theater, Brooklyn, NY, 1995; *Cloud Tectonics,* Playwrights Horizons, New York City, then La Jolla Playhouse and Actors Theatre of Louisville, all 1997; *The Berlin Circle,* Steppenwolf Theatre Company, Chicago, IL, 1998; *Space,* Steppenwolf Theatre Company, 1998 then Mark Taper Forum, Los Angeles, 1999 then Public Theater, New York Shakespeare Festival, New York City, 1999; and *Dream True,* Vineyard Theater, New York City, 1999. Also directed *The Trojan Woman: A Love Story,* En Garde Arts, New York City; *Orestes,* En Garde Arts; *Marisol,* La Jolla Playhouse; *Cloud Tectonics,* La Jolla Playhouse; and *1969,* Actor's Theatre of Louisville, Louisville, KY. Other work as director includes *Time of Your Life; Maria Arndt; The Ballad of Little Jo; Time to Burn; Bells Are Ringing;* and *Saturn Returns.*

AWARDS, HONORS: Princess Grace Award; Theater Communications Group/National Endowment for the Arts Director Fellowship; Pew, J. Alton Jones, and Rockefeller awards.

WRITINGS:

(With Adam Guettel; book and additional lyrics only) *Floyd Collins* (musical; produced by American Music Theater Festival, Philadelphia, PA, 1993, then Playwrights Horizons, New York City, 1996, then Bridewell Theater, London, England, 1999), Rodgers and Hammerstein Theatre Library (New York, NY), 1997.

Stonewall: Night Variations (play), produced by En Garde Arts, Pier 25, New York City, 1994.

Space (play), produced by Steppenwolf Theatre Company, 1998, then Public Theater, New York Shakespeare Festival, New York City, 1999.

(With Ricky Ian Gordon) *Dream True,* produced by Vineyard Theater, New York City, 1999.

Also wrote additional dialogue for *Friday the 13th—A New Beginning,* 1985. Other plays include *States of Independence,* American Music Theater Festival, Philadelphia, PA; and *1969 (or Howie Takes a Trip),* Actors Theatre of Louisville's Humana Festival.

Contributor to *Humana Festival '94: The Complete Plays,* edited by Marisa Smith, Smith and Kraus (Lyme, NH), 1994; *The Best Men's Stage Monologues of 1994,* edited by Jocelyn Beard, Smith and Kraus (Newbury, VT), 1994; and *Anne Bogart: Viewpoints,* edited by Michael Bigelow Dixon and Joel A. Smith, Smith and Kraus (Lyme, NH), 1994. Wrote foreword for *Marisol and Other Plays,* edited by Jose Rivera, Theatre Communications Group (New York, NY), 1997.

SIDELIGHTS: Discussing her work in *American Theatre,* playwright Tina Landau said, "Right now I'm really interested in connecting with an audience, and defining the difference between that and pandering." She went on to note that "I used to be more interested in dance-theatre pieces, highly conceptual abstract work. I now am interested in storytelling, and pushing the envelope in terms of form. I would never purposefully want to write something that is inaccessible."

Landau's most well-known and oft-staged work is *Floyd Collins,* for which Adam Guettel wrote the music. Staged in a number of locales on both sides of the Atlantic during the 1990s and early 2000s, *Floyd Collins* is based on a real-life saga that gripped the nation's attention for a few days in 1925. The protagonist of the title, a Kentuckian confronted by poverty, descended into a cave one night in January in hopes of finding a route to the much larger Mammoth Cave, which would thus create a tourist attraction that would make his family wealthy. Instead, a loose boulder pinned him in place sixty feet beneath the surface, and sixteen days later, the cavern became his tomb.

In the meantime, the event had attracted nationwide attention, and became one of the first truly modern news stories, with reporters on the scene relating events to the readers (and, thanks to the new medium of radio, listeners) back home. Nor was this the only aspect of Floyd Collins's story that makes it seem eerily like events from the present day: in addition to the media circus, there was what one reporter at the time called the "Deathwatch Carnival," as a fair-like atmosphere developed around the entrance to the tunnel where searchers tried unsuccessfully to rescue Collins. Landau, wrote Rachel Shteir in *American Theatre,* "was gripped by images of rural mountebanks selling overpriced, dime-sized hamburgers and cure-all sassafras elixirs while, in the earth below, a man shriveled hopelessly away. 'Like all modern American tragedies, Floyd's personal tragedy diminished in proportion to the number of people drawn to it,' she comments wryly."

Stonewall: Night Variations also plays off of real events, in this case a 1969 protest that marked the beginnings of modern gay activism. "As the evening arcs from repression to liberation," wrote Phyllis Goldman in *Back Stage,* "closets will open and the audience will be confronted with a 'healing spirit more powerful than any darkness we may encounter.' It's a fitting coda to the remarkable event that was Stonewall." Less immediately tied to actual events, *Space,* which contemplates the possibility of extraterrestrial intelligence, is certainly topical. More personal is the story in *Dream True,* which concerns two boys who begin as friends in Wyoming, and eventually lose touch with one another. Yet they maintain spiritual contact through their dreams, which keep them closer than they can be in real life.

BIOGRAPHICAL AND CRITICAL SOURCES:

BOOKS

Contemporary Theatre, Film, and Television, volume 32, Gale (Detroit, MI), 2000.

PERIODICALS

American Theatre, April, 1994, Rachel Shteir, review of *Floyd Collins,* pp. 8-9; March, 1998, Thomas Connors, review of *Space,* pp. 42-43; September, 1998, Sarah Schulman, "Tina Landau: The Rest Is Metaphor" (interview), pp. 68-70.

Back Stage, July 1, 1994, Phyllis Goldman, review of *Stonewall: Night Variations,* p. 36; March 15, 1996, David A. Rosenberg, review of *Floyd Collins,* p. 60; April 23, 1999, Irene Backalenick, review of *Dream True,* p. 41.

Back Stage West, October 7, 1999, Scott Proudfit, "Star Struck" (interview), p. 3.

New York, March 18, 1996, John Simon, review of *Floyd Collins,* pp. 52-53.

New York Times, April 18, 1994, Jon Pareles, review of *Floyd Collins,* p. B1; June 25, 1994, Ben Brantley, review of *Stonewall: Night Variations,* p. N11; July 3, 1994, Vincent Canby, review of *Floyd Collins,* p. H3; February 25, 1996, Sam Roberts, review of *Floyd Collins,* p. H5; March 4, 1996, Ben Brantley, review of *Floyd Collins,* p. B5; March 17, 1996, Margo Jefferson, review of *Floyd Collins,* p. H8.

Variety, April 25, 1994, Toby Zinman, review of *Floyd Collins,* p. 39; June 27, 1994, Greg Evans, review of *Stonewall: Night Variations,* p. 98; March 4, 1996, Jeremy Gerard, review of *Floyd Collins,* p. 82; April 26, 1999, Charles Isherwood, review of *Dream True,* p. 56; July 19, 1999, Matt Wolf, review of *Floyd Collins,* p. 35; December 13, 1999, Charles Isherwood, review of *Space,* p. 119.

Wall Street Journal, December 18, 1997, Joel Henning, review of *Space,* p. A20; May 17, 1999, Joel Henning, review of *Floyd Collins,* p. A24.

OTHER

Steppenwolf Theatre Company Web site, http://www.steppenwolf.org (October 26, 2002).*

*   *   *

LANDERS, Ann
See LEDERER, Esther Pauline (Friedman)

LAUTER, Geza Peter 1932-2002

OBITUARY NOTICE—See index for *CA* sketch: Born November 26, 1932, in Bad-Lauterberg, Germany; died of a heart attack March 30, 2002, in Washington, DC. Educator and author. Lauter was a professor of international business who was an expert in global market competition. Educated at the University of California, Los Angeles where he received his Ph.D. in 1968, Lauter was an instructor at Cornell during the mid-1960s; he joined George Washington University in 1968, where he remained for the rest of his career, becoming a professor of business administration in 1975 and the director of doctoral programs for the business department. He was the chair of the Department of International Business from 1997 to 2001. His writings discuss such issues as economic development in Eastern Europe and the Japanese influence on global markets. Lauter's books include *The Manager and Economic Reform in Hungary* and the coauthored books *Multinational Corporations and East European Socialist Economies* and *The Internationalism of the Japanese Economy.*

OBITUARIES AND OTHER SOURCES:

PERIODICALS

Washington Post, April 20, 2002, p. B7.

*   *   *

LAVERS, Chris(topher) P. 1965-

PERSONAL: Born May 15, 1965, in London, England; son of Peter (an accountant) and Rita (in retail sales) Lavers. *Ethnicity:* "White." *Education:* City of London Polytechnic, B.Sc. (earth science), 1987; University of Nottingham, Ph.D. (ecology), 1994. *Religion:* "Agnostic." *Hobbies and other interests:* Natural history, basketball.

ADDRESSES: Office—School of Geography, University Park, University of Nottingham, Nottingham, England NG7 2RD. *Agent*—Patrick Walsh, Conville and Walsh Ltd., 118-120 Wardour St., London W1F 0TU, England.

CAREER: University of Nottingham, Nottingham, England, lecturer, 1994—.

WRITINGS:

Why Elephants Have Big Ears: Nature's Engines and the Order of Life, Gollancz (London, England), 2000, published as Why Elephants Have Big Ears: Understanding Patterns of Life on Earth, St. Martin's Press (New York, NY), 2001.

Regular contributor of book reviews to *Guardian*. Also contributor to *New Scientist, New Statesman,* and *Spectator.*

WORK IN PROGRESS: Research on vertebrate ecology and energetics, ancient natural history texts, and the ecology of Sherwood Forest.

SIDELIGHTS: "I am motivated by the desire to share with others my love of science and the natural world," Chris Lavers told *CA*. One of the products of this desire is *Why Elephants Have Big Ears: Nature's Engines and the Order of Life,* published in the United States as *Why Elephants Have Big Ears: Understanding Patterns of Life on Earth.* In this book Lavers seeks to answer common questions about animals in a manner that is scientifically accurate yet accessible to the general reader. He discusses not only why elephants have big ears—they help the animals get rid of excess body heat—but why mammals are large and live on land, why most reptiles are small and often live in wetlands, the advantages and disadvantages of being warm-blooded or cold-blooded, and numerous other topics, delving into prehistoric times to explain how the blueprints for evolution of future species were laid out in this period.

"Understanding all of these whys becomes easy under the author's tutelage," commented Nancy Bent in *Booklist.* A *Kirkus Reviews* contributor remarked that Lavers takes "provocative stabs at answering the really big questions about wildlife biology" and provides "entertaining erudition" in prose that "is as comfortable as flannel sheets on a cold night and as crisp as starlight." *Geographical* reviewer Chris Martin, though, deemed *Why Elephants Have Big Ears* "a mixed bag . . . rather blandly answering questions

that have been in the back of everyone's minds since childhood" while also "wrestling with some serious and fascinating issues." Jeff Hecht, writing in *New Scientist,* noted that "some of Lavers's interpretations may be controversial," but found the book overall "both fascinating and illuminating."

BIOGRAPHICAL AND CRITICAL SOURCES:

PERIODICALS

Booklist, February 15, 2001, Nancy Bent, review of *Why Elephants Have Big Ears: Understanding Patterns of Life on Earth,* p. 1095.
Ecologist, July, 2000, Lucinda Labes, review of *Why Elephants Have Big Ears,* p. 70.
Geographical, August, 2000, Chris Martin, review of *Why Elephants Have Big Ears,* p. 94.
Kirkus Reviews, February 1, 2001, review of *Why Elephants Have Big Ears,* p. 166.
New Scientist, June 24, 2000, Jeff Hecht, "Heat Strokes," p. 48.*

*   *   *

LEDER, Mary M(ackler) 1916(?)-

PERSONAL: Born c. 1916, in the United States; married Abram Leder (died, 1959); children: one daughter (deceased). *Education:* Attended University of Moscow.

ADDRESSES: *Home*—New York, NY. *Agent*—c/o Indiana University Press, Bloomington, IN 47405.

CAREER: Worked as proofreader, editor, and translator for a branch of TASS (Soviet news agency) and at a foreign-language publishing house, both in Moscow, USSR.

WRITINGS:

My Life in Stalinist Russia: An American Women Looks Back, edited by Laurie Bernstein, Indiana University Press (Bloomington, IN), 2001.

BIOGRAPHICAL AND CRITICAL SOURCES:

PERIODICALS

Kirkus Review, February 1, 2001, review of *My Life in Stalinist Russia: An American Woman Looks Back,* p. 167.
Publishers Weekly, February 26, 2001, review of *My Life in Stalinist Russia,* p. 76.*

*   *   *

LEDERER, Eppie
   See LEDERER, Esther Pauline (Friedman)

*   *   *

LEDERER, Esther Pauline (Friedman) 1918-2002
(Eppie Lederer; Ann Landers, a pseudonym)

OBITUARY NOTICE—See index for *CA* sketch: Born July 4, 1918, in Sioux City, IA; died of multiple myeloma, June 22, 2002, in Chicago, IL. Columnist and author. Lederer only had one full-time job in her life, and it made her famous around the world. Known to her family and friends as Eppie, the world knew her as Ann Landers. In 1955 she won a job at the *Chicago Sun-Times* as a replacement for the recently deceased author of the "Ann Landers" advice column. For nearly fifty years Lederer offered guidance to troubled people on every topic imaginable. She was outspoken about her sometimes controversial views, such as support of legalized abortion and gun control, but her advice was grounded in her firm belief in conventional family values. She did not hesitate to consult with experts as needed, nor did she hesitate to beg her correspondents to seek professional help when she believed they were truly at risk. Lederer wrote straightforward advice tinged with empathy, unsophisticated humor, and occasionally a streak of sarcasm. Over the years her topics changed with the times, but the one thing that endured was her genuine interest in the people who sought her help. In 1987 Lederer moved her column to the *Chicago Tribune.* At the height of syndication, the column appeared in more than a thousand newspapers, reaching an estimated ninety million readers; she received as many as two thousand letters per week.

Lederer also supported a number of educational, medical, and charitable causes. Her many awards included more than thirty honorary degrees, the Robert T. Morse Award of the American Psychiatric Association, the National Service Award of the American Cancer Society, and the Public Service Award of the Albert and Mary Lasker Foundation. Lederer also gave public lectures and wrote books and pamphlets. Her books include *Ann Landers Talks to Teenagers about Sex, The Ann Landers Encyclopedia: Improve Your Life Emotionally, Medically, Sexually, Spiritually,* and *Wake up and Smell the Coffee! Advice, Wisdom, and Uncommon Good Sense,* the last published in 1996. Lederer was the identical twin of Pauline Phillips, another popular advice columnist under the name Abigail Van Buren. She owned the rights to the name Ann Landers, and it was Lederer's wish that her column would die with her.

OBITUARIES AND OTHER SOURCES:

BOOKS

Grossvogel, David, *Dear Ann Landers: Our Intimate and Changing Dialogue with America's Best-Loved Confidante,* NTC Publishing Group, 1987.

PERIODICALS

Los Angeles Times, June 23, 2002, obituary by Kristina Sauerwein, pp. A1, A24.
New York Times, June 24, 2002, obituary by Margalit Fox, p. A20.
Times (London, England), June 24, 2002.
Washington Post, June 23, 2002, obituary by Martin Weil, pp. A1, A10.

*   *   *

LEHMAN, John 1941-

PERSONAL: Born June 8, 1941, in Chicago, IL; son of Edward H. (an engineer) and Grace (Solway) Lehman; married Pat Whyte, 1967 (marriage ended, 1986); married Talia Schorr, August 22, 1991; children: (first marriage) John K., Pamela. *Ethnicity:* "German." *Edu-*

cation: University of Notre Dame, B.A., 1963; University of Michigan, M.A., 1971. *Hobbies and other interests:* Classic automobiles, travel.

ADDRESSES: Home—315 East Water St., Cambridge, WI 53523. *Office*—Strategic Sales Support, 100 Riverplace, Suite 250, Milwaukee, WI 53716. *E-mail*—santerra@aol.com.

CAREER: Lehman Advertising and Marketing, Madison, WI, president, 1981-91; *Rosebud,* Cambridge, WI, publisher, 1994—. Also affiliated with Strategic Sales Support, Madison, WI. Member of Wisconsin Governor's Poet Laureate Commission. *Military service:* U.S. Army, 1963-70; became captain; received Bronze Star and Army Commendation Medal.

MEMBER: Council of Wisconsin Writers (director), Federation of Wisconsin Poets, Wisconsin Regional Writers Association.

AWARDS, HONORS: Christopher Latham Sholes Award, Council of Wisconsin Writers, 2001.

WRITINGS:

Shrine of the Tooth Fairy (poetry), Cambridge Book
    Review Press, 1999.
Dogs Dream of Running (poetry), Salmon Run Press,
    2001.
Making Good Writing Great, Zelda Wilde Publishing,
    2002.
Lorine Niedecker: America's Greatest Unknown Poet,
    Zelda Wilde Publishing, 2002.

Poetry editor, *Wisconsin Academy Review,* 1999—.

WORK IN PROGRESS: The Big Metaphor: Verse Noir, for Salmon Run Press, completion expected in 2003.

SIDELIGHTS: John Lehman told *CA:* "Besides writing poetry I've spent many years in advertising. With advertising there is always a strong sense of an audience. And the idea isn't to teach that audience or entertain them, but get them to do something, *to buy something!* Poetry is that way. The poet wants to move you, get you to be a different person in some way at

the end of the poem than you were when you began it. That's hard. You've got to pull readers in, get them to forget their own worlds for a few moments. You have to challenge them, yet not lose them in the process, and then send them back to face their lives in a more meaningful and artistic way. But there is a difference. Advertising seeks to eliminate choice, poetry to give us choices where we didn't think we had any.

"On the other hand, what I've learned in more commercial realms has helped market my magazine *Rosebud,* market my books, and market myself. I don't apologize for that; we live in a marketing age. I contend that writers need some successes in order to continue, whether that's being in the *Paris Review* or having someone you know tell you how he or she relates to a piece you write. I advise others: 'Figure out what is unique about your writing or yourself and go with that.' I read people like Dylan Thomas and Gerard Manley Hopkins—to drop a few names—but I know I could never write like them. I don't live in their world, either, and neither do my readers. My stuff is closer to Richard Brautigan with a little Philip Levine thrown in. No, I take that back. It's pure John Lehman."

*   *   *

LEITH, John H(addon) 1919-2002

OBITUARY NOTICE—Born September 10, 1919, in Due West, SC; died August 12, 2002, in Greenville, SC. Theologian, minister, educator, and author. Leith was ordained a Presbyterian minister in 1943 and served pastorates in Tennessee and Alabama for several years. In 1959 he was appointed Pemberton Professor of Theology at Union Theological Seminary in Richmond, Virginia, a position he retained until 1990. Leith served the church in many capacities, including nearly ten years as board chair of the Presbyterian Survey and nearly forty years as a board member for the magazine *Presbyterian Outlook.* In more than a dozen books, Leith expounded his views on Reformed theology; he is said to have influenced multiple generations of future pastors and theological scholars. Leith's writings include *The Church: This Believing Fellowship, The Reformed Imperative: What the Church Has to Say that No One Else Can Say, John Calvin's Doctrine of the Christian Life, From Generation to Generation: The Renewal of the Church according to*

Its Own Theology and Practice, Crisis in the Church: The Plight of Theological Education, and most recently *The Pilgrimage of a Presbyterian: Collected Shorter Writings,* the last published in 2000.

OBITUARIES AND OTHER SOURCES:

PERIODICALS

Greenville News, August 14, 2002, p. 4B.

OTHER

Presbyterian News Service, http://www.pcusa.org/ (August 13, 2002), obituary by Alexa Smith.
Union Theological Seminary and Presbyterian School of Christian Education Web site, http://www.union-psce.edu/ (August 13, 2002).

*　　*　　*

LEW, Alan 1943-

PERSONAL: Born 1943, in Brooklyn, NY; married Sherril Jaffe (a novelist); children: Steven, Hannah, Malka. *Ethnicity:* "Jewish." *Education:* University of Pennsylvania, B.A., 1965; University of Iowa Writers Workshop, M.F.A., 1970; Jewish Theological Seminary, ordained as rabbi, 1988. *Religion:* Judaism.

ADDRESSES: Home—San Francisco, CA. *Office*—Kodansha American Inc., 575 Lexington Ave., 23rd Floor, New York, NY, 10022.

CAREER: Rabbi of congregation Beth Shalom, San Francisco, CA, 1991—. Rabbi of Congregation Eitz Chaim, Monroe, NY; Jacob Perlow Hospice of Beth Israel Medical Center, New York, NY, first chaplain. KPIC-TV, San Francisco, CA, moderator of Mosaic television program.

MEMBER: Board of Rabbis of Northern California (past president), Religious Witness with the Homeless (member of steering committee), Jewish Community Federation (member, board of directors), Jewish Bulletin of Northern California (member, board of directors).

WRITINGS:

Eight Monologues (poetry), Open Books (Berkeley, CA), 1978.
(With Sherril Jaffe) *One God Clapping: The Spiritual Path of a Zen Rabbi,* Kodansha International (New York, NY), 1999.

Author of two other books of poetry. Contributor of articles, stories, and poems to periodicals, including *Life, National Reporter,* and *Naropa Journal of Poetry.*

SIDELIGHTS: Rabbi Alan Lew is the coauthor with his wife, Sherril Jaffe, of *One God Clapping: The Spiritual Path of a Zen Rabbi,* which traces Lew's own personal spiritual journey from the Judaism of his youth, through Eastern spirituality, and back again to Judaism. "It is part of the American anthropology, that we seem to leave the religion we are born to behind at a certain point, and to cast out on our own—to try to find our own spiritual path," Lew confided in a document posted on the *USCJ Web site.* "This was certainly my experience. I had no unfriendly feelings toward Judaism then; at this point in my life, Judaism seemed to me, to be a minor wing of the Democratic Party." Lew explored hatha yoga and Tibetan Buddhism before encountering a Zen master at a lecture in San Francisco. The master, he said on the *USCJ Web site,* made an impression on him through the sense of discipline he brought with him to his work. "Zen, or at least the Zen I began to do that week, was essentially a practice—an extremely disciplined practice. It wasn't a theology, and it wasn't a home, and it wasn't spiritual consumerism. . . . It was a practice characterized by rigorous discipline—by what we did, and how thoroughly and regularly we did it." "Lew's inviting memoir," wrote a *Publishers Weekly* contributor, "offers a glimpse of one man's integration of Eastern wisdom and Western spirituality."

BIOGRAPHICAL AND CRITICAL SOURCES:

PERIODICALS

Publishers Weekly, May 31, 1999, p. S21.

OTHER

USCJ Web site, http://www.uscj.org/ncalif/sanfracb/yk15759.html (July 29, 1999), "Practice, Practice, Practice."*

LEWIS, Flora 1922(?)-2002

OBITUARY NOTICE—See index for *CA* sketch: Born July 29, c. 1922 (some sources cite 1923), in Los Angeles, CA; died of cancer, June 2, 2002, in Paris, France. Journalist and author. As one of very few female correspondents in Europe after World War II, Lewis interpreted events for numerous U.S., British, and French periodicals. For ten years, beginning in 1956, Lewis worked for the *Washington Post,* including stints as bureau chief in Bonn, London, and New York City. In 1956 she covered the anti-communist uprisings in Poland and Hungary. Later, as a syndicated columnist for *Newsday,* Lewis covered the Arab-Israeli war of 1967 from the Middle East and produced eyewitness accounts from Vietnam. In 1972 she was appointed chief of the Paris bureau of the *New York Times,* a notable achievement for a female journalist at the time. She served the newspaper until 1994, as European diplomatic correspondent and ultimately as senior columnist. During all these years, Lewis absorbed a deep understanding of European affairs and accumulated a substantial number of high-level contacts, both achievements that contributed to her successful fifty-year career. She also garnered respect for her sophisticated analysis of complex events based on her ability to collect disparate minutiae and synthesize them into a comprehensive picture. Lewis was cited for her grasp of the continuity of history throughout the sprawling continent and for her ongoing optimism for the future, as much at the beginning of the cold war as at the end. Two of her books were titled *A Case History of Hope: The Story of Poland's Peaceful Revolutions* and *Europe: Road to Unity.* A member of the elite Council on Foreign Relations and a council member of the International Institute for Strategic Studies, Lewis won many accolades for her reportage, including a lifetime achievement award from the Overseas Press Club of America and the Fourth Estate Award of the National Press Club. Lewis's other nonfiction writings include *One of Our H-Bombs Is Missing, Red Pawn: The Story of Noel Field,* and *Europe: A Tapestry of Nations.*

OBITUARIES AND OTHER SOURCES:

PERIODICALS

Guardian (London, England), June 2, 2002.
International Herald Tribune, June 3, 2002, obituary by Craig R. Whitney.

Los Angeles Times, June 3, 2002, p. B9.
New York Times, June 3, 2002, obituary by Craig R. Whitney, p. A17.
Times (London, England), June 3, 2002, p. 29.
Washington Post, June 3, 2002, obituary by Richard Pearson, p. B4.

*   *   *

LEWIS, R(ichard) W(arrington) B(aldwin) 1917-2002

OBITUARY NOTICE—See index for *CA* sketch: Born November 1, 1917, in Chicago, IL; died June 13, 2002, in Bethany, CT. Educator, biographer, critic, editor, and author. In his writings, Lewis combined literary criticism with historical biography, an interdisciplinary effort that resulted in literary biography. He examined not only the influence of events on an author's writing, but the way in which the writing reflected and defined the life. Lewis's renown as a literary scholar was assured by the publication of *Edith Wharton: A Biography,* which first emerged during a resurgence of interest in Wharton in the 1970s. The work was acclaimed by many critics for the rigorous research behind it as well as Lewis's penetrating literary analysis, and it earned the author many prestigious awards, including a Pulitzer Prize for biography, the Bancroft Prize for American history, and the first nonfiction prize awarded by the National Book Critics Circle. Originally trained as a historian, Lewis developed an interest in literature, particularly the work of American authors, after World War II. He taught English at Yale University for nearly thirty years, but his specialty was the growing field of American studies, based on an interdisciplinary approach for which Lewis was well trained. His first book was *The American Adam: Innocence, Tragedy, and Tradition in the Nineteenth Century,* a work of literary criticism in which Lewis maintained that America represented an unspoiled new land where the innocence lost in Eden could be reborn, and he analyzed what he saw as evidence of the archetypal Adam in the writings of various American authors. Lewis wrote nearly a dozen books and edited as many more, including the novels, short stories, and correspondence of Wharton. His numerous awards included a nomination for the National Book Award for *The Jameses: A Family Narrative* and the gold medal of the American Academy of Arts and Letters.

OBITUARIES AND OTHER SOURCES:

PERIODICALS

Chicago Tribune, June 17, 2002, pp. 2-6.
Los Angeles Times, June 16, 2002, p. B19.
New York Times, June 15, 2002, obituary by Michael Anderson, p. A27.
Times (London, England), July 2, 2002.
Washington Post, June 17, 2002, p. B4.

*   *   *

LIBAW, William H. 1923-

PERSONAL: Born April 10, 1923, in New Jersey; son of Oscar and Millie (Silver) Libaw; married Norma Yates, December 13, 1972 (deceased); children: Oliver Yates. *Education:* University of California, Berkeley, B.S., 1948.

ADDRESSES: Home—427 South Lapeer Dr., Beverly Hills, CA 90211.

CAREER: Worked as a design engineer for Northrop, Magnavox, Planning Research, and Mesa Scientific, all Los Angeles, CA.

WRITINGS:

How We Got to Be Human: Subjective Minds with Objective Bodies, Prometheus Books (Amherst, NY), 2000.

WORK IN PROGRESS: Picasso to Warhol: Why Art Fell Apart.

BIOGRAPHICAL AND CRITICAL SOURCES:

PERIODICALS

Publishers Weekly, July 10, 2000, review of *How We Got to Be Human: Subjective Minds with Objective Bodies,* p. 56.
Skeptical Inquirer, May, 2001, Kendrick Frazier, review of *How We Got to Be Human,* p. 62.

LUKE, Helen M. 1924-1995

PERSONAL: Born 1924, in England; immigrated to the United States, 1949; died 1995; married, 1929 (marriage ended, 1949). *Education:* Oxford University, M.A.; further studies at the Jung Institute, Zurich, Switzerland.

CAREER: Author and Jungian analyst. Founder, Apple Farm Community, Three Rivers, MI.

WRITINGS:

Dark Wood to White Rose: A Study of Meanings in Dante's Divine Comedy, Dove Publications (Pecos, NM), 1975.
The Life of the Spirit in Women: A Jungian Approach, Pendle Hill Publications (Wallingford, PA), 1980.
Woman: Earth and Spirit, the Feminine in Symbol and Myth, Crossroad (New York, NY), 1981.
The Inner Story: Myth and Symbol in the Bible and Literature, Crossroad (New York, NY), 1982.
The Voice Within: Love and Virtue in the Age of the Spirit, Crossroad (New York, NY), 1984.
Old Age, Parabola Books (New York, NY), 1987.
Kaleidoscope: "The Way of Woman" and Other Essays, edited by Rob Baker, Parabola Books (New York, NY), 1992.
The Way of Woman: Awakening the Perennial Feminine, Parabola Books (New York, NY), 1992.
Such Stuff as Dreams Are Made On: The Autobiography and Journals of Helen M. Luke, Parabola Books (New York, NY), 1999.
The Laughter at the Heart of Things, Parabola Books (New York, NY), 2001.

Also author of *The Way of Story: Myths and Stories for the Inner Life,* Parabola Audio Books (New York, NY), two cassettes.

SIDELIGHTS: Helen M. Luke's life was an ongoing journey, both intellectually and geographically. Luke attended Somerville College of Oxford University in the early 1920s, a time when the student population there was still overwhelmingly male. In 1949 Luke left her marriage and moved to the United States, where she began to practice as a Jungian analyst in Los Angeles. In 1962 she founded Apple Farms Community in Three Rivers, Michigan, described as a center for people seeking to discover and appropriate the transforming power of symbols in their lives. It was at Apple Farms that Luke began to write and publish.

Luke's first book, *Dark Wood to White Rose: A Study of Meanings in Dante's Divine Comedy,* combines her academic work in Italian literature with her Jungian studies into a Jungian interpretation of Dante's famous work. A reviewer writing in *Choice* described the book as one that "offers many original and personal insights into the poem, particularly as it sheds light on contemporary concerns (e.g., women's liberation, liturgical reform), for she treats the poem as contemporary and relevant." Her next work, *The Inner Story: Myth and Symbol in the Bible and Literature,* used ten topics drawn from the Bible or other literature as points of departure for discussion of myth and symbol.

She returned to the theme of women's spiritual life in subsequent works, the first of which was *Women, Earth and Spirit: The Feminine in Symbol and Myth.* Here Luke weaves together Jungian thinking with myths, fairy tales, and Christian interpretation. She deals with what she views as the fundamental differences between men and women. The book was published at a time when the feminist movement was fighting the notion that women are, in spirit and character, fundamentally different from men, and that they are best suited to traditional female nurturing roles. This debate is reflected in contemporary reviews of Luke's book. Mary A. Trainor, writing in *Best Sellers,* noted, "Some feminists may interpret Helen Luke's ideas as a return to passive subjugation. This is not the case. She acknowledges the long history of women's oppression by men. But she is concerned that today's values will destroy the creative genius of the feminine." In contrast, Judith Plaskow, writing in the *Religious Studies Review,* described the book as using myth and the like as "starting points for numerous unsupported and apolitical generalizations about the 'feminine' and 'womanhood.'"

Luke's writings about the spiritual lives of women were collected in an anthology, *Kaleidoscope: "The Way of Woman" and Other Essays.* W. C. Buchanan, writing in *Choice,* praised the collection for its "fresh and lively" language and for its insights, "not the fruits of academic study; they grew out of living the symbolic life in community and counseling with people who have seriously undertaken the way of individuation," the Jungian term for the quest for self. The material Luke uses is eclectic, ranging from the writings of J. R. R. Tolkien to the Bible. At the same time, the collection revives Luke's earlier interpretations of roles for men and women, particularly her concept of "feminine energy," which she believed would suffer deep were women to perform male roles.

The Voice Within: Love and Virtue in the Age of the Spirit brings together Luke's Jungian scholarship with Christian thinking on the question of sin. James E. Milord, writing in *America,* cited Luke's central question as one posed earlier by Jung: "How do I relate to the fact that I cannot escape sin?" Luke chose to discuss this "human predicament"—that sin is inescapable—by looking at it in terms of love, vows, and symbols rather than traditional good and evil.

As she aged, Luke turned to the subject of growing older and drew on classical authors whose characters confront aging and death. The result is a work that garnered praise both for its blending of literature and experience and for its insights. In the first four of five chapters, *Old Age* integrates passages from Homer's *Odyssey,* Shakespeare's *King Lear* and *The Tempest,* and T. S. Eliot's "Four Quartets" with Luke's own thoughts about the meaning of age. As a reviewer described in *Choice,* Luke "imagines old age not as a decline but as a potentially culminating stage of life, a time of preparation for death." She did not overlook the travails and sufferings that old age may bring, but rather described them as a "fire that can incinerate the ego." Old age, Luke contends, is a stage of life, not a defect or a pathological state against which we should battle.

Luke's final works were published after her death in 1995. The first, *Such Stuff as Dreams Are Made On* (the title is also taken from *The Tempest*), was published in 1999, although she wrote the first part when she was seventy. The work is in two parts, the first straightforward autobiography, the second derived from journals she kept about her dreams during her final decades. According to Luke, this process of looking deep within our selves and our dreams allows us to "know and accept and live the next thing with devotion." In 2001 *The Laughter at the Heart of Things* brought together a collection of her essays, some previously unpublished. The Jungian outlook runs through these works. This final work was described by a reviewer in *Publishers Weekly* in terms that sum up Luke's lifelong quest: "a world made orderly by myth."

BIOGRAPHICAL AND CRITICAL SOURCES:

PERIODICALS

America, May 18, 1985, James A. Milord, review of *The Voice Within: Love and Virtue in the Age of the Spirit,* p. 417.

Best Sellers, August, 1981, Mary A. Trainor, review of *Woman: Earth and Spirit,* p. 183; July, 1982, Robert Hauptman, review of *The Inner Story: Myth and Symbol in the Bible and Literature,* p. 159.

Booklist, July, 1992, Pat Monaghan, review of *Kaleidoscope: "The Way of Woman" and Other Essays.*

Choice, July-August, 1976, review of *Dark Wood to White Rose: A Study of Meaning in Dante's Divine Comedy,* p. 670; November 15, 1987, review of *Old Age;* January, 1993, W. C. Buchanan, review of *The Way of Women and Other Essays,* p. 794.

Christian Century, March 10, 1982, Rita M. Gross, review of *Women, Earth, and Spirit: The Feminine Symbol and Myth,* pp. 2276-2277.

Kirkus Reviews, September 15, 1987, review of *Old Age,* p. 1386.

Library Journal, March 15, 1992, review of *Old Age;* October 15, 1995, Susan Hamburger, review of *The Way of Story: Myths and Stories for the Inner Life,* p. 105.

Publishers Weekly, December 6, 1999, review of *Such Stuff as Dreams Are Made On: The Autobiography and Journals of Helen M. Luke,* p. 62.

Religious Studies Review, July, 1983, Judith Plaskow, review of *Women, Earth, and Spirit,* p. 250.*

M

MacDONNELL, Lawrence J. 1944-

PERSONAL: Born May 9, 1944, in Buffalo, NY; son of Wilfred D. and Evelyn Elizabeth (Cronin) MacDonnell; married Margaret Stevenson; children: Megan, Sandy, Kate. *Ethnicity:* "Scotch-Irish." *Education:* University of Michigan, B.A., 1966; University of Denver, J.D., 1972; Colorado School of Mines, Ph.D., 1976. *Politics:* Democrat. *Hobbies and other interests:* The outdoors.

ADDRESSES: Home—2160 Linden Ave., Boulder, CO 80304. *Office*—929 Pearl St., Suite 300, Boulder, CO 80302. *E-mail*—lmacdonnel@aol.com.

CAREER: Attorney and author. University of Colorado, Boulder, director of Natural Resource Law Center at School of Law, 1983-94; attorney in private practice, Boulder, 1995—. Stewardship Initiatives, president, 1997—. National Research Council, member of committee on riparian system functioning; City of Boulder, member of board of trustees of Open Space, 1999-2004. *Military service:* U.S. Air Force, 1967-71.

MEMBER: Colorado Riparian Association (president, 1996).

WRITINGS:

(With Bates, Getdor, and Wilkinson) *Searching out the Headwaters,* Island Press, 1993.
(Editor with Bates) *Natural Resources Policy and Law,* Island Press, 1993.

Also author of *From Reclamation to Sustainability,* University Press of Colorado (Boulder, CO).

WORK IN PROGRESS: A casebook, *Environment and Natural Resources Law,* completion expected in 2002.

SIDELIGHTS: Lawrence J. MacDonnell told *CA:* "My primary motivation for writing is a strong interest in education. The importance of well-informed understanding is the basis of decision making and action. My writing is influenced by my love of place, especially the natural environment. I am coming to grips with living in the arid American West."

*   *   *

MACKELPRANG, Romel W. 1955-

PERSONAL: Born April 24, 1955, in Kanab, UT; son of Romel J. (a certified public accountant) and Barbara J. (White) Mackelprang; married Susan Layton, August 19, 1977; children: Rachel, Romel D., Emily, Rebecca. *Ethnicity:* "Caucasian." *Education:* University of Utah, B.S., 1978, M.S.W., 1980, D.S.W., 1986. *Politics:* "Democrat/Liberal." *Religion:* Church of Jesus Christ of Latter-day Saints (Mormons). *Hobbies and other interests:* Soccer, backpacking, golf, running, reading.

ADDRESSES: Home—2304 East 60th Ave., Spokane, WA 99223. *Office*—School of Social Work, Eastern Washington University, 526 Fifth, Cheney, WA 99004; fax: 509-359-6475. *E-mail*—rmackelprang@mail.ewu. edu.

CAREER: University of Utah, Medical Center, Salt Lake City, UT, social worker, 1980-87; Eastern Washington University, Cheney, WA, assistant professor, then professor of social work, 1987—. Private practice as health care consultant and legal consultant; also expert witness; member of Washington Governor's Advisory Council on HIV/AIDS.

MEMBER: Council on Social Work Education, American Association of Spinal-Cord-Injury Psychologists and Social Workers.

WRITINGS:

(Editor, with D. Valentine) *Sexuality and Disabilities: A Guide for Human Service Practitioners,* Haworth Press, 1993.
(With Richard Salsgiver) *Disability: A Diversity Model Approach in Human Service Practice,* Brooks-Cole, 1999.

WORK IN PROGRESS: Life Transitions for Youth with Disabilities.

SIDELIGHTS: Romel W. Mackelprang told *CA:* "From a young age, I've always wanted to work with people. Early in my professional career I began working with people with disabilities. As I have counseled with them, worked with them, and developed lasting friendships, I have realized that the perceptions of disability are as important as the condition itself. Societal attitudes lead to social policy and conditions that keep people with disabilities at a disadvantage. These attitudes set in motion actions similar to actions precipitated by racism, sexism, ageism, et cetera. Thus a sense of social responsibility has prompted me to engage in much of the research and writing in which I have participated. By broadening perceptions of disability beyond sick, helpless, invalid, hand-i(n)-cap, I hope we can promote a more socially just society.

"Recently I have started expanding my ideas beyond disability and have begun work on a book that addresses human development generally. It will be interesting to see how those generalizations are accepted in the world beyond disability."

MacLAREN, Roy 1934-

PERSONAL: Born October 26, 1934, in Vancouver, British Columbia, Canada; son of Wilbur and Anne (Graham) MacLaren; married Alethea Mitchell June 25, 1959; children: Ian, Vanessa, Malcolm. *Education:* University of British Columbia, B.A., 1955; University of Cambridge, M.A., 1957; postgraduate studies at Harvard University, 1974; University of Toronto, M.Div., 1991.

ADDRESSES: Agent—c/o Author Mail, Pantheon Inc., 2100 Syntex Ct., Mississauga, Ontario, Canada L5N 3X4. *E-mail*—roy.maclaren@dfait-mdeci.qc.ca.

CAREER: Canadian government official, publisher, writer. Foreign service officer for the Canadian Diplomatic Service in Vietnam, Czechoslovakia, Switzerland, and the United Nations, 1957-69; director of public affairs for Massey-Ferguson, Ltd., 1969-74; Ogilvy & Mather, Ltd., Canada, president, 1974-76; Canadian Business Media, Ltd., chairman, 1976-93; Broadview Press, Ltd., director on the board, 1979-84; Deutsche Bank, Ltd. (Canada), director on the board, 1984-93; also served as director for London Insurance Group and Royal LePage, Ltd. Liberal member of parliament of Canada, 1979-84, 1988-96, parliamentary secretary to minister of energy, mines, and resources, 1980-82, minister of state, 1983-84, minister of national revenue, 1984, minister of international trade, 1993-96, high commissioner for Canada to the United Kingdom, 1996-2000. University of Toronto, Toronto, Canada, special lecturer, 1970-76; chairman, Canadian Government Task Force on Relations between Government and Business, 1976. Publisher, *Canadian Business.*

MEMBER: Royal Society of Arts (fellow), Royal Canadian Yacht Club (Toronto, Ontario), Athenaeum Club, Toronto Club, Rideau Club (Ottawa, Ontario), White's Club.

AWARDS, HONORS: D.S.L., University of Toronto, 1996.

WRITINGS:

Canadians in Russia, 1918-1919, Macmillan of Canada (Toronto, Ontario), 1976.
Canadians behind Enemy Lines, 1939-1945, University of British Columbia Press (Vancouver, British Columbia), 1981.

Consensus: A Liberal Looks at His Party, Mosaic Press (New York, NY), 1984.

Honourable Mention: The Uncommon Diary of an MP, Deneau, 1986.

(Editor) *African Exploits: The Diaries of William Stairs, 1887-1892,* Liverpool University Press (Liverpool, England), 1999.

Also author of *Canadians on the Nile, 1882-1898: Being the Adventures of the Voyageurs on the Khartoum Relief Expedition and Other Exploits,* University of British Columbia Press (Vancouver, British Columbia).

SIDELIGHTS: Roy MacLaren has long been involved in Canadian business and government and has written several books about Canadian military history and politics. His *Canadians in Russia, 1918-1919* discusses Canadian involvement in the Soviet revolution, particularly in three areas: the Caspian, where Canadians fought to keep the Turks and Germans from taking control of the Baku oil fields; North Russia, where they fought because the British believed they were more suited to a harsh, cold climate; and Siberia, where British, Japanese, and American goals came into conflict.

In *Canadians on the Nile, 1882-1898* MacLaren describes the 1884 Wolseley Expedition, which was sent by the British government to Khartoum, Sudan. The expedition recruited voyageurs, backwoods Canadian men used to canoeing and rafting on Canadian rivers. *American Historical Review* contributor R. J. D. Page described the book as a "popular history written with some flair but more concerned with colorful detail than historical analysis."

Canadians behind Enemy Lines, 1939-1945 tells the story of the small number of Canadians who were involved by the British Special Operations Executive in spying missions in France, Eastern Europe, and Asia. Many of these Canadians were originally from the countries where they were involved in espionage, and were therefore native speakers of the languages there. Records of these missions are thin because many of them have been destroyed, and access to the remaining ones is restricted to those with a security clearance. In *Quill and Quire* J. L. Granatstein wrote that this is the fullest account yet available of these missions, and that "as a record of courage and service, this book is very impressive." In *Saturday Night,* David Stafford

noted the patchy nature of the source material, and wrote, "Despite the book's modest scope MacLaren provides us with some instructive material about Canada's past. If he does not always explain much, he teaches us a great deal."

Honourable Mention: The Uncommon Diary of an MP is MacLaren's own account of his life in politics, beginning in 1977, when he decided to seek election as a liberal member of the Canadian parliament for suburban Toronto, to the defeat of Prime Minister John Turner's government in 1984. Because MacLaren decided against writing a "tell-all" book exposing others' secrets, the book reveals little about other politicians but much about MacLaren himself. J. L. Granatstein wrote in *Quill and Quire* that the book is "most revealing for what it says about its author, a man who seemed to prefer good wine and ripe Brie to the hard work of campaigning."

African Exploits: The Diaries of William Stairs, 1887-1892 is the most complete collection ever published of the diaries of a Canadian involved in the European expansion into Africa in the 1880s. The book records William Strain's participation in two African expeditions during the fight for European colonization and control over Africa. Stairs was a member of Henry Stanley's final trans-African expedition to rescue Emin Pasha. Three years later, leaving a trail of violence and suffering, the group succeeded in the rescue. After this, Stairs was involved in an expedition to take Katanga for King Leopold II of Belgium. The expedition was successful, but like the previous one it left a wake of devastation behind it, including the loss of Stairs's own life; he died of malaria when he was twenty-eight years old. MacLaren presents the diary with his own introduction and conclusion, providing the historical, psychological, and cultural context for Stairs's exploits.

BIOGRAPHICAL AND CRITICAL SOURCES:

PERIODICALS

American Historical Review, April, 1979, R. J. D. Page, review of *Canadians on the Nile, 1882-1898,* p. 596.

Books in Canada, November, 1986, p. 9.

Canadian Historical Review, September, 1987, p. 461.

Maclean's, September 21, 1998, p. 31.

Quill and Quire, January, 1982, p. 32; July, 1983, p. 6; November, 1986, p. 24.

Saturday Night, February, 1982, David Stafford, review of *Canadians behind Enemy Lines, 1939-1945,* p. 55.*

*   *   *

MAKOWSKI, Elizabeth

PERSONAL: Female. Education: University of Wisconsin—Milwaukee, B.A. (summa cum laude), 1973, M.A., 1976; Harvard University, A.M., 1977; Columbia University, Ph.D., 1993.

ADDRESSES: Office—Department of History, Taylor-Murphy 206, Southwest Texas State University, San Marcos, TX 78666. *E-mail*—em13@swt.edu.

CAREER: Educator. University of Wisconsin—Waukesha, lecturer, 1977-78; University of Wisconsin—Washington County, West Bend, lecturer, 1978-80; University of Wisconsin—Parkside, Kenosha, adjunct assistant professor, 1981; University of Mississippi, University, instructor in history and in curriculum and instruction, 1982; State University of New York College at Old Westbury, visiting assistant professor of comparative humanities, 1991-92; Southwest Texas State University, San Marcos, assistant professor, 1993-98, associate professor of history, 1998—.

WRITINGS:

(With Katharina Wilson) *Wykked Wyves and the Woes of Marriage: Misogamous Literature from Juvenal to Chaucer,* State University of New York Press (Albany, NY), 1989.

Canon Law and Cloistered Women: "Periculoso" and Its Commentators, 1298-1545, Catholic University of America Press (Washington, DC), 1999.

Contributor to books, including *Equally in God's Image: Women in the Middle Ages,* edited by Julia Bolton Holloway and others, Peter Lang (New York, NY), 1990. Contributor of articles, essays, and reviews to periodicals, including *Catholic Historical Review, Catholic Southwest, Journal of Medieval History, North American Review,* and *Mississippi Monograph.*

*   *   *

MALIN, Jo (Ellen) 1942-

PERSONAL: Born September 25, 1942, in St. Louis, MO; daughter of Louis and Bernice (Lasky) Malin; children: David Malin-Roodman, Sarah Malin-Roodman. *Education:* Washington University, St. Louis, MO, B.A., 1964; Indiana University—Bloomington, M.A., 1968; State University of New York at Binghamton, Ph.D., 1995. *Hobbies and other interests:* Morris dancing.

ADDRESSES: Office—School of Education and Human Development, State University of New York at Binghamton, P.O. Box 6000, Binghamton, NY 13902-6000.

CAREER: Worked as public relations coordinator in Binghamton, NY, 1979-80; South Tier Women's Services, Binghamton, assistant to medical director, 1980-84; Good Shepherd-Fairview Home, Binghamton, director of public relations and development, 1983-86; State University of New York at Binghamton, project director for educational talent search, 1987—, assistant to vice provost for undergraduate studies, 1996—.

MEMBER: Educational Opportunity Association (member of national council; founder of Women's Network), Association for Equality and Excellence in Education (member of board of directors), New York State Financial Aid Administrators Association.

AWARDS, HONORS: President's Award, Association for Equality and Excellence in Education, 1991-92; Mary McLeod Education Award, Broome County Urban League, 1992.

WRITINGS:

The Voice of the Mother: Embedded Maternal Narratives in Twentieth-Century Women's Autobiographies, Southern Illinois University Press (Carbondale, IL), 2000.

Member of editorial board, journal of Equal Opportunity Association.*

*   *   *

MANESS, Lonnie (E.) 1929-

PERSONAL: Born July 30, 1929, in Wildersville, TN; son of Lonnie (a brakeman and flagman) and Ruby Jewll (a homemaker; maiden name, Fowlkes) Maness; married Brooksie Nell Altom, May 4, 1951 (deceased); children: Barbara Nell Maness Staford, David Lonnie. *Ethnicity:* "White." *Education:* Attended University of Tennessee Junior College; University of Wisconsin-Milwaukee, B.S. and M.S.; University of Memphis, Ph.D. *Politics:* "Independent; tending toward Republican Party." *Religion:* Church of Christ.

ADDRESSES: Home—100 Burchard St., Martin, TN 38237. *Office*—University of Tennessee, Martin, TN 38238. *E-mail*—lmaness@utm.edu.

CAREER: Standard Oil Company, Milwaukee, WI, cashier, 1952-64; University of Tennessee, Martin, joined faculty, 1965, professor of history, 1981—. Presenter at conferences, and speaker at numerous events and on television. Member, Southeast Conference on Latin-American Studies. *Military service:* U.S. Air Force, 1951, aviation cadet.

MEMBER: Tennessee Historical Society, West Tennessee Historical Society (vice president and executive board member), Jackson Purchase Historical Society, American Legion (commander, 1989-91), Lions Club, Phi Kappa Phi, Phi Alpha Theta.

AWARDS, HONORS: National Alumni Outstanding Teacher Award, University of Tennessee, 1984; Marshall Wingfield Award, *West Tennessee Historical Society Papers,* 1993, for article "Henry Emerson Etheridge and the Gubernatorial Election of 1867: A Study in Futility."

WRITINGS:

An Untutored Genius: The Military Career of General Nathan Bedford Forrest, Guild Bindery, 1990, second edition, 1991.

Contributor to books, including *Tennessee Encyclopedia of History and Culture,* Rutledge Hill (Nashville, TN), 1998, and to periodicals, including *Colonial Courier, West Tennessee Historical Society Papers, Journal of the Jackson Purchase Historical Society,* and *Tennessee Historical Quarterly.* Contributor of book reviews to periodicals, including *Colonial Courier, Tennessee Historical Quarterly, Journal of Mississippi History, Register of the Kentucky Historical Society,* and *Journal of the Jackson Purchase Historical Society.*

WORK IN PROGRESS: Congressman Henry Emerson Etheridge: Aspects of His Life and Times.

*   *   *

MARSHALL, Robert O. 1939-

PERSONAL: Born 1939; married; wife's name, Maria (deceased, 1984); children: John, Robert, Christopher.

ADDRESSES: Home—New Jersey State Prison, Trenton, NJ. *Agent*—c/o Algora Publishing, 222 Riverside Dr., Suite 16D, New York, NY 10025-6809

CAREER: Former insurance salesman, Toms River, NJ.

WRITINGS:

(With Oakleigh Valentine) *Tunnel Vision: Trial & Error,* Algora (New York, NY), 2002.

WORK IN PROGRESS: A survival guide for prisoners.

SIDELIGHTS: In 2002, as his appeal options for release from death row in a New Jersey prison dwindled, Robert O. Marshall, convicted of hiring hit men from Louisiana to kill his wife at a rest area off the Garden State Parkway in 1986, published *Tunnel Vision: Trial & Error.*

Marshall's trial was a major news story in the mid-1980s; author Joe McGinniss has since given it notoriety with his best-selling book *Blind Faith,* which became a television movie starring Robert Urich and Joanna Kerns. Marshall, an insurance salesman who was having an affair with a school administrator in his hometown of Toms River, New Jersey, was accused of using hit men to kill his wife, Maria, and collect on a $1.5 million insurance policy.

Soon after his arrival on death row in 1986, Marshall began writing *Tunnel Vision*, his response to *Blind Faith*. In *Tunnel Vision*, written with his sister, Oakleigh Valentine, Marshall writes about his arrest for his wife's murder, his experiences in the New Jersey courts, and his efforts to appeal his conviction and win a new trial.

He describes the isolation and anxiety of life on death row. "The book offers no stunning revelations but puts forth Marshall's side of the case and describes the distress of being separated from his family," Emilie Lounsberry wrote for *Knight-Ridder/Tribune News Service*. Calling the book a "disturbing plea for relief," a *Publishers Weekly* contributor described it as a "grim narrative of murder, misfortune, and—to hear Marshall tell it—official thirst for retribution."

The New Jersey Supreme Court, in a 5-1 ruling on July 30, 2002, rejected Marshall's request for a new trial, saying his appeal raised no new evidence. Marshall, who exhausted his appeals through New Jersey courts, planned to appeal through the federal courts.

BIOGRAPHICAL AND CRITICAL SOURCES:

PERIODICALS

Knight-Ridder/Tribune News Service, February 1, 2002, Emilie Lounsberry, "As Death-Row Appeals Dwindle, Inmate Makes Case in New Book," p. K7822.
Publishers Weekly, February 25, 2002, review of *Tunnel Vision: Trial & Error,* pp. 49-50.

OTHER

Canadian Coalition against the Death Penalty, http://www.ccadp.org/robertmarshall.htm/ (March 24, 2002), "Robert Marshall—Death Row, New Jersey."
Nj.com, http://www.nj.com/ (July 30, 2002), "Final State Appeal for 'Blind Faith' Killer Rejected."*

MASCARENHAS, Margaret

PERSONAL: Born in Ann Arbor, MI. *Politics:* Green.

ADDRESSES: Home—California and Goa. *Agent*—Sterling Lord Literistic, 65 Bleeker St., New York, NY 10012. *E-mail*—mmasc@goatelecom.com.

CAREER: Freelance writer and editor.

WRITINGS:

Skin (fiction), Penguin-India, 2001.

Columnist for *Gomantak Times* and *Freenewsgoa.* Contributor to periodicals, including *Verve, Femina, India Today, Times of India,* and *Outlook.* Book editor for Goa Foundation publications.

Author's work has been translated into French.

WORK IN PROGRESS: Two novels, with working titles *Passion Fruit* and *The French Club.*

SIDELIGHTS: Margaret Mascarenhas told *CA:* "Although I was born in the United States, I was raised in Venezuela. My mother is American, my father is from Goa, India, a former Portuguese colony, which explains my last name. Currently I divide my time between the United States—Northern California mostly—and Goa, which is a tropical paradise that retains an Old World colonial charm.

"My first novel, *Skin,* is set in Goa, Angola, and California. It is about cultural identity, with a subtext on the Portuguese slave trade in Goa. My writing is predominately influenced by contemporary Latin-American authors—Gabriel García Marquez, Jorge Luis Borges, Mario Vargas Llosa, etc.—and my second book—in progress—is set in Venezuela. My third book, also in progress, is set mostly in California, where I went to college. I am mainly preoccupied with relationships between family members and friends and lovers, and their resolutions, in my writing. I am also somewhat obsessed with cultural identity since, as a hybrid myself, I have had to struggle with this issue."

MATZ, Marc

PERSONAL: Married; wife's name, Maritha. *Education:* Attended schools in the United States and abroad, including the University of California—Los Angeles, and Universita del Bella Arte, Florence, Italy.

ADDRESSES: Home—San Diego, CA. *Agent*—c/o Tor Books, 175 Fifth Ave., New York, NY 10010.

CAREER: Writer.

MEMBER: Science Fiction Writers of America.

WRITINGS:

Nocturne for a Dangerous Man (science fiction novel), Tor Books (New York, NY), 1999.

Also contributor to periodicals, including *Tomorrow* and *Magazine of Fantasy & Science Fiction.*

SIDELIGHTS: Marc Matz's first novel, *Nocturne for a Dangerous Man,* "combines near-future intrigue with hard-boiled detection," wrote Jackie Cassada in *Library Journal.* The book traces the search of detective Gavilan Robie for kidnap victim Siv Mattheissen through the high-tech, globally warmed world of the twenty-first century. Robie has to use a variety of techniques to find Siv and even more to understand her place in the corporation for which she works. He also has to understand the goals of the kidnappers, a self-proclaimed terrorist cell focusing on eco-terrorism who call themselves Erinyes. Curiously, they have not made any ransom demands of Siv's lover, the lesbian head of a major international corporation.

Robie eventually traces the kidnappers to a Chinese-owned bank in Chile and confronts them. "Matz comfortably balances action and contemplation," stated Roberta Johnson in *Booklist,* "and intersperses brief glimpses of the kidnappers with Robie's search and his encounters with wildly varied colleagues, mentors, and enemies." "Overall," a *Publishers Weekly* critic declared, "this is an excellent debut, and one featuring a sensitive protagonist certain to appeal to intelligent action."

BIOGRAPHICAL AND CRITICAL SOURCES:

PERIODICALS

Booklist, May 15, 1999, p. 1682.
Library Journal, June 15, 1999, p. 112.
Publishers Weekly, May 31, 1999, p. 71.*

*   *   *

MAUSHART, Susan 1958-

PERSONAL: Born 1958, in New York, NY; married twice; divorced twice; children: Anna, William, Suzannah. *Education:* New York University, Ph.D. (communication theory). *Hobbies and other interests:* Pug dogs.

ADDRESSES: Home—Perth, Western Australia. *Agent*—c/o Bloomsbury Publishing, 175 Fifth Ave., Suite 300, New York, NY 10010. *E-mail*—s. maushart@curtin.edu.au.

CAREER: Author and educator. Curtin University, Perth, Western Australia, instructor in social science. Columnist; comedy writer.

AWARDS, HONORS: Festival Prize for Non-Fiction, Adelaide Writer's Festival, 1994, for *Sort of a Place like Home: Remembering the Moor River Native Settlement.*

WRITINGS:

Sort of a Place like Home: Remembering the Moor River Native Settlement, Fremantle Arts Centre Press (South Fremantle, Australia), 1993.
The Mask of Motherhood: How Becoming a Mother Changes Everything and Why We Pretend It Doesn't, New Press (New York, NY), 1999.
Wifework: What Marriage Really Means for Women, Bloomsbury (New York, NY), 2002.

Contributor of syndicated weekly column to *The Weekend Australian Magazine.*

SIDELIGHTS: Susan Maushart, a social science professor at Curtin University in Australia, a columnist syndicated nationally in that country, and a single mother of three children, has made a name for herself writing about motherhood.

"In my research as a social scientist, and in my experience as the mother of three young children, I have been struck again and again by two observations that women without children seem disturbingly unprepared for the challenges of motherhood, and women with children seem disturbingly unprepared to discuss those challenges," Maushart stated in an interview on *Ann Online.*

The Mask of Motherhood: How Becoming a Mother Changes Everything and Why We Pretend It Doesn't is Maushart's effort to debunk romantic myths about motherhood. She discusses birth, breast-feeding, sleep deprivation, and domestic inequality. Moreover, she discusses how the lack of control with which mothers must cope shocks high-achieving women who are used to being in control, and how mothers hide the challenges of motherhood from non-mothers.

"Maushart's own pessimistic reading of feminism has had a powerful resonance with women readers, myself included," Julie Stephens wrote in *Arena.* According to *People's* Kim Hubbard, Maushart "writes engagingly and persuasively about the fact that, with so many options open to them, today's mothers feel more pressure than ever to defend their choices by donning a happy face."

Stephens added, "Aside from documenting some of the effects of this earth-shattering transition which is experienced as so enormous in personal terms but remains socially invisible, Maushart is at her most controversial when she points to women's own complicity in masking the substance of their maternal lives." In *Publishers Weekly,* a reviewer commented that although Maushart makes some "valuable points" about motherhood, she is "less convincing" when discussing such topics as childbirth and breast-feeding and is overall not "breaking any new ground." Conversely, Bethan Roberts, writing in *Spike Magazine,* considered Maushart "particularly incisive on the problems facing older working mothers" and called *The Mask of Motherhood* overall a "welcome addition in the face of the relentless, brainless optimism of most women's magazines and daytime television."

Critic Ann Marlowe characterized *Wifework: What Marriage Really Means for Women,* as "a brief against a caricature of contemporary dual—career marriage, Australian-style." Maushart maintains that women continue to do most domestic work even when both spouses work outside the home, that women do most of the organizational chores, and that women give most of the emotional support. While Marlowe said "too much of Maushart's analysis and rhetoric are stale," a *Publishers Weekly* contributor found the work to be an "often funny dissection of modern marriage; it is 100% honest—like the rest of this smart and witty book."

Maushart also wrote the award-winning *Sort of a Place like Home: Remembering the Moor River Native Settlement,* in which she presents the oral literature of the Australian Aboriginals along with official documents dealing with area natives. Jackie Huggins wrote in *Australian Book Review,* "It is commendable that the rich oral literatures are placed at the beginning of the book. . . . This gives the book impetus and authenticity, particularly as it is organised by non-Aboriginals." Huggins added, "The Aboriginal content is good; however the official documents are tedious and a little overambitious in the range of information and time."

BIOGRAPHICAL AND CRITICAL SOURCES:

PERIODICALS

Arena, June-July, 1998, Julie Stephens, review of *The Mask of Motherhood: How Becoming a Mother Changes Everything and Why We Pretend It Doesn't,* pp. 51-52.
Australian Book Review, November, 1993, Jackie Huggins, "Read between the Lines," pp. 42-43.
People, February 22, 1999, Kim Hubbard, review of *The Mask of Motherhood,* p. 44.
Publishers Weekly, January 25, 1999, review of *The Mask of Motherhood,* p. 83; February 25, 2002, review of *Wifework: What Marriage Really Means for Women,* p. 54.

OTHER

Ann Online, http://www.annonline.com/interviews/ (May 8, 2002).
Australian, http://theaustralian.news.com/ (May 8, 2002), "Susan Maushart."

Book Page, http://www.bookpage.com/ (May 8, 2002), Linda Stankard, review of *Wifework.*

Salon.com, http://wwwsalon.com/ (May 8, 2002), Ann Marlowe, "Why Do Women Wed?"

Spike, http://www.spikemagazine.com/ (May 8, 2002), Bethan Roberts, "Body Electric."*

*   *   *

MAUSSER, Wayne

PERSONAL: Male. *Hobbies and other interests:* Collecting sports memorabilia (especially baseball items), collecting old radios, racquetball, golf, boating, brewing beer.

ADDRESSES: Office—WPKR-Radio, 2401 West Waukau Ave., Oshkosh, WI 54904; fax 920-236-4240.

CAREER: Journalist. WPKR-Radio, Oshkosh, WI, news and sports director, 1990—, host of *WPKR Monday Night Tailgate Party,* 1991—, cohost of *The Terry and Wayne Show,* 1999—, and reporter assigned to cover Green Bay Packers games. Former cohost of nationally syndicated talk show.

MEMBER: Society of Oshkosh Brewers.

WRITINGS:

(With Larry Names and Milt Pappas) *Out at Home: Triumph and Tragedy in the Life of Milt Pappas,* LKP Group (Oshkosh, WI), 2000.

Coauthor of sports trivia and facts books.

BIOGRAPHICAL AND CRITICAL SOURCES:

OTHER

WPKR-Radio Web site, http://www.wpkr.com/ (March 21, 2000).*

*   *   *

MAY, Gerald Gordon 1940-

PERSONAL: Born June 12, 1940, in Hillsdale, MI. *Education:* Wayne State University, M.D., 1965.

ADDRESSES: Home—9490 Dawn Blush Ct., Columbia, MD 21045.

CAREER: Psychiatrist and writer. Grant U.S. Air Force Hospital, intern, 1965-66; Wilford Hall U.S. Air Force Hospital, in psychiatric residency, 1966-69; Andrews Air Force Base, Washington, DC, chief of inpatient services, 1969-71; Lancaster General Hospital, Lancaster, PA, director of addictive disorders program; Pennsylvania State University, PA, clinical associate professor of psychiatry, 1972-73; Temple University, Philadelphia, PA, clinical associate professor of family medicine, 1972-73.

WRITINGS:

Simply Sane: Stop Fixing Yourself and Start Really Living, Paulist Press (New York, NY), 1977, expanded edition published as *Simply Sane: The Spirituality of Mental Health,* Crossroad (New York, NY), 1993.

The Open Way: A Meditation Handbook, Paulist Press (New York, NY), 1977.

Pilgrimage Home: The Conduct of Contemplative Practice in Groups, Paulist Press (New York, NY), 1979.

Care of Mind, Care of Spirit: Psychiatric Dimensions of Spiritual Direction, Harper (San Francisco, CA), 1982, published as *Care of Mind, Care of Spirit: A Psychiatrist Explores Spiritual Direction,* HarperSanFrancisco (San Francisco, CA), 1992.

Will and Spirit: A Contemplative Psychology, Harper (New York, NY), 1982.

Addiction and Grace, Harper (New York, NY), 1988.

The Awakened Heart: Living beyond Addiction, HarperSanFrancisco (San Francisco, CA), 1991, published as *The Awakened Heart: Opening Yourself to the Love You Need,* HarperSanFrancisco (San Francisco, CA), 1993.

SIDELIGHTS: Gerald Gordon May is a prominent psychiatrist and writer who is known for promoting self-realization techniques. In *Simply Sane: Stop Fixing Yourself and Start Really Living,* he recommends positive, productive self-awareness and the understanding that change, while inevitable, need not be negative. Barbara Zelenko, writing in *Library Journal,* accused May of providing few "concrete examples of how to 'go sane,'" but R. V. Williams, writing in *Best Sellers,* declared that *Simply Sane* constitutes "a clear, unpretentious, highly readable work" by a "sensible and compassionate human being."

In *The Open Way: A Meditation Handbook,* May provides basic instructions in developing a meditation practice, and he relates various relaxation and breathing techniques. *Library Journal* reviewer J. S. Bagby proclaimed *The Open Way* "lively" and affirmed that it offers useful information "for both the beginner and the experienced mediator." A *Critic* reviewer, meanwhile, acknowledged that "any prospective mediator could probably use this manual with profit."

May distinguishes between psychological and spiritual methods of psychotherapy in *Care of Mind, Care of Spirit: Psychiatric Dimensions of Spiritual Direction,* and he emphasizes the invigorating, restorative nature of enhanced spiritual awareness. Timothy A. Curtin wrote in *America* that *Care of Mind, Care of Spirit* "is a book that breathes . . . practical comprehension and a grasp of the mysterious and difficult ways of the spirit.," and John Kotre wrote in *Commonweal* that May's book would prove useful to psychotherapists.

May continued to address issues and aspects of spirituality in *Will and Spirit: A Contemplative Psychology,* in which he recommends greater spiritual awareness as a corrective to the demands and distractions of modern living. Carolyn M. Craft noted in *Library Journal* that May demonstrates "extraordinary perception and sensitivity," and a *Choice* reviewer lauded *Will and Spirit* as "a ground-breaking book." James L. Empereur, meanwhile, observed in *America* that May's study provides "an intelligent and clear presentation of the relationship between psychological and spiritual growth." He added, "For many spiritual directors it will be heartening to find a psychiatrist relativizing the claims of that profession in favor of the workings of God in the human soul."

In *Addiction and Grace,* May probes the psychological and spiritual facets of substance abuse and articulates the notion that addictions are prevalent aspects of human behavior. Elise Chase wrote in *Library Journal* that May's book "guides readers from attachment to non-attachment," and James Alsdurf wrote in *Christianity Today* that the volume leads readers "to a new experience of the 'most powerful force in the universe.'" May also addresses extreme depen-

dency in *The Awakened Heart: Living beyond Addiction,* where he contends that addiction can be overcome through trust and love. Kenneth Wray wrote in *Christian Century* that the book "could stimulate spirited discussion."

May has worked as chief of the Andrews Air Force Base's inpatient services program and as director of Lancaster General Hospital's addictive disorders program. In addition, he has taught as a clinical associate professor at both Pennsylvania State University and Temple University.

BIOGRAPHICAL AND CRITICAL SOURCES:

PERIODICALS

America, October 30, 1982; March 26, 1983.
Best Sellers, June, 1977.
Choice, May, 1983.
Commonweal, November 5, 1982.
Christian Century, January 29, 1992.
Christianity Today, May 12, 1989.
Critic, July, 1978.
Library Journal, December 1, 1976; June 15, 1977; March 1, 1983; January, 1989.
New York Times Book Review, January 17, 1977.
Washington Post Book World, April 3, 1977.*

*   *   *

McCARRISTON, Linda 1943-

PERSONAL: Born July 30, 1943, in Chelsea, MA; daughter of William Thomas and Leona Marie (a grocery store clerk; maiden name, Parent) McCarriston; married Michael La Combe, August 21, 1965 (divorced, July, 1977); married Tom Absher, January 19, 1979 (marriage ended); children: (first marriage) Michael, David; (second marriage; stepchildren) Robin, Shannon, Matthew. *Education:* Emmanuel College, B.A., 1965; Goddard College, M.F.A., 1978; further study at Boston University, 1985.

ADDRESSES: Home—1746 Alder Drive, Anchorage, AK 99508. *Office*—Department of Creative Writing and Literary Arts, University of Alaska—Anchorage, 3211 Providence Drive, Anchorage, AK 99508. *E-mail*—afljm@uaa.alaska.edu.

CAREER: Poet, 1984—. Goddard College, Plainfield, VT, faculty member, summer writing program, 1978, 1979, undergraduate program, 1982; Vermont College, Montpelier, faculty member, adult degree program, 1979-91; Bunting Institute, Radcliffe College, Cambridge, MA, visiting writer, c. 1991-92; George Washington University, Washington, DC, Jenny McKean Moore Visiting Writer, c. 1992-93; University of Alaska Anchorage, assistant professor of creative writing, 1993—.

MEMBER: AWP, New England American Studies Association.

AWARDS, HONORS: Grolier Prize, Grolier Bookshop, Cambridge, MA, 1982; Vermont Council for the Arts fellow, 1982; AWP Award Series Selection, 1984, for *Talking Soft Dutch;* National Endowment for the Arts fellow, 1984, 1988; Terrence Des Pres Prize, *TriQuarterly Review,* 1991, for *Eva-Mary;* Chancellor's Award for Excellence in Creative Activity, University of Alaska—Anchorage.

WRITINGS:

POETRY

Talking Soft Dutch, Texas Tech Press (Lubbock, TX), 1984.
Eva-Mary, TriQuarterly Books/Northwestern University Press (Chicago, IL), 1994.
Little River: New and Selected Poems, Salmon Publishing (Cliffs of Moher, County Clare, Ireland), 2000, TriQuarterly Books (Evanston, IL), 2002.

Work represented in numerous collections and anthologies, including *The Vermont Experience,* edited by Tom Slayton, Vermont Life Books, 1987; *To Woo and to Wed: Contemporary Poets on Love and Marriage,* edited by Michael Blumenthal, Poseidon, 1992; and *Women in the Trees,* edited by Susan Koppleman, Beacon Press, 1996. Contributor of poems and essays to periodicals, including *Atlantic Monthly, Boston Review, Calyx, George Washington Review, Georgia Review, Green Mountain Review, Kalliope, New England Review, Ohio Review, Ploughshares, Poetry, Sojourner,* and *TriQuarterly Review.*

SIDELIGHTS: Much of Linda McCarriston's poetry draws on the pain of her childhood, when she was sexually abused and beaten by her father, which shaped her life for many years to come. She had two stifling marriages in which filling the traditional role of wife failed to bring her happiness, and she suffered from depression and alcoholism for many years. Her experiences brought her an acute awareness of gender issues, and also of economic class—she comes from a working-class background, labored for years as a poorly compensated adjunct professor, and has waited tables to support her writing. Her first book of poetry, *Talking Soft Dutch,* includes poems she wrote while working on her master's degree in her thirties, "but many written later, informed gradually by the differences in voice and world view that I was reclaiming," she wrote in *Contemporary Authors Autobiography Series (CAAS). Talking Soft Dutch,* with many poems about horses, dogs, and the ordinary tasks of rural life, "is impressive for its lyricism, balance and clarity, but it is also a personally reticent book," remarked Alison Townsend in *Women's Review of Books.* "McCarriston refers only occasionally to traumatic events in her own childhood; one has the sense that a curtain has been drawn over troubling material she is not yet ready to process."

In *Eva-Mary,* however, McCarriston deals fully with her childhood and its repercussions. This collection, she wrote in *CAAS,* is "the culmination of years of struggling with issues of class, gender, love, silence, voice, power and powerlessness, the impossibility of 'traditional' (read 'permanent inequality') marriage." She further explained, "When, finally, I began to write the poems of *Eva-Mary,* fifteen years after I first entered therapy, the fact of my violent childhood was neither more nor less a burden in itself than it had been on any of the days of its occurrence. The unbearable burden that the book addresses (speaking, as it does, 'to the judge') was the continuing denial—no inversion—of its reality by all the order-sustaining social institutions: church and state, law and medicine, psychiatry especially, as it occupied, pretty much, the shoes of the 'Dead God' of 'sophisticated' folks. In the family, the family facts were acknowledged. *Eva-Mary,* then, was to realize not my need to 'share,' and certainly not any need to 'be analyzed,' but the moral imperative of speaking, to my world, a truth about itself that all of its forces had long been mobilized to deny."

McCarriston describes her father's abuse in poems such as "A Castle in Lynn." The title refers to her hometown, Lynn, Massachusetts, and her father's assertion that his home was his castle. The poem portrays him as an old man remembering "the hard bottom of the girl," "the full new breast," and "split[ing] the green girlwood," and concludes, "in a lifetime of used ones, second-hand, one girl he could spill like a shot of whiskey, the whore only he could call *daughter.*" This poem, Townsend pointed out, has a "quiet fury." In another poem, "October 1913," McCarriston imagines her father as an infant and her paternal grandmother, an impoverished Irish immigrant with a large family, contemplating infanticide. "Remarkable for its insight, this poem does not forgive her father, but recognizes the bleakness and horror of his origins," Townsend observed, adding that, moreover, it sheds light on "the terrible lot of Irish immigrant women." McCarriston's father was also violent toward his wife; the poem "To Judge Faolain, Dead Long Enough: A Summons" curses the judge who denied McCarriston's mother protection from her husband's abuse. The poet "sentences the judge and all he stands for to the fate her mother (and women like her mother) have lived," related Townsend.

Stephen Corey, critiquing *Eva-Mary* for *Georgia Review,* remarked that "questions of excess and didacticism surface easily when a writer is confronting such deeply emotional and moral content as appears throughout *Eva-Mary,* but much of this book succeeds because of McCarriston's unflinching determination to *force* subject matter and a fever-pitched voice to be the prime carriers of her art." There is a lighter side to the collection as well: "McCarriston also gives us, interspersed with her tales of the brutal and the brutalized, several poems about the saving grace of animal innocence and beauty—especially that of horses," noted Corey. "The Apple Tree," the first poem in the book, repeated at the end, further derives images of peace and healing from nature. The poem is dedicated to McCarriston's mother, "the hero of this nightmare," commented James Finn Cotter in *Hudson Review,* as she "fought to save her children when priest, judge, and doctor failed to help, and who finally, at fifty-three, divorced the ogre she had been chained to." Cotter pronounced *Eva-Mary* a "fine, brave volume."

Little River: New and Selected Poems features poems from McCarriston's previous collections along with new work. Dealing often with human relationships, both beneficial and not so, the volume's message is "clearly feminist" but "never heavy-handed," in the words of a *Kirkus Reviews* critic. Written in a simple, spare style, the poems "yet are musical, containing voices calling and answering to each other despite all obstacles," observed *Booklist* contributor Patricia Monaghan. The *Kirkus Reviews* critic summed up *Little River*'s contents as "provocative, finely wrought poems packing thematic punch with rare imagistic beauty."

BIOGRAPHICAL AND CRITICAL SOURCES:

BOOKS

Contemporary Authors Autobiography Series, Volume 28, Gale (Detroit, MI), 1998, pp. 189-229.

PERIODICALS

Booklist, November 1, 2000, Patricia Monaghan, review of *Little River: New and Selected Poems,* p. 513.

Georgia Review, spring, 1992, Stephen Corey, review of *Eva-Mary,* pp. 184-185.

Hudson Review, autumn, 1992, James Finn Cotter, "Prized Poetry," pp. 518-524.

Kirkus Reviews, October 1, 2000, review of *Little River,* p. 1397.

Poetry, April, 1985, Vernon Shetley, review of *Talking Soft Dutch,* pp. 38-39.

Publishers Weekly, September 20, 1991, review of *Eva-Mary,* p. 126.

Sojourners, July, 2000, Rose Marie Berger, "Got Poetry?," p. 62.

Tri-Quarterly Review, fall, 1991, "Linda McCarriston: The Terrence Des Pres Prize Winner," pp. 15-16.

Women's Review of Books, March, 1992, Alison Townsend, "Poetry Out of Pain, "pp. 11-12.*

*   *   *

McCARTEN, Anthony (Peter Chanel Thomas Aquinas) 1961-

PERSONAL: Born April 28, 1961, in New Plymouth, New Zealand; married Fiona Mathieson, 1988 (divorced, 1992); children: one son. *Education:* Francis Douglas Memorial College, New Plymouth, New Zealand, graduated, 1979; Victoria University, Wellington, New Zealand, B.A., 1987.

ADDRESSES: Home—London, England. *Agent*—Playmarket, P.O. Box 9767, Wellington, New Zealand; and, Casarotto Ramsay, National House, 60-66 Wardour St., London W1V 3HP, England.

CAREER: Taranaki Herald, New Plymouth, New Zealand, journalist, 1979-82; musician. Director of short films *Nocturne in a Room*, 1992, and *Fluff*, 1995.

AWARDS, HONORS: Queen Elizabeth II Arts Council grants, 1989, 1990, 1991; New Zealand *Listener* award and Wellington Theatre Critics award, both 1991, both for *Via Satellite;* Mollière Comedy Prize, France, 2001, for *The English Harem.*

WRITINGS:

Cyril Ellis, Where Are You? (play), first produced in Wellington, New Zealand, 1984.

Invitation to a Second-Class Carriage (play), first performed in Wellington, New Zealand at the Depot Theatre, 1984.

Yellow Canary Mazurka (play), first produced in Wellington, New Zealand at the Circa Theatre, 1987.

(With Stephen Sinclair) *Ladies Night* (play), first produced in Auckland, New Zealand at the Mercury Theatre, December, 1987.

Pigeon English (play), first produced in Wellington, New Zealand at the Playwrights' Workshop, 1989.

Weed (play), first produced in Wellington, New Zealand at the Circa Theatre 1990.

A Modest Apocalypse (short stories), Godwit Press (Auckland, New Zealand), 1991.

Via Satellite (play), first produced in Wellington, New Zealand at the Circa Theatre, 1991.

Hang on a Minute, Mate! (play; adapted from the novels by Barry Crump), first produced in Wellington, New Zealand, 1992.

Let's Spend the Night Together (play), first performed at the Bats Theatre, 1994.

FILTH (Failed in London, Try Hong Kong) (play), first performed in Wellington, New Zealand at the Circa Theatre, 1995.

Four Cities (play), produced in Los Angeles, CA, 1996.

Via Satellite (film screenplay; based on his play of the same title), 1999.

Spinners (novel), William Morrow (New York, NY), 1999.

The English Harem (novel), Vintage (Auckland, New Zealand), 2001.

Also author of plays *Ladies' Night 2* and *Legless,* with Stephen Sinclair. *Ladies Night* has been translated and performed in Germany, Austria, Spain, and Italy.

SIDELIGHTS: Anthony McCarten is a well-known New Zealand playwright who has also written short stories and a novel, as well as trying his hand at film directing. His characters are often small-town, rural people who are confronted with extraordinary situations. In his first play, the comical *Cyril Ellis, Where Are You?*, a group of people travel by train on the anniversary of the Tangiwai Disaster in which many travelers were killed when a train ran into a swollen river. As Patricia Cooke noted in *Contemporary Dramatists,* this first effort marked McCarten as a "promising new talent."

In McCarten's next play, *Yellow Canary Mazurka,* he explores the lives of the lonely and rejected tenants of high-rise apartment buildings whose private lives are spent in virtual isolation. He collaborated with Stephen Sinclair on his next work, *Ladies Night.* This play is about five young men who are desperate for money and who will do anything to earn it, including work as strippers at a nightclub, a job that leads to great financial success. "*Ladies Night* has had numerous productions and resists critical disapproval," commented Cooke, "quickly becoming the most widely seen New Zealand play ever."

McCarten's *Pigeon English* was less successful, however. A satire on government bureaucrats who must remove roosting pigeons from the town hall clock, the play took almost four years to complete only to receive disappointing reviews. Positive reviews returned with the playwright's fifth play, *Weed,* which explores the plight of New Zealand farmers who, faced with severe disadvantages in the global economy, turn to raising profitable marijuana crops. The play was extremely popular in New Zealand and has had several revivals around the country.

Comical plays have continued to flow from McCarten's pen, among them *Via Satellite* and *Four Cities.* The former is about a family consisting of a mother, four daughters, and the husband of one of the daughters, who are all awaiting the televised appearance of the fifth daughter as she competes for the gold in the Olympics. The play explores family dynamics through the reaction of each member to the fifth daughter's success. *Four Cities* follows June Ramsey, a forty-five-year-old, highly cultured woman who feels she has yet to experience all that life has to offer. To add a little interest to her life, she takes a tour of four foreign cities and begins an affair with her tour guide.

McCarten's characteristic sense of humor is readily apparent in his first novel, *Spinners,* which is about strange goings on of an extraterrestrial sort in a small New Zealand town. The main character, Delia Chapman, after working three split shifts at a meat packing plant, is abducted by aliens who impregnate her using heat waves. She reports the event and is thought to be suffering from overwork and stress-induced insanity. The tabloids and town gossips get a hold of the story, but rumors really begin to fly when two of Delia's factory friends also become pregnant. Reviewers generally enjoyed McCarten's sense of humor in the story, but there was some criticism of the novel's conclusion in which Delia gives birth to a son. Because of the sterile way in which she was impregnated, the birth could be interpreted as a virgin birth, and parallels between this event and the birth of Christ are continued with the visitation of three "wise men."

A *Publishers Weekly* contributor wrote of *Spinners* that McCarten's "fresh dialogue and keen, devilish sense of humor make the facile resolution this novel's only disappointing moment." And *New York Times Book Review* contributor David Finkle wondered of the conclusion: "Was this development in McCarten's plan? He may have set out to amuse himself by wondering how a town of fools would react in an outlandish what-if predicament." However, although McCarten's characters are clearly flawed, the author treats them sympathetically, and some reviewers saw this as a strength in the book. As Leonie Reynolds pointed out in an *SF Site* review, "Here is the point that distinguishes McCarten from some of his contemporaries; he never forgets that you get out of people only what goes into them, and explains the minor character flaws as human."

BIOGRAPHICAL AND CRITICAL SOURCES:

BOOKS

Contemporary Dramatists, St. James Press (Detroit, MI), 1993.

PERIODICALS

Library Journal, January 1999, Christine Perkins, review of *Spinners,* p. 154.
New York Times Book Review, May 16, 1999, David Finkle, review of *Spinners,* p. 32.
Publishers Weekly, December 7, 1998, review of *Spinners,* p. 50.

OTHER

SF Site, http://www.sfsite.com/ (June 30, 1999), Leonie Reynolds, review of *Spinners.**

*　　*　　*

McCONNELL, Jane

PERSONAL: Married T. Jeff Heyman; children: Lucy, Henry, Jack. *Education:* Stanford University, graduated 1985.

ADDRESSES: Home—Boulder, CO. *Office*—c/o *Mothering: Natural Family,* P.O. Box 1690, Santa Fe, NM 87504.

CAREER: Women's Sports and Fitness, editor; currently freelance writer. Fund-raiser and marketing representative for agency for the prevention of homelessness.

WRITINGS:

(With Peggy O'Mara) *Natural Family Living: The Mothering Magazine Guide to Parenting,* Pocket Books (New York, NY), 2000.

Contributor to periodicals. Associate editor, *Mothering: Natural Family Living.*

BIOGRAPHICAL AND CRITICAL SOURCES:

PERIODICALS

Denver Post, April 2, 2000, Claire Martin, "Boulder Mom Co-authors Book on Parenting Ideas."

Kirkus Reviews, February 15, 2000, review of *Natural Family Living: The Mothering Magazine Guide to Parenting,* p. 235.

Stanford, July-August, 2001, Kathy Christie Hernandez, "Class Notes."*

* * *

McFALL, Lynne 1948-

PERSONAL: Born 1948. *Education:* University of Pittsburgh, Ph.D., 1982.

ADDRESSES: Agent—c/o Author Mail, Peter Lang Publishing, 275 Seventh Ave., 28th Fl., New York, NY 10001. *E-mail*—luckymcfal@aol.com.

CAREER: Author. Syracuse University, Syracuse, NY, associate professor of philosophy.

WRITINGS:

The One True Story of the World, Atlantic Monthly Press (New York, NY), 1990.

Dancer with Bruised Knees, Chronicle (San Francisco, CA), 1994.

Happiness, Peter Lang (New York, NY), 1996.

SIDELIGHTS: Lynne McFall's first book, *The One True Story of the World,* was called "that rare thing, a philosophical novel that also manages to be accessible and dramatically gripping," by Ralph Sassone in the *New York Times Book Review.* As a child, narrator Jesse Walker had played a game with her father. Each night he would begin a different version of "the one true story of the world," and Jesse would finish it. As an adult she tries to deal with his abandonment when she was ten. Jesse is an obituary writer for a New England newspaper. At thirty-four she loses her job and heads home to California, hoping to find the ending to her own story. Jesse suffers car accidents and homelessness, and lives for a time in a women's shelter. While in Iowa, she has an affair with a hog farmer. In her quest, Jesse learns more about herself and also the real circumstances surrounding her father's disappearance. "Characterization and metaphor are impressively handled," wrote Elizabeth Guiney Sandvick in *Library Journal.* A *Publishers Weekly* reviewer commented that McFall ends the chapters "with piercing observations, framed with such grace they go straight to the heart, as will the quirky heroine we meet in these pages."

Lisa Zeidner wrote in the *New York Times Book Review* that McFall's *Dancer with Bruised Knees* is "a very funny look at the nature of depression." Sarah Blight is a forty-year-old photographer. Her mother, who suffers from agoraphobia, has not left the house in ten years and hangs laundry, while naked, by the light of moon. Her father is an alcoholic, and her brother Morgan is accused of murdering his wife and stuffing her into a trash barrel. Sarah believes he may have done it, because when they were children he had a sadistic streak. In a game of Russian roulette, he killed Sarah's twenty-six cats. After Sarah's boyfriend, Jake, leaves her, his new girlfriend puts out one of Sarah's eyes with a pool cue in a barroom brawl. Sarah takes a temporary job typing, but is fired when she refuses to wear an eye patch. Zeidner wrote that Sarah "celebrates her deformity when she realizes that 'I was no longer homely; I now had the capacity to terrify.'"

"What most distinguishes this novel is Sarah's straight-shooting, deadpan voice," wrote Zeidner of *Dancer with Braided Knees.* "She avoids drowning in self-pity even when she's falling-down drunk and weeping to country-and-western ballads about lost love." Zeidner called the ending "both slam-bang and subtle." *Booklist* reviewer Ron Antonucci said McFall's "lean, strong prose rings an affirmative, resonant echo amid the bleakness," calling *Dancer with Bruised Knees* "a rich, mordant novel." A *Publishers Weekly* reviewer called McFall "a remarkably talented writer who makes Sarah's voice—wry, cynical, and bitter, yet capable of poignant tenderness—so mesmerizing that one comes under the spell of her bleak view of life."

BIOGRAPHICAL AND CRITICAL SOURCES:

PERIODICALS

Booklist, October 15, 1994, p. 402.

Kirkus Reviews, July 15, 1994, p. 940.

Library Journal, May 15, 1990, p. 95; August, 1994, p. 130.

New York Times Book Review, June 3, 1990, p. 22; November 6, 1994, p. 12; December 4, 1994, p. 70; June 2, 1996, p. 32.
Publishers Weekly, April 6, 1990, p. 103; August 1, 1994, p. 69.*

*   *   *

McKAY, Gardner 1932-2001

PERSONAL: Born June 10, 1932, in New York, NY; died of prostate cancer, November 21, 2001, in Oahu, HI; son of Deane (an advertising executive) and Catherine (a homemaker) McKay; married Madeleine Madigan (an artist), 1983 (one source says 1980, another 1984); children: Tristan, Liza. *Education:* Attended Cornell University.

CAREER: Actor and writer. Appeared in television series *Boots and Saddles,* 1957, and *Adventures in Paradise,* 1959-62, and in films *Raintree County,* 1957, *The Pleasure Seekers,* 1964, and *I Sailed to Tahiti with an All-Girl Crew,* 1968. *Los Angeles Herald Examiner,* Los Angeles, CA, drama critic and theater editor, 1977-82. Teacher of playwriting at University of California—Los Angeles, University of Alaska, and University of Hawaii.

AWARDS, HONORS: Los Angeles Drama Critics Circle Award for *Sea Marks.*

WRITINGS:

Sea Marks (play), first produced in Los Angeles, 1972, adapted by McKay for Public Broadcasting Service (PBS) television production, 1976.
Toyer (play), first produced at Kennedy Center, Washington, DC, 1983, adapted by McKay into novel, Little, Brown (Boston, MA), 1999.

Author of numerous other plays, including *Masters of the Sea, This Fortunate Island,* and *Untold Damage,* which McKay adapted for television in 1971. Writer and reader of stories on radio program *Stories on the Wind,* Hawaii Public Radio, 1995-2000.

SIDELIGHTS: Gardner McKay was an up-and-coming film and television actor when he decided he would rather pursue a career as a writer. An exceedingly handsome young man, he became a star with the television series *Adventures in Paradise,* in which he played the captain of a schooner in the South Pacific. After the series ended in 1962, McKay turned down an opportunity to make a film with Marilyn Monroe. He then traveled extensively, explored jungles and deserts, and finally began devoting himself to writing. His play *Sea Marks,* about a love affair carried on mostly by correspondence between an Irish fisherman and a Welsh career woman who lives in England, received praise when it premiered in the 1970s and was still being revived in 2002. Another play, *Toyer,* about a psychopath who performs grisly surgery on young women, was adapted by McKay into his first published novel. McKay, who settled in Hawaii in 1987, also wrote other plays, numerous short stories, poetry, and as-yet unpublished novels, and at his death was working on his autobiography.

Sea Marks is "a poignant and poetic love story," wrote *Washington Post* critic Michael Toscano, reviewing a 2002 production. The male protagonist, Colm, begins writing letters to Timothea, a woman he has seen but once and who does not remember him. They lead contrasting lives: he makes his living by fishing on an isolated Irish island, while she works in publishing in Liverpool. They form a bond through their letters, however—her company publishes his as poetry—and eventually they decide to meet. Walter Kerr, commenting on a 1981 off-Broadway staging in *New York Times,* found the play somewhat predictable but added, "Nonetheless, it's the work of an able man, a writer with sufficient command of unpretentious metaphor to bring off the difficult feat of making you believe that his 'primitive's' casual comments might be construed as natural verse. There is abundant humor—a surprisingly honest humor—in the relationship that grows up between impossible partners." *Chicago Tribune* writer Richard Christiansen, discussing a 1988 Chicago production, though McKay "tells this fragile story delicately and with some eloquence."

Toyer is far different type of story. Set in Los Angeles, it concerns a man who seduces attractive women, then subjects them to a medical procedure called a spinal chordotomy, which leaves them comatose. A newspaper calls him "the Toyer" for the way he toys with his victims. Eventually he chooses as his next mark Maude, a doctor who has been treating some of the women he has attacked. The stage version is a two-character drama with the Toyer confronting Maude in her home, to which he gains access by posing as a friendly young man and helping her start her car. This is "the old woman-in-peril routine," wrote *Chicago Tribune* reviewer Christiansen of a 1997 Chicago production. "Creaky as the old formula is," Christiansen continued, "it continues to wield its power over a willing audience. Peeping Toms that we are, we just love to look in on the mayhem." The novel also involves a journalist, Sara Smith, who is attacked but released by the Toyer. Her newspaper publishes letters from him as well as writings by Maude as she and Sara seek to track him down. In addition to being a thriller, the book is a commentary on media exploitation of tragedy, although some reviewers thought it unlikely that any newspaper would print Toyer's letters. One of them was Chicago *Tribune Books* critic Chris Petrakos, who added that despite its unbelievable elements, *Toyer* "has its moments"; it is "sometimes gripping, sometimes ludicrous," he remarked. *New York Times Book Review* contributor Marilyn Stasio likewise thought the novel's plot defied logic and credibility, but she allowed that McKay's prose has a "bizarre beauty" and features "gorgeous imagery." *Booklist* reviewer Budd Arthur deemed the novel "powerfully written" and "a chiller of a thriller," while *Library Journal*'s Nancy Paul called it "well written, interesting, and interestingly offbeat."

BIOGRAPHICAL AND CRITICAL SOURCES:

PERIODICALS

Booklist, November 15, 1998, Budd Arthur, review of *Toyer* (novel), p. 568.
Chicago Tribune, August 4, 1988, Richard Christiansen, "Romance Sweetly Acted, but Theater's a Bit Too Intimate," Tempo section, p. 5; August 6, 1997, Christiansen, "Creep Within: Chilling 'Toyer' Tells Familiar Tale of Suspense," Tempo section, p. 2.
Kirkus Reviews, November 1, 1998, review of *Toyer* (novel), pp. 1556-1557.
Library Journal, May 15, 1999, Nancy Paul, review of *Toyer* (novel), p. 147.
Los Angeles Times Book Review, January 17, 1999, Eugen Weber, "L.A. Confidential," p. 4.
New York Times, October 4, 1981, Walter Kerr, "High Marks for 'Sea Marks' and a Fizzle at the Phoenix," section 2, p. 5.
New York Times Book Review, January 24, 1999, Marilyn Stasio, review of *Toyer* (novel), p. 24.

People, April 19, 1999, William Plummer and Ron Arias, "Riding High: Gardner McKay, Former TV Hunk, Gets Back into the Swim, as a Novelist," p. 135.
Tribune Books (Chicago, IL), February 21, 1999, Chris Petrakos, review of *Toyer* (novel), p. 8.
Washington Post, February 4, 1983, Lloyd Grove, "'Toyer': Playing for Cheap Thrills," Weekend section, p. 7; May 23, 2002, Michael Toscano, "'Sea Marks' Both Intense, Serene," p. T10.

OBITUARIES:

PERIODICALS

Los Angeles Times, November 22, 2001, Dennis McLellan, "Gardner McKay, 69: Left Acting Career to Be Writer," p. B10.
New York Times, November 24, 2001, "Gardner McKay, 69, TV Heartthrob Who Turned to Writing," p. A13.
People, December 10, 2001, "Born to Run: For '60s TV Heartthrob Gardner McKay, Life Was an Adventure in Paradise," p. 155.*

*   *   *

MEDAVOY, Mike 1941-

PERSONAL: Born January 21, 1941, in Shanghai, China; immigrated to United States, 1957, naturalized U.S. citizen, 1962; son of Michael and Dora Medavoy; married Patricia Duff (marriage ended); married Irena Medavoy (a charity executive); children: Brian, Melissa, Michael, Nicholas. *Education:* University of California—Los Angeles, B.A., 1963.

ADDRESSES: Home—Los Angeles, CA. *Office*—c/o Simon and Schuster, 1230 Avenue of the Americas, New York, NY 10020.

CAREER: Talent agent and motion picture executive. Universal Studios, Los Angeles, CA, with casting department, 1963; Bill Robinson Associates, Los Angeles, CA, agent, 1963-64; General Artist Corp./ Creative Management Agency, Los Angeles, CA, vice president, motion picture department, 1965-71;

International Famous Agency, Los Angeles, CA, vice president, motion picture department, 1971-74; United Artists Corp., Los Angeles, CA, senior vice president, 1974-78; Orion Pictures, Burbank and Los Angeles, CA, founder and executive vice president, 1978-90; Tri-Star Pictures, Culver City, CA, chairman, 1990-94; Phoenix Pictures, Culver City, CA, chairman, 1995-2001; independent film producer, 2001—. St. Petersburg (Russia) Film Festival, honorary co-chair, 1992; Tokyo Film Festival, jury chair, 1994; American Cinematheque, co-chair, 1997; Film Roman, member, board of directors, 2000—; Cinema Entertainment Group, member, board of advisors, 2000—. Shanghai Film Conference, member of advisory board; Sundance Institute, member, board of governors. Gary Hart for President Campaign, national finance chair, 1984; and Bill Clinton Presidential Campaign, member of Western Finance Committee, 1992; Boston Museum of Fine Arts, chair of visiting committee; Los Angeles Museum of Science and Industry, member, board of directors; University of California, Los Angeles, Center for International Relations, chair.

MEMBER: Academy of Motion Picture Arts and Sciences (governor, 1977-81), UCLA Foundation, UCLA Chancellors Association.

AWARDS, HONORS: Academy Award for Best Picture, 1975, for *One Flew over the Cuckoo's Nest,* 1976, for *Rocky,* 1977, for *Annie Hall,* 1984, for *Amadeus,* 1986, for *Platoon,* 1990, for *Dances with Wolves,* and 1991, and for *The Silence of the Lambs*; Motion Picture Pioneer Award, 1992; UCLA Alumni Career Achievement Award, 1997; Producers Award, Cannes Film Festival, 1998; Neil H. Jacoby Award, 1999; Lifetime Achievement Award, Israel Film Festival, 2002.

WRITINGS:

(With Josh Young) *You're Only as Good as Your Next One: 100 Great Films, 100 Good Films, and 100 Films for Which I Should Be Shot,* Pocket Books (New York, NY), 2002.

SIDELIGHTS: Mike Medavoy details his adventures in the movie business in *You're Only as Good as Your Next One: 100 Great Films, 100 Good Films, and 100 Films for Which I Should Be Shot,* written with journalist Josh Young. Through his executive positions with such companies as United Artists, Orion Pictures, Tri-Star Pictures, and Phoenix Pictures, Medavoy has been involved in the production of about 300 films, including Best Picture Academy Award winners such as *One Flew over the Cuckoo's Nest, Amadeus,* and *Dances with Wolves,* other prestigious releases including *Network* and *Philadelphia,* and popular successes such as *The Terminator.* Medavoy came to the business from an unusual background; he was born to Russian Jewish immigrants in China and grew up in Chile, finally coming to the United States while in his teens. His first job in the motion-picture business was in the mailroom of Universal Studios, but he rose quickly, working in casting and as a talent agent before becoming a production executive. In *You're Only as Good as Your Next One,* he details both his successes and failures in filmmaking, offers behind-the-scenes gossip, and denounces forces in the business who put financial considerations ahead of quality.

Medavoy's memoir is "a decent, intelligent book about a business that is often neither," commented *Los Angeles Times Book Review* contributor Kenneth Turan, who noted that Medavoy comes across in the book "like the kind of executive he has the reputation for being: determined, no-nonsense, sure of himself." Laura Landro, though, writing in *Wall Street Journal,* found the memoir "a self-aggrandizing saga" that "is as much as anything a plea for recognition and a settling of old scores. . . . Mr. Medavoy's breezy, conversational style does convey a sense of Hollywood's mix of great talent and cutthroat ethics, but he places too much of the blame for his failures on others." Turan, however, thought that "this strictly business autobiography is at its best and most readable when Medavoy comes down from the mountaintop and gives in to his irritation with those he feels have done somebody wrong." These include "the former Sony Pictures triumvirate of Peter Guber, Jon Peters and Mark Canton, who he claims made his life a living hell when he was running Tristar Pictures," Turan reported.

Landro liked some aspects of the book, saying that Medavoy's "yarns about the machinations behind the making of movies . . . are entertaining enough," providing insights about such stars as Kevin Costner and Madonna. Medavoy also offers valuable information "on the complex business deals, negotiations with distributors, and political exigencies necessary to make a successful motion picture coalesce," observed Richard W. Grefrath in *Library Journal.* A *Publishers Weekly* reviewer noted that Medavoy's "insider anecdotes . . . are revelatory," while *People*'s Mark O'Donnell termed the book "a frank and fond insider's memoir" filled with "fun facts about some great films . . . and some dogs." The *Publishers Weekly* reviewer concluded that Medavoy has succeeded in "documenting decades of filmmaking with authoritative ease" in this "solid memoir."

BIOGRAPHICAL AND CRITICAL SOURCES:

BOOKS

Medavoy, Mike, and Josh Young, *You're Only as Good as Your Next One: 100 Great Films, 100 Good Films, and 100 Films for Which I Should Be Shot,* Pocket Books (New York, NY), 2002.

PERIODICALS

Booklist, February 1, 2002, Mike Tribby, review of *You're Only as Good as Your Next One,* p. 915.
Library Journal, February 1, 2002, Richard W. Grefrath, review of *You're Only as Good as Your Next One,* p. 101.
Los Angeles Times Book Review, March 10, 2002, Kenneth Turan, "Executive Privilege," p. 5.
People, February 18, 2002, Mark O'Donnell, review of *You're Only as Good as Your Next One,* p. 41.
Publishers Weekly, January 28, 2002, review of *You're Only as Good as Your Next One,* p. 282.
Variety, May 12, 1995, Dan Cox, "Medavoy Rises Atop Phoenix," pp. 66-67.
Wall Street Journal, February 15, 2002, Laura Landro, "An Insider Disses Hollywood," p. W6.*

*   *   *

MERCADO, Tununa 1939-

PERSONAL: Born 1939, in Cordoba, Argentina; married.

ADDRESSES: Home—Argentina. *Agent*—c/o Author Mail, University of Nebraska Press, P.O. Box 880484, Lincoln, NE 68588-0484.

CAREER: Author, journalist, and translator. Wrote for *La Opinión,* Argentina, c. 1970s.

AWARDS, HONORS: Guggenheim fellowship.

WRITINGS:

Celebrar a la mujer como una pascua (stories; title means "To Celebrate Woman like a Fiesta"), 1967.
Canon de alcoba (stories; title means "Bedroom Canon"), Ada Korn Editora (Buenos Aires, Argentina), 1988.
En estado de memoria (novel), Ada Korn Editora (Buenos Aires, Argentina), 1990, translation by Peter Kahn with introduction by Jean Franco published as *In a State of Memory,* University of Nebraska Press (Lincoln, NE), 2001.
Le letra de lo mínimo ("El escribiente" series), B. Viterbo Editora (Rosario, Argentina), 1994.
La madriguera ("Colección Andanzas" series), Tusquets Editores (Buenos Aires, Argentina), 1996.

SIDELIGHTS: Tununa Mercado is one of Latin America's leading female writers whose first translated volume is her autobiographical novel *In a State of Memory.* Mercado spent two periods—from 1966 to 1970 and 1974 to 1976—in exile. These exiles were prompted by hostile military regimes and the social disorganization of the mid-1970s. *World Literature Today*'s Naomi Lindstrom wrote that this narrative "evokes the continual struggle with memory that characterized the exile experience of one frequently bitter and cranky but wonderfully sharp-eyed and eloquent observer."

The book is described by the publisher as a "novelistic memoir," and Nan Levinson noted in *Women's Review of Books* that "Mercado's strategy reflects this inbetweenness. She is writer and written-about, as in a memoir, creator and created subject, as in a postmodern novel. Facts, details, and context are slipped in obliquely, if at all, and though the narrator shares the author's name and biography, they may or may not be the same person. All this forces the reader to join in the writer-narrator's dislocation, unsure what has happened and what has been imagined or exaggerated."

Mercado married her literature professor when she was twenty-two and published her first collection of stories six years later. In 1966 the couple embarked on their first exile by moving to France. After returning in 1970, Mercado worked as a journalist for four years. Following the death of Argentine dictatorJuan Perón and threats to Mercado's husband, the family began a twelve-year exile in Mexico to avoid persecution by the military, which was killing or causing the disappearances of approximately 30,000 people. Mercado returned to Buenos Aires in 1983, three years after democracy was restored.

"These are the details," wrote Levinson, "but in the telling, everything turns filmy, ephemeral, dislodged. In sixteen mostly short chapters, Mercado offers fragmentary scenes, flashbacks, and recollections of people, many of them gone, and places stained with tragic associations."

The book opens with the narrator sitting in the waiting room of a psychiatric clinic. Another patient demands to be seen, but the doctor will not take him out of turn. The man, Cindal, later hangs himself and "is lodged in the narrator's consciousness," said Levinson, "as her and not-her, as metaphor and harsh actuality, as object of envy for being able to suffer with such conviction, and as embodiment of misery, imagined and real, for which the only 'cure' is self-annihilation. And so, the tone is set."

The narrator learns of deaths of friends in Argentina as she observes, in embarrassment, other Argentine exiles adopting a superficial version of Mexican style and culture in an effort to fit in. *In a State of Memory* reflects the feelings of those who stayed in Argentina and who criticized the exiles for leaving and for their easy lives in Mexico. Mercado balances this by revealing the loss and disorientation experienced by the exiles, which often became even more difficult upon returning to Argentina as they tried to catch up with all that had occurred while they were away.

Levinson praised Mercado's storytelling and continued by saying that her book "is full of sensuous, luxuriant, lapel-grabbing writing, exciting to read, but also, at times, smothering as tropical growth." Lindstrom called Mercado's writing "not necessarily easy to appreciate at first. . . . So it was an excellent idea to include a foreword by Jean Franco that helps readers understand why Mercado is a very significant and innovative writer."

BIOGRAPHICAL AND CRITICAL SOURCES:

PERIODICALS

Women's Review of Books, May, 2001, Nan Levinson, review of *In a State of Memory,* pp. 9-10.
World Literature Today, summer-autumn, 2001, Naomi Lindstrom, review of *In a State of Memory,* p. 226.*

*   *   *

MERRILL, Lisa

PERSONAL: Female. *Education:* New York University, Ph.D.

ADDRESSES: Office—Department of Speech Communication and Rhetorical Studies, Hofstra University, 100 Fulton Ave., Hempstead, NY 11549. *E-mail*—spclgm@hofstra.edu.

CAREER: Hofstra University, Hempstead, NY, associate professor of speech communication and rhetorical studies. Northwestern University, Chicago, IL, visiting professor of performance studies.

AWARDS, HONORS: Joe A. Calloway Prize for Best Book in Theatre of Drama, Peter Herman Literary Award, both for *When Romeo Was a Woman: Charlotte Cushman and Her Circle of Female Spectators.*

WRITINGS:

(With Deborah Borisoff) *The Power to Communicate: Gender Differences as Barriers,* Waveland (Prospect Heights, IL), 1985, 3rd edition, 1998.
(Editor with Linda Longmire) *Untying the Tongue: Gender, Power, and the Word,* Greenwood Press (Westport, CT), 1998.
When Romeo Was a Woman: Charlotte Cushman and Her Circle of Female Spectators, University of Michigan Press (Ann Arbor, MI), 1999.

Also book review coeditor for *Text and Performance Studies.* Editorial board member for "Theatre of the Americas" series, Southern Illinois University Press.

BIOGRAPHICAL AND CRITICAL SOURCES:

PERIODICALS

Gay & Lesbian Review, summer, 2000, Tim Miller, interview with Lisa Merrill, p. 16.
Library Journal, December, 1998, p. 110.*

*   *   *

METZGER, Lois 1955-

PERSONAL: Born December 22, 1955, in New York, NY; daughter of David and Ilse (Stern) Metzger; married Tony Hiss, February 22, 1986; children: Jacob. *Education:* State University of New York, Buffalo, B.A. (English and psychology), 1976; Johns Hopkins University, M.A., 1978.

ADDRESSES: Home and office—22 East 8th St., New York, NY 10003.

CAREER: Author of children's books.

MEMBER: Authors Guild, Authors League of America.

AWARDS, HONORS: Best Books award, *Parents Magazine,* 1992 for *Barry's Sister.*

WRITINGS:

Barry's Sister (for children), Atheneum (New York, NY), 1992.
Ellen's Case (for children), Atheneum (New York, NY), 1995.
Missing Girls (for children), Viking (New York, NY), 1999.

Contributor to periodicals, including *Omni, New Yorker, Nation, Harper's Bazaar,* and *North American Review.*

SIDELIGHTS: Children's books author Lois Metzger has been writing since she was nine; when she was nineteen, she published her first work, a science-fiction short story. She still enjoys writing science fiction, but she feels more comfortable writing fiction for young adults because the topics are more similar to things with which she still concerns herself.

Metzger's first novel, *Barry's Sister,* opens with eleven-year-old Ellen Gray upset about her mother's pregnancy. When her brother is born with ataxic cerebral palsy due to asphyxiation from a prolapsed umbilical cord during his delivery, Ellen feels responsible for Barry's condition because she had wished he would die before he was born. Initially, Ellen reacts with anger and jealousy. She is repulsed by Barry and resents the special attention he gets from their mother and father, an officer on a nuclear submarine whose work frequently requires him to be away from home. However, when Ellen realizes that Barry loves her and is comforted by her presence, she changes her attitude dramatically and becomes preoccupied with his well-being. She also begins working daily with Barry's therapist.

Readers of *Barry's Sister* can benefit by learning more about ataxic cerebral palsy, family and social relations, and empathy. While *New Yorker* critic Cynthia Zarin described Metzger's debut as "excellent," Hazel Rochman gave the book a more mixed review in the *New York Times:* "The emotional therapy talk in *Barry's Sister* is occasionally overdone—this is a young-adult problem novel in that sense—and Ellen's neat stages of anger, depression, overcompensation and equilibrium have little to do with the messy adjustments of real life." However, Rochman added that "the information that Ms. Metzger presents about cerebral palsy is precise and accurate."

Sparked by Metzger's witnessing of a malpractice trial, the sequel to *Barry's Sister, Ellen's Case,* takes place when Barry is four years old and Ellen is sixteen. The family is involved in a medical malpractice case with the doctors who delivered Barry, and Ellen falls in love with Jack Frazier, the lawyer representing the Grays. Like its predecessor, *Ellen's Case,* is informative about the causes of cerebral palsy. However, *Voice of Youth Advocates* critic Dorie Freebury complained that the characterization in the book is weak. Once Ellen falls in love with Frazier, Freebury said, she "evolves into . . . a fickle and shallow individual," and the love story threatens to minimize the importance of the malpractice suit in the plot.

The themes of family guilt and grief and otherness continue in Metzger's third novel. *Missing Girls* is set in 1967, when two girls feel like the "missing girls" they see on the news. Since Carrie Smith's mother's death four years before, Carrie has felt like a runaway in her own home. She lives with her immigrant grandmother, "Mutti," but longs to have an "American" family like that of her friend Mona Brockner, an outcast at school whom Carrie befriends. When Mona's family turns out not to be the picture of happiness Carrie thought it was, she turns to Mutti to find out more about her own history. Mutti tells her about her survival in nine concentration camps during World War II and Carrie's mother's separation from her during the Nazi years in Germany, when she was sent away on the Kindertransport to live with a visiting Scotsman. Although a *Publishers Weekly* critic felt that the novel contains many promising elements, the reviewer concluded that, "unfortunately, their combination doesn't add up." Hazel Rochman and Jack Helbig, writing in a *Booklist* review, further complained that the "metaphors and parallels are overexplained" in the story. However, they concluded, "Like Metzger's fine novel *Barry's Sister* . . . this is a candid story of family guilt and grief."

BIOGRAPHICAL AND CRITICAL SOURCES:

PERIODICALS

Booklist, August, 1995, Hazel Rochman, review of *Ellen's Case,* p. 1941; February 1, 1999, Hazel Rochman and Jack Helbig, review of *Missing Girls,* p. 975.

Horn Book, March-April, 1996, Nancy Vasilakis, review of *Ellen's Case,* p. 232.

New Yorker, November 23, 1992, Cynthia Zarin, review of *Barry's Sister,* p. 80.

New York Times, May 17, 1992, Hazel Rochman, "Children's Books; He's My Brother," p. 29.

New York Times Book Review, February 25, 1996, Molly E. Rauch, "New Kids on the Block," p. 25.

Publishers Weekly, March 23, 1992, review of *Barry's Sister,* p. 72; January 11, 1999, review of *Missing Girls,* p. 72.

School Library Journal, October, 1995, p. 158.

Voice of Youth Advocates, December, 1995, Dorie Freebury, review of *Ellen's Case,* p. 306.*

MEYER, Henry Cord 1913-2001

PERSONAL: Born February 12, 1913, in Chicago, IL; died of cancer, September 30, 2001, in Claremont, CA; married Helen Meyer; children: Henry, Christopher, Dallas. *Education:* University of Colorado, A.B., 1935; University of Iowa, A.M., 1937; Yale University, Ph.D., 1941.

CAREER: Pomona College, Pomona, CA, professor of history, 1946-64; University of California—Irvine, professor of history, 1964-81, department chair, 1964-69, emeritus professor, 1981-2001. Stanford University, Stanford, CA, and University of Wisconsin, visiting professor, 1953-54; Advanced Placement Program, College Entrance Examination Board and Educational Testing Service, Princeton, NJ, chairman of European history committee, 1968-71. *Military service:* Office of Strategic Services, resident analyst, 1941-45.

AWARDS, HONORS: Social Science Research Council award, 1954-55; Beer Prize, 1956; Fulbright award and Guggenheim fellowship, 1960-61; Rockefeller residency at Villa Serbelloni, 1972.

WRITINGS:

Mitteleuropa in German Thought and Action, Nijhoff (The Hague, Netherlands), 1955.

Five Images of Germany: Half a Century of American Views on German History, Service Center for Teachers of History (Washington, DC), 1960, second edition, 1966.

(Editor) *The Long Generation: Germany from Empire to Ruin, 1913-1945,* Harper (New York, NY), 1973, published as *Germany from Empire to Ruin, 1913-1945,* Macmillan (London, England), 1973.

Collected Works, Volume I: *Essays and Articles, 1937-1960,* C. Schlacks, Jr. (Irvine, CA), 1986.

Airshipmen, Businessmen, and Politics, 1890-1940, Smithsonian Institution Press (Washington, DC), 1991.

Drang Nach Osten: Fortunes of a Slogan-Concept in German-Slavic Relations, 1849-1990, P. Lang (New York, NY), 1996.

Count Zeppelin: A Psychological Portrait, Tiola Consolidated (Auckland, New Zealand), for Lighter-than-Air Institute, 1998.

(With John Duggan) *Airships in International Affairs, 1890-1940,* Palgrave (New York, NY), 2001.

SIDELIGHTS: Henry Cord Meyer, founding chairman of the history department at the University of California—Irvine, wrote extensively about nineteenth- and twentieth-century European history, especially that of Germany. Later in his career he wrote about the development and use of the rigid airship known as the zeppelin, a type of craft that fell out of favor after the *Hindenburg* crash in the late 1930s but played a significant role in the evolution of aviation. Meyer was a "distinguished scholar of modern German history," noted *Choice* contributor C. Ryant in a review of *Airshipmen, Businessmen, and Politics, 1890-1940.*

Meyer's contributions to German historical scholarship include editing *The Long Generation: Germany from Empire to Ruin, 1913-1945,* which covers a period that began with Kaiser Wilhelm II's twenty-fifth anniversary on the throne and ended with Germany's defeat in World War II. It includes writings by German government officials of the period, such as selections from the diary of Nazi propagandist Joseph Goebbels, records of a meeting between Adolf Hitler and his top military officers concerning the invasion of Poland, newspaper articles, and a firsthand account by a prisoner in a concentration camp. A *Choice* reviewer remarked that the book places the Nazi era and the period of the Weimar Republic "within a larger context of German history than is common," and praised Meyer's selection of contents and the quality of his translations. Another of Meyer's books on German history is *Drang Nach Osten: Fortunes of a Slogan-Concept in German-Slavic Relations, 1849-1990,* tracing the use of the slogan *drang nach osten,* which means the "eastward thrust" of Germany. Meyer explains that the term, often believed to be of German origin, was first used by Eastern Europeans who feared that Germany would take over their lands; Germans adopted the saying as their own when the Nazis came to power. In this "admirable brief monograph," Meyer "demonstrates clearly the historical importance of slogans of this kind," commented Norman Rich in *Central European History.*

Meyer's interest in rigid airships developed after he retired from teaching. "It began as a hobby really, and then developed into a genuine research interest," his widow, Helen Meyer, told a writer for *Los Angeles Times* in 2001. *Airshipmen, Businessmen, and Politics, 1890-1940,* which collects ten essays by Meyer, discusses how nationalistic sentiment contributed to the airship industry in Germany, England, and the United States; the industry's economic impact on cities where its major factories were located; German use of airships for espionage; and numerous other topics. It also provides portraits of the industry's leading personalities, including Count Ferdinand von Zeppelin, Hugo Eckner, Johann Schütte, and Alfred Colsman. Meyer explains the role they played within "the complex web of airship development and politics," observed John H. Morrow, Jr. in *Journal of American History.* adding that this phenomenon is worth studying because it "occasioned the rise of the 'military-industrial complex.'" William F. Trimble, writing in *Technology and Culture,* thought Meyer's book offers "considerable insight" but fails to "fully develop" its "persistent theme of the symbolism of the airship and how it represented for many a brave new world in the air." Eric Schatzberg, a contributor to *Isis,* believed Meyer's "focus on the individual prevents him from asking a fundamental question: Why did the zeppelin lend itself so readily to technological fanaticism and nationalist propaganda, especially in Germany?" Schatzberg also, however, praised "the strength of the research"—Meyer interviewed many people who had been involved in developing airships, and he consulted numerous archival sources—and "the quality of the prose." Moreover, the critic remarked, the book "deserves an audience beyond zeppelin enthusiasts."

BIOGRAPHICAL AND CRITICAL SOURCES:

PERIODICALS

Central European History, fall, 1997, Norman Rich, review of *Drang Nach Osten: Fortunes of a Slogan-Concept in German-Slavic Relations, 1849-1990,* pp. 607-608.

Choice, January, 1974, review of *The Long Generation: Germany from Empire to Ruin, 1913-1945,* p. 1173; April, 1992, C. Ryant, review of *Airshipmen, Businessmen, and Politics, 1890-1940,* p. 1278.

Isis, March, 1993, Eric Schatzberg, review of *Airshipmen, Businessmen, and Politics, 1890-1940,* pp. 185-186.

Journal of American History, December, 1992, John H. Morrow, Jr., review of *Airshipmen, Businessmen, and Politics, 1890-1940,* p. 1203.

Technology and Culture, April, 1993, William F. Trimble, review of *Airshipmen, Businessmen, and Politics, 1890-1940,* pp. 443-444.

Washington Post Book World, August 26, 1973, review of *The Long Generation: Germany from Empire to Ruin, 1913-1945,* p. 15.

OBITUARIES:

PERIODICALS

Los Angeles Times, October 4, 2001, Jeff Gottlieb, "Henry Meyer, 88; Historian, Zeppelin Expert," p. B15.*

*   *   *

MEYER, June
See JORDAN, June (Meyer)

*   *   *

MIDDLETON-MURRY, John (Jr.) 1926-2002
(Richard Cowper, Colin Murry)

OBITUARY NOTICE—See index for *CA* sketch: Born May 9, 1926, in Bridport, Dorsetshire, England; died of a stroke April 29, 2002. Educator and author. Middleton-Murry was best known as a science-fiction writer who published works under the pseudonym Richard Cowper. The son of a prominent literary critic, he developed an interest in writing while attending Rencomb College in the late 1930s. During World War II he served in the Royal Navy, returning to study at Brasenose College, Oxford, where he received his B.A. in English in 1950. He also studied to be a teacher at Leicester University, and then Whittinge-hame College, where he was an English master from 1952 to 1967. Middleton-Murry became the English department head at Atlantic College in South Wales before retiring from teaching in 1970 to devote himself to writing. At this point, he had already published several mainstream novels under the pseudonym Colin Murry, including *The Golden Valley* (1958), *Recollections of a Ghost* (1960), and *A Path to the Sea* (1961). Some of these books contain streaks of fantasy, and some critics were not surprised when he later turned to science fiction. Published under the Cowper pseudonym, Middleton-Murry's science fiction is not so much concerned with fantastic technology as it is

with his characters' emotions. Some of his notable sci-fi novels include *Breakthrough* (1967), *The Twilight of Briareus* (1974), *The Road to Corlay* (1978), which won the British Fantasy Award in 1979, and the satirical work *Clone* (1972). He was also the author of numerous sci-fi short story collections, such as *Out There Where the Big Ships Go* (1980) and *The Magic Spectacles and Other Tales* (1986), as well as the autobiographies *One Hand Clapping: A Memoir of Childhood* (1975), which was published in the United States as *I at the Keyhole,* and *Shadows on the Grass* (1977).

OBITUARIES AND OTHER SOURCES:

PERIODICALS

Guardian (London, England), May 3, 2002, p. 20.
New York Times, June 1, 2002, p. B15.
Times (London, England), May 31, 2002, p. 40.

*   *   *

MONTVILLE, Leigh

PERSONAL: Male. *Education:* Graduated from University of Connecticut.

ADDRESSES: Home—Winthrop, MA. *Office*—c/o Bantam Dell Doubleday Publishing Group, 1540 Broadway, New York, NY 10036.

CAREER: New Haven Journal-Courier, New Haven, CT, reporter, 1965-68; *Boston Globe,* Boston, MA, sportswriter and columnist, 1968-89; *Sports Illustrated,* senior writer, 1989-c. 2000.

WRITINGS:

Manute: The Center of Two Worlds (biography), Simon and Schuster (New York, NY), 1993.
(With Jim Calhoun) *Dare to Dream: Connecticut Basketball's Remarkable March to the National Championship,* Broadway Books (New York, NY), 1999.

At the Altar of Speed: The Fast Life and Tragic Death of Dale Earnhardt, Doubleday (New York, NY), 2001.

WORK IN PROGRESS: A biography of baseball great Ted Williams, to be published by Doubleday.

SIDELIGHTS: Veteran journalist Leigh Montville has written about a wide variety of sports, including basketball, baseball, football, and auto racing. A highly unusual pro basketball player is the subject of *Manute: The Center of Two Worlds.* This book chronicles the experiences of Manute Bol, a native of a rural village in the Sudan who attracted the attention of college recruiters and later the National Basketball Association (NBA) because of his remarkable height—seven feet, seven inches. Bol's skill proved less remarkable as he played for a succession of NBA teams, but his low scoring average was balanced out somewhat by his shot-blocking ability and the fact that "his mere presence on the court requires adjustments by opposing teams," noted a *Kirkus Reviews* commentator. Bol also has faced the challenge of living in an environment very different from that of his homeland, and this is a major focus of Montville's book. Bol's tribe, the Dinka, has no written language and few material possessions; in the United States, the athlete was plunged into a world of money and luxury. "Montville masterfully re-creates the cultural shock Bol experienced," remarked Wes Lukowsky in *Booklist.* The author also "shows how Bol is able to fit into both worlds simply by being himself," reported a *Publishers Weekly* reviewer, who further commented that *Manute* "is a most unusual sports biography." The *Kirkus Reviews* critic summed up the book as "oddly touching and funny; a captivating look at a unique individual," and Lukowsky deemed it of "high caliber."

At the Altar of Speed: The Fast Life and Tragic Death of Dale Earnhardt came out just a few months after Earnhardt, a star NASCAR driver, was killed at age forty-nine during the Daytona 500 race on February 18, 2001. Earnhardt, a North Carolina native and son of a locally renowned racer, dropped out of school in the ninth grade to begin his racing career and eventually became a driver of great ability and daring, dubbed "The Intimidator," a moniker he disliked. He won seven Winston Cup championships and helped boost the popularity of stock car racing as well as pol-

ish the image of what had been considered a "hillbilly" sport. He had some difficulty with personal relationships, with two failed marriages before he was able to establish a satisfying family life, but he tended to talk little about such private matters—so there is little about them in Montville's book. Aside from that, "Montville skillfully unspools the story of Earnhardt's life," related Charles Hirshberg in *Sports Illustrated,* adding that "the story of Earnhardt's racing career is richly told, too." *New York Times Book Review* contributor Dave Caldwell found the biography "treacherously thin in spots, especially Earnhardt's family life," but also "rich in anecdotes, particularly when it comes to recounting his hardscrabble early days as a driver." A *Kirkus Reviews* critic thought Montville uses "what approaches an idolatrous voice" in discussing Earnhardt; however, the reviewer concluded that the author "draws a forceful portrait, letting the evolving atmosphere of NASCAR and Earnhardt's achievements speak for themselves."

BIOGRAPHICAL AND CRITICAL SOURCES:

PERIODICALS

Booklist, February 1, 1993, Wes Lukowsky, review of *Manute: The Center of Two Worlds,* p. 966.
Kirkus Reviews, December 15, 1992, review of *Manute,* p. 1559; September 1, 2001, review of *At the Altar of Speed: The Fast Life and Tragic Death of Dale Earnhardt,* p. 1271.
New York Times Book Review, October 28, 2001, Dave Caldwell, "Amazing Racer," p. 20.
People, March 15, 1993, Tim Whitaker, review of *Manute,* p. 31.
Publishers Weekly, December 14, 1992, review of *Manute,* p. 49.
Sports Illustrated, September 3, 2001, Charles Hirshberg, "Compassion Drives a Paean to Dale Earnhardt and His Legions of Grieving Fans," p. R10.*

*   *   *

MORAN, Daniel Keys 1962-

PERSONAL: Born 1962.

ADDRESSES: Agent—c/o Author Mail, Random House, 1540 Broadway, New York, NY 10036.

CAREER: Writer.

WRITINGS:

The Armageddon Blues: A Tale of the Great Wheel of Existence, Bantam (New York, NY), 1988.
The Ring (based on a screenplay by William Stewart and Joanne Nelsen), Doubleday (New York, NY), 1988.
Terminal Freedom, Quiet Vision (Sandy, UT), 2002.

"TALES OF THE CONTINUING TIME" SERIES

Emerald Eyes, Bantam (New York, NY), 1988.
The Long Run, Bantam (New York, NY), 1989.
The Last Dancer, Bantam (New York, NY), 1993.

"KEYS TO PARADISE" SERIES

The Flame Key, Tor (New York, NY), 1987.
The Skeleton Lord's Key, Tor (New York, NY), 1987.
(With Robert E. Vardeman) *Key of Ice and Steel,* Tor (New York, NY), 1988.

SIDELIGHTS: Daniel Keys Moran, an American writer who began publishing science fiction in the early 1980s, expanded upon a short piece titled "All the Time in the World" to write his first novel. *The Armageddon Blues* was published as the first volume of the "Tales of the Great Wheel of Existence" series, which placed Moran as "a talent to watch," according to one *Publishers Weekly* reviewer. The debut novel begins in a post-holocaust, twenty-eighth-century United States and features a mutant female named Jalian. One day she discovers a time machine designed by some non-human beings. Jalian uses the time machine to travel back before the time of the holocaust in order to try to prevent the disaster from happening.

A second series, "Tales of the Continuing Time," includes the books *Emerald Eyes, The Long Run,* and *The Last Dancer.* The series is about a group of people who have been genetically engineered to have telepathic and other amazing abilities, and how they must fight to survive in a world of non-engineered people who are hostile towards them. Moran also published *The Ring* as a stand-alone futuristic fantasy. Based on a screenplay by William Stewart and Joanne Nelsen, this "ambitious, imaginative saga of cosmic intrigue,"

according to reviewer Randy M. Brough in *Voice of Youth Advocates,* takes place a millennium after a nuclear holocaust destroys planet Earth. Protagonist Cain builds armies and gains control of a powerful weapon called the Ring, which he must keep by battling other races who claim ownership of the weapon.

Although some critics claim that Moran's novels do not progress with increasing intensity and talent, according to a writer for *The Encyclopedia of Science Fiction* Moran "displays very considerable energy and some humor, shows a fine [author A. E.] Van Vogt-style recklessness with superman plots, and has demonstrated a copious ambition."

BIOGRAPHICAL AND CRITICAL SOURCES:

BOOKS

Clute, John, and Peter Nicholls, editors, *The Encyclopedia of Science Fiction,* St. Martin's (New York, NY), 1993.
Reginald, Robert, *Science Fiction & Fantasy Literature, 1975-1991,* Gale (Detroit, MI), 1992.

PERIODICALS

Analog Science Fiction and Fact, October, 1988, p. 187; May, 1989, pp. 183-184; January, 1990, p. 305; June, 1994, p. 161.
Kirkus Review, August 15, 1988, p. 1199.
Locus, July, 1989.
Publishers Weekly, March 11, 1988, p. 98; June 3, 1988, pp. 82-83; August 19, 1988, pp. 61-62; July 28, 1989, p. 215; October 11, 1993, p. 84.
San Francisco Chronicle, March, 1989, p. 37.
Voice of Youth Advocates, April, 1989, p. 44.*

*   *   *

MORRISON, Danny 1953-

PERSONAL: Born 1953, in Belfast, Ireland; married.

ADDRESSES: Home—Belfast, Ireland. *Agent*—c/o Roberts Rinehart, 5455 Spine Rd., Mezzanine W., Boulder, CO 80301.

CAREER: Former editor of the *Republican News,* beginning c. 1975; elected to Northern Ireland Assembly, 1982; Sinn Fein, director of publicity, 1979-90, former vice president.

WRITINGS:

Ireland: The Censored Subject, Sinn Fein Publicity Department (Belfast, Northern Ireland), 1989.

West Belfast (novel), Mercier Press (Cork, Ireland), 1989, Roberts Rinehart (Boulder, CO), 1995.

On the Back of the Swallow (novel), Mercier Press (Cork, Ireland), 1994, Roberts Rinehart (Boulder, CO), 1996.

The Wrong Man (novel), Roberts Rinehart (Boulder, CO), 1997.

Then the Walls Came Down (novel), Mercier Press (Cork, Ireland), 1999.

Also contributor of articles and reviews to periodicals, including *Irish Times,* London *Observer,* London *Guardian, Washington Post, Boston Globe, Andersonstown News* and *An Phoblacht/Republican News.*

WORK IN PROGRESS: Adapting *The Wrong Man* for the stage.

SIDELIGHTS: Danny Morrison is a writer who was a former publicity director and vice president of Sinn Fein, the political voice of the Irish Republican Army (IRA), which opposes the British occupation of Northern Ireland and which has been blamed for much of the violence there. Because of his political activities, Morrison was arrested twice by English authorities; he was charged with being a member of the IRA in 1978, but defended himself successfully against accusations that he conspired to obstruct justice, and in 1990 he was sentenced to eight years in prison for allegedly abducting IRA informer Sandy Lynch.

After his release from prison, Morrison left active involvement in Sinn Fein behind and devoted himself to his writing. Although he was banned from expressing his views on radio or television, he learned that he could also reach an audience through his fiction. His first novel, *West Belfast,* debuted in 1990. Set in turbulent Northern Ireland during the 1960s, the novel follows the fortunes of the McCann family as their sons John and Jimmy become involved in the growing political upheaval. Kevin Toolis, a reviewer for *New*

Statesman and Society, called the book "a rare first novel" that is "the first attempt to tell the other side of the story in fictional form." Toolis added that the book is "a consciously didactic work" that "carefully interweaves Republican milestones . . . into the narrative to explain and justify the Republican viewpoint." Toolis further noted, "Morrison has flipped the mores of the 'Troubles' thriller to present the IRA man as hero." *Booklist* critic Mary Banas similarly felt that *West Belfast* is didactic, calling it "less a work of literature than a deeply felt expression of the author's own political views."

In Morrison's novel *The Wrong Man* the author tells the story of Raymond Massey, a "clean-cut, new man hero," according to *Irish Times* critic Eugene McEldowney, whose alter ego is that of a determined assassin for Northern Ireland's cause. Although McEldowney criticized the novel's lack of "craft," he added that it "will undoubtedly draw fire from certain quarters for being republican propaganda . . . but this will be to miss the point," which is to promote the author's political cause.

Morrison's views have been strongly expressed in venues other than his fiction. Even when reviewing another Irish writer's work or when creating an obituary, Morrison's own passions surface. In one issue of *An Phoblacht/Republican News,* for example, he reviewed Gerry Adams's autobiography, *Before the Dawn,* as a testimony of Adams's truth and heroism. Some events discussed in the book took place in West Belfast in 1981 during Morrison's own childhood. It was a time Morrison described as "the trauma of ten men dying and ten and more heartbroken families being cynically twisted this way and that by those in power, before being emotionally gutted for life." Morrison added, "We'll never get over it. We never will."

BIOGRAPHICAL AND CRITICAL SOURCES:

PERIODICALS

An Phoblacht/Republican News, September 26, 1996, Danny Morrison, review of *Before the Dawn: An Autobiography.*

Booklist, July, 1990, Mary Banas, review of *West Belfast,* p. 2072.

Economist, January, 1990, pp. 52, 57.

Irish Times, March 25, 1997, Eugene McEldowney, "Hearts of Gold, Bullets of Lead."

New Statesman and Society, January 13, 1990, Kevin Toolis, "Novel Weapon," pp. 36-37.

OTHER

Danny Morrison Web site, http://www.iol.ie/
~neylonm/ (January 2, 2001).*

*   *   *

MUEGGLER, Erik 1962-

PERSONAL: Born 1962, in Montana; married Min
Kim; children: Max. *Education:* Cornell University,
B.A., 1987; Johns Hopkins University, M.A., 1990,
Ph.D., 1996.

ADDRESSES: Office—Department of Anthropology,
University of Michigan, Ann Arbor, MI. *E-mail*—
mueggler@umich.edu.

CAREER: Taught English in China; University of
Michigan, Ann Arbor, member of faculty in the
Department of Anthropology, 1996-2001, associate
professor of anthropology, 2001—; faculty associate,
Center for Chinese Studies.

AWARDS, HONORS: National Academy of Sciences
grant for advanced study in China, 1991; National
Endowment for the Humanities fellowship, 1996; John
D. and Catharine T. MacArthur Foundation Fellowship, 2002.

WRITINGS:

*Age of Wild Ghosts: Memory, Violence, and Place in
Southwest China,* University of California Press
(Berkeley, CA), 2001.

Contributor to periodicals, including *Cultural Anthropology, Comparative Studies in Society and History,
Journal of Asian Studies,* and *Modern China.*

WORK IN PROGRESS: Research for an ethnography
of the poetics of grief in Yi regions and a history of
nineteenth- and early-twentieth-century botanical
exploration in the Great Rivers area of Yunnan.

SIDELIGHTS: Erik Mueggler is a cultural anthropologist known for his research on the politics of ethnicity
in China. With a methodology that is both historical
and anthropological, Mueggler studies minority communities in provincial China and analyzes their political, social, and cultural relationships to the State.

Mueggler became interested in China after spending a
year there teaching English. While working on his
doctorate, he studied how the Cultural Revolution
impacted the everyday lives of Chinese citizens. The
research later became the basis for *The Age of Wild
Ghosts: Memory, Violence, and Place in Southwest
China,* an ethnography of the impoverished and politically marginalized Yi people who inhabit the Yunnan
Province. The book explores how the Yi's experience
as an ethnic minority at the periphery of a nation-state
relates to their history of violence, their understanding
of justice, and their sense of community. A reviewer
for *Choice* called *The Age of Wild Ghosts* "a fascinating and disturbing tale of guilt," adding, "the anguish
of the Yi in a world out of control is well captured."

Sheryl James of the *Detroit Free Press* called the book
"an academic yet haunting portrayal of the forces that
shaped the impoverished Yi ethnic community in
southwest China."

In 2002 Mueggler was named one of twenty-four Mac-
Arthur fellows by the John D. and Catherine T. Mac-
Arthur Foundation. According to information released
by the MacArthur Fellows Program, Mueggler was
honored for producing "new and persuasive conclusions about the distinctive relationship between
China's minorities and the State." The release concluded, "Mueggler has set a benchmark for original
and imaginative ethnography in provincial China."
Fellows receive a grant of $500,000 over five years to
use as they see fit. Mueggler told the *Detroit News*
that the money would allow him to dedicate more
time to research in China.

BIOGRAPHICAL AND CRITICAL SOURCES:

PERIODICALS

Ascribe Higher Education News Service, September
    25, 2002, "University of Michigan Anthropologist
    Receives MacArthur Foundation Award."
Choice, October, 2001, E. N. Anderson, review of *The
    Age of Wild Ghosts,* p. 352.

Detroit Free Press, September 25, 2002, Sheryl James, "Unwelcome Call Carries News of a Dream Come True for U-M Anthropologist."

Detroit News, September 25, 2002, "U-M Anthropologist Gets $500,000 for Studies," p. 1.

Salt Lake Tribune, September 28, 2002, Hilary Groutage Smith, "Logan Native's Love for China Is a Pot of Gold."

OTHER

MacArthur Foundation Web site, http://www.mac found.org/ (August 19, 2002), biography of Erik Mueggler.

University of California Press Web Site, http://www. ucpress.edu/ (September 30, 2002), review of *The Age of Wild Ghosts.*

University of Michigan Web site, http://www.umich. edu/ (September 30, 2002), biography of Erik Mueggler.*

*   *   *

MURRY, Colin
See MIDDLETON-MURRY, John (Jr.)

N

NAIR, Anita

PERSONAL: Born in Shoranur, Kerala, India; married; husband's name Suresh; children: one son. *Education:* NSS Ottapalam (Kerala, India), B.A. *Hobbies and other interests:* Gourmet food, painting, piano, Kathakali dancing.

ADDRESSES: *Home*—Bangalore, India. *Agent*—Laura Susijn, The Susijn Agency, 820 Harrow Road, London NW10 5JU, England. *E-mail*—info@anitanair.net.

CAREER: Novelist and journalist. Wrote for *ASIDE* and *City Tab;* later worked in real estate and exhibition design. Wrote advertising copy for twelve years, working for Contract, Clarion, O&M Direct, MAA, and MASS, Bangalore, India.

AWARDS, HONORS: Virginia Center for Creative Arts fellowship.

WRITINGS:

Satyr of the Subway: And Eleven Other Stories, Har-Anand Publications (New Delhi, India), 1997.
The Better Man, Picador (New York, NY), 2000.
Ladies Coupé: A Novel in Parts, Penguin (London, England), 2001.

Nair's poem "Happenings in the London Underground" was published in a poetry anthology by the Poetry Society of India, 1992; other poetry published in a British Council Poetry Workshop anthology. Contributor to the *Times of India, Man's World,* and *India Today.* Columnist for *New Indian Express.*

Nair's work has been translated into French, German, Italian, Lithuanian, Spanish, and Dutch.

WORK IN PROGRESS: *Magical Indian Myths* for Puffin India, and an anthology of writing about Kerala for Penguin India; plans to write a trilogy connected to *The Better Man.*

SIDELIGHTS: Novelist Anita Nair worked for twelve years writing advertising copy before she was able to devote herself to the self-described addiction of writing. The author of *Satyr of the Subway: And Eleven Other Stories, The Better Man,* and *Ladies Coupé: A Novel in Parts* was born in the remote region of Kerala, India, and raised in Madras (now Chennai). She returned to Kerala at seventeen and attended a small college there. Though she is now based in Bangalore, it is Kerala that serves as the most frequent setting for her work. Nair has said that she loves to immerse herself in the experiences of characters unlike herself, such as the retired businessman in *The Better Man* or the spinster in *Ladies Coupé.* The earlier book became the first novel by an Indian-based writer to be published by Picador. Nair declined to make changes to *Ladies Coupé* in order to tailor it for American readers.

Nair's debut novel, *The Better Man,* centers on the bachelor Mukundan Nair, who retires to his birthplace in a remote village in Kerala. He once left to avoid his abusive father, but now hopes to prove his worth to the village elders. He lives in a house inherited from his mother and now inhabited by her ghost, who mourns that he did not save her from his father or from falling down the stairs to her death. A house painter and healer called One-Screw-Loose Bhasi befriends Mukundan and quietly helps him overcome the emotional scars of his childhood. As a result, Mukundan begins a secret relationship with schoolteacher Anjana, who is divorcing the husband who deserted her. But the relationship falls under the critical eye of local leaders, who also hope that Mukundan will help them gain control of land owned by Bhasi.

A popular and critical hit in India, *The Better Man* earned mostly positive critical response in the United States. In a review for the *New York Times,* Kit Reed found that the novel is hampered by an aimless manner and disjointed components. He called it "a genial, meandering tale filled with false alarms and diversions" and concluded, "Charming as it is, the novel gathers momentum only at the end, when Bhasi and Mukundan find themselves at odds just in time for the drama of conflict and resolution." *Library Journal* contributor Faye A. Chadwell, however, was riveted by the question of whether Mukundan or Bhasi is the "better man." Chadwell enthused that "this imaginative debut will delight with its remarkable grace, unforced humor, and elegantly descriptive prose." She also credited the novel with proving its declaration that "within everything rests a power to ignite." In *Booklist,* Bonnie Johnston called *The Better Man* a "vibrant first novel" and "a passionate yet introspective story." A *Publishers Weekly* reviewer who admired the "charming" novel, said, "Nair has the magical ability to make all of her readers feel, briefly, like Kaikurussi villagers in this humorous, imaginative, and gracefully written novel."

Reviewer Bharti Kirchner, writing for the *Seattle Times,* questioned "why Nair develops the male players more patiently than the female ones who, for the most part, are voluptuous providers of bodily comforts, sought mainly as passive companions and lovers." This is a concern Nair responded to in an interview with *Café Dilli* online's Bindu Menon. "Some reviewers thought [the women] were all props and not essential to the point of the story but the book was written from a man's point of view and what his needs are—women had no importance in his life, so the book reflected that," she explained.

Another kind of reply was made with Nair's second novel, *Ladies Coupé.* In this story, the author immerses the reader in a place exclusively for women, the now nonexistent ladies' compartment or coupé on Indian trains. Protagonist Akhila is a forty-five-year-old tax department employee who has taken care of her family since her father's early death. Her responsibilities as the first-born have caused her to abandon her own aspirations and interests in order to nurture her siblings. Ungrateful, they now dismiss her as an ineffectual spinster. Feeling trapped by her life, she impulsively embarks on a trip to a resort at the farthest point in India. She finds herself traveling overnight in a ladies coupé with five other women. Each proves to have a radically different life story, with a variety of social, economic, and family pressures.

Several reviewers recommended the work for its deft portrayal of ordinary lives. Urvashi Butalia commented in a review for the *Hindustan Times* online, "Nair's low-key, sometimes funny and sometimes hard-hitting book, is not earthshaking but is definitely worth a read." In an article for *Masala.com,* A. Nayak remarked on the wide range of personal stories told in the coupé, concluding that "all are poignant and indelible." Nayak observed that given its premise, the book could "easily become a treatise on the social status of women, but Nair's story-telling style saves it from becoming a commentary on women's lib." Geeta Doctor, writing for *India Today on the Net,* also found a delicate balance in the novel, in which Nair illuminates the struggle of a typical middle-class family as well as the revelations of Akhila and her companions. "The manner in which Nair relates these transformations is in turn revelatory and redeeming," Doctor concluded.

BIOGRAPHICAL AND CRITICAL SOURCES:

PERIODICALS

Booklist, May 15, 2000, Bonnie Johnston, review of *The Better Man,* p. 1730.

Library Journal, July, 2000, Faye A. Chadwell, review of *The Better Man,* p. 141.

New York Times, August 13, 2000, Kit Reed, review of *The Better Man,* p. 23.

Publishers Weekly, April 24, 2000, review of *The Better Man,* p. 56.

Seattle Times, August 20, 2000, Bharti Kirchner, "'Obedient Father,' 'Better Man' Portray Very Different Indian Men."

OTHER

Anita Nair's Home Page, http://www.anitanair.net (February 21, 2003), Bindu Menon, "'Ladies Coupé' Was Harder to Write" (interview with Nair).

Hindustan Times, http://www.hindustantimes.com/ (June 3, 2001), Urvashi Butalia, review of *Ladies Coupé.*

India Today on the Net, http://www.india-today.com/ (June 4, 2001), Geeta Doctor, review of *Ladies Coupé.*

Masala.com, http://www.masala.com/ (July 8, 2001), A. Nayak, review of *Ladies Coupé.**

*   *   *

NAUM, Gellu 1915-2001

PERSONAL: Born August 1, 1915, in Bucharest, Romania; died of a heart attack, September 29, 2001, in Bucharest, Romania. *Education:* Sorbonne, Ph.D., 1939.

CAREER: Poet, playwright, novelist, and translator.

AWARDS, HONORS: Union of Writers prize, 1964, 1969; award from Belgian government, 1967; European Prize for Poetry, 1999.

WRITINGS:

Poeme alese, Cartea Românesca (Bucharest, Romania), 1974.

Insula, Ceasonricaria Taus, and *Poate Eleonora,* Cartea Românesca (Bucharest, Romania), 1979.

Partea cealalta, Cartea Românesca (Bucharest, Romania), 1980.

Zenobia, Cartea Românesca (Bucharest, Romania), 1985, English translation by James Brook and Sasha Vlad published by Northwestern University Press (Evanston, IL), 1995.

My Tired Father, translated by James Brook, Inkblot (Oakland, CA), 1986.

Malul albastru: poeme, Cartea Românesca (Bucharest, Romania), 1990.

Fata si suprafata: Urmat de Malul albastru: poeme, 1989-1993, Editura Litera (Bucharest, Romania), 1994.

Focul negru, Editura Eminescu (Bucharest, Romania), 1995.

Sora fântânâ, Editura Eminescu (Bucharest, Romania), 1995.

Ascet la baraca de tire: poeme, Editura Fundatiei Culturale Râmne (Bucharest, Romania), 2000.

Copacul-animal urmat de avantajul vertebrelor, Editura Dacia (Bucharest, Romania), 2000.

Also author of *The Incendiary Traveller,* 1936; *The Liberty of Sleeping on a Forehead,* 1937; *Vasco da Gama,* 1940; *The Hall of Sleep,* 1944; *Castle of the Blinds,* 1945; *Medium,* 1945; *The Calm Sun,* 1961; *Athanor,* 1969; *The Tree-Animal,* 1971; *Poetise, Poetise,* 1972; *The Description of the Tower,* 1975; *The Other Side,* 1980; *The Blue Shore,* 1990; *The Face and the Surface,* published in German as *Rede auf derm Bahndamm an die steine,* 1994; and *The Forbidden Terrible.*

SIDELIGHTS: Gellu Naum was one of Romania's most prominent and prolific surrealist writers, with a body of work that included poetry, plays, and novels. "Naum's poetry relies on contradictions and contrasts, welds the mythical to the actual, the farcical to the solemn, and leads playful moments into dramatic ones," noted *World Literature Today* contributor Marguerite Dorian in her critique of a German translation of the poetry collection *The Face and the Surface.* She called him a "wanderer of an oneiric realm, for which he sets out, intending to explore and to map its territory, but he is constantly—at times delightfully so—distracted and diverted from the task by a protean landscape which keeps rotating around him like an overloaded kaleidoscope and by encounters and adventures of great imagination." Another *World Literature Today* reviewer, Nicholas Catanoy, dubbed Naum "an endlessly experimenting surrealist" in an assessment of *Partea cealalta,* also a book of poems.

Studying in Paris before World War II, Naum became acquainted with André Breton and other French surrealists. Returning to his hometown of Bucharest, he joined with other surrealist writers in drafting a manifesto, published in 1945. He worked for much of his career, however, in a climate inhospitable to his imaginative style, under the Communist Party, which came to power in Romania in 1947. He was able to publish very little of his poetry and other creative work, only rarely getting approval from government censors, until the regime relaxed somewhat in the late 1960s. During its most repressive period he supported himself largely as a translator; among the authors whose works he translated into Romanian were Samuel Beckett and Franz Kafka.

As so few of his writings have been translated from Romanian to English, perhaps Naum's best-known and most widely available work in the United States is the novel *Zenobia*, published in Romania in 1985 and in English translation ten years later. In *Zenobia*, Naum casts himself as protagonist and narrator; he tells of his travels with an imaginary woman, Zenobia, who offers love and support through a sometimes dreamlike, sometimes nightmarish series of encounters, including conversations with corpses. His journey is "a labyrinthine search for truth," and the novel is "an imaginary poetic narrative under the surrealist spell of love and hazard, magic and fairy tale," commented Jeanine Teodorescu-Regier in *World Literature Today*. *Library Journal* contributor Olivia Opello called *Zenobia* "an existentialist antinovel" full of "experiments with style and vocabulary." A *Kirkus Reviews* critic found the book "a perversely inventive and amusing portrayal of alienation and despair." The critic praised the author's "eloquently cadenced prose" and the quality of the translation, by James Brook and Sasha Vlad, which "effectively conveys Naum's penchant for abstraction." Teodorescu-Regier observed that the translators "succeed superbly" in portraying the story's "anguished atmosphere" while maintaining its humor. Opello also had positive words for the translators' work, saying it allows readers to "enjoy the language fully." The *Kirkus Reviews* commentator concluded that "in its strongest moments," Naum's novel "recalls the best of Beckett, Gombrowicz, and Ionesco." Teodorescu-Regier summed up by saying, "Any reader would find in *Zenobia* a rewarding attempt to go beyond the power of worlds, images, and logic. . . . It seeks to narrate the unnarratable and challenges its readers to comprehend the incomprehensible."

BIOGRAPHICAL AND CRITICAL SOURCES:

BOOKS

Laville, Rémy, *Gellu Naum: Poête roumain, prisonnier au château des aveugles,* Institut Français Bucarest (Bucharest, Romania), 1994.

PERIODICALS

Choice, January, 1996, review of *Zenobia,* p. 799.
Kirkus Reviews, June 15, 1995, review of *Zenobia,* p. 805.
Library Journal, August, 1995, review of *Zenobia,* p. 119.
World Literature Today, autumn, 1981, Nicholas Catanoy, review of *Partea Cealalta,* p. 660; summer, 1996, Jeanine Teodorescu-Regier, review of *Zenobia,* p. 679; autumn, 1998, Marguerite Dorian, review of *Rede auf dem Bahndamm an die Steine (The Face and the Surface),* pp. 819-820.

OBITUARIES:

PERIODICALS

Independent, November 16, 2001, obituary by Adrian Dannatt, p. S6.
Variety, October 29, 2001, p. 40.*

*   *   *

NEGASH, Tekeste

PERSONAL: Born in Ethiopia; immigrated to Sweden, 1977; married Berit Sahlström; children: three daughters. *Education:* Uppsala University, Ph.D., 1987.

ADDRESSES: Office—Box 7005, 750 07, Uppsala, Sweden. *E-mail*—Tekeste.Nagash@lbutv.slu.se.

CAREER: Swedish University of Agricultural Sciences, Uppsala, Sweden, with Department of Rural Development Studies, 1997-98; Dalarna University College, Falun, Sweden, associate professor of modern history, 1999—.

WRITINGS:

Italian Colonialism in Eritrea, 1882-1941: Policies, Praxis, and Impact, Uppsala University (Uppsala, Sweden), 1987.

The Crisis of Ethiopian Education: Some Implications for Nation-building, Uppsala University (Uppsala, Sweden), 1990.

(Editor, with Lars Rudebeck) *Dimensions of Development with Emphasis on Africa: Proceeding from the Interdisciplinary Conference on Third World Studies, Uppsala, March 1994,* Nordiska Africainstitutet (Uppsala, Sweden), 1995.

Rethinking Education in Ethiopia, Nordiska Africainstitutet (Uppsala, Sweden), 1996.

Eritrea and Ethiopia: The Federal Experience, Transaction Publishers (New Brunswick, NJ), 1997.

(With Kjetil Tronvoll) *Brothers at War: Making Sense of the Eritrean-Ethiopian War,* Ohio University Press (Athens, OH), 2000.

SIDELIGHTS: Tekeste Negash, a native of Ethiopia who is now a Swedish citizen, has focused his scholarship on his country of origin and its neighbors in the Horn of Africa. His doctoral dissertation at Uppsala University served as the basis of his first published book, *Italian Colonialism in Eritrea, 1882-1941: Policies, Praxis, and Impact.* Italy established Eritrea in 1890 by joining "disparate regions with different historical and ecological characteristics," Negash explains in this work. Although conceived as a colony where Italians could settle and farm, Eritrea in reality served as a beachhead for Italy's efforts to further expand its holdings in Africa, and the Eritrean people provided a source of personnel for the colonial army in its wars with Ethiopia and Libya. The British occupied Eritrea during World War II; the nation subsequently became part of Ethiopia, then gained independence in 1993.

Negash's book "is an important contribution to the literature on Eritrea and Italian colonialism in general," commented James C. McCann in *Journal of African History.* He continued, "The author does an admirable job of providing a scholarly account of the development of a colonial system with a flavor quite different from French, British, and Portuguese variations on the imperial theme." The Italians, unlike some other colonial powers, failed to offer the indigenous people comprehensive Western-style educational opportunities. Such an education usually had the consequence—no doubt unintended on the part of the colonizers—of giving rise to independence movements. But in Eritrea, according to Negash, because of the Italians' disregard for educating their subjects, the cause of independence did not attract many adherents until long after Italy had pulled out. "His evidence is well marshalled and convincing," McCann remarked. Alan Cassels, writing in *American Historical Review,* thought Negash's book stands apart from other works on Italy's colonial pursuits in Africa because "it is written from the perspective of the colony." It is well researched and provides "useful scholarship," Cassels added, while McCann concluded that the book "is a major step forward" in the study of Eritrea.

Rethinking Education in Ethiopia takes up a key problem in the nation. Negash argues that the formal education system of Ethiopia has served its population poorly; access is limited, classes are large, educators disdain rural Ethiopian culture, and there are few jobs for graduates. "It is morally wrong and economically unjustifiable to invest scarce resources on the formal education system whose contribution to the development of society is at best tenuous and at worst irrelevant," he writes. He calls instead for an emphasis on "non-formal education," such as vocational training and adult literacy programs. David Styan, a contributor to the journal *Africa,* wished for a more extensive definition of non-formal education and discussion of how it could help rural Ethiopians. However, he said, this does not "invalidate the importance of [Negash's] basic criticisms of the contradictions at the heart of Ethiopia's educational system."

Eritrea and Ethiopia: The Federal Experience looks at the union of these two countries, "a critical period in Eritrea's history" in the worlds of *Journal of African History* reviewer Richard Reid. After years of Italian and then British rule, in 1952 Eritrea became, under a federation agreement, a self-governing region within Ethiopia. A decade later, Ethiopia completely absorbed Eritrea, a situation that remained until the overthrow of Ethiopian leader Mengistu Haile Mariam in 1991. The new government endorsed Eritrean independence, which became a reality in 1993. Many Eritreans have viewed their country as a pawn in the hands of Western powers and Ethiopia, but "Negash makes a convincing case that the demand for union [with Ethiopia] came from Eritreans—mostly but not entirely from the Christian community," commented Christopher Clapham in *African Affairs*. Reid, though, was not convinced, saying, "The author actually suggests that Ethiopia did not even want Eritrea, an argument not supported by any serious evidence and which in any case the author himself repeatedly disproves." Jon S. Ebeling, a critic for *Perspectives on Political Science*, noted that Negash is offering "entirely new interpretations" of Eritrean history, but found his book "an important addition to the scholarship on Eritrea and its development as an independent country today." Clapham, while praising the work generally, voiced the opinion that Negash had downplayed "the astonishing military, organizational and ideological feats" of the Eritrean People's Liberation Front in the struggle for independence. "He would have been better advised to end his account in 1962," Clapham remarked. "His reinterpretations of the two decades preceding that date must however be taken seriously."

The post-independence period was marked by the war that broke out between Eritrea and Ethiopia in 1998 and continued until 2000. Many outsiders were amazed that the two countries, apparently friendly after the split, would engage in a war that resulted in perhaps upward of 40,000 deaths. Negash and coauthor Kjetil Tronvoll attempt to explain the clash in *Brothers at War: Making Sense of the Eritrean-Ethiopian War*. Although the fighting commenced over a border dispute, the root causes were more historical and economic in nature, they conclude. They also portray the conflict as to some extent civil strife among the Tigrinya-speaking people, who have produced the rulers of both countries. The authors "consider both Eritrean and Ethiopian national interests and objectives as fueling the war but do not assess any responsibility," reported T. Natsoulas in *Choice*. Similarly, Clapham, writing in *Times Literary Supplement*, called their account "scrupulously impartial." Natsoulas also noted that Negash and Tronvoll believe further conflict is "a strong possibility."

BIOGRAPHICAL AND CRITICAL SOURCES:

BOOKS

Negash, Tekeste, *Italian Colonialism in Eritrea, 1882-1941: Policies, Praxis, and Impact*, Uppsala University (Uppsala, Sweden), 1987.
Negash, Tekeste, *Rethinking Education in Ethiopia*, Nordiska Africainstitutet (Uppsala, Sweden), 1996.

PERIODICALS

Africa, winter, 1998, David Styan, review of *Rethinking Education in Ethiopia*, p. 135.
African Affairs, July, 1998, Christopher Clapham, review of *Eritrea and Ethiopia: The Federal Experience*, p. 419.
African Studies Review, September, 1998, Patricia S. Kuntz, review of *Rethinking Education in Ethiopia*, pp. 205-207.
American Historical Review, December, 1989, Alan Cassels, review of *Italian Colonialism in Eritrea, 1882-1941: Policies, Praxis, and Impact*, p. 1450.
Choice, November, 2001, T. Natsoulas, review of *Brothers at War: Making Sense of the Eritrean-Ethiopian War*, p. 568.
Ethnic and Racial Studies, January, 2001, Alemseged Abbay, review of *Eritrea and Ethiopia*, pp. 144-147.
Foreign Affairs, September-October, 2001, Gail M. Gerhart, review of *Brothers at War*.
Journal of African History, August, 1988, James C. McCann, "The Eritrean Adventure," pp. 554-556; January, 2000, Richard Reid, review of *Eritrea and Ethiopia*, p. 166.
Perspectives on Political Science, winter, 1999, Jon S. Ebeling, review of *Eritrea and Ethiopia*, p. 48.
Times Literary Supplement, November 23, 2001, Christopher Clapham, "The Price of Land," p. 20.*

*   *   *

NEILL, William 1922-

PERSONAL: Born 1922, in Ayrshire, Scotland.

ADDRESSES: Home—Burnside, Crossmichael, Castle Douglas, Kirkcudbrightshire DG7 3AP, Scotland.

CAREER: Poet and translator.

WRITINGS:

Four Points of a Saltire, Reprographia (Edinburgh, Scotland), 1969.
Scotland's Castle, Reprographia (Edinburgh, Scotland), 1969.

Poems, Akros (Lancashire, England), 1970.

Despatches Home, Reprographia (Edinburgh, Scotland), 1972.

Galloway Landscape and Other Poems, URR Publications (Scotland), 1981.

Cnu a Mogaill, Glasgow University (Glasgow, Scotland), 1983.

The Jolly Trimmers: or, Love of Slavery: A Satirical Cantata, Luath Press (Barr, Ayrshire, Scotland), 1985.

Wild Places: Poems in Three Leids, Luath (Barr, Ayrshire, Scotland), 1985.

Making Tracks: And Other Poems, Gordon Wright (Edinburgh, Scotland), 1988.

Blossom, Berry, Fall, and Selected Works, edited by Gary Maclean-Quin, Brackenridge & Air (St. Andrews, Scotland), 1989.

Straight Lines, Blackstaff (Belfast, Northern Ireland), 1991.

Tales frae the Odyssey o Homer, Saltire Society (Edinburgh, Scotland), 1992.

A Caledonia Canto and Other Poems, Spectrum Poetry (Kilmarnock, Ayrshire, Scotland), 1993.

Selected Poems, 1969-1992, Canongate Press (Edinburgh, Scotland), 1994.

(Translator) Giuseppe Gioachino Belli, *A Hantle of Romanesco Sonnets bi Giuseppe Gioachino Belli, 1791-1863,* Burnside Press (Castle Douglas, Scotland), 1995.

Just Sonnets, Burnside Press (Castle Douglas, Scotland), 1996.

(Translator) Giuseppe Gioachino Belli, *Twa Score Romanesco Sonnets bi Giuseppe Gioachino Belli, 1791-1863,* Burnside Press (Castle Douglas, Scotland), 1996.

Galloway Landscapes, Previous Parrot Press (Whitney, Scotland), 1997.

The Tungs o Scots: An Essay, Akros (Kirkcaldy, Scotland), 1997.

Caledonian Cramboclink: The Poetry of William Neill, Luath (Edinburgh, Scotland), 2000.

Contributor to periodicals.

SIDELIGHTS: William Neill was born in Ayrshire, Scotland, in 1922, and has lived most of his life in Galloway, Scotland. He writes in Scots, Gaelic, and English, and has published many works in Gaelic and Scots literary magazines. He has also translated older works, such as those of Dante and Giuseppe Gioachina Belli, into Scots.

BIOGRAPHICAL AND CRITICAL SOURCES:

OTHER

Scottish Book Trust, http://www.scottishbooktrust.com/ (October 19, 2000).*

*   *   *

NELSON, Marcia Z.

PERSONAL: Female. *Education:* University of Chicago, graduate degree in English; Northwestern University, graduate degree in journalism.

ADDRESSES: Office—c/o Sheed & Ward Publishing, 30 Amberwood Parkway, Ashland, OH 44805.

CAREER: Writer.

WRITINGS:

The God of Second Chances: Stories of Lives Transformed by Faith, Sheed & Ward Publishing (Franklin, WI), 2001.

Come and Sit: A Week inside Meditation Centers, SkyLight Paths (Woodstock, VT), 2001.

Contributor of articles on religion books to *Publishers Weekly.*

SIDELIGHTS: Marcia Z. Nelson deals with her religious experiences and those of others in *The God of Second Chances: Stories of Lives Transformed by Faith* and *Come and Sit: A Week Inside Meditation Centers.* In the former, Nelson interviews people who have been able to recover from drug and alcohol addictions, leave lives of crime, and bravely face illness because of religious faith. Information about the role religion has played in her life also appears throughout the book. Nelson shows herself to be "a tough, well-traveled, sophisticated believer in a God whose mercy is the source and substance of hope," commented Phyllis Tickle in her foreword to *The God of Second Chances,* adding, "The fact that we come to know and like her as a human being while we profit from her as a journalist is no small part of the adventure as we go with her on this journey."

Come and Sit deals with meditation as practiced in Christianity, Judaism, Hinduism, Sufism, and three forms of Buddhism. Nelson visited meditation centers for each religion; she provides insight into her experiences there as well as information she gleaned from interviews with other meditators and their teachers. Her book also includes a glossary and a list of meditation centers. A *Publishers Weekly* reviewer praised Nelson's understanding of the faiths covered in the book and her explanation of their respective approaches to meditation "in non-threatening layperson's terms." The reviewer summed up *Come and Sit* as "the quintessential work for anyone who is commencing meditation practice."

BIOGRAPHICAL AND CRITICAL SOURCES:

BOOKS

Nelson, Marcia Z., *The God of Second Chances: Stories of Lives Transformed by Faith,* Sheed & Ward Publishing (Franklin, WI), 2001.
Nelson, Marcia Z., *Come and Sit: A Week inside Meditation Centers,* SkyLight Paths (Woodstock, VT), 2001.

PERIODICALS

Publishers Weekly, January 28, 2002, review of *Come and Sit: A Week Inside Meditation Centers,* p. 287.*

*   *   *

NEWMAN, Mildred (Rubenstein) 1920-2001

PERSONAL: Born 1920, in New York, NY; died of a pulmonary embolism, November 6, 2001, in New York, NY; married second husband, Bernard Berkowitz (a psychologist and psychiatrist), 1962; children: Sandy and Neal Newman (first marriage), Bob Berkowitz (stepson). *Education:* Hunter College,

bachelor's degree, master's degree (psychology), 1943; further study with National Association for Psychoanalysis.

CAREER: Psychologist.

WRITINGS:

(With husband, Bernard Berkowitz, and Jean Owen) *How to Be Your Own Best Friend: A Conversation with Two Psychologists,* Random House (New York, NY), 1973.
(With Bernard Berkowitz) *How to Be Awake and Alive,* Random House (New York, NY), 1975.
(With Bernard Berkowitz) *How to Take Charge of Your Own Life,* Harcourt (New York, NY), 1977.

SIDELIGHTS: Mildred Newman enjoyed great popularity in the 1970s as the author, with husband Bernard Berkowitz, of best-selling self-help books that made complicated psychological concepts understandable to average readers. The couple, who counted celebrities such as actor Anthony Perkins and playwright Neil Simon among their clients, gained fame in their own right with the publication in 1973 of *How to Be Your Own Best Friend: A Conversation with Two Psychologists.* The book is "a slender volume of practical advice, simply expressed," commented Wolfgang Saxon in a *New York Times* obituary of Newman. It sold millions of copies and was still in print at the time of Newman's death, even though some critics disdained it as "pop psychology." The book takes the form of a question-and-answer session between the psychologists and interviewer Jean Owen. Newman and Berkowitz exhort her and their readers to get rid of self-defeating attitudes, to give themselves credit for their accomplishments, and in general to feel good about themselves. "This little book is a kind of psychiatric pep talk," observed Harry Schwartz in *New York Times.* He also, however, called it "pablum" and a "sort of child's introduction to elementary psychotherapy." *Atlantic* reviewer Richard Todd saw "partial wisdom" in some of the authors' advice, but thought the book has a trivializing effect, tending to "denature the conflict between our need to change and to create a life whose narrative makes some sense." Fred Wright, writing in *Library Journal,* saw the book's prescriptions as "accurate but sometimes oversimplified"; he praised its accessible style and recommended it as a supplement to psychotherapy, not a substitute for it.

Newman and Berkowitz's follow-up, *How to Be Awake and Alive,* is again structured in question-and-answer style, although this time the questioner is not named. The psychologists put forth the view that many adults lead their lives under the influence of childhood fantasies, even though they may not realize it. Adults need to recognize these fantasies and let go of them if they are to be fully awake and alive. This all makes "reasonably sound, if somewhat elementary sense," related Christopher Lehmann-Haupt in *New York Times.* But, he said, the recognition of childish dreams, and other factors not conducive to good mental health, does not generally occur as automatically as it does in the book's case histories. "In my understanding, psychotherapy is not so much a series of leaps to high mountaintops as a slow climb toward one . . . you don't realize how far you've come until you get to the top." A *Publishers Weekly* reviewer described the work as "low key and affirmative," remarking that the authors "transcend banality by virtue of their unaffected simplicity."

How to Take Charge of Your Life makes points similar to those in the previous two books: adults need to have self-esteem, to get rid of negative thoughts, to take responsibility. It differs from the earlier books, though, by dispensing with the question-and-answer structure. Newman and Berkowitz's advice is delivered "warmly, supportively, and epigrammatically," wrote Mary Pradt Ziegler in *Library Journal.* A *Booklist* contributor thought the new style more like "bland blank verse," but nevertheless found much "common-sense advice" in the volume.

BIOGRAPHICAL AND CRITICAL SOURCES:

PERIODICALS

Atlantic, November, 1973, Richard Todd, review of *How to Be Your Own Best Friend,* pp. 109-111.

Booklist, June 1, 1977, review of *How to Take Charge of Your Life,* p. 1462.

Library Journal, September 1, 1973, Fred Wright, review of *How to Be Your Own Best Friend,* p. 2451; May 15, 1975, Martha Cornog, review of *How to Be Awake and Alive,* p. 993; May 1, 1977, Mary Pradt Ziegler, review of *How to Take Charge of Your Life,* p. 1027.

New Republic, September 3, 1977, Roberta Tovey, review of *How to Take Charge of Your Life,* pp. 36-37.

New York Times, October 13, 1973, Harry Schwartz, "New Hope for the Immature," p. 33; July 4, 1975, Christopher Lehmann-Haupt, "How Not to Feel Better," p. 21.

Publishers Weekly, March 17, 1975, review of *How to Be Awake and Alive,* p. 52.

OBITUARIES:

PERIODICALS

Los Angeles Times, November 11, 2001, Myrna Oliver, "Mildred Newman, 81; Psychologist, Author," p. B17.

New York Times, November 9, 2001, Wolfgang Saxon, "Mildred R. Newman, 81, Psychologist and Popular Author," p. C12.*

*   *   *

NEWMAN, Phyllis 1933-

PERSONAL: Born March 19, 1933, in Jersey City, NJ; daughter of Arthur (a handwriting analyst) and Rachael (a fortune teller) Newman; married Adolph Green (a playwright, lyricist, and actor), January 31, 1960; children: Adam, Amanda. *Education:* Attended Western Reserve University.

ADDRESSES: Agent—Harris M. Spylios, The Spylios Agency, 250 West 57th St., New York, NY 10107.

CAREER: Actress and writer. Stage appearances include *Wish You Were Here,* Imperial, NY, 1953; *I Feel Wonderful,* Theatre de Lys, NY, 1954; *Bells Are Ringing,* Shubert, NY, 1956; *First Impressions,* Alvin, NY, 1959; *Moonbirds,* Cort, NY, 1959; *Subways Are for Sleeping,* St. James, NY, 1961; *Pleasures and Palaces,* Fisher, Detroit, 1965; *Princess Barbara,* Ella/Passionella, The Apple Tree, Shubert, NY, 1967; *On the Town,* Imperial, NY, 1971; *Last of the Red Hot Lovers,* Westbury Music Fair, NY, 1972; *The Prisoner of Second Avenue,* Eugene O'Neill, NY, 1972; *Gala Tribute to Joshua Logan,* Imperial, NY, 1975; *My Mother Was a Fortune Teller,* Hudson Guild, NY, 1978; *The Madwoman of Central Park West,* 22 Steps, NY, 1979; and *Unicorn,* Berkshire Theatre Festival,

Stockbridge, MA, 1982. Other stage appearances include *Red Rover, Red Rover; Rocket to the Moon; Light Up the Sky; Annie Get Your Gun;* and *I Married an Angel.* Major tours include *I'm Getting My Act Together and Taking It on the Road,* Chicago, NY; and *Vamps and Rideouts,* 1982. Stage work as director includes *Straws in the Wind,* American Place, NY, 1975; *Walking Papers,* Circle in the Square, NY; *Area Code 212,* Public Theatre, NY; and *Façade,* for Leonard Bernstein; and *Franklin D.*

Film appearances include *Picnic,* Columbia, 1955; *The Vagabond King,* Paramount, 1956; *Let's Rock,* Columbia, 1958; *To Find a Man,* Columbia, 1972; *Mannequin,* 1987; *Saying Kaddish,* 1991; *Only You,* 1994; *The Beautician and the Beast,* 1997; *A Price above Rubies,* 1998; *A Fish in the Bathtub,* 1999; *Just for the Time Being,* 2000; and *It Had to Be You,* 2000. Television appearances include *Diagnosis: Unknown,* CBS, 1960; *That Was the Week That Was,* NBC, 1964-65; *The Wild, Wild West,* 1966; "Olympus 7-0000," ABC Stage 67, ABC, 1967; *The People Next Door* (movie), 1968; *The Bob Hope Show,* 1971; *Follies in Concert,* 1986; *The Equalizer,* 1986; *One Life to Live,* 1987; *Coming of Age,* CBS, 1988; *thirtysomething,* 1989, 1990; and *Murder, She Wrote,* 1991. Other TV appearances include *The Madwoman of Central Park West* and *The Tonight Show.*

AWARDS, HONORS: Antoinette Perry Award, 1962, for *Subways Are for Sleeping.*

WRITINGS:

My Mother Was a Fortune Teller (play), produced at Hudson Guild, NY, 1978.
(With Arthur Laurents) *The Madwoman of Central Park West* (play), produced at 22 Steps, NY, 1979.
Just in Time: Notes from My Life, Simon and Schuster (New York, NY), 1988.

Wrote song, "Brand New Dreams," for *Destined to Live: 100 Roads to Recovery* (television special), NBC, 1988.

ADAPTATIONS: The Madwoman of Central Park West was adapted for audio by DRG Records, 1990.

SIDELIGHTS: In a career that began with her 1953 stage debut in *Wish You Were Here,* Phyllis Newman has accumulated an impressive resume as a performer.

Though the stage has been her principal creative outlet—she won a Tony Award in 1962—she has also appeared in a number of films, beginning with *Picnic* in 1955. Her husband, the lyricist Adolph Green, is also a widely known and respected figure in the world of entertainment.

The title of Newman's 1978 play *My Mother Was a Fortune Teller* is more than just a catchy line: her mother, Rachael, told fortunes under the name Marvelle, while her father, Arthur, was a handwriting analyst who billed himself as "Gabel the Graphologist". Discussing her childhood with Marian Christy of the *Boston Globe,* Newman said, "My mother was a great encourager. She thought I was the greatest thing that ever happened. . . . Growing up, I looked at her and knew she believed I was the best. That steady look in her eyes made me want to be the best."

Her relationship with her mother is among the topics Newman discussed in her 1988 autobiography *Just in Time: Notes from My Life.* Of particular importance in the narrative is Newman's bout with breast cancer, which forced her to undergo two separate mastectomy operations, followed both times by rigorous chemotherapy. Asked how she survived during this difficult time, she told Christy, "I made a list of reasons I was going to be well. I wrote in longhand on yellow paper. I framed that list. I looked at the list every day. I thought about the specifics on the list."

Newman confessed to worrying that she would be accused of penning her autobiography as a means of cashing in on her illness, and went on to indicate that women needed a book that discussed breast cancer frankly. At the time she suffered from it, she said, she drew strength by looking at public figures, such as former First Lady Betty Ford, who had endured breast cancer and lived. While she was undergoing chemotherapy, she continued to work: "Work was the best revenge. I put on a public face. I did not want to look like a cancer victim." Concluding the interview with Christy, Newman said, "I don't have a secret of life except to enjoy it every day. I really believe the best of times is now."

BIOGRAPHICAL AND CRITICAL SOURCES:

BOOKS

Contemporary Theatre, Film, and Television, volume 33, Gale (Detroit, MI), 2001.

PERIODICALS

Boston Globe, August 28, 1988, Marian Christy, "How Phyllis Newman Fought the Big Fight," p. A11.

New York Times Book Review, November 27, 1988, Arnold Aronson, review of *Just in Time: Notes from My Life,* p. 23.

Publishers Weekly, June 24, 1988, Genevieve Stuttaford, review of *Just in Time,* pp. 99-100.

US, August 22, 1988, review of *Just in Time,* p. 60.*

*   *   *

NICHOLSON, Geoff 1953-

PERSONAL: Born April 3, 1953, in Sheffield, England; son of Geoffrey Howell (a carpenter) and Violet Theresa (a bookkeeper; maiden name, Moore) Nicholson. *Education:* Gonville and Caius College, Cambridge, B.A., 1975, M.A., 1978; University of Essex, M.A., 1978.

ADDRESSES: Home—23 Sutherland Ave., London W9, England. *Agent*—Derek Johns, c/o A. P. Watt, 20 John St., London WC1, England.

CAREER: Writer. Worked as chef, gardener, furniture salesman, dustman, and driving instructor.

AWARDS, HONORS: Winner of *Custom Car* short story competition, 1985, for "Boy-raced from Oblivion"; *Street Sleeper* was shortlisted for the *Yorkshire Post* first work award; Whitbread Prize finalist, for *Bleeding London.*

WRITINGS:

NOVELS

Street Sleeper, Quartet (London, England), 1987.

The Knot Garden, Hodder & Stoughton (London, England), 1989.

What We Did on Our Holidays, Hodder & Stoughton (London, England), 1990.

Hunters and Gatherers, Hodder & Stoughton (London, England), 1991, Overlook Press (Woodstock, NY), 1994.

The Food Chain, Hodder & Stoughton (London, England), 1992, Overlook Press (Woodstock, NY), 1993.

The Errol Flynn Novel, Sceptre (London, England), 1994.

Still Life with Volkswagens, Quartet (London, England), 1994, Overlook Press (Woodstock, NY), 1995.

Everything and More, Gollancz (London, England), 1994, St. Martin's (New York, NY), 1995.

Footsucker, Gollancz (London, England), 1995, Overlook Press (Woodstock, NY), 1996.

Bleeding London, Gollancz (London, England), 1997, Overlook Press (Woodstock, NY), 1997.

Flesh Guitar, Gollancz (London, England), 1998, Overlook Press (Woodstock, NY), 1999.

Female Ruins, Gollancz (London, England), 1999, Overlook Press (Woodstock, NY), 2000.

Bedlam Burning, Gollancz (London, England), 2000, Overlook Press (Woodstock, NY), 2002.

OTHER

Sleeping Dogs (radio play), first broadcast by British Broadcasting Corp. (BBC), 1982.

Big Noises: Rock Guitar in the '90s, Quartet (London, England), 1991.

Day Trips to the Desert: A Sort of Travel Book, Hodder & Stoughton (London, England), 1992.

Andy Warhol: A Beginner's Guide, Hodder & Stoughton (London, England), 2002.

Frank Lloyd Wright: A Beginner's Guide, Hodder & Stoughton (London, England), 2002.

SIDELIGHTS: Geoff Nicholson aims to be "a serious comic writer," as he once told *CA.* His protagonists frequently take their interests to the point of obsession. The characters in *Hunters and Gatherers,* for instance, are consumed by collecting; a husband and wife collect cars and extramarital lovers, respectively, while another character, a writer, is obsessed with chronicling collectors. *New York Times Book Review* critic Eric Kraft called the novel "a humorous but serious study of people who collect things, with ruminations on the psychological, sociological, and philosophical aspects of their obsession. It is also about people who tell stories, with ruminations on the nature of their obsession." Nicholson treats these subjects in a manner that is "clever, entertaining and intriguing . . . literate and rich, with references to culture high and low," Kraft said, although he found fault with the handling of the characters and their emotions: "Though they bump into one another now and then, they don't feel much when they do." To *Time* reviewer John Skow, the book "is not so much a novel as a collection of loosely related fiction riffs, but it does not suffer at all from its lack of connective tissue." Nicholson's narrative, he added, is "always peculiar, frequently droll, and on several occasions funny."

In *Everything and More,* Nicholson turns a jaundiced eye on materialism, with a tale centering on a fictional London department store, Haden Brothers, which a *Publishers Weekly* critic described as "a combination of Harrod's, Kafka's Castle, and the Marx Brothers' *The Big Store.*" The primary characters are Vita Carlisle, a seemingly ideal salesperson who eventually tries to blow up the store; Charlie Mayhew, a would-be artist who takes a low-level job at Haden Brothers and falls in love with Vita; and Arnold Haden, the last of the brothers, who also longs for Vita. Quirky supporting players include a blind elevator operator who tells Charlie he smells right for the store and disgruntled workers who take their revenge on management by shoplifting. "The book bristles with energy, the plot moves quickly and there's a great sense of life and movement to all the characters," observed Susan Jeffreys in *New Statesman and Society.* "There are also (a real bonus in a comic novel) some terrifically sensual passages, particularly when the store is being described. . . . It is riddled with secret passages, underground chambers, and even a tomb." The *Publishers Weekly* reviewer found *Everything and More* "a highly literate and bawdy assault on the principle that all things, including people, have exchange values."

In *Bleeding London,* the focus is again on obsessions, with one character, Mick Wilton, determined to avenge his girlfriend's rape; another, Stuart London, so obsessed with the city whose name he shares that he intends to walk every one of its streets; and a third, Judy Tanaka, driven to accumulate sexual partners. All use the same London city guide as an aid in their quests. "Nicholson constructs his plot lines to intersect like crossroads," noted J. D. Biersdorfer in the *New York Times Book Review,* adding that the result will "keep readers comfortably hooked." A *Publishers Weekly* commentator praised the novel's "delightfully

cynical sense of humor" and many "vivid vignettes," finding fault only in the amount of time that it takes for the characters to meet. "Even so, getting there's most of the fun," the reviewer concluded.

Flesh Guitar looks at a rock music fan's obsession with a guitarist named Jenny Slade, whose instrument appears to be made of human flesh. Slade is portrayed as an influence on many famed rockers, such as Frank Zappa, Jimi Hendrix, and Kurt Cobain. According to *New York Times Book Review* contributor Anthony Bourdain, *Flesh Guitar*'s concept is promising, but its execution is lacking; the novel, while "always clever, is seldom fun," he wrote. A *Publishers Weekly* reviewer, however, deemed *Flesh Guitar* "a clever montage rife with signature black humor and ultrahip self-consciousness."

Nicholson mixes architectural theory with fiction in *Female Ruins.* Kelly Howell, daughter of the late English architect Christopher Howell, agrees to be a tour guide for American Jack Dexter. Dexter is actually an admirer of her father's, and wants to get close to Kelly in order to find out more about the man who was a great architect and a lousy father. Barbara Love of *Library Journal* called *Female Ruins* an "entertaining read . . . enlivened by scattered riffs on architecture." A contributor to *Publishers Weekly* considered it "a complex, subtle story with equally intricate and modulated characters." Chris Jones of *Book* wrote that *Female Ruins* "is a gripping tale with potent ideas that linger long in the mind."

In *Bedlam Burning,* narrator Mike Smith is both attractive and aimless. When his friend Gregory Collins enlists Mike to pose for the jacket photo for Gregory's first novel, Mike agrees. Gregory convinces Mike to stand in for him at an author reading as well, and soon Mike, posing as Gregory, finds himself accepting a writer-in-residence position at an insane asylum. The psychiatrists at the asylum first lock him up (the disorientation will help him identify with the patients). Once he is released, he steps into the role of writer-in-residence, and although he's not sure what to do with it, he eventually sets the inmates to writing their own pieces. In the meantime, he discovers that Kincaid's method for curing madness is to deprive his patients of visual images, and he beds psychiatrist Alicia Crowe, who is aroused by foul language. Nicholson "knows how to catch your interest from Page 1," wrote Marcel Theroux in his review for the *New York Times*

Book Review, continuing, "Mike is good company as a narrator: bright, engagingly straightforward, and yet virtually clueless about what's going on around him." A *Publishers Weekly* contributor wrote that *Bedlam Burning* "delightfully stretches sanity to its farcical breaking point."

AUTOBIOGRAPHICAL ESSAY:

Geoff Nicholson contributed the following autobiographical essay to *CA:*

My favourite misguided description of the life of the writer comes from William Burroughs in *The Adding Machine.* He writes,

> "As a young child I wanted to be a writer because writers were rich and famous. They lounged around Singapore and Rangoon smoking opium in a yellow pongee silk suit. They sniffed cocaine in Mayfair and they penetrated forbidden swamps with a faithful native boy and lived in the native quarter of Tangier smoking hashish and languidly caressing a pet gazelle."

My own imagination wasn't nearly so feverish. When I was about ten years old, at a family gathering, my Aunty Daisy, in front of everybody, asked me what I wanted to be when I grew up. I reduced the room to laughter (some of it no doubt derisive) by answering that I wanted to be "a scientist."

Naturally I didn't know what was involved in being a scientist any more than I knew what was involved in doing any other job, though I think I already had an intuition that working in a factory or on a building site, which was what most of the men in my family did, wasn't going to be very much fun.

The reason I'd said I wanted to be a scientist was because I was already a great reader, and I was in the middle of a science-fiction phase, enjoying books, and indeed comics and movies, in which the heroes, the men who went into space and battled with aliens and renegade robots, were invariably scientists. They emerged from their well-ordered laboratories to have fantastic adventures, save the world, and get the girl. That was pretty much what I wanted for my future.

The author and his father, Sheffield, England, c. 1957

I suppose even at the age of ten a little thought would have told me that I was better suited to adventures of the imagination than to the adventures of science. From the very earliest age I had written little stories and plays, and although I suppose all children do this at school, I had also done it at home on my own time, and I always did it in, so to speak, "book form." I'd go along to the local Woolworth's and buy small hardback notebooks so that my efforts looked as much like "real" books as possible. The fact that they had to be handwritten was a cause of great frustration. I knew there were such things as typewriters in the world, but in my home, in a working-class family in Sheffield, in the north of England in the late 1950s, for a young boy to aspire to owning a typewriter would have been as bizarre and fanciful as wanting Meissen pottery or a harp.

My parents were good, solid, respectable working people. They thought that education was a very good thing, though they'd had precious little of it themselves. Poverty, low expectations, and the Second World War had had predictably damaging effects on their lives. My father had joined the navy at the age of sixteen, in 1941, and had found it such a terrible experience that he never spoke of it for the rest of his life. My mother was far less reticent. She talked a lot about the German bombing of Sheffield, and her stories gave me nightmares.

By the time I was born, in 1953, my father was a joiner and my mother an office clerk. My mother's family was Irish Catholic, my father's Protestant, Lincolnshire farmers. Having married in a Catholic church, they had been forced to promise that their children would be brought up in the Catholic faith. I imagine some stormy parental debate had taken place before I was born (though it was never referred to), and it had been agreed that if I wasn't going to be brought up a Catholic I would be brought up as nothing at all. Consequently my childhood was remarkably free of religion, and the first time I went to a proper church service was when I was twenty-one, having been taken there by a girlfriend. I didn't feel that I'd been missing anything.

My parents apparently also ignored the Catholic church's teachings on birth control, since I was an only child. My mother was one of seven, and of her siblings, four would also have one-child families. When I first realized this I wondered if there was some odd genetic trait in the family, but there was a far simpler explanation. They had learned that money simply went further if there were fewer mouths to feed.

I suspect that being an only child is not a bad preparation for a life as a writer. You are forced to tolerate your own company, you have to use your imagination, and you come to think of yourself as something of an outsider. I suspect too that an unhappy childhood is another "advantage" for a writer, and unhappy I certainly was. I can give no absolute reason for it. My parents loved me (though they were careful not to show it too conspicuously), I had friends, I was bullied no more than average, I did well enough at school, and yet I was a lonely and melancholy kid, and this seems to have been something in-built, something that has never entirely gone away. I remember a parent saying to my mother as they stood outside the school gates watching the children, "These are the happiest days of their lives if they did but know it," and I hoped passionately that this would prove not to be true.

In these circumstances a retreat into books seems natural enough. I read a lot, though not very well or widely. I devoured dozens of books by Enid Blyton—especially the "Famous Five" and the "Secret Seven" series. I read "Just William," the "Hardy Boys," and a lot of science fiction short stories.

Later there were the "Billy Bunter" books by Frank Richards, and the "Jennings and Derbyshire" series by

The author as a child in a toy store in Sheffield in the late 1950s

Anthony Buckeridge, which are set in the world of all-male English public schools. Today I find it hard to believe that I had any interest in, or even understood, these stories of closed, privileged societies, but the fact remains that I enjoyed them well enough at the time.

This world was perhaps less alien than it might otherwise have been since by then (at the age of eleven) I'd passed the Eleven Plus, a make-or-break examination that blighted the lives of all English children at that time. I was, supposedly, one of the lucky ones. I'd been selected to go to a rather prestigious grammar school, King Edward VII's, or King Ted's as it was generally known, a place that for better or worse shared most of the values of public schools, but at least the boys were sent home to their families at the end of each day.

King Ted's was a dour, joyless place that was far more concerned with passing exams than with offering a broad education, though perhaps for this very reason it was extremely good at getting boys into university, especially Oxford and Cambridge. Sports and corporal punishment were also a large part of the school culture. I didn't much like sport, though I was surprisingly good at rugby, and I avoided being caned, though I did it by keeping my head down and remaining anonymous, rather than by actually behaving well. This is pretty much how I've dealt with institutions ever since.

For all that I disliked school, I wanted to do well, and I could see that there were some good, eccentric, and inspirational teachers there, especially of English, my best subject and the only one I really enjoyed. We were introduced early to Shakespeare, Swift, Lewis Carroll, Edgar Allan Poe, H.G. Wells. One of the teachers brought in John Lennon's *A Spaniard in the Works* and I thought it was wonderful.

We were encouraged to write as well as read. I seem to remember writing a very short play called *Waiting for God,* about soldiers trapped in a cellar in France in World War I. I'd certainly never read any Samuel Beckett at the time, but evidently I'd heard of him and his most famous play.

Under my own steam I discovered Ian Fleming and the "James Bond" novels, and at the age of thirteen or so I began writing a spy novel of my own, called *Half an Agent Is Better Than None.* It was exactly the sort of thing likely to be written by a thirteen-year-old boy who had read a lot of Ian Fleming and not understood very much of it. Needless to say, it was very short, but for a thirteen year old, the writing of it had required a lot of discipline and commitment, and I discovered I had these. I wrote every day, a habit that's stayed with me.

I didn't show the resulting "novel" to many people, but I didn't keep it a secret, and at school and among friends and family I was known to be "good at English." The teachers at my school thought I might get in to university. I certainly had no idea what university would involve or might be like, and neither did anybody else in my family. Everyone we knew had left school as soon as they could and immediately started work. My parents, to their credit and on what basis I'm not sure, accepted that going to university was a very desirable thing. They encouraged me, but they were as vague as I was about what they were actually encouraging.

At around this time I read David Lodge's novel *The British Museum Is Falling Down,* about the lives of various university teachers and students. It was a revelation, and the world it depicted was as strange and unlikely as anything I'd come across in science fiction. People spent their days in libraries reading books and writing about them. It even appeared you might do this for the whole of your life, make a career out of it. I was amazed, and even though I was still entirely naive about the realities of this world, I felt that I wanted very much indeed to be part of it. Whether this was a realistic ambition, I had no idea.

*

Unlikely as it seemed to me at the time, I was duly accepted by Gonville and Caius College, at Cambridge University to study English. I was both pleased and surprised. As part of the selection process I endured a grueling interview with the director of studies at the college, the poet and academic Jeremy Prynne. For large parts of the interview I didn't really understand what either he or I was saying, and my part of the discussion proceeded by a kind of desperate free association, but if I was talking nonsense, apparently it was interesting nonsense. My acceptance, I learned later, was largely because of that interview.

I think some sort of positive discrimination was probably going on at Cambridge at that time. The colleges were trying to become more socially diverse, and they were keen to accept students who didn't come from typical, middle-class, public-school backgrounds. This wasn't simple altruism. The colleges realized that cleverness didn't have much to do with social class, and that by drawing from a wider pool they would end up with more clever people than if they only recruited from the middle class. I was certainly prepared to find Cambridge a hotbed of effete snootiness, and a part of me was perhaps disappointed to discover that it was one of the least snobbish places I've ever been; elitist no doubt, but never pettily snobbish. It simply didn't allow me to carry a chip on my shoulder, and for that I was very grateful.

In my first year at university I worked very hard and very ineffectually. I enjoyed the subject well enough, reading Shakespeare, Chaucer, Langland, and doing a lot of practical criticism, but I did badly in the end-of-year exams, not badly enough to be told to leave, but badly enough that it occurred to me I might be better off elsewhere doing something else, though I wouldn't have known what. With all the academic work, I hadn't found much time to do any creative writing of my own.

However, at the beginning of the second year a college friend said that if I wrote a one-act play it was almost guaranteed to be performed by the college drama society. I was skeptical but it proved to be true. I stitched together a fifty-minute play called *Everly Happy After* (a title that now makes me cringe) which was performed in the college, and was very well received, at least by other students. After that I spent the rest of my time at university putting at least as much energy into writing and producing plays and comedy revues as I did into studying English. There was quite a social life that went with being part of the drama crowd, and that was certainly an attraction.

Despite these apparent distractions, my academic grades improved considerably. In my final year I wrote a dissertation on Henry Miller, William Burroughs, and Jack Kerouac, which I greatly enjoyed doing and got high marks for. I also wrote about Harold Pinter and an obscure English playwright called Heathcote Williams.

In a moment of bravado I set up a theatre group called the Misfit Theatre as a vehicle for my own work. Even as I was doing it I knew that thereafter I'd always be able to say, "By the time I was twenty-one I was running my own theatre group." We performed around the university and then on tour at the Edinburgh Festival Fringe. The Misfit Theatre presented an uneasy mixture of rock music, performance art, comedy sketches, and philosophical monologues, and we put on rock shows with titles like *Amateur Traumatics* and *The Siegfried Follies* (more callow, embarrassing titles), combining anarchy with well-drilled virtuoso performances and, I hoped, well-written material. I also wrote and directed a more conventional play called *Oscar.*

If we had lived up to our ambitions the group would have been something between the Living Theatre and The Mothers of Invention, but I suspect it all came across as a group of students trying far too hard. It was important to us at the time, we took it seriously,

and we certainly entertained our audiences but it was hard to see where it might lead. A couple of London agents came to watch us perform and assured us there was no way in the world that we could ever make a living doing this sort of thing. The Misfit Theatre came to a natural end.

Consequently I wrote at least two straight plays and although they were read by various managements, including the National Theatre, who were encouraging to a certain extent, nobody ever looked like offering me a production. I returned to full-time education, largely as a delaying tactic, enrolling for a one-year master's degree in European Drama at the University of Essex, in Colchester. The big attraction for me was the option of writing and directing a play as part of the course work. This I duly did, a play called *Angst for the Memory,* which was performed in the university theatre and then at a tiny fringe theatre in London.

In fact Margaret Ramsay, the legendary literary agent who represented, among many others, Joe Orton, Eugene Ionesco, and Alan Ayckbourn, came along to see the show. Afterwards she told me candidly (since she was never anything other than perfectly candid) that it was the worst production she had seen in several years, and she described the leading lady, who I thought I'd coaxed into giving quite a winning performance, as "that creature." Perhaps I should have been far more deterred than I actually was, but I reasoned that she had condemned the production rather than the play, and I had only become a director by default because nobody else was offering to direct my work. I decided to concentrate on *writing* plays rather than directing or producing them.

By then I had completed my M.A., moved to London, and was supporting myself with a variety of menial jobs, while trying to put my real energies into writing plays. One of these was broadcast on BBC radio, an important outlet for drama at the time, and this felt like considerable progress, but chiefly I wrote for the London fringe, or possibly the fringe of the fringe. And I did find a couple of small theatre groups who performed my plays in very small rooms, often above pubs, to minute audiences. It was "professional theatre" to some degree in that the performers were fully trained professional actors, who preferred to work for no money than not to work at all, but I found it hard to convince myself that there was really any

Rehearsing with fellow members of the Misfit Theatre at Cambridge University, 1974

demand for what we were doing. By this time, in the late 1970s, such audience as there was for even mildly adventurous or experimental theatre in England seemed to be evaporating rapidly.

During this period I also began writing material for a stand-up comedian, and subsequently for a few radio and television comedy programmes. I had sketches performed by well-known English performers such as Lenny Henry, Chris Tarrant, and Tracey Ullman. On occasions this work was quite well paid, and it was an area very welcoming to new writers. If the material was funny it really didn't matter whether or not you were a "name." But writing comedy to order is fiendishly difficult. I wasn't bad at it, but I wasn't great, and although I enjoyed the discipline of having to get up in the morning, sit down, and write something funny, ultimately the satisfaction that came from doing it just wasn't enough. With some notable exceptions, the audience that watches comedy seldom knows or cares who writes the material. I was arrogant enough, and perhaps needy enough, to want to see my name above the title.

*

The difference between success and failure is seldom very clear-cut for a writer. To have written anything at all can always be considered quite an achievement. To have had my work performed on stage, TV, and radio was, in one way, as much success as I had ever dared hope for. It was certainly more success than a lot of would-be authors will ever know. On the other hand I could hardly consider myself much of a success when I couldn't find an audience for my writing and certainly couldn't make a living from it.

By this time I was thirty years old and married to a woman called Tessa. We met while we were both working at Harrods, the exclusive English department

In London, 1978

store (rather more exclusive then than now), where I had a job as a furniture salesman and invoice clerk; another fill-in job. This gave me the best line of my wedding speech, "Some marriages are made in heaven, but ours was made in Harrods." It would also eventually give me plenty of material for my novel *Everything and More,* set in a vast and allegorical department store, but at the time it just seemed like hard, dreary work.

Shortly after we were married I did some writing of the sort that only happens once in a lifetime. At the time I had an intense, and vaguely ironic, interest in classic and customized cars. This interest was also largely theoretical. I didn't intend to own one of these

vehicles, not least because I couldn't possibly have afforded one. Instead I just bought magazines, read them, and dreamed.

Then one of the magazines, called *Custom Car,* ran a short story contest for which the prize was a customized Ford Escort. The story had to be very short indeed—just a hundred words—and I decided to enter. I spent a Sunday afternoon writing the story, in which you had to imagine that you'd won the car and describe the first night you took it out. I reasoned that I could probably write a better short story than most of the readers of *Custom Car.* This was no doubt terribly arrogant of me, but it turned out to be correct. I won the car. My story was a loose parody of J. G.

Ballard's *Crash,* though I've never been sure whether the judges recognized this.

It was the most effective, and undoubtedly the most profitable afternoon's writing I have ever done. It hardly proved that I had what it took to be a "real" writer, but it was an incredible boost to my confidence.

*

While Tessa had no problem with me being an aspiring writer, I certainly felt some pressure to prove that my writing wasn't just an indulgence. I had never expected writing to make me rich, but for my own self-respect it had to be more than a hobby. I needed to prove myself. In these circumstances, writing a novel was, in some ways, an extremely obvious idea, though it took me a long time to come up with it.

One of the biggest problems facing any writer at the start of his career is knowing what kind of writer he actually is; whether he's a populist, an avant-gardist, an intellectual, an old-fashioned storyteller. For my own part I had some trouble deciding whether I wanted to be Samuel Beckett or Jack Kerouac, Thomas Pynchon or Tom Sharpe, J. G. Ballard or S. J. Perelman. Of course I'd have settled for being any of these, for being anything at all, and naturally I wanted above all to be entirely myself, but this is always so much harder than most people ever imagine. A lot of young writers assume that originality comes out of naivety or ignorance, but the reverse is true; the more you know, the more knowing you become, the greater your chances of being original.

I had always had a gift for pastiche and parody and when I came to write my first novel it seemed natural enough to take an existing literary form as a jumping-off point. I selected the road novel. My love of Jack Kerouac came into play, and also a summer I'd spent hitchhiking around the United States when I was a student, and no doubt my success in winning the Ford Escort played its part. I was writing this in 1985, when the road novel genre was rather less worked over than it is now. My idea was simply to transfer the grand American ideas and ideals about freedom, self-discovery, and the open road, and see how they could possibly work in a country as small and confined as England.

What made the book come together was buying a Volkswagen Beetle. I have always had a tendency to over-research things, so when my wife and I were looking for a used car I began to read about the Volkswagen, to discover its history, its origins in Nazi Germany, its resurrection at the hands of the occupying British troops, its acceptance by 1960s American hippies as a symbol of rebellion against consumerism and planned obsolescence. The fact that it was sold to America via one of the slickest-ever Madison Avenue advertising campaigns was all part of the fascination.

And so I wrote my first novel, *Street Sleeper.* To have written it at all was a source of some satisfaction, since when I started I hadn't been sure I could even get the required number of words down on paper. I then showed it to the only contact I had in English book publishing, and after some editorial give and take, the book was duly accepted for publication.

I was ecstatic, and again surprised. As a writer of plays I had spent a long time knocking on doors that were closed to me. Here I had knocked on a door that was opened immediately. I couldn't help wondering if I'd been wasting my time for the previous decade or so, that I should have been writing novels all along. I could take some consolation from telling myself that writing for the stage had taught me how to write dialogue, but there remained the feeling that I might have been barking up the wrong tree all the time. Perhaps as a result of this, I experienced a great outpouring of creativity. I wrote a novel a year for the next seven years.

Street Sleeper was as well received as any first novelist could possibly expect. It got good reviews, though not as many of them as I'd have liked, and it was short-listed for the Yorkshire Post First Work Award. The paperback rights were sold immediately, and then someone bought an option on the film rights. In fact, over the fifteen or so years since publication, movie producers have always been interested in this book, but I'll talk more about my dealings with the film world later.

The public regularly reads stories about novelists who receive vast, life-changing amounts of money for their first novels. However, the fact that it's deemed newsworthy only goes to prove how rare it is. Even though I was now making some money from writing, it was scarcely enough to live on, and it occurred to me that my earnings would go much further if I lived outside of London. Tessa and I moved to Yorkshire. This was a mistake in all sorts of ways. We had (all too romantically) imagined living in a small cottage in some remote bit of the Yorkshire countryside. In the event we finished up living in a suburban bungalow in Sheffield, my home town. I suppose this was a homecoming of a sort, but not at all as we'd envisaged.

In fact I was able to write perfectly well there in suburbia. I rapidly completed two more novels, *The Knot Garden,* which is a kind of shaggy-dog whodunnit, where the mystery of who committed the murder becomes more and more unfathomable as the book goes on. Then *What We Did on Our Holidays,* a broad slapstick farce set in a seaside caravan park, a milieu I knew all too well from the family holidays of my childhood.

Any writer who uses humour always runs the risk of not being taken seriously, and although these books certainly contained much more humour than my later ones, I never had the sense that they were light or easy works. All too often my work at this time was described as "zany" and that drove me crazy. It seemed to me that my books were far too dark, savage, and violent to be thought of that way.

These books did well enough to just about make me a living and allow me to continue to think of myself as a writer. In many ways it was exactly what I'd always wanted. I was very content, but my wife was not. It seemed she was much happier being married to a failing, would-be writer than to a somewhat successful one. She said she wanted to get divorced. I said I didn't. This wasn't a debate in which there was much room for development, and since there were no children, nor anything else to keep us together, before long I agreed to a divorce. In retrospect I think this was a very good decision, but it was not mine.

My fourth novel, *Hunters and Gatherers,* is about a writer living in Sheffield who has recently divorced his wife. In fact most of the book was written some time before Tessa and I ever discussed breaking up, but perhaps I knew instinctively that it was coming and I was already trying it on for size. By the time the novel was published I was divorced, had left Sheffield, and was living in London again, and although I was

not, and am still not, part of any London literary scene, it did seem that a writer, at least one like me, is going to be more at home in a metropolis than in the Sheffield suburbs.

Hunters and Gatherers felt like a considerable step forward. It was a bigger, more complex, and more obviously serious novel than anything I'd written before. The characters were more fully drawn and, even though there was still plenty of wit and humour in the book, it was not by any definition a "comic novel."

People have told me it's the archetypal Geoff Nicholson novel. It concerns a number of obsessive collectors who are only connected to each other via the protagonist who interacts with them all. The characters try to make order by assembling their own private collections, but the essential anarchy and randomness of the universe constantly defeats them. It is also the first of my novels that deals directly with the relationship between people and objects, a theme to which I have regularly returned. I'm not entirely sure why this subject appeals to me so much, but the question of materialism, of having and not having, seems like a very relevant one at this point in history.

*

In the late 1980s, in England, there was a vogue (rather short-lived) for books of travel writing. If you were an author with a certain amount of track record it wasn't too hard to get a commission to go traveling and then write about it. This felt too good to be true, and in some ways it probably was. I'm not sure how many of these books were ever really very good. But of course I joined the bandwagon. Who wouldn't? I submitted a proposal to travel to a number of the world's deserts, the ones in Morocco, Egypt, the United States, and Australia. I made no claims to be a great or intrepid traveler so I called the book *Day Trips to the Desert.*

My enthusiasm for deserts was perfectly genuine, and indeed still is. As a tourist I'd done a certain amount of exploring the American desert in California and Arizona and I found it a wonderful and moving place. I imagined my book would be a wry meditation on bleak landscapes, desolation, emptiness, and why people, myself included, were so strongly drawn to such things. I also thought it might be quite a funny book.

However, shortly before I set off on my first trip, to the deserts of Australia, my father was diagnosed as having terminal cancer. The best estimate was that he had six to nine months left to live. My trip to Australia was only for five weeks, so there seemed no reason not to go, indeed every reason to do it sooner rather than later so that I would be back in England for the last and worst phase of his illness.

So for five weeks or so I found myself in bleak terrain, in hostile but beautiful stretches of the Australian Outback, making notes, keeping a diary, taking photographs, and constantly trying to find a working phone box so that I could call England and ask my mother how things were. Things were never good, but I didn't realize quite how bad until I got back to England.

Tired and jet-lagged I went up to Sheffield. My father was still at home, rather than in a hospital or hospice where he clearly belonged. The disease had progressed much faster than anybody had ever imagined. My father just about managed to say hello to me, and then he gave up the ghost. For a few intolerably long days he suffered unbearably, hallucinating, fighting us, unable to get any relief from pain. There were vast quantities and many forms of morphine in the sickroom, but we couldn't find any way of getting him to take it. When my mother and I couldn't cope anymore, my father was taken, much against his will, into hospital and he died that same night. I have often imagined that some compassionate doctor or nurse speeded his departure.

I felt that all this experience of my father's death had to go into the book I was writing. Indeed, how could I have written about my experiences in the desert without mentioning the extent which this was affected by knowing that my father was dying at home? *Day Trips to the Desert* is therefore a rather strange, emotionally naked, and inconsistent book, and certainly one that is untypical of my writing. It is a book that has been much enjoyed and much criticized by readers and critics, which may be an indication that there's something quite interesting going on in it. It is certainly a book that I wouldn't write today, and there are moments when I perhaps wish I hadn't written it at all, or at least wish that I had written it very differently. But that is the nature of writing. You make mistakes, you wish you'd made different decisions, but in the end you have to live with them and stand by the work

*

I returned to writing novels. In quick succession I completed *The Food Chain,* a novel about sex, food, English gentlemen's clubs, and cannibalism; then *The Errol Flynn Novel,* about several characters who are obsessed with Flynn, one a filmmaker, one an actor with a physical resemblance to the Hollywood star; and then *Still Life with Volkswagens,* a sequel to *Street Sleeper,* my first novel, though I think it is better and a good deal more sophisticated than the original.

The English publishing industry was going through a particularly volatile period while I was writing and publishing these books. There were many personnel changes and each novel was ushered into print by a different editor and/or publisher. It's pointless to complain about this; publishing is a business and therefore subject to the vagaries that affect any other business. Most writers do hope for a stable and enduring relationship with an editor, someone who knows their work, whose opinion they can trust, and who is firmly on their side. However, this is a surprisingly rare thing, and apparently getting rarer. These days a writer's most important relationship is likely to be with his agent rather than his editor. After *Still Life* I found a new agent with whom I continue to have a good professional relationship, while all around us a great many editors have come and gone, and plenty of publishing companies have changed ownership or sunk completely.

Fortunately, by this time I was also enjoying a more enduring relationship with an American publisher. It hadn't been easy for me to get published in the United States. My early novels had been rejected by American editors on the grounds that English humour didn't "translate." Having spent a lot of time in the United States in recent years, this seems to me rather more understandable than it did then. The best writing may be universal, but humour often relies on very local references. There are plenty of American readers who are Anglophiles but even the best of them are unlikely to grasp the kind of detailed references to English cricket or English soap operas which are present in my early novels. *Hunters and Gatherers* was the first novel of mine to be published in the United States, and although that book is set in a very specific English locale, as I have said, it deals with much broader issues. Certainly nobody has ever complained about being unable to understand its local references.

To be published in America felt like a great step forward. Ever since the Beatles (or possibly even since Charles Dickens) every Englishman wants to conquer America. A lot of English writers have a love/hate relationship with American culture, but I have always been a fairly straightforward admirer of the best of it. My favourite novelists, rock bands, movies, have always been American. I wanted America to like my work, and to a large extent it has.

My books were immediately taken far more seriously in America than they ever had been in England. They were reviewed at greater length, in more depth, and in more prestigious publications. I was declared to be a serious literary writer, not just a comic novelist, which was what I'd been saying all along. Consequently I began to make at least an annual pilgrimage to the States, partly to promote my books, and partly because I simply liked it there.

*

That's why I was not in England when my mother died. I was in the desert again, in Nevada and Arizona, but just on holiday this time rather than on a writing commission. My mother was in reasonably good health for a woman in her late sixties, with a slight but (as far as we knew) perfectly manageable heart condition. But I got back home to England and found a message on my answering machine from an uncle who would never normally have phoned me. Even so, this didn't seem especially strange. But I called him back and discovered that my mother had died the previous weekend, alone in a chair in her living room, apparently on Saturday afternoon, quickly if not exactly painlessly, and had been discovered the next morning by a neighbour.

Talking to doctors afterwards it appears there was nothing anybody could have done to save her, even if they had been in the same room, even if they'd had medical expertise. Her heart had simply stopped working. These things, apparently, sometimes happened.

Nevertheless, to have been so far away when it happened did leave me with a sense of guilt. I tried to remember the last conversation we'd had, but there was nothing remotely poignant or ominous about it. I was also surprised, and perhaps disappointed, that I hadn't intuited that something was wrong, hadn't felt a severing across the ether when she died, but I had felt nothing, had not had the slightest inkling.

I think writers must be careful not to regard everything that happens in their life simply as raw material. In fact I have tried to write a fictional account of my mother's death and my feelings about it, but somehow I haven't been able to make it work. There is a part of me that thinks this is only right and proper. Writing for me is seldom a matter of self-revelation or self-discovery. It is about creating something that stands quite apart from its creator.

Nevertheless, I sometimes wonder if I would and could have written my next book if my mother had been alive. It was called *Footsucker,* and it is a novel about a fetishist who is obsessed with women's feet and shoes. It is by no means a dirty book, and it is in only the vaguest sense autobiographical, but it does deal directly with sexuality, and it's probably not a book that a man, at least a man like me, would want his mother to read.

Footsucker is a book that received a lot of attention, both in the books pages and elsewhere. Foot fetishism is the kind of sexual aberration that can be discussed openly in a way that more extreme fetishes or sexual obsessions obviously cannot. Some people also find the subject inherently comic or absurd, though again this isn't a comic novel, and it certainly does not make fun of fetishists. I think that would be far too easy.

I was, and continue to be, interviewed more about *Footsucker* than about any other book I've ever written. The question I'm asked repeatedly is, "Are you a foot and shoe fetishist?" I used to say that this was an inappropriate question. In previous novels I'd written about muggers, murderers, terrorists, Fascists, Nazis, but nobody had ever asked if I was any of these things. So why was I now being asked if I was a foot fetishist? This strikes me as a perfectly reasonable response, but I'm also aware that it doesn't really answer the question.

So the simple answer is no, I am not a fetishist like the hero of my book. Indeed, I'm nothing like him at all. For one thing, I'm a writer and he's not. Another answer, however, is that obviously nobody devotes a year or so of his life to writing about a subject that doesn't in some way move or intrigue him. The more complicated answer, if still a little evasive, and one I think inherent in the book, is that we are all fetishists to a greater or lesser extent, and the corollary is that fetishists are by and large perfectly "normal."

Footsucker took me to America again, on a short publicity tour. There was a launch party for the book at a club in New York, and there I met someone who changed my life radically. Her name was (and is) Dian and she was the editor of a "fetish" magazine, and we experienced a real "across a crowded room" moment. We talked a little and it instantly became clear to both of us that we had the chance of an intense and, we hoped, permanent relationship. We took that chance, and we've been together ever since. This means that, in the phrase loved by blurb writers, I "divide my time" between London and New York. It's not an entirely easy or straightforward life but it works.

In some ways it seems a rather corny idea; fetish novelist meets fetish magazine editor and both find what they're looking for. All I can say is that we saw something more than that in each other and, need I add, that fetishism does not loom very large in our day-to-day lives. I have never written another novel about fetishism, and Dian now works in mainstream publishing. But the story of how we met still causes a great deal of amusement, and our relationship fully establishes my status as an Americophile.

*

Footsucker was a long way from being a bestseller but it helped to make my name better known. My next novel, *Bleeding London,* continued the process, and is probably my best known and most popular work to date, a book that speaks to a lot of people.

It is partly a revenge story; a petty criminal from the north of England travels to London to punish six men he believes have raped his girlfriend. He arrives in London and finds it a strange, alienating, and in many ways disappointing place, though ultimately he comes to love it. This is not precisely my own experience of London, but it's not far off, and this model of the relationship between the provincial man and the

metropolis is evidently recognizable to people who know very little about London or even England. Readers have told me the story would work if the book were set in Tokyo or Berlin.

And yet it is definitely a book about London. Another of its characters, called Stuart London, is attempting to walk down every one of its streets, crossing them out on a map as he goes, and he intends to commit suicide once he has finished and the map is finally all blacked out. This provided me with a great opportunity to indulge my fascination with the darker and more extraordinary parts of London. Some of the most favourable reviews say that the city emerges as a character in its own right.

Bleeding London was a book that got me invited to a number of literary festivals, in Toronto and Munich among others. It seemed to presage a new level of success and even fame, but progress in these areas is rarely straightforward for a writer. I felt that my next two novels, *Flesh Guitar* and *Female Ruins,* were somewhat neglected. I'm not saying this is entirely incomprehensible, they undoubtedly weren't such attention-grabbing books, and weren't about such obviously appealing subjects. *Flesh Guitar* is the story of a female rock guitarist, told through a series of parodies of Melville, Borges, and Bruce Chatwin, among others. *Female Ruins* concerns a woman coming to terms with the death of her late father, "the greatest English architect never to have built a building." These books have their fans but I have to accept that they're a minority taste. So it was not until my next and most recent novel, *Bedlam Burning,* that my work again received the kind of attention I had been hoping for.

The novel, set mostly in the mid-1970s, concerns a man who, under false pretenses, gets a job as a writer-in-residence in a very unorthodox and dubious lunatic asylum. The book examines a number of clichés about art being a form of madness, and about it being also a sort of therapy. I don't have a great deal of time for either of these ideas, but I could see there was great sport to be had with them. For what it's worth, my personal view is that yes, some writers are troubled by madness, but then so are some plumbers. It seems to me that ultimately madness is no more helpful to writers than it is to plumbers.

The book was widely perceived as a satire on the worlds of writing and publishing, as well as of academia and the psychiatric professions, and in certain critical circles this seemed to reinforce the idea that I am primarily a "satirist." I wasn't sure that this really describes what I do until I found a passage written by the literary critic C. Northrop Frye. He says that satire requires, "fantasy, a content recognized as grotesque, moral judgments (at least implicit), and a militant attitude to experience." And yes, I think that sounds very much like what I do in my writing, especially the part about the militant attitude to experience. It seems to me that every writer worth his or her salt has to have a robust militancy about them.

I also think that all good writers are at heart subversives; they want to point out that the emperor is wearing no clothes. I'm inclined to do this in life as well as in writing. It means that one always has an edgy, somewhat combative relationship to the world, but I'm not sure what other type of relationship is desirable, or even available. If that makes me a satirist, then I suppose I'm perfectly happy to accept that title.

*

As I write, a Hollywood movie studio owns an option on *Bedlam Burning;* indeed over half of my novels have been optioned for the movies at one time or another, although none of them has as yet been made into a film, and I'm not entirely convinced that one ever will be.

I'm not naive enough to think that the relationship between films and novels is a simple or easy one, but like most writers I would very much like to see at least one of my books turned into a film, to see my "vision" turned into actual images. The novelist tells himself that he can't really lose in this arrangement. If the film is good and popular he gets some reflected glory and perhaps some extra book sales. If the film is a complete disaster this is unlikely to do his reputation much harm. The public knows how often filmmakers mangle novels, and aren't generally inclined to blame the novelist. The shrewd writer is probably also aware however (and this is bound to cause him some profound ambivalence), that the best books almost never make the best movies.

No novelist wants to think that he's simply providing raw material for the movie industry. If he did, he'd presumably be writing screenplays. In my own case it seems that there's something in most of my books that attracts movie makers. I often deal with things that have a strong visual element; shoes, Volkswagens, architecture, electric guitars, for instance; and my novels tend to be strong on dialogue rather than, say, internal monologue or abstract stream of consciousness. Filmmakers appreciate this.

Nevertheless, there's often something distinctly unfilmic about my work; multiple unreliable narrators, people who keep diaries, oblique but crucial scenes set in different historical periods. These elements don't fit in with the typical movie model of conflict, complication, and resolution, but simply to leave them out means that you lose the essential nature of my works.

I love the movies. I've had some dealings with movie people, which have generally proved to be hilarious, frustrating, and the source of much wry anecdote. I've written a couple of unproduced (and probably unproducable) movie scripts, but it is rather unsatisfying work for a novelist. Film is a collaborative art and I think most novelists aren't very good at collaborating. Furthermore, at some point, the writer of a screenplay hands his words over to somebody else and gives up control. This is a painful procedure. When I write a novel I'm completely in control. I'm the director, the costume designer, the dialogue coach, the location manager, everything. This suits me very well, although I'm aware that there are times when giving up control may be no bad thing.

*

I said earlier that it's very hard for a writer to know what constitutes success. Failure I suppose is easier to measure; you remain unpublished and/or unread. Being published and finding a readership are obviously basic requirements for any version of success, but genuine success seems to be about something other than big advances and selling a lot of books.

We would all write bestsellers if we could, but we know that certain types of book, because of form or content, will never find a mass audience, but they're still worth writing, and that doesn't mean that they or their authors are failures. Money, of course, is a different matter. I don't think I've ever met an author who wrote simply for money, but I've also never met one for whom money wasn't vitally important. It's a measure of achievement, a sign of professionalism, proof that your work is wanted and has value. It also, of course, bears very little relation to your imagined worth. I tend to agree with Rudyard Kipling that failure and success are both impostors, but success is the kind of impostor that at least enables you to pay your bills.

I think that anyone who makes even the humblest form of art is always saying "look at me." I suspect that most of us are also saying, "look at me and love me." Clearly there's a contradiction here. By definition, not everyone who reads my work is going to love it. Indeed, some are going to positively hate it. Publishing your work involves putting yourself on the line, exposing your most intimate thoughts and feelings, and as Bette Davis said about growing old, it's not for wimps. Every author gets bad as well as good reviews, and the good ones never quite make up for the bad ones. A writer needs to be open, sensitive, aware, and self-aware, but he also needs to be as tough as old boots. I have personally known two novelists who killed themselves because their work was neglected or ignored, and frankly I'm surprised it's not more.

*

The longer you survive as a writer the more you find yourself compared to an ever-growing group of other writers. There's nothing wrong with that. Reviewers need a shorthand, new readers understandably want to know what they're getting before they start to read your books, and comparisons aren't always odious. One of the reviews of my first play, *Oscar,* compared me to Ben Jonson. This was unbelievably flattering and, of course, wholly absurd.

As a novelist I have been compared to Evelyn Waugh, Tom Robbins, George Perec, Vladimir Nabokov, both Martin and Kingsley Amis. One of the most satisfying comparisons came when the critic Robert Sandall compared my novel *Flesh Guitar* to Thomas Pynchon's *The Crying of Lot 49.* For me it really doesn't get much better than that. Whether it's true in any meaningful way is another question altogether.

I've also had certain of my novels compared to the work of David Lodge, and that was best of all, considering how alien and unapproachable his world seemed when I first read *The British Museum Is Falling Down* all those years before. It gets better still. A

few years ago I was invited to a literary festival and found myself on a stage with David Lodge, discussing how hard it is for male writers to create convincing female characters and vice versa. We understandably came to no very firm conclusion. After the event we went for a cup of coffee together, and as we sat there who should be passing but Malcolm Bradbury, the other great author of English campus novels—who asked if he could join us. The wheel seemed to have come more than full circle.

If you had tried to tell me when I was a sixteen-year-old boy in Sheffield, making my first attempts to write, that this kind of meeting might await me somewhere in the future, not only wouldn't I have believed you, I'd have thought you were making cruel fun of me. Back then I assumed that authors—even the humblest of them—inhabited some ethereal plain where mere mortals didn't tread. I'm glad that I no longer have that illusion, but I'm equally glad to be among their number.

From time to time I do some book reviewing for the *New York Times Book Review* and early on I was invited into the office to meet Chip McGrath, the editor. Rather formally he thanked me for the work I'd done and I said I was more than happy to do it, that I liked to write.

"Well that makes a change," said Chip McGrath. "Because most writers just like to *whine.*"

I did my best to assure him that I wasn't that sort of writer, that I try, at least so far as my working habits are concerned, to emulate Anthony Burgess, who once said that he never turned down any reasonable offer of work, and that he didn't turn down many *unreasonable* ones either.

I am much the same. Consequently, in recent times I have found myself asked to write about photography, chair design, gardening, cricket, collecting, food, and chaos theory. I've written a couple of beginners' guides to Andy Warhol and Frank Lloyd Wright. I did it because I was asked to. These are topics that I'm basically interested in but writing to someone else's brief, for a newspaper or magazine that has specific requirements, can be very refreshing. It never feels like hack work, and at some point it all feeds back into the novels and enriches them.

Geoff and Dian, New York, 2001

Yes, writing is a mysterious and spiritual process, but it is also the daily activity that writers simply have to get up every morning and do. It is a job, and it is certainly hard work. The mystery and spirit come about as a *result* of that hard work, not in spite of or separately from it.

When you begin writing a novel you think you're building a great Gothic cathedral, full of light and air, craftsmanship and spirituality, something that embodies all humanity's greatest achievements and aspirations. After you've been working on it for a while you realize you were being absurdly overambitious and presumptuous, and at this point you'd settle for constructing something serviceable and not too ugly, something that people might like and find a use for, like a sports hall or a museum. By the very end of

the process you're happy if you've built something that stands up and keeps out the wind and rain; a bus shelter or a greenhouse.

Then the public arrives, professional and amateur alike, the critics and the readers. They look at what you've done, and tell you that you haven't built a greenhouse at all, but rather a brick air raid shelter. You console yourself with the thought that at least you haven't built an instant ruin.

*

In one sense writing has given me everything; a living, my friends, my self-respect, my self-definition. It's allowed me to do things and go to places that I could once only have dreamt of. In another way, however, it's been limiting. For most of my career my income has been both small and irregular. I often seemed to be surviving by the skin of my teeth. I used to tell myself that I couldn't possibly support a family, and that is at least partly why I have never had children. Sometimes this is a cause of great regret. But the truth is, I know that people with lower incomes than mine have still found ways of having a family, and I suspect it may have more to do with my belief that family life is one of the great "enemies of promise." Raymond Carver has written movingly about the resentment he felt towards his own children, who prevented him from writing, and I imagine I might have had very similar feelings. I'm not sure that creation and procreation are completely antithetical, but I chose the former over the latter, and it was a very deliberate choice. And if this sounds like a selfish choice I couldn't deny that.

I have arranged my life so that I spend the majority of every day alone in a room, reading and writing. It's a lonely life in many ways, and often leads to an unhealthy degree of self-absorption and solipsism. It's also essentially a very repetitious life; putting words down on paper, editing and rearranging them, sometimes throwing them away and starting again. Distractions in the form of meetings, phone calls, and the occasional public appearance are always welcome, but they have nothing to do with the real task of writing. On the other hand, I'm completely aware that it's a very easy life indeed compared with working in a factory or on a building site.

In my novels I have regularly written about characters who are obsessed and obsessive. They tend to be fixated on ideas, objects, and people, with sex and love, and sometimes with obsession itself. To the extent that I have created these characters, I know them very well, sympathize with them, and understand the nature of obsession. My own personal obsession, however, is only with writing. It's mine, and I appear to be sticking to it.

BIOGRAPHICAL AND CRITICAL SOURCES:

PERIODICALS

Book, September, 2000, Chris Jones, review of *Female Ruins,* p. 81.

Booklist, May 1, 2000, Brendan Dowling, review of *Female Ruins,* p. 1653.

Library Journal, May 1, 2000, Barbara Love, review of *Female Ruins,* p. 154; February 1, 2002, Barbara Love, review of *Bedlam Burning,* p. 132.

Magazine of Fantasy and Science Fiction, February, 2000, Charles De Lint, review of *Flesh Guitar,* p. 23.

New Statesman and Society, October 7, 1994, p. 47.

New York Times, February 27, 2002, Richard Eder, "When the Imposter Tries to Do the Job in Earnest," p. B7.

New York Times Book Review, February 5, 1995; January 4, 1998; March 14, 1999; July 23, 2000, Matthew Klam, "A Doll's House," p. 11; February 10, 2002, Marcel Theroux, "Insanity Clauses," p. 10.

Publishers Weekly, September 6, 1993, p. 83; May 1, 1995, p. 41; August 21, 1995, p. 46; August 12, 1996, p. 63; August 4, 1997, p. 62; December 14, 1998, p. 56; April 3, 2000, review of *Female Ruins,* p. 61; November 19, 2001, review of *Bedlam Burning,* p. 47.

Time, January 23, 1995, p. 59.

Washington Post, February 19, 2002, Chris Lehmann, "Into the Cuckoo's Nest," p. C04.

*   *   *

NOE, Randolph 1939-

PERSONAL: Born November 2, 1939, in Indianapolis, IN; son of Clem Moffat and Bernice (maiden name, Baker; later surname, Reiley) Noe; married Anne Will, March 2, 1968 (divorced); married, September 11, 2000; wife's name Marsha (a hospital director); children: Reiley, Anne Will, Randolph, Jr., Jonathan Baker. *Nationality:* American. *Ethnicity:* "Anglo-French-Native American." *Education:* Attended Franklin College, Indiana State University, B.S., 1964; Indiana University, J.D., 1967. *Politics:* Democrat. *Religion:* Roman Catholic. *Hobbies and other interests:* Legal and literary history.

ADDRESSES: Home—3242 Crossbill Rd., Louisville, KY 40213. *Office*—Tilford, Dobbins, Alexander, Buckaway & Black, 1400 One Riverfront Plaza, Louisville, KY 40202. *E-mail*—rnoe@tilfordlaw.com.

CAREER: Attorney. Citizens Fidelity Bank, Louisville, KY, trust officer, 1968-70; partner of various law firms and attorney in private practice, Louisville, KY, 1971-

93; Tilford, Dobbins, Alexander, Buckaway & Black (law firm), Louisville, KY, attorney, 1994—. Holy Rosary Academy, member of board of trustees, 1978-81; Tekawitha Conference of Native American Catholics, member.

MEMBER: American College of Probate Counsel (fellow), American Society for Legal History.

WRITINGS:

Kentucky Probate Methods, Bobbs-Merrill (New York, NY), 1976, supplement, 1990.
The Shawnee Indians: An Annotated Bibliography, Scarecrow Press (Lanham, MD), 2001.

Editor, *Kentucky Law Summary,* 1986—.

WORK IN PROGRESS: Stout, Bold, and Cunning: A History of the Shawnee Indians; a bibliography of the English legal profession to the end of the nineteenth century; research on other aspects of Shawnee history and culture.

*   *   *

NORDSTROM, Byron J. 1943-

PERSONAL: Born August 30, 1943, in Minneapolis, MN; son of Alvin L. (in business) and Bernice B. (a homemaker) Nordstrom; married Janet Larson (a physical therapist), June 8, 1968; children: Kristian, Hans. *Ethnicity:* "Scandinavian American." *Education:* Lawrence University of Wisconsin, B.A., 1965; University of Minnesota, M.A., 1968, Ph.D., 1972. *Hobbies and other interests:* Cabinetry, playing the lute.

ADDRESSES: Office—Department of History, Gustavus Adolphus College, St. Peter, MN 56082. *E-mail*—byron@gac.edu.

CAREER: Educator. Gustavus Adolphus College, St. Peter, MN, professor of history and Scandinavian studies, 1974—. University of Washington, Seattle, visiting assistant professor, 1977; University of East Anglia, visiting professor, 1984. Consultant to Swedish Council of America.

MEMBER: Society for the Advancement of Scandinavian Study, Swedish-American Historical Society.

WRITINGS:

Swedes in Minnesota, Swedish Council of America, 1976.
Dictionary of Scandinavian History, Greenwood Press (Westport, CT), 1986.
Scandinavia since 1500, University of Minnesota Press (Minneapolis, MN), 2000.
Sweden: A History, Greenwood Press (Westport, CT), 2002.

WORK IN PROGRESS: Scandinavia between the World Wars.

O

O'CONNELL, Mary

PERSONAL: Female; Children: two. *Education:* University of Kansas, B.A.; attended Iowa Writer's Workshop.

ADDRESSES: Home—Lawrence, KS. *Agent*—c/o Author Mail, Atlantic Monthly Press, 841 Broadway, 4th Floor, New York, NY 10003-4793.

CAREER: Lawrence Arts Center, Lawrence, KS, teacher.

WRITINGS:

Living with Saints, Atlantic Monthly Press (New York, NY), 2001.

Contributor of stories to literary magazines, including *The Sun* and *Mid-American Review.*

WORK IN PROGRESS: A novel about three friends.

SIDELIGHTS: Mary O'Connell made her literary debut in 2001 with *Living with Saints,* a collection of ten short stories about women living in a complex world. Inspired by the autobiography of Therese of Lisieux, *Story of a Soul,* and seeing a painting of the martyrdom of Saint Agnes, O'Connell wrote her first "saint" story, "The Patron Saint of Girls."

"I didn't set out to write a collection of saint stories," O'Connell admitted to Chuck Leddy of *Book Reporter.* "But I was so struck by the girl saints. I kept making the deal with myself: I'll just write one more and then move on, I'll just write one more. . . ." As it happened, a literary agent read the story "Saint Ursula and Her Maidens" in *The Sun,* a small magazine, and contacted O'Connell, asking if she had enough stories for a book. *Living with Saints* was the result.

Living with Saints contains stories that draw parallels between the lives of contemporary women and Christian women saints. The content, however, might surprise some reasons. "I wasn't concerned about being pegged as a religious writer, but I definitely worried that very pious people would find the stories a bit satanic," O'Connell said. "But, in my mind at least, the book is more generally about women and struggling and hoping and love and longing, which is the story of the saints, too."

For example, in "Saint Therese of Lisieux," a Catholic high school girl keeps the secret that her father is molesting her, and wishes she could escape the world. In "Saint Anne" (patron saint of mothers), a single mother tries to make ends meet, and in "The Patron Saint of Travelers" several American women share a London apartment.

"It is hard to believe that this is the author's first published collection," Aisling Foster remarked in *Times Literary Supplement.* "O'Connell writes superb dialogue, a bracing mix of modern vernacular and eternal spiritual longings," wrote a critic for *Kirkus Reviews,* who cited "Sister Ursula with Her Maidens,"

"Saint Therese of Lisieux," and "Saint Dymphna." In *Publishers Weekly,* a critic wrote, "O'Connell has an uncanny ear for dialogue and an otherworldly communion with the hearts and minds of adolescent girls in particular." *Library Journal*'s Debbie Bogenschutz liked the humor, which she called "often biting but never malicious, authentic and never forced."

Yet under O'Connell's humor lies something more. "Although the lives of Mary O'Connell's characters may seem light years away from her original inspiration," Foster said, "their various journeys towards enlightenment and apotheosis are not only sinfully funny but curiously uplifting." Leddy observed, "Whether you're religious or not, these stories resonate in their profound search for meaning." *Booklist*'s Mary Carroll said the tales in *Living with Saints* are "sure to enchant some readers and enrage others."

BIOGRAPHICAL AND CRITICAL SOURCES:

PERIODICALS

Booklist, September 15, 2001, Mary Carroll, review of *Living with Saints,* p. 193.
Kirkus Reviews, August 1, 2001, review of *Living with Saints,* p. 1057.
Library Journal, August, 2001, Debbie Bogenschutz, review of *Living with Saints,* p. 168.
Los Angeles Times, November 25, 2001, Mark Rozzo, review of *Living with Saints,* p. 10.
New York Times Book Review, November 18, 2001, Meghan O'Rourke, "Girl Saints," p. 59.
Publishers Weekly, August 27, 2001, review of *Living with Saints,* p. 47.
Times Literary Supplement, February 8, 2002, Aisling Foster, review of *Living with Saints,* p. 24.

OTHER

BookBrowser, http://www.bookbrowser.com/ (May 8, 2002), Jonathan Shipley, review of *Living with Saints.*
Bookreporter, http://www.bookreporter.com/ (May 8, 2002), interview.
Network Chicago, http://www.networkchicago.com/ (May 8, 2002), Linda Bubon, review of *Living with Saints.**

O'CONNER, Patricia T.

PERSONAL: Married Stewart Kellerman (an author). *Education:* Graduate of Grinnell College. *Hobbies and other interests:* Reading, photography, gardening, walking in the woods.

ADDRESSES: Home—CT. *Agent*—c/o Author Mail, Harcourt, 15 East 26th St., New York, NY 10003-4793.

CAREER: Writer. *New York Times,* New York, NY, editor, 1982-97. Also worked as a reporter/editor for the *Waterloo Courier,* beginning 1973, and as editor for the *Des Moines Register* and the *Wall Street Journal.*

WRITINGS:

Woe Is I: The Grammarphobe's Guide to Better English in Plain English, Putnam (New York, NY), 1996.
Words Fail Me: What Everyone Who Writes Should Know about Writing, Harcourt (New York, NY), 1999.
(With husband, Stewart Kellerman) *You Send Me: Getting It Right When You Write Online,* Harcourt (New York, NY), 2002.

SIDELIGHTS: Patricia T. O'Conner was an editor with the *New York Times* who has written three books about writing. In *Woe Is I: The Grammarphobe's Guide to Better English in Plain English* O'Conner addresses parts of speech, proper usage, and common errors in such chapters as "Woe Is I: Therapy for Pronoun Anxiety,""Plurals Before Swine: Blunders With Numbers," "Yours Truly: The Possessives and the Possessed," "They Beg to Disagree: Putting Verbs in Their Place," "Verbal Abuse: Words on the Endangered List," "Comma Sutra: The Joy of Punctuation," and others. Daniel Pinkwater wrote in the *New York Times Book Review* that the book is "lighthearted and funny. . . . [and] useful. There is precisely enough (and no more) wit and illustrative humor." *Kliatt* reviewer Claire Rosser observed that "O'Conner's friendly approach may be just what will help many flounderers. . . . This one wins for clarity and quiet charm." Charles R. Crawley wrote in *Technical Communications* that "in addition to O'Conner's ability to do clear technical writing, her use of examples is superb. She uses many well-known fictional personalities, such as the Kramdens, the Cleavers, and Jane Marple. . . . She alludes to old prize fighters Jack Dempsey and Gene Tunny to describe how people used to write. . . . She also has a very good sense of humor, which definitely helps her voice come through. You begin to think how much fun it would be to sit in on a seminar of hers." Crawley noted that the book's glossary "is good enough to be read narratively, and the bibliography is instructive enough except for the conspicuous absence of *The Chicago Manual of Style,* which disagrees with some of her grammatical stances."

Kimberly B. Marlow wrote in the online edition of the *Seattle Times* that in O'Connor's *Words Fail Me: What Everyone Who Writes Should Know about Writing* she "covers all manner of writerly challenges: ways to avoid cliches and passive writing, tips for saying tough stuff with honesty, ideas for getting organized and staying on track with a project." Chapters include "Pompous Circumstances: Hold the Baloney," "The Life of the Party: Verbs That Zing," "Lost Horizon: What's the Point of View," "Smothering Heights: Misbehaving Modifiers," and "Everybody's Favorite Subject: I, Me, My." A reviewer for the online *Writers Write* commented that *Words Fail Me* "is a superb reference for student and professional writers alike, with practical advice, relevant examples, and O'Conner's brand of witty humor. . . . Think of it as a user's manual for words." Roxianne Moore reviewed the book for *Suite 101* online and noted that it is "aimed at nonfiction writers" but felt O'Conner's suggestions "will also be useful for fiction writers." Moore particularly liked O'Conner's chapter titled "Get with the Program: The Organized Writer," saying "she covers everything from how to keep track of your ideas before they get lost to tacking those ideas and tidbits onto the bones of your project." Diane Cole wrote in the *New York Times Book Review* that O'Conner "prefers jesting to scolding and dispenses wisdom with a light touch." Cole called O'Conner "a self-styled 'Grammar Moses.'"

In 2002, O'Conner and husband Stewart Kellerman published *You Send Me: Getting It Right When You Write Online,* a guide for writing on the Internet. Focused particularly on writing e-mails, O'Conner and Kellerman dispense suggestions for getting to the point, getting facts correct, and e-mail etiquette.

In an interview with Claire E. White on the *Writers Write* Web site, O'Conner was asked about the tendency in e-mails to avoid basic sentence structure and use slang. O'Conner replied, "Email seems to fall somewhere between speech and formal writing. But when you're writing an electronic message of any kind, you should first consider your audience. . . . If you're emailing your Senator, your professor, or a prospective employer, be just as careful as you would in a written letter—that is, do your best with grammar, spelling, punctuation, and composition. If you're emailing your best friend, you can relax a bit, just as you would in speaking to that person. But don't send anything that could be hurtful or embarrassing if it fell into the wrong hands. Especially at work!"

BIOGRAPHICAL AND CRITICAL SOURCES:

PERIODICALS

Kliatt, September, 1998, Claire Rosser, review of *Woe Is I: The Grammerphobe's Guide to Better English in Plain English,* p. 32.
Library Journal, June 15, 2002, Herbert E. Shapiro, review of *You Send Me: Getting It Right When You Write Online,* p. 76.
Technical Communication, November, 1997, Charles R. Crawley, review of *Woe Is I,* p. 439.
New York Times Book Review, September 15, 1996, Daniel Pinkwater, review of *Woe is I,* p. 31; August 9, 1998, p. 28; December 6, 1998, p. 97; September 19, 1999, p. 20.

OTHER

Seattle Times Web Site, http://www.seattletimes.com/ (April 13, 2000),"A Few Choice 'Words' To Help Struggling Writers,".
Suite 101, http://www.suite101.com/ (April 13, 2000).
Writers Write, http://www.writerswrite.com/ (April 13, 2000), review of *Words Fail Me: What Everyone Who Writes Should Know about Writing*; (December, 1999), "A Conversation with Patricia O'Conner."*

*   *   *

O'DONNELL, Ruan

PERSONAL: Male. Education: National University of Ireland, B.A., M.A.; Australian National University, Ph.D.

ADDRESSES: Office—Department of Government and Society, University of Limerick, Limerick, Ireland; fax +35-36-133-0316. *E-mail*—Ruan.Odonnell@ul.ie.

CAREER: University of Limerick, Limerick, Ireland, lecturer in modern history.

WRITINGS:

(Editor of revision) *Insurgent Wicklow: The Story as Told by Brother Luke Cullen, O.C.D.,* Kestrel Books (Bray, Ireland), 1998.

1798 Diary, Irish Times Books (Dublin, Ireland), 1998.

The Rebellion in Wicklow, 1798, Irish Academic Press (Dublin. Ireland), 1998.

Aftermath: Post-Rebellion Insurgency in Wicklow, 1799-1803, Irish Academic Press (Dublin, Ireland), 1999.

Exploring Wicklow's Rebel Past, 1799-1803: History, Folklore, and Sites of the Wicklow Rebellion, [Dublin, Ireland], 1999.

BIOGRAPHICAL AND CRITICAL SOURCES:

PERIODICALS

American Historical Review, April, 2001, Marianne Elliott, review of *The Rebellion in Wicklow, 1798,* p. 648.

Choice, December, 1998, C. W. Wood, Jr., review of *The Rebellion in Wicklow, 1798,* p. 746.

English Historical Review, September, 2001, Paddy McNally, review of *Aftermath: Post-Rebellion Insurgency in Wicklow, 1799-1803,* p. 979.

History Today, October, 1997, review of *The Rebellion in Wicklow, 1798,* p. 55.

OTHER

University of Limerick, http://www.ul.ie/ (November 15, 1999).*

*   *   *

OEFFINGER, John C. 1952-

PERSONAL: Born October 30, 1952, in Ft. Sill, OK; son of Jack (an attorney) and Sally (Lehman) Oeffinger; married Kathryn Pourteau (an e-learning consultant), May 11, 1975; children: J. Clayton II. *Education:* Texas A & M University, B.A. (anthropology), 1976, graduate work, 1976-77. *Politics:* Democrat. *Religion:* Catholic. *Hobbies and other interests:* Photography.

ADDRESSES: Home and office—11508 Gunfight Lane, Austin, TX 78748. *E-mail*—john@oeffingers.com.

CAREER: Texas Hospital Association, Austin, senior vice president, 1988-96; HealthExec, Inc., Houston, TX, vice president, 1997-98; Healthway Interactive, Inc., Austin, director of e-learning and marketing, 1998-99; ArticuLearn, Inc., Austin, director of Internet applications development, 2000-01; Oeffingers.com, Austin, principal, 2001—. Texas Hospital Education and Research Foundation, board member, 1988-95; member, UNIDO Consultative Group and Informatics Technology for Development, 1988.

MEMBER: Writer's League of Texas, Austin Civil War Round Table, American Society for Training and Development.

AWARDS, HONORS: Diploma de Honor, Hospital Clinico Universitario Jose Joaquain Aguirre, Universidad de Chile, 1986; Media award, American Academy of Nursing, and Presidential Award, Texas Nurses Association, both 1992, both for McMurphy nursing project.

WRITINGS:

A Soldier's General: The Civil War Letter of Major General Lafayette McLaws, University of North Carolina Press (Chapel Hill, NC), 2002.

WORK IN PROGRESS: Research leading to a biography of Major General Lafayette McLaws; research leading to a division history of the McLaws Division.

SIDELIGHTS: John C. Oeffinger told *CA:* "I spent a weekend in the University of North Carolina's special collections library to answer a simple research question. I stumbled upon an untapped historical resource that historians have neglected. During his service in the Confederate Army, Major General Lafayette McLaws (1821-1897) served under and alongside such famous officers as Robert E. Lee, Joseph E. Johnston, James Longstreet, and John B. Hood. He played a significant role in some of the most crucial battles of the U.S. Civil War, including Harpers Ferry, Antietam, Fredericksburg, Chancellorsville, and Gettysburg. A prolific letter writer, McLaws left behind a wealth of handwritten material documenting his experiences before and during the war. Despite all this, no biography of McLaws or history of his division has ever been published.

"*A Soldier's General* gathers ninety-five letters written by McLaws to his wife and other family members between 1858 and 1865, making these rich sources available to a wide audience for the first time. The letters, transcribed from McLaws's notoriously poor handwriting, contain a wealth of opinion and information about life and morale in the Confederate army, Civil War-era politics, the impact of war on the Confederate home front, the Southern press, and one man's efforts to advise and remain connected with his wife and children while engaged in a distant conflict. Among the fascinating threads woven through the letters is the story of McLaws's fractured relationship with childhood friend Longstreet, who had McLaws relieved of command in 1863. (McLaws ultimately demanded a court-martial to restore his honor.) The introduction traces McLaws's life from his beginnings in Augusta, Georgia through his days at West Point, his experiences in the U.S. Army and the war with Mexico, his marriage to Emily Taylor (a niece of former President Zachary Taylor), his Civil War exploits, and his postwar years. The next step will be a biography and articles on McLaws's family and the role they played in his life.

"I have always had a researcher's heart. Working on the Internet pays the bills so that I can add new insights and information to the historical record. My approach to writing has changed substantially, especially in moving from passive to active voice. Editors and reviewers have challenged me to pay attention to the details and be accurate. Most importantly, they have encouraged the research to bring the characters to life using their own words. *A Soldier's General* is a terrific story that has as much meaning today as it did in the 1800s."

*   *   *

OLLESON, Philip

PERSONAL: Male. *Education:*Cambridge University, M.A.; University of Nottingham, Ph.D.

ADDRESSES: Office—School of Continuing Education, University of Nottingham, Jubilee Campus, Wollaton Road, Nottingham, England NG8 1BB. *E-mail*—philip.olleson@nottingham.ac.uk.

CAREER: School of Continuing Education, University of Nottingham, Nottingham, NG8 1BB England, senior lecturer.

WRITINGS:

(Editor) *The Letters of Samuel Wesley: Professional and Social Correspondence, 1797-1837,* Oxford University Press (New York, NY), 2001.
(With Michael Kassler) *Samuel Wesley (1766-1837): A Source Book,* Ashgate (Aldershot, England), 2001.

Also author of *The Rise of the String Quartet,* 1974.

WORK IN PROGRESS: Another collection of Samuel Wesley's letters.

SIDELIGHTS: Philip Olleson has done extensive scholarly research on the life and work of Samuel Wesley, a prominent English composer and musician of the late eighteenth and early nineteenth centuries. Wesley was the nephew of John Wesley, who founded the Methodist church, and the son of Charles Wesley, who wrote numerous hymns. Samuel, however, scandalized his family by embracing Roman Catholicism and engaging in illicit love affairs. He also suffered from mental illness, alternating manic and depressive periods, and he spent time in an asylum. Furthermore, he had chronic financial problems, which at one point put him in a debtors' prison. Despite his troubles, Wesley "worked with exceptional energy on all possible fronts—composing, performing, proselytizing and writing about music—but achieved only moderate success in an English musical world which did not yet sustain enough professional activity to make full use of his potential contributions to concert life," related Judith Weir in a *Times Literary Supplement* review of Olleson's edition of *The Letters of Samuel Wesley: Professional and Social Correspondence, 1797-1837.* Additionally, the composer's personal difficulties may have been held against him in some quarters, Weir reported, as "he was passed over for many important appointments as an organist for which he was evidently well qualified."

Weir noted that letters dealing with Wesley's rather fascinating private life are largely absent from Olleson's volume; the focus is on his musical career. The letters begin with those written when Wesley was thirty-one years old, and the only family letters included are those touching on music. *The Letters of Samuel Wesley* contains only about half of his existing letters, which total about 600, and more family letters are to be published in another book. Such a separation has precedent, Weir pointed out: "Wesley himself drew a firm line between his personal troubles and his professional enthusiasms." His letters and Olleson's supplemental material, she and other reviewers observed, offer significant insight into the life of a professional musician and the musical topics that most interested Wesley; for instance, he was an early enthusiast of J. S. Bach. "A brief chronology and biography provide a helpful framework for the letters, which are thoroughly annotated," J. Girdham commented in *Choice*, while Weir remarked, "The editor's copious footnotes explaining the endless allusions to now forgotten musicians and events are welcome." A companion volume, *Samuel Wesley (1766-1837): A Source Book*, which Olleson prepared with Michael Kassler, offers further details on Wesley's family, as well as lists of his compositions, a bibliography, and much other information; this is "an important reference source," K. A. Abromeit wrote in *Choice*. Weir concluded her review of the letters collection with praise for Olleson's efforts as editor. "Wesley," she said, "whose own publishing ventures came to little, and whose contributions to musical learning were never given their due value . . . would have been amazed and delighted to see this beautifully produced book, doubtless pausing only a moment before dashing off a long and genial letter of approbation to its precise and literate editor, Philip Olleson."

BIOGRAPHICAL AND CRITICAL SOURCES:

PERIODICALS

Choice, February, 2002, J. Girdham, review of *The Letters of Samuel Wesley: Professional and Social Correspondence, 1797-1837*, p. 1058; March, 2002, K. A. Abromeit, review of *Samuel Wesley (1766-1837): A Source Book*, pp. 1208, 1210.
Times Literary Supplement, November 23, 2001, Judith Weir, "All Is up or Down: Samuel Wesley's Life of Passionate Penury," pp. 5-6.*

OSBORNE, Eliza 1946-

PERSONAL: Born 1946.

ADDRESSES: Home—Northampton, MA. *Agent*—c/o Author Mail, Soho Press, 853 Broadway, New York, NY 10003.

CAREER: Author.

WRITINGS:

The Distance Between, Soho Press (New York, NY), 2000.

Contributor to anthologies, journals, magazines, and newspapers.

SIDELIGHTS: Eliza Osborne's novel, *The Distance Between,* documents its protagonist's four hundred-mile journey home. *Seattle Times* reviewer Wingate Packard wrote that this "sure-footed first novel is an enjoyable picaresque . . . I admire Osborne's witty marriage of an old style of story . . . with a heroine focused on motherhood." When Mattie Welch, married and the mother of two sons, learns from her sister that her parents have been badly injured in a car accident, she leaves Massachusetts for Pennsylvania on a trip that allows her to examine her fragile relationship with her mother and observe other mother-daughter relationships along the way. *Library Journal* contributor Jan Blodgett called Osborne's characters "at once fragile and angry, giving and distant, and lovable and unlikable."

The story opens with Mattie picking up a pregnant teen and taking her to the hospital to deliver and wait for the arrival of her own mother. While still on the road, Mattie learns that her mother has died, and she takes a side trip with a mother and daughter to an airport where a second daughter is arriving. After making a stop, Mattie finds a small girl asleep in her back seat. A *Publishers Weekly* reviewer called this scene "the novel's most moving and illuminating encounter." The reviewer observed that Osborne "strikes a resonant emotional chord." Mattie's mother had been a different person, a country singer, before Mattie was born—a fact Mattie discovered when she found newspaper clippings and old Gibson guitars in the attic. She wonders if it was her birth that changed her mother into the person she had become, a woman who had been hard to love. Neal Wyatt, reviewing the novel in *Booklist*, called Osborne's language "spare but enlivened with flashes of purely joyful writing." Charles Wyrick wrote for *BookPage* online that Osborne "is a writer of such inestimable talent one cannot help but hear poems in her prose."

BIOGRAPHICAL AND CRITICAL SOURCES:

PERIODICALS

Booklist, December 1, 2000, Neal Wyatt, review of *The Distance Between,* p. 686.
Library Journal, December, 1999, Jan Blodgett, review of *The Distance Between,* p. 188.
Publishers Weekly, November 8, 1999, review of *The Distance Between,* p. 48.
Seattle Times, January 30, 2000, Wingate Packard, "*The Distance Between* Is Enjoyable, Thoughtful," p. M5.

OTHER

BookPage, http://www.bookpage.com/ (November 16, 2000).*

* * *

O'TOOLE, James M. 1950-

PERSONAL: Born 1950. *Education:* Boston College, Ph.D., 1987.

ADDRESSES: Office—Department of History, Boston College, 140 Commonwealth Ave., Chestnut Hill, MA 02467. *E-mail*—james.otoole@bc.edu.

CAREER: Boston College, Chestnut Hill, MA, associate professor of history. Has worked as archivist for New England Historic Genealogy Society, Massachusetts State Archives, and Roman Catholic Archdiocese of Boston, and taught courses on archives at University of Massachusetts, Boston.

WRITINGS:

Guide to the Archives of the Archdiocese of Boston, Garland (New York, NY), 1982.
Understanding Archives and Manuscripts, Society of American Archivists (Chicago, IL), 1991.
Basic Standards for Diocesan Archives: A Guide for Bishops, Chancellors, and Archivists, Association of Catholic Diocesan Archivists (Chicago, IL), 1991.
(Editor) *The Records of American Business,* Society of American Archivists (Chicago, IL), 1997.
Militant and Triumphant: William Henry O'Connell and the Catholic Church in Boston, 1859-1944, University of Notre Dame Press (Notre Dame, IN), 1992.
Passing for White: Race, Religion, and the Healy Family, 1820-1920, University of Massachusetts Press (Amherst, MA), 2002.

SIDELIGHTS: Archivist turned history professor James M. O'Toole attracted wide attention with *Militant and Triumphant: William Henry O'Connell and the Catholic Church in Boston, 1859-1944,* a study of the longtime archbishop of Boston. O'Connell is "one of the least attractive figures in U.S. Catholic history," commented Gerald P. Fogarty in a review of the biography for *America.* Born to Irish immigrants in Lowell, Massachusetts, in 1859, O'Connell was ordained as a priest in 1884. He rose through the ecclesiastical ranks to become bishop of Portland, Maine, in 1901 and archbishop of Boston in 1907. O'Connell was a voice for the absolute authority of the Vatican over U.S. Catholics, some of whom, in the late nineteenth century, were seeking to make the church more democratic and pluralistic. He became known for his iron-fisted rule and his appetite for travel and luxurious living, but Boston's Irish Catholics did not seem to mind, as they saw him as an example of upward mobility for their people.

"While Boston's Catholics have long stated that O'Connell gave them a sense of pride, there was another side to his story and that is the one O'Toole tells so well," observed Forgarty. O'Connell, for instance, demanded detailed and accurate financial reports from his subordinates but was known to appropriate church funds for his personal use. And while exhorting Catholics to adhere to the church's moral teachings, O'Connell tolerated the breaking of celibacy vows by his nephew, Monsignor James P. E. O'Connell, and another priest, both of whom were married in secret. The exposure of their arrangements, in the 1920s, cost the archbishop a great deal of his power, according to O'Toole. He also suggests that William O'Connell had homosexual experiences. James Carroll, writing in *Atlantic,* thought O'Toole tended to "adopt the breathlessness of expose" in dealing with sexual matters, but added that "his thorough documentation of sordid and secret decadence speaks volumes about what outwardly repressive regimes like O'Connell's really mean."

Jon K. Reynolds, reviewing *MIlitant and Triumphant* for *New England Quarterly,* found the biography "a balanced and readable study that presents the man, warts and all, without dwelling on the sensational." Meanwhile, Thomas J. Rowland remarked in *Journal of American Culture* that "even if one comes away from reading this work, failing to discover any measurable sympathy for the man or any redeemable qualities of note in his character, O'Toole has shown that historical biography remains a vital way to gain insight into the life and times of the cardinal's contemporaries." The book, he continued, is also "useful in that it succeeds in redirecting American Catholic history towards a more healthy and honest evaluation of the past."

Another fascinating episode from the history of the Catholic Church in America is explored in *Passing for White: Race, Religion, and the Healy Family, 1820-1920.* This book recounts the story of Irish immigrant Michael Morris Healy, who owned a plantation in Georgia and married his African-American slave, Eliza Clark. The union produced nine children who were born slaves but were smuggled to the North before the U.S. Civil War. With the help of the Catholic Church, the Healys were able to pass for white and acquired solid educations. Many became priests or nuns, going on to serve in high position in Church organizations.

O'Toole has received praise as well for his writings on the archivist's craft. His *Guide to the Archives of the Archdiocese of Boston* is a "meticulous" work that "rivals the care [the archives'] administrators have taken to preserve the record," in the opinion of *Church History* contributor John P. Marschall. Francis J. We-

ber, writing in *Catholic Historical Review,* characterized the work as well-organized and featuring "detailed historical explanations," and he further called it "magnificent" and "monumental." *The Records of American Business,* edited by O'Toole, is a "valuable book" dealing with issues surrounding "the state and role of business archives in the United States," reported Geoffrey Jones in *Business History.* To *American Archivist* reviewer Michael Moosberger, the points made in the book on business archives are equally relevant to other archives, so the work constitutes "an important resource, not only for the business historian, business archivist, or corporate executive, but for all of us involved in the archival enterprise."

BIOGRAPHICAL AND CRITICAL SOURCES:

PERIODICALS

America, April 3, 1993, Gerald P. Fogarty, review of *Militant and Triumphant: William Henry O'Connell and the Catholic Church in Boston, 1859-1944,* p. 19.

American Archivist, summer, 1991, Peter J. Wosh, review of *Basic Standards for Diocesan Archives: A Guide for Bishops, Chancellors, and Archivists,* pp. 429-430; spring, 1999, Michael Moosberger, review of *The Records of American Business,* pp. 177-181.

Atlantic, July, 1992, James Carroll, review of *Militant and Triumphant,* p. 90.

Business History, April, 1999, Geoffrey Jones, review of *The Records of American Business,* p. 158.

Business History Review, autumn, 1998, Albert F. Bartovics, review of *The Records of American Business,* p. 519.

Catholic Historical Review, January, 1983, Francis J. Weber, review of *Guide to the Archives of the Archdiocese of Boston,* pp. 119-120.

Church History, March, 1984, John P. Marschall, review of *Guide to the Archives of the Archdiocese of Boston,* p. 150.

Journal of American Culture, spring, 1994, Thomas J. Rowland, review of *Militant and Triumphant,* pp. 96-97.

New England Quarterly, March, 1993, Jon K. Reynolds, review of *Militant and Triumphant,* pp. 137-139.*

OWEN, John M(alloy) 1962-

PERSONAL: Born 1962.

ADDRESSES: Office—Cabell Hall, Room 232, University of Virginia, P.O. Box 400787, Charlottesville 22904-4787. *E-mail*—jmo4n@virginia.edu.

CAREER: University of Virginia, Charlottesville, VA, on faculty of government and foreign affairs department.

WRITINGS:

Liberalism and War Decisions: Great Britain and the U.S. Civil War, Center for International Security and Arms Control (Stanford, CA), 1996.
Liberal Peace, Liberal War: American Politics and International Security, Cornell University Press (Ithaca, NY), 1997.

SIDELIGHTS: John M. Owen is a political scientist at the University of Virginia and the author of *Liberal Peace, Liberal War: American Politics and International Security.* Owen explains why liberal or democratic states that encompass free speech and open elections rarely go to war with each another, although they do engage states with other political systems, often in an attempt to liberalize them. *Choice* reviewer J. M. Scolnick, Jr. wrote that Owen "clearly presents his analysis, combining it with well-conducted case studies that generally support his hypotheses." Owen examines ten war-threatening crises in which the United States was involved between 1790 and 1900. He notes that the war between the states is an example of an exception to his general rule.

Adam Roberts wrote in the *Times Literary Supplement* that Owen "also shows something else, which is more disturbing for theorists of democratic peace; military factors, including calculations of the cost of going to war, were often influential in tipping the balance against war. In other words, democratic peace does not mean the end of power politics. Owen hints at, but never addresses directly, a sinister aspect of democratic peace theory: its assumption that there would be peace if only everybody else was like us." Roberts concluded that Owen's book "will help take the idea of democratic peace out of the land of political and academic hype, and into the realm of serious study." In a *Foreign Affairs* review, David C. Hendrickson called *Liberal Peace, Liberal War* an "illuminating work."

BIOGRAPHICAL AND CRITICAL SOURCES:

PERIODICALS

Choice, July-August, 1998, p. 1927.
Foreign Affairs, May-June, 1998, p. 139.
Times Literary Supplement, November 6, 1998, p. 23.
Virginia Quarterly Review, summer, 1998, p. 97.*

P

PAGIS, Dan 1930-1986

PERSONAL: Born October 16, 1930, in Raduz, Bukovina, Romania; died July 29, 1986; son of a chemist. *Education:* Hebrew University, Jerusalem, Israel, Ph. D., 1972.

CAREER: Hebrew University, professor of Hebrew literature, 1972; Jewish Theological Seminary of America, New York, NY; visiting professor; University of California at San Diego, lecturer; Harvard University, lecturer.

WRITINGS:

POETRY

She'on Ha'tzel (title means "Shadow Dial"), [Merhavya, Israel], 1959.
Shahut me'uheret: shirim (title means "Late Leisure") Sifriyat po'alim (Merhavyah, Israel), 1964.
Gigul (title means "Transformation"), Agudat hasofrim ha-'Ivrim be-Yisra'el le-yad hotsa'at Mosadah (Ramat Gan, Israel), 1970.
Poems, translated by Stephen Mitchell, Carcanet Press (Oxford, England), 1972.
Moah, Hotsa'at ha-Kibuts ha-me'uhad (Tel Aviv, Israel), 1975.
Selected Poems of T. Carmi and Dan Pagis, translated by Stephen Mitchell, Penguin (Baltimore, MD), 1976.
Perakim ba-shirah ha-'Ivrit be-Italyah: hoveret 'ezer le-shi'uro shel, ha-Universitah ha-'Ivrit bi-Yerushalayim (Jerusalem, Israel), 1980.

Shneim Assar Panim, Hakibbutz Hameuchad (Tel Aviv, Israel), 1981.
Points of Departure (bilingual edition), translated by Stephen Mitchell, introduction by Robert Alter, Jewish Publication Society of America (Philadelphia, PA), 1982.
Milim nirdafot: Shirim, ha-Kibuts ha-me'uhad (Tel Aviv, Israel), 1982.
'Al sod hatum: le-toldot ha-hidah ha-'Ivrit be-Italyah uve-Holand, Hotsa'at sefarim 'a sh. Y. L. Magnes, ha-Universitah ha-'Ivrit (Jerusalem, Israel), 1986.
(With Ludwig Strauss and Gad Ulman) *Ha-Kad ha-'atik: agadot* (juvenile), [Tel Aviv, Israel], 1986.
Shirim aharonim, (title means "Last Poems"), ha-Kibuts ha-me'uhad (Tel Aviv, Israel), 1987.
Variable Directions: The Selected Poetry of Dan Pagis, translated by Stephen Mitchell, North Point Press (San Francisco, CA), 1989.
Kol ha-shirim (title means "Collected Poems"), ha-Kibuts ha-me'uhad (Tel Aviv, Israel), 1992.
The Selected Poetry of Dan Pagis, translated by Stephen Mitchell, University of California Press (Berkley, CA), 1996.

Poetry represented in several anthologies, including *Quarterly Review of Literature Poetry Series XI* and *'Anaf: me'asef le-sifrut tse'irah,* Shoken (Jerusalem, Israel), 1963. Author's work has been translated into English and German.

CRITICISM

Hidush U'masoret Be'shirat Ha'hol (title means "Change and Tradition: Secular Hebrew Poetry in Spain and Italy"), Keter Publishing House (Jerusalem, Israel), 1976.

Mekamot 'ivriyot: ve'sipurim aherim bi'ferozah mehu-rezet (title means "Hebrew Poetry, Medieval and Modern"), ha-Universitah ha'ivirt bi'Yerushalayim (Jerusalem, Israel), 1977.

Sugim be-shirat ha-hol ha-'Ivrit bi-Sefarad: leket shirim, ha-Universitah ha-'Ivrit, ha-Fakultah le-mada'e ha-ruah, ha-Hug le-sifrut 'Ivrit (Jerusalem, Israel), 1978.

(With E. Fleischer and Y. David) *Kitve profesor Hayim Shirman (1904-1981)* (title means "A Bibliography of the Writings of Professor Jefim (Haim) Schirmann"), Mosad Byalik (Jerusalem, Israel), 1983.

Hebrew Poetry of the Middle Ages and the Renaissance (essays in English), University of California Press (Berkeley, CA), 1991.

(With E. Fleischer) *ha-Shir davur 'al ofnav: mehkarim u-masot ba-shirah ha-'lvrit shel Yeme ha-benayim,* Magnes, ha-Universitah ha-lvrit (Jerusalem, Israel), 1993.

OTHER

(Editor)*Shire ha-hol shel Mosheh Ibn'Ezra* (title means "The Secular Poems of Moses ibn Ezra"), Hebrew University (Jerusalem, Israel), 1967.

(Editor) *Shirat Levi Ibn Altabban of Saragossa* (title means "Poems of Levi ibn al-Tabban"), ha-Akademyah ha-Le'umit ha'Yisra'elit le'Madam'im (Jerusalem, Israel), 1967.

Ha'beitzh She'hithapsa (juvenile; title means "The Egg Who Masqueraded"), 'Am 'oved (Tel Aviv, Israel), 1973.

(Editor) *Shire ha-hol* (title means "Secular Poems"), Hotsa'at Makhon Shoken le-mehkar ha-Yahadut le-yad Bet ha-midrash le-rabanim be-Amerikah (Jerusalem, Israel), 1977.

(With Shirley Kaufman and Henry Moore) *Hitbonenut be-tahrite gulgolet ha-pil me-et Henri Mur bi-Yerushalayim bi-zeman ha-milhamah* (title means "Looking at Henry Moore's Elephant Skull Etchings in Jerusalem during the War"), ha-Kibuts ha-me'uhad (Tel Aviv, Israel), 1980.

SOUND RECORDINGS; POETRY

Transformations, Jeffrey Norton Publishers (Guilford, CT), 1980.

(With Yehuda Amichai, Nathan Yonathan, and Karen Alkalay-Gut), *Contemporary Israeli Poetry,* recorded at Whittall Pavilion and Coolidge Auditorium, Library of Congress, April 2, 1985.

Milim nidafot pegishah 'im ha'meshorer Dan Pagis: ha-tokhnit shudrah yamim ahadim le-ahar moto shel ha-meshorer Dan Pagis (recording of radio program), Kol Yisra'el (Jerusalem, Israel), 1993.

ADAPTATIONS: Points of Departure was reproduced in Braille by the Jewish Braille Institute of America.

SIDELIGHTS: An immigrant to Israel, a poet, and a scholar of medieval Hebrew poetry, Dan Pagis remains known for providing fresh insights into the study of ancient Hebrew poetic texts. He is a poet of displacement and survival and was a leading modernist. Intellectual and ironic detachment characterize his work. Although Pagis is often referred to as a poet of the Holocaust, critic Robert Alter argued instead that Pagis's "imaginative landscape extends from the grim vistas of genocide to the luminous horizon of medieval Hebrew poetry in the Iberian peninsula." Alter pointed out in his introduction to *The Selected Poetry of Dan Pagis* that although the theme of displacement remains the central concept in his poems, Pagis's poetry also reveals playfulness. Alter wrote, "The same poetic force that juggles ontological categories in the Holocaust poems, transforming Creator and victim alike into faceless smoke, or a fleeing refugee into 'imaginary man' (in 'Instructions for Cross the Border'), is also behind the metamorphosis of armchairs and balloons into strange and wonderful animals in the delightful group of poems, 'Bestiary.'" In addition to the five books of poetry published during his lifetime, Pagis also published numerous scholarly texts, and one children's book, *Ha'beitzh She'hithapsa.*

Pagis's association with displacement was both political and personal. He was born in the politically destabilized province of Bukovina, which at the time of his birth was part of Romania. It had once been part of Austria and was later claimed by Russia. When he was four, Pagis's mother died, and his father immigrated to Israel (then Palestine). Pagis was raised by his non-religious Jewish grandparents in a German-speaking environment that emphasized German culture. At the age of eleven, Pagis was imprisoned in a Nazi concentration camp in Ukrainia for four years. Upon his release in 1946, he followed his father to Palestine. Although the two met up, they did not establish a close relationship. Pagis was enrolled in a kibbutz boarding school. In 1949, after only three years of studying Hebrew, Pagis published his first poem in that language. Alter commented, "This rapid determination to become a poet in Hebrew, I venture to guess, was not only a young person's willed act of adaptation but also the manifestation of a psychological need to seek expression in a medium that was itself a radical displacement of his native language."

His teaching career began when he taught on a kibbutz he had joined. In 1956 he began his studies at Hebrew University in Jerusalem, noted as a center of research in Hebrew literature from the period of the mid-tenth century through the nineteenth centuries. While there, Pagis studied with revered Hebrew literary scholar, Jefim Hayyim Schirmann, and in 1983, published a bibliography of Schirmann's work.

In 1976, Pagis published his own study of medieval Hebrew poetry, *Hidush U' masoret Be'shirat Ha'hol* The study is divided into three major chronological-geographical units: Muslim Spain, Christian Spain, and Italy. Like other books by Hebrew medievalists publishing around the same time, Pagis's book examines several fundamental poetic elements, including language, form, subject, and style rather than a history of the poets and their work. Beginning with the emergence of Hebrew secular poetry in Spain in the tenth century, known as the Golden Age of Hebrew poetry, the book examines the impact of Muslim civilization on Hebrew texts. Looking to models in Arabic poetry, Hebrew poets of the period appropriated metrical techniques, rhyme schemes, genres, themes, and conventions. However, they always wrote in Hebrew and used the Torah as their standard for excellence. Marc Saperstein, in the *Journal of the History of Ideas* praised Pagis for his study, which is "amply illustrated by quotations from the poetry itself. Sometimes, as in the discussion of the relationship between poet and patron, the quotations are self-explanatory; where necessary, as in the discussion of ornamentation, imagery, and metaphor, the passages are elucidated by a superb literary analysis."

In his book Pagis considers the shift from Muslim to Christian Spain and the influence of the Arabic poetic *maqama* form on the development of narrative in rhymed prose during the period. He discusses the classical form of Hebrew maqama as shown in the work of the poet, Judah Alharizi. Pagis then examines more than twenty pieces of rhymed prose from the period, ranging from popular stories to social satire, in order to establish the parameters of the genre. Again analyz-

ing stylistic features Pagis makes the distinction that the poets were aligning themselves with the *maqama* tradition, rather than merely the structural framework of the form, which employs a hero and a narrator.

The final section of the book addresses the origins of secular Hebrew poetry in Italy. While Hebrew poetry written in Spain is relatively well known, that written in Italy is less familiar to students of Hebrew poetry, despite its uninterrupted one-thousand-year-old tradition. A key poet examined in Pagis's book is Immanuel of Rome whose work exhibits elements of Spanish Hebrew poetry, including the use of Arabic metrical patterns, as well as contemporary Italian poetics, most notably the sonnet form. Immanuel was the first to work in the sonnet form in a language other than Italian. Pagis examines the thirty-eight sonnets in Immanuel's ouvre. Saperstein praised Pagis's analysis, noting, "his primary concern remains to clarify the aesthetic foundations of Italian Hebrew poetry . . . As the material is both far more diffuse and far less familiar than the poetry of Spain, Pagis's achievement in this respect is considerable."

Pagis's second major scholarly work, *Hebrew Poetry of the Middle Ages and the Renaissance,* appeared in English translation in 1991. The text was met with enthusiastic critical acclaim when it was published posthumously in English with an introduction by well-known poetry critic Robert Alter. Judith Kates wrote in *Speculum,* "The publication of Dan Pagis's Taubman Lectures on secular Hebrew poetry of the Middle Ages and Renaissance provides a wide-ranging, yet incisive, critical introduction in English to this extraordinary body of literature. . . . This small volume . . . grows out of meticulous scholarship in the whole range of secular poetry and rhymed prose in Hebrew from the tenth to the eighteenth centuries. In addition, Pagis brings to his readings of single texts and to his synthesizing arguments the acute ear and sympathetic sensibility of the practicing poet, widely read in European poetry and literary theory."

Pagis examines the vexed question of individuality in the poetry. He analyzes the relationship between poetic convention and personal experience as it is played out in the use of conceits. Revisiting his earlier work, he revises his earlier assertions regarding expressive features in the poetry of medieval Hebrew poets. Kates wrote, "Now, he says with disarming candor . . . that this poetry allowed much more room for individuality than has been generally supposed and the 'modern scholars have been sometimes more conventional in their views than medieval poets were in their works.'"

Identifying a range of individual expression within love poetry, Pagis places the genre somewhere between conventional model and personal expression. He suggests that in later periods, personal experience rather than poetic convention provided the impetus for the crafting of love poetry. Pagis traces the origin of the love poetry of the medieval Hebrew poets to conventional Arabic frameworks and motifs. Educated Jews learned Arabic language and literary frameworks, and synthesized them with their own tradition using biblical language. They relied upon stock situations, characters, and imagery. Eventually all these conventions became open to question. Unique experiences of the poets rather than poetic convention defined the genre. Even in early classical examples, Pagis identifies individual expression as part of an historical movement toward openness and innovation. Judith Kates praised the quality of Pagis's scholarship: "Pagis delineates a picture of a medieval poetry deeply satisfying to a modern sensibility with no sacrifice of scholarly integrity, remaining true to the understanding of convention and tradition of which he himself was the major exponent. . . . all students of medieval literature are the beneficiaries of this brilliant and far-ranging critical account of a poetry little known to English-speaking scholarship."

Highly respected for his scholarship, Pagis was equally extolled as a poet despite his relatively small output. The themes he wrote about—displacement, recovery of self, memory, and history—touched a nerve with critics. Ammiel Alcalay wrote in *Parnassus,* "The body of Pagis' poetry may seem small . . . but its scope is enormous. He goes far in 'redeeming the memory' of areas of experience that seem beyond not only redemption but comprehension. His strength as a poet is such that, once beyond these areas, he is able to fashion poems of brilliant elegance and wit without ever compromising the totality of his vision, a vision whose intensity, urgency, and sheer power are constant but never shrill or staccato."

Pagis's first book of poetry, *She'on ha-tsel,* was published in Hebrew in 1959. In 1981, he republished six poems from his first book as part of a special series of modern Hebrew poetry known as the "Zuta" miniature series. Titled *Shneim Assar Panim,* the collection includes autobiographical poems with emphasis on memory, childhood, and the mysteries of life. The poems use imagery from science and the cosmos. They range in tone from lighthearted playfulness with images of elephant chairs and safaris to the intense invocation of the figures of Cain and Abel and the Holocaust. Wrote Dov Vardi in *World Literature Today,* "an Israeli critic remarked that Pagis was a cold poet. It is true that he does not howl or shout, that there is no passion. But he is not cold. He is controlled and displays exquisite poetic taste, clarity and sense of proportion."

His first book-length publication to appear in English, *Points of Departure,* caused Ammiel Alcalay to write in *Parnassus* that "few come to mind whose stature as both a poet *and* scholar/critic is so high." The bilingual edition, with translations by Stephen Mitchell, centers on the theme of displacement that Pagis explored throughout his career as a poet. The poem most often cited from the collection, "Written in Pencil in the Sealed Railway-Car," harkens back to Pagis's early adolescent experiences in the Nazi concentration camp. Only six lines long, the poem is thought to capture the entire Holocaust epoch through biblical referencing and palpable imagery. Alcalay commented on Pagis's sense of displacement, noting "it may precisely be Pagis' initial distance that affords his poetry its profound intimacy." A *Choice* critic observed, "Dan Pagis has the gift to sound simple while suggesting great depth. . . . Despite the tragedies Pagis has witnessed, there is no self-pity; a healthy irony makes life bearable. . . . This is excellent poetry, worthy to be carefully read, taught, and fully enjoyed."

Pagis characteristically employed multiple voices in his poetry, sometimes of biblical characters, more often of "nameless, hunted figures," as Rochelle Ratner pointed out in a *Library Journal* review. Recurring motifs, in addition to the theme of displacement, include time, scientific imagery, and metaphors of space. Critic Sharon Dunn, wrote of the posthumously translated *Variable Directions* in *Massachusetts Review,* "Pagis' poems are so lucid, so clear—they are like the coldest winter night lit by starlight. They seem to be written from some faraway place, somewhere Pagis has arrived (and we've not), some vantage from which our world looks scarred, murderous, and mad." Citing Pagis's poem, "A Lesson in Observation," in which the speaker in the poem admonishes the reader to "Pay close attention" to what is going on both in and out of the world, Dunn mused, "for Pagis there must be inner peace at the contemplation of and the fact of outer space. But it is peace that acknowledges the terror of history." Called "surreal" by a *Publishers Weekly* critic, the poems included in *Variable Directions* tend to be written in "propulsive, staccato sentences, commanding, denying, questioning, at times almost a pedagogic stance. . . . Death-camp memories are distorted to fit a postwar world. . . . Pagis casts an ironic eye on his environment, accepting survival as a question of chance and point of view."

Sidra DeKoven Ezrahi of *New Republic* observed, "Pagis' unraveling of the chronological order, his free-floating images that are referential in origin but unmoored from historical context, denote a radical exercise of the poetry prerogative." He predicted that "the real conversation with Pagis is likely to begin when his collected works appear posthumously," which is exactly what happened. The publication, in English, of *The Selected Poetry of Dan Pagis* caused great excitement among scholars and readers of Hebrew poetry. Leon I. Yudkin wrote in *World Literature Today*, "Much of Pagis's verse indeed revolves around issues of what it is possible to articulate and how. His language is both learned and colloquial, and attempts to come to grips with the raw life-and-death issues of destruction and revival. . . . The poetry is obsessed and determined by the past but refuses to be limited by it." Praised for his ability to write in the present but retain a sense of the traditions of the past, Pagis has created work that was described by Robert Alter as "wry and shrewdly colloquial . . . on occasion delights in the texture of language and the feel of experience this texture is made to match . . . in its distinctly modern idiom it, too, is a self-conscious demonstration and affirmation of what the poetic imagination can do." Ammiel Alcalay wrote in *Parnassus* simply, "Pagis is the quietest and most modest of poets."

BIOGRAPHICAL AND CRITICAL SOURCES:

BOOKS

Panim, Shneim Assar, *Dan Pagis,* Hakibbutz Hameuchad (Tel Aviv, Israel), 1981.

PERIODICALS

Choice, September, 1982, review of *Points of Departure,* p. 93.

Encounter, December, 1972, Anthony Thwaite, "A Matter of Survival," pp. 76-78.
Journal of the History of Ideas, January, 1979, Marc Saperstein, "Current Israeli Scholarship on Medieval Hebrew Literature," p. 159.
Judaism, fall, 1996, Robert Alter, "Dan Pagis and the Poetry of Displacement," p. 399.
Library Journal, July, 1982, Rochelle Ratner, review of *Points of Departure,* p. 1329.
Massachusetts Review, spring-summer, 1990, Sharon Dunn, "American Poetry, 1989," pp. 287-307.
New Republic, February 25, 1991, Sidra DeKoven Ezrahi, review of *Variable Directions,* p. 34.
Parnassus, spring, 1983, Ammiel Alcalay, review of *Points of Departure,* p. 85.
Publishers Weekly, May 12, 1989, review of *Variable Directions,* pp. 285-286.
Speculum, January, 1994, Judith A. Kates, review of *Hebrew Poetry of the Middle Ages and the Renaissance,* pp. 231-234.
Translation Review Supplement, July, 1997, review of *The Selected Poetry of Dan Pagis,* p. 6.
World Literature Today, winter, 1983, Dov Vardi, review of *Dan Pagis,* by Shneim Assar Panim, p. 167; summer, 1997, Leon I. Yudkin, review of *The Selected Poetry of Dan Pagis,* p. 643.*

*   *   *

PAKENHAM, Valerie 1939-

PERSONAL: Born November 13, 1939, in England; daughter of R. G. (a writer) and M. C. (a homemaker) McNair Scott; married Thomas Pakenham, July, 1964; children: Maria, Eliza, Edward, Frederick. *Education:* St. Anne's College, Oxford, degree (with honors). *Religion:* Church of Ireland. *Hobbies and other interests:* Gardening, building, design, music.

ADDRESSES: Home—Tullynally Castle, Castlepollard, County Westmeath, Ireland. *E-mail*—tpakenham@ecrcom.net.

CAREER: Worked as a journalist prior to 1964; freelance writer.

WRITINGS:

Out in the Noonday Sun: Edwardians in the Tropics (nonfiction), Random House (New York, NY), 1985.

Dublin: A Traveller's Companion, Constable (London, England), 1988.

The Big House in Ireland, Cassell (London, England), 2001.

BIOGRAPHICAL AND CRITICAL SOURCES:

PERIODICALS

Birmingham Post, January 13, 2001, "Poverty and Laughter," p. 53.

History Today, January, 1986, Denis Judd, review of *The Noonday Sun: Edwardians in the Tropics,* p. 56; January, 2001, review of *The Big House in Ireland,* p. 58.

New York Times Book Review, January 5, 1986, Jonathan Rose, review of *Out in the Noonday Sun,* p. 16.

Times Literary Supplement, January 6, 1989, Anne Haverty, review of *Dublin: A Traveller's Companion,* p. 7; March 16, 2001, Toby Barnard, review of *The Big House in Ireland,* p. 31.

*   *   *

PALMER, Noreen E. 1960-

PERSONAL: Born November 24, 1960, in Columbus, OH; daughter of Alfred and Lurlena White; married Charles Edwin Palmer, April 18, 1991; children: Charles, Jr., Arianna. *Education:* Ohio University, B.S., 1983; Ohio State University, M.A., 1986, M.S.W., 1988. *Hobbies and other interests:* Reading, cooking, walking.

ADDRESSES: Home—3163 Arrowsmith Dr., Reynoldsburg, OH 43068-5000. *Office*—Grantl Riverside Health Center, 475 Hill Rd., North Pickerington, OH 43147-1157.

CAREER: Psychotherapist. Ohio State University, Columbus, social work program coordinator, 1988-89; St. Stephen's Community House, Columbus, OH program director, 1989-92; National Medical Care, Columbus, social worker, 1992-96; Curative Health Services, Columbus, professional liaison, 1997—; psychotherapist in private practice, 1995—. Black-

board Literacy Initiative, founder and executive director, 1995-97; Homeless Families Foundation, Columbus, volunteer clinical director, 1996-99, vice president, 1997-99.

MEMBER: American Diabetes Association (member of board of directors, Heartland chapter), Continental Societies.

AWARDS, HONORS: Commendation, Canton, OH, City Council, 1988; appreciation awards, Pathways Mentors, 1989, and Continental Societies, 1997; volunteer award, Homeless Families Foundation, 1999.

WRITINGS:

(With Faye Childs) *Going Off: A Guide for Black Women Who've Just about Had Enough,* St. Martin's Press (New York, NY), 2001.

Contributor to periodicals, including *Black Expressions.*

BIOGRAPHICAL AND CRITICAL SOURCES:

PERIODICALS

Publishers Weekly, April 23, 2001, review of *Going Off: A Guide for Black Women Who've Just about Had Enough,* p. 65.*

*   *   *

PALMER, R(obert) R(oswell) 1909-2002

OBITUARY NOTICE—See index for *CA* sketch: Born January 11, 1909, in Chicago, IL; died June 11, 2002, in Newtown, PA. Historian, educator, translator, and author. Palmer's lasting achievement may be his popular textbook, *A History of the Modern World,* which has gone through nine editions since its original appearance in 1950. The weighty tome has been in continuous use at hundreds of colleges and universities and has been widely translated as well. For most of his career, Palmer was a professor of history at Princeton University. He taught at Washington

University in Saint Louis in the mid-1960s, then moved to Yale University in 1969. Much of Palmer's research focused on France, the French Revolution in particular, with special attention paid to the complex political events that shaped the history of France and, therefore, the rest of the modern world. He received the Bancroft Prize for American history from Columbia University for *The Democratic Revolution: A Political History of Europe and America, 1760-1800.* Other writings included *Catholics and Unbelievers in Eighteenth-Century France, Twelve Who Ruled: The Year of Terror in the French Revolution,* and *The World of the French Revolution.* Palmer also translated and edited the writings of several French scholars and authors.

OBITUARIES AND OTHER SOURCES:

PERIODICALS

New York Times, June 18, 2002, obituary by Douglas Martin, p. A23.

*   *   *

PALS, Daniel L. 1946-

PERSONAL: Born October 28, 1946, in South Holland, IL; son of Herbert H. and Margaret B. (Vanderas) Pals; married Phyllis Ross Balzer, August 11, 1973. *Education:* Calvin College, A.B., 1968; Calvin Theological Seminary, B.D., 1971; University of Chicago, M.A., 1973, Ph.D., 1975.

ADDRESSES: Home—1239 Dickinson Drive, Miami, FL 33146-1298. *Office*—University of Miami, Department of Religion, P.O. Box 248264, Miami, FL 33124-8264. *E-mail*—dpals@miami.edu.

CAREER: Trinity College, Deerfield, IL, assistant professor of history, 1976-77; Centre College, Danville, KY, assistant professor of religion and history, 1977-80; University of Miami, Miami, FL, professor and chair of religion department, 1980—, interim dean, College of Arts and Sciences, c. 2001—.

MEMBER: American Society for Church History, American Academy of Religion, Presbyterian Church (USA).

AWARDS, HONORS: Max Orovitz Award, University of Miami, 1980, 1984, 1990; Freshman Teaching Award, 1989.

WRITINGS:

The Victorian "Lives" of Jesus, Trinity University Press (San Antonio, TX), 1982.
Seven Theories of Religion, Oxford University Press (New York, NY), 1996.

Church History, editorial assistant, 1973-76. Contributor of articles to professional journals.

SIDELIGHTS: Religion scholar Daniel L. Pals's first book, *The Victorian "Lives" of Jesus,* grew out of his doctoral dissertation. In it, he deals with the nineteenth-century vogue in England for biographies of Jesus Christ. These include *Ecce Homo: A Survey of the Life and Work of Christ* by John Robert Seeley, published in 1866; Frederic William Farrar's two-volume *Life of Christ,* which came out in 1874; and Cunningham Geikie's *The Life and Work of Christ,* from 1882. These biographers sought to reconcile the Bible's varying accounts of Christ's life and "to tell a dramatic story," noted Rosemary Booth in *Christian Century.* Trying to reach a wide audience, the most popular biographers drew readers in by portraying an idealized Holy Land and by making Christ accessible, emphasizing that he was human as well as divine, but they did not challenge mainstream Christian beliefs. They were responding in part to such a challenge—the assertion that the Gospels were mythical, put forth by David Friederich Strauss in *Das Leben Jesu,* published in 1835. Because Strauss was German, and many of his countrymen were also producing biographies of Christ, the English writers were additionally motivated by national pride—they had to answer and attempt to outdo the Germans.

Pals's "fascinating volume reads in livelier fashion than most books born of doctoral dissertations," commented Horton Davies in *Theology Today.* "Its unusual interest comes from its theological, historical, and sociological probes into the various Victorian attempts to write biographies of Jesus, orthodox, liberal, or rationalist." He continued, "This book is important for its comprehensiveness, and also for the light it shows on religion in Victorian England," adding that "Pals has taken us on an important, well mapped journey, and he is a reliable travel guide." Booth observed that Pals's "style, while careful and scholarly, is also fluent. . . . The book is a nice reminder that religious scholarship can be thorough without being remote."

Seven Theories of Religion examines ideas formulated about faith by such disparate observers as Karl Marx, Sigmund Freud, Victorian anthropologists E. B. Tyler and Sir James Frazer, and religion historian Mircea Eliade. Pals explains how each theory reflects the theorist's field of specialization, looks at the influence their opinions have had, and discusses the possibility of developing a broader theory of religion. "Together the seven theories offer impressive witness to the power of religion to create meaning, invite critical investigation, and spark sustained and sometimes heated controversy," remarked Walter H. Capps in *Christian Century*. Pals treats each theory in a "thorough yet succinct" manner, noted Laura S. Grillo in *History of Religions*. "More than masterful summaries," she went on, "Pals's expositions are lively vignettes that leave the reader with the impression of having entered the world and reasoning of each author." What's more, she said, "Pals writes with elegant simplicity," giving his work "astonishing" accessibility as well as a "formidable scope" of scholarship. She summed up the volume as a "welcome book" with much to offer both beginning and advanced students of religion.

BIOGRAPHICAL AND CRITICAL SOURCES:

PERIODICALS

Choice, May, 1983, review of *The Victorian "Lives" of Jesus,* pp. 1306-1307.
Christian Century, March 23, 1983, Rosemary Booth, review of *The Victorian "Lives" of Jesus,* pp. 285-285; June 19, 1996, Walter H. Capps, review of *Seven Theories of Religion,* p. 665.
History of Religions, August, 1997, Laura S. Grillo, review of *Seven Theories of Religion,* p. 90.
Religious Studies Review, October, 1983, Leander E. Keck, review of *The Victorian "Lives" of Jesus,* p. 378.
Theology Today, July, 1983, July, 1983, Horton Davies, review of *The Victorian "Lives" of Jesus,* pp. 242-244.*

PARAL, Vladimír 1932-

PERSONAL: Born 1932, in Czechoslovakia (now Czech Republic).

ADDRESSES: Home—Marianské Lazne (Marienbad), Czech Republic. *Office*—c/o Catbird Press, 16 Windsor Road, North Haven, CT 06473.

CAREER: Research chemist and writer.

WRITINGS:

Milenci & vrazi, Mladá Fronta (Prague, Czechoslovakia), 1970, translated by Craig Cravens as *Lovers & Murderers: A Novel,* Catbird Press (North Haven, CT), 2001.
Profesionální zena: Román pro kazdeho, Melantrich (Prague, Czechoslovakia), 1974, English translation by William Harkins published as *The Four Sonyas,* Catbird Press (North Haven, CT), 1993.
Radost az do rána: O kreccích a lidech, Melantrich (Prague, Czechoslovakia), 1975.
Generální zázrak: Roman nadje, Severoces nakl (Usti nad Labem, Czechoslovakia), 1977.
Tri ze zoo, Veletrh splnenych prání, Soukromá vichrice, and *Katapult* (omnibus volume; previously published separately), Melantrich (Prague, Czechoslovakia), 1977.
Muka obraznosti, Ceskoslovensky spisovatel (Prague, Czechoslovakia), 1980.
Pokusení A—ZZ, Melantrich (Prague, Czechoslovakia), 1982.
Romeo & Julie 2300, Práce (Prague, Czechoslovakia), 1982.
Válka s mnohozvíretem: Památce Karla Capka s pokorou a láskou, Ceskoslovensky spisovatel (Prague, Czechoslvakia), 1983.
Zeme zen, Ceskoslovensky spisovatel (Prague, Czechoslvakia), 1987.
Catapult: A Timetable of Rail, Sea, and Air Ways to Paradise (originally published in Czechoslovakia as *Katapult*), translated from the Czech and with a critical introduction by William Harkins, Catbird Press (Highland Park, NJ), 1989.
Dekameron 2000, aneb, Láska v Praze, Ceskoslovensky spisovatel (Prague, Czechoslvakia), 1990.
Lniha rozkosí, smíchu a radosti, Dialog (Prague, Czech Republic), 1992.

Playgirls, Dialog (Prague, Czech Republic), 1994.
Tam za vodou, Dialog (Prague, Czech Republic), 1995.

Author of several other novels.

SIDELIGHTS: Vladimír Páral is one of the most successful literary novelists in the Czech Republic (formerly Czechoslovakia). Páral, who is also a scientist, has more than twenty novels to his credit; they take place largely in the northern Czech city of Usti nad Labem, where he lived for many years. With the publication of his first novel, *Veletrh splnenych prání* in the 1960s, Páral "became almost overnight one of the country's most discussed writers and has since then achieved a considerable reputation abroad, notably in West Germany," according to a *Times Literary Supplement* contributor in a review of *Milenci & vrazi.* "Here at last was a novelist who was not trying to write out of his system a traumatic wartime experience nor the romanticized nostalgia of adolescence, but who instead dealt with the most controversial and, in the circumstances, most risky subject there was—contemporary life." Comparing Páral with another leading Czech novelist of the time, *World Literature Today* contributor Karen von Kunes, reviewing *The Four Sonyas,* wrote, "If Milan Kundera's novels make the reader laugh and think, Vladimír Páral's books entertain him and make him feel. Kundera's characters are victims of political oppression. Páral's characters become products of the bureaucracy; all melted together produce unforgettable characters of communist Czechoslovakia." Páral is also "one of the most erotic of Czech writers," commented *World Literature Today*'s B. R. Bradbrook in a piece on *Lniha rozkosí, smíchu a radosti.*

Works by Páral that have appeared in English translation, besides *Lovers & Murderers,* include *Catapult: A Timetable of Rail, Sea, and Air Ways to Paradise* and *The Four Sonyas.* Critiquing *Catapult* and *The Four Sonyas* for *Bloomsbury Review,* Thomas S. Edwards remarked that in these books Páral "reminds us that freedom is, at best, an elusive concept" and that both works "are darkly humorous attempts to uncover what that freedom actually entails in our modern lives, and whether the `timetables to paradise' will actually take us where we want to go." *Catapult* is the story of a thirtyish engineer, Jacek, bored with his marriage, who embarks on affairs with seven women at different points along the route of his commuter train. Juggling

them all, however, soon becomes problematic, and Jacek is unable to choose among them and eventually decides he was better off with his wife. "Liberty becomes torment in Páral's world, and torment liberty," observed Richard Lourie in *Washington Post Book World.* Páral manages, Lourie added, to make "the most banal and fantastical elements blend harmoniously so that we both recognize the hero's life as highly improbable and also accept his emotions as real and legitimate." *Atlantic* contributor Dennis Drabelle called *Catapult* "a book to look back on admiringly"; it is, he explained, "a witty, headlong merger of stream of consciousness and the novel of midlife male angst."

The Four Sonyas is, like *Catapult,* a "preposterous comed[y] of rampant desire," related Lourie. The title refers to the four aspects of one young woman, barmaid Sonya Cechova. With the four identities quarrelling within her, Sonya enters into a series of exploitive relationships with men; once she is able "to achieve the integration of the four separate parts of her personality . . . she emerges as a complete and independent woman," remarked Edwards. Von Kunes deemed the novel "amusing, entertaining, and well written"; to Lourie, it has the "rollicking energy" of a bawdy eighteenth-century novel placed in a late-twentieth-century setting. Edwards thought Sonya an underdeveloped character, but saw "several great moments of comedy" in her story. Similarly, Drabelle described Sonya as "a bonbon without a center," but added, "Even so, *The Four Sonyas* provides capital entertainment."

Lovers & Murderers revolves around the intertwining lives of the residents of an apartment complex owned by a chemical company in Usti nad Labem. They hop into and out of one another's beds, and compete for prime space in the building. "It is a picture of the incessant battle between the haves and the have-nots . . . with the familiar cycle of the poor becoming corrupt as soon as they make it and then defending their positions against a new onslaught," related a *Times Literary Supplement* reviewer of the original Czech edition in 1970, who also praised Páral's "dazzling technique of repeating words, phrases and even whole passages in mirror-like situations." A *Publishers Weekly* contributor, critiquing the translation, described *Lovers & Murderers* as "Rabelasian" and noted that its "playful, relentless energy combines with sexual and political candidness to make grand, cartoonish comedy of a bleak situation." *Library Journal's* Andrea Caron Kempf thought Páral "shows an impressive mastery of literary technique" in this "vitriolic" but "very funny" novel.

BIOGRAPHICAL AND CRITICAL SOURCES:

BOOKS

Páral, Vladimír, and Heda Bartíková, *Profesionál muz: Vladimír Páral o sobe a jinych, zajímavejsích vecech* (interview by Bartíková with Páral), GABI (Cesky Tesín, Czech Republic), 1995.

PERIODICALS

Atlantic, May, 1993, Dennis Drabelle, review of *Catapult: A Timetable of Rail, Sea, and Air Ways to Paradise* and *The Four Sonyas,* p. 122.

Bloomsbury Review, May, 1993, Thomas S. Edwards, review of *Catapult* and *The Four Sonyas,* p. 11.

Kirkus Reviews, February 1, 2002, review of *Lovers & Murderers: A Novel,* p. 142.

Library Journal, April 1, 1989, Marie Bednar, review of *Catapult,* p. 100; January, 1993, Ruth M. Ross, review of *The Four Sonyas,* p. 166; February 1, 2002, Andrea Caron Kempf, review of *Lovers & Murderers,* p. 132.

New York Review of Books, May 18, 1989, D. J. Enright, review of *Catapult,* pp. 37-39.

New York Times Book Review, June 18, 1989, Olga Wickerhauser, review of *Catapult,* p. 20.

Publishers Weekly, February 17, 1989, review of *Catapult,* p. 68; January 4, 1993, review of *The Four Sonyas,* p. 59; January 28, 2002, review of *Lovers & Murderers,* p. 272.

Times Literary Supplement, February 7, 1970, "The Conquerors and the Besieged," p. 702; February 2, 1986, Igor Hajek, "Making an Enemy of Man," p. 150.

Washington Post Book World, March 7, 1993, Richard Lourie, "Czechs and Mates," p. 11.

World Literature Today, summer, 1993, Karen von Kunes, review of *The Four Sonyas,* pp. 631-632; autumn, 1993, B. R. Bradbrook, review of *Lniha rozkosí, smíchu a radosti,* pp. 854-855.*

PAYNE, John 1842-1916

PERSONAL: Born August 23, 1842, in England; died February 11, 1916; son of John Edward Haskins Payne (a linguist and inventor).

CAREER: Poet, translator, and attorney.

WRITINGS:

POETRY

The Masque of Shadows and Other Poems, Pickering (London, England), 1870.

Intaglios: Sonnets, Pickering (London, England), 1871.

Songs of Life and Death, King (London, England), 1872.

Lautrec: A Poem, Pickering (London, England), 1878.

New Poems, Newman (London, England), 1880.

The Descent of the Dove and Other Poems, privately printed (London, England), 1902.

The Poetical Works of John Payne, two volumes, Villon Society (London, England), 1902.

Vigil and Vision: New Sonnets, Villon Society (London, England), 1903.

Twelve Sonnets de Combat (supplement to *Vigil and Vision*), privately printed (London, England), 1903.

Songs of Consolation, Simkin, Marshall, Hamilton, Kent (London, England), 1904.

Sir Winfrith and Other Poems, Thomas Wright (Olney, England), 1905.

Selections from the Poetry of John Payne, edited by Tracy and Lucy Robinson, Lane/Bodley Head (New York, NY), 1906.

Verses for the Newton-Cowper Centenary, Cowper Press (Olney, England), 1907.

The Quatrains of Ibn et Tefrid, privately printed (London, England), 1908.

Carol and Cadence: New Poems, Villon Society (London, England), 1908, republished in part as *Nature and Her Lover and Other Poems from "Carol and Cadence,"* John Payne Society (Olney, England), 1922.

Flower o' the Thorn: A Book of Wayside Verse, Villon Society (London, England), 1909.

Humoristica three series, privately printed (London, England), 1909-10.

The Way of the Winepress, John Payne Society (Olney, England), 1920.

OTHER

(Translator) *The Poems of Master François Villon*, Villon Society (London, England), 1878.

(Translator) *The Book of the Thousand Nights and One Night: Now First Completely Done into English Prose and Verse, from the Original Arabic*, nine volumes, Villon Society (London, England), 1882-84, parts republished as *Book of the Thousands Night and One Night*, privately printed (London, England), 1906, and *Abou Mohammed the Lazy, and Other Tales from the Arabian Nights*, John Payne Society (Olney, England), 1906.

(Translator) *Tales from the Arabic*, three volumes, privately printed (London, England), 1884, enlarged and expanded to four volumes, Villon Society (London, England), 1884-89.

(Translator) *Alaeddin and the Enchanted Lamp; Zein ul Asnam and the King of the Jinn*, privately printed (London, England), 1885, Villon Society (London, England), 1889.

(Translator) *The Decameron of Boccaccio*, three volumes, Villon Society (London, England), 1886, published as *The Decameron; or, Ten Days' Entertainment*, World Publishing (Cleveland, OH), 1947.

(Translator) *The Novels of Matteo Bandello*, six volumes, Villon Society (London, England), 1890.

(Translator) *The Quatrains of Omar Kheyyam of Nishapour*, Villon Society (London, England), 1898.

(Translator) *The Poems of Shemseddin Mohammed Hafiz of Shiraz*, three volumes, Villon Society (London, England), 1901.

(Translator) *Flowers of France: The Romantic Period, Hugo to Leconte de Lisle*, two volumes, Villon Society (London, England), 1906.

(Translator) *Flowers of France: The Renaissance Period, from Ronsard to Saint-Amant*, Villon Society (London, England), 1907.

(Translator) *The Poetical Works of Heinrich Heine*, three volumes, Villon Society (London, England), 1913.

(Translator) *Flowers of France: The Latter Days, Ackerman to Warnery*, two volumes, Villon Society (London, England), 1913.

(Translator) *Flowers of France: The Classic Period, Malherbe to Millevoye*, Villon Society (London, England), 1914.

The Autobiography of John Payne of Villon Society Fame, Poet and Scholar, edited by Thomas Wright, Thomas Wright (Olney, England), 1926.

Also contributor of reviews, articles, and essays to periodicals, including *Bookman, Cosmopolitan, Independent*, and *Munsey's Magazine*.

SIDELIGHTS: Writing in the *Dictionary of Literary Biography*, C. W. Willerton noted that, while it was John Payne's desire to be remembered as a great poet, his "best legacy" was his translations for the Villon Society, including *The Decameron, The Arabian Nights*, and a number of other classic poems and tales. Though Willerton stated that Payne "left behind hundreds of pages of poems as well as a worshipful John Payne Society," neither his poetry nor the Society has endured.

During his lifetime, however, much of Payne's early poetry received positive reviews. *The Masque of Shadows and Other Poems*, for example, which contains "The Rime of Redemption," "The Building of a Dream," "The Romaunt of Sir Floris," and the title poem, received critical acclaim at the time of the collection's release. As Willerton noted, even over three decades after the publication of *Masque* A. C. Swinburne praised "The Rime of Redemption" as a "masterpiece." Payne's second poetry collection, *Intaglios*, was also well received, with such noted literary figures as Matthew Arnold and Dante Gabriel Rossetti issuing their praise. Regardless of the favor Payne's work was accorded by his contemporaries, Willerton argued that his verses has fallen into relative obscurity due to their lack of real originality. Willerton went on to catalogue a series of "observations" that characterize "virtually all his original poetry." Among Willerton's complaints are Payne's "obsessive" combination of love and death in his ballads and sonnets, as well as his use of imagery, which he feels "runs to opulence, often dragging down the action." Willerton concluded that Payne's poems are "best when they emphasize plot and worst when they emphasize description."

Though Payne's poetry did not have the lasting impact for which he had hoped, his translations have had a lasting effect on literary scholarship. Willerton felt that his body of translated works is especially "impressive in bulk and in range of languages." His translation of *The Poems of Master François Villon*, which received praise from Theodore de Banville and Matthew Arnold, among others, resulted in the founding of the Villon Society, which provided a publishing outlet for much of Payne's work. Also of note is his nine-volume translation of *The Arabian Nights*.

Willerton noted that even though Tracy and Lucy Robinson, two of Payne's friends, founded the Payne society in an effort to promote his work, Payne's poetry did not survive him for long. The Society published two small collections after his death, including *Selections from the Poetry of John Payne,* which *Critic* reviewer Edith M. Thomas felt was "profoundly impressive." Thomas Wright also prepared *The Life of John Payne* and edited *The Autobiography of John Payne of Villon Society Fame, Poet and Scholar,* but neither of these works received a great deal of attention. Willerton argued that perhaps the reason Payne never achieved lasting status in literature is that he thought himself the equal of the writers he translated, yet "neither his poems nor Wright's adoring biography has persuaded modern readers to agree."

BIOGRAPHICAL AND CRITICAL SOURCES:

BOOKS

Dictionary of Literary Biography, Volume 35: *Victorian Poets after 1850,* Gale (Detroit, MI), 1985.
Williams, C. R. McGregor, *John Payne,* Presses Modernes (Paris, France), 1926.
Wright, Thomas, *The Life of John Payne,* Unwin (London, England), 1919.

PERIODICALS

Critic, August, 1906, Edith M. Thomas, review of *Selections from the Poetry of John Payne.*
Dial, May 16, 1906, William M. Payne, review of *Selections from the Poetry of John Payne.*
Nation, April 19, 1906, review of *Selections from the Poetry of John Payne.*
Outlook, February 24, 1906, review of *Selections from the Poetry of John Payne.**

* * *

PEAKE, Thomas H(arold) 1947-
Tom H. Peake

PERSONAL: Born November 1, 1947, in Kansas; son of Thomas B., Jr. (a minister) and Maurine (an educator; maiden name, Snyder) Peake; married December 27, 1968; wife's name Victoria L.; children: Lisa, Katie. *Ethnicity:* "Caucasian." *Education:* Northwest Missouri State University, B.A., 1969; University of Missouri—Kansas City, M.A., 1970; University of Memphis, Ph.D., 1976; University of Virginia, postdoctoral study, 1984-86.

ADDRESSES: Home—3195 Concours Rd., Melbourne, FL 32934. *Office*—School of Psychology, Florida Institute of Technology, 150 West University Blvd., Melbourne, FL 32901-6975; fax: 321-674-7105. *E-mail*—tompeake@rr.cfl.com.

CAREER: Psychologist and educator. Missouri Western College, St. Joseph, instructor in psychology, 1970-72; Memphis State University, Memphis, TN, psychologist at Speech and Hearing Center, 1972-74, instructor in psychology, 1973-74; Topeka State Hospital, Topeka, KS, clinical doctoral intern, 1974-75; Pine Rest Christian Hospital, Grand Rapids, MI, clinical psychologist, 1975-81, director of early adolescent unit, 1975-77, director of neuropsychological services, 1975-81; Eastern Virginia Medical School, Norfolk, associate professor of psychiatry and behavioral sciences and of physical medicine and rehabilitation, 1981-86, and codirector of Neuropsychology Center; Florida Institute of Technology, Melbourne, professor of psychology, 1986—, director of counseling and psychological services, 1986-93, director of behavioral medicine and neuropsychology services for psychology clinic, 1993—, associate dean for practice development, 1999—. American Board of Professional Psychology, diplomate and fellow; American Board of Medical Psychotherapy, diplomate and fellow; American Association for Marriage and Family Therapy, approved supervisor; British Psychological Society, chartered clinical psychologist; St. Joseph State Hospital, clinical psychologist, 1970-72; Whitehaven Community Mental Health Center, staff psychologist, 1973-74; Norfolk Mental Health Center and Psychiatric Institute, staff member, 1981-86; Norfolk General Hospital, staff member, 1981-86; Children's Hospital of the King's Daughters, staff member, 1981-86; private practice of clinical psychology, 1986—; Wüsthoff Medical Center, staff member, 1987—; Holmes Regional Medical Center, staff member, 1987—; Florida Department of Elder Affairs, director of behavioral medicine and neuropsychology services for East Central Florida Memory Disorders Clinic, 1993—. Aquinas College, adjunct assistant professor, 1977-81; Michigan State University, clinical assistant professor, 1977-81; University of South Florida, adjunct professor at Florida Mental Health Institute, 1989—; guest lecturer and workshop presenter. *Military service:* U.S. Army Reserve, 1970-76; medic and neuropsychiatric specialist.

MEMBER: International Neuropsychology Society, American Psychological Association (fellow; chair of committee on aging, Division of Family Psychology, 1992-95, 1999-2001), American Association for Marriage and Family Therapy, American Society on Aging, National Academy of Neuropsychology, Society for Clinical and Experimental Hypnosis, Society for Psychotherapy Research, British Psychological Society, Southeastern Psychological Association, Southern Gerontological Society, Florida Psychological Association, Virginia Psychological Association, Virginia Academy of Clinical Psychologists.

AWARDS, HONORS: Tregaskis grant, University of London, 1992-93; named teacher of the year, Florida Institute of Technology School of Psychology, 1994.

WRITINGS:

(Editor, as Tom H. Peake, with Robert P. Archer) *Clinical Training in Psychotherapy,* Haworth Press (New York, NY), 1984.
(With Charles M. Borduin and Robert P. Archer) *Brief Psychotherapies: Changing Frames of Mind,* Sage Publications (Newbury Park, CA), 1988, revised edition, J. Aronson (Northvale, NJ), 2000.
(Editor, with John D. Ball) *Psychotherapy Training: Contextual and Developmental Influences in Settings, Stages, and Mind Sets,* Haworth Press (New York, NY), 1991.
Healthy Aging, Healthy Treatment: The Impact of Telling Stories, Praeger Publishers (Westport, CT), 1998.
Cinema and Life Development: Healing Lives and Training Therapists, Praeger Publishers (Westport, CT), in press.

Contributor to books, including *Family Therapy Techniques for Problem Behaviors in Children and Teenagers,* edited by C. E. Schaefer and others, Jossey-Bass (San Francisco, CA), 1984; *Psychiatry and Mental Health Science Handbook,* edited by C. Thomas, W. H. Green Publishers (St. Louis, MO), 1988; *Treating the Changing Family,* edited by M.

Harway, Wiley (New York, NY), 1996; and *Handbook of Couple and Family Forensic Issues,* edited by F. Kaslow, Wiley (New York, NY), 2000. Contributor to professional journals, including *Cross-Cultural Psychology Bulletin, Journal of Psychotherapy with College Students, Journal of Mental Health, Administration in Mental Health, Journal of Clinical Psychology, Psychotherapy in Private Practice, Medical Psychotherapist, Journal of Contemporary Psychotherapy, International Journal of the Addictions,* and *Journal of Psychology and Theology.* Guest editor, *Clinical Supervisor,* 1984-93; member of editorial board, *Medical Psychotherapy: International Journal;* editorial consultant, *Journal of Family Therapy,* 1993— .

*   *   *

PEAKE, Tom H.
  See PEAKE, Thomas H.

*   *   *

PERLMUTTER, Amos 1932(?)-2001

PERSONAL: Born c. 1932, in Bialystok, Poland; died of cancer, June 12, 2001, in Washington, DC; son of Berta Perlmutter; married; first wife's name, Nina (divorced); married Sharon Watts. *Education:* University of California, Berkeley, bachelor's, master's, and doctoral degrees.

CAREER: Israeli atomic energy commissioner; Israeli Defense Forces, political advisor to chief of staff; member of Israeli delegation to the United Nations; Woodrow Wilson International Center for Scholars, fellow, 1971-72; School of Advanced International Studies, John Hopkins University, Washington, DC, adjunct professor, 1982-90; *Journal of Strategic Studies,* founder and coeditor; School of Public Affairs, American University, professor of political science, 1972-2001. Also taught at Harvard University, the Massachusetts Institute of Technology, and the Free University of Berlin. *Military service:* Served in Israeli military during Israeli War of Independence, 1948, Suez War, 1956, and Yom Kippur War, 1973.

WRITINGS:

Military and Politics in Israel: Nation-building and Role Expansion, Praeger (New York, NY), 1969.

Anatomy of Political Institutionalization: The Case of Israel and Some Comparative Analyses, Center for International Affairs (Cambridge, MA), 1970.

Egypt, the Praetorian State, Transition Books (New Brunswick, NJ), 1974.

The Military and Politics in Modern Times: On Professionals, Praetorians, and Revolutionary Soldiers, Yale University Press (New Haven, CT), 1977.

Politics and the Military in Israel, 1967-1977, F. Cass (Totowa, NJ), 1978.

(Compiler, with Valerie Plave Bennett) *The Political Influence of the Military: A Reader,* Yale University Press (New Haven, CT), 1980.

Modern Authoritarianism: A Comparative Institutional Analysis, Yale University Press (New Haven, CT), 1981.

Political Roles and Military Rulers, F. Cass (Totowa, NJ), 1981.

(Editor, with John Gooch) *Strategy and the Social Sciences: Issues in Defence Policy,* F. Cass (Totowa, NJ), 1981.

(With Michael Handel and Uri Bar-Joseph) *Two Minutes over Baghdad,* Vallentine, Mitchell (London, England), 1982.

Israel, the Partitioned State: A Political History since 1900, C. Scribner's Sons (New York, NY), 1985.

The Life and Times of Menachem Begin, Doubleday (Garden City, NY), 1987.

FDR and Stalin: A Not So Grand Alliance, 1943-1945, University of Missouri Press (Columbia, MO), 1993.

Making the World Safe for Democracy: A Century of Wilsonianism and Its Totalitarian Challengers, University of North Carolina Press (Chapel Hill, NC), 1997.

Also contributor to periodicals, including the *Jerusalem Post, Washington Times, New York Times, Los Angeles Times, Wall Street Journal,* London *Times,* and *Jewish World Review.*

SIDELIGHTS: Born in Bialystok in northern Poland, and raised in Palestine and Israel, Amos Perlmutter was an expert on the Middle East and a frequent contributor to the *Jerusalem Post.* He was a professor of political science at American University from 1972 until his death in 2001, and is the respected author of fifteen books and many articles about the Middle East and U.S. foreign and security policies.

Perlmutter's best-known work is *The Life and Times of Menachem Begin,* which became a bestseller. Begin,

a former Israeli prime minister, resigned in 1983, after making peace with Israel and returning the Sinai Peninsula to Egyptian control. Perlmutter concentrates on Begin's early life, beginning with his experiences as a struggling law student and committed Zionist in Poland just before World War II. In *Washington Post Book World,* Peter Grose wrote, "Evocation of this throbbing Jewish society, now irrevocably destroyed, holds great fascination, and alone can explain the man who ended up, almost by chance, in faraway Palestine." In *New Republic,* Shlomo Avineri commented that Perlmutter's portrait of Begin is "incisive," and observed, "This is the best book on Begin to have appeared."

FDR and Stalin: A Not So Grand Alliance, 1943-1945 examines the relationship between Franklin Delano Roosevelt and Soviet dictator Josef Stalin. According to Perlmutter, Roosevelt sacrificed Eastern European and American interests in order to pursue his goal of an alliance between the United States and the Soviet Union. In addition, Perlmutter contends, Roosevelt and Stalin agreed to leave British Prime Minister Winston Churchill out of the alliance. According to John C. Chalberg in *Reviews in American History,* the book is "an indictment of the whole of Rooseveltian wartime diplomacy from the vantage point of the post-Cold War era." In *National Review,* Peter W. Rodman wrote that the book is "one of the pioneering scholarly efforts in the field" of cold war history.

Making the World Safe for Democracy: A Century of Wilsonianism and Its Totalitarian Challengers presents Perlmutter's interpretation of twentieth-century politics based on his reading of the conflicting goals of Hitler, Stalin, and Wilson. Perlmutter argues that ideology was a driving force in world politics throughout the twentieth century. In the *Review of Politics,* Michael J. Francis wrote, "Perlmutter's historical account of Hitlerism and Stalinism is provocative and illuminating." William C. Widenor, writing in the *Historian,* also found the book "thought provoking," though he noted it was "alternately enlightening and infuriating" due to the fact that the work "is guided by a contemporary question . . . and relies on a very selective reading."

In an obituary in the *Washington Post,* Jay Winik, who collaborated with Perlmutter on several articles, is quoted by Louie Estrada as saying, "He really had his finger on the pulse of the Middle East. He had a keen grasp of the Arab mind in one hand and shrewd insightfulness about the complexities of getting things done in Israel on the other."

BIOGRAPHICAL AND CRITICAL SOURCES:

PERIODICALS

American Historical Review, February, 1978, Peter Paret, review of *The Military and Politics in Modern Times: On Professionals, Praetorians, and Revolutionary Soldiers,* pp. 133-134; April, 1979, Elmer B. Scovill, review of *Politics and the Military in Israel, 1967-1977,* pp. 511-512; June, 1983, Michael Curtis, review of *Modern Authoritarianism: A Comparative Institutional Analysis,* pp. 652-653.

American Political Science Review, June, 1982, Dale R. Herspring, review of *Political Roles and Military Rulers,* p. 438.

Economist, August 29, 1987, review of *The Life and Times of Menachem Begin,* p. 81.

Historian, spring, 1999, William C. Widenor, review of *Making the World Safe for Democracy: A Century of Wilsonianism and Its Totalitarian Challengers,* p. 680.

Jewish Social Studies, January, 1971, Charles S. Kamen, review of *Military and Politics in Israel: Nation-Building and Role Expansion,* pp. 77-79.

London Review of Books, July 1, 1982, Malise Ruthven, "Fundamentalisms," p. 6.

Middle East Journal, summer, 1971, Marver H. Bernstein, review of *Military and Politics in Israel,* pp. 415-416; spring, 1982, L. B. Ware, review of *Political Roles and Military Rulers,* pp. 258-259.

National Review, May 2, 1994, Peter W. Rodman, review of *FDR and Stalin: A Not So Grand Alliance, 1943-1945,* pp. 57-58.

New Republic, October 11, 1982, Stanley G. Payne, "The Authoritarian Century," pp. 32-37; June 8, 1987, Shlomo Avineri, review of *The Life and Times of Menachem Begin,* p. 48.

New York Times Book Review, December 1, 1985, Paul Johnson, review of *Israel, the Partitioned State: A Political History since 1900,* p. 7.

Publishers Weekly, August 16, 1993, review of *FDR and Stalin,* p. 95.

Reviews in American History, June, 1994, John C. Chalberg, review of *FDR and Stalin,* p. 305.

Review of Politics, summer, 1999, Michael J. Francis, review of *Making the World Safe for Democracy,* p. 572.

Times Higher Education Supplement, October 16, 1992, Len Scott, "A War-Torn Peace," p. 29.

Times Literary Supplement, July 31, 1969, "Arming the Jews," p. 860; February 17, 1978, S. E. Finer, "The Statesmanship of Arms," p. 217.

Washington Post Book World, February 23, 1986, J. Robert Moskin, review of *Israel,* p. 8; July 5, 1987, Peter Grose, review of *The Life and Times of Menachem Begin,* pp. 1, 8-9; January 23, 1994, Kenneth Adelman, "Who Blinked at Yalta," p. 4.

OBITUARIES:

PERIODICALS

Chicago Tribune, June 17, 2001, pp. 4, 7.
Los Angeles Times, June 15, 2001, p. B14.
New York Times, June 16, 2001, Wolfgang Saxon, p. A15.
Washington Post, June 14, 2001, Louie Estrada, p. 807.*

*   *   *

PETERSON, Eugenie Vasilievna
See DEVI, Indra

*   *   *

PEZESHKZAD, Iraj 1928-

PERSONAL: Born 1928, in Tehran, Iran; immigrated to France. *Education:* Educated in Iran and France; earned law degree in France.

ADDRESSES: Home—Paris, France. *Agent*—c/o IBEX Publishers, P.O. Box 30087, Bethesda, MD 20824; fax: 301-907-8707.

CAREER: Journalist and author. Iranian judiciary, judge; Iranian foreign service; writer and journalist, early 1950s—.

WRITINGS:

My Uncle Napoleon: A Novel, translated from Persian by Dick Davis, Mage Publishers (Washington, DC), 1996.

Asemun Rismun, IBEX Publishers (Bethesda, MD), 1997.

ADAPTATIONS: My Uncle Napoleon was made into an Iranian television series in the mid-1970s.

SIDELIGHTS: Iraj Pezeshkzad was born in Tehran, Iran, and was educated in Iran and France. He spent five years as a judge in the Iranian Judiciary, and then joined the Iranian foreign service. Pezeshkzad began writing in the early 1950s, translating works by Voltaire and Moliere into Persian and writing short stories for magazines. He has also written several plays and articles on the Iranian Revolution, the French Revolution, and the Russian Revolution. He lives in France, where he works as a journalist.

My Uncle Napoleon: A Novel, which was published in Iran in the early 1970s and rapidly became an Iranian bestseller, tells the story of three families living under the rule of a demanding and paranoid patriarch obsessed with Napoleon Bonaparte, earning him the nickname "Uncle Napoleon." Uncle Napoleon models himself after his namesake, identifies with him, and invents a heroic past based on the real Napoleon's exploits. His extended family becomes increasingly tired of these endless self-aggrandizing tales, and devises numerous schemes to outwit or placate Uncle Napoleon. The story is told from the point of view of an unnamed teenage narrator, who is in love with his cousin Layli. His pursit of love is constantly interrupted by the intrigues, conspiracies, and goofs of his extended family members.

My Uncle Napoleon is presented as social satire; most of the characters are broadly drawn caricatures, and as Julie Scott Meisami wrote in the *Times Literary Supplement,* it "narrates a series of improbable and farcical situations in which mountains are routinely made out of molehills and straightforward behaviour is rejected in favour of duplicity and intrigue." Although Meisami noted that the novel is occasionally anachronistic—set in the 1940s, it uses slang of the 1970s, for instance—on the whole, it is "a very funny book," with "earthy humour" and a "swift pace."

In the *Washington Post Book World,* Gelareh Asayesh wrote that *My Uncle Napoleon* is "a surprising novel, a raunchy, irreverent, hilarious farce wrapped around a core of quiet sorrow." Asayesh further observed it is "like one long party, building from one absurd crisis to the next." "Pezeshkzad, like any author of substance, transcends his cultural boundaries," said Asayesh. A

Publishers Weekly reviewer commented that the satire of specific elements of Iranian society may be unclear to non-Iranian readers unfamiliar with that society.

In 1976 *My Uncle Napoleon* was adapted for Iranian television, and was widely popular. According to Meisami, Iranians "were entertained by its running gags, its caricatures of various character types, and the convolutions of its plot."

In an interview published with the online *Iranian,* Pezeshkzad told Tara Taghizadeh that he wrote the book during a stint in Switzerland while he was in the Iranian foreign service, and that the inspiration for the novel came from "a desire to capture humorously the typical Iranian trait of consistently refusing to accept responsibility, and habitually blaming the rest of the world for Iran's woes." He also said that the character of Uncle Napoleon is loosely based on one of his own uncles, who became obsessed with the French ruler.

BIOGRAPHICAL AND CRITICAL SOURCES:

PERIODICALS

Christian Science Monitor, February 12, 1997, review of *My Uncle Napoleon: A Novel,* p. 12.
Library Journal, November 15, 2001, Andrea Kempf, "The Rich World of Islam: Muslim Fiction," p. 128.
Middle East Journal, autumn, 1997, review of *My Uncle Napoleon,* p. 618.
Publishers Weekly, June 3, 1996, review of *My Uncle Napoleon,* p. 64.
Times Literary Supplement, November 1, 1996, Julie Scott Meisami, "The Teller of Tehran," p. 25.
Washington Post Book World, September 29, 1996, Gelareh Asayesh, "Frolicking in a Persian Garden," p. 4.

OTHER

Atlantic unbound, http://www.theatlantic.com/ (August, 1996), Phoebe-Lou Adams, review of *My Uncle Napoleon.*
Iranian, http://www.iranian.com/ (April 19, 2002), Tara Taghizadeh, "The Myths of a Classic."*

POLLAN, Michael

PERSONAL: Born on Long Island, NY; married Judith Belzer (a painter); children: Isaac. *Education:* Bennington College, B.A.; attended Mansfield College, Oxford; Columbia University, M.A. *Hobbies and other interests:* Gardening.

ADDRESSES: Home—Cornwall Bridge, CT. *Agent*—c/o Random House, Inc., 299 Park Ave., New York, NY 10171.

CAREER: House and Garden, former contributing editor and columnist; *New York Times Magazine,* former contributing editor; *Harper's,* former editor-at-large, contributing editor; freelance writer.

AWARDS, HONORS: Named among the Best Gardening Books of the Twentieth Century, American Horticultural Society, for *Second Nature: A Gardener's Education.*

WRITINGS:

(With Eric Etheridge) *The Harper's Index Book,* illustrated by Martim Avillez, introduction by Lewis H. Lapham, Holt (New York, NY), 1987.

(With Stephen M. Pollan and Mark Levine) *The Field Guide to Home Buying in America: A Home Buyer's Companion from House Hunting to Moving Day,* Simon & Schuster (New York, NY), 1988.

Second Nature: A Gardener's Education, Atlantic Monthly Press (New York, NY), 1991.

A Place of My Own: The Education of an Amateur Builder, Random House (New York, NY), 1997.

The Botany of Desire: A Plant's Eye View of the World, Random House (New York, NY), 2001.

Also series editor of the "Modern Library Gardening" series. Contributor to periodicals, including *Esquire, Conde Nast Traveler, Vogue,* and *Gardens Illustrated.*

SIDELIGHTS: Michael Pollan is a freelance writer and editor who resides in Connecticut with his wife and son. The three books he has authored—*Second Nature: A Gardener's Education, A Place of My Own: The Education of an Amateur Builder,* and *The Botany*

of Desire: A Plant's Eye View of the World—are all "set in, and concerned with, the outdoor classroom that is his five wooded acres in northwestern Connecticut," according to William L. Hamilton in the *New York Times.* Pollan told Hamilton that he "plant[s] certain things because I want to learn certain things," and observed that modern humans have become "divorced from the operations of nature."

Pollan, who has been compared to Thoreau, is an avid gardener who has a disliking for "conventional, neatly mowed suburban lawns," as noted by Kathleen Courrier in *Sierra. Second Nature* "is a brilliant analysis of the relationship between garden and nature," according to Jane Barker Wright in *Horticulture.* Written as Pollan meditated on the garden he was attempting to grow on the land of the Connecticut dairy farm he had purchased, *Second Nature* "isn't so much a how-to on gardening as a how-to on thinking about gardening," observed a *Publishers Weekly* critic, who praised Pollan's witty writing, stating it is "never ponderous." "Pollan's observations are so fresh and well argued that the reader feels transformed," said Wright.

In *A Place of My Own,* Pollan describes his quest to build a small hut on his Connecticut property in which he could write and which would have electricity but no running water. Along with his description of the process, he describes the insights he gained along the way, and he includes bits of architectural history and theory as well as little-known information about building. In Chicago's *Tribune Books,* Karen E. Klages commented, "Pollan has created a glorious piece of prose that speaks to everyone of the built environment, how it shapes us and we it." "One of the things that makes Mr. Pollan such an attractive writer," wrote Verlyn Klinkenborg in the *New York Times Book Review,* "is the modest way he presents his discoveries." A *Publishers Weekly* reviewer called the book "a very special armchair adventure."

The Botany of Desire, which was a *New York Times* bestseller, presents Pollan's theory that domesticated plants have shaped humans as much as humans have shaped them. He writes, "We automatically think of domestication as something we do to other species. But it makes just as much sense to think of it as something certain plants and animals have done to us." For example, he notes, the potato has reshaped the economies of South America and Europe, and the tulip was the subject of such an intense fad in Holland in the 1630s that some people went mad trying to acquire particular types. The book is divided into four parts, each examining a particular plant cultivated by humans: apples, tulips, potatoes, and marijuana.

In he *New York Times Book Review,* Burkhard Bilger wrote that the subject of plant domestication in *The Botany of Desire* is "absorbing," and although at times Pollan's prose is overdone or redundant, in general Pollan "brings a clutch of quirky talents to the task of exploring [his subject]. . . . His prose both shimmers and snaps, and he has a knack for finding perfect quotes in the oddest places." Todd Seavey commented in *Reason* that Pollan sometimes "engages a bit too freely in metaphorical talk about plants planning and strategizing and `wanting' their genes spread," even though evolution is not a conscious process, but noted that Pollan "provides more than enough enlightenment to compensate for any minor drawbacks." In *School Library Journal,* Barbara A. Genco wrote that the book "is a perfect choice for those long winter nights spent longing for spring," while a *Publishers Weekly* reviewer called the work "erudite, engaging and highly original."

BIOGRAPHICAL AND CRITICAL SOURCES:

PERIODICALS

Booklist, February 15, 1997, Kevin Grandfield, review of *A Place of My Own: The Education of an Amateur Builder,* p. 986; January 1, 2002, review of *The Botany of Desire: A Plant's Eye View of the World,* p. 760.

Horticulture, October, 1995, Jane Barker Wright, review of *Second Nature: A Gardener's Education,* p. 71.

Library Journal, February 15, 1997, Jonathan Hershey, review of *A Place of My Own,* p. 160.

New York Times, June 28, 2001, William L. Hamilton, "Sex, Drugs, and Seed Catalogs," p. F1.

New York Times Book Review, March 16, 1997, Verlyn Klinkenborg, "Mr. Pollan Builds His Dream House," p. 8; June 3, 2001, Burkhard Bilger, "For the Love of Potatoes," p. 13.

Publishers Weekly, April 26, 1991, review of *Second Nature,* p. 62; January 13, 1997, review of *A Place of My Own,* p. 61; April 9, 2001, review of *The Botany of Desire,* p. 59.

Reason, February, 2002, Todd Seavey, "The Potato Whisperer: Surprising Wisdom from a Greenish Gardener," pp. 61-62.

School Library Journal, December, 2001, Barbara A. Genco, review of *The Botany of Desire,* p. 59.

Sierra, March-April, 1992, Kathleen Courrier, review of *Second Nature,* p. 80.

Tribune Books (Chicago, IL), May 25, 1997, Karen E. Klages, "Craftsmanship," pp. 6-7.

Whole Earth Review, summer, 1991, Kathleen O'Neill, review of *Second Nature,* p. 116.

Wilson Quarterly, summer, 2001, Christopher Hewat, review of *The Botany of Desire,* p. 122.

World Watch, January-February, 2002, Curtis Runyan, review of *The Botany of Desire,* p. 39.*

*   *   *

POLLARD, Arthur 1922-2002

PERSONAL: Born 1922, in Lancashire, England; died June 2, 2002; married; wife's name, Phyllis; children: John, Andrew. *Education:* University of Leeds, B.A.; University of London, B.D.; University of Hull, B.Th.; Oxford University, B.Litt.; universities of Lincolnshire and Humberside, L.L.D. *Religion:* Church of England.

CAREER: Professor, politician, author, and lecturer. Congleton Council, Lancashire, England, leader, beginning 1952; Hull University, England, professor of English, beginning late 1967. Humberside County Council, elected official; Beverly Rural Ward, East Riding of Yorkshire Council, representative. GCE A-Level chief examiner for thirty-two years; Secondary Examination Council member; University of Buckinghamshire, consultant professor; universities of Leeds, Lincolnshire, Humberside, and the Open University, council member.

WRITINGS:

English Hymns, Longmans, Green (London, England), 1960.

English Sermons, Longmans, Green (London, England), 1963.

Mrs. Gaskell: Novelist and Biographer, Manchester University Press (Manchester, England), 1965.

Richard Hooker, Longmans, Green (London, England), 1966.

(Editor, with J. A. V. Chapple) *The Letters of Mrs. Gaskell,* Harvard University Press (Cambridge, MA), 1967.

Charlotte Brontë, Humanities Press (New York, NY), 1968.

Trollope's Political Novels, University of Hull Press (Hull, England), 1968.

(Editor) *The Victorians,* Barrie and Jenkins (London, England), 1970, P. Bedrick Books (New York, NY), 1987.

Satire, Methuen (London, England), 1970.

(Editor) *Crabbe: The Critical Heritage,* Routledge and Kegan Paul (London, England), 1972.

(Editor) *Webster's New World Companion to English and American Literature,* World Publications (New York, NY), 1973.

(Editor and author of; introduction and notes) *Silver Poets of the Eighteenth Century,* Rowman and Littlefield (Totowa, NJ), 1976.

Anthony Trollope, Routledge and Kegan Paul (Boston, MA), 1978.

(Editor) *Thackeray, Vanity Fair: A Casebook,* Macmillan (London, England), 1978.

(Editor) *Andrew Marvell Poems: A Casebook,* Macmillan (London, England), 1980.

(Editor and author of; introduction and notes) George Crabbe, *New Poems,* Greenwood Press (Westport, CT), 1986.

(Editor, with Norma Dalrymple-Champneys) George Crabbe, *The Complete Poetical Works,* 3 volumes, Clarendon Press (New York, NY), 1988.

The Landscape of the Brontës, with photographs by Simon McBride, E. P. Dutton (New York, NY), 1988.

(Editor) Hugh Latimer, *The Sermons,* Carcanet Press (Manchester, England), 2000.

Also literary editor of *Anglican Hymn Book,* 1966.

SIDELIGHTS: Arthur Pollard wrote or edited dozens of books and authored more than sixty articles on theology, church history, and English literature. He established Commonwealth literature studies at the University of Hull, was a worldwide lecturer, and counseled local governments on education matters. According to Lucy Oates at the *ERiL* Web site, "Pollard's other great interest was the Church of England and he was a reader from 1951." Jeremy Wilcock wrote at the *Beverley & Holderness Liberal Democrats* Web site that Pollard was "a devout Christian, an eminent academic, and a long-standing servant of the community."

In *Crabbe: The Critical Heritage,* Pollard presents a collection of criticism on George Crabbe's works drawn from critics who wrote during Crabbe's lifetime. Although a *Times Literary Supplement* reviewer commented that much of this criticism was "absurdly prejudiced and deadeningly repetitive," the reviewer also noted that the volume contains some commentaries on Crabbe that "touch on the most fascinating and complex aspects of Romantic and Victorian poetic theory." A *Booklist* reviewer wrote that the opinions expressed in the collection are as varied as the contributors, who include "Johnson, Austen, and Tennyson."

In George Crabbe's *The Complete Poetical Works,* which Pollard coedited, the editors present a three-volume edition of the poet's works, including twenty-five previously unpublished poems as well as numerous fragments. In *Essays in Criticism,* Gavin Edwards wrote that the collection's most important feature is that "it gives us a reliable text, and provides clear and detailed justification for its often difficult editorial decisions." He also noted that Pollard and Champneys "are at their best on the scientific, theological and literary contexts of Crabbe's work," although their interpretation of its social and political context is "more often open to question." In the *Review of English Studies,* Peter New noted that Crabbe's works have "at last been accorded the appropriate respect of meticulous editing," and commented that the volumes meet a high standard of "detailed scholarship and general excellence." New concluded, "this is a fine edition, the well-shaped fruit of many years' dedicated scholarship."

Silver Poets of the Eighteenth Century is a collection of poetry by lesser-known poets of that century, including Swift, Johnson, Goldsmith, Gray, and Collins. In *Books and Bookmen,* Derek Stanford praised Pollard's "balanced introduction" to the poets and their work, as well as his wealth of clear explanatory notes on the poems.

BIOGRAPHICAL AND CRITICAL SOURCES:

PERIODICALS

Booklist, November 15, 1972, review of *Crabbe: The Critical Heritage,* p. 272.

Books and Bookmen, February, 1977, Derek Stanford, "A Little of What You Fancy," pp. 49-50.

Criticism, spring, 1979, Linda K. Hughes, review of *Anthony Trollope,* pp. 167-171.

Essays in Criticism, January, 1989, Gavin Edwards, "The Essential Crabbe," pp. 84-91.

Modern Language Review, January, 1983, Paulina Palmer, review of *Andrew Marvell Poems: A Casebook,* pp. 141-143.

Modern Philology, February, 1980, R. C. Terry, "Pinning Trollope Down," pp. 310-314; February, 1991, O. M. Brack, Jr., review of *The Complete Poetical Works,* pp. 333-336.

Review of English Studies, February, 1989, Peter New, review of *The Complete Poetical Works,* pp. 127-128.

Times Literary Supplement, February 2, 1973, review of *Crabbe,* p. 117; September 30, 1988, Donald Davie, review of *The Complete Poetical Works,* p. 1063.

OTHER

Beverley & Holderness Liberal Democrats Web Site, http://www.bevandholdlibdems.org.uk/ (June 4, 2002), Jeremy Wilcock, "Councillor Arthur Pollard: A Tribute."

ERiL, http://www.eril.net/ (June 6, 2002), Lucy Oates, "Death of Councillor Arthur Pollard."*

*   *   *

PRAMOJ, M(on) R(ajawong) Kukrit 1911-1985

PERSONAL: Born April 20, 1911, in Sing Buri, Thailand; died of heart disease, October 9, 1985, in Bangkok, Thailand; son of Prince Khamrob and Mom Daeng Pramoj; married Pakpring Tongyai, 1936; children: Rongrit, Visumitra. *Education:* Attended Queen's College, Oxford.

CAREER: Banker, statesman, and journalist. Elected to the Thai parliament, 1946; elected prime minister of Thailand, 1975-76; *Siam Rath* (newspaper), founder.

Actor and director in theatre productions; film appearances include *The Ugly American* (film), 1963.

WRITINGS:

Top panha pracham wan: chut mai, Kaona (Phranakhon, Thailand), 1950.

Kep lek phasom noi, Khlang Witthaya (Phranakhon, Thailand), 1950.

(With William J. Gedney) *Panha pracham wan,* Rongphim Borisat Khana Chang Chemkat (Phranakhon, Thailand), 1951.

Si phaendin, Siamrat (Krungthep, Thailand), 1956, reprinted, Duang Kamol (Bangkok, Thailand), 1981, published as *See pandin,* Syam Rath (Bangkok, Thailand), 1980, translation by Tulachandra published as *Four Reigns,* Silkworm Books (Chiang Mai, Thailand), 1998.

Phai Daeng, Nakhon Khasem Buksato (Phranakhon, Thailand), 1957.

Kwampenma khong Mutsalim nai Prathet Thai, Phak Kitchasangkhom (Bangkok, Thailand), 1958.

Khu'krit wichan, Klang witthaya (Krungthep Thonburi, Thailand), 1959.

(With Prayun Chanyawong) *Sapda chon,* Phadung Su'ksa (Phranakhon, Thailand), 1960.

Lai chiwit, Khlangwithaya (Krungthep, Thailand), 1960, translated by Meredith Borthwick as *Many Lives,* Silkworm Books (Chiang Mai, Thailand), 1996.

Sawatdi rudu ron, Kaona (Phranakhon, Thailand), 1961.

Khu'krit Pramoj top panha pracham wan, Kaona (Phranakhon, Thailand), 1961.

(With others) *Pathakatha ru'ang kansadet phraratchadamnoen yu'an Saharat 'Amerika lae Yurop,* 'Unao Thong'urai (Bangkok, Thailand), 1962, reprinted, 1988.

Pramuan towathi ru'ang samkhan 10 ru'ang: raila'iat Mom Ratchawong Khu'krit to kap Luang Thamrong—nai yatti 'Lok samai ni charoen khu'n', Kaona (Phranakhon, Thailand), 1962.

Phu'an non chut mai, Kaona (Phranakhon, Thailand), 1962.

Khu'krit wa, Kaona (Phranakhon, Thailand), 1962.

Huannang, Khlangwittaya (Phranakhon, Thailand), 1962.

Chocho, nayok, talot kan: samkok chabap naithun, Rongphim Kasemsamphan Kanphim (Phranakhon, Thailand), 1962.

Chak Yipun, Kaona (Phranakhon, Thailand), 1962.

(With Prayun Chanyawong) *Thok Khamen,* Kaona (Phranakhon, Thailand), 1963.

Phrachedi Chiayhamongkhon, Rongphim Phrachan (Phranakhon, Thailand), 1963.

Panha prachamwan chut phiset, Sansawan (Phranakhon, Thailand), 1963.

Huang mahnnop, Kaona (Phranakhon, Thailand), 1963.

'Anuson nai ngan chalong khrop ro 50 pi haeng kitchakan khong Borisat Punsimen Thai chamkat Phutthasakkarat 2456-2506, Thai Watthaena Phanit (Phranakhon, Thailand), 1963.

Wiwatha rawang Mo.ro.wo. Khukrit Pramoj kap Than Phuttathat Phikkhu, 'Asom 'Akson (Phranakhon, Thailand), 1964.

(With others) *Wiwatha,* 'Ongkan Fu'nfu Phuttasatsana (Phranakhon, Thailand), 1964.

Phu'an non: chabap somnun, Kaona (Phranakhon, Thailand), 1964.

Phraphutthasatsana samrap saman chon, Kaona (Phranakhon, Thailand), 1964.

Lok kap khon, Bannakhan (Phranakhon, Thailand), 1966.

(With Narong Chanru'ang) *Yot nu'ng khont thale,* Praphan San (Phranakhon, Thailand), 1967.

Yiu, Kaona (Phranakhon, Thailand), 1967.

Sangkhom samai 'Ayutthaya, Rongphim Mahawittayalai Thammasat (Phranakhon, Thailand), 1967.

Raingan lae khamchichaeng ru'ang kankosang Phiphitthaphan Sathan haeng Chat Sawanworanayok, privately printed (Bangkok, Thailand), 1967.

Mu'ang Thai nai sanghhom lok: pramuan chak raikan hu'an Non, Praphan San (Phranakhon, Thailand), 1967.

Mu'ang Thai kap Khu'krit, Kanoa (Phranakhon, Thailand), 1967.

Khu'krit kap sangkhom Mu'ang Thai, Praphan San (Phranakhon, Thailand), 1967.

Khon Khong Lok: pramuan chak "Phuan non," Bannakhan (Bangkok, Thailand), 1967.

Ru'ang Phraphutthasatasana, Hanghunsuan Chamkat Siwaphon (Bangkok, Thailand), 1968, reprinted, 1989.

Songkhram Wiatnam, Bannakhan (Phranakhon, Thailand), 1968.

Songkhram phiu: pramuan chak raikan Phu'an non thang withayu, Bannakhan (Phranakhon, Thailand), 1968.

Sawatdi lom ron, Bandan (Phranakhon, Thailand), 1968.

Poet kru phi, Praphan (Phranakhon, Thailand), 1968.

Pisat kanmu'ang: nam khabuan nakkhian chu' kong, Bandan (Phranakhon, Thailand), 1968.

Kukrit Pramoj kap panha khong thai samai lu'aktang mai riaproi, Kasembannakit (Phranakhon, Thailand), 1968.

'Amerika nai 'Esia 'Akhane: pramuan chak raikan Phu'an non, Bannakhan (Phranakhon, Thailand), 1968.

Sathanakan rop ban rao, Bannakhan (Phranakhon, Thailand), 1969.

Ru'ang khong lok tawan Tok, Bannakhan (Phranakhon, Thailand), 1969.

Prachum phongsawadan prachathipatai: pramuan chak raikan "Phu'an non" thang witthayu, Bannakhan (Phranakhon, Thailand), 1969.

Phama sia mu'ang, Kaona (Phranakhon, Thailand), 1969.

Lok suan tua khong Khommunit: pramuan chak raikan "Phu'an non" thang witthayu, Bannakhan (Phranakhon, Thailand), 1969.

Chak na 5 nangsu'phim Sayamrat, Praphan San (Phranakhon, Thailand), 1969.

Songkhram yen, Bannakhan (Phranakhon, Thailand), 1970.

Songkhram ron, Bannakhan (Phranakhon, Thailand), 1970.

Khamen Sihanu, Chawa Kukano, Bannakhan (Phranakhon, Thailand), 1970.

Chao lok, pramuan chak "phuan non" thang witthayn khong M. R. W. Khukrit Pramoj, Bannakhan (Phranakhon, Thailand), 1970.

Songkhram pak: Parmauan raikan chak phu'annon, Bannakhan (Phranakhon, Thailand), 1971.

Sen lae nikai Watcharayan, Kaona (Phranakhon, Thailand), 1971.

(With others) *Samnao khamfong ru'ang lamoet Patinya Sakon klao duai Sitthimanutsayschon lae minprmat doi sai khwam tham hai chot siahai rawang Nai Pridi Phanomyong doi Nai Wicha Kantamara, phurpmop 'amnat chot,* Pru'ang Siriphat (Bangkok, Thailand), 1971.

Phu'nthan thang watthanatham Thai, Mahawittayalai Thammasat (Phranakhon, Thailand), 1971.

Mu'ang nai-mu'ang nok: pramun chak raikan phu'annon, Bannakhan (Phranakhon, Thailand), 1971.

Khu'krit thok Mu'ang Thai: pramuan raikan "Phu'an non," Akson Borikan (Phranakhon, Thailand), 1971.

Kan'aphiprai ru'ang setthakit khong Thai 71, sawan hai ching ru'?, Khana Setthasat (Bangkok, Thailand), 1971.

Khrong kraduk nai tu, Rongphim Chaiyarit (Phranakhon, Thailand), 1971.

Sayamrat na 5, Kaona (Phranakhon, Thailand), 1972.

Sayam mu'ang yim, [Thailand], 1972.

Khrop chakkrawan: pramuan chak raikan 'phu'an non' kkhong Mo. Ro. Wo., Bannakhan (Nakhon Luang, Thailand), 1972.

Khambanyai wicha phu'nthan 'arayatham Thai, ru'ang Phraphuttasatsana kap sanghom Thai, Mahawittayalai Thammasat (Bangkok, Thailand), 1972.

(With others) *Kansadaeng khon somphot Somdet Phraboromma'orasathirat Sayammakutratchakuman doi naksu'ksa Mahawitthayalai Thammasat na hoprachum yai, Mahawitthalyali Thammasat, wan this 27 Thanwakhom 2515: suchibat,* Mahawitthalalai Thammasat (Bangkok, Thailand), 1972.

Huan Nang, Kao Na (Nakhon Luang, Thailand), 1972.

Khu'krit kap prachathipatai: Phonngan lae chiwit thang kanmu'ang khong Khu'krit Pramoj, Bannakhan (Krungthep Mahanakhon, Thailand), 1973.

(Translator) Richard Bach, *Chonathan Livingsatan Nangnuan* (translation of *Jonathan Livingston Seagull*), Kaona (Krungthep, Thailand), 1973.

Khu'krit thok panha chaona chaorai, Kaona (Krungthep, Thailand), 1975.

Su Si Thai Hao, Kaona (Krungthep, Thailand), 1976.

Soi Suan Phlu, Kaona (Bangkok, Thailand), 1976.

Kritsadaphinihan 'an botbang midai, Sayamrat (Krungthep, Thailand), 1976.

Ru'ang khong khon rak ma, Nosopho (Krungthep, Thailand), 1977.

Ruam ru'ang san, Sayamrat (Krungthep, Thailand), 1977.

Phraphutthasatsana; lae, Lok nai Phraphutthasatsana, Phim thi Rongthim Sayamrat (Krungthep, Thailand), 1977.

Khui kan ru'and kao kao, Sayamarat (Krungthep, Thailand), 1977.

Khao nok na, Sayamrat (Krungthep Mahanakhon, Thailand), 1977.

Kansu'ksa kap kansu'pthot lae soemsang watthanatham, Kong Witthanatham (Bangkok, Thailand), 1977.

—Phana—Hoi, Phi.Chi. (Krungthep, Thailand), 1978.

Khu'krit Pramot-phut, Sayamrat (Krungthep, Thailand), 1978.

Yim kap Khu'krit, Sayamrat (Krungthep, Thailand), 1979.

Top panha huachai, Rongphim Sayamrat (Krungthep, Thailand), 1979.

Thunniyom, Samayrat (Krungthep, Thailand), 1979.

Ruchak phu'anban: Kahmen, Yuan, Sayamrat (Krungthep, Thailand), 1979.

Khu'krit phokhruahua pa, Sayamrat (Krungthep, Thailand), 1979.

(With Phichan Tangkhaphaisan) *Watthanatham lae kasaitham,* Sayamrat (Bangkok, Thailand), 1980.

Wairun, Sayamrat (Krungthep, Thailand), 1980.

Tawan chai saeng, 'Ongkankha khon Khurusapha (Krungthep, Thailand), 1980.

(With Chattawa Klinsuthon) *Yu kap Kurit,* Piyasan (Bangkok, Thailand), 1980.

Khu'krit kap phuttasatsana, Sayamrat (Krungthep, Thailand), 1980.

Ban Khu'krit lae Do Khun Tan, Bannakit (Krungthep, Thailand), 1980.

Latthi lae nikai, Sayamrat (Krungthep, Thailand), 1981.

Laksana Thai, Thai Watthana Phanit (Krungthep, Thailand), 1981.

Khu'krit 70, Saphan chatchamnai (Bangkok, Thailand), 1981.

(With He Fang) *Keli Bamo duan pian feng ci xiao shuo xuan* (in Chinese), Wai yu jiao xue yu yan jiu chu ban she (Beijing, China), 1981.

Sam nakhon, Sayamrat (Krungthep, Thailand), 1982.

(With others) *Rabop ratchakan Thai: saphap panha lae khosanoe chak fai kanmu'ang, kharatchakan, nakwichakan, lae thurakit 'ekkachon,* Khana Ratthaprasasanasat (Bangkok, Thailand), 1983.

Panha kankhlu'anyai khong khon Thai, Rongphim Rungru'ang (Krungthep, Thailand), 1983.

(With Witsanu Suwanphoem) *Khu'krit Pramoj, sao 'ek prachathipatai,* Manthana Sathapat (Bangkok, Thailand), 1983.

'Ekkalak khong chat, Samnak Nayok Ratthamontri (Krungthep, Thailand), 1983.

Banthu'k phap chiwit Mo. Ro. Wo. Khu'krit Pramoj— 'atchariya lae puchaniyabukkhon: nuangnai wara 'okat chalong 'ayu khop 6 rop (72 pi), Sayamrat (Krungthep, Thailand), 1983.

Thitthang khong ratthasat Thai, Samakhom Nisit Kao Ratthasat (Krungthep, Thailand), 1985.

Khu'krit 2528, Kongbannanathikan Sayamrat Raiwan (Krungthep, Thailand), 1985.

Pi ni maimi 'arai mai, Rongphim Sayamrat (Krungthep, Thailand), 1986.

Farang sakdina, Sayamrat (Bangkok, Thailand), 1986.

Phayathi katha, Rongphim Sayamrat (Krungthep, Thailand), 1987.

Mu'ang maya, Borisat Sayamrat Chamkat (Krungthep, Thailand), 1987.

Ru'ang khong lathi lae nikai, Sayamrat (Bangkok, Thailand), 1988.

Khun Chang Khun Phaen: chabap 'an mai (with audio cassette), Sayamrat (Bangkok, Thailand), 1988.

(With Vilas Manivat) *Khu'krit yam rak,* Kokya (Krungthep, Thailand), 1988.

Khon lai salok, Sayamrat (Krungthep, Thailand), 1988.

Khu'krit '89/ Happy Birthday 78th Anniversary, Thanaban chatchamnai (Bangkok, Thailand), 1989.

Khon kap suan, Sayamrat (Krungthep, Thailand), 1989.

Kawao thi Bang Phleng, Sayamrat (Bangkok, Thailand), 1989.

Wikrit nai phra Phutthasatsna, Sathaban Wichai Phuttasatasana (Chiangmai, Thailand), 1990.

Lakhon Khu'krit, Sayamrat (Krungthep, Thailand), 1990.

Chomsuan duai kan, Rongphim Sayamrat (Krungthep, Thailand), 1990.

Phikhro Khu'krit phinit si phaendin, Borisat Samnakphim Kokya (Krungthep, Thailand), 1991.

Namphrik, Sayamrat (Bangkok, Thailand), 1992.

Wiwatha ru'ang chit wang, Thammasapha (Krungthep, Thailand), 1991.

Soi Suan Phlu, Rongphim Saysmrat (Bangkok, Thailand), 1993.

Ru'ang san Khu'krit, Sayamrat (Krungthep, Thailand), 1993.

(With others) *M. R. Kukrit Pramoj, His Wit and Wisdom: Writings, Speeches, and Interviews,* Duang Kamol (Bangkok, Thailand), 1983.

Sathaban Thaikhadisu'ksa, Mahawitthayalai Thammasat ruamkap Thanakhan Krung Thep—Phanitchayakan Chamkat, Mahachon chat ngan 84 pi Sattrachan Phontri Mo. Ro. Wo. Khu'krit Pramoj na hoprachum yai-lik, Mahawitthalyai Thammasat, Tha Phrachagn, 19-23 Mesayon 2538 (souvenir book with memoir), Sathaban Thaikhadisu'ksa (Bangkok, Thailand), 1995.

Mong mum prat khon khitlu'k Khu'krit Pramoj, Island (Bangkok, Thailand), 1995.

Photchananukrom chabap Khu'krit, Sayamrat (Krungthep, Thailand), 1996.

Nangsu' 'anuson Khu'krit Pramoj, Munnithi Khu'krit 80 (Bangkok, Thailand), 1996.

Botlakhon ru'ang Si phaendin lae Susi Thaihao: datplaeng chak botpraphan khong So. Phontri Mo. Ro. Wo., Na Ban Wannakam (Krungthep, Thailand), 1996.

Khu'krit, nakleng klon, Borisatphi (Krungthep, Thailand), 1998.

Khu'krit, Sisara (Krungthep, Thailand), 1998.

Kharom Khu'krit, Namfon (Krungthep, Thailand), 1999.

Pramuan ru'angrao kieokap Phraphutthasatasana, Nai Nat Pawinwiwat (Krungthep, Thailand), 2000.

Also author of *The King of Siam Speaks,* 1948; and Phamà sia (in Burmese), 1969.

SIDELIGHTS: "There are certain institutions which a Thai respects," former Thai prime minister M. R. Kukrit Pramoj once said in a speech. "There are his religion, which is mostly Buddhist, his King and his parents. If you say to a Thai that his politicians are rotten he will kiss you on both cheeks. . . . If you call his wife a bitch he will agree with you completely and ask you to have a drink to that. But as for those three institutions which I have already mentioned, I would advise you to leave well alone." The humor and insight of those remarks were characteristic of Pramoj, a longtime writer and politician who became one of his country's most respected figures by guiding Thailand through political turbulence at the end of the Vietnam War. Pramoj, according to a *New York Times* obituary by Barbara Crossette, was also "one of Thailand's most colorful, outspoken and versatile characters."

Though seemingly born to the ruling classes, Pramoj nurtured a sense of humility—no doubt reinforced by his Buddhist leanings—and a self-deprecating sense of humor. The son of a Thai prince, he held the title "mon rajawong," which he abbreviated to M. R., joking that it stood for "minor royalty." "He might have spent his life as a courtier, dispensing wit and wisdom," wrote an *Economist* reporter. "However, as a young man, he was sent to Britain to discover the world outside." Armed with an Oxford University education, Pramoj returned to Thailand to find that the monarchy had bowed to a new form of constitutional government. "He was overjoyed," noted the *Economist* writer. Although embarking on a life in the private sector, where he worked in banking and the civil service, in 1946 Pramoj felt the pull of public service. He ran for and was elected to the Thai parliament, thus embarking on a political career. Some years later he founded the newspaper *Siam Rath,* through which he published editorials opposing the military dictators who rose to power in Thailand in the years after World War II.

In 1975 Pramoj was elected Thailand's prime minister. The concurrent takeover of Vietnam, Laos, and Cambodia sparked concerns that other Asian nations would follow suit and succumb to Communist domination. Pramoj, "rejecting the domino theory, established diplomatic relations with China and asked American troops to leave the huge bases from which they had mounted much of the war in Vietnam," explained Crossette. These were bold steps that endeared the politician to Thai intellectuals; conservatives, however, voted Kukrit Pramoj out of office in 1976 and put in his place his elder brother, Seni Pramoj, as prime minister.

For all his progressive political thinking, Pramoj was a traditionalist when it came to Thai culture. He advocated the teaching of classical language, art and architecture, even opening a school of Thai dancing. A trained stagecrafter, he was even lured by Hollywood, appearing in the role of a fictional prime minister in the 1963 feature film *The Ugly American*. Still, the writer-statesman was determined to honor his country's traditions. "We don't have to live in Western houses or employ Western methods in our daily lives," he was once quoted as commenting in the *New York Times*. "If we were to limit ourselves to just being Thai people, I think we would be happier all around."

Though better known as a politician, Pramoj was also "a world-class writer," according to *New York Review of Books* contributor Richard West, "equipped with imagination, humor, narrative skills, and keen understanding of human nature." One of his few works translated into English, *Si phaendin* follows a woman, Ploi, from her childhood in the 1880s to her death in 1946. Ploi lives through the reigns of four kings, Rama V through VIII, during an historic period in Thai history, as her country moves from monarchy to constitutional government. Noting that "Kukrit never preaches," West added of the novel that it "is clearly meant to explain and extol to a new generation of Thais the customs and faith of their ancestors." In this novel, which appeared in translation as *Four Reigns*, "it is the family that is paramount. This partly explains why Thai women especially love *Four Reigns*."

BIOGRAPHICAL AND CRITICAL SOURCES:

Encyclopedia of World Literature in the Twentieth Century, St. James Press (Detroit, MI), 1999.

Pramoj, M. R. Kukrit, and others, *M. R. Kukrit Pramoj, His Wit and Wisdom: Writings, Speeches, and Interviews*, Duang Kamol (Bangkok, Thailand), 1983.

PERIODICALS

Booklist, June 15 1982, p. 1360; December 15, 1990, p. 807; January 30, 1992, p. 917; November 1, 1992, p. 583; January 1, 1994, p. 812; February 1, 1995, p. 994.
New York Review of Books, January 30, 1992, Richard West, "Royal Family Thais," p. 35.
Translation Review Supplement, December, 1999, review of Four Reigns, p. 7.

OTHER

Things Asian, http://www.thingsasian.com/ (April 22, 2002), Kenneth Champoen, "The Four Reigns of Kukrit Pramoj."

OBITUARIES:

PERIODICALS

Economist, October 21, 1995 p. 109.
Independent (London, England), October 11, 1995, p. 16.
New York Times, October 10, 1995, p. A21.*

Q-R

QUIROS, Armando 1925-

PERSONAL: Born October 28, 1925, in Phoenix, AZ; son of Joseph and Aurelia Quiros; married Lois Fancher (divorced May 29, 1991); married Ruth Bobrov Glater, June 20, 1992. *Ethnicity:* "Mex-American (Latino)." *Education:* San Luis Rey College, B.A., 1948; Old Mission Theological Seminary, M.Div., 1952; Catholic University of America, J.C.L., 1964; Santa Clara University, M.A., 1972.

ADDRESSES: Home—718 North Voluntario St., Santa Barbara, CA 93103. *Office*—1129 State St., Ste. 19, Santa Barbara, CA 93101. *E-mail*—mandquiros@aol. com.

CAREER: Member of Franciscan Fathers of California, 1944-74; Catholic priest, 1951-74; Graduate Theological Union, Berkeley, CA, taught ethics and canon law; Zona Seca Alcohol and Drug Abuse Center, Santa Barbara, CA, clinical supervisor; Klein Bottle Youth Program, Lompoc, CA, clinical supervisor.

MEMBER: California Association of Marriage and Family Therapists.

WRITINGS:

Spiritual Homecoming: A Catholic Priest's Journey to Judaism, Fithian Press (Santa Barbara, CA), 2001.

SIDELIGHTS: Armando Quiros was a Franciscan priest and theology professor before converting to Judiasm. Quiros told *CA* that his primary motivation has been "to speak to the sources of anti-Semitism in the relation to the Bible and Catholic theology. . . . To provide an 'ethical will,' my bequest to those on a spiritual quest." Quiros added that he was inspired by what he termed "a late (very late) awakening to anti-Semitism in my spiritual upbringing."

*   *   *

REDDAWAY, W(illiam) Brian 1913- 2002

OBITUARY NOTICE—Born January 8, 1913, in Cambridge, England; died July 23, 2002, in Cambridge, England. Economist, statistician, educator, and author. Reddaway achieved respect for his skill at applying theoretical or "academic " economics to the practical economic issues of his day. As a young man he turned to economics to help him understand the poverty and depression of the 1930s; his approach was, and would remain, empirical. Reddaway was educated at Cambridge University; in 1938 he was appointed a fellow of Clare College, Cambridge, and there he remained for the rest of his career. He directed the Department of Applied Economics from 1955 to 1969 and retired as a professor of political economy in 1980. Reddaway spent a substantial amount of his time outside the academy as well. During World War II he worked as a government statistician for the Board of Trade, involved among other assignments with developing rationing systems for clothing and gasoline. In the 1950s he was an advisor to the Organization for European Economic Cooperation and the European Coal and Steel Community; in the 1960s it was the Royal Commission on the Press and the National Board for Prices and Incomes; in the 1980s the

Confederation of British Industry. Reddaway also conducted research abroad, including trips to the then-Soviet Union, Australia, and India, which led to books on foreign economies and financial systems. At home, Reddaway's research and writing was often related to taxes and currencies; he was praised for his skill at calculating the empirical and sometimes unexpected ramifications of national policy. His writings include *The Economics of a Declining Population, Measurement of Production Management, Effects of the Selective Employment Tax,* and, as a coauthor, *Companies, Incentives, and Senior Managers.*

OBITUARIES AND OTHER SOURCES:

PERIODICALS

Independent (London, England), July 31, 2002, obituary by Martin Weale, p. 16.
Times (London, England), August 2, 2002.

*　　*　　*

REICH-RANICKI, Marcel 1920-

PERSONAL: Born June 2, 1920, in Wloclawek, Poland; son of David and Helen (Auerbach) Reich; married Teofila Langnas, July 22, 1942; children: Andrew. *Education:* Attended Prussian Gymnasium, Berlin. *Religion:* Jewish.

ADDRESSES: Home—Gustav-Freytag-Strasse 36, 60320, Frankfurt on Main, Germany.

CAREER: Die Zeit, literary critic, 1960-73; *Frankfurter Allgemeine Zeitung,* literary editor, 1973-88; ZDF (public television), host of *Das Literarische Quartett,* 1988-2001. Visiting professor at Washington University, St. Louis, 1968, Middlebury College, 1969, and University of Stockholm and Uppsala, 1971-75; honorary professor, University of Tübingen, 1974. *Military service:* London's Polish consul general and spy, 1948-49.

MEMBER: Group 47, PEN Club.

AWARDS, HONORS: Heine-Plakette, 1976; Ricarda Huch Prize, 1981; Goethe-Plakette, 1984; Thomas-Mann-Preis, 1987; Ludwig-Börne-Preis, 1995; Goethe Prize, 2002.

WRITINGS:

Auch dort erzählt Deutschland; Prosa von "Drüben", P. List (Munich, Germany), 1960.
Deutsche Literatur in West und Ost. Prosa seït 1945, R. Piper (Munich, Germany), 1963.
Literarisches Leben in Deutschland. Kommentare und Pamphlete, Piper (Munich, Germany), 1965.
Literatur der kleinen Schritte. Deutsche Schriftsteller, Piper (Munich, Germany), 1967.
Die Ungeliebten; sieben Emigranten, Neske (Pfullingen, Germany), 1968.
Gesichtete Zeit. Deutsche Geschichten 1918-1933, Piper (Munich, Germany), 1969.
Lauter Verrisse. Mit einem einleitenden Essay, Piper (Munich, Germany), 1970.
Anbruch der Gegenwart; deutsche Geschichten 1900-1918, R. Piper (Munich, Germany), 1971.
Verteidigung der Zukunft; deutsche Geschichten seit 1960, R. Piper (Munich, Germany), 1972.
Über Ruhestörer; Juden in der deutschen Literatur, Piper (Munich, Germany), 1973.
Zur Literatur der DDR, Piper (Munich, Germany), 1974.
Entgegnung: zur deutschen Literatur der siebziger Jahre, Deutsche Verlags-Anstalt (Stuttgart, Germany), 1979.
(With Friedrich von Müller) *Betrifft Göete: Rede (1832) und Gegenrede (1982),* Artemis (Zurich, Switzerland), 1982.
The King and His Rival: The Expanded New Edition of the Correspondence Between Thomas and Henrich Mann, translated by Timothy Nevill, Inter Nationes (Bonn, Germany), 1985.
Zwischen Diktatur und Literatur: Marcel Reich-Ranicki im Gespräch mit Joachim Fest, edited and introduced by Karl B. Schnelting, Fischer Taschenbuch (Frankfurt on the Main, Germany), 1985.
Mehr als ein Dichter: über Heinrich Böll, Kiepenheuer & Witsch (Cologne, Germany), 1986.
Herz, Arzt, und Literatur: zwei Aufsätze, Ammann (Zurich, Switzerland), 1987.
Thomas Mann und die Seinen, Deutsche Verlags-Anstalt (Stuttgart, Germany), 1987.
Der doppelte Boden: ein Gespräch mit Peter von Matt, Ammann (Zurich, Switzerland), 1992.
Günter Grass: Aufsätze, Ammann (Zurich, Switzerland), 1992.
Heine und die Liebe (bound with *Streit und Humanität,* by Walter Jens), edited by Helmut Koopmann and Henning Krauss, Vögel (Munich, Germany), 1992.

Die Anwälte der Literatur, Deutsche Verlags-Anstalt (Stuttgart, Germany), 1994.

Martin Walser: Aufsätze, Ammann (Zurich, Switzerland), 1994.

Die verkehrte Krone: uber Juden in der deutschen Literatur, L. Reichert (Wiesbaden, Germany), 1995.

Vladimir Nabokov: Aufsätze, Ammann Verlag (Zurich, Switzerland), 1995.

Ungeheuer oben: über Bertolt Brecht, Aufbau-Verlag (Berlin, Germany), 1996.

Wolfgang Koeppen: Aufsätze und Reden, Ammann (Zurich, Switzerland), 1996.

Der Fall Heine, Deutsche Verlags-Anstalt (Stuttgart, Germany), 1997.

The Author of Himself: The Life of Marcel Reich-Ranicki, Mein Leben: Autobiographie, translated by Ewald Osers, Princeton University Press (Princeton, NJ), 2001.

Vom Tag gefordert: Reden in deutschen Angelegenheiten, Deutsche Verlags-Anstalt (Stuttgart, Germany), 2001.

EDITOR

In Sachen Böll: Ansichten u. Einsichten, Deutscher Taschenbuch Verlag (Munich, Germany), 1968, published as *In Sachen Böll: Ansichten und Aussichten,* Kiepenheuer & Witsch (Cologne, Germany), 1986.

Wolfgang Koeppen, *Die elenden Skribenten: Aufsätze,* Suhrkamp (Frankfurt on Main, Germany), 1981.

Alfred Polgar, *Kleine Schriften* (selections), Rowohlt (Reinbek bei Hamburg, Germany), 1982.

(With Dagmar von Briel and Hans-Ulrich Treichel) Wolfgang Koeppen, *Gesammelte Werke in sechs Bänden,* Suhrkamp (Frankfurt on Main, Germany), 1986.

Meine Schulzeit im Dritten Reich: Erinnerungen deutscher Schriftsteller, Kiepenheuer & Witsch (Cologne, Germany), 1988.

Horst Krüger, ein Schriftsteller auf Reisen: Materialien und Selbstzeugnisse, Hoffmann und Campe (Hamburg, Germany), 1989.

Romane von Gestern, Heute Gelesen, S. Fischer (Frankfurt on the Main, Germany), 1989.

Hermann Burger, *Erzählungen* (stories), S. Fischer (Frankfurt on Main, Germany), 1994.

Rainer Maria Rilke, *Und ist ein Fest geworden: 33 Gedichte mit Interpretationen,* Insel (Frankfurt on Main, Germany), 1996.

Frauen Dichten Anders: 181 Gedichte mit Interpretationen, Leipzig: Insel (Frankfurt on Main, Germany), 1998.

Heinrich Hein, *Ich hab im Traum Geweinet: 44 Gedichte mit Interpretationen* (poems), Insel (Frankfurt on Main, Germany), 1998.

Hundert Gedichte des Jahrhunderts: mit Interpretationen, Insel (Frankfurt, Germany), 2000.

OTHER

Contributor to Polish journals and newspapers; author of introductions to Polish editions of works by Goethe, Raabe, Storm, Borne, Fontane, Mann, and Hesse. Reich-Ranicki's works have been translated into English and Polish.

SIDELIGHTS: Also known as "der Literaturpapst," or the pope of literature, Marcel Reich-Ranicki is a literary critic whose highbrow intellect, irreverent manner, and unforgiving reviews have made him a household name in Germany. He is also the author of numerous volumes of criticism about German and Polish literature. Well known for disparaging books written by Günter Grass, Heinrich Böll, and other literary giants, Reich-Ranicki admits to losing friends as a result of speaking his mind. Even so, he remains a popular figure in Germany, a fact some attribute in part to his heritage. In an article for London's *Sunday Telegraph,* Daniel Johnson said the author embodies the German "idea of a Jewish intellectual." Johnson theorized, "the Germans embrace Reich-Ranicki as a talisman to ward off the evil spirits of the Nazi past. But he is also seen as a reincarnation of another past, the German-Jewish culture of public intellectuals . . . whose loss the Germans now lament."

Reich-Ranicki first achieved recognition as a literary critic for *Die Zeit,* then as the literary editor of the *Frankfurter Allgemeine Zeitung.* He became popular as the outspoken host of *Das Literarische Quartett,* a televised forum for conversations about contemporary literature. His autobiography, *The Author of Himself* spent fifty-three weeks on the bestseller lists in Germany and was well received by his fellow critics.

The Author of Himself begins with Reich-Ranicki's account of his childhood in Poland and his experience as a young Jew during World War II. Early chapters of the book detail life in the Warsaw Ghetto, where

Reich-Ranicki lived with his family and worked as an interpreter for the Nazi Party. A reviewer for *Library Journal* remarked, "Reich-Ranicki's accounts of life in the Polish ghetto are some of the most vivid and compelling ever written." A *World Literature Today* reviewer called Reich-Ranicki's descriptions of the ghetto "sober, matter-of-fact, without comments." He added, "Reich-Ranicki is brilliant: He knows that the extreme cannot tolerate intensification. He does not weep, for he has no intention to do his reader's work. The reader weeps."

The Author of Himself also chronicles Reich-Ranicki's postwar experience, with chapters on his work as a Polish consul and spy in London, his affiliation with the Communist Party, and his arrival in West Germany in 1958. It concludes with a segment on postwar German intellectual life. Jacob Heilbrunn of the *Los Angeles Times* praised the book for its "deceptively simple and beautifully wrought German," adding, "it is one of the most poignant and important memoirs of the twentieth century." In the *Partisan Review*, Elaine Margolin concluded, "Reich-Ranicki's first-person narrative is written with subtlety and intelligence, and is an unforgettable piece of Holocaust literature that forces the reader to consider the long-term effects of unimaginable loss."

In addition to *The Author of Himself*'s literary merit, many critics note the cultural significance of Reich-Ranicki's background and his readiness to return to the nation behind the Holocaust. Anne Applebaum remarked in *Spectator* that both characteristics reflect the author's complicated relationship to Germany, its language, and its literature. "He addresses the question," she wrote, "of how it was possible for a nation with a culture such as Germany's to carry out the Holocaust, and of how it was possible, after Auschwitz, for a Jew to reconcile himself to Germany. The answers are sometimes tangled, and certainly not complete, but almost no one else will ever be in a better position to provide them."

Reich-Ranicki has published more than twenty works of critical literature in addition to his autobiography, and is considered by many to be Germany's preeminent literary critic. In 2002 he was honored with the prestigious Goethe Prize in recognition of his life's work.

BIOGRAPHICAL AND CRITICAL SOURCES:

BOOKS

Hage, Volker, editor, *Golo Mann, Marcel Reich-Ranicki: Enthusiasten der Literatur: ein Briefwechsel, Aufsätze und Portraits*, S. Fischer (Frankfurt, Germany), 2000.

Jens, Walter, editor, *Literatur und Kritik: aus Anlass d. 60. Gerburtstages von Marcel Reich-Ranicki*, Deutsche Verlags-Anstalt (Stuttgart, Germany), 1980.

Koeppen, Wolfgang, *Ohne Absicht: Gespräch mit Marcel Reich-Ranicki in der Reihe "Zeugen des Jahrhunderts,"* edited by Ingo Hermann, Lamuv (Göttingen, Germany), 1994.

Wapnewski, Peter, editor, *Beatrifft Literatur: über Marcel Reich-Ranicki*, Deutsche Verlags-Anstalt (Stuttgart, Germany), 1990.

PERIODICALS

Choice, January, 2002, R.C. Conard, review of *The Author of Himself*, p. 885.

Independent (London, England), May 11, 2001, Martin Chalmers, review of *The Author of Himself*, p. 5.

Independent Sunday (London, England), April 29, 2001, Robin Buss, review of *The Author of Himself*, p. 33.

Library Journal, September 1, 2001, review of *The Author of Himself*, p. 180.

Los Angeles Times, July 28, 2002, Jacob Heilbrunn, review of *The Author of Himself*, p. R13.

New York Review of Books, April 11, 2002, Neal Ascherson, "Surviving for Art," p. 55.

New York Times, November 25, 1984, James M. Markham, "Frankfurt Critic Sees Unity in German Literature," p. 38; August 31, 2002, Desmond Oates Butler, "Holocaust Survivor Wins Goethe Prize," pp. A21, B15.

Partisan Review, summer, 2002, Elaine Margolin, review of *The Author of Himself*, p. 490.

Publishers Weekly, July 2, 2001, review of *The Author of Himself*, p. 67.

Spectator, May 26, 2001, Anne Applebaum, review of *The Author of Himself*, p. 49.

Sunday Telegraph, April 22, 2001, Daniel Johnson, review of *The Author of Himself*, p. 16.

Time International, July 10, 2000, "Erudite Everyman," p. 54.

Times (London, England), April 18, 2001, John Ardagh, review of *The Author of Himself,* p. 15.

Times Literary Supplement, October 10, 1997, T.J. Reed, review of *Der Fall Heine,* p. 3; December 17, 1999, Peter Graves, review of *Mein Leben: Autobiographie,* p. 25.

Wall Street Journal, July 22, 1983, Amity Shlaes, "German Book Czar: A Survivor from Warsaw," p. 17; July 5, 2002, Ian Johnson, "A Novel Piques Old German Anxieties," p. A7.

World Literature Today, summer, 1991, review of *Thomas Bernhard: Aufsatze und Reden,* p. 483; fall, 1991, review of *Romane von Gestern-heut Gelesen: 1933-1945,* p. 706; summer, 1992, review of *Ohne Rabatt: uber literatur aus der DDR,* p. 511, *Max Frisch: Aufsatze,* p. 515; winter, 1995, review of *Die Anwalte der Literatur,* p. 133; summer, 1997, review of *Wolfgang Koeppen: Aufsatze und Reden,* p. 584; spring, 2001, review of *Mein Leben,* p. 370.

OTHER

DasErste Web site, http://daserste.de/ (September 12, 2002), interview with Marcel Reich-Ranicki.

Princeton University Press Web site, http://www.pup.princeton.edu/ (August 20, 2002), review of *The Author of Himself.**

*   *   *

REISS, Julie H. 1962-

PERSONAL: Born April 27, 1962, in New York, NY; daughter of James S. and Johanna (an author) Reiss. *Education:* Reed College, B.A., 1984; City University of New York, Ph.D., 1996.

ADDRESSES: Agent—c/o MIT Press, Five Cambridge Center, Cambridge, MA 02142-1493. *E-mail*—jhmrtrf@aol.com.

CAREER: Author.

MEMBER: College Art Association.

WRITINGS:

From Margin to Center: The Spaces of Installation Art, MIT Press (Cambridge, MA), 1999.

WORK IN PROGRESS: "Researching the role of the viewer in contemporary art."

SIDELIGHTS: Julie H. Reiss told *CA:* "I am interested in the interaction between the viewer and the work of art. I write on aspects of art that most directly address this issue."

*   *   *

RICE, Patricia 1949-

PERSONAL: Born 1949, in NY; married; children: two.

ADDRESSES: Home—Charlotte, NC. *Agent*—c/o Ivy Books Publicity, 1540 Broadway, New York, NY 10036. *E-mail*—readers@patriciarice.com.

CAREER: Former certified public accountant; full-time writer.

MEMBER: Romance Writers of America, Authors Guild, Novelists, Inc.

AWARDS, HONORS: Romantic Times Reviewer's Choice Award, 1988, for *Indigo Moon; Romantic Times* Career Achievement Award, Historical Fantasy, 1991; *Romantic Times* Reviewer's Choice Award, Best Regency Comedy, 1992, for *Mad Maria's Daughter; Romantic Times* Career Achievement Award, Historical Storyteller of the Year, 1993; Bookrak Bestselling Paperback Award, 1994, for *Texas Lily; Romantic Times* Career Achievement Award, Best British-Set Historical Romance, 2000.

WRITINGS:

Love's First Surrender, Zebra (New York, NY), 1984, reissued as *Surrender,* Zebra Books (New York, NY), 1998.

Lady Sorceress, Signet (New York, NY), 1985.

Moonlight Mistress, Zebra (New York, NY), 1985.

Love Betrayed, Onyx (New York, NY), 1987.

Lord Rogue, New American Library (New York, NY), 1988.

Indigo Moon, Signet (New York, NY), 1988.

Silver Enchantress, Onyx (New York, NY), 1988.

Cheyenne's Lady, Onyx (New York, NY), 1989.

Love Forever After, Onyx (New York, NY), 1990.

Rebel Dreams, Onyx (New York, NY), 1991.

Moon Dreams, Onyx (New York, NY), 1991.

Devil's Lady, Onyx (New York, NY), 1992.

Artful Deceptions, Signet Regency (New York, NY), 1992.

Mad Maria's Daughter, Signet Regency (New York, NY), 1992.

Touched by Magic, Onyx (New York, NY), 1992.

Shelter from the Storm, Onyx (New York, NY), 1993.

The Genuine Article, Signet Regency (New York, NY), 1994.

Texas Lily, Topaz (New York, NY), 1994.

Paper Roses, Topaz (New York, NY), 1995.

Paper Tiger, Topaz (New York, NY), 1995.

Denim and Lace, Topaz (New York, NY), 1997.

Paper Moon, Topaz (New York, NY), 1996.

The Marquess, Topaz (New York, NY), 1997.

Wayward Angel, Topaz (New York, NY), 1997.

Garden of Dreams, Fawcett Gold Medal (New York, NY), 1998.

Blue Clouds, Fawcett Gold Medal (New York, NY), 1998.

Volcano, Fawcett Gold Medal (New York, NY), 1999.

Impossible Dreams, Ivy Books (New York, NY), 2000.

Merely Magic, Signet (New York, NY), 2000.

All a Woman Wants, Signet (New York, NY), 2001.

Nobody's Angel, Thorndike Press (Waterville, NY), 2001.

Almost Perfect, Ivy Books (New York, NY), 2002.

Must Be Magic, Signet (New York, NY), 2002.

McCloud's Woman, Ivy Books (New York, NY), 2003.

Contributor of novellas to anthologies, including *The Kissing Bough,* in *A Regency Christmas,* Signet, 1989; *Deceiving Appearances,* in *Full Moon Magic,* Signet, 1992; *Midnight Lovers,* in *Moonlight Lovers,* Signet, 1993; *Keeping the Fire Hot,* in *Secrets of the Heart,* Topaz, 1994; *A Golden Crocus,* in *Blossoms,* Signet, 1995; *Friends Are Forever,* in *A Country Christmas,* Onyx, 1999; and *Fathers and Daughters,* in *Captured Hearts,* Topaz, 1999.

SIDELIGHTS: Romance writer Patricia Rice has published numerous novels, and has won several career achievement awards from *Romance Times* magazine. She began writing when she was very young, having become devoted to books after her family moved from New York to Kentucky, which left her with "culture shock," she noted in *Romantic Hearts.* As her new neighborhood did not have a library or bookstore, she tried writing her first book at age nine, so she would have something to read.

She continued to write during her teens; in *Romantic Hearts,* she described her early work as "wildly romantic books about misunderstood teens who died tragically." She eventually married, had children, and earned an accounting degree, while continuing to write.

Her move into serious writing came when her husband took a job in a small town where she did not know anyone and could not find a job. In a bookstore, she discovered historical romances, and decided to write her own. She went on to earn a name for herself as a respected writer of both historical and contemporary romances. At her Web site, Rice noted that she "create[s] different types of experiences" in the two genres. "Historicals can be purely imaginary within the realm of the setting and period," she said. "But creating contemporaries requires a great deal more attention to detail and pragmatics," she later continued.

All a Woman Wants features Victorian spinster Bea Cavendish, who has just lost her father and inherited his heavily mortgaged estate. Bea runs into seafaring Lachlan Warwick McTavish, and despite his coarse ways, hires him to teach her about estate management. He agrees, as long as she finds a nanny for his nephew and niece—but he does not tell her that he has kidnapped them from their neglectful father, the Viscount Simmons. As they work to repair the estate, romance blooms between them, made tense by McTavish's plan to leave and immigrate to America with the two children. In *Publishers Weekly,* a reviewer praised the novel's "complex, sympathetic characters" and its "moving but inevitable conclusion."

In *Almost Perfect* Cleo Alyssum moves to a small South Carolina beach town to restart her life and regain custody of her nine-year-old son after battling drug addiction and a criminal past. She uses a small inheritance to buy some beachfront property, and soon meets Jared McCloud, who wants to rent a small house on the property. Initially, Cleo is standoffish, but eventually she comes to trust Jared after they endure a hurricane together. *Booklist* reviewer Megan Kalon wrote that *Almost Perfect* is "perfectly captivating."

At her Web site, Rice commented, "I love the stories of the people behind closed doors and shuttered windows." She said she usually begins her stories with two strong characters in mind—characters with problems they need to overcome and needs they want to satisfy. Often she finds her characters are looking for home, and "as I build the characters and their relationships, I tend to build homes around them."

BIOGRAPHICAL AND CRITICAL SOURCES:

BOOKS

Jaegly, Peggy J., *Romantic Hearts: A Personal Reference for Romance Readers,* Scarecrow Press (Lanham, MD), 1997.

PERIODICALS

Booklist, January 1, 2001, Diana Tixier Herald, review of *Nobody's Angel,* p. 927; February 1, 2002, Megan Kalan, review of *Almost Perfect,* p. 928.
Library Journal, August, 1998, Kristin Ramsdell, review of *Blue Clouds,* p. 73.
Publishers Weekly, November 25, 1988, review of *Lord Rogue,* p. 63; November 30, 1990, Penny Kaganoff, review of *Moon Dreams,* p. 68; August 10, 1992, review of *Devil's Lady,* p. 67; February 12, 1996, review of *Paper Moon,* p. 74; March 27, 2000, review of *Impossible Dreams,* p. 57; May 14, 2001, review of *All a Woman Wants,* p. 58; January 28, 2002, review of *Almost Perfect,* p. 276.

OTHER

Patricia Rice Web site, http://www.patriciarice.com (June 27, 2002).
Romance Reader, http://www.theromancereader.com/ (February 2, 1998), Ann McGuire, review of *Garden of Dreams;* (July 31, 1998) Linda Mowery,

review of *Blue Clouds;* (July 26, 1999) Cathy Sova, review of *Volcano;* (March 18, 2000) Susan Scribner, review of *Impossible Dreams;* (February 27, 2001) Jean Mason, review of *Nobody's Angel.**

*   *   *

RICHARDS, Vernon 1915-2001

PERSONAL: Original name, Vero Benvenuto Constantino Recchioni; born July 19, 1915, in London, England; died December 10, 2001; son of Emidio (some sources say Ernidio; an anarchist) and Constanza Recchioni; married Marie Louis Berneri (a writer), 1937 (died 1949); companion of Peta Hewetson (died 1997). *Education:* King's College London, degree, 1939. *Politics:* Anarchist. *Hobbies and other interests:* Organic gardening, photography, violin.

CAREER: Political activist, publisher, and writer. *Italia Libera* (newspaper), founder; *Freedom* (anarchist newspaper; previously called *Spain and the World, Revolt!,* and *War Commentary*), founder, 1936; Freedom Press Group, member, 1949-52; Freedom Press, editor, 1952-64, contributing writer and editor, 1964-1990s; organic gardener, 1968-2001. Also railway construction engineer, tour leader, photographer, manager of his father's London-based wine and pasta store.

WRITINGS:

(Editor) *Marie Louise Berneri: A Tribute,* Freedom Press (London, England), 1949.
(Editor) *Neither East nor West,* Freedom Press (London, England), 1952.
Lessons of the Spanish Revolution, 1936-1939, Freedom Press (London, England), 1953, reprinted, 1983.
(Editor and compiler) *Errico Malatesta: His Life and Ideas,* Freedom Press (London, England), 1965.
The Impossibilities of Social Democracy, Freedom Press (London, England), 1978.
Protest without Illusions, afterword by Gillian Fleming, Freedom Press (London, England), 1981.
(Editor) Betrand Russell, and others, *Why Work?: Arguments for the Leisure Society,* Freedom Press (London, England), 1983.

The Left and World War II, Freedom Press (London, England), 1989.

(Editor) *British Imperialism and the Palestine Crisis,* Freedom Press (London, England), 1989.

(Editor) *Neither Nationalisation nor Privatisation,* Freedom Press (London, England), 1989.

(Editor) *World War—Cold War,* Freedom Press (London, England), 1989.

(Editor) *Spain: Social Revolution—Counter Revolution (1936-1939),* Freedom Press (London, England), 1990.

The Anarchist Revolution, Freedom Press (London, England), 1995.

Weekend Photographer's Notebook, Freedom Press (London, England), 1996.

George Orwell at Home, Freedom Press (London, England), 1998.

Violence and Anarchism, Freedom Press (London, England), 1998.

Beauty Is More than in the Eye of the Beholder, Freedom Press (London, England), 1999.

Part-time Photographer's Portrait Gallery, Freedom Press (London, England), 1999.

Also authored many articles and pamphlets.

SIDELIGHTS: Vernon Richards was for more than sixty years one of the most significant figures in the anarchist movement in Britain and beyond, according to his obituary writer in the London *Times.* He was a writer and political activist, contributing to newspapers, anthologies, and pamphlets, and authoring several books on anarchist themes. The *Times* obituary writer noted that Richards "did more than almost anyone else to sustain and propagate anarchist ideas."

Richards was born Vero Benvenuto Constantino Recchioni in 1915 in the Soho district of London, England. His father, Emidio Recchioni, was an anarchist who had been incarcerated in the 1890s in the Italian prison on the island of Pantelleria and who subsequently escaped and immigrated to England. Between World War I and World War II Emidio was involved in plots to assassinate Italian dictator Mussolini. Thus, Richards grew up with anarchist ideals and role models.

Richards, like his father, became active in the fight against Mussolini, and in 1935 was deported from France. He returned to London, changed his name to Vernon Richards, and began publishing an anarchist/anti-fascist paper called *Italia Libera* ("Free Italy").

In 1936, when the Spanish Civil War began, Richards worked to promote British support of Spanish anarchists. He founded a newspaper, *Spain and the World,* which provided first-hand accounts of the war in Spain. Eventually, however, the paper's focus broadened and it became the most influential anarchist paper in Great Britain, the successor to the previous paper *Freedom,* originally founded in 1886 and suspended in 1932.

Spain and the World was renamed *Revolt!* when the Spanish Civil War ended, and then renamed *War Commentary* when World War II began. In 1944 Richards, his wife, and two friends were arrested for producing anti-war propaganda. In 1945 they were put on trial. Richards's wife was found not guilty because the law stated that legally a wife cannot be considered to conspire with her husband, but Richards and his two friends were sentenced to twelve months in prison.

When World War II ended, Richards renamed his newspaper *Freedom,* and expanded his activities to publishing anarchist books and pamphlets under a book-publishing wing of the paper called Freedom Press. In 1965 Richards moved from London to the countryside of Suffolk, where he grew organic vegetables and continued to contribute to the operation of Freedom Press.

Richards's writings included two books about his wife: *Marie Louise Berneri: A Tribute* and *Neither East nor West;* an analysis titled *Lessons of the Spanish Revolution;* and a biography, *Errico Malatesta: His Life and Ideas.* He also produced two collections of his own articles, *The Impossibilities of Social Democracy* and *Protest without Illusions. Why Work?: Arguments for the Leisure Society* was an anthology of works by many writers, including Bertrand Russell and William Morris.

Colin Ward noted in an obituary for the London *Guardian* that "at the end of the 1990s, admirers sponsored the publication by Freedom Press of four books of Richards's photographs. In 1999, the Centre for Catalan Studies produced an album of his pictures, taken after 1957 while he was escorting holidaymakers to the then poverty-stricken Catalan village of L'Escala."

BIOGRAPHICAL AND CRITICAL SOURCES:

PERIODICALS

New Statesman, July 28, 1972, Edward Blishen, "Incarcerated," pp. 131-132.

OBITUARIES:

PERIODICALS

Guardian (London, England), February 4, 2002, Colin Ward, p. 16.
Independent (London, England), December 13, 2001, John Pilgrim, p. S6.
Times (London, England), December 12, 2001, p. 19.*

* * *

RICKEY, George Warren 1907-2002

OBITUARY NOTICE—Born June 6, 1907, in South Bend, IN; died July 17, 2002, in St. Paul, MN. Sculptor, artist, educator, and author. Rickey's abstract kinetic sculptures have enchanted viewers all over the world. He specialized in large geometric sculptures, frequently of stainless steel, which were designed to move with the wind. What interested him most, he claimed, was not the shape of the objects he created, but the patterns of motion he could see when they were activated by the air around them. Rickey's works have been compared to the mobiles of Alexander Calder and identified with the Constructivist style that emerged in Russia early in the twentieth century. The sculptor was educated at Oxford University; he studied art in Paris and in England at the Ruskin School of Drawing and Fine Art. He began his career as a painter, but his fascination with movement drew him increasingly toward sculpture. By the end of his career, Rickey's work had been exhibited all over the world and housed in permanent collections, including those of the Museum of Modern Art, the Corcoran Gallery of Art, and the Tate Gallery. Rickey was also an educator, teaching at colleges in Pennsylvania and throughout the Midwest. He was a professor at Tulane University from 1955 to 1962, then at Rensselaer Polytechnic Institute in New York until 1965. He was an active sculptor until shortly before his death, with studios in East Chatham, New York, Santa Barbara, California, and Berlin, Germany. Rickey's work has been published in several collections in the United States and Germany, and he was the author of the book *Constructivism: Origins and Evolution.* Rickey was awarded the gold medal for sculpture of the American Academy of Arts and Letters in 1995.

OBITUARIES AND OTHER SOURCES:

BOOKS

Contemporary Artists, 4th edition, St. James Press (Detroit, MI), 1996.

PERIODICALS

Los Angeles Times, July 23, 2002, p. B11.
New York Times, July 21, 2002, obituary by Ken Johnson, p. A21.

* * *

RIGG, Patricia Diane 1951-

PERSONAL: Born September 3, 1951, in London, England; married. *Education:* University of Calgary, Ph.D.

ADDRESSES: Home—62 Silver Terr., Bedford, Nova Scotia, Canada B4A 3R8. *Office*—Department of English, Acadia University, Wolfville, Nova Scotia, Canada B0P 1X0; fax: 908-585-1070. *E-mail*—patricia.rigg@acadiau.ca.

CAREER: Acadia University, Wolfville, Nova Scotia, Canada, assistant professor of English, 1995—.

WRITINGS:

Robert Browning's Romantic Irony in "The Ring and the Book," Fairleigh Dickinson University Press (Madison, NJ), 1999.

WORK IN PROGRESS: Research on nineteenth-century women poets.

* * *

RIVERA, Edward 1939(?)-2001

PERSONAL: Born c. 1939, in Puerto Rico; died of a heart attack, August 25, 2001, in New York. *Education:* City College of New York Columbia University, M.F.A.

CAREER: Writer and educator. City College of New York, assistant professor of English, 1969-2001.

WRITINGS:

Family Installments: Memories of Growing up Hispanic, Morrow (New York, NY), 1982.

Also contributed short stories and essays to literary magazines and anthologies, including *New American Review, Bilingual Review,* and *New York Magazine.*

SIDELIGHTS: Edward Rivera was born in Puerto Rico, but grew up in New York City. He was an assistant professor at the City College of New York, where he taught English and worked at the college's Center for Worker Education. He is the author of an autobiographical novel, *Family Installments: Memories of Growing up Hispanic.* He also served as a mentor for other writers, including Abraham Rodriguez, Jr. and Junot Diaz.

Rivera took ten years to write *Family Installments,* which tells how a young boy noted for producing what *Nation* reviewer Elena Brunet called "the best-spelled graffiti in Spanish Harlem" became a writer. Brunet praised the book's "cadenced, mythlike" beginning, which describes the narrator's ancestors in Puerto Rico. From Puerto Rico, the novel moves to New York and follows the journey of young Santos as he grows up and tries to find his place in American culture.

The book describes culture clashes, as Santos's family tries to fit into American culture. For example, when a teacher assigns Shakespeare's *Julius Caesar* as required reading in an English class, narrator Santos and his Puerto Rican friends are confused and offended by the behavior of Shakespeare's characters. As Udo Nattermann explained in *International Fiction Review,* "The pupils regard the behavior of the Roman characters as an insult to Puerto Rican values, even as an expression of sexual perversion, and the Elizabethan language as an arrogant assumption of class superiority."

In another scene, Santos and his friend Pannas are playing in Central Park when they are harassed by four African-American boys who demand to know to what racial group they belong. In this way, Nattermann noted, Santos "learns that the United States is a racially segregated country compelling its citizens to decide with which ethnic group they want to be associated."

According to Rivera's obituary in the *New York Times,* the novel was viewed as "a groundbreaking book" about Latino culture in Puerto Rico and New York City. In the obituary, Rivera's brother Richard is quoted as saying the book was "a way of documenting the importance of our family in [Rivera's] life, and the pain of culturation [sic]." In *Newsweek,* Jean Strouse praised the novel's "generosity" and remarked, "Rivera does not steer Santos along any narrow path of self-definition. Instead, he uses him to bring out the full textures and colors of everything he sees. By telling his story so well, Rivera turns it into a gift—both to the people he writes about, and to the rest of us."

BIOGRAPHICAL AND CRITICAL SOURCES:

PERIODICALS

International Fiction Review, January, 2001, Udo Nattermann, "International Fiction vs. Ethnic Autobiography: Cultural Appropriation in Mark Twain and Edward Rivera," p. 13.
Library Journal, September 1, 1982, review of *Family Installments: Memories of Growing up Hispanic,* p. 1654.
Ms., July, 1983, Madeline Lee, review of *Family Installments,* p. 76.
Nation, December 25, 1982, Elena Brunet, review of *Family Installments,* p. 693.
Newsweek, August 30, 1982, Jean Strouse, "Hispanic Gift," p. 66.
New York Times Book Review, September 5, 1982, Philip Lopate, review of *Family Installments,* p. 5; December 5, 1982, review of *Family Installments,* p. 15; September 18, 1983, review of *Family Installments,* p. 43.
Publishers Weekly, June 18, 1982, review of *Family Installments,* p. 66.
Yale Review, summer, 1983, Carlos R. Hortas, review of *Family Installments,* p. 622.

OBITUARIES:

PERIODICALS

New York Times, September 1, 2001, p. A13.
Washington Post, September 2, 2001, p. C6.*

ROCK, Peter 1967-

PERSONAL: Born 1967, in Salt Lake City, UT; married Ella Vining (a medical student), August 8, 1998. *Education:*Attended Deep Springs College, Deep Springs, CA; Yale University, B.A., 1991.

ADDRESSES: Office—Reed College, 3203 S.E. Woodstock Blvd., Portland, OR 97202.

CAREER: Writer and teacher. Has taught at Deep Springs College, Deep Springs, CO, Yale University, New Haven, CT, San Francisco State University, San Francisco, CA, and University of Pennsylvania, Philadelphia. Reed College, Portland, OR, visiting assistant professor of creative writing, 2001—.

AWARDS, HONORS: Henfield Award, 1996; Wallace Stegner fellowship, Stanford University, Stanford, CA, 1995-97.

WRITINGS:

NOVELS

This Is the Place, Anchor Books (New York, NY), 1997.
Carnival Wolves, Anchor Books (New York, NY), 1998.
The Ambidextrist, Context Books (New York, NY), 2002.

Contributor to periodicals, including *New York Times Magazine, Philadelphia Inquirer, Philadelphia Weekly, Epoch, Tin House, Zoetrope,* and *ZYZZYVA.*

SIDELIGHTS: Peter Rock's novels focus on the misfits of the world. *This Is the Place,* set in a Nevada gambling town just across the state line from strait-laced Utah, deals with the obsessive love of an aging blackjack dealer for a teenage Mormon girl. *Carnival Wolves* follows a burned-out security guard and his dog as they meet a succession of bizarre characters while traveling across the United States. *The Ambidextrist* centers on a homeless young man who becomes an unwittingly malignant influence in the life of a thirteen-year-old boy.

In *This Is the Place,* the dealer, commonly called "Pyro," becomes fixated on nineteen-year-old Charlotte, who has left Bountiful, Utah for the gambling resort of Wendover, Nevada in search of a less circumscribed life than was available among the devout Mormons of her hometown. Pyro is old enough to be her grandfather, and was once the lover of her aunt. Eventually she loses interest in him and departs with a race-car driver, going to Las Vegas and then Salt Lake City, but Pyro, unable to forget her, tracks her down. "The novel we read is the story he tells to justify the terrible crime he commits in the name of love," related Nancy Pearl in *Library Journal.* A *Kirkus Reviews* contributor praised Rock's "vivid vignettes" of Nevada and Utah, but deemed the story "forced," with "an uncertain focus" and much left unclear. A *Publishers Weekly* reviewer thought Rock "misses out on the humanity to be examined in this ill-fated romance." Pearl, however, maintained that the novel offers "an intriguing plot, and fully nuanced characters."

The central character of *Carnival Wolves,* Alan Johnson, is bored with his life as a museum security guard in upstate New York. He decides to take off on a cross-country trip, accompanied by a Dalmatian that he had aided after it fell but that belongs to someone else. Along the way Alan and the dog meet a sadistic taxidermist, a mad chimpanzee, a wife fleeing a polygamous marriage, and an assortment of other strange characters, including an offbeat young woman who finally offers him an emotional connection. Pearl, again reviewing for *Library Journal,* considered *Carnival Wolves* "disappointing" after *This Is the Place.* While "Rock does a superb job of conveying a sense of paranoia and uneasiness," she wrote, ultimately Alan and his story are uninvolving. *Booklist* critic Brian Kenney also saw little of interest in the protagonist or his encounters, but allowed that the novel is "well-written" and that Rock "is definitely an author worth watching." In *Philadelphia Inquirer,* however, Harriette Behringer faulted *Carnival Wolves* for sensationalism and superficiality, observing that, despite occasional "flashes of insight," the narrative "gives way to a mere freak show" and "only shocks." A *Publishers Weekly* commentator, on the other hand, found in the book "considerable depth of characterization and an unerring sense of detail and atmosphere" and called it "a beautifully written, funny, deliberately twisted travelogue."

The Ambidextrist's protagonist, Scott, is a vagabond who earns his living by taking part in medical experiments. He drifts back to his hometown, Philadelphia, with the intention of building a more mainstream sort of life. He seeks to establish friendships with Ruth, a young woman who works in airline security, and her teenage brother, Terrell, who has become involved with a gang. Scott's comment to Terrell about the need to test friendship leads Terrell and his friends to test one another's loyalty in increasingly dangerous and violent ways. Joshua Cohen, writing in *Library Journal,* thought Rock's characters unsympathetic; because of that, he said, "the book never reaches its potential." A *Publishers Weekly* critic also had reservations about the characters, remarking that the "direct and unsentimental" depiction of them "distances the readers from Rock's protagonists." The upside of this approach, the critic reported, is its "documentary immediacy." The reviewer concluded, "The novel is best appreciated for its taut, spare prose, which skillfully evokes the isolation of listless lives."

BIOGRAPHICAL AND CRITICAL SOURCES:

PERIODICALS

Booklist, August, 1998, Brian Kenney, review of *Carnival Wolves,* p. 1969.

Kirkus Reviews, February 15, 1997, review of *This Is the Place,* p. 251.

Library Journal, March 1, 1997, Nancy Pearl, review of *This Is the Place,* p. 104; July, 1998, Nancy Pearl, review of *Carnival Wolves,* p. 138; December, 2001, Joshua Cohen, review of *The Ambidextrist,* p. 175.

Philadelphia Inquirer, August 23, 1998, Harriette Behringer, review of *Carnival Wolves.*

Publishers Weekly, February 24, 1997, review of *This Is the Place,* p. 64; June 22, 1998, review of *Carnival Wolves,* p. 83; December 10, 2001, review of *The Ambidextrist,* p. 52.

OTHER

PhiladelphiaWeekly.com, http://www.philadelphia weekly.com/ (February 8, 2001), Maura Johnston, "City Writs."*

*   *   *

ROMAINE, Suzanne 1951-

PERSONAL: Born 1951. *Education:* Bryn Mawr College, A.B. (magna cum laude), 1973; University of Edinburgh, M.Litt., 1975; University of Birmingham, Ph.D., 1981.

ADDRESSES: Office—Merton College, Oxford OX1 4JD, England. *E-mail*—Suzanne.romaine@ling-phil. ox.ac.uk.

CAREER: Max Planck Institute für Psycholinguistik, Nijmegen, Netherlands, senior research scientist in linguistic anthropology; University of Birmingham, Birmingham, England, lecturer in English; Merton College, Oxford, England, Merton Professor of English Language, 1984—.

AWARDS, HONORS: Honorary doctorate, University of Troms , Norway, 1998; honorary doctorate, University of Uppsala, Sweden, 1999; Rotary International Foundation fellowship; Canadian Commonwealth scholarship; Kerstin Hesselgren professor, University of Uppsala, Sweden, 1991-92; Book of the Year Award, British Association of Applied Linguistics, 2001, for *Vanishing Voices: The Extinction of the World's Languages.*

WRITINGS:

Socio-Historical Linguistics: Its Status and Methodology, Cambridge University Press (New York, NY), 1982.

The Language of Children and Adolescents: The Acquisition of Communicative Competence, Oxford University Press (New York, NY), 1984.

(Editor) *Sociolinguistic Variation in Speech Communities,* E. Arnold (London, England), 1982.

Pidgin and Creole Languages, Longman (New York, NY), 1988.

Bilingualism, B. Blackwell (New York, NY), 1989.

(Editor) *Language in Australia,* Cambridge University Press (New York, NY), 1991.

Language, Education, and Development: Urban and Rural Tok Pisin in Papua New Guinea, Oxford University Press (New York, NY), 1992.

Language in Society: An Introduction to Sociolinguistics, Oxford University Press (New York, NY), 1994.

(Editor, with John R. Rickford) *Creole Genesis, Attitudes, and Discourse: Studies Celebrating Charlene J. Sato,* J. Benjamins Publishers (Philadelphia, PA), 1999.

Communicating Gender, L. Erlbaum Associates (Mahwah, NJ), 1999.

(With Daniel Nettle) *Vanishing Voices: The Extinction of the World's Languages,* Oxford University Press (New York, NY), 2000.

Also edited volume 4 of *The Cambridge History of the English Language,* Cambridge University Press (New York, NY), 1992-2001.

SIDELIGHTS: Suzanne Romaine is a professor and linguist. Her primary areas of interest are historical linguistics and sociolinguistics, including language change, diversity in languages, language acquisition in children, and language and gender.

Language, Education, and Development: Urban and Rural Tok Pisin in Papua New Guinea, based on Romaine's fieldwork among Tok Pisin speakers in Papua New Guinea, examines the use of this language by schoolchildren in Papua New Guinea, and describes how these younger speakers are bringing about change in the language as a whole. These changes involve a split between rural and urban speakers, an increased number of words borrowed from English, and the development of new grammatical rules. In the journal *Language in Society,* Jeff Siegel wrote, "This is an important work for anyone interested in language variation and change, or in pidgin and creole languages."

Communicating Gender explores how gender is communicated in language, and notes that concepts of gender, which vary greatly from culture to culture and across different periods in history, are largely based in linguistic constructs. Romaine combines her linguistic knowledge with forays into sociology, psychology, history, anthropology, feminist studies, economics, and communications, and notes that in any society, there are continually competing versions of reality. The dominant group's interests are usually served by language; thus, there is often a power struggle among groups regarding the proper names for people or things. For example, many minority groups have chosen what label they will take for themselves in order to assert their power; women in our culture may use the title "Ms." or change the title "chairman" to "chair." In *Contemporary Sociology,* Kari Lerum wrote, "No new theoretical ground is forged with this work, but Romaine has amassed one of the largest and most integrative literature reviews on this topic to date." Paula Steward Bush, writing in *Contemporary Psychology,* called the book an "outstanding achievement."

In *Vanishing Voices: The Extinction of the World's Languages,* Romaine and coauthor Daniel Nettle describe how almost half of the world's languages may become extinct in the twenty-first century. For example, Native Americans in California used to speak over one-hundred different languages, and Aboriginal people in Australia had over 250 languages. Both groups of languages are almost completely extinct now, as are thousands of languages all over the world. In 1999 there were fifty-one languages in the world for which there was only a single speaker still living. Five hundred of the world's languages now have less than one-hundred speakers.

Romaine and Nettle argue in *Vanishing Voices* that this loss is part of a larger pattern of loss that is taking place in the earth's ecosystem; they say that the struggle to save particular ecosystems, such as the rain forest, is tied in with the struggle for indigenous people in those ecosystems to save their culture and language. In researching the book, the authors interviewed several people who were the last speakers of particular languages, such as Red Thundercloud, a Native American in South Carolina; Ned Maddrell, the last speaker of Manx, a language of the British Isles; and Arthur Bennett, an Australian who was the last person to speak the Aboriginal language Mbabaram.

Preston Jones praised *Vanishing Voices* in *Books and Culture* for its "theoretical and descriptive" text, which is "less activist" in tone than some other books on the subject. In *Library Journal,* Marianne Orme noted that the authors "persuasively present the scientific value of saving endangered languages," and "provide useful background information and tackle underlying issues."

BIOGRAPHICAL AND CRITICAL SOURCES:

PERIODICALS

Books and Culture, March, 2001, Preston Jones, "Endangered Species," p. 26.
Contemporary Psychology, August, 2000, Paula Stewart Bush, review of *Communicating Gender,* p. 387.
Contemporary Review, February, 2000, Edward Bradbury, "How We Got Modern English," p. 106.
Contemporary Sociology, May, 2000, Kari Lerum, review of *Communicating Gender,* pp. 506-507.

Language, June, 1994, Frances Ingemann, review of *Language, Education, and Development: Urban and Rural Tok Pisin in Papua New Guinea,* pp. 404-405; March, 2000, Zdenek Salzmann, review of *Communicating Gender,* p. 201.

Language in Society, March, 1994, Jeff Siegel, review of *Language, Education, and Development,* pp. 144-149; June, 1996, Felice Ann Coles, review of *Language in Society: An Introduction to Sociolinguistics,* pp. 283-286.

Library Journal, June 15, 2000, Marianne Orme, review of *Vanishing Voices: The Extinction of the World's Languages,* p. 83.

Modern Language Journal, winter, 1994, David James Silva, review of *Language in Society,* pp. 560-561.

USA Today, January, 2001, Steven G. Kellman, review of *Vanishing Voices,* p. 79.*

*   *   *

RONSON, Jon

PERSONAL: Male; Children: Joel. *Religion:* Jewish.

ADDRESSES: Home—London, England. *Office*—c/o Simon and Schuster, 1230 Avenue of the Americas, New York, NY 10020. *E-mail*—jon@jonronson.com.

CAREER: Documentary filmmaker and writer. Maker of television programs *Tottenham Ayatollah, New Klan, New York to California (A Great British Odyssey), Dr. Paisley, I Presume,* four-part series *Critical Condition,* talk show *For the Love Of . . . ,* and five-part series *The Secret Rulers of the World,* all for Channel 4, and six-part series *The Ronson Mission* for BBC2. Producer of radio documentary *Hotel Auschwitz* for BBC Radio 4. Contributor to *All Things Considered* and *This American Life,* both for National Public Radio.

WRITINGS:

Clubbed Class (travel writings), Pavilion Books (London, England), 1994.

Them: Adventures with Extremists, Picador (London, England), 2001, Simon and Schuster (New York, NY), 2002.

Regular contributor to *Guardian Weekend.* Writer of "Human Zoo" column for *Guardian.* Former columnist for *Time Out.*

WORK IN PROGRESS: The nonfiction book *Mystery Project X,* a follow-up to *Them;* a documentary on the Jesus Christians; and a sequel to *The Secret Rulers of the World* for Channel 4.

SIDELIGHTS: British writer and filmmaker Jon Ronson profiles members of numerous fringe political movements in *Them: Adventures with Extremists,* which had a companion five-part documentary series, *The Secret Rulers of the World,* broadcast in the United Kingdom in May, 2001. Among his subjects are Omar Bakri Mohammed, a Muslim fundamentalist who dubs himself "Osama bin Laden's man in London;" Rachel Weaver, daughter of conspiracy theorists Randy and Vicki Weaver, who saw her mother killed by U.S. marshals in a shootout at Ruby Ridge, Idaho in 1992; militant Northern Irish Protestant leader Ian Paisley; the Grand Wizard of the Knights of the Ku Klux Klan; former sportscaster David Icke, who believes the world is ruled by giant lizards disguised as humans; and those who believe the world is ruled by a secret cabal of international financiers, all Jewish, the shadowy "them" from which the book takes its title. He also takes a look at some of those accused of being in the cabal, such as the business and political leaders who get together annually at the Bohemian Grove retreat in Northern California; he portrays the gathering as—far from a plotting session for world domination—a raucous fraternity-style party with a few overtones of New Age spirituality.

Along the way, Ronson manages to humanize the "extremists," in the opinion of several critics. "I've never read such a delightful book on such a serious and important topic," remarked Jon Wiener in *Nation.* "Somehow he's written a warm and humane account of some of the most objectionable people on the planet. And he's got a lot of insight into their picture of us—and our picture of "them." For instance, there is a good deal of humor in his depiction of Omar Bakri, whose claim to be bin Laden's primary London operative appears to be mere puffery and who appears to have had no part in the September 11, 2001 attacks on the United States. "Ronson's portrayal of this Muslim fundamentalist as a comic figure rather than a frightening one is part of his larger project: to demystify the people we call 'extremists,' to de-demonize the demons," Wiener observed. Ronson seeks to understand and explain their thinking, and to allow them to correct some assumptions made by mainstream media—for instance, he gives space to Rachel

Weaver's denial that her parents were white supremacists or anti-Semites. *New Statesman* contributor Bryan Appleyard found Ronson's book "a funny, superbly controlled account of his wanderings through the wonderland of fanaticism and delusion." Appleyard noted that "The writing is carefully understated. He avoids too much comment, offers little analysis, and lets the material speak for itself. In fact, his material is so good that it would be madness to do otherwise."

The author's understated, humorous tone troubled some reviewers. "Ronson's idiosyncratic reporting method leads him into uncomfortable situations," commented Ron Rosenbaum in *New York Times Book Review.* "He plays down, when he doesn't conceal, his own Jewishness, and adopts a chipper British version of the faux-naïf pose, `Yes, how very interesting, tell me more.' But not all Ronson's characters, alas, are harmless eccentrics." For instance, Rosenbaum pointed out, there is Klan leader Thom Robb, with whom Timothy McVeigh, convicted of killing hundreds in the bombing of the Oklahoma City federal building, was once allied. "Robb was by this account part mentor to a mass murderer whose only quarrel with Robb's racist doctrine was its cosmetic overlay," Rosenbaum related. Matt Nesvisky, writing in the *Jerusalem Report,* had a similar problem with the book: "Ronson's subject—right-wing fanatics, conspiracy theorists, Jihad supporters and other assorted anti-Semites—is not, at least to some of us, exactly a thigh-slapping topic. Many of the individuals involved in such activities are either patently ridiculous or otherwise worthy targets for derision. But just as many are truly menacing, and the lies they disseminate can do immeasurable damage." *Spectator* critic Anthony Daniels, however, thought laughing at the truly menacing might not be such a bad idea. Calling Ronson's book "amusing," Daniels added, "His style is relentlessly jocular, as if nothing is to be taken too seriously, and the paranoid in me began to wonder whether, had he attended a Munich beer hall in 1923, he would have written a jocular account of a certain gentleman with a toothbrush mustache. Then again, if people had been able to laugh at him, perhaps the world would have been saved a lot of pain."

BIOGRAPHICAL AND CRITICAL SOURCES:

PERIODICALS

Booklist, November 1, 2001, Gavin Quinn, review of *Them: Adventures with Extremists,* p. 449.

Jerusalem Report, June 3, 2002, Matt Nesvisky, "Fringe Humor."

Kirkus Reviews, October 1, 2001, review of *Them,* p. 1408.

Library Journal, October 15, 2001, Lee Arnold, review of *Them,* p. 99.

Nation, February 18, 2002, Jon Wiener, "Politically Incorrect," p. 32.

New Statesman, May 7, 2001, Bryan Appleyard, "A Wandering Jew," p. 56.

New York Times Book Review, January 13, 2002, Ron Rosenbaum, "Beyond the Fringe," p. 10.

Publishers Weekly, November 12, 2001, review of *Them,* p. 48.

Spectator, April 14, 2001, Anthony Daniels, review of *Them,* p. 33.

U. S. News & World Report, February 11, 2002, Holly J. Morris, "Face to Face with *Them,*" p. 12.

Washington Monthly, January-February, 2002, Alex Heard, review of *Them,* p. 51.

Washington Post, January 3, 2002, Jonathan Yardley, "Way out There: Peering through the Fringe," p. C2.

OTHER

Jon Ronson's Web site, http://www.jonronson.com (July 1, 2002).

Salon.com, http://www.salon.com/ (March 14, 2002), Joanna Smith Rakoff, interview with Jon Ronson.*

*   *   *

ROSE, H(orace) E(dgar) 1913-1999

PERSONAL: Born May 30, 1913, in Fowey, Cornwall, England; died January 19, 1999; married, 1947; wife's name Yda; children: three sons, one daughter. *Education:* City and Guilds College (now Imperial College of Science and Technology), B.S., M.S., D.Sc.; Manchester University, Ph.D. *Hobbies and other interests:* Restoring and building clocks.

CAREER: King's College, London, England, faculty member, beginning 1944, professor of powder technology, 1961-78. During early career, lectured at Manchester University.

MEMBER: Worshipful Company of Clockmakers.

AWARDS, HONORS: Institute of Mechanical Engineers awards, 1946, 1950; Hal Williams Hardinge Prize, American Institute of Mining, Metallurgical, and Petroleum Engineers, 1965; King's College, London, fellow, 1974; Institute of Civil Engineers fellowship.

WRITINGS:

The Measurement of Particle Size in Very Fine Powders, Constable (London, England), 1953, Chemical Publishing (New York, NY), 1954.

(With A. J. Wood) *An Introduction to Electrostatic Precipitation in Theory and Practice,* Constable (London, England), 1956, 2nd edition, 1966.

(With R. M. E. Sullivan) *A Treatise on the Internal Mechanics of Ball, Tube, and Rod Mills,* Chemical Publishing (New York, NY), 1958.

(With R. M. E. Sullivan) *Vibration Mills and Vibration Milling,* Constable (London, England), 1961.

Subrecursion: Functions and Hierarchies, Oxford University Press (New York, NY), 1984.

A Course in Number Theory, Oxford University Press (New York, NY), 1988, revised edition, 1995.

Also contributor to periodicals.

SIDELIGHTS: H. E. Rose was a professor of powder technology at London's King's College. The field of powder science includes the study of particulates as pollutants, and Rose's work has been applied in mining and other industries that have recognized his contributions with a number of awards.

Rose left his village school in Devon at age fourteen to become an printers apprentice in London. At night he attended classes at Regent Street Polytechnic before earning a college scholarship. After earning his Ph.D., he began a long academic career at King's College, where his research into powders gained him wide recognition; he also started a program in powder science at King's for undergraduate and graduate students.

Rose wrote a number of textbooks on powders and other studies in physics and engineering, as well as the mathematics book *A Course in Number Theory. American Scientist* contributor Neal Koblitz praised this mathematics book for covering "a lot of ground," including "algebraic number theory" and "analytic number theory." Although *Choice* critic D. V. Feldman felt that the book lacked a "strong point of view," the reviewer said it was "quite competently executed." And Maurice Machover added in *Mathematics Teacher* that the book "contains excellent problems" and that "Rose's second edition can serve as a good textbook or a fine reference book."

After retiring in 1978, Rose pursued his personal interest in building and restoring clocks, becoming a liveryman in the Worshipful Company of Clockmakers.

BIOGRAPHICAL AND CRITICAL SOURCES:

PERIODICALS

American Scientist, March, 1990, Neal Koblitz, review of *A Course in Number Theory,* p. 182.

Choice, January, 1989, D. V. Feldman, review of *A Course in Number Theory,* pp. 834-835.

Mathematics Teacher, October, 1996, Maurice Machover, review of *A Course in Number Theory,* p. 606.

OBITUARIES:

PERIODICALS

Times (London, England), February 19, 1999.*

*   *   *

ROSS, Charles D. 1958-

PERSONAL: Born September 2, 1958; children: Dylan, Caryn. *Education:* University of Virginia, B.S., 1980, M.S., 1983, Ph.D., 1987.

ADDRESSES: Office—Department of Natural Sciences, Longwood College, Farmville, VA 23909. *E-mail*—cross@longwood.edu.

CAREER: Physicist and author. Longwood College, Farmville, VA, associate professor of physics and director of pre-engineering programs.

AWARDS, HONORS: Maria Bristow Starke Faculty Excellence Award, Longwood College, 2002.

WRITINGS:

Trial by Fire: Science, Technology, and the Civil War, White Mane Publishing Company, Inc. (Shippensburg, PA), 2000.
Civil War Acoustic Shadows, White Mane Publishing Company, Inc. (Shippensburg, PA), 2001.

SIDELIGHTS: Charles D. Ross is a professor of physics at Longwood College in Farmville, Virginia. He is the author of books that combine U.S. Civil War history with scientific reasoning and knowledge.

Trial by Fire: Science, Technology, and the Civil War examines how scientific knowledge and the growth of new technologies influenced events of the Civil War. The war occurred during the Industrial Revolution, when scientific knowledge was being applied to almost every aspect of life, transforming American culture. The first part of the book discusses three colonels who used scientific knowledge to their advantage: Union Colonel Henry Pleasants dug a 510-foot-long tunnel under Confederate lines and exploded a bomb in their midst; Colonel Joseph Bailey created a series of dams on the Red River, saving an entire Union fleet; and Confederate Colonel George Washington Rains created the best gunpowder factory in the world. The second part of the book discusses the use of submarines, aircraft, and the telegraph, all new technologies at the time.

In *Civil War Acoustic Shadows,* Ross examines acoustics on the battlefield, and shows how acoustic properties often had a decisive influence on the outcome of battles. For example, in 1862 at the Battle of Seven Pines, Confederate General Joseph E. Johnston's troops outnumbered Union troops, and Johnston seemed sure to win; but the battle ended up as an indecisive draw. According to Ross, the acoustic properties of the battlefield were the reason. Ross combed through weather records, soldiers' diaries, and historic reports to recreate six battles, showing how weather, terrain, and other factors diverted sound, creating an "acoustic shadow" in which battle sounds could not be heard. In *Choice,* R. E. Bilstein called the book "a useful study, imaginatively researched."

BIOGRAPHICAL AND CRITICAL SOURCES:

PERIODICALS

Choice, January, 2002, R. E. Bilstein, review of *Civil War Acoustic Shadows,* p. 902.
Discover, September, 2001, Fenella Saunders, review of *Civil War Acoustic Shadows,* p. 79.
History Today, April, 2000, Robert Pearce, review of *Trial by Fire: Science, Technology, and the Civil War,* p. 58.

*   *   *

RUNCIMAN, Lex 1951-

PERSONAL: Born February 13, 1951, in Portland, OR; son of Alec (a businessman) and Geneva (a homemaker; maiden name, Martindale) Runciman; married Deborah Berry (a political staffer), September 11, 1971; children: Elizabeth Helen, Jane Christine. *Education:* Santa Clara University, B.A. (English), 1973; University of Montana, M.F.A. (creative writing), 1977; University of Utah, Ph.D. (English), 1981.

ADDRESSES: Home—P.O. Box 268, McMinnville, OR 97128. *Office*—Linfield College Department of English, 900 Southeast Baker St., McMinnville, OR 97128. *E-mail*—lruncim@linfield.edu.

CAREER: Oregon State University, Corvallis, instructor and writing center director, 1981-90, assistant professor of English, 1990-92; Linfield College, McMinnville, OR, associate professor of English, 1992—.

AWARDS, HONORS: Oregon Book Award in Poetry, Literary Arts Inc., 1989, for *The Admirations;* Edith Green Distinguished Professor, Linfield College, 1993.

WRITINGS:

(Editor, with Richard Robbins) *Where We Are: The Montana Poets Anthology,* SmokeRoot Press (Missoula, MT), 1979.
Luck (poetry), Owl Creek Press, 1981.

(Editor, with Steven Sher) *Northwest Variety: Personal Essays by Fourteen Regional Authors,* Arrowood Books (Corvallis, OR), 1987.

The Admirations (poetry), Lynx House Press (Amherst, MA), 1989.

The St. Martin's Workbook, St. Martin's Press (New York, NY), 1989.

(With Chris Anderson) *A Forest of Voices: Reading and Writing the Environment,* Mayfield Co. (Mountain View, CA), 1995.

(With Chris Anderson) *Asking Questions: A Rhetoric for the Intellectual Life,* Allyn & Bacon (Boston, MA), 2000.

WORK IN PROGRESS: Continuo (poetry), for Salmon Publishing, Ltd., County Clare, Ireland.

*   *   *

RUSSO, J. Edward

PERSONAL: Male. *Education:* California Institute of Technology, B.S. (mathematics), 1963; University of Michigan, M.S. (probability and statistics), 1966, Ph.D (cognitive and mathematical psychology), 1971.

ADDRESSES: Office—443 Sage Hall, Johnson Graduate School of Management, Cornell University, Ithaca, NY 14853-6201. *E-mail*—jer9@cornell.edu.

CAREER: Johnson Graduate School of Management, Cornell University, Ithaca, NY, S. C. Johnson Family Professor of Management. WiseUncle (business consulting firm), chief scientific advisor; General Motors Research Laboratories, automobile design advisor; Procter & Gamble, market research advisor; consultant to numerous companies and agencies, including Royal Dutch/Shell, Eli Lilly, IBM, T. Rowe Price, General Motors, U.S. Federal Trade Commission, and National Institute of Technology.

MEMBER: American Psychological Society (fellow).

WRITINGS:

(With Paul J. H. Schoemaker) *Decision Traps: Ten Barriers to Brilliant Decision-making and How to Overcome Them,* Doubleday (New York, NY), 1989.

(With Paul J. H. Schoemaker) *Winning Decisions: Getting It Right the First Time,* Currency (New York, NY), 2002.

SIDELIGHTS: J. Edward Russo has collaborated with Paul J. H. Schoemaker to produce two books aimed at helping business managers make decisions. In *Decision Traps: Ten Barriers to Brilliant Decision-making and How to Overcome Them,* they identify such common pitfalls as "plunging in," "overconfidence," and "shortsighted shortcuts," and offer advice on how to avoid them. A *Kirkus Reviews* critic summed up the book's content as "slickly packaged (if deadly earnest) tips and reminders on staying out of harm's way when making important decisions." In *Winning Decisions: Getting It Right the First Time,* Russo and Schoemaker provide further guidance on decision-making, including how to gather comprehensive information and interpret knowledge gained from past decisions. They include worksheets, case studies, and anecdotes from the experiences of large companies such as Pepsico and British Airways. The authors "offer a clear, straightforward explanation" of how to make decisions and "even show an occasional humorous side," commented a *Publishers Weekly* reviewer, adding, "This book will prove valuable to managers at all levels of an organization." Meanwhile, Paul B. Brown, writing in *Inc.,* called *Winning Decisions* "one of the few business books published in 2001 that's worth the cover price."

BIOGRAPHICAL AND CRITICAL SOURCES:

PERIODICALS

Inc., February 1, 2002, Paul B. Brown, "The Tip: Decision Time."

Kirkus Reviews, October 1, 1989, review of *Decision Traps: Ten Barriers to Brilliant Decision-making and How to Overcome Them,* pp. 1456-1457.

Management Review, March, 1990, review of *Decision Traps,* p. 62.

Publishers Weekly, November 5, 2001, review of *Winning Decisions: Getting It Right the First Time,* p. 56.

OTHER

WiseUncle Web site, http://www.wiseuncle.com/ (July 1, 2002).*

RUTH, Elizabeth 1968-

PERSONAL: Born March 8, 1968, in Windsor, Ontario, Canada. *Education:* University of Toronto, B.A. (English literature; with honors), 1993, M.A. (counseling psychology), 1997; attended Humber School for Writers.

ADDRESSES: Home—Toronto, Ontario, Canada. *Agent*—c/o Author Mail, Dundurn Press Ltd., 8 Market St., Suite 200, Toronto, Ontario, Canada M5E 1M6. *E-mail*—eruth100@hotmail.com.

CAREER: Writer and educator. George Brown College, Toronto, Ontario, Canada, instructor in short-story writing, 2002—, and member, Writers-in-electronic-residence program.

MEMBER: Writers Union of Canada (Ontario representative).

AWARDS, HONORS: Selected one of top three documentaries of the year, *Out Front* (radio program), 2000, for "Quantum Father"; top ten books of the year designation, *Now* (periodical), and Writers' Trust of Canada Fiction Prize finalist, both 2001, and finalist for City of Toronto Book Award, and Amazon.ca/ Books in Canada First Novel Award, both 2002, all for *Ten Good Seconds of Silence;* grants from Canada Council, 2001, and Ontario Arts Council, 2001, 2002.

WRITINGS:

Ten Good Seconds of Silence (novel), Dundurn Press (Toronto, Ontario, Canada), 2001.
(Editor) *Bent on Writing: Contemporary Queer Tales,* Canadian Scholars Press/Women's Press, 2002.

Author of "Quantum Father" (documentary), broadcast as an episode of *Out Front,* CBC-Radio 1, 2000; and "Lady Godiva" (short documentary film), 2001. Work represented in anthologies, including *She's Gonna Be: Stories, Poems, Life,* McGilligan Books (Toronto, Ontario, Canada), 1998; *Hot & Bothered 3,* Arsenal Pulp Press (Vancouver, British Columbia, Canada), 2001; and *Brazen,* Arsenal Pulp Press (Vancouver, British Columbia, Canada), 2002. Contributor of short stories, articles, and reviews to periodicals, including *Room of*

One's Own, Contemporary Verse 2, Church-Wellesley Review, Intangible: Counter-Realist Journal, and *Globe & Mail* (Toronto, Ontario, Canada). Editor, *Fireweed Literary Journal,* 1999-2002.

WORK IN PROGRESS: Smoke, a novel.

BIOGRAPHICAL AND CRITICAL SOURCES:

OTHER

Elizabeth Ruth Web site, http://www.elizabethruth.com (July 11, 2002).

*   *   *

RYAN, Chris 1945-

PERSONAL: Born 1945.

ADDRESSES: Agent—c/o Author Mail, Routledge, 29 West 35th St., New York, NY 10001-2299.

CAREER: Social scientist and author. University of Saskatchewan, visiting professor.

WRITINGS:

An Introduction to Hotel and Catering Economics, Thornes (London, England), 1980.
Recreational Tourism: A Social Science Perspective, Routledge (New York, NY), 1991.
Researching Tourist Satisfaction: Issues, Concepts, Problems, Routledge (New York, NY), 1995.
Marketing Issues in Pacific Area Tourism, Haworth Press (New York, NY), 1997.
(Editor, with Stephen Page) *Tourism Management: Towards the New Millennium,* Pergamon (New York, NY), 2000.
(With Colin Michael Hall) *Sex Tourism: Marginal People and Liminalities,* Routledge (New York, NY), 2001.

SIDELIGHTS: Social scientist Chris Ryan has written a number of textbooks on the topic of tourism economics. His first publication *An Introduction to*

Hotel and Catering Economics "gives an outline of traditional economics theory," commented David Airey, a reviewer in *British Book News,* as it is put into practice in hotels and catering businesses. Although Airey had some misgivings about the book, including "poor presentation" and "unscholarly language," he did concede that the book offers "a broad picture" of British hotels and catering establishments.

When describing Ryan's book *Recreational Tourism: A Social Science Perspective,* a reviewer in the *Journal of Economic Literature* called the text one with "a holistic view of tourism and the problems associated with it." Kenneth Dauber, a reviewer in *Contemporary Sociology* also noted that the book "draws on a variety of social science disciplines—sociology, economics, psychology, and geography—on the marketing and producing of tourist experiences." Its "scope" according to Dauber "is reflected in an excellent and useful bibliography." S. P. Reynolds, a reviewer in *Choice,* recommended *Recreational Tourism,* claiming the work "surveys much recent social science research on tourism from the English-speaking countries in [an] interdisciplinary text."

BIOGRAPHICAL AND CRITICAL SOURCES:

PERIODICALS

British Book News, November, 1980, David Airey, review of *An Introduction to Hotel and Catering Economics,* pp. 664-665.

Choice, April, 1992, S. P. Reynolds, review of *Recreational Tourism: A Social Science Perspective,* p. 1278.

Contemporary Sociology, May, 1993, Kenneth Dauber, review of *Recreational Tourism: A Social Science Perspective,* p. 436.

Journal of Economic Literature, October 13, 1992, review of *Recreational Tourism: A Social Science Perspective,* pp. 1615-1616.

Times Higher Education Supplement, March 10, 1995, Frank Webster, review of *Researching Tourist Satisfaction: Issues, Concepts, Problems,* p. 24.*

S

SACHS, Harley L. 1931-

PERSONAL: Born January 1, 1931, in Chicago, IL; son of Jack (a furrier) and Miriam B. (an office manager) Sachs; married Ulla D., May 15, 1960; children: Anna-Lena Toledo, Belinda, Cynthia. *Education:* Indiana University, B.A., 1953, M.A. (English), 1956; Indiana Christian University, Ph.D. (language and letters), 1971. *Politics:* "Not a party member." *Religion:* "Jewish." *Hobbies and other interests:* Sailing.

ADDRESSES: Home—113 West Houghton Ave., Houghton, MI. *Office*—IDEVCO, Apt. 222, 2545 Southwest Terwilliger Blvd., Portland, OR 97201. *E-mail*—hlsachs@mtu.edu.

CAREER: Houghton, MI, and Portland, OR, freelance author, 1957—; Southern Illinois University, Alton, instructor, 1963-65; Michigan Technological University, Houghton, professor emeritus, 1965-86; Ålborg University, Ålborg, Denmark, guest professor, 1986-87. Board member, Society for Technical Communication; county commissioner; library board member. *Military service:* U.S. Army, 1953-55, became CPL; earned four medals.

MEMBER: Upper Peninsula of Michigan Writers, Willamette Writers, American Civil Liberties Union.

AWARDS, HONORS: Best of Show, Society for Technical Communication, 1975, for "Communication Gamesmanship"; Writer of the Year, Upper Peninsula of Michigan Writers, 1981; first prize, H. G. Roberts Foundation, 1988, for essay "Alzheimers."

WRITINGS:

Freelance Nonfiction Articles (monograph), Society for Technical Communication, 1987.
Irma Quarterdeck Reports (humor), Wescott Cove (Stamford, CT), 1991.
Threads of the Covenant (short stories), Isaac Nathan (Los Angeles, CA), 1995.
Scratch—Out! (e-book), ElectricUmbrella, 1999.
Conspiracy! (e-book), ElectricUmbrella, 1999.
The Gold Chromosome (e-book), ElectricUmbrella, 2000.

Author of numerous newspaper columns, trade magazine articles, letters to the editor, short stories, and poems, as well as about a dozen novels.

WORK IN PROGRESS: "Ben Zakkai's Coffin" (mystery), to be issued as an audio book; research on medical fraud.

SIDELIGHTS: Harley L. Sachs told *CA:* "Writing is the most fun I know. Authors who have influenced me are John LeCarre, Ernest Hemingway, Mary Higgins Clark, and Sue Grafton. I write a mystery novel every summer when I return to my home in Michigan, writing every morning seven days a week, generally an 800- to 1000-word scene, the day after revising previous pages. I am often inspired by dreams and have a collection of short stories, 'Dreams and Nightmares,' which was sold as an e-book by ElectricUmbrella. The latest novel began as a dream. Each book gets a little better than the last."

SACHS, Margaret 1948-

PERSONAL: Born March 21, 1948, in Hamburg, Germany.

ADDRESSES: Agent—c/o Author Mail, Penguin Putnam, 375 Hudson St., New York, NY 10014.

CAREER: Aerial Phenomena Research Organization, field investigator.

WRITINGS:

(With Ernest Jahn) *Celestial Passengers: UFO's and Space Travel,* Penguin (New York, NY), 1977.
The UFO Encyclopedia, Putnam (New York, NY), 1980.

BIOGRAPHICAL AND CRITICAL SOURCES:

PERIODICALS

Choice, May, 1981.
Fate, December, 1981, George W. Early, review of *The UFO Encyclopedia,* p. 98.
Library Journal, January 1, 1981.
School Library Journal, May, 1981, review of *The UFO Encyclopedia,* p. 94.
Wilson Library Bulletin, June, 1981, Charles Bunge, review of *The UFO Encyclopedia,* p. 782.*

*　　　*　　　*

SACKVILLE-WEST, Edward (Charles) 1901-1965

PERSONAL: Born November 13, 1901, in London, England; died July 4, 1965, in Clogheen, Ireland; son of Charles John (in the military) and Maud Cecilia Bell Sackville-West. *Education:* Attended Christ Church, Oxford, c. 1920s.

CAREER: Novelist, music and literary critic. Music critic for *New Statesman,* mid-1920s.

AWARDS, HONORS: Eton music prize, 1918; James Tait Black Memorial Prize, 1936, for *A Flame in Sunlight: The Life and Work of Thomas de Quince.*

WRITINGS:

Piano Quintet, Knopf (New York, NY), 1925.
The Ruin: A Gothic Novel, Heinemann (London, England), 1926, Knopf (New York, NY), 1927.
The Apology of Arthur Rimbaud: A Dialogue, Woolf (London, England), 1927.
Mandrake over the Water-Carrier: A Recital (novel), Heinemann (London, England), 1928.
Simpson: A Life (novel), Knopf (New York, NY), 1931, revised edition, Weidenfeld & Nicolson (London, England), 1951.
The Sun in Capricorn: A Recital (novel), Heinemann (London, England), 1934.
A Flame in Sunlight: The Life and Work of Thomas de Quincey, Cassell (London, England), 1936, published as *Thomas de Quincey: His Life and Work,* Yale University Press (New Haven, CT), 1936.
Graham Sutherland, Penguin (Harmondsworth), 1943, revised edition, 1955.
The Rescue: A Melodrama for Broadcasting Based on Homer's Odyssey, music by Benjamin Britten, Secker & Warburg (London, England), 1945.
And So to Bed: An Album Compiled from His B.B.C. Feature, Phoenix House (London, England), 1947.
Inclinations, Secker & Warburg (London, England), 1949, Scribner's (New York, NY), 1950.
(With Desmond Shawe-Taylor) *The Record Guide,* Collins (London, England), 1951, revised with contributions by Andrew Porter and William Mann, 1955, Greenwood Press (Westport, CT), 1978.
(With Desmond Shawe-Taylor) *The Record Year: A Guide to the Year's Gramophone Records including a Complete Guide to Long-playing Records,* two volumes, Collins, 1952, 1953.

OTHER

(Translator with Vita Sackville-West) Rainer Maria Rilke, *Duineser Elegien: Elegies from the Castle of Duino,* Hogarth Press (London, England), 1931.
(Translator) *Goya: Drawings from the Prado,* Horizon (London, England), 1947.

(Editor) Thomas De Quincey, *Recollections of the Lake Poets,* Lehmann (London, England), 1948.

(Editor) Thomas De Quincey, *Confessions of an English Opium-eater, Together with Selections from the Autobiography,* Chanticleer (New York, NY), 1950.

Also author of an unfinished novel, *The Eyes of the Statue.*

Contributor to *Little Innocents: Childhood Reminiscences,* Cobden-Sanderson (London, England), 1932; author of introduction to *The Correspondence between Richard Strauss and Hugo von Hofmannsthal,* translated by Hans Hammelmann and Ewald Osers, Collins (London, England), 1961.

SIDELIGHTS: The young Edward Sackville-West was an accomplished pianist, and his family thought he would become a musician. But while he was attending college at Oxford his attentions shifted to literature. During this time, he wrote several stories that were published in the *Oxford Outlook* and his first novel, *The Ruin: A Gothic Novel. The Ruin* contains several autobiographical elements. The story is about a family living in a Tudor mansion called Vair that is reminiscent of Knole, the family home Sackville-West often visited, in Sevenoaks, Kent. When Sackville-West was a child, this house, filled with an impressive collection of art and furniture, was occupied by his great-uncle Lionel, third baron Sackville. In addition, one of the characters in the novel, Marcus Fleming, who visits the family living at Vair, is based on a friend of Sackville-West's from college, Jack McDougal. Sackville-West, who was probably a homosexual, according to those who have studied his life, was infatuated with this fellow student.

Fleming's visit stirs up trouble for the Torrent family living at Vair. The heads of this turbulent household are Lady Torrent, who is ill, and her husband, Sir James Torrent, who spends his time by himself in the attic playing the piano. Their four adult children, Ariadne, Nigel, Denzil, and Helen, all still live at home. Ariadne and Nigel have an unusually obsessive relationship and seem to be having an affair with one another. Denzil becomes intrigued with their visitor, Flemming, as does Helen. The novel ends with the complete ruin of the family—Lady Torrent dies, Nigel kills himself, and Ariadne joins a convent. This unusual crew of characters baffled many reviewers when the book first came out, including Edward Muir, who described them in his *Nation and Athenaeum* review. He wrote, "The minds of the characters are so perverted and paradoxical that it is difficult to find any significance in them."

Although it was the second book he actually wrote, the first Sackville-West novel to be published was *Piano Quintet.* Combining his love of music and literature, this novel follows the three men and one woman of the Poller String Quartet as well as the pianist who joins them as they tour Europe. An ill-fated love affair overtakes the first and second violin players and draws in the other members of the group. Two epigraphs, one by Rainer Maria Rilke and the other by sixteenth-century French poet Maurice Sceve about the connection between love and music are included in the novel and reveal Sackville-West's love of French literature acquired during his visits to France as a young adult, as well as his interest in German poetry.

Piano Quintet helped established Sackville-West's reputation as a writer. Though some found the plot confusing and hard to follow at times, it was generally well received by critics. In Lloyd Morris's review of the novel for the *Saturday Review of Literature,* for example, he praised the author, writing that "in many ways [it is] an exceptional performance. Mr. Sackville-West's first novel introduces a talent disciplined to the exact accomplishment of its intention. His talent is served by a responsible technique and fortified by discriminating intelligence. . . . 'Piano Quintet' has the final effect of irony, civilized and sophisticated and a little wistful."

Sackville-West's third novel, *Mandrake over the Water-Carrier: A Recital,* is a complex look at a number of characters in the Channel Islands who are involved in magic and witchcraft. This was followed by *Simpson: A Life,* the fictional biography of a children's nurse, Ruth Simpson, that some feel may have been based on the life of his own childhood nanny, Ada Annie Hutton. The setting of *The Ruin* reappears as the nanny's first place of employment, where she is to take care of three of Lady Torrent's children. She then continues on, traveling to different places to find jobs in a variety of homes. The story tragically ends when, while trying to return to Germany after World War I to take care of yet another child, Simpson is killed in a Nazi riot. Sackville-West's sensitive portrayal of the main character was highly regarded by critics, including a reviewer for the *New Republic* who wrote that, "'Simpson' bears witness to the fine truth of John Dewey, that 'every existence is an event.'" Sackville-West's last novel is *The Sun in Capricorn: A Recital,* which again references *The Ruin,* as well as *Simpson,* through the appearance of the character Denzil Torrent.

Sackville-West also wrote several works of nonfiction, including a biography of the poet Arthur Rimbaud titled *The Apology of Arthur Rimbaud: A Dialogue.* The book is structured like an imaginary conversation between Sackville-West and Rimbaud as the two discuss topics such as the poet's decision to give up literature as a young adult. Sackville-West's second biographical work is the award-winning *A Flame in Sunlight: The Life and Work of Thomas de Quincey,* which was published in America as *Thomas de Quincey: His Life and Work.* This critical work explores the life and literature of this nineteenth-century English writer who has often been overlooked. Writing in *Books* about this work, S. C. Chew said, "This is an altogether charming book, exquisitely written, informed with an acute and sympathetic perception of De Quincey's character both in its strength and its weakness, admirably proportioned, and maintaining a just balance between the 'life' and the 'work,' as excellent as biography as it is as criticism."

Sackville-West also wrote a number of music reviews, especially during the 1940s. He himself owned a large and impressive record collection, and in 1951 he collaborated with Desmond Shawe-Taylor to produce *The Record Guide.* The first work of its kind in England, it is a collector's guide to buying records. He worked with Shawe-Taylor again in 1952 on a similar work, the two-volume *The Record Year: A Guide to the Year's Gramophone Records including a Complete Guide to Long-playing Records.*

Sackville-West became the fifth baron Sackville after his father's death in 1962. Unfortunately, he did not have long to enjoy the title. He was working on the unfinished novel, *The Eyes of the Statue,* when he died at Clogheen in 1965. Though winning some acclaim in his lifetime, Sackville-West's works did not endure the test of time. His novels of the 1920s and 1930s did not remain in print for long, and the only one to be republished was *Simpson,* which the author revised in

1951. Margaret Crosland considered the author's legacy in the *Dictionary of Literary Biography:* "The subtlety, complexity, and eccentricity of his work have prevented Sackville-West from occupying a major place in twentieth-century fiction, but his few novels reflect an unusual and fascinating mind. Their oblique reflections of life in Britain during the 1920s and 1930s present an image that is different from that found in virtually all other contemporary British writing."

BIOGRAPHICAL AND CRITICAL SOURCES:

BOOKS

De-la-Noy, Michael, *Eddy: The Life of Edward Sackville-West,* Bodley Head (London, England), 1988.

Dictionary of Literary Biography, Volume 191: *British Novelists between the Wars,* Gale (Detroit, MI), 1998.

PERIODICALS

Booklist, September, 1931, review of *Simpson: A Life;* January, 1937, review of *Thomas de Quincey: His Life and Work.*

Bookman, September, 1931, Elizabeth Sanderson, review of *Simpson.*

Books, June 7, 1931, Mary Ross, review of *Simpson,* p. 3; November 29, 1936, S. C. Chew, review of *Thomas de Quincey: His Life and Work,* p. 4.

Boston Transcript, October 10, 1925, review of *Piano Quintet,* p. 2; July 8, 1931, review of *Simpson,* p. 2; November 28, 1936, William Fox, review of *Thomas de Quincey: His Life and Work,* p. 4.

Cleveland Open Shelf, September, 1931, review of *Simpson,* p. 127.

Dial, August, 1927, review of *The Ruin.*

International Book Review, January, 1926, Sidney Shultz, review of *Piano Quintet,* p. 123.

Kirkus Reviews, August 1, 1950, review of *Inclinations.*

Library Journal, January 15, 1952, review of *The Record Guide.*

Literary Review, January 22, 1927, p. 2.

Manchester Guardian, April 21, 1936, H. B. Charlton, review of *A Flame in Sunlight: The Life and Work of Thomas de Quincey,* p. 7; August 24, 1951, review of *The Record Guide,* p. 4.

Music Library Association Notes, March, 1952, R. H. Reid, review of *The Record Guide.*

Nation, September 9, 1931, review of *Simpson;* December 12, 1936, Maxwell Geismar, review of *Thomas de Quincey: His Life and Work.*

Nation & Athenaeum, August 5, 1925, Edwin Muir, review of *Piano Quintet;* October 9, 1926, Edwin Muir, review of *The Ruin.*

New Republic, December 30, 1925, Betsy Greenebaum, review of *Piano Quintet;* March 2, 1927, R. M. Lovett, review of *The Ruin;* July 22, 1931, review of *Simpson.*

New Statesman, July 18, 1925, P. C. Kennedy, review of *Piano Quintet;* November 6, 1926, P. C. Kennedy, review of *The Ruin;* February 21, 1931, review of *Simpson.*

New Statesman & Nation, April 18, 1936, David Garnett, review of *Thomas de Quincey: His Life and Work;* September 1, 1951, Philip Hope-Wallace, review of *The Record Guide.*

New Yorker, November 4, 1950, review of *Inclinations.*

New York Evening Post, June 6, 1931, review of *Simpson,* p. 10S.

New York Herald Tribune Books, February 13, 1927, review of *The Ruin: A Gothic Novel,* p. 12.

New York Times, December 6, 1925, Lloyd Morris, review of *Piano Quintet,* p. 2; December 27, 1925, review of *Piano Quintet,* p. 16; January 9, 1927, review of *The Ruin,* p. 9; June 7, 1931, F. T. Marsh, review of *Simpson,* p. 2; December 13, 1936, Percy Hutchison, review of *Thomas de Quincey: His Life and Work,* p. 7.

New York Tribune, November 1, 1925, Janet Ramsay, review of *Piano Quintet,* p. 15.

Saturday Review, June 20, 1925, Gerald Bullett, review of *Piano Quintet;* September 18, 1926, L. P. Hartley, review of *The Ruin;* February 14, 1931, H. C. Harwood, review of *Simpson.*

Saturday Review of Literature, October 17, 1925, Rebecca West, review of *Piano Quintet;* November 14, 1925, Lloyd Morris, review of *Piano Quintet;* June 20, 1931, Elinor Mordaunt, review of *Simpson;* January 16, 1937, P. V. Stern, review of *Thomas de Quincey: His Life and Work;* September 23, 1950, Leonard Bacon, review of *Inclinations.*

Spectator, July 18, 1925, review of *Piano Quintet;* September 18, 1926, review of *The Ruin;* February 14, 1931, review of *Simpson;* April 17, 1936, Edmund Blunden, review of *Thomas de Quincey: His Life and Work;* January 6, 1950; September 21, 1951, Martin Cooper, review of *The Record Guide.*

Times Literary Supplement, June 4, 1925, review of *Piano Quintet,* p. 382; September 23, 1926, review of *The Ruin,* p. 630; February 12, 1931, review of *Simpson,* p. 114; April 25, 1936, review of *A Flame in Sunlight,* p. 351; February 3, 1950, Monk Gibbon, review of *Inclinations,* p. 72; October 19, 1951, review of *The Record Guide.**

*   *   *

SANDERS, Dori(nda) 1935(?)-

PERSONAL: Born 1935 (some sources say 1934), in York, SC.

ADDRESSES: Home—Filbert, SC. *Agent*—c/o Author Mail, Algonquin Books, P.O. 2225, Chapel Hill, NC 27515.

CAREER: Author, farmer, and banquet manager.

AWARDS, HONORS: Lillian Smith Book Award, 1990.

WRITINGS:

Clover (novel), Algonquin Books (Chapel Hill, NC), 1990.

Her Own Place (novel), Algonquin Books (Chapel Hill, NC), 1993.

Dori Sanders' Country Cooking: Recipes and Stories from the Family Farmstand, Algonquin Books (Chapel Hill, NC), 1995.

The Dori Sanders manuscript collection is maintained at the University of South Carolina.

ADAPTATIONS: Clover has been optioned for filming by Walt Disney.

SIDELIGHTS: Dori Sanders came to writing relatively late in life. The author grew up on a farm in rural South Carolina, and as an adult she continued a life of farming and selling her produce at a roadside stand on her property. But Sanders was encouraged to write by friends who told her that she was good and should try to publish her work. The success of her first novel,

Clover, which stayed on the *Washington Post* best-seller list for ten weeks, established her as an author, even though she insists that she is still a farmer first.

Sanders grew up in a large family in which storytelling was a hobby, and she preferred the world of her dad's words to her mother's "cooking and cleaning world." Sanders recalls World War II as an important time because women (including herself) suddenly had the opportunity to get off the farm and make money at local munitions plants. She suspects that the experience may have given her the courage to write and publish her work later.

The inspiration for *Clover* came to Sanders while she was selling vegetables and fruit at her roadside stand one day and watched two funeral processions pass by—one for an African American family and the other for a white family. A young girl waved at her from the first funeral procession; a white woman simply stared at her from the car of the second procession. Sanders reflected on the differences between the two lives and wondered what might have happened if these two people had gotten together. This became the basis for *Clover,* which features a ten-year-old African American girl named Clover whose father has died hours after his wedding to a white woman. Clover must suddenly learn to live with her white stepmother, Sara Kate, who has promised to remain in town and take care of Clover even though Clover's relatives think her stepmother is strange. Jack Sullivan pointed out in the *New York Times* that the "story is sprinkled with hilarious, highly specific commentary on food which is both Clover's favorite way of describing her world and Sanders' shrewd means of illuminating the subleties of racial conflict." A *Southern Living* reviewer noted that the book is "a perceptive picture of life in the rural New South, an often witty tale of small town American trying to cope with big city situations." *Los Angeles Times Book Review* critic Ursula Hegi called Clover's voice "authentic and clear," but added that overall the novel stays "on the surface, linking a sequence of events without showing the reverberations." However, Hegi added that "Sanders is successful in staying within the immediate language that is accessible to a child, creating a voice that is authentic and clear." And *Kliatt* reviewer Melody A. Moxley praised *Clover* as a "wonderful story" that is "well paced. A good choice for all ages."

Sanders' second novel, *Her Own Place,* is the story of Mae Lee, a bride who is eventually abandoned by her husband and who later becomes a successful farmer. The book takes place during World War II and was inspired by Sanders' own experiences during that time. Mae Lee's character is tenacious and believes that the quality of life is "in the details." Karen Stabiner noted in the *Los Angeles Times Book Review* that the novel "rolls gently along, with a sweet mix of humor and familiarity" and that "nothing really distracts from the book's genuine strength."

The author has also published *Dori Sanders' Country Cooking: Recipes and Stories from the Family Farmstand,* a book that combines recipes from the Sanders' family recipes as well as a narrative that describes the some of the history and stories behind the food. Sanders writes about harvest time, hog butchering, and growing up on the farm. The recipes encompass a variety of foods, including skillet crackling bread, pecan pie with black walnut crust, and pickled pigs lips. A *Publishers Weekly* reviewer noted that the "heart here is in Sanders' memories" and that the "narrative and cookery blend delightfully in this mix of recollection and old fashioned family cooking."

BIOGRAPHICAL AND CRITICAL SOURCES:

BOOKS

Contemporary Black Biography, Volume 8, Gale (Detroit, MI), 1995.

PERIODICALS

African American Review, spring, 1995, p. 166.
American Librarian, June, 1991, p. 600.
American Visions, April-May, 1993, pp. 28, 30.
Booklist, February 15, 1993, Brad Hooper, "The Booklist Interview," pp. 1012-1013; December 15, 1995, Barbara Jacobs, review of *Dori Sanders' Country Cooking: Recipes and Stories from the Family Farmstand,* p. 678.
Book Report, September, 1993, p. 48.
Belles Lettres, winter, 1991, p. 55.
Christian Science Monitor, June 24, 1993, p. 14.
Essence, September, 1990, p. 52; August, 1993, p. 52.
Jet, August 20, 1990, p. 38.
Kirkus Reviews, March 1, 1993, review of *Her Own Place,* p. 255.

Kliatt, July, 1995, Melody A. Moxley, review of *Clover,* p. 42.

Library Journal, November 15, 1995, Judith C. Sutton, "Cookery," p. 94.

Los Angeles Times Book Review, April 15, 1990, Ursula Hegi, "So Who Needs a White Stepmother?," p. 2; May 26, 1991, p. 10; June 6, 1993, Karen Stabiner, review of *Her Own Place,* p. 6; May 8, 1994, p. 8.

Modern Maturity, November-December, 1996, p. 30.

NEA Today, March,1991, p. 18.

New York Times, May 20, 1990, Jack Sullivan, "In Short; Fiction," section 7, p. 30.

New York Times Book Review, May 29, 1990, p. 30; June 16, 1991, p. 28; May 29, 1994, p. 20.

New York Times Magazine, November 12, 1995, Moly O'Neill, "Talking Turkey," pp. 107-108.

People Weekly, July 19, 1993, p. 45.

Publishers Weekly, January 19, 1990, p. 95; April 19, 1991, p. 64; March 8, 1993, p. 66; September 18, 1995, review of *Dori Sanders' Country Cooking,* p. 127.

Southern Living, October, 1990, p. 76; December, 1995, p. 88; June, 1997, pp. 122, 168.

School Library Journal, August, 1990, p. 177; December, 1990, p. 27; September, 1993, p. 262.

Tribune Books (Chicago, IL), April 1, 1990, p. 6; July 28, 1991, p. 8.

Vogue, April, 1990, p. 278.

Voice of Youth Advocates, August, 1990, p. 163.

Virginia Quarterly Review, autumn, 1990, p. 130.

Washington Post Book World, June 9, 1991, review of *Clover,* p. 16; May 9, 1993, David Streitfeld, "On the Roadside," p. 12.

Writer's Digest, August, 1993, p. 7.

World & I, July, 1993, p. 358.*

*　　*　　*

SANKEY, Jay 1963-

PERSONAL: Born 1963.

ADDRESSES: Home—Toronto, Canada. *Agent*—c/o Author Mail, Routledge, 29 West 35th St., New York, NY 10001.

CAREER: Stand-up comic, writer, and cartoonist. Performing credits include *Contents under Pressure,* a one-man television show for the Bravo network, and *Friday Night,* for the Canadian Broadcasting Corporation.

WRITINGS:

Zen and the Art of Stand-up Comedy, Routledge (New York, NY), 1998.

Zen and the Art of the Monologue, Routledge (New York, NY), 2000.

Also author of *When Creators Collide, Sankey Pankey,* and *100% Sankey.* Published a CD, *Odd Little Man* (Attic); and the videos *Sankey-Tized I* and *Sankey-Tized II.*

SIDELIGHTS: Jay Sankey, a stand-up comic, writer, and cartoonist based in Toronto, Canada, earned respectful reviews for his book *Zen and the Art of Stand-up Comedy.* The book presents many practical tips on the nuts and bolts of comedy writing and performing, including how to generate ideas, time the delivery of jokes, and deal with audiences. Yet the book was seen as much more than a simple how-to volume, because it also offered philosophical comments on the nature of comedy and performance. *Library Journal* reviewer Norman Oder found this mix particularly successful, and appreciated Sankey's message that the Zen approach of being "in the moment" can work effectively for comedians on stage. Though Oder noted that the author did not give enough attention to the formidable career hurdles facing stand-up comics today, he welcomed Sankey's insightful approach to the subject of comedy. A reviewer for *Publishers Weekly* expressed similar praise, noting that *Zen and the Art of Stand-up Comedy* offers aspiring stand-up comics "a career's worth of wisdom" that is both thoughtful and provocative.

Sankey has also written *When Creators Collide,* as well as two collections of sleight-of-hand tricks, *Sankey Pankey* and *100% Sankey.* He has also written and recorded a CD, *Odd Little Man.* His close-up magic routines are collected on two videotapes, *Sankey-Tized I* and *Sankey-Tized II.* In 2000, Sankey published a follow-up volume to *Zen and the Art of Stand-up Comedy,* titled *Zen and the Art of the Monologue.* Sankey has performed on the stand-up and the magicians' circuits throughout North American and in

Europe, and has appeared frequently on television. He was seen in seven episodes of the Canadian Broadcast Corp. (CBC)'s *Friday Night,* during which he told eerie bedtime stories. He has also performed in the one-man show *Contents under Pressure* for Bravo.

BIOGRAPHICAL AND CRITICAL SOURCES:

PERIODICALS

Library Journal, May 1, 1998, Norman Oder, review of *Zen and the Art of Stand-up Comedy,* p. 102.
New Theatre Quarterly, August, 2000, Steve Nallon, review of *Zen and the Art of Stand-up Comedy,* p. 303.
Publishers Weekly, May 15, 1998.

OTHER

Ann Online, http://www.annonline.com/ (November 2, 1998), Jay Sankey biography.*

* * *

SATTER, Beryl E. 1959-

PERSONAL: Born 1959. *Education:* Harvard University, M.A.; Yale University, Ph.D.

ADDRESSES: Office—History Department, Rutgers University, 175 University Ave., Newark, NJ 07102. *Email*—satter@andromeda.rutgers.edu.

CAREER: Rutgers University, Newark, NJ, assistant professor of history.

WRITINGS:

Each Mind a Kingdom: American Women, Sexual Purity, and the New Thought Movement, 1875-1920, University of California Press (Berkeley, CA), 1999.

Contributor to scholarly publications, including *American Quarterly, Journal of Social History, New England Quarterly,* and *Reviews in American History.*

WORK IN PROGRESS: New Thought and the Era of Woman, 1875-1920.

SIDELIGHTS: Historian Beryl E. Satter, who teaches at Rutgers University, earned significant attention with the publication of her book, *Each Mind a Kingdom: American Women, Sexual Purity, and the New Thought Movement, 1875-1920.* Critics hailed it as a landmark work of scholarship of interest to both general and academic readers alike. The book offers an analysis of American women's quasi-religious, self-improvement cults in the late nineteenth and early twentieth centuries. In particular, the work discusses the New Thought Movement, which promised religious salvation and material success through positive thinking and the suppression of physical desire. New Thought, Satter shows, led to such organizations as Christian Science and Alcoholics Anonymous and served as a means by which white, middle-class women attempted to reshape society.

A *Publishers Weekly* reviewer found Satter's argument convincing and relevant, hailing *Each Mind a Kingdom* as a "groundbreaking investigation that overturns established paradigms" of women's history. In the *Washington Post,* Hans Johnson praised the book as an "impressive history" to which Satter brings subtle insights, though he pointed out that she does not give sufficient attention to the matter of New Thought's racist and bigoted elements in the early 1900s. Gillian Gill, writing in the *Women's Review of Books,* also found Satter's treatment of the twentieth century movement "slightly cursory." But Gill admired much about the book, noting that it "marks a new chapter in the historiography of New Thought and an awareness of how much our understanding of today's New Age phenomena can be illumined by an informed analysis of alternative health movements in the nineteenth century." *Each Mind a Kingdom,* Gill concluded, is "a superbly researched and organized study that will provoke the general reader to new thinking, and offer valuable assistance to future scholars."

BIOGRAPHICAL AND CRITICAL SOURCES:

PERIODICALS

American Historical Review, October, 2000, Margaret Bendroth, review of *Each Mind a Kingdom: American Women, Sexual Purity, and the New Thought Movement, 1875-1920,* p. 1326.

American Studies International, February, 2001, Shelly McKenzie, review of *Each Mind a Kingdom,* p. 130.

Choice, December, 1999, C. K. Piehl, review of *Each Mind a Kingdom,* p. 786.

Journal for the Scientific Study of Religion, September, 2000, Christel Manning, review of *Each Mind a Kingdom,* p. 390.

Journal of American History, September, 2000, Leslie Fishbein, review of *Each Mind a Kingdom,* p. 682.

Journal of Religion, January, 2002, R. Marie Griffith, review of *Each Mind a Kingdom,* p. 115.

Journal of Women's History, summer, 2001, Cynthia Wilkey, review of *Each Mind a Kingdom,* p. 180.

Modernism/Modernity, April, 2000, Thomas Pavel, review of *Each Mind a Kingdom,* p. 340.

Publishers Weekly, July 5, 1999, p. 52.

Reviews in American History, March, 2001, Patricia R. Hill, review of *Each Mind a Kingdom,* p. 85.

Washington Post, February 22, 2000, p. C02.

Women's Review of Books, November, 1999, p. 27.*

*   *   *

SAUNDERS, Trevor J(ohn) 1934-1999

PERSONAL: Born July 12, 1934, in Corsham, Wiltshire, England; died of cancer, January 24, 1999; son of William John and Phyllis Margaret (Escott) Saunders; married Teresa Mary Louisa Schmitz, September 5, 1959; children: Clare Catherine Anne, Angela Mary Veronica. *Education:* University College, B.A., 1956; Emmanuel College, Cambridge, Ph.D., 1962. *Religion:* Roman Catholic. *Hobbies and other interests:* Railroad history, movies.

CAREER: Bedford College, London, England, assistant lecturer in Latin, 1959-61; University of Hull, Hull, England, from assistant lecturer to lecturer in classics, 1961-65; University of Newcastle, Newcastle upon Tyne, England, lecturer, 1965-72, senior lecturer in classics, 1972-78, reader in Greek philosophy, 1978, professor of Greek, beginning 1978, head of classics department, 1976-82, 1987-92, dean of arts faculty, 1982-85, member of the senate, 1977-80, 1982-85, 1988-91, member of court, 1982-85, council member, 1984-87, 1989-92; Institute for Advanced Study, Princeton University, Princeton, NJ, visiting member, 1971-72, 1986; University of Durham, council member, beginning 1987. Member of Council of University Classics Departments, chairman, 1981-84.

MEMBER: Classical Association, Society for the Promotion of Hellenic Studies, Cambridge Philological Society.

AWARDS, HONORS: Humanities Research Center, Australian National University, Canberra, Australia, visiting fellow, 1986.

WRITINGS:

(Translator and author of introduction) Plato, *The Laws,* Penguin (Harmondsworth, England), 1970.

Notes on the Laws of Plato, University of London (London, England), 1972.

Bibliography on Plato's Laws, 1920-1970, with Additional Citations through May 1975, Arno (New York, NY), 1976.

(Editor and author of introduction) *Early Socratic Dialogues,* Penguin (New York, NY), 1987.

Plato's Penal Code: Tradition, Controversy, and Reform in Greek Penology, Oxford University Press (New York, NY), 1991.

(Translator) Aristotle, *Politics. Books 1 and II,* Oxford University Press (New York, NY), 1995.

Contributor to *The Cambridge Companion to Plato,* edited by Richard Kraut, Cambridge University Press (Cambridge, England), 1993, and of introduction to *Early Socratic Dialogues,* 1987. Also contributor to professional journals.

SIDELIGHTS: Trevor J. Saunders was one of the world's leading experts on Plato and was also a well-known English classicist. During his academic life he taught Greek language and literature, but his main interest was in Greek political, legal, and social thought. He began his studies at University College, London in 1953; it was there that he converted to Catholicism and met his wife of forty years, Teresa Mary Louisa Schmitz. Upon receiving his Ph.D., Saunders held several positions as a lecturer, and in 1965 he began his long career with the University of Newcastle. His pioneering work, the study of Plato's *Laws,* began with his doctoral thesis and culminated with *Plato's Penal Code: Tradition, Controversy, and Reform in Greek Penology.*

In what *Choice* reviewer R. H. Evans called an "extraordinary book" that is "beautifully written and produced," *Plato's Penal Code* devotes much space to pre-Plato penology in Homer and in Greek mythology and literature. *Times Literary Supplement* reviewer Mary Margaret Mackenzie observed that Saunders' goals include discussing "ancient moral values" and Plato's theories about punishment, as well as analyzing "the penal code of the *Laws* against the background of Attic law and forensic oratory." The book, according to Mackenzie, shows that "Plato's penal code . . . is both consistent with his theory of punishment and carefully arranged to modify, rather than to outrage, contemporary legal assumptions."

Michael Gagarin wrote in *Classical Review* that "most scholars see a sharp discontinuity between Plato's radically new penal theory—which starts from the premise that no one does wrong willingly, and concludes that punishment should provide a cure for the offender's morally unhealthy state of mind—and the actual punishments set forth in the Laws, many of which seem quite traditional. . . . Saunders defends Plato and marshals a comprehensive and coherent case against the charge of discontinuity, showing that although many of Plato's punishments continue traditional practices, they could at least potentially embody the radical penology of his curative theory." Gagarin felt that Saunders recognizes the challenges in taking this position. "He admits the weakness of some of his arguments, takes note of conflicting evidence, raises counter-arguments, and assesses the relative merits of both sides."

Plato's Penal Code resulted in more accolades for Saunders among Plato scholars, and he attended two international conferences on the *Laws* shortly before he died on January 24, 1999. A London *Times* obituary writer remarked that his books "combine meticulous scholarship with a sympathetic awareness of non-specialist readers, a ready turn of phrase and a lively sense of humor." The writer concluded, "As a lecturer and teacher, he was admired for his lucidity and wit, and loved for the care and attention he gave to his individual students. One of his chief concerns, in his last days, was that he might be letting them down." Saunders also loved movies and railroads; he explored old stations and tracks and planned family vacations around his interest. The final moments of his cremation were heralded by the sound of a steam engine.

BIOGRAPHICAL AND CRITICAL SOURCES:

PERIODICALS

Choice, October, 1992, R. H. Evans, review of *Plato's Penal Code: Tradition, Controversy, and Reform in Greek Penology,* p. 316.

Classical Review, January 1, 1993, Michael Gagarin, "Plato on Punishment," pp. 82-84.
Classical World, April-May, 1978, John J. Keaney, review of *Bibliography on Plato's Laws, 1920-1970,* p. 471; March, 1993, p. 359.
Ethics, October 1, 1993, p. 198.
Religious Studies Review, April, 1993, p. 162.
Times Literary Supplement, February 21, 1992, Mary Margaret Mackenzie, "Curing the Criminal?," p. 24.

OBITUARIES:

PERIODICALS

Times (London, England), February 24, 1999.*

*   *   *

SCALES, Junius Irving 1920-2002

OBITUARY NOTICE—Born March 26, 1920, in Greensboro, NC; died of heart failure after a stroke, August 5, 2002, in New York, NY. Political organizer and activist, proofreader, and author. Scales has been called the only U.S. citizen ever sent to jail for the crime of belonging to the Communist Party. His imprisonment marked a dramatic contrast to his origins as a child of privilege who grew up within the sheltered environment of a southern mansion. Scales joined the American Communist Party in 1939 as a college student, he once wrote, after his abrupt introduction to the social injustices prevalent in the world at large; the Communist Party promised equality for all. He worked for the party as a civil rights coordinator and labor organizer throughout the South until his arrest in 1954. The charge was the felony, under the Alien Registration Act (or Smith Act) of 1940, of belonging to an organization that advocated violence against the federal government. Though other arrests had involved party leaders, Scales was the only person convicted simply for being a party member. Scales appealed the conviction repeatedly until finally, in 1961, the U.S. Supreme Court upheld the conviction, and he was sent to a federal prison. Ironically, he had resigned from the party some years earlier, disillusioned when he learned of Stalinist atrocities and other horrors. Even more ironically, the Supreme Court itself later declared the Smith Act unconstitutional. Many notable Americans, including former first lady Eleanor Roosevelt, protested Scales's incarceration as a political prisoner, for he had never actually committed a violent act. In 1962 President John F. Kennedy commuted the sentence to time served. Scales spent the rest of his life out of the public eye, as a night-shift proofreader for the *New York Times.* He retired in 1983 and wrote a memoir, *Cause at Heart: A Former Communist Remembers.*

OBITUARIES AND OTHER SOURCES:

BOOKS

Scales, Junius Irving, and Richard Nickson, *Cause at Heart: A Former Communist Remembers,* University of Georgia Press (Athens, GA), 1987.

PERIODICALS

Chicago Tribune, August 8, 2002, p. 2-9.
Los Angeles Times, August 9, 2002, obituary by Dennis McLellan, p. B13.
New York Times, August 7, 2002, obituary by Ari L. Goldman, p. C23.
Washington Post, August 8, 2002, obituary by Adam Bernstein, P. B6.

*   *   *

SCHECHTER, Bruce

PERSONAL: Male. *Education:* Massachusetts Institute of Technology, Ph.D.

ADDRESSES: Agent—c/o Author Mail, Simon & Schuster, 1230 Avenue of the Americas, New York, NY 10020.

CAREER: Writer, c. 1989—. *Discover* magazine, staff writer; *Physics Today,* editor. Frequent guest on radio shows and lecturer on math and science topics.

AWARDS, HONORS: Knight fellow in Science Journalism, MIT.

WRITINGS:

The Path of No Resistance: The Story of the Revolution in Superconductivity, Simon and Schuster (New York, NY), 1989.
My Brain Is Open: The Mathematical Journeys of Paul Erdos, Simon and Schuster (New York, NY), 1998.

Also contributor of articles to popular magazines, including *McCalls, Readers Digest, Science, Scientific American,* and *Omni.*

SIDELIGHTS: Bruce Schechter's *The Path of No Resistance: The Story of the Revolution in Superconductivity* is a history of the search for superconducting materials, which transmit energy without waste of energy. Schechter tells the story of the engineers and scientists who work in this field, which may someday result in levitating cars, new ways of launching missiles, and superfast trains. Bill Sharp wrote in the *New York Times Book Review* that Schechter "opens up their work, revealing the passions, humor, jealousies and brilliance of the people who have taken a quiet back lane of science and transformed it into an international raceway of competitive technology." Schechter follows the development of superconductivity from its origins in 1911 to the 1987 Nobel Prize for physics. As Sharp noted, Schechter "turns theoretical material into enjoyable, understandable prose for lay readers, making it clear that while research into superconductivity requires low temperatures, it is populated with warm-blooded, fascinating people."

In *My Brain Is Open: The Mathematical Journey of Paul Erdos,* Schechter describes the eccentric life and work of research mathematician Paul Erdos, who died in 1996. For over 50 years, Erdos was essentially homeless and jobless, and wandered from place to place, staying in the guest rooms of fellow mathematicians. As Schechter wrote in a press release about the book, "Having no home or job, and incapable of the most ordinary household tasks (such as buttering bread) Erdos was sustained by the generosity of colleagues and by his own belief in the beauty of mathematics." Erdos would show up at his friends' doors with a suitcase that contained everything he owned, and announce "My brain is open!" which meant that he was ready to get to work.

Schechter first became interested in writing about Erdos when he wrote a profile of Ron Graham, a mathematician who was a friend of and frequent collaborator with Erdos. Because Erdos had no home, Graham maintained his correspondence and took care of his files. "While teaching me the rudiments of juggling and walking on his hands down the halls of Bell Labs," Schechter wrote in a press release, "Ron told me stories about his even more astonishing and eccentric friend."

Although Schechter was intrigued by Graham's stories of Erdos and vowed to meet him, he never did; Erdos died before Schechter got the chance. He attended Erdos's funeral with Graham, where he met many of Erdos's friends and collaborators and decided that if he could not meet Erdos in life, he would get to know him by writing a biography. All these people were enthusiastic about Schechter's plan, and offered their help and their memories of Erdos. Many of these people, now middle-aged, had been child prodigies in mathematics, and had been helped in their careers by Erdos, who collaborated more widely than any mathematician ever had. They all praised Erdos for his generosity and kindness.

Erdos specialized in a kind of math that did not require a lot of technical expertise. His main interests were the properties of prime numbers and counting, and was skilled at creating problems that were interesting and intriguing to young people. Because Erdos traveled so widely, he came in contact with and worked with mathematicians of all ages and in many countries. A *Publishers Weekly* reviewer wrote of *My Brain Is Open*, "Readers will be engrossed by his well-crafted chronicle of the eccentric Hungarian and of the mathematical worlds he traversed for eight decades."

BIOGRAPHICAL AND CRITICAL SOURCES:

PERIODICALS

Booklist, September 15, 1998, Gilbert Taylor, review of *My Brain Is Open: The Mathematical Journeys of Paul Erdos,* p. 180.

Library Journal, September 15, 1998, Jack W. Weigel, review of *My Brain Is Open,* p. 109.

Nature, March 11, 1999, Alexander Masters, review of *My Brain Is Open,* p. 120.

New Scientist, August 1, 1998, Robert Matthews, review of *My Brain Is Open,* p. 40.

New York Times Book Review, April 9, 1989, p. 32.

Physics Today, April, 1999, Peter D. Lax, review of *My Brain Is Open,* p. 69.

Publisher's Weekly, August 3, 1998, p. 65.

Reader's Digest, January, 1992, p. 13.

Science Books and Films, January, 1990, p. 32.*

*　　*　　*

SCHELER, Max G. 1928-

PERSONAL: Born December 28, 1928, in Cologne, Germany; son of Max Scheler (a philosopher). *Education:* Attended University of Munich, 1949-51; attended Sorbonne, Paris, France, 1951; studied photography with Herbert List beginning 1949.

ADDRESSES: Home—Bellevue 39A, 22301 Hamburg, Germany.

CAREER: Photographer. *Neue Zeitung* and *Heute* magazines, Munich, Germany, freelance photographer, 1950-52; Magnum Photos cooperative agency, reportage photographer for magazines including *Epoca, Look, Paris-Match,* and *Picture Post,* 1953-58; *Münchner Illustrierte,* Munich, photographer, 1958-59; *Stern* magazine, Hamburg, staff photographer, 1959-75 and photo editor, 1975-76; *Geo* magazine, Hamburg, managing editor, 1976-80; *Merian* magazine, chief editor, 1980-92; Hoffmann und Campe Verlag, Hamburg, editor of photographic books, 1980-92. *Exhibitions:* Group exhibitions include *World Exhibition of Photography: What Is Man?* Pressehaus Stern, Hamburg, 1964; *Ost-West Reportagen,* Museum für Junst und Gewerbe, Hamburg, 1969; *Deutsche Fotografie nach 1945,* Junstverein, Kassel, Germany, 1979; *Fotografie 1919-1979,* Fotomuseum im Stadtmuseum, Munich, 1979; *Fotografische Sammlung,* Museum Folkwang, Essen, Germany, 1983. Works in collections including Museum für Junst und Gewerbe, Hamburg; Fotomuseum im Münchner Stadtmuseum, Munich; Museum Ludwig, Cologne; Museum Folkwang, Essen, Germany.

MEMBER: Gesellschaft Deutscher Lichtbildner; Deutsche Gesellschaft für Photographie.

WRITINGS:

Liverpool Days, [London, England], 1994.

EDITOR

Herbert List: Photographien 1930-1970, [Munich, Germany], 1976.

Herbert List: Portraits, Hoffman und Campe (Hamburg, Germany), 1977.

Portfolio Herbert List: Zeitlupe Null, [Hamburg, Germany], 1980.

Herbert List: Fotografia Metafisica, [Munich, Germany], 1983.

I Grandi Fotografi: Herbert List, [Milan, Italy], 1983.

Junge Männer, Herbert List, [London, England], 1988.

Hellas, Herbert List, Schirmer/Mosel (Munich, Germany), 1993.

Italy, Herbert List, Schirmer/Mosel (Munich, Germany), 1995.

Herbert List: The Monograph, Monacelli (New York, NY), 2000.

EXHIBITION CATALOGUES; ILLUSTRATOR

Fotografie 1919-1979, Made in Germany: Die GDL-Fotografen, text by W. Boje, F. Kempe, B. Lohse, and others, [Frankfurt, Germany], 1979.

Deutsche Fotografie nach 1945, edited by Petra Benteler, Floris M. Neususs, and others, [Kassel, West Germany], 1979.

Museum Folkwang: Die Fotografische Sammlung, introduction by Ute Eskildsen, [Essen, West Germany], 1983.

SIDELIGHTS: Max G. Scheler once commented, "While as a photographer I was mainly interested in social issues, covering such events as political crises, upheaval, revolution, as well as statesmen in their encounters, travels, and campaigns, and later focused on general social conditions all over the world, I have lately been more interested in cultural aspects and the aesthetic side of good reportage—which I produce and publish in *Merian* magazine. While as a young man I thought I could help to improve the world, I am happy now to be able to show what beauty is left in it."

BIOGRAPHICAL AND CRITICAL SOURCES:

BOOKS

Contemporary Photographers, 3rd edition, St. James Press (Detroit, MI), 1996.*

SCHIFF, Stacy

PERSONAL: Female. *Education:* Attended Williams College.

ADDRESSES: Agent—c/o Author Mail, Simon & Schuster, 1230 Avenue of the Americas, New York, NY 10020.

CAREER: Writer. Simon & Schuster, New York, NY, senior editor.

WRITINGS:

Saint-Exupery: A Biography, Random House (New York, NY), 1994.

Vera (Mrs. Vladimir Nabokov): Portrait of a Marriage, Random House (New York, NY), 1999.

SIDELIGHTS: Stacy Schiff's *Saint-Exupery: A Biography* is a detailed study of the life of French aviator and writer Antoine de Saint-Exupery (1900-44), who is best known for his book *The Little Prince.* Saint-Exupery, known to his friends as "Saint-Ex," was born to a family of provincial nobility that had fallen on hard times, and as a young boy he showed both poetic sensitivity and skilled mechanical aptitude. In the 1920s these interests flowered, when he became a pilot and published his first short story.

As a pilot, he delivered mail for a French company, flying over the western Sahara to deliver mail to Dakar. He spent two years in the desert, in charge of rescuing other planes and pilots who had become stranded. As a pilot, he had plenty of time to think, and he began developing the ideas that marked his work: the importance of bonding between friends, shared responsibility, and the importance of an inner spiritual life.

He then went to South America, where he became the manager of operations for a mail route to remote Patagonia, and then worked for Air France. At the same time, he continued to write. In 1942 he was sent to Algiers to fight with the Free French Forces during World war II. In 1944 he flew over German-occupied France, and disappeared in the course of this mission.

Schiff's biography provides a detailed and enthusiastic look at Saint-Ex's life as a flier and as a writer, with most of the emphasis on his experiences as a pilot. In the *New York Times Book Review,* Isabelle de Courtivron wrote that Schiff's book is "welcome and timely," and she praised Schiff's research into the minutiae of Saint-Exupery's life, and her study of pioneering French aviation. In the *New York Review of Books,* A. Alvarez praised Schiff's "subtle, sensitive, and extraordinarily fair-minded" account of Saint-Ex's life.

Vera (Mrs. Vladimir Nabokov): Portrait of a Marriage tells the story of Vera Nabokov and her devotion to her husband and his literary career. The couple were very close; Vera edited, translated, negotiated, and conducted correspondence about her husband's writing, and he dedicated every book "To Vera." A *Publishers Weekly* reviewer noted that the book "offers more than a peek at the famous author through his wife's eyes." In the *New York Times Book Review,* Lyndall Gordon remarked that Schiff "does not attempt to explain away the enigma that Vera presents," referring to the fact that Vera vetoed a proposed book about the love life of Siamese twins, but earnestly supported Nabokov's book *Lolita,* about a man who has an affair with his twelve-year-old stepdaughter. Gordon also praised Schiff's "flair for the succinct" and her ability to show that "the lives of the obscure can be as intriguing as the lives of the famous." In the *London Review of Books,* Jenny Diski remarked that Vera was "well-served by Stacy Schiff who understands mirrors, magicians, and doppelgangers" well enough to understand Vera's double life as "just a wife" and as Nabokov's mainstay and inspiration.

BIOGRAPHICAL AND CRITICAL SOURCES:

PERIODICALS

Booklist, February 15, 1999, Donna Seaman, review of *Vera (Mrs. Vladimir Nabokov): Portrait of a Marriage,* p. 1003.
Choice, October, 1999, C. A. Rydel, review of *Vera (Mrs. Vladimir Nabokov),* p. 336.
Christian Science Monitor, January 5, 1995, Merle Rubin, review of *Saint-Exupery: A Biography,* p. 13.
Entertainment Weekly, May 21, 1999, p. 70.

Library Journal, April 1, 1999, Ronald Ray Ratliff, review of *Vera (Mrs. Vladimir Nabokov),* p. 98.
London Review of Books, July 1, 1999, p. 14.
New Yorker, December 5, 1994, p. 141.
New York Review of Books, February 2, 1995, p. 7; June 21, 2001, Michael Wood, review of *Vera (Mrs. Vladimir Nabokov),* p. 39.
New York Times Book Review, January 8, 1995, p. 33; August 17, 1997, p. 24; April 25, 1999, p. 34.
Publishers Weekly, September 19, 1994, p. 56; March 22, 1999, p. 81.
Spectator, July 24, 1999, John de Falbe, review of *Vera (Mrs. Vladimir Nabokov),* p. 32.
Times Literary Supplement, January 27, 1995, Mavis Gallant, review of *Saint-Exupery: A Biography,* p. 3.
World Literature Today, winter, 2001, John L. Brown, review of *Vera (Mrs. Vladimir Nabokov),* p. 167.

OTHER

Pennsylvania State Library Web Site, http://www.libraries.psu.edu (October 18, 2002).*

*   *   *

SCHINDLER, Emilie 1907-2001

PERSONAL: Born October 22, 1907, in Alt Moletein, Austria-Hungary (now Stary Maletin, Czech Republic); immigrated to Argentina, 1949; died October 5, 2001, in Berlin, Germany; married Oskar Schindler, March 6, 1928.

CAREER: Activist.

AWARDS, HONORS: Righteous among the Nations Award, Yad Vashem, 1993; Order of May (Argentina), 1995; named an Illustrious Citizen, Argentina, 2000.

WRITINGS:

(With Erika Rosenberg) *Memorias,* Planeta (Buenos Aires, Argentina), 1996, translation by Delores M. Koch published as *Where Light and Shadow Meet: A Memoir,* Norton (New York, NY), 1997.

SIDELIGHTS: During World War II, Emilie Schindler, helped her industrialist husband Oskar save over 1,200 Jewish people from being killed in Nazi death camps. Their work was commemorated in the film *Schindler's List,* directed by Steven Spielberg.

Schindler was born Emilie Pelzl in a German-speaking village in a region that is now the Czech Republic, but which at the time was part of the Austro-Hungarian Empire. Her family members were landowners, and she was educated in a convent. When she was twenty, she met her future husband, Oskar Schindler, who arrived at her family's house selling electric generators. In 1928 she married him, and they moved to Krakow, Poland. In Krakow, they ran a factory where the Jewish people they helped save worked during the Holocaust.

In 1949 the Schindlers moved to San Vicente, Argentina. Oskar returned to Germany in 1958, and remained estranged from his wife until his death in 1974. Although they never saw each other again, they never obtained a divorce. Schindler lived on limited means in Argentina, subsisting on a small state pension until Spielberg's film focused media attention on her. In 1995 she received the highest honor Argentina grants to non-Argentinians, the Order of May.

In 1996 Schindler wrote *Memorias,* translated from the original Spanish into English as *Where Light and Shadow Meet: A Memoir.* In the book she describes Oskar as a self-serving womanizer, and presents her own recollections of scavenging food and medicine for the Jewish people whom she and her husband helped. According to her obituary in the *New York Times,* in a 1999 interview on German ARD television, Schindler said of the film, "Oskar is the hero— and what about me? I saved many Jews, too."

In *Library Journal,* Mary F. Salony praised the book's "straightforward, accessible" prose, and in *Kirkus Reviews,* a critic noted that the book is "a stark, strained account of a singularly courageous couple." In *Law Society Journal,* Morag Donaldson wrote of the memoir, "To the eyes of the world, Emilie was just the woman behind [Oskar] Schindler. She has now stepped out from his shadow to tell events as they occurred—in her own, carefully chosen, elegant language. One perceives a sense of relief on her part at having told her story, and a sense of hope that she too might be accorded the esteem in which her husband is held."

Schindler returned to Germany in 2001, saying she wanted to spend her final days in her home country. She moved into a retirement home in Bavaria, but was moved to a Berlin clinic when she became ill. Her papers and other items were given to a history museum in Bonn, Germany.

BIOGRAPHICAL AND CRITICAL SOURCES:

PERIODICALS

Booklist, August, 1997, Mary Carroll, review of *Where Light and Shadow Meet: A Memoir,* p. 1873.
Kirkus Reviews, June 1, 1997, review of *Where Light and Shadow Meet,* p. 859.
Law Society Journal (New South Wales, Australia), April, 1998, Morag Donaldson, review of *Where Light and Shadow Meet,* p. 110.
Library Journal, August, 1997, Mary F. Salony, review of *Where Light and Shadow Meet,* p. 101.
Spectator, November 1, 1997, David Pryce-Jones, review of *Where Light and Shadow Meet,* p. 41.

OTHER

The Holocaust—Crimes, Heroes and Villains, http://Auschwitz.dk/ (September 1, 2002), "Emilie Schindler."
Jewish Bulletin of Northern California, http://www.jewishsf.com/ (November 21, 1997), Anneli Rufus, "Schindler Was a Cruel Do-Gooder, Widow's Memoir Says."

OBITUARIES:

PERIODICALS

New York Times, October 8, 2001, p. A19.*

*   *   *

SCHLEEF, Einar 1944-2001

PERSONAL: Born 1944, in Sangerhausen, German Democratic Republic (now Germany); died of a heart condition, July 21, 2001, in Berlin, Germany; *Education:* Studied at Academy of Arts, East Berlin; studied film direction at the German Film and Television Academy, West Berlin.

CAREER: Theater director, and writer. Director, Berliner Ensemble, East Berlin, German Democratic Republic, to 1976, and c. 1990-96; director, Schauspiel, Frankfurt, Germany, 1985-90; also worked in Du&uumlsseldorf and Vienna.

WRITINGS:

Gertrud, Suhrkamp (Frankfurt, Germany), 1980.

Wezel: Schauspiel, Suhrkamp (Frankfurt, Germany), 1983.

Die Schauspieler, Suhrkamp (Frankfurt, Germany), 1986.

Schlangen: die Geschichte der Stadt Theben, Suhrkamp (Frankfurt, Germany), 1986.

(With Michael Schmidt) *Waffenruhe,* D. Nishen (Berlin, Germany), 1987.

Zigaretten, Suhrkamp (Frankfurt, Germany), 1998.

Einar Schleef: Republikflucht, Waffenstillstand, Argon (Berlin, Germany), 1992.

Droge Faust Parsifal, Suhrkamp (Frankfurt, Germany), 1997.

SIDELIGHTS: According to his obituary in the *New York Times,* Einar Schleef was "one of Germany's best-known theater directors." He was also the author of several plays. Schleef was born in Sangerhausen in the former communist German Democratic Republic (GDR), and studied at the Academy of Arts in East Berlin. In the mid-1970s, he worked at the Berliner Ensemble, which had been founded by playwright Bertolt Brecht.

At the time, Germany was a divided nation, and the GDR was still one of the "Iron Curtain" countries, nations with repressive communist governments in league with the government of the Soviet Union. When Schleef ran into trouble with the East German authorities, he left and went to West Germany.

In West Berlin, he studied film direction at the German Film and Television Academy. His first novel, *Gertrud,* based on the life of his mother, was published in 1980. He also published several plays, including *Wezel: Schauspiel* and *Die Schauspieler.*

Schleef was director of the Schauspiel in Frankfurt from 1985 to 1990. After the reunification of Germany, he went back to Berlin, where he returned to the Berliner Ensemble. According to the *New York Times,* his direction of Brecht's play "Puntila and His Man Matti" was considered "one of the theater's most daring productions."

In 1996, following a dispute with the theater, Schleef left to work in Dusseldorf and Vienna. He died in 2001 as a result of a heart condition.

BIOGRAPHICAL AND CRITICAL SOURCES:

PERIODICALS

New York Times, May 10, 1998.

World Literature Today, summer, 1984, F. P. Haberl, review of *Wezel: Schauspiel,* p. 414.

OBITUARIES:

PERIODICALS

New York Times, August 5, 2001, "Einar Schleef, 57; Author and Director," p. 32.

Variety, August 13, 2001, p. 59.

Washington Post, August 4, 2001, "Einar Schleef, Theater Director," p. B7.*

*   *   *

SCHMITT, Eric-Emmanuel 1960-

PERSONAL: Born 1960, in Lyon, France; son of a boxer and a track and field champion. *Education:* École Normale Supériuere de la rue d'Ulm, graduated 1983; Ph.D., 1987.

ADDRESSES: Agent—Suzanne Sarquier, 24 rue Feydeau, 75002 Paris, France.

CAREER: University of Chambéry, Chambéry, France, master of conferences, c. 1987-93; playwright and novelist, c. 1991—.

AWARDS, HONORS: Moliére Awards for best play, best playwright, and most promising new work, 1993, for *Le Visiteur;* Moliére Award nominations, including best play and best playwright, 2000, for *Hotel des deux mondes;* nominations for Prix de l'Académie Française and Prix Interallié, 2000, for *L'Evangile selon Pilate;* Grand Prix des Lectrices, 2001, for *L'Evangile selon Pilate,*; nominations for Prix de l'Académie Française, 2001, for *La Part de l'autre;* Prix de l'Académie Française, 2002, for life's work.

WRITINGS:

Diderot, ou La philosophie de la séduction (essay; title means "Diderot; or The Philosophy of Seduction"), Albin Michel (Paris, France), 1997.

PLAYS

La nuit de valognes (produced at the Maison de la Culture de Loire Atlantique, 1991), Actes-sud (Paris, France), 1991, translation by Jeremy Sams published as *Don Juan on Trial,* Dramatic Publishing (Woodstock, IL), 1991.

Le Visiteur (produced at the Petit Théâtre, Paris, France, 1993), Actes sud-Papiers (Arles, France), 1994, translation by Jeremy Sams published as *The Visitor* in *Schmitt Plays I* (includes *Don Juan on Trial, Enigma Variations,* and *Between Worlds*), Methuen (London, England), 2002.

Golden Joe (produced by the CADO d'Orléans, 1994), Albin Michel (Paris, France), 1995.

Variations Enigmatiques (produced at the Théâtre Marigny, Paris, France, 1996), Albin Michel (Paris, France), 1996, translation by Jeremy Sams published as *Enigma Variations* in *Schmitt Plays I* (includes *Don Juan on Trial, The Visitor,* and *Between Worlds*), Methuen (London, England), 2002.

Milarepa (produced at Théâtre Vidy, Lauzanne, Switzerland, 1996), Albin Michel (Paris, France), 1997.

Le Libertin (title means "The Libertine"; produced at the Théâtre Montparnasse, Paris, France, 1997), Albin Michel (Paris, France), 1997.

(Translator and adaptor) *Le Nozze di Figaro* (opera), produced at the Opéra de Compiègne, Compiègne, France, 1997.

Frédérick, ou Le Boulevard du crime (title means "Frederick; or, The Crime Boulevard"; produced at the Théâtre Marigny, Paris, France, 1998), Albin Michel (Paris, France), 1998.

Hôtel des deux mondes (produced at the Théâtre Marigny, Paris, France, 1999), Albin Michel (Paris, France), 1999, translation by John Clifford published as *Between Worlds* in *Schmitt Plays I,* Methuen (London, England), 2002.

Monsieur Ibrahim et les fleurs du Coran (title means "Mr. Ibrahim and the Flowers of the Koran"; produced in France, December, 1999), Albin Michel (Paris, France), 2001.

Théâtre (includes *La Nuit de Valognes, Le Visiteur, Le Bâillon,* and *L'École du diable*), Albin Michel (Paris, France), 1999.

NOVELS

La Secte des egoïstes (title means "The Sect of the Egoists"), Albin Michel (Paris, France), 1994.

L'Evangile selon Pilate (title means "The Gospel according to Pilate"), Albin Michel (Paris, France), 2000.

La Part de l'autre (title means "The Share of the Other"), Albin Michel (Paris, France), 2001.

Schmitt has adapted or translated several works for the French stage and screen, including *Sarcophagus* by Vladimir Goubariev, *The Merchant of Venice* and *King Lear* by William Shakespeare, *Nine* by Maury Yeston and Arthur Kopit, *Volpone* by Ben Jonson, *Aurelien* by Aragon, and *Les Liaisons dangereuses.*

ADAPTATIONS: Le Libertin has been adapted as a film directed by Gabriel Aghion.

SIDELIGHTS: Eric-Emmanuel Schmitt is one of France's most prolific and acclaimed playwrights. His plays have been performed in countries all over the world, including the United States. *Enigma Variations,* perhaps Schmitt's best-known stage play, even had a run at Los Angeles's Mark Taper Forum with Donald Sutherland in the starring role in 1999. Schmitt has garnered many of France's premier writing honors, including Moliére awards for individual plays and the Prix de l'Académie Française for the whole of his theatrical work. Schmitt is also a novelist, and his titles in this genre include *L'Evangile selon Pilate* and *La Part de l'autre.* In addition, he is the author of the philosophical essay *Diderot, ou La philosophie de la séduction.*

A former academic specializing in philosophy, Schmitt held a post at the University of Chambéry when his first play, *Don Juan on Trial,* hit the stage in 1991. In it, several characters enter an old Norman castle, including a duchess, a knight, a countess, a nun, and Don Juan and his valet. The suggestion of the countess that all present "denounce their former love relationships," in the words of Bettina L. Knapp in *World Literature Today,* brings about the famed lover's "entry into the play." Knapp went on to praise *Don Juan on Trial* for its "humor and satiric elements."

Schmitt's second play, *The Visitor,* brought him enough success to enable him to leave his academic post and turn to writing full time. *The Visitor* takes place in Vienna, just after the Germans have invaded, and just before one of the play's main characters, psychoanalyst pioneer Sigmund Freud, flees the city. As the play begins, Freud's daughter Anna is trying to warn him of the danger the Nazis bring with them. Eventually, Freud winds up speaking directly to God. *The Visitor* won Schmitt three Moliére Awards—for best play, best playwright, and most promising new work—and it has been performed all over the world. Schmitt eventually re-worked the play as an opera, and it attained success all over again in 2000.

Another of Schmitt's most successful plays is 1996's *Enigma Variations.* The drama has only two characters—one, Abel Znorko, a reclusive, Nobel Prize-winning author; the other, Erik Larsen, a journalist who comes to his remote Arctic hideaway to interview him. At first Znorko, snobbish and superior, has the upper hand. The play contains many twists, however, which led David Mermelstein, reviewing a Los Angeles performance of *Enigma Variations* for *Variety,* to compare it to Ira Levin's *Deathtrap.* Mermelstein went on to praise Schmitt's effort as "relentlessly compelling." Mira Friedlander, critiquing a Toronto performance of *Enigma Variations* for yet another issue of *Variety,* stated that the "play seems profound even as it entertains. It's loaded with clever laugh lines but is just serious enough to leave the impression that great feelings have been unleashed, stroked and tucked away in time for the last line."

Schmitt's *Between Worlds* premiered at Paris's Théâtre Marigny in September, 1999. The play is set in a surrealistic hotel, patrolled by medical personnel. Eventually the audience realizes that the characters are all actually hovering between life and death in comas—except for Dr. S., who announces "imminent departures for the lift and statements about the characters' state of health," according to Nicholas Powell, reviewing a Paris performance for *Variety.* Powell felt that "the central strength of the play is the ever-present uncertainty about imminent death or survival—a dramatization of the doubts that assail all of us, to some extent, every day."

Among Schmitt's novels is *L'Evangile selon Pilate,* published in 2000. The title means "The Gospel according to Pilate," and *L'Evangile* takes as its premise that after Pontius Pilate sentences Jesus to death—and after the sentence is carried out—Jesus appears to Pilate. As a result, Pilate becomes one of the first Christians. Schmitt works with an even stranger possibility in 2001's *La Part de l'autre.* This novel asks the question, "Would history be different if Adolf Hitler had been accepted into art school?" The infamous dictator had originally wanted to become a painter; if he had been encouraged in his artistic endeavors, would the Holocaust have been avoided? Schmitt examines these issues not only with an alternate Hitler who becomes a celebrated artist, but also with a fictional version of the real Hitler, so that readers can compare them side by side. A reviewer for *Economist* concluded of *La Part de l'autre* that "all in all, this makes for a strange book, one which is by turns learned and playful."

In addition to his many original works, Schmitt has adapted or translated many plays by other authors for French stage and screen audiences. His credits in this area include versions of Shakespeare's *The Merchant of Venice* and *King Lear,* as well as the American play *Nine* by Maury Yeston and Arthur Kopit.

BIOGRAPHICAL AND CRITICAL SOURCES:

PERIODICALS

Economist, November 10, 2001, review of *La Part de l'autre,* p. 113.

Spectator, June 10, 2000, Sheridan Morley, "Antipodean Triumph," p. 46.

Variety, May 10, 1999, David Mermelstein, review of *Enigma Variations,* p. 148; November 1, 1999, Nicholas Powell, review of *Hotel des deux mondes,* p. 100; March 6, 2000, Mira Friedlander, review of *Enigma Variations,* p. 50.

World Literature Today, winter, 2000, Bettina L. Knapp, review of *Theatre* and *Hotel des deux mondes,* p. 107.

OTHER

Eric-Emmanuel Schmitt Web site, http://www.eric-emmanuel-schmitt.net/ (June 20, 2002).

Kafkaiens Web site, http://www.kafkaiens.org/ (May 6, 2002), review of *L'Evangile selon Pilate.*

Le Monde, http://www.lemonde.fr/ (May 7, 2002), "Eric-Emmanuel Schmitt se donne tous les droits."

Radio-Canada Web site, http://www.radio-canada.ca/ (May 6, 2002).*

*   *   *

SCHWARTZ, Mimi

PERSONAL: Born in New York, NY; married; two children. *Education:* Rutgers University, Ed.D.

ADDRESSES: Office—Richard Stockton College of New Jersey, P.O. Box 95, Pomona, NJ 08240. *E-mail*—schwartm@stockton.edu.

CAREER: Richard Stockton College of New Jersey, Pomona, NJ, professor of writing, 1980—. Cape May, NJ, Winter Poetry and Prose Getaway, faculty member.

WRITINGS:

(With others) *Writing for Many Roles,* Boynton/Cook Publishers (Upper Montclair, NJ), 1985.

(Editor) *Writer's Craft, Teacher's Art: Teaching What We Know,* Boynton/Cook Publishers (Portsmouth, NH), 1991.

Thoughts from a Queen-sized Bed (memoir), University of Nebraska Press (Lincoln, NE), 2002.

Editor of anthologies *Under Age* (with Lynn Powell), *In Our Own Worlds* (with Kathy Kenfield and Joyce Greenberg), and *Our Stories, Our Selves.* Contributor to periodicals, including *New York Times, Philadelphia Inquirer, Lear's, Creative Nonfiction,* and *Puerto del Sol.* Contributor to radio program *Satellite Sisters.*

SIDELIGHTS: Mimi Schwartz is both a practitioner and teacher of the craft of writing memoirs and personal essays. *Thoughts from a Queen-Sized Bed* collects forty essays covering Schwartz's forty-year marriage. The essays deal with serious topics such as her mastectomy and her husband's stroke and lighter ones such as family gatherings and travel adventures, with the general theme being the evolution of life, love, family, and friends. She also includes stories of her parents, such as her German Jewish father's attendance at a Hitler rally before immigrating to the United States. A *Publishers Weekly* reviewer, finding most of the book a bit too mundane, commented that "a few gems surface amid the quotidian onslaught," with the father's story being one of them. A *Kirkus Reviews* contributor, though, deemed the collection "a gentle, moving celebration" of ordinary life, while *Booklist*'s GraceAnne A. DeCandido praised Schwartz's "light and sure touch," adding that she handles her material "deftly."

BIOGRAPHICAL AND CRITICAL SOURCES:

BOOKS

Schwartz, Mimi, *Thoughts from a Queen-sized Bed,* University of Nebraska Press (Lincoln, NE), 2002.

PERIODICALS

Booklist, December 15, 2001, GraceAnne A. DeCandido, review of *Thoughts from a Queen-sized Bed,* p. 701.

Kirkus Reviews, November 15, 2001, review of *Thoughts from a Queen-sized Bed,* p. 1606.

Publishers Weekly, November 26, 2001, review of *Thoughts from a Queen-sized Bed,* p. 49.*

*   *   *

SCHWEIZER, Niklaus R. 1939-

PERSONAL: Born August 24, 1939, in Zurich, Switzerland; son of Rudolf Alexander (a judge) and Hedwig Louise (Ulrich) Schweizer. *Ethnicity:* "Caucasian." *Education:* Attended University of Zurich, 1960-64; University of California, Davis, M.A., 1966, Ph.D., 1968. *Hobbies and other interests:* Hawaiian history and language, amateur radio.

ADDRESSES: Home—4231 Pāpū Circle, Honolulu, HI 96816. *Office*—Department of European Languages and Literature, University of Hawaii at Manoa, 1890 East-West Rd., Suite MH 483, Honolulu, HI 96822; fax: 808-956-9536. *E-mail*—niklaud@hawaii.edu.

CAREER: Teacher of German at a school in Honolulu, HI, 1968-70; University of Hawaii at Manoa, Honolulu, part-time visiting assistant professor, 1969-70, assistant professor, 1970-74, associate professor, 1974-83, professor of German, 1983—. Honorary consul of Switzerland in Honolulu, 1972—; Friends of the Royal Hawaiian Band, president, 1979-99, board chair, 1999—; Hui Hānai, member of council, 1981-87, council president, 1987; Friends of Iolani Palace, member of board of directors, 1982—; Consular Corps of Hawaii, dean, 1986, historian, 1988—; Ahahui Ka'iulani, member of board of directors, 1990—; Moanalua Gardens Foundation, member of board of directors, 1994—.

MEMBER: PEN Center USA West, Pacific Translators, German-Hawaiian Communication and Friendship Club (honorary member).

AWARDS, HONORS: Annual Award, German-Hawaiian Communication and Friendship Club, 1998.

WRITINGS:

The Ut pictura poesis Controversy in Eighteenth-Century England and Germany, Herbert Lang (Berne, Switzerland), 1972.

A Poet among Explorers: Chamisso in the South Seas, Herbert Lang, 1973.

Hawaii and the German-Speaking Peoples, Topgallant Publishing (Honolulu, HI), 1982.

(Editor) Curtis Piehu Iaukea and Lorna Kahilipuaokalani Iaukea Watson, *By Royal Command: Biographical Notes on Curtis Piehu Iaukea,* Hui Hānai (Honolulu, HI), 1988.

His Hawaiian Excellency, Peter Lang Publishing (New York, NY), 1987, 2nd edition, 1994.

(Editor) *Journal des Malers Ludwig York Choris,* Peter Lang Publishing (New York, NY), 1999.

Turning Tide: The Ebb and Flow of Hawaiian Nationality, Peter Lang Publishing (New York, NY), 1999.

Contributor to books, including *Hawaiian Music and Musicians,* edited by George S. Kanahele, University of Hawaii Press (Honolulu, HI), 1979; *East Meets West: Homage to Edgar C. Knowlton, Jr.,* edited by Roger L. Hadlich and J. D. Ellsworth, Department of European Languages and Literature, University of Hawaii at Manoa (Honolulu, HI), 1988; and *Across the Oceans: Studies from East to West in Honor of Richard K. Seymour,* edited by Irmengard Rauch and Cornelia Moore, College of Languages, Linguistics, and Literature, University of Hawaii at Manoa (Honolulu, HI), 1995. Contributor of articles to periodicals, including *Merian, Geo Special, Swiss Review of World Affairs,* and *Hawaiian Journal of History.*

WORK IN PROGRESS: Editing *The Memoirs of the Honorable Robert Wilcox,* translated by Nancy Morris, for Kupa'a (Honolulu, HI); *Kahaunani: "Snow White" and Other German Fairy Tales in Hawaii.*

BIOGRAPHICAL AND CRITICAL SOURCES:

PERIODICALS

Contemporary Pacific, spring, 2001, Kanalu G. Terry Young, review of *Turning Tide: The Ebb and Flow of Hawaiian Nationality,* p. 292.

*   *   *

SCITOVSKY, Tibor 1910-2002

OBITUARY NOTICE—See index for *CA* sketch: Born November 3, 1910, in Budapest, Hungary; died of complications following surgery, June 1, 2002, in Stanford, CA. Economist, educator, and author. One of Scitovsky's most controversial books at the time of its publication in 1976 was *The Joyless Economy: An Inquiry into Human Satisfaction and Consumer Dissatisfaction.* In that work, he postulated that the U.S. economy took the joy out of life by overzealous focus on safety at the expense of risk and on comfort at the expense of challenge. By the end of the twentieth century, however, the book was being called one of the most important books of its age. He later wrote *Human Desire and Economic Satisfaction: Essays on the Frontiers of Economics.* Scitovsky immigrated to the United States after World War II and settled immediately at Stanford University, joining the economics faculty during a period of growth and development. He later taught at Harvard University and Yale University, and at various institutions in California. The bulk of his writings address conventional issues in economics. They included *Welfare and Competition, Economic Theory and Western European Integration,* and *Money and the Balance of Payments.*

OBITUARIES AND OTHER SOURCES:

PERIODICALS

Los Angeles Times, June 7, 2002, p. B12.
San Francisco Chronicle, June 7, 2002, p. B12.
Times (London, England), June 20, 2002, p. 37.
Washington Post, June 8, 2002, p. B7.

*   *   *

SHALEV, Zeruya 1959-

PERSONAL: Born 1959, in Israel. *Education:* Earned a master's degree in biblical studies.

ADDRESSES: Home—Jerusalem, Israel. *Agent*—c/o Author Mail, Grove/Atlantic Inc., 841 Broadway, New York, NY 10003-4793.

CAREER: Chief literary editor for an Israeli publisher; writer.

WRITINGS:

Love Life, translated by Dalya Bilu, Grove/Atlantic (New York, NY), 2000.

SIDELIGHTS: When Israeli writer and editor Zeruya Shalev penned her first novel, it became a best-selling book in her home country and was translated into English as *Love Life.* Shalev's writing in this work has been described as dense, sensual, and emotional. The story is narrated in stream-of-consciousness fashion by Ya'arah, a graduate student who lives in Jerusalem with her kind but sexually unappealing husband, Yoni.

When she meets Aryeh, an old childhood friend of her father's, she jumps into an affair with the much older man, being attracted to him despite his callous ways. The relationship hurts her marriage and her studies, leading her to act impulsively. A crisis comes when Ya'arah decides to comfort her lover following the death of his wife rather than go on a late honeymoon with her husband. She comes to realize that she has recreated her parents' dysfunctional relationship, and that her interest in Aryeh is tied to their history together.

American reviewers expressed a full range of opinions about the novel. In *Library Journal,* Molly Abramowitz took note of the author's use of "biblical allusions and . . . psychological underpinnings," but decided that *Love Life* is in essence "a tedious sexual romp." A *Kirkus Reviews* contributor was frustrated by the novel's narrative style and philosophical departures, but also marveled at its "complex architecture, built on a series of slowly disclosed revelations of the past connections between her parents and her lover," which was described as possessing "a certain fascinating force." Adding that it is a remarkably good translation, the critic advised that the novel is "oddly unpleasant and yet somehow riveting."

Stronger reviews for *Love Life* included Bonnie Johnston's appraisal in *Booklist.* She judged that Shalev succeeds in "deftly revealing the complex passions of a woman" as she discovers that she has repeated her parents' mistakes. Johnston felt that the book's "sexual explicitness is completely appropriate" in order to show how very unhappy the lovers are. A *Publishers Weekly* writer described the "sexy, densely written" story as an Erica Jong-like creation, having a smart heroine who loses control of her life but is still able to make insightful commentary. The critic noted that in various situations, Ya'arah "explodes with ingenuity and eventually insight as she comes to understand her mother's choices and, to some extent, Israeli society, with its visceral ties to the past." Critic Roland Merullo admired the author's work in *Washington Post Book World,* where he also commended the translation. While Merullo agreed that the stylistic density and Ya'arah's unpredictability made the reader impatient, he remarked that the novel "moves with a naturalness and grace that mirror life's complexity." Pleased with the author's "brutally honest and often brilliant tour of individual and family psychology," he called Shalev "a wise and sophisticated talent."

BIOGRAPHICAL AND CRITICAL SOURCES:

PERIODICALS

Booklist, January 1, 2000, Bonnie Johnston, review of *Love Life,* p. 880.

Library Journal, January, 2000, Molly Abramowitz, review of *Love Life,* p. 163.

Kirkus Reviews, January 15, 2000, review of *Love Life,* p. 79.

Publishers Weekly, December 20, 1999, review of *Love Life,* p. 52.

Washington Post Book World, April, 2000, Roland Merullo, review of *Love Life,* p. 7.*

*   *   *

SHAND, Rosa 1937-

PERSONAL: Born May 8, 1937, in Wilmington, NC; daughter of Gadsden Edwards (an engineer) and Mary Boykin (a homemaker; maiden name, Heyward) Shand; married Philip Williams Turner III, September 13, 1958 (divorced, April 22, 1986); children: Philip Gadsden Turner, Mary Cantey Meigs, Kristin Shand Turner. *Ethnicity:* "Caucasian." *Education:* Randolph-Macon Woman's College, B.A., 1958; University of Texas at Austin, M.A., 1981, Ph.D. (English literature), 1983. *Politics:* Democrat. *Hobbies and other interests:* Reading, foreign films, music, painting.

ADDRESSES: Home—189 Clifton Ave., Spartanburg, SC 29302. *Office*—Converse College, Spartanburg, SC 29302; fax: 864-596-9202. *Agent*—Michael Cone Don, Don Cong Don Agency, 156 Fifth Ave., Ste. 625, New York, NY 10010. *E-mail*—rosashand@mindspring. com.

CAREER: Virginia Public Schools, English teacher, 1958-61; Bishop Tucker College, Mukono, Uganda, English teacher, 1962-68; University of Texas, Austin, instructor, 1984-85; Converse College, Spartanburg, SC, assistant professor of English, associate professor, then Larrabee Professor of English, 1985—. Gives readings, 1991—; South Carolina Governors School, interviewer, 1993-99; South Carolina Academy of Authors, member of board of governors, 1990-95; Emrys Foundation, member of board of governors, 1994-95; Hub City Writing Project member, 1995—; judge of contests; teacher at workshops and conferences; featured on radio programs, including the National Public Radio programs *Sound of Writing* and *Southwords.*

MEMBER: Author's Guild, AWP, Poets-Writers, Amnesty International, Phi Beta Kappa, Phi Kappa Phi.

AWARDS, HONORS: Katherine Anne Porter Fiction Prize, *Nimrod,* 1991; fellowships from Virginia Center for the Creative Arts, 1992-99, Yaddo, 1993, Mac-Dowell Colony, 1995 and 2000, Sewanee Writers Conference, 2000, and National Endowment for the Arts, 2000; South Carolina fellow in fiction, 1994-95; Willa Cather Prize finalist, 1999, for *The Gravity of Sunlight;* first place, South Carolina Academy of Authors fiction fellowships, 1999; Elizabeth Simpson Smith Award for writers from both Carolinas, 1999, for short story "The Saluda Grade;" Independent Publishers Prize for best short fiction (co-recipient), 1999, for *New Southern Harmonies;* twice winner of PEN Syndicated Fiction Project.

WRITINGS:

The Gravity of Sunlight (novel), Soho, 2000.
(Contributor) *New Southern Harmonies: Four Emerging Fiction Writers,* Holocene, 1998.

Contributor of short stories to journals, including *Virginia Quarterly Review, Massachusetts Review, Shenandoah, Southern Review, Nimrod, Chelsea, American Fiction, Witness, Northwest Review, New Southern Harmonies, Indiana Review,* and *Chariton Review.* Contributor of book reviews and other articles to *Christian Century, Ball State University Forum, Outposts,* and the books *Hub City Anthology,* 1996, and *Hub City Christmas,* 1997, both published by Hub City Writers.

WORK IN PROGRESS: "Pawleys Island," a novella to be published with a collection of Southern stories, for Soho; *Happiness, Oh That,* a novel, for Soho, 2003; *The Uganda Bookshop Coffeeshop,* a collection of linked African stories.

SIDELIGHTS: Rosa Shand told *CA:* "Why do I write? For one thing, it strikes me from time to time that life is too fragile to be left to nature, whereas a work of art can give the illusion of permanence. For another thing, as someone—I forget who—says, 'We need food, shelter, and story' (it's Conrad who pulls those needs together, talking of the 'sheltering power of words'). Our minds insist on traveling with words, escaping, on the simplest level, so that our imaginations can come back refreshed (surely as important as sleep). Books provide escape, and an often-subtle reconfiguration of the world to which we return. Books lend body and weight and a third dimension to what would otherwise be flat. More personally, I suppose that since books have remained a good part of my life, trying to enter the world of books by writing has seemed a natural goal, or perhaps that ambition comes more easily to a certain shy and dreamy—or perhaps I should say impractical—temperament.

"Influences? Of course influences are myriad—from fiction, poetry, film, oh anything. But some of the more conscious ones: as a young girl in the South, one who assumed artistic aims would have to be explored undercover, the appeal of the Emilies (Dickinson and Brontë), who wrote behind closed doors, took strong hold on my imagination—they held out a possibility. Also, as a student of literature, I fell primarily under the spell of the modernists, Joseph Conrad and Virginia Woolf, for their style as much as for what they say. Woolf puts her finger on the mysterious way that writing communicates far beyond its reasoned meaning when she says of Conrad: 'One source of difficulty and disagreement is, of course, to be found, where men have at all times found it, in his beauty. . . . That beauty teaches, that beauty is a disciplinarian, how are we to convince them, since her teaching is inseparable from the sound of her voice.' I later fell in love with, and remain in love with, Chekhov, for the living ambiance of his world. The style of Jean Rhys and Marguerite Duras have captivated me; as has Faulkner with the atmosphere of his *Absalom, Absalom!* A few of the living American writers would have to be Joy Williams (in her stories) and Marilynn Robinson's (with her strange *Housekeeping*) and James Salter (in the stunning beauty of much of his *A Sport and a Pastime*). I tried, in the dissertation I had to write for the doctorate, to analyze why certain works of fiction hold such power; and it seemed to me to be largely related to their atmosphere, which often means the space in which they are set as well in their imagery and rhythm. I found that the Frenchman, Gaston Bachelard, had figured it out as well as anybody; he penetrates that mystery of how language communicates so far below the reasoning mind, in ways of which we are scarcely conscious.

"As for my own writing process, I wish I had one that I understood and could stick to. Of course it's necessary to write everyday. But I don't. Almost everything else seems to be more pressing (I try to use the excuse that I'm teaching full-time, but I know it's a rationalization). For me, the artists' colonies—the MacDowell Colony, Yaddo, and most frequently, the Virginia Center for the Creative Arts—have been extremely important, particularly in the hellish work of hammering out first drafts; because what else can you do but write in such a place. But if I ever manage to get a first draft down, then I can begin to have fun; genuine writing, for me, seems always to lie in the re-writing and re-writing.

"Do I know where I'm going when I begin to write a story or a novel? Although I envy and respect those writers who make no plan, who simply let sentence follow sentence, I compromise. I've usually thought out what I would call a loose structure—not an outline, and not a rigid plan, because a writer has to be open to what always comes along in the course of writing itself. When you've finally inserted yourself in a house of fiction, you are bound to feel its inner workings a whole lot better than you did when you stood in the doorway. That seems to be inevitable; to know all beforehand would also be deadly boring to the writer as well as to the reader."

BIOGRAPHICAL AND CRITICAL SOURCES:

PERIODICALS

Austin American-Statesman, June 11, 2000, Nadia Uddin, review of *The Gravity of Sunlight.*

Book, May-June, 2000, Amy Timberlake, review of *The Gravity of Sunlight.*

Booklist, May 1, 2000, Bonnie Johnston, review of *The Gravity of Sunlight.*

Charlotte Observer, August 23, 1998, Polly Paddock Gossett, "Spartanburg's Literary Voices Begin to Boom."

Creative Loafing, May 7, 1999, James Scott, *"New Southern Harmonies* Ranked Best Short Fiction Collection in North America."

Newsday, July 23, 2000, John Leonard, review of *The Gravity of Sunlight.*

New York Times Book Review, June 18, 2000, Margot Livesey, "Loving Africa."

Publishers Weekly, March 13, 2000, review of *The Gravity of Sunlight.*

State (Columbia, SC), August 2, 1998, William W. Starr, "Stunning Collection Spotlights S.C. Writers"; April 30, 2000, William W. Starr, "Shand's Talent Illuminates *Gravity of Sunlight,* Her First Novel."

Tribune Books (Chicago, IL), May 7, 2000, Sandra Scofield, review of The Gravity of Sunlight.

*　　*　　*

SHERLOCK, Dame Sheila
See SHERLOCK, Sheila (Patricia Violet)

*　　*　　*

SHERLOCK, Sheila (Patricia Violet) 1918-2001

PERSONAL: Born March 31, 1918, in Folkstone, England; died December 30, 2001, in Marylebone, England; daughter of Samuel Philip and Violet Mary Catherine (Beckett) Sherlock; married David Geraint James (a physician), 1951; children: Auriole Sherlock Davis, Amanda Sherlock James. *Education:* Edinburgh University, medical degree, 1941. *Hobbies and other interests:* Cricket, tennis, travel.

CAREER: Physician. Royal Postgraduate Medical School, Hammersmith Hospital, London, England, consulting physician and lecturer in medicine, 1948-59; Royal Free Hospital Medical School, London, England, chair of the department of medicine, 1959-2001.

AWARDS, HONORS: William Cullen Prize, 1962; named Dame of the British Empire, 1978; Jimenz-Diaz Prize, 1980; Thannhauser Prize, 1980; Fothergill Gold Medal, Medical Society of London, 1983; Gold Medal, British Medical Association, 1985; Distinguished Service Award, American Association for the Study of Liver Disease, 1986; one of ten most cited woman scientists of the previous decade, *Scientist,* 1990; Royal Society, fellow. Also recipient of numerous honorary degrees, including degrees from universities in Mexico; Barcelona, Spain; Lisbon, Portugal; Sweden; and Oslo, Norway.

WRITINGS:

Diseases of the Liver and Biliary System, Blackwell Scientific (Oxford, England), 1955, (with James Dooley), 11th edition, Blackwell Science (Malden, MA), 2002.

(Editor, with Nicola Dioguardi) *Proceedings of the International Symposium on Liver Reactivity: September 18, 1969,* Carlo Erba Foundation (Milan, Italy), 1969.

(Editor, with Fenton Schaffner and Carroll M. Leevy) *The Liver and Its Diseases,* Intercontinental Medical Book Corp. (New York, NY), 1974.

The Human Liver, Carolina Biological Supply Co. (Burlington, NC), 1978.

(As Dame Sheila Sherlock; with John A. Summerfield) *Color Atlas of Liver Disease,* Year Book Medical Publishers (Chicago, IL), 1979.

(Editor) *Alcohol and Disease,* Churchill Livingstone (London, England), 1982.

(Editor, with James Dooley, Robert Dick, and Manuel Viamonte, Jr.), *Imaging in Hepatobiliary Disease,* Blackwell Scientific (Oxford, England), 1988.

SIDELIGHTS: Sheila Sherlock was a professor of medicine and a world authority on the liver. She was the first woman to be appointed professor of medicine in the United Kingdom, and was the first female vice president of the Royal College of Physicians. Sherlock was also the author of the first textbook on the liver and biliary system, *Diseases of the Liver and Biliary System,* which was published in 1955 and has gone through numerous editions since. The eleventh edition was published in 2002.

Because Sherlock was female, she was not allowed to attend medical schools in England, so she went to Scotland and earned her medical degree in 1941 from Edinburgh University. When she was only thirty years old, she was appointed lecturer and consulting physician at the Hammersmith Hospital Postgraduate Medical School. Five years later, she was known all over the world for her work on liver disease.

When Sherlock began her medical career, little was known about liver disease, and the specialty of hepatology did not yet exist. Sherlock's work in research and teaching led to improvements in the diagnosis and treatment of liver disease and helped form the specialty of hepatology. Her innovations included the introduction of the needle biopsy; this technique was much less invasive and risky than the traditional open biopsy and could be used in patients who were too ill to undergo the general anesthesia that open surgery required. Sherlock's use of the needle biopsy helped to determine the causes of jaundice, a liver condition common in World War II troops. In 1966 Sherlock helped create a test to diagnose primary cirrhosis of the liver, and later showed that this disease was caused by an autoimmune problem.

In Sherlock's obituary in the *New York Times,* Anahad O'Connor quoted Dr. Eugene Schiff, former president of the American Association for the Study of Liver Diseases, as saying that when Sherlock began her medical career, "it was unimaginably difficult for a woman to advance in medicine. But she became a renowned doctor. . . . Her books were very popular because, in the beginning, she was the only author on the subject and loaded them with concise and easy to read information." In 1951 Sherlock became a fellow of the Royal College of Physicians, the youngest woman ever to be elected to the position.

In 1951 Sherlock moved to the Royal Free Hospital and Medical School, where she established a center for research on the treatment of liver disease. Physicians came from all over the world to study with her. According to Sherlock's obituary in the *British Medical Journal,* there was a time when all the liver physicians in the world visited her unit. The obituary writer reported, "She was a mother hen to those working under her and in her department, and did all she could to teach them and advance their careers, pushing them out of the nest when she felt they were ready."

In addition to textbooks, Sherlock wrote over six hundred papers on liver disease. In recognition of her achievements, Sherlock was created a Dame of the British Empire in 1978. In 1990, *Scientist* published a list of the ten most-cited woman scientists of the previous decade; Sherlock was one of them.

Diseases of the Liver and Biliary System was called "the foremost liver book in the world by only one or two authors" by Frank Iber in a review of the tenth edition of the book in the *Journal of the American Medical Association.* Iber also stated the book is "delightfully readable and mercifully brief in its prose." It has been translated into Spanish, German, Greek, Portuguese, Japanese, and Italian. "The references are always appropriate and current," noted Juan Rodes in a review of the tenth edition in *Lancet,* referring to the book as "the classic hepatology text."

Sherlock's other works have also been well received by medical journals. *Color Atlas of Liver Disease* is a gem," wrote Marshall M. Kaplan in the *New England Journal of Medicine,* noting that it "provides a useful overview of clinical liver disease." *Imaging in Hepatobiliary Disease* contains "clear and concise" text, observed John M. Braver in the *New England Journal of Medicine.* "The book does not pretend to be exhaustive," said Braver, "but in the space available the major clinical topics are well covered."

BIOGRAPHICAL AND CRITICAL SOURCES:

PERIODICALS

Annals of Internal Medicine, September 1, 1992, William D. Corey and Bradford C. Gelzayd, review of *Color Atlas of Liver Disease,* p. 447; November 1, 1993, Douglas Simon, review of *Diseases of the Liver and Biliary System, 9th ed.,* p. 961.
Journal of the American Medical Association, August 18, 1993, Frank Iber, review of *Diseases of the Liver and Biliary System,* p. 886; December 17, 1997, Frank Iber, review of *Diseases of the Liver and Biliary System,* p. 2116.
Journal of Occupational Medicine, July, 1983, Henry R. Herbert, review of *Alcohol and Disease,* p. 507.
Lancet, February 13, 1993, Ian A. D. Boucher, review of *Diseases of the Liver and Biliary System, 9th ed.,* p. 422; December 13, 1997, Juan Rodes, review of *Diseases of the Liver and Biliary System,* p. 1786.
New England Journal of Medicine, August 11, 1988, John M. Braver, review of *Imaging in Hepatobiliary Disease,* pp. 380-381; January 18, 1990, Charles Trey, review of *Diseases of the Liver and Biliary System,* p. 211; February 6, 1992, Marshall M. Kaplan, review of *Color Atlas of Liver Disease,* p. 421.

OBITUARIES:

PERIODICALS

British Medical Journal, January 19, 2002, p. 174.
Guardian (London, England), January 19, 2002, p. 20.
Independent (London, England), January 8, 2002, p. S6.
New York Times, January 10, 2002, Anahad O'Connor, p. B9.

OTHER

Hampstead & Highgate Express, http://www.hamhigh. co.uk/ (January 11, 2002), Sarah Harrison, "Liver Doctor Was World-Famous."

Yale Medicine, http://info.med.yale.edu/external/pubs/ (spring, 2002), "In Memoriam."*

* * *

SHINOHARA, Kazuo 1925-

PERSONAL: Born April 2, 1925, in Shizuoka, Japan; married Kumiko Sasaki, 1951; children: Miwako, Rieko, Hikaru. *Education:*Tokyo School of Physics, graduate, 1947; Tohoku University, studied mathematics; Tokyo Institute of Technology, B.Eng., 1953, D.Eng., 1967.

ADDRESSES: Home—Tokyo, Japan. *Office*—1622 Futoo-cho, Kohoku-ku, Yokohama, Japan.

CAREER: Architect and writer. Private practice, Tokyo, Japan, 1954—; Tokyo Institute of Technology, Tokyo, Japan, instructor, 1953-61, established studio, 1962, associate professor, 1962-69, professor, 1970-85, professor emeritus, 1986—. Yale University, New Haven, CT, visiting professor of architecture, 1984; Technische Universität, Vienna, Austria, visiting professor of architecture, 1986. *Military service:* Served in Japanese Army in Japan and Korea, 1945.

AWARDS, HONORS: Architectural Institute of Japan Prize, 1972; Medal with Purple Ribbon, government of Japan, 1980; honorary fellow, American Institute of Architects, 1988; Ministry of Education Prize, Japan, 1989.

WRITINGS:

Residential Architecture, [Tokyo, Japan], 1964.
Theories on Residences, [Tokyo, Japan], 1970.
Kazuo Shinohara: Sixteen Houses and Architectural Theory, [Tokyo, Japan], 1971.
Theories on Residences II, [Tokyo, Japan], 1975.

Kazuo Shinohara II: Eleven Houses and Architecture Theory, [Tokyo, Japan], 1976.
(With Yasumitsu Matsunaga) *Kazuo Shinohara: Essays by Yasumitsu Matsunaga and Kazuo Shinohara,* Institute for Architecture and Urban Studies and Rizzoli International Publications (New York, NY), 1982.

SIDELIGHTS: Kazuo Shinohara is a noted Japanese architect who is best known for the houses he has designed. Often simple in plan, they employ principles of traditional Japanese architecture.

Shinohara was born in Shizuoka Prefecture in Japan, and graduated from the Tokyo School of Physics in 1947. He studied mathematics at Tohoku University, and then became an assistant professor at Tokyo Medical College. He earned a degree in architecture at the Tokyo Institute of Technology in 1953, and remained at that school, where he taught architectural design from 1953 to 1986.

In the 1950s and 1960s, Shinohara designed small, simple houses that drew on the qualities of traditional Japanese architecture, using wooden walls, tiled roofs and *tatami* mat flooring, but also added new concepts of symmetry/asymmetry, and division/connection. During the 1970s, Shinohara's work became more abstract and geometric, and he began using concrete instead of wood. He further emphasized simplicity; for example, one of the houses he designed had a floor of pounded earth that followed the slope of the site it was built on.

From the mid-1970s, Shinohara began emphasizing "primitive" qualities, with heavy wooden beams and large concrete columns, as well as fragmentation, using "gaps" or "thresholds" between areas of order and disorder. Shinohara designed larger buildings as well as private houses. One of his best-known works is the Tokyo Institute of Technology Centennial Hall, built in 1987. Shinohara's work has had a profound influence on the work of other architects in Japan and other countries.

BIOGRAPHICAL AND CRITICAL SOURCES:

PERIODICALS

House and Garden, August, 1984, Martin Filler, "High Wire Act: A Tokyo House by Master Architect Kazuo Shinohara Attains a More Delicate Balance between Modernity and Tradition," p. 74.

Los Angeles Times, December 12, 1982, John Dreyfuss, review of *Kazuo Shinohara,* p. 5.

Progressive Architecture, May, 1983, Hiroshi Watanabe, "New Japanese Architecture," p. 135.*

* * *

SHORTER, Dora Sigerson 1866-1918

PERSONAL: Born August 16, 1866, in Dublin, Ireland; died January 6, 1918; daughter of George (a surgeon and scholar) and Hester (a writer; maiden name, Varian) Sigerson; married Clement Shorter (an editor), 1895.

CAREER: Poet, author, painter, and sculptor.

WRITINGS:

Verses, Elliot Stock (London, England), 1893.

The Fairy Changeling and Other Poems, John Lane (New York, NY), 1898.

Ballads and Poems, James Bowden (London, England), 1899.

My Lady's Slipper, and Other Verses, Dodd, Mead (New York, NY), 1899.

The Father Confessor, Stories of Danger and Death, Ward, Lock (New York, NY), 1900.

The Woman Who Went to Hell, and Other Ballads and Lyrics, De la More (London, England), 1902.

As the Sparks Fly Upward, Moring (London, England), 1903.

The Country-House Party, Hodder and Stoughton (London, England), 1905.

The Story and Song of Black Roderick, Moring (London, England), 1906.

The Collected Poems of Dora Sigerson Shorter, Hodder and Stoughton (London, England), 1907.

Through Wintery Terrors, Cassell (London, England), 1907.

The Troubadour and Other Poems, Hodder and Stoughton (London, England), 1910.

New Poems, Maunsel (London, England), 1912.

Do-Well and Do-Little, A Fairy Tale, Cassell (London, England), 1913.

Madge Lindsey and Other Poems, Maunsel (London, England), 1913.

Comfort the Women. A Prayer in Time of War, privately printed, [London, England], 1915.

Love of Ireland: Poems and Ballads, Maunsel (London, England), 1916.

An Old Proverb, privately printed [London, England], 1916.

Poems of the Irish Rebellion, Constable (Edinburgh, Scotland), 1916.

Kittie's Toys, Gaelic Press (Dublin, Ireland), 1917.

The Sad Years, Constable (London, England), 1918.

A Legend of Glendalough, and Other Ballads, Maunsel (Dublin, Ireland, and London, England), 1919.

Sixteen Dead Men and Other Poems of Easter Week, Kennerley (New York, NY), 1919, published as *The Tricolour: Poems of the Irish Revolution,* Maunsel and Roberts (Dublin, Ireland), 1922.

A Dull Day in London, and Other Sketches, Eveleigh Nash (London, England), 1920.

New Poems, Maunsel and Roberts (London, England), 1921.

The Augustan Books of Poetry, Benn (London, England), 1926.

Contributor to periodicals, including *Irish Monthly.* The manuscript department of the library at Trinity College, Dublin, Ireland, holds notebooks, manuscripts, and letters in the Papers of Dora Sigerson Shorter. Letters are also held by the National Library of Ireland, including those to T. Dawson and Mary Thompson.

SIDELIGHTS: Dora Sigerson Shorter was born in Dublin, Ireland to parents who were at the hub of the political and artistic culture of their time. She was educated at home and greatly influenced by William Butler Yeats. "As a mentor and colleague," noted Deborah A. Logan in *Dictionary of Literary Biography,* "Yeats shared with Sigerson a love for their impoverished and strife-torn country, a desire to recover traditional Celtic culture as a body of lore worthy of artistic legitimation, and a determination to fight for Irish independence through poetic eulogies to the growing list of patriots willing to die for the Irish cause."

Two years after the publication of *Verses,* her first collection of poetry, the writer married Clement Shorter, editor of the *Illustrated London News.* Upon moving to London, she expanded her circle to include such literary figures as A. C. Swinburne, Thomas Hardy, and George Meredith, and produced an impressive output of work. "Yet," wrote Logan, "the pain of leaving the beloved land of her birth and witnessing from a distance its escalating political conflicts was one she never overcame. As a result, much of her work thematically conveys her longing for a mythical Celtic twilight, the remoteness of which increased dramatically with each Irish freedom fighter's death."

Another influence on Shorter's poetry was John O'Leary, who believed that her work lacked focus and discipline. He gave her a copy of Thomas Percy's *Reliques of Ancient English Poetry,* which showed her a way in which her primary themes of Celtic lore, Irish politics, family, and gender issues could be unified. Logan wrote that "although her "undisciplined" style has been compared with that of the young Robert Browning, her simplicity with Oliver Goldsmith, her naiveté with Samuel Taylor Coleridge, and her natural imagery with William Wordsworth, Shorter's poetry is better assessed in terms of her ability to synthesize Celtic, Romantic, and Victorian influences in a modernist perspective. For all her links with a mythical past, Shorter's political sensibility unmistakably casts her a poet of the modern age."

Shorter's themes were established beginning with her *Verses.* "The Changeling" is about an infant stolen by fairies who leave a spiritless substitution in its place and demonstrates a conflict between Catholicism and pagan mythology. *The Fairy Changeling and Other Poems* adds Gaelic influences to mythology and features maidens and spinsters, priests and black hounds. Included are poems about pagan holidays, as in "All Hallow's Eve," and others that focus on Christian holidays, as in "The Skeleton in the Cupboard," wherein the plea is made to put aside differences for the one day of Christmas. *Ballads and Poems* and *My Lady's Slipper, and Other Verses* are comprised mainly of previously published poems, and the imagery ranges from bridal and religious to witches and banshees.

The Woman Who Went to Hell, and Other Ballads features a poem that begins with a wedding and the mother of the groom confessing that she made a pact with the devil in exchange for her son, Dermod's, soul, which Satan is to take on his wedding day. When Satan arrives, the bride offers to serve in Hell for seven years in exchange for her groom's soul. Logan wrote that "Shorter's novel recasting of the biblical Jacob

and Rachel story—with gender roles reversed; of the Virgin Mary's pact with God, the mother's pact with the Devil; of the `true' bride's associations with Christ the redeemer; and of Satan, rather than God, exacting service—is Dantesque in its blending of Catholicism with elements of Celtic myth." *The Story and Song of Black Roderick* has a similar theme and is about a warrior who marries the daughter of the leader of a rival clan to secure the peace. Although she truly loves him, Roderick ignores her once they are married, and she wanders the moors, growing weak and ill, until she dies of grief. It is then that he regrets his treatment of the woman who loved and had faith in him.

Logan called *The Collected Poems,* with an introduction by George Meredith, Shorter's "most comprehensive volume," and wrote that Meredith "suggests that the poet's work should be read with `some consideration of the Celtic mind' while taking into account Shorter's preference for ballads, `which are rather in disfavour now.' Meredith defines `the Celtic mind' as `fantastical, remote, divorced from reality'; yet, he reminds readers that although poetic symbolism `swallows Reality. . . . Reality is read through it.' Shorter's Celtic mind, in other words, is as perfectly suited to poetic symbolism as her lyricism is to the musical demands of the ballad form."

The poems in *Madge Linsey and Other Poems* explore gender inequities. In "The Sister", the narrator queries men about their occupations, which are forbidden to her. "The Two Laws," an examination of the double standard, is about the union of a squire's son and a peasant maid. He goes on to marry well and have a legitimate son, while the maid and her son become outcasts. The title poem is also about a fallen woman, loved by two men—John who sacrifices his life and soul to save hers, and Ben, whose faith is never tested. "Although 'Madge Linsey' is notable for reversing the genders of worthy and unworthy lovers of Shorter's earlier poems," wrote Logan, "the poem also recalls the issues of religious hypocrisy raised by Jeanne Bras.'"

An Old Proverb is Shorter's privately printed, limited-edition work on themes inspired by World War I. It was posthumously followed by *Sixteen Dead Men and Other Poems of Easter Week,* which Logan called "the crowning and final poetic achievement of her life." The volume was inspired by the 1916 Easter week execution of Irish rebels. Shorter spent her last days writing the dedication and arranging the poems for the book's publication. She directed that the profits from this and her earlier works be used to construct a monument to the men killed in the Easter massacre, the sculpture for which she designed and created herself. Logan said that the prose introduction, titled "The Tricolour," "deals less with the flag of a nation than with a set of values—'Labour,' 'Idealism,' and "Peace"— each `shot down' along with the men representing the values."

Shorter sensed that she was dying. "Perhaps Shorter's frustration over the passive role assigned to her as a woman manifests itself in the idea that her death vicariously contributed to the cause of Irish freedom," wrote Logan. Katharine Tynan, a friend who contributed "Dora Sigerson: A Tribute and Some Memories" to Shorter's volume *The Sad Years,* said Shorter attributed her own death "to her intense and isolated suffering over the events following Easter week, 1916, in Dublin. . . . She broke her heart over it all; and so she died, as she would have chosen to die, for love of the Dark Rosaleen," Ireland. Logan concluded by saying that Shorter's "finest dedication to 'the Dark Rosaleen,' *The Tricolour,* speaks enduringly and compellingly of the struggle that continues long after her death."

BIOGRAPHICAL AND CRITICAL SOURCES:

BOOKS

Dictionary of Literary Biography, Volume 240: *Late Nineteenth- and Early- Twentieth-Century British Women Poets,* Gale (Detroit, MI), 2001.
In Memoriam Dora Sigerson, privately printed, 1923.
Kelley, John, and Eric Domville, editors, William Butler Yeats, *Collected Letters,* Volume 1, *1865-1895,* Clarendon Press (Oxford, England), 1986.*

*   *   *

SILBERMAN, Robert (Bruce) 1950-

PERSONAL: Born 1950.

ADDRESSES: Office—Department of Art History, University of Minnesota, 271 19th Ave. S., Heller-338, Minneapolis, MN 55455-0121. *E-mail*—silbe001@ umn.edu.

CAREER: University of Minnesota, Minneapolis, MN, associate professor of art history. Frederick R. Weisman Art Museum, Minneapolis, guest curator for "World Views: Maps and Art" exhibit, 1999-2000; senior consultant, with Vicki Goldberg, for PBS series *American Photography: A Century of Images,* broadcast 1999.

WRITINGS:

(With Colleen Sheehy) *Metroscapes: The Minneapolis Gateway Photographs of Jerome Liebling and Robert Wilcox: Suburban Landscapes of the Twin Cities and Beyond,* Frederick R. Weisman Art Museum/University of Minnesota (Minneapolis, MN), 1998.
(With Vicki Goldberg) *American Photography: A Century of Images,* Chronicle Books (San Francisco, CA), 1999.
World Views: Maps and Art (exhibit catalog), essay by Yi-Fu Tuan, Frederick R. Weisman Art Museum (Minneapolis, MN), 1999.

Contributor to periodicals, including *Burlington Magazine* and *American Craft.*

WORK IN PROGRESS: Collaborating on the Garrison Diversion in North Dakota with photographer Wayne Gudmundson; studying photographic portraits of cities.

BIOGRAPHICAL AND CRITICAL SOURCES:

PERIODICALS

New York Times Book Review, December 19, 1999, Rosemary Ranck, "Click! Click! For a Century," p. 23.*

*   *   *

SKEMPTON, A(lec) W(estley) 1914-2001

PERSONAL: Born June 4, 1914, in Northampton, England; died August 9, 2001; son of Alec and Beatrice Skempton; married Mary ("Nancy") Wood, 1940 (died, 1993); partner of Beverley Beattie; children: two daughters. *Education:* Imperial College, London

University, B.S. (first-class honors), 1935, M.Sc., 1936, D.Sc., 1949. *Hobbies and other interests:* Playing the flute and croquet.

CAREER: Imperial College, London, England, lecturer and founder of soil mechanics, 1946-55, chair of soil mechanics, 1955-57, professor of civil engineering and head of department, 1957-76, professor emeritus and senior research fellow, 1976-2001.

AWARDS, HONORS: Royal Society fellow; Geotechnical Engineering Hall of Fame incipient; Royal Academy of Engineering founder fellow; knighted, 2000.

WRITINGS:

Early Printed Reports and Maps (1665-1850) in the Library of the Institution of Civil Engineers, Thomas Telford Ltd. (London, England), 1977.

(With Charles Hadfield) *William Jessop, Engineer,* David and Charles (North Pomfret, VT), 1979.

(Editor) *John Smeaton, FRS,* Thomas Telford Ltd. (London, England), 1981.

A Bibliographical Catalogue of the Collection of Works on Soil Mechanics, 1764-1950, Imperial College (London, England), 1981.

Selected Papers on Soil Mechanics, Thomas Telford Ltd. (London, England), 1984.

British Civil Engineering, 1640-1840: A Bibliography of Contemporary Printed Reports, Plans, and Books, Mansell Publications (New York, NY), 1987.

Civil Engineers and Engineering in Britain, 1600-1830, Variorum (Brookfield, VT), 1996.

(Editor, with others) *A Biographical Dictionary of Civil Engineers, Volume 1: 1500-1830,* Thomas Telford Ltd. (London, England), 2001.

SIDELIGHTS: Peter Vaughan called A. W. Skempton "one of the most influential British civil engineers of the twentieth century," in a London *Independent* obituary. "It is largely due to... [Skempton] that soil mechanics became a key discipline in civil engineering," a reporter noted in a London *Times* obituary. Skempton, a former professor at Imperial College in London, was a scholar of geology, soil mechanics, and the history of civil engineering, authoring several

books on the latter subject. His research included the areas of effective stress, pore pressures in clays, bearing capacity, and slope stability.

In 1936 Skempton joined the Building Research Station (BRS) in Garston, England, to work first on reinforced concrete and then soil mechanics, starting in 1937. His work for the BRS included Waterloo Bridge, the Muirhead dam in Scotland, Gosport Dockyard, and the Eau Brink Cut channel. In 1946 he was invited by a former professor, Sutton Pippard, to start a soil mechanics program at Imperial College.

In 1947 Skempton was a founding member of the soil mechanics and foundations committee for the Institution of Civil Engineers (ICE), "first contributing to the Rotterdam international conference and then establishing what is today the British Geotechnical Association," according to Joseph Dwyer in an obituary for the London *Guardian.* Dwyer also noted that Skempton worked with the ICE for twenty-one years, overseeing "a reorganization of the archive's collections," and raising "the professional standards of its work and publications." Skempton also served as president of the International Society of Soil Mechanics and Foundation Engineering from 1957 to 1961.

Skempton "played a guiding role in developing intellectual and academic rigour in his field," said Dwyer. He was well respected for editing works on previously ignored civil engineers such as John Smeaton and William Jessop. "He did a lot of bibliographic research himself," wrote Vaughan, "producing, for example, *Early Printed Reports and Maps (1665-1850) in the Library of the Institution of Civil Engineers.*"

Civil Engineers and Engineering in Britain, 1600-1830 is a collection of papers that Skempton wrote over a forty-five-year period; most of them were previously published in technical journals. In *Technology and Culture,* George Atkinson wrote, "This collection of papers makes an invaluable contribution to the history of a period when civil engineering first took on a modern form in a free-enterprise society." Geoff Timmins, writing in *Business History,* commented, "To those specialising in the history of science and technology and in transport history, this volume will be particularly welcome."

"Skempton dealt with the full range of engineering problems," noted Vaughan. "His synthesis of engineering and geology was particularly noticeable."

BIOGRAPHICAL AND CRITICAL SOURCES:

PERIODICALS

Business History, October, 1998, Geoff Timmins, review of *Civil Engineers and Engineering in Britain, 1600-1830,* p. 170.
Technology and Culture, January, 1999, George Atkinson, review of *Civil Engineers and Engineering in Britain, 1600-1830,* p. 148.

OBITUARIES:

PERIODICALS

Guardian (London, England), October 4, 2001, Joseph Dwyer, p. 24
Independent (London, England), August 21, 2001, Peter Vaughan, p. S6.
Times (London, England) September 10, 2001, p. 17.*

                        *   *   *

SLOCUM, Robert Boak 1952-

PERSONAL: Born May 21, 1952, in Macon, GA; son of James Robert (a professional engineer) and Sara Lila (a homemaker; maiden name, Bell) Slocum; married Sheryl Stephanie Walter, May 15, 1982; children: Claire Marie, Rebecca Bell, Jacob Robert. *Ethnicity:* "Caucasian." *Education:* Vanderbilt University, B.A. (cum laude), 1974, J.D., 1977; Nashotah House Seminary, M.Div. (cum laude), 1986; University of the South, D.Min., 1992; Marquette University, Ph.D., 1997. *Hobbies and other interests:* Running, tai chi, photography.

ADDRESSES: Home—1325 Madison St., Lake Geneva, WI 53147. *Office*—Church of the Holy Communion, 320 Broad St., Lake Geneva, WI 53147; fax: 262-248-8767. *E-mail*—rbslocum@genevaonline.com.

CAREER: Ordained Episcopal priest, 1987; vicar of Episcopal churches in Louisiana, 1987-91; rector of Episcopal church in Waukesha, WI, 1991-92; Church of the Holy Communion, Lake Geneva, WI, priest in

charge and rector, 1993—. Marquette University, lecturer in theology, 1997—; Nashotah House Seminary, visiting professor, 2000. Episcopal Diocese of Louisiana, member of executive council; Episcopal Diocese of Milwaukee, cochair of clergy day and clergy retreat planning committee, 1999—. Milwaukee Veterans Administration Hospital, part-time Protestant chaplain, 1993-98. Lake Geneva Library Board, president, 1995—; Geneva Lakes Area United Way, president, 1998-2000. *Military service:* U.S. Air Force, judge advocate, 1978-83; became captain; received Meritorious Service Medal.

MEMBER: American Academy of Religion, American Association of University Professors, College Theology Society, Society of Anglican and Lutheran Theologians, Society for the Study of Christian Spirituality.

WRITINGS:

(Editor, with Don S. Armentrout) *Documents of Witness: A History of the Episcopal Church, 1782-1985,* Church Hymnal Corp. (New York, NY), 1994.
(Editor) *Prophet of Justice, Prophet of Life: Essays on William Stringfellow,* Church Publishing (New York, NY), 1997.
(Editor and contributor) *A New Conversation: Essays on the Future of Theology and the Episcopal Church,* Church Publishing (New York, NY), 1999.
(Editor, with Don S. Armentrout) *An Episcopal Dictionary of the Church,* Church Publishing (New York, NY), 2000.
The Theology of William Porcher DuBose: Life, Movement, and Being, University of South Carolina Press (Columbia, SC), 2000.

Work represented in anthologies, including *Wisconsin Poets' Calendar,* 2000. Contributor of articles and reviews to journals, including *Sewanee Theological Review, Journal of Ecumenical Studies, Anglican and Episcopal History, Living Church, Anglican Digest,* and *St. Luke's Journal of Theology.* Book notes editor, *Anglican Theological Review,* 1999-2000.

WORK IN PROGRESS: A Heart for the Future, personal reflections on the Christian hope; a systematic theological study of the work of Austin Farrer.

SIDELIGHTS: Robert Boak Slocum told *CA:* "I seek to write in a way that combines depth of reflection with lived experience so that all kinds of people may be engaged by what I write. Most of my writing is theological, including both pastoral reflections and academic analysis as separate but related areas of interest for my work. In both of these areas of writing, I try to present material that has a strong substantive foundation of meaning and insight. But I believe strongly that it is possible to convey this foundation of meaning through examples, illustrations, and stories in a way that will reach an audience that is not limited to specialists in the field. My method of writing theology was influenced by the Episcopal theologian William Porcher DuBose, whose theology was deeply rooted in his life experience. I have also been touched by writers who have written spiritual autobiographies—including Augustine, Thérèse of Lisieux, C. S. Lewis, William Stringfellow, and Thomas Merton. I hope to use and draw from stories of faith to break open the meaning of Christian believing."

*   *   *

SMILEY, Tavis 1964-

PERSONAL: Born September 13, 1964, in Gulfport, MS; son of Emory G. (an Air Force noncommissioned officer) and Joyce M. (an associate Pentecostal minister) Smiley. *Education:* Indiana University, B.A., 1986.

ADDRESSES: Office—Smiley Group, Inc., 3870 Crenshaw Blvd., Suite 391, Los Angeles, CA 90008. *Agent*—Babette Perry, International Creative Management, 8942 Wilshire Blvd., Beverly Hills, CA 90211.

CAREER: Television talk show host, radio commentator, and author. City Council president Pat Russell, Los Angeles, CA, aide, 1987; SCLC, Los Angeles, CA, special assistant executive director, 1988; Mayor Tom Bradley, Los Angeles, CA, administrative aide, 1988-90; *BET Tonight with Tavis Smiley,* Black Entertainment Television, commentator/host, 1996-2001; ABC Radio Network, *The Tom Joyner Show,* Washington, DC, political commentator; ABC Radio Network, *The Smiley Report,* commentator, 1990—; *The Smiley Report* newsletter, publisher; *USA Weekend* (magazine), contributing editor; *Tavis Talks,* National Public Radio, Washington, DC, host, 2002—. Contributor to *PrimeTime Thursday* and *Good Morning America* for ABC News and to several CNN shows, including *Inside Politics.*

United Way of Greater Los Angeles, steering committee, 1989-90; Inner City Foundations for Excellence in Education, advisory board, 1989-91; After Class Scouting USA, advisory board, 1991; Martin Luther King, Jr. Center for Non-Violent Social Change, advisory board, 1992-93; Challengers Boys and Girls Club, board of directors, 1989—; Los Angeles Black College Tour, board of directors, 1991—; Tavis Smiley Foundation, founder.

MEMBER: Los Angeles Young Black Professionals (chair, operations committee, 1988-90), Kappa Alpha Psi.

AWARDS, HONORS: Dollars and Sense Outstanding Business and Professional Award, 1992; *Time's* 50 Future American Leaders, 1994; *Vanity Fair* Hall of Fame, 1996; NAACP President's Award, 2000; NAACP Image Award, Best News Talk or Information Series, three times, including 1999; National Association of Minorities in Communications, Mickey Leland Humanitarian Award, 1998.

WRITINGS:

Just a Thought: The Smiley Report, Pines One Publications, 1993.
Hard Left: Straight Talk about the Wrongs of the Right, Anchor Books/Doubleday (New York, NY), 1996.
On Air: The Best of Tavis Smiley on the Tom Joyner Morning Show, Pines One Publishing, 1998.
Doing What's Right: How to Fight for What You Believe—And Make a Difference, Vintage Anchor Publishing (New York, NY), 2000.
(Editor) *How to Make Black America Better: Leading African Americans Speak Out,* Doubleday (New York, NY), 2001.
Keeping the Faith: Stories of Love, Courage, Healing, and Hope from Black America, Doubleday & Company, Inc. (New York, NY), 2002.

Also foreword author, K. Thomas Oglesby, *What Black Men Should Do Now,* Carol Publishing Group (New York, NY), 1999.

SIDELIGHTS: A television and radio personality as well as an author, Tavis Smiley is known for his commentary on social and political issues, particularly those affecting African Americans. Smiley grew up in a large family of ten children. When he was two years old, his father was transferred to Grissom Air Force Base in Bunker Hill, Indiana, and the family moved to a mobile home in Kokomo, Indiana. Smiley's father often worked several jobs to support all the children, and although the family was poor, they never went hungry. Smiley's mother worked at the church the family attended, so Smiley and his siblings were often in church every day.

At age thirteen, Smiley became interested in politics when he attended a campaign speech by U.S. Senator Bird Bayh. Realizing that politicians had more influence and ability to change the world in a positive way than the baseball players he had previously idolized, Smiley decided that night to become involved in politics. Although Smiley was one of only a few African-American students in the predominantly white high school he attended, he was elected class president and voted "most likely to succeed."

During Smiley's college years at Indiana University, he became active in student government and on the debate team. He worked as an intern for Bloomington mayor Tomilea Allison. Although he considered dropping out of college because he had achieved his goals, a friend persuaded him to stay in school. Smiley then got a position as an intern in the office of Los Angeles mayor Tom Bradley. He later worked as an administrative aide for Bradley.

In 1991 Smiley ran for city council in Los Angeles. In a field of fifteen candidates, he came in fourth, a respectable performance for a political newcomer. He wrote in *Hard Left: Straight Talk about the Wrongs of the Right,* "I realized I was most fulfilled when I was helping educate, empower, and encourage people who live in the indigenous community." Thus, despite his defeat, he decided to run for office again in four years.

In order to keep his name in the public consciousness, Smiley decided to enter the field of talk radio, and developed a sixty-second syndicated program, called *The Smiley Report,* on social and political issues. The show was eventually aired nationwide, and Smiley published a collection of his commentaries titled *Just a Thought: The Smiley Report* in 1993.

In 1994 Smiley moved into television and began co-hosting an evening talk show with Ruben Navarette. The show was aimed at people in their twenties, an audience largely neglected by talk radio. That year, *Time* magazine included Smiley on its list of 50 Future American Leaders, but when Smiley, who was politically liberal, noticed that many of the other honorees were from the conservative end of the political spectrum, he wrote the book *Hard Left.* Smiley comments, "Those of us who are left of center have allowed the Right to take control of the dialogue." As a result, he continued, conservatives have had free rein to assert that they are they only group who believe in the value of religion and family.

Hard Left "is the culmination of more than a decade of running on the political fast track and winning a network of friends and allies among power brokers impressed by his infectious enthusiasm and intelligence," wrote Edward J. Boyer in the *Los Angeles Times.* A *Publishers Weekly* reviewer felt the book was "a hard-hitting intellectual counterpunch that liberals will endorse."

In 1996 President Bill Clinton introduced Smiley to Tom Joyner, host of a nationally syndicated radio show, and Joyner invited Smiley to do commentaries on his show. In the fall of that year, Smiley was chosen to host *BET Tonight,* a newsmagazine show on Black Entertainment Television. In 1998 Smiley published *On Air: The Best of Tavis Smiley on the Tom Joyner Morning Show.* For readers in search of "something short and quick on contemporary political issues from a notable analyst," wrote Charles Brooks in *Black Issues Book Review,* this book is a good choice.

In 2001 Smiley was fired from his position at Black Entertainment Television when the network was sold to a much larger company, Viacom, and its focus changed from offering potentially controversial content to providing more neutral content that would sell to a wide variety of viewers. However, Smiley's fans were outraged by the decision, and viewers flooded Viacom with phone calls, faxes, and mail expressing their support for Smiley. Despite this, the decision to let Smiley go was unchanged. According to an interview in *Jet,* Smiley said of his dismissal, "You can't have a life and be successful and not encounter some setbacks here and there."

After his dismissal from Black Entertainment Television, Smiley signed deals to be a commentator for National Public Radio, ABC News, and CNN, and also sold a two-book deal to Random House. In 2001 Smiley published *How to Make Black America Better: Leading African Americans Speak Out,* a collection of essays by leading African Americans that discussed ten "challenges" to the African-American community, including issues of health, education, money, and political power. Glenn Townes, writing in *Black Issues Book Review,* found the work to be "a must read for anyone interested in getting the best advice from those people who are indeed making life better for black Americans."

BIOGRAPHICAL AND CRITICAL SOURCES:

BOOKS

Carney, Jessie, editor, *Contemporary Black Biography,* Gale Group (Detroit, MI), 2000.

PERIODICALS

American Journalism Review, July, 2001, Kathryn S. Wenner, "Keep on Smiley," p. 9.
Black Issues Book Review, July, 1999, Charles Brooks, review of *On Air: The Best of Tavis Smiley on the Tom Joyner Morning Show,* p. 54; March, 2001, Glenn Townes, review of *How to Make Black America Better: Leading African Americans Speak Out,* p. 63.
Booklist, June 1, 1996, Mary Carroll and Gilbert Taylor, review of *Hard Left: Straight Talk about the Wrongs of the Right,* p. 1640; February 1, 2001, Lillian Lewis, review of *How to Make Black America Better,* p. 1025.
Broadcasting and Cable, June 4, 2001, Susanne Ault, "Smiley's Face at ABC," p. 8.
Ebony, April, 2001, review of *How to Make Black America Better,* p. 16.
Jet, June 18, 2001, "Talk Show Host Tavis Smiley Signs Multimillion-Dollar TV, Radio and Book Deals," p. 10.
Kirkus Reviews, April 15, 1996, review of *Hard Left,* p. 587.
Library Journal, November 1, 2000, Ann Burns and Emily Joy Jones, review of *How to Make Black America Better,* p. 104.
Los Angeles Times, July 22, 1996, Edward J. Boyer, "Fast Track, Left Lane," p. B1; August 21, 2001, John L. Mitchell, "A Painful Failure in Politics Clears a Pathway to Success," p. B3.

Nation, May 14, 2001, Makani Themba, "Black Entertainment Television's `Lifestyle' Choice," p. 18.
Publishers Weekly, May 27, 1996, review of *Hard Left,* p. 63; January 8, 2001, review of *How to Make Black America Better,* p. 63.
Washington Post, June 22, 1998, Esther Iverem, "Driving on the Left," p. C1; January 19, 2000, Natalie Hopkinson, "From Talk Show Host, A Challenge to Fight," p. M30; March 22, 2001, Lisa De Morales, "BET Bumps Host Tavis Smiley," p. C1; March 23, 2001, Lisa De Morales, "Smiley's Person: His Friend Tom Joyner Attacks BET's Boss," p. C5; March 24, 2001, Lisa De Morales, "BET Terminates Contract of Talk Show Host Tavis Smiley," p. C7; June 1, 2001, Lisa De Morales, "Tavis Smiley Finds Work with ABC, CNN, NPR," p. C5.*

*　　*　　*

SMITH, Barbara 1929-

PERSONAL: Born March 21, 1929, in Milwaukee, WI; daughter of Arthur A. (a mill representative) and Gladys (a teacher; maiden name, Campbell) Atkeson; married Donald A. Smith (an educational administrator), December 28, 1957; children: Jean, Carolyn Smith Burggraf, David. *Ethnicity:* "Caucasian." *Education:* Carroll College, B.A.; University of Wisconsin, M.A.; also attended University of Minnesota, West Virginia University, American University, Rensselaer Polytechnic Institute, and University of Kentucky. *Politics:* Democrat. *Religion:* American Baptist. *Hobbies and other interests:* Arts, music, sports, social activism.

ADDRESSES: Home and office—16 Willis Lane, Philippi, WV 26415.

CAREER: American Baptist Churches U.S.A., director of National Baptist Student Movement, 1952-60; Alderson-Broaddus College, professor of literature and writing, 1960-96, chair of Division of Humanities, 1975-96; freelance writer and editor, 1996—. Davis and Elkins College, instructor and consultant, 1997-99. Acquisitions evaluator and editor for publishing companies, including University of Tennessee Press and Mountain State Press, 1997—. West Virginia

Humanities Council, member of steering committee and program committee, 1985—. Southern Appalachian Writers' Cooperative, member, 1970—; Barbour County Writers' Workshop, director, 1973-96; West Virginia Writers, judge of annual award program, 1988—; workshop leader; gives readings from her works. Little Learners Kindergarten, cofounder and codirector, 1960-75; Sugar Creek Children's Center, president, 1975-87, member of board of directors, 1975-90; Literacy Volunteers of America, member of board of directors of West Virginia chapter, 1992—. West Virginia Public Radio, cohost of the weekly broadcast, *Party Line,* 1979-82; EcoTheater, Inc., member of board of directors, 1979-89. Heart and Hand Ministries, member of board of directors, 1960-65, 1989—; West Virginia Baptist Foundation for Campus Ministry, secretary of board of trustees, 1968-75; American Baptist Churches U.S.A., member of planning committee for national ministries, 1988-95. Concerned Citizens of Barbour County, vice president, 1990-93; Mountain Hospice, Inc., member of board of directors, 1991—, president, 1991-95, 1998—.

MEMBER: Appalachian Writers' Association (member of board of directors, 1978—), Appalachian Women Writers (member of board of directors, 1975-84), West Virginia Writers (vice president).

AWARDS, HONORS: Named woman of the year for West Virginia, Delta Kappa Gamma, 1984; West Virginia Writers, first prize for biography and autobiography, 1984, first prize for narrative poetry, 1985, first prize for lyric poetry, 1987; James Still Fellow at University of Kentucky, Appalachian Colleges Association, 1986; Alderson-Broaddus College, named outstanding woman of the year, 1986, Apollo Award, 1996; Pushcart Prize nomination, short fiction category, 1993; Dennis C. Plattner Award, *Appalachian Heritage,* 1993, for excellence in writing of fiction; humanities fellow, West Virginia Network of Ethics Committees, 1995—; Annual Award for Service to the Arts and the Community, Barbour County Arts and Humanities Council, 1997.

WRITINGS:

Six Miles Out (novel), Mountain State Press (Charleston, WV), 1981.

(Editor) *What the Mountains Yield: A Collection from West Virginia Writers,* Jalamap Publications (South Charleston, WV), 1986.

Work for Today: Ministering with the Unemployed, American Baptist Churches U.S.A., 1990.

Community Ministries, American Baptist Churches U.S.A., 1991.

Profiles of West Virginia Spirit (biography for new adult readers), West Virginia Humanities Council, 1994.

(Editor and contributor) *Coming Together* (poetry), 1995.

Philip Pendleton Barbour: "The Pride of the Democracy of Virginia," Barbour County Historical Society, 1997.

The Chenoweth Family: Builders of Bridges, Barbour County Historical Society, 1997.

(Editor and contributor) *Weep with Those Who Weep* (poetry), Trillium Press, 1998.

For the Record (play), producer in Philippi, WV, 1999.

The Circumstance of Death (novel), Mountain State Press (Charleston, WV), 2001.

(Editor, with Kirk Judd, and contributor) *Wild Sweet Notes: Fifty Years of West Virginia Poetry, 1950-1999,* Publishers Place (Huntington, WV), 2000.

The Barbour County Courthouse: Justice, Honor, and Service in the Heart of West Virginia (chapbook), Barbour County Commission, 2002.

Work represented in anthologies, including *Sense of Place in Appalachia,* edited by S. Mort Whitson, Office of Regional Development Services (Morehead, KY), 1988; and *Populore,* 1997. Contributor of articles, short stories, and poetry to periodicals, including *Arete, Aethlon, Appalachian Heritage, Antietam Review, Fish Psalms, Goldenseal, New River Review, Advocate, Potomac Review,* and *Phoenix Press Runners.* English editor, *Glorious Hope,* 1990-2000.

WORK IN PROGRESS: Three novels; poetry; local history books; research on local history.

SIDELIGHTS: Barbara Smith told *CA:* "I know it sounds hokey, but I write because I care, and I care a lot about people whose voices are not usually heard. I care about the region in which I have been located for almost all of my adult life: Appalachia, West Virginia in particular. I care about ecology and the deteriorating condition of our world. I care about world hunger and injustice—all of that good stuff. My caring stems from my religious convictions and from my tendency to snoop—watch and, especially, listen. For instance, I overheard someone yesterday talking about a woman who is raising seven grandchildren while living in a house that has no heat and no glass in the windows. This family has become a subject of investigation and prayer and action and will soon be worked, in disguise, into something I am writing.

"Writers who affect me most are those who seem to share or oppose my concerns. I read almost everything I can put my hands on, from Tolstoy to the cereal box. I am finally learning, however, that I am not morally obligated to finish everything I have started. So many books and so little time! I am highly influenceable and, thus, whatever author I am currently agreeing or disagreeing with is like to appear on my 'affects me most' list—for the moment.

"I write in spurts, mainly because I do not have large blocks of time free from other obligations. I write very fast and minimally, to the point that I depend on a few of my reliable reader-friends to tell me what is *not* on the page. Writing is hugely satisfying, and I don't mind revision, but I loathe rewriting, and I am absolutely the pits at peddling my material. Thus, I have about six book-length manuscripts and over 200 poems and short stories that should be coming or going in the mail, but instead are sitting on the shelf or standing on edge in a file drawer. My one consolation is that I understand that I am in good company!"

*   *   *

SMITH, Barbara Dawson

PERSONAL: Married; children: two daughters. *Hobbies and other interests:* Collecting research books.

ADDRESSES: Home—Houston, TX. *Agent*—c/o St. Martin's Press, 175 Fifth Ave., New York, NY 10010. *E-mail*—bsmith@barbaradawsonsmith.com.

CAREER: Writer and instructor at writing seminars.

MEMBER: Romance Writers of America.

AWARDS, HONORS: Golden Heart Award, Romance Writers of America; Best Historical Romantic Suspense Award and Best Regency Historical Award, *Romantic Times;* RITA Award, Best Short Historical, 2002, for *Tempt Me Twice.*

WRITINGS:

No Regrets, Silhouette (New York, NY), 1985.
Defiant Embrace, Zebra (New York, NY), 1985.
Defiant Surrender, Zebra (New York, NY), 1987.
Stolen Heart, Avon (New York, NY), 1989.
Dreamspinner, Avon (New York, NY), 1990.
Candle in the Snow, included in *Avon Christmas Romance,* Avon (New York, NY), 1990.
Fire on the Wind, Avon (New York, NY), 1992.
Fire at Midnight, Avon (New York, NY), 1992.
A Glimpse of Heaven, St. Martin's Press (New York, NY), 1995.
Never a Lady, St. Martin's Press (New York, NY), 1996.
Once upon a Scandal, St. Martin's Press (New York, NY), 1997.
Her Secret Affair, St. Martin's Press (New York, NY), 1998.
Beauty and the Brute, included in *Scandalous Weddings,* St. Martin's Press (New York, NY), 1998.
Too Wicked to Love, St. Martin's Press (New York, NY), 1999.
Seduced by a Scoundrel, St. Martin's Press (New York, NY), 1999.
Romancing the Rogue, St. Martin's Press (New York, NY), 2000.
Tempt Me Twice, St. Martin's Press (New York, NY), 2001.
With All My Heart, St. Martin's Press (New York, NY), 2002.

SIDELIGHTS: Two weeks after romance writer Barbara Dawson Smith sent her first historical romance novel to a publisher, the publisher bought it. Smith, who lives in Houston, Texas, with her husband and two daughters, has been writing ever since.

In *Once upon a Scandal,* Marquess of Wortham Lucas Coulter is angered when he finds out on his wedding night that Lady Emma tricked him into the marriage because she is pregnant by another man. He abandons her, leaving the country, but eventually returns. Lady Emma asks for a divorce, but in revenge for her betrayal, he refuses to free her and insists that she move in with him and be his wife. He enforces this by blackmailing her with the fact that he has discovered she is a jewel thief. In time he learns that Lady Emma's pregnancy was the result of a rape, but his gentle love for her eventually overcomes her resistance to him.

In *Her Secret Affair,* Smith tells the story of Venus Isabel Darling, who is on a search for her father's identity as well as that of the man who murdered her mother. Her mother had written a tell-all memoir that scandalized society, and one of the men named in it is the father of Justin Culver, Earl of Kern. Justin wants to stop Venus from publishing the memoir. A *Publishers Weekly* reviewer praised the novel, saying the characters' "warring wills and sexual tension . . . sizzles throughout." Ellen Hestand, in a review for *Romance Reader,* commented, "*Her Secret Affair* is a skillfully written book. It's lively and interesting, the characters are well-developed, and the plot is credible."

Seduced by a Scoundrel features Lady Alicia Pemberton, who must take care of her aging mother and her irresponsible brother. When her brother gambles away the last of the family funds, Alicia offers herself to Drake Wilder, a gambling hall owner, in order to pay debts. He refuses, but proposes marriage to her. Desperate, she unwillingly agrees to marry the apparently odious Wilder, but eventually succumbs to his charms and falls in love with him. In *Publishers Weekly,* a reviewer commented that Smith "brings a refreshing twist to a familiar plot" in this historical romance.

In *Romancing the Rogue,* Smith tells the story of Gypsy beauty Vivien Thorne, who is actually of noble descent, and her love affair with Marquess of Stokeford Michael Kenyon. In *Publishers Weekly,* a reviewer commended Smith for taking a storyline that is well-worn and making it fresh, commenting, "plots and subplots contrive to make this an entertaining novel."

Tempt Me Twice, which won a 2002 RITA award for best short historical, stars artist Gabriel Kenton—who plans to travel to Africa in search of a lost city—and Kate Talisford, who tries to prevent him from leaving by seducing him. She is unsuccessful, but when he returns to England, he is appointed her guardian after her father is murdered. Kate is suspicious of Gabriel, whom she suspects of being involved in her father's death, but eventually he is exonerated and she and Gabriel fall in love.

In *With All My Heart,* Smith tells the story of Lord Joshua Kenyon, who is stunned when he discovers his dueling opponent is a beautiful woman in disguise. Anna despises Kenyon, but her life is at stake because a mysterious man is trying to kill her, so she must join forces with Kenyon, and eventually she finds that she is in love with him.

BIOGRAPHICAL AND CRITICAL SOURCES:

PERIODICALS

Publishers Weekly, November 13, 1995, review of *A Glimpse of Heaven,* p. 58; March 16, 1998, review of *Her Secret Affair,* p. 61; November 29, 1999, review of *Seduced by a Scoundrel,* p. 57; August 14, 2000, review of *Romancing the Rogue,* p. 333; July 9, 2001, review of *Tempt Me Twice,* p. 52.

OTHER

Barbara Dawson Smith Web site, http://www.barbaradawsonsmith.com/ (August 18, 2002).
Romance Reader, http://www.theromancereader.com/ (May 7, 2002), Ellen Hestand, review of *Her Secret Affair.*
Romantic Times, http://www.romantictimes.com/ (April 21, 2002).*

*   *   *

SMITH, David G. 1948-

PERSONAL: Born March 22, 1948, in Melbourne, Victoria, Australia; son of Stephen (a printer) and Edna (a secretary; maiden name, Gardner) Smith; married Robin Spicer (divorced); married Maureen Kane (personal assistant to a chief executive), January 13, 1990; children: Denby, Jessica. *Education:* University of Melbourne, B.S. (honors), Ph.D., 1976. . *Hobbies and other interests:* Scuba diving, flight simulation, guitar.

ADDRESSES: Office—imaginACTION Pty. Ltd., Melbourne, Victoria, Australia. *Agent*—Peg McColl, Penguin Books Australia, Whitehorse Rd., Ringwood, Victoria, Australia. *E-mail*—imaginac@bigpond.net.au.

CAREER: Novelist, filmmaker, and entrepreneur. University of British Columbia, Vancouver, British Columbia, Canada, postdoctoral fellow in zoology,

1976; University of Melbourne, Melbourne, Victoria, Australia, lecturer in zoology, 1978-82; Australian Broadcasting Corporation, Melbourne, host, writer, and researcher, 1982-88; imaginACTION Pty. Ltd., Melbourne, owner and director, 1988—; Museum Victoria, Melbourne, director of human mind and body program. Associate producer, *Australia: Land beyond Time* (IMAX documentary), 2001-02; creative director and videographer of *Waypoint One* (CD-ROM); speaker and lecturer.

MEMBER: Royal Society for the Encouragement of Arts, Manufactures, and Commerce, Independent Scholars Association of Australia.

AWARDS, HONORS: ATOM International awards for Most Innovative Product and Best Video in Multimedia, both 1996, and Silver Apple, Apple Computers, 1998, all for *Waypoint One* (CD-ROM); Royal Society for the Arts fellow, 2001.

WRITINGS:

Animal Tales (natural history), Penguin Books Australia (Melbourne, Victoria, Australia), 1988.
Continent in Crisis, Penguin Books Australia (Melbourne, Victoria, Australia), 1990.
Freeze Frame (thriller), Penguin Books Australia (Melbourne, Victoria, Australia), 1992.
Total Containment (thriller), Penguin Books Australia (Melbourne, Victoria, Australia), 1993.
(With others) *Biology* (textbook), McGraw-Hill, 1994.
Saving a Continent: Toward a Sustainable Future, UNSW Press, 1994.

Contributor to periodicals. Coauthor, with B. Daum, of catalogue based on Museum of Victoria's natural history collection.

WORK IN PROGRESS: Several television documentaries; two thrillers; international CD-ROM for trauma surgery education.

SIDELIGHTS: David G. Smith told *CA:* "I trained as a comparative physiologist and conducted research in that field for a decade. Since childhood I had nurtured a fascination for film and television production and when an opportunity arose to discuss matters physi-

ological on a national Australian television variety show I began a career shift that led to me working on several major television series—*Nature of Australia* and *David Smith's Earthwatch,* both for ABC-TV. Gradually I moved toward fiction and on the strength of two nonfiction books was encouraged by Penguin to tackle two thrillers. These were critically acclaimed, which was extremely rewarding. I found fiction astonishingly easy and rewarding to write.

"I have tried in all of my writing and film work to celebrate the wonder of the natural world. My belief is that through understanding will come a deep respect for our extraordinary planet and that this will motivate a new sense of integration between humans and our underlying biology. I am most contented in two circumstances: when writing, and when I am behind my camera filming a one-off event. Highlights would have to include celebrating my fortieth birthday at Corbett National Park while filming a TV documentary called *Project Tiger* and working as associate producer on the 2002 giant-screen documentary *Australia: Land beyond Time.*"

* * *

SPECTOR, Craig 1958-

PERSONAL: Born 1958, in Virginia. *Education:* Berklee College of Music, B.A. (with honors).

ADDRESSES: Office—Stealth Press, 128 East Grant St., 4th Floor, Lancaster, PA 17602-2854.

CAREER: Film and television project developer, 1983—; freelance writer, 1985—; Stealth Press, founder. Also composes, performs, and records music.

WRITINGS:

(With John Skipp) *Fright Night,* Tor (New York, NY), 1985.
(With John Skipp) *The Light at the End,* Bantam Books (New York, NY), 1986.
(With John Skipp) *The Cleanup,* Bantam Books (New York, NY), 1987.

(With John Skipp) *The Scream,* Spectra (New York, NY), 1988.

(With John Skipp) *Dead Lines: A Novel of Horror,* Bantam Books (New York, NY), 1989.

(Editor, with John Skipp) *The Book of the Dead,* Mark V. Ziesing (Willimantic, CT), 1989.

(With John Skipp) *The Bridge: A Horror Story,* Spectra (New York, NY), 1991.

(Editor, with John Skipp) *Still Dead,* Mark V. Ziesing (Shingletown, CA), 1992.

(With John Skipp) *Animals,* Bantam Books, 1993.

To Bury the Dead, HarperCollins (New York, NY), 2000.

SIDELIGHTS: Craig Spector is a horror writer. He began publishing with coauthor John Skipp in 1986. Their first novel was *The Light at the End,* followed by five more books and two anthologies. Their works are part of a relatively new genre in the horror genre known as "splatterpunk." Spector's partnership with Skipp ended in 1983, and Spector went on to develop feature film and television projects for ABC, NBC, Fox, Hearst Entertainment, Davis Entertainment, and Hometown Films. He also went on to found Stealth Press, "a new publishing venture that, in essence, is producing high quality hardcovers and marketing them directly to readers via the Internet," Spector explained at the press's Web site.

Spector's first solo novel, *To Bury the Dead,* was born during a time of both professional and personal change in Spector's life. He commented at the Stealth Press Web site: "I decided to do something very different. My previous body of work was largely concerned with trying to inject a level of "hyper-reality" into unreal or supernatural situations. So I decided to take a very 'real' situation—nothing supernatural or otherworldly at all—and try to make it get so strange that reality begins to unravel for the main character."

The novel features Paul Kelly, a firefighter and paramedic whose life is turned upside down when he answers an ambulance call and finds that the victim is his sixteen-year-old daughter Kyra, who has been brutally murdered by another teenager. Kelly, who does not seek blood or vengeance, wants to know why the teen sociopath committed the murder, and follows this obsession to the limit. Spector "is a strong writer who convincingly re-creates the dark, often gruesome world of paramedics and firefighters," wrote a *Publishers Weekly* reviewer.

BIOGRAPHICAL AND CRITICAL SOURCES:

PERIODICALS

English Journal, December, 1986, John W. Conner and Kathleen M. Tessmer, review of *Fright Night,* p. 60.

Library Journal, June 1, 2001, Michael Rogers, review of *The Light at the End,* p. 226.

Publishers Weekly, December 20, 1985, John Mutter, review of *The Light at the End,* p. 63; January 30, 1987, review of *The Cleanup,* p. 279; January 8, 1988, John Mutter, review of *The Scream,* p. 75; December 9, 1988, Penny Kaganoff, review of *Dead Lines,* p. 58; October 23, 2000, review of *To Bury the Dead,* p. 62.

OTHER

Feo Amante's Horror HomePage, http://www.feoamante.com/ (August 18, 2002), Paul V. Wargelin, interview with Craig Spector.

Stealth Press Web si, http://www.stealthpress.com/ (August 18, 2002).*

*   *   *

SPENDER, Humphrey 1910-

PERSONAL: Born April 19, 1910, in London, England; brother of poet Stephen Spender; married; wife's name, Margaret (died, 1946); married; second's wife's name, Pauline (marriage ended); partner of Rachel; children: (second marriage) Quentin. *Education:* Attended University of Freiburg, 1927-28; studied at Architectural Association, 1929-33.

ADDRESSES: Agent—c/o Author Mail, Yale Museum of British Art, 1080 Chapel St., New Haven, CT 06520.

CAREER: Photographer, artist, textile designer, and draftsman. Worked for *Daily Mirror, Picture Post* (magazine), and *Mass Observation,* all London, England. Royal College of Art, London, lecturer. *Exhibitions:* Since 1975, Spender's work has been displayed, in both individual and group exhibits, in England, France, and the United States.*Military service:*Military photographer during World War II.

WRITINGS:

PHOTOGRAPHY

(With Tom Harrisson and Charles Madge) *Mass Observation,* [London, England], 1937.

(With Tom Harrisson) *Mass Observation: The First Year's Work,* [London], 1938.

(With Tom Harrisson) *Britain by Mass Observation,* [London, England], 1939.

(With Tom Harrisson) *Britain Revisited,* [London, England], 1961.

(With Tom Harrisson) *Britain in the Thirties: Photographs by Humphrey Spender,* Lion and Unicorn Press (London, England), 1975.

Thirties: British Art and Design before the War (exhibition catalogue), edited by Ian Jeffrey, William Feaver, Brian Lacey, and others, [London, England], 1979.

Modern British Photography, 1919-1939 (exhibition catalog), edited by David Mellor, [London, England], 1980.

(With Jeremy Mulford) *Worktown People: Photographs from Northern England 1937-38,* Falling Wall Press (Bristol, England), 1982.

Humphrey Spender: People (exhibition catalog), [London, England], 1984.

From Worktown to Our Town: Photographs of Bolton (exhibition catalog), edited by John McDonald, Bolton Museum and Art Gallery (Bolton, England), 1993.

Humphrey Spender's Humanist Landscapes: Photodocuments, 1932-1942 (exhibition catalog), edited by Deborah Frizzell, Yale Center for British Art (New Haven, CT), 1997.

SIDELIGHTS: Humphrey Spender is the most influential photographer of the British documentary movement of the 1930s and 1940s. Because of his interest in Germany, he studied art history and German in that country there during the 1920s, a period during which he was also exposed to the New Objectivity movement and had access to the major German visual magazines. Spender's brother, Michael, who was employed by the makers of the Leica camera, gave Spender his first lessons in shooting and developing,

and this furthered Spender's interest in photography and the German style, which he brought back to England with him.

Spender studied architecture for three years, but the faltering construction industry offered no work when he was qualified. His job as a draftsman lasted just three days, and he became a freelance photographer on the Strand. His photographs were in demand by such slick magazines as *Vogue* and *Harper's Bazaar,* but he found little satisfaction in this type of work. But because it paid well, he was able to take on the type of project that would fascinate him for the rest of his career. He began pictorially recording the lives of the poorest of children in London's East End.

He was offered, and accepted, a job with the *Daily Mirror,* for which he was to photograph and note urban life. What the paper was looking for were pictures of gardens, cottages, and other noncontroversial subjects; what Spender wanted to shoot were the struggles of the working class and other "humanist" subjects, like the Jarrow Hunger Marchers, which he documented in 1936.

He found the perfect outlet beginning in 1937, working with Tom Harrisson, the founder of Mass Observation. Harrisson applied his skills as an anthropologist to studying the lives of the people of Bolton, or "Worktown," and Spender became the organization's primary photographer. His pictures came to represent the project more than anyone else's. The *Daily Mirror* finally fired him, but he soon signed on with *Picture Post,* edited by Oxford graduate Tom Hopkinson and Hungarian exile Stefan Lorant, and this team quickly became the pioneers of a new form of British documentary photojournalism.

"It proved an ideal home for Spender," noted Kevin Jackson in the London *Independent,* "who set to work on a series of large-scale photo essays on life in Britain's industrial centres and slums, from Whitechapel to Tyneside: often angry, damning, muckraking narratives which prompted shrieks of disapproval from local authorities."

With the onset of war, *Picture Post* assigned Spender to stories about the fighting forces in an effort to boost morale. "One of these, 'Life on a Destroyer,'" said

Jackson, "is among the most atmospheric of all his assignments, though his single most dramatic image, splashed across the cover on September 5, 1942, was the bandaged profile of a handsome British commando wounded in a disastrous raid on Dieppe." Spender became an official photographer for the British army and later was assigned the task of producing maps from Royal Air Force photographs to be used for the D-Day landings.

When the war ended, Spender spent less time on journalism and more on painting and textile design. Although he was well known among his peers, his work was offered to a wider audience when *Britain in the Thirties: Photographs by Humphrey Spender* was published. Spender's work continues to be featured in exhibitions and made available by accompanying catalogs.

The *Guardian*'s Sabine Durrant, who interviewed Spender at his home in 2000, wrote that "he has an extraordinary soft, clear voice. His elder brother [British poet laureate Stephen Spender] may have been the poet, but the younger brother has a way with language too—conjuring his life in snapshots, unflinching in self-criticism, dispassionate in his observation of others." Durrant noted Spender "doesn't think the Mass Observation project did much to disclose anything, most of his pictures sat, undeveloped in a drawer until the 1970s. And he has always felt he failed in his fundamental aim to be invisible."

Spender, who has been nearsighted for most of his life, developed a cataract and was given lens implants that have nearly corrected his vision. He told Durrant, "I'm not that pleased about it." "It comes down to texture," said Durrant. "Spender has always liked to look at things close up. . . . It is the expressions on his subjects' faces—the unemployed of Tyneside, the housewives of Stepney—that tell you as much about the deprivation of their lives as the state of their clothes or houses." Spender mourns the end of *Picture Post* telling Durrant, "If there was [still a publication], I would do a feature on mobile phones or backpackers. They present such marvelous sorts of visual things in mainline stations."

BIOGRAPHICAL AND CRITICAL SOURCES:

BOOKS

Contemporary Photographers, Gale (Detroit, MI), 1996.

Rosenblum, Naomi, editor, *A World History of Photography,* [New York, NY], 1985.

PERIODICALS

British Journal of Photography, June, 1992, Michael Hallett, interview.

Guardian (London, England), July 24, 2000, Sabine Durrant, "The Sabine Durrant interview: The lensman: He Is Recognized as One of the Most Important British Photographers of the Last Century, Has a Devoted Companion Fifty-four Years His Junior, and Recently Acquired Full Sight for the First Time in his Life. So Why Is Humphrey Spender So Grumpy?" p. 4.

Independent (London, England), July 14, 2000, Kevin Jackson, "The Arts: Still Looking for a new England," p. 9.

New York Times, October 10, 1997, John Russell, "Exploring the Misery of a Desperate Era," p. B34.

Times (London, England), December 13, 1997, David Driver, review of *Humphrey Spender's Humanist Landscapes,* p. 19.*

*   *   *

SPOERRI, Elka (Zagaroff) 1924-2002

OBITUARY NOTICE—See index for *CA* sketch: Born July 27, 1924, in Sofia, Bulgaria; died of cancer May 17, 2002, in Bern, Switzerland. Art historian and author. Spoerri was best known as an expert on the art of Adolf Wölfli. A student of art history at Stanford University and the University of Berne during the 1950s, Spoerri was an assistant at the Museum of Fine Arts in Berne during the late 1960s and early 1970s, becoming a lecturer there from 1973 to 1981. She was introduced to the world of Wölfli's work through her husband, a psychiatrist who was interested in the artist and author, who suffered from schizophrenia and spent much of his life in a mental institution. When her husband died in 1973, Spoerri continued his work in deciphering the complex work and encoded language of Wölfli and revealing him to be a brilliant artist. In 1975 she became the founding curator of the Adolf Wölfli Foundation Museum of Fine Arts, organizing exhibitions of Wölfli's work until her retirement in 1996. Spoerri was the author of *Adolf Wölfli* (1976) and coauthor of *The Other Side of the Moon: The World of Adolf Wölfli* (1988). She also edited several books about the artist.

OBITUARIES AND OTHER SOURCES:

PERIODICALS

New York Times, June 3, 2002, p. A17.

*   *   *

SPRING, Matthew

PERSONAL: Male. *Education:* Attended Keele University; Magdalen College, Oxford, D.Phil.; studied lute at the Royal College of Music.

ADDRESSES: Office—49 Pitts Rd., Oxford OX3 8BA England; fax: 01865 761966. *Agent*—c/o Oxford University Press, Great Clarendon St., Oxford OX2 6DP England. *E-mail*—hurdy-gurdyman@matspring. demon.co.uk.

CAREER: Lutenist/hurdy-gurdy player and musicologist. Birmingham University, Birmingham, England, musicologist; Bath Spa University College, Bath, England, associate lecturer in early music. Sirinu (Early Music Network Tours), cofounder, 1992-94; musical performer in duo with Sara Stowe, 1986—.

AWARDS, HONORS: Three-year Leverhulm Trust fellowship, London Guildhall University; Radcliff fellowship in musicology, 1995-96.

WRITINGS:

The Lute in Britain: A History of the Instrument and Its Music, Oxford University Press (Oxford, England), 2001.

Contributor to music journals and books.

SIDELIGHTS: Musicologist and lute player Matthew Spring has published numerous articles on musicology. His book *The Lute in Britain: A History of the Instrument and Its Music* explores the history of this stringed instrument, which was an important instrument from late medieval times to the eighteenth century in Europe. In addition to discussing the instrument's history, Spring also considers the lute in concert, lute song accompaniment, and its use in Scotland, as well as the slow decline in its use resulting from the fact that it is a very quiet instrument with a limited range. In the *Times Literary Supplement,* Curtis Price wrote that the book "draws together . . . a wealth of recent scholarship" and "enlivens the narrative with practical comments on technique, instrument design and construction."

Spring plays the lute, baroque guitar, and hurdy-gurdy, among other instruments. He has performed with musician Sara Stowe for many years, and has appeared on radio and television in Great Britain. He and Stowe have recorded their performances on the Hyperion and Chandos labels. Spring also performs with a musical ensemble called Chalemie.

BIOGRAPHICAL AND CRITICAL SOURCES:

PERIODICALS

Times Literary Supplement, November 23, 2001, Curtis Price, review of *The Lute in Britain: A History of the Instrument and Its Music,* p. 13.*

*   *   *

STANLEY, Debby
See STANLEY, Deborah B.

*   *   *

STANLEY, Deborah B. 1950-
(Debby Stanley)

PERSONAL: Born May 5, 1950, in Richmond, VA; daughter of Robert Caldwell, Jr. (a Presbyterian pastor) and Constance (a technical editor; maiden name, Kistler) Bradford; married John Malcomb Thoens (divorced, 1989); married David Charles Stanley, August, 1994; children: (first marriage), Jonathan Bradford. *Ethnicity:* "Caucasian." *Education:* Mary Washington College, B.A., 1972; Trenton State College, art teacher certification, 1975; Fresno State College, additional teacher certifications, 1985; University of San Francisco, preliminary certification in educational administration, 1988; Fresno Pacific College, library media teacher certification, 1994. *Politics:* Democrat. *Religion:* Presbyterian. *Hobbies and other interests:* Technology and computers, reading, fine art and antiques.

ADDRESSES: Home—27490 Englewood St., Moreno Valley, CA 92555. *Office*—Central Middle School, 4795 Magnolia Ave., Riverside, CA 92506; fax: 909-276-2028. *E-mail*—debdavest@aol.com and dstanley@rusd.k12.ca.us.

CAREER: Advertising artist for agencies in New Jersey, 1972-82; elementary school art teacher in East Windsor, NJ, 1982-83; elementary school teacher at Clovis, CA public school, 1985-90, and library media teacher, 1990-96; library media teacher at San Diego, CA public middle school, 1996-97, and Glendale, CA public high school, 1997-98; Riverside Unified School District, Riverside, CA, library media teacher at Central Middle School, 1998—. California Consortium for Visual Arts Education, resource specialist, 1991-96.

MEMBER: Computer-Using Educators, California School Library Association, Phi Beta Kappa.

AWARDS, HONORS: "Good Ideas" Awards, California School Library Association, 1994, for integrating visual arts into a school library, and 1999, for standards integration into a school library.

WRITINGS:

Practical Steps to the Research Process for High School, Libraries Unlimited (Englewood, CO), 1999.
Practical Steps to the Research Process for Middle School, Libraries Unlimited (Englewood, CO), 2000.
Practical Steps to the Research Process for Elementary, Libraries Unlimited (Englewood, CO), 2001.

Some writings appear under the name Debby Stanley.

WORK IN PROGRESS: Hands-on Lessons for the Research Process, a compact disc.

SIDELIGHTS: Deborah B. Stanley told *CA:* "I was busy setting up a workshop I was presenting at the California School Library Association state conference in Pasadena in 1997, when a friendly looking lady came into my as-yet-empty room. She watched me bustling around for a minute and then came right to the point, 'Have you ever thought about writing a book?' 'Yes!' I replied. 'I've been teaching about research for years, and though this is my first conference presentation about it, I've tried this method at elementary, middle school, and now high school. I know it works!

"Thus was born my adventure in authoring. After the conference, I followed Betty Morris's instructions to go online and apply to write a book about research, actually a professional trade book. The steps of the application process included writing a summary of proposed chapters, then writing full-length versions of the first three chapters. After eight years of teaching research, I knew exactly what I wanted to say and do. The summaries for fifteen chapters divided into four sections literally tumbled from my gray matter. Unfortunately for the publisher, my experience in fine arts and advertising also meant that the format, the style of presentation of what I needed to say, was an inseparable part of my message. But I also appreciated both my lack of expertise and the publisher's talents, and we easily wove our ideas into a pattern that accomplished our mutual purposes. I wanted a hands-on, very visual, bullet-style guidebook that would be readily accessible for busy teachers. I even wanted a spiral binding so teachers could flop the book's many teaching templates over the copy machine and create transparencies in their five minutes of 'prep time' before class. Oh well, I couldn't have everything!

"*The Research Process* . . . is a Cinderella-type process. It is so intuitive that no one really owns it. The main difference from previous methods is that this was truly born from the bottom up. It came from students! It was then honed by the critical demands of busy teachers: lack of time to meet the diverse needs of students while preventing the plague of plagiarism. Here is how the research process came about. One of my early library media teacher training classes required that we graduate students each plan and teach a research unit with another teacher at our school site. In the course of completing this assignment, I observed what students were doing as they performed research. It was immediately apparent that there were distinct steps. Over time I identified basic strategies that students were doing to accomplish each step. As they did something, I wrote it down. I then designed my first simple teaching templates so that I, as a library media teacher, could turn around and teach those strategies. A motto has always been, 'Keep it do-able!

"Over the next ten years of collaborative planning and teaching information literacy skills (research) embedded in content-area units of study (collaboration), some of the early teaching templates remained remarkably intact. Many others have been refined or designed to meet the specific needs of teachers, students, and curriculum requirements. Therefore, I can never quite stop writing, designing, and teaching research steps and strategies. I, myself, am a work in progress. I never tire of the twinkle I see when a student understands that research is like a jigsaw puzzle that is actually easier to do and much more rewarding than plagiarism. Information literacy is not only possible to learn in simple ways; it is even fun!"

*   *   *

STEFFEN, Lloyd H. 1951-

PERSONAL: Born November 27, 1951, in Racine, WI; son of Howard and Ruth (Rode) Steffen; married Emmajane S. Finney (a minister and agency director), February 14, 1981; children: Samuel Atticus, Nathan Lloyd, William Henry II. *Education:* New College, B.A. (history), 1973; Yale Divinity School, M.Div. (cum laude), 1978; Brown University, Ph.D. (religious studies), 1984. *Religion:* United Church of Christ. *Hobbies and other interests:* Guitar, music, playing with band Religion & Cash.

ADDRESSES: Home—1349 Woodland Circle, Bethlehem, PA 18017. *Office*—Lehigh University, 36 University Dr. Johnson Hall 110, Bethlehem, PA 18015. *E-mail*—lhs1@lehigh.edu.

CAREER: Educator and author. Lehigh University, Bethlehem, PA, professor, chair, department of religion studies, and university chaplain, 1990—; Northland College, Ashland, WI, professor of philosophy and religion and chaplain, 1982-90. Member, board of directors, Religious Coalition for Reproductive Choice, 2000—, vice chair, 2002—; board of directors, As-

sociation for College and University Religious Affairs, 1991-92, 1993-96. Professional firefighter, Bradenton, FL, 1973-74. Common Ground of the Lehigh Valley, 1994-97, chair, 1995-97; board of directors, Center City Ministries, 1992-96; Institute for Jewish Christian Understanding, program committee for Day of Dialogue, 1993—.

MEMBER: American Academy of Religion, American Philosophical Association, Society for Values in Higher Education.

AWARDS, HONORS: Faculty research grant, Lehigh University, 1998, for death penalty research support; First Church and Society Award, Pilgrim Press, 2001, for *Executing Justice: The Moral Meaning of the Death Penalty;* United States observer to "Project Europe: European University Chaplain's Conference," United Church of Christ, 1999; certificate, President's Office, United Church of Christ, 1998, for *Life/Choice: The Theory of Just Abortion.*

WRITINGS:

Self-Deception and the Common Life, Peter Lang (New York, NY), 1986.
(Editor) *Abortion: A Reader,* Pilgrim Press (Cleveland, OH), 1998.
Executing Justice: The Moral Meaning of the Death Penalty, Pilgrim Press (Cleveland, OH), 1999.
Life/Choice: The Theory of Just Abortion, Pilgrim Press (Cleveland, OH), 1994.

Contributor to journals including *Journal of the American Academy of Religion, Christianity and Crisis, Environmental Ethics, Philosophy East-West, Christian Century, ILIFF Review, Books and Religion, Sacred Heart Review, Pulpit Digest, Cross Currents, Ethics, Theology Today,* and *Review of Books in Religion.* Regular columnist for "Spiritual Journeys," *Express-Times* (Easton, PA).

WORK IN PROGRESS: Ethical Reach: On Moral Vision and Personal Disorder, for Georgetown University Press; "Religion and the Restraint of Violence: An Essay on the Demonic, Holy War, and Just War"; research on problems of personal disorder, self-deception, and the demonic application of just-war model to other ethical issues and current events.

SIDELIGHTS: Lloyd H. Steffen told *CA:* "My purpose in writing is to address and clarify the significant moral issues of our time. By arguing for moral moderation and articulating the basis for common ground in the moral enterprise, I seek to open up new possibilities for conversation. My constructive work in ethics respects complexity, pluralism, and the context of uncertainty, and thus opposes moral absolutism and the contradictions to which absolutism inevitably leads."

* * *

STEIMBERG, Alicia 1933-

PERSONAL: Born July 18, 1933, in Buenos Aires, Argentina; daughter of Gregorio (a teacher) and Luisa (a dentist; maiden name, Imas) Steimberg; married Abraham Sokolowicz (divorced, 1967); married Abraham Svidler (an industrial engineer; deceased); children: (first marriage) Estela, Victor; (second marriage) Martin. *Ethnicity:*"Latin American-Jewish." *Education:* Graduate of Instituto Nacional del Profesorado en Lenguas Vivas, Buenos Aries, Argentina. *Politics:* "Apolitical-centrist." *Religion:* "Jewish Family." *Hobbies and other interests:* Music, film, theater.

ADDRESSES: Home—Don Bosco 3820, 7 , 1206 Buenos Aires, Argentina. *Agent*—Julia Popkin, Los Angeles, CA; Guillermo Schavelzon, Buenos Aires, Argentina. *E-mail*—steimber@sinectis.com.ar.

CAREER: Writer, teacher, and translator. National Ministry of Culture, Buenos Aires, Argentina, director of books, 1995-97.

AWARDS, HONORS: Literary prize, Argentine Society of Writers, 1979; Fulbright award, 1983; winner of Tusquets Competition, 1988, for *Amatista;* Planeta Biblioteca del Sur prize, 1992, for *Cuando digo Magdalena.*

WRITINGS:

Músicos y relojeros, Centro Editor de América Latina (Buenos Aires, Argentina), 1971, translation by Andrea G. Labinger published as *Musicians and Watchmakers,* Latin American Literary Review Press (Pittsburgh, PA), 1998.

La loca 101 (novel; title means "Madwoman 101"), Ediciones de la Flor (Buenos Aires, Argentina), 1973.

Su espíritu inocente (novel; title means "Her Innocent Spirit"), Editorial Pomaire (Buenos Aires, Argentina), 1981.

Como todas las mañanas (stories; title means "Just Like Every Morning"), Editorial Celtia, 1983.

El árbol del placer (novel; title means "The Tree of Pleasure"), Emecé Ediciones, 1986.

Amatista (novel), Tusquets (Barcelona, Spain), 1989.

(With others) *Salirse de madre,* Croquiñol Ediciones (Buenos Aires, Argentina), 1989.

El mundo no es de polenta (young adult; title means "The World Is Not Made of Polenta"), El Quirquincho, 1991.

Cuando digo Magdalena (title means "When I Speak the name of Magdalena"), Planeta (Buenos Aires, Argentina), 1992, translation by Andrea G. Labinger published as *Call Me Magdalena,* University of Nebraska Press (Lincoln, NE), 2001.

Vidas y vueltas (stories), edited by Adriana Hidalgo, [Buenos Aires, Argentina], 1999.

La Selva (novel; title means "The Rainforest"), Alfaguara (Buenos Aires, Argentina), 2000.

Una tarde de invierno un submarino (young adult novel; title means "In a Winter Evening, a Submarine"), Alfaguara (Buenos Aires, Argentina), 2001.

Contributor to Argentine periodicals, including *Clarin and El Cronista;* work represented in anthologies, including *Landscapes of a New Land,* edited by Marjorie Agosin, White Pine Press, 1989.

WORK IN PROGRESS: A diary of stories, fantasies, and dreams.

SIDELIGHTS: Alicia Steimberg is an award-winning Argentine author of short stories and novels, who bases much of her writing on her own life. Her first autobiographical novel, translated as *Musicians and Watchmakers,* was inspired by stories she heard from her maternal grandmother, a Jewish Ukranian immigrant who arrived in Buenos Aires in 1890, when she was eleven years old. It is from her that Steimberg learned about her family's history, the cold and snow she had never experienced, and the growth of Argentina's capital in the twentieth century. Steimberg's character is also Alicia Steimberg, and the author fictionalizes parts of her childhood in an eccentric family that includes a domineering widowed mother, vegetarian atheist grandfather, hypochondriac grandmother, a number of feisty aunts, and an uncle who molests her. When Alicia is harassed by her anti-Semitic fifth grade teacher, she adopts the Catholicism of a friend, and she develops her political awareness during the regime of Juan Peron. A *Publishers Weekly* contributor called the book a "small gem of a novel," and said that Andrea G. Labinger's translation "is a delight, conveying the sights, sounds, misconceptions, and dreams of an intensely experienced youth."

Steimberg's *La Loca 101* is an experimental novel, based on her experiences with the people and city of Buenos Aires, and in which she generously uses dreams and fantasies. *Su espíritu inocente* is a novelized continuation of her childhood and young adult memories, and *Como todas las mañanas* is a book of short stories.

El árbol del placer is a novel based on the popularity of psychoanalysis in Buenos Aires in the 1960s and 1970s, fueled in part by the large numbers of professionals who arrived from Europe, who then treated a great many patients, often complementing analysis with the use of hallucinogenic drugs. Steimberg wrote *Amatista* as an entry in a competition for erotic literature held by Editorial Tusquets, in part to test the success of her Argentine Spanish with the editors in Spain.

Steimberg has written two books for young teens. *El mundo no es de polenta* is a book of stories, anecdotes, and recipes that teach readers how to cook simple, healthy meals. Steimberg was prompted to write the book because her own children would ask for food money when they were on holiday, that she knew they were spending in restaurants and for take-out. She hopes the book will sway teens away from relying on junk food.

La Selva is a novel about an older woman who spends time at a Brazilian spa recuperating from the painful illness and death of her husband and escaping from a son who is ruining his life with alcohol and drugs. While there, she meets a man who will give her life a new direction.

Call Me Magdalena is the translation of Steimberg's award-winning *Cuando digo Magdalena,* inspired by a few days spent with friends. It is narrated by Magdalena, a woman who reflects on her life as an Argentine Jew and who searches for her identity through stories of faith and love. This exercise takes place in a mind control session where participants attempt to learn to deal with modern life, and which is sponsored by the wealthy Juan Antonio, whose own life provides the subplot. *Library Journal*'s Lee McQueen wrote that Magdalena's "confusion over how to define herself as an Argentine Jew is playfully and effectively drawn." A *Publishers Weekly* reviewer said the novel is distinguished by Steimberg's "simple and evocative prose." A *Kirkus Reviews* contributor called Steimberg "one of Latin America's best writers," and the novel, "intricate, sensuous, and frequently hilarious."

Steimberg told *CA* that "there is more than one" reason why she started writing. "At the beginning, I think I just wanted to know if I could do it, I mean if I was able to produce the kind of writing we call 'literature' or 'fiction.' At the time, I was nineteen or twenty years old. There were, and there have always been, two principal currents in my writing: autobiography and experiment."

"I may have previous ideas, but usually schematic. Even when they are rather elaborate, I never know for certain what I am about to write. It is a process of association. Sometimes it is just a word, a phrase that captures my fantasy. My texts undergo a process of 'cleaning up,' additions and discardings that take no less time than the writing itself. What remains in my memory of a dream, recollections of the past, or sheer invention, everything is good enough to trigger a text.

"Apart from giving pleasure and entertainment to the reader, I never had any specific purpose. I certainly never expected to change the world with my books, though some readers have told me that they discovered things in them that helped to change some of their ideas. I am deeply satisfied with giving them something to think about, or simply to enjoy."

Steimberg has been influenced by the work of Argentines Jorge Luis Borges, Julio Cortázar, and Manuel Puig; Americans John Cheever and Raymond Carver; British writers Saki (H.H. Munro), Somerset Maugham, and Martin Amis; and Italian Natalia Ginzburg. "This list could be interminable," said Steimberg. "I like honest writers, I hate opportunists."

BIOGRAPHICAL AND CRITICAL SOURCES:

BOOKS

Flori, Monica S., *Streams of Silver: Six Contemporary Women Writers from Argentina*, Bucknell University Press (Lewisburg, PA), 1995, pp. 147-184.

PERIODICALS

Americas (English edition), May-June, 1984, Cecilia Delacre Capestany, review of *Como todas las mañanas*, p. 59.
Belles Lettres, summer, 1993, Susana Conde, review of *Cuando digo Magdalena*, p. 12.
Kirkus Reviews, September 15, 2001, review of *Call Me Magdalena*, p. 1324.
Library Journal, September 1, 2001, Lee McQueen, review of *Call Me Magdalena*, p. 236.
Publishers Weekly, July 6, 1998, review of *Musicians and Watchmakers*, p. 52; August 13, 2001, review of *Call Me Magdalena*, p. 282.
Virginia Quarterly Review, spring, 2002, review of *Call Me Magdalena*, p. 61.*

* * *

STEIN, Leon 1910-2002

OBITUARY NOTICE—See index for *CA* sketch: Born September 18, 1910, in Chicago, IL; died May 9, 2002, in Laguna Woods, IL. Composer, conductor, educator, and author. Stein was a prolific musical composer who had his works performed by orchestras around the United States. He was a graduate of De Paul University, where he received his Ph.D. in 1949 after serving in the U.S. Naval Research during World War II. He remained at De Paul throughout his academic career, beginning as an instructor in 1931 and becoming a professor and chairman of the music department by 1948. He also served at various times as the director of the graduate school, founder and conductor of the university's chamber orchestra, and the dean of the School of Music, retiring in 1976. When not in the classroom, Stein was directing orchestras, including the Community Symphony of Chicago from 1945 to 1965 and the City Symphony of Chicago from 1964 to 1984. As a composer, Stein completed over one hundred original pieces, including four symphonies and two operas. He was also the author of *The Racial Thinking of Richard Wagner* (1950) and *Structure and Style: The Study and Analysis of Musical Forms* (1962), as well as the editor of *Anthology of Musical Forms* (1962). For his contributions to music, Stein was inducted into Chicago's Hall of Fame in 1982.

OBITUARIES AND OTHER SOURCES:

BOOKS

Slonimsky, Nicolas, *Baker's Biographical Dictionary of Twentieth-Century Classical Musicians,* Schirmer Books (New York, NY), 1997.
Who's Who in Entertainment, third edition, Marquis (New Providence, NJ), 1997.

PERIODICALS

Los Angeles Times, May 11, 2002, p. B19.
San Francisco Chronicle, May 11, 2002, p. A22.

* * *

STEVENS, Felton, Jr. 1970-

PERSONAL: Born October 24, 1970, in Baton Route, LA; son of Felton (a warehouse engineer) and Helen J. (a homemaker; maiden name, Mosley) Stevens; married June 23, 2001; wife's name Jeanette B.; children: (stepchildren) Jeremy Ransom, Kiara Ransom. *Ethnicity:* "African American." *Education:* University of Texas—Arlington, B.A., 1996. *Politics:* "Former Democrat." *Religion:* Baptist. *Hobbies and other interests:* Reading, weight training.

ADDRESSES: Home—P.O. Box 535351, Grand Prairie, TX 75053. *Office*—c/o AWM Publishing, P.O. Box 3716, Arlington, TX 76007. *E-mail*—felton@awmpub.org.

CAREER: University of Texas Southwest Medical Center, Dallas, TX, research assistant, 1999—. Affiliated with AWM Publishing, Arlington, TX. Worked in collections at Aetna U.S. Healthcare.

MEMBER: Small Publishers Association of North America, American Heart Association.

WRITINGS:

Changing Faces (nonfiction), AWM Publishing (Arlington, TX), 2001.
Hell with a Badge, 2002.

WORK IN PROGRESS: Your Gift Will Make Room; research on adultery and its effects, causes, and consequences.

SIDELIGHTS: Felton Stevens, Jr. told *CA:* "My primary motivation for writing is God, because I trust that He is the reason behind my talent for writing. Through my spiritual gift of service, combined with writing, He is allowing me to touch the lives of others. Honestly, I don't consider myself to be a Stephen King or Max Lucado when it comes to the art of writing, but I do my best to write from the heart. My past experiences and relationships with others influence my writing, and prayer prepares me for each session.

"I begin each writing task with prayer, for the simple fact that God's glorification is my main purpose for writing. I pray for guidance, wisdom, and perseverance concerning this process of writing, whether I'm penning a poem, a short story, or even an entire book.

"Besides the fact that my writing will help others, what also inspires me is that by putting my feelings on paper, I am also helping myself. For years I kept a journal of past experiences, and one day while reading through it, I noticed a pattern. Whenever my situations and circumstances were at a major high, or low (in most cases), I would simply write about the issues. For example, in my past relationships with women, I noticed, after reading my journal, that there were certain cycles I would go through. Once these cycles were broken (through a relationship with God), my entire life began to change. So ultimately it is God who inspires me to write, because through Him I've learned more about myself."

*   *   *

STOESZ, David 1947-

PERSONAL: Born May 25, 1947, in Omaha, NE; children: Julio. *Ethnicity:* "Anglo." *Education:* Ohio State University. M.S.W., 1974; University of Maryland, Ph.D., 1980. *Hobbies and other interests:* Whitewater kayaking, making furniture, weaving.

ADDRESSES: Home—8110 Carlyle Pl., Alexandria, VA 22308. *Agent*—c/o Author Mail, University of Wisconsin Press, 1930 Monroe St., 3rd Fl., Madison, WI 53711-2059. *E-mail*—dstoesz@vcu.edu.

CAREER: Social worker, educator, and author. Hood College, Frederick, MD, assistant professor, 1979-84; San Diego State University, San Diego, CA, professor, 1986-95; Virginia Commonwealth University, Arlington, professor, 1995—, Samuel Wurtzel Chair in Social Work, 1995-2000; policyAmerica, Alexandria, VA, associate, 2001—.

MEMBER: Council on Social Work Education, Association of Public Policy Analysis and Management.

AWARDS, HONORS: San Diego Social Worker of the Year, 1993.

WRITINGS:

(With Howard Jacob Karger) *American Social Welfare Policy: A Structural Approach,* Longman (New York, NY), 1990, 4th edition published as *American Social Welfare Policy: A Pluralist Approach,* Allyn and Bacon (Boston, MA), 2002.
(With Howard Jacob Karger) *Reconstructing the American Welfare State,* Rowman and Littlefield (Lanham, MD), 1992.
(With Mark W. Lusk and Ken R. Patterson) *Family Self-Sufficiency: Welfare Reform in Idaho,* Dept. of Social Work, College of Social Sciences and Public Affairs, Boise State University (Boise, ID), 1995.
(With Lela B. Costin and Howard Jacob Karger) *The Politics of Child Abuse in America,* Oxford University Press (New York, NY), 1996.
Small Change: Domestic Policy under the Clinton Presidency, Longman (White Plains, NY), 1996.
(With Charles Guzzetta and Mark Lusk) *International Development,* Allyn and Bacon (Boston, MA), 1999.
A Poverty of Imagination: Bootstrap Capitalism, Sequel to Welfare Reform, University of Wisconsin Press (Madison, WI), 2000.

Contributor to periodicals, including *Virginian Pilot.*

WORK IN PROGRESS: Quixote's Ghost: Theory and Social Welfare, University of Wisconsin Press, 2004.

SIDELIGHTS: Social worker David Stoesz has written a number of volumes on welfare in the United States and the ways in which it might be improved. One of these is *Reconstructing the American Welfare State,* written with Howard Jacob Karger, which explains its evolution and what factors have influenced change. Stoesz notes that conservative groups encouraged criticism of social welfare, giving legs to the Reagan administration's containment policy and the resulting Omnibus Budget Reconciliation Act. This legislation caused many to fall off the welfare roles and into poverty.

Loretta Muller reviewed the book in *Public Administration Review,* saying that Karger "describes the liberal reaction to the conservative assault on social welfare as one of bewilderment." The authors contend that rather than confront the conservatives, the liberals reconsidered their own ideology, resulting in neo-liberalism, which espouses reduced costs to government and increased costs and responsibility for business. The authors argue that social policy should be driven by international competitiveness, one of the planks in their social policy platform. They feel that positive change could be accomplished by solidifing families through education, employment, and community unity; promoting more interaction between social classes; strengthening pride and promotion of civic responsibility; and by having various social programs offer choices to clients.

The authors propose that a "civic welfare state" should include a family conservation program, community revitalization initiative, and national service program. Muller wrote that Stoesz and Karger "argue that previous reforms were insufficient to deal with postindustrial America and provide a plausible alternative plan for reconstructing the welfare state. . . . Whether this plan is feasible or not, the book makes it clear that there is a consensus on the need for and desire for change."

Stoesz wrote *The Politics of Child Abuse* with Karger and Lela B. Costin. "Especially insightful is their discussion of the historical emergence of 'child savers' in the late nineteenth century," noted Anthony N. Maluccio in *Social Service Review,* "that is, the child

rescue movement represented by the early Societies for the Prevention of Cruelty to Children.... . In clear, forceful, and hard-hitting language [the authors] describe many aspects of the child rescue movement— from its origin to the present, the decline and rediscovery of child abuse between 1920 and 1960, the transformation of child abuse from the 'battered child' syndrome to the 'battered psyche' syndrome after 1960, and the breakdown of the child abuse service delivery system as it became overwhelmed by increasing demands."

Social Service Review's Malcolm Bush noted that "while physical and sexual abuse appear in families at every income level, they are more prevalent in lower-income families. Is abuse, then, a side effect of poverty? Or is the behavior that may keep some families in poverty a contributing factor to abuse? Or, given the comparatively low incidence of abuse and neglect even in poor families, are such harms evidence that poverty is merely one among many contributing factors?" Bush said that these questions, as well as others relating to drug abuse in poor communities, poverty and minority status, the increase in single-parent families and the attendant difficulties, and strained state budgets, are not addressed by the authors. Nor, said Bush, do they discuss "political opinions about child abuse. Civil rights attorneys complain about children removed from their homes for what amounts to poverty. Crusading attorneys generally rail against soft-hearted liberals who refuse to call assault by name. Family preservationists, pointing to the disaster that foster care is for many children, argue the merits of keeping families intact as long as possible. . . . Journalists make careers out of heart-rending stories of one particular child abuse case. All the while, social workers and courts are overwhelmed by the sheer number of children needing attention."

The authors propose a cabinet-level department with the power to create local authorities to oversee the traditional functions of child welfare programs. Robert E. Cosner observed in the *Annals of the American Academy of Political and Social Science* that *The Politics of Child Abuse* "lets no one off the hook. . . . The classical struggle between the fundamentalist right-wing groups that seek to abolish all state intervention into family life and the liberal social interventionists who advocate for continued social program expansion at all costs has resulted in a polarization of attitudes that has benefited no one. At continued risk are the victims, children of all classes and races who find themselves enmeshed in ideological issues that they can neither understand nor care about."

In A Poverty of Imagination: Bootstrap Capitalism, Sequel to Welfare Reform, Stoesz recommends the replacement of public welfare with his "bootstrap capitalism" approach to relieving poverty, which employs wage supplements, asset building, and community capitalism. The *Progressive*'s Marya Sosulski commented that his ideas are "unrealistic," in that Stoesz doesn't suggest where the money to implement them would come from, and because he doesn't offer "a convincing argument for why big business would allow this kind of competition to succeed when it has muscled small business out of the picture at every other conceivable point."

Stoesz documents the decline of the welfare system that has protected the poor but also kept them financially dependent in order to survive. He notes that although it has been obvious for some time that reform is necessary, the groups who would have been expected to conduct the research and develop the solutions—social workers and liberals—were absent from the dialogue that consisted mainly of conservative complaint. Liberals defended the poor, but they failed to take real responsibility for change. From the 1970s forward, the conservative think tanks received huge sums from corporations that was used to shift public sentiment away from liberal policy and toward conservative ideas. Sandra S. Smith noted in the *American Journal of Sociology* that "gone was the common perception that the welfare system merely acted to ease the poverty of those who simply lacked cash (Old Materialism). In its wake lay the popular perception that the welfare system, as structured, encouraged dependency. . . and that only by instituting major reforms relating to assistance to behavior, could the government discourage deviancy among the poor (New Paternalism)."

Consequently, in August 1996, President Clinton signed into law the Personal Responsibility and Work Opportunity Reconciliation Act (PRWORA), which replaced Aid to Families with Dependent Children (AFDC) with Temporary Assistance to Needy Families (TANF), a program that raised poverty ceilings, incorporated work requirements, and was time limited. Caseloads dropped, but poverty did not significantly decline as recipients left the welfare roles to work at low-wage jobs. In effect, the non-working poor became the working poor.

Smith felt Stoesz could have elaborated more on the reasons why social workers and liberals failed to make a stronger commitment to the poor, and why conservatives so closely followed their own agenda. She also felt Stoesz might have included an analysis of how race influenced both sides, but concluded by saying that the book "does make a substantive contribution to poverty literature generally and to welfare reform literature specifically. Well written and timely, Stoesz's analysis is informative, engaging, and powerful. What's more, his suggestions for continued reforms are inspired." A writer for *Policy and Practice of Public Human Services* said *A Poverty of Imagination* "sets the stage for the next act in poverty policy."

Stoesz told *CA:* "Having held direct service as well as administrative appointments in mental health, public welfare, and higher education, I write about the future of American social welfare. The American welfare state is an industrial era construct that has been animated by capitalism and conservatism. A policy context typified by a dynamic information sector situated in a burgeoning post-industrial society necessitated the exploration of policy options that are as post-liberal as they are post-conservative. Accordingly, my work reflects a 'third way' in social policy as that pertains to the United States. A theoretical exploration of my thinking is in preparation as *Quixote's Ghost: Theory and Social Welfare,* a book that should be published by the University of Wisconsin Press in 2004."

"Since American universities are largely reactive to social policy events, I have collaborated on the development of policyAmerica to promote innovations in social policy."

BIOGRAPHICAL AND CRITICAL SOURCES:

PERIODICALS

American Journal of Sociology, September, 2001, Sandra S. Smith, review of *A Poverty of Imagination: Bootstrap Capitalism, Sequel to Welfare Reform,* p. 513.

Annals of the American Academy of Political and Social Science, July, 1993, Stewart Tolnay, review of *Reconstructing the American Welfare State,* p. 194; March, 1998, Robert E. Cosner, review of *The Politics of Child Abuse in America,* p. 221.

Choice, November, 2001, B. A. Pine, review of *A Poverty of Imagination,* p. 599.

International Social Work, January, 2001, Wes Shera, review of *International Development,* p. 129.

Journal of Social History, winter, 1997, Steven Mintz, review of *The Politics of Child Abuse in America,* p. 461.

Journal of Sociology and Social Welfare, March, 2000, Anthony Hall, review of *International Development,* p. 182; September, 2001, review of *A Poverty of Imagination,* p. 242.

Policy and Practice of Public Human Services, December, 2000, review of *A Poverty of Imagination,* p. 50.

Progressive, August, 20001, Marya Sosulski, review of *A Poverty of Imagination,* p. 44.

Public Administration Review, March-April, 1994, Loretta Muller, review of *Reconstructing the American Welfare State,* pp. 216-217.

Social Service Review, March, 1997, Anthony N. Maluccio, review of *The Politics of Child Abuse in America,* p. 135; June, 1997, Malcolm Bush, review of *The Politics of Child Abuse in America,* p. 317; September, 2001, review of *A Poverty of Imagination,* p. 532.*

*   *   *

STRELOW, Liselotte 1908-1981

PERSONAL: Born September 11, 1908, in Redel bei Polzin, Lower Pomerania; died September 30, 1981, in Hamburg, Germany. *Education:* Studied photography, Lette-Verein, Berlin, Germany, 1930-32.

CAREER: Photographer. Worked in the photo studio of Sys Byk, Berlin, 1932-33; Kodak AG, Berlin, staff photographer, 1933-38; freelance portrait and magazine photographer, magazines included *Frankfurter Allgemeine Zeitung, Rheinisches Post, Die Welt, Der Spiegel, Die Zeit,* and *Theater der Zeit;* Schauspielhaus, Düsseldorf, Germany, Staff theater photographer, 1947-54; official photographer, Richard Wagner Festival, Bayreuth, 1952-61; City Theatres, Cologne,

Germany, chief photographer, 1959-62. Created photograph used for 1959 stamp of German president Heuss. *Exhibitions:* Individual exhibitions include Galerie Mutter Ey, Düsseldorf, Germany, 1949; Galerie de Parnass, Wuppertal, Germany, 1952; German Pavilion, World's Fair, Brussels, Belgium, 1958; Deutsche Gesellschaft für Photographie, Cologne, 1961; Kunstverein, Düsseldorf, 1962; Münchner Stadtmuseum, Munich, 1973; Galerie Kuhling, Hamburg, 1977; Galerie Nagel, West Berlin, 1977; Liselotte Strelow: Portäts 1933-72, Rheinisches Landesmuseum, Bonn, 1977. Selected group exhibitions include *World Photo Exhibition,* International Museum of George Eastman House, Rochester, NY, 1935; *Photo-Kino Ausstellung (Photokina),* Cologne, Germany, 1950; *Subjektive Fotografia,* Saarbrucken, 1951; Biennale *de Fotografia,* Venice, Italy, 1957; *World Exhibition of Photography: What Is Man?,* Pressehaus Stern, Hamburg, 1964; *50 Jahre GDL,* Museum für Kunst und Gewerbe, Hamburg, 1989; *Fotografinnen,* Museum Folkwang, Essen, 1970; Deutsche *Fotografie nach 1945,* Kasseler-Kunstverein, Kassel, West Germany, 1979; *Lichtbildnisse: Das Porträt in der Fotografie,* Rheinisches Landesmuseum, Bonn, Germany, 1982; and *Sammlung Gruber,* Museum Ludwig, Cologne, 1984. Works in collections include Museum Folkwang, Essen, Germany, International Museum of Photography, George Eastman House, Rochester, NY; and Museum Ludwig, Cologne, Germany.

MEMBER: Gesellschaft Deutsche Lichtbildner, 1959-61 and 1979-81, Deutsche Gesellschaft für Photographie.

AWARDS, HONORS: Silver Medal, World Photo Exhibition, 1935; Handwerkskammer Prize, 1938; International Art Photo Diploma, 1950; Plaque, Photokina, 1951, 1952; City of Hamburg Prize, 1951; Diploma, *Camera* magazine, 1951; Diploma, World Exhibition of Photography, Photographen-handwerke, 1952; Gold Medal, Biennale de Fotografia, 1957; Honor Award, World's Fair, 1958; Adolf-Grimme Prize, with S. Mohrhof, WDR Boradcasting, 1966; David Octavius Hill Prize, Gesellschaft Seutsche Lichtbildner, 1969; Culture Prize (with R. Clausen and R. Relang), Deutsche Gesellschaft für Photographie, 1976.

WRITINGS:

(Photographer) *Gustaf Grundgens,* text by Werner Vielhaber, [Bad Honnef, West Germany], 1953.

Das Manipulierte Menschenbildnis, Econ-Verlag (Düsseldorf, Germany), 1961, translated and adapted by L.A. Mannheim and published as *Photogenic Portrait Management,* Focal P. (London, England), 1966.

(Photographer) *Liselotte Strelow: Porträts 1933-1972* (exhibition catalogue), text by Klaus Honnef, Halbet (Bonn, Germany), 1977.

(Photographer) *Sammlung Gruber, Photographie des 20. Jahrhunderts.* (exhibition catalogue), foreword by Siegfried Gohr, [Cologne, Germany], 1984.

Contributed articles to periodicals *Photo-Graphik, Suddeutscher Zeitung, Die Welt, Foto magazine,* and *Frankfurter Illustrierte.* Author's archives are housed in a permanent collection at the Rheinisches Landesmuseum in Bonn and in the Dumont-Lindemann Archiv/Theatre Museum in Düsseldorf.

SIDELIGHTS: A *Contemporary Photographers* writer wrote that "Liselotte Strelow [was] one of the last great practitioners of portrait photography in the classical sense."

BIOGRAPHICAL AND CRITICAL SOURCES:

BOOKS

Contemporary Photographers, 3rd edition, St. James Press (Detroit, MI), 1996.

OTHER

Hausder Geschichte der Bundesrepublik Deutschland, http://www.hdg.de (May 8, 2002), "Liselotte Strelow."*

*   *   *

SUDA, Issei 1940-

PERSONAL: Born April 24, 1940, in Tokyo, Japan; married Sachiko Nakagawa 1969. *Education:* Attended Tokyo University, 1960-61; Attended Tokyo College of Photography, 1962.

ADDRESSES: Home—4-5-9 Tendai, Inage-ku, Chibashi, Chiba 263, Japan.

CAREER: Tenjo Sajiki Stage Production, Tokyo, staff photographer, 1967-70; Freelance photographer contributing to magazines including *Asahi Camera, Camera Mainichi, Nippon Camera,* and *Camerart;* Tokyo College of Photography, Yokohama, Japan, tutor, 1979—. *Exhibitions:* Individual exhibitions include *Fuski Kaden,* Nikon Salon, Tokyo, Japan, 1977; *A Photographic Exhibition of Issei Suda,* CAMP Gallery, Tokyo, 1978; *Original Prints of Issei Suda,* Tsukaido Gallery, Fukuoka, Japan, 1979; *My Tokyo,* SICOF, Milan, Italy, 1981; *Taipei White Heat,* Doi Photo Plaza, Tokyo, 1988; *4chome, Ginzo, Tokyo 1983-1986,* Ginzo Nikon Salon, Tokyo, 1989; *Yokohama,* Frog, Tokyo, 1991; *Hakodate,* Hakodate History Plaza, Hokkaido, Japan, 1992; *Family Diary,* Hiranga-cho Bridge Gallery, Tokyo, 1993; *Trance,* Zeit Photo Salon, Tokyo, 1994; *Flow of People,* Hiranaga-cho-bashi Gallery, Tokyo, 1995; *Eclipse,* Konica Plaza, Tokyo, 1996; *Vietnam Night Seen,* Gallery Art Graph, Tokyo, 1997; *Snap Landscape,* Gallery Furushima, Chiba, 1998; *New Area,* Konica Plaza, Tokyo, 1999; *Infancy Days,* Konica Plaza, Toyko, 2000; and *Rubber,* Gallery Past Rays, Yokohama, 2001. Selected group exhibitions include *Neue Fotografie aus Japan,* Kulturhaus, Granz, Austria (touring exhibition), 1977; *Photokina '78,* Cologne, Germany, 1978; *Japanese Photography Today and Its Origin,* Galleria d'Arte Moderna, Bolgna, Italy (touring exhibition), 1979; *39 Japanese Photographers,* Zeit-Foto Salon, Tokyo, 1982; *A Day in the Life of Japan,* Tokyo, 1985; *8 Japanese Photographers,* Photo Gallery International, Toyko, 1988; *The Hitachi Collection of Contemporary Japanese Photography,* Center for Creative Photography, University of Arizona, Tucson, 1989; *Glances at the City, Tokyo,* Tokyo Municipal Museum of Photography, Tokyo, 1990; *Japanese Photographs: the 1970s,* Tokyo Municipal Museum of Photography, Tokyo, 1991; and *What Did Photographers Express? 1960-1980,* Konika Plaza, Tokyo, 1992. Works included in collections at Tokyo College of Arts and Crafts, Museum für Kunst und Gewerbe, Hamburg, Germany; Yamaguchi Prefectural Art Museum, Yamaguchi, Japan; and Paris Museum of Photography, Paris, France.

AWARDS, HONORS: New Photographer of the Year Award, Japan Photographic Society, 1976; annual award, Photographic Society of Japan, 1983; domestic artist prize, Higashikawa Award, Higashikawa International Photography Festival, 1985; Kendomon Award, 1997.

WRITINGS:

Dog's Noses, [Tokyo, Japan], 1991.

PHOTOGRAPHER

Fushi Kaden, edited by Tatsuo Shirai, [Tokyo, Japan], 1978.

My Tokyo, edited by Yusaku Kamekura, [Tokyo, Japan], 1979.

A Day in the Life of Japan—June 7, 1985 (exhibition catalogue), edited by Rick Smolan and David Cohen, [New York, NY], 1985.

SIDELIGHTS: Issei Suda once commented, "The act of taking a picture is just one of the many manifestations of being alive.

"My confrontations with life are like a pendulum—to be touched, not to be touched, to be betrayed not to be betrayed, the progress of which seems to me to constitute my photography.

"My sense of sight usually takes precedence over my sense of tough; it is, at any rate, difficult to know all of one's senses. However, in everyday occurrences, that to which I respond, I often feel a kind of strangeness about me of feel attracted to some object. In trying to take pictures as within the perspective and response to such feelings, I verify myself and try to practice according to a certain model of Japanese action and spirit."

BIOGRAPHICAL AND CRITICAL SOURCES:

BOOKS

Contemporary Photographers, 3rd edition, St. James Press (Detroit, MI), 1996.*

*   *   *

SWARD, Robert (Stuart) 1933-

PERSONAL: Born June 23, 1933, in Chicago, Ill.; son of Irving Michael (a doctor) and Gertrude (Huebsch) Sward; married second wife, Diane Kaldes, February, 1960 (divorced, 1969); married Judith Essenson, March 21, 1969 (divorced, 1972); children: (second marriage) Cheryl Ann, Barbara Anne, Michael Paul; (third marriage) Hannah, Nicholas. Education: University of Illinois at Urbana-Champaign, B.A. (with honors), 1956; Middlebury College, Bread Loaf School of English, graduate study, summers, 1956-58; University of Iowa, M.A., 1958; University of Bristol, graduate study, 1960-61. Religion: Jewish. Hobbies and other interests: Swimming, meditating, yoga, computers, photography.

ADDRESSES: Home—P.O. Box 7062, Santa Cruz, Calif. 95061-7062. E-mail—sward@cruzio.com.

CAREER: Connecticut College, New London, instructor in English, 1958-59; Cornell University, Ithaca, NY, instructor in English, 1962-64; University of Iowa Writers' Workshop, Iowa City, writer-in-residence, 1967; University of Victoria, British Columbia, Canada, assistant professor of English and writer-in-residence, 1969-73; editor and publisher, Soft Press, Victoria, British Columbia 1970-77; Hancock House Publishers, Victoria, British Columbia, senior book publisher, 1976-79; freelance writer, editor, and technical writer, 1979—. Visiting writer, University of California, Santa Cruz, 1986—, and Monterey Peninsula College, Monterey, Calif., 1986—. Associate fellow, Strong College, York University, Canada, 1984—. Freelance broadcaster for Canadian Broadcasting Corporation (CBC-Radio). Participant, writers-in-the-schools program, 1979—, Ontario Arts Council, 1979-85; visiting writer-in-the-schools, Cultural Council of Santa Cruz County, 1986—. Sward has exhibited his poetry, stories, photographs, and lithographs on occasion. Worked previously as a gardener. Military service:U.S. Navy, Korean War, 1951-53.

MEMBER: Modern Poetry Association, National Writers' Union, Writers' Union of Canada, League of Canadian Poets, Committee of Small Magazine Editors and Publishers, Periodical Writers Association, Poetry Santa Cruz, Phi Beta Kappa.

AWARDS, HONORS: Dylan Thomas Poetry Award; poetry fellow, Bread Loaf Writers' Conference, 1958; Fulbright scholar, 1960-61; Guggenheim fellowship, 1964-65; D. H. Lawrence fellowship, University of New Mexico, 1966; Canada Council grants, 1973-74 and 1981; Explorations grant, 1982; MacDowell Colony, Djerassi Foundation, and Yaddo fellowships.

WRITINGS:

The Jurassic Shales (novel), Coach House Press (Toronto, Ontario, Canada), 1975.

The Toronto Islands: An Illustrated History (also see below), Dreadnaught Press (Toronto, Ontario, Canada), 1983.

A Much-Married Man: A Novel, Ekstasis Eds. (Victoria, British Columbia, Canada), 1996.

POETRY

Advertisements, introduction by Fred Eckman, Odyssey Chapbook Publications, 1958.

Uncle Dog and Other Poems, Putnam (London, England), 1962, published as *Kissing the Dancer and Other Poems,* introduction by William Meredith, Cornell University Press (Ithaca, NY), 1964.

The Thousand-year-old Fiancee and Other Poems, Cornell University Press (Ithaca, NY), 1965.

Horgbortom Stringbottom, I Am Yours, You Are History, Swallow Press, 1970.

Hannah's Cartoon, Soft Press, 1970.

(With Mike Doyle) *Quorum/Noah,* Soft Press, 1970.

Gift, Soft Press, 1971.

Songs from the Jurassic Shales, Soft Press, 1972.

Five Iowa Poems and One Iowa Print, Stone Wall Press, 1975.

Honey Bear on Lasqueti Island, B.C. (contains photographs and prints), Soft Press (Victoria, British Columbia, Canada), 1978.

Six Poems, League of Canadian Poets (Toronto, Ontario, Canada), 1982.

Twelve Poems, Island House Books (Toronto, Ontario, Canada), 1982.

Movies: Left to Right, South Western Ontario Poetry (London, Ontario, Canada), 1983.

Half a Life's History, Poems: New and Selected, 1957-1983, introduction by Earle Birney, AYA Press (Toronto, Ontario, Canada), 1983.

(With Robert Priest and Robert Zend) *The Three Roberts: Premiere Performance,* HMS Press (Scarborough, Ontario, Canada), 1984.

(With Robert Priest and Robert Zend) *The Three Roberts on Love,* Dreadnaught Press (Toronto, Ontario, Canada), 1984.

(With Robert Priest and Robert Zend) *The Three Roberts on Childhood,* Moonstone Press (St. Catharines, Ontario, Canada), 1985.

Four Incarnations: New and Selected Poems, 1957-1991, Coffee House Press (Minneapolis, MN), 1991.

(With Bernice Lever, Roger Nash, James Raney, Caroline Davidson, and Sonja Dunn) *Uncivilizing: A Collection of Poetry,* Insomniac Press (Toronto, Ontario, Canada), 1997.

Three Dogs and a Parrot, Select Poets Series (Pleasant Hill, CA), 2001.

(With David Swanger, Charles Atkinson, and Tilly Shaw) *Family,* foreword by David Alpaugh, Select Poets Series (Pleasant Hill, CA), 1994.

Rosicrucian in the Basement, introduction by William Minor, Black Moss Press (Windsor, Ontario, Canada), 2001.

Heavenly Sex, Black Moss Press (Windsor, Ontario, Canada), 2002.

EDITOR

Vancouver Island Poems (poetry anthology), Soft Press (Victoria, British Columbia, Canada), 1973.

Cheers for Muktananda (poetry anthology), Soft Press (Victoria, British Columbia, Canada), 1976.

Edythe Hembroff-Schleicher, *Emily Carr: The Untold Story,* Hancock House, 1978.

Allen T. Denison and Wallace K. Huntington, *Victorian Architecture of Port Townsend, Washington,* Hancock House, 1978.

Phil J. Thomas, *Songs of the Pacific Northwest,* Hancock House, 1979.

Leslie Drew and Douglas Wilson, *Agillite: The Art of the Haida,* Hancock House, 1980.

(With Penny Kemp) *Contemporary Verse Two: Spiritual Poetry in Canada,* Volume VI, numbers 1-2, University of Manitoba, 1981-82.

Also editor of *Writers Friendship,* an ongoing feature of the literary eZine *Web Del Sol/Perihelion.*

RADIO BROADCASTS

Spiritual Poetry in Canada (contains interviews with Margaret Atwood, Earle Birney, John Robert Colombo, Joy Kogawa, David McFadden, and others), CBC-Radio, April, 1983.

Poetry as Performance, CBC-Radio, June, 1984.

Also author of a radio anthology with singer-songwriter Leonard Cohen for CBC-Radio, December, 1984.

OTHER

(contributor) Ursula Heller, compiler, *Village Portraits* (collection of photographs and interviews; contains edited versions of interviews from Sward's *The Toronto Islands: An Illustated History*), Methuen (Toronto), 1981.
Earthquake Collage (multimedia), Blue Moon Review, 1989.

Contributor to anthologies, including *John F. Kennedy Memorial Anthology: Of Poetry and Power,* edited by Edwin Glikes and Paul Schwaber, Basic Books, 1964; *A Controversy of Poets: The Anchor Book of Contemporary American Poetry,* edited by Robert Kelly and Paris Leary, Doubleday Anchor, 1965; *Where Is Vietnam?,* edited by Walter Lowenfels, Doubleday, 1967; *The Contemporary American Poets: American Poetry since 1940,* edited by Mark Strand, World Publishing, 1970; *Some Haystacks Don't Even Have Any Needle and Other Modern Verse,* Scott, Foresman, 1970; *New: American and Canadian Poetry,* edited by John Gill, 1973; *The Oxford Book of American Light Verse,* edited by William Harmon, Oxford University Press, 1979; *The Face of Poetry: 101 Poets,* edited by LaVerne Harrell Clark, foreword by Richard Eberhart, Heidelberg Graphics, 1979; *Here Is a Poem,* edited by Florence McNeill, League of Canadian Poets, 1983; *X-Connect, Writers of the Information Age,* edited by David Diefer, University of Pennsylvania, 1996; *I Want to Be the Poet of Your Kneecaps: Poems of Quirky Romance,* edited by John B. Lee, Black Moss Press, 1999; *Following the Plow: Recovering the Rural: Poems on the Land,* edited by John B. Lee, Black Moss Press, 2000; *Southern California Anthology,* edited by James Ragan, University of Southern California, 2002.

Also author of the holograph *Letter to a Straw Hat,* (uncredited), Soft Press, 1976. Sward's poetry is featured in the premiere issue of the journal *Santa Cruz,* 1985. Contributor of poems, reviews, stories, and features to over two hundred periodicals in the United States, Canada, South America, England, Germany, Switzerland, New Zealand, and Australia, including *Poetry, Paris Review, Alsop Review, Transatlantic Review, New Yorker, Poetry Canada, Out of Sight, Web Del Sol,* and *Neue zuercher.*

"The Islanders," a traveling exhibition of Robert Sward's poems on the Toronto Island community, accompanied by the photographs of Ursula Heller, opened in the Toronto City Hall in November, 1980. Collections of Sward's manuscripts are housed in the Washington University Libraries, St. Louis, Mo., in the City Hall Archive, Toronto, Ontario, the University of Victoria Special Collections Library, British Columbia, and in the National Library of Canada, Ottawa, Ontario. Additional material of Sward's is housed in the Special Manuscript Collection in the Rare Books Library at the University of Victoria, British Columbia, Canada.

ADAPTATIONS: The Thousand-year-old Fiancee and Other Poems, read by Sward, was recorded by Western Michigan University Aural Press in 1965 and by New Letters on the Air, University of Missouri, Kansas City, March, 1985; *Rosicrucian in the Basement* was recorded by Uncle Dog Audio, 2001. Interviews and readings from *Rosicrucian in the Basement* were collected on the audio recording *Robert Sward: Poetry, Interview, Review,* with Jack Foley, Uncle Dog Audio, 2002.

WORK IN PROGRESS: Collected Poems; Toronto Island Suite, a collection of poems, interviews, stories, and photographs focusing on the Toronto Island community; *How to Cure a Broken Heart,* short stories; *Adventures with Authors and Eagles,* a comic novel; *Journey to Ganeshpuri,* a nonfiction work discussing the experience of living in a spiritual community in India; editor with Pat Keeney Smith of a work tentatively titled *From Impulse to Art: Interviews with Twenty Poets and Novelists* which will contain interviews with Margaret Atwood, Saul Bellow, Leonard Cohen, Ted Hughes, Mark Strand, and D. M. Thomas.

SIDELIGHTS: Robert Sward began his writing career at sea during a four-year stint with the U.S. Navy. A United States citizen by birth, Sward lived in Canada for a number of years and considers himself "a North American poet." "I don't feel bound to any one particular place," he told *Excalibur*'s Stuart Ross. "If it's possible to belong to both places, I do."

In a review of Sward's *Kissing the Dancer and Other Poems,* John Malcolm Brinnin of the *New York Times Book Review* noted, "many of [the author's] poems are honed to a spareness that recalls the vernacular simplicity of William Carlos Williams. To his credit, the endeavor reveals a voice and not a repetition. . . .

[Sward] is fierce, new-minted and convincing." Though he writes primarily in idiomatic American English, Sward does give his poetry a "sinewy linguistic texture," according to the *Carleton Miscellany*'s Lawrence Lieberman. Describing this as "the most singular quality of his poetry," Lieberman went on to say that "the word-thickness . . . revives a tradition in English that many critics feel reached a dead end in the work of Hopkins and Hart Crane, two poets who . . . cultivated special vocabularies while retaining a large measure of literary or 'poetical' vocabulary."

Pulitzer Prize winner William Meredith speculated in the preface to *Kissing the Dancer and Other Poems* that Sward's poems have been turned down by many publishers "because they are so original as to be unrecognizable as poetry by a conventional eye. They have gone off to respectable publishers with praise from Stanley Kunitz, Louise Bogan, even Robert Lowell, and come back with the embarrassed confession that they simply escaped the respectable editors. . . . Like other good works of art, these poems have the air of having been made for people rather than for other artists. They contain high-toned gossip rather than aesthetics, or the aesthetics are hidden and acted out like charades. A lot of the poems are unpleasant in places, like life itself, but none of them contains any fashionable despair. . . . There is that humility about them that comes from paying a blasphemous attention, God's own attention, to oneself."

There is also in these poems an attention to things which results in a kind of mysticism. "The mysticism of objects, of thingness," observed Lieberman, "is an inversion and, in a way, a bizarre parody of conventional mysticism. With Wordsworth, we 'see into the life of things.' In Sward's world, things work their way inside *our* life, become parts of our psyche, dominate our minds and take us over, *make* us over, entirely." Meredith commented, "I have come to the conclusion that when [Sward] works on [his poems] he is paying perfect, slightly mystical attention to . . . (1) himself as an example of a man; (2) his vocabulary as a butterfly net to catch the experiences the man has; and (3) a passion for simplicity. His simplicity is not that of Zen . . . or of Thoreau, but something more like that of Blake or Emily Dickinson."

Much of the mysticism in Sward's poetry can be traced to his practice of yoga. In fact, the poet regards the connection between poetry, yoga, and meditation as "the whole process of communication between two people, an intermingling of one consciousness with another. I guess I'm constantly trying to simplify my language and my approach. I write primarily for myself, but the next inclination is to see whether other people can connect with it. I don't think there's anybody who poetry cannot reach."

Sward's ability to mythologize is again apparent in his 1991 title, *Four Incarnations*. In the collection, the poet describes the stages of life he has traveled through to become who he is; he identifies these stages as four different incarnations of himself. "Poets, to a certain extent, mythologize themselves and Sward—in his Robert incarnations—is no different," wrote Christine Watson of the *Santa Cruz Sentinel*. Watson continued, "But [Sward has] said, 'mythologizing your life is merely attaching meaning to what is true.'" Ann Struthers, in her review for the *Des Moines Sunday Register,* commented that Sward "remains an unregenerate humorist, intent on poking fun at himself and determined to take the pompousness out of poetry and the aura of mystery out of the writing process." *Poetry Flash* contributor Richard Silberg noted, "Robert Sward has a zany sense of humor; he has the concentrated powers of a serious child." Tina Barr of *Harvard Review Poetry Room* commented, "His best poems lack self-consciousness, are inventive rather than being carefully wrought. They are fluid in texture so we are caught in an experience which prefers to resist analysis."

Commenting on Sward's poetry, a contributor to *Contemporary Poets* wrote, "Sward's delight with language is evident in all of his poetry, and the reader senses a healthy dose of play at work in every poem." The contributor concluded, "[Sward] can move up off the page, out of the words, like a man coming into sunlight."

AUTOBIOGRAPHICAL ESSAY:

Robert Sward contributed the following autobiographical essay to *CA:*

Part I

Four Incarnations--An Overview

Born on the Jewish North Side of Chicago, bar mitzvahed, sailor, amnesiac, university professor (Cornell, Iowa, Connecticut College), newspaper editor, food reviewer, father of five children, husband to four wives, my writing career has been described by critic Virginia Lee as a "long and winding road."

1. Switchblade Poetry: Chicago Style

I began writing poetry in Chicago at age fifteen, when I was named corresponding secretary for a gang of young punks and hoodlums called the Semcoes. A social athletic club, we met at various locations two Thursdays a month. My job was to write postcards to inform my brother thugs—who carried switchblade knives and stole cars for fun and profit—as to when, where, and why we were meeting.

Rhyming couplets seemed the appropriate form to notify characters like light-fingered Foxman, cross-eyed Harris, and Irving "Koko" of upcoming meetings. An example of my switchblade juvenilia:

> The Semcoes meet next Thursday night
> at Speedway Koko's. Five bucks dues, Foxman,
>   or fight.

Koko was a young boxer whose father owned Chicago's Speedway Wrecking Company and whose basement was filled with punching bags and pinball machines. Koko and the others joked about my affliction—the writing of poetry—but were so astonished that they criticized me mainly for my inability to spell.

2. Sailor Librarian: San Diego

At seventeen, I graduated from high school, gave up my job as soda jerk, and joined the navy. The Korean War was underway; my mother had died, and Chicago seemed an oppressive place to be.

My thanks to the U.S. Navy. They taught me how to type (sixty words a minute), organize an office, and serve as a librarian. In 1952, I served in Korea aboard a three-hundred-foot-long, flat-bottomed Landing Ship Tank (LST). A yeoman third class, I became overseer of twelve hundred paperback books, a sturdy upright typewriter, and a couple of filing cabinets.

The best thing about duty on an LST is the ship's speed: eight to ten knots. It takes approximately one month for an LST to sail from Pusan, Korea, to San Diego. In that month I read Melville's *Moby Dick,* Whitman's *Leaves of Grass,* Thoreau's *Walden,* Isak Dinesen's *Winter's Tales,* the King James Version of the Bible, Shakespeare's *Hamlet* and *King Lear,* and a biography of Abraham Lincoln.

While at sea, I began writing poetry as if poems, to paraphrase Thoreau, were secret letters from some distant land.

I sent one poem to a girl named Lorelei, with whom I was in love. Lorelei had a job at the Dairy Queen. Shortly before enlisting in the navy, I spent fifteen dollars of my soda-jerk money taking her up in a single-engine, sight-seeing airplane so we could kiss and—at the same time—get a good look at Chicago from the air. Beautiful Lorelei never responded to my poem. Years later, at the University of Iowa Writers' Workshop, I learned that much of what I had been writing (love poems inspired by a combination of lust and loneliness) belonged, loosely speaking, to a tradition—the venerable tradition of unrequited love.

3. Mr. Amnesia: Cambridge

In 1962, after ten years of writing poetry, my book *Uncle Dog and Other Poems* was published by Putnam in England. That was followed by two books from Cornell University Press, *Kissing the Dancer* and *Thousand-year-old Fiancee.* Then in 1966, I was invited to do fourteen poetry readings in a two-week stretch at places like Dartmouth, Amherst, and the University of Connecticut.

The day before I was scheduled to embark on the reading series, I was hit by a speeding MG in Cambridge, Massachusetts.

I lost my memory for a period of about twenty-four hours. Just as I saw the world fresh while cruising to a war zone, so I now caught a glimpse of what a city like Cambridge can look like when one's inner slate, so to speak, is wiped clean.

4. Santa Claus: Santa Cruz

In December 1985, recently returned to the U.S. after some years in Canada, a freelance writer in search of a story, I sought and found employment as a Rent-A-

Santa Claus. Imagine walking into the local community center and suddenly, at the sight of four hundred children, feeling transformed from a skinny, sad-eyed self into an elf—having to chant the prescribed syllables, Ho, Ho, Ho.

What is poetry? For me, it's the restrained music of a switchblade knife. It's an amphibious warship magically transformed into a basketball court, and then transformed again into a movie theater showing a film about the life of Joan of Arc. It is the vision of an amnesiac, bleeding from a head injury, witnessing the play of sunlight on a redbrick wall. Poetry comes to a bearded Jewish wanderer, pulling on a pair of high rubber boots with white fur, and a set of musical sleigh bells, over blue, fleece-lined sweatpants. It comes to the father of five children, bearing gifts for four hundred and, choked up, unable to speak, alternately laughing and sobbing the three traditional syllables— Ho, Ho, Ho—hearing at the same time, in his heart, the more plaintive, tragic, Oi vay, Oi vay, Oi vay.

Part II

From the Kitchen Floor to the Kitchen Table

At age three, before I knew the alphabet, I would kneel or lie on the kitchen floor and draw pictures on large sheets of colored craft paper. One night, as she was preparing dinner, my mother turned and pointed to some of my scribblings.

"Those look like letters of the alphabet."

"What's 'alpha-bet' ?"

"A, B, C . . . it's like what you're drawing right now. One day you'll write words and make up stories on paper."

What my mother was suggesting seemed to me beyond magic, beyond anything . . . I'll wait and see if she's right, I thought. She could just be making it up.

That was my earliest memory.

My interest in literature began with the linoleum on the floor of my bedroom. Imprinted on this linoleum and, as a consequence, on my mind, were a half-dozen Mother Goose rhymes with illustrations of Jack and Jill, Old King Cole, Little Jack Horner, the Old Woman Who Lived in a Shoe, Little Bo Peep, and Humpty Dumpty. One reason I mention the linoleum is that in the 1960s, I used Humpty Dumpty as a persona, a stand-in for Uncle Sam and America itself as I saw the country during the Vietnam War. Humpty Dumpty became Horgbortom Stringbottom, the title character in a book-length poem, *Horgbortom Stringbottom, I Am Yours, You Are History* (Swallow Press, 1970).

But I'm getting ahead of myself. At age five or six, going to bed at night, and waking up in the morning, I'd lean over the side of my bed and dreamily reflect on the linoleum as, years later, I would contemplate Hindu and Buddhist mandalas. In any case, I began reading linoleum Mother Goose rhymes before I began reading books. Indeed, I began reading books in order to escape the linoleum, which had begun to embarrass me.

My mother supplemented the linoleum with real books. I remember her reading aloud from *Gulliver's Travels, Thousand and One Nights, Alice in Wonderland, Pinocchio,* and *The Jungle Book.* After being run over by the MG in 1966 and my subsequent memory loss, some of this literature stayed with me. For example, a year after the accident, I began thinking of myself as something of an amnesiac Gulliver, an ingenuous new arrival in a strange land, when I worked on my novel *The Jurassic Shales.* In fact, there are elements of all five "children's" books in the novel.

*

At birth I weighed twelve pounds and, right from the beginning, my father complained I was more than my poor mother could handle. Fifty years later, my sister, Betty, and Aunt Leah recall stories of a drunken obstetrician, unsterilized forceps, an infected ear, and a generally mangled-at-birth Bobby Sward. At eight, I was healthy, though a pain in the neck. I was moody, shy, and yet prone to "talk back." In addition, while my blonde, blue-eyed, five-year-old sister, Betty, earned money modeling tricycles and clothes for Montgomery Ward catalogs, I developed eczema on my hands, face, and legs. The condition grew so bad, I sometimes wore cotton gloves to school so I'd remember not to scratch myself. I had inherited my mother's large, hazel-brown eyes and so was nick-

Braving a Chicago winter day, age nine months, 1934

named "Banjo Eyes," after the singer Eddie Cantor. Friends joked about my name: "The Sward is mightier than the Sword." And because I had a zany imagination, I had only to say, "Hey, I have an idea," and other eight-year-olds would collapse laughing. I was regarded as an oddball, an outsider. I had few friends. To this day I can remember the names of my grade three buddies: Junior Pucklewartz, Alan Stencil, and Eddie Greenberg.

Twelve years later, in 1952, home on leave from the Korean War, I sat down at the kitchen table and wrote a poem called "Pozzolana" about volcanoes in Italy and strong, slow-hardening cement. That was my first published poem. On the table or on the floor, kitchens are still my favorite place to write.

Part III

A Long and Winding Road

My mother, Gertrude (née Huebsch), was born into a wealthy Chicago family and grew up on the South Side, pampered and protected. She had three brothers,

Richard, the unlucky-in-love, tormented violinist; Harry, the finagling liquor salesman who always lived in hotels; and Irwin, an embittered, wounded-in-action, World War I veteran.

A tall, striking brunette with enormous, hazel-brown eyes, champion swimmer and diver, my mother was runner-up for Miss Chicago in the 1920s. Her father, Max Huebsch, grew up in Vienna, Austria, was an inventor, a speculator in the Chicago real estate market, and, for a time, a millionaire.

Like H. L. Mencken, the so-called Sage of Baltimore, Max Huebsch complained his way through the 1930s and '40s. He was narrow-minded, cantankerous, and looked down on any person who happened to be less fortunate than himself. Again, like Mencken, whom he resembled physically, Grandpa had a go-it-alone approach to living. His impassive, dry, bourbon-colored face would become purple-red, hot, and sticky at the mention of any social welfare program. Grandpa would foam at the mouth and sputter in English, with lapses into German, as he heaped invective on Franklin Roosevelt and the New Deal. He blamed Roosevelt for all that was wrong with the world.

In 1953, before my discharge from the navy, I visited Grandpa Huebsch. Neatly groomed in a well-ironed uniform, I told stories of my experiences in the Korean War and managed to pass the old man's inspection. He had known me as a dreamy, moody, "difficult child," and had urged my mother to send me to a military academy so I could learn discipline. She resisted. Max Huebsch was Teutonic, implacable, anti-youth, anti-life, anti-poetry.

I must have redeemed myself in his eyes by joining the navy and going to war. When Max Huebsch died in 1957—at age ninety-nine, after chain-smoking Camels and drinking straight shots of bourbon for over twenty years—he remembered me in his will. I inherited enough money to buy a used 1954 Plymouth, to attend the Bread Loaf School of English in Middlebury, Vermont, and to buy time to complete some of the poems included in *Advertisements* (Odyssey Chapbook Publications, 1958), *Uncle Dog and Other Poems* (Putnam and Company, London, 1962), and *Kissing the Dancer* (Cornell University Press, Ithaca, New York, 1964).

Family portrait, about 1912: (clockwise, from bottom right) The author's father, Irving Michael Sward, age eight; Grandmother Bessie; Aunt Leah, age six; Grandfather Hyman David Swerdloff; and Uncle Morris

What's in a Name?

Poltava, Russia--New York City

My grandfather, Hyman David Swerdloff (1880-1929), was an orthodox Jew, father of my father, and the first Sward. In 1905, in the company of other survivors of government-sponsored pogroms, Hyman and his family journeyed from Poltava, Russia, to New York City. There the Russian "Swerdloff" became the more American "Sward," a word meaning "greensward, turf green with grass." In Sir Walter Scott's *Ivanhoe,* for example, the poet speaks of "A thick carpet of most delicious greensward." So it was that a twenty-five-year-old Russian-Jewish tailor immigrated to America to have thrust upon him a poetic name with Old English roots dating back to A.D. 900.

Leah Gold, my aunt, describes her father as a humorous, generous, but cautious man. "He loved making us laugh, never let us leave the house without asking if we had money in our pockets, and, if he noticed something too near the edge of a table, he'd pick it up and place it in the middle."

An entrepreneur with limited resources, Hyman Swerdloff employed several apprentices. He used to joke about having people work for him, "You've got to hire someone to take the blame."

In 1903, Hyman was conscripted and forced to serve in the Russian army as a quartermaster. His humor stood him in good stead with his fellow soldiers. Hyman, however, kept silent about his sympathies for the anti-czarist revolutionary movement. For decades, Jews in Poltava had been terrorized—many were killed—by czarist troops. On one occasion, Hyman's wife Bessie narrowly escaped death while waiting outside a prison for her brother, a revolutionary, to be released. In 1905, fearing they would become victims of the Russo-Japanese War, the Swerdloffs joined the stream of emigrants to the United States.

The Immigrant and the Beauty Queen

My parents met in 1927 and married in 1929, just in time for the Depression. My sister, Betty, jokes they simply fell in love with one another's good looks. In photographs from the 1920s, my father looks like a cross between Charlie Chaplin and Errol Flynn. Ambitious and hardworking, he longed to become a physician, but because of the Depression and family responsibilities, he cut short his studies and became a podiatrist. Dad was a poor businessman and, though he loved his work, he had to struggle to make a living in Chicago. Late in life, he moved to Palm Springs, California. At age seventy-six, still a workaholic, he passed the state board exam to practice in California. Even in his eighties, after open-heart surgery, he continued to work.

Part IV

Uncle Dog: The Poet at 9

There was never a time, growing up in Chicago, when I didn't own a dog. There was Fluffy the golden cocker spaniel, Spot the wirehaired terrier with eczema worse than mine, gentle, unassuming crossbreeds and curs, dogs and dog-dogs, some of whom I found on the streets of Chicago without collars or identification and introduced to my parents saying, "He followed me home and we're going to keep him." I even fantasized about dogs, dogs like the garbageman's sharp-looking, fox-eared cur who I nicknamed "Uncle Dog." Cocky, aristocratic in manner, Uncle Dog appeared to laugh on occasion.

Certainly he carried himself with dignity and wore an ever-alert, amused expression on his face. In 1957, I wrote a thirty-nine-line poem for him titled "Uncle Dog: The Poet at 9."

First published in the *Chicago Review,* "Uncle Dog: The Poet at 9" served as title poem for a collection of my work brought out by Putnam in England in 1962. "Uncle Dog" was reprinted in Robert Kelly's *A Controversy of Poets,* Mark Strand's *The Contemporary American Poets,* George MacBeth's *The Penguin Book of Animal Poetry,* and a dozen other anthologies and textbooks.

At nine, I read books on the care and feeding of dogs and once, out of curiosity, fed Fluffy a can of Campbell's vegetable beef soup while I sampled Fluffy's horsemeat Rival dog food. Indeed, my interest in health foods began in the 1940s when, shopping for dog food, I began reading labels. Who would have guessed that this early interest in dogs, dog food, and soup would lead me, years later, to become not only a vegetarian, but a professional food-reviewer?

There's a photo of me at age nine with thirty-nine other Peterson Elementary fourth-graders. All the kids in the photograph are smiling at the camera over their left shoulder. I'm the only one in the photograph facing in the wrong direction. And, instead of a cheerful, cheesy smile, I have a dreamy, abstracted look on my face. I was nearsighted, had a bad overbite, and, when crimes or misdemeanors were committed around the school, was the kid most likely to be punished. Guilty of some offenses, not guilty of others, I spent more than one period outside the classroom sitting in my locker.

One thing I liked about Peterson Elementary School was the library. What a relief to escape harassed teachers and Depression-era classrooms crowded with forty

Mother, Gertrude Huebsch, and father, Dr. Irving M. Sward, before their marriage, Elkhart Lake, Wisconsin, about 1928

or more students. The library is where I discovered Albert Terhune's *Lad: A Dog* and Jack London's *Call of the Wild.* As author of "Uncle Dog," "Alpha the Dog," "Clancy the Dog," "Letter to His First Dog," "Classified—Pets," "Pet Shop," "I Have Just Bought a House," and other poems in which dogs play a central role, I have to acknowledge Terhune and London as two of my early mentors. London's ability to get inside the mind of Buck the dog, and to write convincingly from an animal's point of view, struck me as uncanny. I found I cared more for Buck the dog than I did for Lou Gehrig and the sports heroes my friends read about. However, I didn't want to be laughed at and so kept quiet about my affection for Jack London and his ability to turn dogs into true heroes of fiction.

Bells, Bells, Bells . . .

In grade five, our teacher asked us to memorize two poems, "The Raven" and "The Bells," by Edgar Allan Poe. At age ten, standing up in class and reciting lines like "Tintinabulations of the bells bells bells" was enough to make us enemies of poetry forever. Further, to hear a teacher with no feeling for poetry announce that "Edgar Allan Poe is a great, great poet" aroused in us a feeling of contempt for the melancholy, tubercular versifier. Without a word to anyone, full of confidence, I decided to rewrite "The Raven" and "The Bells" and improve them. After going through those two poems line by line, word by word, I had to admit that even the verses that most embarrassed me could not be improved upon. I came away from the experience with a grudging respect for my adversary, the no-longer-boring Edgar Allan Poe. After that, I surrendered to the task at hand and memorized the two poems. Next, I began reading more of Poe and making up verses of my own. If you can't beat 'em, join 'em.

Part V

Switchblade Truman Cold War

Rhapsody in Blue

In 1947, I began attending Chicago's Von Steuben High School on the city's North Side. Von Steuben? Right. Our largely Jewish high school was named after a German general, Baron Friedrich Wilhelm Von Steuben, Washington's military advisor during the Revolutionary War. Germany had been our enemy since the rise of Hitler in the early 1930s. Two years after the war, many of my classmates continued to have nightmares about Nazi death camps. Little surprise that the name *General Friedrich Wilhelm Von Steuben* made us vaguely uncomfortable.

Von Steuben was then an academically lax, "country club" high school with a student body of first- and second-generation Americans. Many of my classmates had moved up to conservative, middle-class Albany Park from Chicago's West Side. In the late 1950s and '60s, as these people prospered, they bought homes in suburbs like Skokie and Highland Park. In 1947, my mother said, "Bobby, you'd better start studying and come home with good grades. Don't you want to become a doctor or lawyer so you can live in Highland Park?" Ambitious for me, she wanted me to take music lessons. A fan of Gene Krupa, I asked for a set of drums. She suggested I try an accordion. Eventually we settled on a piano.

In upwardly striving, postwar Albany Park, we experienced the Truman years as no less hypocritical,

conservative, and stifling than the grin-and-wave Eisenhower era that followed. At fourteen, I wanted no part of Skokie or Highland Park. Like my buddies, I got myself a ducktail haircut, wore Levi's, blue suede shoes, and navy blue "hoodlum" shirts purchased at Smokey Joe's on the South Side. I listened to singers like Chicago-born Frankie Laine ("Mule Train") and Vaughn Monroe ("Racing with the Moon") and, when no one else was around, I'd play classical music, including recordings of George Gershwin's *Rhapsody in Blue* and *An American in Paris*. I also read Irving Shulman's *The Amboy Dukes* and carried a switchblade knife. Anti-Semites started fights after Von Steuben basketball games and, sometimes, at Sonny Berkowitz's Lawrence Avenue pool hall. At fourteen, I was already 6'1" and weighed 160 pounds. Because of my size, I was obliged to fight several times on my friends' behalf with my fists—I never used a knife. Invited to join a club called The Regular Fellas, I made a fateful decision. I chose, instead, to become a member of a gang called the Semcoes.

One rainy evening, after a seven-day initiation ritual, ten teenagers—I among them—raced on hands and knees across a muddy football field. As we raced, we were pelted with hell-night, week-old fruit and vegetables. Covered with tomatoes and mud, but winner of the race, I was told to flag down the Chicago Transit Authority's Foster Avenue bus. Ah, the rewards of winning! As the bus pulled to a stop, I leapt aboard and, pretending to carry a gun, shouted, "This is a holdup. Stick 'em up!" I believed myself to be well-disguised. The driver and bug-eyed passengers put their hands in the air. Some older, more experienced riders, used to being robbed, began removing their wristwatches and rings. As they held out their wallets and valuables, I made a quick career decision. I wanted to be in the Semcoes, but understood I was no Billy the Kid. I jumped off the bus as the driver sped into the night. My friends were suitably impressed and I became a gang member in good standing.

The mud, tomatoes, and filthy clothes proved to be an inadequate disguise. At school the next day, a girl asked me, "Robert, wasn't that you last night on the Foster Avenue bus?"

As a gang member, I spent hours hanging out with my friends, eating Twinkies, drinking soda pop, and playing billiards at the poolhall. One night we drove to Gary, Indiana, to a brothel. I was impressed both by the sex I enjoyed that night, an unexpectedly tender initiation, and the near-visionary experience of seeing fire erupting from the local steel mills. Excited by my first sexual escapade and the sight of the Indiana sky exploding with hellfire and brimstone, I tried to explain to my friends that seven-eighths of everything is invisible. I argued that there is a difference between appearance and reality, and that we Semcoes were just punks who didn't know anything about anything. A messenger bringing unwelcome news, my days as a gang member were numbered.

*

In early 1948, my athletic, vivacious, forty-two-year-old mother began taking medication for a goiter condition. As months passed, she became morose and irritable. Then she told me she had to undergo some "routine" surgery. On July 3, 1948, my mother died while being operated on for an enlarged thyroid gland. I know she was concerned about having a dreamy, abstracted son. Hence her last words to my father: "Keep his [Robert's] feet on the ground." Gertrude Sward died ten days after my fifteenth birthday and, for what it's worth, my height (6'1") and weight (160 pounds) have remained constant from that day to the present.

Addressing my father at the funeral service, the rabbi said, "Now, Irving, you're going to have to be both a father and a mother to your children." Seeing my father wince with confusion, I understood that my sister and I were, in fact, going to have to raise ourselves. I asked myself, Were my mother and father ever who I thought they were? Who were my parents, really? I knew for certain that my mother had been an agnostic. Following her death, I felt anger with God, with my mother, with my father, and myself.

My mother's death turned me into a scholar. From 1948 to 1951, I devoted myself to my studies and began earning straight *A*'s. At sixteen, I decided I really did want to go to college. I wrote to Harvard to find out what I had to do to get into law school. Their reply: Be first in your class and come with lots and lots of money. My father, meanwhile, had begun drinking and his practice had fallen off. I realized I would have to work my way through college. At the same time, I was trying to make whatever sense I could of my life. I found myself making up song lyrics and

poems. However, I was too embarrassed to write them down. I took on the position of corresponding secretary for a gang of hoodlums because it offered me what seemed a legitimate opportunity to write. I became the gang's resident mad poet. And, the truth is, no member of the Semcoes objected to receiving rhyming reminders of meetings.

I wrote an original rhyming message to each Semcoe—no two alike! I didn't care that I was assured of only one reader for any given poem. Better an audience of one than none, I thought.

After my mother's death, I began taking long walks along the lakefront near Navy Pier. I felt drawn to Michigan Boulevard and often visited Chicago's Art Institute. Sometimes I'd go read and warm myself in the Chicago Public Library. Entering the library one winter afternoon, I passed through the Art Room on the main floor. There I saw a number of men browsing in the works of the great masters. They resembled figures out of the opera *La Bohème*. I fantasized that they were Bohemians, brooding geniuses, the neglected artists of America. Most likely they were homeless men from West Madison Street. However, I saw them as artist-monks who had risked everything, who had taken vows of poverty on behalf of their calling. Could I do that? I wondered. Could I take a vow of poverty and dedicate myself to writing or painting? And live in a garret as these people did, to be discovered only in the last years of my life? I wasn't so sure.

Part VI

The Korean War (1950-1954)

Growing up in Chicago during World War II, I felt elated but also oddly disappointed when the war ended. I was a patriotic twelve-year-old in 1945, and had expected to go overseas as a sailor or marine. In 1941, the Japanese had caught us unawares and bombed Pearl Harbor. The murderous Nazis had plans to conquer the world. There was a captured German U-boat tied up at the dock by Navy Pier that caught my imagination. I once toured that submarine and a U.S. destroyer escort tied up nearby. Each evening our family listened to the radio for news of the war. I had grown up with visions of German troops marching into Chicago. If that happened, I planned to work with some resistance group and perform acts of sabotage against the enemy.

Seaman Sward, age eighteen, Great Lakes Naval Training Center, 1951

In 1949, ten months after my mother died, my father remarried. My stepmother immediately began telling my father, my sister, and me how to live our lives. It was as if, with the death of my mother, I had lost my father too. To make matters worse, I had two stepbrothers and their dog Satin, a dog I disliked, sharing my bedroom. It was time to think about leaving home. At seventeen, I enlisted in the naval reserve and began attending weekly meetings at Navy Pier. In 1950, the Korean War started, and in 1951, 1 graduated from Von Steuben. Fearing I would be drafted, I visited a navy recruiter who promised if I volunteered I'd get the G.I. Bill to pay my way through college. I signed up.

In 1952, stationed on Coronado Island, working at the headquarters of the commander of the Amphibious Fleet, I was feeling safe and secure. I mulled over stories I'd heard of servicemen in World War II who had done "easy duty" for four years and grown fat and lazy.

A few months later, bored with filing and sorting mail for the admiral, restless to see the world, I volunteered to go to Korea to serve in the combat zone. I expected weeks to pass before my application was approved.

Surprise! Twenty-four hours after I filed my request, I was on the USS *Menard,* an attack transport heading for Korea. In addition to the regular crew, we were carrying two thousand combat-ready marines.

Two weeks later, I was designated editor of the ship's newspaper. My job was to select and edit from a mass of incoming news dispatches those likely to be of interest to sailors and marines. Once I included a story about the launching of a nuclear-powered submarine. President Dwight D. Eisenhower had termed the submarine "a weapon for peace." I felt obliged to editorialize on the cold war. I wrote that there was something contradictory in the president's phrase "weapon for peace." Having uncovered that contradiction, I busied myself rewriting all news reports that contained evidence of "newspeak." There was much to do. Unfortunately, this was also the time of Senator Joseph McCarthy's crusade against communism. One evening, when the executive officer found me writing poetry on the ship's typewriter, he coolly asked if I was a communist.

A few weeks later, on maneuvers off the coast of Red China, the ship's radar operator noted an unidentified aircraft. I happened to be out on deck reading a World War II Armed Forces edition of the poetry of Edgar Allan Poe. When the battle alarm sounded, everyone seemed to disappear at once. All the ship's hatches clanged shut and the *Menard* began steaming into some combat formation. Alone on deck, unable to reach my position in the radio tower, I began pounding on the watertight hatches yelling to be let in. No one heard me. Seeing the *Menard* was in no immediate danger, I curled up outside the ship's radio tower and continued reading poetry.

The day after we arrived in Japan, I was transferred to Landing Ship Tank (LST) 914, an ugly, three-hundred-foot-long, flat-bottomed relic from World War II. Crew members joked that the price of a modern missile was greater than the price of a recommissioned LST. We drew reassurance from the fact it would be uneconomical for an enemy submarine to sink us.

Again I was made editor of the ship's newspaper (readership: 110). And, as yeoman third class, I found myself typing up "clean" copies of the ship's deck log with notations on weather conditions and cloud formations. I became the vessel's chronicler, a nineteen-year-old diary-keeper for an amphibious warship. But best of all, I became overseer of twelve hundred World War II surplus books—stashed in one of the holds. One incredible day the commanding officer told me to haul out the books and create a library of the ship's Armed Forces Editions.

U.S. servicemen and women in World War II were among the first readers of quality paperback books. Realizing many military people *(a)* have a certain amount of spare time, and *(b)* enjoy reading books, the government began providing "little paper books to fit in a soldier's pocket," as Isak Dinesen put it. In 1956, in her interview with the *Paris Review,* she remarks, "The book [*Winter's Tales*] had been put into Armed Forces Editions . . . suddenly I received dozens of charming letters from American soldiers and sailors all over the world." I am proud to say I was one of those sailors.

In 1958, at the Bread Loaf Writers Conference, I heard publishers crediting the Armed Forces Editions with preparing the way for what has become known as the paperback revolution. In 1952, before I even heard of Lawrence Ferlinghetti and his City Lights Paperback Bookstore (founded in 1953), I was one of many librarians managing a City Lights at sea, a City Lights Quality Library in a War Zone—and I was my own best customer.

I had a few friends, access to a desk, a typewriter, paper, and all the books I could read. On the other side of the bulkhead was the ship's kitchen. Each day I enjoyed the fragrance of coffee, fresh-baked bread, down-and-dirty (but generally edible) meat and potatoes. Evenings, restless and lonely, oddly stirred, I'd write letters or wander about on deck, looking at the stars. New to poetry, a raw recruit to literature, I scribbled away my months at sea, happy and madly productive, as I'd be years later at the MacDowell Colony, at Yaddo, and the Djerassi Foundation. In 1958, William Meredith, my colleague at Connecticut College, suggested a poet could do worse than spend twenty years sailing around the world with all expenses paid by the U.S. government. Meredith himself had served as a navy pilot during World War II.

It took thirty years for me to begin writing about my experiences in the Korean War. In 1986, I sent the poem "On My Way to the Korean War" to Dr. Martin Bax in London, England. Martin, a physician and magazine editor, ran the poem in *Ambit* 106.

On my way to the Korean War,
I never got there.

One summer afternoon in 1952,
I stood instead in the bow
of the Attack Transport *Menard,*
with an invading force
of 2,000 battle-ready Marines,
watching the sun go down.
Whales and porpoises,
flying fish and things jumping
out of the water.
Phosphorescence—
Honolulu behind us,
Inchon, Korea, and the war ahead . . .

The poem goes on to tell how a half-dozen sailors, I among them, converged on the bow of the ship, where each evening, composed and silent, we'd maintain our vigil until sunset. One evening, suddenly, unaccountably, I felt extraordinarily joyful, peaceful, secure in a way I had never felt before. At the same time I seemed to lose all sense of personal history. I felt myself merging with every atom, every visible and invisible thing. I felt if I chose, I could simply step out into space and, sink into the ocean or soar into the sky, all would be well. I'd joined the navy to see the world. One thing I hadn't counted on was achieving union with the world I'd gone to see. I came out of the experience believing I had been initiated in some way, that I was beginning to wake up.

In-breathe, out-breathe, and leave,
in-breathe, out-breathe, and leave.
Leave your body, leave your body,
leave your body, leave your body,

We sang as we went out
to where the light went,
and whatever held us to that ship
and its 2,000 battle-ready troops, let go.
So it was, dear friends, I learned to fly.

And so in time must you
and so will the warships,
and the earth itself,

and the sky,
for as the prophet says, the day cometh
when there will be no earth left to leave.

Oh me, O my
O me, O my

goodbye earth, goodbye sky.
Goodbye, goodbye.

My association with Dr. Martin Bax goes back to 1961. As editor of *Ambit* and a fan of "Uncle Dog: The Poet at 9," Martin arranged several poetry readings for me in London pubs and coffeehouses. Thirty years later, Martin says he still uses "Letter to his First Dog" and other poems of mine "when we do Jazz Recital." It was Martin who, in 1961, suggested I contact John Pudney, then senior editor at Putnam in London. I had been unable to find a publisher in the States. As William Meredith wrote in his introduction to *Kissing the Dancer* (1964), "These poems are unusual . . . in a number of ways, but what strikes me first about them is that they are the only book of poems I know about . . . that has been turned down by a lot of publishers over a good many years because they are so original as to be unrecognizable as poetry by a conventional eye. They have gone off to respectable publishers with praise from Stanley Kunitz, Louise Bogan, even Robert Lowell, and come back with the embarrassed confession that they simply escaped the respectable editors."

I was fortunate. Putnam published *Uncle Dog and Other Poems* in 1962, about the same time John Pudney took on the writer Jeff Nuttall, another indication of his open-minded approach to poetry.

But I'm getting ahead of myself.

Part VII

Iowa Writers' Workshop (1956-1967)

In 1956, the year I graduated from the University of Illinois, Paul Engle offered me a fellowship to attend the Iowa Writers' Workshop. A year later, at the University of Iowa, I was writing up to ten poems a day and assaulting *Poetry Northwest,* the *Chicago Review,* and the *New Yorker* with an almost constant barrage. In 1957, Carolyn Kizer published three of my poems in *Poetry Northwest* and George Starbuck accepted "Uncle Dog: The Poet at 9" for the *Chicago Review.* I became a regular contributor to the *Antioch Review,* the *Beloit Poetry Journal, Best Articles & Stories, Carleton Miscellany, Chelsea Review, Epoch,* the *Nation, New Orleans Poetry Journal,* and *Poetry Chicago.* I persevered, and eventually even the *New Yorker,* and the *Paris Review* printed my poems.

For a period of about ten years, from 1957 to 1967, I typically had twenty "packets" of poems (five or more poems per packet) circulating at any one time. Only rarely did I send the same poems out to two magazines at the same time.

In 1957, I submitted satires on *New Yorker* advertisements to two Chicago-based magazines, Rob Cuscaden's *Mainstream* and Ron Offen's *Odyssey.* Rob had begun his mimeographed effort in 1955, and Offen later joined him as coeditor.

Originally, as Ron tells it, the outlook of *Mainstream* was to "present poetry that was in the 'mainstream,' poetry that was being written by 'real' poets rather than academics. Later, when we became *Odyssey,* this changed somewhat. Then our inclination was to feature poets that were neither 'neat' nor 'beat.' So we published people who didn't seem to be part of either school, like Charles Bukowski, Imamu Amiri Baraka (then LeRoi Jones), Michael Benedict, Judson Crews, Fred Eckman, Curtis Zahn, and Robert Sward."

When I began work on this autobiography, I contacted Ron Offen, who, after all, published *Advertisements* (Odyssey Chapbook Publications) in 1958. I asked Ron how it was that he and Cuscaden chose to invest money and energy in producing a collection of my satires at a time when I was "odd man out" in Iowa City and little known outside the Midwest. I also wanted to know how they, as magazine editors, viewed the literary climate at that time.

Ron Offen replied:

Both of us had a profound distrust of poems about poems, poems about myths, and poems with cryptic Greek epigraphs. On the other hand we had a certain respect for form—we were close to the Angry Young Men of England in that respect—and were suspicious of the Beats' insistence on spontaneity, a freedom from artistic control that seemed too often "typewriting" rather than "writing," to paraphrase Capote's criticism of Kerouac's work.

Robert Sward, like most of the poets we published, seemed to fit somewhere between the two influences. As a quasi-academic, he was studying at Iowa . . . he was very conscious of craftsmanship (although he rarely used conventional forms), and his stance was ironic rather than engage. But like the Beats he wrote about his own experiences as a kid in Chicago or aimed satiric barbs at the last phase of the Eisenhower beehive-hairdo-and-airhead culture.

In addition, we were enthralled with Sward's wacky and marvelous sense of humor (something most of the arid academics and earnestly spiritual Beats lacked). And the spirit of humor carried beyond his work into his life. For example, he once wrote us that the reason we couldn't reach him by phone was that Ma Bell had yanked out his phone when he offered to pay his bill with a sonnet sequence (syllabic sonnets, mind you!).

Because Cuscaden and Offen had already published some of my poems on *New Yorker* magazine advertisements, and knew I had others, in 1958 they offered to publish a chapbook titled *Advertisements*. Poet Fred Eckman wrote an introduction, Ron Offen designed the cover, and, availing themselves of a 1250 Multilith press, Odyssey Chapbook Publications printed 368 copies of the book. "My guess is we sold about 25 at a buck a pop," says Offen, who now runs a California-based magazine called *Free Lunch: A Poetry Journal*. Offen hasn't given up on me yet. After thirty years, he still publishes my quirky poems.

A jazz aficionado, I drew on funky blues, gospel music, and Middle America speech rhythms. I wrote in a variety of forms—including sonnets—but most of my work was in unrhymed syllabics and free verse. I loved poets as diverse as e. e. cummings, Marianne

With sister, Betty, Chicago, about 1967: "The house in the background was 'home' when I attended Von Steuben HS and belonged to the Semcoes"

Moore, Wallace Stevens, and W. H. Auden, writers who found it in their souls to integrate "seriousness" with playfulness and humor. But the Iowa cornbelt metaphysicals took themselves very seriously. In those years, 1956-58, all the Iowa poets seemed to be jabbering about Franz Schubert, German art songs of the nineteenth century, Baudelaire, the Flowers of Evil, the fountains of Rome, and the well-wrought urn. I was reading Whitman's *Leaves of Grass,* Mark Twain's *Life on the Mississippi,* and the *Des Moines Register.*

*

In 1967, George Starbuck invited me to teach at the Iowa Writers' Workshop. I was privileged to have students like James Tate, Alan Soldofsky, Michael Dennis Browne, Jon Anderson, and Michael Culross in my classes. I no longer have a beard, but I do live now in a beautiful, exotic land—dangerous, mad Santa Cruz, after a 7.1 earthquake. And, as my second, third, and fourth wives will testify, I've overstepped the boundaries and, yes, have flung myself "across life-size pages / in uneven lines."

Have I become "endless, unlikely, remarkable"? Perhaps it's time, dear Michael, dear friends, for us to become better acquainted.

Part VIII

Recollections of an Amnesiac: The New England Poetry Circuit

The best thing that ever happened to me
  besides everything else
    was briefly having amnesia and enjoying it
    at least briefly.
How instructive are our illnesses. How
  instructive is madness and
    losing one's mind precisely the moment one
    had begun
    overvaluing that mind . . .
        (from "Scarf Gobble Wallow Inventory")

                 *

Cornell published *Thousand-year-old Fiancee and Other Poems* in 1965. In the winter of 1966, I was at the MacDowell Colony writing poems and preparing to embark on the New England Poetry Circuit. Holly Stevens, coordinator of the series, had made arrangements for me to visit fourteen colleges and universities in Connecticut, Massachusetts, Maine, and New Hampshire. The day before I was scheduled to give my first reading, I trekked around Cambridge seeing friends and visiting bookstores. Early in the afternoon, I stepped out from between two snowbanks to cross a street and was run over by a student driving an MG. I regained consciousness in the backseat of the car as we drove to Massachusetts General Hospital. Looking at the young man and woman in the front seat, I wondered, Who are these people? Seeing blood on my jacket, I touched my head and realized my ear had come loose. I didn't know my name or the names of the driver and his beautiful female companion. But look at that blue sky and the sunlight on that redbrick wall, I remember thinking. Amazing. Unfortunately, I didn't know what city I was in. I didn't know the day, year, or anything to do with my personal history. Was I married or single? Were there children to be notified? How had I become a bloodied passenger in the cramped backseat of a classy green sports car?

At the hospital, a doctor sewed my ear back onto my head. I was conscious the entire time. Next, I was transferred to a ward filled with heart-attack and gunshot victims, a three-hundred-pound man with a bleeding ulcer, and others, like myself, with less dramatic ailments. Once I settled in, I rang for a nurse. "I've been run over by a car and I've lost my memory," I said. "I'd like someone to talk to." She looked into my eyes, glanced at the bandage holding my ear in place, turned and walked away without a word. Moments later she returned with a giant television set mounted on an enormous tripod. The television set was wheeled to the front of the ward so all the patients could watch. The program she selected was a movie, *The Three Faces of Eve.* She cranked up the volume. Again, I rang for a nurse and explained I wanted someone to talk to. Looking frightened, the second nurse also disappeared. Then my survival instinct must have kicked in. Slowly I began to remember things.

Early the next morning, I convinced the doctors I was ready to leave. Released from the hospital, my head wrapped in bandages, I went to see a lawyer. "Don't do the poetry readings," he advised me. "Cancel the poetry tour. Go home and have yourself a rest. Claim you were too badly injured to perform. That way you can sue for lots and lots of money. If you don't take my advice, there's not much I can do for you."

"I've committed myself to all those colleges," I said, blinking as my memory continued to return. "I'm primed to do the readings. So I'm going to go ahead and give them."

The lawyer shrugged and turned away. But I was thinking of Holly—Wallace Stevens's daughter—and the work she did to make the series possible. Memory or no memory, stitches in the head or no stitches in the head, I made up my mind to give those readings.

You may ask, How can you remember back to a precise time in 1966 and recall so many details, particularly if you had been run over by a car and lost your memory?

Good question. One of the first things I wanted to do after recovering my memory was to write about the experience. For whatever reason, I'm happy to say, I can recall more details about that particular day than any other day in my life—with the possible exception of October 17, 1989, when Santa Cruz experienced a

7.1 earthquake. Nothing like a near-death experience to wake one up, to shake loose all those mental cobwebs. Where was I? Oh, yes, I did all fourteen readings. The New England Poetry Circuit proved to be an intense and, certainly, a memorable experience.

In 1989, I did a reading at the Berkeley YMCA. Ruth and Artie Daigon, editors of *Poets On,* came to the reading and laughed as they recalled my visit to the University of Connecticut in 1966. "You had an audience of 225 people waiting for you. You arrived late. You trotted into the hall smiling and wearing a big white bandage on your head. You had a beard and you were waving your arms. You were very physically active in your reading."

Following the New England Poetry Circuit, I returned to the MacDowell Colony, where I worked on my journals. "I find myself perplexed at my sexual response at a time when I was physically injured," I wrote. "What is the connection between sex and violence? There I was, unconscious in the backseat of the MG that had nearly killed me. Then, as I regained consciousness, I found myself physically attracted to the young woman seated in front of me. I didn't know then that it had been she who had run me over. After a brief fantasy in which she was my partner, I realized I was bleeding. Even as an amnesiac I couldn't go five minutes without a sex thought. Only after that fantasy did it occur to me that I didn't know my own name. Otherwise, if I had been able to remember my name, I might have introduced myself."

What does it say about me that in this instance, as in many other instances in my life, the sexual impulse overrode everything else?

Once is enough, of course, but I have never regretted being an amnesiac. I know I'm lucky to be alive. I know too I was fortunate to be at the MacDowell Colony to recover. There I sought answers to the question: Who am I?

I spent hours walking in the woods, reading Dag Hammarskjold's *Markings,* and listening to Bob Dylan, the Beatles, and the Mamas and the Papas. A year or two later, I began work on the novel *The Jurassic Shales* and the longish "Scarf Gobble Wallow Inventory." The latter is a poem of personal stock-taking, a way of dealing with amnesia, loss, marriage and the family, space exploration, and the afterlife.

How hungry and for WHAT are the people this
  season
    predicting the end of the end of the end of
I've only just come home after having been
  away
The world sends its greetings and the greetings
  send
    greetings
Hello goodbye, hello goodbye . . .

The experience of being run over by a car still haunts me. In the early 1980s, living in Toronto, I wrote another poem about losing my memory. It's called "Mr. Amnesia," and it starts:

Even an amnesiac remembers some things better than others.
In one past life I was a subway conductor
for the Chicago subway system.

In another I was . . . . Gosh, I forgot!

. . . I don't know about you, but I hardly
  unpack
and get ready for this life and it's time

To move on to the next . . .

Part IX

Welcome to Victoria, B.C. (1969-1979)

During the late 1960s and early '70s, American men arriving in Canada were automatically assumed to be Vietnam War protestors, draft dodgers, or deserters. American veterans of World War II, Korean War veterans, even bona fide academics and unsuspecting tourists were regarded with disapproval.

In 1969, I was a married, thirty-six-year-old, honorably discharged and decorated Korean War veteran. I was also the father of four children. I was not subject to the draft and had been specifically invited to the University of Victoria to teach. However, the circumstances of my arrival meant nothing to anti-American nationalists.

Canada is a beautiful, wonderfully raw, exciting country, an inspiringly sane, peaceable kingdom compared to America. There are many valid reasons for citizens of the country to be nationalistic. But why the prejudice against foreigners? Why the fear? Why so little generosity of spirit? Why believe that invited guests, for example, come for dishonorable rather than honorable reasons?

At a faculty party in September 1969, I found myself in conversation with a portly, red-faced, rather jowly steak-and-kidney-pie academic, the head of the university's freshman English program. "Well, what do you think of Victoria?" he asked, pouring me a drink. "It's dull, provincial, quiet, friendly, and clean," I replied. "I'm amazed that every house I've seen so far has a flower garden."

Then I told him how English poet Michael Dennis Browne laughed when he saw Victoria. "England hasn't looked like this for over twenty years," he said. "Victoria is a facsimile of an England that exists now only in peoples' imaginations."

I felt angry with Michael for saying this. Who wants to live in an imitation of someone else's homeland, garden city of Canada or not? But maybe Michael was right. I wanted to hear what the steak-and-kidney-pie Canadian had to say. The professor harrumphed with annoyance. He ignored my question. Instead he asked me, "What brought you to British Columbia? Are you a Vietnam War draft dodger?"

"I was invited to read my poetry here in February. This was the last stop for me on the Northwest Poetry Circuit. Your colleagues said Victoria was narrow and self-centered. They said they wanted an 'intense American-type, someone whose adrenalin is moving,' to replace Robin Skelton. They even paid my moving expenses. What brought *you* here?" I asked. "My family moved here from New England. We left because of the Revolution."

At first I thought the professor was saying he too was a new arrival. Maybe an older, more established person fed up with Lyndon Johnson and the Vietnam War. Maybe someone who decided America was a violent country on the brink of revolution? Or was he perhaps an individual so outraged at the 1968 police riot in Chicago that he had left the country? Science-fiction writer Judith Merril, and others, had left America for that reason.

"What do you mean, Revolution?" I asked.

"The American Revolution. My ancestors left America after the Boston Tea Party. We're United Empire Loyalists," he said proudly. He was very impressed with himself.

"Professor, you mean you've been here for over two hundred years? That's incredible. By the way, how long does it take to get tenure at UVic?"

It never occurred to me there existed in this world an outpost of people who, more than two hundred years after the event, still regarded the dumping of tea into Boston Harbor as a criminal act, who believed Paul Revere to be "the enemy," and who, though they lived twenty minutes from Seattle, felt an emotional bond with King George III (the crazy one) and Queen Elizabeth II.

And here I was, a Chicago-born, bearded, academic hippie drinking Bristol cream sherry with United Empire Loyalists in a city named after dowager Queen Victoria. A couple years earlier, I had written, "Iowa, what am I doing in Iowa?" Now the question was, "Canada, what am I doing in Canada?"

Suddenly America seemed very far away.

"Is anything wrong?" asked the chairman. "All the color's left your face."

Oh, my God, I thought.

*

I came to Victoria to give a fifty-minute poetry reading. I accepted a teaching position that was supposed to keep me in British Columbia for nine months. I wrote poems about Canadian alligator matrons, prehistoric English crocodiles, tea-drinking Royalists, Tories in their glory. To my surprise, I was rehired to teach a second year. My daughter Hannah was born in 1970, and I purchased a three-story, tudor-style home in quiet, stodgy Oak Bay for $18,500. In 1971, I was promoted to assistant professor, given a bonus, a new two-year contract and other inducements, and so stayed on two more years. In 1973 I met, and in 1975,

With daughter Cheryl Cox, Vancouver Island, Canada, 1978

married, a French-Canadian artist (see "Barbara Walters Interviews a Much-Married Man"). What started out as a fifty-minute, Northwest Poetry Circuit appearance led to my living in Canada for fifteen years.

Part X

Soft Press, Canada (1970-1979)

"The spirit in man is soft.

It can go anywhere."

I am in debt to William Stafford for the name Soft Press. It was Stafford who said, "The spirit in man is

soft. It can go anywhere." I am also indebted to Ram Dass (Dr. Richard Alpert), who, in 1968, was living an hour or two from Peterborough, New Hampshire. I was in residence at the MacDowell Colony when I learned that Ram Dass, recently returned from India, was now a "neighbor." I immediately phoned asking if I could visit.

Ram Dass reportedly lost his job at Harvard for experimenting with LSD. In one of his experiments, he included the sons of a Harvard dean. The afternoon of my visit, Ram Dass spoke of how he had gone back to Harvard and, by chance, encountered the two young men.

"What was it like running into them?" I asked.

"They were soft," he said, meaning gentle, at peace with themselves.

For some reason I was struck by the positive emphasis he placed on the word "soft." Up until then I tended to think of "soft" in a negative way.

Months later, when I arrived in Victoria, B.C., to begin teaching, there was a letter waiting for me.

"I have consecrated Vancouver Island in advance of your arrival. Many beautiful people with much light," it read. And was signed, "Ram Dass."

Soon after Ram Dass's letter arrived, poet and publisher Larry Raferty asked if he could store a one-hundred-year-old treadle-operated Cropper platen letterpress in the basement of our Oak Bay home. I said yes and, a few weeks later, purchased two thousand pounds of lead printing type. A novice, it took me up to eight hours to prepare the press, set the type, and print one page of poetry. Nonetheless, for about seven years that press was the heart of our 1050 Saint David Street house.

I reflected on the meanings of the word "soft." Could I accept the challenge of using the word when I named a publishing company? That, briefly, is how Soft Press came into existence.

In 1973, we produced a hand-set, signed limited edition of William Stafford's *In the Clock of Reason.* Stafford's poems were followed by our most ambitious project, an anthology titled *Vancouver Island Poems.* Canadian artist Pat Martin Bates contributed cover artwork and our poets included Dorothy Livesay, Earle Birney, P. K. Page, Susan Musgrave, Victor Coleman, and Gary Geddes.

Soft Press published twenty-one books of poetry, most of which were well received, and won some small grants from Canada Council. From 1970 to 1979, I supported the Press with my salary as a university professor and, later, as an editor for a commercial publishing house.

I was publishing widely in the early 1970s, was popular with my students, but some of my colleagues complained: "Isn't four years long enough for a visit-

ing [American] poet, particularly one who has been much-married, whose poetry is incomprehensible, and who employs controversial teaching methods?" In truth, my colleagues had a point. One day the chairman of the English department visited my classes. I describe the experience in "Mr. Amnesia":

An instructor in Modern Poetry, I once lectured

For four weeks as if each class was the first
   class
of a new year. When the genial Chairman,
manifesting polite alarm,

Visited my classes the occasion of his being
   there
gave me the opportunity to teach
as if those classes, too, were new classes.

Promoted, given a raise, a bonus and a new
   two-year contract,
even I was confused. Each class I taught
   became one
in an infinite series of semesters, each semester

Lasting no more than fifty minutes.
I don't know about you, but I hardly unpack
and get ready for this life and it's time

To move on to the next . . .

"Mr. Amnesia" stretches the truth. In 1973, my appointment ran out and I decided to devote myself to writing poetry, managing Soft Press, and working for a commercial publishing house.

                                        *

Why is it that hard-nosed businesspeople are regarded as the embodiment of sanity? Because they dedicate their lives to a quest for money and power? Because in our society we believe rational behavior and the possession of money and power go hand in hand? The question intrigues me because, in my experience, businesspeople—publishers, for example—are often more idiosyncratic, if not notably irrational, than the people they publish.

In 1976, I became senior editor for a commercial book publisher. I accepted the position because I was going broke publishing poetry with Soft Press. I had another reason for taking the job: I wanted to learn all I could about the day-to-day operation of a nitty-gritty, seemingly successful publishing house. I had, and still have, dreams of starting a new publishing firm.

I was a loyal, hardworking employee. On one occasion, I learned that the company owed money to a printer. Therefore, I introduced my employer to a literary agent. The agent was ready to negotiate a fifteen-thousand-dollar purchase of some old letters and manuscripts the publisher regarded as "worthless, space-consuming garbage." A certain university library was prepared to buy this material.

"What's the agent like?" the publisher asked.

"He's honest and reputable, but he can be rude," I replied.

"Rude," bellowed the book publisher. "I'm rude. I'm the rudest man in Canada. There's no one ruder than I am."

I wasn't prepared for this response.

It's true I knew he was rude. It's true that once we'd argued over a manuscript I didn't want to publish. It's true he insulted me. It's true I lost my temper and hit him over the head with the three-hundred-page manuscript. But after two years of working in the industry, I assumed such unpleasantness was normal. He never protested being hit. I kept my job as editor and, some months later, asked for and received a raise.

So I'd forgotten how much he prided himself on being uncivilized. A self-proclaimed wild-and-wooly, businessman bully, bush airplane pilot, and "outback" filmmaker, he had a reputation to uphold. For some reason he needed to believe he was the rudest man in

Canada. For me to suggest that there might be a rival, an individual more uncouth, more uncivilized, more barbarous than himself, was unacceptable. The publisher felt threatened.

I knew what was coming and made a point of being present when the two businessmen met. The publisher immediately accused the agent of being a swindler. The agent responded that the publisher was a noted boor with a reputation for publishing crap. The publisher counterattacked by ridiculing the agent for overvaluing the manuscripts he himself wanted to sell. Though the two were meeting for the first time, they were attacking one another's reputations with glee. If the stakes had been higher, would more insults and profanities have been exchanged? Who won? The publisher. He was more aggressive, threw out more damaging remarks, and, in the end, still managed to collect his fifteen thousand dollars.

What did I get out of it? A day off.

Part XI

Survivor of Four Marriages, Father of Five Children

I practised the Lamaze method and assisted at the birth of two of my children, Hannah and Nicholas. People speak of the "bonding" that occurs when one is present at the birth of a child. I know I felt it. It's somewhat ironic, in fact, that two years after her birth, I became both a father and a mother to Hannah. In 1972, Hannah's mother underwent a fit of wanderlust. "Robert, you can have legal custody," she said. "I think you'll be a better parent to Hannah than I can be."

So it happened that in my last full year of teaching at the University of Victoria, I became a single parent. I remember the first day that two-year-old, blonde, blue-eyed Hannah and I were alone together. We sat on the floor of a kitchen from which all the furniture had been removed. I had nothing original to say. "It's just you and me, kid," I joked.

From the time of her birth in Victoria, B.C., to her graduation from Santa Cruz High in 1988, Hannah lived and travelled with me continuously.

It's difficult to concentrate four or five hours at a time on poetry when there are children around. As father of five, I had to come up with a solution. One day in Peterborough, New Hampshire, my son Michael—then four years old—was playing in the attic with my six-year-old stepdaughter. Concerned for their safety, I didn't want to leave them alone. So instead of turning on the TV or yelling for them to shut up, I listened and took notes on what they were saying. That's how I began writing poetry with children.

"Monster Poem—Lagoon Goon"; "For Michael"; "Doctor in the Horse, House, Mouse"; "Elementary Fire Alarm"; and others were written for, and in some cases, with, my children. "Bebop a Rock"; "Blind Poet;" and "Lakes Can Die, Too" were inspired by teaching in elementary and high schools for the Ontario Arts Council in Canada, and the Cultural Council of Santa Cruz County in California. In 1979, when I first began participating in a Poet-in-the-Schools program, schoolchildren responded to my free verse poems by saying, "Poetry rhymes. If it doesn't rhyme, it's not poetry." For these students, my credibility as a poet and teacher depended on my ability to write poetry that rhymed. Assonance and consonance left them cold. *Scream-dream* was a rhyme. *Leaves-lives* was not. Alliteration was acceptable. Say *Ding-dong*, and you had their attention. Try to establish a musical connection between *steel* and *chill*, and you lost it. I could read a poem like "Honey Bear,"

> A pale blue light
> surrounds her toes as she waltzes

> By the clover and the mint.
> Lighter than air, heavier
> than a bear. Clear-skinned lady
> O fairest of the fair

> I bow to my honey bear.

and they were ready to write poems of their own.

In 1984, I learned how to operate a computer and began to do some desktop publishing. Since that time, I have worked with elementary, junior-high, and college students to produce inexpensive anthologies of the best of their prose and poetry.

How I Learned to Stand on My Head and

Marry My Third and Fourth Wives

In December 1968, shortly before my third marriage, I began to find it difficult to breathe and went to see a physician. After an examination he said, "You have asthma. You need to reduce the stress in your life."

At that time I was in my fifth or sixth residence at the MacDowell Colony. I was working on my novel *The Jurassic Shales*. I didn't know it in 1968, but it was the fear of an impending marriage that was making it difficult for me to breathe.

Wayne Boohors, a New York painter—and a fellow Colonist—introduced me to some basic yoga postures.

When it comes to breathing, I'm a pragmatist. I did the assigned bends and stretches and soon I was breathing normally. Okay, so yoga works, I decided. If yoga can help me breathe, what else can it do for me?

In 1969, 1 began taking yoga classes with a former British army officer who had spent twenty years in India studying meditation. I went to yoga retreats with Indra Devi, Swami Radha, Muktananda, and others. I studied Sanskrit. I read and reread Paramahansa Yogananda's *Autobiography of a Yogi*, the *Bhagavad Gita*, *The Upanishads*, W. Y. Evans-Wentz's *The Tibetan Book of the Dead*, Robert Payne's *The White Pony*, John Blofeld's *The Zen Teaching of Zen Huang Po*, Lao Tzu's *Tao Te Ching*, and everything else I could find on Eastern literature and religion.

When the British army officer retired from teaching, he asked me to take over his classes. So I began working as a book editor at the Authors and Eagles publishing house by day, and teaching hatha yoga to British Columbia Civil Service employees at night. From 1976 to 1979, I also led a Siddha Yoga meditation center.

When the pressure became too much, I'd go off to a weekend yoga retreat. When that didn't work, I'd go off to a seven-day yoga retreat. After that I began attending month-long yoga retreats. Eventually—in my fourth marriage—I went to live in an ashram in Ganeshpuri, India.

My third wife disliked my involvement in yoga. She wasn't too keen on my writing poetry either. Each morning I'd get up at dawn, stroll outside, and stand on my head. Then I'd write in my journal. An hour or two later, I'd come into the house hungry for breakfast. She'd be waiting for me. "Have you taken out the garbage yet? How much money do we have in the bank? What kind of a husband are you?"

Once my third wife picked up a copy of Richard Wilhelm's translation of the *I Ching: Book of Changes,* the one with an introduction by Carl Jung, and threw it at me.

Well, imagine sharing your life with someone who scribble scribble scribbles every chance he gets. Imagine living with a partner who, when he isn't scribbling, is standing on his head. From her point of view, I was insufferable.

Ars longa, vita brevis. Art is long. Marriage is short.

Part XII

The Much-Married Man Moves to Toronto

In 1975, Toronto's Coach House Press sponsored a two-week workshop for small-press publishers. As publisher of Soft Press, and as organizer of a poetry-reading series at Open Space, Victoria, B.C., and at the University of Victoria, I had already met a dozen or more Coach House authoRS: Margaret Atwood, Douglas Barbour, George Bowering, Victor Coleman, Gerry Gilbert, Roy Kiyooka, Robert Kroetsch, Dorothy Livesay, David McFadden, Fred Wah, Phyllis Webb, David Young, and others. I had hopes of getting a book of my own published, a novel called *The Jurassic Shales.* In addition, I dreamed of moving to Toronto—Canada's answer to New York City—and the Coach House workshop was an opportunity to check it out.

One day, Coach House Press editor Victor Coleman invited me to a party. Victor lived in a community of about seven hundred people on the Toronto Islands, a

With daughter Hannah, age nine, and son, Nicholas, age two, Toronto Island, Canada, 1979

mile-and-a-half ferry ride from downtown Toronto. Cars are not allowed on the Islands, and the main mode of transportation is the bicycle. The residents, a unique mix of writers, painters, musicians, workers in Canada's business and entertainment industry, all commuted to the city together on a ferry boat. A number of American expatriates live on the Islands, along with people from England, France, Germany, and Switzerland.

The Coach House Press party went on late into the night. It was two days before I got back to Toronto and, by that time, I had made up my mind to move to the Big City, and to live in the Island community.

Canadian poet Penny Kemp invited me to rent her house while she wintered in South America. Penny's house featured a staircase made out of tree branches and a full-size, indoor swing suspended from a swaybacked thirty-foot ceiling. Overly energetic swingers tended to crash into walls or against a stove, which sometimes set the house on fire.

I was living in Penny's house in 1980 when Swiss photographer Ursula Heller arrived on assignment for

Neue Zurcher Zeitung, a German-language newspaper published in Zurich. Ursula invited me to interview twenty longtime residents of the community for a five-page feature story. My interviews were translated into German and published—with Ursula's photographs—on Valentine's Day, 1981. Meanwhile, *The Islanders,* a traveling exhibition of my poems and Toronto Island interviews, accompanied by Ursula's photographs, opened in Toronto City Hall. Specially typeset, enlarged, mounted on large, transportable panels, *The Islanders* exhibit was subsequently seen by more than sixty thousand people.

A year later, I received a Canada Council Explorations Grant to develop the interviews and to produce a book, *The Toronto Islands: An Illustrated History.* I spent weeks in the Toronto City Archives reading diaries from the eighteenth and nineteenth centuries, including accounts of the invasion of the Toronto Islands, and the burning of Toronto, by American troops in the War of 1812. The *Toronto Star* published numerous sections of *The Toronto Islands.* David Crombie, former mayor of Toronto and a member of Parliament, contributed an introduction and, in 1983, Dreadnaught Press published the book.

Torontonians generally support the community. But Metro Council and suburban politicians were mounting their forces at that time, as they had off and on for thirty years, to tear down the Islanders' homes and destroy the "Bohemian" enclave. In Canada, the Islanders have established a reputation for themselves as people who enjoy life. In cold climates, particularly, the enjoyment of life is sometimes subject to persecution.

When the book appeared, I was invited to appear on numerous radio and TV shows. I shared what I learned about the history of the Islands and talked about the controversy. Dreadnaught Press seized the opportunity to sponsor a publication party which was attended by several hundred people—and a TV crew. I became, by Canadian standards, a best-selling author.

The Three Roberts

Robert Priest, Canadian poet, rock musician, and singer-songwriter, was also a Dreadnaught author. Robert and I were both active in the Ontario Arts

The Three Roberts: (from left) Robert Sward, Robert Zend, and Robert Priest, 1984

Council's Poet-in-the-Schools program. Both of us were involved in writing a series of children's poems. Robert Priest, with Bongo Herbert and the illustrator Rudi McToots, had even formed a performance group for children, the Boinks.

Robert and I met for lunch one afternoon at a Bloor Street falafel restaurant. I joked, "Let's do a stand-up comic poetry reading and call ourselves The Two Roberts." "No, no, that doesn't sound right," said Priest. "How about The Three Roberts?" "Good idea, but who's going to be the third Robert?" I asked. "There's this mad poet I heard the other night who writes in Hungarian and in English. He's also a radio broadcaster and film editor. We could combine poetry, music, and visuals."

According to Glenn Gould, Robert Zend [was] "unquestionably Canada's most musical poet." Immanuel Velikovsky said of him, "Robert Zend's feet are planted on the ground, his heart is forgiving, his head is in the clouds." William Ronald said of him, "Zend is a split personality, and I love him both."

I too came to love Robert Zend. Because I lived on the Islands, we talked often on the phone. One day Robert called me. I described the experience in a poem called, appropriately enough, "The Three Roberts":

Ring, ring.
"Robert, this is Robert."

"Is this Robert?" "This
is Robert, Robert." "Yes,
Robert?" I say, "This
Is Robert, too." "Ah,
excuse me, I need
to find a match,"

says Robert Zend putting
down the telephone
and rummaging for matches,

granting me, a non-smoker,
the status of accessory
to his addiction.

All this occurring a few
seconds into an otherwise
scintillating conversation . . .

The three of us began to meet and rehearse. We spent
hours playing together, establishing themes, introducing and juxtaposing poems. "This is the way musicians rehearse," said Priest. And that was the way we
rehearsed for each of our readings.

On January 29, 1984, we read together at Grossman's
Tavern, a few blocks from the University of Toronto.
This reading, our first as a group, was arranged by Elliot Lefko, "founder of poetry concerts in Toronto,
'the mastermind of poetry cabaret,'" according to the
Globe and Mail. Elliot, one of Canada's literary
entrepreneurs, did well by us. It was a cold, gray,
miserable Sunday afternoon, but over three hundred
people turned out. Priest led off with a musical set.
We read individually, then as a group, alternating
poems, playing out a series of variations.

In response to the demand for the poems we read,
Robert Zend designed an edition titled *The Three
Roberts, Premiere Performance.* HMS Press published
and distributed the book in conjunction with a Toronto
music magazine called *Shades.* Writers Judith Merril,
Elizabeth Smart, and Sheila Wawanash praised the
little publication and it sold well.

Next we did a reading at Major Robert's Restaurant
near the intersection of Major and Robert Streets in
Toronto. Our theme was Love and, in response to the
demand for the poems we read, Dreadnaught Press
published an edition titled *The Three Roberts on Love.*

Our third reading was on the theme of Childhood. We
read at a small church a few steps from the Eaton
Center in Toronto. Again, there was demand for our
work. In 1985, Peter Baltensperger and Brenda Kre-
wen issued *The Three Roberts on Childhood* with
Moonstone Press (St. Catharines, Ontario). We did a
fourth reading on the theme of War, but that "book" is
as yet unpublished.

The group dissolved in 1985 about the time we were
scheduled to appear on a Canadian Broadcasting
Corporation radio show. Robert Zend, a one-man literary renaissance, underwent heart surgery and died a
few months later. That same year I returned to the
U.S.

Part XIII

*How Whitman, Thoreau, and John Robert Colombo
Sent Me Back to America*

I met John Robert Colombo, Canadian poet and editor
of *Colombo's Canadian Quotations,* in 1971. Friends
for nearly twenty years, we sometimes browsed
together in Queen Street, Toronto, bookstores. On one
occasion, Colombo introduced me to a volume titled
*Walt Whitman's Diary in Canada, with Extracts from
Other of His Diaries and Literary Notebooks.* There's
a certain irony in the fact Colombo, the "Master
Gatherer of Canadiana," helped set me on a course
which led me back to my American roots.

In any case, I learned that Whitman visited Toronto in
1880, and was favorably impressed. "The city made
the impression on me of a lively dashing place," he
wrote in a thick pocket journal he carried with him.
Whitman went sightseeing on an omnibus and (as one
might expect) rode on top with the driver. He wrote of
"blue Ontario's waters, sunlit, yet with a slight haze,
through which [I saw] occasionally a distant sail."

When I learned of Thoreau's visit to Canada ("What I
got by going to Canada was a cold," wrote Thoreau), I
began imagining what it might be like to live abroad
for many years and then, homesick for one's native
land, to be visited by two dear friends—albeit from
the nineteenth century. How could one resist packing
one's bags and returning with them? I wanna go home,
I wanna go home. That was my underlying thought as
I wrote a feature for the *Toronto Star* titled "Whitman
Loved (But Thoreau Hated) Toronto."

Since 1969 I had lived exclusively on islands—Vancouver Island for ten years and Toronto Island for five. Reading Whitman's journals, rereading *Leaves of Grass,* I felt I was waking up after a long sleep. I was an expatriate Rip Van Winkle. "It's time to go home," I said. But my French-speaking Canadian wife and two children, Hannah and Nicholas, didn't want to leave the safe and secure Toronto Islands and the "no automobiles allowed" community of seven hundred people. "Why leave?" they protested. "We own a home in an idyllic park with a view of Lake Ontario. Downtown Toronto is ten minutes away by ferry. We have everything we need right here."

But I was fifty years old and pining away for my American friends and children who still lived in the States. In addition, I missed the language. I missed the humor. Canadian speech is subtly different from American speech. As a writer, I craved the language I had grown up with. My French-speaking Canadian wife told me I resembled some extraterrestrial being, a Chicago-born E.T. destined to return to his home. I knew it was put up or shut up. Now or never. I began making plans to return to America and to bring my family. It was a less-than-democratic decision, and I paid a price.

"Where are we going to live? What about school? All our friends are here. America's a violent country. People shoot one another in the street for no reason. And what about money? Where are you going to get a job?"

"I'll meditate on it," I said.

In 1984, in the Hart House Debates Room at the University of Toronto, I went to see a white-clad yogi with an untrimmed beard who hadn't spoken a single word in more than thirty years. He understood English, but used a young "interpreter" to field questions and read aloud from a chalkboard on which he, the yogi, wrote the answers.

"What is the function of a master?" I asked.

As befits a man who has kept his mouth shut for three decades, the yogi had developed a skill for saying a great deal in the fewest possible words. "The function of a master is to show the path and leave," he wrote on his chalkboard.

"This is like having a conversation with a Chinese fortune cookie," I whispered to my wife.

The next day, I confronted my editor at the *Toronto Star* with former Harvard University professor Richard Alpert's (aka Ram Dass) description of the yogi in his book *Be Here Now:*

> His arms are . . . tiny. But this little ninety-pound fellow . . . architecturally designed . . . temples and schools, supervised . . . the buildings and grounds . . . He slept two hours a night. His food intake for the last fifteen years had been two glasses of milk a day . . . yet when the workmen can't lift a particularly heavy rock, they call for "the little great king." As in a comic strip, he goes over and lifts the rock, just with one-pointedness of mind.

That did the trick. The editor came up with $300.00 so I could attend, and write about, a week-long yoga retreat at Sparrow Lake, about one hundred miles north of Toronto. My wife and children came with me. A week later, the *Star* ran an illustrated two-page feature under the heading, "He hasn't spoken for thirty years, but the wise words of Baba Hari Dass and five peaceful days at his yoga camp helped relieve a frazzled Toronto family's daily stresses."

Baba Hari Dass did more than relieve us of our stresses. As things turned out, he also proved to be my ticket back to America. Soon after the piece was published, I received a letter from the Mount Madonna Center inviting me to teach a couple of writing courses at Mount Madonna School in the Santa Cruz Mountains. The author of the letter neglected to mention that the school is located on the San Andreas Fault. In any case, my family and I were provided with a house, meals, a decent school for the children, and an opportunity to get reoriented to life in the U.S.A.

As my friend Mort Marcus wrote in his introduction to *Poet Santa Cruz,*

> Now he has moved from Canada to California, taken up residence at Santa Cruz County's Mount Madonna . . . and the physical and

psychical environment has taken him by the tongue to new spiritual heights, which have slowed his responses to a meditative stillness and (surprisingly) eased him back into such closed forms as sonnets and villanelles . . . This change shows in his new poems, "A Monk on the Santa Cruz Mountains"; "Castroville—California"; "A Coffee Shop . . . "; "Li Po"; and "The Emperor . . ."

*

In Part II of this autobiography, I write of my progress in moving from the kitchen floor to the kitchen table—a milestone. In January 1986, I moved from the mountains overlooking Monterey Bay to Santa Cruz, a seismically active community of forty-five thousand people located seventy-five miles south of San Francisco. Another milestone. Right, I was a wife-less, risk-taking man in his early fifties with little money in the bank. Back in the real world working as a free-lance writer and teacher, it was time to do some stocktaking, time for another inventory.

Sometimes I imagine myself being interviewed by Barbara Walters.

Part XIV

Barbara Walters Interviews a Much-Married Man

INT: Robert, why four marriages?

RS: You mean, why four successful marriages? I know I may sound defensive, but I regard all my marriages as successful. They may have dried up in the end, but they weren't miserable marriages. I learned from each one. And they've produced five beautiful children.

INT: I stand corrected. Would you tell us what you were looking for in each of your marriages? Then, would you tell us what they were like and what went wrong?

RS: I wanted a devoted wife and muse, a nurturer and a general factotum all in one person. I was looking for the perfect partner—sexually, emotionally, intel-

lectually. Because I came into my first two marriages with the traditional male script, I caused pain for the women, for my children, and for myself. It's sad, but true.

My first, an Iowa Writers' Workshop marriage, ended because of my immaturity. At some level, I didn't know what I wanted. My first wife and I had both grown up in the 1940s on the North Side of Chicago. There was something wonderfully warm and familiar about her. I remember how, on Saturday afternoons, we'd open all the windows in our two-room, Iowa City apartment, turn up the volume on the phonograph, and clean house while playing schmaltzy recordings of *La Boheme* and *Madame Butterfly*.

Then we'd invite friends over and make a big spaghetti dinner. I was happy but, at the same time, I feared I had lost my freedom. I was afraid I was being pressured into getting a regular job. In those days men who married instantly gained twenty or thirty pounds. I was afraid I was going to develop a potbelly and stop writing poetry. So I began willfully scribbling poetry all the time. I was a jerk.

INT: The late 1950s and early 1960s were a productive time for you.

RS: I wrote "Uncle Dog: The Poet at 9" and many of the poems included in the Odyssey Chapbook *Advertisements,* the Putnam, England, edition of *Uncle Dog and Other Poems,* and *Kissing the Dancer.* I associate one, a zany poem titled " . . . I Have Just Bought a House," with my first marriage. That poem is in the form of a letter:

> Dear George—George, I have just bought a
>   house,
> an eighty-seven room house. Also,
> a twenty-one room house. And many
> little houses. And eighteen trailers,
> and nineteen cars (six with beds in them);
> and wives for all the rooms, the trailers
> the little houses, and the six cars
> with beds in them,
>   . . . and they all love me,
> all my wives love me. They do, George . . .

INT: You must know that line from Emily Dickinson: "Is there not a sweet wolf in us that wants what it wants?"

RS: Yes, and there's a connection between that hot, aggressive, sweet wolf in me and the patriarchal role.

INT: And then, Robert, you married a second time.

RS: In an age when there weren't other alternatives, at a time when it was the right thing to do, my second wife and I were propelled into marriage by an unexpected pregnancy. She came from a well-to-do Washington, D.C., Greek Orthodox family. She was a fine mother, a fantastic cook. She loved to entertain. She created a terrific home. In fact, I didn't realize how important home was until the marriage ended. That was one thing I learned from the marriage: that I sincerely wanted a home, family, and children. I learned too that I tended to impose a script on women and limited their growth.

As much as I loved these women, I was callow, shallow, and disloyal, not ready for marriage. All the time I was going scribble scribble scribble. That wasn't so bad. But I was also pant pant panting around. I'd ask myself, What else is out there? What am I missing? I was like a heat-seeking cocky mocky poetry missile. I was a low-down, self-involved dirty dog. Woof, woof. I want. I want. That part of me that needed stability to write was at war with the part that needed to have adventure. And I thought the adventure would help my writing.

INT: In 1967, you left your second wife and ran off to London, England, to live with the British novelist Ann Quin, author of Berg *and* Three. *By all accounts, you were very much in love with Ann. But then you decided to return to the States to be with your children. After all that, what possessed you to marry a third time?*

RS: After being run over by an MG, my reason was swept away by a gorgeous peaches-and-cream New York German-Jewish American stoned sardonic architect princess with a lovely sense of humor and the features of a playboy bunny. I was goo goo, ga ga, a love-hungry yummy dummy. And what a price I paid for that one! At once entertaining and informative, it was like being married for four years to a living technicolor Kama Sutra psychedelic fleshtone get-it-while-it's-hot chapter of American history, all the best and worst aspects of the sexual revolution.

A friend describes the marriage as a combination of thunder, lightning, and intercity rivalry: her New York The Big Apple First City Master Race Center of the Universe versus my pip squeak bourgeois Chicago Second City midwestern Eastern European origins. In her view, people who grew up in Manhattan and attended Music and Art High School are privileged humans, wiser, tougher, and more deserving than anyone else in America. So right from the beginning there was some tension.

In addition, I was formed by the 1940s and cautious 1950s. She was formed by the zipless encounters of the 1960s. "I want an open marriage," she said. Wowwy powwy. "I want a subscription to the *Saturday Evening Post,*" I replied. You know, Barbara, I'm more conventional than my resume might lead you to think. And after four marriages, I find each divorce hurts hurts hurts just as much, maybe more, than the one before.

INT: Hmm. You're referring of course to your marital resume. What goes around, comes around. It sounds to me as if you got what you deserved. But tell us, Robert, after all these years, are you for monogamy?

RS: Yes, I am. I have come to agree with Robert Graves, who says, the act of love is a metaphor of spiritual togetherness, and if you perform the act of love with someone who means little to you, you're giving away something that belongs to the person you do love or might love. The act of love belongs to two people in the way that secrets are shared . . . promiscuity seems forbidden to poets, though I do not grudge it to any non-poet.

I feel I've done some of my best writing when I've been faithful, solid, and secure in a relationship. I need conventional, nitty gritty practicality in my life in order to write zany surreal crazy goofy musical moving tuneful poems and stories and to have a place, a faithful goddess, a base to come back to. All that mindless careless joysticking didn't lead to much readable, let alone memorable, poetry.

INT: What poem of yours do you associate with your third marriage?

RS: There's one called "Scarf Gobble Wallow Inventory," which George Hitchcock published in *Kayak* 21. Robert Vas Dias reprinted "Scarf Gobble . . ." in

Inside Outer Space: New Poems of the Space Age (Doubleday-Anchor). I mention the anthology because the poem is now out of print.

INT: How about a sample?

RS: All I am really hungry for is everything
   The ability to hibernate and a red suitcase go-
      ing off
      everywhere
   Every cell in your body and every cell in my
      body is
      hungry and each has its own stomach . . .

Is the universe a womb or a mouth?
And what *is* hunger, really?
And is the end of the world to be understood in
   terms of
      hunger or gifts, or the tops of peoples'
         heads coming off?

The most complex dream I've ever dreamed I
   dreamed in
   London.
It involved in its entirety taking one bite of an
   orange . . .

Even now we are all saying, over and over,
I've never been so hungry in my life.
I want one more bacon-lettuce-and-tomato
   sandwich,
to make love and kiss everyone I know
   goodbye . . .

INT: Inside Outer Space . . . There's a science-fiction aspect to that poetry anthology, isn't there?

RS: Yes, and there was a science-fiction, War-of-the-Worlds aspect to my third marriage.

INT: Which leads us to your fourth marriage. You were heavily into yoga in 1975, weren't you?

RS: Yes, and Wife Number Four was raised in the Russian Orthodox tradition. She agreed to be married by a yogi. I thought maybe that would help. Mantras,

incense, and a California marriage license. Who knows, all that chanting and meditation may have done some good. That marriage lasted what was, for me, a record-setting twelve years.

When we married, I was forty-two and she was thirty, an artist and a feminist. This time I became the devoted spouse, muse, nurturer, and general factotum. This time, while she complained of being shackled and unfree, I did all I could to make the marriage work. As much as I loved poetry, for example, I began writing articles and features to make money so we could survive and so she could devote herself to her art.

INT: Then what happened?

RS: How does one support a family of four as a freelance writer? As much as I loved her, I was frustrated: I had less and less time to write poetry. And she was fed up living off my marginal income. She was also bored and restless. Fortunately, when the marriage ended, we were living in a spiritual community in the Santa Cruz Mountains. I thought, What good is a spiritual community if it can't help you through a busted marriage? I began by seeking advice from a yogi.

"How come she left?" I asked the yogi.

"She found you boring. She wants fun," he wrote on a small chalkboard.

"Am I boring?"

"No. You have different natures. Women leave you because they want excitement. You are a writer. You live in an abstract world which doesn't excite them."

Then he told me to get a job and make money. He also told me that she had moved in with another man and asked if I could accept that the marriage was over. Well, it turned out he was right on all counts. That happened in August 1985.

Daughter Hannah and son Michael, 1988

INT: After tying and untying the knot four times what did you feel?

RS: I felt ready to jump out of my skin. I was burning up and, at the same time, I felt I had just stepped out of a freezer. When the yogi told me my fourth wife found me boring, I thought, Here's a man who's never been married. Would I trade places with him? I thought, If I had to choose between never marrying and paying the price one pays for breaking up, no, no, better celibacy, better the life of a monk than a much-married man singing the blues.

INT: Fair enough. And how long did that resolution last?

RS: It wasn't exactly a resolution. I lived in a cabin in the Santa Cruz Mountains for six months looking after a seventy-nine-year-old blind woman, a hat-maker known as Mountain Mama. And I worked on my *Collected Poems* and a novel, *How to Cure a Broken Heart*. In 1986, I was ready to move back to civilization.

INT: Santa Cruz is civilization?

RS: Santa Cruz is an exciting place to live. There's lots going on. And, if nothing else, one can count on a little geologic activity. In any case, I needed a job. I found work as a newspaper editor and food reviewer. I taught some poetry courses and continued working on the *Collected Poems*.

INT: And what about your children? How have they turned out?

RS: My oldest daughter, Cheryl, is now a scientist. She does research in limb regeneration and teaches at University College in London, England.

Barbara is a graduate of Berkeley, where she finished first in her class. Barbara lives near San Francisco and works full-time as an environmental scientist. She writes about air pollution and acid rain issues. She's also married and has two children.

Barbara and my oldest son, Michael, are children from my second marriage. Michael is a student at Arizona University in Flagstaff.

Hannah's a dancer and actress. She's working for a degree at Florida International University.

Nicholas, my youngest, is a junior-high student living on Toronto Island. Nicholas's dream is to play professional hockey.

Expensive as it is to travel, we do manage to see one another—though not as often as the old man would like. Nicholas, of course, is with me every summer.

INT: What were the worst and best times in your life?

RS: Before going to India, working for the Authors and Eagles publishing house, I used to jog every day on the beach. One day I found myself jogging and sobbing at the same time. I'd been in Canada since 1969. I was sobbing out of homesickness, out of love for America and my family and friends in the U.S.A. I was sobbing because I felt trapped and didn't know how to get back. I was sobbing because I was grieving for a marriage that had turned sour. I was sobbing because I was working at a stupid, ill-paying job to support a wife and two children and my writing career had gone off the track.

INT: And the best of times?

RS: Now. Being with Gloria. Finding time to write. Because writing is my passion. And teaching, because I love teaching and feel I'm giving more to it now than I ever did in the past.

Erica Jong writes, "At forty-five, you either perish or recreate yourself like a phoenix. I was chosen for the latter course." Barbara, I'm fifty-six years old, but I believe I too was chosen for the latter course. And this is the best of times, no doubt about it.

INT: Coffee House Press plans to publish your Collected Poems in 1991. We'll have to have you back when the book is in the stores.

End of fantasy.

Daughter Barbara Austin and granddaughter Robin, 1990

Part XV

Compatibility Plus (1987--)

In October 1986, I was named editor of a weekly Santa Cruz County newspaper. As editor, I wrote a regular column, the lead news story, back-up stories, features, and profiles. In addition, I took photographs, wrote captions, and worked with the art department to lay out and produce the paper.

In February 1987, the publisher asked me to do a feature on "The Business of Love" for a special Valentine's Day edition. I began my story by phoning Allan Gleicher, a former Westinghouse engineer, and now director of services for Compatibility Plus, an introduction service for "selective single people."

Allan agreed to meet me at a coffee bar in the Capitola Book Cafe, "good neutral ground for a first date." Busy, successful people don't have time to date around, he said. Where are they going to meet other successful people on their own level?

For $495, the matchmaker said he would personally screen a client, and their prospective mates, in order to save everyone time.

Going the Extra Mile for Love

Later, doing more research on love, I learned that the secret of the marriage-broker business (according to Genkichi Ishizaka, the most successful matchmaker in

Japan) is "to get the right boy for the right girl so that their sexual energies will go bang and keep on going bang." To achieve this end, Genkichi Ishizaka says he seeks a combination of the opposites in temperament together with similarity in backgrounds.

To make a long story short, my Valentine feature was published. In March, now an honorary member of Compatibility Plus, I received a complimentary computerized printout with the phone numbers of three well-to-do, upwardly mobile clients. I called one of the three, but my heart wasn't in it.

In June 1987, Allan Gleicher phoned to say he had someone new, someone special he wanted me to meet, a beautiful, warmhearted, emotionally stable, talented woman, recently separated from her spouse. She too was from Chicago. Opposites in temperament, similarities in background, I thought.

"If she's been separated from him for less than a year, I don't want to meet her," I said.

"They've been separated over a year," Allan assured me. "Her name is Gloria Alford. She's an artist, and you were the very first person I thought of."

I decided I wanted to meet this woman.

According to Gloria, I appeared at her door looking like a *Saturday Evening Post* cover. "You were carrying a bouquet of flowers and a poetry book. You had a big innocent smile, and you were all dressed up . . . you had rosy cheeks and a bald spot surrounded with dark, curly hair like a monk . . . and that very first night you told me you had been married four times."

I handed Gloria one of my poetry books—*Half a Life's History*—and she handed me a copy of *Monterey Life* magazine with a profile of her and her artwork. So there we sat in her living room reading about one another. I liked what I read: "If an accepted belief doesn't make sense to her, Gloria will ignore it." Gloria was quoted as saying, "Why not take up new challenges in mid-life, or even in old age? Who determines that youth is the only worthwhile life stage?"

"Gloria majored in social sciences at Berkeley . . . taking a few art classes . . . [and, later] decided to cut her own path [as a sculptor] and make use of new techniques and materials—vacuumformed plastic, screen printing, computer graphics, and printed circuit boards . . . she's now in demand by museums and galleries across the country."

"I knew that night, I had no doubt at all that something very special had happened," Gloria says.

"Why would you be interested in a man who's been married four times?" I asked.

"You make a convincing case you've learned something from your marriages. You know what mistakes you made . . . and you made them all. You're a man who's had some of his rough edges smoothed out. Yet you seem not so much worn down with your four marriages as shined up. So to my eyes, you're more valuable . . . you know, the way certain antiques have a patina on them?"

In *Four Incarnations,* there's a sequence written for Gloria. One of the poems is titled "For Gloria on Her 60th Birthday, or Looking for Gloria in Merriam-Webster." The last two stanzas read:

> She has chestnut-colored hair,
> old fashioned Clara Bow lips,
> moist brown eyes . . .
>   Arms outstretched, head thrown back
> she glides toward me and into her seventh
>   decade.

Her name means "to adore,"
"to rejoice, to be jubilant,
to magnify and honor as in worship, to give or
    ascribe glory—"
    my love, O Gloria, I do, I do.

POSTSCRIPT

Robert Sward contributed the following update in 2002:

Part XVI

Compatibility Plus (2002--)

Fifteen years later Gloria and I are still together. Gloria says, "The matchmaker did good."

Four Incarnations and Counting

In 1989 I lost my job as a technical writer for the Santa Cruz Operation. After about a year of writing software user manuals it was determined that my writing style was too "literary" for a Silicon Valley manufacturer that supplied software to large corporations—and the U.S. military. My chief accomplishment was to help develop an SCO Style Guide, which remained in use until the company, for a variety of reasons, ceased to exist. In any case, my employer and I parted on good terms.

But I brooded on my limitations as a technical writer. After all I was hired, in part, because I was confident I could write anything, including reference guides and user manuals.

After years of writing poetry, assessing and revising my work, sounding every syllable over and over in my mind, exploring the etymology of all words in a given stanza, including basic articles like "and" and "the," I found it difficult to compose a simple prose sentence like "Insert disk A into slot B" without sounding it aloud and considering alternative phrasings.

It is a joke among technical writers that the manuals they produce are out of date almost as soon as they are released. A year or two later I was to hear something similar from Coffee House Press publisher Allan Kornblum. Speaking on the longevity of books, Allan observed, "Volumes of poetry, like user manuals, have a shelf life of something between yogurt and cottage cheese." Anyway, given the slowness with which I compose, my user manuals were out of date weeks, if not months, before they were completed.

I consoled myself: The manuals may be out of date, but when read aloud they sound terrific. Even when I worked as "Mr. Taste Test," a food reviewer for a Santa Cruz County newspaper, I had to sound everything aloud. To this day, when the muse appears, she speaks slowly and distinctly, typically employing the rhythms of everyday speech. She seems to understand that, for this writer, inspiration is an aural event.

Overall, working in Silicon Valley was a humbling and frustrating experience. Sitting in a small, windowless cubicle learning XENIX and UNIX, utterly abandoned by the muse, unable to write anything for nine months except technical manuals, I was genuinely glad to leave.

On the plus side, I left SCO a passionate aficionado, a believer, a devotee of computers. In 1988, a fifty-five-year old naïve user, scarcely able to manage a pull down menu, I would sit in front of some of the most powerful machines then available and fantasize about how one might be able to use the Internet for poetry and fiction: What would it be like to edit or contribute to a literary eZine with tens of thousands of readers? What would it be like to communicate online with fellow writers anywhere in the world? What would it mean to work with graphic images and sound files in an online literary community? Of course scientists, the U.S. military, educators, and even some writer-editors, like Doug Lawson at *Blue Penny Quarterly* and Mike Neff at *Web Del Sol,* had been communicating online for years. A late arrival, in 1988 all this was news to me.

As it turned out, a number of the software engineers and programmers I worked with also proved to be talented writers. Once in a while after hours we'd get together to read aloud our own creations—or the work of others—and good-naturedly critique whatever was being presented. One way and another, pushing sixty, I began to feel part of the online community. Living in Santa Cruz with a beautiful, heartful, emotionally stable, talented woman, I felt I had found a home.

Why I Publish in eZines (1994—)

From the time of my first publications in the late 1950s—in Henry Rago's *Poetry* (Chicago), George Starbuck's *Chicago Review,* and Carolyn Kizer's *Poetry Northwest*—my poetry and book reviews appeared largely in hardcopy literary quarterlies. When, in 1994, my work began to appear online in *Blue Penny Quarterly* (now *Blue Moon Review*), *Web Del Sol, Realpoetik, Recursive Angel, Zero City* and other eZines, I became known as a "bridge person," a poet-teacher with a literary track record crossing over from the world of hardcopy print publications to some rapidly emerging electronic outlets.

Publishing on the Net was a liberating experience. In 1996 I explained why in an essay, "Why I Publish in eZines." A few brief excerpts:

> Computer-phobic writers, teaching cronies and fans of old style litmags ask why I have chosen to publish in eZines like *Alsop Review, Blue Penny Quarterly, X-Connect, eSCENE,* and *Fiction Online* . . .

> 1. I publish on the Net because it's cheap—e-mail after all is free.

> 2. It's more efficient—no SASEs, no International Reply Coupons; fewer trips to the office supply store.

> 3. It saves time—I don't have to wait eighteen months to hear back and the rejections, when they come, are less annoying because a) I've invested less in the submission process and b) it's easy enough to send the work somewhere else.

> 4. It gives me the opportunity to improve on what I write and make changes even after publication. Zen Buddhists say First thought, best thought. I say, Think again.

5. It allows for interaction—timely feedback from fellow writers, editors, publishers, agents, and students.

One quiet afternoon in 1994 I sent a poem to *Realpoetik* ("rpoetik, the little magazine of the Internet, a moderated listserv . . ."), got an e-mail acceptance message and saw the poem published, all within twenty-four hours. Editor Robert Salasin claims he has approximately one thousand subscribers. All I know is that over the next few days I got more responses ("fine work . . . ," "wish you continued success in Cyberspace . . . ," "would like to use excerpts from *A Much-Married Man* . . .") from that single appearance than I got from thirty years of publishing in magazines like the *Antioch Review,* the *Hudson Review,* the *Nation,* the *New Yorker,* the *Transatlantic Review,* etc.

Yes, it's a form of instant gratification. Just what the world needs, right? In my opinion, instant gratification has gotten a bad rap. Or maybe I'm late to the game and am just beginning to catch on. Anyway, I write for myself and always have, but I still agree with Whitman: it doesn't hurt to have an audience.

I still use pen and pencil to write and revise and turn to my fifty-year-old Olympia portable to type envelopes. I'm still doing what I did in my twenties: writing, revising, and sending the best work I have to the editors of the journals I admire.

Writing is rewriting and I spend just as much time revising now as I ever did. To this day I send poems and stories to traditional print journals and, when the publication appears, sometimes long to remove a line or two or correct a typo or printer's error. A while back the *Transatlantic Review* published *Thousand-Year-Old Fiancée* and destroyed the poem, made it meaningless with a record thirteen typographical errors. They never sent me page proofs and, once the poem was printed, there was nothing I could do except rage at the editor, the inattentive, lackadaisical schmuck.

Now, when I submit work to an e-journal, there is no typographer involved because there is no type to set. And if an error occurs or I change my mind, voila!, I can e-mail corrections and see the fix made promptly and at no expense. I like that . . .

*

I'm doing multimedia stuff now combining poetry, fiction and nonfiction with photographs, paintings and—

soon—music and the human voice. I'm collaborating with visual artists, computer scientists, and other writers . . .

My first computer was an Apple IIe and my first word processing program was Magic Window. Today I use Microsoft Word on a Mac Performa supercharged by my eighteen-year-old son. How does it all work? I have no idea. I just switch on my modem, gaze into cyberspace, and type away. It's still Magic Window to me.

"So what's the point?" my partner wants to know. "Isn't this just one big ego trip? Who really reads those e-journals? Do you actually think you're going to sell copies of your book on the Net? What about copyright? How do you know someone isn't going to rip off that new book of yours?"

Of course she's right, but I have all those virtual magazines and editors on the Net waiting for me to check in.

"Gee, honey, I don't know," I say. "I'm just gonna go upstairs for a moment and check my mail."

*

Much has changed since 1996, but reading eZines and checking email are still obsessions.

Money, Inspiration, and the Muse

In a capitalist country, money is oxygen. As someone plagued by asthma, I find an inverse relationship between the amount of money I have in the bank and the need for inhalers. When I'm in debt, I struggle for breath. When I am free of debt, I breathe easy. Money is oxygen. Question: What is the relationship between money and the muse?

Still, speaking as a writer, I find the only thing better than being employed is being unemployed. SCO paid well and offered any number of benefits to departing employees. I was virtually given a Macintosh computer and with that, plus unemployment benefits, I set to work on *Four Incarnations: New and Selected Poems,* which was published in 1991.

At a bookstore reading with poet and jazz critic **William Minor** *(left), who wrote the introduction to* **Rosicrucian in the Basement,** *1991*

"Ah, that reminds me of a joke," said a computer engineer at my farewell party. "A man goes to the doctor and the doctor says, 'You have a book in you and I'm afraid it's going to have to come out.'"

As William Stafford once observed, "Every emergency is also an opportunity."

The end of every story is the beginning of another. That may also be a cliché, but it's true.

*

Anyway, apart from writing a book—and what led, or may have led, to the writing—there is always the story of the author's adventures in seeing the volume through the editing, design and production stages and into print. Founder of a Canadian publishing house (Soft Press, Victoria, B.C.) and, later, production

manager at a commercial publishing firm, I like to be as involved as possible in all aspects of a book's creation. My podiatrist father used to say that it takes as many as thirty people to produce a good pair of shoes. Quality book production is also a collaborative process. Still, no matter how involved an author has been, at one stage or another, it is necessary to surrender control and simply pray for the best. Like a mother in labor, you never really know what your creation is going to look like until you hold it in your hands.

Four Incarnations, Four Incarcerations,

Four Incantations . . .

In 1991, shortly before *Four Incarnations* appeared, prematurely celebrating its publication, I phoned Allan Kornblum in Minneapolis. "Robert, I need to tell you, your book was typeset, laid out, shipped to the printer, but it never arrived. It seems to have been lost en route," he said, preparing me for the worst. Later, the book did, in fact, arrive at the printer, but it turned out that someone along the way had gotten it into his or her head that the title was not meant to read *Four Incarnations* but, rather, *Four Incarcerations.* That meant the cover needed to be redone.

No book appears without mishaps and I am grateful to Allan and Coffee House Press for producing and enthusiastically promoting what turned out to be a very attractive and well-received little volume.

One gains self-knowledge in the course of writing a book. One learns something further when one promotes it. So it was that this anxious author, waiting for the volume to arrive, again jumped the gun and dropped off the press kit at a local newspaper. Noting the facsimile cover on the envelope, the author photo, and heft of the package, the editor remarked, "I'll look forward to reading your poems, Robert. An envelope, *Four Incantations,* hmm . . . makes an unusual cover, doesn't it?"

"Wait, wait, Mr. Editor. Look again, this is the *press kit.* The book is still at the printer."

To this day I still see occasional newspaper references to "Four Incarcerations" and "Four Incantations."

Coming up to the Big "7-0"

I'm not there yet, but soon enough I'm going to turn seventy. The Big "7-0."

A wise man says, "It takes several lives to make one person." I believe that and that we are also, all of us, phoenixes rising daily from the ashes of our old selves, the ashes of the many lives we have lived in our one lifetime.

The fin-de-siècle Viennese writer Arthur Schnitzler wrote, "The soul is a vast domain . . . So many contradictions find room in us . . . We try our best to maintain order in ourselves, but this order is really just synthetic. Our natural condition is chaos."

Speaking of chaos, one reviewer wrote that "*Four Incarnations* is named for four distinct periods in Sward's writing career . . . shaped by four marriages

and four dramatic changes . . ." I wonder sometimes: does that peculiar use of the word *and* suggest that my four marriages were something less than dramatic?

If I have learned anything as a much-married man it is that there is a very thin line between drama, divorce, and complete disorder and confusion. For what it's worth, in my experience, it usually takes twelve to eighteen months to heal from that sort of drama. That's if one's lucky. And apart from the emotional price, there's the financial cost and the horrendous toll such things take on one's children. Yes, I feel guilty. How could I not?

Friends ask, "Does it get easier . . . does getting divorced and getting divorced again . . . does it get easier, the second or third time around?"

No. One feels like a loser, one feels like a jerk. Life is change, but how much drama, chaos, and disorder does a person need? I've noticed, by the way, that the books that have been best received—*Kissing the Dancer, Four Incarnations, Rosicrucian in the Basement,* and *Heavenly Sex*—were written not in times in chaos, but when I felt more or less secure and, dare I say, happy in my home life?

In the '60s and '70s I took pride in being called "wild man," "crazy," a "zany." I experimented with psychedelics and bought into the Romantic notion that to carouse, to indulge, to play Dionysian "mad poet" would help me tap into what I believed to be a rich source of poetry. So it was I tried—and tried again—writing under the influence. It may have worked for Coleridge, Baudelaire, and Ginsberg, but I was seldom happy with the results. To this day my drug of choice is freshly ground premium coffee.

Blake suggests that the way to wisdom is through excess. Maybe, maybe not. These days I'm paying more attention to Ben Franklin and less to Blake. "Early to bed, early to rise, makes a man healthy, wealthy and wise." Whatever works. Whatever furthers the writing.

As for incarnations, I believe most of us live more than one life in a lifetime. For an American, there's nothing special about this. Multiple incarnations are simply a condition of our time, especially in California where reinventing oneself is now a virtual industry.

Looking back I see that, without intending to do so, I spent most of the 1990s writing poetry and fiction having to do almost entirely with Marriage and the Family.

Four Incarnations, in fact, was followed by a book titled *Family* (Select Poets Series, 1994), described by publisher David Alpaugh as "a fresh look at family life by four award-winning Northern California poets and writers, Charles Atkinson, Tilly Shaw, David Swanger, and Robert Sward. All four of the contributors to *Family* teach at the University of California at Santa Cruz."

Atkinson, Shaw, Swanger, and I are part of a writing group that has met once or twice a month for the past ten years (1992—) to critique one another's work. Our little volume grew out of working sessions where we noticed how many of our poems had to do with love, divorce, incest, multiple marriage, aging, loss, and the challenge of bringing up children in a highly unstable world. For the record, since 1994 the writing group has also included the visual artist Douglas McClellan and the brilliant critic and poet Dion Farquhar.

Family was followed by *Uncivilizing* (Insomniac Press, 1997), a collection of poetry by six Canadian, American and British writers: Bernice Lever, Caroline Davidson, Roger Nash, Sonja Dunn, James Reaney, and myself. Why *Uncivilizing*? Because that volume was intended as a response by the six to the shake, rattle, and roll of one century as, in a time of mindless violence and greed—Post-Civilization—it gave birth to the next.

While evidence of uncivilizing continues to mount, the Insomniac Press collection bears testimony to some generosity of spirit and resiliency. How else might these poems come to have been written?

Hope is apparent, too, I feel, in my wife Gloria's cover art, a vision of the future, of the Twenty-first Century as a time of balance and harmony, a peaceable kingdom, a lion asleep in the lap of a woman reading, the world, at last, re-civilized.

Computers, Artists' Colonies, and *Heavenly Sex*

Teaching eleven years for University of California Extension and Cabrillo College, largely self-sufficient, working out of my little redwood tower—with a nearby community of friends—I had little urge to spend time, as I once did, at blessed places like the MacDowell Colony and Yaddo.

The truth is, much of my best early work, I feel, was done at those artists' colonies. So it was in 1993, recalling what it was like to work in a supportive environment without distraction, ready to move forward on my second novel, *A Much-Married Man,* and some other projects, I applied—with the encouragement of two longtime friends, Carolyn Kizer and Diane Johnson—for residency at Dr. Carl Djerassi's "colony" in Woodside, CA.

A ninety-minute drive up the rugged coast from Santa Cruz, the Djerassi Foundation was within easy reach of "home." Weekends I'd spend with Gloria. Weekdays I'd work eight to ten hours, forty hours a week, at the writing. Yes, my podiatrist father was a nine-to-five workaholic and set an example for me with his ethic. Nutty as it may sound, I apply my podiatrist father's work rhythms to staring at my computer monitor and, every couple years, producing a new book of poetry or fiction.

Among the poems I generated at Djerassi were some that, later revised, found their way into *Rosicrucian in the Basement* (Black Moss Press, 2001) and *Heavenly Sex* (Black Moss Press, 2002).

Robert Bly, whom I had met in 1962 when I was teaching at Cornell University, was particularly helpful and encouraging with respect to developing the Rosicrucian podiatrist father poems and the relationship between father and son. Once, when I was struggling with a key poem in the sequence, Bly wrote, "I like the wide sweep of it. There are many mysteries between father and son that people don't talk about . . . There's much leaping, but each line, so to speak, steps firmly on something solid . . . The father figure comes through consistently, there's a lot of buoyancy, and the son is consistent and fine too."

I am deeply grateful, too, to poet and critic Dana Gioia, for his inspired suggestion that I develop the dramatic and narrative elements in both books and even include additional characters. Prior to *Rosicrucian,* I had not thought of myself as a narrative poet. In *Heavenly Sex,* the sexy, silvery-blonde stepmother, Lenore, and the talking, voyeuristic Catahoula Leopard Dog now fill out the cast of characters.

New, too, are the audio CDs: *Rosicrucian in the Base-ment* (Uncle Dog Audio, 2002) and the KPFA Radio (San Francisco) *Poetry, Review and Interview with Jack Foley* (Uncle Dog Audio, 2002). I worked for several years for CBC Radio in Toronto and have always enjoyed listening to and producing shows with writers and musicians. The new series of audio CDs is a step further in this direction. Including sound files that may be downloaded from literary eZines like Jaimes Alsop's *Alsop Review* is another.

Certainly I was heartened when Dana said of the *Rosicrucian* audio CD that it "unfolds perfectly at its own pace and never loses the listener."

The Rosicrucian One Dollar Bill

Following my mother's death in 1948, my father suf-fered greatly, wailing and howling for days. My eleven-year-old sister and I had no idea what to do for him or how to ease his—or our own—sense of loss and pain. Young as I was, my father asked me to ac-company him on some of his drinking and carousing expeditions along Rush Street on the near north side of Chicago. At fifteen I was a very unhappy, puzzled fellow, drinking highballs, smoking cigarettes, and conversing with what seemed to me equally unhappy and confused hookers.

Later Dad sought consolation in a number of self-help books, starting with Dr. Norman Vincent Peale's *The Power of Positive Thinking* and Dale Carnegie's *How to Win Friends and Influence People*. For all his good intentions, Dad's outlook remained negative and, if anything, he seemed to lose what few friends he had rather than gain new ones.

Then, following a heart attack, Dad transformed, seemed "to find himself," as he put it. Expressing great annoyance at my reservations and questions, he became a strict and devout member of what he called "the true and invisible Rosicrucian Order."

With his study of the "invisible," my father, though outwardly loving, became ever more secretive and, so it seemed to me, inaccessible. That was the year I flunked algebra and trained for the Von Steuben High School track team by running late at night up and back the couple miles from our home to Sonny

Father, Irving M. Sward, a central figure in several of the author's works

Berkowitz's pool hall on Lawrence Avenue. I hung out at the pool hall, read all I could of Chicago's James T. Farrell, gorged myself on Twinkies, Hershey bars and what, in those days, was called soda pop.

For my podiatrist father, Rosicrucianism is allied with Kabbalah—Jewish mysticism—and he sought to put himself "on the right track for union with the Higher Self." So here he was, a poor immigrant to the U.S., a small businessman, an Eisenhower and Nixon Repub-lican living in a conservative neighborhood on the far North Side of Chicago thinking and talking—in the privacy of our suburban home—like the New Age hip-pies and yogis I came to meet a decade or two later.

Naturally, under the circumstances, we quarreled, and I remember more than one period in which we went days without speaking to one another. We had some religious and philosophical differences. Just as parents typically wish for their children to remain true to the family's religion, so children wish for their parents to do the same. In the poem "Rosicrucian in the Base-ment" I ask:

"What is it with the cross? You believe in Jesus, dad?"

"What?"

"Are you still a Jew?"

He turns away.

"Damnit, it's not a religion, *verstehst*?"
        Brings fist down on the altar.
"We seek the perfection of metals," he says,
        re-lighting stove,
                "salvation by smelting."

"But what's the point?" I ask.

"The point? Internal alchemy, *shmegegge. Rosa
    mystica*," he shouts.
"Meat into spirit, darkness into light."

The poem goes on:

Seated now, seated on bar stools.
Flickering candle in a windowless room.
Visible and invisible. Face of my father
        in the other world.
I see him, see him in me
my rosy cross
            podiatrist father.
"I'm making no secret of this secret," he says,
turning to the altar.
"Tell me, tell me how to pray," I say.
"Burst," he says, "burst like a star."

Later, when I ask him, "What is a Rosicrucian,"
    he replies,

"Franklin was a Rosicrucian.
He made it. He made
    the one dollar bill.
Open your wallet, take out a dollar.
Money talks, in pictures
    it talks. See,
            Egyptian pyramid.
Money, American money
    with a pyramid.

The eagle, that you understand,
        thunderbolts in one hand,
olive branch in the other.
So, the pyramid,
        what does *that* say?
'You have no idea,' it says,
'you don't know the value of money.
Money is to remind you
what's important in life.' Look:
see, a halo with lines . . .
        above the pyramid,
'Glory,' that's what they call it,
a 'Glory,' burst of light
with the eye of God inside.
But the pyramid is unfinished,
it needs work, like you.

"'Ach, enough! Enough with money,' says
    money.
Just remember, God has His eye on you.
And the sun and the moon and the stars are
    inside you.
So listen, listen to the pyramid.
You can't buy your way into heaven, it's true,
but you need to know money to get there."
        (From "The Rosicrucian One Dollar Bill")

Something like that really happened. Yes, that is indeed the way my father introduced me to Rosicrucianism. As he went on to explain, in 1776 the Continental Congress asked Ben Franklin, the quintessential American, Thomas Jefferson, and John Adams to come up with a design for America's Great Seal. America, after all, was a new country and needed to create its own currency. Franklin, then a member of a worldwide society, the Free and Accepted Masons, was, my father believed, also a Rosicrucian. Jefferson and Adams may also have shared these beliefs and that is why the American one dollar bill includes the curious image of a pyramid, the Egyptian "eye of God," and the Latin phrase *e pluribus unum,* "out of many, one." Occult wisdom always leads away from the diversity and distraction of the outer world, my father explained, to the unity at the heart of being.

Patriotic, my father also invoked Ralph Waldo Emerson, who claimed that, following the Revolution, all succeeding generations could see God only at second hand, while Franklin, Jefferson, and Adams had seen Him face to face. "So, Bobby, you too want to see

God face to face? Then look, look into the eye of God on the one dollar bill. Tell me, son, when will you learn? When will you learn the value of money?"

In Jungian psychology the mandala is believed to be a symbol representing the self and harmony within the individual. My father never used the word "mandala," but, for him, the "Rosicrucian One Dollar Bill" represented everything he needed to know about the Self and the universe and how to survive in this world and find one's way to the next.

Born in Russia at the turn of the twentieth century, an Orthodox Jew, the son of a poor tailor, my father, too, it seems, went through more than one incarnation.

Part XVII

The Blue Gum Eucalyptus and the Chain-Saw Solution

I am not a political person. I'm a poet, a writer who basically likes to be alone. Every two or three years I have a book come out and travel and do some readings, after which I retreat back into my shell and go on writing. I like it like that.

Now suddenly, in my sixty-ninth year, everything has changed. Fifty years after my first publication, about to embark on a tour with my twentieth book, *Heavenly Sex,* I have become momentarily newsworthy, but not for my poetry. On September 17, 2002, the *Los Angeles Times* ran a front-page "Column One" feature, "Tempest in the Treetops," in which I was identified as a "tree-killing poet" for resorting to what the reporter called a "botanical form of civil disobedience."

Widely syndicated some weeks before by Ted Williams, a writer from *Audubon Magazine,* the story ("How to Get Busted for Arboricide in California"), now illustrated and expanded on in the *Los Angeles Times,* was quickly picked up by CBC Radio's "As It Happens" and other print and electronic media in the U.S. and Canada.

Whatever media interest Black Moss Press and Firefly, their distributor, may have won for *Heavenly Sex* and *Rosicrucian in the Basement,* now gave way to this flurry of attention on "California's Eucalyptus Wars."

As I write this, I am at the center of what seems to be a national controversy involving (a) people who would protect native plants and (b) others, the pro-eucalyptus faction, that would protect the highly invasive, recently introduced, flammable blue gum. Ironically, I find myself the enemy of some concerned citizens who have formed a group called P.O.E.T. (Preserve Our Eucalyptus Trees), dedicated to stopping people like me from removing the blue gum eucalyptus.

A poet accused of arboricide, not a pleasant way to be labeled in the media, I have also been called a philistine ("Anyone who wants to cut a tree of any size is regarded as a philistine," *Los Angeles Times,* September 17, 2002) and an individual with a "pathological fear" of trees.

Now I think of Annie Dillard who wrote, "Writing in the first person can trap the writer into airing grievances . . . while literature is an art, it is not a martial art."

She's right, of course. And I'm aware, as I'm sure the reader is, of a subtle shift in tone as my agitation begins to show. A sort of "before your very eyes, watch now as this mild-mannered, somewhat reclusive septuagenarian, this laid-back temperate man of letters, begins to loose his cool."

The good news is I got to read poetry on a nationally broadcast radio show, but it was doggerel, a four-line, previously unpublished verse that served to cap an interview and make a point:

Blue Gum Euc

Deadly beauty,
Much to admire
Until it falls
Or catches on fire.

And, as I acknowledged on CBC's "As It Happens," the poem was written by my wife, not by me. There's good doggerel and there's bad doggerel. Gloria's little verse meets the aesthetic standard of "less is more" and in twelve words manages to capture the essence of our eleven-year fight with city hall, one summarized nicely, by the way, in another headline, "The Killer of

Killer Trees out on a Limb in Santa Cruz." The lead in that story read: "Robert Sward, 69, of Santa Cruz, doesn't look, sound or act like a tree murderer."

Facing a fine and costs of up to $10,000, my wife and I took pleasure where we could find it. For example, a local newspaper, alluding to my poem "Uncle Dog," ran the headline, "Barking up a Eucalyptus Tree."

Though initially disinclined to write about our prolonged involvement in the eucalyptus wars—what does it have to do with poetry?—I find it impossible to speak of the last decade or so without at least some mention of how and why I have spent so much of my time fighting city hall.

Our war with those Santa Cruz city fathers who ferociously defend all trees—no matter where they come from or how deadly they may be in an urban environment—began in 1987, when Gloria and I first got together.

It peaked May 18, 2002, when I removed two of eight diseased blue gum eucs from our property. Our trees, our property, our danger.

Danger? What Danger?

On March 5, 1996, during a fierce storm, one of several eucalyptuses on a neighboring parcel nearly took out a Pacific Gas & Electric substation. My wife went outside to inspect. As she gazed into the churning sea of foliage, a nearby PG&E worker called out a warning.

Gloria took a few steps backward just as the swollen green-gray mass of another blue gum eucalyptus slammed to the ground nearby.

As the *Los Angeles Times* put it, "In its descent, the tree took out electrical lines on both sides of the street and snapped a telephone pole like a toothpick. [Santa Cruz's] local newspaper put this near-miss story on its front page."

Later, one of the city's own certified arborists told me, "Robert, there are two people on city council who would not move a eucalyptus off the body of a small child."

I am not a political person, but when my wife, our children, our grandchildren, and our home are endangered by elected officials whose version of political correctness is more important than public safety, I rebel.

In 1991, following the Oakland Hills fire, I began boning up on our foe, the grove of shallow-rooted, 200-foot, bark-shedding trees that overhang our home. In short, my crusade against the eucs began when I watched TV news reports of the 1991 eucalyptus-fueled fire, ninety miles north of our home, a fire that claimed twenty lives and caused more than $5 billion damage. That fight picked up some steam in 1996 following my wife's near death-by-eucalyptus episode.

My research led me write my own poem on the subject, "Ten Years under the Eucalyptus—The Tree That Destroyed California." Not something I would include in a book, excerpts may be appropriate here because the material does, after all, summarize something of the conditions under which we have lived since 1987:

Ten Years under The Eucalyptus—
The Tree That Destroyed California

It was all a mistake.

The tree that destroyed California
stands to burn down our house.
Came from Australia,
its oily, reddish bark
a clothing of finest fluffy timber.

A dream, the California dream:
    drought resistant,
    resistant to insects,
    fast-growing . . .

But no good for lumber ("too brittle"),
no good for windbreak ("blasting crown of fire
    torching everything around it"),
no good in a city,
no good in the country ("secreting toxins,
    it destroys all native plants")

Gee, let's bring it to California and see how it
  does.
Ta da! The tree from hell,
tree that needs fire to propagate,
    seeds, little eucalypts
shooting off in all directions.
Good news for pyromaniacs,
a whole tree, oily sap a boil,
exploding in one big Whoosh!

. . . Climax vegetation, end-of-the-line tree,
death to the host vegetation,
death without regeneration.

"I rise in flame," says the Blue Gum Eucalyptus,
"I rise in flame, but you don't."

So it was, after a decade of unsuccessfully fighting for
permission to ax our grove—our trees, our property,
our home—a retired college professor and a staunch
environmentalist, I hired a roustabout tree cutter to
take them out.

The eucalyptus police, as locals call them, were quick
to arrive.

Suddenly we were faced with a fine of $2500, payable
within forty-eight hours or else, the "else" being an
additional fine of $2500 for each day we delayed and,
if we didn't pay up as required, a lien on our house.
Senior citizens on a limited income, we are currently
fighting a "mitigation" plan that stands to cost
thousands more.

"That's enough about the trees," says my wife,
"enough already."

Death Is What Happens When All You Have Left Is
    The Life That Was There All Along

Some of the poems in *Heavenly Sex* are sexy. Some
are heavenly or concerned with heavenly matters. Others are both heavenly and sexy. The poem "After the
Bypass," written after my father's surgery, focuses on
death, loneliness, and fear. At the same time, it touches
on sex, what it means to be invisible, the Talmud,
money, and the pleasures of hospital food.

According to Mutlu Konuk Blasing, the subject of
autobiography is "the self becoming conscious of itself
in and as history. The recognition of one's identity as
consciousness attests to one's identity with all
conscious beings."

As I worked on the final section of "After the Bypass,"
a dialogue between a presumably departed father and
his grieving son, I reached a point in the piece where
the deceased remarks,

". . . I have a treasure now, it's true,
but no body.
And you, you meshugge, you have a body,
but no treasure.
You should take a year off. Spend some time
at the Invisible College."

For many days I was stuck. I couldn't go forward
until I knew how to end the poem. Thank God for
swimming. Two or three times a week I swim in an
outdoor heated pool at UC Santa Cruz. One afternoon
while swimming laps, I seemed to go into an altered
state. The muse had a line for me: "Death is what happens when all you have left is the life that was there
all along."

What the hell does that mean? I thought.

That we bring with us, that is, that we come into this
life with consciousness, take on some physical form
and, when we die, all there is left is the life, the
consciousness that was there all along.

Continuing to swim laps I thought, That's interesting.
Meanwhile, the water ceased to be water. I don't know
how to say this, but I went on swimming, lap after
lap, without a body. More to the point, it was as if my
physical form and the water in the pool had become
one. This was accompanied by a sense of incredible
well-being.

Then I thought, Gee, that's a good line. But I was
feeling so good I didn't want to get out of the pool to
write it down. I wanted to continue swimming. If I got
out of the pool I knew I would lose the intense physical pleasure I was having. I also knew that if I
continued swimming I stood a good chance of losing
an interesting line.

With wife, artist Gloria Alford, Santa Cruz, 2002

So I called for help, motioned to the lifeguard who clambered down from her perch and I heard myself say, "I'm sorry, but please, I need your help . . . I need a pen and some paper."

With a puzzled expression, shaking her head, God bless her, she obliged.

So it was I was able to complete "After the Bypass," the final section of which reads (in my father's voice):

"Now I'll tell you about death.
Life has an eye to see, says Talmud,
    but what do you think Death has?
Death is made of eyes,
    made of eyes, dressed in eyes.

And when she comes, she comes with a knife
    in her hands.
And you go through the wall and it's a flaming
    word.
Death is what happens when all you have left
    is that life that was there all along.
But remember: you're still gonna need money
    when you die."

BIOGRAPHICAL AND CRITICAL SOURCES:

BOOKS

Contemporary Poets, 7th edition, St. James Press (Detroit, MI), 2001.
The Face of Poetry, Heidelberg Graphics, 1979.

Sward, Robert, *Kissing the Dancer and Other Poems,* introduction by William Meredith, Cornell University Press, 1964.

Sward, Robert, *Half a Life's History, Poems: New and Selected, 1957-1983,* introduction by Earle Birney, Volume IV, AYA Press, 1983.

Sward, Robert, *Rosicrucian in the Basement,* introduction by William Minor, Blackmoss Press, 2001.

PERIODICALS

Canadian Literature, spring, 1985.

Carleton Miscellany, spring, 1967, Lawrence Lieberman, review of *Kissing the Dancer and Other Poems.*

Chicago Sunday Tribune, April 12, 1992, "Literary Events," p. 3.

Des Moines Sunday Register, May 10, 1992, Ann Struthers, "Off-the-wall Approach Energizes Sward's Poetry."

Excalibur, April 2, 1981, Stuart Ross, interview.

Harvard Review Poetry Room, June, 1992, Tina Barr, review of *Four Incarnations: New and Selected Poems, 1957-1991.*

Monday Magazine (Victoria, British Columbia, Canada), October 13, 1975.

New York Review of Books, March 31, 1966.

New York Times Book Review, October 25, 1964, John Malcolm Brinnin, review of *Kissing the Dancer and Other Poems;* April 17, 1966.

Pacific Northwest Review of Books, April, 1978.

Poetry, April, 1963.

Poetry Flash, February, 1992, Richard Silberg, review of *Four Incarnations.*

Publishers Weekly, October 18, 1991, review of *Four Incarnations.*

Santa Cruz Sentinel, November 18, 1991, Christine Watson, "A Poet Knows It: Poet Robert Sward Finds His Inspiration in Life's Incarnations," pp. A9-A10.

Times Literary Supplement, August 18, 1966.

Washington Times, December 15, 1991, Susan Shapiro, review of *Four Incarnations.*

OTHER

Blue Moon Review, http://www.thebluemoon.com/oldtime.shtml (November 27, 2002).

Cabrillo College, http://www.cabrillo.cc.ca.us/divisions/english/engl/rsward/quake/ (1998).

Robert Sward's Web Page, http://www.robertsward.com (November 27, 2002).

University of California Santa Cruz McHenry Library Special Collections, http://library.ucsc.edu/ (November 27, 2002).

Washington University's Olin Library, http://library.wustl.edu/ (November 27, 2002).

Web del Sol, http://www.webdelsol.com/ (November 27, 2002).

T

TABLADA, José Juan 1871-1945

PERSONAL: Born April 3, 1871, in Mexico City, Mexico; died August 2, 1945, in New York, NY; married wife, Evangelina, c. 1908 (divorced); married Nina Cabrera, 1918. *Education:* Attended military school.

CAREER: Writer. Worked as railroad clerk, 1890s; reporter for *El Universal;* member of Mexican Department of Education, c. 1908; wine merchant; Mexican diplomat in Colombia, Ecuador, and Venezuela. Founded Librería de los Latinos, 1920.

WRITINGS:

IN ENGLISH

Contributor to periodicals, including *International Studio, Shadowland,* and *Survey Graphic.* Editor, *Mexican Art and Life,* 1938-39.

IN ENGLISH TRANSLATION

Work represented in anthologies, including *Anthology of Mexican Poetry,* edited by Octavio Paz, [Bloomington, IN], 1958; and *New Poetry of Mexico,* edited by Octavio Paz and others, [New York, NY], 1970.

OTHER

El florilegio (poetry; title means "Floral Wreath"), [Mexico City, Mexico], 1899, revised edition, 1904.

La epopeya nacional: Porfirio Díaz (poetry; title means "The National Epic Poem: Porfirio Díaz"), [Mexico City, Mexico], 1909.

Tiros al blanco (Actualidades políticas) (articles; title means "Shots at the Target"), [Mexico City, Mexico], 1909.

Madero-Chantecler (verse play), 1910.

La defensa social: Historia de la campaña de la división del norte (essay; title means "The Social Defense: A History of the Campaign of the Northern Division"), [Mexico City, Mexico], 1913.

Hiroshigué: El pintor de la nieve y de la lluvia, de la noche y de la luna (title means "Hiroshige: Painter of the Snow and the Rain, of the Night and the Moonlight"), 1914.

Los días y las noches de París (journalism; title means "Parisian Days and Nights"), 1918.

Al sol y bajo la luna (poetry; title means "In the Sun and under the Moon"), [Mexico City, Mexico], 1918.

Un día . . . Poemas sintéticos (poetry; title means "One Day . . . Synthetic Poems"), 1919.

En el país del sol (vignettes; title means "In the Land of the Sun"), [Mexico City, Mexico], 1919.

Li-Po y otros poemas (poetry; title means "Li-Po and Other Poems"), 1920.

Cultura mexicana: Artes plásticas—Periodos precortesiano, colonial, y moderno (lecture; title means "Mexican Culture: Plastic Arts—Pre-Cortez, Colonial, and Modern Periods"), 1920.

Antología general de José Juan Tablada (collected works), edited by Enrique González Martinez, [Mexico City, Mexico], 1920.

El jarro de flores: Disociaciones líricas (poetry; title means "The Flower Vase"), 1922.

La resurrección de los ídolos (novel; title means "The Resurrection of the Idols"), [Mexico City, Mexico], 1924.

Intersecciones (poetry), [Mexico City, Mexico], 1924.

(Editor and translator) *El arca de Noé* (children's book; title means "Noah's Ark"), 1926.

Historia del arte en México (title means "History of Art in Mexico"), [Mexico City, Mexico], 1927.

La feria (Poemas mexicanos) (poetry), [New York, NY], 1928.

La feria de la vida (memoirs; title means "The Fair of Life"), [Mexico City, Mexico], 1937.

Los mejores poemas de José Juan Tablada (title means "The Major Poems of de José Juan Tablada"), [Mexico City, Mexico], 1943.

Del humorismo a la carcajada (vignettes and jokes; title means "From Humor to a Peal of Laughter"), [Mexico City, Mexico], 1944.

Obras (collected works), edited by Jorge Ruedas de la Serna and Esperanza Lara Velázquez, Volume 1: *Poesía*, [Mexico City, Mexico], 1971; Volume 2: *Satira política*, [Mexico City, Mexico], 1981.

Work represented in anthologies, including *Antología de jóvenes poetas mexicanos* (title means "Anthology of Young Mexican Poets"), 1922.

Author of column "Rostros y máscaras" (title means "Faces and Masks") in *El Universal*, c. 1890. Contributor to periodicals, including *El Pais, El siglo XIX, La Patria Ilustrada, Revista de Revistas,* and *Revista Azul.* Chief editor, *El Imparcial*, 1912-13. Founded *La Revista Moderna*, 1898.

SIDELIGHTS: José Juan Tablada was a notable Mexican diplomat and writer who produced more than twenty publications during a literary career that spanned the first half of the twentieth century. Tablada published his first poem in 1889, when he was still in his teens, and issued his first collection, *El florilegio,* ten years later. In his early poems, Tablada demonstrated his affinity for both the French symbolists, notably Charles Baudelaire, as well as more modernist modes of expression.

A second edition of *El florilegio,* appearing in 1904, also serves as evidence of Tablada's longtime interest in Japanese culture, including the haiku form. That interest led him to Japan in 1900, and that journey, in turn, inspired him to produce a series of vignettes that were eventually collected as *En el país del sol,* which was published in 1919. His interest in Japanese art and culture also led him to write *Hiroshigué: El pintor de la nieve y de la lluvia, de la noche y de la luna,* a study—replete with reproductions—of the master painter Hiroshige.

After returning to Mexico and expanding *El florilegio,* Tablada occupied himself by writing newspaper articles, some of which he collected in 1921 as *Tiros al blanco.* He allowed fourteen years to pass before he issued another sizeable poetry collection, *Al sol y bajo la luna.* In this volume, Tablada once again evokes Asian places and culture, but he also demonstrates his grasp of developing Dadaism. Two years later, Tablada produced *Li-Po y otros poemas,* a collection in which he proved himself a master of visual poetry, wherein the structure resembles the shape of various objects. "Although Tablada is generally credited with having introduced Latin American poets to the Japanese *haiku,*" wrote Willard Bohn in the *Hispanic Review,* "he was also responsible for encouraging them to experiment with visual poetry." Bohn described Tablada's work as "surprisingly original" and accorded him "an important place in the history of modern visual poetry today."

In the 1920s, Tablada followed *Li-Po y otros poemas* with such publications as *La resurrección de los ídolos,* a mystical novel, and *El arca de Noé,* a children's book including both original material and Tablada's translations of works by French writers. An imposing study, *Historia del arte en México,* followed in 1927, and another poetry collection, *Intersecciones,* appeared in 1928.

While pursuing a literary career, Tablada also served the Mexican government by working as a diplomat in South America. In 1920, however, ill health compelled him to end his diplomatic career. He thereupon moved to New York City, where he managed his own bookstore before moving upstate and becoming editor of *Mexican Art and Life,* which promoted Mexican culture to American readers. Tablada stayed in the United States until 1936, when he returned to Mexico and worked on *La feria de la vida,* a volume of memoirs that appeared the next year. After a heart ailment prompted his return to New York City for medical treatment, Tablada accepted an appointment as vice-consul to the Mexican consulate there. He died, though, before he could fill the post.

BIOGRAPHICAL AND CRITICAL SOURCES:

PERIODICALS

Hispanic Review, spring, 2001, Willard Bohn, "The Visual Trajectory of José Juan Tablada," pp. 191-208.*

*   *   *

TADEMY, Lalita

PERSONAL: Female. *Education:* University of California—Los Angeles, B.A., 1970; M.B.A., 1972.

ADDRESSES: Agent—c/o Author Mail, Warner Books, 1271 Avenue of the Americas, New York, NY 10020.

CAREER: Writer. Sun Microsystems, former vice president and general manager.

WRITINGS:

Cane River, Warner Books (New York, NY), 2001.

ADAPTATIONS: Cane River was recorded as an audiobook by Time Warner.

WORK IN PROGRESS: A second historical novel.

SIDELIGHTS: Lalita Tademy earned her bachelor's and master's degrees at the University of California—Los Angeles, and went on to a successful business career, eventually becoming vice president and general manager of Sun Microsystems, a computer firm. However, despite the job's high pay and prestige, she had little time for friends or other interests, so after three year, she quit. At first, she told Heather Knight in *SFGate,* she was not sure what to do with herself. However, she had always had an interest in her family's history, and after eighteen months, she began writing *Cane River.*

Cane River, based on Tademy's research into her own family history, is a multigenerational novel tracing the connections among four generations of African-American women, from before the U.S. Civil War to the 1930s. In the initial stages of her genealogical research, Tademy visited the National Archives and Records Administration building in San Bruno, California, but when she exhausted the resources there, she knew she had to go to her family's ancestral home of Cane River, Louisiana. Over the next few years, she took six trips there, visiting colleges, libraries, courthouses, and the historical society and reading old letters, newspapers, wills, and land claims. In addition, she talked to anyone who could tell her stories about the past.

Tademy's research made her realize that there were no easy answers to some of the questions she had about her family's past. She told Knight, "My perceptions when I started were: Slavery? Bad. White people? Evil. Black people? Victims. [But] there was so much gray in Cane River that I had to step back." Much of the confusion came from the fact that her own family was a mix of slaves and owners; some unions were the result of love, and others of rape. Although Tademy searched exhaustively, she was unable to trace her family farther back than 1850, and could not discover where in Africa her ancestors came from.

Eventually, in 1997, she began writing. She told Knight, "In my head, I lived on the plantation, and then I lived through the Civil War, and then I lived in Reconstruction and then I lived in the Jim Crow South. . . . I was these women, but on the flip side, they were me. I really felt them as ancestors, not just characters I made up." Tademy took writing courses at Stanford and the University of California—Berkeley to help her learn to write effectively.

Reviewing the book in *People,* David Cobb Craig called it a "strongly written first novel about determined women in seemingly hopeless situations." Brenda Richardson, writing in *Black Issues Book Review,* praised Tademy's use of original documents such as newspaper reports, photographs, deeds, and wills, which Tademy includes in the book. Richardson commented, "Folded into the story, like egg whites that allow a cake to rise, these documents enrich the blend of fact and fiction." A *Good Housekeeping* reviewer called the novel "a unique and absorbing historical novel that opens a window onto a disturbing period of American history." In *Booklist,* Vanessa Bush wrote, "This fascinating account of American slavery and race-mixing should enthrall readers who love historical fiction."

BIOGRAPHICAL AND CRITICAL SOURCES:

PERIODICALS

Black Issues Book Review, May, 2001, Brenda Richardson, review of *Cane River,* p. 17.

Booklist, February 15, 2001, Vanessa Bush, review of *Cane River,* p. 1086.

Fortune, July 3, 1989, Carol Davenport, "Lalita L. Tademy, 40," p.138.

Good Housekeeping, June, 2001, "On My Mind," p. 24.

New York Times, July 26, 2001, Martin Arnold, "Books by Blacks in Top 5 Sellers," p. E3.

People, May 28, 2001, David Cobb Craig, review of *Cane River,* p. 45.

Publishers Weekly, March 12, 2001, review of *Cane River,* p. 62; August 6, 2001, review of *Cane River* (audiobook), p. 33.

Times (London, England), April 16, 2001, Penny Wark, "A Love in Black and White," p. S12.

Washington Post, June 12, 2001, Jabari Asim, "Families Torn Asunder," p. C03.

OTHER

Lalita Tademy Web site, http://www.lalitatademy.com/ (September 16, 2001).

SFGate, http://www.sfgate.com/ (June 1, 2001), Heather Knight, interview with Lalita Tademy.*

*   *   *

TAYLOR, Alan 1955-

PERSONAL: Born 1955, in Portland, ME. *Education:* Colby College Brandeis University, Ph.D., 1986.

ADDRESSES: Office—3208 Social Sciences and Humanities, UC-Davis, Davis, CA 95616. *E-mail*—astaylor@ucdavis.edu.

CAREER: Historian and author. University of California, Davis, professor of history.

AWARDS, HONORS: Bancroft Prize, Albert J. Beveridge Award, and Pulitzer Prize in American history, all 1996, all for *William Cooper's Town;* Arthur H. Cole Prize, 1999-2000.

WRITINGS:

(With Roger N. Parks and David P. Hall) *New England: A Bibliography of Its History,* University Press of New England (Hanover, NH), 1989.

Liberty Men and Great Proprietors: The Revolutionary Settlement on the Maine Frontier, 1760-1820, University of North Carolina Press (Chapel Hill, NC), 1990.

William Cooper's Town: Power and Persuasion on the Frontier of the Early American Republic, A. A. Knopf (New York, NY), 1995.

American Colonies, Viking Penguin Books (New York, NY), 2001.

WORK IN PROGRESS: A borderlands history of Canada and the United States in the aftermath of the American Revolution.

SIDELIGHTS: Alan Taylor is a historian and professor at the University of California, Davis. His areas of interest include early American and colonial history, the history of the American West, and the history of Canada.

Liberty Men and Great Proprietors: The Revolutionary Settlement on the Maine Frontier, 1760-1820 "will be a landmark in the 'new' history of the early American frontier," according to Richard D. Brown in *New England Quarterly.* Taylor tells the story of the settlement of Maine after the American Revolution, and the conflicts between settlers who cleared the land and politically powerful proprietors who tried to "sell" them—at hugely inflated prices—the land they had already settled. Taylor examines the political, cultural, and economic issues that led to this conflict, as well as the events of the conflict itself. Brown wrote, "The power of Taylor's richly detailed, eloquent analysis lies in his convincing explanation of how political and social processes combined with ideas and cultural values to produce violent conflict first and then a revolutionary settlement in Maine"—a settlement where, in contrast to American ideals, competition and inequality became fundamental parts of the fabric of society. In the *Journal of Economic History,* Peter C. Mancall wrote that the book contains "a well-constructed narrative spiced with the stories of real people" that explains how "the creation of a `liberal social order' proved a difficult task in Maine and no doubt throughout much of America as well."

William Cooper's Town: Power and Persuasion on the Frontier of the Early American Republic, which won 1996 Bancroft, Beveridge, and Pulitzer prizes, provides both a biography of William Cooper, a frontier land developer and political leader of the 1780s and 1790s, and a study of Cooperstown, New York, which Cooper founded in 1786. Taylor also analyzes the novel *The Pioneers,* set during the founding of Cooperstown and written in 1822 by Cooper's son, James Fenimore Cooper.

"This extraordinary saga charts the partisan battles for supremacy in the new America republic," along with the competition among religious institutions for members and the attempt by "American writers to create a distinctive national literature," wrote a *Publishers Weekly* critic about *William Cooper's Town.* "This engaging, prize-winning chronicle . . . has much to offer," said Graham Russell Hodges in *Agricultural History.* In the *Times Literary Supplement,* Jack P. Greene wrote, "This is a moving and historically important story told with insight, analytic intelligence and profuse detail." Gordon S. Wood noted in the *New York Review of Books* that Taylor's analysis of the actual history of Cooperstown in comparison to the fictionalized events of *The Pioneers* is particularly fascinating. Wood wrote that although the book at times has more detail than many readers probably need, Taylor's research is "prodigious." In sum, Wood commented, "It is an extraordinary story that Taylor has told—an American tragedy, involving a man's family and his entire community," further observing that "the book is worthy of all the acclaim and prizes it has received."

American Colonies is the first volume of a five-volume series of books on American history. In the *New York Times Book Review,* Andrew R. L. Cayton wrote that in the book, Taylor "expertly weaves together the arguments and evidence of dozens of historians and anthropologists, especially those interested in indigenous peoples, environments and the nature of the Atlantic world." In doing so, he places early American history within the context of other world events, particularly in Africa, Europe, and the Americas. A *Publishers Weekly* reviewer noted that *American Colonies* "offers a balanced understanding of the diverse peoples and forces that converged on this continent early on and influenced the course of American history." "Most interesting," wrote Allen Weakland in *Booklist,* "is the manner in which the early

colonists . . . were aided by the Native Americans . . . [and] African slaves." Taylor also "vividly describes the harsh realities of colonial life," observed Robert Flatley in *Library Journal,* noting the book is "well written and documented." Taylor discusses other issues in *American Colonies* as well, including some Americans still face, such as global trade, cross-cultural encounters, and diversity.

BIOGRAPHICAL AND CRITICAL SOURCES:

PERIODICALS

Agricultural History, winter, 1997, Graham Russell Hodges, review of *William Cooper's Town: Power and Persuasion on the Frontier of the Early American Republic,* p. 92.

Booklist, September 15, 1995, Patricia Hassler, review of *William Cooper's Town,* p. 139; October 15, 2001, Allen Weakland, review of *American Colonies,* p. 380.

Historian, winter, 1998, review of *William Cooper's Town,* p. 365.

Journal of American History, June, 1991, Jackson Turner Main, review of *Liberty Men and Great Proprietors: The Revolutionary Settlement on the Maine Frontier, 1760-1820,* p. 303.

Journal of Economic History, September, 1991, Peter C. Mancall, review of *Liberty Men and Great Proprietors,* p. 753.

Kirkus Reviews, September 1, 2001, review of *American Colonies,* p. 1278.

Library Journal, October 15, 2001, Robert Flatley, review of *American Colonies,* p. 94.

New England Quarterly, December, 1991, Richard D. Brown, review of *Liberty Men and Great Proprietors,* p. 643.

New York Review of Books, August 8, 1996, Gordon S. Wood, review of *William Cooper's Town,* p. 36.

New York Times Book Review, December 2, 2001, Andrew R. L. Cayton, review of *American Colonies,* p. 61.

Publishers Weekly, August 28, 1995, review of *William Cooper's Town,* p. 100; October 29, 2001, review of *American Colonies,* p. 48.

Sacramento Business Journal, December 15, 2000, "*Journal of Economic History,*" p. 40.

Times Literary Supplement, February 28, 1997, Jack P. Greene, review of *William Cooper's Town,* p. 8.*

THOMAS, Lew(is) (Christopher) 1932-

PERSONAL: Born December 19, 1932, in San Francisco, CA; married Natalie Joyce Simon, 1960; children: Kesa Louize. *Education:* University of San Francisco, B.A., 1963; self-taught in photography.

ADDRESSES: Home—1441 West Alabama, Houston, TX 77007. *Agent*—Fraenkel Gallery, 55 Grant Avenue, San Francisco, CA 94108; Asher/Faure, 612 North Almont, Los Angeles, CA 90069.

CAREER: Independent photographer, San Francisco, CA, 1967-85; independent photographer, Houston, TX, 1985—; Legion of Honor Bookstore, San Francisco, manager, 1963-82; NFS Press, San Francisco, publisher and editor, 1975-83; Joseph Gross Gallery, University of Arizona, Tucson, director, 1983-84; Houston Center of Photography, Houston, executive director, 1985—; *Spot* quarterly, Houston, editor, 1985—. San Francisco Art Institute, San Francisco, visiting artist, 1977, artists' committee member, 1979-83, photography instructor, 1981; City College of San Francisco, San Francisco, photography instructor, 1982-83; San Francisco State University, lecturer in photography, 1983; University of Arizona, Tucson, lecturer in photography, 1983-85. Worked as a clerk and warehouseman in San Francisco, 1952-59.

MEMBER: College Art Association of America, Society for Photographic Education.

AWARDS, HONORS: Ilo Liston Publications Award, Mills College/Western Association of Art Museums, 1974; Graphic Arts Award, Printing Industries of America, 1974, 1980; publications grant, SECA/San Francisco Museum of Modern Art, 1976; photography fellowship, National Endowment for the Arts, 1975, 1980, 1981; exhibitions grant, Ellison Books Award, University of Cincinnati, 1979; National Endowment for the Arts grant, 1980.

WRITINGS:

The Thinker (exhibition catalog), [San Francisco, CA], 1974.
8 X 10, [San Francisco, CA], 1975.

(Editor) *Photography and Language,* Camerawork Press (San Francisco, CA), 1976.
(Coeditor) *Eros and Photography,* Camerawork/NFS Press (San Francisco, CA), 1976.
(Editor) *Photography and Ideology,* [Los Angeles, CA], 1977.
(Editor) *Gay Semiotics,* [San Francisco, CA], 1978.
Structuralism and Photography, NFS Press (San Francisco, CA), 1979.
(Editor) *18th near Castro Street X 24,* [San Francisco, CA], 1979.
(Coauthor) *Pages from a Child's Documentary,* [San Francisco, CA], 1980.
(Coeditor) *Still Photography: The Problematic Model,* NFS Press (San Francisco, CA), 1981.
(Editor) *The Restless Decade: John Gutmann's Photographs of the Thirties,* Abrams (New York, NY), 1984.*

*   *   *

THORNHILL, John 1929-

PERSONAL: Born May 13, 1929, in Brisbane, Australia; son of William Joseph (a librarian) and Mary Teresa (a nurse; maiden name, Fox). *Ethnicity:* "Anglo-Irish." *Education:* Attended Catholic schools and seminary in Queensland and New South Wales; University of St. Thomas (Rome, Italy), S.T.L., 1955, Ph.D., 1958. *Religion:* Catholic.

ADDRESSES: Home—6/180 Butterfield St., Herston, Queensland, 4006, Australia; fax: 07-3252-1185. *E-mail*—jethornhill@hotmail.com.

CAREER: Roman Catholic priest and educator in theology and philosophy. Ordained in Rome, 1955; St. Peter Chanel Seminary, Sydney, New South Wales, Australia, lecturer, 1959-74, rector, 1969-74; Aquinas Academy, Sydney, director, 1975-80; Catholic Theological Union, Sydney, head of theology department, 1981-93, lecturer, 1981-94. Member of International Theological Commission (appointed by Pope John Paul II), 1980-85, and Anglican Roman Catholic International Commission, 1983-90; represented the Catholic Church in Australian Lutheran-Roman Catholic dialogue, 1992-95.

MEMBER: Australian Theological Association (president, 1989-93), Marist Society of Mary.

WRITINGS:

The Person and the Group: A Study, in the Tradition of Aristotelian Realism, of the Meaning of Human Society, Bruce Publishing Co. (Milwaukee, WI), 1967.

Sign and Promise: A Theology of the Church for a Changing World, HarperCollins (London, England), 1988.

Christian Mystery in the Secular Age: The Foundation and Task of Theology, Christian Classics (Westminster, MD), 1991.

Making Australia: Exploring Our National Conversation, Millennium Books (Newtown, New South Wales, Australia), 1992.

Modernity: Christianity's Estranged Child Reconstructed, W. B. Eerdmans Publishing Co. (Grand Rapids, MI), 2000.

Questions Catholics Ask in a Time of Change: Understanding the Hope We Must Share, St. Paul's Publications (Strathfield, New South Wales, Australia), 2001.

WORK IN PROGRESS: Research into the Christian faith and the world's authors.

SIDELIGHTS: John Thornhill is a Catholic priest and retired educator and the author of several books, including *Modernity: Christianity's Estranged Child Reconstructed.* Ronald Marstin, who reviewed the volume in *Cross Currents,* wrote that "while many are ready to abandon modernity as an exhausted project, John Thornhill believes the movement which has shaped Western culture for the past 500 years may be just about to come of age. If he is right, future historians will assess our current travails as only a painful transition between early modernity and its mature phase." Marstin commented that Thornhill "acknowledges that Western civilization had to get out from under the heavy hand of medieval Christendom to assert the legitimate autonomy of the secular order; the old authorities could no longer command unquestioning submission; any authority would now have to give an account of itself before the bar of a shared understanding."

Marstin continued, "We can find a way out of our dilemma, Thornhill says, if we take another look at the assumptions on which the intellectual project of modernity was founded, especially at its indiscriminate rejection of the Greek and Judeo-Christian traditions that had shaped the medieval world. Those traditions presume to offer transcendent standards against which any human project must be measured." As a reaction to Medieval authoritarianism, the Enlightenment saw science as the only means by which truth could be measured. "If we have long grown suspicious of any but mechanistic explanations of the cosmos, it is time to raise anew questions that the Enlightenment rejected . . . if the project of modernity is to be advanced," noted Marstin.

Interpretation's Gloria H. Albrecht observed that Thornhill puts forth the idea that religion and traditions "offer to modernity what it needs to succeed: a narrative account of existential meaning and purpose for human life," and "presents well one side of the critique of modern Western societies: the loss of unifying cultural traditions."

Nancy Hawkins noted in *America* that Thornhill "argues that modernity must be conceived as an ideological movement of reaction against medievalism. As an ideology it needs to be understood as a search for truth and to be appreciated as one of the essential characteristics of our Western cultural tradition. To prove his point the author calls upon the 'great ones,' such as Descartes, Locke, and Nietzsche. He also offers the reader an extremely useful broad sketch of the various inspirations behind modernity." Thornhill looks at the nature of modernity, its problems, the issues it raises, and its creation of a "free society." He concludes that modernity has made us more aware of a variety of religions and cultures. Both Albrecht and Hawkins noted that the book contains no mention of the writings or views of women or the peoples of third-world countries, those traditionally marginalized, exploited, and oppressed by modern societies. Hawkins felt that in this regard, "Thornhill's world view is severely limited." She did, however, conclude that "while it has its flaws . . . the book is an important contribution to scholarship." William M. Shea wrote in Theological Studies that in addressing the tensions of Western religion within its culture, Thornhill "has written a particularly good map . . . . It deserves careful reading."

Thornhill told *CA:* "My primary motivation for writing is to find answers to the big questions (often arising from my work as an educator): the nature of human society, Vatican II's vision for the Church, whether theology can balance fidelity to tradition and an openness to the present, what culture united Australians as they faced their bicentenary, why the modern world is disintegrating, despite its immense achievements.

"I have been influenced by an interest in history and culture, and most of my works have evolved as I sought to create a text useful to my students. My doctoral thesis was on Toynbee's *A Study of History.* Living in Rome for five years made me aware of human culture and its diversity down through the ages. The interaction between culture and Christian faith has always been a focus of interest in my thought."

BIOGRAPHICAL AND CRITICAL SOURCES:

PERIODICALS

America, November 18, 2000, Nancy Hawkins, review of *Modernity: Christianity's Estranged Child Reconstructed,* p. 26.
Cross Currents, fall, 2001, Ronald Marstin, review of *Modernity,* p. 431.
Interpretation, April, 2001, Gloria H. Albrecht, review of *Modernity,* p. 214.
Theological Studies, September, 2001, William M. Shea, review of *Modernity,* p. 655.
Theology, January, 2001, Richard Arrandale, review of *Modernity,* p. 49.*

*   *   *

TOMLINSON, Gary (Alfred) 1951-

PERSONAL: Born December 4, 1951, in West Point, NY; son of John Gibson and Norma (Cerino) Tomlinson; married Lucy Eve Kerman, June 15, 1977; children: David, Laura, Julia. *Education:* Dartmouth College, B.A., 1973; University of California—Berkeley, M.A., 1975, Ph.D., 1979.

ADDRESSES: Office—University of Pennsylvania, Department of Music, 201 South 34th St., Philadelphia, PA 19104-6313. *E-mail*—gatomlin@sas.upenn.edu.

CAREER: University of Pennsylvania—Philadelphia, assistant professor of music, 1979-84, associate professor, 1984-89, professor, 1989-96, Annenberg Professor in the Humanities, 1996—, chairman, department of music, 1986-89. Visiting professor, Duke University, 1983, Princeton University, 1993, Folger Shakespeare Library, 1993; Housewright eminent visiting scholar, Florida State University, Tallahassee, 1994; visiting scholar, Phi Beta Kappa, 1997-98.

MEMBER: American Musicological Society (executive board, 1988-90), Renaissance Society of America (executive board, 1989-91).

AWARDS, HONORS: Guggenheim fellowship, 1982; Alfred Einstein prize, American Musicological Society, 1982; MacArthur fellowship, 1988-93.

WRITINGS:

(Editor) *Italian Secular Song, 1606-1636: A Seven-Volume Reprint Collection,* Garland (New York, NY), 1986.
Monteverdi and the End of the Renaissance, University of California Press (Berkeley, CA), 1987.
Music in Renaissance Magic: Toward a Historiography of Others, University of Chicago Press (Chicago, IL), 1993.
Metaphysical Song: An Essay on Opera, Princeton University Press (Princeton, NJ), 1999.
(Editor) *Strunk's Source Readings in Music History: The Renaissance,* 1998.
(Editor, with Joseph Kerman and Vivian Kerman), *Listen,* Bedford (Boston, MA), 1999.

SIDELIGHTS: Musicologist Gary Tomlinson, Annenberg Professor in the Humanities at the University of Pennsylvania, specializes in the late Renaissance and early Baroque periods. Strongly influenced by the writings of cultural theorist Michel Foucault, Tomlinson brings to his work a distinctly postmodernist approach. He gained critical attention in 1987 with the publication of *Monteverdi and the End of the Renaissance,* a reworking of his doctoral dissertation. *Times Literary Supplement* reviewer Denis Stevens found the book deeply flawed by self-conscious and jargonish writing, but noted that Tomlinson discusses several issues "with skill and insight." Other critics, however, considered the book more commendable. In *Library Journal,*

Philipa Kiraly judged the book "fluent, attractive, and intelligible in style," and in *Modern Language Review,* F. W. Sternfeld enthused that its "analysis . . . is so trenchant that I have no hesitation in recommending this volume."

In *Music in Renaissance Magic: Toward a Historiography of Others,* Tomlinson explores the connections between music and magic in the Renaissance within a wide cultural context. Many critics admired the book's analysis and methodology. Blake Wilson, in *American Historical Review,* hailed it as an "immensely complex and challenging book" that "must be viewed as one of the most eloquent and sophisticated applications of postmodern critical theory to Renaissance culture" as well as "a provocative challenge to . . . the field of musicology." Though Julie Robin Solomon, in *Modern Language Review,* criticized Tomlinson's "monolithic" dependence on Foucault in structuring his argument, she deemed *Music in Renaissance Magic* nothing less than a "stunning book."

In *Metaphysical Song: An Essay on Opera,* Tomlinson takes an integrative rather than a chronological approach, integrating history, philosophy, and drama to explain how elements of an operatic work are used to convey meaning. *Library Journal*'s Timothy J. McGee considered *Metaphysical Song* a "well-written, wide-ranging, and thought provoking" work.

A recipient of Guggenheim and MacArthur fellowships, Tomlinson has also received the Alfred Einstein prize of the American Musicological Society.

BIOGRAPHICAL AND CRITICAL SOURCES:

PERIODICALS

American Historical Review, October, 1988, p. 1080; June, 1994, Blake Wilson, review of *Music in Renaissance Magic: Toward a Historiography of Others,* p. 931.
Choice, May, 1994, P. G. Swing, review of *Music in Renaissance Magic: Toward a Historiography of Others,* p. 1447; September, 1999, K. Pendle, review of *Metaphysical Song: An Essay on Opera,* p. 155.
Library Journal, May 15, 1987, Philipa Kiraly, review of *Monteverdi and the End of the Renaissance,* p. 87; April 15, 1999, Timothy J. McGee, review of *Metaphysical Song: An Essay on Opera,* p. 99.

Modern Language Review, October, 1988, F. W. Sternfeld, review of *Monteverdi and the End of the Renaissance,* pp. 1009-1010; January, 1995, Julie Robin Solomon, review of *Music in Renaissance Magic: Toward a Historiography of Others,* pp. 137-138.
Review of Metaphysics, September, 2000, Gerard Casey, review of *Metaphysical Song: An Essay on Opera,* p. 174.
Times Literary Supplement, August 7, 1987, Denis Stevens, "Verbal Engagements," p. 845.*

* * *

TRAISTER, Barbara Howard 1943-

PERSONAL: Born December 18, 1943, in Blytheville, AR; daughter of Ralph (a farmer) and Eleanor (a professor; maiden name, Ross) Howard; married Daniel Traister, June 12, 1965; children: Rebecca, Aaron. *Ethnicity:* "Caucasian." *Education:* Colby College, B.A., 1965; Yale University, M.Phil., 1968, Ph. D., 1974. *Hobbies and other interests:* Reading, theater, art.

ADDRESSES: Home—321 Elm Ave., North Hills, PA 19038. *Office*—Department of English, Lehigh University, 35 Sayre Dr., Bethlehem, PA 18015; fax: 610-758-6616. *E-mail*—bht0@lehigh.edu.

CAREER: Kalamazoo College, Kalamazoo, MI, assistant professor of English, 1968-73; Lehigh University, Bethlehem, PA, professor of English, 1973—, department chair, 1994-2000. Medical College of Pennsylvania, adjunct professor, 1986-93. Colby College, member of board of trustees, 1988-94.

MEMBER: Shakespeare Association of America, Renaissance Society of America, Phi Beta Kappa.

AWARDS, HONORS: Fellow of National Endowment for the Humanities, American Council of Learned Societies, Rockefeller Foundation, and Folger Shakespeare Library.

WRITINGS:

Heavenly Necromancers: The Magician in English Renaissance Drama, University of Missouri Press (Columbia, MO), 1984.

The Notorious Astrological Physician of London: Works and Days of Simon Forman, University of Chicago Press (Chicago, IL), 2001.

WORK IN PROGRESS: Research on the use of anecdote in early modern chronicle history.

BIOGRAPHICAL AND CRITICAL SOURCES:

PERIODICALS

Library Journal, January 1, 2001, Eric D. Albright, review of *The Notorious Astrological Physician of London: Works and Days of Simon Forman,* p. 146.

Shakespeare Survey, annual, 1998, Richard Dutton, review of *Heavenly Necromancers: The Magician in English Renaissance Drama,* p. 231.

Times (London, England), January 31, 2001, Peter Ackroyd, "Doctor to Will's Dark Lady Books," p. 10.

Times Literary Supplement, March 9, 2001, Ann Geneva, review of *The Notorious Astrological Physician of London,* p. 10.

*   *   *

TRAPP, J. B. 1925-

PERSONAL: Born July 16, 1925, in Carterton, New Zealand; son of Henry Mansfield Burney (an accountant) and Frances Melanie (a homemaker; maiden name, Wolters) Trapp; married Elayne Margaret Falla, June 9, 1953; children: Michael Burney, James Stephen. *Education:* Victoria University of Wellington, M.A., 1947.

ADDRESSES: Home—London, England. *Office*—Warburg Institute, University of London, Woburn Sq., London WC1H 0AB, England; fax: 00-44-7862-8955. *E-mail*—joseph.trapp@sas.ac.uk.

CAREER: Librarian. Alexander Turnbull Library, Wellington, New Zealand, assistant librarian, 1946-50; Victoria University College, Wellington, New Zealand, junior lecturer, 1950-51; University of Reading, Read-

ing, Berkshire, England, assistant lecturer, 1951-53; Warburg Institute, University of London, London, England, assistant librarian, 1953-66, librarian, 1966-76, director, 1976-90, honorary fellow, 1990—.

MEMBER: British Academy (fellow; vice president, 1983-85; foreign secretary, 1988-95), Society of Antiquaries (fellow), Royal Swedish Academy (foreign member).

WRITINGS:

Medieval English Literature (anthology), Oxford University Press (New York, NY), 1973, 2nd edition, 2002.

(Editor) *Apology for Thomas More,* Yale University Press (New Haven, CT), 1979.

Erasmus, Colet, and More (monograph), British Library (London, England), 1991.

(Editor, with L. Hellinger) *History of the Book in Britain,* Volume 3: *1400-1557,* Cambridge University Press (New York, NY), 1999.

E. H. Gombrich: A Bibliography, Phaidon Press (New York, NY), 2001.

WORK IN PROGRESS: Research on illustrations of Petrarch.

*   *   *

TROTTA, Liz

PERSONAL: Female. *Education:* Attended College of New Rochelle for two years; Boston University, B.A.; Columbia University, Graduate School of Journalism, 1958.

ADDRESSES: Agent—c/o Author Mail, HarperCollins, 10 East 53rd St., 7th Fl., New York, NY 10022.

CAREER: Newspaper reporter, television journalist, teacher, and novelist. NBC, New York, NY, 1965-79; covered presidential campaign of George McGovern, 1984; worked for CBS, 1985; worked for Hillman Periodicals, Inter-Catholic Press Agency, *Long Island*

Press, Chicago Tribune, and *Newsday;* taught journalism at Stern College of Yeshiva University; *Washington Times,* New York bureau chief.

AWARDS, HONORS: Three Emmys; two Overseas Press Club Awards.

WRITINGS:

Fighting for Air: In the Trenches with Television News, Simon & Schuster (New York, NY), 1991.
Jude: A Pilgrimage to the Saint of Last Resort, HarperCollins (New York, NY), 1998.

SIDELIGHTS: Liz Trotta, a news journalist, was the first woman to cover a war for broadcast news. After starting a career in print journalism, Trotta switched media to rise through the ranks of television broadcast journalism to eventually win a network position. Her biggest and toughest assignment was to cover the Vietnam War in 1968 for NBC. When Trotta was first given the assignment, the bureau chief in Saigon threatened to resign if NBC followed through with their plans of having a woman cover the war. Instead of the assignment being taken away from Trotta, the bureau chief in Saigon was replaced and Trotta carried out the assignment for which she won the 1968 Overseas Press Club Award.

Trotta's experience as a female broadcast journalist in a male-dominated industry is the subject of her book *Fighting for Air: In the Trenches with Television News.* As Marjorie Williams wrote in the *Washington Post Book World,* "*Fighting for Air* is a healthy reminder of how recently and reluctantly the major media let women join their ranks." The book describes Trotta's news career with NBC and CBS, her analysis of the network managers and news anchormen, and her own assignments covering stories in Tehran, London, and Bangladesh. The center of her book recounts the war stories in Vietnam, including events of the time she spent in Saigon and on the front lines. "She conveys with immediacy the terrifying nature of war reporting, the strange allure it has for those who do it, and the great dedication it took for correspondents, in the age before videotape and instantaneous satellite feeds, to bring us the 'living room war' from southeast Asia," commented Williams.

Even with her meritorious coverage of the Vietnam War, Trotta's career at NBC didn't last; she was fired in 1979. She was then hired by CBS, but her assignments were mediocre and she was fired shortly after when the look of television news took on a younger profile. Trotta attributes her earlier success in television journalism to the pioneers of broadcast news that tutored her as well as Huntley, who managed NBC in the early 1960s. In her book, Trotta suggests that her troubles with NBC management began when Chet Huntley left the network. Sam Donaldson wrote in the *Washington Monthly,* "Trotta blames her problems on sex discrimination, management philistines, and the everyday incompetence of many NBC staff members."

Trotta's second book, *Jude, Pilgrimage to the Saint of Last Resort,* is an exploration and travelogue into the devotion of St. Jude Thaddeus, the patron saint of lost causes and desperate cases. Trotta's investigations into the life of St. Jude, the least known of the Twelve Apostles of Christ, took her to the ruins of Edessa, Turkey, where King Abgar was cured of leprosy, and ended at St. Jude's burial site in St. Peter's Basilica in Rome. She interviewed ordinary people from all walks of life and religious background who are devout believers in the powers of St. Jude from all over the world. Patrick H. Samway, reviewing Trotta's book in *America,* praised it as "rich in detail," and observed "this book looks carefully" at St. Jude "who leads the faithful on journeys of recovery and hope."

BIOGRAPHICAL AND CRITICAL SOURCES:

BOOKS

Sherrow, Victoria, *Women and the Military,* ABC-CLIO (Santa Barbara, CA), 1996.

PERIODICALS

America, September 19, 1998, p. 24.
Kirkus Reviews, May 15, 1998, p. 728.
National Review, August 12, 1991, pp. 48-51.
New York Times Book Review, November 8, 1998, p. 23.
Publishers Weekly, May 25, 1998, p. 81.
Washington Monthly, June, 1991, pp. 57-58.
Washington Post Book World, June, 2, 1991, p. 7.*

TRUPP, Philip (Zber)

PERSONAL: Married; wife's name, Sandy.

ADDRESSES: Home—Washington, DC. *Agent*—c/o Author Mail, Fulcrum Publishing, 350 Indiana St., #350, Golden, CO 80401-5093. *E-mail*—pzbar@aol. com.

CAREER: Writer, c. 1972—. *Washington Times,* jazz critic. Worked with Project Mercury for National Aeronautics and Space Administration; has produced a television series for National Broadcasting Corporation and is a frequent guest on talk radio.

WRITINGS:

New York Bar and Grill, Arbour Press (New York, NY), 1972.
The Art of Craftsmanship: An Examination of the Historical Values Which Have Shaped the American Spirit, Acropolis Books (Washington, DC), 1976.
Tracking Treasure: Romance and Fortune Found beneath the Sea and How to Find it!, Acropolis Books (Washington, DC), 1986.
(With Kenneth J. Karpinski) *The Winner's Style: The Modern Male's Passport to Perfect Grooming,* Acropolis Books (Washington, DC), 1986.
Divers Almanac Guide to the Florida Keys, Triton, 1991
Oceans: A Voyage of Discovery, Fulcrum Publishing (Golden, CO), 1998.
Sea of Dreamers: Travels with Famous Ocean Explorers, Fulcrum Publishing (Golden, CO), 1998.
Ancient Wisdom I: The Spiritual Tale of the Scholar Chu Shui Hu, Capital Books (Sterling, VA), 2001.

WORK IN PROGRESS: Islands of Desire, a book of adventures.

SIDELIGHTS: Philip Trupp is an author, journalist, and adventurer. He has been a newspaper reporter and magazine feature writer. He was associated with Project Mercury in the early days of the space program and is an official aquanaut of the National Oceanic and Atmospheric Administration, and led a team of journalists who lived and worked below the surface of the sea in Hydrolab II.

In *Sea of Dreamers: Travels with Famous Ocean Explorers,* Trupp makes the point that most people know more about the moon than about the mysterious world of the ocean. Trupp has long been associated with ocean researchers and explorers, and in this book he presents these fascinating people: Maurice Ewing, who maps the world's seas and oceans; Harold Edgerton, the Massachusetts Institute of Technology scientist who brought light to the dark depths with his invention of stroboscopic photography; Cindy Van Dover, who discovered sources of light in the deep sea; and Eugenie Clark, whose amazing research with sharks showed that they are smarter than had previously been thought. A *Publishers Weekly* reviewer noted that the book makes a "serious, worthy point": that ocean researchers will only be able to obtain funds for their work if they can explain their research in interesting, engaging ways that ordinary people can understand.

Tracking Treasure: Romance and Fortune Found beneath the Sea and How to Find It! is a guidebook for undersea treasure hunters. Trupp includes advice on how to find funding for a treasure hunt, how to dig for treasure, and where treasure is likely to be in Caribbean and North American waters. He also presents the case of Mel Fisher, who spent sixteen years looking for the *Atocha,* a Spanish ship that wrecked near Key West in 1622, and who eventually found its treasure, a hoard of silver and gold worth 400 million dollars. Trupp adds a brief discussion of ethics: should treasure be solely the property of the finder, or do finders have a responsibility to society when they find priceless archeological treasures? Trupp sides with the treasure finders on this issue.

In *Divers Almanac: Guide to the Florida Keys,* Trupp provides an introduction to scuba diving in Florida, divided into sections describing different regions: the Panhandle, the Sun Coast, the East Coast, the Keys, and Southwest Florida. Trupp provides information for divers at all levels of experience and ability, and also provides hints for treasure hunters and beachcombers by describing Spanish shipping routes and other places where treasure is most likely to be found.

BIOGRAPHICAL AND CRITICAL SOURCES:

PERIODICALS

Library Journal, October 15, 1998, Jean E. Crampon, review of *Sea of Dreamers: Travels with Famous Ocean Explorers,* p. 94.
Publishers Weekly, June 20, 1986, p. 95; November 2, 1998, p. 62.

OTHER

Philip Z. Trupp's Home Page, http://members/aol.com/Pzbar/.*

*   *   *

TURCO, Mary

PERSONAL: Female. *Education:* Harvard University, Ed.D.

ADDRESSES: Office—Women's Studies Program, Dartmouth College, Hanover, NH 03755.

CAREER: Dartmouth College, Hanover, NH, professor of women's studies.

WRITINGS:

Crashing the Net: The U.S. Women's Ice Hockey Team and the Road to Gold, HarperCollins (New York, NY), 1999.

BIOGRAPHICAL AND CRITICAL SOURCES:

PERIODICALS

New York Times Book Review, May 2, 1999, p. 20.
Publishers Weekly, March 29, 1999, p. 77.*

U

UNDERHILL, Evelyn 1875-1941
(John Cordelier)

PERSONAL: Born December 6, 1875, in Wolverhampton, England; died June 15, 1941; daughter of Arthur (a barrister) and Alice Lucy (maiden name, Ironmonger) Underhill; married Hubert Stuart Moore (a lawyer), 1907. *Education:* Attended King's College (London, England).

CAREER: Poet, author, lecturer and social worker.

WRITINGS:

A Bar-Lamb's Ballad Book, Kegan Paul, Trench, Trübner (London, England), 1902.

The Gray World (novel), Century (New York, NY), 1904, published as *The Grey World,* Heinemann (London, England), 1904.

The Miracles of Our Lady Saint Mary Brought out of Divers Tongues and Newly Set Forth in English, Heinemann (London, England), 1905, Dutton (New York, NY), 1906.

The Lost Word (novel), Heinemann (London, England), 1907.

The Column of Dust (novel), Methuen (London, England), 1909.

Mysticism: A Study in the Nature and Development of Man's Spiritual Consciousness, Dutton (New York, NY), 1911, revised edition, 1930.

(As John Cordelier) *The Path of Eternal Wisdom: A Mystical Commentary on the Way of the Cross,* Watkins (London, England), 1911.

(As John Cordelier) *The Spiral Way: Being Meditations upon the Fifteen Mysteries of the Soul's Ascent,* Watkins (London, England), 1912, revised edition, 1922.

A Franciscan Mystic of the Thirteenth Century: The Blessed Angela of Foligno "British Society of Franciscan Studies," extra series number 1), Aberdeen University Press (Aberdeen, Scotland), 1912.

Immanence: A Book of Verses, Dutton (New York, NY), 1912.

The Mystic Way: A Psychological Study in Christian Origins, Dutton (New York, NY), 1913.

Practical Mysticism: A Little Book for Normal People, Dutton (New York, NY), 1914.

(Translator, with Rabindranath Tagore) *One Hundred Poems of Kabir,* India Society (London, England), 1914, published as *Songs of Kabir,* Macmillan (New York, NY), 1916.

Mysticism and War, Watkins (London, England), 1915.

Ruysbroeck, Bell (London, England), 1915.

Theophanies: A Book of Verses, Dutton (New York, NY), 1916.

(Editor) Jan van Ruysbroeck, *The Adornment of the Spiritual Marriage. The Sparkling Stone. The Book of Supreme Truth,* translated by C. A. Wynschenck, Dutton (New York, NY), 1916.

Jacopone da Todi: Poet and Mystic, 1228-1306: A Spiritual Biography, Dutton (New York, NY), 1919.

The Essentials of Mysticism and Other Essays, Dutton (New York, NY), 1920.

The Life of the Spirit and the Life of To-Day, Dutton (New York, NY), 1922.

The Mystics of the Church, Clarke (London, England), 1925, Doran (New York, NY), 1926.

Concerning the Inner Life, Dutton (New York, NY), 1926.

Prayer, YWCA (London, England), 1926.

A Franciscan Poet: Jacopone da Todi, [London, England], 1926.

Man and the Supernatural, Methuen (London, England), 1927, Dutton (New York, NY), 1928.

Life as Prayer, United Free Church of Scotland (Edinburgh, Scotland), c. 1927.

The Teacher's Vocation, St. Christopher's (London, England), 1928.

The House of the Soul, Methuen (London, England), 1929, Dutton (New York, NY), 1930.

Worship, Mowbray (London, England), 1929, Harper (New York, NY), 1937.

The Philosophy of Contemplation, Burrow (Cheltenham, England), 1930.

The Inside of Life, Mowbray (London, England), 1931.

Evelyn Underhill ("Benn's Augustan Books of Poetry" series), Benn (London, England), 1932.

The Golden Sequence: A Fourfold Study of the Spiritual Life, Methuen (London, England), 1932, Dutton (New York, NY), 1933.

Mixed Pasture: Twelve Essays and Addresses, Longmans, Green (New York, NY), 1933.

The School of Charity: Meditations on the Christian Creed, Longmans, Green (New York, NY), 1934.

(Editor) *A Book of Contemplation, the Which Is Called The Cloud of Unknowing in the Which a Soul Is Oned with God,* Watkins (London, England), 1934.

What Is Mysticism?, Mowbray (London, England), 1936.

Education and the Spirit of Worship, Headly (London, England), 1937.

The Spiritual Life: Four Broadcast Talks, Harper (New York, NY), 1937.

The Parish Priest and the Life of Prayer, Mowbray (London, England), 1937.

The Mystery of Sacrifice: A Meditation on the Liturgy, Longmans, Green (New York, NY), 1938.

A Meditation on Peace, Fellowship of Reconciliation (London, England), 1939.

A Service of Prayer for Use in War-Time, Church Literature Association (London, England), 1939.

(Editor) *Eucharistic Prayers from the Ancient Liturgies,* Longmans, Green (New York, NY), 1939.

Spiritual Life in Wartime, Christian Literature Association (London, England), 1939.

Abba: Meditations on the Lord's Prayer, Longmans, Green (New York, NY), 1940.

The Church and War, Anglican Pacifist Fellowship (London, England), 1940.

The Fruits of the Spirit, Longmans, Green (New York, NY), 1942.

The Letters of Evelyn Underhill, edited by Charles Williams, Longmans, Green (New York, NY), 1943.

Light of Christ: Addresses Given at the House of Retreat, Pleshey, in May, 1932, Longmans, Green (New York, NY), 1944.

Collected Papers of Evelyn Underhill, edited by Lucy Menzies, Longmans, Green (New York, NY), 1946, published as *Life as Prayer and Other Writings of Evelyn Underhill,* Morehouse (Harrisburg, PA), 1991.

Meditations and Prayers, Longmans, Green (New York, NY), 1949.

Shrines and Cities of France and Italy, edited by Lucy Menzies, Longmans, Green (New York, NY), 1949.

The Wisdom of Evelyn Underhill: An Anthology from Her Writings, edited by John Stobbart, Mowbray (London, England), 1951.

An Anthology of the Love of God from the Writings of Evelyn Underhill, edited by Lucy Menzies and Lumsden Barkway, Mowbray (London, England), 1953, McKay (New York, NY), 1954.

The Mount of Purification, Longmans (London, England), 1960.

Selections from the Writings of Evelyn Underhill, Upper Room (Nashville, TN), 1961.

The Evelyn Underhill Reader, edited by T. S. Kepler, Abingdon (Nashville, TN), 1962.

Lent with Evelyn Underhill: Selections from Her Writings, edited by G. P. Mellick Belshaw, Morehouse-Barlow (New York, NY), 1964.

Evelyn Underhill: Modern Guide to the Ancient Quest for the Holy, edited, with an introduction, by Dana Greene, State University of New York Press (Albany, NY), 1988.

Evelyn Underhill on Prayer ("Christian Spirituality" series), edited by Tony Castle, Marshall Pickering (London, England), 1989.

The Ways of the Spirit, edited, with an introduction, by Grace Adolphsen Brame, Crossroad (New York, NY), 1990.

Daily Readings with a Modern Mystic: Selections from the Writings of Evelyn Underhill, edited by Delroy Oberg, Twenty-third Publications (Mystic, CT), 1992.

Given to God, edited by Delroy Oberg, Darton, Longman and Todd (London, England), 1992.

Heaven a Dance: An Evelyn Underhill Anthology, edited by Brenda Blanch and Stuart Blanch, Triangle (Chicago, IL), 1992.

Fragments from an Inner Life: The Notebooks of Evelyn Underhill, Morehouse (Harrisburg, PA), 1993.

The Soul's Delight: Selected Writings of Evelyn Underhill, edited, with an introduction, by Keith Beasley-Topliffe, Upper Room (Nashville, TN), 1998.

Contributor to works by others, including the introduction to *The Scale of Perfection,* by Walter Hilton, Watkins (London, England), 1923, and to periodicals, including *Fortnightly Review.* Underhill's personal papers are in the King's College archives, London, England (sixty-two items); the May Sinclair Collection at the University of Pennsylvania, Philadelphia, (fourteen letters); St. Andrews University archives, St. Andrews, Scotland (fifty-three letters); and the Fawcett Library, City of London Polytechnic, (one letter).

SIDELIGHTS: Evelyn Underhill's religious poetry and books on mysticism led to her being the first laywoman to conduct retreats in the Anglican Church and the first woman to lecture on religion at Oxford University. Since 1988 she has been commemorated in the Episcopalian Calendar, "the closest that denomination comes to canonization," noted James Whitlark in *Dictionary of Literary Biography.* Underhill's influence was such that in 1932 Ernest Benn Limited reprinted a number of her devotional lyrics in its "Augustan Books of Poetry" series. Her poems are not so much appreciated for themselves as they are appreciated as an expression of her view of mysticism. "She herself abandoned writing poetry," wrote Whitlark, "saying that it was too easy. Poetry, nonetheless, was her primary avenue to the aesthetic, and coupled with the social work she did in the slums, it formed, she believed, a foundation for the highest level of human activity: the mystical, or the perception of ultimate reality."

Underhill's parents moved to London when she was very young, and she was educated privately until the age of thirteen when she continued her studies at Sandgate House near Folkestone. With the exception of one uncle who became an Anglican priest, Underhill's family was not particularly religious, but she was confirmed, at age sixteen, on March 11, 1892, at Christ Church in Folkestone, and took her first communion at St. Paul's, Sandgate, on Easter Sunday. That same year she won first prize in a short-story contest in *Hearth and Home* magazine.

Underhill's father founded the Royal Cruising Club, and her parents spent much of their time on their vessel, the *Amoretta,* with Underhill joining them during her vacations. It was there that she met her future husband, Hubert Stuart Moore, one of their frequent guests, who later became a specialist in marine law. At King's College Underhill studied Latin, French, Italian, philosophy, history, and botany. Beginning in 1898, her mother took her on annual trips to Europe. Her letters to Moore reflect her reactions to Catholic art, especially in Italy, which increased her admiration of that faith. Moore was indifferent, and Underhill was pulled in two directions. On the one hand she wanted to marry Moore, and on the other she was leaning toward conversion.

A Bar-Lamb's Ballad Book, Underwood's first volume, in which she makes religious allusions, was called "amateurish" by Whitlark, who noted that it is an imitation of Sir William Gilbert's *The "Bab" Ballads.* "Throughout her life her sense of humor always tempered her otherwise overwhelming piety," wrote Whitlark. "At this period, her modernist theology was close to Unitarian, with Jesus no more than a conventional symbol, so she did not worry that her humor was slightly tinged with blasphemy."

The Gray World is dedicated to Alice Herbert, wife of J. A. Herbert, who was in charge of manuscripts at the British Museum and who wrote *Illuminated Manuscripts* with help from Underhill. In this novel the protagonist "becomes a medievalist illuminator of books," said Whitlark, "but his story derives from sources in the Oriental as well as the Occidental past." At first the ghost of a child of the London slums, Willie Hopkinson is reincarnated in an Eastern setting as the son of a mother who wants him to be a poet. There are allusions to Chinese Taoist philosopher Chuang Tsu, who wondered if he might actually be a butterfly. The protagonist joins an ecumenical group that includes Buddhists and a Shintoist and becomes a bookbinder, a craft that Underhill practiced somewhat successfully. "This orientalism is typical of fin-de-siècle narratives," wrote Whitlark, "as is the presentation of art as a kind of religion and meaningful life as being derived from work at traditional crafts." Whitlark also remarked on the volume's "effeminate" main character, "another convention of the Aesthetic period." Willie is attracted to Stephen Miller, who then transfers his affection for Willie to Willie's materialistic sister Pauline. Willie is disgusted when he hears of their engagement and finds a woman who is similarly inappropriate, but after a time she breaks off their relationship, following which Willie chooses to live a chaste life that combines the artistic and the spiritual. Whitlark wrote that "he enunciates Underhill's most persistent theme: poets and mystics 'all speak a different language, but what they are trying to say is substantially the same'—they are devoted to eternal, divine Beauty."

The Miracles of Our Lady Saint Mary Brought out of Divers Tongues and Newly Set Forth in English was Underhill's first scholarly book. *The Lost Word* is a harsh commentary on heterosexuality, but in spite of the issues Underhill raises in the novel, she finally married Moore and began her most productive period. She was upset when he refused to let her join the Catholic Church, but she discarded that plan altogether after Pope Pius X issued the encyclical *Pascendi Dominici Gregis,* which condemned modernists for their controversial attempts to combine religion and science. Underhill's main interest in the Catholic Church was the modernism she found in the writings of Maud Petre and George Tyrrell.

"By then," said Whitlark, "she knew that she could not find a substitute religion as an artisan or as a member of an esoteric society. She became a religious exile, a situation she explores powerfully in *The Column of Dust,* the only one of her narratives to have the developed plot and characterization expected of a novel. The book explores a paradox . . . that occultism might prepare the way for conversion to 'true' (in other words mystical) Christianity." The strong female character is Constance Tyrrel, who wanted a child and doesn't even know the name of the man who fathered her daughter. Constance, who is in love with another woman, is possessed by a spirit and keeps the "Holy Graal" in her cupboard. Other eccentric characters populate the satire that "lays out a partly original scheme of deliverance from the wasteland it ridicules," wrote Whitlark. "According to this scheme, one need not accept conventional sexual orientation or orthodox faith. Salvation comes from 'selfless adoration,' which can be leaned by following such controversial activities as ritual magic and fornication to their ultimate results."

Mysticism: A Study in the Nature and Development of Man's Spiritual Consciousness, the first substantial and accessible work on the subject, brought Underhill considerable acclaim. It transcends mysticism's categorization as superstition and show it to be a broadly human experience. Whitlark said the volume "could be read as relatively friendly to both Catholic and Protestant Christianity, a reconciliation of Christian faith with the latest in philosophy, comparative religions, and psychology." Reacting to criticism of *Mysticism,* Underhill cautiously composed her next two books, *The Path of Eternal Wisdom* and *The Spiral Way,* under the pseudonym John Cordelier.

Her next major scholarly work was her controversial *The Mystic Way: A Psychological Study in Christian Origins,* in which she psychoanalyzes Jesus. "Underhill presents him as the supreme mystic," wrote Whitlark, "a status that is significantly less exalted than Christian orthodoxy posits. Furthermore, following historical criticism, she presumes that the words of Jesus in the Bible were 'put into his mouth' by the evangelists who shaped his legend into a myth."

Immanence: A Book of Verses contains autobiographical references that provide a clearer picture of Underhill's developing Christianity. Whitlark wrote that "like *Mysticism, Immanence* is divided between two aspects of the divine: God's manifestation in the world . . . and God's transcending the physical." Because of the poetic merit of *Immanence,* Underhill had the opportunity to collaborate with Nobel Prize-winning poet Rabindranath Tagore on translating *One Hundred Poems of Kabir,* poems mistakenly attributed to that fifteenth-century mystical poet. Whitlark noted that other poems published at about the same time, notably *Practical Mysticism: A Little Book for Normal People* and *Mysticism and War,* evidence Underhill's "concern to show that her subject had pragmatic value in helping the British summon the spirituality to persevere during World War I." Underhill and Moore saw their neighbor's house bombed. He turned to designing artificial limbs and working with the hospital board, and she become more involved with social work. Beginning in 1916, Underhill also worked in the Admiralty's intelligence branch.

Underhill rejoined the Anglican Church after the death of her friend Ethel Baker, who had been her connection to the Catholic Church. Underhill was not completely entrenched in the Anglican faith, however, and her 1921 Upton lectures, published as *The Life of the Spirit and the Life of To-Day,* were delivered at Oxford's Unitarian-affiliated Manchester College rather than at an Anglican school. Whitlark noted that her spiritual advisor, Catholic modernist Barton Friedrich von Hügel, "complained that she was little more than a deist. . . . Like her books that precede and follow *The Life of the Spirit and the Life of To-Day*, the lectures are ecumenical, finding the same spiritual path in 'Hindu, Buddhist, Egyptian, Greek, Alexandrian, Moslem, and Christian' faiths."

After von Hügel's death in 1925, Underhill looked to Walter Frere, bishop of Truro, for spiritual direction, and also consulted with Benedictine abbot Dom John Chapman. She herself become a spiritual advisor to others, leading retreats and speaking on the radio. She opposed the ordination of women, seeing that step as an obstacle to reunification with the Catholic Church. On Frere's advice she studied Russian Orthodoxy and joined the Fellowship of St. Alban and St. Sergius in 1935. But she was ultimately influenced by Anglican Reginald Somerset Ward, who had given up his pastorate in favor of traveling to hold retreats. It was his views and her reading of Aldous Huxley's *What Are You Going to Do about It?*, published in 1936, that reenforced her pacifism, which was reflected in "Postcript," written just before she died.

Underhill was not only a prolific author, but also one who brought attention to other visionaries. "Her poetic reputation has dimmed," wrote Whitlark, "but her argument that poetry and mysticism explore the same reality made the latter seem more familiar and encouraged such poets as T. S. Eliot to investigate the numinous. Popularized by her, the status of mysticism rose from an obsolete relic of monasticism to a respectable element of modern culture. . . . Instead, she turned more and more to a balance between the two that anticipated New Age holism while she remained close enough to Christianity to become a virtual saint to the Episcopal Church of America."

BIOGRAPHICAL AND CRITICAL SOURCES:

BOOKS

Allchin, A. M., and Michael Ramsey, *Evelyn Underhill: Two Centenary Essays*, SLG (Oxford, England), 1977, enlarged edition published as *Evelyn Underhill: Anglican Mystic: Eight Letters of Evelyn Underhill and Essays by A. M. Ramsay and A. M. Allchin*, 1996.

Armstrong, Christopher J. R., *Evelyn Underhill (1875-1941): An Introduction to Her Life and Writings*, Eerdmans (Grand Rapids, MI), 1975.
Armstrong, Christopher J. R., *Evelyn Underhill*, Masters of Prayer, Church Information Office (London, England), 1986.
Cropper, Margaret, *Evelyn Underhill*, Longmans, Green (New York, NY), 1958.
Dictionary of Literary Biography, Volume 240: *Late Nineteenth- and Early Twentieth-Century British Women Writers*, Gale (Detroit, MI), 2001.
Greene, Dana, *Evelyn Underhill: Artist of the Infinite Life*, Crossroad (New York, NY), 1990.
Underhill, Arthur, *Change and Decay: The Recollections and Reflections of an Octogenarian Bencher*, Butterworth (London, England), 1938.*

* * *

UNDERHILL, Paco

PERSONAL: Male. *Education:* Attended Ehwa University; Vassar College, graduated, 1975.

ADDRESSES: Office—Envirosell, Inc., 907 Broadway, 2nd Floor, New York, NY 10010. *E-mail*—p.underhill@envirosell.com.

CAREER: Environmental Analysis & Planning Consultants (became Envirosell, Inc.), New York, NY, founder, 1979—; writer. Member of Project for Public Space, New York, NY, 1975—. Instructor at City University of New York, 1977-78.

WRITINGS:

Why We Buy: The Art and Science of Shopping, Simon & Schuster (New York, NY), 1999.

SIDELIGHTS: Paco Underhill is a consultant who advises retailers on methods and means for generating sales. Patricia T. O'Conner, writing in the *New York Times Book Review*, described Underhill as "a former urban geographer who has made it his business to lurk in supermarkets and bookshops and department stores to observe 'shoppers in situ.'" She added, "His idea of a good time is to stalk the cereal aisle or the produce section and count the number of men . . . who check the price of an item before tossing it into the grocery cart. Teams of 'trackers' from his consulting firm catch consumers in the act of looking, touching, sniffing, weighing, comparing, trying on, buying. Armed with this information, Underhill advises businesses on how to increase sales." Likewise, Jean E. Palmieri wrote in *Daily News Record* that Underhill "studies how people shop." Palmieri called Underhill "a student of retail design, shopper behavior and checkout-counter dynamics."

Underhill's company, Envirosell, tracks consumers to determine their shopping habits and preferences. The researchers' findings are then used to determine ways to enhance profits. Underhill discovered, for example, that shoppers tend to turn right upon entering a store. This information, coupled with the knowledge that most shoppers are women, led him to suggest that stores display appropriately appealing items in the areas initially frequented by those women shoppers.

Underhill is the author of *Why We Buy: The Science of Shopping,* in which, according to Linda Kulman in *U.S. News & World Report,* he "shares secrets he has gleaned through in-store trackers and video cameras." Alberto Mobilio wrote in *Fortune* that *Why We Buy* "scrupulously maps the familiar realm of retail to serve up sales-pumping tips on dressing-room décor." Paula Dempsey, writing in *Library Journal,* contended that the title of *Why We Buy* is "misleading," but a *Publishers Weekly* critic affirmed that the book "should aid those in business while intriguing urban anthropologists, amateur and professional." Barbara Jacobs, meanwhile, declared in *Booklist,* "It is fascinating, this business of how and why people shop."

BIOGRAPHICAL AND CRITICAL SOURCES:

PERIODICALS

Booklist, May 1, 1999, Barbara Jacobs, review of *Why We Buy: The Art and Science of Shopping.*
Daily News Record, October 29, 1997, Jean E. Palmieri, "Retail Consultant Paco Underhill on the State of the Store."
Fortune, June 21, 1999, Alberto Mobilio, review of *Why We Buy,* p. 52.

Library Journal, April 1, 1999, Paula Dempsey, review of *Why We Buy,* p. 120.
New York Times Book Review, Patricia T. O'Conner, review of *Why We Buy.*
Publishers Weekly, April 5, 1999, review of *Why We Buy.*
U.S. News & World Report, June 21, 1999, Linda Kulman, "Why Buy Kazoos You Can't Use?"*

*   *   *

UNWIN, Simon 1952-

PERSONAL: Born January 26, 1952, in the United Kingdom; son of David James Douglas and Jerrie (Inman) Unwin; married Gillian Norma Evans, October 5, 1974; children: Mary, David, James. *Education:* University of Cardiff, B.Sc. (with first class honors), 1975, B.Arch., 1977, Ph.D., 1988. *Hobbies and other interests:* Music.

ADDRESSES: Home—Cardiff, Wales. *Office*—Welsh School of Architecture, University of Cardiff, Cardiff CF10 3NB, Wales. *E-mail*—unwins@cf.ac.uk.

CAREER: University of Cardiff, Cardiff, Wales, senior lecturer at Welsh School of Architecture, 1984—. British Council, associate advisor; Historic and Buildings Council for Wales, member.

MEMBER: Royal Society of Arts (fellow), Royal Institute of British Architects, Institute for Historic Building Conservation.

WRITINGS:

Analysing Architecture, Routledge (New York, NY), 1997.
An Architecture Notebook: Wall, Routledge (New York, NY), 2000.

WORK IN PROGRESS: An Architecture Notebook: Place; An Architecture Notebook: Ideas; architectural analysis.

SIDELIGHTS: Simon Unwin told *CA:* "My writing is motivated by a desire to understand the workings of architecture. I see architecture as one of the media by which we make sense of the physical world. I define it as giving intellectual structure to the places we use in our lives. As such architecture may be thought of as equivalent to language and philosophy. And just as everyone is to some extent a philosopher, so everyone is also to some extent an architect.

"My writing explores the way architecture works, the means, powers, and strategies available to architects in configuring places. I started writing to try to build a bridge into architectural education for students. My first book *Analysing Architecture,* grew from my work in the Welsh School of Architecture. It has subsequently come to be used in many schools of architecture across the world. Since its publication I have been looking at specific aspects of the workings of architecture in more detail. My second book was *An Architecture Notebook: The Wall,* and I am presently working on further notebooks on 'place' and 'ideas.'"

*   *   *

URSU, Anne

PERSONAL: Born in Minneapolis, MN. *Education:* Graduate of Brown University.

ADDRESSES: Agent—c/o Author Mail, Hyperion Books, 77 West 66th St., 11th Fl., New York, NY 10023.

CAREER: Writer. Worked in a bookstore; *City Pages,* Minneapolis, MN, theater critic; *Phoenix,* Portland, ME, arts writer.

WRITINGS:

Spilling Clarence, Theia (New York, NY), 2002.

WORK IN PROGRESS: A novel.

SIDELIGHTS: Anne Ursu's debut novel, *Spilling Clarence,* was called "imaginative and charming" by Susan Larson in the New Orleans *Times-Picayune,* "a must for fans of such writers as Anne Tyler and Alice Hoffman. . . . Ursu does a wonderful job."

The novel is set in fictional Clarence, Minnesota, a town that boasts a college and a psychopharmaceutical plant. When an employee of the plant uses the old microwave in the break room, it sparks and starts a fire that releases a chemical cloud into the air, followed by the blast of air raid sirens. The townspeople are told to stay indoors as men in yellow hazard suits appear outside. Several of the characters are stranded in the Davis and Dean bookstore and café as they wait for the all-clear signal. They include Professor Bennie Singer and his nine-year-old daughter Sophie, and Susannah Korbet, who moved to Clarence to be with her fiancee, Todd, a graduate student who is working with Bennie in the field of memory studies.

Although an assurance of safety is made, the mind-altering drug deletrium begins to cause the townspeople's memories to become extremely keen, and even the animals are affected. Bennie is tormented by memories of his dead wife who was killed in a car crash. Christine Perkins commented in *Library Journal* that Ursu's descriptions of these recollections and his interactions with his daughter, "are very moving. . . . Ursu is a writer who cares deeply about her characters." Susannah constantly thinks of her mother, whose mental illness has driven a wedge between her and Todd. She moves into the Sunny Shadows Estates Elegant Living Retirement Community, where she has been working, and where Bennie's author mother Madeline finds regret in memories of her marriage. She has just begun a relationship with Clarence, the town's oldest veteran, who is haunted by recollections of Nazi prison camps. As each of these characters recalls the past, he or she realizes that decisions must be made for the future.

A *Kirkus Reviews* contributor felt that the character of Sophie "is perhaps the most interesting. . . . As a girl too young to have abundant memories of her own, her sturdy handling of the crises around her belies the fact that, as she puts it, 'I'm just little.'" *USA Today's* Jackie Pray noted that Ursu's "charming portrayal of precocious Sophie keeps the tone light."

A *Publishers Weekly* reviewer called *Spilling Clarence* "lightly engaging." *Booklist's* Kristine Huntley wrote that "with compelling, scarred characters and a cleverly rendered setting, Ursu's debut is both thought-provoking and enjoyable." *US Weekly* reviewer Janet Steen felt that "this whimsical, bittersweet debut suggests that the stories of our lives are what save us."

Carlin Romano, who reviewed the novel for the *Philadelphia Enquirer*, wrote that Ursu "impressively keeps the story of Clarence's encounter with its past marching on four generational levels. . . . *Spilling Clarence* unfolds dimensions of how our pasts and presents intermingle, how our dreams and memories feed off one another." Kate Ayers reviewed *Spilling Clarence* for *Bookreporter.com*, which also interviewed Ursu. Ayers said that "this book leaves you chuckling, grinning, tearful, thoughtful, warmed, chilled, and, not surprisingly, reminiscent. Your good fortune, however lies in the fact that you can control where your mind wanders. Your good fortune also lies in the fact that you have had the opportunity to read a brilliant first novel."

BIOGRAPHICAL AND CRITICAL SOURCES:

PERIODICALS

Booklist, December 1, 2001, Kristine Huntley, review of *Spilling Clarence,* p. 631.

Kirkus Reviews, November 15, 2001, review of *Spilling Clarence,* p. 1578.

Library Journal, November 15, 2001, Christine Perkins, review of *Spilling Clarence,* p. 99.

Philadelphia Inquirer, January 6, 2002, Carlin Romano, review of *Spilling Clarence.*

Publishers Weekly, November 12, 2001, review of *Spilling Clarence,* p. 34.

Times Picayune (New Orleans, LA), June 17, 2002, Susan Larson, review of *Spilling Clarence.*

USA Today, January 30, 2001, Jackie Pray, review of *Spilling Clarence.*

US Weekly, January 7, 2002, Janet Steen, review of *Spilling Clarence,* p. 64.

OTHER

Anne Ursu Home Page, http://www.anneursu.com/ (June 9, 2002).

Bookreporter.com, http://www.bookreporter.com/ (January 2, 2002), Kate Ayers, review of *Spilling Clarence* and interview with Ursu.*

V

VALENCIA, Guillermo 1873-1943

PERSONAL: Born in 1873, in Popayán, Antioquia, Colombia; died July 8, 1943; son of Joaquín Valencia Quijano (a lawyer and politician) and Adelaida Castillo (maiden name, Caicedo) Valencia. *Education:* Attended University of Cauca.

CAREER: Writer. Member, Colombian House of Representatives, 1896-99; Colombian first secretary in Europe, 1899; member, Colombian House of Representatives, 1903, and Colombian Senate, 1908-43.

WRITINGS:

IN ENGLISH TRANSLATION

Anarkos (poetry), [Bogota, Colombia], 1941, translation by Cecil Miles published as *Anarkos,* [Medellín, Colombia], 1945.

Contributor to periodicals, including *Pan American, Poet Lore,* and *Poetry.*

OTHER

Ritos (poetry; title means "Rites"), 1899, expanded edition, 1914.
A Popayán (poetry), [Popayan, Colombia], 1906.
Poesías (poetry), [Bogota, Colombia], 1912.
Oraciones panegíricas, [Bogota, Colombia], 1915.
Alma Mater, [Popayan, Colombia], 1916.

Poemas selectos (title means "Selected Poems"), introduction by M. Toussaint, [Mexico City, Mexico], 1917.
Poemas (title means "Poems"), [Buenos Aires, Argentina], 1918.
Sus mejores poemas, [Madrid, Spain], 1919.
Polémica sobre la pena de muerte, [Bogota, Colombia], 1925.
Job, [Bogota, Colombia], 1927.
Catay, [Bogota, Colombia], 1929.
A San Antonio de Padua en el séptimo centenario de su muerte, [Papayan, Colombia], 1931.
Panegíricos, discursos, artículos, edited by A. Villa Ramirez and G. Martin, [Armenia, Colombia], 1933.
Discursos (title means "Speeches"), [Bogota, Colombia], 1935.
El vengador de Wilde, [Popayan, Colombia], 1936.
Himno a la raza, [Popayan, Colombia], 1938.
Obras poéticas completas (collected works), introduction by Baldomero Sanín Cano, [Madrid, Spain], 1948.
Poesías y discursos (title means "Poetry and Speeches"), edited by Carlos García Prada, [Madrid, Spain], 1959.
Josefina Valencia de Hubach, editor, *Poemas* (collected works), [Bogota, Colombia], 1973.
Discursos (three volumes; title means "Speeches"), introduction by José M. Rivas Sacconi, [Bogota, Colombia], 1973-74.

Translator of works by numerous writers, including Heinrich Heine, Victor Hugo, John Keats, Oscar Wilde, and Olavo Bilac.

SIDELIGHTS: Guillermo Valencia was a Colombian political figure and writer whose publications include various volumes of poetry. He was born in Popayan, Colombia, in 1873, and he grew up in a family that emphasized an appreciation of literature. He eventually entered the University of Cauca, where he intended to earn a degree in law. At age twenty, however, he turned to politics, and in 1896 won election to the Colombian house of representatives. Three years later he obtained appointment to the Colombian legation in Europe.

By this time, Valencia had already produced his debut publication, *Ritos,* which includes poems written during his first stint as a representative. He issued a second book, *A Popayán,* in 1906, and a third volume, *Poesías,* appeared in 1912, by which time he had become a member of the Colombian senate, where he continued to serve until his death in 1943.

Despite his longtime tenure in the senate, Valencia managed to maintain his literary career. In 1914 he produced an expanded edition of *Ritos,* and in the ensuing years he issued further volumes of poetry. Such works aptly demonstrate his flair for expressing both alienation and a withdrawal into fantasy, but they also serve to express his religious faith and his interpretations of Biblical tales.

Valencia managed to fuse his political and literary concerns in the numerous speeches that he delivered during the course of his tenure in the Colombian congress. Many of these speeches were later collected and issued in the posthumous publication *Discursos,* which appeared in three volumes during the mid-1970s.

BIOGRAPHICAL AND CRITICAL SOURCES:

BOOKS

Oxford Companion to Spanish Literature, Clarendon Press (Oxford, England), 1978.*

*   *   *

VAN CROMPHOUT, Gustaaf

PERSONAL: Male. *Education:* University of Minnesota, Ph.D.

ADDRESSES: Office—Department of English, Northern Illinois University, DeKalb, IL 60115. *E-mail*—gustavan@niu.edu.

CAREER: Northern Illinois University, DeKalb, IL, professor of English.

WRITINGS:

Emerson's Modernity and the Example of Goethe, University of Missouri Press (Columbia, MO), 1990.
Emerson's Ethics, University of Missouri Press (Columbia, MO), 1999.

Contributor to academic journals, including *ESQ: A Journal of the American Renaissance.*

SIDELIGHTS: Northern Illinois University professor of English Gustaaf Van Cromphout is a scholar in the field of American transcendentalism, and has written two books on the works of Ralph Waldo Emerson. In *Emerson's Modernity and the Example of Goethe,* Van Cromphaut examines the influence of the German philosopher on Emerson. Susan L. Roberson, in *Southern Humanities Review,* found Van Cromphout's argument flawed, pointing out that his failure to consider Emerson's early works caused him to overemphasize Emerson's debt to Goethe. Roberson also faulted the book for its lack of "explication and interpretation." In *Nineteenth Century Literature,* however, Thomas Wortham hailed the book as a work of "rare knowledge and understanding" that enhances understanding of Emerson's thinking. "I doubt that once reading it," he concluded, "one would ever forget its valuable lessons, or its beautiful style and modest manner."

Van Cromphout followed this volume with *Emerson's Ethics,* which the University of Missouri Press identified as the "first comprehensive study" to consider Emerson's ethics within a wider theoretical context. The book examines the philosopher's search for a moral self at a time when the concept of "self" was being questioned, and considers Emerson's college essays on ethics, his interest in Kant's moral thinking, and his views on nature, language, and the moral responsibility of writers.

BIOGRAPHICAL AND CRITICAL SOURCES:

PERIODICALS

Choice, September, 1999, p. 148.
College Literature, February, 1991, p. 113.

Ethics, July, 2001, William Day, review of *Emerson's Ethics,* p. 830.

Nineteenth-Century Literature, June, 1991, Thomas Wortham, review of *Emerson's Modernity and the Example of Goethe,* pp. 141-143.

Southern Humanities Review, winter, 1992, Susan L. Roberson, review of *Emerson's Modernity and the Example of Goethe,* pp. 80-83.

OTHER

University of Missouri Press Web Site, http://www.system.missouri.edu/ (spring, 1999).*

*   *   *

van der VYFER, Thuys
    See de VRIES, Abraham H.

*   *   *

VIBERT, Elizabeth 1962-

PERSONAL: Born 1962. *Education:* Oxford University, D.Phil.

ADDRESSES: Office—c/o University of Victoria, P.O. Box 1700, STN CSC, Victoria, BC V8W 2Y2, Canada.

CAREER: University of Victoria, Victoria, British Columbia, Canada, assistant professor of history.

WRITINGS:

(Editor, with Jennifer S. H. Brown) *Reading beyond Words: Contexts for Native History,* Broadview Press (Orchard Park, NY), 1996.

Traders' Tales: Narratives of Cultural Encounters in the Columbia Plateau, 1807-1846, University of Oklahoma Press (Norman, OK), 1997.

SIDELIGHTS: Elizabeth Vibert is an historian whose area of special expertise is the Columbia Plateau, a region the area of which now comprises parts of Washington, Oregon, Idaho, Montana, and British Columbia. Vibert's account of the region, published as *Traders' Tales: Narratives of Cultural Encounters in the Columbia Plateau,* ends in 1846, the year when land disputes between Great Britain and the United States finally ended and forty-nine degrees north latitude was established as the division line between the United States and British Columbia. Vibert is most interested in the encounters between European and white American fur traders and the native peoples of the region: such groups as the Nez Perces, Umatillas, Yakamas, Cayuse, Salish, and Kutenai.

Vibert begins *Traders' Tales* by establishing what was at stake in the standing of these early fur traders' accounts of the land and people of the region; even today, traders' tales, often the only extant written documents of the region's history, are held up as factual accounts and used as evidence in court cases. Some native people's claims to territory in British Columbia have been denied on the basis of traders' characterizations of native groups. Vibert's aim is to bring in "an array of other evidence (especially linguistic, archeological, biological, and anthropological sources) to refute, augment, or support observations by the traders," according to an *H-Net* reviewer. Vibert points out that it is problematic to treat the accounts of the traders—nearly all of whom were male and European or Euro-American—as objective fact; instead, she analyzes the assumptions and biases that underlay their perceptions of the natives of the region. "Not only did the Columbia Plateau traders possess significant cultural baggage along gender, class, and racial lines, but they attempted to describe Indian cultures and natural environments that they poorly understood at best," continued the *H-Net* critic.

For instance, because native women performed much of the agricultural work of their communities—work that was most often performed by men in Europe—while their husbands fished nearby rivers, the traders characterized these women as "overworked drudges" and the men as "indolent", "weak", and "primitive," since river-fishing was mainly a sport in Europe. Because the fur traders' livelihoods depended on the pelts supplied by native hunters, they tended to characterize hunters as "manly", "robust", "full-bodied", and "brave". They associated meat-eating with robustness and good-health, whereas a vegetarian diet of grains, and vegetables unsuitable for a man of fortitude.

The fur traders often deplored "begging Indians" who asked for clothing, food, and other necessities at the trading posts. The natives would ask the trading officials to take "pity" on them by offering these gifts. Vibert supplies a good deal of linguistic and cultural evidence that the term "pity" as used by the native groups had a very different meaning for them than for their European neighbors. "To seek pity is the `polite' way of asking . . . requests for pity on many occasions appear to have signified not fear or awe, but the desire to forge a relationship," Vibert writes.

Reviewers were impressed with Vibert's subject and research in *Traders' Tales,* and the book was widely recommended for use in undergraduate- and graduate-level courses in history and gender studies.

BIOGRAPHICAL AND CRITICAL SOURCES:

PERIODICALS

American Historical Review, June, 1997, p. 949.

OTHER

H-Net, http://www.h-net.msu.edu/ (January 29, 1999).*

*   *   *

VIDMER, Richards 1898-1978

PERSONAL: Born October 7, 1898, in Washington, DC; died of heart failure, July 23, 1978, in Murray-Calloway County Hospital, Murray, KY; son of George (a general in the U.S. Army and superintendent of West Point) and Carol (maiden name, Richards) Vidmer; married Miriam Miller, June, 1922 (divorced); married Elizabeth Brooke (divorced); married Mary Field; children: (first marriage) two sons, one daughter. *Education:* George Washington University, graduated, 1921.

CAREER: Sportswriter. *Washington Herald,* Washington, DC, reporter, 1921-22; *Washington Daily News,* Washington, DC, sports editor, 1922-24; *New York Times,* New York, NY, sportswriter, 1924-29; *New York Morning Telegraph,* New York, NY, sportswriter, 1929; *New York Herald Tribune,* New York, NY, sportswriter, 1929-33, columnist, 1933-40s, foreign correspondent, 1940s-51; golf pro in Barbados, 1951-60s; Dun and Bradstreet, New York, NY, editor, 1960s-70s. *Military service:* U.S. Army Air Corps, pilot, 1910s. Commissioned as a major, 1940s, served as an intelligence staff officer, Washington, DC, and a fighter pilot with the Eighth Air Force.

WRITINGS:

Wrote nationally syndicated column "Down in Front" for the *New York Herald Tribune;* contributor to periodicals, including the *Saturday Evening Post* and *Current History.*

SIDELIGHTS: Richards Vidmer was a colorful sportswriter who worked for newspapers in Washington, D.C., and New York City for more than two decades. He was born in Washington, D.C., and his father was a cavalry captain with the U.S. Army at the time of his birth. George Vidmer was a career officer who reached the rank of general and become superintendent of the army's military academy at West Point. As the son of an army officer, Vidmer traveled widely. While still a child he lived in Japan, Cuba, the Phillippines, and several states, including Texas. He grew up around horses and played polo, a sport he later covered for the *New York Times.* While in Texas he also played professional baseball under the name "Widmeyer," in order to protect his college eligibility. Although he was accepted at West Point, Vidmer chose to serve in World War I and enlisted in the Army Air Corps. He earned his wings but never experienced combat. During a routine training flight over Long Island, his plane crashed with another. He spent nearly a year undergoing surgery and recovering in Walter Reed Hospital.

After his release, Vidmer enrolled in George Washington University. He had recovered enough from his injuries to play football and baseball, experiences that would also prepare him for his future career. Upon graduating from college in 1921, Vidmer met the managing editor of the *Washington Herald* who offered him a job as a general assignment reporter and occasional feature writer. The following year Vidmer left the *Herald* for a position as sports editor at the *Washington Daily News,* covering the Washington Senators baseball team, football, and boxing. In 1924, while covering a heavyweight boxing match in New York, Vidmer visited the offices of the *New York Times,* where he met managing editor Carr Van Anda and sports editor Bernard Thomson. He was offered a job within weeks. Vidmer was unsure as to whether he should make the big step to New York, but on the advice of his friend Walter Johnson, who pitched for the Senators, he accepted.

Vidmer reported on football each fall but preferred covering baseball. He himself enjoyed bridge—he was a master bridge player—and golf, and he played under par for most of his life. He could cover nearly any sport with skill, often reporting on polo matches, horse shows, track and field events, boxing, tennis, and rowing. Vidmer was the model used by author Katharine Brush in creating the protagonist for her novel *Young Man of Manhattan.* In the book, Toby McLean is a playboy sportswriter who frequents the speakeasies of the Roaring Twenties. The best-selling novel further enhanced Vidmer's reputation.

In 1929 a group of investors who had purchased the *New York Morning Telegraph* were hiring the best writers at top wages in an effort to make the newspaper the leader in reporting on politics, sports, and the arts in New York City. They brought in big talent to fill spots on the writing staff, including Walter Winchell, Ring Lardner, Ben Hecht, and Westbrook Pegler, and managing editor Gene Fowler approached Vidmer with an offer he couldn't refuse. But the paper quickly began to fail. Vidmer had also been courted by the *New York Herald Tribune,* and he took a position as a sportswriter with the *Tribune* during the same year.

At about this time, sportswriters were moving away from sensationalism in reporting their stories, and Vidmer was criticized for continuing to write in that style. In his book *City Editor,* Stanley Walker gave an example of what he considered the outdated approach in Vidmer's coverage of the championship heavyweight fight between champion Primo Carnera and challenger Max Baer. Vidmer wrote, "The Baer went over the mountain and brought the heavyweight championship of the world back to the United States in his right hand. With audacious confidence, smiling surety, and a sledgehammer punch developed slaughtering cattle, Max Baer whittled Primo Carnera, the man, down to the size of a Singer midget in the Madison Square Garden Bowl last night, toyed with him like a mongoose teasing a cobra, and made his final strike in 2:16 of the eleventh round scoring his eleventh knockdown." Walker felt that the reader had

to read half a column before getting the details of the fight and said that "this sort of thing, even when it is understandable and apt, soon becomes meaningless, even obnoxious."

Bernard J. Crowley wrote in *Dictionary of Literary Biography* that Vidmer "believed in respecting the privacy of the athletes he covered. . . . On the road he was a golfing partner to various players, including Babe Ruth, who also drank and played bridge with Vidmer. Vidmer only reported on his on-field performance. He afforded a similar measure of privacy to another player he respected, Lou Gehrig, after he pulled himself from the Yankee lineup in 1939. Vidmer spoke with Gehrig's doctors in the Yankee clubhouse but declined to report that he was suffering from an untreatable creeping paralysis out of consideration for the player."

In 1933 the *Herald Tribune*'s Bill McGeehan died. McGeehan had written the column "Down the Line," and although there were several well-qualified writers available to replace him, the column was offered to Vidmer because of his ability to cover more than just football and baseball. The column was renamed "Down in Front" and was syndicated to more than a hundred newspapers. The column gave Vidmer the option of writing on various subjects. He provided readers with histories of teams and their traditional rivalries and of some of the rituals that took place on campuses. He created his "Baseball's Gallery of Goats" and added to it the names of players who had dropped balls or missed hits at critical moments in a game. Vidmer even wrote verse, including his 1936 poem "Girl at the Game," in which he honors female football fans.

After World War II Vidmer and his wife divorced, and he met Elizabeth Brooke, daughter of the rajah of Sarawak, a British protectorate in northwest Borneo. They married in England, Vidmer left the *Herald Tribune,* and the couple moved to Barbados. There Vidmer worked as a golf pro and helped golfer Bobby Jones design courses. After a decade, Vidmer returned to the United States, a decision that ended his second marriage. While working as an editor for Dun and Bradstreet in New York, he met and married Mary Field, and in the mid-1970s they retired to Kentucky. He died soon after from heart failure brought on by complications from emphysema.

BIOGRAPHICAL AND CRITICAL SOURCES:

BOOKS

Berkow, Ira, *Red: A Biography of Red Smith,* Times Press (New York, NY), 1986.

Breslin, Jimmy, *Damon Runyon—A Life,* Ticknor and Fields (New York, NY), 1991.

Cooke, Bob, editor, *Wake up the Echoes, from the Sports Pages of the New York Herald Tribune,* Hanover House (Garden City, NY), 1956.

Corum, Bill, *Off and Running,* edited by Arthur Mann, Holt (New York, NY), 1959.

Dictionary of Literary Biography, Volume 241: *American Sportswriters and Writers on Sport,* Gale (Detroit, MI), 2001.

Fowler, Gene, *Skyline: A Reporter's Reminiscence of the 1920s,* Viking (New York, NY), 1961.

Frank, Stanley, editor, *Sports Extra: Classics of Sports Reporting,* Barnes (New York, NY), 1944.

Holtzman, Jerome, *No Cheering in the Press Box,* Holt, Rinehart, and Winston (New York, NY), 1974.

Kluger, Richard, *The Paper: The Life and Death of the New York Herald Tribune,* Knopf (New York, NY), 1986.

Walker, Stanley, *City Editor,* Stokes (New York, NY), 1934.

Woodward, Stanley, *Sports Page,* Simon and Schuster (New York, NY), 1949.*

*   *   *

VILE, John R. 1951-

PERSONAL: Born April 29, 1951, in Wilmington, DE; son of Ralph (a teacher) and Joanna (a teacher; maiden name, Griffith) Vile; married Linda Christensen (a teacher), June 26, 1976; children: Virginia, Rebekah. *Ethnicity:* "Caucasian." *Education:* College of William and Mary, B.A., 1973; University of Virginia, Ph.D., 1977. *Politics:* Republican. *Religion:* Baptist. *Hobbies and other interests:* Collecting and selling books and American art, pottery.

ADDRESSES: Home—2010 Greenland Dr., Murfreesboro, TN 37130. *Office*—Political Science Dept., Middle Tennessee State University, P.O. Box 29, Murfreesboro, TN 37132; fax: 615-898-5460. *E-mail*—jvile@mtsu.edu.

CAREER: McNeese State University, Lake Charles, LA, 1977-89, began as assistant professor, became professor of government, department chair, 1981-89; Middle Tennessee State University (MTSU), Murfreesboro, TN, professor of political science and department chair, 1989—, chairs council president, 1999. Sunday school teacher and deacon.

MEMBER: American Mock Trial Association (board member, 1995-2002), Tennessee Political Science Association (president, 1995), American Association of University Professors (chapter president, 2000), American Political Science Association.

AWARDS, HONORS: Distinguished research awards, MTSU, 1993, 1999; Neal Smith Award for law-related education, American Mock Trial Association, 2000; *Encyclopedia of Constitutional Amendments, Proposed Amendments, and Amending Issues, 1789-1995* was chosen as a best reference book of 1996 by *Library Journal* and by *Booklist,* one of the thirty best reference books of 1996 by the Reference and User's Association of the American Library Association, one of the best legal references of 1996 by *Law Library Journal,* and as an Honor Book for social studies, grades seven to twelve, by the Society of School Librarians International.

WRITINGS:

Rewriting the United States Constitution: An Examination of Proposals from Reconstruction to the Present, Praeger (New York, NY), 1991.

The Constitutional Amending Process in American Political Thought, Praeger (New York, NY), 1992.

A Companion to the United States Constitution and Its Amendments, Praeger (Westport, CT), 1993, 3rd edition, 2001.

Contemporary Questions surrounding the Constitutional Amending Process, Praeger (Westport, CT), 1993.

Constitutional Change in America: A Comparative Study of Constitutional Amendments, Judicial Interpretations, and Legislative and Executive Actions, Praeger (Westport, CT), 1994.

Encyclopedia of Constitutional Amendments, Proposed Amendments, and Amending Issues, 1789-1995, ABC-CLIO (Santa Barbara, CA), 1996, revised and expanded, 2003.

The United States Constitution: Questions and Answers, Praeger (Westport, CT), 1998.

The History of the American Legal System: An Interactive Encyclopedia (CD-ROM), ABC-CLIO (Santa Barbara, CA), 1999.

Pleasing the Court: A Mock Trial Handbook, Houghton Mifflin (Boston, MA), 1999.

Presidential Winners and Losers: Words of Victory and Concession, Congressional Quarterly Press (Washington, DC), 2002.

(With Mark Byrnes and David Carleton) *On Common Ground: Framework for Democracy* (study guide), McGraw Hill (Boston, MA), 2002.

EDITOR

The Theory and Practice of Constitutional Change in America: A Collection of Original-Source Materials, Peter Lang (New York, NY), 1993.

(With Mark Byrnes) *Tennessee Government and Politics: Democracy in the Volunteer State,* Vanderbilt University Press (Nashville, TN), 1998.

Great American Lawyers: An Encyclopedia, two volumes, ABC-CLIO (Santa Barbara, CA), 2001.

Student's Guide to Landmark Congressional Laws, seven volumes, Greenwood (Westport, CT), 2001-02.

Proposed Amendments to the U.S. Constitution, 1787-2001, three volumes, Law Book Exchange, 2002.

Great American Judges, two volumes, ABC-CLIO, 2003.

Contributor to books, including *The Oxford Companion to the United States Supreme Court,* edited by Kermit L. Hall, Oxford University Press (New York, NY), 1992; *Oxford Companion to Politics of the World,* edited by Joel Krieger, Oxford University Press (New York, NY), 1993; *Congressional Quarterly's Guide to the Presidency,* edited by Michael Nelson, Congressional Quarterly Press (Washington, DC), 1996; and *A History of the Tennessee Press,* edited by James W. Ely, Jr., University of Tennessee Press (Knoxville, TN), 2002; and to periodicals, including *McNeese Review, Insights on Law and Society, Christian Century, Journal of the Georgia Political Science Association, South Carolina Law Review, Constitutional Commentary, Southeastern Political Review, Cumberland Law Review, Tennessean, Education Law Reporter, News for Teachers of Political Science, Journal of Law and Politics, Publius, Journal of Political Science, Boardmember,* and *Eternity.*

WORK IN PROGRESS: (Coeditor) *Encyclopedia of American Civil Liberties,* M. E. Sharpe, 2004.

SIDELIGHTS: John R. Vile is a professor of political science and a constitutional scholar who has written and edited a number of volumes, including the *Encyclopedia of Constitutional Amendments, Proposed Amendments, and Amending Issues, 1789-1995.* This two-volume reference contains more than five hundred alphabetical entries and studies the twenty-seven amendments that have been ratified and the hundreds that have been proposed. Vile also discusses related Supreme Court decisions and issues that include right to life, prayer in public schools, equal rights, term limits, and electoral politics.

James Carl Duram noted in *History* that although Vile favors limited use of the amending process, "his entries are evenhanded, judicious assessments of each amendment or proposed amendment, its significance, and the individuals involved in its creation." Duram felt the encyclopedia to be well organized and clearly written, so much so that it can be used by a broad audience, from high school students to constitutional scholars. A *Booklist* reviewer also noted its "readability" and called it "an excellent, up-to-date reference source on an important and fascinating aspect of our national governmental framework."

Great American Lawyers: An Encyclopedia profiles prominent trial lawyers, both living and deceased. Attorneys, historians, and political scientists have contributed essays that run three to nine pages in length and are accompanied by photographs. Vile includes his own colorful anecdotes. Each of the subjects is placed in an historical context, and the appendixes list them by year and place of birth, as well as where they studied law and later practiced. *Library Journal's* Henry Charles called the volume "entertaining and informative."

Vile told *CA:* "I began writing because I thought it was a way to professional advancement, because I thought it would enhance my teaching, and because, as a department chair, I thought that I should set an example for others in my department. I have continued because I have come to enjoy the challenge that writing poses (especially when it needs to be balanced around many other activities), the satisfaction of seeing my name in print and earning some extra money, and the opportunity to make a contribution to scholarship that will reach far beyond my own classrooms.

"I teach American constitutional law, and I have done most of my writing on the U.S. constitution and related issues. I am a great admirer of the American founders and of the constitutional system that they established and the principles that under gird it. I regularly update my *Companion to the United States Constitution and Its Amendments,* which is designed both as a reference work and as a supplement to classes in American constitutional law. I am especially interested in the constitutional amending process, and issues related to this process, and I have written a number of scholarly monographs on this topic, including my first book, *Rewriting the United States Constitution,* as well as the *Encyclopedia of Constitutional Amendments, Proposed Amendments, and Amending Issues,* a second expanded edition of which will be published in 2003. In recent years, I have also become interested in biography—I have edited the two-volume works *Great American Lawyers* and *Great American Judges.* Unlike previous works, the latter primarily focuses on the contributions of state and lower federal judges rather than on U.S. Supreme Court justices.

"Although many of my recent works are designated as reference works, it is my hope that they will direct attention to areas of study that have not previously received adequate attention. Although it is outside my main teaching interests, I am especially excited about my book *Presidential Winners and Losers: Words of Victory and Concession.* This is the first book of its kind to deal with the reactions of presidential candidates to their victories and defeats and what these reactions teach us about our republican form of government. I have also begun work on an Encyclopedia of American civil liberties, and I am currently writing a book titled *Heroes All around Us.* It deals with individual citizens whom presidents have recognized in speeches to Congress since President Reagan inaugurated this practice in 1982."

BIOGRAPHICAL AND CRITICAL SOURCES:

PERIODICALS

American Journal of Legal History, October, 1993, Richard B. Bernstein, review of *The Constitutional Amending Process in American Political Thought,* p. 511.

Booklist, December 1, 1996, review of *Encyclopedia of Constitutional Amendments, Proposed Amendments, and Amending Issues, 1789-1995,* p. 684.

Book Report, May-June, 1997, Terri Duncko, review of *Encyclopedia of Constitutional Amendments, Proposed Amendments, and Amending Issues, 1789-1995,* p. 57.

Choice, October, 1992, R. A. Strickland, review of *The Constitutional Amending Process in American Political Thought,* p. 384; December, 1993, C. P. Chelf, review of *Contemporary Questions Surrounding the Constitutional Amending Process,* p. 673; February, 1995, C. P. Chelf, review of *Constitutional Change in America: A Comparative Study of Constitutional Amendments, Judicial Interpretations, and Legislative and Executive Actions,* p. 1005; February, 1999, Q. Kidd, review of *Tennessee Government and Politics: Democracy in the Volunteer State,* p. 1137; April, 2002, M. G. Pufong, review of *Great American Lawyers: An Encyclopedia,* p. 1406.

History, fall, 1997, James Carl Duram, review of *Encyclopedia of Constitutional Amendments, Proposed Amendments, and Amending Issues, 1789-1995,* p. 9.

Library Journal, November 15, 1996, Joan Pedzich, review of *Encyclopedia of Constitutional Amendments, Proposed Amendments, and Amending Issues, 1789-1995,* p. 56; June 1, 2001, Harry Charles, review of *Great American Lawyers,* p. 139.

Review of Politics, summer, 1995, Samuel B. Hoff, review of *Constitutional Change in America,* p. 544.

School Library Journal, February, 1997, Lawrence Kapture, review of *Encyclopedia of Constitutional Amendments, Proposed Amendments, and Amending Issues, 1789-1995,* p. 133.

Trial, February, 1992, Paul A. LeBel, review of *Rewriting the United States Constitution: An Examination of Proposals from Reconstruction to the Present,* p. 81.

*   *   *

VOLKMAN, Karen 1967-

PERSONAL: Born 1967, in Miami, FL. *Education:* Attended New College, Syracuse University, University of Houston, and the University of Iowa.

ADDRESSES: Home—Brooklyn, NY. *Agent*—c/o Author Mail, University of Iowa Press, 119 West Park Rd., 100 Kuhl House, Iowa City, IA 52242-1000.

CAREER: Poet and educator. New York University, adjunct lecturer; University of Chicago, Springer Poet-in-Residence. Has also taught at Syracuse University, University of Houston, and through Poets in Public Service.

AWARDS, HONORS: National Endowment for the Humanities younger scholars grant, 1989; Hillsborough County emerging artist grant, 1990; *Prairie Schooner*'s Reader's Choice Award, 1993; National Endowment for the Arts fellowship, 1993; Isabella Gardner fellowship, 1994; Bread Loaf scholarship, 1995; National Poetry Series selection, for *Crash's Law,* 1995; has received fellowships from MacDowell Colony and Yaddo.

WRITINGS:

Crash's Law, W. W. Norton (New York, NY), 1996.
Spar, University of Iowa Press (Iowa City, IA), 2002.

Contributor of poems to periodicals, including *Poetry, Paris Review, Partisan Review, American Poetry Review, Western Humanities Review, Boston Review,* and *Voice Literary Supplement.* Contributor to anthologies, including *The Best American Poetry* and *The Pushcart Prize Anthology.*

SIDELIGHTS: Award-winning poet Karen Volkman had to overcome a youthful distaste for her craft before realizing it was to be her calling in life. As a teen growing up in southern Florida, Volkman, author of the critically acclaimed *Crash's Law,* and *Spar,* was more likely to be seen reading a novel or short story than she was a collection of poems. According to her, poetry was just too "boring" to grasp her attention. However, her interest in the form dramatically changed when, in one of her classes, she was introduced to the book *Western Wind* written by Frederick Nims. The book helped her understand the motivations of a poet, and poetry began to make sense to her. Soon thereafter, at the age of twenty, Volkman began writing poems, and she has never looked back. In the subsequent years, she has also become a writing instructor and an adjunct lecturer at New York University, Syracuse University and the University of Houston. Her goal as an instructor is to bring the same type of awakening to her students Nims's book brought to her. "I work to give a sense of poetry as something written by real

people with pleasure and some skill," the Brooklyn-based Volkman has said. That statement seems to justly apply to Volkman's own poetry. Throughout the 1990s her work was featured in such publications as *Poetry, Boston Review, American Poetry Review,* and others, and she has earned a multitude of awards.

Crash's Law, Volkman's debut collection, caught the eye of many critics and was recognized as a 1995 National Poetry Series selection. "From its very first words, *Crash's Law* bespeaks a mind attuned no less to the accidents than to the orders of sensual life," wrote Heather McHugh, one of the judges who selected the collection for the 1995 National Poetry Series. Stephen Burt, a critic for the *Yale Review,* called the collection's opening poem, "Infernal," the "poem of the year." Volkman's motivation for the collection was the "hope to blend a depiction of contemporary consciousness with the oldest conventions of cry and song."

The book's poems explore childhood memory and the conception of home, a place of comfort and "nearness." Vibrant images of gardens where tulips and lilies flourish fill the pages, as do scenes of myth and folklore. "I am all eye," she writes in the poem "Looking Back," searching through her memory to find a "daughter's footsteps / on the bare swept floor." In "Red Shoes," Volkman writes, "Not red, she said, but the dark / of pure desire, as bright and private / as the space beneath the rib cage. / They shine! said the blind old woman. / Yes, they shine." "Infernal" is a piece that examines the southern Florida city of Miami from various viewpoints. "The revenant sprawls by the pool / assessing opulent stucco and glossy indigo," Volkman writes. "In traffic, the shunt and pull / of engines, exhaust like cirrus scudding . . . earth only lighter. / Sun, triumphant, muscled between clouds, / heat for a moment the nearness we weep for./ I stay close to the water, / you stay close to the shore."

Los Angeles Times Book Review critic Ralph Angel called Volkman "a poet of consciousness" who "orchestrates the rhythms and sounds of conscious living." Patricia Monaghan of *Booklist* was also impressed with the collection, referring to *Crash's Law* as "riveting" and "fresh." Monaghan felt Volkman's writing style to be "dense, tense, allusive, and alliterative."

In 2002, Volkman released a second collection of poems, titled *Spar.* A *Publishers Weekly* contributor wrote about the collection that "these poems are involved, elusive and often startling performances."

BIOGRAPHICAL AND CRITICAL SOURCES:

BOOKS

Volkman, Karen, *Crash's Law,* W. W. Norton (New York, NY), 1996.

PERIODICALS

Booklist, June 1, 1996, p. 1668.
Los Angeles Times Book Reviews, April 13, 1997, p. G.
Publishers Weekly, April 29, 2002, review of *Spar,* p. 66.
Yale Review, July, 1997, p. 148.*

*   *   *

VU, Tran Tri

PERSONAL: Born in Vietnam; married; children: one daughter.

ADDRESSES: Agent—c/o Author Mail, University of California Press, 2120 Berkeley Way, Berkeley, CA 94720.

CAREER: Writer. *Military service:* Former officer in South Vietnamese army.

WRITINGS:

The Lost Years: My 1,632 Days in Vietnamese Reeducation Camps, University of California Press (Berkeley, CA), 1989.

SIDELIGHTS: Tran Tri Vu's *The Lost Years: My 1,632 Days in Vietnamese Reeducation Camps* tells the story of the author's sentence to a prison camp in Vietnam, almost day by day, with detailed clarity. Vu was a South Vietnamese military officer and was arrested and detained by the North Vietnamese in "reeducation" camps from 1975 until 1979. Although Vu intended to make readers aware of the plight of political prisoners in the camps, he is relatively unbiased in his account, and clearly saw his captors as real people struggling under their Communist system. Vu describes the brutal treatment of prisoners, including punishment, hunger, sickness, dangerous working conditions, and the loneliness and homelessness of those, who, when moved from cell to cell, are at "home" when their small sack of clothes is with them. Vu also makes clear that what the "reeducation" camps were supposedly intended for is merely an excuse for punishing those who hold views different from those of their captors: soldiers from the wrong side of the war, intellectuals, and others who are perceived as a threat to the totalitarian government. A *Publishers Weekly* reviewer praised the book, noting that Vu's calm, restrained detailing of events in the camp is a "wrenching contrast" to the actual experience of being imprisoned there.

BIOGRAPHICAL AND CRITICAL SOURCES:

PERIODICALS

Far Eastern Economic Review, November 23, 1989, p. 52.
Publishers Weekly, June 9, 1989.*

W

WAGNER, Tony

PERSONAL: Male. *Education:* Harvard University, Ed.D.

ADDRESSES: Office—Change Leadership Group, Programs in Professional Education, Harvard Graduate School of Education, 14 Story St., 4th Fl., Cambridge, MA 02138. *E-mail*—tony_wagner@harvard.edu.

CAREER: Educator and author. Classroom teacher and principal; Public Agenda Foundation, project director; University of New Hampshire, assistant professor of education; Graduate School of Education, Harvard University, Cambridge, MA, co-director of the Change Leadership Group, leader of Harvard Seminar on Public Engagement; senior advisor on education to Bill and Melinda Gates Foundation. Educators for Social Responsibility, co-founder and first executive director; Institute for Responsive Education, president and CEO.

WRITINGS:

How Schools Change: Lessons from Three Communities, Beacon Press (Boston, MA), 1994, revised and published as *How Schools Change: Lessons from Three Communities Revisited,* Routledge-Falmer (New York, NY), 2000.
Making the Grade: Reinventing America's Schools, RoutledgeFalmer (New York, NY), 2002.

Contributor to periodicals, including *Education Week, Phi Delta Kappan,* and *School Administrator.*

SIDELIGHTS: Tony Wagner is an educator whose *How Schools Change: Lessons from Three Communities* is a study of ninth grades in three Boston-area schools, one private and two public, that were implementing reforms. These schools were influenced by the programs of Theodore Sizer of Brown University, founder of the Coalition of Essential Schools. Sizer promotes in-depth learning in smaller and fewer classes, teachers as coaches, and graduation based on knowledge rather than credits.

Wagner was president of the Institute for Responsive Education in Boston when he undertook this study as a researcher and consultant. He spent several years in three very different schools. They include Hull Junior-Senior High School, located in a small, economically struggling community near Boston where the local superintendent had convinced voters to raise property taxes in order to improve their school, and Rindge and Latin High School, a Cambridge, Massachusetts school in which teachers had established "the Academy," an innovative program within the school. At the former, the Hull superintendent eventually left when his program failed, as Wagner notes, because he neglected to fully involve both the community and the teachers. In the latter school, the teachers were not granted the authority to expand the program to other grades and make additional improvements to the curriculum, and the project director resigned out of frustration.

The third school in the study was Brimmer and May, a small private school in Chestnut Hill, a very affluent section of Boston. Because of its manageable size and less bureaucracy, the Sizer methods were successful here. Values were established and respected, older students positively influenced younger students, and teachers and parents met frequently to discuss concerns.

The final chapter of *How Schools Change* contains Wagner's suggestions for reform. He writes that state and local governments should collect and disseminate studies that document what students should know, develop more performance-based assessments, establish a national network of schools, promote more research to show how change can happen, and foster forums for the discussion of educational goals. "Although there's nothing wrong with this list," observed Joe Nathan in *Issues in Science and Technology*, "it omits a great deal. Having spent millions of dollars over the past decade on school reform, haven't we learned at least some approaches that work well? If so, why don't schools pay attention? There are questions Wagner barely considers. But we must examine them, or we'll spend another decade covering much of the same ground again."

Booklist's Brian McCombie called *How Schools Change* "enlightening, and radical, in the most progressive sense of the word." A *Publishers Weekly* reviewer felt that "Wagner's compelling appraisal of dedicated educators at work delivers a strong message." In an *Antioch Review* article, Hazel M. Latson commented that school systems that are planning to modify curriculum, prepare a mission statement, or implement a number of other reforms, would be benefitted by this volume. Latson also felt it could be helpful in the "School Choice" debate, in which, noted Latson, advocates propose that "schools with the competitive edge of quality educational programs would be in greater demand and flourish, while schools that do not compete will have significantly decreased enrollments and will go out of business."

In *Making the Grade: Reinventing America's Schools*, Wagner introduces his prototype, the "New Village School," which he says is organized around the "four Cs," competency-based curriculum, core values, collaboration, and community—and cites schools that most closely follow that concept. Wagner feels children are not being served when they are judged by standards and tests without regard to their problem-solving and critical-thinking skills. A *Publishers Weekly* reviewer noted that "teachers teach to the test, students become scores, and everyone feels less motivation to learn and achieve," and continued, say-

ing that Wagner "offers a number of solutions that move the dialogue beyond tired debates." William J. Leary noted in School Administrator that Wagner points out "that many public school students today are very much at risk, particularly those who are poor and nonwhite, echoing the 1983 National Commission on Excellence in Education report." A *Kirkus Reviews* contributor felt that "Wagner's most valuable contribution here is reporting on his own work with communities whose school systems were in disarray and how . . . common goals were established and successfully implemented." *Library Journal*'s Scott Walter called *Making the Grade* an "engaging, readable study."

BIOGRAPHICAL AND CRITICAL SOURCES:

PERIODICALS

Antioch Review, spring, 1995, Hazel M. Latson, review of *How Schools Change: Lessons from Three Communities,* p. 242.
Booklist, July, 1994, Brian McCombie, review of *How Schools Change,* p. 1903.
Issues in Science and Technology, fall, 1994, Joe Nathan, review of *How Schools Change,* p. 90.
Choice, July, 2001, B. L. Nourie, review of *How Schools Change,* p. 2011.
Kirkus Reviews, September 15, 2001, review of *Making the Grade: Reinventing America's Schools,* p. 1346.
Library Journal, August, 1994, Arla Lindgren, review of *How Schools Change,* p. 99; August, 2001, Scott Walter, Review of *Making the Grade,* p. 128.
Publishers Weekly, June 27, 1994, review of *How Schools Change,* p. 62; November 5, 2001, review of *Making the Grade,* p. 59.
School Administrator, April, 2002, William J. Leary, review of *Making the Grade,* p. 49.
Teachers College Record, fall, 1995, Andrew Gitlin, review of *How Schools Change,* p. 138.
Washington Post Book World, November 6, 1994, Colman McCarthy, review of *How Schools Change,* p. ER25.*

*   *   *

WALBRIDGE, John 1950-

PERSONAL: Born April 28, 1950, in Lake Forest, IL; son of John, Jr. (a businessman) and Mary Lou (a businesswoman; maiden name, Sailor) Walbridge; married May 27, 1972; wife's name Linda S. (an academic); children: John T., IV. *Education:* Yale University, M.A., 1973; Harvard University, Ph.D., 1983; *Religion:* " Anglican."

ADDRESSES: Office—Near Eastern Languages, Indiana University, Bloomington IN 47405. *E-mail*—jwalbrid@indiana.edu.

CAREER: Yarmouk University, Irbid, Jordan, lecturer, 1979; Northern Land & Lumber Co., Escanaba MI, vice president, 1980-87; Baha'i Encyclopedia Project, Wilmette, IL, general editor, 1987-91; Columbia University, New York, NY, assistant editor, 1991-93; Indiana University, Bloomington, professor of Near Eastern languages, 1993—.

WRITINGS:

Sacred Acts, Sacred Time, Sacred Space, George Ronald, 1996.
(Translator, with Hossein Ziai) *Suhrawardi's Philosophy of Illumination,* Brigham Young University Press, 1999.
The Leaven of the Ancients: Suhrawardi and the Heritage of the Greeks, State University of New York Press (Albany, NY), 2000.
The Wisdom of the Mystic East: Suhrawardi and Platonic Orientalism, State University of New York Press (Albany, NY), 2001.
(Translator) Kahlil Gibran, *The Storm: Stories and Prose Poems,* White Cloud Press (Ashland, OR), 1993.
(Translator) Kahlil Gibran, *The Beloved: Reflections on the Path of the Heart,* White Cloud Press (Ashland, OR), 1994.

WORK IN PROGRESS: Translation of Galen, *Medicine for the Students of Alexandria;* translation of *The Platonic Forms in Islamic Philosophy;* research on a social history of logic in Pakistan; the roles of rationalism in education in Islamic India, British India, and Pakistan.

SIDELIGHTS: John Walbridge told *CA:* "My earlier work mostly dealt with the role of mysticism in Islamic philosophy. My current research is inspired by two years I have recently spent living, researching, and teaching in Lahore, Pakistan.

WALKER, David J.

PERSONAL: Married; wife's name, Ellen.

ADDRESSES: Agent—c/o Author Mail, St. Martin's Press, 175 Fifth Ave., New York, NY 10010. *E-mail*—dvdjwlkr@aol.com.

CAREER: Member of the Society of Jesus (Jesuit) order of Roman Catholic priests; later became a lawyer and investigator with the Chicago Police Department.

AWARDS, HONORS: Edgar Award nomination, Mystery Writers of America, for *Fixed in His Folly.*

WRITINGS:

"MALACHY FOLEY" MYSTERY SERIES

Fixed in His Folly, St. Martin's Press (New York, NY), 1995.
Half the Truth, St. Martin's Press (New York, NY), 1996.
Applaud the Hollow Ghost, St. Martin's Press (New York, NY), 1998.
No Show of Remorse, St. Martin's Press (New York, NY), 2002.

"WILD ONION, LTD." MYSTERY SERIES

A Ticket to Die For, St. Martin's Press (New York, NY), 1998.
A Beer at Bawdy House, St. Martin's Press (New York, NY), 2000.
The End of Emerald Woods, St. Martin's Press (New York, NY), 2001.

SIDELIGHTS: David J. Walker's detective fiction has won praise for its humor and likable protagonists. A former Roman Catholic priest, Walker left religious life to become an attorney. He also worked as an investigator with the Chicago Police Department, which inspired him to create his "Malachy Foley, P.I." series. "Foley is a likable protagonist with a sharp tongue and enough tough to back it up," noted Wes Lukowsky in *Booklist.*

The first of Walker's Foley novels, *Fixed in His Folly,* appeared in 1995, and introduces the memorable detective who sometimes moonlights as a jazz pianist. Once an attorney, Foley became mixed up in a situation involving a friend, and was disbarred for his loyalty. As *Fixed in His Folly* opens, a successful attorney named Harriet "Happy" Mallory comes to Foley for help: she confesses that she gave a child up for adoption thirty years before, and now wants to find him. Foley discovers he is now a troubled alcoholic priest, Father Kevin Cunningham, who is missing. Several of his friends and family have disappeared or died since Cunningham's adoptive mother, a doctor, went to prison. Foley delves into the case, trying to unlock Cunningham's family secrets and decipher hidden identities. "A tangled, moody debut with a decidedly dark view of religion and the religious," noted a *Kirkus Reviews* contributor. Walker was nominated for an Edgar award, the genre's top honor, for this first effort.

Walker's second novel, *Half the Truth,* begins when Sharon Cooper, a violin virtuoso, contacts Foley after a rat turns up in her instrument case. She fears for her life, and that of her missing younger brother Jason, as she tells Foley about the two suspicious characters who visited her to inquire about Jason's whereabouts. Jason is a college hoops star who dreams of a professional career, and Sharon fears that he has become mixed up in something far more serious. Before Foley can get to Wisconsin to talk to Jason's former coach, the man dies. He finds Jason eventually, but then Sharon disappears, along with Foley's estranged wife. *Armchair Detective* reviewer Ronald C. Miller praised the Mal Foley character as "persistent and resourceful," and declared that "wonderful characters abound in this deftly plotted tale." Walker's "prose is lively," noted a *Publishers Weekly* reviewer, "and Foley, with a mouth as quick as his hands, has some interesting edges."

In the 1998 novel *Applaud the Hollow Ghost,* Walker depicts a more sentimental side of the clever urban detective. Foley learns that his onetime high school classmate, Lambert Fleming, has been accused of assaulting a neighbor girl. Developmentally disabled, Lammy was the target of mean classroom pranks, and Foley recalls an incident when Lammy's eyes looked with pleading to him for help, and he turned away. Guilt-stricken, Foley bails Lammy out of jail and sets out to prove him innocent. Cutting through the spate of notoriety surrounding the case, Foley comes to believe that the girl may be lying to cover up an assault by a family member, and the plot becomes more complicated when he learns her family has ties to organized crime. *Applaud the Hollow Ghost,* noted a *Kirkus Reviews* contributor, "does a manful job of tacking between fisticuffs and sensitive stuff, though violence will win out, in an operatic finale." A *Publishers Weekly* reviewer felt that the finale "stretches credibility, but otherwise Walker sets questions of morality in a believable context."

Walker began a second series in 1998 that focused on the partners of a Chicago detective agency, Wild Onion Ltd. One of them, Kirsten, is a former police officer who dropped out of law school. Her husband, Dugan, is a lawyer who once dropped out of the police academy. The first novel in the series, *A Ticket to Die For,* revolves around their client Larry Candle, a less respectable lawyer who has been accused of appropriating one of his clients' settlements. Kirsten and Dugan set out to take a deposition from a witness, but a sudden murder is followed by a mysterious disappearance, and the pair soon find themselves in a thicket of the anti-pornography movement and mob activity. A *Publishers Weekly* writer termed the plot "complex and memorable," and praised the Kirsten-and-Dugan team, "whose interplay is wry but not cutesy." A *Kirkus Reviews* contributor termed it "as richly plotted" as Walker's previous books, and "good for a lot more laughs—and a perfect introduction to the talented author."

The next in the "Wild Onion" series, *A Beer at Bawdy House,* once again brings together elements from the author's own career history. Here, Bishop Peter Keegan comes to the agency for help when a stalker threatens to make public a secret the respected cleric has been hiding for years. He claims that he once visited a bawdy house, and was reprimanded by his superiors for it. Kirsten and Dugan believe that Keegan's half-brother Walter, who heads Chicago's organized crime division, is the nemesis. A meeting is arranged, but Walter becomes the target of assassination attempt before it takes place. "Just when everything seems cut-and-dried, up comes a stunning twist," stated a *Publishers Weekly* reviewer, who also praised Walker's ability to craft "well-drawn characters, serpentine plots and atmospheric settings." *Booklist* reviewer Wes Lukowsky praised Kirsten and Dugan's "witty, civilized banter" and predicted that the "Wild Onion" books will "be a long-running, intelligent series."

In *The End of Emerald Woods*, John Hurley, an unethical real estate developer, wants to turn beautiful Emerald Woods into a shopping mall. Eudora Ragsdale, treasurer of a group opposed to Hurley, has some of the organization's funds stolen from her home. She enlists the aid of Kirsten and Dugan, who assume it will be a simple job. Things turn complicated when they get no help from the local police and discover a burned body in a house belonging to Eudora's best friend. A *Booklist* reviewer noted the "clever plots, great Chicago settings, . . . sparkling dialog and . . . sexual tension."

Walker returned to his "Malachy Foley" series with *No Show of Remorse* in 2002. The repercussions of an old case that caused him to lose his license to practice law suddenly surface again in his life. The case involved crooked police, missing money, and cocaine. Now, as he attempts to reinstate his license, someone is determined make sure that doesn't happen. A *Publishers Weekly* reviewer called the book "a solid read."

BIOGRAPHICAL AND CRITICAL SOURCES:

PERIODICALS

Armchair Detective, spring, 1997, Ronald C. Miller, review of *Half the Truth*, p. 242.
Booklist, November 1, 1996, Wes Lukowsky, review of *Half the Truth*, p. 483; February 1, 1998, Wes Lukowsky, review of *Applaud the Hollow Ghost*, p. 905; October 1, 1998, Emily Melton, review of *A Ticket to Die For*, p. 312; January 1, 2000, Wes Lukowsky, review of *A Beer at Bawdy House*, p. 886; October 15, 2000, Wes Lukowsky, review of *The End of Emerald Woods*, p. 425; February 15, 2002, Connie Fletcher, review of *No Show of Remorse*, p. 996.
Kirkus Reviews, April 1, 1995, review of *Fixed in His Folly*, p. 431; January 1, 1998, review of *Applaud the Hollow Ghost*, p. 25; October 1, 1998, review of *A Ticket to Die for*, p. 1419.
Library Journal, January, 2000, Rex E. Klett, review of *A Beer at Bawdy House*, p. 167.
Publishers Weekly, April 17, 1995, review of *Fixed in His Folly*, p. 42; September 30, 1996, review of *Half the Truth*, p. 65; January 19, 1998, review of *Applaud the Hollow Ghost*, p. 375; September 21, 1998, review of *A Ticket to Die For*, p. 77; December 20, 1999, review of *A Beer at Bawdy*

House, p. 58; November 6, 2000, review of *The End of Emerald Woods*, p. 74; February 4, 2002, review of *No Show of Remorse*, p. 56.*

*   *   *

WALLACE, Patricia M.

PERSONAL: Female. *Education:* University of Texas at Austin, Ph.D.

ADDRESSES: Home—Silver Spring, MD. *Office*—Center for Knowledge and Information Management, Robert H. Smith School of Business, University of Maryland, College Park, MD 20742.

CAREER: University of Maryland University College, associate vice president and chief information officer, Center for Knowledge and Information Management, Smith School of Business, executive director, 2000—. Clarion University, associate professor; Asian Division, University of Maryland, Tokyo, Japan, director of information services and faculty member.

WRITINGS:

(With Thomas S. Brown) *Physiological Psychology*, Academic Press (New York, NY), 1980.
(With Jeffrey H. Goldstein and Peter Nathan), *Introduction to Psychology* (textbook), William C. Brown (Dubuque, IA), 1987, 4th edition (with Jeffrey H. Goldstein), published as *An Introduction to Psychology*, Brown & Benchmark (Madison, WI), 1997.
Psych Online' 97, Brown & Benchmark (Madison, WI), 1997, 2nd edition, McGraw-Hill (New York, NY), 1999.
The Psychology of the Internet, Cambridge University Press (New York, NY), 1999.

SIDELIGHTS: Psychologist and information specialist Patricia M. Wallace is the author of *Psychology of the Internet*, *Psych Online 97*, and an introductory psychology textbook that appeared in its fourth edition in 1997.

Written for a general college readership, *Introduction to Psychology* covers a broad array of topics, including life-span development, biological causes of behavior, learning processes, abnormal psychology, and psychotherapy. Since its 1987 debut, Wallace has revised *Introduction to Psychology,* improving its readability and built-in study guide and updating descriptions of research. Terri Gullickson, writing in *Contemporary Psychology,* called the third edition a "solid introductory text" that is "written in a reader friendly style." Likewise, Gary B. Nallan, also writing in *Contemporary Psychology,* praised the built-in study guide of the fourth edition and described the whole as a "handsome product" that is "readable and mostly accurate."

In *The Psychology of the Internet* Wallace, relying on the most current research about the Internet and its users, as well as classic psychological studies, outlines the behavior patterns of Internet users. In addition to analyzing the so-called addictive qualities of the Internet, Wallace discusses such topics as deception, aggression, romance, and altruism by users. "This is a well-organized and accessible primer on the impact of the Internet on social and workplace dynamics," praised a *Publishers Weekly* reviewer.

In 2000 Wallace was hired to head the Center for Knowledge and Information Management at the University of Maryland's Smith School of Business. University leaders created the center to study the impact of information management in the modern business world in such areas as knowledge and learning networks, electronic commerce, and Internet economics.

BIOGRAPHICAL AND CRITICAL SOURCES:

PERIODICALS

Contemporary Psychology, January, 1991, Charles L. Brewer, review of *Introduction to Psychology,* 2nd edition, p. 81; September, 1995, Terri Gullickson, "Also of Interest," p. 910; June, 1998, Gary B. Nallan, "Introductory Psychology Textbooks," p. 413.
Library Journal, November 15, 1999, David E. Valencia, review of *The Psychology of the Internet,* p. 90.
Psychology Today, September-October, 2001, Paul Chance, review of *The Psychology of the Internet,* p. 74.
Publishers Weekly, October 18, 1999, review of *The Psychology of the Internet,* p. 61.

OTHER

Robert H. Smith School of Business Web Site, http://www.rhsmith.umd.edu/ (February 8, 2000).*

*   *   *

WALLACH, John P(aul) 1943-2002

OBITUARY NOTICE—Born January 18, 1943, in New York (some sources cite Scarsdale), NY; died of lung cancer, July 10, 2002, New York, NY. Journalist and author. Wallach spent much of his career reporting on war and violence; he spent the rest of his life working for peace. Wallach joined the Hearst newspaper syndicate as a reporter in 1968 and remained there as a foreign editor until about 1995. For nearly thirty years he covered international events, including reports documenting U.S. covert intelligence operations in Nicaragua, which earned him the Edwin M. Hood Award of the National Press Club in 1989, and he worked frequently as a foreign correspondent from the conflict-torn Middle East. Wallach spearheaded a series of exploratory meetings between Soviet and U.S. officials in the 1980s that earned him the Soviet Medal of Freedom. In 1993, however, the bombing of the World Trade Center in New York City prompted Wallach to begin a new career. Retiring from journalism, he became the executive director of the Elie Weisel Foundation for Humanity and, in 1993, founded the summer camp called Seeds for Peace. Wallach's mission was to bring young people from Egypt, Israel, and Palestine together at a neutral campsite in Maine, where they could learn to see one another as human beings before all hope of peaceful coexistence was lost. The camp, which began with forty-five children in 1993, hosted ten times that many in the year 2002, drawing campers from all over the Middle East as well as Cyprus, the Balkans, the Far East, and Afghanistan. In 1997 Wallach became a senior fellow of the United States Institute of Peace, which published his book, *The Enemy Has a Face: The Seeds of Peace Experience.* For his work on behalf of peace, Wallach received the UNESCO Prize from the United Nations and the Legion of Honor of the Hashemite Kingdom of Jerusalem. His other writings include *The New Palestinians: The Emerging Generation of Leaders* and, with his wife Janet Wallach, *Still Small Voices: The Human Story behind the Intifada.*

OBITUARIES AND OTHER SOURCES:

BOOKS

Wallach, John P., and Michael Wallach, *The Enemy Has a Face: The Seeds of Peace Experience,* photographs by James Lukoski, U.S. Institute of Peace (Washington, DC), 2000.

PERIODICALS

Chicago Tribune, July 12, 2002, pp. 2,10.
Los Angeles Times, July 12, 2002, p. B13.
New York Times, July 12, 2002, obituary by Paul Lewis, p. A17.
Times (London, England), July 18, 2002.
Washington Post, July 12, 2002, obituary by Adam Bernstein, p. B6.

*　　*　　*

WARING, Anna Letitia 1823-1910

PERSONAL: Born April 19, 1823, in Plas-y-Velin, Neath, Glamorganshire, Wales; died May 10, 1910; daughter of Elijah (a writer and journalist) and Deborah Waring.

CAREER: Poet and author.

WRITINGS:

Hymns and Meditations, Charles Gilpin (London, England), 1850; eigth enlarged edition, Shaw (London, England), 1883.
"What Can't Be Cured Must Be Endured"; or, Christian Patience and Forebearance in Practice, Nisbet (London, England), 1854.
"Early to Bed, and Early to Rise, Makes a Man Healthy, Wealthy and Wise"; or, Early Rising, a Natural, Social, and Religious Duty, Nisbet (London, England), 1856.
Additional Hymns, Bennett (London, England), 1858.
Lizzie Weston's Mission, American Tract Society (Boston, MA), 1864.

The Wasted Grain and Other Poems, Orphans' Printing Press (Leominster, England), 1867.
(Compiler) *Days of Remembrance: A Memorial Calendar,* Hodges (Dublin, Ireland), 1886.

Contributor to periodicals, including *Sunday Magazine.* Work represented in hymn books, including the *Leeds Hymn Book,* 1853, the American Unitarian *Hymn Book for Church and Home,* 1868, and *Hymns of Praise and Prayer,* collected by James Martineau, 1873.

SIDELIGHTS: Anna Letitia Waring, an author of devotional writings with readers in both England and the United States, is best remembered for her *Hymns and Meditations.* The Right Reverend F. D. Huntington, Episcopal bishop of central New York, who provided the introduction for the eighth edition published in 1863, described Waring's work as "a class of devotional writings having a peculiar ministry and a peculiar value." Waring's audience was largely working class. Huntington praised her "tone of spiritual feeling," her "inventive thought," her "fine discriminations in the application of terms," and her "certain reserve and self-command in the use of fancy."

Waring was born in Wales, one of seven children of Elijah and Deborah Waring. Her father had campaigned for parliamentary reform in their home of Hampshire, England, through *The Cambrian Visitor,* a journal he founded and edited. When the family relocated to Wales, he became a journalist. Elijah Waring later published a biography of his friend Iolo Morganwg (Edward Williams), *Recollections and Anecdotes of Edward Williams, the Bard of Glamorgan.* In her biography *In Remembrance of Anna Letitia Waring,* Mary S. Talbot noted that Waring's mother was supportive of her daughter's writing, as was her uncle Samuel Miller Waring, the author of *Sacred Melodies.* Waring, said Talbot, spoke of her happy childhood and a house often visited by friends.

The family belonged to the Society of Friends, or Quakers, and in 1840 Waring left the sect for the Church of England. Crys Armbrust noted in *Dictionary of Literary Biography* that "her resolve to do so was strengthened by her reading of a document left behind by her uncle Samuel, who had died in 1827, in which he said that he had converted to Anglicanism because he felt a need for the sacraments; Waring had the same need." Her family did not oppose her, and she was baptized on May 15, 1842, by the Reverend Anthony Crowdy at the Parish Church of St. Martin's, Winnall, Winchester. Waring studied scripture and learned Hebrew in order to read the Old Testament in the original language. She also read the Hebrew Psalter on a daily basis.

Hymns and Meditations consists of nineteen poems based on biblical texts. Armbrust wrote that the "most memorable ones are taken from the Psalms, such as 'Father, I know that all my life,' `In Heavenly Love abiding,' and `Go not far from me, O my God.' Waring's vision of sin is terrible, but it is accompanied by the promise of salvation by a merciful Supreme Being. Divine revelation, stoic resignation, and spiritual redemption figure in each of the poems." Many of Waring's poems were included in popular hymn books of the time.

Two volumes that reflect Waring's involvement during the 1860s with prison reform and the temperance movement are *Lizzie Weston's Mission* and *The Wasted Grain and Other Poems.* When Alexander Strahan published the eleventh enlarged edition of *Hymns and Meditations* in 1870, Waring joined his list of mainstream authors, including Alfred Tennyson, William Ewart Gladstone, and Anthony Trollope. She also began writing for Strahan's *Sunday Magazine,* which boasted a readership of 90,000. From 1883, the Society for Promoting Christian Knowledge (which was also the publisher of Talbot's biography of Waring) took over the various republications of *Hymns and Meditations.* Some of Waring's unpublished poems are included in an appendix to Talbot's biography. Waring's only other publication was *Days of Remembrance: A Memorial Calendar,* a collection of scriptural texts. From the 1890s until her death she wrote only for her friends.

Waring spent her later years in Bristol, where she was involved with the Discharged Prisoners Aid Society and visited inmates at Horfield Prison. Talbot noted that "in her own conversation there were no conventional sayings, no vain repetitions; each thought came slowly, clothed in graphic and appropriate language. There was always an extraordinary directness of approach in all her dealings with her fellows, and her gravity of manner had in it no sternness. Those who knew her well took much delight in the fund of merry quiet humour which lay concealed under her grave demeanor." Waring died in 1910 after a brief illness.

At her request, most of her unpublished work and her letters were destroyed.

BIOGRAPHICAL AND CRITICAL SOURCES:

BOOKS

Huntington, Right Reverend F. D., author of introduction, *Hymns and Meditations* by Anna Letitia Waring, Dutton (Boston, MA), 1863.

Dictionary of Literary Biography, Volume 240: *Late Nineteenth- and Early Twentieth-Century British Women Poets,* Gale (Detroit, MI), 2001.

Miles, Alfred H., *The Sacred Poets of the Nineteenth Century,* Volume 11, Routledge (London, England), 1905.

Talbot, Mary S., *In Remembrance of Anna Letitia Waring,* Society for Promoting Christian Knowledge (London, England), 1911.*

*   *   *

WARREN, Kay B(arbara) 1947-

PERSONAL: Born 1947, in Stanford, CA; daughter of Bruce G. and Elva C. (Ristal) Warren; married Loy McGee Carrington, March 21, 1988; children: Camie, Buddy. *Education:* University of California, B.A., 1968; Princeton University, Ph.D., 1974.

ADDRESSES: Office—Department of Anthropology, Harvard University, William James Hall 320, 33 Kirkland St., Cambridge, MA 02138.

CAREER: Mount Holyoke College, Holyoke, MA, lecturer in anthropology and sociology, 1973-74, assistant professor of anthropology and sociology, 1974-80, associate professor of anthropology and sociology, 1980-82; Princeton University, Princeton, NJ, professor of anthropology, 1982-98, founding director of program in women's studies, 1982-88, chair of anthropology department, 1994-98; Harvard University, Cambridge, MA, professor of anthropology, 1998—.

AWARDS, HONORS: Fellowships from Wenner-Gren Foundation (1992-93), Institute for Advanced Study (1994-98), and John Simon Guggenheim Foundation (1996-97).

WRITINGS:

The Symbolism of Subordination: Indian Identity in a Guatemalan Town, University of Texas Press (Austin, TX), 1978.

(With Susan C. Bourque) *Denial and Reaffirmation of Ethnic Identities: A Comparative Examination of Guatemalan and Peruvian Communities,* International Area Studies Programs/University of Massachusetts (Amherst, MA), 1978.

(With Susan C. Bourque) *Women of the Andes: Patriarchy and Social Change in Two Peruvian Towns,* University of Michigan Press (Ann Arbor, MI), 1981.

(With Krishna Ahooja-Patel and Susan C. Bourque) *Women's Access to Technology: Myths and Realities,* INSTRAW (Santo Domingo, Dominican Republic), 1990.

(Editor) *The Violence Within: Cultural and Political Opposition in Divided Nations,* Westview Press (Boulder, CO), 1993.

Indigenous Movements and Their Critics: Pan-Maya Activism in Guatemala, Princeton University Press (Princeton, NJ), 1998.

(Editor, with Carol J. Greenhouse and Elizabeth Mertz) *Ethnography in Unstable Places: Everyday Lives in Contexts of Dramatic Political Change,* Duke University Press (Durham, NC), 2002.

SIDELIGHTS: Harvard University Anthropologist Kay B. Warren has made the study of ethnic identities in Mesoamerica her field of specialty. Warren is the author or contributing author of numerous works. Her first book, 1978's *The Symbolism of Subordination: Indian Identity in a Guatemalan Town,* was the result of her field study in San Andrés Semetabaj, home to both an indigenous population of Cakchiquel natives and Latinos descended from the Spanish conquest. Warren focuses her research on the meek Cakchiquel, a group whose mythology and self-identity made them easily subdued by the Europeans in the early 1500s, and has since kept them in the role of second-class citizens in their own land. As *The Symbolism of Subordination* recounts, a turning point came in 1952, when a missionary group called Catholic Action began winning converts and attempting to foster in the Cakchiquel a more assertive new group identity—one not based upon their ethnicity. They were urged to assimilate and demand equal treatment, but the Latino population opposed this movement. "This is a meaty,

fascinating, and sharply focused study," asserted *American Anthropologist* reviewer Philip D. Young, who concluded by calling it "a valuable contribution to our knowledge of the politics of identity."

Warren has also contributed to two titles with Susan C. Bourque: *Denial and Reaffirmation of Ethnic Identities: A Comparative Examination of Guatemalan and Peruvian Communities,* which appeared in 1978, and *Women of the Andes: Patriarchy and Social Change in Two Peruvian Towns,* published in 1981. She served as editor for the collection of seven essays in 1993's *The Violence Within: Cultural and Political Opposition in Divided Nations,* before publishing another work on ethnic identity in Guatemala. *Indigenous Movements and Their Critics: Pan-Maya Activism in Guatemala* appeared in 1998 and was the result of Warren's investigation into a relatively recent renaissance of ethnic pride in the country. This development was partially incited by years of devastating civil war in which military governments and leftist insurgencies battled for the people's allegiance. Eschewing this have been small, but growing Pan-Mayan movements that arose more than four hundred years after the Spanish conquered the area. Such groups call for educational reform, a revival of the Mayan language, and a multicultural democracy. Warren's book concentrates on the years between 1987 and 1996, and sets out to disprove the notion that such movements are isolated and insignificant. Warren's "analysis and insight," wrote James C. Harrison in *Multicultural Review,* "make this book a significant contribution to the literature on indigenous social movements."

BIOGRAPHICAL AND CRITICAL SOURCES:

PERIODICALS

American Anthropologist, September, 1980, Philip D. Young, review of *The Symbolism of Subordination,* pp. 656-657.

American Ethnologist, November, 1999, George A. Collier, review of *Indigenous Movements and Their Critics: Pan-Maya Activism in Guatemala,* p. 1009.

American Historical Review, April, 2001, David McCreery, review of *Indigenous Movements,* p. 618.

Choice, October, 1993, M. Curtis, review of *The Violence Within,* p. 363.

Foreign Affairs, May, 1999, Kenneth Maxwell, review of *Indigenous Movements*, p. 143.

Hispanic American Historical Review, May, 2000, Stefano Varese, review of *Indigenous Movements*, p. 378.

Journal of Politics, May, 2000, Roderic Ai Camp, review of *Indigenous Movements*, p. 622.

Latin American Politics and Society, spring, 2002, Beverly Nagel, review of *Indigenous Movements*, p. 189.

Library Journal, April 1, 1979, Susan Hamburger, review of *The Symbolism of Subordination*, p. 845.

Multicultural Review, September, 1999, James C. Harrison, review of *Indigenous Movements*, pp. 84-85.*

*   *   *

WATERS, Sarah 1966-

PERSONAL: Born 1966, in Wales. *Education:* Ph.D. in English literature.

ADDRESSES: Home—London, England. *Office*—c/o Riverhead Books, 375 Hudson Street, New York, NY 10014.

CAREER: Author. Has been an associate lecturer with the Open University.

AWARDS, HONORS: Somerset Maugham Award; *Sunday Times* Young Writer of the Year Award; shortlisted twice for the *Mail on Sunday*/John Llewellyn Rhys Memorial Prize; shortlisted for Orange Prize for Fiction, 2002, and Booker Prize, 2002, both for *Fingersmith.*

WRITINGS:

Tipping the Velvet, Riverhead Books (New York, NY), 1999.

Affinity, Riverhead Books (New York, NY), 2000.

Fingersmith, Virago (London, England), 2002.

SIDELIGHTS: Sarah Waters is the author of *Tipping the Velvet*, a book exploring female sexuality in Victorian England, and *Affinity*, a story set in Victorian London. *Tipping the Velvet*, published in 1999, is a complex book, exploring the unorthodox life of Nancy King, a budding lesbian, and her search for true love. Nan is initially portrayed as an innocent, simple girl, enjoying a night out at the local music hall where she sees and becomes infatuated with Miss Kitty Butler, a cross-dressing lounge singer. The following chapters trace the young girl from innocence to young love and heartbreak, on to the requisite loneliness of a common streetwalker and into true love. Waters presents the material with a compassionate sensitivity. Miranda Seymour of the *New York Times Book Review* wrote of *Tipping the Velvet*, "Waters has captured it beautifully—not only the seediness of the hall and the transforming spell cast by the jaunty cross-dressing girl but the star struck innocence of Nancy's first love, the breathless passion she can hardly find words to describe." Overall, the reaction to *Tipping the Velvet* was strong and positive, although a few critics found a somewhat redundant re-stressing of Waters's lesbian political ideals rather tiring.

In 2000, Waters published *Affinity*. Critics found this work to be much darker than her previous book. Following the death of her father and the marriage of her best friend (and secret lover) to her brother, Margaret Pryor becomes a "Lady Visitor" in a prison in order to recover from these losses. During her rounds, Margaret meets Selina Dawes, a spiritualist in prison for fraud and assault, with whom she falls in love. "*Affinity* is a powerful yet detailed Victorian tale centering on relationships, especially [those] forbidden by society between two women," wrote a *Bookbrowser.com* reviewer. Although a *Publishers Weekly* reviewer found, "lugubrious historical detail and awkward pacing," Sarah Chinn, of the *Advocate*, wrote, "Waters has created a compelling character in a deeply absorbing book."

BIOGRAPHICAL AND CRITICAL SOURCES:

PERIODICALS

Advocate, June 22, 1999, Anne Stockwell, review of *Tipping the Velvet*, p. 124; May 23, 2000, Sarah Chinn, review of *Affinity*, p. 107.

Booklist, June 1 & 15, 1999, Margaret Flanagan, review of *Tipping the Velvet*, p. 1787.

Lambda, July, 2000, Sarah Van Arsdale, "An Affinity for the Past," p. 6.

New York Times Book Review, June 13, 1999, Miranda Seymour, "Siren Song," p. 9.

Publishers Weekly, April 12, 1999, review of *Tipping the Velvet,* p. 53; May 29, 2000, review of *Affinity,* p. 51.

Seattle Times, June 25, 2000, Michael Upchurch, review of *Affinity.*

OTHER

Bookbrowser.com, http://www.bookbrowser.com/ (May 30, 2000), Harriet Klausner, review of *Affinity.**

*   *   *

WATTS, Jerry Gafio 1953-

PERSONAL: Born May 17, 1953, in Washington, DC; son of James S. and Maria (Wright) Watts. *Ethnicity:* "Afro-American." *Education:* Harvard College, B.A., 1975; Yale University, M.A., 1977, M.Phil., 1978, Ph. D., 1985. *Politics:* Democrat-Socialist. *Religion:* Methodist. *Hobbies and other interests:* Watching sports.

ADDRESSES: Home—P.O. Box 340297, Hartford, CT 06134. *Office*—American Studies Program, Trinity College, 300 Summit St., Hartford, CT 06106-3100. *E-mail*—Jerry.Watts@Trincoll.edu.

CAREER: Educator, author and lecturer. University of California—Davis, acting assistant professor of Afro-American studies, 1982-84; Wesleyan University, Middletown, CT, instructor, 1984-85, assistant professor of government and Afro-American studies, 1986-90; Trinity College, Hartford, CT, associate professor of American studies, 1990—.

MEMBER: American Studies Association, American Sociological Association, American Political Science Association.

AWARDS, HONORS: Ford Foundation postdoctoral fellowship, 1987; American Council of Learned Societies fellowship, 1987; National Endowment for the Humanities research travel grant, 1990.

WRITINGS:

Heroism and the Black Intellectual: Ralph Ellison, Politics, and Afro-American Intellectual Life, University of North Carolina Press (Chapel Hill, NC), 1994.

Amiri Baraka: The Politics and Art of a Black Intellectual, New York University Press (New York, NY), 2001.

Contemporary Sociology, member of editorial board, 1994-97. Contributor of articles, reviews, and essays to periodicals, including *Hartford Courant, Boston Review, Nation, Democratic Left, Contemporary Sociology, New Politics, Humbolt Journal of Social Relations, Phylon, Social Research, Emerge, New York Times Book Review, Dissent, Radical America, Urban Affairs Quarterly, Z, Christianity and Crisis, Journal of Black Studies, Social Text,* and *Common Quest: The Magazine of Black and Jewish Relations.* Contributor to books, including *Higher Education under Fire,* edited by Michael Berube and Cary Nelson, Routledge (New York, NY), 1994; *The Politics of Minority Coalitions: Race, Ethnicity, and Shared Uncertainties,* edited by Wilbur Rich, Praeger (Westport, CT), 1996; and *Teaching Matters: Essays on Liberal Education at the Millennium,* edited by Mark Warren McLaughlin, Drew Hyland, and J. Ronald Spencer, Trinity College (Hartford, CT), 1999.

WORK IN PROGRESS: The Crisis of the Negro Intellectual Revisited, contributor and coeditor with James Miller, Routledge.

SIDELIGHTS: Jerry Gafio Watts, who has taught both American and Afro-American studies, is a frequent contributor to periodicals and books and reviewer of works by others that focus on race, class, culture, politics, civil rights, economics, and prominent blacks whose work and lives have impacted the African-American community. Watts is also the author of books that include *Amiri Baraka: The Politics and Art of a Black Intellectual,* a study rather than a biography of the life of Baraka, known as LeRoi Jones during the time of the Beat generation of the late 1950s, but best known for his militancy and activism and association with the Black Power movement of the 1960s. Watts describes his subject as an "apocalyptic loose cannon" who has been guilty of "ethnic cheerleading." A. O. Edmonds said in *Library Journal* that this is "a massive study of the political and intellectual career of the poet and activist."

Justin Driver wrote in *New Republic* that *Amiri Baraka* "is the most thorough and reliable assessment of Baraka's work so far. Watts approaches his subject with a healthy degree of skepticism, criticizing Baraka roundly for the unbridled hatred that runs throughout much of his work. The problem is that Watts is too close to his subject. . . . Watts also occasionally allows jargon ('social marginality facilitator') to intrude into the narrative." "Still," continued Driver, "Watts' criticisms of Baraka are usually on target. He rightly skewers his subject for the condescending ways in which Baraka simplified his theatrical writing in an effort to make his work more accessible to the black masses. . . . In a novel assessment, Watts contends that the homophobia and the sexism in Baraka's work stem from an effort to cover up his own gay encounters during his Beat days."

A *Publishers Weekly* contributor noted that Watts did not interview Baraka or anyone close to him in writing this book, "which may explain why Baraka remains something of an enigma here. Still, Watts takes a decisive step toward deciphering the persona of a leading American writer." *Booklist*'s Vernon Ford observed that as Baraka became more involved in politics, his creative efforts suffered, and added that "through it all, despite Baraka's warts, Watts assesses him to be, at heart, the same individualistic Beat poet."

BIOGRAPHICAL AND CRITICAL SOURCES:

PERIODICALS

Booklist, September 15, 2001, Vernon Ford, review of *Amiri Baraka: The Politics and Art of a Black Intellectual,* p. 182.

Choice, April, 1995, C. Werner, review of *Heroism and the Black Intellectual: Ralph Ellison, Politics, and Afro-American Intellectual Life,* p. 1306.

Contemporary Sociology, March, 1996, Lewis A. Coser, review of *Heroism and the Black Intellectual,* p. 264.

Dissent, summer, 1997, Gerald Early, review of *Heroism and the Black Intellectual,* p. 114.

Journal of American Studies, August, 1995, Gavin Cologne-Brookes, review of *Heroism and the Black Intellectual,* p. 321.

Journal of Southern History, May, 1996, Charles Pete Banner-Haley, review of *Heroism and the Black Intellectual,* p. 420.

Library Journal, October 1, 1994, Anthony O. Edmonds, review of *Heroism and the Black Intellectual,* p. 100; August, 2001, A. O. Edmonds, review of *Amiri Baraka,* p. 124.

New Republic, April 29, 2002, Justin Driver, review of *Amiri Baraka,* p. 33.

New York Times Book Review, February 5, 1995, Charles Johnson, review of *Heroism and the Black Intellectual,* p. 15.

Publishers Weekly, August 6, 2001, review of *Amiri Baraka,* p. 74.*

*   *   *

WEAVER, Courtney 1965-

PERSONAL: Born 1965, in San Francisco, CA. *Education:* Brown University; New York University, M.A.

ADDRESSES: Agent—c/o Author Mail, Random House, 1540 Broadway, New York, NY 10036.

CAREER: Worked for British Broadcasting Corporation; *and San Francisco Chronicle,* San Francisco, CA; freelance writer.

WRITINGS:

Unzipped: What Happens When Friends Talk about Sex—A True Story, Doubleday (New York, NY), 1999.

Contributor to *Salon.com, Restaurant and Hospitality* and *San Francisco Examiner.*

SIDELIGHTS: Courtney Weaver spent several years as a journalist before finding success with her 1999 debut work, *Unzipped: What Happens When Friends Talk about Sex—A True Story.* A graduate of Rhode Island's Brown University, Weaver went on to earn a graduate degree in creative writing from New York University.

She lived in Northern Ireland, worked for the British Broadcasting Corporation, and wrote for the *San Francisco Chronicle.* But it was her column for the online magazine *Salon.com,* titled "Unzipped," that garnered industry attention, and Weaver decided to use "Unzipped"—which chronicled the romantic travails of her friends in San Francisco—as the basis for her first book.

Unzipped details the lives, both public and private, of a cast of twenty-something characters. These include a former punk rocker whose marriage has recently ended and now finds herself a single mother back in the dating pool, and a nanny who likes to visit bondage clubs. Commitment-phobic women and tales of vengeful exes also appear in *Unzipped*'s pages, and Weaver even discusses her dating habits candidly. She writes about the difficulty of the freelancer's isolated lifestyle, and in passages commended by a *Publishers Weekly* reviewer, depicts "herself in her darker moments as that most solitary of creatures: the Internet addict." Other reviews offered mostly positive assessments of Weaver's debut. "Her portraits are vivid, and the book is an entertaining read," wrote *Library Journal*'s Martha Cornog. "Ultimately, 'Unzipped' feels less like a book than a conversation," noted *New York Times Book Review* critic Jenny Lyn Bader. "At least it's a conversation with a charming person. And its conclusion, as Weaver musters some compassion for herself, has an unexpected sweetness."

BIOGRAPHICAL AND CRITICAL SOURCES:

PERIODICALS

Library Journal, October 15,1999, Martha Cornog, review of *Unzipped,* p. 89.
New York Times Book Review, December 26, 1999, Jenny Lyn Bader, "How Was It for You?," p. 9
Publishers Weekly, November 8, 1999, review of *Unzipped,* p. 57.*

*　　*　　*

WEAVER, Richard 1910-1963

PERSONAL: Born March 3, 1910, in Weaverville, NC; died April 3, 1963; son of Richard Malcolm and Carrie (Embry) Weaver. *Education:* University of Kentucky, graduated, 1932; Vanderbilt University, M.A., 1934; attended Harvard University, Sorbonne, and University of Virginia; Louisiana State University, Ph.D., 1943.

CAREER: Writer, literary critic, and scholar. Alabama Polytechnic Institute (now Auburn University), Auburn, AL, instructor, 1936; Texas A & M University, College Station, TX, assistant professor, 1937-40; Army Specialized Training Corps, North Carolina State College, Raleigh, NC, special instructor, 1944; University of Chicago, Chicago, IL, professor of English, 1945-63.

AWARDS, HONORS: Quantrell Award, 1949, for excellence in undergraduate teaching.

WRITINGS:

Ideas Have Consequences, University of Chicago Press (Chicago, IL), 1948.
The Ethics of Rhetoric, H. Regnery Company (Chicago, IL), 1953.
Composition: A Course in Writing and Rhetoric, Holt (New York, NY), 1957.
Visions of Order: The Cultural Crisis of Our Time, Louisiana State University Press (Baton Rouge, LA), 1964, new edition, foreword by Russell Kirk, preface by Ted J. Smith III, Intercollegiate Studies Institute (Bryn Mawr, PA), 1995.
Life without Prejudice, and Other Essays, introduction by Eliseo Vivas, H. Regnery Co. (Chicago, IL), 1965.
(With Richard S. Beal) *Rhetoric and Composition: A Course in Writing and Reading,* 2nd edition, revised, Holt (New York, NY), 1967.
A Rhetoric and Handbook, Holt, Rinehart, and Winston (New York, NY), 1967, (with Richard S. Beal), revised edition published as *A Rhetoric and Composition Handbook,* Quill (New York, NY), 1981.
The Southern Tradition at Bay: A History of Postbellum Thought, edited by George Core and M. E. Bradford, Arlington House (New Rochelle, NY), 1968, new edition, Regnery Gateway (Washington, DC), 1989.
A Concise Handbook (revision of part four of Weaver's *A Rhetoric and Handbook*), Holt, Rinehart, and Winston (New York, NY), 1968.

Language Is Sermonic: Richard M. Weaver on the Nature of Rhetoric, edited by Richard L. Johannessen, Rennard Strickland, and Ralph T. Eubanks, Louisiana State University Press (Baton Rouge, LA), 1970.

The Southern Essays of Richard M. Weaver, edited by George M. Curtis III and James J. Thompson, Jr., Liberty Press (Indianapolis, IN), 1987.

The Vision of Richard Weaver, edited by Joseph Scotchie, Transaction, 1996.

Was a regular contributor to *National Review.* Also contributed to *Modern Age, Intercollegiate Review,* and *Southern Partisan.*

SIDELIGHTS: Richard M. Weaver was a writer, literary critic, and social and intellectual historian. "He is a critic first," wrote Bernard K. Duffy in the *Quarterly Journal of Speech,* "a theorist second. He defends a rhetoric that manifests the conservative characteristics he admires so that his theory of rhetoric is, in one sense, a theory of conservative rhetoric."

Although Weaver was a relatively prolific writer, only three of his books were published during his lifetime, with others appearing after his death. In the four years since his death, his work has continued to be discussed by academics.

Writing in *Modern Age,* John R. E. Bliese called Weaver one of "the most important figures in the post World War II conservative movement," observing that "many of Richard Weaver's works are sustained critiques of materialism and the consumer culture." Weaver believed that American culture, particularly its moral and ethical principles, was in a state of decay, largely caused by the culture's emphasis on science, materialism, and self, and its de-emphasis on spiritual values, discipline, and sacrifice. Although Weaver believed in the importance of spiritual values, he did not defend any particular religion or creed. As Ben C. Toledano wrote in *National Review,* "His was a non-creedal faith, an ethical vision of life's verities, virtues, and truths. A close friend described him as 'religious in his devotion to high principles and to spiritual values as opposed to materialism.'" Weaver decried the fact that American culture tended to glorify wealth and those who accumulated it, and to ignore those with wisdom, integrity, and generosity.

In works such as *Ideas Have Consequences* and *Language Is Sermonic: Richard M. Weaver on the Nature of Rhetoric,* "Weaver argued the case for language,

language as revealed by the great poets, philosophers, and statesmen," wrote Thomas D'Evelyn in the *Christian Science Monitor.* D'Evelyn noted that Weaver did not care for minimalism in writing, believing, in Weaver's words, that "language is intended to be sermonic. Because of its nature and of its intimacy with our feelings, it is always preaching." In a *Modern Age* review of *Ideas Have Consequences,* Regis A. Factor noted that "Weaver's diagnosis and prescriptions have lost little currency in fifty years."

Some of Weaver's thought was derived from his experiences as a southerner; he believed that the culture of the South before the U.S. Civil War was "the last non-materialist civilization in the Western World," in the words of Bliese. Weaver wrote many essays describing and defending the fine points of southern culture, some of which were collected in *The Southern Tradition at Bay: A History of Postbellum Thought* and *The Southern Essays of Richard M. Weaver.* At times, according to Carl N. Degler in *American Historical Review,* Weaver's stand is far outdated; for example, in *The Southern Tradition at Bay,* Weaver comments that women should not work and should not have the vote. Degler also noted that Weaver's commentary on African Americans is so outdated that it is "of interest only as a historical source, not as a modern commentary on southern thought." "It is not the novelty of his themes but the ingeniousness of his arguments and his imaginative use of the language that make Weaver's writing worthwhile," commented Duffy in his review of *The Southern Essays of Richard M. Weaver.*

The Vision of Richard Weaver, published more than thirty years after Weaver's death, includes articles he published in journals, along with other writings from his studies. "The selections are a representative overview of Weaver's work and thought," observed Joseph M. Canfield in *Modern Age,* noting that while "there is some duplication of vignettes," it merely "helps to emphasize the influences which helped in the development of Weaver's ideas." Canfield also commented that, at least by everyday folks in Weaver's hometown, Weaver's "ideas seem to be lost in the rush of modernity, which Weaver deplored," including the "banal culture disseminated by the electronic media" and a "plethora of shopping malls where mass-produced merchandise is sold on credit cards."

George A. Panichas in *Modern Age* called Weaver, along with Irving Babbitt, "modern American teachers and critics who can now be honored as Sages and, indeed, included among the *Sacri Vates*," noting that Weaver's "*Visions of Order,* in its remarkable way, pays tribute to Babbitt's enduring legacy and relevance." Panichas felt Weaver was a man "of vision" who is "quintessentially" a man "of wisdom." M. E. Bradford in *National Review* commented that Weaver "was in all likelihood the foremost student of rhetoric as a living force writing in English in our time."

BIOGRAPHICAL AND CRITICAL SOURCES:

PERIODICALS

American Historical Review, June, 1969, Carl N. Degler, review of *The Southern Tradition at Bay: A History of Postbellum Thought,* pp. 1735-1736.
Christian Science Monitor, June 11, 1986, Thomas D'Evelyn, "The Power and Purpose of Language," p. 23.
Modern Age, summer, 1996, George A. Panichas, "Irving Babbitt and Richard Weaver," pp. 267-276; winter, 1996, John R. E. Bliese, "Richard M. Weaver, Russell Kirk, and the Environment," pp. 148-158; spring, 1997, Joseph M. Canfield, review of *The Vision of Richard Weaver,* pp. 173-177; fall, 1998, Regis A. Factor, "*Ideas Have Consequences* Revisited," pp. 375-383.
National Review, April 8, 1969, Jeffrey Hart, "The Dignity of the South," pp. 340-341; November 17, 1970, M. E. Bradford, "Weaver and the Web of Words," pp. 1223-1225; June 28, 1985, Carl R. Schmahl, review of *Ideas Have Consequences,* p. 51; January 29, 1996, Ben C. Toledano, review of *The Vision of Richard Weaver,* pp. 64-65.
Quarterly Journal of Speech, April, 1971, Robert L. Scott, review of *Language Is Sermonic: Richard M. Weaver on the Nature of Rhetoric,* pp. 249-250; August, 1988, Bernard K. Duffy, review of *The Southern Essays of Richard M. Weaver,* pp. 392-395.
Sewanee Review, July, 1991, Ward Allen, "Saving the Sum of Things," pp. 490-498.
Southern Humanities Review, spring, 1989, Eugene Current-Garcia, review of *The Southern Essays of Richard M. Weaver,* pp. 185-189.

OTHER

Intercollegiate Studies Institute Web Site, http://www.isi.org/ (April 22, 2002), "Weaver Fellowship."*

WEEMS, Carrie Mae 1953-

PERSONAL: Born 1953, in Portland, OR. *Education:* California Institute of the Arts—Valencia, B.A., 1981; University of California—San Diego, M.F.A., 1984; University of California—Berkeley, M.A., 1987.

ADDRESSES: Agent—P.P.O.W., 532 Broadway, New York, NY 10012.

CAREER: Photographer. University of California—San Diego, teaching assistant, 1983-84; San Diego City College, San Diego, CA, teacher, 1984; Visual Studies Workshop, Rochester, NY, artist-in-residence, 1986; University of California—Berkeley, teaching assistant, 1987; Hampshire College, Amherst, MA, assistant professor, 1987-91; Light Work, Syracuse, NY, artist-in-residence, 1988; Hunter College, New York, NY, visiting professor, 1988-89; Art Institute of Chicago, Chicago, IL, artist-in-residence, 1990; Rhode Island School of Design, Providence, RI, 1990; California College of Arts Crafts, Oakland, CA, assistant professor, 1991.

AWARDS, HONORS: Los Angeles Women's Building Poster Award, 1981; University of California fellowship, 1981-85; California Arts Council grant, 1983; Louis Comfort Tiffany Award, 1992; Photographer of the Year, Friends of Photography, Ansel Adams Center, San Francisco, 1994; National Endowment for the Arts Visual Arts grant, 1994-95.

WRITINGS:

In These Islands: South Carolina and Georgia, Sarah Moody Gallery of Art (Tuscaloosa, AL), 1995.
And 22 Million: Very Tired and Very Angry People, San Francisco Art Institute (San Francisco, CA), 1992.
Constructing Masculinity (picture essay) Routledge (New York, NY), 1995.
Carrie Mae Weems: Recent Work, 1992-98, George Braziller in association with Everson Museum of Art (New York, NY), 1998.

BIOGRAPHICAL AND CRITICAL SOURCES:

PERIODICALS

Artforum International, February, 1993, Kate Linker, "Went Looking for Africa: Carrie Mae Weems," p. 79.
Art in America, May, 1999, Ernest Larsen, "Between Worlds," p. 122.*

WEINER, Andrew D(avid) 1943-

PERSONAL: Born June 29, 1943, in New York, NY.

ADDRESSES: Office—Department of English, University of Wisconsin—Madison, 600 North Park St., Madison, WI 53706. *E-mail*—adweiner@facstaff.wisc. edu.

CAREER: University of Wisconsin, Madison, professor of English literature, 1969—.

WRITINGS:

Sir Philip Sidney and the Poetics of Protestantism: A Study of Contexts, University of Minnesota Press (Minneapolis, MN), 1978.*

*   *   *

WEISS, Julian

PERSONAL: Male. *Education:* Westfield College, University of London, B.A., 1978; Oxford University, Ph.D., 1984.

ADDRESSES: Office—Spanish and Spanish-American Studies, King's College, The Strand, London WC2R 2LS, England. *E-mail*—julian.weiss@kcl.ac.uk.

CAREER: University of Liverpool, Liverpool, England, instructor; University of Virginia, Charlottesville, VA, instructor; University of Oregon, Eugene, OR, associate professor of Spanish; King's College London, London, England, professor of literature.

WRITINGS:

The Poet's Art: Literary Theory in Castile, c. 1400-60, Society for Medieval Languages and Literature, 1990.

(Editor, with E. Michael Gerli) *Poetry at Court in Trastamaran Spain: From the Cancionero de Baena to the Cancionero General,* Medieval and Renaissance Studies (West Tempe, AZ), 1998.

SIDELIGHTS: Julian Weiss specializes in medieval and early modern Spanish literature and cultural materialism. According to the King's College London Web site, "his current projects concern Renaissance literary and textual criticism and the ideological formation of the intellectual in the thirteenth century."

Weiss's *The Poet's Art: Literary Theory in Castile, 1400-60* is a revision of his 1984 doctoral thesis. The book analyzes various texts from medieval Spain, including both aristocratic and professional writers, and examines literary attitudes in fifteenth-century Castile. Weiss points out that there was no single authority of fifteenth-century style; a variety of styles, authors, and traditions existed at the time. In *Hispanic Review,* Ivy A. Corfis wrote, "Weiss offers a reliable and intelligently drawn portrait of literary style and tastes in the first sixty years of the 1400s," and that he "accurately identifies the major theoretical concerns of the period, placing them within their historical frame and tradition." "Julian Weiss's study must be considered obligatory reading for all serious students of fifteenth-century Spain," observed Derek C. Carr in *Modern Language Review,* "and especially for those approaching the subject for the first time." In *Medium Aevum,* David Hook called *The Poet's Art* "an impressively wide-ranging and well-documented study," and noted "Weiss has presented us with an essential foundation for present understanding, and future investigation, of the culture and intellectual life of fifteenth-century Spain."

Poetry at Court in Trastamaran Spain: From the Cancionero de Baena to the Cancionero General is comprised of a selection of essays presented at a conference held from February 11-14, 1993, at Georgetown University in Washington, D.C. According to Weiss in the book's introduction, the work includes "a representative cross-section of current work, produced by scholar's writing at different stages in their careers." "*Poetry at Court in Trastamaran Spain* [is] a necessary volume for scholars interested in coming to a deeper understanding of *cancionero* verse, the *cancioneros* themselves, and court culture in fifteenth-century Spain," observed Vincent Barletta in *Hispanic Review.*

BIOGRAPHICAL AND CRITICAL SOURCES:

PERIODICALS

Hispanic Review, winter, 1992, Ivy A. Corfis, review of *The Poet's Art: Literary Theory in Castile,*

1400-60, pp. 81-82; winter, 2001, Vincent Bar-
letta, review of *Poetry at Court in Testamaran
Spain: From the Cancionero de Baena to the Can-
cionero General,* pp. 93-95.
Medium Aevum, fall, 1991, David Hook, review of
The Poet's Art, pp. 322-324.
Modern Language Review, October, 1993, Derek C.
Carr, review of *The Poet's Art,* pp. 1009-1011.

OTHER

King's College London Web site, http://www.kcl.ac.uk/
(September 2, 2002), "Dr. Julian Weiss."*

* * *

WEISS, Julian M. 1952-2001

PERSONAL: Born 1952, in NY; died of cancer,
December 11, 2001, in Washington, DC; married
Karen Peacock (divorced); children: Jeremy. *Education:* State University of New York, New Paltz,
graduate.

CAREER: Writer and Asian affairs scholar. Freelance
writer, 1977-83; *Asiaweek,* Washington correspondent,
1981-90; Georgetown University Center on International Business, senior fellow, 1981-91; Washington
Roundtable for the Asia-Pacific Press, executive director, 1986-90, 1993-2001; Heritage Foundation,
international communications fellow, 1993-2001;
University of Maryland Institute for Global Chinese
Affairs, senior fellow.

WRITINGS:

*The New Hegemony: Deng Xiaoping's China Faces
the World,* Council for Social and Economic Stud-
ies (Washington, DC), 1988.
The Future of Manufacturing, Facts on File (New York
NY), 1989.
*The Asian Century: The Economic Ascent of the
Pacific Rim—And What It Means for the West,*
Facts on File (New York, NY), 1989.
(Editor) *Tigers' Roar: Asia's Recovery and Its Impact,*
M. E. Sharpe (Armonk, NY), 2001.

Contributor to periodicals, including *Asiaweek,* the
Economist, the *Journal of Commerce,* the *Christian
Science Monitor,* and the Asian *Wall Street Journal.*

SIDELIGHTS: Julian M. Weiss was a journalist who
specialized in Asian economic and political affairs. He
was a frequent speaker at conferences and seminars,
and lectured to a wide variety of audiences, including
the Japananese Ministry of Foreign Affairs, and the
Federation of Korean Industries.

Weiss first traveled to Asia in 1979 as part of an assignment for the *Christian Science Monitor,* and
became fascinated with Asian culture and politics during the trip. He founded the Washington Roundtable
for the Asia-Pacific Press in 1986; it lapsed in 1990,
but Weiss began directing it again in 1993, when he
began working for the Heritage Foundation, a conservative think tank. The Roundtable eventually grew to
include over four hundred print and broadcast journalists from nineteen countries, and was the largest
organization of its kind in the United States.

At the Heritage Foundation, Weiss continued to
analyze and write about Asian economic issues. He
warned of Japan's coming economic troubles years
before other analysts did. In 1997 he wrote that several
East Asian economies were on the verge of trouble,
months before economic problems struck the region.

In *The Asian Century: The Economic Ascent of the
Pacific Rim—and What It Means for the West,* Weiss
provides a review of the political history, as well as
the strengths and weaknesses, of the economies of
Japan, China, Korea, Taiwan, Hong Kong, Singapore,
Malaysia, and the Association of Southeast Asian
Nations. Focusing on technologies such as computers,
electronics, robots, and biotechnology, Weiss discusses
economic prospects for these nations. He also considers how various issues influence the economy throughout Asia; some of these issues are the increasing
population of aging people, dwindling resources, and
the role of women in various Asian cultures. According to a reviewer in the *Futurist,* Weiss views the four
recently industrialized nations—South Korea, Taiwan,
Hong Kong, and Singapore, known as the "four
tigers"—as a "rising tide washing the shores of the
global economy." Weiss discusses whether these
countries can live up to this reputation, given the
problems they face. He also discusses how their
economies are affected by events in the United States
and other countries.

The *Futurist* reviewer remarked that *The Asian Century* is "authoritative for anyone interested in conducting business in Asia or the Pacific Rim region." In *School Library Journal,* Barbara Weathers called the book "a rich, invaluable, and accessible resource." A *Publishers Weekly* critic praised Weiss's "balanced analysis" and commented the work was a "sober, fact-filled volume."

Tigers' Roar: Asia's Recovery and Its Impact is a collection of articles by forty-five authors on Asian nations and their cultural and economic situation. Covering a wide range of topics, including the role of the Internet, cultural values, urbanization, environment, international integration, and security issues, the articles provide background for an understanding of Asian economies. In *Choice,* S. J. Gabriel noted, "readers can find all sorts of interesting papers in the volume," and observed that the language is generally "easily accessible to the lay reader."

BIOGRAPHICAL AND CRITICAL SOURCES:

PERIODICALS

Choice, March, 2002, S. J. Gabriel, review of *Tigers' Roar: Asia's Recovery and Its Impact,* p. 1291.

Futurist, September-October, 1990, review of *The Asian Century: The Economic Ascent of the Pacific Rim—and What It Means for the West,* p. 43.

Journal of Social, Political and Economic Studies, fall, 1989, review of *The New Hegemony: Deng Xiaoping's China Faces the World,* p. 350.

Library Journal, August, 1989, Steven I. Levine, review of *The Asian Century,* p. 142.

Publishers Weekly, September 15, 1989, review of *The Asian Century,* p. 105.

School Library Journal, June, 1990, Barbara Weathers, review of *The Asian Century,* p. 148.

OBITUARIES:

PERIODICALS

Washington Post, December 14, 2001, p. B6.*

*   *   *

WEITZ, Mark A. 1957-

PERSONAL: Born December 13, 1957, in Marianna, FL; married, February 21, 1990; wife's name, Patricia. *Ethnicity:* "Anglo." *Education:* University of Texas, Austin, B.A., 1979; Baylor University School of Law, J.D., 1983; Southwest Texas State University, M.A., 1994; Arizona State University, Ph.D., 1998.

ADDRESSES: Home—465 Clanton Ave., Montgomery, AL 36104; fax: 334-264-7306. *Office*—Auburn University, P.O. Box 244023, Montgomery, AL 36124; fax: 334-244-3740. *E-mail*—Drweitz@aol.com or mweitz@ mickey.aum.edu.

CAREER: Historian, educator, and attorney. Admitted to the Bar, State of Texas, 1983; Auburn University, Montgomery, Montgomery, AL, professor of history.

MEMBER: American Historical Association, Organization of American Historians, Society of Historians of the Gilded Age and Progressive Era.

AWARDS, HONORS: History Associates Award, Arizona State University, 1998, for excellence in graduate studies; Michael A. Steiner Award, Arizona State University, 1998, for best dissertation; new faculty grant-in-aid, Auburn University, Montgomery, 2001-04, for *More Damning than Slaughter: Desertion in the Confederate Army.*

WRITINGS:

A Higher Duty: Desertion among Georgia Troops during the Civil War, University of Nebraska Press (Lincoln, NE), 2000.

Clergy Malpractice in America, Nally v. Grace Community Church of the Valley ("Landmark Law Cases and American Society" series), University Press of Kansas (Lawrence, KS), 2001.

(Editor, with Janet Correll Ellison) John Hill Ferguson, *On to Atlanta: The Civil War Diaries of John Hill Ferguson, Illinois Tenth Regiment of Volunteers,* University of Nebraska Press (Lincoln, NE), 2001.

Served on the editorial board of *Making Sense of Women's Lives,* Collegiate Press (San Diego, CA), 2000. Contributor to and reviewer for periodicals, including *Journal of Military History, Civil War History, Tennessee Historical Quarterly, Western Legal History, Historian, Georgia Historical Quarterly, Montana, the Magazine of Western History, Appalachia Studies,* and *Mississippi Journal of History.* Contributor to volumes, including the *Encyclopedia of the American Civil War,* edited by Jeanne and David Heidler, ABC-Clio Press (Santa Barbara, CA), 2000; and *Rebellion, Repression, Re-invention: Mutiny in a Comparative Perspective,* edited by Jane Hathaway, Praeger/Greenwood (New York, NY), 2001.

WORK IN PROGRESS: More Damning than Slaughter: Desertion in the Confederate Army, University of Nebraska Press (Lincoln, NE), 2003.

SIDELIGHTS: Mark A. Weitz is an historian and educator in the fields of U.S. history, the Civil War and Reconstruction, Southern history, and U.S. Constitutional history. His books include *A Higher Duty: Desertion among Georgia Troops During the American Civil War,* in which he makes the case that Southern soldiers fought not in the name of "nationalism," but to protect and defend their families. Henry M. McKiven, Jr. wrote in *Journal of Southern History* that Weitz "argues that a hegemonic 'planter class' brought Georgia into the war with 'little support from non-slaveholders' . . . and the ambivalence of non-slaveholders toward secession, he maintains, is the key to understanding desertion."

Weitz draws on a register housed in the National Archives that was kept from 1863 to 1865 by the Union Army, noting the names of Southern soldiers who had deserted, pledged their allegiance to the United States, and then were allowed to either stay in the North for the remainder of the war or go home. The Georgian deserters tended to be from households who depended on their own labor to survive, and their absence left many of their families destitute. The soldiers became increasingly afraid for their families as General Sherman's army advanced into Georgia in the spring of 1864.

Weitz claims that North Georgia soldiers also deserted because of class tension, angered that the Black Belt planter class, who stood to benefit most from the war, did not take an active role in the fighting. Keith S. Bohannon said in *Civil War History* that although comments to this effect appear in the writings of civilians and soldiers from the upcountry and upper Piedmont region, "they are too infrequent to support Weitz's sweeping claim. His assertion that the planter class really didn't support the war contradicts his own evidence that units raised from the Black Belt,

comprised in large part of planters and their kin, had the lowest desertion rates of any Georgia Confederate organizations." Bohannon pointed to the fact that the number of Georgia deserters noted in the register represented only about three percent of the total of 120,000. "Nonetheless," he concluded, "*A Higher Duty* is noteworthy as one of the few book-length studies of Confederate desertion, a topic that needs to receive far more attention."

BIOGRAPHICAL AND CRITICAL SOURCES:

PERIODICALS

Choice, September, 2000, M. L. Tate, Review of *A Higher Duty: Desertion among Georgia Troops during the American Civil War,* p. 207.
Civil War History, September, 2001, Keith S. Bohannon, review of *A Higher Duty,* p. 271.
Journal of American History, June, 2000, Kevin Conley Ruffner, review of *A Higher Duty,* p. 207.
Journal of Military History, April, 2002, Christopher C. Meyers, review of *A Higher Duty,* p. 570.
Journal of Southern History, November, 2001, Henry M. McKiven, Jr., review of *A Higher Duty,* p. 874.*

*   *   *

WELCH, Martha McKeen 1914-

PERSONAL: Born May 17, 1914, in Easton, PA.

ADDRESSES: Agent—c/o Author Mail, Penguin Putnam, 375 Hudson St., New York, NY 10014.

CAREER: Freelance photographer, beginning 1947, including photographs for greeting cards, book jackets, and catalogs; Bookseller, Bedford Village, NY, owner, beginning 1974.

AWARDS, HONORS: Younger honor, New York Academy of Sciences, 1981, for *Sunflower!*

WRITINGS:

CHILDREN'S BOOKS

Saucy, illustrated by Unada, Coward (New York, NY), 1968.
Pudding and Pie, Coward (New York, NY), 1969.

Nibbit, Coward (New York, NY), 1969.

Just like Puppies, Coward (New York, NY), 1969.

Sunflower!, Dodd (New York, NY), 1980.

Close Looks in a Spring Woods, Dodd (New York, NY), 1982.

Will That Wake Mother?, Dodd (New York, NY), 1982.

BIOGRAPHICAL AND CRITICAL SOURCES:

PERIODICALS

Appraisal, fall, 1982.

Bulletin of the Center for Children's Books, May, 1982.

Horn Book, June, 1981.

Publishers Weekly, November 19, 1982, review of *Will That Wake Mother?,* p. 76.

School Library Journal, February, 1981; September, 1982; January, 1983, review of *Will That Wake Mother?,* p. 68.

Science Books and Films, January/February, 1981.

Wilson Library Bulletin, March 1983, Olga Richard and Donnarae MacCann, review of *Will That Wake Mother?,* p. 591.*

* * *

WELZENBACH, Michael 1953(?)-2001

PERSONAL: Born c. 1953, in Iowa; died of congestive heart failure and liver failure resulting from hepatitis C, December 18, 2001, in Arlington, VA; married Jane Loftus (divorced); married Gael Jacques (divorced); married Melanie Graham (divorced); married Suzanne Shackley (divorced); children: (with Loftus) Kerry Margaret. *Education:* Attended Old Dominion University.

CAREER: Art critic, painter, sculptor, poet, and musician. Art gallery, Washington, DC, framer; *Los Angeles Times,* Los Angeles, CA, art critic, 1983-85; *Washington Post,* Washington, DC, art critic, 1985-88; *Calypso* (Jacques Cousteau's magazine), Norfolk, VA, editor, 1988-90; Jacques Cousteau, Europe, staff member, 1990; *Reader's Digest,* Europe and later London, Ontario, Canada, staff writer, 1990s-2001. Also participated on WETA-TV's *Around Town* program, Washington, DC, mid-1980s.

WRITINGS:

Conversations with a Clown, Atlantic Monthly Press (New York, NY), 1991.

SIDELIGHTS: Art critic Michael Welzenbach's novel *Conversations with a Clown* features Pierrot, a harlequin figure who has appeared in the works of artists from Jean-Antoine Watteau to Pablo Picasso. In Welzenbach's book, Pierrot is an eccentric older man living under the name Gilles Pedrolino in the East Village neighborhood in New York City. Michiko Kakutani commented in the *New York Times* that Pierrot "emerges as a cranky, garrulous pedant . . . continually launching into long-winded speeches about the creative process and reminiscing about famous artists he has known." As in traditional art and folklore, he is constantly battling his archrival Harlequin for the affections of the beautiful Columbine. He is no lightweight, however; as Kakutani noted, he is "a fiercely opinionated fellow with a quick temper and an even quicker tongue."

Pierrot becomes friends with art critic Corey Peters, the narrator of the tale. Peters is fed up with the art scene, disgusted by the politics and commercialism that infest it, and saddened by many artists' self-indulgence and lack of devotion to craft. Pierrot takes Peters in hand and reminds him of the true nature and purpose of art, reminiscing about the good old times he had with artists, including Picasso, Amedeo Modigliani, Francisco Goya, and Mary Cassatt; they even visit the Japanese artist Katsushika Hokusai through a form of time travel. By the end of the book, the formerly jaded critic has a renewed sense of art's regenerative powers, and has learned lessons on art history and aesthetics.

Although Sybil Steinberg wrote in *Publishers Weekly* that the story is "tedious," she also commented that "as a meditation on art's truth and purpose, it soars." Lori D. Kranz wrote in *Bloomsbury Review,* "How an ageless clown restores a cynical art critic's faith in art makes *Conversations with a Clown* fascinating reading, especially for art lovers," and commented that the novel should "be read slowly and thoughtfully by those who still believe in magic."

In addition to his writing, Welzenbach enjoyed painting, sculpting, poetry, and music. He traveled to South America for the Smithsonian Institution, and was involved in the discovery of a whale head fossil off the lower Potomac River.

BIOGRAPHICAL AND CRITICAL SOURCES:

PERIODICALS

Arts Magazine, April, 1991, Lois E. Nesbitt, review of *Conversations with a Clown,* p. 111.

Bloomsbury Review, April-May, 1991, Lori D. Kranz, review of *Conversations with a Clown,* p. 16.

Library Journal, December, 1990, Doris Lynch, review of *Conversations with a Clown,* p. 166.

New York Times, January 22, 1991, Michiko Kakutani, "Modern Art in the Eyes of Commedia dell'Arte," p. C15.

Publishers Weekly, October 19, 1990, Sybil Steinberg, review of *Conversations with a Clown,* p. 48.

OBITUARIES:

PERIODICALS

Washington Post, December 22, 2001, p. B5.*

* * *

WERT, Jeffry D.

PERSONAL: Male. *Education:* Lock Haven University, B.A. (cum laude), Pennsylvania State University, M.A.

ADDRESSES: Agent—c/o Author Mail, Simon & Schuster, 1230 Avenue of the Americas, New York, NY 10020.

CAREER: Writer, and historian. Penns Valley Area High School, Spring Mills, PA, history teacher.

AWARDS, HONORS: Alan Nolan-Iron Brigade Award, 2000.

WRITINGS:

From Winchester to Cedar Creek: The Shenandoah Campaign of 1864, South Mountain Press (Carlisle, PA), 1987.

General James Longstreet: The Confederacy's Most Controversial Soldier: A Biography, Simon & Schuster (New York, NY), 1993.

Custer: The Controversial Life of George Armstrong Custer, Simon & Schuster (New York, NY), 1996.

A Brotherhood of Valor: The Common Soldiers of the Stonewall Brigade, C.S.A., and the Iron Brigade, U.S.A., Simon & Schuster (New York, NY), 1999.

Gettysburg, Day Three, Simon & Schuster (New York, NY), 2001.

Contributor of articles to periodicals.

SIDELIGHTS: Civil War historian Jeffry D. Wert has illuminated America's most turbulent years in the nineteenth-century with histories of both the Union and the Confederate sides. In *From Winchester to Cedar Creek: The Shenandoah Campaign of 1864,* he provides a blow-by-blow account of the eighth Vermont Infantry's campaign in the Shenandoah Valley, beginning with the 1864 Third Winchester Battle. Wert also analyses the commanders, Philip H. Sheridan and Jubal A. Early, and their subordinates. Stephen F. Austin wrote in the *Journal of Southern History,* "Readers who have an appetite for learning the placement and activities of virtually every unit and many individuals in the three battles will be gratified, as will those who want an analysis of the generals and their goals." A second edition, with a new introduction by Wert, was published in 1997.

Mosby's Rangers narrates the campaign of what Wert calls "probably the most renowned combat unit of the Civil War," the 43rd Battalion of Virginia Cavalry. Led by Colonel John Singleton Mosby, the Raiders were formed in January of 1863. The guerrillas executed strategic raids on Union railroads, pickets, wagon trains, troop detachments, and outposts. But, according to Wert, the Rangers did not delay the Union victory as much as they thought; in fact, they merely brought unnecessary suffering upon their own people. *Washington Post*'s Robert A. Webb wrote that Wert's "fresh, unromantic look at Mosby's band" is valuable as a history and as a "guide for day trips to dozens of towns and villages where Mosby operated, each with a story or two to tell." Wert does a similar analysis in *A Brotherhood of Valor: The Common Soldiers of the Stonewall Brigade, C.S.A., and the Iron Brigade, U.S.A.*

Wert sets about redeeming an often maligned historical figure in his *General James Longstreet: The Confederacy's Most Controversial Soldier.* This was a difficult subject for a biography because all of Longstreet's private papers were destroyed in two different house fires. Wert relies on military facts to narrate Longstreet's career, which began in the Mexican War. Longstreet was blamed for the Confederate defeat at Gettysburg when he opposed Lee's determination to make a frontal assault. Whether or not he is responsible, Longstreet must also bear the infamy of engaging in conspiracy under Braxton Bragg in Tennessee, receiving pay as a Confederate officer before resigning his U.S. commission. Still, he was a tactically brilliant soldier. John Eisenhower commented in the *New York Times Book Review* that "Mr. Wert . . . feels that criticisms of Longstreet have been largely unfair, and he attempts to restore Longstreet's reputation to what he considers its rightful place. Yet he does not do so at the expense of Longstreet's `competitors,' notably Jackson. . . . despite Longstreet's faults, the reader comes away with sympathy and respect for a general treated unfairly in conventional history."

Wert discusses another provocative historical figure in his book, *Custer: The Controversial Life of George Armstrong Custer,* based on archival research and recent scholarship. One the Union's youngest generals, Custer had an unsurpassed record as a cavalry officer. His tremendous self-confidence helped ensure his victories, but his flamboyant personal style alienated many other soldiers. After the Civil War, Custer allowed himself to take too many chances, and he fell in the famed battle at Little Bighorn with the Plains Indians. Wert also examines Custer's marriage with Elizabeth (Libbie) Clift Bacon Custer. Comparing Wert's biography with that by Louise Barnett (*Touched by Fire,* 1996), *New York Times* reviewer Robert V. Remini declared Wert's the better biography, "with a fuller and more exciting description of the Last Stand."

In *Gettysburg, Day Three,* Wert examines the final day of the famous Civil War battle. Seen from both the Union and Confederate sides, Wert, using diaries and letters, shows the battle in all its confusion from the point of view of the individual soldiers, and the generals, including George Meade, Winfield Scott Hancock, James Longstreet, and Robert E. Lee. Wert recounts the battlefield decisions and motivations, including Pickett's charge on the Northern encampment, and switches from one venue to another to capture the battle in all its scope. *Booklist*'s Jay Freeman wrote that *Gettysburg, Day Three* "will be an excellent addition to Civil War collections."

BIOGRAPHICAL AND CRITICAL SOURCES:

PERIODICALS

Atlantic Monthly, January, 1994, Phoebe Lou Adams, review of *General James Longstreet,* pp. 122-123.
Booklist, October 15, 1993, Roland Green, review of *General James Longstreet,* p. 416; May 15, 1996, Gilbert Taylor, review of *Custer: The Controversial Life of George Armstrong Custer,* p. 1566; June 1, 2001, Jay Freeman, review of *Gettysburg, Day Three,* p. 1833.
Civil War Times, October, 2001, Mark L. Bradley, review of *Gettysburg, Day Three,* p. 14.
Journal of Southern History, August 1998, Archie P. McDonald, review of *From Winchester to Cedar Creek,* p. 557.
Kirkus Reviews, August 1, 1990, review of *Mosby's Rangers,* p. 1076.
Los Angeles Times Book Review, December 30, 1990, Chris Goodrich, review of *Mosby's Rangers,* p.6.
New Republic, July 29, 1996, James M. McPherson, review of *Custer: The Controversial Life of George Armstrong Custer,* pp. 38-41.
New York Times Book Review, November 28, 1993, John Eisenhower, "The Goat of Gettysburg," p. 34; July 14, 1996, Robert V. Remini, "Furious George."
Publishers Weekly, April 22, 1996, review of *Custer: The Controversial Life of George Armstrong Custer,* p. 53; December 7, 1998, review of *A Brotherhood of Valor,* p. 41.
Virginia Quarterly Review, winter, 2002, review of *Gettysburg, Day Three.*
Washington Post, October 14, 1990, Robert A. Webb, review of *Mosby's Rangers,* p. 8.
Washington Post Book World, November 28, 1993, review of *General James Longstreet,* p. 13.
Wild West, December, 1996, review of *Custer: The Controversial Life of George Armstrong Custer,* p. 76.*

*   *   *

WHITFIELD, Eileen 1951-

PERSONAL: Born 1951.

ADDRESSES: Agent—c/o Author Mail, University Press of Kentucky, 663 South Limestone St., Lexington, KY 40508-4008.

CAREER: Film critic, actress, and author.

WRITINGS:

Pickford: The Woman Who Made Hollywood, University Press of Kentucky (Louisville, KY), 1997.

SIDELIGHTS: Toronto film critic and former actress Eileen Whitfield is the author of *Pickford,* a critically acclaimed biography of silent film actress Mary Pickford, one of the seminal figures of the U.S. film industry. The book's subtitle, *The Woman Who Made Hollywood,* does not miss the mark. Pickford, arguably the best-known actress—and financial draw—of her day, also had a head for business. In addition to negotiating ever bigger salaries for herself, she also formed—along with Charlie Chaplin, D. W. Griffith, and Douglas Fairbanks—the first artist-owned Hollywood studio, United Artists. Her marriage to Fairbanks, a matinee idol in his own right, only added to her pop culture sheen as "America's Sweetheart."

Whitfield writes that Pickford grew up impoverished—her alcoholic father died when she was just six years old. To help the family financially, Pickford began working as a stage actress at the age of eight. She went to Broadway and worked for the famous theater impresario David Belasco and from there she went to Hollywood. Throughout her movie career (1910-29), she played adolescent roles and was rarely able to win an adult role. Additionally, her marriage to Fairbanks eventually turned sour and they divorced. Unable to make the transition to talking pictures, Pickford ended up like the Nora Desmond character in *Sunset Boulevard:* a former movie star wondering through her large mansion lost in a haze of alcohol. Ironically, Pickford auditioned for the role of Desmond, and was turned down. The saddest irony of all, though, is that no copies of Pickford's best films have survived.

M. S. Mason of the *Christian Science Monitor* found Whitfield's book to be a "gripping biography." "Whitfield's own love for silent film is palpable, and her defense of it graceful and true," Mason wrote. Charles Taylor of *Salon.com* noted that "If Whitfield is everything you'd want in a biographer, she's also everything you could ask for in a film historian. *Pickford* is as good a history on the origins of the movies as I've ever read." Rosellen Brewer commented in *Library Journal,* "Though there have been other biographies of Pickford, [Whitfield's] will stand as the definitive one."

BIOGRAPHICAL AND CRITICAL SOURCES:

PERIODICALS

Booklist, September 1, 1997, p. 50.
Entertainment Weekly, September 26, 1997, L. S. Klepp, review of *Pickford: The Woman Who Made Hollywood,* p. 74.
Kirkus Reviews, July 1, 1997, p. 1021.
Library Journal, July 1997, p. 86.
Newsweek, July 14, 1997, Ray Sawhill, review of *Pickford: The Woman Who Made Hollywood,* p. 69.
New Yorker, September 22, 1997, Arlene Croce, review of *Pickford: The Woman Who Made Hollywood,* p. 130.
Publishers Weekly, July 14, 1997, review of *Pickford: The Woman Who Made Hollywood,* p. 73.

OTHER

Salon.com, http://www.salonmagazine.com/ (September 10, 1997).*

*   *   *

WILLEY, Gordon R(andolph) 1913-2002

OBITUARY NOTICE—See index for *CA* sketch: Born March 7, 1913, in Chariton, IA; died of heart failure April 28, 2002, in Cambridge, MA. Archeologist, anthropologist, educator, and author. Willey was an expert on archaeology in the Americas and was considered by many to be the "dean" of his field. Willey earned his master's degree at the University of Arizona and a Ph.D. at Columbia, where he also taught for a year. From 1943 to 1950 he worked as an anthropologist for the Smithsonian Institute, and it was during this period that he wrote his classic *Archaeology of the Florida Gulf Coast* (1949). His excavation work in Peru led to his creation of "settlement pattern studies," in which he developed theories about social, political, and economic interactions in cultures by analyzing ruins and other remains of civilizations. Joining Harvard University as the Bowditch Professor of Archaeology in 1950, where he was also dean of the department in the 1950s, Willey became a senior professor in 1983, retiring in 1987; he also taught for a time at Boston University. While at Harvard, Willey became a noted expert on the Mayan civilization and wrote such important works as *Method and Theory in American Archaeology* (1958), written with Philip Phillips, *Prehistoric Maya Settlements in the Belize Valley* (1965), the two-volume *An Introduction to American Archaeology* (1966, 1971), and *Portraits in American Archaeology* (1989). Some of his other works include *The Artifacts of Seibal, Guatemala* (1978), *Essays in Maya Archaeology* (1987), *New World Archaeology and Culture History* (1990), and *Excavations at Seibal: Summary and Conclusions* (1990). A former president of the American Archeological Association, Willey earned many awards and honors during his career, including a Huxley Medal from the Royal Anthropological Institute, the Order of the Quetzal from Guatemala, and a gold medal from the Archaeological Institute of America. He was also the first-ever honorary vice president of the Society of Antiquaries and was active in many other scientific and academic organizations.

OBITUARIES AND OTHER SOURCES:

BOOKS

Who's Who in America, 55th edition, Marquis, 2001.

PERIODICALS

Los Angeles Times, May 1, 2002, p. B11.
New York Times, May 1, 2002, p. C13.
Times (London, England), May 1, 2002, p. 31.
Washington Post, May 1, 2002, p. B5.

*   *   *

WILLIAMS, Daniel H(arrison) 1955-

PERSONAL: Born May 11, 1955, in St. Louis, MO; married Cindy Breece, April 28, 1979; children: Ryan, Chad. *Education:* Northeastern Bible College, B.A., 1978; Trinity Divinity School, M.Div., 1981; Princeton Theological Seminary, Th.M., 1984; University of Toronto, M.A., Ph.D., 1991. *Politics:* Republican. *Religion:* Baptist. *Hobbies and other interests:* Raising and farming with horses.

ADDRESSES: Agent—c/o Author Mail, William B. Eerdmans Publishing Co., 255 Jefferson Ave. SE, Grand Rapids, MI 49503. *E-mail*—dwilli1@orion.it. luc.edu.

CAREER: Minister, and educator. Ordained 1981; West Side Baptist Church, Rochester, NY, associate pastor, 1981-84; University of Toronto, Toronto, Ontario, Canada, instructor, 1987-91; First Baptist Church of Crafton, Pittsburgh, PA, pastor, 1991-94; University of Pittsburgh, Pittsburgh, research fellow; Loyola University, Chicago, IL, assistant professor, 1994, associate professor of theology in patristics and historical theology, 1999, professor of religion in patristics, 2002—. First Baptist Church of Wheaton, Wheaton, IL, teacher and counselor, 1996—; participant in the Evangelical-Roman Catholic Dialogue, 2000—. External examiner, consultant, and journal referee.

MEMBER: America Council of Church History, Ecclesiastical History Society, Groupe Suisse d'Etudes Patristiques, International Association for Patristic Studies, Midwest Patristics Seminar, North American Patristic Society (board of directors).

AWARDS, HONORS: Publication grant, Centre for Religious Studies, University of Toronto, 1990; American Academy of Religion grant, 1990, summer stipend, Loyola University Endowment for the Humanities, 1997; university teacher fellowship; National Endowment for the Humanities, 2000.

WRITINGS:

(Editor, with Michel R. Barnes, and contributor) *Arianism after Arius: Essays on the Development of the Fourth-Century Trinitarian Conflicts,* T & T Clark (Edinburgh, Scotland), 1993.
Ambrose of Milan and the End of the Nicene-Arian Conflicts, Oxford University Press (New York, NY), 1995.
Retrieving the Tradition and Renewing Evangelicalism: A Primer for Suspicious Protestants, William B. Eerdmans Publishing Co. (Grand Rapids, MI), 1999.
(Editor and contributor) *The Free Church and the Early Church: Essays in Bridging the Historical and Theological Divide,* William B. Eerdmans Publishing Co. (Grand Rapids, MI), 2002.

(Editor and contributor) *The Church's Bible: Commentary on Matthew,* William B. Eerdmans Publishing Co. (Grand Rapids, MI), 2002.

Contributor to books, including *Christian Origins: Theology, Rhetoric, and Community,* edited by L. Ayre and G. Jones, Routledge (London, England), 1998; *Recent Studies in Early Christianity: A Collection of Scholarly Essays,* edited by E. Ferguson, Garland (New York, NY), 1999; and *Dictionary of Christian Theologians,* edited by P. Carey and J. Lienhard, Greenwood, 2000. Contributor to and reviewer for periodicals, including *Journal of Early Christian Studies, Religion, Interpretations, Journal of Religion, Anglican Theological Review, Journal of Theological Studies, Church History,* and *Journal of Ecclesiastical History.*

WORK IN PROGRESS: English translation and annotation, Hilary of Poitiers, *Commentarium in Matthaeum,* Catholic University of American Press, 2002-03; editor, *Evangelical Ressourcement: Ancient Sources for the Church's Future,* Baker Academic; coeditor, *Early Hymns for Today's Church,* Hope Publishing, 2003; *The Early Christian Tradition: Resources for All Protestants,* Baker Academic, 2003; coeditor, *Triadic Confessions to Trinitarian Doctrine in the Early Church,* Catholic University of America Press.

SIDELIGHTS: Daniel H. Williams is a minister who has written or edited a number of volumes, including *Arianism after Arius: Essays on the Development of the Fourth-Century Trinitarian Conflicts,* which he coedited with Michel R. Barnes. T. A. Kopecek noted in *Journal of Theological Studies* that six of the eleven contributors also can be found in an earlier collection that resulted from the Ninth Oxford Conference on Patristic Studies in 1983. Kopecek noted that as in Oxford, Eastern topics dominate, with only one essay discussing the West. "The major difference," he said, "is that the most interrelated of the Oxford papers . . . were about Arianism's early stages; the papers on the latter stages were written by scholars who were not sharing in a common conversation. The present collection is evidence that such a conversation is now taking place and that a consensus about the sorts of research and discussion needed to clarify later Arianism is being achieved. This volume provides an excellent introduction both to some of the leaders in the conversation and to the kinds of issues being explored."

Ambrose of Milan and the End of the Nicene-Arian Conflicts is Williams's study of Nicene and Arian perceptions of the Trinity in the fourth century. Barnes said in the *Journal of Religion* that the book "has three tasks: to reveal the existence of a vigorous Latin anti-Nicene theology in the second half of the fourth century, to show that Ambrose's own anti-'Arian' position was one that he developed over time as bishop of Milan, and to conclude that Ambrose's triumph over Homoian theology in Milan constituted the end of the conflict between pro-and anti-Nicene theologies. Each of these represents a fresh consideration of the events in question, although it may be said that as Williams moves from the first to the third task, his take on the events becomes more original."

Williams first summarizes the traditional view of the tensions between the two, writing that "the Western Church was generally committed to the Nicene faith, or 'orthodoxy,' at an early date, and that Arianism posed little . . . serious threat to its final domination as the Christian faith of the Roman Empire." *Historian*'s Jan T. Hallenbeck noted that "much to the contrary, Williams argues, the anti-Nicene position was supported by numerous clergy as well as by Valentinian II; it was often presented in deceptive manners and was not struck down until A.D. 386-387." Hallenbeck, who called this study "complex and challenging," continued by calling Williams's coverage "thorough, nicely organized, and well written. His introduction establishes both the work's subject matter and his thesis. Eight chapters follow, treating the material in considerable depth."

David G. Hunter noted in *Theological Studies* that "one of the great virtues of Williams's book is its attempt to draw attention to little-known defenders of Nicaea who preceded Ambrose: Hilary of Poitiers and Eusebius of Vercelli. Williams carefully charts the careers of both men and their efforts to restore to the Nicene faith those bishops who had capitulated at the Western Council of Ariminum." John Currant wrote in *Journal of Ecclesiastical History* that "Williams's strengths are very evident in the close study of the texts. Readers will be indebted to him in particular for his valuable work on the opponents of Ambrose. . . . He has made accessible a compelling fusion of theological and political analysis and he has fleshed out impressively some of the most impassioned dissenters of late antiquity. And if some of his own theories do not find acceptance elsewhere . . . he has given us a new point of departure for understanding the enemies of Ambrose of Milan."

Neil McLynn wrote in *Journal of Theological Studies* that Williams's thesis "is bold and powerfully stated, and is entirely successful in its criticism of easy assumptions about an inevitable 'triumph of orthodoxy,' and of the traditional hagiographical portrait of Ambrose. Williams's own explanation of the Nicene victory and his presentation of Ambrose, meanwhile, are certain to provoke vigorous discussion." McLynn felt Williams's "two great strengths" to be "the detailed exposition (covering nearly half the book) of the doctrinal controversies of the two decades before Ambrose became bishop, and the methodical presentation of each separate issue, with full discussions—and determined criticism—of previous interpretations." McLynn concluded by saying, "That Williams ultimately poses more questions than he answers does not detract from his achievement. . . . By providing Ambrose with such worthy opponents, moreover, he allows us to appreciate the bishop's achievement in surviving."

A *Publishers Weekly* reviewer called *Retrieving the Tradition and Renewing Evangelicalism: A Primer for Suspicious Protestants* "an informed, well-written appeal for historical foundations." Timothy George wrote in *First Things,* that the book is "at once a protest and a lamentation against what might be called the tradition of traditionless evangelicalism." George noted that Williams's earlier writings "have established him as a careful scholar of doctrinal development in the early Church. He draws on that research in this book as he seeks to reengage his own evangelical community with the Great Tradition of historic Christian orthodoxy embodied in the conciliar decisions of the fourth and fifth centuries." *Interpretation*'s Donald G. Bloesch called the *Retrieving the Tradition* "an important contribution to the current ecumenical discussion on the interrelation of scripture and church tradition."

BIOGRAPHICAL AND CRITICAL SOURCES:

PERIODICALS

Catholic Historical Review, April, 1997, Joseph T. Lienhard, review of *Ambrose of Milan and the End of the Nicene-Arian Conflicts,* p. 295.

Church History, June, 1997, Charles M. Odahl, review of *Ambrose of Milan and the End of the Nicene-Arian Conflicts,* p. 310.

First Things, October, 2000, Timothy George, review of *Retrieving the Tradition and Renewing Evangelicalism: A Primer for Suspicious Protestants,* p. 71.

Historian, spring, 1996, Jan T. Hallenbeck, review of *Ambrose of Milan and the End of the Nicene-Arian Conflicts,* p. 704.

Interpretation, April, 2001, Donald G. Bloesch, review of *Retrieving the Tradition and Renewing Evangelicalism,* p. 220.

Journal of Ecclesiastical History, July, 1996, John Curran, review of *Ambrose of Milan and the End of the Nicene-Arian Conflicts,* p. 555.

Journal of Religion, April, 1997, Michel Rene Barnes, review of *Ambrose of Milan and the End of the Nicene-Arian Conflicts,* p. 293.

Journal of Theological Studies, April, 1995, T. A. Kopecek, review of *Arianism after Arius: Essays on the Development of the Fourth-Century Trinitarian Conflicts,* p. 333; April, 1997, Neil McLynn, review of *Ambrose of Milan and the End of the Nicene-Arian Conflicts,* p. 270.

Publishers Weekly, September 27, 1999, review of *Retrieving the Tradition and Renewing Evangelicalism,* p. 97.

Theological Studies, March, 1997, David G. Hunter, review of *Ambrose of Milan and the End of the Nicene-Arian Conflicts,* p. 158.

Theology Today, October, 2001, John R. Franke, review of *Retrieving the Tradition and Renewing Evangelicalism,* p. 480.*